INTERNATIONAL CHAMBER of COMMERCE ARBITRATION

Third Edition

W. Laurence Craig
William W. Park
Jan Paulsson

Oceana®

International Chamber of Commerce ·
The world business organization

OXFORD
UNIVERSITY PRESS

Oxford University Press, Inc., publishes works that further Oxford University's objective of excellence in research, scholarship, and education.

Copyright © 2000 by Oxford University Press, Inc.; ICC Publishing, SA;
W. Laurence Craig; William W. Park; Jan Paulsson
Published by Oxford University Press, Inc.
198 Madison Avenue, New York, New York 10016

Oxford is a registered trademark of Oxford University Press
Oceana is a registered trademark of Oxford University Press, Inc.

Library of Congress Cataloging-in-Publication Data

Craig, W. Laurence (William Laurence)
International Chamber of Commerce arbitration / by W. Laurence Craig, William
W. Park, Jan Paulsson. — 3rd ed.
p. cm.
Includes bibliographical references and index.

ISBN 978-0-379-21392-8 (alk. paper)
1. Arbitration and award, International. 2. International Chamber of Commerce.
Court of Arbitration. I. Park, William W. II. Paulsson, Jan. III. Title.
K2400.C725 1998
341.5'22—dc21   97-47674
CIP

Third Edition
ICC Publication No. 594; ISBN 92-842-1251-0

Printed in the United States of America on acid-free paper.

Note to Readers:

This publication is designed to provide accurate and authoritative information in regard to the subject matter covered. It is based upon sources believed to be accurate and reliable and is intended to be current as of the time it was written. It is sold with the understanding that the publisher is not engaged in rendering legal, accounting, or other professional services. If legal advice or other expert assistance is required, the services of a competent professional person should be sought. Also, to confirm that the information has not been affected or changed by recent developments, traditional legal research techniques should be used, including checking primary sources where appropriate.

(Based on the Declaration of Principles jointly adopted by a Committee of the American Bar Association and a Committee of Publishers and Associations.)

ABOUT THE AUTHORS:

W. Laurence Craig
Member of the Bars of New York and the District of Columbia
Avocat, Paris
A.B., Williams College; J.D., Harvard University
Doctor of Law of the University of Paris
Partner, Coudert Frères, Paris

William W. Park
Professor of Law, Boston University
Member of the Bars of Massachusetts and the District of Columbia
B.A., Yale University; J.D., Columbia University; M.A., Cambridge University
Counsel, Ropes & Gray, Boston

Jan Paulsson
Member of the Bars of Connecticut and the District of Columbia
Avocat, Paris
A.B., Harvard University; J.D., Yale University
Diplôme d'études supérieures spécialisées, University of Paris
Partner, Freshfields, Paris

TABLE OF CONTENTS

Introduction to the Third Edition xiii

Abbreviations xv

PART I
THE INSTITUTION

Chapter 1 General Characteristics 1

1.01 Basic principles. 1

1.02 Volume of cases 2

1.03 The stakes 3

1.04 Typical parties to ICC arbitrations 4

1.05 Typical subject matter of ICC cases. 6

1.06 Delocalization. 7

1.07 Trends in choosing venue and arbitrators 9

1.08 Length of proceedings. 13

1.09 General conclusions 14

Chapter 2 The Organizational Framework 17

2.01 Introduction. 17

2.02 The ICC and its National Committees 17

2.03 The Court 19

2.04 The Secretariat 24

2.05 The Arbitrators 26

Chapter 3 Costs 29

3.01 Principles of assessment 29

3.02 Is ICC arbitration too expensive? 29

3.03 The problem of advances on costs 33

3.04 Consequences of failure to contribute 34

3.05 Cost reforms 35

PART II
THE AGREEMENT TO ARBITRATE

Chapter 4 Types of Arbitration Agreements **37**

4.01 Special submission ("compromis") 37

4.02 Contractual clause 37

4.03 Ad hoc (non-administered) arbitration 38

4.04 Institutional arbitration 40

4.05 Supervised institutional arbitration 41

Chapter 5 The Validity of The Arbitration Agreement **43**

5.01 Introduction 43

5.02 Capacity of the parties 44

5.03 Authority to represent parties 46

5.04 Autonomy of the arbitration clause 48

5.05 Law applicable to the arbitration agreement 52

5.06 Form of the agreement to arbitrate 54

5.07 Arbitrability 60

5.08 Incorporation by reference 73

5.09 Related parties not having signed the arbitration agreement 74

5.10 Related agreements not containing the arbitration clause 79

5.11 Multi-party disputes 81

Chapter 6 Indispensable Elements **85**

6.01 Unambiguous reference to ICC arbitration 85

6.02 Scope of the dispute to be arbitrated 86

6.03 The ICC Model Clause 88

Chapter 7 Generally Recommended Additional Elements **91**

7.01 Number, nationality, and qualification of arbitrators 91

7.02 Place of arbitration 93

7.03 Language of arbitration 96

7.04 Law applicable to the merits of the dispute. 97

Chapter 8 Occasionally Useful Elements. 105

8.01 Negotiation, conciliation, or mediation as precondition 105

8.02 Rules or law of procedure 106

8.03 Law governing the arbitration agreement 107

8.04 Rules of conflict of laws. 108

8.05 Powers of amiable compositeur 110

8.06 Powers to adapt the contract 114

8.07 Powers and procedures for provisional relief 116

8.08 Procedural details. 117

8.09 Use of discovery. 118

8.10 Apportionment of costs 118

8.11 Entry-of-judgment stipulations 119

8.12 Waiver of appeal. 121

8.13 Waiver of sovereign immunity. 122

8.14 Accommodation for multi-party disputes. 125

Chapter 9 Pathological Elements 127

9.01 Introduction. 127

9.02 Equivocation: the cardinal sin. 128

9.03 The case of the missing authority 129

9.04 The case of the disastrous compromise 132

9.05 Overdoing the search for institutions 133

9.06 The illusory arbitration clause. 134

9.07 Suffocating the process with specificity 135

9.08 Haste makes waste 135

PART III
ICC ARBITRATION IN PRACTICE

Chapter 10 Bringing Arbitration Under the Rules 137

10.01 Introduction. 137

10.02 Business disputes of an international character 138

10.03 Which edition of the ICC Rules applies? 142

10.04 The Request for Arbitration 145

10.05 Answer and Counterclaim 150

10.06 Failure or refusal to answer and other defaults: ex parte proceedings ... 151

10.07 Notifications and communications and calculation of periods of time ... 153

Chapter 11 Arbitral Jurisdiction 155

11.01 The Court of Arbitration's preliminary prima facie determination
of existence of agreement to arbitrate 155

11.02 Procedure for raising jurisdictional issues before the Court of
Arbitration 158

11.03 Arbitrators' authority to determine their jurisdiction. 161

11.04 Recognition by national courts of arbitrator's power to determine
his own jurisdiction... 167

11.05 Jurisdiction over parties who have not signed the arbitration
agreement 171

11.06 Intervention, joinder and consolidation 179

**Chapter 12 Constituting the Arbitral Tribunal and Determining
the Place of Arbitration 185**

12.01 Place of arbitration 185

12.02 Number of arbitrators................................... 189

12.03 Appointment of sole arbitrator or chairman 191

12.04 Party-nominated arbitrators 194

12.05 Failure of a party to nominate an arbitrator 197

12.06 Constituting the arbitral tribunal in multi-party arbitrations 198

Chapter 13 Arbitrator Disqualification or Incapacity 203

13.01 Rejection of nomination, challenge, and disqualification............ 203

13.02 The Court's standards and their source....................... 207

13.03 Independence required of arbitrator......................... 209

13.04 Arbitrator's duty of disclosure 213

13.05 Grounds for challenge.................................. 223

13.06 Removal of an arbitrator by the Court....................... 237

13.07 Standards of conduct for arbitrators during the proceedings 240

13.08 Replacement of arbitrators................................ 242

13.09 Non-replacement of arbitrators: the "truncated tribunal" 245

13.10 Time limits for challenge 249

Chapter 14 Advance To Cover Costs 253

14.01 Determination of advances 253

14.02 Consequences of default by one party 263

14.03 The use of bank guarantees for the advance on costs 266

14.04 Other consequences of default by a party to pay advance on costs 267

Chapter 15 Terms of Reference 273

15.01 Rationale 273

15.02 Contents 276

15.03 Default by party 284

15.04 Entry Into effect 285

15.05 Legal Effect 286

Chapter 16 Rules Governing the Proceedings 295

16.01 Freedom of parties and arbitrators 295

16.02 Mandatory procedural requirements of national law 297

16.03 Effect of choice of an a-national procedure 299

16.04 Procedural rulings 300

16.05 Representation and Rights of Audience 303

16.06 Confidentiality 311

Chapter 17 Choice of Substantive Law 319

17.01 Freedom of arbitrators to apply "appropriate" rules of law 319

17.02 Choice of law criteria most frequently used in ICC arbitration 323

17.03 Application of contractual terms, relevant trade usage, and
"lex mercatoria" 330

17.04 Influence of public law and international public policy 338

Chapter 18 "Amiable Composition" 347

18.01 Definition 347

18.02 "Amiable Composition" and deciding "ex aequo et bono" under
the ICC Rules 351

18.03 Scrutiny and review of awards rendered by amiables compositeurs 353

Chapter 19 Arbitral Awards **355**

19.01 Time limits for awards 355

19.02 Awards by consent 358

19.03 Interim and partial awards 359

19.04 Form of award 364

19.05 Majority awards and awards rendered by the chairman 368

19.06 Dissenting opinions 371

Chapter 20 The Court's Scrutiny of Awards **375**

20.01 The Court's role 375

20.02 Review of procedural defects 377

20.03 Modification of the form of awards 378

20.04 Comments on points of substance 379

20.05 Court's scrutiny of awards as seen by national courts 380

Chapter 21 Determination of Costs **385**

21.01 General principles 385

21.02 ICC administrative costs 386

21.03 Arbitrators' fees 387

21.04 Arbitrators' allocation of costs between the parties 391

Chapter 22 Entering Into Effect of the Award **397**

22.01 Signature of the award by arbitrators 397

22.02 Payment of costs and notification of award to parties 399

22.03 Finality and enforceability of award 400

22.04 Deposit of award and assistance of Secretariat 404

22.05 Termination of arbitrators' powers 406

22.06 Exclusion of Liability 410

PART IV
HEARINGS, PROOF, AND ANCILLARY PROCEEDINGS

Chapter 23 ICC Arbitrators' Approach to Fact Finding **415**

23.01 Arbitrators' power to establish facts "by all appropriate means" 415

23.02 Civil-law procedures 418

23.03 Common-law procedures 419

23.04 Generally recognized procedural principles 422

Chapter 24 Written Proof and Arguments **427**

24.01 Emphasis on written submissions in ICC arbitration 427

24.02 Documents 429

24.03 Memorials and briefs 430

24.04 Timeliness of submissions 431

24.05 Written statements of witnesses 432

Chapter 25 Hearings **435**

25.01 Arbitrators' power of subpoena and to administer oath 435

25.02 Testimony 437

25.03 Party experts 442

25.04 Demonstrative evidence 443

25.05 Oral argument 444

25.06 Closing the proceedings 446

Chapter 26 Fact Finding and Interlocutory Measures Ordered by Arbitrators **449**

26.01 Production of documents 449

26.02 Depositions 457

26.03 Site visit 458

26.04 Experts appointed by the tribunal 458

26.05 Interim measures and other interlocutory relief ordered by arbitrators . . 460

Chapter 27 Ancillary Proceedings Before National Courts **471**

27.01 Article 23(2) of the Rules: interim or conservatory measures 471

27.02 Injunction, expertise, and other urgent measures 473

27.03 Other interlocutory relief 480

27.04 Attachments 482

27.05 Court ordered discovery and production of evidence 486

PART V
THE IMPACT OF NATIONAL LAW

Chapter 28 National Constraints on ICC Arbitration **495**

28.01 Private Consent and Public Power 495

28.02 Matters Affected by National Arbitration Law 496

28.03 The Arbitral Situs 497

28.04 Award Annulment: Why and to What Effect.................... 500

28.05 Multiple Procedural Norms 507

28.06 Keeping National Law in Perspective 510

28.07 Courts and Arbitral Jurisdiction 512

28.08 The Special Status of International Arbitration 516

Chapter 29 The Uncitral Model Law **519**

29.01 Statutory Framework.................................. 519

29.02 The Agreement to Arbitrate............................. 523

29.03 Interlocutory matters 526

29.04 Review of awards 528

Chapter 30 English Law **531**

30.01 Statutory Framework.................................. 531

30.02 The Agreement to Arbitrate............................. 537

30.03 Interlocutory Matters 539

30.04 Review of Awards 542

Chapter 31 French Law **549**

31.01 Statutory framework.................................. 549

31.02 The Agreement to Arbitrate 551

31.03 Interlocutory Matters................................. 555

31.04 Review of Awards 557

Chapter 32 Hong Kong Law **563**

32.01 Statutory Framework.................................. 563

32.02 The Agreement to Arbitrate............................. 567

32.03 Interlocutory Matters 569

32.04 Review of Awards 570

Chapter 33 Swiss Law **575**

33.01 Statutory Framework.................................. 575

33.02 The Agreement to Arbitrate............................. 577

33.03 Interlocutory Matters 579

33.04 Review of Awards 582

Chapter 34 United States Law. 591

34.01 Statutory Framework. 591

34.02 The Agreement to Arbitrate 596

34.03 Interlocutory Matters 607

34.04 Review of Awards 610

PART VI
TRENDS IN INTERNATIONAL COMMERCIAL ARBITRATION

Chapter 35 Lex Mercatoria. 623

35.01 Three concepts of lex mercatoria 623

35.02 ICC awards as precedents 639

35.03 An illustration of the emergence of transnational norms: the issue
of force majeure. 651

35.04 Toward a concept of arbitral justice 657

Chapter 36 State Contracts 661

36.01 International arbitration as a perceived menace to sovereignty 661

36.02 Arbitration without privity 663

36.03 Sovereign immunity and acts of State 670

36.04 The ability of developing countries to deal with transnational disputes. . . 676

Chapter 37 ICC Arbitration and the New York Convention 679

37.01 Background 679

37.02 Framework. 680

37.03 Scope 681

37.04 Defenses to Recognition and Enforcement. 684

37.05 Interaction with Other Treaties. 686

Chapter 38 Additional ICC Dispute Resolving Mechanisms. 697

38.01 Conciliation. 697

38.02 Expertise. 701

38.03 Pre-arbitral Referee 706

38.04 Adaptation of contracts. 709

38.05 Maritime and aviation arbitration 712

38.06 Specialized commissions 713

38.07 Appointing authority. 714

38.08 Supervising arbitration applying non-ICC rules. 715

38.09 Documentary Credit Disputes. 715

APPENDICES

Appendix I: Statistics and General Information

Table 1 Composition of ICC Commissions and Working Groups 721

Table 2 Composition of the Court of Arbitration 724

Table 3 Nationalities of Arbitrators. 727

Table 4 Nationalities of Arbitrators Selected in 1989-1999 (11 Years) 728

Table 5 Nationalities of Parties to Arbitration Filed in 1989-1999 (11 Years). . 732

Table 6 Regional Leaders 737

Table 7 Places of Arbitration Established in 1989-1999 (11 Years) 738

Table 8 Amounts In Dispute. 743

Table 9A Calculating ICC Administrative Expenses and Fees of Arbitrators
According to the ICC Schedule 744

Table 9B Estimating Costs and the Advance on Costs 745

Table 10 Signatories to the 1958 New York Convention on the Recognition
and Enforcement of Foreign Arbitral Awards 748

Appendix II:

Rules of Optional Conciliation 753

Rules of Arbitration of the International Chamber of Commerce 756

Statutes of the International Court of Arbitration of the ICC 771

Internal Rules of the International Court of Arbitration of the ICC 773

Arbitration Costs and Fees 776

Destination table: From 1975 Arbitration Rules to 1998 Arbitration Rules . . . 781

Derivative table: From 1998 Arbitration Rules to 1975 Arbitration Rules 784

Appendix III:

ICC Rules for Expertise 789

ICC Rules for Documentary Credit Dispute Resolution Expertise
DOCDEX Rules 793

Appendix to the ICC DOCDEX Rules 798

ICC/CMI Rules for International Maritime Arbitration 800

ICC Rules for a Pre-Arbitral Referee Procedure 808

APPENDIX: Costs and Payment for the ICC Pre-arbitral Referee Procedure 813

TABLES

Table of Cases 815

Table of Arbitral Awards 859

Table of Authorities 873

Table of Articles of the 1998 ICC Arbitration Rules 911

INDEX

Subject Index 919

INTRODUCTION TO THE THIRD EDITION

With the advent of the 1998 ICC Rules of Arbitration, the Second Edition of ICC ARBITRATION became obsolete. Even with respect to the many matters which the revision left unchanged, the fact that the Rules were comprehensively reorganized meant that previous references to particular articles perforce became inaccurate.

Released two years after the entry into effect of the 1998 Rules, this Third Edition benefits from early experiences in applying them. The statistics are up to date as of January 2000, and we were able to include a discussion (in Chapter 13) of the much-awaited judgment of the English Court of Appeal in *AT&T v. Saudi Cable Co.*, dealing with the issue of ICC arbitrators' duties of disclosure, impartiality and independence, which was handed down on 15 May 2000.

We maintain our original resolution that this book remain a practical reference work providing solutions to concrete problems. To save the reader from a wild goose chase of cross-references, information is occasionally repeated when it is germane to more than one of our simply subdivided topics.

We owe a special thanks to colleagues who advised us with respect to particular chapters: Neil Kaplan, Q.C. (Hong Kong), Laurent Lévy (Switzerland) and Johnny Veeder, Q.C. (England), as well as to young lawyers and legal assistants who helped us produce this edition, principally Toshiki Enomoto, Andrea Maass, Christine Meller, Andrew Said, and Christopher Chinn.

Finally, we need to point out that this is not an authorized publication of the ICC Court of Arbitration. We have benefitted from the comments of a number of ICC officials, but we alone are responsible for the opinions expressed herein.

Paris and Boston, July 2000

ABBREVIATIONS

ARBITRATION

The journal of the Chartered Institute of Arbitrators, London

ARB. INT.

ARBITRATION INTERNATIONAL (LCIA)

DERAINS & SCHWARTZ

YVES DERAINS & ERIC SCHWARTZ, A GUIDE TO THE NEW ICC RULES OF ARBITRATION (Kluwer, 1998)

I ICC AWARDS

COLLECTION OF ICC ARBITRAL AWARDS 1974-1985 (SIGVARD JARVIN & YVES DERAINS, eds., Kluwer, 1990)

II ICC AWARDS

COLLECTION OF ICC ARBITRAL AWARDS 1986-1990 (SIGVARD JARVIN, YVES DERAINS & JEAN-JACQUES ARNALDEZ, eds., Kluwer, 1994)

III ICC AWARDS

COLLECTION OF ICC ARBITRAL AWARDS 1991-1995 (JEAN-JACQUES ARNALDEZ, YVES DERAINS & DOMINIQUE HASCHER, eds., Kluwer, 1994)

ICC BULL.

THE ICC INTERNATIONAL COURT OF ARBITRATION BULLETIN

ICC PROCEDURAL DECISION

COLLECTION OF PROCEDURAL DECISIONS IN ICC ARBITRATION (DOMINIQUE HASCHER, ed., Kluwer 1997)

ILM

INTERNATIONAL LEGAL MATERIALS (American Society of International Law)

JDI

JOURNAL DU DROIT INTERNATIONAL

J. INT. ARB.

JOURNAL OF INTERNATIONAL ARBITRATION

ICCA HANDBOOK	INTERNATIONAL HANDBOOK ON COMMERCIAL ARBITRATION (International Council for Commercial Arbitration/Kluwer, updated periodically since 1976)
MEALEY'S INT. ARB. REP.	MEALEY'S INTERNATIONAL ARBITRATION REPORT
REDFERN & HUNTER	ALAN REDFERN & MARTIN HUNTER, LAW AND PRACTICE OF INTERNATIONAL COMMERCIAL ARBITRATION (Sweet & Maxwell, 3d ed. 1999)
REV. ARB.	REVUE DE L'ARBITRAGE
RIV. DIR. INT. P. P.	RIVISTA DI DIRITTO INTERNAZIONALE PRIVATO E PROCESSUALE
Rules	The 1998 Rules of Arbitration of the ICC (reproduced in Appendix 1)
SWISS BULL.	BULLETIN, Swiss Arbitration Association
YEARBOOK	YEARBOOK COMMERCIAL ARBITRATION (International Council for Commercial Arbitration/ Kluwer, annually since 1976)

PART I

THE INSTITUTION

CHAPTER 1

GENERAL CHARACTERISTICS

1.01 Basic principles

Arbitration under the Rules of the International Chamber of Commerce has the following essential features:

Universality: the type of transnational commercial dispute that may be resolved by ICC arbitration is not limited by the nature of the parties' business, nor their nationality, nor indeed by whether they are in the private or public sector.

Geographic adaptability: although the ICC's headquarters are in Paris, ICC arbitrations may be conducted anywhere in the world. In two out of three cases, the seat of arbitration in fact is not in Paris; during the past decade, seat of arbitrations were established in more than 80 different countries.

Openness: there is no in-group of counsel or arbitrators with which parties must cast their fate. Lawyers from all over the world represent their clients directly, without having to resort to any specialized "ICC bar." Parties may choose arbitrators whom they know and trust: 98 nationalities were represented among the arbitrators appointed to ICC tribunals during the eleven-year period from 1989 to 1999 (Appendix I, Table 4).

Institutional supervision: awards rendered by ICC arbitrators are final. The ICC Rules exclude appeal on substantive questions of law or fact, as opposed to the two-tiered systems of some arbitration institutions. On the other hand, the attitude of the institution is not *laissez-faire.* For one thing, the ICC staff relieves the arbitrators of having to deal with the parties regarding payment of fees and expenses. More importantly, although the ICC Court of Arbitration will never substitute its judgment for that of the arbitrators on matters of substance, it will insist that the arbitrators respect rules of form, in order that the award have maximum legal enforceability. It is the Court, not the arbitrators, that finally notifies the award to the parties. Thus an institutional balance is struck between interference and neglect.

Procedural flexibility: how the arbitrators organize hearings, submission of proof, and presentation of arguments is largely left to the discretion of the arbitrators, provided always that they keep the arbitration confidential.[1] The ICC Rules are brief, and express generalities. They impose neither a "continental" nor a "common-law" manner of conducting the proceedings; the parties, and failing them the arbitrators, are free to decide what fits the particular case.

This approach to the resolution of disputes has clearly responded to the needs and preferences of transnational commerce, for the ICC's Court of Arbitration has become the dominant general-purpose institution—as opposed to single trade associations—in the field of international commercial arbitration. This preeminence is manifest whether one refers to the volume of cases, or to the magnitude of amounts in dispute. Furthermore, and once again on both accounts, the business of the ICC Court has accelerated over the past decade. The statistics reviewed in Section 1.02 reflect these observations.

1.02   Volume of cases

Founded in 1919, the ICC adopted its first rules of arbitration in 1922, with the Court of Arbitration being established in 1923. By 1976, 3000 requests for arbitration had been filed with the ICC. In 1998, the Secretariat of the International Court of Arbitration received the 10,000th case. Thus, more than two-thirds of all cases brought to ICC arbitration arose in the last 20 years of its 75-year existence. The Secretariat of the Court can currently expect to receive more than 500 requests for arbitration each year, although a number of the claims are later withdrawn or settled.[2] The registration of claims occurs before they are submitted to the Court for the constitution of the particular arbitral tribunal which will decide the case, which in turn of course precedes disposition by the arbitrators. Cases are not submitted to the Court for further processing unless a payment of US $2000 as the required advance against administrative expense has been made by the claimants. In the records of the

---

1   Article 21(3) of the ICC Rules of Arbitration (reproduced in Appendix II and sometimes referred to below only as "the Rules") excludes third parties from hearings; Article 28(2) makes clear that copies of awards are made available by the ICC to parties alone. Article 1 of the Internal Rules of the Court of Arbitration further stresses the confidential character of the administration of the arbitration. These provisions explain why the ICC authorizes publication of awards only on the condition that it is done is such a manner as to preclude identification of the parties.

2   The statistics which are set forth in Appendix I and analyzed hereafter were first presented in this form by the authors in the first edition of this text in 1983, having been culled from various ICC documents made available to them over the years. In examining the statistics for a given year in the Tables contained in Appendix I, one must bear in mind that the ICC arbitral process is continuous, with the result that different categories of statistics do not necessarily reflect the same group of cases. For example, a request for arbitration filed toward the end of 1997 will be reflected in the statistics regarding the nationality of the parties, but the arbitrators and the place of arbitration may not have been known until 1998, thus falling outside the tables for 1997. Similarly, an arbitrator named in 1997 may have been chosen by a party whose case was brought in 1996.

ICC, a case takes on a "profile" at the time it is submitted to the Court, because it is at this time that arbitrators are named, a place of arbitration is fixed, and basic features of the disputes are recorded. There were 529 requests submitted to the Court in 1999. The number of arbitrations pending at any one time within the ICC system exceeds the annual number of requests considerably. As of 1 January 1998 there were 935 arbitrations pending on the docket maintained by the ICC Secretariat.

No other institution approaches the ICC's universality and volume of cases. Attempted comparisons are transparently unconvincing. For example, the China International Economic and Trade Arbitration Commission (CIETAC) has for several years reported an annual number of requests for arbitration well in excess of that of the ICC. Almost all of these cases involve one Chinese and one non-Chinese party. But the proposition that CIETAC administers the largest number of international arbitrations cannot be taken seriously. For one thing, until CIETAC reveals the amounts in dispute observers will assume that most of its cases involve modest sums of money. Secondly and more importantly, CIETAC is a recognizably *Chinese* institution; most foreigners accept CIETAC arbitration with considerable reluctance, as a matter of negotiating pressure. Until CIETAC can point to cases where *both sides* are non-Chinese, and the dispute is unconnected with China, it is not even in the running with the ICC. Of course, similar criteria should apply to other institutions as well. Thus, while the London Court of International Arbitration at the end of 1997 had 89 pending cases involving at least one non-UK party, and the International Center for Dispute Resolution of the American Arbitration Association registered 280 cases in the 12-month year ending May 1997, these numbers would look far more modest if one eliminated cases involving any U.K. or U.S. party, respectively. As truly international institutions go, there simply is nothing like the ICC Court.

1.03 The stakes

34.9% of the cases submitted to the ICC Court in 1999 involved amounts in excess of US $1 million; 19.8% of these in excess of US $10 million (*see* Appendix I, Table 8).

As for "mega-cases" in which the amounts in dispute exceed US $1 billion, in their practice the authors have come across a dozen in the last decade, and there are doubtless more. These cases generally involve large infrastructure or natural-resources projects, and often implicate a State or another public-sector entity as a contracting party.

It should be noted that parties are effectively dissuaded from claiming astronomical amounts with the intent, for example, to strike terror in the hearts of their adversaries. ICC arbitration costs are related to the amounts in dispute; for that reason, claims in ICC arbitration tend to reflect seriously contested amounts.

The ICC has become the forum for the settlement of some of the more difficult and delicate contemporary international commercial conflicts. Not infrequently, the atmosphere is politically charged and there is little mutual desire to co-operate. Litigation between State entities of countries in which there has just been a revolution and their suddenly disfavored suppliers comes to mind. Or, to take a situation of lesser political tension but nonetheless great difficulty, consider the numerous large claims arising in the wake of the massive excess orders of material—cement in particular—by the Nigerian government in the mid-1970's.[3] There, it turned out that the country simply could not absorb the goods, or even take delivery in its congested ports; refusal to accept contracted shipments was established as a matter of governmental policy (exchange authorizations were rescinded or refused). Even in a perfectly routine ICC case, say between two European companies and involving "only" US $1 million, the international elements of the case nevertheless require skilled professional handling in order to assure the legitimacy of the process and the international currency of the award.

These difficulties should be kept in mind when reflecting on the performance of the ICC and its arbitrators. While the great majority of cases are resolved without a hitch, it is a fact that now and then a party seeking to rely on an award has a difficult time in enforcing it. If the non-respect for the ICC award in such a case is to be considered a casualty of the system, it is to be recalled that in warfare the troops with the highest casualty rates are elite assault forces who are given the most difficult tasks. The U.S. Marines in World War II may have had higher losses than any other service, but that was not a valid ground to judge them less effective. Like elite troops, the ICC's Court of Arbitration gets the hardest jobs; and like them, it cannot always operate unscathed.

1.04   Typical parties to ICC arbitrations

More than half (54%) of the 11,143 parties involved in requests for ICC arbitration during the eleven-year period from 1989 to 1999[4] (Appendix I, Table 5) came from Western Europe; 1,387, or in other words about 12% were from France alone. Among the parties, the fifteen nationalities most frequently represented were, in order, those of: 1) France, 2) the U.S., 3) Germany, 4) Italy, 5) the U.K., 6) Switzerland, 7) Spain, 8) the Netherlands, 9) India, 10) Belgium, 11) Austria, 12) Canada, 13) Mexico, 14) Japan, 15) Sweden.

Comparing the regional origins of parties, over the last eleven years there has been a significantly decreased prevalence of parties from Western Europe. In

---

3   *See e.g.*, Ipitrade International S.A. v. Federal Republic of Nigeria, 465 F. Supp. 824 (D.D.C. 1978); Verlinden B.V.v. Central Bank of Nigeria, 647 F.2d 320 (2d Cir. 1981).

4   Because of the incidence of joint claimants and defendants, there is no fixed correlation between numbers of cases and numbers of parties.

1996, for the first time in the Court's history, they represented less than 50% of the parties involved. Concurrently, there is an important increase from the Far East, Latin America, and Eastern Europe's recently independent states. For instance, over the last eleven years parties from the Far East, who constituted only 3% in 1980, and 6.6% in 1988, now represent 11.2% of ICC users on the eleven year average, and 13.5% in the year 1999.

Latin American countries seem to be overcoming much of their traditional resistance to international arbitration. Parties from Latin America, who constituted only 3.8% of the ICC users in 1987, represented 9.8% in 1999. Latin America is now the fourth most frequently represented region in ICC arbitration after Western Europe, North America and the Far East. This included twelve countries with more than five nationals represented in ICC arbitral proceedings. Overall, the percentage of parties from outside Western Europe in 1999 (48.9%) may be compared with the 41.6% and 33% figures in 1982 and 1977.

Governments occasionally participate in ICC proceedings. Their signature of the contract containing an ICC arbitration clause is held to constitute a waiver of immunity of jurisdiction. More frequently, governments participate in international business through various public-sector entities possessing their own separate legal personalities. Precise statistics concerning these entities are difficult to establish, since many public-sector entities do business under names that cannot be distinguished from those of private-sector companies. 10.1% of the requests filed in 1998 visibly involved a State or a public entity.

One of the challenges facing any international arbitral institution is to establish and maintain universal recognition of its legitimacy. Its usefulness would be limited if it were perceived as biased in favor of parties coming from a certain region, or representing a certain socio-economic system. From the ICC's point of view, it is encouraging that a significant number of cases involve East-West disputes. The ICC Court has a Working Party, established several years ago, which maintains contacts with East block trade organizations in order to examine, establish and promote procedures acceptable to the latter and their non-East block trading partners.

In the nine-year period from 1980 to 1988, approximately the same number of East block parties were claimants and defendants (201 claimants, 159 defendants). A similar observation may be made with respect to Third World parties. While Third World parties had historically been defendants in the overwhelming majority of cases, in 1980-1988 about one-third of Third World parties were claimants, and in 1989-1999 the proportion rose to nearly 50%. This bespeaks increased confidence in and awareness of the system. It may be that this development was helped by the fact that in two of the most publicized ICC awards, Ethiopian and Egyptian claimants not only obtained monetary relief, but were able to enforce those awards in the United States against American defendants.[5] Recent cases increasingly demonstrate the capacity of parties who in the past were seldom active in ICC arbitration to make the system work to their benefit. (*See generally* Section 36.04.)

1.05   Typical subject matter of ICC cases

ICC arbitration can be classified into five categories. The following summary shows the percentage of cases in each category submitted to the Court during the period 1989-1998.[6]

Category (*Percentage*)	1989	1990	1991	1992	1993	1994	1995	1996	1997	1998
1) Foreign trade	39.0	44.2	42.5	40.9	42.1	51.4	45.0	43.8	36.2	32.9
2) Joint venture and construction	26.4	25.4	26.5	13.7	20.3	17.9	20.3	17.2	18.9	26.4
3) Licensing	18	16.4	19.6	23.6	12.1	15.9	15.4	14.4	17.3	19.7
4) Finance	6.0	5.8	2.3	9.8	17.7	11.7	13.0	17.0	14.8	10.8
5) Other (labour, maritime, advertising and real estate)	10.6	8.2	9.1	12	7.8	3.1	6.3	7.6	12.8	10.2

ICC disputes thus maintain their great variety. Maritime disputes fall within the seventh catch-all category; these cases appear to remain largely within the traditional maritime *milieux*, rather than being brought to ICC arbitration.

It would be interesting to have statistics concerning the amounts in dispute correlated by category. It would not be surprising if category 2 ("joint venture and construction"), with less than 20 percent of the case volume, accounts for half of the amount in dispute in all ICC proceedings—and half of the total costs thereof. Such data, however, are unavailable.

As noted above, a substantial number of cases submitted to ICC arbitration concerned governments or governmental entities directly. This fact reflects one particularly salient feature of the ICC process: it is frequently chosen as part of the contractual framework of large investment projects involving the local government and in which neither side is willing to accept the jurisdiction of the other's national courts. Illustrations of highly significant and visi-

---

5   *See* Parsons & Whittemore Overseas Co. Inc. v. Société Générale de l'Industrie du Papier (RAKTA) (Egyptian State-owned company), 508 F.2d 969 (2d Cir. 1974); Imperial Ethiopian Government v. Baruch v. Foster Corporation, 535 F. 2d 334 (5th Cir. 1976); *see generally*, Jan Paulsson, *Third World Participation in International Investment Arbitration*, 1987 ICSID REVIEW—FOREIGN INVESTMENT LAW JOURNAL 19.

6   These statistics are now made available by the Secretariat of the Court of Arbitration and published in the last issue of each annual volume of the JDI. In the previous edition of this book, the authors identified seven categories of cases. Since 1993, the categories presented as "Joint venture and industrial cooperation" and "Construction" are now presented as one category. The category previously presented as "Agency" is now included within the "Foreign Trade".

ble European projects in which contractual relationships subject to ICC arbitration have implicated governments include Eurodisneyland (France) and the Eurotunnel (the U.K. and France).

1.06   Delocalization

While Paris is the seat of the ICC Court, it is not necessarily the seat of ICC arbitrations. Of the 3,393 cases with respect to which the Court in the eleven-year period 1989-1998 either confirmed contractual choices, or fixed seats of arbitration, France—in all but a handful of cases Paris—was the situs in only 1,056, or 31%, of the cases. Indeed, the seats of ICC proceedings were situated in ten Middle Eastern countries, nine African countries, seventeen Asian countries and ten Latin American countries, not to mention the United States (247 times) and Canada. Altogether, ICC arbitrations were held in 83 different countries during the 1989-1999 period.

Nevertheless, as Table 7 of Appendix I shows, the great majority of ICC arbitrations—85%—have their seat in Europe. This fact is hardly surprising, for at least three reasons:

— given the ICC's own location in Paris, parties generally stipulate a European situs for ICC arbitration both as a matter of tradition and as a matter of common sense between the European litigants who in fact are a substantial majority;

— the Paris-based Secretariat can most readily "service" tribunals sitting in Europe within 48-hour mail delivery;

— the ICC Court of Arbitration has an obligation to the parties who rely on it not to embark on adventures that may be politically attractive to the ICC as an institution, but may jeopardize a party's legal position. No matter how much the Court would like to point to its adaptability to locales around the world and extend its acceptance of previously seldom-involved countries, it cannot justify sending parties to countries where international arbitration has not been adequately assimilated by the local legal system.

That ICC arbitrations may take place virtually anywhere means that ICC proceedings have a degree of geographic adaptability which only the International Centre for Settlement of Investment Disputes (ICSID) comes close to duplicating. ICSID, however, was created by a treaty that obliges the signatory States to recognize an ICSID award as though it were a final judgment of their own national courts. Because ICC awards have no such foundation, significant attention must be given to the potential impact of the law of the place of arbitration: by the parties in stipulating a situs; by the Court in fixing the situs absent a contractual stipulation; and by the arbitrators in conducting the proceedings and in drafting their award. All must be concerned to avoid places where international arbitration is legally hazardous and not to proceed in a manner that may give grounds for the local courts to interfere with the proceedings or the award.

As an institution, the ICC has promoted the delocalization of the international arbitral process. The ICC does not want the result of ICC arbitration to differ depending on the situs; the choice of a neutral forum should not be a trap for the unwary. ICC representatives have traditionally combatted any international requirement of double *exequatur*: the obligation to register an award in its country of origin before registration in a second country where enforcement is sought. The 1958 New York Convention on the Recognition and Enforcement of Foreign Arbitral Awards, which had been signed by 121 countries as of October 1999 (*see* Appendix I, Table 10), reflects the ICC view by requiring only that the award be "binding on the parties."

Whether ICC awards may be "a-national" and whether the enforcement jurisdiction may and should execute an award despite the pendency of a challenge in the country where it was rendered are questions which have generated considerable scholarly controversy. One of the present authors has expressed the view that the courts of the place of arbitration should assume a role in international commercial arbitration as one designed to control the *bona fides* of the award on an international, rather than a national, level and that they accordingly should function

> only as an instrument for the control of the conformity of the award to transnational minimum standards such as those embodied in the major international conventions. Unless the parties have agreed otherwise, the judge at the place of arbitration has no mission or capacity to apply his own national criteria to the award.[7]

Whatever one's doctrinal views as to the limits of freeing an award from the authority of the courts at the arbitral situs, it is still the case that parties, the ICC Court, and arbitrators all seek to conform to local strictures as a practical matter: it would be irresponsible to ignore local law simply to demonstrate one's passionate attachment to the principle of delocalization of the international arbitral process. This implies that all concerned must be well informed of the legal consequences that flow from the choice of the seat of arbitration. Does one want interventionist or *laissez-faire* local judges? Does local law give one the freedom to choose procedural rules other than the local ones? For example, under the provisions of French law applicable to international arbitration, one may have arbitration in Paris but subject to the German rules of procedure, or those of the West Gronkshire Traders' Association, or any other rules agreed upon by the parties. Such freedom would be consistent

---

7   *See* Jan Paulsson, *Arbitration Unbound*, 30 INTERNATIONAL AND COMPARATIVE LAW QUARTERLY 358 (1981); *see also*, by the same author, *Enforcing Arbitral Awards Notwithstanding an LSA (Local Standard Annulment)*, 9 ICC BULL. No. 1 (May 1998); *Compare*, William L. Craig, *Uses and Abuses of Appeals from Awards*, in 4 ARB. INT. 174 (1988).

with Article 15 of the ICC Rules which provides that the parties or—failing them—the arbitrators may agree to any rules governing the proceedings "whether or not reference is thereby made to the rules of a procedure of a national law to be applied to the arbitration." In other places, however, local law may hold arbitral proceedings to be invalid unless they conform to local rules. To be cavalier in this respect is to play with fire; if an award is set aside in the country where it was rendered, its international currency is severely impaired.

In addition to the degree of acceptance of arbitral procedural autonomy in the local legal system, it is important to determine the constellation of multilateral and bilateral relationships between the country under consideration as the seat of arbitration and the country or countries where it may become important that the award be effective.

The conclusion here is clear: when in doubt, stipulate a traditional situs. Routine transactions are generally best served by routine solutions. Unusual situations require extensive technical expertise to find tailor-made solutions. A pathological arbitration clause imperils the whole foundation of the contract no matter how carefully the rest of the document has been drafted. Great attention at the time of contracting is certainly merited.

If a party does get into difficulties, however, it may well benefit from the fact that the ICC Court has a stake in assuring that its awards are recognized. While the ICC is neutral during the course of the proceedings, it is no longer neutral once the award has been rendered; it is, after all, an ICC award. The ICC prides itself on the fact that approximately 90% of all awards are complied with voluntarily.[8] If losing parties thought that ICC awards could be resisted, this situation undoubtedly would change. Accordingly, the ICC Court and Secretariat actively seek to assure the *bona fides* of ICC awards, as they are supposed to do under Article 35 of the Rules. And parties seeking to rely on an ICC award quite properly find an ally in the ICC Court and Secretariat.

1.07   Trends in choosing venue and arbitrators

A number of factors suggest that parties choose ICC arbitration because it represents an international and neutral system for the resolution of commercial disputes. Furthermore, there is evidence that the consumers of international arbitration services have certain preferences both as to the kinds of arbitrators and the places of arbitration best suited for ICC arbitrations.

By using the term "international," the authors do not suggest that there is a tidy solution to the problem of delocalization (Section 1.06, *supra*) nor that private parties may by their own agreement alone create public international

---

8   The frequency of voluntary compliance cannot be determined with certainty, since parties do not
     systematically inform the Court as to what happens after awards are rendered; however, this es-
     timate appears consistently in ICC publications.

law obligations devoid of any relationship to national laws. By agreeing to ICC arbitration, however, the parties indisputably give an international dimension to their contract and to its dispute resolution system.[9]

The fact that parties from 168 countries have participated in ICC arbitration in the last eleven years is evidence of the breadth of its appeal. To some extent, this appeal is based on negative factors. The prime motivation of businessmen and sovereign states who agree to ICC arbitration is that it does not possess the potential menaces of national courts, and particularly the national courts of the opposing party. What contracting parties fear is less the application of the adversary's substantive law than the application of foreign procedures, which are based upon foreign language, foreign manners, and foreign policies. Sometimes a party fears, whether justifiably or not, that the courts of the other contracting party's state will favor its own nationals or be subservient to national interests. Parties are sometimes concerned that judicial proceedings may be not only strange and alien, but also simply inappropriate for the resolution of international commercial disputes.

National arbitration associations do not provide solutions in this respect. In the minds of foreign parties, they frequently have the same disadvantages—being foreign and not necessarily neutral—as foreign national court proceedings. This is especially true, of course, where the national arbitration association is that of the adversary's nationality. Thus, there has frequently been a reluctance among non-United States parties contracting with Americans to agree to arbitration under the auspices of the American Arbitration Association, even though this body has established rules especially applicable to international disputes, maintains lists of arbitrators having other than United States' nationality, and indeed ensures that presiding arbitrators must, if the non-US party so requests, be of a neutral nationality. Usually, foreigners accede to arbitration before national arbitration institutions only when they recognize that the body of law and customs of that nation should customarily and naturally be applied.[10]

The unwillingness of a party to leave the merits of a dispute to the national courts of its opposing party is reflected to a substantial, albeit lesser, degree in its unwillingness to have an arbitration take place in its adversary's country of origin. Environmental factors, including the possibility of national court interference with, or review of, the arbitral proceedings, may be imag-

---

9   For further examination of the fit between this international dimension and the requirements of national laws, *see* William L. Craig, *International Ambition and National Restraint in ICC Arbitration*, 1 ARB. INT. 49 (1985), reprinted in Appendix VII.

10   This is the case, particularly as to custom, in respect to the many commodities disputes which are referred to arbitration in London under the Rules of the *Grain and Feed Trade Association* (GAFTA) or the *Federation of Oils, Seeds and Fats Association* (FOSFA); *see* B. Chapman, *FOSFA International Arbitration*, 4 ARB. INT. 323 (1986). It is also true with respect to the resolution of maritime disputes by arbitration in London under English law.

ined to disadvantage the foreign party. It is largely for these reasons that ICC arbitrations frequently take place in neutral countries. Sometimes these fears have no justification, and reasons of language, applicable law, and convenience make the adversary's venue an acceptable choice. When they do not, the third country chosen as the seat of arbitration should have a legal framework which permits and encourages ICC arbitration and the procedural flexibility endorsed by its Rules. Such a venue should also have not only appropriate physical facilities but also a historical background, or at least an expressed governmental interest, of encouraging neutral dispute resolution on its territory. One of the trends that one can witness in ICC arbitration is the development and growth of a number of venues which nationals of the 145 countries participating in ICC arbitration find acceptable.

When the parties choose the site of arbitration in their agreement (a choice which they should always try to make; see Section 7.02 *infra*), they make a positive choice of the legal and physical environment in which their arbitration will take place. In the eleven-year period 1989—1999, 80.7% of all arbitration at sites designated by the parties took place in just five countries: France (31.1% of the sites so chosen), Switzerland (22.7%), the United Kingdom (9.3%), the United States (7.3%) and Germany (4%) (see Appendix I, Table 7).

When the parties fail to agree on a site of arbitration, the ICC Court of Arbitration will make the determination pursuant to Article 14 of the Rules, using criteria discussed later herein (*see* Section 12.01, *infra*). The difficulty in the Court's mission, seeking principally to ensure the enforceability of any award rendered, but also taking into consideration geographical convenience and other factors, leads to a somewhat greater diversity of choice. In the eleven-year period 1989—1999, 76% of all arbitration sites designated by the Court took place in eight countries: France (34.4% of the sites so chosen), Switzerland (13.9%), the United Kingdom (7.8%), the United States (5.9%), Germany (4.7%), Italy (3.3%), the Netherlands (3.1%), and Canada (2.9%) (*see* Appendix I, Table 7). As can be seen, included in these eight are the five countries most frequently chosen by the parties themselves. Switzerland has been frequently chosen because of its reputation for neutrality and its long arbitration history (*see* Chapter 32, *infra*). The choice of Cyprus (never chosen by the parties but 10 times by the Court of Arbitration) seems to be based purely on geographical considerations (*i.e.* an intermediary point between Western Europe and the Middle East/Asia/Africa). In recent years, Singapore, Mexico and Tunisia have, as venues, enjoyed the particular confidence of not only parties but also the ICC Court (*see* Appendix I, Table 7).

The ICC and its Secretariat are aware of the importance of developing countries as consumers of ICC arbitration services, and have been ready to cooperate with national and international organizations to promote ICC arbitration at an appropriate site or sites in the developing world.

It may be that the search has been motivated more by political consideration than by any felt need of the participants in international trade. Except for cases where a party from a developing country has been able to impose its own domicile on its co-contractant as the site for arbitration, it is not clear that parties from developing countries necessarily prefer to have an ICC arbitration in a neutral developing country rather than in a neutral capital exporting country. State entities, which have a great deal of bargaining leverage in negotiating contract terms, including the place of arbitration, may have used that leverage to avoid venues in the capitals of old colonial powers, but not to insist on arbitration in the developing world. Indeed several well known state entities from developing countries regularly and repeatedly choose to hold their ICC arbitration at a neutral site in Western Europe.

This is not to say that ICC arbitrations do not take place in developing countries. During the eleven-year period 1989-1999, 258 ICC arbitrations took place in the Third World. 26 of these arbitrations were at developing world sites chosen by the ICC Court of Arbitration because the parties had not themselves made a choice. Included among the 14 developing world sites chosen by the Court of Arbitration in addition to Singapore, Mexico City and Tunis, were Kuala Lumpur and Kuwait City, each of which was chosen several times (Appendix I, Table 7). The growth of ICC arbitration in the Third World generally is reviewed in Chapter 36.

Just as ICC statistics may be helpful to discern a trend in the sites chosen for arbitration, so may they be useful in examining the criteria used to choose arbitrators. Unless the parties have agreed otherwise (*see* Section 7.01), each party may nominate an arbitrator having its own nationality. It is surprising to note, however, the frequency with which arbitrators from certain countries are nominated by parties having a *different* nationality. These included, in the period 1989-1999, the following numbers of appointed arbitrators having a nationality different from the nominating party: Switzerland (320), the United Kingdom (246), France (238), Germany (222), and the United States (177).

Some of these appointments may have been inspired by the place of arbitration, and some by the language of the contract or its applicable law. It is also most likely that parties conclude that experienced arbitrators with the requisite practical, legal and commercial background can be found in these *milieux*.

The ICC Court's choice of nationality of the presiding or sole arbitrator is frequently based upon the assumption that it is wise to rely on an arbitrator having knowledge of the law and the environment of the seat of arbitration. Where the parties have agreed to the venue, and where it is not the domicile of one of the parties, there is a permitted inference that the parties would not find unacceptable an arbitrator having the nationality of that country. Where the ICC itself picks the seat of arbitration (because the parties have failed to do so), it seeks a country that is an acceptable neutral location for both parties, and a choice of a presiding or sole arbitrator may follow these criteria.

It is for these reasons that the breakdown of nationalities of the arbitrators chosen by the Court bears some resemblance to that of the venues of ICC arbitration:[11]

Swiss	387	(18.2%)
French	315	(14.8%)
British	234	(11.0%)
German	167	(7.9%)
Belgian	144	(6.8%)
U.S.A.	108	(5.0%)

It is notable that the Court of Arbitration has made significant efforts to identify experienced arbitrators from developing countries having the appropriate neutral profile and has named sole or presiding arbitrators with some frequency from Singapore, Mexico, Lebanon and Tunisia (25, 24, 20 and 20 times respectively).

1.08   Length of proceedings

Article 24(1) of the Rules provides that ICC arbitrators are to make their awards within six months of the signature of the Terms of Reference. This rarely happens. The extensions contemplated in Article 24(2) have become commonplace. Nevertheless, in the average case, ICC proceedings are remarkably rapid.

Compilation of statistics in this respect would be rather meaningless. First of all, ICC cases are exceedingly varied. There are enormously difficult cases involving great geographic displacements in which defendants, aided by an oversympathetic arbitrator, do absolutely everything to delay matters. On the other extreme, there are cases in which the parties simply have a gentlemanly disagreement that they would like someone to settle fairly and expeditiously. Indeed a number of ICC awards are nothing but amicable settlements that are formalized—and thus take on a *res judicata* character—just as proceedings were getting under way. One should not blame the ICC Court for failing to act with blinding speed in the former category, nor give it any particular credit for the dispatch with which the latter category is resolved. Second, it often happens that the parties agree to go slowly either because they are involved in settlement discussions or because they simply agree that the preparation of their respective cases is a difficult matter and they prefer to go about it at a measured pace. Obviously, these practices extend the average time of proceedings without any fault attributable to the institution.

---

11   Appendix I, Table 4. It should be noted that in a number of cases the parties jointly nominate an arbitrator to serve as chairman or sole arbitrator. The three most frequent nationalities of such arbitrators are Swiss, French and English. *Id.*

Given these obstacles to meaningful statistics, it would appear sufficient to know that the average duration of an ICC arbitration is between one and two years. When one considers that this result is achieved in international proceedings and that the merits are not subject to review, the record is truly outstanding. One might simply contrast the ICC's performance with that of a national legal system. How long does it take to get a final disposition in a civil case, including appeals? The ICC Court of Arbitration comes out looking rather good in comparison, despite the fact that its clientele and its cases present more complications than those dealt with by ordinary national courts.

1.09   General conclusions

Notwithstanding the emergence of a considerable number of arbitral institutions offering their services to settle international commercial disputes, the ICC has dominated this field since World War II. This means that all types of mistakes committed in the area of international commercial arbitration probably have occurred within the ICC framework. If a party has been sorely disappointed by the process, chances are that its negative experience was with the ICC. There are some institutions with a perfect record—but no cases.

Moreover, the international arbitral process is far from simple, particularly with respect to defendants who have lost all interest in maintaining good relations with the claimants and thus adopt tactics of relentless obstreperousness. Great care and ability are required to give a binding character to a process which has a purely consensual foundation. The frustration one occasionally feels in these difficult cases perhaps is attributed too readily to the institution, which cannot realistically be expected to eradicate the inherent difficulties of the process.

The ICC has the most significant track record, and it is natural that scholarly attention has been focused on points at which the process snags; instances where awards are resisted, arbitrators are asked to be removed, the arbitral clause itself is contested before ordinary courts, and injunctions are sought to stop the arbitrators from proceeding. However interesting they may be, these cases are marginal and should not obscure the fact that the vast majority of ICC proceedings are concluded smoothly and quietly. The result is respected if for no other reason than the growing awareness that resistance is ultimately doomed to failure, given the increased international recognition of the process of commercial arbitration.

ICC arbitration is not a panacea. Dealing in the art of the possible, however, the ICC Court of Arbitration has proved its effectiveness in making resolution of international commercial disputes a matter of routine. This alone is a major accomplishment. As for the very difficult cases, ICC arbitration offers potential solutions in situations which might otherwise have been utterly intractable.

Finally, it bears noting that ICC arbitrators are rarely concerned about being reversed on appeal, or setting bad precedents, or about technicalities which unfortunately require an unfair result in a particular case. Apart from the sheer professional quality of the arbitrators who preside ICC tribunals, who are generally well-known and respected international jurists, these factors go a long way towards explaining why, although of course parties often feel they should have fared better, there is a wide acceptance that ICC arbitral decisions generally do justice on the merits.

CHAPTER 2

THE ORGANIZATIONAL FRAMEWORK

2.01 Introduction

When it is said that a dispute is to be resolved by "ICC arbitration," people often vaguely surmise that the ICC as an institution will decide the case. In fact, the merits of the litigation may be decided by arbitrators without any prior ICC experience, and the proceedings may take place in a city in which no ICC arbitration has ever taken place.

The various tasks for putting into motion, conducting, supervising, and concluding an ICC arbitration are attributed to different institutional organs. The ICC approach to arbitration can therefore be understood only if one analyzes the identity and roles of: the ICC and its National Committees, the Court of Arbitration, the Secretariat of the Court, and the arbitrators chosen for each case.

2.02 The ICC and its National Committees

The International Chamber of Commerce, founded in 1919, is an association of internationally-oriented enterprises and their national organizations. Some 7264 enterprises and organizations in 136 countries are members of the ICC. The purpose of the ICC is to "promote international commerce worldwide," for example by encouraging favorable actions by international organizations and governments. It also seeks to inform the public, quite naturally with a special emphasis on the international business community. In most countries, ICC members have created National Committees which serve as an interface between the members and the ICC headquarters in Paris.

The ICC acts through these National Committees, of which there are now 70 (some of which have become significant organizations in their own right), as well as through a General Secretariat in Paris, which employs some 100 persons. The ICC's Secretary General, Maria Livanos Cattaui, was elected in 1996 after 19 years with the World Economic Forum in Geneva. The supreme organ of the ICC is the Council, which generally meets twice a year. Its President is elected for a two-year term. Members of the Council are appointed by the National Committees, each of which may appoint from one to three members according to its contribution to the ICC budget.

The ICC holds Congresses every three years. These are general assemblies to which all member companies and organizations are invited to send senior representatives. Total attendance in recent Congresses has averaged some 1000 participants. The last four Congresses were held in Hamburg (1990), Cancun (1993), Shanghai (1997), and Budapest (2000).

The annual Conference meets in years when no Congress is held. Conferences are held in collaboration between the ICC Conference Department created in 1996 and national committees. As with Congresses, a different venue is chosen on each occasion at the invitation of a National Committee. Recent Conferences have been held in Madrid, Marrakech, New Delhi, and (in 1998) Geneva.

The ICC has created numerous Commissions (often divided into Steering Groups and Working Parties) appointed by the President and Secretary General in consultation with National Committees. Joint Working Parties are formed occasionally by representatives of more than one Commission. In addition, Special Committees may be designated by the President or Secretary General. The *raison d'être* of Commissions and Special Committees is to consider major policy areas relevant to international commerce, and where appropriate to make recommendations to international organizations and governments.[1]

The ICC's work is thus a mixture of action and reflection. As to the latter, the considerable output of the Commissions and Committees is occasionally published by the ICC. An example of this work is the development of the widely used ICC Incoterms, adopted in 1936, fundamentally revised in 1953, and expanded in 1967, 1976, 1980, 1990, and most recently in 2000, to cover new terms reflecting the evolution of the tools of trade, particularly transport. The Incoterms have become a most useful instrument in drafting international contracts.

A body founded in 1979 and independent from the general ICC structure is the Institute of International Business Law and Practice, the Academic Council of which, while appointed by the President of the ICC, has full independence on policy matters. Led by eminent lawyers (mostly practitioners and professors) of various nationalities, none of whom is employed by the ICC, the Institute

---

1   In addition to the ICC Commission on International Arbitration, there are 15 policy commissions, as listed in Table 1 of Appendix 1, which cover a wide range of sectors such as banking, energy, environment, extortion, insurance, intellectual and industrial property, international trade, marketing, taxation, telecommunications, transport. There are composed of working parties temporarily constituted to undertake specific projects which are afterwards submitted to their parent body.

sponsors and promotes seminars, round-table conferences, research and publications, and holds an annual meeting on a specific theme.

2.03 The Court

The arbitration mechanism has been developed primarily to further the ICC's purpose of facilitating international trade, not to raise revenue. The settlement and prevention of disputes is a natural part of any effort to remove barriers to transnational commerce and investment. ICC arbitration is administered and supervised by the Court of Arbitration, which is one of four ICC bodies concerned with the settlement of international commercial disputes. The other three are:

− the Commission on International Arbitration, which advises on the development of the ICC Rules of Conciliation and Arbitration;

− the International Maritime Arbitration Organization (IMAO); and

− the International Centre for Expertise.

The International Centre for Expertise may be relevant in conjunction with arbitration. It may be called upon to produce independent evaluations and recommendations which might assist the parties in reaching a *modus vivendi*. Knowing what an expert outsider has concluded might temper unreasonable expectations of arbitral proceedings and induce a conciliatory attitude. (*See* Section 38.02).

The Court itself is in fact not a court at all in the ordinary sense of the word; it does not decide cases. Parties never appear before the Court. At the most, they may make written submissions which will be presented to the Court, often with a recommendation, by the Secretariat. The average ICC case comes to the collective attention of the Court for a matter of minutes only. (The Court members individually have full opportunity to study relevant files submitted to them prior to Court sessions.) This distance from the battle reflects the fact that the Court merely supervises the work of arbitrators, who are appointed on a case-by-case basis.

The Court meets in plenary session once a month. In each such session, the Court designates two of its members to sit with the Chairman as a Committee of the Court. Depending on when the Chairman chooses to convene it, this Committee typically sits once a week until the following plenary session. Under Article 5(5)(a) of its Internal Rules, the Court may without restriction "determine the decisions that may be taken by the Committee." Prior to 1998, there were statutory restrictions on this delegation. Given the quantitative evolution of the ICC's caseload, it became unrealistic to require, for example, that all awards be scrutinized in plenary session. Now, the Court is free to expand the scope of the Committee's decision-making as it sees fit. For example, the Committee may henceforward approve draft awards that appear straightforward, but might prefer to hold them over for the plenary session if there is a powerful dissenting opinion. (For the time being, however, the Court proceeds under guidelines, issued in September 1997, which do not allow the Committee to rule on applications to remove arbitrators.)

Article 1(3) of the Rules authorizes the Chairman (or a designated Vice-Chairman) "to take urgent decisions on behalf of the Court" subject only to the duty to report the decision to the full Court. The fact that the scope of this authority is co-extensive with that of the Court itself (and therefore in principle broader than that of the Committee) should be understood in light of the fact that a context of urgency may mean that any formal deliberation would be a purely academic exercise. In practice, decisions of the Chairman alone are likely to be exceptional; decisions of the Committee a matter of routine.

Unlike the Secretariat's officials, the members of the Court are not ICC employees. This goes as well for the Chairman, who bears ultimate responsibility for the work of the Court.[2] Since 1997, the Chairman is Robert Briner, a member of the Geneva bar and notably a former President of the Iran-U.S. Claims Tribunal as well as former Chairman of the International Bar Association's Section on Business Law. Dr Briner's extensive experience as an international practitioner was welcomed by users of ICC arbitration who like to feel that the Court is led by someone who understands practical problems.

The members of the Court are nominated by National Committees.[3] They receive no remuneration, and their reimbursement for expenses is largely symbolic (500 French francs per session attended and per half-day). While the quorum under Article 4 of the Court's Statutes is six, a minimum of fifteen members is generally present, assisted by the Secretary General, the General Counsel and the six Counsel directly responsible for the case files (*see* Section 2.04).

---

2   The great authority of the Chairman is striking when one considers his powers to "take urgent decisions on behalf of the Court" under Article 1(3) of the ICC Rules. Such decisions, according to a former General Counsel of the Court, Sigvard Jarvin, *"Comments on a September 1982 Decision by the Chairman,"* VIII YEARBOOK 206 (1983) are "merely reported to the Court at its next session, but not subject to revision, at least not as a normal measure." Under the Rules, there is no limit to the Chairman's power to take urgent decisions. He has the power to approve awards and, it would appear, even to remove an arbitrator. This may be compared with the power of the Committee of the Court under Article 4(5) of the Court's Internal Rules, which provides that: "The Court shall determine the decisions that may be taken by the Committee." The Court has decided, for the implementation of the 1998 ICC Rules, that the Committee may approve certain awards, although awards raising particular problems will be reserved for consideration by the Court in plenary sessions. The Committee has not been delegated power to deal with the status of an arbitrator (challenge, replacement, removal).

3   The present membership of the ICC Court is listed in Table 2 of Appendix 1.

Detailed treatment of the Court's activities will be given in Part III. For present purposes, they may be summarized as follows:

(i) Determination of the existence of a prima facie agreement to arbitrate

Under Article 6(4) of the Rules, the arbitral tribunal as constituted for each particular case decides questions relating to its own jurisdiction. Article 6(2) provides, however, that in the event one of the parties challenges the existence or validity of the agreement to arbitrate, the Court will allow the case to reach the arbitrators only if it is satisfied of the *prima facie* existence of such an agreement.

Furthermore, in the event an unfounded attempt is made to set an ICC arbitration in motion, a tribunal need not be formed even if the defendant fails to react. This result is obtained by Article 6(2) of the Rules, which provides that if there is no documentary evidence whatsoever of the existence of an agreement to arbitrate, or if the ICC is not sufficiently identified, the Court will inform the claimant that the arbitration cannot proceed even if the defendant has not answered. From time to time, there are clauses specifying arbitration under the rules of non-existent institutions, and parties are tempted to explain that they really meant to refer to the ICC. The Court will refuse to allow arbitration to proceed unless there is at least a possible basis to infer that the parties intended to have recourse to the ICC Rules.

In the event the defendant answers on the merits and does not object to the proceedings, the Court will allow the arbitration to proceed irrespective of a flawed or even nonexistent agreement to arbitrate. A new agreement to arbitrate is deemed to have arisen, the Request constituting an offer and the non-objecting Answer, the acceptance.

Article 6(2) of the Rules makes clear that a decision by the Court to decline the case is of an administrative nature, and that "any party retain the right to ask any court having jurisdiction whether or not there is a binding arbitration agreement."

(ii) Appointment of arbitrators

Chairmen, Sole Arbitrators, or arbitrators in cases in which a party refuses to make a nomination, are appointed by the Court. This does not mean, however, that the Court actually chooses individual arbitrators. There is no in-group of arbitrators who figure on an ICC list. Such a list has no *raison d'être,* because, with respect to Chairmen or Sole Arbitrators, the Court simply determines that a particular nationality is desirable (generally that of the place of arbitration), and requests the relevant National Committee to make a recommendation. With respect to the nomination of arbitrators "on behalf of" recalcitrant parties, the Court turns to the National Committee (assuming one exists) of that party, on the grounds that this most closely conforms to legitimate expectations, although under Article 9(6) of the Rules, the Court is free to make any appointment it deems appropriate if the National Committee fails to make an acceptable recommendation within the time limit set by the Court.

The Court rarely rejects a recommendation from a National Committee. In exceptional cases, the Court will refuse a nomination on the grounds that the proposed arbitrator does not have demonstrated ability and experience to preside an international arbitration. (The Secretary General of the Court endeavors to review with each National Committee the performance of arbitrators proposed by it to avoid recommendations of persons unlikely to be confirmed by the Court.) The Court would, in such a case, ask the National Committee in question to suggest another name. In a word, the way to selection as an arbitrator by the ICC (as opposed to by a party) is generally through various National Committees rather than through the Secretariat of the Court.

How each National Committee goes about its selection process is beyond the scope of this book. Some ICC National Committees have very dynamic arbitration sub-committees which participate actively in the development of ICC arbitration and have a procedure in place for proposing well-qualified arbitrators (the National Committees of France, the United Kingdom and the United States are good examples). Other National Committees have handed over the function of proposing arbitrators to their respective national arbitration associations, thus leaving the matter to specialists and avoiding the possibility that a group of favorite nominees emerge around national committees whose primary business is not arbitration. The choices made by National Committees are not always ideal. It is generally useful and appropriate, provided the parties agree, to allow the two party-appointed arbitrators a short period in which to agree on a chairman. Frequently parties have expressly so provided in their arbitration clause.

Prospective arbitrators are required to inform the Secretariat of any facts which might have a bearing on their independence vis-à-vis the parties (Article 7(2) of the Rules). The reasons for the Court's decision to confirm or reject a nominee are not communicated (Article 7(4)).

A significant addition to the Court's authority was made by the introduction of Article 10 of the 1998 Rules, which provides a workable solution to the vexing problem of multiparty arbitrations. Where the dispute is to be referred to three arbitrators and where there is more than one Claimant or more than one Respondent, each group is required to make jointly any nomination to which it may be entitled. Should the members of a group of Claimants or Respondents fail to make such a joint appointment, the Court may, under Article 10, appoint all members of the Tribunal and designate one of them to act as Chairman.

(iii) Determination of the place of arbitration

Many contracts specify the place of arbitration. In the absence of such a provision, the Court will choose an appropriate place of arbitration given the particular context of each case.

(iv) Determination of fees and expenses of the arbitrators, and establishment of the amount of deposits

The arbitrators may give indications as to the amount of time they have spent on the case and list their expenses. The Court fixes the amount of advances on costs as well as the costs of the arbitration with reference to the ICC Schedule of Costs.

(v) Approval of arbitrators' Terms of Reference

Before hearing a case, ICC arbitrators prepare Terms of Reference defining the issues to be resolved and establishing basic matters of procedure. Technically, under Article 18 of the Rules, the Court needs to approve the Terms of Reference only if one of the parties has refused to sign them. In practice, the Court examines the Terms of Reference even in cases in which they are agreed, thus giving the arbitrators added assurance that they are on the right track. In the event that the agreed Terms of Reference seem deficient, the Court will suggest that they be revised. As always, the Court will not interfere with respect to matters of substance; it seeks to assure compliance with formal requirements.

(vi) Deciding challenges against arbitrators

Prejudiced, biased, incompetent, or non-performing arbitrators may be challenged before the Court. If, after having considered the concerned arbitrator's comments, the Court decides he should be replaced, the initial appointing procedure is repeated. This means that theoretically a party could nominate a never-ending series of clearly challengeable arbitrators in an effort to sabotage the proceedings. In practice, the authors have not encountered this phenomenon. Under Article 7(4) of the Rules, no reasons are given for the Court's decision on challenge motions.

(vii) Extension of time limits

Deadlines for the parties' initial submissions (such as the Answer to the Request for Arbitration) and for the submission to the Court by the arbitrators of Terms of Reference and draft awards may be extended for good cause by the Court. The two-month limit for Terms of Reference (Article 18(2) of the Rules) and the six-month time limit for awards (Article 24(1) of the Rules) are extended if the Court "decides it is necessary to do so." In practice such extensions (at least for awards) have become routine. This is hardly surprising given the unrealistic nature of these deadlines in many, if not most, international proceedings. The process of extending the deadlines does, however, trigger a review mechanism; the status of *every* pending case is thus re-examined at regular intervals.

(viii) Authorizing two arbitrators to conclude an arbitration

Another important addition to the Court's authority by virtue of the 1998 Rules relates to situations where an arbitrator has died or been removed at a late stage of the proceedings. This is known as a "truncated tribunal." It is especially important to provide a safeguard against a partisan arbitrator-*saboteur* who might be tempted to resign in order to derail an arbitration which shows signs of not heading toward the outcome he favors. Article 12(5) of the Rules allows the Court to decide that the remaining two arbitrators may go forward without replacing the disappearing arbitrator.

(ix) Approval of awards

Under the 35th and final Article of the ICC Rules, entitled "General Rule," the Court has the duty to "make every effort to make sure that the Award is enforceable at law." This is an important concern when the Court "scrutinizes" draft awards proposed by tribunals as it is required to do under Article 27. Once again, for better or for worse, the parties must live with the decision of the arbitrators on matters of substance; this is what they accept in agreeing to ICC arbitration. The Court never corrects alleged errors of fact or law; it simply acts to assure the formal sufficiency of the award. Most experienced ICC arbitrators can be counted on to render irreproachable awards. But no one is perfect, and it is at this stage of scrutiny that an illogical, incomprehensible, or incomplete draft might be sent back to the arbitrators for clarification; here the quality control of the ICC arbitral process is exercised.[4]

This function seems to have been successfully carried out for a long time. According to one study,[5] only four awards were set aside by local courts during the 1972-1975 period, which corresponds to approximately 0.5% of the awards rendered. Only around 6% of ICC awards, according to the former Director of the Court a few years later, were even challenged.[6] This is a commendable record indeed given the multinational complexities of the cases submitted to ICC arbitration.

2.04   The Secretariat

The Secretary General of the Court heads the Secretariat and has overall responsibility for all of its work. Since 1996, the Secretary General is Horacio Grigera Naón, an Argentine lawyer qualified both in his own country and in the United States. Mr Grigera Naón began his career in an internationally-oriented law firm in Buenos Aires, and subsequently worked as senior counsel

---

4   The Court also reviews any corrections or interpretation given by the arbitral tribunal pursuant to Article 29 of the Rules, a provision introduced with the 1998 reform.

5   *See* Gillis Wetter, II THE INTERNATIONAL ARBITRAL PROCESS, 153 (1979)

6   Remarks of Tila Maria de Hancock, *in* Alan Shilston, *A View from the 1981 Annual Conference of the Chartered Institute of Arbitrators*, 47 ARBITRATION 255 (1982).

at the International Finance Corporation in Washington. He is also a former member of the ICC Court, representing the Argentine National Committee.

The Secretary General's authority has been significantly expanded by virtue of the 1998 ICC Rules. For example, under Article 9(8), he may confirm arbitrators who have filed unqualified statements of independence, or qualified statements which have not given rise to objections. (If he considers that the nominee should *not* be confirmed, he refers the matter to the Court.) The objective of this innovation was to save time, avoiding the necessity of waiting for a session of the Court to confirm nominations that appear trouble-free.

An even more important innovation is that of the provisional advance, introduced by Article 30(1) of the 1998 Rules. It provides that the Secretary General may establish an amount to be paid entirely by a claimant who wishes to have the arbitration commence without waiting for the respondent to determine whether and when it will pay its share. (The provisional advice is intended to cover the costs of the proceedings until the Terms of Reference have been drawn up; *see* Chapter 15.)

The Secretary General may also, after consultation with the arbitral tribunal, direct the latter to suspend its work if advances have not been paid. This function becomes particularly important in circumstances where he sets a time-limit (of not less than 15 days) after which relevant claims or counter-claims are considered withdrawn. (Article 30(4); Article 1(3) of Appendix III.)

The Secretary General is assisted by an American Deputy Secretary General, Anne-Marie Whitesell, and a Canadian General Counsel, Fabien Gélinas.

Immediate responsibility for the progress of each case falls on the Counsel, generally young lawyers. They are identified to litigants as being responsible for the file. As of early 2000, there were six Counsel: Denis Bensaude (France), Andrea Carlevaris (Italy), Brooks Daly (U.S.), Katherine Gonzalez-Arrocha (Panama), Detlev Kühner (Germany), and Edouardo Silva Romero (Colombia).

The Secretariat routinely handles cases in the English, French, German and Spanish languages.[7] Other languages may require *ad hoc* arrangements. At the level of the Court cases are discussed in one of the two working languages: English or French.

When a Request for Arbitration is filed with the Court, the Secretary General assigns the case to one of the Counsel. The decision is based on language capacity, experience with similar cases, and of course availability given existing case load.

---

[7]   Forty percent of the cases that arose in 1980 required the French language, 40% English, 15% German and 5% others; remarks of Tila Maria de Hancock, *id*. Although the authors are not aware of updated statistics, it is safe to assume that the English proportion has expanded significantly in the course of the 20 intervening years.

With the help of an Assistant and a secretary (who together form a permanent "team"), each Counsel takes responsibility for all aspects of each case assigned to him or her. Accordingly, the members of these teams become persons with whom the parties or their representatives are in touch. As a matter of day-to-day operations, practitioners of ICC arbitrations are likely to have all their dealings with one of the Counsel and his or her team.

Upon receipt of a Request for Arbitration, the parties are informed not only of the identity of the Counsel assigned to the case, but also that of the Assistant and of the secretary, and the telephone extension numbers of all three. Counsel and Assistants on the same team may *not* take vacation or otherwise be absent at the same time. There is even a "duty officer" during the Christmas holidays.

Routine matters have been expedited by recruiting and training capable Assistants and secretaries who may give perfectly reliable information as to the status of the case.

In addition to dealing with the parties, the Counsel prepare reports for the Court on the cases entrusted to them. These reports are particularly important in regard to specific action required of the Court. During the sessions of the Court or of the Committee of the Court, the Counsel are present as well as the Secretary General and the General Counsel, and may be called upon for oral explanations.[8]

In one respect the 1998 Rules have reduced the role of the Secretariat. Under the previous Rules, the Secretariat drew the attention of claimants to the lack of a *prima facie* agreement to arbitrate, and the Claimant would then have the right to require that issue to be determined by the Court itself. Under Article 6(2) of the 1998 Rules, in order to save time any issue as to the *prima facie* existence of an agreement to arbitrate is directly and immediately submitted to the Court.

Last but not least, the Secretariat plays an active role in connection with constituting the arbitral tribunal: liaising with National Committees about prospective candidates, obtaining statements of independence, and soliciting comments from parties about nominees. Similarly, the Secretariat organizes the flow of comments of parties and arbitrators in the event of a challenge to an arbitrator.

2.05   The Arbitrators

High-quality arbitrators are the *sine qua non* of a satisfactory arbitral process. In the event a three-man tribunal is used, two arbitrators are generally named by the parties. The ICC's ability to control the quality of these

---

8   *See generally* Horacio A. Grigera Naón, *The Role of the Secretariat of the International Court of Arbitration*, ICC BULL. SPECIAL SUPPLEMENT: THE NEW 1998 ICC RULES OF ARBITRATION 18 (1997).

party-nominated arbitrators is limited. The ICC Rules do not require that an arbitrator have a nationality different from the party who nominated him, nor that he have particular professional qualifications. This means that the Court can intervene only negatively, by refusing to confirm an arbitrator who is not "independent" of the parties as required by Article 7(1) of the Rules. The grounds for challenge, as well as an in-depth analysis of the meaning of the word "independent," are beyond the scope of this discussion (*see* Section 13.03). Suffice it to say that a current or even former employee or consultant (such as a lawyer) of a party should not be nominated without the informed consent of the other party.

The chairman of the tribunal (or the sole arbitrator) sets the professional tone of arbitral proceedings; it is here that the quality of an institution is put to the test. The ICC can point to its extensive experience in large, complex, and varied transnational litigation from which it has developed an institutional capacity to provide suitably experienced international arbitrators.[9]

The Court itself does not generally choose arbitrators unless the arbitration clause specifically so requires. In most instances it merely decides which National Committee should propose a name. If the arbitral clause specifies Copenhagen as the place of arbitration, the Court will generally request (unless one party is Danish) that the Danish Committee nominate a chairman or sole arbitrator. Unless he appears unfit, the Court will then formally *appoint* him; just as it formally *confirms* arbitrators nominated by parties. If no situs is specified, the Court will decide on a place, taking into account factors of convenience, fairness, and above all local rules conducive to arbitral efficacy. The Court will then typically ask the National Committee of that country to propose an arbitrator.

Over the years, certain National Committees have been solicited more consistently than others. As a result, these National Committees have developed significant expertise in choosing dependable arbitrators suitable for various kinds of disputes. Table 4 of Appendix I indicates the most frequent nationalities of ICC arbitrators in the period 1989-1999. These statistics show that certain nationalities appear more frequently as ICC nominees than as party nominees; such is the case particularly for Switzerland, Austria and Belgium. This is hardly surprising, since these countries are frequently chosen as the neutral seat of arbitration; it makes sense for the ICC to appoint a local arbitrator.

A reverse pattern applies to US national arbitrators. Relatively few are appointed by the ICC. Such a result also is predictable since circumstances in which a US national is named by the ICC ordinarily would require that there be two non-US party litigants. (It is exceedingly rare that a US party defaults

---

9   For a discussion concluding that "references to an international arbitration 'mafia' not only lack a solid evidentiary basis, but in fact do not seem to reflect any probing reflection," *see* Jan Paulsson, *Ethics, Eligibility, Elitism*, 14 J. INT. ARB. 13, 19 (1997).

in nominating an arbitrator, which means that the US National Committee is seldom called on to appoint a US national on a defaulting party's behalf.) If both parties were US nationals, they would only rarely use ICC arbitration. If only one were a US national, a US Chairman or Sole Arbitrator would ordinarily be out of the question. It is unlikely that two non-US parties would want arbitration in the United States, and this for geographic reasons alone. Accordingly, cases in which US nationals act as Chairmen or Sole Arbitrators are rather few, and generally involve a US national residing in Europe or parties who exceptionally find the US to be a convenient situs—such as South American and European adversaries who might want an arbitral situs in Miami.

CHAPTER 3

COSTS

3.01   Principles of assessment

Parties often complain about the costs of ICC arbitrations: both the amount of the advance they must pay at the outset of the proceedings and the amount of the final reckoning. Table 9A of Appendix I illustrates the costs with differing amounts in dispute. For instance, a dispute involving $1 million will result in an administrative charge of $16,800, and fees per arbitrator ranging from a minimum of $11,250 to a maximum of $53,500. If the dispute involves $100 million, the figures are $75,800 (administrative charge) and $61,750 minimum / $260,000 maximum (arbitrators' fees).

The arbitrators' fees are established with reference to a Sole Arbitrator. Where three arbitrators are involved, Article 2(3) of Appendix III to the Rules (Costs and Fees) provides that the Court has the discretion, rather than the obligation, to increase the fee. In practice, the minimum assessment for three arbitrators tends to approach a trebling of the minimum for one arbitrator. On the other hand, it is rare in large cases that the fees approach the theoretical maximum of three times the highest amount for a Sole Arbitrator.

It may be useful in some cases to contact the Secretariat, before filing a Request for Arbitration, to determine what the assessments are likely to be. The Secretary General will often suggest that a Sole Arbitrator, rather than a three-man panel, be used to save costs. With very small cases, parties are even advised to consider an alternative means of resolving their dispute, as the stakes may not warrant the expense of setting international machinery in motion.

3.02   Is ICC arbitration too expensive?

Statements that ICC arbitration is expensive are meaningless in the abstract; the cost must be evaluated in relation to the alternatives. Certainly, ICC arbitration seems cheaper than abandoning one's rights altogether. Litigation, even in one's own home courts, is not necessarily a less expensive alternative, given the possibility of one or more appeals. More importantly, it simply is not always reasonable to expect that one's home forum will be acceptable to a foreign contracting party. ICC arbitration is too often compared—unrealistically and unfairly—with a perfect world in which there are no administrative difficulties, no judicial prejudice against foreign parties, no language problems, no uncooperative parties, and where the just always prevail at no cost to themselves.

Those who are interested in a more practical approach might simply ask whether what the ICC provides is worth its price. The question can never be put to rest definitively. The following observations, however, are relevant to an assessment of the cost-efficiency of ICC arbitration.

(i) Complex litigation results in expensive proceedings

A promissory note should not ordinarily be made subject to ICC arbitration. If the face amount of the note is substantial, the cost will be high even though the case is easily managed and the legal and factual issues very limited. National legal systems often have special procedures to expedite claims under financial instruments. International disputes subject to ICC arbitration are usually more complicated and the stakes are often high. It is not startling to find that the costs of such cases are substantial. In fact, the costs of litigation in complex cases are high even in national courts where the court costs are small and the judge is paid by the taxpayer.

The most expensive international arbitration the authors have encountered in practice was not an ICC case, but an *ad hoc* proceeding involving many weeks' hearings, simultaneous translation by a team of expert translators, and bilingual overnight verbatim transcripts by equally proficient court reporters. The cost of these hearings, independent of arbitrator or counsel fees, approached US $1 million. Even more astonishing costs were projected in an arbitration that was not international at all, but an "ordinary" English arbitration between U.K. companies. After 120 days of hearings, the costs in that case, which involved a controversy as to a shipbuilder's compliance with technical specifications, exceeded one million pounds sterling, with an estimated 100 days of hearings remaining.[1]

From time to time at the end of a case—particularly if there is a settlement—parties write to the ICC Court requesting reconsideration of assessments. (Fees are in fact often reassessed in the event of early settlement.) They go into great detail about how relatively little time was spent by the arbitrators and the Secretariat on the matter and conclude that, say, a cost of $200,000 is unjustified. These vociferous protests, of course, may be formulated by counsel who have generated fees in excess of $1 million, doing—and

---

1   Succula Ltd. and Pomona Shipping Co. Ltd. v. Harland and Wolff Ltd., [1980] 2 LLOYD'S L. REP. 381.

perhaps quite properly so—everything in their power to bring out every document, every witness, every piece of evidence and certainly not concentrating on keeping the case simple and economical. When the case is large, it is fair to say that one gets what one pays for if the following is provided: experience, quality, and the promise of a first-class product—a legally solid award having international currency.

(ii) It is very difficult to make meaningful comparisons

For large cases, ICSID arbitration is probably less expensive than ICC arbitration, primarily because the parties stand to benefit from the World Bank's infrastructure, and because arbitrators' fees are calculated on a per day rate. Such a general statement, however, cannot be advanced with respect to any other arbitral institution equipped to handle complex international arbitration. As for *ad hoc* proceedings arranged outside an institutional framework, they often turn out to be frighteningly expensive. The parties think they avoid administrative expenses, but in point of fact the tribunal they set up must create its own *sui generis* administration. In addition, the back-up insurance of a Secretariat experienced in hundreds of proceedings is absent; there is the danger of an "incidental" procedural oversight which might result in a challengeable award.

(iii) The payment-for-services-rendered approach is more complex than it might seem

There are no easy answers, no obvious reform which the ICC "ought" to adopt. The one most often suggested is that arbitrators' fees should be based on services actually rendered, on the basis of a daily rate. The choice (in the form of a rebuttal) appears to be rather straight-forward: a plodding arbitrator who allows the proceedings to go on and on with little direction, but who charges only a modest $1,000 a day for his 40 days of confused efforts; or a dynamic and incisive arbitrator who manages to lead the parties to defining, presenting, and arguing the case rapidly, spending only a few working days but expecting an "outrageous" remuneration of $20,000. The adoption of a rigid *per diem* system would tend to make such dynamic arbitrators disappear, and bring out the plodders. To work properly, the system must reward efficiency—not create an incentive for arbitrators to make the game last longer. In international arbitration, the danger exists that if only one of three arbitrators decides he wants the proceedings to be prolonged, he will find ready means to do so.

It is worth noting that the London Court of International Arbitration (LCIA) has chosen to fix arbitrators' fees on the basis of time spent on the case. The LCIA's 1998 Schedule of Fees and Costs provides that arbitrators' fees should fall within "bands" of £800 to £2,000 "per normal working day" and £100 to £250 per hour for fractional or overlong days.

With a three-man tribunal in a complex case, it is clear that arbitrators' fees may quickly become substantial. It is impossible to make categorical statements about the relative costs of ICC arbitrators as opposed to LCIA arbitrators, just as it is impossible to assert that one approach or the other is the best for all cases. Each method has its advantages and disadvantages, and each may, if well administered, be applied with sufficient flexibility to achieve reasonable solutions.

(iv) Windfalls to arbitrators could and should be avoided

Whenever a case has been settled early or was resolved far more easily than anticipated, or when the amount in dispute is enormous, the Court should disregard the Schedule in order to avoid unjustifiably high arbitrators' fees. An example of this occurred some years ago when a large case was settled before any issue had been argued; there had been a single day-long meeting to draft the Terms of Reference. Even after partial refund of the deposit, each arbitrator was given a fee of some $40,000.

This kind of jackpot approach has no place in international commercial arbitration; it corresponds more to the image of the occasionally lucky business "finder" than to that of a reputable profession. A *garde-fou* was needed. Article 18 of the Court's 1988 Internal Rules introduced the notion, reiterated in Article 2(2) of Appendix III of the 1998 Rules, that arbitrators' fees should reflect "the time spent, the rapidity of the proceedings and the complexity of the dispute" irrespective of the Schedule; had this rule been in effect at that time, one might assume that the arbitrators' windfall described above would not have occurred. Stephen Bond, the Court's Secretary General, stated in an unpublished speech given in 1989 that "the ICC Court has the discretion to go above or below the scale itself when circumstances would so require in order to prevent either unjust enrichment or an insufficient recompense for work done in a particular case." (This discretionary authority finds a textual basis in Article 31(2) of the 1998 Rules). Such a clear statement of policy should reassure litigants, and calm the ardor of the occasionally-tempted arbitrator who feels that the ICC Schedule gives him a set of personal acquired rights.

(v) Paying to go first-class gives the right to expect first-class service

The ICC Secretariat should provide a degree of responsiveness, efficiency, and general service-mindedness commensurate with the considerable rates it charges for its services.

(vi) Foresightful parties can minimize costs by intelligent drafting

It is a fallacy to think that ICC arbitration cannot be streamlined to suit small cases. Indeed, even an international dispute involving well less than $100,000 can be handled cost-effectively if the parties draft an arbitration clause providing that:

– there will be a sole arbitrator;

– the arbitrator will be directly appointed by the President of the ICC Court; and

−the parties accept that the arbitrator may decide without holding any hearings (documents only).

3.03   The problem of advances on costs

Interests from advances on costs made by parties are not credited to them and have become an important source of revenue for the ICC. As a result, parties to ICC arbitrations subsidize ICC operations which may have little direct relation to their particular arbitration. By way of justification, the ICC points out that its arbitration process is not limited to its Paris-based staff and a mass of files in an office. The process is linked to the ICC as a whole. Court members are nominated by ICC National Committees, which also frequently play a significant role in the selection of arbitrators, and sometimes assist in encouraging a losing party to honor an award. The arbitration Rules are elaborated in consultation with the ICC Commission on Arbitration. Various ICC personnel, from the Secretary General to the accounting department, spend time on arbitration matters. There is no doubt that the prestige of the ICC lends a special cachet to awards rendered under its aegis, and thus enhances compliance with them—whether voluntary or otherwise. In brief, ICC arbitration is not disassociable from the rest of the ICC, and the ICC therefore considers it justifiable that income from arbitrations contributes to general overheads. Finally, if it is correct, as the ICC maintains, that the administrative costs charged to parties in arbitrations do not balance the expenses of running the Secretariat, those charges would have to be increased if the ICC were not to benefit from interest income from advances.

Initially, advances on costs, which until 1988 were referred to as "deposits" (*see* Chapter 14, *infra*), were conceived as a means of ensuring that neither the Secretariat nor the arbitrators incurred out of pocket expenses on the parties' account. The advance was fixed as a function of anticipated actual costs; a simple case involving three Paris-based arbitrators sitting in Paris would require a lesser advance than a case to be heard in Athens, with a New York lawyer, a London Q.C., and a Greek professor, and with an anticipated site visit to a factory in Mombasa.

Over the years, however, the purpose of the advances has demonstrably changed. The amounts have increased to such a degree that the advance evidently corresponds to the ICC's estimation of the total costs and fees of the arbitration. In other words, the advance has become a *security device* rather than a fund from which running expenses are met. Advances of several hundred thousand dollars have been requested and paid in; these obviously do not represent an estimate of actual outlays. On this footing, the ICC has no reason to resist the concept of alternative security devices, in particular bank guarantees.

That it once did so can be explained only by the fact that interests from advances constituted a significant and independent source of ICC revenues.[2] Aware of criticism of the system, the ICC, as a result of several studies, introduced in 1986 measures permitting a spreading out over time of the payments required as security for fees and expenses and permitting in limited circumstances the use of bank guarantees.

In their 1998 revision, the ICC Rules have introduced the notion of a *provisional* advance, entirely payable by the claimant and intended only "to cover the costs of arbitration until the Terms of Reference have been drawn up" (Article 20(1)). This provisional advance should "as soon as practicable" be replaced by the ordinary advance (the provisional advance then being considered as a partial payment of the latter). The point of this innovation—which is applied in individual cases at the discretion of the Secretary General—is to speed up the constitution of the arbitral tribunal, especially in cases where urgent measures are required and it appears counterproductive to allow a respondent to slow the process down by taking its time in responding to requests for payment of its share of the ordinary advance. (This and other aspects of the financial aspects of the process are explained further in Chapter 14.)

The ICC's incentive to maintain a reasonable costs structure is its knowledge that if the parties find the ICC's practices unacceptable, they may amend their arbitration clause at any time, and, wisely or not, opt for an alternative mechanism for settling their dispute.

3.04 Consequences of failure to contribute

Three questions are often asked about the relationship between ICC arbitration costs and procedure:

> (i) What happens if the defendant refuses to advance its share of the costs? Under Article 30(3) of the Rules, the claimant must advance the entire sum—and indeed *must* do so if the case is to go forward. This does not mean that the defendant is foreclosed from presenting its case (although it may not present a counterclaim if a separate advance has been established for it and not paid). If the claimant prevails and recovers all costs under the award and the defendant does not pay the award voluntarily, the advance nevertheless will be used to pay the fees and costs. At this point, the possibility of forcible execution by ordinary courts becomes paramount for the unhappy claimant—unless moral satisfaction is enough.

---

2   At the end of 1977, the total amount of arbitration deposits held by the ICC exceeded 38 million French francs. *See* Gillis Wetter, II THE INTERNATIONAL ARBITRAL PROCESS 152 (1979). The ICC has not publicized the amount since then, but it is safe to assume it has increased by several multiples.

(ii) If the claim is for $1 million, and the defendant counterclaims for $100 million, must the claimant pay half of the large deposit triggered by the large counterclaim? A substantial disproportion between claim and counterclaim is one of the elements that may cause the Court to accede to the claimant's request for the establishment of separate advances under Article 30(2) of the Rules. Such requests are examined by the Court on a case-by-case basis, taking account of all relevant circumstances. Should separate advances be established, each party is requested to pay all of the advances relating to its claim. If the defendant refuses to pay the advance on account of its counterclaim, the claim would then be heard alone.

(iii) What happens if the arbitrators have decided the case and drafted the award, but the final assessment has not been paid by the parties? The Secretariat will not "notify" the award to the parties under Article 28(1) of the Rules. Indeed, the draft award would probably not even be submitted to the Court for scrutiny under Article 27 of the Rules until the full advance has been paid in.

3.05 Cost reforms

Any suggestion that the ICC is impervious to the concerns of users would be wrong. To take an important example, in the years 1984-1986 studies were made by financial experts and by arbitration "user" groups. These groups were formed after consultation with National Committees, and were comprised principally of lawyers from various countries having long experience with ICC arbitration, and of outside accounting and management consultants. These studies resulted in modifications of the Schedule of Arbitration Costs in 1986 (the Schedule is published as Appendix III of the ICC Rules). These changes were confirmed and reinforced by the modifications of the ICC Rules which entered into effect on 1 January 1988.

The 1988 reforms consisted of four principal measures, of which the following three have been maintained under the 1998 Rules:

(i) Each Request for Arbitration must be accompanied by an advance payment of $2,000 with respect to the administrative expenses (Article 3, Schedule of Conciliation and Arbitration Costs). The sum had previously been $500. Accordingly, nuisance claims were discouraged, and a more realistic minimum charge for processing the Request was established. As of 1998, the amount is $2,500.

(ii) The administrative charge which is used to defray the expenses of the ICC Secretariat and of the Court of Arbitration was made subject to a "cap" or flat rate. As of 1998, the rule, as set down in Article 4(2) of Appendix III to the Rules, is that "where the sum in dispute is over US$ 80 million, a flat amount of US$ 75,800 shall constitute the entirety of the administrative expenses." Even when the amount in dispute exceeds this sum, the administrative expense to which the ICC is entitled is not increased.

(iii) Bank guarantees for up to 50% of the advance to cover estimated costs of arbitration are accepted by the Court of Arbitration in lieu of a further cash deposit in cases where one party has fully paid in cash its 50% share, and must then also cover a defaulting party's share of the costs. The acceptability of bank guarantees is intended to lighten the burden of a party who must make up the default of the opposing party in order for the arbitration to proceed. The 1998 edition of Appendix III to the Rules includes more precise details of this mechanism in Articles 1(5), 1(6), 1(8) and 1(9).

The fourth of the mechanisms relating to cost devised in 1986 was founded on a commendable intention, but turned out to be burdensome. The idea was to provide for staggered advances in order to counter criticism that the ICC was unjustifiably benefitting from a full up-front deposit of the entirety of costs which in fact corresponded to services rendered and disbursements made well into the future. So instead of requiring each party to advance 50% of the costs at the outset, the ICC in 1986 called for 25% to be paid initially by each side, and the remaining 50% in equal shares prior to the entering into effect of the Terms of Reference. In practice, this system of staggered advances produced unwanted complications and delays, especially since the file could not be transmitted to the arbitral tribunal until the first set of staggered deposits had been paid in. (The process appeared particularly formalistic and unnecessary when a hurried claimant was perfectly prepared to provide sufficient initial funds, but the Secretariat nonetheless had to go through the process of giving the defendant an opportunity to pay its share—occasionally declined after somewhat tactical hesitation.)

In 1998, as stated in Section 3.03, the Rules introduced the mechanism of Provisional Advances (Article 30(1)), by which the Secretary General may in appropriate cases allow the claimant to advance all funds required to take the case to the stage of the Terms of Reference, the notion being that full (not staggered) advances should be paid in equal shares "as soon as practicable" (Article 30(2)). The transmission of the file to the arbitral tribunal no longer necessarily awaits payment of advances; rather, the file goes unimpeded to the arbitral tribunal but the Secretary General (after consultation with the tribunal) may direct that the proceedings be suspended if funds are not paid in. The test of this flexible method will doubtless be the pragmatism with which it is applied.

The impact of these mechanisms is considered *infra* in Chapter 14, "Advance to Cover Costs" and Chapter 21, "Determination of Costs."

PART II

THE AGREEMENT TO ARBITRATE

CHAPTER 4

TYPES OF ARBITRATION AGREEMENTS

4.01 Special submission ("compromis")

A dispute may be referred to arbitration by the means of a specific agreement to that effect, reached after the dispute has arisen. In continental parlance, such a special submission to an arbitral jurisdiction is referred to as a *compromis*, as opposed to the *clause compromissoire* (arbitration clause) contained in the agreement which has given rise to disagreement, and therefore necessarily drafted before the particulars of the future dispute are known.

It is rare that a case comes to ICC arbitration by way of a special submission. ICC arbitral jurisdiction is almost invariably based on an arbitration clause contained in the initial contract. On the other hand, it is not infrequent, even where ICC arbitration has been stipulated in the contract, that the parties reach agreement after a given dispute has arisen with respect to certain particulars of the proceedings (place of arbitration, identity of the presiding arbitrator, mutually convenient procedural rules, and the like). Such agreements may better conform to the specific character of the case having arisen than the original arbitration clause. They are perfectly valid. (After all, the parties could at any time agree to cancel the arbitration clause and bring the matter before an ordinary court.) They are more realistically defined as amendments to the arbitration clause rather than as special submissions reflecting a partial novation of the arbitration clause. The new agreement will relate to modalities rather than the principle of arbitration; it is because the parties know they cannot escape arbitration that they both have an incentive to make ac commodations.

4.02 Contractual clause

Arbitration clauses inserted in broader agreements are the typical means by which the jurisdiction of international arbitral tribunals is created.

The principal agreement frequently incorporates the arbitration clause by reference, for example, to standard rules providing among other things a system

of arbitration (see Section 5.08). Occasionally, the agreement to arbitrate results from a simple exchange of letters or telexes comporting such a reference. The key feature of the arbitration clause, as opposed to special
submission, is that it is entered into before any dispute has arisen. Accordingly, the issue of consent may be more controversial than in the context of a
special submission, where both parties specifically agree to the scope and
procedure of an arbitration tailored to an existing conflict.[1]

Arbitration agreements are typically categorized as referring to either "ad hoc
arbitration" or "institutional arbitration." The latter category may be subdivided to distinguish institutions that supervise the proceedings from those
that merely appoint arbitrators.

4.03   Ad hoc (non-administered) arbitration

Parties wishing to provide for arbitration but also to avoid a supervising institution sometimes draft so-called *ad hoc* clauses, intended to be self-executing in the sense that they oblige the parties to initiate and proceed with
arbitration without the assistance of a permanent institution.

In recent years these clauses have tended to become longer and longer, and
are frequently drafted with great care and intelligence.

Nevertheless, parties should generally be cautioned *against* adopting *ad hoc*
arbitration clauses in an international contract, no matter how well drafted.

In practice, once litigation ensues, agreements for *ad hoc* arbitration have created adversity (and in some cases disaster)[2] for the claimant. It is impossible
to foresee and provide for all the procedural issues which may come up. (In
the case of institutional arbitration, such issues are handled by reference to a
pre-established body of rules.) Moreover, every time the defendant creates delays, or fails to file pleadings or evidence, or refuses to participate in hearings, the claimant has an unattractive choice: A) to ask a judge to intervene,
thus ending up in an ordinary court, which is exactly what one wanted to
avoid by drafting the arbitration clause, or B) to ask the arbitrators to proceed
by default, which will increase the risk that their award would be challenged
by the losing party. Although ICC arbitrations on occasion proceed by default
(*see* Section 15.03), ICC arbitrators are rather more comfortable in such a case
than would be *ad hoc* arbitrators, because their mandate to proceed would be
backed up by clear institutional practice. More importantly, the presence of
the ICC Court of Arbitration as a supervising authority, and the deference of

---

1   As a result, the formal requisites may be greater for a contractual clause than for a special sub-
    mission. *Compare* Articles 1443 and 1449 of the French New Code of Civil Procedure, discussed
    in RENÉ DAVID, ARBITRATION IN INTERNATIONAL TRADE 198 (1985).

2   For a case where a Belgian party, having opted out of ICC arbitration in favor of an *ad hoc* ar-
    rangement, lost even the possibility of taking its Iranian cocontractant to arbitration, *see* ICC
    Case 3383, I ICC AWARDS 100, 394.

national courts to its administrative supervision as agreed by the parties, makes it almost unheard of for a party to ask a judge to intervene in matters of procedure.

Whatever its merits in a purely domestic situation, the *ad hoc* arbitration clause in an international setting (where potential means of creating delays are innumerable) frequently frustrates the party seeking to enforce the contract.

It is understandable at the negotiation stage, when both sides are cooperative, that the parties wish to provide a highly informal (and, they imagine, inexpensive) arbitration "within the family." But once relations are empoisoned, only the defendant is happy with the *ad hoc* clause—and its enjoyment increases in direct proportion with its bad faith. At that point in time, the imagined savings of the fees of an institution like the ICC seems small indeed when compared with the loss of effective litigation procedures.

In this connection, it is instructive to refer to a Report to the International Law Association's Montreal Conference of 1982 which concluded that:

> in the vast majority of cases . . . arbitration with parties from developing countries are dealt with on the basis of those few arbitration rules and arbitration institutions which have found wide acceptance in international commerce. Indeed especially in commercial relations between parties from developing countries and from industrialized countries, in view of the fundamentally different economic and legal backgrounds of the parties, the necessary legal security which one tries to achieve for both parties will not be achieved in *ad hoc* arbitration, but only institutionalized arbitration because only there can answers normally be found to the many sometimes complicated questions of procedural and substantive law that may have to be solved during a dispute.[3]

One feature of *ad hoc* arbitration which occasionally leads to unpleasant situations is that the arbitrators typically set their own fees. This creates an inherently delicate tension in that the person who is about to judge the merits of a controversy first asks the litigants for payment. Experienced and reputable arbitrators generally handle this situation well, but there are instances of over-reaching which can leave a party feeling dismayed, particularly if its adversary for tactical reasons instantly accepts an unreasonable fee structure. Such situations do not arise in ICC arbitration, where the parties' only discussion about fees and costs is conducted with the Secretariat.

Institutional arbitration clauses are thus generally to be favored. The authors are aware of Professor Pierre Lalive's views to the contrary,[4] but in this in-

---

3   Professor Karl-Heinz Böckstiegel, *rapporteur, Arbitration between Parties from Industrialized and Less Developed Countries*, 60 INTERNATIONAL LAW ASSOCIATION, REPORT OF CONGRESS 269.

4   *See Avantages et inconvénients de l'arbitrage ad hoc, in* ETUDES OFFERTES À PIERRE BELLET 301 (1991).

stance beg to differ. If it appears useful to opt for an *ad hoc* mechanism *after* a dispute arises, this can readily be done if one's adversary is reasonable.[5] If he is not, it will be a relief that he cannot play on the strings of mischief available in an *ad hoc* setting.

4.04 Institutional arbitration

Many institutions are involved in the field of arbitration, whether they merely appoint arbitrators or also administer practical and financial aspects of the process. An even greater number of institutions *purport* to carry out such tasks. For a number of years, the ICCA Yearbook contained a special section listing individual arbitral institutions. By 1998 (Volume XIII), the list had grown to 75 entries. Most of them had little if any real experience. It is dangerous to entrust inexperienced institutions with important problems, and even worse to select an organisation which turns out to lack staying power and ceases to exist. An undiscriminating list may create false impressions. Accordingly this feature of the Yearbook was discontinued. Faced with a proposal to refer to an unfamiliar institution, the contract drafter must be exceedingly wary. (In this connection, it should be understood that UNCITRAL is not an arbitral institution. Reference to the UNCITRAL Arbitration Rules therefore leads to *ad hoc* arbitrations (*see* Section 4.03).)

Institutional arbitration implies the existence of a permanent institution that administers rather than merely promotes arbitration. (To refer in an arbitration clause to an organization that supervises research and seminars, but does not conduct arbitration, would be a classic example of the pathological clauses discussed in Chapter 9.) Such institutions will set the arbitral process in motion by constituting an arbitral tribunal, sometimes from an exclusive list of arbitrators, more often giving the parties some liberty in selecting the members of the tribunal. In case of disagreement, the institution will invariably appoint the necessary arbitrator.

Some institutions provide for two-member tribunals, with an umpire to be called in only after the two arbitrators have heard the entire case and found themselves unable to agree. Many institutions have a "two-tiered" system comprising a board of appeals capable of modifying an initial award. Indeed, under the European Wholesale Potato Trade Rules ("RUCIP" under its French acronym), the arbitral appeals tribunal may sit in a different country than the

---

5   If it is not done correctly, an agreement to opt out of ICC arbitration in favor of an *ad hoc* procedure may lead to disaster. *See supra,* Note 2.

first tribunal.[6] Under some rules, if the defendant fails to name an arbitrator, the arbitrator named by the claimant becomes the sole arbitrator.[7]

It is vital to have an understanding of the basic functioning of an institution before entrusting it with all future disputes under an international contract. It is a very different thing to agree to arbitration run by an institution that requires that all arbitrators be chosen from its internal list comprising only nationals of a given country,[8] than to submit to a process where one may be certain that a majority of the arbitrators will not be of the nationality of one's adversary. Although the former procedure might yield a fair result, the same is true of the national courts of one's adversary, which often are nonetheless viewed as insufficiently neutral.

Typically, institutions that administer arbitrations fade into the background, and are intended to do so, once the arbitral tribunal has been constituted. The arbitrators proceed as they wish, and render their award, completely unfettered by the institution. In the presumably rare instances where the arbitrators have done something fundamentally wrong, it is left to national courts to intervene.

4.05 Supervised institutional arbitration

Supervised arbitration is a special type of institutional arbitration. One might say that it is a mechanism designed to reduce the supervisory role of national courts by creating an autonomous supervisory capacity within the arbitral institution. Since by hypothesis parties opting for international arbitration are seeking to stay out of national courts, the development of such autonomous supervisory functions appears justified and, as described in Chapter 2, characterizes the ICC approach to arbitration.

As stated in Chapter 2 and analyzed in greater detail in Chapter 20, the ICC Court of Arbitration does not decide cases and never substitutes its judgment for that of arbitrators acting under its aegis. ICC arbitration is not two-tiered.

---

6   In a decision of March 9, 1978 the German Supreme Court upheld against a German buyer an award by the RUCIP appeals tribunal seated in Brussels, in favor of a Dutch buyer whose claim had at first been rejected by a first-level RUCIP tribunal seated in Hamburg, 1978 WERTPAPIER-MITTEILUNGEN 573, extracts in English *in* IV YEARBOOK 264 (1979).

7   An award, rendered under such a rule in London in accordance with the English Arbitration Act 1950, was enforced against an Italian company by the Court of Appeal of Venice, decision of 21 May 1976. 1976 RIV. DIR. INT. P.P. 850; extracts in English *in* III YEARBOOK 277 (1978).

8   Awards rendered by East European arbitral tribunals comprising only local nationals have been upheld abroad. For example, an award rendered by three Czech nationals, acting as arbitrators at the Czechoslovak Chamber of Commerce, against a German company and in favor of a Czech company, was enforced by the German Supreme Court in a decision of 6 March 1969, 1969 WERTPAPIER-MITTEILUNGEN 671; extracts in English *in* II YEARBOOK 235 (1977). The *Bundesgerichtshof* stated, id. at 236, that the German party could not complain about the composition of the tribunal, as it should have realized that the arbitrators would all be Czech nationals and that the German party could not influence their selection.

On the other hand, ICC awards are not issued by the arbitrators themselves, but by the Secretariat of the Court, and only upon the Court's approval. The Court comprises jurists from many countries, experienced with the recurring task of obtaining awards that are valid internationally. The Court is therefore in a position to give advice and make suggestions to the arbitrators with respect to matters of form, and to keep them from committing procedural errors endangering the validity of awards. The ICC is jealous of its awards; nothing is less pleasing to the ICC Court than to have one of its awards set aside by a national court. This institutional self-interest benefits parties seeking to rely on the process. There is hardly one of the ICC Rules that has not been tested by disappointed losers before the French courts (Paris is a common site for ICC arbitration, *see* Appendix I, Table 7); all have stood the test.[9] In sum, with supervised arbitration the parties benefit from the *cachet* of the supervising institution; a presumption of legitimacy attaches to an award by virtue of its having been issued by the ICC, and which it would not have if the three arbitrators acted alone. For example, an American judge faced with a request to enforce an ICC award has a significant number of precedents of ICC awards being enforced in the U.S; in such a situation, he may feel more at ease ordering an American party to respect a multi-million dollar award than if it had simply been rendered by three individuals, two of whom were unheard-of foreigners and the third—the American—having written an outraged dissent.[10]

The ICC Rules are flexible with respect to issues of procedure. In fact, as will be seen in Part Three, they are very general, leaving it up to the parties (or, failing them, the arbitrators) to establish procedural rules. This feature of ICC arbitration makes it appropriate for parties to consider making a certain number of points clear in the arbitration clause itself, and the essential purpose of this Part Two is to call attention to those points. Occasionally, parties wonder why the ICC Rules are not more detailed, and whether this would not save time for negotiators. (Such questions will survive the 1998 reform, for although the new Rules are more detailed, they still leave most practical issues to be dealt with in light of the circumstances of individual cases.) The answer is that the ICC cherishes the flexibility of its Rules, which makes it possible to adapt custom-made rules to a given contract. In this manner, parties from different cultural and economic systems may reach accommodation with respect to their arbitration clause. This flexibility has made it relatively easy to propose ICC arbitration to parties from State-directed economies, who otherwise tend to find objectionable details in the rules of other institutions located in the industrialized West.

---

9   The REVUE DE L'ARBITRAGE since the mid-1960's has published many of these cases, for too numerous to cite here. Issues relating to the 1998 ICC Rules will be considered in their respective contexts in Part III.

10 *See* Parsons & Whittemore Overseas Co Inc. (U.S.) v. Société Générale de l'Industrie du Papier (RAKTA) (Egypt), 508 F.2d 969 (2nd Cir. 1974); summarized *in* I YEARBOOK 205(1976).

CHAPTER 5

THE VALIDITY OF THE ARBITRATION AGREEMENT

5.01   Introduction

Part Five explores the legal principles that give the arbitral process its obligatory force: the rules of law that give authority to the actions and decisions of international arbitrators. The present Chapter examines how parties may validly establish such authority by contract.

Article II(1) of the 1958 New York Convention on the Recognition and Enforcement of Foreign Arbitral Awards provides that:

> Each Contracting State shall recognize an agreement in writing under which the parties undertake to submit to arbitration all or any differences which have arisen or which may arise between them in respect of a defined legal relationship, whether contractual or not, concerning a subject matter capable of settlement by arbitration.

This language does not limit the body of laws to which an arbitrator might refer to determine whether a case is "capable of settlement by arbitration"; it certainly does not forbid his looking to a law chosen by the parties themselves.

One interpretation, giving the widest possible effect to the contractual stipulation of arbitration, would be for the arbitrator to accept the agreement to arbitrate if the dispute is "capable of settlement by arbitration" under any relevant law. This *favor validitatis* approach is reflected in Article 178(2) of the Swiss Federal Law on Private International Law ("LDIP") which provides that:

> an arbitration agreement is valid if it complies with the conditions of either the law chosen by the parties, the law applicable to the substance of

the dispute, in particular the law applicable to the main contract, or Swiss law.[1]

Arbitrators do in fact look first and foremost to the agreement of the parties in assessing the validity of the reference to arbitration. Thus, a Swedish arbitrator, asked to hold that his nomination had been ineffective because not made by the third party defined in the agreement but by the ICC Court of Arbitration (at said third party's request), stated:

> I agree so far with the defendants that an arbitration clause may have, as to its scope, to be interpreted strictly. Such maxim, however, may not have the same effect when it comes to the appreciation of the validity or the effectiveness of an arbitration clause. On the contrary when inserting an arbitration clause in their contract the intention of the parties must be presumed to have been willing to establish an effective machinery for the settlement of disputes covered by the arbitration clause.[2]

The present Chapter should be read with this presumption of the validity of the parties' agreement in mind. We shall necessarily review a number of issues with respect to which arbitrators and judges have questioned the effectiveness of the parties' agreement to arbitrate. These issues are important theoretically, but their intellectual complexity should not obscure the fact that in most arbitrations the validity of the agreement is not an issue.

5.02   Capacity of the parties

Normally speaking, whether parties have the capacity to agree to arbitration depends on their own national law.[3]

---

1   The U.S. Supreme Court has stated that the parties' intentions are foremost, and any doubts to be resolved in favor of the arbitrability of disputes; Moses H. Cone Memorial Hospital v. Mercury Construction Corp., 460 U.S. 1 (1982); Mitsubishi Motors Corp. v. Soler Chrysler-Plymouth Inc., 473 U.S. 614 (1985). *Cf.* Article 59(c) of the World Intellectual Property Organization Arbitration Rules of 1994:

> "An Arbitration Agreement shall be regarded as effective if it conforms to the requirements concerning form, existence, validity and scope of either the law or rules of law applicable [to the substance of the dispute] or the [arbitration law of the place of arbitration]".

2   Preliminary Award in ICC Case 2321/1974, I ICC AWARDS 8. *Accord*, Interim Award in ICC Case 4145/1983, I ICC AWARDS 558; Interim Award in ICC Case 5029/1986, II ICC AWARDS 69; Amco Asia Corp. *et al.* v. Indonesia, ICSID award on jurisdiction of 25 September 1983 (three unanimous arbitrators), 23 ILM 351, at 359 (1984); Oriental Commercial and Shipping Co. *et al.* v. Rosseel N.V., 609 F. Supp. 75 (SDNY, 1985); Renusager Power Co. v. General Electric Co. and the International Chamber of Commerce, judgment of the Supreme Court of India of 16 August 1984; unpublished, excerpts *in* X YEARBOOK 431, at 433-4 (1985); *contra*, ICC Case 4392/1983, I ICC AWARDS 473 (sole arbitrator sitting in Zürich).

3   Article V(1)(a) of the New York Convention makes clear that capacity is to be determined not by the law chosen by the parties, but by the law applicable to them; it is accepted that this refers to their "personal" law (that of their nationality or domicile). Thus, the tribunal sitting in Stockholm in ICC Case 4381/1986, II ICC AWARDS 264 (a dispute between a French claimant and an Iranian public law company), stated, at 1104, that "each party's capacity to agree to arbitration is governed by that party's personal law."

An important exception to this general rule is the situation where the capacity to arbitrate may be directly or indirectly affected by the party claiming lack of capacity. Specifically, it would be contrary to fundamental principles of good faith for a state party to an international contract, having freely accepted the arbitration clause, later to invoke its own legislation to contest the validity of its agreement to arbitrate.

This principle of good faith has been applied by ICC arbitrators as an imperative norm perceived without reference to any specific national law. A leading precedent in this connection is a 1971 award[4] dealing with a claim by a state not to be bound by the arbitration clause, where the tribunal stated that:

> international *ordre public* would vigorously reject the proposition that a State organ, dealing with foreigners, having openly, with knowledge and intent, concluded an arbitration clause that inspires the cocontractant's confidence, could thereafter, whether in the arbitral proceedings or in execution proceedings, invoke the nullity of its own promise.

The Swiss Federal Law on Private International Law specifically provides in Article 177(2) that a state party to an arbitration agreement "cannot rely on its own law to contest the arbitrability of a dispute or its own capacity to be a party to an arbitration;" the same holds for State enterprises.[5]

"All problems concerning the legal status of a legal entity are governed by the law of the State in which it has its seat (*siège*) and from which it derives its legal capacity," Swiss Federal Tribunal, decision of 5 May 1976, Société des Grands Travaux de Marseille (France) v. People's Republic of Bangladesh *et al.*, ARRÊTS DU TRIBUNAL FEDERAL 102 IA 574; summarized *in* V YEARBOOK 217 (1980).

Accord under Italian law, decision of the *Corte di Cassazione* of 27 April 1979, Compagnia Generale Construzione "COGECO" S.p.A. v. Piersanti, 15 RIV. DIR. INT. P.P. 565 (1979); summarized *in* VI YEARBOOK 229 (1981) (Italian company's employment contract with an Italian bricklayer to work in Saudi Arabia; *held*, the employer could not oblige the employee to arbitrate in Saudi Arabia because Italian law does not allow for the settlement of labor disputes by arbitration, the status and capacity of persons being defined by the law of the State of which they are nationals.)

4   ICC Case 1939/1971, cited by Yves Derains, 1973 REV. ARB. 145. *See also* ICC Cases 7263/1994, XXII YEARBOOK .92 (1997); 1803/1972, I ICC AWARDS 40; 3327/1981, I ICC AWARDS 433; 3896/1982, I ICC AWARDS 161, 481; 4381/1986, II ICC AWARDS 264; 5103/1988, II ICC AWARDS 361; as well as the American Arbitration Association award, Revere Copper and Brass v. Overseas Private Investment Corporation, 17 ILM 1321 (1978), summarized *in* V YEARBOOK 202 (1980).

5   The French Supreme Court has held that legal incapacity of French State-owned entities to submit to arbitration is inapplicable in the context of international contracts, *in* the *Galakis* case, 1966 BULLETIN CIVIL I-199; the motive for this exceptional freedom being the recognition of the "needs" and "usages" of international commerce. *See* Henri Battifol, *Arbitration Clauses Concluded between French Government-Owned Enterprises and Foreign Private Parties*, 7 COLUMBIA JOURNAL OF TRANSNATIONAL LAW 32 (1968). The Courts of Tunisia have followed this example in holding Tunisian State enterprises to their agreements to arbitrate; *see* Société Tunisienne d'Electricité et de Gaz (STEG) v. Société Entrepose, *Tribunal de grande instance* of Tunis, 22 March 1976, published *in* French in 1976 REV. ARB. 268; summarized in English *in* III YEARBOOK 283 (1978); BEC-GTAF v. State of Tunisia, *Tribunal de premiere instance* and *Cour d'appel* of Tunis, 17 October 1987 and 1 February 1988, both published in French in 1988 REV. ARB. 732. *Ac-*

Obviously, it is always advisable to ascertain the capacity of one's cocontractant to agree to arbitration.

National laws may for this purpose make a distinction between domestic and international contracts. Thus, for example, persons who do not qualify as merchants under the law of a given country may, as a general proposition, be considered unable to make a prospective waiver of judicial remedies (i.e., by accepting to arbitrate), but an exception may be made for cases where their contract is of an international character.[6]

5.03   Authority to represent parties

The notion of *capacity* to agree to arbitration is different from the question of power to *represent* and bind a party. The former is an enquiry as to what the parties are able to do in the contract; the latter concerns the very presence of a party in the relationship (*see also* Section 5.09).

Doubtless in most cases the question whether the person signing on behalf of a party has the authority to do so would not be treated differently depending on whether one were examining the main contract or the agreement to arbitrate. It nevertheless merits mention in this discussion of the validity of agreements to arbitrate simply to call attention to the problem.

It is difficult to accept that the law "chosen" by a Mr. X to be applicable to a purported contract would determine whether Company ABC is bound by Mr. X's signature. Whether or not there is a valid agency with respect to the repre-

---

cord as for Greece, see case No. 565 of 1965 of the Supreme Court, 1966 EPHIMÉRIS ELLION NOMIKON 289; discussed *in* ANGHELOS C. FOUSTOUCOS, L'ARBITRAGE INTERNE ET INTERNATIONAL EN DROIT PRIVÉ HELLÉNIQUE 263 (1976); as for Algeria, M. Issad, 1977 REV. ARB. 236; as for Spain, BERNARDO CREMADES, ESTUDIOS SOBRE EL ARBITRAJE 105-113.

See generally Jan Paulsson, *May a State Invoke Its Internal Law to Repudiate Consent to International Commercial Arbitration?* 2 ARB. INT. 90 (1986). The Italian Supreme Court in 1996 upheld an ICC award that rejected a contention by Tunisian defendants that as public sector entities they could not under their own law enter into binding arbitration agreements, SAEPA & SIRPE v. Germanco srl, XXII YEARBOOK 737 (1997).

For the purposes of enforcement of arbitral awards against foreign sovereigns in countries that have legislation dealing with immunity, such as the U.S. and the U.K., acceptance of an arbitration clause may be deemed to constitute waiver of immunity irrespective of the internal law of the foreign State. *See. e.g.*, Ipitrade International S.A. (France) v. Federal Republic of Nigeria, 465 F. Supp. 824 (D.C. 1978); 13 ILM 1395 (1978); summarized *in* IV YEARBOOK 337 (1979). In the United States, amendments introduced in 1988 to the Arbitration Act, 9 U.S.C. § 15, and the Foreign Sovereign Immunities Act, 28 U.S.C. § 1605(a)(6), made this principle a matter of statute.

6   In French law, *see* the leading *Hecht* case. *Cour de cassation*, decision of 4 July 1972; 1972 JDI 843; 1974 REVUE CRITIQUE DE DROIT INTERNATIONAL PRIVE 82; 1974 REV. ARB. 67. *See also* the 21 May 1997 judgment of the Court of Cassation in the *Jaguar France* case, BULL. CIV. 1, no. 159, 107; 1997 REV. ARB. 537 with a favorable comment by Emmanuel Gaillard; 1998 REVUE CRITIQUE DE DROIT INTERNATIONAL PRIVÉ 87 with a strongly critical comment by Vincent Heuzé. Similar reasoning has been used in recent Belgian cases to overcome a law which had previously been held to invalidate arbitration agreements in exclusive distributorship agreements; *see* XXII YEARBOOK 631 and 637 (1977).

sentative is therefore not to be determined by reference to the proper law of the contract between the two principals, but by reference to the law that determines the relationship between the alleged representative and the principal sought to be bound. Courts throughout Europe have in this respect followed the principle of *locus regit actum*. Thus, two Italian parties were held by their own courts to be obliged to arbitrate on the basis of an agreement concluded in Paris through a broker and providing for arbitration in London, although Italian law requires that a power of attorney be in writing and the authority of the broker in question was established by oral proof only. The fact that such proof was acceptable under French law satisfied the Italian *Corte di cassazione* that the Italian principals should be obliged to honor the agreement to arbitrate.[7]

It is likely that international arbitrators will interpret questions of authority of representatives liberally, on the grounds that international trade usages demand that one overlook formal flaws in corporate action if as a matter of fact corporate consent is evident. This may be determined by conduct or communications which implicitly but clearly ratify the acts of the representative, and induce the confidence of the cocontractant.[8]

---

[7]   Decision of 25 January 1977, Total Soc. It. p.a. (Italy) v. Achille Lauro (Italy), 17 Rassegna dell'Arbitrato 94 (1977); summarized *in* IV Yearbook 284 (1979). *See also* the following decisions: *Spain*, decision of the *Tribunal superior* (Supreme Court) of 11 February 1981, La Ley, 27 April 1981, No. 146; summarized *in* VII Yearbook 356 (1982) (award rendered in London in favor of Finnish shipowner enforced against a Spanish charterer despite latter's argument that the power of attorney given by the Finnish party to its party solicitor was insufficient under Spanish law; Finnish law should apply as the place where the power of attorney had been granted). *Germany*, decision of the *Landgericht* of Hamburg of 16 March 1977, summarized *in* III Yearbook 274 (1978) (award rendered in Hamburg in favor of a German party against an Italian party set aside on the grounds that German law should not have determined the question whether an Italian broker had the authority to represent the Italian principal; given that that was the place where the power of attorney was granted and the place of residence of the representative, Italian law, which unlike German law requires a written power of attorney, should be applied).

But see the decision of the Greek *Areios Pagos* (Supreme Court) of 14 January 1977, Agrimpex S.A. (Greece) v. J.V. Braun & Sons, Inc. (U.S.) 25 Nomikon Vima (1977) 1126: summarized *in* IV Yearbook 269 (1979) (New York agent for Greek party could not bind the latter to arbitration on grounds that Greek law required powers of attorney to take the same form as the act for which it is intended; since the arbitration agreement must be in writing under the New York Convention, the same was true for the power of attorney; the Court noted, however, that the Greek party could have validly ratified the agreement if it, rather than only the agent, had participated in the arbitration).

The Court of Appeal of Naples has held, decision of 17 March 1979, Scheepvaartkantoor Holwerda (Netherlands) v. S.p.A. Esperia di Navigazione (Italy), 1979 Il diritto marittimo 377; summarized *in* VII Yearbook 337 (1982), that a broker's authority is satisfactorily established under Italian law if it is granted by telex.

[8]   *See* to this effect the award rendered in 1996 by a five-member tribunal operating under the rules of the Paris Chamber of Arbitration in a case where an Egyptian corporate defendant alleged that the chairman of its board did not have the authority to accept an arbitration clause since such an act requires a "special mandate" under the Egyptian Civil Code. The arbitrators dismissed this objection on the "principle of presumptive mandate," given that "the claimant concluded a contract in good faith with the official representative of the defendant, and the latter let it be under-

The Supreme Court of Italy has stated that the absence of a valid power of attorney is a defense that should be raised by the principal who contests the agent's authority; it cannot be invoked by the other party in situations where the represented principal does not contest the representative's acts.[9]

An ICC arbitrator has noted that lawyers' powers of attorney to represent a party in arbitration may entitle them only

> to act in the framework of the ICC arbitral tribunal, and . . . not expressly authorize them to renounce from the arbitral clause on behalf of their clients.[10]

It should be recognized that the issue of authority of agents and other representatives tends to be a question of private law, involving neither the interests of the State nor those of third parties. This makes the matter easier to deal with than the question of capacity to agree to arbitration, which is an area where national laws have set forth policies limiting the realm of freedom to provide for arbitral jurisdiction. Of course, as noted in Section 5.02, national laws often provide for wider possibilities of referring to arbitration in an international context than in a purely domestic contractual relationship.

5.04   Autonomy of the arbitration clause

Normally, the arbitration agreement is to be deemed separate from and independent of the contract in which it is contained. This autonomy (or severability[11]) of the arbitration clause is a conceptual cornerstone of international arbitration. It is often confused with the notion of *compétence-*

---

stood that its Chairman may enter into an arbitration agreement," XXII YEARBOOK 30 (1997). *See also* ICC Cases 7263/1994, XXII YEARBOOK 92 (1997); 4667/1984, unpublished, quoted *in* Yves Derains, Comment, II ICC AWARDS 297, 338; 5065/1986, II ICC AWARDS 330; the 5 March 1980 award of the Arbitration Court of the Chamber of Commerce and Industry of Czechoslovakia, unpublished; extracts *in* XI YEARBOOK 112 (1986). *But see* ICC Case 5832/1988, ICC CASES 352, 536 (arbitrators sitting in Switzerland held that an Austrian defendant was not bound by an agreement to arbitrate proposed by its duly authorized representatives as part of the conditions of an "order letter" when the final contract was signed by employees lacking written formal powers of representation as required under Austrian law, rejecting the argument that there could be ratification by conduct), and the unenthusiastic commentary by Guillermo Aguilar Alvarez, II ICC AWARDS 356.

U.S. courts have held principals bound to arbitrate under notions of estoppel, Sunkist Soft Drinks, Inc. v. Sunkist Growers, Inc., 10 F. 3d 753 (11th Cir. 1993), *cert. denied*, 115 S. Ct. 190 (1994); Usina Costa Pino S.A. v. Louis Dreyfus Sugar Co., 933 F. Supp. 1170 (S.D.N.Y. 1996), and apparent authority, Republic of Nicaragua v. Standard Fruit Co., 937 F. 2d 469 (9th Cir. 1991), *cert. denied*, 503 U.S. 919 (1992).

9   Decision of 19 November 1978, Metallgesellschaft A.G. (FRG) v. Motosi Aldo (Italy) *et al.*, summarized *in* VI YEARBOOK 232 (1981).

10   ICC Case 3383/1976, I ICC CASES 100, 394.

11   It may be argued that the word "severability" reflects a more modest vision than "autonomy," in that it denotes merely *potential* or *occasional* as opposed to *invariable* distinctness. The fact is however that the French *autonomie* is making inroads with its English cognate whereas

compétence, which relates to the authority of an arbitral tribunal itself to decide, although generally only in the first instance, whether it has jurisdiction. But unlike *compétence-compétence*, which in most situations is a matter of procedure, the autonomy of the arbitration clause is a substantive principle. Thus, in a legal system which did not accept *compétence-compétence* but upheld the autonomy principle, a contention that a contractual claim could not be heard in arbitration because the entire contract was void would have to be decided by a judge, but the latter would then send the matter to arbitration if it appeared that the autonomous arbitration clause itself was not necessarily affected by the invalidity of the contract. By the same token, arbitrators applying the usual rule of *compétence-compétence* would have to declare themselves without jurisdiction if they found the contract to be void and if the applicable law (unusually) did not recognize the autonomy principle.

Whether applied by courts or arbitrators, the autonomy principle presumes that even though the parties may have signed an invalid contract they nevertheless expressed a separate and valid intent that any dispute arising in connection with the contract should be resolved by arbitration. That intent is then viewed as extending to cover the consequences of the invalidity of the contract (assuming the arbitral tribunal in fact finds it to be invalid).

It follows that as long as a national court called upon to rule on a challenge to the award does not consider that there was a case of invalidity going to the arbitration clause itself, the arbitrator's finding as to the validity of the main contract is as conclusive as any other element of his decision on the merits.

The motivating force behind the establishment of the autonomy of the arbitration clause in international contracts is the plain desire to uphold the validity of the agreement to arbitrate. The principle is not easy to justify as a matter of pure logic. In a comprehensive and often cited essay in support of the autonomy of the arbitration clause[12] Judge Stephen Schwebel reached the conclusions that 1) the theory is sound, 2) as a matter of practice, the principle "has been sustained by the terms and implications of arbitration conventions and rules, and by the case law, whether of public international law, international commercial arbitration, or national arbitration," and 3) scholarly support for the principle is "broad and compelling." Nevertheless, it is difficult to maintain that the autonomy principle is satisfactorily justified by reference to the parties' presumed intent. (As Judge Schwebel puts it, parties

---

"*séparabilité*" is not gaining currency in French. (For an effort in this direction, *see* however Pierre Mayer, *Les limites de la séparabilité de la clause compromissoire*, 1998 REV. ARB. 359.) The latter may be more correct, but for present purposes the words are treated as interchangeable.

At any rate, the very title chosen by two Australian authors, Andrew Rogers & Rachel Launders, *Separability—the Indestructible Arbitration Clause*, 10 ARB. INT. 77 (1994), suggests that the notion of severability per se is not necessarily conceived in a guise of modesty.

12 Stephen Schwebel, *The Severability of the Arbitration Agreement*, *in* INTERNATIONAL ARBITRATION: THREE SALIENT PROBLEMS 1 at 60 (1987).

"typically . . . intend to require arbitration of *any* dispute not otherwise settled, including disputes over the validity of the contract or treaty."[13]) One might well retort, to the contention that the parties should be presumed to have intended that validity issues be finally determined by the arbitral tribunal, that it is more plausible to presume that the parties intended to create a valid contract, and if that was not the case all bets are off. In this light, the theoretical construct that an arbitration clause is to be viewed as a second and independent agreement ("when the parties to an agreement containing an arbitration clause enter into that agreement, they conclude not one but two agreements, the arbitral twin of which survives any birth defect or acquired disability of the principal agreement"[14]) is not in fact a justification for the autonomy principle but simply a way of describing the result one wishes to reach. In other words, the true justification for the autonomy principle is practical rather than theoretical.

As an important official study underlying the English Arbitration Act concluded:

> "Whatever degree of legal fiction underlying the doctrine, it is not generally considered possible for international arbitration to operate effectively in jurisdictions where the doctrine is preclude . . . international consensus on autonomy has now grown very broad."[15]

The autonomy principle is not inconsistent with national courts' control of arbitrators' decisions with respect to their jurisdiction. On the contrary, since arbitration is an exceptional remedy, with claims to the same efficacy as an ordinary judgment, judges may, should, and indeed must, before enforcing

---

13   *Id.*, at 3.

14   *Id.*, at 5. *See also* William W. Park, *The Arbitrability Dicta in First Options v. Kaplan*, 12 ARB. INT. 137 (1996).

15   U.K. Department of Trade and Industry Consultation Document on Proposed Clauses and Schedules for an Arbitration Bill, reprinted *in* 10 ARB. INT. 189, 227 (1994). As evidence of the international consensus, the study cited, *id.*, leading cases from Switzerland, Sweden, France, the U.S., Germany, and Russia; it considered that English law "fits firmly into the mainstream of this international consensus," and recommended the statutory recognition of the doctrine which ultimately took the form of Sec. 7 of the Arbitration Act 1996.

Similar statutory language has been enacted in Belgium, where Article 1697(2) of the Judicial Code provides: "A ruling that the contract is invalid shall not entail ipso jure the nullity of the arbitration agreement contained in it"; in Switzerland, where Article 178(3) of the Federal Statute on Private International Law states simply that "[t]he validity of an arbitration agreement cannot be disputed on the grounds that the main contract is not valid . . . " and the Netherlands, where Article 1053 of the Code of Civil Procedure reads as follows:

> "An arbitration agreement shall be considered and decided upon as a separate agreement. The arbitral tribunal shall have the power to decide on the validity of the contract of which the arbitration agreement forms part or to which the arbitration agreement is related."

Most importantly, Article 16 of the UNCITRAL Model Law on International Commercial Arbitration establishes the principle that "the arbitral tribunal may rule on its own jurisdiction," and then goes on to affirm: "A decision by the arbitral tribunal that the contract is null and void shall not entail *ipso jure* the invalidity of the arbitration clause."

an award, ascertain that the arbitrator had valid jurisdiction. A more contro-versial question is whether national judges should interfere with arbitral pro-ceedings before they are concluded, for example by issuing an injunction to stay the arbitration for want of jurisdiction. This topic will be encountered throughout Part Five.

Under the autonomy principle, however national courts may not control the arbitrators' decisions as to the validity of the main contract, as they would verify arbitral jurisdiction.

Thus, in the leading American case of *Prima Paint Corp. v. Flood and Conklin Mfg. Co.* the US Supreme Court clearly expressed the autonomy principle in a case where one party had hidden its financial situation and declared bank-ruptcy one week after signing the contract. Even though the other party claimed there had been fraud vitiating its consent, the Court held that the ar-bitral tribunal was to decide the dispute, stating:

> Except when the parties otherwise intend, arbitration clauses as a mat-ter of federal law are "separable" from the contracts in which they are embedded ... where no claim is made that fraud was directed to the arbi-tration clause itself, a broad arbitration clause will be held to encompass arbitration of the claim that the contract itself was induced by fraud.[16]

The concept of the autonomy of the arbitration clause is embraced by the ICC Rules, which set forth in Article 6(4):

> Unless otherwise agreed, the Arbitral Tribunal shall not cease to have ju-risdiction by reason of any claim that the contract is null and void or al-legation that it is non-existent provided that the Arbitral Tribunal upholds the validity of the arbitration agreement. The Arbitral Tribunal shall continue to have jurisdiction to determine the respective rights of

---

16 Prima Paint Corp. v. Flood and Conclin Mfg. Co., 388 U.S. 395 (1967). For a discussion of the dis-tinction between claims of fraud that contaminate the arbitration clause itself and those that do not, *see, e.g.*, Campaniello Imports Ltd. v. Saporiti Italia S.p.A., 117 F. 3d 655 (1997); Twi Lite International, Inc. v. Anam Pacific Corp. *et al.*, USND Calif., 11 MEALEY'S INT. ARB. REP. E-1 (No-vember 1996). For a case where the insertion of the arbitration clause in the main contract was induced by fraud, *see* the discussion by the Swiss Cantonal Tribunal of Vaud in its decisions of 20 November 1946 ("X v. Y"), JOURNAL DES TRIBUNAUX 1947 III 59.

It is instructive to compare the various National Reports that make up the INTERNATIONAL HAND-BOOK ON COMMERCIAL ARBITRATION. Under the outline imposed by Professor Pieter Sanders, all contributors must deal with whether the arbitration clause is separable. In some cases the an-swer is clearly yes such as the countries referred to in Note 15 *supra* or in those having adopted the UNCITRAL Model Law and its Article 16; in others it is clearly no. But most of these Reports give a clear impression that this area is yet to be dealt with by the national courts in question, and many of them appear not to grasp the fact that there may be *compétence-compétence* as a matter of arbitral procedure without any necessary implication that arbitration clauses are sev-erable.

the parties and to adjudicate their claims and pleas even though the contract itself may be non-existent or null and void.[17]

It should finally be noted that since the arbitration agreement is conceived as independent of the main contract in which it is contained, its own validity is not necessarily determined by the law applicable to the main contract.[18]

5.05   Law applicable to the arbitration agreement

Even when a contract is expressly subject to a particular law, as by a stipulation for example that "any difference arising hereunder shall be settled . . . according to Belgian law," it is not certain that the validity, scope, and effects of the arbitration clause would be determined by reference to Belgian law.

This is so because of the autonomy of the arbitration clause, recognized by the ICC Rules (*see* Section 5.04). By referring to ICC arbitration, the parties have accepted that the arbitrators are to decide upon challenges to their jurisdiction and to the validity of the main contract. In so doing, ICC arbitrators need not apply the law applicable to the merits of the dispute.

An arbitral tribunal comprising three leading scholars of international arbitration (namely Professors Sanders of Holland, Chairman, and Goldman and Vasseur of France), in a 1982 award which became a matter of public knowledge as a result of a challenge before the Court of Appeal of Paris,[19] specifically held that their determination of the scope and effect of the arbitration clause would not be based on the law chosen by the parties as applicable to the merits (French law), but on 1) the common intent of the parties as re-

---

17   For a review of the notions of separability of the arbitration clause and arbitral *compétence-compétence* as reflected in various institutional rules and international treaties, *see* Pieter Sanders, *Commentary on UNCITRAL Arbitration Rules*, II YEARBOOK 172, 197-200 (1977).

For an award holding that an arbitration clause was effective although the contract was generally subject to an approval of equipment which had not materialized, *see* ICC Case 4555/1985, I ICC AWARDS 536; English translation *in* II ICC AWARDS 24.

In ICC Case 4145/1983, I ICC AWARDS 559, English translation *in* II ICC AWARDS 53, the arbitrators held, at 100, that: "the question of validity or nullity of the main contract, for reasons of public policy, illegality or otherwise, is one of merits and not of jurisdiction, the validity of the arbitration clause having to be considered separately from the validity of the main contract (*see* Art. 8(4) ICC Rules)."

The French Supreme Court has held that the novation of a contract by a subsequent settlement agreement did not neutralize the ICC arbitration clause in the original contract, Cosiac (Italy) v. Luchetti (Italy) *et al.*, decision of 10 May 1988, 1988 REV. ARB. 639.

18   Some ramifications of this observation are illustrated *infra* Note 22.

19   Isover St. Gobain v. Dow Chemical France *et al.*; ICC Case 4131/1982, I ICC AWARDS 146, 465, upheld by the Paris Court of Appeal, decision of 21 October 1983; 1984, REV. ARB. 98; extracts in English *in* IX YEARBOOK 132 (1984).

vealed by the circumstances of the negotiation and performance of the contract, and 2) usages conforming to the needs of international commerce.[20]

It may be queried whether application of French law as such would have led to a different result, since reference to the common intent of the parties and to trade usages are consistent with, and indeed encouraged by, French law.[21]

An arbitrator who does not refer to a particular national law to determine the validity, scope, and effects of the arbitration clause gives himself a particularly wide berth to apply the growing body of published international awards, if not as precedents reflecting general principles of an international law merchant, then at least as evidence of usages.[22]

This development increases the significance of published ICC awards as evidence of generally accepted practice relating to the validity and effects of the arbitration clause.

Under Article V (1)(a) of the New York Convention for the Recognition and Enforcement of Foreign Arbitral Awards, the agreement to arbitrate is examined either by reference to the law stipulated by the parties or, failing such a stipulation, to the law of the place of arbitration. Given the fact that the law applicable to the arbitration clause is rarely the subject of a specific stipulation, it is hardly surprising to find that most national court decisions under the New York Convention have applied the law of the country where the award was

---

20 Other awards holding that the arbitration clause is not subject to the governing law of the main contract include: ICC Cases 4381/1986, II ICC AWARDS 264 (specifying that ICC arbitrators may rule on the validity of the arbitration clause without referring to any national law whatsoever); 4695/1984, II ICC AWARDS 33; 4604/1984, I ICC AWARDS 546 (Italian law governed the contract, but arbitrability under Italian and ECC competition law is decided under the law of the place of arbitration: Geneva).

21 As of 1981, Article 1496 of the French Code of Civil Procedure reads:

"The arbitrator shall decide the dispute according to the rules of law chosen by the parties; in the absence of such a choice, he shall decide according to the rules of law he deems appropriate. In all cases he shall take into account trade usages."

22 As Professor Lalive, sole arbitrator, stated in ICC Case 1512/1971, I ICC AWARDS 3, 33, 37 at 39, the usages of international commerce are that an arbitration:

"shall only be governed by the rules of arbitration chosen by the parties . . . Once the parties have agreed to . . . the ICC Rules, there is no possibility to rely against the ICC Rules, upon any provision of the law of Pakistan or the law of India."

Since the leading case of Hecht v. Buismans, decided by the Paris Court of Appeal in 1970, 1972 REV. ARB. 67, by virtue of the autonomy principle the French courts will not, in international cases, apply a prohibition of arbitration under the substantive applicable law of a contract to invalidate an arbitration clause contained in it. (In the *Hecht* case, a French law invalidating arbitration agreements by commercial agents was disregarded.) *See also* the authorities cited *supra* Note 2.

In its much-heralded judgment in the *Dalico* case, Khoms El Mergeb v. Société Dalico, 1994 JDI 432, 1994 REV. ARB. 116, the French Court of Cassation declared that as a result of the autonomy principle the "existence and effectiveness" of an arbitration clause are to be assessed "according to the common intention of the parties, with no necessary reference to a national law."

rendered.[23] What this means is that prudent ICC arbitrators, although free to decide on the validity of the arbitration clause without reference to a national law[24] should also deem themselves bound, under Article 35's exhortation that they "shall make every effort to make sure that the Award is enforceable at law," to take account of the law of the place of arbitration.[25]

Since the law applicable to the merits of the dispute does not necessarily govern the arbitration clause, parties may specifically stipulate the law governing the arbitration clause, whether or not they opt for the same law as applicable to the merits (*see* Section 8.03). The following Sections 5.06—5.11 suggest the legal questions that might have to be resolved in relation to the arbitration clause.

5.06   Form of the agreement to arbitrate

Article 6(3) of the ICC Rules—which provides that unless the defendant accepts to appear, the request for arbitration will be denied unless the Court is *prima facie* satisfied that an arbitration agreement under the Rules may exist—seems to suggest that at a minimum some written proof must be given confirming the existence of that agreement.

The New York Convention expressly recognizes, in Article II(2), that an exchange of letters or telegrams may constitute an "agreement in writing." The notion of an "exchange" would seem to preclude that acceptance of a proposal to submit to arbitration could occur passively (by failure to protest).[26]

---

23   See Commentary, XI YEARBOOK 450 (1986); *see also* Deutsche Shachtbau-und Tiefbohrgesellschaft mbH v. Ras Al Khaimah National Oil Co. *et. al.*, decision of the Court of Appeal of England, of 24 March 1987, [1987] 2 LLOYD'S L. REP. 246, [1987] 2 ALL E.R. 769; extracts *in* XIII YEARBOOK 522 (1988), holding that even if the proper law of a contract calling for ICC arbitration were that of Ras Al Khaimah, the "proper law of the arbitration is Swiss; "reversed on other grounds by the House of Lords, [1988] 2 LLOYD'S L. REP. 293, 2 ALL E.R. 833.

24   As in ICC Cases 4131/1982, I ICC AWARDS 146, 465; 4381/1986, II ICC AWARDS 264.

25   *Cf.* ICC Case 4472/1984, I ICC AWARDS 525 (sole arbitrator sitting in Zürich, referring to local authorities in holding that to decide upon his own jurisdiction he "must verify that the arbitration agreement is valid under the law applicable at the seat of the arbitral tribunal").

By a judgment of 21 March 1995, the Swiss Federal Tribunal held that the scope of an arbitration clause should, in order to achieve consistency with the New York Convention, be determined by reference to the law of the seat of arbitration; excerpts *in* XXII YEARBOOK 800 (1997).

26   A letter appointing an arbitrator was considered sufficiently responsive to telexes proposing arbitration that it was held to constitute agreement; Swiss Federal Supreme Court decision of 5 November 1985, Tracomin S.A. (Switz.) v. Sudan Oil Seeds Co. (U.K.) 1985 ARRÊTS DU TRIBUNAL FÉDÉRAL 3IB 253, summarized *in* XII YEARBOOK 511 (1987). The failure to respond to a letter, written one and a half months after signature of a contract not containing any arbitration clause and stating that the contract was subject to standard conditions which did contain a reference to arbitration and had applied to a previous contract between the same parties, was held by the French Supreme Court not to constitute tacit acceptance, Confex (Rum.) v. Ets. Dahan (France), decision of 25 February 1986, 1986 JDI 735; summarized *in* XII YEARBOOK 484 (1986). *See also* the award of the Hamburg Commodity Exchange Grain Merchants' Association Arbitral Tribunal dated 7 December 1995, XXII YEARBOOK 55 (1997) (no jurisdiction in absence of defendant's sig-

German courts have held an arbitration agreement *valid* under Article II of the New York Convention in one case where a French seller had written to the German buyer that he wished to submit their dispute to arbitration under the International Wool Agreement of 1965 (which in fact localizes arbitration in the country of the seller) and the latter had written back affirmatively, but later refused to participate in arbitration on the grounds that he had not specifically agreed to arbitration in France,[27] and in another case where the agreement to arbitrate was contained in a broker's confirmation sent by the broker to each party, signed and returned by each party to the broker, but not directly exchanged between the parties,[28] but *invalid* under the Convention in cases where the arbitration agreement was contained in a sales confirmation to which the buyer did not object.[29]

---

nature or other expression of intent to conclude an arbitration agreement). *Cf.* Hill v. Gateway 2000, 105 F. 3d 1147 (7th Cir. 1997) (arbitration clause enforceable even though included in a computer purchase contract which was sent to a buyer who ordered the computer by telephone but did not return the contract, the terms of which indicated that they would apply if the computer was kept for more than 30 days); Kahn Lucas Lancaster, Inc. v. Lark International, Ltd., 1997 WL 458785 (S.D.N.Y.) (arbitration clause in purchase order). *See generally* Section 29.02, as well as Neil Kaplan, Is the Need for Writing as Expressed in the New York Convention and the Model Law Out of Step with Commercial Practice? 12 ARB. INT. 27 (1996); Richard Hill, *Formal Requirements for Arbitration Agreements: Does Kahn Lucas Lancaster v. Lark International Open Pandora's Box?* 12 MEALEY'S INT. ARB. REP. 18 (October 1997); and Paul Friedland, *U.S. Courts' Misapplication of the Agreement in Writing Requirement for Enforcement of an Arbitration Agreement under the New York Convention*, 13 MEALEY'S INT. ARB. REP. 21 (May 1998).

27 Decision of the *Landgericht* of Bremen of 8 June, 1967, DIE DEUTSCHE RECHTSPRECHUNG AUF DEM GEBIETE DES INTERNATIONALEN PRIVATRECHTS IN DEN JAHREN 1966 UND 1967, 860, published with an English summary *in* ICA NY CONVENTION V. 46; summarized *in* II YEARBOOK 234 (1977).

28 Decision of the *Landgericht* of Hamburg of 19 December 1967, 1968 ARTBITRALE RECHTSPRAAK 139; published with an English summary *in* ICA NY CONVENTION V. 47; summarized *in* II YEARBOOK 235 (1977). (The broker did not forward the confirmation of each party to the other party. However, the court noted that under German law the broker is authorized to record the intent of both parties.)

See also P.E.P. Shipping v. Noramco Shipping Corp., 1997 WL 358118 (E.D. La.); Overseas Cosmos Inc. v. NR Vessel Corp., 97 Civ. 5898 [DC] (SDNY), 13 MEALEY'S INT. ARB. REP. B-11 (May 1998).

29 Decision of the *Bundesgericht* (Supreme Court) of 25 May 1970, 1970 WERTPAPIER MITTEILUNGEN 1050; published in French translation in 60 REVUE CRITIQUE DU DROIT INTERNATIONAL PRIVÉ 88 (1971); summarized *in* II YEARBOOK 237 (1977); decision of the *Oberlandesgericht* of Düsseldorf of 8 November 1971, DIE DEUTSCHE RECHTSPRECHUNG AUF DEM GEBIETE DES INTERNATIONALES PRIVATRECHTS IN DEM JAHRE 1971 (1971) 492; published with an English summary *in* ICA NY CONVENTION V. 50; summarized *in* II YEARBOOK 238 (1977) (in both cases, awards nonetheless enforced because tacit agreements to arbitrate were acceptable under national laws).

Awards were also rejected by courts in Italy and Switzerland because the agreement to arbitrate was contained in unreturned sales confirmations: decision of the Court of Appeal of Naples of 13 December 1974, Ditte Frey, Milota, Seitelberger (Austria) v. Ditte F. Cuccaro e figli (Italy), 11 RIV. DIR. INT. P.P. 552 (1975); published with an English summary *in* ICA NY CONVENTION V. 22; summarized *in* I YEARBOOK 193 (1976); decision of the *Tribunal cantonal de Genève* of 6 June 1967, J.A. van Walsum N.V. (Netherlands) v. Chevelines S.A. (Switzerland), 64 SCHWEIZERISCHE JURISTEN-ZEITUNG 56 (1968); published with an English summary *in* ICA NY CONVENTION V. 2; summarized *in* I YEARBOOK 199 (1976).

Arguments that telexes are not sufficient evidence of an agreement in writing have not persuaded national judges, who have readily extended the notion of "telegram," explicitly accepted under Article II (1) of the New York Convention, to cover telexes. As the Court of Appeal of Geneva put it, Article II "contemplates in a general way the transmission by telecommunication of messages which are reproduced in a lasting format."[30]

Standard conditions are often used in international contract practice, and they may raise delicate problems in determining whether they constitute a sufficient agreement in writing to arbitrate. Such conditions may be part of a printed form contract, or may be found printed on the back of a contract, or may be contained in a separate document to which the contract refers *en bloc* without specifically mentioning arbitration. Parties seeking to avoid arbitration sometimes argue that they should not be bound by what they consider to be an adhesion contract, or that the mechanism of incorporation by reference did not adequately put them on notice that they would be deemed to have made an indirect stipulation in favor of arbitral jurisdiction. Whether the facts of a specific case sufficiently demonstrate the existence of an agreement in writing is to be determined by the law applicable to the putative arbitration agreement. While usages of international trade should be upheld wherever they create reasonable inferences that contradict formalistic denials of jurisdiction, one should not necessarily believe that any scrap of written evidence of a reference to arbitration is sufficient.[31]

But see decision of the *Rechtbank* (court of first instance) of Rotterdam of 26 June 1970, Israel Chemicals Phosphates Ltd. v. N.V. Algemene Oliehandel, 1971 NEDERLANDSE JURISPRUDENTIE 1372; published with an English summary *in* ICA NY CONVENTION V.9; summarized *in* I YEARBOOK 195 (1976) (a liberal interpretation of Article II(2) of the New York Convention, holding that where the Israeli buyer had sent a purchase order in writing to the Dutch seller, and the latter returned a sales contract containing an arbitration clause, and the buyer did not object to the clause until two months after delivery of the goods in Haifa, the latter was bound to arbitrate by "an exchange of written documents.")

For a case dealing with arbitration clauses in bills of lading and their effect on consignees (or lack thereof), *compare* the decision of the French Court of Cassation *in* Mediterranean Shipping Co. v. GALF Assurance *et al.*, 1995 REV. ARB. 622 (consignee not held to clause), *with* that of the U.S. Supreme Court *in* Vimar Seguros y Reaseguros SA v. M/V Sky Reefer, 115 S. CT. 2322, XXI YEARBOOK 773 (1996) (consignee so held); for a commentary on the contrasting decisions, *see* Jean-Louis Goutal, *La clause compromissoire dans les connaissements*, 1996 REV. ARB. 605.

30 Carbomin S.A. (Switz.) v. Ekton Corp. (Pan.), decision of the *Cour de justice* of 14 April 1983, 106 LA SEMAINE JUDICIAIRE 37 (1984); summarized *in* XII YEARBOOK 502 (1987); *accord*, Tracomin v. Sudan Oil Seeds, *supra* Note 26.

For a demonstration that e-mail systems may produce information that satisfy rules of evidence, *see* R. Horning, *Has HAL Signed a Contract?* 12 SANTA CLARA COMPUTER & HIGH TECH. L. J. 290 (1996). *Cf.* Jasana Arsic, *International Commercial Arbitration on the Internet—Has the Future Come Too Early?* 14 J. INT. ARB. 209 (September 1997).

31 *Compare* Cerealsarda di A. Casillo & Co. S.a.S. (Italy) v. Ditta Otello Mantovani (Italy), decision of the Court of Appeal of Venice of 26 January 1983, 68 RIV. DIR. INT. P.P. 204 (1985), summarized *in* XII YEARBOOK 493 (1987); *with* Cereali Mallozzi S.p.A. (Italy) v. Agenzia Marittima Albano e Avallone (Italy) *et al.*, decision of the *Tribunale* (court of first instance) of Naples of 7 April 1982,

In a case in which a Canadian claimant suing two Italian defendants wanted to rely on a standard form contractual stipulation of arbitration in New York,[32] a U.S. federal court ordered the arbitration to proceed despite an argument that the arbitration clause was formally deficient. The defendants contended that while the contract was expressly governed by New York law, the validity of the arbitration clause should be determined under Italian law. This point was not academic; under Italian law, it was argued, the arbitration clause would be valid only if it appeared *above* the signature of the parties, which it did not.

The Court rejected this argument, citing an observation of the U.S. Supreme Court that the thrust of the New York Convention was not to decline enforcement of arbitration agreements "on the basis of parochial views . . . in a manner that would diminish the mutually binding nature of the agreements."[33] It added that this concern would seem "equally compelling whether the `parochial view' is that of the forum or of another State with an alleged interest in the controversy."

The Court went on to say that its reading of the New York Convention was that arbitration agreements should be given effect unless to do so would offend the law or public policy of the forum. It noted that this result is consistent with the notion that the enforceability of an agreement to arbitrate relates to the law of remedies and is therefore governed by the law of the forum. Thus arbitration was compelled.

Looking at Italian case law, one finds that the views of U.S. and Italian courts appear to be in harmony as regards eschewing parochialism. When the latter began to apply the New York Convention, Italian law notably contained the following potential stumbling blocks for international arbitration: Article 2 of the Code of Civil Procedure declares invalid any agreement by an Italian citizen and resident, whether concluded with another Italian or with a foreigner, to submit to arbitration outside Italy; and Article 1341 of the Civil Code requires specific approval of arbitration clauses contained in contracts of adhe-

---

90 IL DIRITTO MARITTIMO 341 (1983), summarized *in* XII YEARBOOK 492 (1987). *See also* Confex v. Dahan, *supra* Note 26, and S.p.A. Carapelli v. Ditta Otello Mantovani, *infra* Note 37, and JMA Investments *et al.* v. C. Rijkaart B.V. *et al.*, unpublished decision of 18 June 1985, USDC, E.D. Wash.; extracts *in* XI YEARBOOK 57 (1986), where the U.S. federal district court, upholding an agreement to arbitrate in the Netherlands against the complaint of a U.S. defendant that it would not have agreed to such an "onerous" condition as the obligation to arbitrate in a foreign country had it known that such an obligation was part of the "Conditions" referred to in an "Offer" it had accepted, stated, at 580: "Parties, especially commercial parties, are generally held to their contracts whether they have read them or not. Were this not the law, there would be no certainty in contracts."

32 Ferrara S.p.A. *et al.* v. United Grain Growers Ltd., 441 F. Supp. 778 (S.D.N.Y. 1977); ICA NY CONVENTION V. 84; extracts *in* IV YEARBOOK 331 (1979).

33 Scherk (FRG) v. Alberton-Culver Company (U.S.) 417 U.S. 506 (1974) at 520, n.15; ICA NY CONVENTION V.54; summarized *in* I YEARBOOK 203 (1976).

sion or contracts incorporating standard conditions. It would seem that no other country has had as much litigation under the New York Convention as Italy,[34] frequently concerning these issues of form. After some hesitations and inconsistent results,[35] it now seems clearly established that the New York Convention's simple requirement in Article II(2) of "an arbitral clause in a contract or an arbitration agreement, signed by the parties or contained in an exchange of letters or telegrams,"

> constitutes a special law which prevails not only over the general principle of Article 2 of the Italian Code of Civil Procedure, but also over the general principles of Articles 1341 and 1342 of the Italian Civil Code. These principles have an imperative nature, but do not pertain to a principle of international public policy, and, hence, can be derogated from by international conventions.[36]

Accordingly, the Italian Supreme Court has declared that Article II of the New York Convention constitutes a *lex specialis* rendering inapplicable the general Italian rules of form concerning arbitration agreements,[37] and that it "exclusively regulates the form of the arbitration agreement without requiring what Article 1341 prescribes."[38]

---

34   146 Italian cases dealing with the New York Convention have been summarized in the first 22 volumes of the YEARBOOK, *see* XXII YEARBOOK 737 (1997).

35   *See* G. Mirabelli, *Application of the New York Convention by the Italian Courts*, IV YEARBOOK 362 (1979).

36   Decision of the Court of Appeal of Bari of 28 November 1977, Getreide Import Gesellschaft mbH (FRG) v. Fratelli Casillo (Italy), 61 RIV. DIR. INT. P.P. 820 (1978); summarized *in* VII YEARBOOK 342 (1982) (allowing execution of an award rendered in Germany on the foundation of grain-trade arbitration as provided for by standard conditions accepted by the losing Italian party). Reaffirmed by the Italian Supreme Court's decision of 15 March 1986, Orazio Torrisi (Italy) v. Friedrich Kern (Austria), summarized *in* XII YEARBOOK 497 (1987). *Accord*, decision of the Swiss Federal Supreme Court of 5 November 1985, Tracomin v. Sudan Oil Seeds, *supra* Note 26.

37   So held in affirming the decision of the Court of Appeal of Bari cited in the preceding Note, *Corte de Cassazione*, 7 October 1980, 1980 RIV. DIR. INT. P.P. 176; summarized *in* VII YEARBOOK 342 (1982).

      Reference to a standard contract of the Grain and Feed Trade Association (GAFTA) was held sufficient to bind two Italian parties to GAFTA arbitration in London as provided for in the standard contract, S.p.A. Carapelli v. Ditta Otello Mantovani, decision of 26 April 1980 of the Court of Appeal of Venice, 82 IL DIRITTO MARITTIMO (1980) 256, summarized *in* VII YEARBOOK 340 (1982).

38   S.A. di Assicurazioni e Riassicurazioni "Lloyd Continental" (France) v. S.p.A. Navigazione Alga (Italy), decision of 11 September 1979, 1980 RIV. DIR. INT. P.P. 425; summarized *in* VI YEARBOOK 230 (1981).

      Accord, decision of 17 November 1971 of the Austrian *Oberster Gerichtshof* (Supreme Court) 96 JURISTISCHE BLÄTTER 629 (1974); published with an English summary *in* ICA NY CONVENTION V.29 ("[I]n view of the international matter involved,. . . the requirement of a written form for the arbitral agreement is exclusively defined by Article II(2) of the UN (i.e. New York) Convention"); also summarized *in* I YEARBOOK 183 (1976).

      Professor Sanders approves this principle, *Consolidated Commentary on Court Decisions on the New York Convention 1958*, IV YEARBOOK 231, 240 (1979).

It should be recognized that formal flaws in the arbitration agreement may be cured by the simple fact that the parties participate in the arbitral proceedings.[39] This may indeed happen in ICC arbitration; under Article 6(2) of the Rules, the formal insufficiency—or even nonexistence—of an arbitral agreement may be overcome if the defendant answers without contesting arbitral jurisdiction. On the other hand, in the absence of a written agreement to arbitrate, the ensuing award would not be entitled to the protection of the New York Convention irrespective of the parties' participation.[40] Under the ICC system, however, the signing of Terms of Reference should be sufficient for this purpose.

The issue occasionally arises whether an arbitration agreement in writing may be validly extended without a specific writing to that effect. The District Court of Yokohama was faced with this question in a 1980 case where a Japanese distributor sued an American chemical company for wrongful termination of the contract. The U.S. defendant requested that the suit be dismissed on the grounds that the action should be heard in ICC arbitration in New York. The Yokohama court agreed with the American party. In deciding that ICC arbitration was in fact the exclusive forum, the Japanese court recognized the fact that the implicit renewal of the agreement to arbitrate was not in writing (the original agreement having expired but the parties having continued to deal under the same conditions), but held that since such a tacit extension was valid under the law applicable to the arbitration agreement (the law of New York), the arbitration clause was specifically enforceable under the New York Convention.[41]

Failure to meet the formal requirements of the New York Convention need not be fatal; as the German Supreme Court has held, the Convention itself does not preclude enforcement of foreign awards under more lenient national requirement of form than those of the Convention.[42]

---

39 See case No. 12, 1974, decided between a GDR party and a Spanish party by the Arbitration Court attached to the GDR Chamber of Foreign Trade, Berlin, summarized *in* I YEARBOOK 127 (1976).

40 *See* the decision of the *Oberlandesgericht* of Düsseldorf of 8 November 1971, DIE DEUTSCHE RECHTSPRECHUNG AUF DEM GEBIETE DES INTERNATIONALEN PRIVATRECHTS IN DEM JAHRE 492 (1971); summarized *in* II YEARBOOK 238 (1977) (n.b. the award was enforced although the Convention did not apply; *supra* Note 42), and the decision of 18 September 1978 of the Supreme Court of Italy, Gaetano Butera (Italy) v. Pietro e Romano Pagnan (Italy), 15 RIV. DIR. INT. P.P. 525 (1979); summarized *in* IV YEARBOOK 296 (1979).

41 Kabushiki Kaisha Ameroido Nihon v. Drew Chemical Corp., 1981 JAPANESE COMMERCIAL ARBITRATION ASSOCIATION QUARTERLY 81-82; summarized *in* VIII YEARBOOK 394 (1983).

42 In a decision of 25 May 1970, 1970 WERTPAPIER-MITTEILUNGEN 1050, *supra* Note 29, the *Bundesgerichtshof* enforced an award based on an oral agreement to arbitrate in Vienna, given the fact that German law allows oral arbitration agreements between merchants. *See also* the decision of the *Oberlandesgericht* of Düsseldorf, *op. cit.* Note 40, enforcing an award rendered in Holland against a German party (holding that although the New York Convention was inapplicable in the absence of a written agreement to arbitrate, the award could be enforced under

5.07   Arbitrability

U.S. courts unfortunately use the word *arbitrability* interchangeably with the word *jurisdiction*.[43] Of course the law is a field where words often take on whatever meaning may gain acceptance. And one may concede that it is logical to say that if the arbitral tribunal does not have jurisdiction the dispute is not arbitrable. To allow this overlap is however to blur a useful distinction. For our purposes, the concept of arbitrability is limited to the inquiry whether the claims raised are prohibited by law from being resolved by arbitration—irrespective of the otherwise undoubted jurisdiction of the arbitral tribunal.

Whether or not such a prohibition applies in a given case is a question which may variously confront contract drafters (wondering whether they can rely on an arbitral mechanism with respect to issues likely to arise if the envisaged contract leads to dispute), arbitrators (inquiring whether they may proceed to decide the merits), the judge at the place of arbitration (asked to set aside the award), and the judge in an execution forum (asked to refuse to recognize the award), as well as judges who are asked to assert initial jurisdiction of the dispute and thus disregard the agreement to arbitrate.

This is a difficult and constantly evolving area. The general trend, however, unmistakably expands the scope of arbitrability.

Arbitrators are perhaps in a more comfortable position than parties or judges, because when in doubt arbitrators can legitimately proceed to decide the merits on the basis that in so doing they are giving effect to the joint intent of the parties;[44] if a judge disregards or overrules their findings that is not a matter for which they should be blamed.[45] (On the other hand, arbitrators may be

---

Sec.1044 of the German Code of Civil Procedure (ZPO) on the ground that the award was operative under the law applicable to the arbitral proceedings; Dutch law acknowledges arbitration agreements made orally or by failure to protest reference to arbitration); the decision of the *Oberlandesgericht* of Celle of 5 June 1981, summarized *in* VII YEARBOOK 322 (1982) (award rendered in Holland enforced against German party whose argument as to the non-existence of an arbitration agreement was barred on the ground that the German party had failed to seek annulment in Holland within the deadline established by Dutch law; i.e. the German courts accepted the final *res judicata* effect of the award under Dutch law); and the following statement of an arbitral tribunal of Hamburg Friendly Arbitration; summarized *in* III YEARBOOK 212 (1978):

> "[T]he (New York) Convention does not prevent the parties from concluding an arbitration agreement orally or in another form; insofar as the national laws do not require a specific form for the arbitral clause even an enforcement pursuant to the Convention is possible."

43   The Supreme Court set the example *in* First Options of Chicago, Inc. v. Kaplan, 1995, 514 U.S. 938. The fuzziness of the Court's terminology is exposed *in* William Park, *supra* Note 14. Before making its choice of words, the Court would have done well to consider REDFERN & HUNTER, at 138.

44   *Accord*, Bernard Hanotiau, *What Law Governs the Issue of Arbitrability?* 12 ARB. INT. 391, at 398 (1996).

45   The fact that arbitrators may thus substantively apply public law does not however necessarily enable them to grant the full range of remedies provided under such legislation, such as exemp-

blamed for having *failed* to decide on the merits by taking an overly timid view of arbitrability[46]) Parties are in a different situation; even if they can expect that arbitrators will arbitrate, it may be very difficult for them to predict the extent to which various judges potentially seized with a dispute, and applying unforeseeable notions of arbitrability, will defer to an arbitration agreement or to an award based on it. As for judges, they may have understandable apprehensions about the attitude of their own appellate jurisdictions. Under the "second-look doctrine" of the famous *Mitsubishi* case, for example, although it was clear that U.S. courts would allow foreign arbitral tribunals to deal with claims based on U.S. antitrust laws, doubts subsisted with respect to the possible examination of the ensuing award by U.S. courts asked to enforce it—were they only to verify that the arbitrators had *considered* the Sherman Act, or were they to *review the merits* of the decision?[47]

To understand the difficulties of this topic, one may usefully begin with asking what law applies to issues of arbitrability.

Under the ICC Rules, it is clear that parties may choose the rules of procedure (Article 15(1)) and substance (Article 17(1)) to be applied. On the other hand, while the Rules make clear that the arbitral tribunal may decide whether an arbitration agreement is valid (and the tribunal thus has jurisdiction), the relevant Article 6(4) does not specify that the parties may stipulate the law or rules to be applied in determining jurisdictional issues. The question then arises whether the arbitral tribunal may and should seek the solution to issues of arbitrability by reference to the rules chosen by the parties.

That the parties may themselves determine what law applies to the question of the validity of their agreement to arbitrate may appear somewhat like Baron Von Munchhausen lifting himself out of a bog by his own pigtail. However, in the international context it appears a necessity for contractual security. Indeed, Article 6(2) of the European Convention of 1961 specifically lists

---

tions and negative clearances under EC law or treble damages under U.S. antitrust rules. *See* Jan Dalhuisen, *The Arbitrability of Competition Issues*, 11 ARB. INT. 151 (1995); Joseph McLaughlin, *Arbitrability: Current Trends in the United States*, 12 ARB. INT. 113 (1996). This may lead to concurrent public and private (arbitral) proceedings.

46 *See supra* Note 66.

47 *See* Mitsubishi Motors Corp. v. Soler Chrysler-Plymouth, 473 US 614, at 638 (1985) (at the enforcement stage, courts may "ascertain that the [arbitral] tribunal took cognizance of the antitrust claims and actually decided them.") *See* William Park, *National Law and Commercial Justice: Safeguarding Procedural Integrity in International Arbitration*, 63 TULANE LAW REVIEW 647 (1989).

For a general analysis of judicial review of arbitral rulings with respect to matters of public policy, *see* Pierre Mayer, *La sentence contraire à l'ordre public au fond*, 1994 REV. ARB. 615. In a judgment of 27 October 1994, LTDC v. R.J. Reynolds Tobacco Int., 1994 REV. ARB. 695, the Court of Appeal of Paris stated that in order not to review the merits of awards, judicial control should "affect, not the arbitrators' evaluation of the parties' rights by reference to the invoked legal provisions of *ordre public*, but rather the result reached with respect to the dispute; there is no grounds for annulment unless its execution violates *ordre public*."

the law chosen by the parties as having the first priority in determining arbitrability. This provision is consistent with the New York Convention (Article II(1); *see* Section 5.01) and represents an evolution from the Geneva Protocol of 1923, which required in its Section 1 that arbitrability be determined by each relevant national system of conflict of laws.[48]

If it is true that the arbitral tribunal should look to the intent of the parties in determining whether a claim is arbitrable, there must be a heavy presumption in favor of arbitrability.[49] If anything is clear, it is that the very existence of the arbitration clause proves that the parties wanted disputes arising under it to be resolved in the manner provided. That is why international arbitrators are generally unsympathetic to respondents, whether corporate or public bodies, who sign contracts including arbitration clauses only to invoke some alleged legal restriction on arbitrability when a dispute arises. Such an objection is particularly difficult to accept when the rule of non-arbitrability is allegedly derived from a national law other than the one stipulated as applicable to the substance of the dispute—but even when it is the same law it is doubtful that a rule of non-arbitrability, even if it can be shown that it would be applied by national courts with respect to internal transactions, should be effective in an *international context*. For example, the fact that a contract between an executive and a company establishing the terms of an assignment in country X is subject to the law of country Y does not mean that a rule of non-arbitrability of employment contracts under the law of Y should defeat the relevant arbitration clause. In disregarding such restrictions, arbitrators and judges often give a theoretical justification founded on the autonomy of the arbitration clause.[50] Another way of putting it is that the effect of domestic legislation should be attenuated—if not neutralized—with respect to international transactions to which they were not intended to apply (or in the

---

48   In an unpublished award quoted by a former Secretary General of the ICC Court as "a good example of a typical approach to this problem," the arbitrators held: "*In the absence in this arbitration of an express or tacit choice by the parties of a law governing the arbitration clause*, the Tribunal will apply Swiss law." *See* Eric Schwartz, *The Domain of Arbitration and Issues of Arbitrability: The View from the ICC*, 9 ICSID REVIEW—FOREIGN INVESTMENT LAW JOURNAL 17, at 27-28 (1994). As he often did, Gillis Wetter may have put the matter as well as it can be in the current state of the law: "the law governing an arbitration agreement is crucial (but not exclusively determinative) in assessing the arbitrability of disputes," *in The Internationalization of International Arbitration*, 11 ARB. INT. 117, at 121 (1995). *Accord*, Bernard Hanotiau, *What Law Governs the Issue of Arbitrability?* 12 ARB. INT. 391 (1996).

49   *See generally* Bernard Hanotiau, *L'arbitrabilité et la favor arbitrandum : un réexamen*, 121 JDI 899 (1994).

50   *See e.g.* the 1970 landmark judgment of the Court of Appeal of Paris *in* Hecht v. Buismans, 1972 REV. ARB. 67, holding that the rule under French law to the effect that a commercial agent cannot enter into a binding arbitration agreement may not be invoked to nullify an arbitration clause in a contract between a French agent and a Netherlands company, irrespective that the stipulated proper law of the contract was that of France, because "in international arbitration, the agreement to arbitrate, whether concluded separately or within the legal document to which it relates, always has a complete juridical autonomy, save exceptional circumstances, from the latter."

context of which the domestic legislation may violate international law, which is preeminent even within the national sphere), while the security of contractual stipulations requires an especially high degree of recognition, free of national protectionism, in an international context.[51]

Arbitrators' decisions as to arbitrability are however subject to the control of national judges, who will not necessarily resolve the issue by reference to the law applicable to the arbitration agreement. (Hence the salutary tendency of ICC arbitrators to "seek to ensure that the claim before them is, in fact, arbitrable under all of the laws that may be relevant to that determination."[52]) Indeed, Article V(2)(a) of the New York Convention expressly authorizes enforcement judges to look at their own law in this respect. As explained above, and as held in many cases in many jurisdictions since 1974 when the U.S. Supreme Court ruled that claims arising under securities legislation could be heard if in the context of international commerce[53] judges may consider that their national laws permit a wider scope of arbitrable claims in connection with international disputes than with domestic ones.

Considering the multiplicity of the laws that may define arbitrability, one can make only general comments with respect to the following categories that have given rise to difficulties. In case of doubt as to the arbitrability of potential future disputes relating to a contract being negotiated, there is no substitute for an examination of the specific potential applicable national laws.

Contracts contra bonos mores. In one of the early ICC cases, the Swedish Judge Gunnar Lagergren, sitting as sole arbitrator, decided that the object of the contract had been the bribery of high government officials. Although both parties wanted him to rule on the merits, he concluded that he had no jurisdiction to hear the case. He stated:

> Parties who ally themselves in an enterprise of the present nature must realize that they have forfeited any right to ask for the assistance of the machinery of justice (national courts or arbitral tribunals) in settling their disputes.[54]

---

51   For a particularly didactic articulation of this approach by Professor Pierre Lalive, sitting as sole arbitrator, *see* ICC Case 1512 1970, summarized *in* V YEARBOOK 174 (1980); final award held enforceable by the Court of Appeal in England, National Bank of Pakistan v. Dalmia Dairy Industries Ltd., [1978] 2 LLOYD'S L. REP. 287. *See also* Klaus Peter Berger, *Exchange Control Regulations, in* ACTS OF STATE AND ARBITRATION 99 (Karl-Heinz Böckstiegel, Ed., 1997).

52   Schwartz, supra Note 48 at 27.

53   Scherk v. Alberto-Culver Co., 417 US 506, *rehearing denied*, 419 US 885 (1974).

54   *See* ICC Case 1110/1963, published as an annex *in* Gillis Wetter, *Issues of Corruption before International Tribunals: The Authentic Text and True Meaning of Judge Gunnar Lagergren's 1963 Award in ICC Case No. 1110*, 10 ARB. INT. 277 (1994); *accord*, ICC Case 3916/1982, I ICC AWARDS 507; and the ICC arbitration decided in 1981, erroneously referred to as also bearing number 3916, extensively quoted *in* 1985 JDI at 988-9. In ICC Case 1677/1975, I ICC AWARDS 20, the arbitral tribunal stated that even if it has the power of *amiable compositeur* (*see* Section

This solution may not always be very practical. In cases where the contravention of *bonos mores* is not obvious, or was obvious only to one party, the arbitral tribunal may, if it simply washes its hands of the matter, be criticized for failing to settle accounts.[55] An alternative approach achieving this result is to declare the contract unenforceable, but nevertheless assert jurisdiction to establish the consequences of unenforceability. Thus, in an ICC case decided in 1982, a three-member tribunal held that an export contract which it deemed to be fictitious and designed to violate Yugoslavian foreign exchange regulations was an "absolute nullity." It stated that "all agreements contrary to mandatory provisions and *bonos mores* are null and void," adding that "this principle is recognized in all countries and in all legal systems. It is an element of generally accepted contract law in the international field."[56]

8.05), it was not:

> "[A]ccording to general principles . . . authorized to take a decision contrary to an absolutely constraining law, particularly the rules concerning public order or morals."

55 In the just-quoted decision, Judge Lagergren did say, *id.* at 294: ". . . before invoking good morals and public policy as barring parties from recourse to judicial or arbitral instances in settling their disputes care must be taken to see that one party is not thereby enabled to reap the fruits of his own dishonest conduct by enriching himself at the expense of the other." The arbitrator was satisfied that this "cannot happen in the case before me."

56 ICC Cases 2930/1982, IX YEARBOOK 105, at 107 (1984); 2730/1982, 1984 JDI 914. *See also* Awards Nos. 2068A and 2068 of the Society of Maritime Arbitrators of New York, rendered on 28 August 1981 and 5 September 1984, respectively, XI YEARBOOK 205 (1986); Northrop Corp. v. Triad International Marketing S.A., 811 F. 2d 1265 (9th Cir. 1987); Sea Dragon, Inc. v. Gebr. Van Weelde Scheepvaartkantoor B.V., decision of the U.S. District Court (SDNY) of 6 October 1983; *extracts in* X YEARBOOK 94 (1985); Continaf BV v. Polycoton S.A., decision of the *Tribunal de première instance* of Geneva of 21 May 1987, XIII YEARBOOK 516 (1988). Société Ganz *et al.* v. SNCFT (Tunisian national railways), judgment of the Court of Appeal of Paris of 29 March 1991, 1991 REV. ARB. 478; European Gas Turbines S.A. v. Westman Int. Ltd., judgment of the Court of Appeal of Paris of 30 September 1993, 1994 REV. ARB. 359; the 1993 award reproduced *in* 16 SWISS BULL. 210 (1998).

The much-publicized case of large claims by intermediaries in connection with a sale of French military vessels to Taiwan, which resulted in criminal convictions in France and indeed the investigation of a former Minister of Foreign Affairs, also involved an ICC arbitration in Geneva; an award of some US $35 million was rendered against the seller, who sought annulment on the ground that the award had upheld a contract for influence-peddling and was therefore against public policy. The Federal Tribunal rejected the complaint, noting that it had been raised before the arbitrators and dismissed by them, and stating that "the grounds invoked by the applicant, which are supported only by its own version of the facts, are entirely at odds with the situation as finally established in the challenged award," Thomson C.S.F. v. Frontier AG Bern, 28 January 1997, 16 SWISS BULL. 118 (1998). The facts related to the arbitral tribunal (and the Federal Tribunal) were that the intermediaries had undertaken to use their "relations" to procure withdrawal of PRC opposition to the sale; this did not involve corruption of Taiwanese authorities, who had been willing buyers from the start. The story that later came out in France, to the effect that the intermediaries had fronted for French embezzlers, was never heard by the arbitrators. *See generally* Ahmed El Kosheri and Philippe Leboulanger, *L'arbitre face à la corruption et aux trafics d'influence*, 1984 REV. ARB. 3.

The arbitral tribunal then went on to order restitution of payments made under the contract despite its nullity; thereby illustrating the principle of the autonomy of the arbitration clause (*see* Section 5.07).[57]

In 1977, the Council of the ICC adopted Rules of Conduct to Combat Extortion and Bribery which were revised in 1996. Article 1 of which states: "No one may, directly or indirectly, demand or accept a bribe."[58]

Claims sounding in tort (delictual liability). Since the very mechanism of arbitration is created by contract, and since the judicial sanction of tortious conduct does not contemplate a contractual relationship between plaintiff and defendant, claims based on alleged torts are generally not arbitrated. That does not, however, necessarily mean that they may never be arbitrated. One may perfectly well conceive a special submission to arbitration, for example, by two insurance companies connected by no contractual relationship before the occurrence of an accident involving their respective insured parties. Most ICC arbitrations, however, arise from arbitration clauses contained in contracts antedating the dispute; such clauses may or may not, depending to great extent on their wording, be deemed to cover claims of wrongful behavior that does not constitute breach of contract but is nevertheless connected with the contractual relationships. The French *Cour de cassation* has held in the affirmative.[59] Indeed, the wording of the ICC Model Clause (*see* Section

---

57 In ICC Case No. 6401 Westinghouse v. National Power Corp. of the Philippines, 7 MEALEY'S INT. ARB. REP. B-1 (1992-1), a tribunal presided by Prof. Claude Reymond observed in *dictum* at B-13/14,

"There may be instances where a defect going to the root of an agreement between parties affects both the main contract and the arbitration clause. An obvious example is a contract obtained by threat. With regard to the impact of bribery, it would remain to be seen whether bribery, if proved, affects both the main contract and the arbitration clause and renders both null and invalid."

58 ICC Publication, 1977. Accusations to this effect are not readily proved; *see* ICC Case 4145/1984, I ICC AWARDS 559, English translation *in* II ICC AWARDS 53; Iran-US Claims Tribunal Award in Case No.43 of 8 October 1986, XII YEARBOOK 287, at 288 (1987). In ICC Case 3916/1982, I ICC AWARDS 507, however, presumptions were sufficient to lead the sole arbitrator to the conclusion that an agency agreement had an illicit purpose. In the notorious *Hilmarton* case, an initial ICC award rejected a claim for fees on account of consultancy services under a contract subject to Swiss law but to be performed in Algeria on the grounds that the fees in question contravened Algerian anti-corruption laws, but was set aside by the Geneva cantonal court; whereupon a new ICC arbitral tribunal upheld the claim (*see* Section 28.04). *See also* United Nations Declaration against Corruption and Bribery in International Commercial Transactions, adopted 16 December 1996, 36 ILM 1044 (1997).

59 *Chambre commerciale*, 11 October 1954, "fully approved" by the *Avocat général* Lecante, 1982 RECUEIL DALLOZ SIREY 388 (1982). Similar holdings were made by the English High Court of Justice *in* Lonrho Ltd. *et al.* v. Shell Petroleum Company Ltd. *et al.*; summarized *in* IV YEARBOOK 320 (1979), and by the Court of Appeal of Florence, decision of 22 October 1976, S.A. Tradax Export (Panama) v. S.p.A. Carapelli (Italy); summarized *in* III YEARBOOK 279 (1978) (tort claim may be heard by an arbitrator even though it is also potential grounds for a criminal law action). *See also* ICC Cases 5477/1988, II ICC AWARDS 358 and 5103/1988, II ICC AWARDS 361.

6.03) has specifically been acknowledged by the Paris Court of Appeal[60] as covering a claim of fraudulent avoidance of contractual conditions.

Under Article II(1) of the New York Convention, arbitration agreements must be recognized *whether the dispute arises out of a contractual relationship or not*. So, if the Convention applies, the arbitrability of claims sounding in tort must be held to be granted,[61] and the question then remains whether the wording of the arbitration agreement covers such claims[62] (*see* Section 6.02).

Competition law. When it is claimed that a contract is unenforceable due to its alleged violation of competition law, should the arbitral tribunal rule on that objection, or should he wait for the issue to be resolved by the courts having jurisdiction over such questions? To avoid sabotage of the arbitral process by spurious anti-trust arguments, the trend has evolved for arbitrators not to interrupt proceedings but to proceed and rule on the anti-trust issue.[63] In the landmark *Mitsubishi* case, the U.S. Supreme Court specifically held that the U.S. courts cannot take jurisdiction over a dispute governed by an arbitration clause even if it raises issues under the Sherman Act (the main U.S. antitrust law); the arbitrators irrespective of their nationality and qualification are to decide such issues as well.[64]

---

60   Decision of 11 December 1981; 1982 RECUEIL DALLOZ SIREY 389. *Accord*, LARS HJERNER, INTERNATIONELLA HANDELSKAMMARENS FÖRLIKNINGS—OCH SKILJEREGLER 15 (1981). *Cf*. S.A. Mineracao da Trinedade-Samitri v. Utah International Inc., 745 F.2d 190 (2nd Cir. 1984).

61   The *Landgericht* of Hamburg, in its decision of 20 April 1977, summarized *in* IV YEARBOOK 261 (1979), referring specifically to this provision of the New York Convention, reasoned that the parties' choice of forum related to both contractual claims and statutory claims sounding in tort, it being "illogical" to suppose the parties had intended their relationship to be subject to different jurisdictions. *Accord*, Canada Packers Inc. *et al.* v. Terra Nova Tankers Inc. *et al.*, Ontario Court of Justice, XII YEARBOOK 669 (1997).

62   In Genesco Inc. (US) v. T. F. Kakiuchi Co. (Japan) and T. Kakiuchi America Inc., 815 F. 2d 840 (2d Cir. 1987), the court confronted a number of claims connected with a series of sales agreements, including a claim for tortious interference with the buyer's relationship with one of its executive officers, who was alleged to have been bribed to approve inferior goods. The relevant arbitration clauses used the expressions "arising under" or "relating to" the relevant sales agreement. The court held that the claim of tortious interference was not subject to arbitration.

63   *See* ICC Cases 1397/1966, I ICC AWARDS 179; 2811/1978, I ICC AWARDS 164, 456; 4604/1984, I ICC AWARDS 546; 6106/1990, ICC BULL. SPECIAL SUPPLEMENT: INTERNATIONAL COMMERCIAL ARBITRATION IN EUROPE 34 (1994); 7097/1993, *id*. at 39; 7673/1993, *id*. at 36; 6475/1994, 6 ICC BULL. 52 (May 1995); and also the extensive ad hoc award dated 30 June 1994 published *in* 13 SWISS BULL. 269 (1995).

      For an unsuccessful attempt by the Government of New Zealand to avoid ICSID arbitration by maintaining that the dispute involved the Commerce Act 1986 prohibiting contracts that lessen competition, *see* The Government of New Zealand v. Mobil Oil New Zealand Ltd. *et al.*, June 1987 decision by the High Court of Wellington, XIII YEARBOOK 638 (1988). *See generally* Andrew Rogers, *Arbitrability*, 10 ARB. INT. 263 (1994), John Beechey, *Arbitrability of Anti-trust/Competition Law Issues—Common Law*, 12 ARB. INT. 179 (1996).

64   Mitsubishi Motors Corp. v. Soler Chrysler-Plymouth, Inc., 473 U.S. 614 (1985). For an illustration of how the *Mitsubishi* holding has been applied, *see* George Fischer Foundry System, Inc. v. Adolph H. Hottinger Maschinenban GmbH, 1995-1 TRADE CASES (CCH), § 70019, at 74772 (6th

If the arbitrator rejects the claim of unenforceability, the matter does not necessarily stop there; the aggrieved party would not be foreclosed from making its claim to the appropriate public court by way of challenging or resisting an award.[65]

This practical approach by arbitrators has been vindicated at least in the European setting, the European Court itself having ruled that arbitrators, unlike judges, may not obtain answers to preliminary questions on European Community law.[66]

Patents and trademarks. Disputes relating to the validity of patents and trademarks raise a problem of arbitrability, because they are likely to affect the interests of third parties who have not agreed to arbitration. One way of dealing with this problem without rejecting the contractual remedy is to hold that such issues of validity may be decided by arbitrators as concerns relations *between the parties*, but that such an award is not binding on third parties.[67] (In other words, a third party could challenge the validity of a patent

---

Cir. 1995). The French cognate of *Mitsubishi* is the 1993 *Labinal* judgment of the Court of Cassation, 1993 Rev. Arb. 645, 120 JDI 957 (1993), 8 Mealey's Int. Arb. Rep. 7 (July 1993). *See* Antoine Kirry, *Arbitrability: Current Trends in Europe*, 12 Arb. Int. 373, at 376 (1996).

65 Examining the authority of an arbitrator to decide the validity of a contract under Article 85 of the EEC Rome Treaty, a Swiss court applied the following concept. When the outcome of a dispute before one court depends on the answer to an issue with respect to which another court has, in principle, jurisdiction, the first court may nonetheless decide that issue, it being understood that its ruling:

"[I]s but a grounds for its judgment on the principal dispute; it does not have the effect of *res judicata.*"

Accordingly, the contested award comported neither an authoritative disposition of the issue of the validity of the litigious contract under EEC law nor an encroachment of the prerogatives of the European Communities' Court of Justice. The Swiss court noted finally the need to:

"[D]istinguish the object of the arbitration, which is a dispute concerning a right that may freely be created by the parties, from the rules of law that are applicable to the outcome of the litigation."

Decision of the *Chambre des recours* of the Canton of Vaud of 28 October 1975, Ampaglas S.p.A. v. Sofia S.A., extracts *in* Journal des Tribunaux 1981 III 61-127.

66 Judgment of 23 March 1982 in Case 102/1981, (Nordsee); reported *in* 1982 European Court Reports 1112; summarized *in* VIII Yearbook 183 (1983). In a particularly important judgment of 28 April 1992, the Swiss Federal Tribunal annulled an award for having failed to rule on a claim of invalidity under European competition law. 9 Swiss Bull. 368 (1992), 1993 Rev Arb 124, XVIII Yearbook 143 (1993). (This case resulted in a new arbitration; the subsequent award appears *in* 13 Swiss Bull. 269 (1995).)

67 In the United States since 1983 a broad range of patent disputes, including questions of validity and infringement, may thus be decided by arbitrators; Public Law 97-247, 35 U.S.C. §294; *see* Michael Hoellering, *Arbitration of Patent Disputes*, Arbitration & the Law 1987-88 163 (AAA General Counsel's Annual Report). *See generally*, Yves Derains, *L'expérience de la Chambre de commerce internationale en matière de propriété industrielle*, 1997 Rev. Arb. 40; Julian Lew, *ICC Working Party on Intellectual Property Disputes and Arbitration*, Swiss Arbitration Association Special Series No. 6, 44 (1994); Marc Blessing, *Arbitrability of Intellectual Property Disputes*, 12 Arb. Int. 191 (1996).

even if such a challenge by another party had failed before an arbitral tribunal.) Under this approach, the arbitrability of infringement actions is more readily acceptable yet.[68] As for disputes relating to the assignment, performance, or termination of a patent license, their arbitrability has become commonplace.[69]

Bankruptcy. National public policy in some countries may dictate that courts are exclusively competent to hear claims against companies in bankruptcy—especially with respect to disputes arising *after* the bankruptcy petition—presumably in order to avoid the temptation of collusive arbitral proceedings designed to spirit assets away from general creditors.[70] Even then, however, it is not certain that an international arbitrator would be bound by domestic laws or decisions to that effect.[71]

If the dispute requires a ruling on the basis of bankruptcy laws, the award will not necessarily be the final disposition of the matter, but be subject—along the lines of the *Mitsubishi* approach—to some form of substantive control by the bankruptcy court at the stage of enforcement. As the Court

---

68   PHILIPPE FOUCHARD, EMMANUEL GAILLARD & BERTHOLD GOLDMAN, TRAITE DE L'ARBITRAGE COMMERCIAL INTERNATIONAL 358-9 (1996).

69   *See, e.g.*, ICC Case 6709/1991, 119 JDI 998 (1992) as well as other ICC awards *in* 4 ICC BULL. 73 *et seq.* (1993) and 5 ICC BULL. 66 *et seq.* (1994). In Roussel-Uclaf v. G.D. Searle & Co. Ltd. *et al.*, [1978] 1 LLOYD'S L. REP. 225, summarized *in* IV YEARBOOK 317 (1979), the Chancery Division of the English High Court had little difficulty in referring a French company's action for alleged infringement of a U.K. patent to ICC arbitration in Sweden.

70   The French Court of Cassation has twice affirmed, with respect to insolvency proceedings initiated in France: "The principles of the halting of individual claims by creditors, of the exclusion of the debtor and of the interruption of actions in the case of bankruptcy are a matter of both internal and international *ordre public*." *See* the *Thinet* and *Almira* cases, 1989 REV. ARB. 473 and 1991 REV. ARB. 625, respectively.

71   For an ICC award where the arbitrators retained jurisdiction over a defendant company even though it was dissolved and struck from the Registry of Commerce of its domicile during the arbitral proceedings, *see* ICC Case 2139/1974, I ICC AWARDS 23, 237. In ICC Case 4415/1984, I ICC AWARDS 530, an arbitral tribunal sitting in Paris asserted jurisdiction although a defendant had been declared bankrupt by an Italian Court. For a case where an award rendered in Japan against a U.S. company in bankruptcy was enforced by the U.S. federal courts, *see* Copal Co. Ltd. (Japan) v. Fotochrome Inc. (U.S.), 337 F. Supp. 26 (EDNY 1974); *aff'd* 517 F. 2d 512 (2d Cir., 1975); summarized *in* I YEARBOOK 202 (1976); extracts of the underlying award *in* XII YEARBOOK 149 (1987). *Accord*, the reasoning of the *Landgericht* of Bremen in case involving an unnamed Portuguese party having prevailed in arbitration in London against an unnamed German company which was declared bankrupt after the commencement of arbitration; unpublished, extracts *in* XII YEARBOOK 486 (1987). But in Victrix Steamship Co. (Panama) v. Salen Dry Cargo AB (Sweden), the U.S. Federal Court for the Southern District of New York refused to enforce an arbitral award rendered in London which it considered to be part of an attempted "end run around . . . Swedish bankruptcy proceedings," decision of 28 August 1986, XIII YEARBOOK 537, at 542 (1988); *aff'd*, 825 F. 2d 709 (2d Cir. 1987), XV YEARBOOK 534. In République de Côte d'Ivoire *et al.* v. Société Norbert Beyrard, 1994 REV. ARB. 685, the Paris Court of Appeal came to the contrary conclusion: the ICC arbitrators had the right to disregard a bankruptcy judgment invoked by a state-controlled corporation as a purported justification for disregarding contractual obligations. *See also* Casa v. Cambior, ICC Case 6697/1990, 1992 REV. ARB. 135; *and generally* Fernando Mantilla Serrano, *International Arbitration and Insolvency Proceedings*, 11 ARB. INT. 51 (1995).

of Appeal of Paris put it in a judgment in 1989, "the arbitrability of a dispute as a matter of public policy (*ordre public*) is not to be understood as a prohibition against applying mandatory laws, but only against rendering decisions which are intrinsically within the exclusive authority of a state jurisdiction, or rendering decisions that approve conduct that violates public order."[72] Accordingly, the arbitrators were held entitled to apply mandatory rules of bankruptcy law (relating specifically to limitations of share transfers by managers of a company facing bankruptcy) subject to annulment of their award if they failed to respect rules that are part of "French and international" public policy.

Securities law. In the United States, federal laws governing the sale of corporate stocks and bonds were, under a 1953 precedent, to be exclusively applied by federal courts.[73] In a 1974 landmark Supreme Court decision, however, this prohibition against arbitration in the domain of securities law was not applied to an international contract.[74] In 1989, the Supreme Court extended this holding to a purely domestic series of transactions.[75]

Trade boycott. The arbitrability of contracts whose object is a transaction prohibited by national policies against trade boycott is also a matter of controversy. Once again, the possibility arises that domestic prohibition of arbitration is held inapplicable in an international context.[76]

Employment agreements, consumer transactions and matters of personal status. National legislatures set down rules designed for the protection of individuals, and entrust the application of these rules to the judiciary. They generally do not accept that this domain be subjected to decisions by arbitrators, since this may lead to abuse by parties in a dominant negotiating position. Accordingly, an arbitrator will not generally have the authority to decide whether a marriage is dissolved, or whether a will is valid.

---

72 Almira Films v. Pierrel, 1989 REV. ARB. 711, upheld by the Court of Cassation, 1991 REV. ARB. 625.

73 Wilco v. Swan, 346 U.S. 427 (1953). Overruled in Rodriguez de Quijas v. Shearson/American Express, 490 U.S. 477 (1989).

74 Scherk v. Alberto-Culver Co., *supra* Note 33.

75 Rodriguez de Quijas, *supra* Note 73. *See generally* John Kerr, *Arbitrability of Securities Law Claims in Common Law Nations*, 12 ARB. INT. 171 (1996); Hans van Houtte, *Arbitrability Involving Securities Transactions*, 12 ARB. INT. 405 (1996).

76 In Antco Shipping Co. Ltd. (Bahamas) *et al. v.* Sidermar S.p.A. (Italy), 417 F. Supp. 207 (SDNY 1976); summarized *in* II YEARBOOK 251 (1977), arbitration was allowed under a contract for the transport to and from Mediterranean ports "excluding Israel," the court holding that notwithstanding U.S. public policy against restrictive trade practices and boycotts, reflected *inter alia* in the U.S. Export Administration Act of 1969, an international contract could be subject to arbitration, unless the "essence" of the contractual undertaking, or the remedy sought, were expressly and "entirely" forbidden by "a pertinent statute or other declaration of public policy." *See generally* Jean-Hubert Moitry, *L'arbitre international et l'obligation de boycottage imposée par un Etat*, 1991 JDI 349.

Similarly, given the public policy reflected in legislation protecting employees and consumers, arbitration is frequently prohibited in employment agreements[77] and consumer transactions.

More generally, there are a number of civil-law countries in which a distinction is made between commercial and non-commercial transactions. Thus, the sale of a car between two dealers would be commercial, between a dealer and a non-dealer would be mixed, and between two non-dealers non-commercial. Only the commercial transaction could be subject to arbitration. The existence of this distinction explains why Article 1(3) of the New York Convention contemplates the possibility for adhering States to exclude applicability of the Convention to non-commercial matters; 40 States have made that reservation.[78]

Individual countries occasionally identify other domains where, in seeking to protect certain categories of parties, they also prevent such parties from agreeing, whether out of ignorance or weakness, to waive their rights to have contractual disputes heard by their national courts. The Belgian Law on Exclusive Distributorships of 27 July 1961, for example, has enabled some Belgian distributors to escape arbitration clauses.[79] More recent lower court decisions have however sought to reverse this trend, relying particularly on the freedom of parties to international contracts to choose a foreign applicable law, as well as the primacy of the New York Convention over national law.[80]

---

77   In a decision of the *Pretore* of Genoa of 30 April 1980, 16 RIV. DIR. INT. P.P. 458 (1980); summarized *in* VII YEARBOOK 342 (1982), the Italian magistrate having exclusive jurisdiction under Italian law to decide labor disputes refused to recognize an arbitration agreement entered into between an Italian national and his German employer. The Pretore erred in basing this refusal on the fact that the New York Convention should be applied only to "commercial" disputes, because Italy did not so limit its ratification of the Convention. He may not have been aware of the reasoning of the Italian Supreme Court in its decision of 27 April 1979, described in Note 3 *supra*, justifying disregard of an Italian bricklayer's undertaking to arbitrate in Saudi Arabia on the principle that the status and capacity of persons is defined by the State of which they are nationals. *Contra* the 1993 judgment of the Court of Appeal of Grenoble in the *Dechavanne* case, 1994 REV. ARB. 337.

78   For an explanation of the ramifications of France's withdrawal of its commerciality reservation, *see* Philippe Fouchard, *Comment*, 1990 REV. ARB. 571.

79   *See* decision of 28 June 1979 of the Belgian *Cour de cassation*, Audi NSU Auto Union A.G. v. S.A. Adelin Petit & Cie, summarized *in* V YEARBOOK 257 (1980) (German company's agreement with its Belgian distributor to resolve disputes by ICC arbitration held ineffective); *reaffirmed* in S.A. Agima (Belgium) v. Smith Industries Ltd. (UK), decision of the *Tribunal de commerce* of Brussels; summarized *in* VIII YEARBOOK 360 (1983).

80   *See* Pierreux NV v. Transportmaschinen Handelshaus GmbH, Commercial Court of Brussels, 6 May 1993, XXII YEARBOOK 631 (1997); Van Hopplynus S.A. v. Coherent Inc., Commercial Court of Brussels, 5 October 1994, 1995 REV. ARB. 311, XXII YEARBOOK 637 (1997). Bernard Hanotiau has opined that the Belgian prohibition does not involve international public policy, *in What Law Governs the Issue of Arbitrability?* 12 ARB. INT. 391, at 401 (1996). The prohibition was in fact disregarded in ICC Case 6379/1990, III ICC AWARDS 134.

The question is thus whether such national prohibitions should also apply to international contracts. A further question is whether such prohibitions should bind international arbitrators, or courts other than those of the country whose law is at issue.[81]

Agreements to arbitrate that would have been illegal under national law have been accepted by national courts, for example in France,[82] Italy,[83] Tunisia,[84] and the United States,[85] in the context of international contracts. Thus has evolved a concept of international public order as overriding national laws which are mandatory with respect to internal relations.[86]

---

81 For examples of ICC arbitrations in which tribunals rejected the imposition of national laws of one of the parties to the extent that they were "incompatible with the ICC Rules" and "designed to apply only to domestic arbitrations," *see* Cases 4589/1984, II ICC Awards 32, 454; 4695/1984, II ICC Awards 33. The courts of India at one point demonstrated some reluctance to uphold arbitration agreements under the New York Convention because India, in signing the Convention, had made the reservation under Article I(3) that the Convention would apply only to "commercial" legal relationships, and there had been no precise legislative definition of that expression. Subsequent decisions have abandoned this narrow view; *see* citations *in* XII Yearbook 420 (1987).

82 *See* decisions reported *in* Jan Paulsson, *Arbitration Unbound*, 1981 International and Comparative Law Quarterly 358, 369. In a 1993 judgment (*Dechavanne*). 1994 Rev. Arb. 337, the Court of Appeal of Grenoble held that an arbitration clause in an international employment agreement was valid.

    For a controversial decision of the French Supreme Court, *see* Meglio v. Société V2000 *et al.*, Bull. Civ. 1, no. 159, p. 107; Rev. Crit. 1998.87 (with a sceptical commentary by Vincent Heuzé), 1997 Rev. Arb. 537, involving an agreement by a Frenchman to order a limited-edition Jaguar automobile from the company V2000 (Jaguar France). The vehicle was to be manufactured by a UK entity entitled Project XJ 220 Ltd. Stating that he had been misled with respect to the characteristics of the vehicle, Mr Meglio sued both the French and UK entities in the French courts, seeking cancellation of the sale and restitution of his deposit. Noting that the contract contained a clause calling for ad hoc arbitration in London, the defendants asked the French courts to decline to hear the case. The Paris Court of Appeal accepted the objection, and its decision was upheld by the Court of Cassation, which observed that the contract involved international commerce (in particular, it called for a transfer of funds from France to England) and therefore did not fall under the French law applicable to domestic arbitration. If Mr Meglio had contracted with a French manufacturer, the result would have been the opposite, because under the French law application to domestic arbitration, clauses calling for the arbitration of future disputes, contained in contracts between professionals and non-professionals, are not enforceable.

83 *See, e.g.,* the decision of the *Corte di Cassazione* of 7 October 1980, Getreide Import Gesellschaft v. Fratelli Casillo, *supra* Note 37.

84 *See* the three decisions cited in *supra*. Note 5.

85 *See, e.g.,* Scherk v. Alberto Culver Company, *supra* Note 33.

86 Article 1502 of the French Code of Civil Procedure, defining the cases in which awards rendered in international arbitration may be set aside, refers to violations of international public policy. *See* Chapter 30. The Italian Court of Appeal of Bari, in Getreide Import Gesellschaft mbH v. Fratelli Casillo *supra* Note 36, *held* that even though certain formal requirements (*see* Section 5.06) were imperative as a matter of Italian law, they did not pertain to international public order and could therefore be overridden by international conventions.

    Accord, Jacques el-Hakim, *National Report, Syria,* VII Yearbook 35, (1982); M. Issad, *L'arbitrage en Algérie*, 1977 Rev. Arb. 219.

International arbitrators may accordingly in some circumstances disregard national norms on the basis that only the imperative rules of international public order are relevant.[87]

For this reason, it is doubtful that such legislation as Article 139 of the Constitutional Law of the Islamic Republic of Iran (forbidding State entities to agree to arbitration with foreign parties in "significant" cases without the approval of the *Majlis* (Parliament))[88] or the Saudi Arabian Council of Ministers' Decision no. 58 of 25 June 1963 (forbidding State entities to accept international arbitration)[89] would be taken into account by international arbitrators.[90]

The freedom of parties concluding international contracts to agree to arbitration in contexts where under national law they would be unable to arbitrate[91] may, in sum, be viewed as an autonomous substantive rule of public policy favoring the security of international contracts.[92]

---

87   Thus Professor Pierre Lalive, sole arbitrator in ICC Case 1512, refused to excuse a Pakistani bank's non-payment to an Indian claimant irrespective of Pakistani emergency legislation forbidding such payments to be made to Indian nationals, excerpts of the award *in* I YEARBOOK 128 (1976); in French *in* 1974 JDI 904.

88   Cited *in* VI YEARBOOK 193 (1981).

89   Translated *in* 3 ILM 45 (1964). It would appear that the 1963 Decision reflects a mistrust of international arbitration that has been at least partially overcome. In 1979, Saudi Arabia adhered to the Convention on the Settlement of Investment Disputes between States and Nationals of Other States.

90   For authority, see cases cited in Section 5.02. For example, an arbitral tribunal sitting in Holland rejected a jurisdictional defense raised by an Iranian party on the grounds of Article 633 of the Iranian Civil Code, which invalidates arbitration agreements between Iranians and foreigners with respect to future disputes if the arbitrators may include nationals of the same country as the non-Iranian party, the tribunal reasoning that Iranian law did not govern the agreement to arbitrate. Award of 5 September 1977 under the Rules of the Netherlands Oils, Fats and Oilseeds Trade Association (NOFOTA), summarized *in* IV YEARBOOK 218 (1979). *See generally* Serge Lazareff, *Mandatory Extraterritorial Application of National Law*, 11 ARB. INT. 137 (1995).

91   The French cases have particularly involved contracts concluded by nonmerchants; thus, an ICC arbitration clause was held to preclude a court action in France by a French party which had agreed with another French party to distribute its products in North America, even though under French law one of the parties was a non-merchant unable to bind itself to arbitration of future disputes, on the grounds that the contract was "international"; Menicucci v. Mahieux, judgment of the Court of Appeal of Paris of 13 December 1975, 1976 JDI 106.

92   In Meadows Indemnity Co. Ltd. v. Baccala & Shoop Insurance Services, Inc., *et al.*, 760 F. SUPP. 1036 (1991) (EDNY), XVII YEARBOOK 686 (1992), the U.S. federal District Court rejected a contention to the effect that a dispute was not "capable of settlement by arbitration" for the purposes of the New York Convention and stated:

    "The determination of whether a type of claim is not capable of settlement by arbitration under Article II(1) [of the Convention] must be made *on an international scale*, with reference to the laws of the countries party to the Convention." (Emphasis added.)

    See also Quintette Coal Ltd. v. Nippon Steel Corp., British Columbia Court of Appeal, (1990) 50 BCLR (2d) 207, 1991 1 WWR 219: "… it will be necessary for national courts to subordinate domestic notions of arbitrability to the international policy favoring commercial arbitration."

5.08   Incorporation by reference

Cases brought to international arbitration frequently involve complex situations where numerous contractual documents relate to one organic relationship, and it appears inappropriate for different jurisdictions to deal with necessarily interrelated issues in a piecemeal and potentially inconsistent manner. On occasion, however, complicated issues arise if one contract contains an arbitration clause, but other documents do not. For example, is a subsequent agreement not containing a reference to arbitration to be deemed a novation or an amendment? The survival of the arbitration clause may depend on the answer.

The obvious solution is to incorporate the arbitration clause contained in the central contract by reference in subsequent documents. Careful and experienced practitioners will know how to keep a contractual relationship intended to be subject to arbitration from slipping into a hybrid state, half- in, half-out, which makes the arbitral mechanism unworkable.

The mechanism of incorporation by reference is also important in types of trading where standard conditions are frequently used. Thus commodities dealers may simply create a contract by an exchange of telexes containing no more than mention of price, quantity, and manner of delivery, and reference to the standard conditions of a trade association. Those standard conditions may include arbitration. While Italian courts in particular long wrestled with the problem of such references, it now seems clear, at least when the New York Convention is applicable, that incorporation by reference may create a binding agreement to arbitrate.[93]

ICC cases tend not to be based on the arbitration provisions of such standard conditions, which more frequently are employed in certain specialized trading *milieux* where the parties have a high volume of transactions and cannot take the time to negotiate complex agreements.[94] The type of arbitration provided for is handled within a trade association. It is expeditious and well-re-

---

93   *See, e.g.,* the decision of the *Corte di Cassazione* of 7 October 1980, Getreide Import Gesellschaft v. Fratelli Casillo, *supra* Note 37; Ferrara S.p.A. v. United Grain Growers Ltd., *supra* Note 32; Mauritius Sugar Syndicate (Mauritius) *et al.* v. Black Lion Shipping Co. S.A. (Panama) *et al.* (*The "Rena K"*, Queen's Bench Division (Admiralty)), [1978] 1 LLOYD'S L. REP. 545; summarized *in* IV YEARBOOK 323 (1979). Article 1443 of the French Code of Civil Procedure explicitly accepts as binding arbitration clauses contained in documents to which the principal contract refers. *See generally* ALBERT JAN VAN DEN BERG, THE NEW YORK ARBITRATION CONVENTION OF 1958, 208 (1981).

94   For a case where Dutch arbitrators held that they had jurisdiction with respect to three contracts, only the first of which was in writing, but where because of the similarity of the transactions (printing of travel posters for a tour operator) the Belgian defendant was presumed to have accepted the maintenance of reference to the original terms of delivery (which in turn referred to arbitration in Holland), *see* the Graphic Industry Award of 6 March 1973, summarized *in* III YEARBOOK 224 (1978). *But see* Société Confex (Romania) v. Etablissements Dahan (France), decision of the French *Cour de cassation,* 25 February 1986, 1986 JDI 735, XII YEARBOOK 484 (1987).

spected by parties careful not to harm their reputation within a tight-knit branch.

ICC arbitration is not of the summary "look-sniff" type, in which experienced tradesmen quickly examine a cargo of oranges or a shipment of cowhides, and which of course is eminently suited for certain routine contracts. For this reason, reference to ICC arbitration is generally made by means of a clause included in the contract established between the parties. A notable exception arose in the *Bomar Oil* case, which involved an agreement (for the sale of crude oil) by exchange of telexes referring to the general conditions of the seller's standard contract. These general conditions stipulated ICC arbitration. The buyer rejected ICC jurisdiction, and a series of arbitral and judicial decisions ensued, culminating in a judgment of the Court of Cassation which held that there had been a valid agreement to arbitrate.[95]

5.09   Related parties not having signed the arbitration agreement

ICC arbitrators are frequently asked to join in the proceedings parties not signatory to the arbitration agreement.

A distinction should be made between the case where the party whose participation is at issue *desires* to be included from the case where it *resists* being joined.

The first case might involve companies subject to common control, where Company A formally signed the contract containing the arbitration clause but Company B in fact suffered loss as a result of the defendant's alleged breach. Company A and Company B jointly request the arbitrator to allow Company B to participate as claimant.

The second category includes, for example, situations where claimant's contract (containing the arbitration clause) was with Company X, but claimant wants to hold Company Y responsible for the alleged breach.

Common sense would suggest that the former request is more likely to succeed than the latter, since the objecting party did sign the arbitration clause and since the dispute concerns a contract to which it is a party and which it is alleged to have breached.[96] In the latter case, the objecting party has nei-

---

95   Bomar Oil (Netherlands Antilles) v. ETAP (Tunisia), judgment of 9 November 1993, 1994 REV. ARB. 108; XX YEARBOOK 660 (1995). The French courts consider the issue to be one of fact, focussing on whether the defendant did understand or should have understood that it was agreeing to arbitration. Most businessmen are held to this understanding. *But see* the *Psichikon* judgment of 7 January 1992, 1992 REV. ARB. 553 (bill of lading signed by the captain of a ship). *Cf.* Article 1201 of the Netherlands Code of Civil Procedure; and Article 7(2) of the UNCITRAL Model Law. *See generally* Section 29.02.

96   The case of Roussel-Uclaf v. G.D. Searle & Co. Ltd. (U.K.) and G.D. Searle & Co. (U.S.). *Supra* Note 69, lends some support for this proposition. There, the French plaintiff brought a patent infringement action before the courts of England against both Searle & Co. and its U.K. subsidiary. Searle & Co. requested that the matter be referred to ICC arbitration in Sweden as agreed by con-

ther agreed to the arbitration clause nor indeed been a party to the relevant agreement.[97]

Much of the debate has focussed on the so-called group of companies doctrine, which became a familiar topic following the publication of the interim award in the *Dow Chemical* case decided in 1982 by an ICC tribunal presided by Prof. Pieter Sanders. The arbitrators rejected the request of the defendant, the French company Isover St. Gobain, that claimant Dow Chemical (U.S.), the parent company, and claimant Dow Chemical (France), a subsidiary, be dismissed as parties to the arbitration on the grounds that the contract containing the arbitration clause had been signed between claimant Dow Chemical (Switzerland), another subsidiary, and the defendant.[98]

Seeking to obtain the result they perceived to conform to the intent of the parties and to the good usages of international commerce (*see* Section 5.05), the arbitrators accepted Dow Chemical (U.S.) and Dow Chemical (France) as parties to the arbitration. To reach this decision, they reviewed the record of correspondence between the parties and concluded that it had not made the

---

tract, and requested a stay of the English court action in deference to the arbitration. The question arose whether the stay should also apply to Searle & Co. (U.K.), even though it was a separate legal entity and not a party to the arbitration agreement. The court stated that:

> "The two parties and their actions are . . . so closely related on the facts of this case that it would be right to hold that the subsidiary can establish that it is within the purview of the arbitration clause, on the basis that it claiming 'through or under' the parent to do what it is in fact doing whether ultimately held to be wrongful or not."

A stay was granted in favor of both defendants.

The English House of Lords was willing to assume, in *dictum,* that an arbitration clause contained in a partnership agreement would apply to disputes between partners as well as to disputes between the partnership and individual partners, and furthermore that a party entering into the partnership could avail itself of the arbitration agreement, Nova (Jersey) Knit Ltd. v. Kammgarn Spinnerei GmbH (FRG), 16 February 1977, [1977] 1 LLOYD'S L. REP. 163; summarized *in* IV YEARBOOK 314 (1979). The 1985 Rules of the London Court of International Arbitration provided in Article 13 that the arbitral tribunal has the power to "allow other parties to be joined in the arbitration with their express consent, and make a final award determining all disputes between them." Such power is neutralized only if *all* the parties to the arbitration agreement wish to exclude such willing intervening parties; *see* Martin Hunter and Jan Paulsson, *Commentary on the 1985 Rules of the LCIA,* X YEARBOOK 167, 169 (1985). This provision reappears in slightly modified wording as Article 22.1(h) of the 1998 LCIA Rules.

97 In Coastal States Trading Inc. (U.S.) v. Zenith Navigation S.A. (Panama), 446 F. Supp. 330 (SDNY, 1977); summarized *in* IV YEARBOOK 329 (1979), a U.S. company, seeking to compel a Panamian company to submit their dispute to arbitration although the two parties had not together signed any agreement whatsoever, failed to convince the court that the latter was the alter ego of another company having signed an agreement with the U.S. party containing an arbitration clause. The court was not satisfied that the Panamian company was so controlled by another company that it had "no separate mind, will or existence of its own." (Nevertheless, arbitration was ordered between the parties on an alternate ground: a bill of lading for a cargo of oil, of which the party seeking arbitration was consignee—the Panamian company being the shipowner—and which incorporated the terms of a charter party containing a broadly drafted arbitration clause.)

98 *Supra* Note 19.

slightest difference which entity within the Dow group had formally signed the contract; the defendant had maintained correspondence with personnel of both Dow Chemical (U.S.) and Dow Chemical (France), specifically pertaining to the performance of the contract formally signed with Dow Chemical (Switzerland). The tribunal concluded that the defendant had in fact intended to contract with the Dow group as a whole, and that accordingly they could deem Dow Chemical (U.S.) and Dow Chemical (France) to be parties to the contract.

This holding is consonant with that made in a U.S. arbitral decision rendered under the auspices of the Society of Maritime Arbitrators, where the arbitrators reviewing the industry practice of operating through multiple subsidiaries at various stages (chartering, shipping and consigning) and expressing their loathness "to narrowly restrict the parties' apparent intention to arbitrate their differences." stated that it was "neither sensible nor practical" to exclude from the arbitration claims of companies "having an interest in the venture and who are members of the same corporate family."[99]

In neither the *Dow Chemical* ICC case nor the Society of Maritime Arbitrators case were the arbitrators required to say whether their conclusion implied A and B could have been made unwilling defendants under the contract signed by C. (It will be noted that as defendants to a counterclaim, they could hardly be characterized as unwilling parties before the arbitral tribunal.) This more difficult question was raised in ICC Case 2138 of 1974 where the tribunal refused to extend the effects of the arbitration clause signed by one entity in a group of companies to another member of that group, stating that with respect to the company not party to the litigious agreement that:

> it was not demonstrated that (it) would have accepted the arbitration clause if it had signed the contract.[100]

A proponent of the "group" approach has acknowledged that it would be excessive to hold that the moment a company signs an agreement containing an arbitration clause, all entities it may control are also bound by that clause, but maintains that incipient proof that controlled companies are subject to arbitral jurisdiction may be

> confirmed by the effective participation of such companies in the performance of the contract. Only those companies of the group that played a part in the negotiation, conclusion, or termination of the contract may

---

99   1980 Award, MAP Tankers, Inc. v. MOBIL Tankers, Ltd., extracts *in* VII YEARBOOK 151 (1982).

100   I ICC AWARDS 242. *Accord*, ICC Cases 3742/1983, I ICC AWARDS 486; 4402/1983, I ICC AWARDS 153; 4504/1985, II ICC AWARDS 279; Oriental Commercial and Shipping Co. *et al.* v. Rosseel N.V., 609 F. SUPP. 75 (SDNY 1985); excerpts *in* XII YEARBOOK 532 (1987).

For the special context of contracts signed by State entities but implicating the State itself, *see* SPP *et al.* v. Arab Republic of Egypt, decision of the Court of Appeal of Paris of 12 July 1984, 1984 JDI 124, English translation *in* 23 ILM 1048 (1984); affirmed by the *Cour de cassation* on 6 January 1987, 1987 JDI 638; English translation *in* XIII YEARBOOK 152 (1988).

thus find themselves bound by the arbitration clause, which, at the time of the signature of the contract, virtually bound the economic entity constituted by the group. Beyond the general principle, the arbitrators should thus appreciate on a case by case basis not only the existence of an intention of the members of the group to bind it as a whole, but also and especially, if such an intent is established, its practical effects vis-a-vis each of the companies of the group considered separately.[101]

It may be instructive to consider how some ICC arbitrators have sought to apply the group theory as a justification to extend arbitral jurisdiction beyond the signatories of the agreement to arbitrate.

ICC Case 2375/1975[102] resulted in both the acceptance of a claimant and the inclusion of a defendant against the joint defendants' wishes. The defendants were two Spanish companies, one the subsidiary of the other. The sole claimant was a French company, which had not signed the relevant agreement. The agreement had in fact been signed by a French company of which the claimant had been at the time, but was no longer, a subsidiary. The agreement had been signed only between the two original parent companies. The dispute concerned an alleged debt relating to costs of preparing tenders for a public-works project in Spain. The former French mother company had no interest in the litigation.

The defendants contended that claimant had no standing to sue in arbitration, not having signed the arbitration agreement with them; and even if this were not so, the Spanish subsidiary could not be a defendant in arbitration, because it had not even signed the agreement with the then French parent company. The ICC arbitral tribunal rejected the defense on both points, noting that the French parent company had expressly reserved its part in the project "for its subsidiary" (the claimant-to-be), that the parties' correspondence referred to the Spanish entities as a "group," and that members of the board of a joint-venture promoting company had been appointed "on behalf of" the Spanish subsidiary rather than its parent company. Holding that:

> the concept of a group is not to be found in the formal independence created by the establishment of separate legal entities, but in the single economic orientation given by a common authority,[103]

the arbitral tribunal took jurisdiction over the parties in the manner requested by the claimant.

---

101 Yves Derains, Note, 1983 JDI 905, at 906. The judgement of the Court of Appeal of Paris *in* the *Kis France* case followed similar reasoning in extending the effect of an arbitration clause to subsidiaries of the signatories, 1992 REV. ARB. 90; XVI YEARBOOK 145 (1991).

102 1 ICC AWARDS 257.

103 *Id.* at 258 (our translation).

A similar result was obtained in ICC Case 1434,[104] where the concept of the corporate group was likewise applied to hold corporate entities bound to an arbitration clause contained in a contract they had not signed. The case involved a complex project in a developing country. A number of contractual documents related to specific elements of the project: technical assistance, supply of productive machinery, financing, and so forth. Some entities of the group of defendants had signed one agreement and not the other; some agreements contained an arbitration clause, others not. In one instance, a document expressly referred to the defending companies as a "group." Faced with this state of confusion, the arbitral tribunal looked to the intent of the parties, which it considered to be the creation of an integrated contractual relationship subject to one single arbitration, and held the defendants bound by the arbitration agreement.[105]

It must be recognized that the assertion of arbitral jurisdiction over parties not having signed the agreement to arbitrate is a controversial matter, and that the enforceability before national courts of awards rendered against protesting third-party non-signatory defendants is open to doubt.[106]

With respect to *assignments* of contract, the general rule is that the assignee may invoke an arbitration clause contained in an assigned contract (i.e. *Both the main contract and the agreement to arbitrate are assigned*) unless the agreement to arbitrate is inseparable from the assignor.[107] Naturally the is-

---

104 I ICC AWARDS 263. *Accord*, ICC Case 5103/1988, II ICC AWARDS 361. *See also* further examples extracted *in* 2 ICC BULL. 20 *et seq.* (1991).

105 For a further discussion of this case, *see* Jan Paulsson, *Third World Participation in International Investment Arbitration*, 1987 ICSID REVIEW FOREIGN INVESTMENT LAW JOURNAL 19 at 25. For an assessment of the parties' intention to the contrary effect, *see* ICC Cases 5721/1990, 117 JDI 1020 (1990); and 6610/1991, XIX YEARBOOK 162 (1994).

106 The perceived "rigorousness" of Swiss law in this respect was a principal factor in the arbitrators' refusal to assert jurisdiction under the group approach in ICC Cases 4402/1983, I ICC AWARDS 153 and 4504/1985-86, II ICC AWARDS 279.

The extension of arbitration agreements to cover non-signatories is explored in six different essays published *in* THE ARBITRATION AGREEMENT—ITS MULTIFOLD CRITICAL ASPECTS, SWISS ARBITRATION ASSOCIATION SPECIAL SERIES NO. 8 (December 1994).

107 For a decision of the Italian Supreme Court upholding the validity of an arbitral clause in respect of a receiver of goods as holder of a bill of lading containing said clause, *see* the decision of 11 September 1979, S.A. Assicuriazioni e Riassicurazioni "Lloyd Continental" S.p.A. v. Navigazione Alga (Italy), summarized *in* VI YEARBOOK 230 (1981). The *Corte di cassazione* stated, *id.* at 232:

"The endorsement of the bill of lading entitled the endorsee to the exercise of all the rights deriving from the contract of transportation, including the right to act against the transporter for damages incurred to the cargo."

Accord, Tradax Export S.A. (Panama) v. Amoco Iran Oil Co. (US), decision of Swiss Federal Tribunal of 7 February 1984, XI YEARBOOK 532 (1986). *See also* ICC Case 7154/1993, III ICC AWARDS 555.

sue should be examined under the applicable law prior to assignment in any particular case.[108]

In the U.S., courts have allowed corporate officers acting as agents of the entity to invoke arbitration agreements in order to prevent circumvention of the arbitral remedy and to uphold the intent of the signatories "to protect individuals acting on behalf of the principal in furtherance of the agreement."[109]

5.10 Related agreements not containing the arbitration clause

Occasionally, disputes arise involving documents ancillary to the main contract, such as a guarantee of performance of the main contract. If such a guarantee contains X's engagement to stand behind Y's contractual performance vis-a-vis A, but does not explicitly state that X also commits itself to the arbitral mechanism contemplated in the main contract, the question arises whether the general reference to the main contract is sufficient to bind X to arbitration.

The answer depends to a considerable extent on the wording of the guarantee.

Quite often, the guarantor is a company related to the principal obligator, and for that reason both parties will accept to join in the same proceedings rather than having to face two litigations with complicated, uncertain, and possibly contradictory results, whether in or outside arbitration. For the same reason, even when a perfectly self-contained arbitration clause is included in the guarantee itself, the guarantor will not attempt to create separate proceedings, for example by naming a different arbitrator than the one chosen by the principal obligator.

In one ICC case, *Universal Pictures v. Inex Film and Inter-Export,*[110] a Yugoslav government entity, Inter Export, had guaranteed the obligations of another State entity, Inex Film. The guarantee took the form of a brief sentence and signature added at the bottom of the signature page of the agreement between Inex and Universal, which contained an arbitration clause. The sentence, immediately under the signatures on behalf of Inex Film and Universal, was in handwriting and read: "The undersigned guarantees per-

---

108 There are of course a number of situations where third parties may seek to rely on, or ignore, arbitration clauses in documents in which they come to have a stake. *See* Pascal Ancel, Case comment, Parodi v. Annecy et France Boissons, Court of Appeal of Lyon, 1997 REV. ARB. 402.

109 Hirschfeld Productions Inc. v. Edwin Mirvich, *et al.*, N.Y. Court of Appeals, 11 MEALEY'S INT. ARB. REP. B-1 (Nov. 1996).

110 This case is in the public domain because the award was filed in execution proceedings before the French courts, and was confirmed by the Court of Appeal of Paris, 1978 REV. ARB. 515, and the COUR DE CASSATION; JURISCLASSEUR PÉRIODIQUE No. 27-28, 9 JULY 1980, PART IV, 257. *See also* Antco v. Sidermar S.p.A., *supra* Note 76.

formance by Inex Film of the above contract." On the basis of this sentence, Inter-Export was held subject to the arbitration clause.[111]

The English House of Lords, reversing the Court of Appeal, has held by a majority opinion,[112] in a dispute between English and German parties, that an arbitration clause contained in a partnership agreement and referring to "all disputes arising hereunder" did *not* extend to cover claims under bills of exchange issued in favor of the English party, which had sold machinery to the partnership in which it participated. Accordingly, the English party was allowed to pursue its claim under the bills of exchange irrespective of the German party's insistence that the action be stayed in deference to arbitral proceedings initiated in Germany under the partnership agreement.[113]

International arbitrators have extended the effect of arbitration clauses to related contracts on the basis that the latter pertained to the same project or transaction and thus were part of a united or interrelated contractual scheme, or that they were otherwise ancillary to the document containing the arbitration clause; such determinations tend to involve a case-by-case analysis of facts and legitimate expectations.[114]

---

111 *Accord,* award of 1 October 1980 of the Court of Arbitration at the Chamber of Commerce and Industry in Sofia, extracts *in* XII YEARBOOK 84 (1987). *But see* ICC Cases 3896/1982, I ICC AWARDS 161, 481; 4392/1983, I ICC AWARDS 473; and Josef Meissner GmbH & Co. v. Kanoria Chemicals & Industries Ltd., decision of the High Court of Calcutta, 1986, 1986 ALL INDIA REPORTS CAL. 45; excerpts *in* XIII YEARBOOK 497 (1988). For a case where a U.S. court held that a guarantor having signed a guarantee worded in general terms is deemed to have accepted the arbitration clause by reference, *see* Compania Espanola de Petroles S.A. v. Nereus Shipping S.A., 527 F. 2d 99 (2d Cir. 1975). *Accord*, United States Fidelity Co. v. West Point Construction Co., 837 F. 2d 1507 (11th Cir. 1988); *contra* Oddmund Grundstad v. Joseph Ritt *et al.*, 106 F. 3d 201 (7th Cir. 1997).

112 Nova (Jersey) Knit Ltd. v. Kammgarn Spinnerei GmbH (FRG), *supra* Note 96. *Accord,* Renusagar Power Co. v. General Electric Co. and the International Chamber of Commerce, supra Note 2; SGS S.A. (France) v. Raytheon (US), 643 F. Rep. 2d. 863 (1st Cir. 1981).

113 *Cf.* Primex International Corp. v. Wal-Mart Stores, Inc., 89 N.Y. 2d 594, 657 N.Y.S. 2d 385 (1997) (merger clause in contract not containing arbitration clause held to enable enforcement of arbitration clauses in prior, expired agreements).

   See generally, PHILIPPE FOUCHARD, EMMANUEL GAILLARD & BERTHOLD GOLDMAN, TRAITÉ DE L'ARBITRAGE COMMERCIAL INTERNATIONAL 317 *et seq.* (1996).

114 *Compare* SOABI v. Republic of Senegal, ICSID Case No. ARB/82/1, XVIII YEARBOOK 42, esp. 51 ss (1992) ("a single project" involving construction of a pre-fabrication plant and construction of 15,000 dwellings, the performance of the latter pursuant to a separate agreement necessarily falling under the scope of the arbitration clause contained in an umbrella agreement) *with* ICC Case No. 7375/1996 (Iran v. Westinghouse Electric Corp., award on preliminary issues), 11 MEALEY'S INT. ARB. REP. A-1 (December 1996) ("a single unified transaction" involving nine contracts for the sale of air defense radar equipment, only one of which contained an ICC arbitration clause).

   The award in ICC Case No. 5651/1988, unpublished, asserting jurisdiction over an amendment to a drilling contract, was upheld by the Swiss Federal Tribunal in KCA Drilling v. Sonatrach, ATF 116 I a 56.

5.11   Multi-party disputes

In its simplest form, the issue of multi-party disputes does not involve non-signatories of the arbitration clause. The parties have indeed agreed to arbitration, but the fact that they are more than two creates difficulties. For example, in a situation with two defendants, each defendant insists on naming an arbitrator, thereby creating the specter of an unworkable (and, under Article 8(1) of the ICC Rules, impermissible) four-member tribunal.

The basic problem in such a situation is how to provide for a manageable multi-party arbitration at the negotiating stage, when it is possible to seek agreement of all parties concerned. This subject will be dealt with in Section 8.14.

However, the multi-party arbitration problem also arises with respect to *non-signatories* of the relevant arbitration clause(s). For example, in ICC Case 2272/1975,[115] an Italian patent holder A brought a claim against a Belgian manufacturer B which A had agreed could produce the patented product exclusively. Their agreement contained an ICC arbitration clause. B in turn made an exclusive distributorship agreement with Belgian company C, under which the *Tribunal de commerce* of Brussels was the chosen forum. The A-B agreement was linked with the B-C agreement inasmuch as B's obligation to A to manufacture the product depended on C's orders under the B-C agreement.

In arbitration, B argued that the arbitrator should decline to take jurisdiction over the case on the grounds that B had sued both A and C before the Brussels court: C could not be brought into the ICC arbitration against its will; the Brussels court was the only one that could hear all three parties in the same proceedings, and such a consolidation was necessary in view of the interconnectedness of the two sets of contractual relationships.

The arbitrator noted that the consolidation before the Brussels court was not required legally, but rather a matter of convenience for B.[116] In fact, C was the sole real defendant in Brussels, and A had obtained B's contractual undertaking to submit to ICC arbitration to the exclusion of any ordinary court of law. The arbitrator accordingly took jurisdiction over A's claim.

It was thus B's problem that it had failed to get C into the ICC proceedings, or A to submit to the jurisdiction of the Brussels court. The solution outside arbitration is that of compulsory joinder, which falls in the domain of courts of general jurisdiction and by definition beyond the scope of the present inquiry,

---

115   1 ICC CASES 11. *See generally* C. Stippl, *International Multi-Party Arbitration: The Role of Party Autonomy*, 7 AMERICAN REVIEW OF INTERNATIONAL ARBITRATION 47 (1996).

116   For another case of a party "in the middle" for whose convenience the English Court of Appeal evidenced solicitousness, *see* Abu Dhabi Gas Liquefaction Company Ltd. v. Eastern Bechtel Corp. and Chiyoda Chemical Engineering & Construction Co. Ltd./Eastern Bechtel Corp. and Chiyoda Chemical Engineering & Construction Co. Ltd. v. Abu Dhabi Gaz Liquefaction Company Ltd., [1982] 2 LLOYD'S L. REP. 425; 21 ILM 1057 (1982); published in French with a commentary by Jan Paulsson *in* 1983 REV. ARB. 119.

which is to assess the validity of mechanisms for dealing with the problem at the contract drafting stage.

Nevertheless, it is useful to review how courts have dealt with the problem, with due attention given to the increased jurisdictional difficulties that often arise in the international context.[117]

For example, in *Dale Metals Corp. v. KIWA*,[118] U.S. Company A and its principal shareholder U.S. Company B signed an agreement for the exclusive sales representation of Japanese companies 1 and 2. The product was delivered for distribution in the U.S. under "confirmations of sale" signed by US-B and Japan-2 only. These "confirmations of sale" contained a clause providing for arbitration in Tokyo.

Alleging that the Japanese manufacturers had violated the original exclusive agreement by dealing with two alternative U.S. distributors, US-A and US-B brought an action before a U.S. federal court in New York against not only Japan-1 and Japan-2, but also the two alternative U.S. distributors. Japan-2 reacted by invoking the arbitration clause contained in the "confirmations of sale," and commenced proceedings against US-B in Tokyo. It next moved for the U.S. court to stay the suit in the U.S. pending arbitration. US-A and US-B retorted that three of the defendants before the U.S. courts were not subject to the arbitration clause and thus not involved in the arbitral proceedings, and that therefore there were no grounds to stay US-A and US-B's suit against them.

The American court noted that the claim against Japan-1 and Japan-2 were identical, and thus the alleged prejudice of US-A and US-B was likewise identical. As for the two alternative U.S. distributors, all defendants were claimed to share responsibility for their alleged wrongdoings. Accordingly, the court concluded:

> it is fair to say that in an arbitration proceeding between (Japan-2) and (US-B) every issue that is raised here will be vigorously pressed. In such circumstances a stay is appropriate even though it affects parties who are not bound to arbitrate.

In essence, on the strength of its conclusions that US-A and US-B had identical interests, the court thus gave all four defendants the benefit of an arbitration agreement signed by only one of them. But if one of the three non-signatory defendants were not happy with the result in arbitration, and rejected any inference of *res judicata* resulting from the arbitration, the six parties' legal relationship might be terribly confused. Accordingly, the court granted the motion to stay on the condition that all four defendants within 30

117　*See generally* Jerry Scowcroft, *Note on Consolidation of Arbitration*, XIII YEARBOOK 128 (1988). Article 1046 of the Netherlands Code of Civil Procedure explicitly empowers the courts to order consolidation of arbitrations, *see* Pieter Sanders, *The New Dutch Arbitration Act*, 3 ARB. INT. 194, at 200 (1987); a possibility that also exists under the Arbitration Ordinance of Hong Kong, *see* Chapter 34.

118　442 F. SUPP. 78 (SDNY, 1977).

days agree in writing not only to be bound by the arbitral proceedings in Tokyo, but also to allow both US-A and US-B to take part in them.

This instance of judicial creativeness brought about a potentially efficacious solution to a complicated problem. It may be that the original exclusive distribution agreement covered more aspects than the "confirmations of sale," and that therefore the arbitral proceedings would not resolve all issues outstanding among the parties. But in that event, as the "confirmations of sale" were a part of the larger distributorship relationship rather than the other way around, the solution would appear appropriate in putting the horse before the cart; that part of the parties' relationship which was subject to arbitration would be carved out of the general dispute, and given a logical precedence.[119]

Another U.S. court ordered consolidation of arbitral proceedings in which an Italian company was claiming against a Bahamian company and the U.S. guarantor of the latter's contractual performance.[120]

The danger of inconsistent arbitration provisions was illustrated by a case before the High Court of Bombay, in which an American group of companies (a parent company and two subsidiaries) had concluded three contracts, of which two provided for arbitration in London, and the third for arbitration in India. The Indian court refused to defer to arbitration.[121] While its essential motivation was the non-commercial nature of the dispute under Indian law, it also took into account the preferability of dealing with all of the issues in one procedure. The result, of course, was that whereas all parties had initially intended for their disputes to be resolved in arbitration, the Indian court allowed none of them to do so.

---

119 For another application of this notion, *see* Sonatrach v. General Tire & Rubber Company, 430 F. SUPP. 1332 (SDNY 1977). *See also* Antco Shipping Co. Ltd. v. Sidermar S.p.A., *supra* Note 76; *Compare* Marathon Oil Company v. Ruhrgas A.G., 115 F. 3d 315 (5th Cir. 1997), rehearing ordered, 129 F. 3d 746 (1997).

120 Antco v. Sidermar, *supra* Note 76.

121 4 April 1977, Indian Organic Chemicals Ltd. v. Chemtex Fibres Inc. (U.S.) *et al.*, 65 ALL INDIA REPORTER, Bombay, Section 106 (1978); summarized *in* IV YEARBOOK 271 (1979).

See *Tribunale de Milano*, 22 March 1976, Sopac Italiana S.p.A. v. Bukama GmbH (FRG) and FIMM (Italy), 12 RIVISTA DI DIRITTO PRIVATO P.P. 574 (1976); summarized *in* II YEARBOOK 248 (1977) (where an Italian party started court action against joint German and Italian defendants, the Italian court retained jurisdiction over the claim as to the Italian defendant irrespective of a clause calling for arbitration in Zürich, contained in a contract between the plaintiff and the German defendant; as the plaintiff alleged breach of a license and distribution agreement, and as the German licensor was a majority shareholder of the Italian defendant which had engaged in parallel manufacture and distribution, the subject matter of the dispute was too inseparable to allow two proceedings with potentially inconsistent results. *Held*, the arbitration clause had become inoperative for the purposes of Article II(3) of the New York Convention.)

See also *Cour d'appel* of Paris, 21 December 1979, Burgmeister & Wain Engineering Co. Ltd. (Denmark) v. Creusot Loire (France) *et al.*, 1981 REV. ARB. 155, sharply criticized by Jacqueline Rubellin-Devichi, *De l'effectivité de la clause compromissoire en cas de pluralité de défendeurs ou d'appel en garantie dans la jurisprudence récente*, 1981 REV. ARB. 29, 44; and reversed by the French *Cour de cassation* on 8 November 1982, 1983 REV. ARB. 177.

CHAPTER 6

INDISPENSABLE ELEMENTS

6.01   Unambiguous reference to ICC arbitration

Under Article 6(2) of the Rules, there can be no ICC arbitration against the defendant's wishes, and the ICC Court will not even establish a tribunal for the limited purpose of ruling on jurisdiction, unless

> it is *prima facie* satisfied that an arbitration agreement under the Rules may exist.

Accordingly, in order to be able to rely on the ICC arbitral mechanism irrespective of the defendant's attitude at the time of dispute, one must have a clear expression of intent not only to arbitrate, but also to have the arbitration take place under the ICC Rules.

It is a fact that when parties refer to arbitration "by the International Chamber of Commerce in Geneva" (or The Hague, or Stockholm), the ICC has taken jurisdiction in spite of the fact that the ICC has no seat in those cities. On the theory that the parties' intent to refer to ICC arbitration is unmistakable, and given the fact that there is no "alternative" ICC in the city named, the ICC's practice is to consider that the ICC has jurisdiction, and that the place of arbitration for the particular dispute in question should be the place stipulated.[1]

In ICC Case 5029/1986, II ICC AWARDS 69, 480, the arbitrators dismissed an objection by the defendant to the effect that a reference to the ICC Rules was

---

[1]   An argument to the effect that reference to the "International Chamber of Commerce in Vienna" was inoperative was dismissed by the Dresden *Oberlandesgericht* (court of appeal) in a judgment of 5 December 1995, excerpts *in* XXII YEARBOOK 266 (1997) on the basis that it should be interpreted as a reference to the ICC Court, Vienna being the place of arbitration, with the comment, *id.* at 268, that "there is no indication that the parties intended to give the arbitral clause a meaning other than the meaning usual in transnational commerce." *But see* the judgment of the *Oberlandesgericht* of Hamm of 15 November 1994, where reference to "the arbitral tribunal of the International Chamber of Commerce in Paris, seat in Zurich" was held to be null and void for failure to indicate a precise choice. It is true that there is a Zurich Chamber of Commerce which has its own rules of arbitration, but the excerpt of the judgment appearing *in* XXII YEARBOOK 707

"abstruse and unintelligible" because it did not make clear that it contemplated the ICC that is based in Paris and "there are, as it is well known, a large number of international chambers of commerce in the world;" the arbitrators did not have "the slightest doubt" but that the ICC was adequately defined. In ICC Case 5103/1988, II ICC AWARDS 361, an arbitral tribunal constituted under an arbitration clause referring imprecisely to the "International Section of the Chamber of Commerce of Paris" rejected an objection to the effect that such a body did not exist.

Needless to say, it is advisable to be quite precise so as to avoid all possible future controversy. Thus caution should be exercised whenever one varies the simple language of the ICC Model Clause (*see* Section 6.03).

6.02   Scope of the dispute to be arbitrated

Parties cannot enter into an unlimited agreement that any controversy that should ever arise between them is subject to arbitration. There must be some degree of specificity in defining the kind of controversy one undertakes to submit to arbitration. The basic approach to be recommended in international commercial relations is to refer to a legal relationship created by one or more contracts. Referring broadly to disputes arising "in connection with" a contract gives the arbitral tribunal latitude to rule on quasi-contractual claims. More generally, it is important that the arbitral tribunal rule not only on disputes as to the performance of the contract (*i.e.* essentially issues of fact), but also on controversies relating to the existence, validity, breach and termination of the agreement (*i.e.* fundamental legal issues), as well as the financial consequences of a determination of any of the above points.

In the *Beira Pipeline* litigation,[2] an English judge was faced with a request for an injunction, as well as damages on account of breach of contract, unlawful interference with contract, conspiracy and negligence. The contract in question comported an undertaking by several oil companies to use only the Beira Pipeline, and contained an arbitration clause. The two plaintiffs, operators of the Pipeline, contended that the defendants had assured the "rebel" Government of Rhodesia that they would be in a position to supply oil despite the closing of the Pipeline as an international sanction for the unilateral declaration of independence made by Rhodesia in 1965, that this assurance had contributed to the declaration of independence, and that defendants in fact supplied oil by alternative means.

(1997) does not reveal how the court dealt with the mention of "Paris," which makes the clause comprehensible as a reference to ICC arbitration but would be aberrant if the parties had been thinking of the Zurich Chamber. The best explanation of the Hamm judgment may be that the party seeking to rely on the arbitration clause conceded unaccountably that the reference was ambiguous; *id.* at 709.

2   Lonrho Ltd. *et al.* v. Shell Petroleum Company *et al.*, summarized *in* IV YEARBOOK 320 (1979).

The defendants argued that an action before the ordinary courts was barred by the arbitration agreement, which covered

> all claims or questions arising out of or in connection with this Agreement...

The judge held that he had no choice but to stay court proceedings in favor of arbitration, reasoning as follows:

> An arbitration clause is no doubt designed primarily to cover claims for breach of contract. Whether it covers claims in tort must *depend on the wording of the clause* ... "If the claim or the issue has a sufficiently close connection with the claim under the contract, then it comes within the arbitration clause" ... In the present case, the claims in tort have the closest possible connection with the Shippers' Agreement. If it is found that Shell and BP have complied in all respects with the terms of the Shippers' Agreement, the Plaintiffs can have no claim in tort against them. (Emphasis added.)[3]

In order to benefit from courts' willingness to presume an intent to submit the widest possible range of issues, it is important not to word the arbitration clause restrictively.

In this connection, it might be mentioned that parties dissatisfied with awards of consequential damages occasionally claim, by reference to a contractual exclusion of such damages, that the arbitral tribunal had no authority to venture into a contractually excluded territory. The arbitrators in such cases have generally determined that the clause is to be disregarded on legal grounds. Similarly, they may have disregarded a limitation-of-liability clause on the grounds that the law provides for unfettered computation of damages in case of aggravated failure of performance (*e.g.*, gross negligence or *faute lourde*). The court decisions known to the authors refuse to disturb the challenged awards, holding that the arbitrators are the final judges of such issues.[4]

Finally, it should be pointed out that controversies with respect to related agreements[5] (*see* Section 5.10) are best avoided by making the appropriate

---

3   IV YEARBOOK 321-2 (1979). The court recognized that there was a possibility of different conclusions in two sets of proceedings, but this was not sufficient to render the arbitration clause inoperative. *Contra*, the decision of 22 March 1976 of the *Tribunale de Milano*, Sopac Italiana S.p.A.v. Bukama GmbH (FRG) and F.I.M.M. (Italy), 12 RIVISTA DI DIRITTO PRIVATO P.P. 574 (1976); summarized *in* II YEARBOOK 248 (1977).

4   *See, e.g.*, Fertilizer Corporation of India *et al.* v. IDI Management, Inc. (U.S.), 517 F. Supp. 948 (1981); summarized in VII YEARBOOK 382 (1982). For an extensive analysis in a large dispute, *see* ICC Case 6320/1992, III ICC AWARDS 336. *But see* Laminoirs-Tréfileries-Cableries de Lens S.A. v. Southwire Co., 484 F. Supp. 1063, summarized in VI YEARBOOK 247 (1981), a 1980 Georgia federal district court decision refusing to enforce what it deemed a penal provision of French Law for late payment of goods; this case is isolated and appears aberrant.

reference in each contractual document one wishes to be able to invoke in arbitration.[6]

6.03   The ICC Model Clause

The ICC recommends the following simple arbitration clause:

> All disputes arising out of or in connection with the present contract shall be finally settled under the Rules of Arbitration of the International Chamber of Commerce by one or more arbitrators appointed in accordance with the said Rules.

The Supreme Court of India has held that expressions such as "arising in connection with" the contract

> are of the widest amplitude and content and include even questions as to the existence, validity and effect (scope) of the arbitration agreement.[7]

For the reasons developed in Section 6.02, it is dangerous to invent elaborate formulations, which in fact may be interpreted as reflecting a desire to limit the scope of arbitration. The ICC Model Clause, with its three key expressions ("all disputes . . . in connection with . . . finally settled") has stood the test of time.[8] When parties now use the Model Clause, it is understood that they in-

---

5   For a dispute regarding the extension of an arbitration clause included in a partnership agreement to cover bills of exchange related thereto, *see* Nova (Jersey) Knit Ltd. v. Kamgarn Spinnerei GmbH (FRG) (House of Lords), [1977] 1 LLOYD'S L. REP. 163; [1977] 2 ALL E.R. 465; summarized *in* IV YEARBOOK 314 (1979).

6   The Netherlands Arbitration Institute attempted to do this by Article 3.1 of its Rules, which suggests the following wording for international contracts:

> "All disputes arising in connection with the present contract or further contracts resulting thereof, shall be finally settled by arbitration in accordance with the Rules of the Netherlands Arbitration Institute."

The interesting question is what would happen in the event such a "resulting" contract provided for another manner of resolving disputes.

7   Renusagar Power Co. (India) v. General Electric Co. (US) and the ICC, decision of 16 August 1984, unpublished, extracts *in* X YEARBOOK 431 (1985). In Pennzoil Exploration and Production Co. *et al.* v. Ramco Hazar Energy Ltd., 13 MEALEY'S INT. ARB. REP. F-3 (May 1998), the U.S. Fifth Circuit Court of Appeals considered the significance of the words "in connection with" as compared with "arising out of." *See also* McDonnell Douglas Corp. v. Kingdom of Denmark, 607 F. Supp. 1016 (E.D. Miss. 1985), extracts *in* XI YEARBOOK at 581-584 (1986).

8   For an example of a case where arbitration was resisted on the grounds that the arbitration clause referred to "disputes regarding performance of the Contract" and that the request raised issues apart from mere issues of "performance," but arbitration was maintained because the clause went on to adopt the ICC language, *see* Omnium francais des petroles v. Giannoti, reported *in* VII ANNUAIRE SUISSE DE DROIT INTERNATIONAL 128 (1950).

In the case of Bureau de recherches geologiques et minieres (BRGM) (France) *et al.* v. Patino Tinto International N.V. (Netherlands Antilles), 11 December 1981, 1982 RECUEIL DALLOZ SIREY 387. The French language of the Model Clause ("tous differends decoulant de") was interpreted by the Paris Court of Appeal to apply to a claim based on fraud, where said fraud was alleged to have been carried out in order to frustrate a condition of the contract containing the arbitration clause.

tended to make a comprehensive reference to the ICC mechanism. Conversely, a different wording may be deemed to signify a different intent.

On the other hand, the Model Clause does not make clear whether the parties are subjecting themselves to future changes of the ICC Rules (*see* Section 10.03), and for that reason some parties prefer to add the words "presently in force" after the word "Commerce" in the Model Clause. Failing to do so is likely, in the authors' experience, to lead arbitrators to conclude that the parties implicitly accepted the possibility that the ICC Rules may evolve.

If the ICC Model Clause appears in a Chapter entitled "indispensable elements," it is not to suggest that parties must slavishly copy this wording, but as a reminder that no variation should be adopted unless one is sure that nothing is lost in the process.[9]

In recommending its Model Clause, the ICC invariably alerts all interested parties (Rules, p.6) to the fact that the national laws of certain countries may impose specific formal requirements of the arbitration agreement. (*See* on this subject Sections 5.05 and 8.03.)

It is astonishing to consider that out of 237 cases submitted to the ICC in 1987, only one precisely followed the Model Clause while no less than 16 were defective.[10] Negotiators all too often content themselves with imprecise references such as "the ICC in London" or "the International Section of the Chamber of Commerce of Paris." While those particular errors have not proved fatal,[11] they have invited needless controversy.

Finally, it should be noted that the fact that the Model Clause is a standard clause does not mean that it leads to a standard interpretation. The scope of the

---

Patino International, a minority shareholder, had the right to be bought out of a French company if the French majority shareholder sold shares to a non-French buyer. Patino International contended that the majority shareholder's creation of a French holding company with a 49% U.S. partner, for the purposes of acquiring part of the shares, was a fraudulent manoeuver designed to deprive Patino International of its contractual right to be bought out.

9 If in a given case the parties expect that the US courts may be asked to interpret an ICC arbitration clause, they may find it advisable to add the words "questions or" to the Model Clause. The reason is that under a 1961 precedent, *In re* Kinoshita, 287 F.2d 951 (2d Cir. 1961), the expression "any dispute or difference . . . arising under [the agreement]" was not broad enough to encompass a claim of fraudulent inducement. In 1984, while recognizing that *Kinoshita* was "inconsistent with federal policy favoring arbitration," the U.S. Court of Appeal for the Second Circuit declined to reverse the precedent, and instead distinguished it in a case where the arbitral clause referred to "any question or dispute arising or occurring under [the agreement]," S.A. Mineracao da Trindade—Samitri v. Utah International Inc., 745 2d 190 (2d Cir. 1984), extracts *in* XI YEARBOOK 572 (1986). *See also* Mediterranean Entreprises Inc. v. Ssangyong Corp., 708 F. 2d 1458 (9th Cir. 1993); J.J. Ryan & Sons Inc. v. Rhone Poulenc Textile S.A., 863 F. 2d 315 (4th Cir. 1988).

10 Stephen Bond, *How to draft an arbitration clause*, 6 J. INT. ARB. 65, at 67 (June 1989).

11 *See* Note 1 *supra*.

Model Clause may vary in light of particular features of the contract of which it is a part. As a unanimous tribunal presided by Lord Wilberforce put it:

> "The arbitration clause (Clause 20) is, with small and irrelevant additions, in the form of a standard clause leading to arbitration under the ICC. But that does not mean that it has to receive a standard, or restrictive interpretation. The clause must always be interpreted as part of, and in the light of, the particular contract in which it appears. Here it is used in a long term contract, with a number of provisions which may require adjustment over the period of that contract. If the conclusion is that the parties contemplated arbitration with a view to their adjustment, and if the language itself of clause 20 is general or wide enough to enable clause 20 to apply to such adjustment, as it certainly is ("all disputes arising in connection with this Contract"), then this clause should be so interpreted even though in other contexts it might be given a narrower scope."[12]

During the drafting of the 1998 Rules, consideration was given to the need to provide explicit indications as to what provisions are deemed by the ICC Court to be mandatory. (For an obvious example, an award will not be given the imprimatur of the ICC Court if the parties purport to exclude formal scrutiny of the award; see Chapter 20. Nor would the ICC follow a stipulation to the effect that the parties are not to advance the costs of arbitration.) It was decided not to do so,[13] with the result that the Court will consider the permissibility of variations of the Rules on a case-by-case basis. In other words, while there is little difficulty in *complementing* the Rules, great prudence is required before seeking to *modify* them—and one must know the difference.[14]

---

12   ICC Case 5754/1988, unpublished.

13   *See* DERAINS & SCHWARTZ at 15. The ICC Rules do not have a cognate to Article 1(1) of the International Arbitration Rules of the American Arbitration Association, which provides that those Rules shall apply "subject to whatever modifications the parties may adopt in writing."

14   For the consequences of the refusal of the ICC to administer an arbitration under a clause calling for the appointment of an "umpire" where the parties were unable to agree that he should in fact act as "chairman" as that function is understood under the ICC Rules, *see* Sumitomo Heavy Industries Ltd. v. Oil and Natural Gas Commission, [1993] 1 LLOYD'S L. REP. 45 (ICC procedures nevertheless "to be followed as far as possible.")

CHAPTER 7

GENERALLY RECOMMENDED ADDITIONAL ELEMENTS

7.01 Number, nationality, and qualification of arbitrators

The ICC Model Clause does not establish whether there will be three or one arbitrators. Predictability is enhanced if the parties are able to make this choice in the arbitration clause. They may reasonably feel, on the one hand, that the speed and cost factors are improved with a sole arbitrator, or, on the other hand, that the dispute will be more thoroughly examined by a three-member tribunal. If so, they may be well advised to opt for a sole arbitrator if disputes are likely to be of modest proportions, and a three-member tribunal for larger cases.

In the event the parties make no such stipulation, the ICC Court has the discretion to determine the number of arbitrators.[1] Article 8(2) of the Rules provides:

> Where the parties have not agreed upon the number of arbitrators, the Court shall appoint a sole arbitrator, save where it appears to the Court that the dispute is such as to warrant the appointment of three arbitrators.

---

1   In a preliminary award of 10 October 1972 in ICC Case 2114, Meiki Co. Ltd. (Japan) v. Bucher-Guyer S.A. (Switzerland), extracts *in* V YEARBOOK 187 (1980), defendant argued it had never agreed to let the ICC Court decide whether one or three arbitrators should be nominated. The ICC Court had named a sole arbitrator to sit in Geneva, the place of arbitration having been chosen by the parties. The sole arbitrator held he had been validly appointed under the ICC Rules, irrespective of the fact that the ICC's recommended arbitration clause had not been used.

The award was subsequently challenged before the Swiss courts. Although it disapproved of the award on other grounds, the Swiss Federal Tribunal found that on this specific point, as the provision for three arbitrators under Swiss law was not mandatory and could therefore be modified by the parties' agreement, the award was not challengeable, ICC Rules overriding the rules of Swiss arbitration law insofar as the latter was not of an imperative nature, decision of 17 March 1976, ARRÊTS DU TRIBUNAL FÉDÉRAL 102 IA 493; summarized *in* V YEARBOOK 220 (1980).

If the number of arbitrators is not stipulated in the arbitration clause, and the parties disagree in this respect, the practice of the ICC in recent years was to call for a three-member tribunal in cases where the amount in dispute exceeds US $1,500,000.

Of course many contractual disputes involve issues of principle that far out-weigh the specific monetary relief sought. (For example, a claimant may call on the arbitrators to terminate a contract whose future performance would involve stakes of millions of dollars, although the currently liquidated damages are only in the thousands.) On the other hand, the parties may consider that although substantial amounts may be at issue, the relationship is perfectly straightforward as a matter of legal analysis, and that the efficiency of a sole arbitrator is therefore the paramount consideration. For this reason, the ICC Court has recently tended to adopt an approach characterized by case-by-case analysis rather than by mechanical application of a monetary threshold rule. Under its current practice, it is thus not surprising to find the Court opting for a sole arbitrator in cases involving amounts of several million dollars, if the issues do not appear particularly complex. It is nevertheless true that the Court is less well placed than the parties to measure the significance of the dispute otherwise than by the simple amount being claimed. There are therefore cases where the parties prefer to fix the number of arbitrators in their contract.

The nationality of either the Sole Arbitrator or the Chairman of a three-member tribunal may be stipulated by contract, and the ICC will respect that stipulation. A potentially more significant possibility is to set forth requirements regarding the party-appointed arbitrators as well. Thus, the arbitration clause may provide that all arbitrators shall be of X nationality or that none of the arbitrators may have the nationality of a party.

On occasion, parties may feel that their co-contractant would, if it could select one of its own nationals as arbitrator, be tempted as defendant to name someone who would accept the mission of obstructing the proceedings.

Of course this might occur even with a national of a different country. To be sure of full neutrality by all arbitrators, the parties might simply provide that all arbitrators are to be named by the ICC.

Experience shows that parties do not often enough take advantage of their opportunity to define the characteristics of the arbitrators in such a way as to reduce the risks of connivance between one's adversary and "its" arbitrator. It is not enough simply to conclude that the other side's nominee will invariably vote partially and resign oneself to having to convince the two other arbitrators. The negative role of a truly partial arbitrator goes beyond the matter of voting. It should be understood that ICC arbitrators are presumed to have judge-like independence, even when they are party-appointed, and that they are treated with some deference by the Secretariat, the Court, and indeed their fellow arbitrators.[2] The result is that a partial arbitrator may cause very substantial delays by being in-disposed to attend hearings on a variety of pretexts, or otherwise to frustrate the course of the proceedings.[3]

Finally, it happens that parties require the arbitrators to possess some qualifications particularly relevant to the contract. They may want to be sure that the tribunal is chaired by someone proficient in certain languages, or trained in the laws of a particular country, or experienced in a particular technical area or geographic region. These kinds of provisions are not to be recommended generally, and in all cases should be drafted with care not to make the arbitration unworkable. If the chairman is supposed to be an English-speaking Austrian with a Brazilian law degree having had experience with Middle East construction projects, the ICC may be forgiven if it does not locate the rare bird. A practical suggestion would be for the parties to express in their contract that the ICC should use its best endeavors to locate a chairman with particular qualifications; this would enable the ICC to provide the next best thing without running the risk of exposing the arbitration to the challenge that it had not been conducted in accordance with the parties' agreement.

Good sense would suggest that one avoid overly precise requirements.

Finally, given that the procedure of international arbitration may present technical legal questions of some difficulty, it is always advisable that a sole arbitrator or chairman be legally qualified. Some years ago, there was an ICC case in which a highly qualified engineer sat as sole arbitrator, and had to appoint a special "legal advisor to the tribunal" when complex questions of law arose. This pragmatic solution worked reasonably well in that case, but is difficult to recommend as a general solution.

7.02 Place of arbitration

The folklore of international arbitration is replete with accounts of how places of arbitration were fixed in City X at the insistence of one of the negotiators, whose sole reason turned out to be the convenience of airline connections. It is a safe bet that anyone who has participated even once in an

---

2   On the other hand, in Fertilizer Corporation of India v. IDI Management, Inc. (U.S.), a U.S. federal court, considering a challenge of an ICC award based on the facts that the Indian party's nominee had previously served as counsel to that party and that this had not been disclosed to the U.S. party, expressed the view that there is a distinction between party-nominated arbitrators and the "supposedly neutral" third arbitrator with respect to the standard of independence to which they should be held, 517 F. Supp. 948 (SD Ohio 1981); summarized *in* VII YEARBOOK 382 (1982); *reconsideration denied*, 530 F. Supp. 542 (1982).

3   For a case where defendant in *ad hoc* proceedings was found by a U.S. court to have prevented the designation of a third arbitrator by directing "its" arbitrator not to select one, *see* Sumitomo Corp. (Japan) *et al.* v. Parakopi Compania Maritima S.A. (Greece), 477 F. Supp. 737 (SDNY 1979); summarized *in* VI YEARBOOK 245 (1981).

international arbitration will never again base the selection of the place of arbitration on such a criterion. The arbitral process is heavily influenced by the legal system of the seat of arbitration, if for no other reason than the procedural habits of the presiding arbitrator, who often is a local jurist (*see* Section 2.05). The courts in some countries intervene heavily in the arbitral process, applying local rules and opening many means of recourse against awards, while other countries are *laissez faire*, especially in international cases. An unwise choice of the place of arbitration may have drastic unintended consequences, even with respect to the contents of the award. If the law at the place of arbitration puts unusually stringent formal requirements on the arbitration agreement,[4] or if (as was the case with respect to the United Kingdom until 1985)[5] it considers that a local statute of limitations mandatorily applies as a matter of the law of the forum irrespective of the absence of such a statute under the substantive law applicable to the contract, a case may be lost before it is begun simply due to the choice of venue.

Some jurisdictions have in the past proved themselves unsuitable for international arbitration because they exclude foreign lawyers (see Section 16.05) or arbitrators, or because they submit them to cumbersome requirements such as work permits.[6]

Parties who are not sure of what they are doing are perhaps best off leaving the choice to the ICC, which, because it has an institutional interest in avoiding judicial disruption of arbitration taking place under its aegis, keeps abreast of legal developments in many countries and avoids localizing arbitrations in jurisdictions where judges have failed to respect the finality of the arbitral process. In fact in the eleven-year period 1989-1999, during which seats of arbitration were selected in 3,393 cases, the parties left the choice to the ICC in 575 cases (17%) (Appendix I, Table 7). It may be surmised that where the contract was silent as to the place of arbitration, leaving the question to the ICC had been a means of avoiding a negotiating deadlock.

Where possible, however, parties should attempt to stipulate an acceptable place of arbitration in the contract, and thus avoid any later disappointment with the ICC's choice. As noted in Section 2.03, the decision of the ICC Court as to the place of arbitration is administrative in nature; no reasons are given, no arguments are heard before the Court; no appeal is allowed. Of course, perusal of Table 7 of Appendix I will be reassuring insofar as it reflects the gen-

---

4   *See* ICC Case 3987/1983, I ICC AWARDS 521.

5   *See* ICC Case 4491/1984, I ICC AWARDS 539; the Foreign Limitation Periods Act 1984.

6   A particularly discouraging example is that of Colombia, where a 1989 decree had opened the way for foreign arbitrators only to be nullified on constitutional grounds by the Supreme Court, which apparently conceived that arbitrators necessarily exercise the imperium of the state; *see* judgment of 21 March 1991, 1991 REV. ARB. 720, with a commentary by Fernando Mantilla-Serrano.

erally predictable choices of venue made by the Court; but it is preferable to have the matter settled in advance.[7]

An additional reason to specify a place of arbitration in the contract is to assure full protection of the New York Convention. By virtue of Article II of the Convention, parties may require a judge to defer to arbitration when asked to rule on a dispute containing an arbitration clause. The Convention is applicable in 121 countries, but most of these countries have stated that their application of the Convention is limited to arbitral awards rendered in other countries having ratified the Convention. If the contract does not specify the place of arbitration, a judge might conceivably conclude that he need not apply Article II of the Convention, as he does not know that the arbitration is to take place in a country having signed the Convention.[8]

How does the negotiator know what place is acceptable? This question, as has already been suggested in the introductory description in Section 1.6 of the potentially delocalized character of ICC arbitration, cannot be treated in general or summary terms. Chapters 29-34 therefore contain a discussion in some detail of the attitude toward international arbitration of six legal systems; the issues raised may be transposed in inquiring about other potential seats of arbitration.

One cannot disregard the possibility that the home courts of one's adversary will deem the place of arbitration so inconvenient that they will refuse to defer to arbitration.[9] Indian courts have refused to stay litigation in favor of arbitrations in Moscow[10] and London[11] respectively, noting *inter alia* the difficulty for the Indian party to obtain foreign exchange for the purpose of transporting witnesses abroad and otherwise conducting proceedings there.

---

7   A contrary view is expressed *in* N. Krishnamurthi, *Some thoughts on a new convention on international arbitration, in* THE ART OF ARBITRATION 207, 210 (*Liber amicorum* for Pieter Sanders, 1982) based on the author's desideratum of having arbitration take place elsewhere than in the western and developed countries as well as on his view that considerations of practicality and fairness as concerns the locale of arbitration may be determinable only once the dispute has arisen.

8   Albert Jan van den Berg, *Commentary of Court Decisions on the 1958 New York Convention*, VII YEARBOOK 290 (1982), raises this possibility at 298.

    For a case where the Italian Supreme Court accepted that an award was to be deemed rendered in Paris, considering that the parties had stipulated arbitration under the *Chambre Maritime* in Paris but "to be held in Genoa," *see* Scheepvaartkantoor Holwerda (Netherlands) v. S.p.A. Esperia di Navigazione (Italy), 1979 IL DIRITTO MARITIMO 377, summarized *in* VII YEARBOOK 337 (1982).

9   *See generally* Andrew Rogers, *Forum Non Conveniens in Arbitration*, 4 ARB. INT. 240 (1988).

10 M/s V/O Tractoroexport (USSR) v. M/s Tarapore and Co. (India), Supreme Court, 58 A.I.R., S.C.I. pt.685, January 1971, summarized *in* 66 AMERICAN JOURNAL OF INTERNATIONAL LAW 637 (1972) and I YEARBOOK 188 (1976), sharply criticized in Indian commentary, as reported *in* R. DAVID, ARBITRATION IN INTERNATIONAL TRADE, 216 (1985).

11 Indian Organic Chemicals Ltd. v. Chemtex Fibres Inc. *et al.*, High Court of Bombay, 1978 ALL INDIA REPORTER 106; summarized *in* IV YEARBOOK 271 (1979).

Of course, in the final analysis the attitude of one's adversary's home courts may not be determinative of the international validity of the award, but as a matter of practically—especially if the other party has no assets abroad—it may be quite important. There are many instances where, for example, it would be more appropriate to have the arbitration take place in a developing country, close to the place of performance of the contract, than in Europe. Parties from industrialized countries are sometimes overly reluctant when faced with a proposal to accept arbitration in a developing country. They do not realize that the essential neutrality of the proceedings may be assured by the manner in which arbitrators are nominated and operate under the ICC Rules.

The fact that the ICC's Court of Arbitration, whose permanent seat is Paris, approves awards does not mean that the award is rendered in Paris.[12] Nor does the fact that hearings are held elsewhere alter the principle that the award is deemed to originate in the city formally designated as the place of arbitration.

7.03   Language of arbitration

The official languages of the ICC are *English* and *French*, but parties may correspond with the Secretariat in other languages; translations will be prepared into one of the official languages if a document is to go before the Court. The fact that the contract is written in English does not prohibit the defendant from answering the Request for Arbitration in French, since the decision with respect to the language of the arbitration is to be taken by the arbitrator and not by the Secretariat or the Court. Once the matter comes before the arbitrator, Article 16 of the Rules applies:

> In the absence of an agreement by the parties, the Arbitral Tribunal shall determine the language or languages of the arbitration, due regard being given to all relevant circumstances, including the language of the contract.

If the contract was drafted in both French and Arabic, the arbitrator, wishing to avoid any semblance of favoritism, may be reluctant to give precedence to either language even though it was used throughout the negotiation and subsequent execution of the contract. The result may be cumbersomeness, confusion, and great expense. Similarly, a contract in English may nonetheless give rise to a bilingual arbitration if it is shown that during the life of the contract, all written communication between the parties was in French.

The language problem may be quite troublesome, particularly if the arbitrator has a personal preference for working in a language other than that desired by one of the parties. Reasons of principle (some would say pride) may also enter the picture. The 1998 Rules may be said to have slightly downgraded

---

12   The High Court of Delhi has specifically so held, in a decision of 28 August 1970, Compagnie Saint Gobain Pont-à-Mousson (France) v. Fertilizer Corporation of India Ltd, summarized *in* II YEARBOOK 245 (1977).

the role of the language of the contract; the prior version of the provision quoted above (Article 15(3) of the 1975 Rules) used the expression "... relevant circumstances and *in particular* to the language of the contract." This is a matter where predictability is especially important, because it is germane to the choice of arbitrators (and indeed advocates). It is therefore wise for contract drafters to define the language to be used in any arbitration.

The clause defining the language of arbitration may furthermore specify that a party wishing to produce a document in a language other than that of the arbitration must provide a translation thereof, but this kind of detail may be handled at the Terms of Reference stage after a dispute has arisen (*see* Section 15.02); an acceptable rule is very likely to be adopted as a function of the basic principle that one language is *the* language of the arbitration.

In other cases, of course, it may be appropriate that the arbitration be bilingual, with or without equal status for the two languages. The authors have encountered the following provision:

> The language of the arbitration shall be English, but either party shall be free to make any submission in either English or French without providing a translation thereof.

7.04 Law applicable to the merits of the dispute

The topic of applicable law comes last in this category of "generally recommended additional elements," because strictly speaking the question of applicable law is independent of the choice of forum. A contract governed by Greek law may give rise to a dispute before any number of jurisdictions: a court in Greece, an arbitral tribunal sitting in Greece, an arbitral tribunal sitting elsewhere, or, for that matter, a court of another country. Indeed, international contracts often have different articles dealing with applicable law and jurisdiction.

In theory at least, there must be one national law that has a paramount claim to determine the obligations arising out of a contract. There are some questions that may not be decided according to general principles, no matter how much confidence the parties have in the fairness of the arbitrator. *See generally* Chapter 35.

Various legal systems may provide different and incompatible solutions for issues such as those relating to the prescription of litigation (statute of limitations), to the transfer of title and risk, to the rate of legal interest,[13] and to the time limit imposed on the buyer to complain about the quality of goods as delivered. (One might note that common-law practitioners are likely to view issues of statutes of limitations and legal interest rates as procedural rather

---

13   For an arbitral award containing an extensive discussion of the law applicable to an agreement between a French seller and a Spanish buyer, concluding with the application of the rate of interest provided by French law in commercial matters, *see* ICC Case 2637, 1 ICC AWARDS 13.

than substantive matters, and look to the law of the forum. In ICC arbitration, it would seem appropriate to hold these issues to be governed by the same law that governs the merits, which is often the only one the parties agreed to.)

Nevertheless, it is rare in ICC arbitration that the primacy of one or another national law turns out to be crucial. This fact may be explained by the comprehensive and detailed nature of the international contracts involved, as well as by the command of Article 17(2) of the Rules which provides that:

> In all cases the Arbitral Tribunal shall take account of the provisions of the contract and the relevant trade usages.

Nevertheless, no matter how careful the contract draftsmen may be in seeking to define the conditions under which they intend contractual obligations to be created, limited, or extinguished, it is always possible that a specific rule of law will be required to dispose of a precise and unpredicted issue.

For this reason, parties are generally not well advised to stipulate expressly that their contract is to be governed by no national law whatsoever. A stipulation of the following kind may therefore be viewed with some misgivings:

> The present contract shall be governed by general principles of law, to the exclusion of any single municipal system of law.

If a dispute turns on a question with respect to which there cannot be a philosophical answer based on fairness as perceived in general principles, and the contract does not contain clear provisions in this respect, the arbitrator's task may become impossible if he cannot refer to a specific national law. Accordingly, it is generally preferable to say nothing about applicable law rather than to exclude expressly all municipal systems.

As will be discussed in more detail in Chapter 17, the absence of a choice of law need not be a handicap. It may well be that as many cases are submitted to ICC arbitration without the parties' stipulation of applicable law as there are with it. Frequently, the parties could not reach agreement as to applicable law and simply left this issue—which in fact may never become relevant—to be determined by the arbitrator.

Nonetheless, to avoid polemics (not to mention the costs and delays that sometimes arise, especially in large cases, when vast written and oral submissions may be required only to reach a preliminary decision on applicable law) it is generally preferable to stipulate applicable law.[14] The provision may be worded quite simply, *e.g.*:

> The present agreement is governed by the laws of _____,
> to the exclusion of its rules of conflict of laws.

---

14   A somewhat different view is expressed by Krishnamurthi, *op. cit.* Note 7, who writes at 211 that "if a particular law is specified by a party with a stronger bargaining position, the opposite party

it seems useful to make clear, as per the final phrase of the above clause, that the law chosen should apply to the merits of the dispute.

This choice of law does not necessarily determine either the *procedure* to be used in the arbitration, which under Article 15 of the Rules is a separate matter (*see* Section 8.02) or the law that gives the arbitration agreement its obligatory character (*see* Section 8.03).

The Indian courts, however, have unfortunately made the choice of Indian law extremely dangerous in cases where the parties have chosen a place of arbitration other than India. They have done so by reasoning that if Indian law is the proper law of a contract, it is also (absent a contrary stipulation) the law governing the arbitration clause, and holding that this means that Indian courts have jurisdiction to examine any complaints about the arbitration under Indian law once the award is rendered—even if it is rendered outside India. It is of course the last proposition which runs entirely counter to the legitimate expectations of contracting parties. The Indian approach also runs counter to the international trend,[15] and has been roundly criticized.[16] It was believed that the Indian 1996 Arbitration Act cured this problem,[17] but in late 1997 the Indian Supreme Court found a way to reassert Indian hegemony over an arbitration having taken place in London.[18]

In *Metex v. T.E.K.* Directorate, unpublished judgment of 1 March 1995, the Turkish Supreme Court took the unfortunate position that a reference to "Turkish laws in force" meant not only substantive law but also the Turkish Code of Civil Procedure, and that therefore an award rendered in Switzerland which did not accept the applicability of Turkish procedural rules could not be enforced in Turkey—although there was no demonstration or even allegation that the losing Turkish party had been prejudiced by the failure to follow any specific procedural rule, or even that it had raised any objection as the arbitration proceeded. When choosing a neutral venue, parties do not expect that annulment proceedings may be brought in two different jurisdictions—particularly when one of them is that of one of the parties' home country.

---

15 The Court of Appeal of Paris set the lead in 1970 *in* Hecht v. Buismans 1972 REV. ARB. 67, holding that the rule under French law to the effect that a commercial agent cannot enter into a binding arbitration agreement may not be invoked to nullify an arbitration clause in a contract between a French agent and a Netherlands company, irrespective that the stipulated proper law of the contract was that of France, because "in international arbitration, the agreement to arbitrate, whether concluded separately or within the legal document to which it relates, always has a complete juridical autonomy, save exceptional circumstances, from the latter."

16 *See* Jan Paulsson, *The New York Convention's Misadventures in India*, 7 MEALEY'S INT. ARB. REP. 3 (June 1992); *International Jurist Flays India for Overstepping Bounds*, THE PIONEER (Delhi), 6 October 1992, at 3, reprinted *in* W. MICHAEL REISMAN, W. LAURENCE CRAIG, WILLIAM PARK & JAN PAULSSON, INTERNATIONAL COMMERCIAL ARBITRATION 1242 (1997).

17 *See* Jan Paulsson, *La réforme de l'arbitrage en Inde*, 1996 REV. ARB. 597.

18 Sumitomo Heavy Industries Ltd. v. ONGC Ltd. *et al.*, (1998) 1 SUPREME COURT CASES 305.

enforced in Turkey—although there was no demonstration or even allegation that the losing Turkish party had been prejudiced by the failure to follow any specific procedural rule, or even that it had raised any objection as the arbitration proceeded. When choosing a neutral venue, parties do not expect that annulment proceedings may be brought in two different jurisdictions—particularly when one of them is that of one of the parties' home country.

The practical consequence is that the well-advised non-Indian drafter in such circumstances should either eschew Indian law as the proper law of the contract, or stipulate that the arbitration clause is subject to the law of the place of arbitration (*see* Section 8.03). The same precaution should be taken with respect to Pakistani law, and perhaps also other neighboring countries which might be influenced by the Indian approach.

Under certain circumstances, when parties are prepared to accept an applicable law but wish to make sure that by such a choice they have not undermined the effect of specific provisions of the contract, the following wording may be adopted:

> All substantive issues in dispute shall be decided by reference to the terms of the present agreement; in the event that it is found to be silent with respect to a particular issue, such issue shall be decided in accordance with the substantive law of (country) _____ .

The purpose of this clause is to avoid that the stipulation of a national law adds obligations to those defined in the contract, or limits rights intended to be created. This type of clause may also be important to the parties' bilateral dialogue before arbitration commences. In other words, it may reduce a party's confidence in its ability to invoke an alleged provision of applicable law that is contrary to the terms of the contract. Arbitrators may be expected to take this stipulation as a reinforcement of the command of Article 17(2) of the Rules. If, to the contrary, the intent to give precedence to the contract is disregarded, one may still argue that nothing was lost in the attempt.

It should not be forgotten that the choice of governing law does not only contribute rules for decision in case the contract is ambiguous or incomplete; it also implies the application of the mandatory rules of the chosen law.[19] (A "mandatory rule" is one that cannot be altered by contractual stipulation.) But if one's subjection to mandatory rules is a matter of volition (*choice* of law), it stands to reason that one may contractually limit that subjection. This argument, comforted by the wide berth given to party autonomy in international arbitration, favors the upholding of clauses that limit applicable law to matters not dealt with by the contract.

It may be posited that giving effect to this kind of clause will favor the contractual acceptance of a wider range of national laws in international con-

---

19   *See* Pierre Mayer, *Mandatory Rules of Law in International Arbitration*, 2 ARB. INT. 274 (1986).

tracts, reducing in particular the reluctance to accept the less well- known laws of new nations.

On occasion, a party's reticence with respect to the proposed applicable law is not based on an unspecified fear of the unknown, but on a perfectly well-understood feature of the law in question. Thus, one may be prepared to accept the law of country X except for the fact that the Civil Code in that country provides that contractual liquidated damages clauses are subject to review and revision by courts as triers of fact. Another example, often seen in practice, is the exclusion of the Swiss Code of Obligations' liberal rules of set-off (*compensation*), which may be unacceptable to a party fearful of having to wait for contractual payment pending long hearings on alleged defects of goods or services it has provided.[20] Accordingly, clauses have been negotiated to the effect that:

> The law of X shall govern, to the express exclusion of Article _____ of its Civil Code.

The practitioner should realize that international party autonomy is put to its test in this context. It is not the authors' purpose to take a doctrinal position, but simply to point out that parties' ingenuity in drafting these types of clauses has limits. Provided, however, that a *fraude à la loi* (a stipulation of law manifestly intended only for the purposes of avoiding legal obligations) is not demonstrated, ICC arbitrators will tend to uphold the parties' agreement. In the exceptional case where the clause is not given full effect, the pragmatist may observe that he is not worse off for having tried.

May "general principles of law" be chosen to govern an international contract? As seen above, such principles can hardly dispose of precise technical legal issues such as prescription of claims (statute of limitations). Even as to matters of interpretation and emphasis, the body of "general principles of law" is neither well-defined nor readily researched (*see* Chapter 35). On the other hand, it is argued in the name of realism that contracts originating and performed in an international *milieu* should not be dealt with in the same manner as contracts having no connection outside a single given country. To apply one national law may yield results that appear capricious and arbitrary when set against the parties' expectations. An ICC arbitrator's task when applying Swedish law to an international contract is not to imagine how a Swedish judge would treat the same issue arising between two Swedish parties. In other words, there appears to be a "common law" of international contracts, having a moderating effect with respect to peculiarities of municipal law. Even within national legal systems it is perfectly acceptable to refer to trade usages, and one body of trade usages may be that of international trade, thus giving application to Article 17(2) of the Rules. Indeed, even the

---

20 The arbitral tribunal in ICC Case 3540/1980, I ICC Awards 105, 399, expressly recognized this possibility.

most vehement opponents of "general principles" as governing law would allow the application of *lex mercatoria* as rules of custom.[21] In sum, without taking sides in a complex academic debate, one may well conclude that in ordinary commercial contracts, the stipulation of "general principles" does not have demonstrably greater positive consequences than those generally flowing from Article 17(2) of the Rules,[22] and still leaves unresolved the question of the ultimately applicable law.[23]

When parties cannot reach agreement, they sometimes stipulate that *both* of their respective national laws are to be applicable to the extent they are in concordance.

To deal with the case of conflict, they may provide that the arbitrator shall somehow determine an intermediate position between the two results mandated by the two bodies of law. This is an unsatisfactory concept, as may be seen if one assumes that Law No. 1 deems the contract to be invalid, and Law No. 2 does not. No "intermediate" position is conceivable. A preferred variant would be to let the arbitrator determine applicable law in the absence of concordance. He would then do so in accordance with Article 17(1) of the Rules. In most cases, at least the *rules of conflict* of the two countries will be in concordance, and the arbitrator would follow predictable conflict of laws reasoning to determine which of the two laws (or even perhaps a third law) will apply.[24]

With respect to the particular case of contracts between States or State entities and private parties, the question of applicable law is particularly pointed: the State generally does not, as a matter of principle, wish to subject its contract to the laws of a foreign co-contractant; the private party is reluctant to submit to a law whose contents may be altered by the State.[25]

Some arbitral tribunals have *presumed* that in such a context the parties did *not* intend for the law of the contracting State to apply because of the unac-

---

21   *See* Wilhelm Wengler, *Les principes généraux du droit en tant que loi du contrat, 1982* REVUE CRITIQUE DE DROIT INTERNATIONAL PRIVÉ 496, n.60.

22   "It is not excluded that ('general principles of law and justice') are, partly, the same as the 'trade usages', which arbitrators have to take into account anyway, according to Article 17(2) of the ICC Rules," award of 29 November 1980 in ICC Case 3380/1980, I ICC AWARDS 96, 413 (Pierre Lalive, Chairman).

23   An examination of the relevant arbitration clauses in 237 cases submitted to the ICC Court in 1987 revealed that only one provided that disputes should be settled "on the basis of international law," and *none* mentioned *lex mercatoria*, Stephen Bond, *How to Draft an Arbitration Clause*, 6 J. INT. ARB. 65 (September 1989).

24   *See* Yves Derains, *L'application cumulative par l'arbitre des systèmes de conflit de lois intéressés au litige*, 1972 REV. ARB. 99.

25   *See generally* Pierre Mayer, *La neutralisation du pouvoir normatif de l'Etat en matière de contrats d'Etat*, 1986 JDI 5.

ceptable possibility that the law would be modified in contradiction with contractual undertakings.[26]

Similar reasoning was applied by the ICC arbitral tribunal in ICC Case 1434/1975, I ICC AWARDS 263. This presumption has not, however, always been accepted by arbitrators.[27] Accordingly, it behooves negotiators on both sides to seek to define a clear understanding of applicable law. Some solutions are as follows:

— Acceptance of the law of the contracting State. Some contracting States require such acceptance (and may invoke regulations prohibiting State subjection to foreign law) and are in a position to impose this preference. In most cases, the fear of legislative change for the sole purpose of achieving an altered legal position in a particular contractual relationship is exaggerated. Even if such an event should occur, the neutrality of an ICC tribunal may be such that it would refuse, as a matter of international *ordre public*, to countenance abuse of legislative power.[28]

— "Freezing" the law of the contracting State as of the date of signature of the contract. It is hardly reasonable to expect that by accepting such a clause a sovereign State has tied its hands with respect to legislation in the public interest. Rather, the clause would constitute an instruction to the arbitrator to consider changes to be inapplicable for the purposes of establishing contractual rights and obligations. In other words, the State may change its laws, but such a change will not add to its co-contractant's contractual obligations, and if it detracts from its contractual entitlements, the consequent loss would be repaired by a corresponding award of damages. Sophisticated long-term

---

26 In the 1963 award rendered by Pierre Cavin, judge of the Swiss Federal Tribunal (Supreme Court), in the *ad hoc* arbitration between Sapphire International Petroleums Ltd. (Canada) and the National Iranian Oil Company, extracts in English *in* 1964 INTERNATIONAL AND COMPARATIVE LAW QUARTERLY 1001, the sole arbitrator viewed the following considerations, "reinforced" by other factors, as paramount in excluding the application of the law of the defendant State entity:

"Under the present agreement, the foreign company was bringing financial and technical assistance to Iran, which involved it in investments, responsibilities, and considerable risks. It therefore seems normal that they should be protected against any legislative changes which might alter the character of the contract and that they should be assured of some legal security. This could not be guaranteed by them by the outright application of Iranian law, which it is within the power of the Iranian State to change." *Id.* at 1012.

27 *See, e.g.*, Saudi Arabia v. Arabian American Oil Company (the *Aramco* award), 1963 INTERNATIONAL LEGAL REPORTS 117.

28 *See* ICC Case 1803/1972 between the Société des Grands Travaux de Marseille and the East Pakistan Industrial Development Corporation, summarized *in* V YEARBOOK 177 (1980), where Andrew Martin, Q.C., sitting as sole arbitrator, had to come to grips with a Presidential Order of Bangladesh which in effect purported to extinguish contractual obligations of the defendant State company. He concluded, *id.* at 181, that:

"It is . . . painfully clear . . . that the Disputed Debts Order was made for the sole purpose of being injected as a spoliatory measure into the present arbitration."

contracts involving States often specifically envisage the possibility of legislative change, and define its financial consequences as between the parties.

— Accepting the law of the contracting State, but only insofar as it is in concordance with the law of the private co-contractant. The potential difficulties of such a clause have been discussed above. A frequent variant is to accept the law of the State insofar as it is in accordance with a non-national body of norms, such as international law, "general principles of law," equity, norms recognized in the international petroleum industry, and the like. This type of reference to more than one system of law was illustrated by the three well-known arbitrations decided in the 1970's and arising out of the Libyan nationalisation of oil concessions. As required by the Libyan Petroleum Code, each of the litigious concession agreements was governed by Libyan law to the extent it was harmonious with international law; all issues with respect to which there was no such concordance should be decided in accordance with general principles of law. While this construct might have benefited from simplification, the fact is that all three arbitral tribunals were able to operate under these provisions.[29]

See also Case No 723 of the Netherlands Arbitration Institute, Setenave v. Settebello; as reported in the FINANCIAL TIMES on 27 February 1986, the otherwise unpublished award unanimously refused to recognize a Portuguese decree designed to procure contractual benefits to a Portuguese State-owned shipyard in detriment to the rights of a foreign purchaser of a supertanker, holding that to do so would be contrary to "concepts of public policy and morality common to all trading nations," and this despite the fact that the contract was in principle governed by Portuguese law. A less drastic way to reach the same result was suggested in 1982 by the distinguished *ad hoc* tribunal in the familiar *Aminoil v. Kuwait* arbitration: " . . . Kuwait law is a highly evolved system as to which the Government has been at pains to stress that 'established public international law is necessarily part of the law of Kuwait,'" IX YEARBOOK 71, at 73 (1984). *See also* Section 35.03(i).

29   The three awards have been published as follows: 53 INTERNATIONAL LAW REPORTS 297 (1979) (the *BP Award*); 1977 JDI 350-389, English translation *in* 17 ILM 3 (1978), (the *Texaco-Calasiatic Award*); 20 ILM 1 (1981) (the *LIAMCO Award*). *See also* the American Arbitration Association award of 24 August 1978, Revere Copper and Brass, Inc. (U.S.) v. Overseas Private Investment Corporation (U.S.), 17 ILM 1321 (1978); extracts *in* V YEARBOOK 202 (1980) (principles of public international law considered applicable to an agreement between the Jamaican Government and a U.S. mining company because it "could be regarded as belonging to the category of long term economic development contracts").

CHAPTER 8

OCCASIONALLY USEFUL ELEMENTS

8.01 Negotiation, conciliation, or mediation as precondition

Contracts often stipulate that in case of dispute, the parties are required to attempt to reach settlement by negotiation, conciliation, or mediation (or a combination thereof) before proceeding to litigation. Occasionally, it is even stated that such settlement efforts must be given a chance for a stated period of time before adversarial proceedings may be commenced.

The attractiveness of such a "cooling-down" mechanism possibly appears greater at the time of negotiating the contract than at the time the dispute arises. If both of the parties feel it is in their interest to settle, negotiations will ensue irrespective of what the contract provides. If one of the parties is convinced of the pointlessness of negotiation, the settlement-efforts precondition may seem to it to be no more than a hypocritical nuisance requiring *pro forma* compliance.[1]

Nonetheless, there are circumstances when such preconditions are called for. One such case is when contractual relationships are so complex and delicate that the parties realize that an adversarial proceeding ending with a cut-and-dried decision (likely to involve termination of contract and the payment of damages) would be deeply unsatisfactory for both sides. In other words, the parties share a profound desire to continue their relationships, and, fearing the disruptive potential of litigation, want to place as many buffers as possible between themselves and face-to-face conflict.

In the latter situation, it would appear useful to give some content to the process of negotiation or mediation. Specific mechanisms for the facilitation of

---

[1] In ICC Case 2478/1974, excerpts *in* III YEARBOOK 222 (1978); 1975 JDI 926, the arbitral tribunal explicitly rejected an argument that the existence of a clause providing for negotiation in the event of currency fluctuation implied an obligation to reestablish the contractual equilibrium if it were altered by such an event.

settlement attempts may be defined. In the ICC context, such a mechanism is ready-made: conciliation under the ICC Rules (*see* Section 38.01).

At any rate, one should be extremely careful not to confuse settlement efforts with arbitration. In particular, it is fatal to the arbitral process to provide that the arbitrators' decision must be acceptable to both sides. This simply is not arbitration. It means that the ordinary courts retain full jurisdiction.[2]

8.02   Rules or law of procedure

When referring to the French notion of the law applicable to the *procédure arbitrale*, one must realize that the expression may mean either of two things: the rules of procedure to be applied by the arbitrator (narrow meaning) or the law applicable to the arbitral proceedings as an institution (broad meaning). The latter concept may be referred to as "the law of the arbitration." It applies to the arbitration agreement, the relationships between the parties and the arbitrator, the rules of procedures to be applied by the arbitrator, and the award itself.

The law of the arbitration may be conceived as "a system of law underlying the proceedings," which in the international context may at different stages of the process implicate several national laws relevant to the determination of the obligatory effect of the arbitral mechanism.[3]

In practice, the important thing to note about the law of international arbitration is that parties have great latitude in choosing rules of procedure. The ICC Rules represent at once a product and an affirmation of this freedom, Article 15(1) providing that:

> The proceedings before the Arbitral Tribunal shall be governed by these Rules and, where these Rules are silent, by any rules which the parties or, failing them, the Arbitral Tribunal may settle on, whether or not reference is thereby made to the Rules of procedure of a national law to be applied to the arbitration.

The concept embodied in the last phrase first appeared in the ICC Rules in 1975. The 1955 Rules had provided that unless the parties agreed otherwise, the rules of procedure of the place of arbitration would apply. Article 15(1) is a manifestation of the possibility open to parties to delocalize ICC arbitration (*see* Section 1.06). It has given rise to academic controversy[4] but in practice

---

2   For a case in point, *see* the decision of the *Landgericht* of Heidelberg (23 October 1972) confirmed by the *Oberlandesgericht* of Karlsruhe (13 March 1973), summarized *in* II YEARBOOK 239 (1977).

3   *See* Jan Paulsson, *Arbitration Unbound: Award Detached from the Law of its Country of Origin*, *in* 1981 THE INTERNATIONAL AND COMPARATIVE LAW QUARTERLY 358, at 376 *et seq*.

4   *See* William W. Park and Jan Paulsson, *The Binding Force of International Arbitral Awards*, in 23 VIRGINIA JOURNAL OF INTERNATIONAL LAW 253 (1983) and the references cited therein.

appears to work without great problems (*see* Chapter 16). Concretely, the parties have a number of choices:

— To say nothing, in which case the arbitrator is free to determine rules of procedure if necessary to resolve issues with respect to which the ICC Rules are silent.

— To adopt the rules of procedure of the municipal law of the seat of arbitration.

— To adopt the rules of procedure of another municipal law. (This possibility is explicitly acknowledged by the New York Convention, as well as by the French Decree of 1981 on International Arbitration.)[5]

— To adopt the rules of procedure established by a body other than a national legislature, such as the UNCITRAL Rules.

— To set forth a number of specific rules in the arbitration clause itself, disposing of the various questions treated throughout this Chapter 8.

The choice of procedural rules may be particularly significant if the place of arbitration has not been stipulated (*see* Section 7.02). Since the chairman will generally be a jurist trained in the country of the seat ultimately chosen, he may be used to rules of procedure different from those with which the parties' counsel are familiar.

Quite often, the parties are able to resolve some issues of procedure at the stage of the Terms of Reference (*see* Chapter 15).

8.03 Law governing the arbitration agreement

As set forth in Section 5.04, the arbitration agreement is analysed as having a legal existence independent of that of the contract in which it appears, and as explained in Section 5.05, the law applicable to the arbitration agreement need not be the same as the one applicable to the main contract.

The parties may therefore seek to stipulate expressly the law to be applied to determine the validity and effect of the arbitration clause. Such stipulations

---

5   Article V of the New York Convention *passim*, particularly paragraph V(1)(e). Article 1491 of the French Code of Civil Procedure.

In an unusual twist on this theme, the English Court of Appeal, in Naviera Amazonica Peruana S.A. v. Compania International de Seguros del Peru, [1988] 1 FTLR 100, excerpts *in* XIII YEARBOOK 156 (1988), held that: "in the absence of some express and clear provision to the contrary, it must follow that an agreement that the curial or procedural law of an arbitration is to be the law of X has the consequence that X is also to be the 'seat' of the arbitration."

In the premises, language to be found in two different documents (general conditions and endorsement) supported contradictory potential venues (Lima and London) but the only specific reference to arbitration spoke of "the conditions and laws of London." The English courts held that the seat should therefore be London. For the articulation of the "potential practical problem" of enforcing an award rendered in London pursuant to the "once-in-a-blue-moon set of circumstances" of this case in the courts of Peru, *see* Martin Hunter, Case comment, 1988 LLOYD'S MARITIME AND COMMERCIAL LAW QUARTERLY REVIEW, at 23.

are rare, perhaps because the parties are satisfied that if such a question arises, their submission to arbitration will not be invalidated by any law likely to be applied. In recent years, however, unfortunate cases in India and Pakistan have given a new importance to this matter. These cases have held that even when an arbitration is conducted outside the country, local courts may control the arbitral process (e.g. by issuing injunctions against arbitrators or setting aside awards) if they consider that their law applies to the arbitration agreement.[6] This approach defeats the objective of neutrality sought by parties to international contracts. It suggests that with respect to legal systems which might follow these examples, foreign parties should not accept their law as applicable to the substance of the contract without carefully isolating the arbitration clause. To this effect, they may be inspired by Article 59(6) of the World Intellectual Property Organization's Arbitration Rules, which provides:

> The law applicable to the arbitration shall be the arbitration law of the place of arbitration, unless the parties have expressly agreed on the application of another arbitration law and such agreement is permitted by the law of the place of arbitration.[7]

Alternatively, the parties simply assume that the law applicable to the main contract also will govern the arbitration clause. If the arbitrator is convinced that this was the mutual understanding of the parties, he would doubtless feel impelled to accept that conclusion.[8]

In circumstances where a competing potentially applicable law is thought unfavorable to arbitration, an explicit stipulation to the effect that the law applicable to the arbitration clause shall be that applicable to the rest of the contract may be useful.

8.04   Rules of conflict of laws

If one has not been able to agree to a substantive law, it may seem somewhat absurd to seek to stipulate that the rules of conflict of a given country (or those invented by resolutions or commentary) shall be applied to determine the substantive law. After all, if one is prepared to accept the rules of conflict in vigor in Country X, why do the parties not simply take legal advice from a jurist of that country? On finding out that the courts of Country X would apply, say, Indonesian law to the envisaged contract, they could then just as

---

6   *See* Sir Michael Kerr, *Concord and Conflict in International Arbitration*, 13 ARB. INT. 137 (1997); Jan Paulsson, *The New York Convention's Misadventures in India*, 7 MEALEY'S INT. ARB. REP. 3 (June 1992); and, regrettably demonstrating that this problem was not overcome by the 1996 Indian Arbitration Act, *Sumitomo Heavy Industries Ltd. v. ONGC Ltd. et al.*, (1998) 1 SUPREME COURT CASES 305.

7   XX YEARBOOK 240, at 361 (1995).

8   It will be recalled, however, that in the ICC award described in Section 5.05 (*Dow Chemical*), the arbitrators applied international usages, to the exclusion of any national law, even though French law was applicable to the main contract.

well make things clear and stipulate directly that Indonesian law is applicable to the contract.

In other words, if the parties cannot agree to a proper law, how can they agree to the rules of conflict that determine the proper law?

Yet it happens. One explanation is that neither side in fact does know the rules of conflict of the neutral country under consideration. Many countries have very little in the way of precedents or learning in the field of conflicts. And even those that do generally favor a "grouping of contacts" approach that leaves room for considerable subjective appreciation. In other words, one really does not know what the applicable law will be until the arbitral tribunal decides.

Even in cases where the result of the application of given rules of conflict is quite predictable (thus, the law of the seller is consistently applied to sales contracts by Western European courts), the "indirect" method of approaching applicable law may be appropriate for formal reasons. For example, negotiators for State trading organizations of some countries occasionally offer the thought that it would be incompatible with the "sovereignty" of their country for them to agree to subject the contract to a foreign law. It may be easier to state that the arbitrators in deciding the case are to apply the rules of conflict of some neutral country. If the result is that a foreign law is applied, this will be the arbitral tribunal's responsibility. The State organization itself will not have yielded "sovereignty" in this respect.

It should be recalled *in fine* if the parties do not agree in this respect, the arbitral tribunal shall, under Article 17(1) of the Rules:

apply the rules of law which it determines to be appropriate.

Much attention has been given to the manner in which arbitrators determine the "appropriate" rules of law, and we shall revert to this issue in Chapter 17. For present purposes, it suffices to say that ICC arbitrators here as in other respects tend to seek solutions in harmony with the parties' legitimate expectations. In one notable award, a sole arbitrator, sitting in Switzerland, found the following succinct expression of his search for a neutral method: "Failing an international convention or a uniform law which is applicable in the States of the contracting parties (France and Spain), the problem must be examined on the basis of certain general rules of connection of international private law."[9]

---

9   ICC Case 2637/1975, I ICC AWARDS 13. ICC arbitrators, particularly in light of Article 17(1) of the Rules, characteristically hold that "the international arbitrator has no *lex fori*, from which he can borrow rules of conflict of laws," award in ICC Case 1512/1971, I ICC AWARDS 3, 33, 37, 207. *Accord*, awards rendered by Judge Lagergren as sole arbitrator in the *ad hoc* B.P. v. Libya arbitration, award of October 10, 1973 on the merits, 53 INTERNATIONAL LAW REPORTS 297, at Section IV.A; by the ICC tribunal presided by Professor Battifol in ICC Case 1250/1964, I ICC AWARDS 30; and by the tribunal in ICC Case 3540/1980, I ICC AWARDS 105, 399.

8.05   Powers of amiable compositeur

The notion of the arbitrator acting as *amiable compositeur* appears to be a creation of French legal thinking. An arbitrator must apply the law, and not his own concepts of fairness, unless the parties give him the power to disregard strict rules of law. If they do so, he becomes an *amiable compositeur*. Literally, the expression could be translated as "author of friendly compromise," but it would be a mistake to conclude from the word "friendly" that this is the same thing as a conciliator or mediator. The *amiable compositeur* remains an *arbitrator*; he renders a decision that is binding on the parties.

On the other hand, the *amiable compositeur* need not take the law as he finds it. He may refashion rules in the interest of fairness as he perceives it. He may thus be said to have the function of legislator as well as judge. It would therefore be wrong to conclude that an ordinary arbitrator acts as an *amiable compositeur* if he applies *lex mercatoria* or even principles of equity. The ordinary arbitrator must determine that such principles in fact exist, and that they may be applied to the case at hand.

The expression *amiable compositeur* does not seem to have an English equivalent, and appears in French in contracts drafted in other languages. Paradoxically, the *amiable compositeur* function is, according to a comprehensive French dissertation by Eric Loquin, in practice more frequently carried out by U.S. arbitrators (who do not think of themselves as doing anything special in so acting) than by French arbitrators.[10] One might surmise that this phenomenon is traceable to the wide awareness in Anglo-American legal development of "equity" as an integral element of "law."

Nevertheless, the fact that *amiable compositeur* arbitration is likely not to be well understood by national judges in certain countries, such as England,[11] makes it unwise to provide for *amiable compositeur* arbitration in such places.

The consequences of giving the arbitrator *amiable compositeur* powers does not include the neutralization of imperative norms of public policy (*ordre public*). The *amiable compositeur* arbitrator cannot have greater freedom than that of the parties at the time they established his mission. Nor does this power mean that the rules of law will necessarily be disregarded. After all, in a given case, the rule of law may indeed coincide with fairness. What it *does*

---

10   L'AMIABLE-COMPOSITION EN DROIT COMPARÉ ET INTERNATIONAL, Librairies Techniques, Paris, 1980. The 1978 version of the Rules of Procedures of the Inter-American Commercial Arbitration Commission (IACAC) contains a recommended clause providing that the "arbitral tribunal shall decide as *amiable compositeur* or *ex aequo et bono*."

11   *See* REDFERN & HUNTER at 37, U.K. Department of Trade and Industry, *Consultation Document on Proposed Clauses and Schedules for an Arbitration Bill*, 10 ARB. INT. 189, at 224-5 (1994). In fact, the English Arbitration Act 1996 did not embrace the concept; *see* Stewart Shackleton, *The Applicable Law in International Arbitration Under the New English Arb* 375, at 379 (1997).

mean is that the arbitrator acting as *amiable compositeur* will not apply the letter of the law unless he is in fact satisfied that it corresponds with fairness.

But when he decides *not* to apply the law, what is the *amiable compositeur* finally doing? To refer to intuition or legal "culture" is to invite the application of subjective values, a dangerous thing in view of the fact that the international framework must fit a world where ethical values are not always shared. Having surveyed a number of awards rendered by *amiable compositeur* arbitrators, Mr. Loquin concludes that it is possible to discern two objective approaches. The first is centered on rules of a general nature, such as (a) a presumption of intended equality in the contractual *quid pro quo*; (b) a presumption of intended equality of risk; and (c) applying the requirement of good faith. The second is more innovative: to work toward the solution which seems to have the best prospects of being accepted by both parties without compromising their potential future dealings.

Are arbitrators acting as *amiables compositeurs* free to temper the application of contractual terms if they feel that this would result in harshness in a particular case? One commentator has suggested[12] that such powers are most likely to be recognized in cases where, at the time they agree to *amiable compositeur* arbitration, the parties recognize that their contract is subject to unforeseeable future events. This may be the case with respect to long-term contracts or with others, such as a motion-picture distribution agreement, whose financial consequences depend on highly unpredictable consumer response. In these situations, one may conclude that the parties specifically intended to reduce the drastic consequences of risk by relying on the wisdom of the arbitrator, and that that was the reason they gave him *amiable compositeur* powers. In an ordinary contract, tempering the contractual provisions would not have such a justification: it would be tampering.

The fact remains, in the international setting, that arbitrators tend to adjust the application of law in favor of giving full effect to the parties' agreement rather than to "adjust" the parties' agreement in order to give effect to a personal evaluation of what would have been a fair bargain. Indeed, international arbitrators are likely to moderate the application of law in favor of the parties' agreement even if they do *not* have *amiable compositeur* authority.[13]

In the specific framework of ICC arbitration, one may well wonder if there are any practical consequences of according *amiable compositeur* powers to the arbitrator. After all, Article 17(2) of the Rules provide that:

> *In all cases* the Arbitral Tribunal shall take account of the provisions of the contract and the relevant trade usages. (Emphasis added.)

---

12   Ernest Metzger, case note, 1982 REV. ARB. 220, at 222.

13   JULIAN LEW, APPLICABLE LAW IN INTERNATIONAL COMMERCIAL ARBITRATION (1978).

If the ordinary arbitrator shall in all cases refer to trade usages, one would expect him rarely, if ever, to disregard settled expectations in a particular type of industry. And it would certainly be unusual that the negotiators not only perceive that the contract is contrary to usage, but want to allow the arbitrator to be able to repair matters as *amiable compositeur* by disregarding what was drafted.

Since it is difficult to conceive that draftsmen suffer from such doubts as to the appropriateness of the contractual rules they have defined that they would—in the same breath, as it were—expressly empower the arbitrators to disregard these rules, one is left with the neutralization of strict rules of law as the fundamental motive for granting *amiable compositeur* powers. There may be complex cases where the impact of one or more potentially applicable laws is difficult for the negotiators to measure, particularly in an unknown country, or negotiating under severe time constraints. Under such circumstances, it may be felt useful and appropriate, by stipulating *amiable compositeur* arbitration, to reduce the risk that unintended technicalities of an imperfectly apprehended applicable law prevent the arbitrator from giving effect to the parties' intent.

In ICC arbitral practice, the *amiable compositeur* question comes up at the time of drafting the Terms of Reference, since Article 18(1)(g) of the Rules invites the parties to specify in that document whether they wish to grant such powers. At this ripe stage of litigation, it is unusual that the parties reach agreement, since it is generally apparent who is favored by a legalistic approach, and who would benefit from giving wide berth to arguments based on equity. Accordingly, if there is to be agreement regarding *amiable compositeur* powers, it generally will occur in the initial arbitration clause.

Is there a difference between giving the arbitrator power to decide "in equity" (or *ex aequo et bono*) as opposed to acting as *amiable compositeur*? This question is a controverted one among scholars.[14]

One rather doubts that it makes a great deal of difference in practice. Whether an arbitrator is asked to act as *amiable compositeur* or to decide in equity, he

---

14   In his commentary to the Swiss Intercantonal Concordat on Arbitration, Andre Panchaud wrote flatly in his note under Article 31: "The award in equity is that rendered by an *amiable compositeur*." The official German text of the 1961 European Convention on International Commercial Arbitration reflects the same perception, translating the decision of an *amiable compositeur* as being one rendered "in accordance with equity".

The 1965 ICSID Convention arguably also assumes the same identity of functions since it refers only to decisions *ex aequo et bono*, and not *amiable compositeur*. Wilhelm Wengler, for his part, insists on the difference between the two concepts, arguing that a decision in equity is but a "refined" application of the law (*i.e.* conscious of fairness in a particular context), whereas the *amiable compositeur* seeks a solution based on considerations independent of legal norms but deemed to be important given the parties' particular dealings and context; *see Les principes généraux du droit en tant que loi du contrat*, 1982 REVUE CRITIQUE DU DROIT INTERNATIONAL PRIVÉ 478-9.

realizes that something more is asked of him than to determine the letter of the law and apply it to the facts. In both cases, the principles of law are inevitably part of the context on the basis of which one may determine what had been the parties' legitimate expectations when entering into contract. In fact, one may safely assume that a quantitative analysis of ICC awards would reveal no significant difference in the number of references to legal rules or principles if they were grouped under the categories of "equity decisions" and *amiable compositeur* decisions, respectively.

Nevertheless, as a matter of contract drafting, it is clear that if the parties desire to give their arbitrator the maximum freedom to fashion his decision according to his personal judgment, they should give him the power of *amiable compositeur* rather than to authorize him to decide in equity. For if there is a difference between the two concepts, it is that the arbitrator is more bound to the law in the latter case.

The question is then whether the parties do not prefer the predictability of application of precise norms laid down by governing law and (more importantly in international contracts, which are generally very complete) agreements as negotiated, on the grounds that this perspective allows one to discern the rules of the game of performance: any future arbitration will be won if one has been more scrupulous than one's co-contractant in respecting legal and contractual obligations.

It should be kept in mind, finally, that while they may disregard certain contractual clauses in order to restore a fair commercial balance to the parties' bargain,[15] *amiable compositeur* arbitrators may not rewrite the contract by creating new obligations. They may adjust or disregard, but not create (*see* generally Chapter 18).

The following clause appeared in an English language contract:

> The arbitral tribunal shall have the broadest powers to decide as an equitable mediator upon the issues submitted to it, without needing to observe legal or procedural rules.

This is a typical *amiable compositeur* clause. However, the expression "equitable mediator" (a clear misnomer inconsistent with the very concept of an arbitrator) should have been replaced by the French expression *amiable compositeur,* which like *force majeure* appears to be the best way to say what

---

15 *Accord,* Philippe Fouchard, Arbitrage Commercial International 404-5 (1965), cited with approval by the ICC arbitral tribunal in Case 3267/1979, excerpts *in* 1980 JDI 961; excerpts in English in VII Yearbook 96 (1982).

Even if acting as *amiables compositeurs*, arbitrators are not, "according to general principles . . ., authorized to take a decision contrary to an absolutely constraining law, particularly the rules concerning public order or morals," award in ICC Case 1677/1975, 1 ICC Awards 20.

one means. If one is truly loath to use a foreign phrase, the following clause covers the concept of *amiable compositeur:*

> The arbitrator shall be entitled to decide according to equity and good conscience and shall not be obliged to follow the strict rules of law.[16]

8.06   Powers to adapt the contract

Arbitration is not invariably the settlement of a dispute. There are situations where the parties simply need to *adapt* their contract in view of factors unknown at the time of contracting. Two categories of adaptation may be involved: filling gaps and modifying the contract.

Filling gaps may be necessary for several reasons. It may be that the missing element is of great importance, but the parties simply were unable to take into account factors imponderable at the time of contracting. The arbitrators may even determine the contractual price, provided applicable law allows this mission to be entrusted to a third party. In this context, the arbitrator is not to decide a dispute, but simply to complete the contract. In other cases, the parties simply did not take the trouble to specify certain details, thinking them to be minor and unlikely to give rise to difficulties. If, to the contrary, a dispute arises, they want the arbitrator to supply the missing term of the contract, naturally in the light of practice in the relevant industry. Thus, the arbitrator may be called on to rule on the type of packaging in which goods ought to be delivered to the buyer, the parties having stipulated without more a certain quantity to be delivered "FOB airport,"[17] or a total number of X deliveries is specified for a total period of Y months without defining the intervals between individual deliveries.

Modifying the contract may be particularly vital to the success of long- term projects, with respect to which the evolution of the product market, rates of currency exchange, technological developments, politics, relative competitive advantages, and the like, may make it highly desirable to provide for an arbitral adjustment of the contract. Otherwise, the sole alternative to a negotiated solution would be the termination of the contract with a possible award of damages. Both parties may agree at the time of negotiating the contract that they must find a way of ensuring better long-term stability for their association.[18]

National laws take different positions with respect to the limits of arbitrators' capacity to adapt contracts.[19]

---

16   Suggested by MICHAEL MUSTILL & STEWART BOYD, COMMERCIAL ARBITRATION 74 (2d ed. 1989).

17   The reader will recognize this term as one of the INCOTERMS developed by the ICC, *see* ICC publication No. 460 (1990 edition of the INCOTERMS).

18   *See generally* WOLFGANG PETER, ARBITRATION AND RENEGOTIATION OF INTERNATIONAL INVESTMENT AGREEMENTS (2d ed. 1995).

19   *See* Section II(3) of the various *National Reports* appearing in the ICCA HANDBOOK; thus, for example, V.V. Veeder writes with respect to England, VOL. II, SUPPL. 23 (March 1997), at 22: "no

Many appear not to have envisaged the problem in legislation or case law. Yet in the practice of international contract negotiation and international arbitration, the adaptation of contracts is a matter of importance, and ICC arbitrators frequently deal with adaptation clauses.[20]

Although ICC arbitrators have on at least one occasion held the language of the ICC Model Clause to be broad enough to allow them to adjust the price of a long-term contract when the parties fail to agree to a periodic price revision as contemplated under the contract,[21] drafters seeking the possibility of arbitral adaptation of contracts should include a specific clause recognizing its need and setting forth as explicitly as possible the elements that are to determine (a) when an adaptation is called for and (b) the extent to which it should be effected.

In response to the apparent needs of international practice, the ICC has attempted to offer a variety of alternative approaches to the matter. These mechanisms—conciliation or technical expertise—may either complement or supplant the device of giving the arbitrators the mission to adapt the contract. They are described in Chapter 38.

---

difficulty arises if the tribunal is authorised to fill such gaps;" Albert Jan van den Berg with respect to the Netherlands, VOL. III, SUPPL. 7 (April 1987) at 7: "the new Act ... explicitly allows parties to authorize an arbitral tribunal to modify or fill gaps in a contract" (Art. 1020(4)(c)); *but* Bernardo Cremades with respect to Spain, VOL. III, SUPPL. 13 (September 1992) at 6 that the situation "needs to be clarified by case law;" Robert Briner with respect to Switzerland, VOL. III, SUPPL. 13 (September 1992) at 12 that "the opinion that arbitrators cannot be entrusted with the power to fill gaps is probably too restrictive, but this question is still undecided." For more detailed discussion, *see* Bernard Oppetit, *Arbitrage juridictionnel et arbitrage contractuel*, 1977 REV. ARB. 315 (expressing doubts as to the situation in France); Peter Schlosser, *Right and Remedy in Common Law Arbitration and in German Arbitration Law*, 4 J. INT. ARB. 27, at 30-32 (1987) (concluding confidently that under German law parties have the freedom to authorize arbitrators to adapt contracts).

The Resolutions of the Working Group on Arbitration and Technology at the 6th International Congress on Arbitration (Mexico City, 1978) included a paragraph 9 that called for "giving to the arbitrators sufficient powers to fill all possible gaps" in order to be able to adjust to technological developments, IV YEARBOOK XXV (1979).

20 In one ICC case, the arbitrators reasoned as follows:

"the price increase was susceptible of objective determination on the basis of available statistics and thus any possibility that it could have been fixed arbitrarily and artificially by one of the parties, which might have rendered the contract illegal or at any rate unenforceable, was avoided . . . The dispute could be submitted to an arbitral tribunal to fix the price increase by reference to objective factors . . ."

ICC Case 4761/1987, II ICC AWARDS 302, at 307. But for an instance where ICC arbitrators *refused* to establish a new indexation clause to replace an industrial index which had ceased to be published, and this although they had the authority to decide as *amiables compositeurs, see* ICC Case 3938/1982, I ICC AWARDS 503.

21 ICC Case 5754/1988, unpublished, quoted in section 6.03. *Contra,* REDFERN & HUNTER at 182.

8.07   Powers and procedures for provisional relief

Until their revision in 1998, the Rules did not explicitly acknowledge the authority of ICC arbitrators to order interim or conservatory measures. Under the prior editions, it was therefore important in certain circumstances to avoid doubt by making contractual provisions in this respect.

Now Article 23(1) entitles the arbitral tribunal, unless the parties have provided otherwise, to order "any interim or conservatory measure it deems appropriate." It also makes clear that such a measure may be conditional upon the requesting party providing security, and that it may take the form of an order or an award.

The appearance of this new feature of the Rules makes it far less important for drafters to complement arbitration clauses in this respect. Indeed, Article 23(2) makes clear that a party may *also* seek judicially granted interim or conservatory measures without thereby being deemed to infringe or waive the agreement to arbitrate. This obviates yet another element of the prudent drafter's kit of yesteryear.

A leading Swiss arbitrator, noting that some countries' laws expressly reserve the judge's prerogatives of granting provisional relief even when the dispute is subject to arbitration, has commented that:

> It is desirable that the arbitrator be able to exercise this power, which will, for example, allow him to order continued performance irrespective of the litigation, or to the contrary, to authorize the taking over of the work site by a new contractor or by the owner, to demand guarantees from one party or the other, and the like.[22]

There have been occasional instances in ICC arbitrations, particularly in large projects for the construction and start-up of industrial plants, where experienced and confident arbitrators have ordered parties to make provisional payments into an escrow account, thereby allowing expenditures to be made occasionally under the control of an expert appointed by the tribunal—to maintain the project at least in suspended animation (if not in progress) pending resolution of the dispute. In appropriate circumstances, an explicit contractual stipulation may be useful, tailor-made to the likely requirements of the works or transactions contemplated, so as to avoid controversy as to the concrete application of Article 23.

Naturally, one should not lose sight of the limited nature of the arbitrators' sanction in this regard. If a party refuses to obey the provisional order, compliance must be secured by enlisting the assistance of ordinary courts. If this may be done only by having the provisional order take the form of an award

---

22   Claude Reymond, *Problèmes actuels de l'arbitrage commercial international*, 1982 REVUE ÉCONOMIQUE ET SOCIALE 5.

approved by the ICC Court and submitted to recognition (*exequatur*) proceedings, one may wish that one had found a way to make the stipulation self-executing, by stipulating the consequences of non-compliance.[23]

Finally, although arbitrators lack powers of enforcement, and cannot grant attachments or hold parties in contempt, all of which powers are reserved for national courts, the effectiveness of provisional orders issued by arbitrators should not be underestimated. Parties do not ordinarily flout procedural orders made by arbitrators under contractually granted powers. To do so would be to risk incurring the disfavor of the tribunal and casting doubt on one's own good faith.

8.08 Procedural details

In view of the fact that the ICC Rules say very little about the specifics of procedure, parties may wish to reach agreement on certain basic questions of procedure. Otherwise, the arbitral tribunal will have very wide discretion under Article 15(1) of the Rules.[24] Since the rules so established depend to great extent on the legal training and habits of the chairman or sole arbitrator, whose nationality may be unpredictable on the date of contracting, it may be useful to set forth some basic principles in the arbitration clause itself.

In practice, however, such matters are usually dealt with in the Terms of Reference established after arbitral proceedings have been commenced. It often appears easier to tailor rules to an existing litigation than to preconceive detailed rules to cover any possible future litigation.

One should always bear in mind that primacy is to be given to the will of the parties. If the parties are agreed that a given procedural issue should be resolved in a particular way, the arbitrators should accede to their wishes in all but the most exceptional situation (such as a request for a procedural step contrary to fundamental principles, or involving the arbitrators in vast efforts they could not have anticipated when accepting their mandate).

---

23 Going somewhat further than Article 23 of the Rules, THE FRESHFIELDS GUIDE TO ARBITRATION AND ADR CLAUSES IN INTERNATIONAL CONTRACTS 88 (2d. edition1999) suggests the following contractual provision:

> Without prejudice to such provisional remedies in aid of arbitration as may be available under the jurisdiction of a competent court, the arbitral tribunal shall have full authority to grant provisional remedies and *to award damages for the failure of a party to respect the arbitral tribunal's orders to that effect*. (Emphasis added.)

24 Arbitrators' exercise of this discretion is generally accepted by national courts asked to rule on challenges to awards. *See, e.g.*, Laminoirs Tréfileries-Cableries de Lens S.A., v. Southwire Co., 484 F. Supp. 1063 (1980); summarized *in* VI YEARBOOK 247 (1981), where ICC arbitrators' refusal to allow cross-examination of an adverse witness on the grounds of irrelevance was held to be within the scope of their authority and did not constitute a ground for the U.S. party to resist execution of the award.

In contracts of a relatively simple nature the parties may in accordance with Article 20(6) stipulate that the arbitral tribunal should (or may) decide on the basis of documents alone. Otherwise, Article 20(6) gives any party the right to insist on a hearing.

8.09   Use of discovery

The opportunities for discovery are far less in ICC arbitration than, for example, in the U.S. federal courts. To many continental practitioners, this fact is a reason to favor ICC arbitration, because they view U.S. discovery practices as overblown, time consuming, and too often abusive.

There may nevertheless be circumstances in which it is appropriate to make a contractual stipulation to the effect that either party shall at the request of the other make available documents or witnesses relevant to the major aspects of the contractual relationship issues. Faced with such contractual language, refusal to comply would not only be defiance of the arbitrator's general authority, but breach of a specific contractual undertaking. Such provisions are particularly self-explanatory in joint venture agreements under which one partner is the operator, and the other is a relatively passive investor who wishes to ensure transparency with respect to financial, technical, and operational matters. Contracts involving intellectual property may also call for explicit provisions to avoid controversy with respect to confidential data.

The International Bar Association's Supplementary Rules Governing the Presentation and Reception of Evidence in International Commercial Arbitration (usually referred to as the IBA Rules of Evidence) represent a compromise between common law and civil law approaches. Intended to supplement the general rules of arbitration chosen by the parties (such as the ICC Rules), they were first promulgated in 1983.[25] A revision is imminent. Well-informed drafters may consider reference to them in arbitration clauses, with the aim of achieving a higher degree of predictability.

8.10   Apportionment of costs

Article 31 of the Rules gives the arbitrator the power not only to allocate the burden of costs of arbitration and arbitrators' fees between the parties, but also to award an amount on account of fees for the prevailing parties' counsel as well as other reasonable outlays. This is common practice in certain countries, unlike the United States where each party is generally required to bear its own attorney's fees.

In the event the parties want either to exclude this possibility or to make it mandatory, they may stipulate to that effect.

---

25   Reprinted *in* X YEARBOOK 145 (1985).

In addition, they may establish a general rule as to the apportionment of costs, for example setting forth that each party shall share equally the costs of arbitration and the arbitrators' fees (on the faith that no vexatious claims will be made) or on the contrary providing that the losing party pays all arbitral cost and fees (in order to discourage frivolous litigation).

This kind of contractual stipulation is relatively unusual.

8.11 Entry-of-judgment stipulations

It has long been the practice in the United States to conclude arbitration clauses with the following words:

> and judgment upon the award rendered by the Arbitrator(s) may be entered in any Court having jurisdiction thereof.[26]

The reason for this practice is to be found in federal court decisions[27] refusing to enforce awards on the grounds that Section 9 of the Federal Arbitration Act requires such an "entry-of-judgment" stipulation. The question therefore arises whether such a stipulation is required with respect to international arbitral awards potentially enforceable in the U.S. These decisions, however, related to purely domestic cases. It is reasonable to conclude that the "entry-of-judgment" stipulation is not necessary in international contracts, and this is for three reasons.

First, recent cases have readily found that the parties' intent that awards be enforceable may be inferred even in the absence of an "entry-of-judgment" stipulation. In one of these cases, an award rendered in Zürich was enforced at the request of a German party by a U.S. federal court in Michigan over an objection of the losing American party based on the absence of an "entry-of-judgment" stipulation. In the contract that had given rise to the dispute, the arbitration clause had included the words "shall be decided finally and binding the parties." The court found this to indicate consent to judgment on the award.[28] In this connection, it bears noting that the ICC Model Clause (*see* Section 6.03) includes the words "finally settled"; moreover, Article 28 of the ICC Rules sets forth the "enforceability" of the award.

Second, the legislation by which the New York Convention was made applicable in the U.S. (the 1970 amendment to the Federal Arbitration Act) does not include the language that had given rise to "entry-of-judgment" stipulation.

---

26 This language is taken from a clause recommended by the American Arbitration Association.

27 *See, e.g.*, Varley v. Tarrytown Associates, Inc., 477 F.2d 208 (2d Cir. 1973).

28 Audi NSU Auto Union A.G. v. Overseas Motors, Inc., 418 F. Supp. 982 (E.D. Mich. 1976), extracts *in* II YEARBOOK 252 (1977). The Second Circuit Court of Appeals has also held that the wording of the arbitration agreement and the conduct of the parties may constitute implicit consent to entry *in National Metal Converters, Inc. v. I/S Stavborg*, 500 F.2d 424 (1974).

Third, U.S. cases have followed a clear policy of enforcing arbitral awards rendered in a transnational context.[29] Indeed, the U.S. delegation to the United Nations Commission on International Trade Law expressed the view that no "entry of judgment" stipulation was called for in the model arbitration clause devised in the context of the UNCITRAL Arbitration Rules:

> particularly because such wording might be confusing to courts in other countries which are not familiar with the American terminology of "entry-of-judgment" and who might misconstrue such wording as authorization for the court to exercise independent judgment on the correctness of the award.[30]

Given the objective of uniform treatment of foreign arbitral awards, it would appear appropriate that national legal systems avoid insisting on peculiar formal requirements. It would seem quite clear that the "entry-of-judgment" stipulation is not required in cases covered by the New York Convention.[31] In a situation where the Convention is not likely to be applicable,[32] the "entry-of-judgment" stipulation still has a role.[33] An effective wording, giving the widest options to the party that will ultimately come to seek to rely on an award, might be the following:

> Judgment on the award may be entered in any court having jurisdiction thereof or having jurisdiction over either of the parties or their assets.

This clause seeks to have an effect both on the court of the place of arbitration, and on the potential courts(s) before which enforcement may be sought. Of course, it is recognized that one of the fundamental accomplishments of the New York Convention is to permit enforcement of an award even if it has not been recognized by a court of the country where the award was rendered; the so-called double-*exequatur* requirement is abolished.[34]

---

29   *See, e.g.*, Scherk v. Alberto-Culver Company, 417 U.S. 506 (1974). Numerous lower federal courts have followed the Supreme Court's lead; for a recent illustration, *see* Fertilizer Corporation of India *et al.* v. IDI Management, Inc., 517 F. Supp. (S.D. Ohio 1981) 948, extracts in VII YEARBOOK 382 (1982); *reconsideration denied,* 530 F. Supp. 542 (1982).

30   Howard M. Holtzmann, *United States*, IV ICCA HANDBOOK, Suppl. September 1992, at 7.

31   *Accord,* Pieter Sanders, *Commentary on Court Decisions on New York Convention 1958, in* I YEARBOOK 207, 217-8 (1976), J.S. McClendon and R. Everard Goodman, eds., INTERNATIONAL COMMERCIAL ARBITRATION IN NEW YORK 29, 135-36, 154 (The World Arbitration Institute New York, 1986).

32   *E.g.*, a provision for arbitration in a country not having ratified the New York Convention, with the result that the enforcement of an award in the U.S. would not be subject to the Convention, since the U.S. has made the so-called reciprocity reservation.

33   In Splosna Plovba v. Agrelak Steamship Corp., 381 F. Supp. 1368 (SDNY 1974), extracts *in* I YEARBOOK 204 (1976), an award rendered in London was not enforced by the federal court in New York, which held that it lacked jurisdiction because of the absence of express contractual language to the effect that the award should be subject to a court judgment of enforcement. The United Kingdom had not at the time ratified the New York Convention.

34   Perhaps because this point is perfectly clear, parties attempting to resist awards covered the New York Convention hardly ever do so on the grounds that *exequatur* has not been obtained in the

8.12   Waiver of appeal

Arbitration does not necessarily imply the definitive resolution of a dispute by a single tribunal. Some arbitral institutions provide for an internal appeal mechanism, giving rise to so-called two-tiered arbitration. Some national legal systems presume that by referring to arbitration, the parties intended to "take their risks" with the arbitrators, and that no appeal may be taken with respect to the substance of the award, whether the error is one of fact or law; others give the ordinary courts jurisdiction to set aside awards felt to be wrong on the merits unless the parties specifically waive the right to appeal to the ordinary courts.[35] Yet other systems may refuse to recognize waivers of appeal (this was the case of England prior to 1979), or to recognize them in certain cases only (this became the law in the United Kingdom by virtue of the Arbitration Act 1979) (*see generally* Section 29.02).

Article 28(6) of the ICC Rules makes clear not only that awards are final, but that by virtue of their reference to ICC arbitration, parties:

> undertake to carry out any Award without delay and to have waived their right to any form of recourse insofar as such waiver can validly be made.

It may be thought that no more need be said. If waivers are accepted, this suffices. If not, presumably it would not do much good to reinforce Article 28(6) by additional contractual language.

In some jurisdictions, however, matters are not that simple. Although the law allows waiver of the right of substantive review by the local courts, it may be argued that the waiver of such a right is of such importance that it must be recorded expressly by the parties: incorporation by reference would not suffice. In the United Kingdom, it is well established that simple reference to the ICC Rules constitutes an acceptable "exclusion agreement" for the purposes of the Arbitration Act 1979 (which permits the ouster of court jurisdiction to review the substance of awards rendered in relation to most types of international contracts; *see* Section 29.02). In Switzerland, to the contrary, the federal law in force since 1989 requires an "express" statement to the effect that judicial recourse is waived, and a general reference to the ICC Rules is not sufficient for this purpose (*see* Section 32.02). Following a Supreme Court decision in Sweden in 1989, the situation appears very similar—and possibly identical—in

---

country of origin. For one case where a French court enforced a German award even though it had not been registered by a German court, *see* Animal feeds International Corporation (U.S.) v. S.A.A. Becker et Cie (France), decision of 9 October 1970, published in 1970 REV. ARB. 166; extracts in English in II YEARBOOK 244 (1977).

35   In France, a dual system exists: generally, a party disappointed by an arbitral award may seek to have it reviewed for substantive error by a court *unless* the parties had waived the right to appeal; but if the parties gave the arbitrators the power to act as *amiables compositeurs* (*see* Section 8.05), they are thereby *presumed* to have waived the right to appeal. *See generally* Section 30.02.

that country.[36] Whether it is desirable to effect such a waiver is quite another question. Given the restricted grounds under which recourse may be sought in Switzerland and Sweden even when there is no waiver, it may well be that many parties would prefer to retain the possibility of having some means of attacking the rare case of arbitral misconduct at its root, *i.e.*, before the courts of the place of arbitration. These illustrations once again point to the importance of carefully considering the legal consequences of the choice of venue.

8.13   Waiver of sovereign immunity

It is not necessary for States or their emanations to waive whatever sovereign immunity they may be entitled to in other contexts in order to effect valid submission to arbitral jurisdiction. An agreement to arbitrate is sufficiently binding in and of itself. It is increasingly rare that a State or a State entity even raises the defense of sovereign immunity before an arbitral tribunal.

The principle of the binding nature of a commitment to arbitrate was noted by the Fifth International Arbitration Congress held in New Delhi in 1975, attended by 483 delegates from 44 countries, including industrialized and developing countries, representing socialist economies as well as market economies. In its plenary concluding session, the Congress:

> noted with satisfaction that States normally carry out arbitral agreements and proceed with arbitration on the basis of equal footing, especially with respect to location of independent arbitrators, the international character of the procedure and the law to be applied.[37]

Nevertheless, in one ICC arbitration, the Republic of Uganda raised the defense of sovereign immunity before a sole arbitrator sitting in Sweden.[38] (It may be relevant that the claimants were two Israeli enterprises, and the dispute arose at a time of great tension between the then Amin regime and Israel.) The Ugandan representatives argued that the State was entitled to sovereign immunity as a matter of Ugandan law, applicable to the legal status of the State. The sole arbitrator rejected this view, stating notably:

> Sovereign immunity may operate as a bar to the exercise of jurisdiction or prevent enforcement measures but does not *per se* interfere with the legal relationship between the parties as defined in a contract or otherwise . . . I doubt very much that the defense of sovereign immunity is a matter of legal status in the sense the defendants have explained but even if it were so I do not agree to the conclusions which the defendants are drawing therefrom. Nor do I see any necessity for relying—as claimants do—upon Swedish law as the law of the place of arbitration . . . I

---

36   *See* Section 31.02 of the 2d Edition of this book (Solel Boneh v. Republic of Uganda).

37   I YEARBOOK 227, 230 (1976).

38   Solel Boneh v. Republic of Uganda, ICC Case 2321/1974, I ICC AWARDS 8, 246.

must admit that I have found some difficulties to follow a line of reasoning that a State, just because of its supreme position and qualities, should be unable to give a binding promise . . . To require or assume then that a promise of a State to submit to arbitration, in order to be binding has to be confirmed in the face of the arbitrator, would probably impair the sovereignty of the State and its dignity more than the arbitrator's performance of his task, conferred upon him in accordance with what the parties once have agreed upon.[39]

Reflecting upon this award in light of prevailing doctrine, a commentator has concluded that since the arbitrator's authority stems only from the agreement of the parties, he cannot implicate, as might a State judge, the responsibility of one State to another:

> That is to say, the foreign State, when called before an arbitral tribunal, cannot fear a violation of its sovereignty.

> [T]he question of waiver of immunity is irrelevant to arbitrators. The State need not waive a right or a prerogative that it does not have.[40]

Nevertheless, international contracts involving States or State entities often comport waivers of immunity. As the above discussion has made clear, these waivers are irrelevant to the arbitral proceedings as such. Their importance is rather with respect to the private party's capacity to bring extra-arbitral sanctions to bear on the contractual relationship.

These sanctions include notably the possibilities of obtaining provisional remedies pending arbitration, such as attachments (*see generally* Section 8.07), of obtaining a confirmation (*exequatur*) of the award, and of forcibly executing the award against assets of the State or State entity.[41]

In addition, the mere existence of waivers may have a stabilizing effect on the comportment of the parties during the performance of the contract.

---

39   I ICC AWARDS at 9-10.

40   Pierre Bourel, *Arbitrage international et immunités des états étrangers*, in 1982 REV. ARB. 119, 124-5. *See also*, STEPHEN SCHWEBEL, INTERNATIONAL ARBITRATION: THREE SALIENT PROBLEMS, Chapter 2 ("Denial of Justice by Governmental Negation of Arbitration") (1987).

41   The Svea Court of Appeal, which sits in Stockholm and is the court of first jurisdiction with respect to foreign awards whose enforcement is sought in Sweden, has flatly held in a case involving an award rendered in favor of an oil company whose concession had been nationalized by the Libyan Government that:

> "Libya—which otherwise in its capacity as a sovereign State has extensive rights to immunity from the jurisdiction of the courts of Sweden—is deemed to have waived the right to invoke immunity by accepting the arbitration clause . . ."

Waiver clauses are therefore of great importance but as they do not concern the arbitration proper they fall outside the scope of this book.[42]

> Suffice it to say that waiver clauses must be carefully drafted in light of the legal system(s) in which their effect may be sought. In some legal systems, like the United Kingdom[43] and the United States,[44] this effort involves attention to specific statutory law; in others, like France,[45] an analysis of caselaw is required.

The preceding discussion should not be misunderstood to the effect that arbitrations involving States or other public-sector entities is no different from other arbitrations. To the contrary, there are three issues frequently raised before arbitrators that are characteristic of arbitrations involving the State: i) the capacity under its own law of the State party to submit to international arbitration, ii) the authority of the persons having represented the State party to bind it to arbitrate, and iii) the arbitrability of issues alleged to be the exclusive domain of the domestic jurisdiction of the concerned State.

These issues have been dealt with in Chapter 5 (and particularly Sections 5.02, 5.03, and 5.07).

At the stage of drafting agreements, it is difficult to eliminate all possibility of these issues arising. As a first step, the parties should determine as far as possible the legal situation of the State party under its own laws. This determination becomes more or less crucial depending on whether the applicable

---

> Decision of June 18, 1980, published in English translation in 20 ILM 893 (1981), in French translation in 1981 JDI 549. A concurring justice added the following general comments with respect to commercial agreements to which States or "State-owned organs" are parties, 20 ILM 895-896; 1981 JDI 550:
>
> > "If such agreements provide for arbitration, it is shocking *per se* that one of the contracting parties later refuses to participate in the arbitration or to respect a duly rendered award. When a State party is concerned, it is therefore a natural interpretation to consider that said party, in accepting the arbitration clause, committed itself not to obstruct the arbitral proceedings or their consequences, by invoking immunity."
>
> With respect to this decision, *see* Jan Paulsson, *L'immunité restreinte entérinée par la justice suédoise dans le cadre de l'exequatur d'une sentence arbitrale étrangère rendue à l'encontre d'un Etat*, 1981 JDI 544.

42   The following clause has been suggested by the International Centre for the Settlement of Investment Disputes (ICSID). Note that it does not cover immunity with respect to conservatory measures:

> The [sovereign party] hereby irrevocably waives any claim to immunity in regard to any proceedings to enforce any arbitral award rendered by a tribunal constituted pursuant to this Agreement, including without limitation, immunity from service of process, immunity from jurisdiction of any court, and immunity of any of its property from execution.

43   State Immunity Act 1978.

44   Foreign Sovereign Immunities Act of 1976, as amended in 1988.

45   *See* Bourel, *op. cit.* Note 40; Jan Paulsson, *Sovereign Immunity from Execution in France*, 11 INTERNATIONAL LAWYER 673 (1977); same author, *Sovereign Immunity: French Caselaw Revisited*, 19 INTERNATIONAL LAWYER 277 (1985).

law is also that of the State party. The problem of intervening inconsistent legislation may be dealt with by excluding the applicability of such legislation, but such a contractual "freezing" of the legal relationship will not always eliminate future argument with respect to capacity, arbitrability and authority to represent. At the stage of litigation, the State party may deny the proposition that such matters could have been governed by contractual stipulation. A more dependable device may be for the State party to make a contractual representation with respect to its capacity to submit to arbitration, and the arbitrability of potential disputes, under its own laws. If the State party's representative also warrants that he is in fact authorized to represent the State in so binding itself, this may not be ultimately conclusive, but will likely be given weight. Certainly a Minister may not, in an international context, be disavowed by the Government he represented.[46] The same may generally be true of the chief executive of a State enterprise.

8.14 Accommodation for multi-party disputes

There seem to be no easy solutions to the problem of multi-party arbitration. The ICC has dealt with a number of cases involving a multiplicity of parties to the same contract (such as joint-venture or consortium contracts) or to a series of contracts involving the same project (such as a construction contract having given rise to subcontracts). The multiplicity of parties might be styled horizontal, vertical or mixed. The avoidance of repetitive proceedings during which the same ground is covered by different arbitrators at great expense, not to mention the danger of inconsistent results, requires consolidation of proceedings. However, the ICC's Guide on Multi-party Arbitration under the Rules of the ICC Court of Arbitration, published in 1982 after several years of study by a working party of the ICC Commission on International Arbitration,[47] refrains from setting forth model clauses and advises parties to consult counsel with respect to particular contracts.

If a uniform-clause approach is adopted (involving an identical clause contained in several documents implicating different sets of parties), it is indeed essential to ascertain that under the applicable law or laws there will be a valid agreement to arbitrate as between parties who are not linked by the same contract.

One of the most useful elements of the ICC Guide on Multi-party Arbitration is its definition of the objectives of the multilateral arbitration agreement:

> 1. The right for any party adhering to the arrangement (the adhering party) to pursue any type of claim by any other adhering party regardless of whether or not they are parties of the same contract.

---

46 *See* citations *in* Jan Paulsson, *May a State Invoke its Internal Law to Repudiate Consent to International Commercial Arbitration*, 2 ARB. INT. 90 (1986), at 102, n. 34.

47 ICC Publication No.404.

2. The right for any adhering party to intervene in any arbitration proceeding between two or more other adhering parties, again, regardless of whether or not they are parties of the same contract.

3. The right of any adhering party who is a defendant in an arbitration proceeding related to the project to involve one or more other adhering parties in the arbitration.

4. The right for any adhering party to obtain the recognition of or compliance with any award on the part of all the adhering parties, whether or not they were parties to the arbitration proceeding, so long as they were given an adequate opportunity to become parties.

As noted, however, to achieve these ends in a specific context is rather more difficult than to define them in a general sense.

The one obviously desirable provision to be obtained in a multi-party setting is one that avoids an unmanageable number of arbitrators. If each of two defendants has the right to insist on naming an arbitrator, the process will quickly derail. One solution is to oblige all parties to the multi-party arrangement to accept the role of an appointing authority (such as the ICC Court) on behalf of all implicated parties.[48]

One of the most significant innovations of the ICC's 1998 Rules is Article 10, which in effect provides a backstop in the event an arbitration involves more than two parties but the drafters of the relevant arbitration clause(s) did not think through the practical consequences. Under Article 10, if there are multiple claimants or defendants and there is to be a three-member arbitral tribunal, each set of claimants or defendants should make a joint nomination of one arbitrator. If there is a failure of joint nomination on *either* side, all three arbitrators will be directly appointed by the Court. The fact that one side has been able to make a nomination is of no moment; the nomination must lapse in order to avoid an unbalanced situation where only one party had the opportunity of freely naming the arbitrator of its choice.

---

48   *See* Gillis Wetter, *A Multi-party Arbitration Scheme for International Joint Ventures*, 3 ARB. INT. 2 (1987).

CHAPTER 9

PATHOLOGICAL ELEMENTS

9.01 Introduction

It would be a mistake to conclude that someone combining all the elements of Chapters 6, 7 and 8 would come up with an ideal arbitration clause. The appropriateness of each of the described elements depends on the specific context of the contract: who are the parties, what do they intend to do, what laws may come to bear on the execution of their contract or on the arbitral proceedings, and where might they want to be certain that an award would be effective? Just as the individual elements of the arbitration agreement depend too much on each contractual context to be definable by a single set of "ideal" clauses, so likewise it is impossible to propose an ideal combination or combinations of the various available options.

If it is impossible to state what one should always do, it is quite easy to give some examples of what one should *never* do. Just as one has concluded that one has seen every kind of incongruity (to use a polite word) that an arbitration clause can contain, or perhaps that at last a new generation of negotiators of international contracts has learned the rules of the game, a new and fascinating pathology[1] is revealed. There is an astonishing contrast between the degree of sophistication reflected in the substance of some voluminous international contracts, prepared by highly competent and resourceful personnel, and the primitiveness of the error to be found in the arbitration

---

1 Frédéric Eisemann, who saw many of them during his 26 years as Secretary General of the ICC Court of Arbitration, is generally credited with coining the expression "pathological arbitration clauses," *in, La clause d'arbitrage pathologique*, ARBITRAGE COMMERCIAL : ESSAIS IN MEMORIAM EUGENIO MINOLI 129 (1974).

This Chapter deals with *mistakes* in drafting arbitration agreements and clauses, not with *fraud*. For an account of how a naively trusting Canadian party became the victim of a scam, *see Severe Sentences for a Bogus Arbitration*, LE MONDE, 5 July 1988, at 18, reprinted in English translation *in* W. MICHAEL REISMAN, W. LAURENCE CRAIG, WILLIAM W. PARK & JAN PAULSSON, INTERNATIONAL COMMERCIAL ARBITRATION 542 (1997).

clause. Since the binding nature of the agreement, and in a real sense its entire legal premise, is to be determined by the forum apparently selected in the last article of the contract, the perfection of the first fifty articles may be for naught if that final matter was neglected. It is true that ICC arbitrators have on occasion rescued technically deficient clauses on the basis that the true intention of the parties was clear,[2] but the fact remains that the controversy gives rise to cost and delay, and, even worse, may cast a continuing doubt on the enforceability of the award.

It would be vain to attempt to give an exhaustive inventory of pathology in international arbitration agreements. It is simply hoped that the illustrations below suggest the most common pitfalls, and how to avoid them.

9.02   Equivocation: the cardinal sin

If the parties want arbitration, they should say so clearly. Some negotiators seem to believe they can remain in limbo, poised timorously somewhere between arbitration and ordinary court action and not needing to strike out on one path or the other until a dispute arises. This is a fallacy. If the arbitration clause does not exclude recourse to the jurisdiction of the ordinary courts, one simply cannot rely on the arbitration agreement.

This seems basic. Yet parties sometimes seem loath to commit themselves to their choice. A savorous example was a clause with which French courts had to deal, headed "Choices (sic) of forum" and which provided that:

> In case of dispute (*contestation*), the parties undertake to submit to arbitration but in case of litigation the *Tribunal de la Seine* shall have exclusive jurisdiction.[3]

Parties may thus lose their ability to arbitrate by treating the mechanism as an option. One must not forget that arbitration is an authoritative disposition of disputes. If parties insert a requirement of mutual consent, they no longer have an arbitration. As a result of the following clause, German courts could properly render a default judgment against a Dutch party without being concerned about deference to arbitration under the New York Convention:

> All disputes arising out of this contract will be submitted in first instance to an arbitral tribunal of the German-Dutch Chamber of Commerce. If the deci-

---

2   *See, e.g.*, ICC Cases 5103/1988, II ICC AWARDS 361; 4472/1984, I ICC AWARDS 525; 4145/1984, I ICC AWARDS 53, 559. *But see* ICC Case 5423/1987, II ICC AWARDS 339, where the arbitrator concluded that reference to arbitration in Paris under the rules of "the Chamber of Commerce" was not sufficient to create jurisdiction under the ICC Rules (there is an entirely separate Chamber of Commerce and Industry in Paris).

3   *See* the decisions of 1 February 1979 (*Tribunal de grande instance* of Paris), 1980 REV. ARB. 97; and 16 October 1979 (*Tribunal de grande instance* of Paris), *id.* 101, as well as the references cited in the commentary of Philippe Fouchard, 1979 REV. ARB. 339.

sion is not acceptable to either party, an ordinary court of law, to be designated by the claimant, will be competent.[4]

This may not be disastrous in a purely national setting, where, for example, a French party with an imperfect arbitration clause will simply have lost the chance to have its case decided by a French arbitrator applying French arbitration rules and ultimately controlled by a French judge, and is left with the prospect of simply having the French judge decide the case as an ordinary court litigation.

But in the international setting, where the parties thought their dispute would be decided by neutral international arbitration conducted in English in Tokyo, but instead become involved in complicated procedures before the courts of Egypt and in Arabic, or the other way around, *mutatis mutandis*, the consequences of a failed arbitration clause can be dramatically disagreeable.

By now, enough has been said that the following clause, taken verbatim from an international contract negotiated and signed after lengthy discussion, may be quoted without comment:

> All disputes arising in connection with the present agreement should be resolved by negotiation and friendly settlement. If this method of resolution should be impracticable (sic), the disputed questions (sic) shall be decided in accordance with the Rules of Arbitration of the ICC in Paris. In the event the proceedings were not able to decide the question (sic) for any reason whatsoever (sic), the judicial courts of the injured party (sic) shall decide the dispute on a legal basis (sic).

9.03 The case of the missing authority

One frequent problem with arbitration clauses is that they define subjective conditions under which the arbitral mechanism is to be triggered or abandoned without specifying who is to determine whether the relevant condition in fact has arisen. To take the example of the clause quoted at the end of Section 9.02, who decides whether i) friendly negotiations are sufficiently "impracticable" for the dispute to be ripe for arbitration, ii) the arbitrator has "for any reason whatsoever" decided the dispute so imperfectly that court proceedings are called for, and iii) one or the other party is to be deemed "injured" and therefore entitled to seize its own national courts? Absent a defined authority, such conditions give one of the parties great opportunity to

---

4 *See* the decision of the *Landgericht* of Heidelberg (23 October 1972), confirmed by the *Oberlandesgericht* of Karlsruhe (13 March 1973), summarized *in* II Yearbook 239 (1977). In *Thiokol Corp. v. Certain Underwriters at Lloyd's of London*, D.C. Utah, North. Div., 1:96-CV-028B, 6 May 1997, an arbitration clause referring to "the London Court of Arbitration" was frustrated by a service-of-suit clause providing that in the event of "the failure of Underwriters hereon to pay any amount claimed to be due hereunder, Underwriters hereon, at the request of the Assured, will submit to the jurisdiction within the United States."

resist arbitration according to its own fiat, a problem to be treated specifically in Section 9.06.

The problem of the missing authority is frequently even more obvious: the parties have failed to make clear who will set the arbitral process in motion. This flaw may not be important in a purely domestic case, where the local judge obviously is the authority to be solicited, but in the international setting an inoperative reference may destroy the possibility of arbitration.

One type of potentially inoperative reference is simply the premature designation of an arbitrator, such as the provision that "Mr. Smith, Deacon of the Church of the Whole Truth in Port-of-Spain, shall act as arbitrator to settle all disputes." If Mr. Smith's days should come to an end before he has an opportunity to act as arbitrator, or even if his faith wanes and he merely discontinues his religious activities, the clause no longer creates an arbitral mechanism on which one may depend for the purposes of an international contract.[5]

Another inoperative reference, and probably the most frequent one, is the specification of a non-existent institution or a non-existent body of rules. It is nothing less than shocking to note how many complicated and painstakingly detailed contracts blithely refer to chambers of commerce that have no arbitration rules, or are not equipped to deal in the language of the contract, or to trade associations that have gone out of existence.

Yet another category of inoperative reference relates to the choice of an appointing authority who turns out to have no obligation and even less desire to get involved in the dispute. Occasionally, parties conceive the idea that while they wish to opt for ICC arbitration, a particular judge or public official or president of a chamber of commerce should select the chairman of the arbitral tribunal rather than the ICC. If so, they are well advised to determine whether the authority so designated in fact will make such appointments, and to reflect on whether that state of affairs can be counted on throughout the life of the contract. It is known that the then President of the International Court of Justice in the early 1970s accepted to appoint sole arbitrators in the arbitrations brought against the Government of Libya by nationalized petroleum concessionaires.[6] It is not known whether the then President of the In-

---

5   *See* Section 9 of the Swedish Arbitration Act of 1929 which provides in part: "If a person who is designated as arbitrator in an arbitration agreement dies, the agreement shall lapse unless otherwise agreed between the parties."

6   *See* references in Note 30, Chapter 7 (Section 7.04). In 1983, the President of the Civil Tribunal of Teheran accepted to play the role defined for him under a contract between French and Iranian companies, and to select among three National Committees of the ICC the one which was to name the chairman of an ICC tribunal; *see* ICC Case 4381/1986, II ICC AWARDS 264. (He chose the Swedish National Committee, which, apparently, had the consequence that Stockholm became the place of arbitration.)

ternational Court of Justice will be so disposed in 2005, or in a case involving private parties.

One authority frequently designated is the President of the Swiss Federal Tribunal. Indeed, Swiss judges traditionally accept to make nominations of arbitrators even in cases where the dispute's sole connection with Switzerland is that the seat of arbitration is in that country, and such acts are—contrary to some mistaken commentary—deemed part of the judge's official duties. However, in several important cases the Federal Tribunal has held that the Swiss judge will *not* make appointments if one of the parties contests the validity of the arbitration clause.[7] It has also been held[8] that the designation will take place over the opposition of one of the parties if said opposition is based on the alleged invalidity of the main agreement as opposed to the arbitration clause. (The theoretical foundation for this distinction is the autonomy of the arbitration clause; *see* Section 5.04.) However, in the context of litigation one prefers not to depend on one's opponent's sense of fair play. To block the mechanism, he need only contest the validity of the arbitration clause. In an international case, colorable grounds to do so are often easy to formulate, and the Swiss judge may be neither prepared nor willing to challenge the *bona fides* of the argument.

It is true that a slight lack of precision may not be fatal to an arbitration clause, as long as the intent to submit to arbitration is unmistakable. It may even be possible to establish a viable arbitral mechanism with the mere mention that: "disputes shall be settled by arbitration in Geneva," since the courts of that city would apply local rules to give effect to the unmistakable agreement to arbitrate.[9] Of course the arbitration could not then be an institutional one. Such a reference would in any event be better than if it also stipulated that the rules of a non-existent institution should apply, for the latter case might give rise to the inference that in the absence of the arbitration they imagined possible under the rules of their supposed institute, the parties would not have wanted arbitration at all. At any rate, in international contexts one is well advised not to count on the intervention of national courts to repair defective arbitration clauses, first because of possible jurisdictional difficulties in approaching said courts, and second because of the difference between the arbitral mechanism they might supply and the mechanisms one might have voluntarily accepted.

---

7   At least two such decisions have been reported: the cases of Paperconsult AG v. CEPAL *et al.*, ARRÊTS DU TRIBUNAL FÉDÉRAL 88.I.100 (1962); and Telefunken v. Cour de Justice de Geneve and N.V. Phillips, ARRÊTS DU TRIBUNAL FÉDÉRAL 78.I.352 (1952).

8   In Motoren-, Turbinen-, und Pumpen AG v. the Ministry of War of Egypt *et al.*, ARRÊTS DU TRIBUNAL FÉDÉRAL 93.I.345 (1967).

9   *See* Libyan National Oil Company v. WETCO, ARRÊTS DU TRIBUNAL FÉDÉRAL 101.III.58 (1975).

If one has clearly referred to the ICC Rules as a fall-back mechanism, the appointing authority will not be missing: it is the ICC Court of Arbitration. If a third party refused to nominate an arbitrator, the ICC Court would step in and make the nomination in regular fashion under the Rules. Its authority for so doing would be Article 8(4), which provides that failing agreement of the parties the Court will effect necessary appointments. The refusal of the third party is thus viewed in effect as a failure of the parties' agreement.[10] The best recommendation, however, is clearly not to implicate an appointing authority outside the ICC, but to rely on the routine mechanisms of the Rules.

9.04   The case of the disastrous compromise

Sometimes parties resolve negotiation deadlocks by compromising on issues where compromise is not appropriate. When traffic in Sweden was directed to move from the left to the right side of public roads in 1967, some citizens regretted the change, but it was never thought that in a spirit of conciliation a "compromise" could be found to allow traditionalists to carry on as before.

So what were the negotiators of the following clause thinking about:

> Disputes hereunder shall be referred to arbitration, to be carried out by arbitrators named by the International Chamber of Commerce in Geneva in accordance with the arbitration procedure set forth in the Civil Code of Venezuela and in the Civil Code of France, with due regard for the law of the place of arbitration.

One surmises that the parties were French and Venezuelan, respectively, and that they wanted neutral ICC arbitration in Geneva. (There is fortunately no alternative ICC in Geneva, so this wording would probably be sufficient for the ICC Court in Paris to decide that it had been given power to constitute a tribunal to sit in Geneva.[11]) On the other hand, each side wanted to be sure that procedures with which it was familiar would be applied, and each accepted the other's point of view. As an afterthought, they acknowledged their concern for the law of the seat of arbitration.

A lengthy analysis could be written about the potential ramifications of this clause, which opens the door to much litigation unrelated to the merits of the dispute. But the fundamental flaw can be stated simply: if there is a contradiction between Venezuelan and French law on any given point of procedure—or indeed if there is an absence of unanimity among Venezuelan, French, and Swiss law and the ICC Rules (the latter relevant presumably only with respect to the constitution of the tribunal)—the resulting award may be attacked (in any jurisdiction where it may be sought to be relied on, in addi-

---

10   *See e.g.* ICC Case 2321/1974, I ICC AWARDS 8, 246.

11   The wording "arbitration by the International Chamber of Commerce in Geneva" posed no problem in ICC Case 2114/1972, I ICC AWARDS 49. *See also* ICC Case 4472/1984, I ICC AWARDS 525.

tion to Venezuela, France, and Switzerland) on the grounds that the procedure as applied failed to conform to the agreement of the parties.[12]

Venezuela was again the locus of a more recent example. In a major dispute between Pepsico and its Venezuelan licensed bottlers, the arbitration clause provided that "this agreement shall be governed by the laws of the Republic of Venezuela" while at the same time calling for ICC arbitration in New York in which "the arbitrators shall apply the substantive law of the State of New York." When the bottlers purported to terminate the agreement, Pepsico demanded payment of some $118 million under a liquidated damages clause. The bottlers took the position that the ensuing dispute should be heard in the courts of Venezuela because the arbitration clause was "inoperative" due to its "obscurity and ambiguity." Pepsico initiated ICC arbitral proceedings while also asking the US Federal District Court for the Southern District of New York to compel arbitration and to enjoin the bottlers from proceeding in Venezuela. The US court decided—notwithstanding the "facially flimsy aspect of the objections to arbitrability"—that the fact that the agreement was stated as governed by Venezuelan law meant that the issue of arbitrability was "plainly a matter of Venezuelan law" and the courts of that country should be offered "the initial opportunity to determine this threshold question."[13] New York law, the court said in a footnote, "comes into play . . . only after the contractual dispute is referred to arbitration."

On the assumption that the parties had originally agreed in good faith to have any disputes resolved by ICC arbitration, one can only comment that the consequence of their confused drafting—namely to generate court litigation in two countries before an arbitration ever got off the ground—was not what they intended.

9.05   Overdoing the search for institutions

One should not be surprised that third parties who are not required to do so are reluctant to implicate themselves even marginally in international disputes. There is no excuse for a cavalier approach to the designation of the authority required to make the arbitration work. The authors have seen an arbitration clause referring to dispute settlement under chambers of commerce in five European cities, "at the election of the claiming party." It turned out in that case that three of the institutions were insufficiently specified (*i.e.* the reference could have implied *more than one* institution, or in fact did not refer to *any* existing institution), and that the two others did not conduct arb-

---

12   *See* Martin Hunter, Case comment, 1988 LLOYD'S MARITIME AND COMMERCIAL LAW QUARTERLY REVIEW, at 23.

13   In this instance, international judicial cooperation was at once coherent and efficient (at least at the first-instance level). Within three months of the US Court decision, the relevant court in Caracas held that the dispute was arbitrable; C.A. Embotelladora Caracas v. Pepsi-Cola Panamericana S.A., 24 Jan. 1997, 12 MEALEY'S INT. ARB. REP. G-3 (Jan. 1997).

itrations. One surmises that the parties were not sure what they were doing, but that with five references they believed one would be sure to work. Such laziness is inexcusable.[14]

9.06   The illusory arbitration clause

The following clause was found in an international contract:

> All disputes arising in connection with the present agreement shall be submitted in the first instance (sic) to arbitration. The arbitrator (sic) shall be a well-known chamber of commerce (like the International Chamber of Commerce) designated by mutual agreement between buyer and seller.

This language affords the defendant unlimited opportunity to resist arbitration. Simply by failing to agree, it may effectively deny any effect to the arbitration clause. Instead of a potential award of wide international currency under the New York Convention, the injured party may end up with a court decision of more limited use.[15]

Worse, the existence of this flawed arbitration clause might hinder the claimant even if he decides after all to abandon the idea of arbitration and take the case to an ordinary court, for then the defendant may invoke the arbitral clause and initiate difficult discussions of fact (who is making unreasonable suggestions?) and law (should the court declare the arbitration clause to be null or should it choose an appropriate institution for the parties and if so on what grounds?).

---

14   For an example of equivocal and therefore inoperative references to two different arbitral institutions (the Bucharest Chamber of Commerce and the ICC), *see* the decision of the Lebanese Supreme Court of 27 April 1987, unpublished, French translation *in* 1988 REV. ARB. 723. *See also* the interlocutory award of 1 September 1981 of the Arbitration Court of the Japan Shipping Exchange, extracts *in* XI YEARBOOK 193 (1986) (arbitral jurisdiction in Japan upheld despite ambiguous reference to arbitration in Japan *and* Korea). For an illustration of the travails that may follow carelessness, including arbitral proceedings in two countries and ultimately a court decision annulling the final arbitral award, in a case where sales confirmations contained a printed reference to 1956 Berlin Rules for the potato trade, which reference had been amended by typewriter to refer to European Rules (RUCIP) (the result of which was to make Hamburg the place of arbitration) but without changing the subsequent printed mentions: "Competent Court, Munich, Arbitral Tribunal: Munich," *see* V YEARBOOK 198, at 260 (1980).

15   A charter party clause stating "General Average and arbitration to be settled in the Netherlands" was held not to be effective as a bar to court action in Hoogovens BV v. MV Sea Catteleya, U.S. District Court SDNY, 3 May 1994, No. 93 Civ. 3859, excerpts in XXII YEARBOOK 881. The court disagreed with a previous decision that upheld a clause reading "Arbitration: If required in New York," and observed that these two clauses were unlike yet another clause where the operative words were "shall be settled by arbitration;" the latter, said the court, "unambiguously imposed compulsory arbitration."

9.07 Suffocating the process with specificity

Overly detailed descriptions of the identity, qualifications and comportment of the arbitrators and the practical functioning of the tribunal may have the effect of making it impossible to constitute the tribunal and to make the process operational in accordance with the parties' stipulations.

9.08 Haste makes waste

Parties are occasionally tempted to stipulate that the arbitrators must render their award within a given brief time period. The intent behind such a provision is to incite the arbitrators to act rapidly. But what may not occur to the contract negotiator is that such a provision may be so constraining as to destroy the entire arbitral mechanism, which in certain cases may play into the hands of a defendant seeking to avoid any responsibility whatsoever.[16] An overly strict time limit may have the unavoidable result that the arbitral tribunal's mandate expires before it is practically possible to conduct an international arbitration.[17]

If nothing is said about time limits, Article 24(1) of the ICC Rules sets forth the principle that awards shall be rendered within six months of execution of the arbitral tribunal's Terms of Reference. In recognition of the practical difficulties of international arbitration, however, Article 24(2) makes clear that the ICC Court may extend this time limit, which it frequently does (*see* Section 19.01). It is a fact that, faced with the reality of litigation, the parties themselves may not be able to go as fast as contract negotiators had imagined, nor even desire to do so.

Parties wishing to insist on the need for speedy resolution of their disputes are doubtless best served by an exhortatory statement of intent coupled with some stipulations of a practical nature, such as opting for a sole arbitrator or a requirement that all three arbitrators be nationals or residents of the country where the arbitration is to take place.

In some cases, involving particularly straight-forward contracts, the parties may stipulate that any dispute shall be decided on documents only, without a hearing. Such a stipulation is not recommended to be used generally, as it is difficult to imagine all parameters of potential litigation at the time of contracting.

Finally, parties interested in speed may well consider the possibilities of alternative and additional dispute resolution procedures developed in recent years (*see* Chapter 38).

---

16 *See, e.g.*, ICC Case 3383/1979, I ICC AWARDS 100, 394.

17 For the difficulties of a reference to arbitration in Roumania followed by the phrase: "Any claim for arbitration formulated after 6 months from the date of arrival of the goods at the final station or port of destination is null," *see* the decision of 12 February 1976 of the German Supreme Court (concerning recognition of an award rendered in Rumania), 1976 WERTPAPIER-MITTEILUNGEN 435; summarized *in* II YEARBOOK 242 (1977).

PART III

ICC ARBITRATION IN PRACTICE

CHAPTER 10

BRINGING ARBITRATION
UNDER THE RULES

10.01   Introduction

The ICC Rules were designed for use in any country where the law allows arbitration. In search of universality, its drafters necessarily relied on simplicity and brevity. A conscious choice was thus made to eschew an elaborate code of procedure containing answers to every conceivable procedural question. Instead, in thirty-five short articles, the ICC Rules provide the skeleton of a procedural code with the intent of defining an arbitral process which may take place in common-law as well as civil-law jurisdictions, and in capitalist as well as State-directed economies.

A complete study of any system of arbitration would require examination of the national laws of the States where the arbitration is to take place, the complex notions of conflict of laws and recognition of foreign awards, and the network of treaties favoring the conduct of international arbitrations and their enforcement. For the practitioner, however, an understanding of the ICC Rules of Arbitration themselves may be the most useful, and frequently an entirely sufficient, approach to the ICC arbitral process. The trouble with many academic studies of international arbitration is that they focus on the review and enforcement of arbitral awards in national courts. Such an approach dwells on the occasional failures rather than the routine successes of arbitration. Arbitrations that reach national courts are there because they are flawed, at least in the opinion of one of the parties. These cases represent only the tip of the iceberg. Below the surface is an untroubled mass of arbitrations which have been finally and successfully resolved according to a succinct set of rules, applied and interpreted by arbitrators with the flexibility inherent in a process designed to cover a wide variety of international commercial disputes.

From the businessman's and the practitioner's point of view, the ICC Rules are frequently the end as well as the beginning of inquiry. The theoretical framework is simple enough. The parties by contract agree to resolve their dispute by private means. The agreed rules are those of the ICC, which are incorporated by reference into the agreement itself. While it is true that the Rules provide a permanent institutional framework for private resolution of disputes, the purpose of the institution is to establish and supervise separate arbitral tribunals on a case-by-case basis as provided in specific contracts between the parties. The principle legitimizing this private process of dispute resolution is that if the parties have the power to create obligations by agreement, they should be able to determine by agreement (subject to the reservations explored in Chapter 5 and reviewed in Section 11.04) how those obligations shall be interpreted, performed, and extinguished. In this sense, ICC arbitration does not rival the public administration of justice by ordinary national courts. As it does not purport to operate in the absence of an agreement between the parties, ICC arbitration does not claim the breadth of authority of courts of general jurisdiction. It aims to provide a process resulting in an award binding upon the contracting parties and enforceable at law.

10.02   Business disputes of an international character

The 1998 ICC Arbitration Rules contain a broad definition of the kinds of disputes which are considered appropriate for resolution by ICC arbitration. Article 1(1), consistent with earlier versions of the Rules, provides that it is the function of the Court of Arbitration:

> . . . to provide for the settlement by arbitration of business disputes of an international character in accordance with the Rules of Arbitration of the International Chamber of Commerce (the "Rules").

The Court has always taken a broad view of what constitutes an international dispute,[1] regularly accepting cases between companies having the same corporate nationality, where the transaction in question might have some effect on international commerce.[2] It has never been considered that the statement

---

1   This view is consistent with the concept of international arbitration under French law. Article 1492 of the French Code of Civil Procedure provides: "Arbitration is international if it implicates international commercial interests." *See* the authors' translation of the French arbitration law, *in* VII YEARBOOK 271 (1982). French law restrains domestic arbitration more than international arbitration. An arbitration between parties domiciled in France will nevertheless be entitled to the international regime if international economic interests are involved. *See* Chapter 30, *infra*.

2   *See, e.g.*, ICC Case 3130/1980, I ICC AWARDS 417 (sales agreement between a Swiss buyer and a Swiss seller calling for delivery in France); ICC Case 5423/1987, II ICC AWARDS 339 (Neither the Court of Arbitration, which found *prima facie* existence of a valid arbitration clause, nor the sole arbitrator found any jurisdictional obstacle to arbitration of a dispute between two French companies, but because of a poorly drafted arbitration clause, which failed to specify the International Chamber of Commerce, the sole arbitrator found that the parties had not intended to designate ICC arbitration at all, and found that he had no jurisdiction.) *See also* ICC Case 5910/1988, 1988 JDI 1216, involving a sale between two Belgian parties; although the arbitra-

of the Court's institutional mission, to provide arbitration services for business disputes of an international character, constrains the jurisdiction of the Court of Arbitration and ICC arbitral tribunals established by it. The overriding consideration is that such jurisdiction is a matter for agreement by the parties. The Court's practice occasioned, in one early case, an unsuccessful attack before the French courts: first against the ICC, for organizing the arbitration; and subsequently against the award rendered by the ICC tribunal, in respect of a dispute between two French companies[3] which was only arguably of an international character.

In order to remove any doubt as to the scope of the Court's arbitral mission, and to avoid any future dispute of its ability to act in disputes arguably of only national character, the Internal Rules of the Court[4] established in 1980 that:

> The Court of Arbitration *may* accept jurisdiction over business disputes not of an international business nature, if it has jurisdiction by reason of an arbitration agreement. (Emphasis added.)

In the process which led to the complete revision of the Rules in 1998, the drafters decided, as a general matter and in the interest of greater transparency, to incorporate into the Rules many of the provisions which had previously existed only as internal rules of the Court. In the process, this sentence was added to Article 1(1) of the Rules:

> If so empowered by an arbitration agreement the Court *shall* also provide for the settlement by arbitration in accordance with these Rules of business disputes not of an international character. (Emphasis added.)

This provision continues to guarantee the power of the Court to act in pursuance of its international mission in matters which are only marginally international, but the modification from "may" to "shall" removes the discretion of the Court to refuse jurisdiction in domestic cases. This desire to make clear to the public that the ICC is available to administer arbitrations dealing with domestic disputes reflects to some degree the fact that, although the ICC has not promoted the use of ICC arbitration clauses for domestic dispute resolution, the number of business disputes of apparently a purely domestic nature submitted to ICC arbitration has increased, to a degree of modest significance,

---

tion was not considered international under Belgian law, the jurisdiction of the ICC tribunal was not subject to question.

3   *Cour d'appel,* Paris, 11 July 1980, Japan Time v. Kienzle France and the International Chamber of Commerce (unpublished.) (*See* section 11.03, note 17.) (The Court dismissed a recourse against the award based on the allegation that the ICC should not have accepted jurisdiction since the arbitration was not international as both parties were French.)

4   Article 1, Internal Rules of the Court, was adopted in 1980 and remained in effect until the adoption of the 1998 Arbitration Rules.

since the late 1980s. Moreover, the compulsory "shall" addressed reservations by some arbitration users who, through National Committees, expressed reluctance to provide for ICC arbitration in agreements having international connotations, but which could be considered under some criteria as domestic if there were any risk that the Court might exercise its discretion not to accept such a case.

In some countries, foreign investments must be realized through joint ventures, with local participation, organized through companies incorporated in the host state. When these joint venture companies contract with the host state, or with other corporations in the host state, it may be argued (or established by laws of the host state) that such contracts are domestic and not international.[5] A number of arbitration users wanted assurances that in such circumstances even if their contractual partners, and the law applicable to the contract, considered a contract as domestic they could nevertheless provide for ICC arbitration, with the assurance that the ICC would administer the arbitration in any event. Article 1(1) of the Rules resolves this issue.

Few questions have been presented to the Court of Arbitration as to disputes alleged not to concern business transactions. In principle, parties could, subject to limitations of national law, create ICC arbitral jurisdiction over non-business disputes. However, the Rules do not provide a basis for extending the mission of the Court to cover non-business disputes, and the Court has demonstrated little inclination to do so. There remains room for interpretation as to what disputes involve business. Certainly, ICC arbitration is not intended for family law or labor matters, both of which are frequently protected by specific mandatory legislation and specially designated tribunals. Nevertheless, members of a family may be involved in international business, and their disputes may be submitted to ICC arbitration. Similarly, while a standard labor agreement for workers might not be accepted for arbitration by the ICC, the case should be different with respect to a specific contract for the services of a senior executive who might insist on the possibility of neutral arbitration as a condition to relocation abroad.[6] Independent personal

---

5   As noted above, the Court in its earlier practice considered contracts of this nature to be international and accepted, as consistent with its functions and mission, to administer arbitrations in accordance with arbitration agreements to this effect.

6   The Court has frequently put into motion ICC arbitrations concerning the employment of international executives, *see* DERAINS & SCHWARTZ, 24. Arbitration clauses in international employment agreements have generally been recognized, and awards concerning them enforced under the New York Convention, despite the agreements not being "commercial". *See, e.g., Cour d'appel*, Grenoble, 13 September 1993, 1994 REV. ARB. 337, note Moreau (employment agreement); Prograph International v. Barhydt, 928 F. Supp. 983 (N.D. Cal. 1996) (employment agreement); *see also* A.J. van den Berg, *Court Decisions on the New York Convention 1958, Consolidated Commentary*, XXI YEARBOOK 394, 408 (1996); *but see Cour de cassation*, 16 February 1999, Société Chateau Tour Saint Christophe v. Astrom (Ch. Sociale), 1999 REV. ARB. 290 (arbitration clause in international employment agreement valid but cannot be enforced by employer to prevent employee from filing labor court suit).

services of commercial representation and distribution are routinely subject to ICC arbitration.[7] In recent years, a few ICC arbitrations are known to have gone forward without having any apparent business connection.[8]

The Court's position in respect to arbitration of non-business disputes is similar to its previous position concerning non-international disputes before it adopted rules specifically permitting it to act: such disputes are not part of its announced mission but there is nothing to prevent it from acting thereon when an arbitration agreement so provides. How it would exercise its discretion to act in a non-business dispute would depend on all of the circumstances. It is one thing for the Secretariat to state, in the abstract, that the ICC would probably not accept to act in a non-business dispute. It is another when the Court is faced by a request for arbitration in an actual dispute, so that refusal to act would result in the frustration of the intention and agreement of the parties to have disputes resolved by neutral independent arbitration. Since it is the mission of the ICC to resolve international disputes and not to frustrate agreements for it to do so, the argument in favor of accepting such cases is strong. Indeed, in such circumstances the Court has accepted to put in motion ICC arbitration of a non-business dispute.[9]

It is quite clear, in any event, that the term "business dispute" is to receive a broad and elastic interpretation. Disputes may be arbitrated under the ICC Rules whether or not they are "commercial" under national law, or under Article I(3) of the New York Convention, which permits states, by reservation, to limit their undertaking to the recognition and enforcement of awards dealing with legal relationships they consider to be commercial. The non-commerciality of a dispute may, in exceptional cases, raise an issue of arbitrability which is to be determined by the arbitrators according to the appropriate rules of law.[10] No restriction to commercial disputes is found in the

---

7   *See, e.g., Cour de cassation*, 4 July 1972, Hecht v. Buismans, 1972 JDI 843.

8   Some years ago the ICC secretariat responded to a query by stating that the Court would probably decline jurisdiction over an inheritance dispute as it would not be considered to be of a "business nature" despite the fact that shares in a company were involved. More recently the Court has formed an arbitral tribunal which issued an award dealing with the financial consequences of a contract for the division of inheritance rights, ICC Case No. 8742/1996, 1999 JDI 1066, note Dominique Hascher. The seat of the arbitration was Switzerland and there was no doubt as to the arbitrability of the dispute since Swiss law permits arbitration of "any dispute involving property." (1987 Swiss Private International Law Act, Article 177)

9   *See* footnote 8 *supra*.

10 An example is found in Article 2061 of the French Civil Code, which has the effect of preventing domestic agreements to arbitrate between individuals who do not have the status of merchants, or concerning a transaction which is not commercial by nature. Under French law the restriction is not applicable to international transactions where agreements to arbitrate are valid without any requirement of commerciality. *Cour de cassation*, 5 January 1999, Zanzi v. De Coninck, 1999 REV. ARB. 260. For a case in which the commercial nature, and hence the arbitrability (under German law), of a publishing agreement was contested before the ICC Court, and ICC arbitral tribunal, and finally a New York State court, *see* International Cultural Property Society Inc. v.

Rules, however, which consciously uses the broader term "business disputes" or, in the French text of the Rules, "différends intervenant dans le domaine des affaires."

10.03   Which edition of the ICC Rules applies?

The ICC Rules have been promulgated in a number of different versions. The 1998 Rules succeeded the 1975 Rules and their 1988 revision. The 1998 Rules effected relatively limited, but nonetheless important, substantive modifications. The organization and wording, however, were entirely re-vamped. Unless otherwise specified, references in this text are to the 1998 Rules.[11] An important issue, which arose in the wake of earlier revisions of the Rules, is what version of the Rules should apply. On the one hand, the Rules are of a procedural nature; it makes good sense for the procedures to be governed by provisions in effect at the commencement of the arbitration. On the other hand, what might be reasonable or self-evident in respect of the date of application of legislative or regulatory measures may be more doubt-ful with respect to consensual rules of arbitration. The institutional rules are, in effect, incorporated by reference when the parties submit to ICC arbitration. For the rules to apply there must be an agreement by the parties—either to the text of the rules, or to the principle of applying future revisions to be made to such rules.

The drafters of the 1998 Rules made clear that in principle the Rules to be ap-plied should be those in effect on the date of commencement of the arbitra-tion. Article 6(1) provides:

> Where the parties have agreed to submit to arbitration under the Rules, they shall be deemed to have submitted *ipso facto* to the Rules in effect on the date of commencement of the arbitration proceedings unless they

---

Walter de Gruyter & Co., N.Y. Sup. Ct., Index No. 121566/99, 14 MEALEY'S INT. ARB. REP. 3 (No. 11, November 1999). On the issue of arbitrability, *see generally* Section 5.07. Commerciality may still be required even in international transactions to validate under some legal systems agree-ments to arbitrate by public bodies. However, any international arbitration concerning a dispute involving an international financial operation has been found to sufficiently involve the inter-ests of international commerce to be arbitrable. *Cour d'appel*, Paris, 13 June 1996, 1997 JDI 151 (unsuccessful recourse on the alleged ground of nullity of the arbitration agreement under the applicable Algerian law by a Kuwaiti public body from a UNCITRAL arbitration award holding it liable to make payments for the construction of the Kuwait embassy in Algiers).

11   To facilitate reference to decisions and comments involving the prior Rules, a table is annexed at Appendix II comparing the numbering of the articles in the present Rules to the articles in the 1975 Rules. For an article-by-article discussion of the modifications, see W. Laurence Craig, Wil-liam W. Park, and Jan Paulsson, ANNOTATED GUIDE TO THE 1998 ICC ARBITRATION RULES, WITH COMMENTARY, (Oceana, 1998); *see also* DERAINS & SCHWARTZ.

have agreed to submit to the Rules in effect on the date of their arbitration agreement.[12]

The rule stated is one of common sense and is consistent with certain needs of administrative practice. Agreements to arbitrate may lie dormant for many years. It is generally desirable to give the parties the benefit of the most up-to-date rules. This is also consistent with the prior practice of the ICC, reflected in a communication of 20 November 1987 from the Secretary General of the Court of Arbitration, and dealing with an earlier revision of the Rules:

> The amended ICC Rules of Arbitration will govern arbitrations which commence on or after January 1, 1988. Parties may also agree to have the amended Rules govern arbitrations initiated prior thereto. Where the parties had provided in an arbitration clause agreed to by them prior to January 1, 1988, to apply the ICC Arbitration Rules then in force, such agreement will be respected regardless of when the arbitration is commenced.

Consistent with the communication of the Secretary General, an arbitral tribunal in ICC case No. 5622[13] of 1992 applied, over the objection of a party, an article of the Rules in effect on the date of commencement of the arbitration in preference to one contained in the Rules at the time of contracting. The new article[14] specifically provided that where an arbitrator was replaced during the proceedings the newly formed tribunal would decide to what extent prior proceedings must be repeated, whereas under the prior version of the Rules it was not clear that such power existed.

The 1998 Rules make clear that, unless the parties specifically agree otherwise, the Rules to be applied are those in effect on the date of commencement of arbitration, including future modifications to the 1998 Rules taking place from time to time. The Rules cannot, however, through their "deeming" provision definitively determine the intent of the parties, particularly where the arbitration agreement pre-dates January 1, 1998, since the prior Rules, incorporated by reference into the arbitration agreement, make no provision for which version of the Rules will apply.

The issue of which version of the Rules applies must be decided as a question of the interpretation of the arbitration agreement and the intent of the parties thereto. This is the province of the trier of fact: the arbitral tribunal. It cannot be resolved, as an administrative matter, by the Court of Arbitration.

---

12   Article 31(1) of the Rules similarly provides that the ICC Court shall, at the end of the arbitral proceedings, determine the fees and expenses of the arbitrators, and the ICC administrative costs "in accordance with the scale *in force at the time of the commencement of the arbitral proceedings.*" (Emphasis added).

13   8 ICC BULL. 52 (May 1997).

14   Article 2(12) of the 1988 revision of the 1975 Rules, corresponding to Article 12(4) of the 1998 Rules. There was no corresponding provision in earlier Rules.

This issue was addressed with respect to conflicts between the 1975 Rules and the 1955 Rules by a distinguished arbitral tribunal chaired by Andrew Martin, Q.C., in the context of a request for discovery. It was alleged that under Article 16 of the 1955 Rules, the procedural rules of the law in force at the place of arbitration (New York) should apply since the Rules themselves were silent on that issue. It was further argued (perhaps erroneously) that under that law the arbitrators could not order discovery or production of documents. Under Article 11 of the 1975 Rules[15], however, the arbitrators were not bound by the municipal procedural law of the place of arbitration. A majority of the arbitral tribunal found (over the dissent of a party-appointed arbitrator, former N.Y. Court of Appeals Judge Van Voorhis) that the 1975 Rules applied and ordered limited production of documents.[16]

As is revealed by the record of the review proceedings before New York State courts, the Court of Arbitration refused to overturn the decision which it considered to be within the jurisdiction of the arbitral tribunal and not that of the Court. It therefore asked the arbitrators to formalize their decision in an interlocutory award. On review of that award, the New York Supreme Court of New York County (a trial court) purported to vacate the preliminary award, sharing the view of the dissenting arbitrator that:

> Incorporating by reference Article 13(1) into the Agreement, the court finds as a matter of law that the parties intended in 1968 to be governed by the 1955 Rules then in existence and not by a set of Rules which might come into existence in the future, with which they were totally unacquainted![17]

On appeal, the higher New York courts reversed and ordered the interlocutory award reinstated on the grounds that such a determination was for the arbitrators and not the courts. The Appellate Division found that there *was* an agreement to arbitrate and that the arbitrators had made a rational determination as to the applicable rules.[18] The Court of Appeals (New York's highest court) took an even more limited view of the court's jurisdiction to review the arbitral tribunal's decision.[19]

Thus the important question of applicability in time of different versions of the ICC Rules has been left to the arbitrators. With increasing frequency,

---

15   Remaining in effect as Article 15(1) of the 1998 Rules.

16   ICC Case 2671, interim award of March 30, 1976, Mobil Oil Indonesia v. Asamera Oil (Indonesia) Ltd., referred to in review proceedings in New York courts. *See* N.Y. LAW JOURNAL, Oct. 28, 1976, p. 10, col. 4.

17   *Id.*

18   Mobil Oil Indonesia v. Asamera Oil (Indonesia) Ltd., 56 A.D. 2d 339; 392 N.Y.S. 614 (N.Y. Supreme Court, Appellate Division 1977).

19   43 N.Y. 2d 276: 372 N.E. 2d 21 (1977).

parties state their specific interest in the arbitration clause. Thus, they may stipulate:

> All disputes arising in connection with the present contract shall be finally settled under the Rules of Arbitration of the International Chamber of Commerce in effect on the date of signature of this contract.

> Or

> All disputes arising in connection with this contract shall be finally settled under the Rules of Arbitration of the International Chamber of Commerce from time to time in effect.

Most often, however, arbitration clauses still give no inkling of the parties' intent on this subject. In such cases, where the arbitration agreement post-dates January 1, 1998 the arbitral tribunal should apply the 1998 Rules, and any future modification thereto, pursuant to the provisions of Article 1(1). Where the agreement pre-dates January 1, 1998, the arbitral tribunal must make an independent finding of the parties' intent. In support of a presumption that the later Rules should apply, the tribunal can rely on previous instructions from the Secretary General of the ICC and on arbitral and national court precedent.[20] There is, however, some authority to the contrary.[21]

In order to avoid controversies of this nature it is recommended that the Terms of Reference, signed by the arbitrators and the parties, provide which version of the Rules applies. In most cases, no difficulty is encountered in having the parties agree to the application of the most recent version of the Rules.

10.04   The Request for Arbitration

Proceedings are commenced by filing a Request for Arbitration pursuant to Article 4 of the Rules which provides, in part:

> 4(1) A party wishing to have recourse to arbitration under these Rules shall submit its Request for Arbitration (the "Request") to the Secretariat, which shall notify the Claimant and Respondent of the receipt of the Request and the date of such receipt.

---

20   *See* ICC Case No. 5622/1992, *supra*, note 11; *Tribunal fédéral Suisse*, 14 June 1990, Komplex v. Voest-Alpine Stahl, 1994 SWISS BULL. 226 (holding 1988 Rules revision applicable to arbitration agreement) note S. Besson (review of Swiss, French, German and English authorities); Offshore International v. Banco Central, [1976] 2 LLOYD'S L. REP. 402 (applying 1975 ICC Rules in force at the time of the Request for Arbitration in preference to 1955 Rules in force at the time of contracting).

21   *See generally*, O'Conor, *Enforcement of Arbitration Awards: Arbitration Rules for the Time Being*, 1 INTERNATIONAL ARBITRATION LAW REVIEW 42 (1997) (reviewing the English cases confirming the presumption that institutional arbitration rules to be applied are those in force at the time of arbitral proceedings and analyzing the possible exceptions).

4(2) The date on which the Request is received by the Secretariat shall, for all purposes, be deemed to be the date of the commencement of the arbitral proceedings.

A party can file its Request with the Secretariat in Paris by any means including registered mail, courier service or, where the party has a correspondent in Paris, by direct delivery.[22] The purpose of the Rule in Article 4(2), that the date of the receipt of the Request by the Secretariat shall be deemed "for all purposes" the date of commencement of arbitral proceedings, is to avoid any conflict with the date, which may be earlier, upon which claimant may have served or delivered the request on respondent. Zeal in notifying respondent will not result in an earlier date; nor will delay by the Secretariat in notifying respondent result in a later one.

The Request should comply with Article 4(3) of the Rules, which provides:

The Request for Arbitration shall *inter alia* contain the following information:

a) the name in full, description and address of each of the parties;

b) a description of the nature and circumstances of the dispute giving rise to the claims;

c) a statement of the relief sought including, to the extent possible, an indication of any amount(s) claimed;

d) the relevant agreements and, in particular, the arbitration agreement;

e) all relevant particulars concerning the number of arbitrators and their choice in accordance with the provisions of Articles 8, 9 and 10, and any nomination of an arbitrator required thereby; and

f) any comments as to the place of arbitration, the applicable rules of law and the language of the arbitration.

This description covers only the minimum requirements of the Request. It does not reflect the fact that in practice ICC tribunals emphasize written documents and pleadings exchanged before hearings rather than development of the facts and the theory of the claim or defense at the hearing.

A comparison may be drawn with the Commercial Arbitration Rules of the American Arbitration Association (AAA) (1999 edition). Under Section R-4 of the AAA Rules, a proceeding is commenced by a party giving written "notice of its intention to arbitrate (the "demand"), which demand shall contain a statement setting forth the nature of the dispute, the names and addresses of

---

22 A communication by fax or e-mail, if receipt can be proved, should be sufficient to establish the date of commencement of an arbitration even though a follow-up filing of the necessary number of hard copies would still be required. ICC Case No. 6784/1990, 8 ICC BULL. 53 (May 1997) (faxed request for arbitration deemed admissible). *See* Section 10.07 "Notifications and communications and calculation of periods of time," *infra*.

all other parties, the amount involved, if any, the remedy sought, and the hearing locale sought." Such a notice may be contained in a few pages. The claim and proof are then developed at a hearing, at which the parties are expected to make statements clarifying the issues, present proofs and witnesses, and provide for the examination and cross-examination of such witnesses (Section R-32 of the AAA Rules). Thus, in theory, although certainly not in practice where large cases are concerned, a party in an AAA proceeding could learn of his adversary's proof and theory of the case for the first time at the hearing or just before it.

The UNCITRAL Rules provide for the commencement of arbitration proceedings by the filing of a simple "Notice of Arbitration" referring to the contract from which the dispute arises and "the general nature of the claim and an indication of the amount involved, if any." (Article 3(3)). This is to be completed at a later stage of the proceedings by the filing of a "Statement of Claim" (Article 18), a more detailed exposition of the facts supporting the claim, the points at issue, and the relief or remedy sought, all accompanied by the documents relied on.

The 1998 ICC Rules, like their predecessors, provide for substantially more than notice of an intention to arbitrate. The Request for Arbitration is designed to inform the other party, and the Court of Arbitration, of the nature and circumstances of the dispute giving rise to the claims and both the nature and, to the extent possible, the relief requested. Nevertheless, there is no requirement that the Request present an exhaustive statement of claim. It is recognized (although the Rules do not require it) that there will be subsequent exchanges of briefs and documents. Documentary evidence (other than the contracts relied on) need not be supplied with the Request as a condition of its validity. An interest in the rapid initiation of the arbitral process is reflected in Article 4(3)(a) of the Rules, which now requires only a "description of the nature and circumstances of the dispute"—not "a statement of the Claimant's case" as required under the prior Rules.[23]

The new language emphasizes the nature of the dispute without insisting on the characterization and specification of the claims. On the other hand, Article 4(3)(f) contains the requirement, not present in prior versions of the Rules, of a statement of the relief sought and, to the extent possible, an indication of the amounts claimed. These indications are important not only to

---

23 Article 3(2)(a) 1975 ICC Rules. In drafting the 1998 Rules the revisers found it was unnecessarily burdensome to require a full statement of the claimant's case at this early stage of the proceedings. Also, some confusion had been observed due to the sentiment of lawyers from civil law countries that a "statement of case" required a detailed reference of what was expected to be proved for each claim and citation to the evidence expected to be submitted therefor. Lawyers from common law countries generally understood the phrase to mean simply the pleading of issues sufficient to give notice of the elements of the claim, with sufficient allegations of fact to make out a claim at law ("notice pleadings").

the other party, but also to the Court of Arbitration, which is required in many cases to determine the number of arbitrators in function of the amount in dispute. That amount is also used in determining the advances on costs.

It helps the Court of Arbitration that Article 4(3)(f) invites the claimant to supply "any comments as to the place of arbitration, the applicable rules of law and the language of the arbitration."

The extent of the claimant's initial submission in the Request will depend upon the nature and size of the case. In a major international construction dispute, the relevant documents ultimately to be considered by the arbitrators may fill several filing cabinets. The initial Request normally includes but a selection of core documents. Further documents will follow in the exchanges of such briefs and documents as the tribunal may order.

It is not clear what procedural remedies would be available if the contents of a Request for Arbitration fell manifestly short of the minimum requirements of the Rules. In several cases respondents have sought to delay or avoid submitting an answer, on the grounds that they were insufficiently informed of the claim made against them. Such positions, which serve to delay the proceedings, are usually viewed with suspicion. While a respondent is entitled to know the nature of the claim, it is not entitled to discovery or a detailed bill of particulars as a condition of its obligation to answer. Attempts of respondents to derail arbitrations in the past, based on allegations that the arbitration had not commenced because the document filed by claimant did not comply with the requirements of a "Request", have failed.[24] Nevertheless, the possibility that such a procedural stance could be taken led to a relaxation of the formal requirements for the Request, and to substantially eliminating the requirement for filing documentary evidence (other than the agreements themselves) in support of the claim at this early stage of the proceedings.

Whatever may be the minimum requirements of Article 4(3), a claimant is generally well advised to make a substantial submission at the outset of the case. First of all, this approach enables the ICC to select an appropriate presiding arbitrator. The Secretariat's description of the case, provided to whichever National Committee is asked to propose a presiding arbitrator, is based only on materials provided by the parties. Furthermore, the initial dossier communicated by the ICC Secretariat to the arbitrators is bound to leave an impression on them. Since the tribunal is formed for the sole purpose of hearing a single case, its members will wish to be informed of the nature of the case prior to the first meeting with the parties and prior to drawing up the Terms of Reference (*see* Chapter 15, *infra*). Furthermore, a full statement of claims allows the Answer to be a more responsive pleading. Hence there is both a real and a psychological advantage to filing a comprehensive Request. There are

---

24   *See, e.g.*, ICC Case 6784, 8 ICC Bull. 53-54 (May 1997).

few disadvantages. Due to the informal nature of the proceedings and the usual requirement of several exchanges of documents prior to the hearing, the tactic of surprise (holding back parts of the case) is seldom successful.

No special form is required for the Request or other documents filed in arbitration. Parties generally present their case in the manner with which their counsel is most familiar. Pleadings and documents tend to be filed in bound volumes. Some practitioners find that exhibits are most easily handled in ring notebooks, which permit particular exhibits to be removed easily by the arbitrators or counsel for examination, and which facilitate subsequent additions (or replacements of poor copies or of texts requiring correction).

Under Article 4(3)(c) of the Rules, the agreement to arbitrate must be submitted with the Request. Typically, this agreement is contained as an arbitration clause in the contract under which the dispute has arisen. If the Request is not accompanied by documentary proof of an agreement to arbitrate, and if the respondent does not respond within the 30-day time limit defined in Article 5 without contesting ICC jurisdiction, the Court of Arbitration may, under Article 6(2) of the Rules, find that there is no *prima facie* agreement to arbitrate and inform the parties that the arbitration cannot proceed. If the issue is contested, it is also disposed of under Article 6(2) (*See* Section 11.01, *infra*).

The claimant must also supply "all relevant particulars concerning the number of arbitrators and their choice." (Article 4(3)(e)). If the arbitration clause does not establish the number of arbitrators, the claimant states a preference for one or three arbitrators, and the Court of Arbitration makes a decision under Article 8(2). If the arbitration clause calls for three arbitrators, the claimant must give the name, address and nationality of an arbitrator for approval by the Court of Arbitration. The claimant may also do so if there is no agreement to a three-member tribunal, but the claimant requests the Court to appoint three arbitrators.

The Request and supporting documents are filed with the Secretariat. Article 3(1) requires that all documents should be submitted in a sufficient number to provide a copy for each respondent, each arbitrator, and the Secretariat. Pursuant to Article 4(5), the Secretariat then sends a copy of the Request and annexed documents to the respondent. Once the tribunal is officially formed, the parties ordinarily provide communications and documents directly to the arbitrators and to the opposing party, while sending an additional copy to the Secretariat. However, if the parties so desire or if the Terms of Reference so provide, the Secretariat can act as a central depository for service of documents and will then forward the documents to the parties by registered mail. Although this procedure generally leads to some delays, it provides security and proof of compliance with deadlines.

10.05   Answer and Counterclaim

Article 5(1) provides that the respondent should file its Answer within thirty days of receipt of the Request forwarded to it by the Secretariat. Thirty days is often manifestly too short a period of time to answer an extensive claim. The Secretariat thus readily grants extensions in appropriate circumstances, as authorized under Article 5(2). Such extensions are ordinarily limited to thirty days, but longer or additional extensions may be granted.

Article 5(1) specifically provides, however, that the postponement of an Answer may not delay forming the arbitral tribunal. The respondent's response to the claimant's proposal for the number of arbitrators and, where appropriate, its nomination of an arbitrator, must in principle be contained in the Answer. If the respondent seeks an extension to answer it must, nevertheless, pursuant to the requirements of Article 5(2), take a position at the time of requesting the extension with respect to the appointment of the arbitral tribunal, so that the Court of Arbitration may proceed without delay to confirm or name arbitrators.

Much of the discussion in Section 10.04 concerning the contents of the Request and the documents to be supplied therewith is also applicable to the Answer.

Article 5(5) provides that if a respondent wishes to file a counterclaim, it should do so at the time of filing the Answer,[25] and the claimant (defendant on the counterclaim) then has an additional thirty days to make an optional Reply to the counterclaim.

The decision whether to file a counterclaim in ICC arbitration is similar to that faced in other litigation, with one important exception: since a counterclaim increases the amount in dispute (which is considered to be the amount claimed *plus* the amount of the counterclaim), the costs of arbitration will be increased (*see* Chapter 14 and Chapter 21, *infra*). So will the amount of the advance on costs required for arbitrators' fees and the administrative charges of the ICC, as well as the amount of the total costs as finally determined at the end of the arbitration.

This increase in costs should deter unrealistic counterclaims since the party making an inflated demand will be called upon to contribute to a substantially increased deposit. Furthermore, if its defense and counterclaim are unsuccessful, such a party may be charged with all, or a major part, of the costs.

---

25   Failure to file a counterclaim with the Answer as provided in Article 5(5) will not bar its subsequent filing. ICC Case 7237/1993, 8 ICC BULL. 65 (May 1997). Article 18 provides that the Terms of Reference will be drawn up in the light of the "most recent submissions." Hence the filing of new claims or counterclaims is authorized up until the signing of the Terms of Reference, and even thereafter, if such counterclaims fall within the limits of the Terms. ICC Case No. 7076/1993, 8 ICC BULL. 66 (May 1997). Article 19 of the 1998 Rules now permits counterclaims falling outside of the limits of the Terms if the arbitral tribunal so authorizes.

Whether or not these considerations have in fact led to reduced counterclaims is difficult to tell. At least it would seem to diminish the incidence of completely baseless *pro forma* counterclaims.

In principle, a respondent may only make a counterclaim against the party who filed the claim and may not seek to add additional defendants to the counterclaim, or make cross claims against other respondents, without the agreement of all parties. Reported as the position of the Court,[26] this policy would leave the claimant as the sole master of who may be parties to the arbitration. This position is easily explicable where joinder of additional parties would cause the problems most usually associated with multi-party arbitration: difficulty in the formation of an arbitral tribunal where each party would have the right to nominate an arbitrator, and the necessity of creating a procedure appropriate to a "three-sided" arbitration instead of the "two-sided" one originally envisaged.[27] Where no such problems exist—because, for instance, the added parties are signatories to the agreement and in fact accept to be considered as part of the claimant or respondent group—it may be appropriate to give weight to the interests of parties who have signed, or are otherwise parties to, ICC arbitration clauses. It is possible that in some circumstances the Court could be persuaded to permit joinder. The Rules do not contain any absolute prohibition on the Court's organisation of arbitral proceedings involving parties not identified in the claimant's request. As this 3d Edition went to press, the Court was studying whether a policy could be defined to allow the Court more fully to use its authority in the interest of fairness and efficiency.

10.06   Failure or refusal to answer and other defaults: ex parte proceedings

One of the principal advantages of an institutional arbitration system such as that provided by the ICC (in comparison with *ad hoc* arbitrations, or those taking place under international rules without an administering authority) is that effective measures may be taken by the supervising authority in the

---

26   By former Secretaries General of the Court, *see* DERAINS & SCHWARTZ 73; Stephen Bond, *The Experience of the ICC International Court of Arbitration*, *in* MULTI-PARTY ARBITRATION, pp. 39, 41-43 (ICC Publishing, 1991). In addition to policy grounds, this can be rationalized on the formal ground that such claims are not counterclaims but cross claims or third party claims. An arbitral tribunal which refused to allow the joinder of an additional member of the Claimant's group of companies as a respondent to the counterclaim relied squarely on this formal ground, even where the member of the group was a signatory to the arbitration agreement. ICC Case 5625/1987, II ICC AWARDS 484. In application of its traditional view that claimant has total control over the parties to arbitration proceedings which the claimant initiates, the Court may refuse to put into motion a counterclaim against an additional party to the arbitration agreement who had not joined as claimant in the original request for arbitration or a cross claim against a party to the arbitration agreement who had not been joined as a respondent in the original claim.

27   *See* Section 5.11, *supra*, "Multi-Party Disputes." For the related problem of consolidation, *see* Section 11.06.

event of dilatory tactics by the parties. Thus, where for instance the respondent refuses to answer or to name an arbitrator, steps may be taken for the arbitration to proceed *ex parte*. Article 6(3) provides:

> If any of the parties refuses or fails to take part in the arbitration, or any stage thereof, the arbitration shall proceed notwithstanding such refusal or failure.

An arbitral tribunal may thus be constituted without the participation of a party, or even over its objection. ICC awards rendered by default are in principle no less enforceable than ones resulting from an active adversarial process.[28]

Where a sole arbitrator either is provided for in the arbitration agreement, or has been determined by the Court to be appropriate, he will be appointed by the Court, and the proceedings will advance, despite the default of one party. If three arbitrators are to be impaneled, the Court of Arbitration will not only appoint the chairman of the tribunal but, in application of Articles 8(4) and 9(6) of the Rules, will also appoint an arbitrator for the defaulting party. In making such appointments, the Court has shown itself to be receptive to the presumed national and political sensitivities of the defaulting parties, while seeking to appoint able and efficient arbitrators (*see* Section 12.05, *infra*).

The Rules also provide power to the Court of Arbitration to deal with the consequences of further default by a party, notably a party's refusal to sign the Terms of Reference. In appropriate circumstances the Court, pursuant to Article 18(3) of the Rules, orders the arbitration to proceed despite the missing signature (*see* Section 15.03, *infra*).

While the Rules provide for and regulate the consequences of default, arbitral tribunals make every possible attempt to induce a defaulting party to participate, even at late stages in the proceedings. They are encouraged to do so by the Secretariat and the Court. The ICC is anxious to ensure the enforceability of its awards, and ensures that even defaulting parties continue to receive notice of every step in the proceedings.

Article 6(3) provides not only for the consequences of a failure to answer—the most common kind of default—but also for a failure of a party to "take part in the arbitration, or any stage thereof," the consequence being that (assuming advances on costs have been made by the parties or one of them)[29] the arbitration will continue through to award. While addressing the

---

28   For a case where the Spanish Supreme Court enforced an ICC award rendered in Geneva against a defaulting Spanish party, *see* Cominco France S.A. v. Soquiber S.L., (unpublished), extracts *in* VIII YEARBOOK 408 (1983). The Spanish court noted that the New York Convention requires only that the defendant be given adequate *notice* of the case, not that it actually appear. Furthermore, it referred to the New York Convention's "clear affirmation" that the burden of proof of lack of notice is on the party resisting the award.

29   Rules, Article 30(4) sets out the procedure for determining that a claim or counterclaim will be withdrawn, without prejudice, for failure to pay the applicable advance on costs. *See infra*, Section 14.02.

consequences of default, the Rules offer no details on the conduct of default proceedings. It is clear, however, that an arbitral tribunal has no authority to enter an award based on accepting as admitted claims which have not been denied. Arbitrators are required to determine whether they have jurisdiction, to receive and evaluate evidence of the claims (or counterclaims), establish the facts by all appropriate means,[30] and render an award stating the reasons upon which it is based.[31]

Article 6(3) applies not only to respondents but to "any party." Accordingly, an arbitral tribunal may be required to rule upon the consequences of the withdrawal of a claimant from the proceedings or its failure to prosecute its claim. Ordinarily such conduct will require the arbitral tribunal to render an award, at least on the issue of costs, which may also include a ruling on the merits of the claims where evidence has been received on the issues, or a dismissal of the claims without prejudice because of failure to prosecute in timely fashion.[32]

10.07   Notifications and communications and calculation of periods of time

Article 3(2) of the Rules provides that notifications and communications from the Secretariat or the arbitrator shall be validly made if they are delivered against receipt, or sent by registered post or courier to the last known address of the party for whom they are intended. They may also be made by facsimile transmission, telex, telegram, or any other means that generates a record.

This provision of the Rules makes clear how official documents may be communicated to a party without possibility of contest, and is particularly relevant at the commencement of the case or in default proceedings. One of the effects of the requirement of Article 4(5) of the Rules that the Secretariat shall send a copy of the Request to the respondent is that the starting date for the respondent's answer is that of receipt (or deemed receipt) of the official notice by the Secretariat. This date may be substantially later than the date on which the Request was received by the Secretariat, for while the Secretariat generally sends on the Request within a few days of receipt (and often by special courier), it may happen that an incorrect address was provided, no sure means of communication exists, or a return receipt is not received. Where the

---

30   Rules, Article 20.

31   Rules, Article 25(2).

32   For an example of arbitration legislation giving the exclusive power to arbitrators, not the courts, to dismiss arbitrations for failure to prosecute, or to make an award based on the evidence before it, *see* the English Arbitration Act 1996, Sec. 41. For the prior history of the issue *see* Gregg and Others (U.K.) v. Raytheon Ltd. (U.S.), [1980] 1 ALL E.R. 420 (Court of Appeal, Opinion of Lord Denning, M.R. and Lord Justice Roskill) (relationship between power of courts and arbitral tribunal to dismiss arbitral proceedings in context of ICC arbitration); Bremer Vulkan (FRG) v. South India Shipping Co., [1981]1 ALL E.R. 298 (House of Lords).

address of the respondent is considered to be proper, but service is refused or the respondent has moved, the Secretariat will often make several efforts to effect a clear service with receipt. Where this is not possible, the claimant must decide whether or not to proceed with the arbitration based on a service that is "deemed" to have been made.[33]

A claimant may send a copy of the Request directly to the respondent at the time of filing with the Secretariat. This will not shorten the time within which the respondent must reply, which runs from the date of receipt or deemed receipt of the document sent by the Secretariat, but may usefully put the respondent on notice of the commencement of proceedings at the earliest possible time.

The general rule for official notices and communications from the Secretariat and the arbitral tribunal does not apply to communications between the parties or from the parties to the arbitral tribunal. Nor does it prevent the arbitral tribunal from agreeing with the parties as to the agreed means of communication. It may be useful for the Terms of Reference to set out the modes of communication agreed by the parties and the arbitral tribunal, thus avoiding any controversy thereafter.

Article 3(4) of the Rules provides that periods of time, wherever specified under the Rules, shall commence running on the day following the date a notification or communication is deemed to be effective as set forth above. The Article sets forth in detail the rules for calculating periods of time in respect of intervening non-working days and holidays.

---

33   Interestingly, the language of Article 3(2) providing the means by which notifications and communications "shall be made" by the Secretariat or the arbitral tribunal to a party replaces the provisions of Article 6(2) of the prior version of the Rules which provided that communications "shall be *validly* made" if not filed according to the means set out. The revisers recognized that the notification according to the means set out constituted "deemed service" for the purpose of continuation of ICC arbitral proceedings, but that the issue of validity of service for the purpose of recognition and execution of an award so rendered was ultimately to be determined by national courts under the relevant applicable law.

CHAPTER 11

ARBITRAL JURISDICTION

11.01 The Court of Arbitration's preliminary prima facie determination of existence of agreement to arbitrate

The international arbitral process would be greatly hampered if a party wishing to resist arbitration could require, prior to the proceedings, that national courts determine the validity of the alleged agreement to arbitrate. However, to leave the issue entirely up to the arbitral tribunal would require the party disputing jurisdiction to participate in the establishment of a tribunal and—in principle—to contribute to the costs thereof even though it contests the obligation to arbitrate.

The ICC Rules stake out a middle ground. Where the respondent does not file an Answer, or where any party raises a plea concerning the "existence, validity or scope" of the arbitration agreement, the Court of Arbitration is given the mission under Article 6(2) of the Rules to determine, as a preliminary matter, whether the arbitration will proceed. The criterion for deciding this issue is whether the Court ". . . is *prima facie* satisfied that an agreement under the Rules may exist." If the Court is so satisfied the arbitration will proceed before the arbitral tribunal. This tribunal, however, is not bound by the Court's provisional decision, and will render a final decision as to arbitral jurisdiction in an interim or final award. If the Court decides that the arbitration will not proceed because it is not convinced, *prima facie*, that an arbitration agreement may exist, the disappointed party is not deprived of all remedies. Under Article 6(2): "In such a case, any party retains the right to ask any court having jurisdiction whether or not there is a binding arbitration agreement."

The power of the ICC Court of Arbitration to decide whether there are sufficient indications of an agreement to arbitrate so that the arbitration should be ordered to proceed is an important feature of ICC arbitration. It was considered by some to be an administrative burden, the elimination of which would lead to economy and time savings. But in fact the Court's powers were confirmed and even broadened in the revision leading to the 1998 Rules.[1] National Committees almost unanimously felt that the procedure was a useful and important protective device.

The previous version of the Rules provided that the Court should make its determination whenever one of the parties contested the "existence or validity of the agreement to arbitrate."[2] The 1998 Rules are broader, providing for the Court to make its determination in respect of pleas concerning "the existence, validity or *scope* of the arbitration agreement."[3] (Emphasis added.) Thus it is made clear that the Court should be *prima facie* satisfied not only that an ICC arbitration agreement may exist, but also that it applies to the parties intended to be made respondents and the disputes on which the claims set out in the Request for Arbitration are based, or some of them.

Article 6(2) also redefines the *prima facie* test. Under the prior Rules, where a jurisdictional issue was raised the Court would permit an arbitration to proceed only when "satisfied of the *prima facie* existence" of an agreement to arbitrate.[4] Article 6(2) now provides that the arbitration shall proceed if the Court "is *prima facie* satisfied that an arbitration agreement . . . may exist." The change in the wording is purposeful. The term "*prima facie* agreement" was a misnomer, since most issues of jurisdiction arise precisely when the formal or *prima facie* existence of the arbitration agreement is put in doubt, at least with respect to one or more of the parties to be charged. A frequent issue is whether an existing agreement may be extended to non-signatories, or to a dispute not specifically provided for in the parties' agreement. What is intended is that the arbitration shall proceed if there is *prima facie* evidence of an agreement to arbitrate, which could reasonably be made out before an arbitral tribunal. In other words, the Court should be convinced that an arbitration agreement "may arguably exist."

The Court's role under Article 6(2) is an important administrative safeguard against the putting into motion of an arbitration procedure when there is no jurisdictional basis for it whatsoever. Nevertheless, the Court seldom exer-

---

1   *See* Section 2.04 for a discussion of the revision's elimination of the Secretariat's role in *prima facie* determination.

2   1975 Rules as amended in 1988, Article 8(3); *see also id.*, Article 7.

3   Under the prior Rules it was said, in respect to the Court's *prima facie* findings when the scope of an arbitration clause was disputed: "The Court has sometimes hesitated on whether the term "existence" in Article 8(3) of the Rules should or not be construed as meaning "existence of a clause which covers the dispute." Viewed from this angle, a clause which would not cover the dispute would have to be considered non-existent. However, the Court has rejected this interpretation of Article 8(3). Consequently, disagreements based on ambiguity of an arbitration clause do not hold an arbitration from being set in motion." Theodore Klein, *Disagreement on the Scope of an Arbitration Clause*, 7 ICC BULL. 24, 25 (December 1996). On the issue generally, see also Serge Gravel and Patricia Peterson, *French Law and Arbitration Clauses—Distinguishing Scope from Validity. Comment on I.C.C. Case No. 6519 Final Award*, 37 MCGILL L.J. 510 (1992).

4   Article 8(3), 1975 Rules, as amended in 1988.

cises this power to prevent an arbitration from proceeding. Where bona fide questions of fact and law are raised concerning the existence, validity or scope of the agreements, they are to be decided by the arbitral tribunal. The Court, which administers and supervises arbitrations, is not well suited to decide such issues which have to be debated, with all the protections of due process, before a body whose mission is to decide disputes in the place and stead of the normally competent national courts.

It is rare that a case comes before the Court where there is no evidence that an arbitration agreement exists at all. More frequently it is argued that the agreement exists but but does not extend to all of the parties sought to be joined. The Court has indeed not infrequently determined that the arbitration may not proceed against some of the named parties, a practice necessitated by the tactics of some claimant parties who seek to join as defendants parties with such tenuous relationships to the arbitration agreement that it is impossible for the Court to be satisfied, even *prima facie*, that an arbitration agreement may exist concerning them. The Court may find that because of pathologies in the arbitration agreement itself it does not constitute a binding agreement to arbitrate, or does not call for arbitration under the ICC Rules,[5] and in such cases will notify the parties that the arbitration may not proceed. It may on rare occasions find that an agreement to arbitrate is clearly null and void. Most of the time, sufficient questions are presented as to require determination by the tribunal. The same is true where it is alleged that conditions precedent to arbitration (exhaustion of negotiation procedures or of conditions required under FIDIC contracts) have not been fulfilled, that jurisdiction is time barred by a statute of limitations or another form of prescription, or that the agreement to arbitrate did not survive the assignment,[6] or termination of the overall agreement in which it is contained.

The ICC Rules do not provide a role for the Court concerning the "arbitrability"[7] of disputes, that is whether the claims are susceptible of arbitration or whether arbitration is excluded on public policy grounds. This determination is to be made by the arbitral tribunal, if so required,[8] under the rules of law it deems applicable.

---

5   The Court has taken an expansive view of what constitutes reference to ICC arbitration and generally will order an arbitration to proceed even where the reference to ICC arbitration is incomplete or inaccurate. The cases are summarized in Jean Benglia, *Inaccurate References to the ICC*, 7 ICC BULL. 11 (December 1996). *See* Section 6.01, *supra*.

6   For a discussion of the respective powers of the Court, the arbitral tribunal, and national courts in the determination of arbitral jurisdiction with respect to assignment by a trustee in bankruptcy of contract claims subject to ICC arbitration, *see* Apollo Computer v. Berg, 886 F. 2d 469 (1st Cir. 1989).

7   For the definition of "arbitrability" and discussion thereof, *see* Section 5.07.

8   *See*, however, A. Dimolitsa, *Issues Concerning the Existence, Validity and Effectiveness of the Arbitration Agreement*, 7 ICC BULL. 14, 21 (December 1996) reporting consideration by the Court of some respondents' inarbitrability arguments (allegations that disputes involving patent law and

11.02   Procedure for raising jurisdictional issues before the Court of Arbitration

Even if there is an evident jurisdictional difficulty, the Request is invariably sent to the respondent to elicit a response. After all, that response may turn out to constitute an unqualified acceptance of ICC arbitration. Even when there is no ICC arbitration agreement at all, a response on the merits which does not contest arbitral jurisdiction is deemed a sufficient indication of acceptance of arbitral jurisdiction to permit the arbitration to proceed, without prejudice to the respondent's right to raise the jurisdictional issue with the arbitral tribunal. But if the respondent contests jurisdiction, or simply remains silent during the 30 day period defined in Article 5(1) of the Rules, the Court will be required to make its *prima facie* determination.

The procedure has been succinctly summarized by the Chairman of the Court of Arbitration:[9]

> If the Respondent contests the existence, validity or scope of the arbitration agreement or if the Respondent does not file an answer, the matter will, after payment by the Claimant of the provisional advance, be submitted to the Court. In clear cases of absence of an arbitration agreement under the Rules, the Court will decide that the arbitration cannot proceed. If the Court is *prima facie* satisfied that an arbitration agreement under the Rules may exist, it will refer the matter to the Arbitral Tribunal, which will then take a decision on its own jurisdiction.

The Court seeks to cut down groundless claims of arbitral jurisdiction intended to pressure an opponent by setting into motion the machinery for appointing an arbitral tribunal. Where there is no agreement to arbitrate, or where the parties have failed to stipulate ICC arbitration, or where there is a pathological arbitration clause, the Court must decline jurisdiction (*see* Chapter 9, *supra*). In determining whether an agreement for ICC arbitration may exist, the Court will limit itself to a review of the contractual documents or the written argument submitted by counsel. No opportunity whatsoever for oral argument is accorded by the Court, whose nature is purely administrative. No lawyer or party has ever appeared to plead a single issue before the ICC Court of Arbitration.

In light of the fact that jurisdictional issues are fully considered by the arbitral tribunal itself, this restriction on presenting arguments to the Court is fully justified. Article 6(2) of the Rules clearly provides that when the Court has determined that the arbitration will proceed ". . . any decision as

---

unfair competition were not subject to arbitration) on the grounds that they went to the "effectiveness" of the arbitration agreement. The author cites, however, no precedents of refusal to allow an arbitration to proceed on this basis.

9   R. Briner, *The Implementation of the 1998 ICC Rules of Arbitration*, 8 ICC BULL. 7 (December 1997).

to the jurisdiction of the Arbitral Tribunal shall be taken by the Arbitral Tribunal itself."

Despite the fact that respondents get "another bite at the apple" on the issue of jurisdiction before the arbitral tribunal, they generally present full arguments before the Court of Arbitration in the hope of terminating the proceedings at the earliest stage. Accordingly, there is often elaborate correspondence between parties and the Court. The most frequent arguments raised to show absence of arbitral jurisdiction are: (i) that the arbitration clause is pathological, typically in the sense of inadequately referring to ICC arbitration; (ii) that there is no arbitration clause or agreement at all; (iii) that respondent neither signed nor acquiesced in the arbitration agreement; (iv) that a party was not bound by an agreement to arbitrate made by an alleged but disavowed representative or agent, or by an affiliated company; and (v) that a party which guaranteed the performance of a contract was not bound by an arbitration clause in the contract whose performance was guaranteed.

The Court's practice in the past was to send even weakly arguable cases of jurisdiction to an arbitral tribunal for determination of the issue. Nevertheless it would on occasion refuse to constitute a tribunal when it was convinced that there was no *prima facie* arbitration agreement.[10] The 1998 revision of the Rules makes it even less likely than in the past that the Court will refuse to order the arbitration to proceed where jurisdiction is doubtful. The replacement of the necessity of finding a "*prima facie* agreement" by the need to be *prima facie* satisfied that an "agreement under the Rules may exist" lowers the bar.[11] Nevertheless, the Court will continue to play an impor-

---

10   In the *Cekobanka* case, the Court declined in 1985 to form an arbitral tribunal where the claimant party alleged that an arbitration agreement had been formed by exchange of telexes. Respondent denied this contention since *inter alia* the offer had been withdrawn prior to acceptance. The Court's determination is reported in subsequent judicial proceedings, *Tribunal de grande instance*, Paris, 8 October 1986, Cekobanka v. ICC, 1987 REV. ARB. 367. In the *R.E.D.E.C.* case in 1987, the Court ordered arbitration to proceed against R.E.D.E.C., the guarantor of a construction contract containing an ICC arbitration clause but, after initially deciding otherwise, refused to order arbitration to proceed against Gaeth Pharaon, the controlling owner and alleged alter ego of R.E.D.E.C. The Court's decision is reported in judicial proceedings, *Tribunal de grande instance*, Paris, 13 July 1988, R.E.D.E.C. et Pharaon v. Uzinexport Import et Chambre de Commerce Internationale, 1989 REV. ARB. 97. *See also*, A. Dimolitsa, *Issues Concerning the Existence, Validity and Effectiveness of the Arbitration Agreement*, 7 ICC BULL. 14 (December 1996), I. Hautot, *Les pouvoirs de la Cour d'arbitrage de la C.C.I. de décider ou non d'organiser l'arbitrage*, 1990 SWISS BULL. 12.

11   The other textual change in Article 6(2), that the Court should not allow an arbitration to proceed if not satisfied that "an arbitration *under the Rules* may exist" (emphasis added) was not intended to make any substantive change from the requirement in the prior Rules that the arbitration should not proceed if the Court found that there was a *prima facie* agreement but "it does not specify the International Chamber of Commerce" (Article 7, 1975 Rules, Article 12, 1980 Internal Rules). In 1998, the first year of application of the new Rules, the Court was required to make an Article 6(2) ruling in 78 cases and found that the *prima facie* test had been satisfied in 76 of the 78 cases. *See* Fabien Gélinas, *The Application of the ICC Rules by the Court: 1998 Overview*, 10 ICC BULL. 11 (Spring 1999).

tant preliminary role not only where it refuses to permit an arbitration to proceed but also where, in appropriate cases, it limits the scope of arbitration by refusing to join non-signatory parties (such as parent companies, guarantors, or states) as additional respondents in otherwise valid arbitrations. *See* section 11.05, *infra*.

When the Court of Arbitration has determined whether or not it is *prima facie* satisfied that an arbitration agreement may exist, the Secretariat notifies the parties and, if appropriate, the arbitral tribunal. No reasons are given for the decision, which is considered administrative in character. The circumstances in which decisions have been taken not to permit an arbitration to proceed are not made public and have only come to light in the very rare case of challenge before national courts.[12]

The power of the Court to act as gate keeper in determining whether ICC arbitrations will proceed has broadly been confirmed by national courts wherever such decisions of the Court have been called into question.[13]

In *Cekobanka v. ICC*[14] the Court of Arbitration determined that the documents exchanged between the parties did not contain an arbitration clause binding the parties to ICC arbitration; accordingly, there was no *prima facie* agreement to arbitrate. The disappointed claimant brought suit before the *Tribunal de grande instance* of Paris seeking to compel the ICC to constitute an arbitral tribunal to hear the affair. The court found that there was no proof that the Court of Arbitration had failed to respect its Rules and that the Court had not committed any wrong in refusing to organize the arbitration solicited by the claimant. Because of the administrative nature of the Court of Arbitration's mission, and the nature of the suit seeking to hold the ICC liable, the French court did not itself consider whether arbitral jurisdiction existed, but only whether the Court of Arbitration had fulfilled its role under the Rules.[15]

---

12   For informed commentary concerning non-public cases of Court refusal to permit arbitrations to proceed, *see* A. Dimolitsa (a member of the Court), *Issues Concerning the Existence, Validity and Effectiveness of the Arbitration Agreement*, 7 ICC BULL. 14 (December 1996); DERAINS & SCHWARTZ, 87-99.

13   For an example of a United States Court's willingness to confirm the ICC Court's role of forwarding cases to arbitral tribunals for determination of jurisdictional issues see Apollo v. Berg, 886 F.2d. 469 (lst Cir. 1989) (discussed *infra* at Section 28.02) where a U.S. Court of Appeals relied on the ICC Rules in holding that the validity of an ICC Arbitration Clause was for the ICC and the arbitrators to determine.

14   *Tribunal de grande instance*, Paris, 8 October 1986, 1987 REV. ARB. 367; P. Fouchard, *Les institutions permanentes d'arbitrages devant le juge étatique*, 1987 REV. ARB. 225, 233.

15   If, following a *prima facie* denial of arbitral jurisdiction by the Court of Arbitration, a suit were brought before a national court on the merits of the dispute between the contracting parties, the court would ordinarily be required to determine, as a preliminary matter, whether there was, in fact, a binding arbitration agreement (despite the ICC Court's *prima facie* negative finding) and the national court's determination of the issue would be binding. *See* 1987 JDI 1039, 1044 (note Y.D.).

In *R.E.D.E.C.*,[16] the French courts faced challenges to both the Court's decision to allow an arbitration to proceed against a non-signatory corporate guarantor of the payment obligations of the respondent signatory to the arbitration agreement, and its decision not to forward to arbitration claims against the owner of the guarantor, a physical person and its alleged *alter ego*. The Paris *Tribunal de grande instance* did not examine the merits of the challenge and found that these decisions were taken in accordance with the Court's proper exercise of its functions in accordance with the ICC Rules.

These typical judgments confirm that a decision by the Court of Arbitration finding *prima facie* arbitral jurisdiction over a dispute and referring the matter to an arbitral tribunal for a determination of all issues (including jurisdiction) retains its administrative character and is not subject to judicial review.[17] Only an award by the arbitrator (whether interim or final) constitutes the exercise of decision-making powers which, depending upon the law at the place of arbitration or execution, may be subject to judicial review.

11.03 Arbitrators' authority to determine their jurisdiction[18]

There are two reasons why an arbitration may proceed despite a challenge by one party to arbitral jurisdiction: first, the Rules enshrine the principle that arbitrators have jurisdiction to determine their own jurisdiction (Article 6(2)),[19] and second, the arbitration clause is severable from the main contract at issue (Article 6(4)) (*see* Section 5.04, *supra*). Even in the face of an ar-

---

16   *Tribunal de grande instance*, Paris, 13 July 1988, 1989 REV. ARB. 97, *see* note 10, *supra*.

17   *See Cour d'appel*, Paris, 11 July 1980, Japan Time v. Kienzle France and the International Chamber of Commerce (unpublished), where the Court of Appeal confirmed the dismissal of a law suit brought against the ICC, contesting its finding of *prima facie* jurisdiction. The court found that the only relief for a party contesting arbitral jurisdiction was recourse against the award, and that allowing a suit against the ICC, based on the Court of Arbitration's finding of *prima facie* jurisdiction, would create unauthorized and disguised judicial review. The court's judgment should be compared with its second decision on the same day in Japan Time v. Kienzle France, which reviewed the award in question, considered the jurisdictional defense (based on the allegation that the ICC should not have accepted jurisdiction since the arbitration was not international, as both parties were French) and dismissed the recourse as not founded. To the same effect is *Tribunal de grande instance* of Paris, 25 June 1980, Organisation de l'Energie Atomique de l'Iran (O.E.A.I.) v. Eurodif S.A., SOFIDIF, *et al.* (unpublished), where respondents contested the Court's decision to send claims involving multiple parties under different contracts to be resolved by a single ICC arbitral tribunal. The court found that the issue as to which parties were bound by diverse arbitration clauses was to be determined by the arbitrators, subject only to the possibility of *ex post facto* control by the court in review or execution proceedings involving an award.

18   *See generally,* Section 28.07, "Courts and Arbitral Jurisdiction."

19   Once the Court has made a positive *prima facie* finding, that article provides that ". . . any decision as to the jurisdiction of the Arbitral Tribunal shall be taken by the Arbitral Tribunal itself."

gument that the principal contract is void or voidable, the arbitrator has the authority to determine his own jurisdiction. Under Article 6(4) of the Rules:

> Unless otherwise agreed, the Arbitral Tribunal shall not cease to have jurisdiction by reason of any claim that the contract is null and void or allegation that it is non-existent provided that the Arbitral Tribunal upholds the validity of the arbitration agreement. The Arbitral Tribunal shall continue to have jurisdiction to determine the respective rights of the parties and to adjudicate upon their claims and pleas even though the contract itself may be non-existent or null and void.

Having agreed to submit their claims to arbitration, the parties are deemed to have given by separate agreement (usually the arbitration clause) power to the arbitrators to rule even upon claims of nullity of the contract in which the arbitration clause is found. Accordingly, when a plea of lack of jurisdiction is raised it is first for the arbitrators to rule on it. Arbitrators are said, by what is sometimes called the *compétence-compétence* rule, to have the power to rule on their own jurisdiction. The effect, subject to *a posteriori* control by national courts, is that the arbitrators rule on jurisdictional questions.[20]

This rule conforms to modern trends and modern treaty practice, as exemplified by Article 21 of the UNCITRAL Rules:

> 1. The arbitral tribunal shall have the power to rule on objections that it has no jurisdiction, including any objections with respect to the existence or validity of the arbitration clause or of the separate arbitration agreement.

> 2. The arbitral tribunal shall have the power to determine the existence or the validity of the contract of which an arbitration clause forms a part. For the purposes of Article 21, an arbitration clause which forms part of a contract and which provides for arbitration under these Rules shall be treated as an agreement independent of the other terms of the contract. A decision by the arbitral tribunal that the contract is null and void shall not entail *ipso jure* the invalidity of the arbitration clause.

> 3. A plea that the arbitral tribunal does not have jurisdiction shall be raised not later than in the statement of defence or, with respect to a counterclaim, in the reply to the counterclaim.

---

20 For a detailed affirmation of this interpretation of the Rules by an English court, *see* Dalmia
·   Dairy Industries Ltd. (India) v. National Bank of Pakistan, [1978] 2 LLOYD'S L. REP. 223 (Court of Appeal, 18 May 1977) where the Court said:

> We think that the Rules, on their true construction as they stand without reference to any particular system of law, do provide, with complete width and generality, for the arbitrators to decide, so as to bind the parties—insofar as any decision of the arbitrator can bind the parties—any question that may be raised as to the arbitrator's jurisdiction when there is a document in writing purporting to constitute an arbitral agreement between the parties under the ICC Rules.

4. In general, the arbitral tribunal should rule on a plea concerning its jurisdiction as a preliminary question. However, the arbitral tribunal may proceed with the arbitration and rule on such a plea in their final award.

This acceptance of the independence of the arbitration clause is also reflected in international treaties dealing with arbitration. Thus, the European (Geneva) Convention of 1961 (*see* Section 37.03, *infra*) provides in Article 5(3):

> Subject to any subsequent judicial control provided for under the *lex fori*, the arbitrator whose jurisdiction is called in question shall be entitled to proceed with the arbitration, to rule on his own jurisdiction and to decide upon the existence or the validity of the arbitration agreement or of the contract of which the agreement forms part.

This trend is further apparent in the 1965 Convention on the Settlement of Investment Disputes Between States and Nationals of Other States, which provides in Article 41:

> (1) The Tribunal shall be the judge of its own competence.

> (2) Any objection by a party to the dispute that that dispute is not within the jurisdiction of the Centre, or for other reasons is not within the competence of the Tribunal, shall be considered by the Tribunal which shall determine whether to deal with it as a preliminary question or to join it to the merits of the dispute.

Even if the parties do not specifically raise any jurisdictional objection, the arbitrators should, for good order's sake and to avoid any needless controversy if the award should later be challenged, articulate the basis of jurisdiction in the award. If jurisdiction is specifically challenged, this will of course be one of the issues which the parties require to be determined in the award. ICC arbitral tribunals have routinely over the last quarter century utilized the powers given to them by the ICC Rules to determine jurisdictional questions.

In ICC Case 1007/1959 between French and German parties, the German company contested the validity of the contract and the arbitration clause based on the failure to obtain required French and German exchange control authorizations.[21] The sole arbitrator in that case found that these shortcomings affected only the execution of the contract—that is, the obligations of performance were suspended—but did not affect the validity of the principal contract nor the arbitration clause.

---

21   Cited *in* P. Sanders, *L'autonomie de la clause compromissoire, in* HOMMAGE À FRÉDÉRIC EISEMANN 39 (ICC Publication No. 321, 1978). For confirmation by French courts that ICC arbitral jurisdiction is not ousted by mere allegations that performance of some of the contractual obligations were contrary to French exchange controls, *see* the decision of the *Cour de cassation*, June 1956, Société Le Gant Nicolet v. SAFIC, 1957 REV. ARB. 14.

In another 1959 award, the sole arbitrator denied a defense of absence of arbitral jurisdiction based on the alleged invalidity of the principal contract. He found that it was:

> without importance that the contract in which the arbitration clause was an integral part was alleged to be void by the defendant.[22]

The often-cited award in ICC Case 1526[23] involved the termination of a concession agreement by an African government. The sole arbitrator held, pursuant to Article 8(4) of the 1975 Rules [Article 6(4) of the 1998 Rules], that he had jurisdiction despite arguments to the contrary by the government, which refused any formal participation in the proceedings. The arbitrator found he had jurisdiction both on the grounds that the government had the capacity to arbitrate and that the dispute was arbitrable. He stated that:

> It is a rule admitted in international arbitration matters that in the absence of a contrary decision of State procedural law, the arbitrator is judge of his own jurisdiction . . . This rule is invalidated neither by French law, law of the headquarters of the International Chamber of Commerce, nor by Swiss law, law of the seat of arbitration, nor by the law of [the African State in question].

> It is also a rule, now generally admitted in international arbitration matters, or in the process of being so admitted, that, according to the expression of the *Cour de cassation* in France, the arbitration agreement, whether it be entered into specially or included in the legal contract to which it applies, apart from exceptional circumstances, has a complete juridical independence, excluding the possibility that it may be affected by the possible invalidity of this contract.

Commenting on the award, Yves Derains, then Secretary General of the Court of Arbitration, expressed regret that the arbitrator had felt compelled to refer to various local procedural laws as support for his finding[24] and did not place more emphasis on the specific power given to the arbitrator by the Rules to determine his own jurisdiction, a power implicitly incorporated by reference into the contract.[25] Since the Rules agreed by the parties give the arbitrator the power to determine his own jurisdiction, why go further? The arbitrator, even in deciding to give full effect to his authority to determine his own jurisdiction, apparently assumed that his jurisdiction was subject to the absence

---

22   ICC Case 1024/1959, cited *in* Sanders, *supra* Note 21, at 39.

23   ICC Case 1526/1968, extracts *in* 1974 JDI 915.

24   *Id.* at 918.

25   The power of the arbitrator to determine his own jurisdiction was set out in Article 13(3) of the 1955 Rules and has been carried forward as Article 8(3) of the 1975 and 1988 Rules and now Article 6(2) of the 1998 Rules. Recent ICC awards rely on the contractual agreement of the parties and the incorporation by reference of the Rules as an independent basis for the arbitrator to determine his own jurisdiction, without the necessity of relying on national law provisions.

of a mandatory national law impediment, despite the fact that it is explicitly provided for in the ICC Rules. In recognizing this potential limitation, the arbitrator demonstrated his concern for the enforceability of his award without having to determine which national law might be applicable to the question. This created no particular difficulty for him, since in fact all the national laws he reviewed supported his conclusion.

That the arbitration clause is deemed severable is a crucial factor when an allegation is made which, if proved, would nullify the principal contract. For example, in an ICC case involving a sales contract in France,[26] the contract would have been null under French law if the price had not been specifically fixed or determinable by objective reference. Despite an allegation of nullity based on the uncertainty of price in the contract, the ICC arbitral tribunal had no difficulty in determining that the arbitration clause was severable and thus unaffected by the alleged nullity. It accordingly affirmed its own jurisdiction, and in fact went on to hold that the sales contract was null.

Arguments that arbitral jurisdiction should be refused on the grounds that the award might not be enforceable at the domicile of the respondent are given no weight in ICC arbitration, and properly so. Thus in a 1976 award concerning a license agreement,[27] Italian defendants argued that their consent to the agreement was vitiated and that in any event the arbitration award would not be enforceable in Italy because under Article 7 of the Italian Code of Civil Procedure an Italian defendant may not be deprived of the right to be heard by his "natural judges," *i.e.*, the Italian courts. The arbitral tribunal rejected both grounds of attack on its jurisdiction, stating that:

> In conformity with . . . the Rules . . . Arbitration of the ICC . . . the claimed nullity or alleged inexistence of the contract does not, unless otherwise so provided, result in the incompetence of the arbitrator.

> If he finds the arbitration clause to be valid, the arbitrator retains his jurisdiction, even in the case of the inexistence or of the nullity of the contract, in order to determine the respective rights of the parties and rule upon their pleadings.

Well-reasoned awards on the issue include ICC Case 7604 and 7610/1995, 1998 JDI 1027, note Dominique Hascher, ICC Case 6437/1990, 8 ICC BULL. 68 (May 1997); ICC Case 4695/1984, XI YEARBOOK 149 (1986); ICC Case 4381/1986, 1986 JDI 1103; and ICC Case 5065/1986, 1987 JDI 1039. The independence of the arbitration clause from any particular national law has also been confirmed by case law in France (in an ICC matter) (see discussion of Dalico decision, Section 31.02(f) and the United States (*see Rhône Méditerranée v. Achille Lauro*, discussed in Section 28.05(a)).

26   ICC Case 1955/1973, cited by Sanders, *supra* Note 21, at 41.

27   ICC Case No. 2476/1976, I ICC AWARDS 289.

After finding that the alleged lack of consent applied only to certain stipulations of the contract but not to the arbitration clause, the arbitrator continued:

> The defendant has, in connection with its challenge to jurisdiction, also pleaded that the award would not be subject to execution in Italy and it reserves the right to invoke, once again, during any possible execution proceedings, the lack of jurisdiction of the Arbitral Tribunal.
>
> In this regard the Arbitral Tribunal states that the question of execution after the award is in no way tied to that of jurisdiction of the Arbitral Tribunal. The two questions are in effect independent, and the jurisdiction of the Tribunal is not conditioned by the fact that the award may not be subject to execution in another country.
>
> Besides, the question of execution of the award does not fall within the powers of the Tribunal which for this reason cannot take it into consideration.[28]

Despite this broad negation of any necessity to look into the possibility of execution, the tribunal referred to the fact that the award would be subject to execution in Switzerland, which was the seat of the arbitration and whose law had been made applicable by the contract. Thus it is safe to say that ICC arbitrators remain concerned about the problem of execution, as they should be (*see* Article 35 of the Rules). But the tribunal was clearly correct in rejecting the argument that the non-enforceability of the award in one state deprives the arbitrator of jurisdiction. Execution of the award may be sought in many other states. Indeed, national legislation may be modified during the arbitration so as to make the award enforceable by the time it is rendered. The jurisdiction of an ICC tribunal depends solely on the ICC Rules, the contract between the parties, and the laws applicable thereto.

In other circumstances, ICC arbitrators have determined that there was no arbitral jurisdiction upon considering evidence and arguments on the issue after the Court of Arbitration had found a *prima facie* agreement to arbitrate. The Court's decision has no influence on the jurisdictional decision of the arbitral tribunal, which is to be taken *de novo*. As one award put it:[29]

> Article 8(3) of the ICC Rules [Article 6(4) of the 1998 Rules] cannot be more clear on the subject: the decision of the Court in no way prejudices the admissibility or the merits of pleas going to the existence or validity of the arbitration agreement. It has for sole and unique effect to transfer to the Arbitral Tribunal the mission of deciding on its own jurisdiction in regard to Defendant No. 2, subject only to the decision of the authority of judicial recourse [in this case the Swiss Cantonal Court of Vaud] which can freely review this jurisdiction . . .

---

28   *Id.* at 290 (author's translation).

29   ICC Case No. 4504/1985/1986, II ICC AWARDS 279 (authors' translation from the French).

In another rather complicated case decided in 1979,[30] an arbitral tribunal found that an ICC arbitration clause had been rescinded by the parties through a subsequent *ad hoc* agreement to arbitrate, and the arbitral proceedings were terminated. The subsequent failure of the alternative procedure could not be used as grounds for reviving the initial ICC arbitration agreement on the basis of which the Court had, in the first place, ordered the arbitration to proceed.

The system set up by the ICC Rules seems reasonable and practical. A jurisdictional objection does not require a separate action before a State court, nor should it delay the formation of the arbitral tribunal. In appropriate cases, the arbitral tribunal may provide for a procedure to have the jurisdictional issue decided preliminarily in an interim award. (*See* Section 19.03 *infra*). Allowing arbitrators to determine their own jurisdiction and providing the initial *prima facie* review by the ICC Court serves to prevent premature intervention by national courts in the arbitral process. The word "premature" here is used intentionally; at the stage of execution, courts under all systems of law and under all international treaties have the authority to verify that the arbitrators had jurisdiction to render the award as a prerequisite to enforcement.

11.04 Recognition by national courts of arbitrator's power to determine his own jurisdiction

Whether national courts will seek to halt an arbitration during the course of the proceedings depends mainly on the laws of the country of the seat of arbitration. The fundamental principles underlying the ICC Rules are generally embraced in most countries under modern arbitration statutes or recent case law involving international commerce (*see generally* Section 5.04, *supra*). Such legal systems have acknowledged that the arbitral tribunal may determine its own jurisdiction.[31]

In Switzerland (*see* Chapter 32, *infra*), the 1987 arbitration law (Chapter 12 of the Swiss Private International Law Act)[32] provides:

Article 186:

The arbitral tribunal shall decide on its own jurisdiction.

Any objection must be raised prior to any defense on the merits.

The arbitral tribunal shall, as a rule, decide on its jurisdiction by a preliminary award.

---

30 ICC Case 3383/1979, extracts *in* 1980 JDI 979; extracts in English *in* VII YEARBOOK 119 (1982), commented on *in* section 4.03 *supra*, Note 2.

31 Sanders, *supra* Note 21.

32 Law of 18 December 1987, in effect as of 1 January 1989. The Swiss Intercantonal Concordat, which remains in effect and is applicable where the parties have expressly so agreed, has a similar provision (Article 8) regarding the power of an arbitrator to determine his own jurisdiction.

As for France, the Code of Civil Procedure provides similar legislation even for domestic arbitrations as of 1980:

> *Article 1458:*
>
> Whenever a dispute submitted to an arbitral tribunal by virtue of an arbitration agreement is brought before a court of the State, such court shall decline jurisdiction.
>
> If the arbitral tribunal has not yet been seized of the matter, the court should also decline jurisdiction unless the arbitration agreement is manifestly null.
>
> In neither case may the court determine its lack of jurisdiction on its own motion.
>
> *Article 1466:*
>
> If one of the parties contests, before the arbitrator, the latter's jurisdiction, whether in principle or scope, it is for the arbitrator to decide on the validity or scope of his mission.

For international arbitration in France (or taking place elsewhere but subject to French procedural law), the possibility of French courts' intervention is even more limited under Article 1494, which provides:

> The arbitration agreement may, directly or by reference to a set of arbitration rules, define the procedure to be followed in the arbitral proceedings. It may also subject it to a given procedural law.
>
> If the agreement is silent, the arbitrator, either directly or by reference to a law or a set of arbitration rules, shall establish such rules of procedure as may be necessary.

Thus specific precedence over French procedural rules is given to the rules to which the parties have agreed, whether by specific contractual stipulations or by incorporation of the rules of an arbitral institution. When viewed together with Article 6 of the Rules, Article 1494 seems to leave no room for intervention by French courts in the arbitral process except on review or execution of an award.

The English Arbitration Act 1996 specifically provides that an arbitral tribunal has jurisdiction to rule on its own jurisdiction (Article 30) and that prior to an arbitral tribunal's decision on this issue a party to arbitral proceedings may seek determination by the court only with the agreement of all parties or of the arbitral tribunal (Article 32).

An award may subsequently be challenged before the court on the ground of lack of substantive jurisdiction by the arbitral tribunal (Article 67). In addition, a party who takes no part in the arbitral proceedings may seek declarations or injunction from the court on the ground that there was no valid arbitration agreement (Article 72).

Embracing this principle as well, the UNCITRAL Model Law on International Commercial Arbitration (*see* Section 28.06), proposed for adoption by states seeking a modern procedural framework for international arbitration, also provides (in Article 16) for the initial determination by the arbitrator of his own jurisdiction.

The clear trend has thus been to favor the arbitrator's power to determine the existence and scope of his own jurisdiction.[33] Nevertheless, some courts, particularly in common law jurisdictions, may reserve the right of intervention where specific claim is made to the effect of nullity or non-existence of the agreement to arbitrate itself (as opposed to the nullity or rescission of the principal contract) particularly in the case of fraud. This point has been made in several cases (which, it should be noted, nevertheless upheld arbitral jurisdiction in the premises).

Thus, in *Flood and Concklin Manufacturing v. Prima Paint*,[34] the U.S. Supreme Court stated:

> [E]xcept where the parties otherwise intend, arbitration clauses as a matter of federal law are "separable" from the contracts in which they are imbedded, and where no claim is made that fraud was directed to the arbitration clause itself, a broad arbitration clause will be held to encompass arbitration of the claim that the contract itself was *induced by fraud*. (Emphasis added.)

Similarly, in its leading decision in *Heyman v. Darwins Ltd*,[35] the English House of Lords stated:

> If the dispute is whether the contract which contains the clause has even been entered into at all, that issue cannot go to arbitration under the clause, for the party who denies that he has ever entered into the contract is thereby denying that he has ever joined in the submission.

There thus seems to be a basis under some laws for national courts to intervene in arbitration proceedings even before an award is rendered (whether it be a final award or an interim award on the jurisdictional claim).[36]

---

33 This is based on the power inherent to the arbitral process. Sections 5.04, *supra* 28.07, *infra*. The most satisfying philosophical rationalisation of *compétence/compétence*—the arbitrator's power to determine his own jurisdiction—is found in P. Mayer, *L'Autonomie de l'arbitre international dans l'appréciation de sa propre compétence*, 217 Recueil des cours 323 (1989); see also W.Michael Reisman, W.Laurence Craig, William W. Park, Jan Paulsson, International Commercial Arbitration: Cases Materials and Notes on the Resolution of International Business Disputes, (Foundation Press, 1997) 525-40, 645-80. In the case of ICC arbitration, this power is strongly reinforced by a specific institutional rule and is broader than, and may be distinguished from, arbitral powers flowing from the independence of the arbitration clause.

34 388 U.S. 395 (1967).

35 1942 A.C. 356; [1942] 1 All E.R. 337.

36 English law remains interventionist on questions of jurisdiction and considers that the court should retain the right, at the request of a party which does not participate in arbitral proceed-

In the United States, a court may in advance of arbitration, upon motion of any party, rule on issues of the existence, validity and scope of the arbitration agreement, as well as the objective arbitrability of claims, as provided in Articles 3 and 4 of the Federal Arbitration Act. *Mitsubishi Motors Corp. v. Soler Chrysler-Plymouth Inc.*, 473 U.S. 213 (1985). Generally speaking, the American approach, where an arbitration agreement exists, has been to allow an arbitration to go forward despite arguments as to the agreement's scope, or its survival of intervening events (e.g., bankruptcy or assignment) so as to let the tribunal originally determine these issues but to step in where the clause is alleged to be void *ab initio* because, for instance, of the lack of authority to bind a party to arbitrate.[37] In ICC cases the fact that the Rules, which the parties have agreed, specifically provides that the arbitrator will decide upon his own jurisdiction favorably influences a court not to intervene to determine most jurisdictional issues until after an award has been rendered.[38] Article 6(4) of the ICC Rules makes it absolutely clear that the arbitrators have a duty to proceed and to determine their own jurisdiction even though parallel action in a State court may have been commenced to nullify the arbitral proceedings. Any other rule would encourage parties to deploy dilatory judicial procedures, often in their own national courts, and to disregard their agreement to arbitrate.

---

ings, to determine, *prior to arbitration*, such issues as authority of the corporate officer or employee to bind his principal to arbitrate, the scope and extent of the clause, and the identity of parties bound by the clause. Arbitration Act 1996, Section 72.

37   *See e.g.*, Apollo Computer v. Berg, 886, F.2d 469 (1st Cir. 1989) (court refused to enjoin ICC arbitration based on allegations that the arbitration agreement had not been validly assigned by trustee in bankruptcy and that any assignment was unenforceable due to non-assignment clause in contract; these issues were for ICC arbitrators.); Three Valleys Municipal Water District v. E.P. Hutton, 925 F.2d 1136 (9th Cir. 1991) (court must determine whether person signing arbitration agreement had authority to do so.). Paine Webber v. Elahi, 87 F.3d 589 (1st Cir. 1996). *See generally*, Section 34.02.

38   In *Apollo*, supra, n. 37, the court stated: "By contracting to have all disputes resolved according to the Rules of the ICC . . . Apollo agreed to be bound by Articles 8.3 and 8.4 [Articles 6.2 and 6.4 of the 1998 Rules]. These provisions clearly and unmistakably allow the arbitrator to determine her own jurisdiction when, as here, there exists a *prima facie* agreement to arbitrate whose continued existence and validity is being questioned." In Andersen Consulting v. Andersen Worldwide Société Coopérative and Arthur Andersen LLP, 1998 WL 122590 (SDNY), claimant's demand for an injunction to compel respondents to arbitrate certain disputed issues in a pending ICC arbitration was denied: "Under the circumstances of this case, the Court declines to order that [respondent] arbitrate all issues relating to the resolution before the ICC. . . the [respondent] correctly argues that it should not be compelled by this Court to arbitrate the validity of the resolution in the pending ICC arbitration because, while it is prepared to litigate that issue in an ICC arbitration, the jurisdictional issue of whether the ICC arbitration is the proper forum is itself subject to resolution before the ICC. The ICC should decide whether these issues are properly litigated in the pending ICC arbitration, in another ICC arbitration, or in another forum under the Swiss Intercantonal Convention." For a discussion of the limits of provisions in the arbitration agreement and arbitration rules to confer jurisdiction on the arbitrator to determine his own jurisdiction, see Sections 28.07 and 34.02. However, even where a state court intervenes to make its own jurisdictional findings prior to the issue having been addressed by the arbitral tribunal the arbitrators must proceed to make their own independent findings.

Because of this duty of the international arbitrator to proceed with the arbitration irrespective of the pendency of a judicial proceeding or injunctions contesting his jurisdiction, only a direct order emanating from a competent court at the seat of the arbitration itself should ordinarily be allowed to affect arbitral proceedings. Thus the arbitrator is bound to proceed with his mission based on the prior agreement of the parties—unless it is clear that such judicial actions have executory force over the arbitral tribunal itself.[39]

The system of ICC arbitration is fundamentally designed to discourage recourse to the courts on jurisdictional issues prior to the award. The parties' rights are not ultimately prejudiced by proceeding with the arbitration. Even after an award is rendered, it is subject to an action to have it set aside by the courts of the place of arbitration if it lacks a jurisdictional foundation. And in any enforcement forum, an arbitrator's decision exceeding his jurisdiction may be resisted.

This system is implemented by Articles 6(2) and 6(4) of the Rules which grant authority to the arbitral tribunal to determine jurisdictional issues. Article 6(4) provides that "the Arbitral Tribunal shall not cease to have jurisdiction by reason of any claim that the contract is null and void or allegation that it is non-existent. . ." In light of the fact that the parties themselves have accepted the ICC Rules (assuming of course that the arbitrator agrees that such is the case), these provisions should effectively reduce the scope for court action on the jurisdictional issue prior to the arbitral award.

11.05 Jurisdiction over parties who have not signed the arbitration agreement

No one contests that arbitration is to be used only where the parties have agreed to arbitrate. There are, however, many ways in which consent may be manifested.[40]

A fundamental jurisdictional issue arises when it is contested that the party named in the arbitral proceeding is bound by, or may benefit from, an admittedly existing arbitration agreement. The issue may be raised first before the Court of Arbitration and subsequently before the arbitral tribunal. The possibility of judicial review may not be excluded.

---

39   See, *e.g.*, ICC Case 6709/1991, III ICC AWARDS 435 (the arbitral tribunal rejected Respondent's request for a stay of the arbitral proceedings until French courts would render a judgement concerning the alleged nullity of the agreement); ICC case 4862/1986, II ICC AWARDS 308 (the arbitral tribunal refused to stay arbitration with seat in Paris despite injunction from the national courts of Yemen (Sanaa)); in a recent case, an English court was able effectively to stay the arbitration, although the seat of the arbitration was Geneva, by extending the effect of an anti-suit injunction not only to the parties but also to two of the arbitrators, English Q.C.'s domiciled in England and subject to such imperative jurisdiction.

40   For a consideration of this issue in the context of drafting arbitration agreements and clauses, *see* Section 5.09.

An example of how the issue may be raised is found in ICC Case 4402/1983 involving a dispute under an oil field operating agreement in which a French company had agreed to act as operator. When disputes arose under the agreement the claimant companies sought to join in the arbitration not only the French operating company but also its French parent company which was not a party to the agreement. In support of ICC jurisdiction it was argued, in pleadings addressed to the Court of Arbitration, that the parent company had previously signed a "Protocole d'Accord No.1" pursuant to which it had entered into commitments concerning operations and had agreed on the key clauses to be contained in the Operating Agreement, including ICC arbitration. The parent company had reserved the option to decide whether it would intervene in the Operating Agreement directly or via a subsidiary. The claimants alleged that the French parent company was the real party in interest and that the Operating Agreement, and its signature by a subsidiary company, was merely the execution of a pre-existing obligation, including the obligation to arbitrate.

The French parent company pointed out that the Protocole d'Accord No.1 was an entirely separate agreement, containing a specific forum selection clause in favor of the ordinary courts of law in Luxembourg, and that its signature of that agreement did not make it a party to the Operating Agreement.

The Court of Arbitration found, however, *prima facie* evidence of an agreement to arbitrate binding not only the French operating company, but also the French parent company, and ordered the arbitration to proceed against both parties in accordance with Article 8(3) of the Rules [Article 6(2) of the 1998 Rules].[41]

To determine the jurisdictional issue, the arbitral tribunal was required to investigate in detail the factual relationships between the parties, their conduct, and the various contractual documents signed by them, as well as the provisions of applicable law. The relevant Swiss Intercantonal Concordat required that an arbitration agreement must be in writing, thus inhibiting any argument that the parent company's consent to arbitration could be implied. In the circumstances, the tribunal found that the officer of the subsidiary who signed the Operating Agreement could not be found to have been acting for and on behalf of the parent company. Nor, in view of the separate legal identity of the related companies, could it be found that the subsidiary was acting as an agent of the group. Claimant had the obligation to prove that the parent company was, in fact, a party to the Operating Agreement, and had failed to carry this burden. The arbitral tribunal rendered a partial award denying arbi-

---

41   VIII YEARBOOK 204 (1983). In this case, under the procedure described in Section 2.03, the decision was taken by the President of the Court of Arbitration exercising the power granted to him

tral jurisdiction over the French parent company,[42] and rejected the argument that the conduct of the parties proved an implicit agreement to arbitrate.

The lengthy briefing of factual and legal issues, and the arbitrators' handing down of a fully reasoned partial award, illustrates the distinction between a finding on arbitral jurisdiction by an arbitral tribunal, and the preliminary administrative decision by the Court of Arbitration of *prima facie* jurisdiction. It is obvious that where the Court of Arbitration is presented with a plausible theory of arbitral jurisdiction over a party which has not signed the arbitration agreement it will favor making a finding of *prima facie* jurisdiction and will leave disputed questions for the arbitral tribunal. It will be for the arbitral tribunal to determine what the parties intended[43] and to rule on all disputed issues of law and fact.

In recent years, ICC arbitral tribunals have been called upon to decide such varied jurisdictional questions as:

(i) whether representatives of a company which initiated an arbitration agreement on behalf of a company to be formed bound the existing company to arbitrate;[44]

(ii) whether a state agency or entity bound the state itself to arbitral jurisdiction;[45]

(iii) whether a member of a group of corporations could appear as a claimant with respect to injury caused to it as seller under the terms of a distribution agreement entered into by another member of its group and containing an arbitration clause;[46]

---

42 IX YEARBOOK 138 (1984). The tribunal, chaired by the Swiss law professor Frank Vischer, cited as authority the *Tribunal fédéral Suisse* decision in Vendome Holding and Cartier v. Horowitz, 10 October 1979, 1981 JOURNAL DES TRIBUNAUX 61—127, holding that only the corporation whose agent and officer had signed the arbitration clause was a proper defendant and that in the circumstances eight other corporations, members of the Cartier group, could not be joined in the arbitration.

43 *See* Sections 5.01—5.10, *supra.*

44 ICC Case 5065/1986, 1987 JDI 1039.

45 *See, e.g.*, ICC Case 1803/1972, V YEARBOOK 177 (1980); ICC Case 3493/1983, Southern Pacific Properties v. EGOTH and the Arab Republic of Egypt, 22 ILM 752 (1983), and subsequent court proceedings, 1986 REV. ARB. 75.

46 ICC Case 4131, interim award of 23 September 1982, Dow Chemical v. Isover-Saint Gobain, 1984 REV. ARB. 137 (full text), IX YEARBOOK 131 (1984) (*supra* Section 5.09). This important award rendered in France by a distinguished tribunal (Professor Pieter Sanders, President, Professors Berthold Goldman and Michel Vasseur) may represent a high water mark in the extension of arbitral jurisdiction to a member of a group of corporations which had not itself signed an arbitration clause. Particularly important was the conduct of the parties to the agreement and the fact that the issue was the intervention of a non-signatory as claimant and not compulsion of a non-signatory respondent.

(iv) whether a member of a group of companies having played a role in the negotiation of the contract containing an arbitration agreement, and signed by a member of its group, could be joined to the arbitration procedings as respondent;[47]

(v) whether a company intended to be the beneficiary of an agreement containing an arbitration clause, but not a signatory thereof, could itself claim the benefit of arbitration;

(vi) whether a corporation was bound by an ICC arbitration clause entered into by an officer and employee having general powers of representation when it was alleged that certain signature formalities required under the law of incorporation had not been respected;

(vii) whether a state was bound by the acts of its Minister when it was alleged that certain formalities required under the law of that state were not complied with;

(viii) whether a sub-contractor which had signed an arbitration clause with the main contractor was also bound to arbitrate in a comprehensive proceeding with the owner of the works due to incorporation by reference of the arbitration clause between the contractor and the owner; and

(ix) whether states which were members of a joint venture consortium, in the nature of a partnership, were individually bound to arbitrate pursuant · to the terms of an arbitration agreement entered into by the consortium entity with a third party contractor.[48]

The solution to such diverse issues may require that the arbitrators resolve complex questions of fact and law. Recognized principles of agency and contract under applicable systems of law supply the basis by which a non-signa-

---

47   ICC Case 4504, interim award of 1985, 1986 JDI 1118. Having brought a claim for breach of an obligation to purchase quantities of oil condensate, the seller sought to add as respondent a corporation affiliated with the buyer which was not a formal party to the purchase agreement and had not signed the arbitration clause. Despite some involvement by the second corporation in the transaction, the tribunal found that there was no cause to pierce the corporate veil, nor could it be found that the employee who signed the clause on behalf of the first respondent was acting at the same time for the second respondent.

48   ICC Case 3879, interim award of 5 March 1984, Westland Helicopters, Ltd. (U.K.) v. A.O.I. *et al.*, 23 ILM 1071 (1984), XI YEARBOOK 127 (1986). An ICC tribunal composed of Dr. Eugene Bucher, President, and Messrs. Pierre Bellet and Nils Mangaard, sitting in Geneva, found that four state parties who were members of a public international law consortium, the A.O.I., were proper parties to an arbitration brought pursuant to an arbitration agreement into by the A.O.I. In review proceedings, the Swiss courts annulled the finding of arbitral jurisdiction as to the Arab Republic of Egypt, the only State party to file a timely action for judicial review, on the grounds that it had not signed the arbitration clause, and therefore was not bound by it. *Tribunal fédéral Suisse*, 19 July 1988, 1988 SWISS BULL. 220.

tory[49] may in some cases be obligated under, or may claim the benefit of, an arbitration clause. Yet those cases are few and the burden of the party claiming under such principles is great, particularly where mandatory procedural requirements in force at the place of arbitration may impose additional formal conditions. Much time and money may be spent arguing these issues, a disadvantage which is compounded by the knowledge that jurisdictional issues decided by the arbitrators are subject to review by national courts, whether in review proceedings at the place of arbitration or in proceedings brought elsewhere to secure execution of the award.

Occasionally, the circumstances which lead to jurisdictional claims on behalf of or against a non-signatory party could not have been foreseen at the time of contracting. Principles of construction and implication may be invoked to effect what must have been the true intent of the original parties to the arbitration agreement and to parties related to them. More frequently, the issue of the rights or liabilities of non-signatory parties arises because of a failure of contract drafters to take the most rudimentary precautions. In such circumstances, the chances are that the arbitral tribunal will find it impossible to make for the parties a contract which they failed to achieve by themselves.

It is difficult to generalize as to the circumstances in which non-signatories will be found to be subject to the terms of an agreement calling for ICC arbitration. A party wishing to assert such jurisdiction should be aware of the different hurdles it may be required to overcome: first the *prima facie* finding of the Court, then the substantive finding of the arbitral tribunal and perhaps finally the involvement of national courts in litigation either to compel arbitration or to enforce an award. The variation in approaches of different national courts is considerable, but the consequence of such variability should not be over-emphasized: a claimant is likely to seek to join a non-signatory party as respondent where justified without excessive concern about enforcement in that party's home court jurisdiction. For instance, where the issue is the liability of a state for the obligations incurred by a public corporation or authority, it is accepted that enforcement against the sovereign in its own courts will be difficult. The issue of determining liability is of great importance in and of itself, however, and has value irrespective of enforceability by the courts of the state in question. Enforcement may, moreover, be achieved elsewhere.

---

49   We use the term "non-signatory" as shorthand to indicate a third party who has not formally entered into the arbitration agreement in the same manner as the principal obligor. See discussion Section 34.02(d). There is nothing in the ICC Rules which requires the principal obligor's agreement to arbitrate to be signed, or even in writing, although applicable rules of law may so require.

A number of points in connection with the exercise of arbitral jurisdiction over non-signatories are worthy of comment (see also Section 5.09):

(i) Exemption from arbitral jurisdiction does not mean exemption from liability. Claimants often seek to establish arbitral jurisdiction over a wealthy parent company, or a solvent affiliate, on some theory of vicarious liability motivated by the desire to be in a position to execute an award against someone who can pay. Such theories require determinations of fact and law. It may well be that a national court in subsequent litigation would find a sister or parent corporation liable if the subsidiary did not execute an award. But these issues will not be for the arbitral tribunal unless it can be proved that the parent or sister corporation agreed (whether directly or by an agent) to be bound by the arbitration agreement itself, and hence to the determination of these issues by arbitrators.

(ii) In the absence of clear proof of contrary intent, it should be presumed that assignees of contract rights will enjoy the benefits and burdens of the arbitration clause[50] in the assigned contract. While the issue arises in a variety of factual contexts and under differing provisions of national law, leading sometimes to conflicting views, the survival of the undertaking to arbitrate after assignment has a strong policy background and is consistent with the needs of modern commerce. Numerous precedents involving ICC arbitration have maintained arbitral jurisdiction in a variety of circumstances following assignment.[51]

(iii) Claiming a right to arbitrate as a third party beneficiary or intended beneficiary of contract rights does not give rise to an equally favorable presumption of arbitral jurisdiction. Every case will depend on the particular contract, the circumstances, and evidence of the intention of the parties.[52]

---

50   The naming of the assignee of an agreement as defendant in an arbitration, even when such assignment has been accepted and acknowledged by the claimant (and other party to the contract), does not necessarily preclude the naming of the original signatory to the contract as an additional Respondent in the arbitration. J. Cremades, *Problems that Arise from Changes Affecting one of the Signatories to the Arbitration Clause*, 7 ICC BULL. 29 (December 1996). *See generally*, Daniel Girsberger and Christian Hausmaninger, *Assignment of Rights and Agreement to Arbitrate*, 8 ARB. INT. 123 (1992).

51   *See, e.g.*, ICC Case 6259/1990, interim award of 20 September 1990, Helge Berg and Lars Arvid Skoog v. Apollo Computer, Inc., (unpublished) (the facts of the case are stated in Apollo Computer, Inc. v. Berg, 886 F. 2d 469 (1st Cir. 1989)).

52   In the landmark *Sofidif* case, (considered *infra* Section 11.06 on the issue of consolidation), an ICC tribunal was not persuaded that Eurodif, a seller of uranium enrichment services, could be considered as a third party beneficiary to be a proper party to an arbitration brought by its purchaser Sofidif against Sofidif's underlying Iranian shareholder which had failed to honor its obligation to take up its share of the long term enrichment services contracted which Sofidif had contracted for in its behalf. ICC Case 3683/1982, interim award of 25 April 1985, reported in *Cour d'appel*, Paris, 19 December 1986, 1987 REV. ARB. 359 (setting aside the award on unrelated grounds); *Cour de cassation*, 8 March 1988, 1989 REV. ARB. 481 (annulling the Paris *Cour d'appel* decision); *Cour d'appel*, Versailles, 7 March 1990, 1991 REV. ARB. 326. While the arbitral tribunal found that Eurodif could not be made a party to the arbitration as an alleged third party

(iv) Arbitral jurisdiction over non-signatory parties is more easily established when they act as claimants than when they are sought to be joined as respondents. The issue may arise in a variety of contexts but is most easily illustrated in the example of groups of companies. In the *Dow Chemical* case,[53] an ICC tribunal found that arbitral jurisdiction could be claimed by Dow's American parent and French subsidiary who had performed the disputed contract even though the arbitration clause had been signed only by Dow's Swiss subsidiary. The respondent, which accepted performance by the non-signatory parties, could show no prejudice if the related companies were accepted as claimants. The argument on which respondent relied—that the party which signed the arbitration clause incurred no loss and the companies which had not signed the agreement to arbitrate should not claim its benefit—lacked equity.

(v) The addition as respondents of non-signatory parties, parent corporations, or members of a group of companies, is justified only where there are special circumstances (including participation in the performance of the contract) from which a contractual intention to include them within the scope of the arbitration clause can be implied.[54] The "alter ego" approach, frequently relied on by United States courts as the basis for holding a parent

---

beneficiary of arbitration agreements binding Sofidif it also found that Sofidif could claim against the Iranian party damages which that party would have caused Eurodif and for which Sofidif would have been responsible contractually. The Versailles decision annulled the award on the ground of impermissible consolidation by the arbitral tribunal of claims under separate contracts involving different parties. In dealing with the scope of arbitral jurisdiction over Sofidif's claims, the Versailles Court stated that Sofidif could claim the benefit of stipulations allegedly made for it prior to its existence only in the event of express provisions in the agreement.

53 ICC Case 4131/1984, interim award of 23 September 1982, 1984 REV. ARB. 137, IX YEARBOOK 131 (1984). *See* full discussion *supra*, Section 5.09.

54 ICC Cases 7604 and 7610/1995, 1998 JDI 1027 (arbitrators found jurisdictional issues to be determined under French law principles which they found governed the arbitral procedure; arbitrators applied the following test to extend the arbitration clause to non-signatory parties: i) participation in the negotiation, execution, and performance of the contract; ii) intention of the parties; iii) willingness of third parties to join the arbitration demonstrated by conduct). ICC Case 8385/1995, 1996 JDI 1061, note Y. Derains (arbitral tribunal, applying *lex mercatoria* principles, pierced corporate veil and extended arbitration clause to parent, holding that the arbitral tribunal must look at the circumstances, the degree of control by the parent or principal shareholder over its subsidiary's activities, the financial situation of the subsidiary, the termination of activities by the subsidiary company, and the influence by the parent on the subsidiary's proper conduct towards third parties.) *See also* ICC Case 7155/1993, 1996 JDI 1037; ICC Case 6519/1991, III ICC AWARDS 420, note Y.D.; ICC Case 6752, III ICC AWARDS 195 (the fact that a parent company and its subsidiary share the same registered office and the same managers does not suffice to extend the contract between the subsidiary and a third party to the parent company). Extracts of other ICC awards dealing with groups of companies are found at 2 ICC BULL. 20 (November 1991). For national court cases dealing with arbitrators' treatment of jurisdiction over members of a group of companies, *see, e.g.,* Carte Blanche (Singapore) Ltd. v. Diners Club Int'l Inc., 2. F. 3d. 24 (2d Cir. 1993); Builders Federal Hong Kong Ltd. v. Turner Construction, 655 F. Supp. 1400 (S.D.N.Y. 1987); Société Nationale v. Shaheen Natural Resources, 585 F. Supp. 57 (S.D.N.Y 1985).

liable for the obligations of its subsidiary (or in some rare cases, an individual for the obligations of a company) has sometimes been used as a basis for positive findings of arbitral jurisdiction by ICC tribunals and by court cases compelling ICC arbitration.[55] Similarly, a non-signatory party may become responsible for a related company's obligations, including its obligation to arbitrate, when the non-signatory's conduct has deceived the opposing party as to the identity and status of the company related to the non-signatory with which the contract containing an arbitration clause was signed.[56]

(vi) A non-signatory parent or related corporation, named as respondent in a national court case concerning the activities of its subsidiary, may sometimes be able to establish the primary jurisdiction resulting from an arbitration clause in a contract between its subsidiary and the claimant party. If successful, the parent would obtain a stay of the court proceeding to have the issues first determined in the arbitration.[57]

(vii) Where a state has not specifically agreed to arbitration, its approval of the agreement of a state entity with a foreign party, and the arbitration

---

55   For cases dealing with the issue (although in the circumstances the alter ego test necessary for lifting the corporate veil was not fulfilled) *see* Wren Distributors, Inc. and Innovative Marketing Concepts, Inc. v. Phone-Mate, Inc., 600 F. Supp. 1576, 1579 (S.D.N.Y. 1985); Roger Jakubowski v. Nora Beverages, Inc. (unpublished) Supreme Court of the State of New York, 21 November 1995, (the New York trial court stayed arbitration against the president of the company, which was a respondent in ICC arbitral proceedings, on the grounds that the president was not the alter ego of the company).

56   ICC case No. 5730, 24 August 1988, Orri v. Société de Lubrifiante Elf Aquitaine, 1992 Rev. Arb. 125 (individual who orchestrated signature of agreement by related company, after having deceived opposing party as to the nature of a group of companies and its composants held liable by ICC arbitrators for debt of company and subject to arbitration clause), setting aside refused, *Cour d'appel*, Paris, 11 January 1991, 1992 Rev. Arb. 95, setting aside confirmed *Cour de cassation civile*, 11 June 1991, 1992 Rev. Arb. 73 (arbitral jurisdiction justified because of fraud of Mr. Orri in dissimulating the real party in interest and orchestrating the signature of the contract and arbitration clause by related company).

57   *See, e.g.,* J.J. Ryan & Sons, Inc. v. Rhone Poulenc Textile S.A. 863 F. 2d 315, 319 (4th Cir. 1988) (ICC arbitration) ("when the charges against a parent company and its subsidiary are based on the same facts and are inherently inseparable, a court may refer claims against the parent to arbitration even though the parent is not formally a party to the arbitration agreement."); Sonatrach v. General Tire & Rubber Co., 430 F. Supp. 1332 (S.D.N.Y 1977) (parent company obtained stay, pending outcome of ICC arbitration against subsidiary, of judicial proceedings brought on grounds of fraudulent inducement to agreement with subsidiary company and its arbitration clause and other tortious conduct); Dale Metals Corp. v. Kiwa Chem. Indus. Co., 442 F. Supp. 78 (S.D.N.Y. 1977) (discussed in Section 5.09) (in somewhat similar circumstances the stay of litigation was conditioned on the acceptance by the defendant corporation to be joined to the pending arbitration and to accept the joinder therein of other related non-signatory corporations); Humetrix, Inc. v. Gemplus SCA, U.S. District Court, California, 11 November 1997 (unpublished) (non-signatory U.S. company brought suit in Federal court litigation in United States against French parent company and controlling individual despite existence of ICC arbitration clause in agency agreement with French company's U.S. subsidiary; French parent may be able to enforce an ICC arbitration agreement entered into by its subsidiary so as to obtain stay of litigation brought against it, but only where claims made against it relate to or arise out of the contract containing the arbitration clause, which was not the case here).

agreement contained therein, does not necessarily subject it to arbitral jurisdiction even if its approval is manifested by signature of the agreement entered into by the state entity.[58] Where the state has not signed the arbitration agreement at all, its consent to arbitration by conduct or behavior is not as easily implied as in the case of corporations in relation to the obligations of their subsidiaries.[59]

11.06   Intervention, joinder and consolidation

The preceding section considered the circumstances in which a party which had not signed the arbitration agreement—an ostensible third party—could nevertheless be considered a party to that agreement and hence to the arbitration based on principles of representation, agency, corporate identity and the like. In this section in issue is whether a person who admittedly is not a party to the original arbitration agreement may nonetheless participate in the arbitration proceedings brought under it by way of joinder of claims brought under another contract between the same parties and subject to arbitration, consolidation of pending arbitral proceedings between the same parties or intervention based on arbitration of the same issues under a related contract with one of the parties.

i) Addition of third parties to the proceedings

Absent agreement of all the parties to the arbitration agreement and of the party to be added to the proceedings (which in effect constitutes a modification of the arbitration agreement) there is no authority under the Rules to permit the intervention of a third party either at its request or at the request of one of the parties to the arbitration.[60] The adding to the arbitration of

---

58   While each case will depend on its facts, and the contractual intent that can be deduced from them, this seems to be the general rule derived from the national court proceedings following the *SPP* arbitration where an ICC tribunal had found that the signature by the Minister of Tourism, with the words "agreed approved and ratified" of a contract entered into by the government organization for tourism and hotels had the effect of making the Egyptian State a party to the agreement. The French courts found that such a signature merely manifested the government's exercise of its control function with no intent to become a party to the agreement. *Cour d'appel*, Paris, 12 July 1984, Southern Pacific Properties Ltd. v. Arab Republic of Egypt, 23 I.L. M. 1048 (1984) (English translation), decision upheld, *Cour de cassation*, 6 January 1987, 26 I.L.M. 1004 (English translation).

59   There is no doubt that the State, like a parent company, can become subject to arbitral jurisdiction by its conduct and the actions and representations of its agents and servants. However, in view of the general principle of sovereign immunity from jurisdiction its waiver of such immunity and acceptance of arbitral jurisdiction, where not specifically expressed, will not be easily implied. *See, e.g.*, S. Jarvin, *Participation à l'arbitrage C.C.I. des Etats et entreprises publiques*, 1995 REV. ARB. 585; P. Cahier, *The Strengths and Weaknesses of International Arbitration Involving a State as a Party*, *in* Julian Lew, ed. CONTEMPORARY PROBLEMS IN INTERNATIONAL ARBITRATION (Martinus, Nijhoff 1987) p. 241.

60   In this respect the Rules are narrower than the LCIA Rules which do not require consent of all the parties as a condition for joinder and which provide in Article 13.1 under the heading "Additional Powers of the Tribunal": "Unless the parties at any time agree otherwise, and subject to

non-signatories as claimants or respondents and the determination of juris-diction by first the Court, on a *prima facie* basis, and then by the arbitral tri-bunal, is a different question: there it is alleged that the party to be added was in fact a party to the arbitration agreement, although not mentioned therein, whether on the ground of representation, performance, corporate status or otherwise. Where one of the grounds does not exist the third party may not be joined to the arbitral proceedings whether or not its presence would be useful or even essential to resolving the underlying dispute or the legal relationship which is the subject of arbitration.

A typical example is found in construction industry practice. Frequently the owner agrees to ICC arbitration with its main contractor who may in turn agree to ICC arbitration with its sub-contractor. The main contractor facing an arbitration dispute with the owner may well wish to have its sub-contractor joined into the proceeding (or the sub-contractor may have an interest to in-tervene). The owner, however, never having agreed to arbitrate with the sub-contractor, may oppose such joinder or intervention. The Court can only accept this position and has no power to make a different contract for the par-ties and order joinder.[61]

ii) De facto consolidation of claims arising under multiple contracts between the same parties

Where successive contracts are made between the same parties concerning the same legal relationship and containing arbitration clauses in the same terms, there is nothing in principle which prevents the claimant from submit-ting its claims under the multiple contracts in a single Request for Arbitration with the intent that they be submitted before a single arbitration tribunal. Nor would a respondent be prevented in defending an arbitration brought against it pursuant to one contract from asserting a counterclaim arising out of a re-lated contract and containing an identical arbitration clause. The Court's con-sideration on a *prima facie* basis that an arbitration agreement may exist between the parties should be satisfied and the issue of whether the parties intended in their arbitration agreements that a single arbitration should be held would be an issue for the arbitrators.[62]

---

any mandatory limitations of any applicable law, the Tribunal shall have the power, on the ap-plication of any party or of its own motion, but in either case only after giving the parties a proper opportunity to state their views, to: . . .

  (c) allow other parties to be joined in the arbitration with their express consent, and make a single final award determining all disputes between them."

61   The reliable way to achieve joinder of a third party, thus creating multi-party arbitration, is by agreements between the parties which effectively foresee, and give prior consent to, such join-ders, or by mandatory provisions of national law providing for joinder and consolidation with-out the consent of all the parties. For discussion of specific arbitration clauses providing for multi-party arbitration, *see* Section 8.14. For discussion of national court powers to order joinder and consolidation, *see* Section 5.1.

62   One member of the Court has expressed the view that disagreements on what he terms the "ex-ternal scope of an arbitration clause", that is the possibility for the arbitration clause in one con-

The factual situation is seldom so clear, however, with related agreements frequently involving additional parties and the arbitration clauses containing different and sometimes contradictory terms.[63] In principle, the claimant should remain free to present its claims under related agreements as it sees fit: whether in consolidated fashion before a single arbitral tribunal or by separate requests for arbitration requiring the constitution of separate arbitral tribunals (whether similarly or differently composed).

Nevertheless the Court, mindful that it lacks any power to order consolidation of arbitrations except to the extent the parties have so agreed, explicitly or implicitly in their arbitration agreement, or as specifically provided in the Rules, continues to exercise some control over *de facto* consolidation. It does not wish to provide for an arbitration to proceed on a consolidated basis if it is apprehensive that such an approach will lead to nullity of the award.

The Court's caution appears to be based on the Sofidif[64] case of an ICC arbitration award rendered in favor of the French company, Sofidif, against an Iranian government authority, the Organisation pour ses Investissements et l'Assistance Economique et Technique de l'Iran (OIAETI), and which was the result of obligations arising out of a complex of agreements between related parties which the Court had permitted to go forward on a consolidated basis.[65] The claims arose out of the Iranian government's cancellation of its nuclear energy policy following upon the 1979 revolution, and its failure to honor its long term obligation to take or pay for long term uranium enrichment services which Sofidif had engaged in the Iranian party's behalf to purchase from Eurodif. The obligations arose from a series of agreements entered into within the framework of Franco-Iranian cooperation in the field of nuclear energy. No "umbrella" arbitration clause provided for a single method of dispute resolution for disputes arising out of any of the related contracts, and

---

tract to cover disputes arising in others, should be decided by arbitral tribunals, not the Court. Theodore Klein, *Disagreement on the Scope of an Arbitration Clause*, 7 ICC BULL. 24, 27 (December 1996). A similar view is expressed in DERAINS & SCHWARTZ, 99: "Indeed, provided that there is at least one arbitration agreement between the parties in question, it may be argued that it should normally be for the Arbitral Tribunal and not the ICC to decide whether all of the matters set forth in the Request for Arbitration fall within a single tribunal's jurisdiction." For a decision by an arbitral tribunal allowing a de facto consolidation by admitting jurisdiction in a single proceeding of claims arising out of related agreements see ICC Case No. 5989/1989, XV YEARBOOK 74 (1990), 1997 JDI 1046, note Hascher.

63 *See* Sections 5.08 and 5.10 for discussion on incorporating a single arbitration clause found in one argreement into ancillary but related agreements.

64 *Cour d'appel*, Versailles, 7 March 1990, OIAETI et Sofidif v. COGEMA, SERU, Eurodif, CEA, 1991 REV. ARB. 326, note Eric Loquin.

65 Even before the final decision of the *Cour d'appel*, Versailles, the award, which had been previously nullified on other grounds by the *Cour d'appel*, Paris, and reinstated by the *Cour de cassation* (see footnote 19, *supra*) had been the subject of substantial critical comment. *See, e.g.,* Emmanuel Gaillard, *L'affaire SOFIDIF ou les difficultés de l'arbitrage multipartite*, 1987 REV. ARB. 275.

the arbitration was brought under the arbitration clauses of two related agreements (both calling for ICC arbitration but one stipulating Paris as the seat of arbitration and the other not defining the seat) involving different but related parties. The ICC arbitral tribunal had found that the complex of contracts formed an economic unit and that the different arbitration clauses were complementary. The reviewing court refused to follow this reasoning. The arbitral tribunal, it found, was not permitted to make an "amalgam" of the arbitral jurisdiction created by the separate arbitration clauses so as to form a general arbitral jurisdiction, based on which it could then determine the substantive obligations of the parties. Rather, it was required to determine initially on the basis of each contract, and as to each party, whether there could be inferred a consent to arbitrate with other parties on a global basis the issues arising under the separate contracts. Because of the failure of the tribunal to meet this requirement (which obviously could only have resulted in a finding of no specific prior agreement to consolidation) the award was nullified.

The award has been said to "confirm in the clearest manner the impossibility in French law to consolidate separate arbitral proceedings, in the absence of a clear agreement by the parties to this."[66]

It may properly be asked, however, whether the Court should permit the authority of this decision, rendered in an extremely complex and special fact situation involving multiple parties, to serve as a basis for hostility to consolidation of related ICC arbitral proceedings in general. The issue should be revisited, particularly where the place of arbitration is elsewhere than France.

Nevertheless, the current view of the Court is that if one of the parties objects to *de facto* consolidation of claims or counterclaims arising out of related agreements and the Court can not find, even on a *prima facie* basis, that there may be an agreement between the parties that claims arising under the various agreements are sufficiently related that they should be heard together, then the Court will order arbitration to proceed separately.

iii) Consolidation of related arbitration proceedings

The Court's relatively cautious approach to *de facto* consolidation may reflect the limited power of *de jure* consolidation—the right to order consolidation of separate pending arbitrations—provided in Article 4(6) of the Rules:

> When a party submits a Request in connection with a legal relationship in respect of which arbitration proceedings between the same parties are already pending under these Rules, the Court may, at the request of a party, decide to include the claims contained in the Request in the pending proceedings provided that the Terms of Reference have not been

---

66   Eric Loquin, note footnote 64, *supra*.

signed or approved by the Court. Once the Terms of Reference have been signed or approved by the Court, claims may only be included in the pending proceedings subject to the provisions of Article 19.

The key limitations are that proceedings may be consolidated only in disputes arising between the same parties and concerning the same legal relationship. Additionally, once the Terms of Reference have been signed by the arbitrators in the proceeding into which the claims are to be consolidated, the consolidation can only take place with the authorization of the arbitrators as provided for in Article 19.[67]

The provision for *de jure* consolidation is of limited consequence since most issues of consolidation will come by attempts to raise claims and counterclaims from related contracts before the originally constituted arbitral tribunal, *i.e., de facto* consolidation.

Accordingly, Article 4(6) consolidation issues will arise only when one of the parties has for tactical or other reasons chosen to bring separate arbitration. The claimant, for instance, may decide to split its claims, or the defendant, instead of filing counterclaims, may elect to act as claimant in new proceedings.

The Court has generally been reluctant to order consolidation of separate proceedings where one of the parties is opposed. To the extent this policy is maintained Article 4(6) loses much of its utility since the pendency of separate arbitrations between the same parties concerning disputes arising in connection with the same legal relationship most frequently is the result of a conscious preference of one of the parties for separate arbitrations.

The Court has been criticized for refusing consolidation and permitting a claimant to split its claims in separate arbitral proceedings, presumably for tactical reasons.[68] It has been urged that joinder of parallel arbitral proceedings arising out of related agreements may be required in the interests of arbitral justice, to preserve equal treatment of the parties and to secure procedural due process. The Court has generally seemed more receptive, however, to the notion that the claimant should be able to determine which claims and under what contracts it wishes to bring its Request for Arbitration.

---

[67] This assumes that the request for consolidation takes place before an arbitral tribunal has been formed in the second case or that the claims have been withdrawn from the second tribunal. More complex questions arise when a request is made for a combination of the two procedures, possibly before a joint, or newly composed, arbitral tribunal.

[68] See Philippe Leboulanger, *Multi-Contract Arbitration*, 13 J. INT. ARB. No. 4 (1996), 43.

CHAPTER 12

CONSTITUTING THE ARBITRAL TRIBUNAL AND DETERMINING THE PLACE OF ARBITRATION

12.01   Place of arbitration

Two of the most important functions of the ICC Court of Arbitration relate to the choice of arbitrators (Articles 8 and 9) and the determination of the place of arbitration (Article 14). Both are subject to stipulations by the parties in the arbitration agreement.

Twenty-five years ago, fewer than half of the cases brought to ICC arbitration involved contracts in which the parties had stipulated the seat of arbitration. This reflected a failure of the negotiation process. Fortunately, the increasing sophistication of practitioners, and the availability of an ever growing literature concerning the arbitral process, has led to recognition of the importance of stipulating the place of arbitration.

The choice of the place of arbitration is fundamental (*see generally* Section 7.02). It is crucial from the perspective of judicial review of, and possible intervention in, the arbitral process by national courts at the seat of arbitration. Moreover, it is important with respect to the conditions of execution of the award in other jurisdictions. It is true that arbitration clauses are frequently the last item discussed in arduous negotiations. Even experienced practitioners at the midnight hour sometimes give in to the temptation to close a deal without agreement on what appears at the time to be a marginal issue - and an agreement is made to arbitrate without stating where. In some of those cases, the parties are subsequently able to agree to the place of arbitration if a dispute arises. Happily, the number of arbitrations where the place of arbitration was agreed by the parties has perceptibly increased. During the period 1980-1988, the place of ICC arbitration was agreed by the parties in 1407 out of 1993 cases (70%), and for the period 1989-1999 in 2818 out of 3393 cases (83%). (*See* Table 7, Appendix I).

If the agreement is silent, the Court of Arbitration determines the place of arbitration (Article 14 of the Rules). In doing so, it takes account of the logistical convenience of the parties, the language and applicable law of the contract, political neutrality, the likelihood of excessive intervention of state courts during the arbitral process, costs of the arbitration in a certain venue, and the legal framework ensuring the award's enforceability.[1] In making its determination, the Court of Arbitration also takes into account factors which suggest an implicit choice of the place of arbitration. Thus, where the arbitration clause is silent as to the place of arbitration but refers to arbitration under the Rules of Arbitration of the International Chamber of Commerce "in Paris" or "of Paris," the Court has often considered that the parties can legitimately be held to an expectation that Paris would be the seat of arbitration. There is only one International Chamber of Commerce; since the words "in Paris" or "of Paris" are not necessary to identify the arbitral institution, they may be given meaning as indicating the seat of the arbitration.[2]

Where the place of arbitration is not stipulated in the arbitration agreement, the parties are permitted, and often encouraged, to make written submissions to the Court of Arbitration on the issue, either in the Request or the Answer, or in separate correspondence to the Court specifically on this point.

During the revision leading to the 1998 Rules, the Court recommended that a provision be added to the Rules that would enable the Court to fix a place of arbitration other than that contained in the agreement, in exceptional circumstances, *e.g.*, war or change in legal regime, after consulting the parties. This was not acted on, as it was believed, particularly where the parties by agreement had themselves chosen the place of arbitration, that it would be an excess of power for the arbitral institution to change such an important contractual term.[3] A similar consideration would apply where the parties had not originally chosen the place of arbitration but had agreed to it when signing

---

1   For a detailed review of the criteria for the fixing of the place of arbitration by the Court, *see* H. Verbist, *The Practice of the ICC International Court of Arbitration With Regard to the Fixing of the Place of Arbitration*, 12 ARB. INT., 347 (1996).

2   The Court of Arbitration would take the same approach where a pathological arbitration clause erroneously refers to the Rules of Arbitration of the International Chamber of Commerce "in Geneva" or "of Geneva" and would assume that the reference to the ICC was self-explanatory and that "Geneva" could only refer to the place of arbitration. This canon of construction has been endorsed by arbitral tribunals and approved by courts. *See* ICC Case 7245/1991, Société Procédés de Préfabrication pour le Béton c/ Libye, setting aside refused, *Cour d'appel*, Paris, 1998 REV. ARB. 399, note B. Leurent; ICC Case 4023/1984, I ICC AWARDS 528; *see generally*, Jean Benglia, *Inaccurate Reference to the ICC*, 7 ICC BULL. 11 (December, 1996).

3   *See* W. Laurence Craig, William W. Park, Jan Paulsson, ANNOTATED GUIDE TO THE 1998 ICC ARBITRATION RULES WITH COMMENTARY (Oceana Publications/ICC Publishing S.A. 1998) 104. Even in the absence of a modification of the Rules to provide express authority to the Court to change a

the Terms of Reference. Lack of institutional power to change the seat of arbitration means that a radical change in the arbitration laws of the seat of arbitration (for instance following a revolution or change in regime) could conceivably result in a radical change in the rights of the parties, or one of them, participating in an arbitration proceeding in that country. The risk would be the greatest, for instance, where one of the parties was a governmental organization of the state within which the seat of arbitration is situated. Such scenarios illustrate the importance of good contract draftsmanship and risk analysis at the outset.

While the drastic power for an arbitral institution to change the seat of arbitration was not adopted, the 1998 Rules did, in Article 14, provide or confirm powers of the arbitral tribunal concerning the locale for various steps in the arbitral proceedings. Thus Article 14(2) allows the arbitral tribunal, after consultation with the parties, to hold meetings and hearings at any location it chooses. The parties have the last word, however, since the tribunal may exercise this power only "unless otherwise agreed by the parties." The second provision added in 1998, at Article 14(3), states that "[T]he Arbitral Tribunal may deliberate at any location it considers appropriate." While this has always been the practice of arbitral tribunals, it has now been incorporated into the Rules.

An important distinction should be made between the official place of arbitration and other geographical locations at which meetings may take place, hearings held, or evidence taken. The official place of arbitration from which legal consequences flow is frequently referred to as the "seat" of arbitration (as, for instance, in Article 3 of the English Arbitration Act 1996) or the *siège d'arbitrage*. Consideration was given at the time of revision of the Rules in 1998 to substituting the word "seat" of the arbitration for "place" to avoid confusion concerning the official domiciliation of the arbitral tribunal with locations at which certain portions of the arbitral proceedings might take place. Much recent legal writing uses "seat" for just this reason. The revisers decided to retain the phrase "place of arbitration", considering that this had not caused any significant problems in the past and that modern arbitration rules in their majority, as is also the case with the New York Convention, have continued to use "place." An opportunity may nevertheless have been missed to harmonize common law and civil law vocabulary, particularly since the French version of the prior Rules had always used the term *siège*.[4]

---

place of arbitration agreed by the parties, it is possible that the court might in exceptional circumstances find that it possesses implicit authority under Article 35, the "General Rule," to make such a change to prevent frustration of the arbitral process and to make possible the rendering of an award enforceable at law.

4   Article 14(1) of the French version of the 1998 Rules now provides: "La cour fixe le lieu de l'arbitrage à moins que les parties ne soient convenues de celui-ci." The earlier Rules used the term *siège de l'arbitrage*.

The distinction between the official domiciliation of the arbitral tribunal and locations at which parts of the arbitral proceedings may take place is clearly recognized in Article 14 of the Rules which provides:

14(1) The place of the arbitration shall be fixed by the Court unless agreed upon by the parties.

14(2) The Arbitral Tribunal may . . . conduct hearings and meetings at any *location* it considers appropriate . . . (Emphasis added)[5]

Since the fixing of the "place" or "seat" of arbitration may establish a certain relationship with the courts and legal system of that place—and notably the possibility of judicial review of the arbitral award in that jurisdiction—the question is sometimes raised whether this situation would be changed if most or all of the arbitral proceedings were held at some other place. The answer, in principle, is no. Arbitration, in concept, and the laws providing for it, emphasize the parties' freedom to choose the laws, procedures and rules to govern their proceedings. If the parties situate their international arbitration in Switzerland so as to obtain the protections of the Swiss Private International Law Act and to obtain a Swiss award, but for convenience hold all meetings at some other location, there is no reason that they should not be able to do so, without changing the character of their arbitration.[6] In *Société Procédés de Préfabrication pour le Béton c/ Libye*[7] the *Cour d'appel* of Paris was faced with an application to set aside an award rendered in an arbitration where the official seat had been determined to be Geneva. After the tribunal had been reconstituted following the resignation of the original three arbitrators, the reconstituted tribunal had held all hearings and issued all procedural orders from Paris. At least one of the members of the tribunal had signed the award in Paris. The theory of the petitioners was that the actions of the tribunal were evidence of a change in the seat of arbitration to Paris, with the consequence that the Paris court would have jurisdiction over judicial recourse from the award. The Court denied this approach, stating:

. . . the seat of the arbitration is purely a legal concept, carrying with it important legal consequences and notably the jurisdiction of state courts over applications for annulment, and depends on the will of the parties; it is not a factual concept depending on the locale of hearings or that of

---

5   Article 14(2) goes on to provide that if *both* parties want the proceedings to be held at the official place of arbitration their choice prevails. The arbitrators are free, however, (pursuant to Article 14(3)), to deliberate elsewhere in their sole discretion.

6   So far no notion has arisen of disregard of a "fictional place of arbitration" ("*siège arbitrale fictive*") by analogy to the jurisprudence regarding disregard of corporate nationality based on a *siège social fictive* (pursuant to which a company duly incorporated and having a registered head office in that country would not be permitted to claim the benefits of that national status when the so-called head office was only a letter box), which had a vogue in France and Europe between the First and Second World Wars.

7   Footnote 2, *supra*.

the effective place of signature of the award, which is liable to vary according to the imagination or maladroitness of the arbitrators.

The Court accordingly declined jurisdiction, which it held to be reserved for the Swiss courts at the seat of arbitration chosen by the parties.[8]

12.02   Number of arbitrators

The number of arbitrators (one or three)[9] may also be agreed by the parties, either in the arbitration clause or by subsequent agreement. The arguments in favor of settling this matter in the arbitration agreement have been set forth in Section 7.01. Where the parties have agreed in advance that there should be three arbitrators the claimant is required to name an arbitrator in its Request for Arbitration and the respondent to name its arbitrator within 30 days thereafter.[10] However, parties often feel that they are not prepared to make in advance the determination of whether one or three arbitrators will be appropriate. Indeed, without modification, the ICC Model Clause, which provides for arbitration "by one or more arbitrators appointed in accordance with the said Rules," anticipates that the parties will be unable to agree on the number in the agreement to arbitrate. The Court must then, at the time a dispute arises, choose the number of arbitrators as per Article 8(2) of the Rules:

> Where the parties have not agreed upon the number of arbitrators, the Court shall appoint a sole arbitrator, save where it appears to the Court that the dispute is such as to warrant the appointment of three arbitrators. In such a case the claimant shall nominate an arbitrator within a period of 15 days from the receipt of the notification of the decision of the Court, and the Respondent shall nominate an arbitrator within a period of 15 days from the receipt of the notification made by the Claimant. (Emphasis added)

Where the Court decides on three arbitrators, Article 8(2) of the Rules maintains the 30 day time limit, within which both parties must have named an arbitrator but by giving each party 15 days to make its nomination keeps intact the defensive advantage of the respondent in naming an arbitrator after

---

8   Footnote 2, *supra* at 402: ". . . le siège de l'arbitrage est une notion purement *juridique*, emportant d'importantes conséquences et notamment la compétence des juridictions étatiques pour connaître des recours en annulation, sous la dépendance de la volonté des parties, et non une notion matérielle dépendant du lieu où l'audience a été tenue ou du lieu effectif de la signature de la sentence, susceptible de varier au gré de la fantaisie ou de la maladresse des arbitres . . ." For further discussion of this case in connection with the interpretation of legislation providing for judicial recourse at the place where an arbitral award is rendered, *see* Section 31.04 (g), *infra*.

9   Article 8(1) of the Rules provides: "The dispute shall be decided by a sole arbitrator or by three arbitrators." The Court has been known, in derogation of this article, to approve tribunals agreed by the parties calling for more than three arbitrators, particularly in multi-party arbitration. *See* Article 10 of the Rules and discussion at Section 12.06.

10   *See* Article 5 of the Rules.

knowing the identity of the arbitrator named by the claimant. This advantage is considered appropriate in an arbitral process.[11]

There is thus a presumption in favor of appointing a sole arbitrator in cases where the parties have not agreed otherwise. If the stakes are large, the presumption will disappear. In smaller cases, the Court encourages the use of a sole arbitrator in order to avoid the greater costs required for three arbitrators which may not be justifiable in relation to the amount in dispute.[12] In the past, the Court has applied the rule of thumb of opting for a sole arbitrator in cases involving less than $1,500,000. More recently, the Court has eschewed such a mechanical approach, and where issues are not complex has preferred a sole arbitrator even where several million dollars have been in dispute. *See* section 7.01, *supra*.[13]

Even if the parties do not establish the number of arbitrators in the arbitration agreement, they will express a view once arbitration commences, typically in the Request and Answer. If both sides agree on the number of arbitrators, the Court's discretion in the matter is removed. Even so, the Court may request the parties to reconsider the matter if they have decided on three arbitrators in a small case. The intent is not to impose the Court's view on the parties, but simply to inform them of the possible disadvantages of a three-member tribunal. As compared to a sole arbitrator, a three-man tribunal is substantially more expensive, and by nature more time consuming (largely due to the difficulty of establishing meeting dates).

If they have not settled the question of the number of arbitrators prior to the commencement of arbitration, parties frequently are unable to agree thereafter. Sometimes such disagreement is based on legitimate and deep-felt preferences. Occasionally it reflects a tactic of one of the parties to dissuade its adversary from proceeding to arbitration. For instance, a respondent may insist on three arbitrators, knowing that if it does not contribute to the advance on costs the claimant will be required to make the entire advance (*see* Chapter 14). Such a party may hope that if the advance is large enough, the claimant will not proceed at all. There are also instances where the claim-

---

11   *See also* Sigvard Jarvin, *The Place of Arbitration—A Review of the ICC Court's Guiding Principles and Practice when Fixing the Place of Arbitration*, 7 ICC BULL. 54 (December 1996).

12   *See* C. Imhoos, *Constitution of the Arbitral Tribunal*, 2 ICC BULL. 3 (November 1991).

13   It may be noted that from 1983 through 1987 approximately 50% of the cases submitted to ICC arbitration involved amounts less than $1,000,000. In new cases set in motion in 1997, the cases submitted to ICC arbitration involving amounts less than $1,000,000 continued to hover around 50%, though there has been a notable increase in cases for which amounts at stake are below $200,000. (*1997 Statistical Report*, 9 ICC BULL. 6 (May 1998)). The Statistical Report stated also that 52% of the arbitrations submitted to the ICC court in 1997 were entrusted to three arbitrators (30.4% by contractual provision, 16.3% by parties' subsequent agreement, 5.3% by decision of the ICC Court) and 48% to a sole arbitrator (11.5% by contractual provision, 16.8% by parties' subsequent agreement, 19.7% by decision of the ICC Court). *Id*, at 8.

ant insists on three arbitrators in order to put economic pressure on an impecunious respondent.

Even where there is a good financial argument for a sole arbitrator, the parties may legitimately favor the collegial judgment of a three-member body. Having three arbitrators may assure a more thorough consideration of all the issues from different points of view. In major arbitrations involving parties from countries that are far apart in terms of geography, culture, politics, and economic development, at least one of the parties usually insists on a three-member panel.

The Court may honor such a request even in cases under the $ 1.5 million threshold referred to above. Its expectation, in an East/West or North/South dispute, is that, for instance, an Eastern European or developing country party would have more confidence in the fairness of a three member tribunal and would be less likely to resist the award if it were to lose.

Where the parties have agreed that the disputes shall be settled by a sole arbitrator, they may, by agreement, nominate the sole arbitrator for confirmation and are encouraged to do so. If the parties fail to nominate a sole arbitrator within 30 days from the date when the claimant's Request for Arbitration has been received by the other party, or within such additional time as may be allowed by the Secretariat, the sole arbitrator is appointed by the Court.

12.03 Appointment of sole arbitrator or chairman

This is where the Court fulfills one of its most important functions: ensuring that the chairman or sole arbitrator is qualified to preside over important international commercial disputes. ICC arbitration finally stands or falls on the success of this mission.

The process of constituting a three-member tribunal begins with each side nominating an arbitrator for confirmation by the Court (Article 8(4)). The third arbitrator (and chairman) is appointed by the Court. If the arbitration agreement specifically provides that the two party-nominated arbitrators will choose the chairman, their choice will be presented to the Court for confirmation if made within the contractual time limits. Since the Court encourages proceedings voluntarily adopted by the parties, it almost invariably confirms joint nominations by parties.

In the absence of joint party nominations, the procedure for appointing a chairman or sole arbitrator is set forth in Article 9(3), under which the Court makes the appointment upon a proposal from a National Committee of the ICC. Proposing arbitrators is one of the most important roles of the National Committees. The most frequently solicited Committees (*e.g.*, Switzerland, France, England, Belgium, Austria and, for the Middle East and Asia, Lebanon; *see* Table 4 of Appendix I) are well organized to propose qualified arbitrators for the dispute at hand. They are informed by the Secretariat of the specific requirements of the case (linguistic, legal, technical, etc.). In making proposals, National Committees provide the Court with all appropriate information concerning the individual.

The Court of Arbitration is not bound to accept the proposal of a National Committee and has, in fact, rejected proposals it does not find appropriate. The consequences are spelled out in the text of Article 9(3) of the Rules:

> If the Court does not accept the proposal made, or if the National Committee fails to make the proposal requested within the time limit fixed by the Court, the Court may repeat its request or may request a proposal from another National Committee that it considers to be appropriate.

Article 9(4) of the Rules empowers the Court to name a chairman or a sole arbitrator from a country where there is no National Committee, provided that neither party objects within the time limit fixed by the Court. This provision, which responds in part to certain criticisms from developing country users as to the exclusivity of the circle of ICC arbitrators, and the fact that ICC appointed chairmen and sole arbitrators tend to originate from developed countries in the West, reinforces the international mission of the Court, and gives it wider powers to deal with particular geographical and political or socio-economic considerations. In view of the express requirement of party consent, it is a limited power, and has been successfully implemented in the past only infrequently.[14]

In choosing the National Committee to propose the chairman or sole arbitrator, the Court most frequently looks to the place of arbitration, particularly if the site was agreed by the parties. A party having accepted a venue can hardly raise an objection to the appointment of a presiding arbitrator from that country. Even where the Court has chosen the place of arbitration, it usually looks to the National Committee there. The reason is that the presiding arbitrator should be aware of any particularities of local law and procedures which might affect the arbitration. In certain circumstances, however, other considerations may militate in favor of a chairman of another nationality: political neutrality, balanced composition of the tribunal, knowledge of the substantive law applicable to the contract, technical or linguistics skills, and the like.

---

14   According to DERAINS & SCHWARTZ, at 159, only 16 of 400 appointments made in 1995-1996 were made under this provision. For a further description of the background of this provision when first adopted in 1988, see Arnaldez and Jakande, *Les amendements apportés au Réglement d'Arbitrage de la Chambre de Commerce Internationale (C.C.I.),* 1988 REV. ARB. 67, at 73.

If one of the parties is a national of the place of arbitration, the Court will not in principle name a chairman or sole arbitrator from that country. Article 9(5) of the ICC Rules provides in part:

> The sole arbitrator or the chairman of an arbitral tribunal shall be chosen from a country other than those of which the parties are nationals.

Thus, for example, the Court could not name a United States citizen as chairman in an arbitration between Italian and American companies to be conducted in New York, even if New York law is applicable to the merits and the language of the contract is English. A more likely choice would be a Canadian or an English arbitrator.

This provision is not inflexible. Article 9(5) continues:

> However, in suitable circumstances and provided that neither of the parties objects within the time limit fixed by the Court, the sole arbitrator or the chairman of the Arbitral Tribunal may be chosen from a country of which any of the parties is a national.

This provision may be applied when both parties are nationals of the same country, or when both arbitrators proposed by the parties are themselves nationals of the same country and it would be advantageous that the arbitration take place in that country.[15]

There is another exception to the general preference for a chairman who is a national of the place of arbitration. The ICC Court generally prefers that the chairman not be of the same nationality as one of the party-nominated arbitrators, in order to ensure a balance of nationalities on the tribunal. Thus, for instance, it may be undesirable in an arbitration in Geneva between French and Moroccan parties that the chairman would be Swiss if there is already a Swiss party-nominated arbitrator. On the other hand, if both parties nominate Swiss arbitrators, there would be no imbalance of nationalities by naming a Swiss chairman as well.

One of the hallmarks of ICC arbitration has been the emergence of a group of arbitrators who, because of special competence in their field, have frequently been named as chairmen or sole arbitrators. Usually they are legal practitioners, retired judges, or law professors. They have come to the attention of National Committees and the ICC Secretariat because of their interest in arbitration and their participation in international commercial transactions for many years. Most have also served as counsel or party-nominated arbitrators in ICC or other arbitrations.

---

15 These examples, cited at the time of the original adoption of the provision in 1975, have been followed frequently by the Court since. *See* ICC Document No. 420/179, INTERNATIONAL ARBITRATION, 1975.05.25, *The Revised ICC Rules of Arbitration*, report of Jean Robert, Rapporteur of the ICC Commission on International Arbitration.

The Court frequently chooses a jurist as chairman of an ICC tribunal because large arbitrations inevitably involve problems of both substantive and procedural law. Party-nominated arbitrators do not always have expertise in these areas. The task of keeping the record of the arbitral proceedings, assuring procedural regularity, and drafting the award usually falls on the chairman. He must be qualified for the task. The chairman must often devote considerably more time to the case than his co-arbitrators. The Court therefore grants the chairman somewhat higher fees than those allocated to the party-nominated arbitrators, the standard ratio being 40/30/30 unless the arbitral tribunal itself proposes to the Court a different division.

12.04   Party-nominated arbitrators

While the Court has taken a very active role to assure consistency in the qualifications of the chairmen and sole arbitrators it appoints, its function in confirming party-nominated arbitrators is in practice quite limited.

If a three-member tribunal is to be constituted, the Rules provide for each party to nominate an arbitrator for confirmation by the Court. According to what has been called the general European concept of arbitration—and what is now accepted as the international one—such a nominee should not be or act as the nominating party's agent or representative.[16]

The required independence of the arbitrators, including party-named arbitrators, is addressed in Article 7(1) of the Rules:

> Every arbitrator must be and remain independent of the parties involved in the arbitration.

In order to assure respect of the principle of independence, the Court requires that prospective arbitrators sign a statement of independence and disclose to the Secretariat any facts or circumstances "which might be of such a nature as to call into question the arbitrator's independence in the eyes of the parties" (Article 7(2)). In addition, arbitrators are asked to submit a resume or curriculum vitae to the Secretariat as a means of detecting and preventing conflicts of interest. (*See* Section 13.04, *infra*). The kinds of facts or circumstances which most usually raise problems are suggested in the form which the ICC requires arbitrators to sign when submitting their declaration of acceptance. In determining whether a particular fact or circumstance needs to

---

16   "There is a question whether a party-appointed arbitrator should be impartial and independent. The general custom in Europe is so to consider a party-appointed arbitrator." R. Straus, *The General Consensus on International Commercial Arbitration*, 68 AMERICAN JOURNAL OF INTERNATIONAL LAW 709, at 714 (1974). Today there is evidence, backed by the contribution of ICC practice, of a general norm requiring independence and impartiality of party- appointed arbitrators in all international commercial arbitrations. The International Bar Association, in its *Ethics for International Arbitration* (1987), reprinted *in* 3 ARB. INT. 72 (1987), takes the position that international arbitrators should be "impartial, independent, competent, diligent and discreet" and makes no distinction in this regard between party-nominated arbitrators and chairmen or sole arbitrators.

be disclosed, the arbitrator should take into account "whether there exists any past or present relationship, direct or indirect, with any of the parties, their counsel, whether financial, professional or of another kind" which might call into question the arbitrator's independence in the eyes of the parties.[17] The importance of the arbitrator's statement of independence is reflected in the fact that where the statement indicates that no circumstances exist which require disclosure, or where disclosed facts have given rise to no objection, confirmation of the nomination may be made by the Secretary General, without having to refer the matter to the Court. Added to the Rules in 1998 to help speed up administrative steps in the arbitration, Article 9(2) provides:

> The Secretary General may confirm as co-arbitrators, sole arbitrators and chairmen of Arbitral Tribunals persons nominated by the parties or pursuant to their particular agreements, provided they have filed a statement of independence without qualification or a qualified statement of independence has not given rise to objections. Such confirmation shall be reported to the Court at its next session. If the Secretary General considers that a co-arbitrator, sole arbitrator or chairman of an Arbitral Tribunal should not be confirmed, the matter shall be submitted to the Court.

The notion of "independent" party-nominated arbitrators has sparked extensive discussion. It would however be impossible to establish specific ICC criteria for determining "independence" without giving rise to criticism from some ICC arbitration consumers, since they represent such a variety of legal and economic systems. Instead of articulating criteria that would inevitably be controversial, the ICC approach is to give the Court wide administrative discretion to refuse, confirm, or remove an arbitrator without stating its reasons.

Article 7(4) of the Rules provides: "The decisions of the Court as to the appointment, confirmation, challenge, or replacement of an arbitrator shall be final and the reasons for such decisions shall not be communicated." Nevertheless, certain criteria of independence have been reflected in the practice of the Court and in judicial decisions in a number of countries. These will be discussed in Chapter 13.

Parties may agree to waive the requirement of independence of party- nominated arbitrators. In the absence of such agreement, a party is clearly not permitted to nominate as arbitrator its own lawyer, or an employee. If, with full knowledge of the circumstances, both parties specifically agree to such an appointment, the nomination may be accepted. In such cases, the nature of the arbitration changes: the party-nominated arbitrators become advocates of

---

17   *See* 6 ICC BULL. 77 (November 1995) (reprinting the form); Stephen Bond, *The Selection of ICC Arbitrators and the Requirement of Independence*, 4 ARB. INT. 300 (1988); D. Hascher, *ICC Practice in Relation to the Appointment, Confirmation, Challenge and Replacement of Arbitrators*, 6 ICC BULL. 4 (November 1995).

their party's position, and the chairman becomes, in essence, an umpire. Such agreements are exceedingly rare in ICC practice.[18]

Even in the usual case where the party-nominated arbitrator must be independent, the parties are still left with a large degree of discretion concerning their choice of the arbitrator. They are generally free to choose a person who is clearly sympathetic to their case. Experience shows, however, that such choices are often counter-productive: a partial arbitrator lacks credibility with his fellow arbitrators. The tribunal will already have heard arguments from counsel. Its other members, and most importantly the chairman, will not want a repeat performance during deliberations. A party-appointed arbitrator staunchly adhering to the positions of the party which nominated him or her will not have much influence on the decision-making process. For this reason, it is generally in a party's own interest to pick a truly independent arbitrator. There is little advantage to having *one* guaranteed vote on a three-person tribunal. The notion of true independence is not illusory; it refers to a professional attitude that would prevent an arbitrator from compromising his convictions and his reputation only to satisfy the party that named him. The authors are pleased to confirm that they have encountered numerous ICC arbitrators, named by the adverse party, who gave every proof of such an attitude.

It is sometimes said that while a party-nominated arbitrator must be "independent," he or she need not be "neutral." The juxtaposition of terms may not be entirely felicitous, but it does reflect a significant distinction. A party is clearly entitled to (and often does) choose an arbitrator of its own nationality. The arbitrator may also come from a similar economic, political and social *milieu*, and may therefore be expected to be sympathetic to positions taken by that party. The arbitrator may also embrace legal doctrines that the nominating party feels are favorable to its case. It is in this limited sense that the party-nominated arbitrator need not be "neutral."

Once the party-nominated arbitrators have been confirmed and the chairman appointed, the parties are informed of the Court's action. The arbitral tribunal is thus officially formed. One obstacle to constitution of the tribunal is the possibility of disqualification of an arbitrator. The procedures and grounds for disqualification are discussed in Chapter 13.

---

18 When there is any question as to the party-appointed arbitrator's independence, it is vital that the opposing party's waiver of objection to the nomination be unmistakable and fully informed; *see* the *Universal Pictures* case discussed in point (v) of Section 13.05. While waiver of a possible ground for objection to an arbitrator occurs with some frequency, a positive agreement that party-appointed arbitrators need not be independent would be highly unusual as the then Secretary General of the Court of Arbitration remarked in a comment on this section. Stephen Bond, *The Experience of the ICC Court of Arbitration in the Selection and Confirmation/Appointment of Arbitrators, in* the ARBITRAL PROCESS AND THE INDEPENDENCE OF ARBITRATORS, Sixth Joint ICC/ICSID/AAA Colloquium on International Arbitration, ICC, Paris, 27 October 1988.

12.05   Failure of a party to nominate an arbitrator

A crucial principle of ICC arbitration is that default by a party at any stage of the proceedings is not allowed to frustrate the arbitral process. The first evidence of a party's failure to cooperate in the arbitral process may be its refusal to nominate an arbitrator.[19] In such a case, Article 8(4) of the Rules provides that the Court of Arbitration will appoint an arbitrator on behalf of the defaulting party. The procedure, as set out in Article 9(6), is that:

> Where the Court is to appoint an arbitrator on behalf of a party which has failed to nominate one, it shall make the appointment upon a proposal of the National Committee of the country of which that party is a national.

The idea behind this provision is simple. Even if a party refuses to participate in the arbitral process, the tribunal should include at least one member having that party's nationality and as he is presumptively sensitive to particular conditions that may be relevant to understanding the situation of the party. Or, put another way, since parties often nominate an arbitrator having their own nationality, the Court of Arbitration, acting to remedy a party's default, tends to use the same national criteria.

An arbitrator is therefore usually named by the Court upon a proposal from the defaulting party's National Committee. However, practice has revealed at least two problems: i) where the defaulting party originates from a country which has no National Committee, and ii) rare cases where the National Committee of the defaulting party is either unable or unwilling to propose a suitable candidate.

Article 9(6) of the Rules provides that in either of these cases where following party default it has been impossible to receive a nomination from a National Committee then ". . . the Court shall be at liberty to choose any person whom it regards as suitable."[20]

The first case has caused the most concern. The ICC proposes an arbitration system of universal application. Consumers of ICC arbitration services—parties who have entered into agreements containing ICC arbitration clauses—may come from anywhere in the world and from any economic system. ICC

---

19 *See* Stephen Bond, *The Constitution of the Arbitral Tribunal*, in ICC Bull. 23 (Supplement, 1997).

20 The full text of Article 9(6) reads:

> Where the Court is to appoint an arbitrator on behalf of a party which has failed to nominate one, it shall make the appointment upon a proposal of the National Committee of the Country of which that party is a national. If the Court does not accept the proposal made, or if the National Committee fails to make the proposal requested within the time limit fixed by the Court, or if the country of which the said party is a national has no National Committee, the Court shall be at liberty to choose any person whom it regards as suitable. The Secretariat shall inform the National Committee, if one exists, of the country of which such person is a national.

clauses are contained in numerous contracts with parties from Russia and other former members of the Soviet Union, Eastern European states and newly developing nations. In many of these countries, National Committees of the ICC have not yet been established (according to the ICC Constitution full membership is restricted to representatives of states having market economies providing conditions of free trade).[21] Also, for other reasons, relatively few National Committees have been established in Latin America. Obviously, a national from any of these countries is free to nominate as party arbitrator a national from its own country, or from any country that it desires, whether or not such country has a National Committee. Article 9(6) assures arbitration users from these countries that under the Rules, even in the case of party default, the Court of Arbitration acting to remedy the default can do so with the same liberty.

The case of the non-cooperative National Committee is fortunately rare. There does exist, however, the possibility that a National Committee may simply be unable to propose an arbitrator having the experience and skills required for the arbitration at hand. Moreover, where an arbitration involves important and sensitive state interests, there is the risk that a National Committee may not have the requisite independence to propose an arbitrator when, in fact, the state is doing all in its power to prevent the arbitration from advancing.

Article 9(6) of the Rules gives to the Court adequate power to deal with any such default by a National Committee in the nominating process.

12.06   Constituting the arbitral tribunal in multi-party arbitrations

We have referred in Section 5.11 to specific problems relating to multi-party arbitrations involving non-signatory parties, and in Section 8.14 to provisions to be made in the arbitration agreement to accommodate multi-party disputes, particularly for the method of appointment of arbitrators. In effect the best solution is to provide in advance for a method of appointment which corresponds to the specificities of the contractual relationships in the multi-party agreement. Frequently, however, the possible problems of constitution of the arbitral tribunal, where multiple parties are involved, will not have been addressed and the issue will be governed by Article 10 of the Rules, added in 1998, which provides:

> 10(1) Where there are multiple parties, whether as Claimant or as Respondent, and where the dispute is to be referred to three arbitrators, the multiple Claimants jointly, and the multiple Respondents, jointly, shall nominate an arbitrator for confirmation pursuant to Article 9.

---

21   In the 1990's, however, China established a National Committee as have the Eastern European states of The Czech Republic, Hungary, Lithuania and Ukraine.

10(2) In the absence of such a joint nomination and where all parties are unable to agree to a method for the constitution of the Arbitral Tribunal, the Court may appoint each member of the Arbitral Tribunal and shall designate one of them to act as chairman. In such case, the Court shall be at liberty to choose any person it regards as suitable to act as arbitrator, applying Article 9 when it considers this appropriate.

Article 10 attempts to resolve the problem (perhaps to be compared to the problem of squaring the circle) of how to give each party the right to nominate "its" arbitrator, while at the same time only providing for a tribunal composed of three members.

Note that Article 10 only applies "where the dispute is to be referred to three arbitrators." Hence it does not apply where the dispute is to be referred to a sole arbitrator who will simply be appointed by the Court, either upon the proposal of a National Committee or as an agreed nomination by all parties. It also would not apply where exceptionally the Court permitted a tribunal to be comprised of more than three arbitrators with the agreement of all the parties.[22]

The solution of Article 10, entirely consistent with prior ICC practice, is to conceive of the dispute as having two "sides": multiple claimants constituting one side and multiple respondents constituting the other side.[23] Each side is to nominate an arbitrator, and the multiple parties within the side are to agree upon the nomination and to make the nomination jointly.

In point of fact this system corresponds to reality and has worked well in many cases. While a substantial number of ICC arbitrations (more than 30%) involve more than two parties they do not necessarily involve any of the special characteristics which have caused problems in multi-party arbitrations. Thus where a group of companies (parent-subsidiary, sister companies, etc.) is named either as claimant or respondent there is no reason why the multiple parties should not be required to agree on an arbitrator jointly, even if the other party is a single party with complete and sole freedom of choice of an arbitrator. In many other cases the members of the claimant side or respondent side have an equally clear affinity of interests. Trouble arises where a conflict of interest exists within the side. Where, on a construction project, the owner brings arbitration against both its contractor and sub-contractor it is by no means certain that the contractor's and sub-contractor's interests are the same and in some cases they may conflict radically.

The same conflicts may exist in a tri-partite joint venture contract containing an arbitration clause. This was said to be the case in *Siemens A.G. and BKMI*

---

22 Any such approval by the Court would be a derogation from Article 8(1) which provides: "The disputes shall be decided by a sole arbitrator or by three arbitrators."

23 This is consistent moreover, with Article 2(ii) which provides: "Claimant" includes one or more claimants and "Respondent" includes one or more respondents."

Industrienlagen GmbH (BKMI) v. Dutco Consortium Construction Co.,[24] hereinafter referred to as the *Dutco* case, where a dispute arose out of a contract
for the construction of a cement plant in Oman. After entering into an agreement to build the plant for an Omani party, the German contractor, BKMI, had
reached a further agreement with two other contractors, Siemens and Dutco.
This consortium contract provided that all disputes would be finally settled
by three arbitrators appointed under the ICC Arbitration Rules. When a dispute arose among the partners, Dutco brought an arbitration against Siemens
and BKMI. Its claims against its partners were separate and quite dissimilar.

In accordance with its practice, the ICC provided that there would be one arbitrator for the claimant and one for the respondents. This meant that either the
two respondents had to agree on their joint arbitrator, or else the ICC would
select an arbitrator for them both. Siemens and BKMI protested. Understandably, each party wanted to maximize its chances of success through nomination of an arbitrator whose background that party believed would make him
sympathetic to its own particular arguments. In this respect, each respondent
wanted the same opportunity as the claimant.

Challenged in court, the ICC practice was upheld by the Paris *Cour d'appel*, but
the *Cour de cassation* held that the ICC practice violated the principle of
"equality of the parties," which the Court held to be a matter of non-waivable
public policy (*ordre public*). Moreover, the Court found this inequality of treatment to violate Article 1502 (2) of the *Nouveau code de procédure civile*, which
provides for the setting aside of an award in cases where the arbitral tribunal
was irregularly constituted.

The *Dutco* case arose under a prior version of the ICC Rules which did not specifically address the requirement of a joint nomination of an arbitrator by
multiple parties claimant or multiple parties respondent, which had only
been a matter of practice. Article 10 cures that defect and parties now agreeing to the Rules will be on notice of the requirements of Article 10(1) that
joint parties shall jointly nominate an arbitrator, which may thus be said to
embody contractually accepted terms.

Article 10(2) offers three possible alternatives where joint parties claimant or respondent are unable or unwilling to make a joint nomination of an arbitrator:

   i) All parties may agree to a method of constituting the tribunal; or

   ii) The Court may independently appoint all three of the members, naming
   one of them chairman (what might be characterized as the ordinary or usual
   method of appointment upon default of a joint appointment); or

---

24   *Cour de cassation, Première chambre civile*, 7 January 1992, France, 1992 REV. ARB. 470, note Pi-
      erre Bellet; see also Jean-Louis Delvolvé, *Multipartisme: the Dutco Decision of the French Cour de
      Cassation*, 9 ARB. INT. 197 (1993).

iii) The Court may appoint an arbitrator for the joint parties claimant or respondent who defaulted in their obligation to make a joint nomination, permitting the other party to the arbitration to nominate the arbitrator of its choice.

The third option is not explicitly spelled out in the Rules but there is absolutely no doubt based on the text of Article 10(2) as well as its drafting history that the Court retains the discretion to permit one party to nominate its arbitrator while itself making the appointment on behalf of the defaulting joint parties.[25] It may be argued that this method permits a certain disequilibrium between the parties in the sense that one party has had free choice of its arbitrator while the others have had their arbitrator picked for them by the Court. On the other hand, such a disequilibrium is true in any case where a party defaults in its arbitrator nomination obligation. As long as the parties have notice of the Court's possible use of its appointment power in this way—as they now do through the text of Article 10(2)—there is little reason to believe that this practice would not be upheld by most national courts,[26] particularly in those jurisdictions which emphasize the contractual rights of parties to resolve disputes in any manner provided they agree.[27]

In France, however, where nearly 25% of ICC arbitrations are held, the Court would feel constrained to appoint all three arbitrators. The *Cour de cassation* held quite clearly in *Dutco* that the parties enjoyed at law an equality of opportunity to appoint an arbitrator and that this right could not be waived in advance in an agreement to arbitrate future disputes. The 1998 Rules modification requiring joint parties to appoint one arbitrator cannot overcome this requirement of *ordre public* as currently interpreted under French law. The Court is not, however, required to let *Dutco* influence its decisions on constituting arbitral tribunals in multi-party arbitrations elsewhere than in France (and in those cases where an award rendered elsewhere might be brought to France for execution). Nevertheless, one may expect that where the multiple parties fail or refuse to make a joint nomination the Court will ordinarily pre-

---

25 An earlier version of Article 10(2) in drafts considered during the 1998 revision process provided that in the event of default of the required joint nomination the Court "shall" appoint each member of the tribunal was rejected, in discussion, at the ICC Commission on International Arbitration. Under the Rules as adopted this method is clearly only an option. Working Party Draft, ICC Doc. No. 420/15-15 of 8 October 1996. See W. Laurence Craig, William W. Park, Jan Paulsson, ANNOTATED GUIDE TO THE ICC ARBITRATION RULES WITH COMMENTARY (Oceana Publications/ICC Publishing 1998) 87-88; *accord* DERAINS & SCHWARTZ, 171, 173; Andreas Reiner, *Le réglement d'arbitrage de la CCI, version 1998*, 1998 REV. ARB. 3, 14.

26 Even before the explicit mention in the Rules of the requirement that multiple parties claimant or respondent make a joint nomination of an arbitrator the Swiss courts had upheld the Court's practice in République arabe d'Egypte v. Western Helicopters Ltd., *Cour de justice de Genève*, 26 November 1982, aff'd *Tribunal fédéral Suisse*, 16 May 1983.

27 For an excellent review of United States practice sustaining contractually agreed methods of arbitrator appointment against allegations of due process violations, see Allan Rau *On Integrity in Private Judging*, 14 ARB. INT. 115, 122-135.

fer to appoint all the arbitrators,[28] reserving its third option only for unusual cases (where, for instance, a group of companies would refuse to make a joint nomination for the express or evident reason of depriving its adversary from making an appointment of a particularly able and respected arbitrator).

---

28 Other recent international arbitration rules also appear to favor preservation of equality between the parties in the appointment of the tribunal over the interest of freedom of a party to choose an arbitrator. See WIPO Arbitration Rules, Article 18 (distinguishing between joint claimants and joint respondents and requiring appointment of all arbitrators by the institution when respondents fail to make a joint appointment); AAA International Arbitration Rules (1997) Article 6(5) (unless parties have agreed otherwise, institution to name all arbitrators if joint claimants or joint respondents named).

CHAPTER 13

ARBITRATOR DISQUALIFICATION OR INCAPACITY

13.01 Rejection of nomination, challenge, and disqualification

The issue of the qualifications or performance of an arbitrator may occur at three different times:

i) By request of a party, after an arbitrator has been nominated by the opposing party, or is being considered for appointment by the Court, but prior to confirmation or appointment.

ii) By challenge, at any time throughout the proceedings after confirmation or appointment by the Court;

iii) By determination of the Court that the arbitrator is not fulfilling his functions, at any time throughout the proceedings.

The Court's authority is derived from Articles 11 and 12 of the Rules which describe the arbitrator's duty to advise the Secretariat of facts concerning his independence, the time periods within which challenges must be made, and the procedures and powers of the Court of Arbitration relating to the composition of the arbitral tribunal at every stage of the proceedings.

The Court has a duty not to appoint or confirm an arbitrator who is not independent of the parties involved in the arbitration,[1] and must rule on any challenge to an arbitrator made by a party "whether for an alleged lack of independence or otherwise."[2] If the challenge is accepted, the arbitrator will be replaced.[3] In addition, the Court has the power to replace any arbitrator at

---

1   "Every arbitrator must be and remain independent of the parties involved in the arbitration." (Article 7(1)).

2   Article 11(1).

3   Articles 11(3) and 12(1).

any time during the proceedings, on its own motion, if the arbitrator is not properly fulfilling his functions.[4]

Questions relating to an arbitrator's qualifications are frequently raised at the earliest stage possible, which is when a party has nominated an arbitrator but he has not yet been confirmed. Early action is facilitated by the provision in Article 7(2) that the Secretariat will provide to the parties information received from the proposed arbitrator relevant to his independence, and will invite comment. Adverse comment technically does not constitute a challenge under Articles 11(1) and (2) since the nominee has not yet become an arbitrator. An objection at this stage is merely an element to be taken into consideration in the confirmation process.

There is substantial evidence that the Court of Arbitration is more likely to refuse the confirmation of an arbitrator than to sustain a challenge once an arbitrator has been appointed. A study of the period 1986-1988 indicated that out of 46 cases where the issue of independence of an arbitrator was raised prior to confirmation or appointment, the arbitrator was not confirmed or appointed in 33 (or 72%) of the cases (out of the 33, seven had been the result of withdrawal by the arbitrator).[5] On the other hand, in respect to challenges of arbitrators subsequent to their being confirmed or appointed by the Court, only seven out of 59 (9%) succeeded.[6] A later study, for the period 1988-1994, confirms a similarly low success rate for challenges of arbitrators already confirmed or appointed by the Court (12%).[7]

Certainly, where an objection is made at the very earliest stage of the proceedings the Court should be more willing to give weight to a party's objection to an arbitrator than it would after the proceedings were well under way. The Court of Arbitration must keep a healthy suspicion of challenges made in the course of proceedings, as they may represent a dilatory tactic of the challenging party. Indeed, challenges at the very end of the proceedings—when the arbitrators are deliberating or the Court scrutinizing the award—seldom succeed because the circumstances lend themselves to the inference that they are made for dilatory or non-meritorious reasons, although this may not always be the case.[8] However, the infrequency of success of challenges is also due to the fact that clear instances of lack of arbitrator independence are often weeded out at the confirmation/appointment stage of the proceedings.

---

4   Article 12(2).

5   Stephen Bond, *The Experience of the ICC Court of Arbitration in the Selection and Confirmation/Appointment of Arbitrators, in* THE ARBITRAL PROCESS AND THE INDEPENDENCE OF ARBITRATORS, ICC Publication No. 472 (1991) 9, 12.

6   *Id*, at 12, reporting on a five-year period.

7   Dominique Hascher, *ICC Practice in Relation to the Appointment, Confirmation, Challenge and Replacement of Arbitrators*, 6 ICC BULL. 11, 12 (November 1995).

8   *Id*. at 16, *see* Emmanuel Gaillard, *Les manoeuvres dilatoires des parties et des arbitres dans l'arbitrage commercial international*, 1990 REV. ARB. 570.

In any event, there is no difference in the standard of independence applied by the Court in the confirmation/appointment stage and in ruling on later challenges when the stage of the proceedings at which the issue arises is fortuitous. For instance, parties have sometimes been provided with an arbitrator's curriculum vitae only after the Court has confirmed his nomination. (Current practice is to communicate such information before confirmation.) If this is the first time a party knows anything about its adversary's nominee, it should not be required to bear a heavier burden to challenge the appointment. After all, one can hardly make an objection to an arbitrator solely on the grounds that he is unknown. Moreover, when a challenge is made on the grounds of lack of impartiality of the arbitrator based on the conduct of the arbitrator during the proceedings, obviously a challenge can only be made from and after the dates of such conduct.

There is, however, a procedural difference between decisions on confirmation and decisions on challenge. The issue of confirmation of a party-nominated arbitrator may be decided by a three-man Committee of the Court or, where the arbitrator's statement of independence has been filed without qualification or a qualified statement has not given rise to objection, by the Secretary General (and in his absence by the General Counsel and Deputy Secretary General).[9] The challenge of an arbitrator pursuant to Article 11(1) of the Rules, on the other hand, is considered of such importance that it can be determined only by the Court in plenary session after consideration of a report by one of its members.[10]

The challenge of an arbitrator under Article 11(1) of the Rules is a serious step in the proceedings, which a party may initiate by filing with the Secretariat of the Court a written statement specifying the facts and circumstances on which the challenge is based. To permit the Court to rule on the admissibility and, if applicable, the merits of the challenge, the Secretariat is required pursuant to Article 11(3) to solicit, for transmission to the Court, the views of the concerned arbitrator, the other members of the tribunal, and the adverse party.[11] The preliminary issue of admissibility principally concerns whether a

---

9   Article 9(2) of the Rules; Article 5, Internal Rules. Approvals by the Secretary General or his delegate are reported to the Court at its next session. In the case where the Secretary General considers that the arbitrator should not be confirmed the matter is referred to the Court.

10   Pursuant to Article 4(5) of the Internal Rules, the Court determines the decisions that may be taken by the Committee of the Court. The Court's President reported that its decision on challenges under the 1998 Rules would be decided only in plenary sessions. Robert Briner, *The Implementation of the 1998 ICC Rules of Arbitration*, 8 ICC BULL. 7, 9 (December 1997). This discretionary practice thus perpetuates what had been a formal limitation of the powers of the Committee in Article 11 of the 1988 Internal Rules, now abolished.

11   Article 11(3) of the Rules requires the Secretariat to afford "an opportunity for the arbitrator concerned . . . and any other member of the Arbitral Tribunal, to comment in writing." This diplomatic and precatory language shows sensitivity to the delicate situation of co-arbitrators, who frequently do not find it necessary to reply.

challenge was timely made. The decision on admissibility, like the decision on the merits, is made in plenary session of the Court.[12]

The mere filing of a challenge does not automatically suspend an ICC arbitral proceeding, and the issue of suspension is not considered by the Court. It is within the discretion of the arbitral tribunal whether to suspend the proceedings or certain parts of it. The tribunal should take into account such factors as whether rulings are about to be made which seriously affect the substance of rights and obligations of the parties, such as the rendering of awards which may be called into question later if arbitrators are replaced. In a November 1999 communication denying a request for suspension of proceedings during the pendency of a challenge, an arbitral tribunal cited Article 14(1) of the Rules as requiring it to "proceed within as short a time as possible . . ." The tribunal deemed that this requirement compelled it to continue the proceedings (in this case, the making of the Terms of Reference) in face of a challenge, although it reserved the right to suspend proceedings if the outcome of those proceedings seriously affected the substance of rights and obligations of the parties.

The challenge procedure is limited to the exchange of documents and written comments. No oral submissions may be made to the Court, whose decision on a challenge, like all of its decisions confirming, appointing or replacing arbitrators, is considered administrative in nature. The written comments submitted by individual arbitrators and parties are communicated by the Secretariat to all the parties and arbitrators, pursuant to Article 11(3) of the Rules, an addition in 1998 which reversed the prior practice that comments from an arbitrator were considered confidential and were not transmitted to the parties and the other arbitrators. The new requirement increases the transparency and fairness of the challenge procedure, and is essential to afford due process to the challenging party. On the other hand, since their comments will be made known, it may also increase the reluctance of arbitrators to comment on the performance of a co-arbitrator.

The role of the Court of Arbitration, accepted by the parties when they agree to arbitration under the Rules, is designed to be expeditious and summary. Article 7(4) of the Rules encourages this by providing that the Court's decision shall be final and that the reasons for the Court's decision shall not be communicated.

Nevertheless, the decisions relating to the composition of the tribunal are so important and sensitive that a very substantial amount of time must be spent by the Court on challenges, in spite of the fact that many of them are clearly made for dilatory purposes.

---

12   Article 11(2).

13.02 The Court's standards and their source

The Rules give the Court administrative power to determine the composition of ICC arbitral tribunals. The Court's decisions on challenges are deemed a matter of administration (establishing acceptable tribunals) rather than the exercise of jurisdictional power (the resolution of a dispute between the parties).[13] This approach is confirmed by the general provisions of Article 1(2) that the "the Court does not itself settle disputes" and of Article 7(4) that the Court does not give reasons for its decisions on challenges.[14]

The drafters of the Rules have thus preserved the administrative discretion of the Court in this area. As a consequence, however, the grounds for its decisions are a matter of conjecture.

Very little indication of the reasons for refusal to confirm arbitrators is given in the ICC Rules. Article 7(1) states that "Every arbitrator must be and remain independent of the parties involved in the arbitration."[15] But Article 11(1)

---

13 Such administrative decisions constitute part of its institutional role of supervising arbitration in a manner agreed to by the parties when they accepted the ICC Rules. As a consequence of the administrative nature of these decisions, French courts have ruled that no interlocutory judicial review will be permitted of the Court of Arbitration's action on a challenge to an arbitrator; nor may the ICC be held liable for damages in respect thereto, as long as it has respected the procedural obligations of the Rules. *Cour d'appel*, Paris, 15 January 1985, 1986 REV. ARB. 87; *Cour de cassation, Deuxième chambre civile*, 7 October 1987, 1987 REV. ARB. 179; *Tribunal de grande instance*, Paris, 28 March 1984, 1985 REV. ARB. 141. *See also*, Dominique Hascher, *ICC Practice in Relation to the Appointment, Confirmation, Challenge and Replacement of Arbitrators*, 6 ICC BULL. 4 (November 1995). However, fundamental issues concerning the composition of the arbitral tribunal may be raised in judicial review of, or execution proceedings concerning, an interim or final award. In addition, mandatory law in effect at the seat of arbitration may in some jurisdictions permit a party to bypass the ICC Court and immediately challenge an arbitrator before the relevant municipal court. Such was the situation in the well-known Swiss case of Westland Helicopters Ltd. v. Arab Republic of Egypt *et al.*, *Tribunal fédéral Suisse*, 10 September 1985, 1986 SWISS BULL. 16, 24 September 1986, 109 LA SEMAINE JUDICIAIRE 1 (1987), XII YEARBOOK 186 (1987); *see* J. Art, *Challenge of Arbitrators: Is an Institutional Decision Final?* 2 ARB. INT. 261 (1986). This situation has been changed for international arbitrations taking place in Switzerland by Article 180 of the Swiss Law on International Private Law of 1987 which provides that a court will decide a challenge in interim proceedings only where "the parties have not determined the procedure for challenge" which is not the case in ICC arbitration. Possibility for post award request for annulment on the grounds of lack of independence or lack of impartiality of an arbitrator subsists in most jurisdictions, however. For consideration of the situation in the United States, see Hunt v. Mobil Oil Corp., 583 F. Supp. 1092 (S.D.N.Y. 1985) (no interlocutory review allowed), 654 F. Supp. 1487 (S.D.N.Y. 1987) (grounds for challenge reviewed and rejected in confirmation proceedings). *See also* A.T. & T. etc., infra. 13.04 (iii).

14 Article 7(4) provides:

The decisions of the Court as to the appointment, confirmation, challenge or replacement of an arbitrator shall be final and the reasons for such decisions as to the appointment, confirmation, challenge, or replacement of an arbitrator shall not be communicated.

15 Note that the arbitrator is required to be independent from all the parties and not just the nominating party. In one matter known to the authors a party succeeded in a pre-appointment objection on the ground that it used, in matters unrelated to the arbitration, the firm of solicitors of which the arbitrator nominated by the other party was a partner, and intended to continue to use it. Although any conceivable lack of independence would have been *favorable* to the objecting

providing for a right of challenge provides no inkling of the grounds therefore. Accordingly, parties may make any argument to support their challenge they feel is consonant with the fair administration of international commercial arbitration and are not limited to the provisions of any particular national law.

Article 7 sets out independence as the defining requirement for ICC arbitrators. The nature of independence is examined in section 13.03 and the extent of required disclosure in the arbitrator's statement of independence is taken up in section 13.04. It must not be forgotten, however, that the independent arbitrator has as his prime duty to act impartially as is set out in Article 15(2) of the Rules providing that

   "[i]n all cases, the Arbitral Tribunal shall act fairly and impartially . . .".

In a certain sense, the duty of independence is only important insofar as it indicates that the arbitrator will be able to act impartially as is required in any system of justice.[16] In these circumstances it may be asked why the Rules, which now provide that the arbitrator shall *act* impartially, do not provide that, as a condition of selection, an arbitrator shall *be* "independent and impartial" as do many other arbitration rules.[17] The answer is rooted in the history of the development of the ICC Rules[18] and in the observation that independence is capable of demonstration by objective criteria (financial and similar ties) while partiality or bias is demonstrated by conduct, which only can take place after appointment. Thus while the Rules do not separately treat impartiality as a condition of the appointment of an arbitrator the Court has the duty of insuring that the parties are afforded fair and impartial proceedings and will sanction partial conduct by an arbitrator which may have a prejudicial effect on the arbitration. This is taken up in Sections 13.05 "Grounds for challenge" and 13.07 "Standards of conduct for arbitrators during the proceedings."

---

party the Court was persuaded that it would be better to have arbitrators with no entanglements at all, at least where the objection was raised at the earliest stage of the proceeding.

16   This point was made clear in the 1996 English Arbitration Act which requires the "impartiality" but not the "independence" of arbitrators. As described in the Departmental Advisory Committee ("DAC") REPORT ON THE ARBITRATION BILL Section 104 (1996): "We should emphasize that we intend to lose nothing of significance by omitting reference to independence. Lack of this quality may well give rise to justifiable doubts about impartiality, which is covered, but if it does not, then we cannot see anything of significance that we have omitted by not using this term."

17   *See, e.g.,* AAA International Rules (1997), Rule 7. LCIA Rules (1998), Article 5.2 WIPO Rules (1994). Article 22.

18   The specific requirement of the "independence" of the arbitrator from the party appointing him was only added in 1975 which was extended in 1980 to include independence from all of the parties. In the 1998 revision process the ICC Commission on International Arbitration discussed adding the requirement of impartiality to Article 7(1) but no consensus was obtained on its definition, and it was recognized that it was difficult to determine in advance what personal characteristics would guarantee future impartial conduct. As one member put it: "At what point does general sympathy and predisposition turn into disqualifying bias or prejudice?"

The Court's mission, under its Statutes, is to ensure the application of the Rules. The Court certainly does not act as an institutional appendage of any national court system when making a determination relating to arbitrators' qualifications. It is not bound by any national laws, and the standard which it seeks to uphold is simply that of the inherent quality of ICC arbitration. In fact, the Court frequently applies more exacting standards than those of the law of the place of arbitration. At the same time, although it is not bound to apply standards of arbitrator qualification in force at the seat of arbitration, the Court is nevertheless mindful of the general mandate of Article 35: "the Court . . . shall act in the spirit of these Rules and shall make every effort to make sure that the Award is enforceable at law." Thus serious consideration is given to arguments that particular arbitrator qualifications are required by mandatory provisions of national law at the seat of arbitration.

Despite the difficulties of determining the Court's criteria of disqualification, a number of cases have become known from information given by parties or by the publication of the record of ICC proceedings in subsequent court actions. Some of the more usual grounds will be examined below.

13.03 Independence required of arbitrator

As discussed in Section 12.04, the ICC's requirements of independence for a party-nominated arbitrator are long standing and existed even under the 1955 Rules, although not explicitly stated there. These requirements were explored in a United States federal court case, where recognition of an ICC award rendered in India under the 1955 Rules was opposed.[19] The grounds for the challenge were newly discovered evidence that the arbitrator, an Indian senior counsel (barrister) appointed by the Indian party seeking enforcement, had in fact previously acted as counsel to that party in several litigations, and had not revealed this fact when the arbitral tribunal was constituted. In an initial decision, the United States District Court held that the award was final and enforceable. It stated, *inter alia*, that the ICC Rules did not at the time require arbitrator independence and thus there was no obstacle to enforcement of the award in the United States.

In proceedings for reconsideration of the decision, the party opposing enforcement submitted an extensive affidavit by Robert Thompson, an English solicitor and a former Secretary General of the Court of Arbitration, concerning the practice of the Court under the 1955 Rules. The affidavit, as quoted in the court's opinion, stated in part:

> It is true that the 1975 rules make it explicit that a party shall nominate only an independent arbitrator. Furthermore, the Court of Arbitration, making use of the biographical data which the arbitrator nominee is to

---

19 Fertilizer Corporation of India *et al.* v. IDI Management Inc., 517 F. Supp. 948 (S.D. Ohio, 1981); extracts *in* VII YEARBOOK 382 (1982).

supply it with has an obligation to approve the nomination only of arbitrators who, *prima facie*, are independent of the party appointing them. Hence, under the 1975 rules, the Court has a more explicit mandate to act on its own initiative to screen party-nominated arbitrators, and to appoint only those who, from the information given to them by the arbitrator, appear to demonstrate sufficient qualities of independence.

However, nothing in the text of Article 2.4 of the 1975 rules, having to do with the nomination and appointment of arbitrators, and the additional burdens of the Court of Arbitration in respect thereto, removes the possibility of disqualification of an arbitrator at the instance of the other party, a provision which remains substantially the same under the 1955 rules (Article 7.4) and 1975 rules (Article 2.7). As it has been pointed out above, lack of independence has been, in the ICC practice, a cause for disqualification under the 1955 rules. It continues to be so under the 1975 rules.[20]

Mr. Thompson went on to conclude that the appointment of an independent arbitrator and the obligation of disclosure by an arbitrator had always been fundamental and accepted rules of ICC arbitration.

The U.S. District Court judge concluded as follows with respect to the affidavit:

This Court is persuaded by Mr. Thompson's reasoning that the ICC rules have always considered that the arbitrators be impartial and/or independent, and that any information bearing on the ability of an arbitrator to be impartial and/or independent must be disclosed.[21] Compare *Commonwealth Coating Corp. v. Continental Casualty Co.*, 393 U.S. 145 (1968) for requirement of any arbitrators to disclose any dealing which might create even "an impression of possible bias."

Despite this finding, the court did not reverse its decision recognizing the award. In light of the fact that the award was unanimous, the court found that the relations between the arbitrator and the party did not render the proceedings so "tainted" that recognition of the award would be contrary to public policy of the United States. Hence the award was recognized under the New York Convention.

While it is undoubtedly established that all ICC arbitrators must be independent, the definition of "independence" remains elusive. An arbitrator may be biased either intellectually or financially. The most classic case of the former is where the arbitrator has previously served as counsel to the party appointing him and has given a legal opinion on points at issue. Some commentators have viewed such participation as an absolute bar to serving as a party-appointed arbitrator, even with the agreement of the other party. Judge Pierre

---

20   Fertilizer Corporation of India *et al.* v. IDI Management Inc., 530 F. Supp. 542, at 543 (S.D. Ohio, 1981); extracts *in* VIII YEARBOOK 419 (1983).

21   530 F. Supp. at 544.

Bellet, a former First President of the French Supreme Court, once said that it is a more serious obstacle to impartiality to have given a prior consultation in a case than to have ties of friendship with the party; ties of friendship may be disregarded as a matter of professional rigor, but pride in adhering to one's earlier opinion is a stronger emotion.[22]

Lack of financial independence is most evident when the nominee is otherwise employed by the nominating party or has some other financial interest in the arbitration. Such economic interests, creating a relationship of subordination between the party and the arbitrator or a pecuniary interest in the outcome, are compelling grounds for challenge.

One of the most difficult tasks of the Court has been to apply these principles in cases involving parties from countries with centralized economies or from developing nations with government controlled economies. If it is clear that an employee of a parent company cannot (without the consent of the other party) be an arbitrator in a case involving a subsidiary, what can be said of the appointment of a government official in a dispute concerning a state enterprise or agency? What of the appointment of the director of one state enterprise in a dispute involving another state enterprise?

These situations raise problems of independence from a different angle than the cases arising in market economies. If in developed East European socialist economies, for instance, the functional separation of different state enterprises may be demonstrated,[23] the same is not true in many developing countries with state controlled economies. The functionary nominated as an arbitrator may in fact be one of a very limited number of trained and experienced jurists. One may surmise that instructions or information will go to

---

22   Pierre Bellet, Intervention, *in* E. Minoli, *Relations entre partie et arbitre*, 1970 REV. ARB. 221, at 233.

23   This was found to be the case by the House of Lords in Czarnikow v. Rolimpex [1978] 2 *All E. R.* 1043, with the result that a Polish state entity could plead *force majeure* based on acts of the Polish State. More recently an *ad hoc* arbitral tribunal has come to a contrary result concerning another Polish enterprise, Award of 9 September 1983, XII YEARBOOK 63 (1987). The issue has been raised in other jurisdictions with varying results. *See, e.g.*, Crédit populaire d'Algérie v. Sapvin, *Cour de cassation,* France, 14 February 1978, 1980 REVUE CRITIQUE DU DROIT INTERNATIONAL PRIVÉ 707, as well as the commentary by Pierre Mayer, id. at 709. For a review of a number of problems arising from the relationship between state agencies and the state in international arbitration, *see generally*, Pierre Lalive, *Arbitration with Foreign States or State Controlled Entities: Some Practical Questions* in Julian Lew, ed. CONTEMPORARY PROBLEMS IN INTERNATIONAL ARBITRATION, (Queen Mary's College, University of London 1986) p. 289 and *Sur la Bonne Foi dans l'Exécution des Contracts d'Etat* in MELANGES OFFERTS À RAYMOND VANDER ELST 425 (Editions Nemesis, Brussels, 1986), p. 425.In this connection, it is interesting to note the following paragraph from Article 2 of the 1982 Rules of Conciliation, Arbitration and Expertise of the Euro-Arab Chambers of Commerce dealing with the Boards set up under those rules to supervise the work of arbitrators:

> The members of the Boards shall be completely independent and undertake not to accept any instruction from any authority. Government officials shall only be eligible for membership of the Boards so long as during their tenure of such positions they have no governmental or official functions.

him directly from other officials involved as litigants. Nevertheless, the Court in these cases has tended not to insist on a degree of separation between the government party and its nominee that the political and economic conditions of the country are simply unable to provide. To insist otherwise would in effect bar parties from some developing countries from naming an arbitrator of their own nationality while parties from developed countries would be able to do so. Such a result would appear to be a greater wrong than that of failure to attain the ideal of independence. To avoid this problem, parties contracting with developing countries may consider proposing an arbitration clause that requires all arbitrators to be of neutral nationality. Such clauses are often seen in practice (*see* Section 7.01).

It has been noted that the parties are free to agree that one or both party-appointed arbitrators need not be independent. In fact, some 30 years ago a Secretary General of the Court of Arbitration favored extending to arbitrations conducted under the ICC Rules such a practice, where each *arbitre-partie* is expected to support his party's position before the neutral chairman, as long as both parties have been informed of the circumstances and have agreed to them.[24]

Frequently, one of the parties nominates an arbitrator it considers truly independent only to find that its adversary names a person with whom it has close links. What should the first party do?

The answer depends upon many factors. Irrespective of one's right in principle to insist that all arbitrators be independent, the advisability of a challenge remains a question of tactics more than one of philosophy. After years of observing international arbitration in practice, the authors have concluded it is best to challenge as infrequently as possible, perhaps on the maxim "better the devil you know than the one you don't." At least for the claimant, little purpose is served by causing one's adversary to have to replace its nominee; the proceedings are delayed, and the replacement nominee may be no more independent than his predecessor. A well-advised challenging party should thus not only be sure of the grounds for challenge, but should also evaluate the ultimate benefits of replacement. Does the challengeable arbitrator in fact present a specific danger to the arbitration, due to his status or prior acts? An arbitrator who shows himself to be the mere agent of a party is probably not worth challenging. His weight within the tribunal will be discounted and the chairman is likely to lend a more attentive ear to his other co-arbitrator.

---

24   F. Eisemann, *La deontologie de l'arbitre commercial international*, 1969 REV. ARB. 217. However, in current ICC practice such an agreement would be extremely unusual as the former Secretary General of the Court of Arbitration has remarked, commenting on this section. Bond, *supra* Note 5. It has been reported that the Court has occasionally refused to approve arbitrators who it did not consider to be sufficiently independent even when no party to the arbitration had objected. *See* DERAINS & SCHWARTZ, 130.

Some practitioners, to the contrary, have a "scorched earth" approach to ICC arbitration. Any motion that can be made will be made. The main result is to cause delay. While the parties do have the right to insist that their adversaries appoint an independent arbitrator, the debate on the issue should not descend to the trivial.

Finally, it should be noted that it is perfectly proper for a party to discuss the case with the potential arbitrator before his nomination.[25] Indeed, it would be irresponsible for an arbitrator to accept nomination without some knowledge of the scope and nature of the dispute. However, this type of preliminary discussion involves the potential arbitrator as a listener only; he should not give advice or express his views of the case. The purpose of such an interview is to permit, on the one hand, the arbitrator to determine whether he has the necessary knowledge and expertise, the time available, and the willingness to accept a nomination and, on the other hand, the party to determine, based on such a face to face meeting, which of several possible candidates is its preferred choice. It is the obligation of the arbitrator to control the scope of any interview, to avoid any discussion of the issues in dispute, and generally assure that the meeting takes place in a controlled environment (generally at the arbitrator's office or premises) for a limited time period (many have recommended that such a meeting should not exceed 30 minutes).

13.04 Arbitrator's duty of disclosure

i) The Rule requirement of disclosure

Article 7(2) and 7(3) of the Rules imposes in the following terms a continuing obligation on the arbitrator to disclose all information relevant to his independence:

> 7(2) Before appointment or confirmation, a prospective arbitrator shall sign a statement of independence and disclose in writing to the Secretariat any facts or circumstances which *might be of such a nature* as to call into question the arbitrator's independence *in the eyes of the parties*. The Secretariat shall provide such information to the parties in writing and fix a time limit for any comments from them. (Emphasis added.)

> 7(3) An arbitrator shall immediately disclose in writing to the Secretariat and to the parties any facts or circumstances of a similar nature which may arise during the arbitration.

---

25 The IBA Code of Ethics, Article 5.1 (1985) allows pre-appointment communications with a prospective party nominated arbitrator and sets out as well guidelines for communications between party nominated arbitrators and their nominating party regarding the choice of the third arbitrator. The subject of arbitrator interviews is canvassed in Doak Bishop and Lucy Reed, *Practical Guidelines for Interviewing, Selecting and Challenging Party-Appointed Arbitrators in International Commercial Arbitration*, 14 ARB. INT. 395 (1998).

The disclosure requirement is intended to be broad. Arbitrators are not only to disclose circumstances which "in their opinion"[26] might call into question their independence "in the eyes of the parties" but circumstances which "might be of such a nature" to raise such a question. Moreover, the necessity of imagining what information might be considered relevant in the eyes of the parties emphasizes the need for the arbitrator to be prepared to disclose information even though he was convinced not only that he was independent but that objectively speaking the facts in issue would not put that independence into question. As a former Secretary General of the Court has put it:

> Because in ICC arbitration the parties are generally of different nationalities and thus at least one party is of a nationality other than that of the prospective arbitrator, it is especially important that the nominee stretch beyond a purely national and domestic perspective and make a special effort to consider the facts and circumstances as the parties might view and construe them.[27]

The arbitrator must disclose not only relationships or interests which he believes might impair his independence, but also those which *any of the parties* might consider as impairing it. He must be able to certify that he is impartial in fact and must also reveal all relevant information which might carry the *appearance* of bias.

In an international arbitration, the duty of disclosure is especially important since a party may not have easy access to information regarding the reputation and relationships of an arbitrator domiciled in a foreign country. As the ICC has not published criteria for the independence required of arbitrators (unlike the American Arbitration Association, which has published a Code of Ethics for Arbitrators in Commercial Disputes),[28] the Secretariat of the Court requests nominees to reveal any personal or financial interest or relationship that might affect their impartiality. The nominee is asked to provide to the Secretariat a curriculum vitae as well as a Statement of Independence. If the nominee is aware of any fact which might lead any party to question his independence, he is required to note it on the Statement, in which case it is considered to be made "with reservations." Pursuant to Article 7(2) of the Rules

---

26   This expression was used in the 1975 Rules. It was abandoned in 1988, this modification being carried over into the 1998 Rules. The prior text suggested that the arbitrator should judge by his own standards what information would be of interest to a party, although even then the ultimate test was whether *the party* would consider the information relevant, not that it necessarily *was* relevant.

27   Stephen Bond, *The Experience of the ICC in the Confirmation/Appointment Stage of an Arbitration in* THE ARBITRAL PROCESS AND THE INDEPENDENCE OF ARBITRATORS, ICC Publication No. 472 (1991), p. 11-12.

28   *See* H. Holtzmann, *The First Code of Ethics for Arbitrators in Commercial Disputes*, 33 BUSINESS LAWYER 309 (1977). Nor has the ICC adopted as a mandatory norm the IBA's articulation of "Ethics for International Arbitrators" (1987), reprinted in 3 ARB. INT. 72 (1987), and 2 MEALEY'S INT. ARB. REP. 287 (1987).

(*see* Section 13.01), the Secretariat provides to the parties any information received relevant to the arbitrator's independence and permits the parties to comment thereon.

ii) Failure of disclosure as a ground for challenge

It may be argued that the failure of an arbitrator to disclose pertinent facts about his relationship to a dispute or to a party is in and of itself sufficient grounds for challenge even though such facts—if disclosed in timely fashion—would not necessarily have been found by the ICC Court to justify disqualification. Such failure of disclosure may be said to constitute evidence of partiality. Such a challenge might be made to the Court on the basis of information discovered during the proceedings. More frequently, they have been made before national courts in review proceedings.

The first duty of an arbitrator to the parties and to the ICC is thus the obligation of disclosure. The challenge mechanism of the ICC Rules can function realistically and effectively only if this obligation is respected. It is furthermore an important guarantee of the trustworthiness of international arbitration to resolve international disputes. As one commentator has put it:

> The challenge of an arbitrator is an important correcting institution in favour of the parties. In the case of a conflict of interest, whether existing before or during the arbitration proceedings, an arbitrator can be challenged. That arbitrator who decides before being officially challenged to give up his functions deserves credit. Even after a challenge procedure has been started, it is laudable for an arbitrator to withdraw voluntarily from his functions as there are certain ethical standards involved. Thus an arbitrator has to avoid any suspicion of being corrupt.[29]

The comment points out a delicate issue: should not an arbitrator be viewed with suspicion if he aggressively rejects any possible implications of partiality from relationships which reasonably trouble a challenging party? To what extent is it acceptable for an arbitrator to insist on remaining in function? It has been observed that in cases involving large amounts, the fee the arbitrator would obtain may be a corrupting influence *per se* and a desire to stay in office, no matter what, may be the result of other than objective considerations.[30]

On the other hand, there are cases where advocates will challenge arbitrators on the slightest pretense as a dilatory tactic rather than as a reflection of a *bona fide* fear of partiality. Acquiescing in insubstantial challenges would lead to the withdrawal or arbitrary disqualification of highly skilled arbitrators, often selected after a careful search. In such cases, the arbitrator should certainly stand firm and await the decision of the Court of Arbitration.

---

29   O. Glossner, *Sociological aspects of international commercial arbitration*, *in* THE ART OF ARBITRATION (Liber Amicorum for Pieter Sanders) 145 (1982).

30   *Id.*

iii) National court precedents regarding the duty of disclosure

In almost all the leading international arbitral centers national courts have confirmed the existence of an arbitrator's duty of disclosure and have been called on to determine the extent of such a duty and the consequences of its breach in a variety of situations.[31] Given the extremely broad range of matters in which a disclosure duty may be implied and the differing concepts of the role of the arbitrator (particularly the party-appointed arbitrator) in different countries and legal systems it is not always easy to generalize from the existing precedents.

Fortunately, the English Court of Appeals has had the occasion to interpret the meaning and effect of the disclosure obligations set out in Article 2 of the ICC Rules in combination with the duties imposed at common law and by English arbitration statutes. In *AT&T Corporation and Lucent Technologies Inc. v. Saudi Cable Company*[32] challenge of the presiding arbitrator (of a three

---

31   The highest courts of France, Switzerland, and the United States have all insisted on the arbitrators' duty of disclosure. In the Consorts Ury v. Galeries Lafayette case, *Cour de cassation*, 13 April 1972, 1975 REV. ARB. 235 and commented on *in* F. Eisemann, *La double sanction prévue par la Convention de la BIRD en cas de collusion ou d'ententes similaires entre un arbitre et une partie qui l'a désigné*, 23 ANNUAIRE FRANÇAIS DE DROIT INTERNATIONAL at No. 16, the French *Cour de cassation* set aside an award in a case where it transpired that the winning claimant's nominee as arbitrator had given a legal opinion regarding the case to the claimant before his nomination. In fact, the French Supreme Court was less troubled by the fact that the opinion had been given than by the fact that the defendant had not been informed thereof, thus leading to the conclusion that its consent to arbitration had been vitiated by "a mistake. . . as to the capacity of one of the persons chosen as arbitrator." In the *Orbis* case, *Tribunal fédéral Suisse*, 26 October 1966, ATF 92 I 271 and commented on *in id.*, the Swiss Federal Tribunal was faced with an award rendered by an arbitral tribunal on which had participated the husband of the assistant of one of the parties' lawyer. In holding that the arbitrator was not sufficiently independent, the Federal Tribunal apparently attached more importance to the fact that the circumstances had not been revealed to the other litigant than to the existence of the double-link "family-employee-lawyer" connection. As Judge Panchaud, himself a well-known arbitrator, was to comment later, "the conclusion to be drawn is that each arbitrator should make known his relationship with the party that named him," *Intervention, Symposium on Qualification de l'arbitre international*, 1970 REV. ARB. 203, at 228. In the United States, the leading case is *Commonwealth Coating Corp. v. Continental Casualty Co.*, 393 U.S. 145 (1968), where the Supreme Court held that courts should be more scrupulous to safeguard the impartiality of arbitrators than of judges since arbitrators have a completely free rein to decide issues of fact and law without appellate review, and that arbitrators are thus required to disclose to the parties any dealings which might create even "an impression of possible bias." In that case, the award of a three-man tribunal was set aside because of the chairman's failure to disclose that he had had previous business relations with one of the parties. Even though the losing party's lawyer freely admitted that he would probably not have objected to the chairman if he had known about his past connection with the other side, even though there was no evidence of intentional concealment (the chairman was simply never asked), even though the business relationship had been sporadic (engineering fees of about $12,000 over four to five years, whereas the chairman was one of the most active consulting engineers in his region), and even though finally there was no evidence—nor even an allegation—that the chairman had not conducted himself "entirely fairly and impartially," the Supreme Court held that "any tribunal permitted by law to try cases and controversies not only must be unbiased but also must avoid even the appearance of bias." Accordingly, the failure of disclosure was fatal to the award.

32   Case No. QBCMF 1999/1200/A3 (Court of Appeal, 15 May 2000). The decision below (Q.B. (Commercial Court) 13 October 1999) is reported in 1 ALL ER (Comm) 201.

person tribunal) arose in a very large commercial case involving the liability, *vel non*, of AT&T to Saudi Cable for failure to negotiate in good faith and agree prices and terms of supply of cable for a $ 4.6 billion telecommunications expansion project ("TEP-6") in Saudi Arabia. The arbitrators had found in a first interim award (in 1996) that AT&T had bound itself in an enforceable pre-bid agreement to undertake negotiations in good faith for such supply and that it had no right to terminate the agreement. In consequence, the parties were instructed to undertake negotiations in fulfilment of their contractual obligations. These negotiations failed and a Second Partial Award (in 1998) determined that AT&T had not negotiated in good faith. Arbitral proceedings continued in the autumn of 1998 for the purpose of determining damages payable by AT&T.

In November of 1998 a fact was uncovered which was to cause considerable surprise, confusion, and concern to the parties and the arbitrators. At that time Saudi Telecom Company was inviting tenders for another telecommunications project in Saudi Arabia ("TEP-8") and competitors tendering for it included Lucent Technologies (the AT&T technology arm which had by this time been spun off as a separate company by means of a public offering) and Nortel of Canada, a competitor of AT&T and the disappointed bidder for the TEP-6 contract with Saudi Cable which had been awarded to AT&T and had become the subject of the arbitration. Nortel was particularly disappointed because it had terminated a 55 year old preferential supply arrangement with Bell Canada in return for a promise of US government support for the TEP-6 project; this support which apparently was neutralized by AT&T's lobbying efforts.

In reviewing Nortel's web site for information pertinent to the TEP-8 project, a Lucent manager found, much to his surprise, that the highly respected and internationally experienced Canadian arbitrator nominated as Chairman of the AT&T/Saudi Cable Tribunal by mutual agreement of the parties (and confirmed by the ICC Court) was in fact a non-executive director of Nortel. (It was later determined that he also owned 474 shares of Nortel and 300 shares of AT&T.)

AT&T's initial surprise that it had not been informed of the arbitrator's ties with an aggressive competitor, especially one that had competed for the same project, soon turned to a conviction that it should seek recusal of the arbitrator based on the confusing circumstances of the failure of disclosure and the fact that AT&T had been concerned from the beginning about the confidential nature of commercial information to be disclosed in the arbitration and had warned the arbitrators about it. Another factor, almost always present in recusal matters and not to be overlooked, was that AT&T had lost the two partial awards made by the tribunal presided by the arbitrator in question, and was awaiting a third award which would establish the amount that it would have to pay as damages to Saudi Cable.

The difficulty of the non-disclosure was that at the time of being considered by the parties for nomination as Chairman the candidate had stated that he

knew of no facts or circumstances which would call into question his independence as an arbitrator (a position which he later confirmed in the Arbitrator's Statement of Independence which he subsequently filed with the ICC as
required). At the same time the arbitrator conveyed to AT&T's lawyers a copy
of his curriculum vitae which listed a number of positions and directorships
which he held but on which there was no mention whatsoever of Nortel. Subsequently, the arbitrator filled out the ICC's Statement of Independence,
checking the box besides the text which indicated no conflicts[33]:

> I am independent of each of the parties and intend to remain so; to the
> best of my knowledge, there are no facts or circumstances, past or pres-
> ent, that need to be disclosed because they might be of such a nature as
> to call into question my independence in the eyes of any of the parties.

At the time of submitting this declaration to the ICC he submitted to the Secretariat as required his curriculum vitae which *did* reveal his non-executive directorship with Nortel. This document was never sent by the ICC Secretariat to the
parties contrary to its usual (and now scrupulously respected) practice. As a result AT&T did not find out that the arbitrator was a director of Nortel until November 1998; nor did it find out that the arbitrator had two c.v.s in circulation,
one of which included the Nortel directorship and the other of which did not.[34]

AT&T filed a challenge with the ICC (after first rejecting the Canadian arbitrator's offer to resign from the Nortel board of directors if that would solve the
problem). On 24 February 1999 the ICC Court rejected the challenge without
(in conformity with its Rules) giving any reason for its decision.[35] On 16 September 1999 the Court released the Tribunal's third partial award which
awarded $ 30,000,000 plus interest as damages against AT&T.[36]

AT&T applied to the English High Court for removal of the Canadian Arbitrator and setting aside the award.[37] Both applications were denied.

The Court of Appeal considered two grounds for appeal: proof of bias and
proof of misconduct (in the technical sense of failure to comply with a proce-

---

33   Slip Opinion, para. 13. In checking this alternative he consciously eliminated the second box
     providing the opportunity, in addition to confirming and asserting his independence, to add "I
     wish to call your attention to the following factors and circumstances which I hereafter disclose
     because I consider that they might be of such a nature as to call into question my independence
     in the eyes of any of the parties."

34   While the circumstances seemed suspicious at the time of initial discovery, by the time of appel-
     late proceedings it "was accepted between the parties that the omission was due to secretarial er-
     ror and was not intentional." No charge of actual bias or impropriety was ever made against the
     arbitrator. (Slip Op., para. 10).

35   Slip Opinion, ¶21.

36   *Id.*

37   The action was brought under Section 1 and 23 of the 1950 Act, the arbitration having been
     commenced prior to the effective date of Arbitration Act 1996.

dure—the disclosure statement required by the ICC Rules— agreed to be binding in the arbitration).

On bias the Court of Appeal quickly eliminated any argument that the arbitrator should be automatically eliminated because he was acting as a judge in his own cause.[38] Nortel was not a party to the arbitration over which the arbitrator presided and hence there was no direct interest. Moreover, if Nortel could be said, because of the size of the TEP-6 and TEP-8 projects, to have some indirect interest in the outcome of the arbitration it was unquestioned that the arbitrator because of his insignificant shareholding in Nortel had no material interest in such outcome. It could not be said that he was acting, even indirectly, in his own cause.

The Court considered more seriously the charge of apparent or unconscious bias. There was no allegation or proof of any actual bias or biased conduct of the arbitrator. Were nevertheless the circumstances such that the court should impute bias to the arbitrator, and if so by what test? The Court first explained, following *R. v. Gough*,[39] that there should be no difference in the test for determination of unconscious bias whether for a judge or an arbitrator, and that AT&T's argument that a lower standard of proof of bias should be required in the case of arbitrators (and accordingly a higher standard of conduct) lacked conviction.[40]

> . . . it would be surprising if a lower threshold applied to arbitration than applied to a court of law. The courts are responsible for the provision of public justice. If there are two standards I would expect a lower threshold to apply to courts of law than applies to a private tribunal whose "judges" are selected by the parties.

The court pointed out that it was in a judicial proceeding[41] and in respect to administration of justice by the courts that Lord Hewart, CJ pronounced his famous aphorism, accepted throughout the common law world, that it is "of fundamental importance that justice should not only be done, but should manifestly and undoubtedly be seen to be done."

The issue before the Court was what words correctly defined the test to be used, in connection with arbitration, to determine whether presumed bias or unconscious bias could be said to exist and action to be required to avoid the appearance of injustice. AT&T sought the application of a lower threshold of proof of indicia of bias and argued that recusal was justified if any "reasonable apprehension" of bias could be said to have existed in the case of the arbitrator.

---

38 Pursuant to the *nemo debet esse judex in propria causa* maxim, see Section 13.05 (iv), *infra*.

39 R. v. Gough, [1993] AC 646.

40 Slip Opinion, ¶40.

41 R. v. Sussex Justices, ex parte McCarthy [1924] 1 KB 256, 259.

The Court declined to depart from the criteria established by the House of Lords in *R. v. Gough*, that it is the duty of the adjudicator in determining whether a judge or arbitrator must be removed or his decision impeached to first ascertain the relevant circumstances and then[42]:

> ... the court should ask itself whether, having regard to those circumstances, there was a real danger of bias on the part of the relevant member of the tribunal in question, in the sense that he might unfairly regard (or have unfairly regarded) with favour, or disfavour the case of a party to the issue under consideration by him.

The Court then considered all the circumstances relevant to the determination whether there was any real danger of bias, including the following:

− the arbitrator was an extremely experienced lawyer and arbitrator who could be relied on to disregard irrelevant considerations;

− the Court accepted the arbitrator's statement that he had been unaware of the TEP-6 project until he was named as arbitrator and did not learn of the TEP-8 project until shortly before the challenge was filed;

− the arbitrator's involvement as Executive Director with Nortel was slight, and his offer to resign showed he did not hold the post in excessive importance; his holding of a few shares was not material;

− there was no suggestion from any quarter that his conduct of his duties as arbitrator betrayed any trace of prejudice.

On the issue of bias the Court found that it was extremely unfortunate that by mistake the information about the Nortel directorship was not disclosed but that the "innocent non-disclosure provides the flimsiest of arguments that the indirect interest of [the arbitrator] in Nortel would or might affect the way he performed his responsibilities as an arbitrator."

Accordingly, the lower court's finding that there was no bias was sustained.

The Court then turned to the second allegation that the arbitrator "misconducted" himself for failure to follow the disclosure requirements of the ICC Rules as he was required to as part of the obligations of the arbitration agreement and incorporated therein.[43]

As a preliminary issue the Court of Appeal disposed of and reversed the finding of the court below that it had no jurisdiction to review any decision by the ICC Court concerning alleged failure of the arbitrator to follow its Rules as to disclosure, and the denial of a challenge based thereon, because of the

---

42   Slip Opinion, ¶ 49, quoting from R. v. Gough.

43   The charge of misconduct was brought under Sections 23(1) and 23(2) of Arbitration Act 1950. The same conduct could be alleged on the ground of "serious irregularity affecting the tribunal, the proceedings or the award" under Section 68 of Arbitration Act 1996.

provisions of Article 2(13) of the Rules [Article 7(4) of the 1998 Rules] that: "Decisions of the Court as to the appointment, confirmation, challenge or replacement of an arbitrator shall be final." The Court of Appeal found that an English court was required to exercise the jurisdiction afforded to it by law to review an award for misconduct (or under Arbitration Act 1996 serious irregularity) without regard to what might be termed the "administrative finality" of the ICC Court's decision on challenge.[44]

Having initially disposed of the bias issue the Court was in a strong position to take a limited view of the scope and effect of the disclosure obligations under the Rules.[45] AT&T maintained that the arbitrator had infringed the rules as to disclosure and had therefore denied to AT&T the right to participate effectively in the choice of the third arbitrator, and to have a third arbitrator of its choice. Moreover, the non-disclosure could not be excused as having been made unknowingly: according to AT&T the arbitrator had a duty to disclose i) at the outset of the arbitration and signature of the Declaration; ii) when during the arbitration it became evident that Nortel had been a disappointed bidder; iii) after the first award when AT&T manifested strongly its concerns about confidentiality and protecting its documents from communication to third parties.

The Court analyzed carefully the obligations of Article 2.7 of the Rules and noted that that disclosure obligation relates to doubts about "independence" of the arbitrator and not, as in the case of Article 12 of the UNCITRAL Model Law, to "impartiality or independence." In most cases it will be a relation with a party which calls into doubt the arbitrator's independence. While not wishing to interpret Article 2.7 in a restrictive manner, the Court noted difficulties in applying the "independence" criteria in respect to relations with third parties but concluded:[46]

> . . . in this case it is not necessary to express any concluded view as to the application of Article 2.7 to a potential arbitrator whose lack of independence is due to a connection with a third party. *If, as I consider the*

---

44   The Court of Appeal expressed a willingness to pay the closest attention to how the ICC Court interpreted its own Rules but noted that since the challenge decision itself was unreasoned it could not be helped by it. It can be predicted, with very little fear of contradiction, that the ICC Court will continue to refuse to give reasons for their decisions on challenges of arbitrators and will continue to maintain that its role on challenges constitutes a fulfillment of administrative rather than adjudicative function.

45   The Court's exercise of its discretionary powers in respect to remedies for any breach of an agreed procedure may also be examined as an issue of the scope of a court's review jurisdiction. For instance, in the absence of proven bias would a failure of disclosure amount to a "serious irregularity" under Arbitration Act 1996 or a procedure "not in accordance with the agreement of the parties" under Article V(1)(d) of the New York Convention?

46   Slip Opinion, ¶51. The Court also rejected the challenge on the grounds that non-disclosure prejudicially affected AT&T's concerns about confidentiality. The disclosure obligation was not aimed at this particular concern.

position to be here, [the arbitrator] is not disqualified from acting as an arbitrator on the grounds of bias at common law, I cannot see how he can be said to lack the necessary independence to which Article 2.7 refers. (Emphasis added.)

The separate opinions of Lord Justices Potter and May cast further doubt, without resolving the issue, on the scope of the obligation of the arbitrator to disclose information regarding relations with third parties under the general obligation of "independence of the parties" under Article 2.7.

In dismissing the appeal on the misconduct point all of the Lord Justices relied at different points in their speeches on the inadvertence of non-disclosure, the lack of prejudice arising out of it, and the inequitable consequences of a setting aside based on formal non-observance of a rule. As Lord Justice Potter stated concerning the misconduct charge:[47]

> [If] breach can be demonstrated, it does not seem to me to be one which could possibly justify the removal of [the Arbitrator] . . ., or the setting aside of any of the awards made. So far as the non-disclosure of [the Arbitrator's] directorship of Nortel was concerned, it was entirely inadvertent. Furthermore, as we have held, no suggestion of real danger of partiality arises or has been substantiated. Nor has any disadvantage in the course of the arbitration been demonstrated . . . To set aside the partial awards or to replace [the Arbitrator] at this stage would be both a costly inconvenience and a substantial injustice to the Respondents.

The English Court of Appeal's decision in *AT&T* is an important contribution to the jurisprudence concerning arbitrator challenge. On the issue of disclosure the Court conditioned the setting aside of the award for a failure of disclosure on some showing of a real danger of bias from the failure, which was lacking in the matter before them. The pragmatism of the approach should serve to preserve the efficacy of awards from attack based on purely formal failures of disclosure.[48] Although the Court found that it was not, in the circumstances of the case, obliged to determine the scope of the concept of an arbitrator's independence under Article 2.7, particularly in respect to relationships with third parties, the case suggests that it was wise of the drafters of the 1998 revision of the Rules not to expand the duty of disclosure to include disclosure of information which a party might consider reflected on the arbitrator's impartiality. While the broadest disclosure is counseled to comply with the spirit of the Rules, the failure to have made the duty more

---

47   Slip Opinion, ¶72, 73.

48   The approach should be contrasted with that of the United States Supreme Court in Commonwealth Coatings v. Continental Casualty Co., 393 U.S. 145 (1968) where it was held that non-disclosure of a relationship with a party would entail setting aside of the award even when it was agreed that if the non-disclosed relationship had been known it would not have occasioned a challenge.

specific may be useful to avoid or limit judicial review based on a party's purely subjective appreciation of the effect on an arbitrator's powers of neutral adjudication of various relationships and contacts. In any event, the Court seemed determined to investigate, in the case of a claim of apparent or unconscious bias, whether in fact that there was any real danger of bias; in the absence thereof the Court would be satisfied that the test not only of justice, but of the appearance of justice, was met.

13.05   Grounds for challenge

i) Grounds not limited to lack of independence

The grounds for challenge under the Rules have never been exhaustively defined. The Court of Arbitration has inherent power to grant a challenge on any grounds it deems appropriate as is specified in Article 11(1) of the Rules:

> A challenge of an arbitrator, whether for an alleged lack of independence *or otherwise*, is made by the submission to the Secretariat of a written statement specifying the facts and circumstances on which the challenge is based. (Emphasis added).

Although the drafting is awkward, it must be concluded, first, that challenges may be made on grounds other than lack of independence and, second, that for such unspecified grounds the wide discretion exercised by the Court in the past is reaffirmed and reinforced. The awkwardness of the text may stem from the ICC's reluctance, due to the particular circumstances of the party-nominated arbitrator, to specify clearly in its rules, as have other institutions, that an arbitrator shall be independent *and* impartial. See Section 13.02, *supra*. In fact, this requirement is implicit, and has been traditionally applied by the Court in its challenge practice to the conduct of all arbitrators, taking into account wherever necessary any special circumstances concerning the party-nominated arbitrator. The practice is reinforced by the addition in 1998 of Article 15(2) of the Rules confirming the evident proposition that the arbitral tribunal is required to act "fairly and impartially." Any ground that would be available to challenge a sitting arbitrator may also be invoked to oppose his or her initial confirmation or appointment.

ii) Party-nominated v. third or sole arbitrators

Except in the case of a challenge on the basis of nationality (*see* point (iii) below), a party-nominated arbitrator may be challenged on the same grounds as a presiding arbitrator. An ICC tribunal should be composed of arbitrators who have the capacity to render a fair and impartial award based on the evidence before them. Although the grounds of challenge are not defined in the ICC Rules, they may be likened to those that apply to the recusation of a judge in a civil matter.

While the general principle is that all ICC arbitrators should be impartial, there is a degree of difference in application of the rule to party-nominated arbitrators as opposed to presiding arbitrators. In the case of a party-nominated arbitrator, the principle of impartiality must be weighed against the right of a party to nominate an arbitrator compatible with its national and economic circumstances. No such counterbalancing interests exist with respect to a chairman or sole arbitrator.

iii) Nationality

A party-nominated arbitrator may not be challenged on the basis of his nationality. In the absence of a contrary agreement, parties are free to nominate arbitrators of their own or any other nationality. Under Article 9(5) of the ICC Rules, however, a presiding arbitrator "shall be of a nationality other than those of the parties."

In choosing the National Committee to name a third or sole arbitrator, the ICC Court will frequently go beyond the minimum requirements of Article 9(5) in order to avoid any appearance of national bias. For instance, in a dispute between a Swedish company and an English company, the Court would not be likely to choose the Norwegian National Committee to propose the third arbitrator since a litigant might believe that Scandinavians have a similar outlook. On the other hand, if the Court had determined for special reasons that a Scandinavian third arbitrator was appropriate, it would not sustain a challenge on the mere basis of nationality.

All other factors being equal, the Court has shown its willingness to replace arbitral chairmen upon perceived lack of neutral nationality by one of the parties, particularly when certain nationalities had been intended to be excluded when terms of the arbitral clause were drawn up.

In proceedings between a British claimant and a Yugoslav respondent where the arbitral seat was Zurich, the Court had named a Hungarian chairman. Upon objection from the British party that in naming Zurich as the seat it had been intended to have a neutral, non-eastern bloc chairman, the Court agreed not to confirm the appointment of the Hungarian national and decided to apply to the Finnish national committee to suggest a chairman.[49]

There are occasions where parties challenge presiding arbitrators on the basis of residence in the state of which one of the parties was a citizen and had cultural or family ties with citizens of that state. Such challenges generally seem to fail. However, in one ICC arbitration, revealed in U.S. court proceedings which reviewed a connected case,[50] the Italian Chairman of an arbitral tribunal was found to have dual citizenship; he was also a U.S. national, as was

---

49   M. Calvo, *The Challenge of ICC Arbitrators—Theory and Practice*, 15 J. INT. ARB, No. 4, (1998) p. 63.

50   Affidavits filed in Fertilizer Corporation of India *et al.* v. IDI Management Inc., *supra* Notes 19 and 20.

one of the parties. On challenge by the non-U.S. party, he was disqualified by the Court of Arbitration.

Problems can also be caused by the issue of corporate nationality. On the face of it, a corporation is deemed to have the nationality of the state in which it is incorporated or, in continental legal systems, has its *siège social*. In exceptional circumstances, however, it is necessary to take into account the nationality of its controlling shareholders. Where, for example, an arbitration involves a French subsidiary of an American multinational enterprise, the Court would generally not ask for a proposal for a third or sole arbitrator from either the French or the U.S. National Committees in order to avoid arguments of conflicting national interest. If either the French or U.S. National Committee had been chosen (perhaps due to lack of adequate information), it is entirely possible that the Court would make a new appointment if a challenge were made. However, no case of this kind appears to have been made public. In one case in the authors' practice, the respondent called the Court's attention to the fact that the claimant, a Liechtenstein entity, was in fact the business vehicle of an Egyptian national. In response, the Court recalled its request for nomination of the chairman by the Egyptian National Committee and redirected its request to the Austrian National Committee. Controversy was thus avoided. The advantage of such early consideration of the nationality problem is that it takes place before a specific individual has been nominated; the discussion focuses on general principles rather than personal attributes.

On the one hand, the Court must as a pragmatic matter take into account the national character of the underlying economic interests at issue. On the other hand, the Court should not permit nor encourage artificial attempts to bar the appointment of neutral arbitrators by invoking a multiplicity of corporate nationalities within a group. Thus, the fact that a corporate party has a branch in the country from which the neutral arbitrator was chosen should not be accepted *per se* as grounds for challenge.

iv) Direct interest in the subject matter of the arbitration: nemo debet esse judex in propria causa (no one should be a judge in his own cause)

It is a legal truism that no man should be a judge in his own cause. Accordingly, where an arbitrator has a direct interest in the outcome of the arbitration, and fails to disclose it, he or she will be disqualified upon the challenge of an interested party. Where an award has been rendered prior to the interest being known, it is subject to being set aside. This practice is entirely consistent with the requirement that an arbitrator must be impartial and the fact that his impartiality will be cast in doubt where he has a pecuniary or other interest in the outcome. The concept goes further in that even when the challenging party admits that it has no suspicion that the arbitrator is biased or partial, the challenge should nevertheless succeed: where an arbitrator has a direct interest in the dispute the appearance of impropriety is such that the arbitration system requires disqualification.[51] Because the remedy is so drastic—removal of an arbitrator who may be guilty of no fault or suspicion of fault whatsoever—it will be limited to cases of direct interest in one of the parties to the arbitration or the subject matter of the dispute keeping in mind the standards of independence pertinent to the jurisdictions which will ultimately execute or affirm the award.[52] Where the financial or other interest is insufficient to consider the arbitrator as if he were a party to the arbitration itself, then partiality or lack of independence must be shown, as indicated below, of which a financial or other relationship will be an element of proof.

v) Continuing financial professional or subordinate relationship with a party

Few things are as great an impediment to impartiality as the possibility that the arbitrator has a financial relationship with one of the parties. The most obvious example is where the nominee has an ongoing employment relationship with the nominating party; not only does such a nominee have a financial interest in keeping his job, but he is also by definition in a subordinate relationship to his employer.

---

51   English cases have particularly developed the *nemo judex* concept, *see* R. v. Bow Street Metropolitan Stipendiary Magistrate and others, ex parte Pinochet Ugarte (No. 2), [1999] 1 ALL ER 577 (H.L.) (extradition proceedings involving former head of state of Chile) where the principle was restated: ". . . once it is shown that a judge is himself a party to the cause, or has a relevant interest in its subject matter, he is disqualified without any investigation into whether there was a likelihood or suspicion of bias. The mere fact of his interest is sufficient to disqualify him unless he has made sufficient disclosure." The principle has been applied to arbitrators on the same basis as applied to judges. Colin Reid Sellar v. The Highland Railway Company & Others [1919] S.C. (H.L.) 19 (award set aside when it was revealed that the arbitrator, whose personal character and independence were found to be above all challenge, had owned a comparatively small number of shares in the railway company that was a party to the dispute). The A.T.& T. case, *supra*, note 32, appears to indicate that nowadays an English court would examine whether a very small shareholding in a company which was a party to the dispute would be sufficient to call for the application of the *nemo debet* principle, following in this respect the leading case of Locabail (UK) Ltd. v. Bayfield Properties [2000] 1 ALL ER 65.

52   The necessity of preserving any system of justice from an appearance of impropriety is said to justify the result where the remedy may in many cases appear to be out of proportion to the wrong. It has been pointed out that the drastic remedy of recusal of the arbitrator or setting aside of the award is most often the result of non-disclosure. Where disclosure is properly made ". . . it is common practice that counsel on each side agree that the existence of the disqualification shall afford no objection to the prosecution of the suit, and the matter proceeds in the ordinary way, but, if the disclosure is not made, either through neglect or inadvertence, the judgment becomes voidable and, may be set aside." Colin Reid Sellar v. The Highland Railway Company & Others, *supra*. 51. While cynics may question whether the gentlemanly conduct among counsel observed in the 1919 decision of the House of Lords is still exercised today, in point of fact in current ICC arbitration practice many issues of potential disqualification of arbitrators are resolved amicably among the parties and their counsel if the issue is brought to the fore at the beginning of the arbitration. The most serious trouble comes when disclosure has not been made, the good will at the commencement of the proceedings has dissolved, and a party who is in the position of losing, or has lost, the arbitration has an incentive to stand on his rights so as to change that position.

It is rare that a party nominates one of its employees as an arbitrator. The rule is so basic as to be recognized in all legal systems. The issue arises more frequently with respect to employment by a related company or individual. In such cases, the Court applies common sense rather than a formal rule. It must determine whether the relationship could affect the impartiality of the arbitrator. Challenges have been sustained in cases where the arbitrator was employed by a company belonging to the group of which the nominating party was also a member. In another instance, the general counsel of a large multinational company withdrew as arbitrator after being challenged on the grounds that he was an employee of a holding company which had an indirect interest in the outcome of the arbitration (it owned shares in an operating company having a joint venture interest with one of the litigants).

In an arbitration involving a state entity, on the other hand, it is less likely that the Court will uphold challenges against arbitrators employed by the state (either directly as government bureaucrats, or indirectly as employees of a state enterprise, agency or university) for reasons described in Section 13.03. Unless the entity employing the arbitrator is directly subordinate to the state agency or enterprise involved in the arbitration, it is unlikely that the Court will take into account the indirect influences that are bound to exist.[53] Such grounds, however, have been the basis of successful challenges in the analogous case of multinational enterprises.

Lawyer arbitrators are on occasion successfully challenged on the grounds that the regular counsel for one of the parties may not serve as an arbitrator in the absence of agreement to the contrary.[54] The Court of Arbitration has recognized this ground for challenge and has thereby confirmed the obligatory rules in effect in most countries (*see* point (vii) below). It is possible, however, that in some cases, the Court may deem the professional relationship to be so occasional or trivial that it rejects the challenge.

---

53 *See generally,* Dominique Hascher, *ICC Practice in Relation to the Appointment, Confirmation, Challenge and Replacement of Arbitrators*, 6 ICC BULL. 4, 7 (November 1995). The ICC practice has survived judicial review, *Cour d'appel*, Paris, 2 June 1989, Gemanco v. S.A.E.P.A. and S.I.A.P.E., 1991 REV. ARB. 92 (amongst other things the Court pointed out that the complaining party had not brought up the conflict in challenge proceedings but only in an attempt to annul the award). Not all commentators approve of the ICC's receptive practice in confirming arbitrators with relation to the state party. *See* Martin Hunter, *Ethics of the International Arbitrator*, 1987 J. CHARTERED INSTITUTE OF ARBITRATORS 219: ". . . time and again, the ICC confirms the appointment of a nominee who is actually manifestly not independent by reason of being an employee of a government where an agency of that government is a party to the arbitration."

54 Berthold Goldman, Intervention, Symposium of 20 November 1970 on *Qualification de l'arbitre international*, 1970 REV. ARB. 203, at 230. Discussing the subject of the independence of arbitrators, Professor Goldman stated:

"I do not think, for my part, that an arbitrator can be impartial in several manners: there is only one way, that of a judge. This is so true that I do not see how the habitual legal counsel of a party can be designated as arbitrator."

A more vexing problem may arise in the context of the nomination as arbitrator of a lawyer who is a partner in a large law firm: even though he or she may be of recognized ability and international reputation and personally independent of both the nominating and opposing parties, the lawyer will in most circumstances not be allowed to serve as arbitrator if one of the other members of that lawyer's firm has counseled the nominating party, even on completely unrelated matters. The general rule appears to be that in most circumstances a challenge to such a person is upheld. While no doubt the arbitrator is *professionally* independent of the party, there remains a theoretical *financial* conflict of interest: the law firm in which the partner has a financial interest will profit from the continued relationship with the party, and an adverse arbitral decision might trouble that relationship.[55] Where there is no profit sharing between lawyers who work in close association, the ground for challenge may no longer hold. In view of the professional relationship of English barristers who share chambers but practice independently and do not share revenue it has been held that it is not a ground for challenge that a barrister acting as an arbitrator shares chambers with a barrister acting for one of the parties to the arbitration.[56]

The situation of the arbitrator who is a partner in a law firm, and the relationship between other members or offices of that law firm with a party to the arbitration, will continue to be a fertile source of challenges and take up a considerable amount of the Court's time. As law firms in international practice merge, expand and consolidate, increasing in size and geographical scope, the problem will no doubt expand as well, at least so long as the members of these firms continue to constitute one of the significant sources for nomination as arbitrators. It is not clear what the Court's reaction is to this phenomenon. It must recognize that in many cases it is beyond the scope of reasonable argument that an arbitrator's independence and impartiality

---

55   In submissions to the court filed in Fertilizer Corporation of India *et al.* v. IDI Management Inc., *supra* Note 19, reference was made to an ICC precedent where the partner in a Washington D.C. law firm, acting as party-appointed arbitrator, discovered during the course of the proceedings that one of his partners had counselled the party's corporate parent on completely unrelated matters, and so informed the parties. A challenge by the opposing party was sustained. A number of similar cases are known.

56   *Tribunal de grande instance*, Paris, 24 February 1992, Ste Icori v. Kuwait Foreign Trading Contracting & Investment Co., 1994 REV. ARB. 557; the same rule has been applied in English courts, *see* Laker Airways Incorporated v. FLS Aerospace Limited, [1999] 2 LLOYD'S L. REP. 45, 26 April 1999 Q.B. (Judgment of Mr. Justice Rix). While the independence of barristers within the same chambers is said to be a generally accepted principle in the practice of English law, it is difficult to say that the practice is not of such a nature as "might call into question the arbitrator's independence" at least in the eyes of a non-British party (a point which was made in commentary heavily criticizing the *Laker Airways* decision, Joanne Riches, Comment, [1999] Sweet & Maxwell, INTERNATIONAL ARBITRATION LAW REVIEW, 175). Accordingly, the circumstances should be disclosed by the barrister arbitrator to the ICC Secretariat and might occasion further questions about the relationship, or even a challenge where there were close ties between the barristers. Standing alone, however, the relationship would not be disqualifying.

would be influenced by the fact that some member of his firm represented, perhaps in a minor way, a party (or a company related to the party) in an unconnected transaction, perhaps in another jurisdiction. It can be suggested that in such cases the *nemo debet* principle leading to automatic disqualification should not be applied, and the Court should determine whether the law firm relationship presented any real likelihood or possibility of bias in all the circumstances.[57]

vi) Prior financial professional or subordinate relationship with a party

If an arbitrator has a continuing financial, professional or subordinate relationship with a party, one may fear (*see* (iv) above) that he will be subject to some pressure to render an award favorable to the party appointing him. If such a relationship is in the past, the analysis is somewhat different. The arbitrator can no longer be said to have a subordinate relationship to the party. Nevertheless, financial or personal interests are not necessarily absent. A person who has had previous business with a party may hope to resume such relations in the future. A long prior employment with a party may have given rise to such a close relationship as to make impartiality difficult. A further risk exists if the arbitrator has had a long employment or professional relationship with a party: he may be cognizant of facts relating to the party or the conduct of its business which are not part of the evidence presented before the arbitral tribunal. His opinion on the controversy may thus be influenced by facts not available to the other arbitrators.

While it is difficult to define specifically prior relationships that are disqualifying, it is safe to state that past relationships generally do not create strong grounds for challenge. The Court will not automatically assume that a nominee should be disqualified because of occasional business relationships in the past with the nominating party. Furthermore, the sensitivity of the issue is considerably attenuated by the fact that it arises most often in connection with party-nominated arbitrators. Due to the diversity of national interests and the requirement that the chairman come from a third country, it is less usual that an ICC chairman will have had any contacts with either party.

---

57 A reasonable approach to dealing with indirect relationships between parties and lawyer arbitrators has been suggested by the English Court of Appeal's 17 November 1999 ruling in *Locabail (UK) Ltd v. Bayfield Properties Ltd* [2000] 1 ALL ER 65, and related applications, dealing with a partner in an English solicitors' firm who acted as a deputy High Court Judge, essentially a part time judge. In proceedings to overturn his decision it was alleged that the law firm of which he was a member, by its representation of a company with interests in another matter adverse to the party before him would be advantaged by the loss by that party of the pending litigation. The court first considered whether "sufficient pecuniary or proprietary interest" resulted in a disqualifying direct interest under the *nemo debet* principle. Finding that it did not, the Court then considered whether there was a real likelihood or possibility of bias. Answering again in the negative, the Court cited the judge's lack of awareness of his law firm's conflicting interest and the tenuous nature of that interest. In determining whether an indirect law firm interest could present a real likelihood or possibility of bias, the court stated that "every application must be decided on the facts and circumstances of the individual case."

The *Universal Pictures v. Inex Films and Inter-Export* case[58] illustrates some issues of disqualification in ICC arbitrations. In that case, the United States party picked as its arbitrator an American lawyer in independent practice in London. The lawyer had, however, been a salaried corporate counsel of the claimant's parent company five years earlier. The defendants had received through the Secretariat the party-nominated arbitrator's resume, which included a statement of his prior employment and the name of the company he had worked for (which, incidentally, was not the same as that of the subsidiary). In addition, counsel for claimant revealed at the commencement of the proceedings before the arbitral tribunal that the party-nominated arbitrator had previously been employed by the parent company of the party. No objection was made to the arbitral tribunal or to the Court of Arbitration, and an award was subsequently rendered in favor of the claimant. In *exequatur* and appeal proceedings in France, the defendants alleged, *inter alia,* that the American arbitrator lacked independence.

The French Court of First Instance, whose decision was upheld on appeal, found (a) that the defendants had been informed of the ties between the arbitrator and the claimant at an appropriate time; (b) that having had the opportunity to protest the confirmation of the arbitrator, they could not claim that they were victims of error or fraud; and (c) that the fact that the party-nominated arbitrator had worked for the parent company of the claimant five years previously was insufficient to justify a conclusion that he was not independent, especially since there had been no proof that he had maintained ties with the corporate group since that time.

It can be concluded that whether a former, but terminated, relationship between an arbitrator and a law firm representing one of the parties will be found to be disqualifying depends on all the circumstances. In several cases the fact that the arbitrator had at one time been an associate in the law firm representing one of the parties was not considered disqualifying. An arbitrator who had formerly been a partner in a large law firm was confirmed despite the fact that one of his former partners was at that time the lawyer of one of the subsidiaries of the party who had appointed him.[59]

vii) Bias or previously expressed opinion

An obvious ground for challenge lies if the arbitrator has previously given his opinion on the matter in dispute: he can no longer address the issues in arbitration with an open mind. Lawyers having previously given their opinion on points at issue in the arbitration to one of the parties should not serve as ICC arbitrators.

---

58   Award examined and upheld by the *Cour d'appel* of Paris, 16 March 1978, 1978 REV. ARB. 501; challenged and sustained on other grounds by the *Cour de cassation,* 28 April 1980; 1982 REV. ARB. 424. The waiver issue is now specifically covered by Article 33 of the Rules which provides: "A party which proceeds with the arbitration without raising its objection to a failure to comply with any provision of the Rules . . . shall be deemed to have waived its right to object."

59   *See* M. Calvo, *The Challenge of ICC Arbitrators*, 15 J. INT. ARB No. 4 (1998) p. 63, 68.

The question may take on a wider dimension. May an arbitrator in a national-ization indemnification case be disqualified because he is an ardent sup-porter and frequent speaker on the necessity of full indemnification, including lost profits? Or because he is a partisan of the Charter of Economic Rights and Duties of States, known to hold the view that no contractual in-demnification is required and only local law compensation provisions should be regarded? Here the distinction between party-appointed arbitrators and the presiding arbitrator once again comes into play. Absent aggravating fac-tors, it seems doubtful that the Court would sustain a challenge in such cir-cumstances against a party appointment; a party should be free to choose an arbitrator of a compatible legal "culture."

On the other hand, the Court would want to avoid appointing a presiding ar-bitrator who had publicly taken extreme and detailed views on political or economic issues central to the arbitration. Nevertheless, the success of a chal-lenge would depend on all the circumstances. The expression of academic views in scholarly publications by a jurist does not necessarily preclude him from deciding a case in a completely impartial manner, based only on the evi-dence, arguments, and applicable law in the case.

Other allegations of bias have been founded on the conduct of an arbitrator in prior, but unrelated, arbitrations involving one of the parties. A challenge will not ordinarily succeed simply because an arbitrator has served in the same capacity in prior proceedings involving one of the parties. Such a claim for recusal would not lie against a judge, and it is hard to see why the rule should be different in arbitral proceedings absent additional factors. One such factor may be the fact that the party-nominated arbitrator has frequently and regu-larly been appointed by that party. He may thus bring to the arbitration supe-rior knowledge concerning one of the parties and his opinion may be influenced by facts outside the arbitration record. Furthermore, the prospect of continued and regular appointment, with the financial rewards that such appointment would bring, could also be of relevance, particularly on the is-sue of independence.[60] In the ordinary case, however, prior service as party-nominated arbitrator is not grounds for disqualification. An open ques-tion, however, is whether the failure of the arbitrator to reveal such prior ap-pointments would be an independent ground of disqualification.[61]

While bias undoubtedly is grounds for challenge, the burden is on the chal-lenger to demonstrate that real bias does in fact exist. For example, bias has been alleged to be reflected by the arbitrator's comportment in prior business relations of a confrontational type, in prior legal proceedings as counsel, and as arbitrator (alleged offensive and prejudicial conduct).

---

60   "When large amounts are involved, . . . the very amount of the arbitrator's fees . . . can be corrup-tive *per se*," Glossner, *supra* Note 30, at 145.

61   *See supra* Note 29.

Such challenges raise delicate problems for the Court of Arbitration. The Court is understandably reluctant to sustain a challenge based on a party's subjective allegation of bias which is denied by the arbitrator. The Court occasionally may seek to avoid ruling on the issue. If it feels that the claims of the challenger, even if somewhat subjective, are *bona fide*, it may instruct the Secretariat to ask the arbitrator whether he wishes to continue in view of the opposition and possible effect thereof on the proceedings. Thus some challenges are settled informally.[62] On the other hand, the Court will not take this approach if it feels that the challenge is unreasonable or made to cause delay.

viii) Serving as arbitrator in related proceedings

The fact that, on the one hand, complex international disputes are more and more frequently covered by arbitration clauses and that, on the other hand, agreements for consolidated multi-party arbitrations amongst conflicting interests are relatively rare increases the probability of the holding of simultaneous or consecutive bilateral arbitrations amongst related parties. Typical have been disputes in the international construction field where for instance a main contractor may have a dispute with a sub-contractor regarding his portion of the works and a related dispute with the owner for payment under the principal contract including for claims arising out of the sub-contractor's works. Related arbitrations might also take place between a main contractor and different sub-contractors in which might be at issue which of the sub-contractors was responsible for delay caused to the main contractor. Other examples may be found where a party would have separate arbitration agreements with a contractor and with another company guaranteeing the performance of the contractor.

In such cases the party faced with several arbitrations may be tempted to choose the same arbitrator for each of the related disputes. The liberty to choose one's arbitrator being such an essential attribute of arbitration, the right to make such a choice has never been questioned. Similarly, on the ground of efficiency and uniformity, the ICC has in some matters in the past accepted to appoint the same president for tribunals in related matters but usually only with the agreement of both parties.[63]

---

62   "Even after a challenge procedure has been started, it is laudable for an arbitrator to withdraw voluntarily from his function . . .," Glossner, *supra* Note 30, at 145.

63   It would appear that the Court is now more concerned with the possible due process argument such appointments may raise and can be persuaded to make an appointment of the same person as president in related arbitrations only in exceptional circumstances. The issue of service in related arbitrations was considered in *Cour d'appel*, Paris, 14 Oct. 1993, Ben Nasser *et al.* v. BNP and Crédit Lyonnais, 1994 REV. ARB. 380 where the French court rejected a manifestly ill founded request to annul an award against guarantors of a debt which had been found to be due in a concurrent arbitration presided by the same chairman, a procedure which had been agreed in advance by the parties.

The fact that an arbitrator also acts as arbitrator in a related dispute involving the same or related issues, does not in itself constitute a ground for challenge although the arbitrator must be careful not to use or refer to in the second arbitration information received privately and confidentially in the first. To do so would risk infringing the *droits de la défense*: a party's right to be informed of and confronted with any evidence used against him.[64]

The situation is different, however, where the arbitrator has come to a substantive determination of issues which remain to be decided in the second arbitration. Having made up his mind before the party in the second arbitration has had the opportunity to be heard, he cannot be expected to be able to eliminate his prior decision from his thoughts: he will be subject to challenge for bias or prejudice by reason of predetermination of an issue.[65]

The issue of the effect of serving in a related arbitration was decided by the ICC Court which rejected the challenge by the Government of the State of Qatar of an arbitrator designated by its American general contractor for works in Qatar. The arbitrator had served concurrently in arbitrations between the American contractor and the State of Qatar and between the American contractor and its Qatari sub-contractor. The final award against Qatar was made the subject of a request for annulment to the French courts. The Paris Court of Appeal rejected the recourse and its decision was confirmed by the *Cour de cassation*. The Court of Appeal reiterated the principle that "prior knowledge of a dispute is not such as to raise doubts as to the impartiality of the arbitrator unless he finds himself in a position of conflict with one of the parties to the dispute, *such as may result from an assessment by the arbitrators of the responsibility of a party that was not a party to the prior arbitration and to the existence of a prejudice against same as a result.*" (Emphasis added)[66] In its decision confirming the Court of Appeal's decision

---

64   The issue is well covered in the leading article of Claude Reymond, *Des connaissances personnelles de l'arbitre à son information privilégiée: reflexions sur quelques arrêts récents*, 1991 REV. ARB. 3.

65   An example is the successful challenge before the French courts in a non-ICC arbitration of an arbitrator who had been named by company A, responsible for the construction of works in Gabon, first in an arbitration against company B to whom A had confided the execution of the works and subsequently against company C whom A had contracted to control the execution of the works. In the first arbitration A was held liable to pay B substantial amounts for completion of the works. In the unanimous award finding A liable, the tribunal responded to the argument that B had been responsible for erroneous decisions concerning execution of the works: "The responsibility seems rather to be that of C which received from A the widest powers . . . and acted as the veritable manager of the affair . . .". The Court accepted C's challenge of the arbitrator who was found to be morally bound to uphold the view expressed in the prior unanimous award in which he had participated. *Tribunal de grande instance*, Paris, 13 January 1986, Setec v. SICCA, 1987 REV. ARB., 63 note Pierre Bellet.

66   *Cour d'appel*, Paris, 12 January 1996, 1996 REV. ARB. 428.

the *Cour de cassation* set out the general principle for determining the validity of an arbitral award where a claim of lack of impartiality is made in annulment proceedings:[67]

> . . . it is the mission of the judge of the regularity of the arbitral award to appreciate the independence and impartiality of the arbitrator, *taking into account any circumstance of a nature to affect his judgment and to provoke in the mind of the parties a reasonable doubt as to these qualities,* which are of the very essence of the arbitral function . . . (Emphasis added).

> . . . the fact of having served as an arbitrator in an arbitration between [the American general contractor] and one of its sub-contractors did not put in doubt his impartiality as long as this dispute did not concern relations between this company and the State of Qatar, owner of the works.

ix) Due process violations

Sometimes during the course of the proceedings a party will become convinced that a tribunal (or a member of the tribunal, usually the Chairman) displays lack of impartiality towards it by failing to accord it equality of procedural treatment with the other party or otherwise manifestly denies it due process rights. Since a manifest violation of due process rights would be a cause for annulment of a final award, it is appropriate that the ICC Court have the power to decide a challenge of the arbitrators for due process violation. The exact content of protected due process rights (and which without doubt include the civil law concepts of *droits de la défense* and *droit de la contradiction)* is nowhere defined in the ICC Rules,[68] but it is assumed to be as broad as the procedural rights guaranteed under the European Convention on Human Rights which is frequently referred to when a challenge is made on procedural grounds.[69] The challenges arise in relation to the procedural conduct of the proceedings by the arbitrators and are characterized by the complainant as unequal or unfair treatment, said to constitute lack of impartiality, finally rising to the level of misconduct. Challenges can relate, for instance, to refusal to receive evidence, refusal to hold a hearing or order an expert investigation

---

67   *Cour de cassation, Première chambre civile,* 16 March 1999, 1999 REV. ARB. 308 (The judicial recourse also made the charge that the arbitrator was not independent because, prior to his appointment, he had assisted the party that appointed him to obtain local counsel in Qatar. This grounds for recourse was also denied.)

68   Article 15(2) of the Rules, added in 1998, does confirm, however, the general principle of due process rights, which had always been implicit in ICC arbitration: "In all cases, the Arbitral Tribunal shall act fairly and impartially and ensure that each party has a reasonable opportunity to present its case."

69   For a review of the procedural rights under the Convention as confirmed by French courts in issues arising before courts and other tribunals *see,* P. Sargos, *Droit à un tribunal impartial,* Report of the *conseiller à la Cour de cassation, Assemblée plénière,* 6 Nov. 1998, J.C.P. II 10198; *see also* C. Jarrosson, *L'arbitrage et la Convention Européenne des droits de l'homme,* 1989 REV. ARB. 573.

or the granting of insufficient or unequal time to file a pleading.[70] While a number of challenges have been made based on the arbitrators' procedural conduct of the hearings, very few have succeeded, because the taking of procedural decisions is precisely within the discretionary powers of the tribunal. It is only in a flagrant case of due process violation causing real prejudice to a party that a challenge based on due process grounds can succeed.[71]

x) The use of national court precedents

A party seeking to justify a challenge will frequently refer to precedents of national courts, since the Court's decisions are kept confidential and the ICC Rules do not define the criteria for challenge. Cognizant of the mandate of Article 35 that all efforts should be made to ensure that an award is enforceable at law, the Court is especially attentive to reasoned arguments that rejecting the challenge may endanger the enforceability of an award in a jurisdiction having some connection with the arbitration. Thus national court precedents, while not binding, can be persuasive arguments for the Court of Arbitration.

It should be noted that most national court decisions arise in appeal or execution decisions after an award has been rendered. Thus some of the cases involving allegations of newly discovered disqualifying facts regarding an arbitrator may be nothing more than last-ditch attempts to avoid honoring duly rendered awards. Challenging an arbitrator during the arbitration may therefore have more chances of success than the same challenge made to a court by a party that has lost the arbitration.

It is clear that national precedents may not be blindly transposed to the international arbitration context. As Swiss arbitration experts have noted, the criteria for disqualification of arbitrators in domestic arbitrations may not automatically be applied to international arbitrations.[72] In some countries, domestic arbitration under local procedural laws is subject to stricter criteria than those of the ICC, requiring complete absence of relation or communication between an arbitrator and the parties. Other countries apply more permissive criteria than the ICC; rather than being independent, party-nominated arbitrators are permitted and in fact expected to become the advocate of a party's cause before the third arbitrator who serves as a type of um-

---

70 *See* M. Calvo, *The Challenge of ICC Arbitrators: Theory and Practice*, 15 J. INT. ARB. No. 4 (1998) p. 63, 71 where a member of the Court describes denial of a challenge based on the fact that the complaining party had only 33 days (instead of the 100 days it had requested or the 39 days given to its adversary) to prepare its case. Due process only requires that each party have a reasonable opportunity to present its case; it does not guarantee exactly the same length of time for each party.

71 *Id*; Dominique Hascher, *ICC Practice in Relation to the Appointment, Confirmation, Challenge and Replacement of Arbitrator*, 6 ICC BULL. 4 (November 1995); E. Schwartz, *The Rights and Duties of ICC Arbitrators*, *in* THE STATUS OF ARBITRATORS, ICC PUBLICATION No. 564 (1995) 67, 87-88.

72 Pierre Lalive, Jean-François Pouchet & Claude Reymond, LE DROIT DE L'ARBITRAGE INTERNE ET INTERNATIONAL EN SUISSE 339 (Lausanne, 1989).

pire. There exist specialized arbitration associations where an enormous number of disputes are arbitrated by a small group of professional arbitrators who are expected to have repetitive and continuing relations with the parties, and which therefore are different from ICC arbitrations. Examples are maritime and commodity arbitrations in London and textile industry arbitrations in New York.

Nevertheless, national courts deal with international and domestic arbitrations in a variety of circumstances that may be relevant to the ICC arbitral process, and national statutes and international conventions set out various criteria for the requirements of independence and impartiality of tribunals.[73] The Court of Arbitration may usefully be referred to precedents relating to the disqualification of arbitrators on the grounds of bias, partiality, or the like. Not only may the reasoning of such precedents be persuasive, but the Court will be attentive to the question whether its action (or more usually its non-action) would hamper execution of the award, with particular care as to the standards which might be brought to bear by a national court at the seat of arbitration.[74]

Finally, national court precedents on disqualification of judges may in many cases provide useful guidance.[75]

---

73   *See* C. Jarrosson, *L'arbitrage et la Convention européene des droits de l'homme*, 1989 REV. ARB. 573, see also P. Sargos, *Droit à un tribunal impartial*, n. 52, *supra*.

74   *See* M. Gaudet (former Chairman of the Court of Arbitration), *La Coopération des jurisdictions étatiques à l'arbitrage institutionnel*, in 1988 SWISS BULL. 90, (text of speech given on 11 March 1988, at the annual meeting of the Swiss Arbitration Association) (referring to a case where the Court of Arbitration, out of respect for the reviewing court in Zurich, and with the authorization of the arbitrators and the parties, communicated to the national court the reasons for its recusal decision); *see also* P. Fouchard, *Les institutions permanentes d'arbitrage devant le juge etatique*, 1987 REV. ARB. 225, 263-271.

75   The 1999 *Pinochet* case in the House of Lords, n. 51, *supra*, is a leading case which sets out principles concerning non-financial conflicts of interest and the duty of disclosure which are of general application and may be expected to directly influence the decisions or challenges of arbitrators for a long time to come. In *Pinochet*, the Appeals Committee of the House of Lords had in a 3-2 decision set aside a lower court decision quashing arrest warrants in the extradition proceeding. The effect of the House of Lord's decision was that the former President of Chile was subject to extradition at the request of Spain for crimes committed in Chile against citizens of Spain during Pinochet's regime. Subsequently, it was revealed that Lord Hoffmann, a member of the House of Lords Judicial Committee, had been a member of the board of directors of Amnesty International Charitable Trust which was affiliated with Amnesty International, the public interest group which had intervened in the Pinochet case as an interested party in favor of extradition. Lord Hoffmann had not disclosed the affiliation. In addition, it was revealed that his wife had worked in an administrative position in the international secretarial of Amnesty International. In the circumstances the House of Lord's determination was annulled. Despite the absence of any charge of actual bias, the participation by a judge in a case where it could be said that he had such an interest that he could be considered to be acting in his own cause was inconsistent with the appearance of justice which was a fundamental requirement of a fair procedure. The case should particularly be noted because the interest in question was a non-financial interest and because it employed the automatic *nemo debet* disqualification principle rather than the possibility for bias principle. See text at n. 51, *supra*.

13.06 Removal of an arbitrator by the Court

In addition to the challenge procedure provided in Article 11 of the Rules, which if successful leads to replacement of the arbitrator[76], Article 12(2) provides:

> An arbitrator shall also be replaced on the Court's own initiative when it decides that he is prevented *de jure* or *de facto* from fulfilling his functions, or that he is not fulfilling his functions in accordance with the Rules or within the prescribed time limits.

This article gives the Court the power to avoid a dysfunctional tribunal by removing an arbitrator who is not fulfilling, or cannot fulfill, his duties and whether or not the reason is for any fault attributable to the arbitrator. Removal may be required in the interest of arbitral justice of which the Court is the guardian under the Rules. The provision that removal under this Article shall be made "on the Court's own initiative" was added in the 1998 revision of the Rules and emphasizes the independent Court role in the matter.

The Court's action under this section, said to be on its own initiative, may nevertheless be the consequence of a complaint to this effect by one or both of the parties. More frequently, however, replacements are the consequence of observations made to the Court by the Secretariat after lengthy correspondence with the arbitrator. It is more likely, furthermore, that the Article 12(2) sanction is used against a chairman or sole arbitrator who has the principal responsibility for ensuring that the arbitration proceed in good order.

Article 12(2) is applied very infrequently.[77] Its very existence reduces the need to invoke it.

The purpose of the Article 12(2) is to avoid tribunal malfunction by giving the Court a weapon to combat unacceptable delays. It is the kind of intervention typical of supervised arbitration (*see* Section 4.05). Sometimes a tribunal's functioning may be greatly hampered by such fundamental disagreement of its members regarding procedure that no agreement, not even a majority agreement, may be reached on even the most basic procedural issues. In such cases, Article 12(2) provides a method for replacement of some or all of the arbitrators.

The ICC Court can use its *ex officio* powers to remove an arbitrator pursuant to Article 12(2) in cases where an arbitral tribunal fails to respect the time limits prescribed by the Rules. As previously noted, extensions are often granted beyond the ordinary requirement of Article 24 that awards are to be made

---

76 Pursuant to Article 12(1) of the Rules as described in Section 13.08.

77 In his statistical report, the former Counsel to the Court reported that from July 1988 through December 1994 only five arbitrators were replaced under the prior version of this article. Dominique Hascher, *ICC Practice in Relation to the Appointment, Confirmation, Challenge and Replacement of Arbitrators*, 6 ICC BULL. 17 (November 1995).

within six months of the signature of the Terms of Reference (*see* Section 19.01). However, arbitral tribunals occasionally fail to take the measures necessary to ensure the orderly progression of the proceedings. The presiding arbitrator has the primary responsibility of assuring procedural compliance, and if he persists in dilatory conduct (for instance, failing to answer correspondence by the Secretariat or refusing to set procedural deadlines) he may be replaced by the Court.

The Court uses its powers with moderation. It will take all necessary steps through the Secretariat to verify that the chairman is at fault before replacing him. Sometimes, many delays are caused by the parties, particularly when neither party desires to proceed rapidly. In such cases, presiding arbitrators frequently feel that the parties should be permitted to be the masters of their procedure. Traditionally the Secretariat permitted such practice to a large extent. More recently it has taken an active role in urging the arbitrators to proceed with reasonable alacrity despite resistance from both parties.

A presiding arbitrator may be prevented from carrying out his function under the Rules when, for example, grave disagreement among the members of the arbitral tribunal brings personal relationships to such a point that further proceedings of the tribunal are jeopardized. In these circumstances, the Court must cautiously use its power to order the replacement of some or all of the members in order to neutralize dilatory tactics. While a chairman may in fact be prevented from carrying out his functions when the comportment of both the party-nominated arbitrators prevents orderly proceedings, this is less likely to be the case if only one of the arbitrators conducts himself poorly.

The Court has the widest discretion to determine that an arbitrator is "not fulfilling his functions" and accordingly should be replaced. The Court can exercise this discretion at any time in the proceedings.[78] The 1988 Rules added for the first time that the Court should determine whether the arbitrator is prevented *de jure* or *de facto* from fulfilling his functions but it is doubtful that phrasing the requirement in Latin adds anything.[79]

It is no doubt true that the Court's powers under Article 12(2) are intended to be different from and independent of the challenge procedure initiated by a party. This is emphasized by the fact that the Court shall replace an arbitrator

---

[78] Even if time limits for a formal challenge by a party has elapsed, the Court may find that an arbitrator is so tainted with bias or inability to perform arbitral duties that it should intervene to preserve the due process integrity of the proceedings.

[79] A Counsel to the Court of Arbitration, writing about the 1988 modifications to the Rules, gave the following examples of disenabling functions: an arbitrator holds or is named to an office which is incompatible with simultaneously holding the office of arbitrator; the arbitrator undergoes surgery requiring a long period of convalescence; an arbitrator nominated by a State, and confirmed by the Court, is named as a Minister of the Government of the State. J.J. Arnaldez, *Les amendements apportés au Règlement d'Arbitrage de la Chambre de Commerce Internationale (C.C.I.)*, 1988 REV. ARB. 67, 817.

on its "own initiative". The fact that there are no specific time limits for Court action under this Article, while there are rigorous time limits within which a party must bring a challenge[80], is another reason why the Court would examine carefully any attempt by a party to circumvent the requirements of the challenge procedure by submitting an application under Article 12(2). This being said, nothing prevents a party from formally advancing an application to the Court for the removal of an arbitrator "on the Court's own initiative". Indeed there may be times when a party does not wish to bring a challenge—either because of the non-existence of formal grounds or because of a reluctance to bring an application which some consider implies a degree of opprobrium—but feels that the arbitrator should be replaced in the interests of arbitral justice.

The interrelation of the Article 11 challenge and Article 12(2) Court removal procedures has been commented on by two former Secretaries General of the Court who opine that Article 12(2) cannot be used as a substitute for the challenge procedure but also observe:

> There have nevertheless been a few, exceptional cases, in which the Court has replaced arbitrators on the basis of former Article 2(11) [the predecessor of Article 12(2)] while simultaneously rejecting a related challenge made by a party. In those cases where this has occurred, the Court preferred to reject the challenge, but nevertheless replace the arbitrator in question because, while prevented from fulfilling his functions, the arbitrator was nevertheless not considered to have acted in a culpable manner.[81]

The same authors report a replacement by the Court of the members of an arbitral tribunal pursuant to the provisions of the predecessor of Article 12(2) (in fact, the replacement of two arbitrators, one having resigned) following upon the annulment by a state court of a partial award rendered by the tribunal, leading to the necessity to make a new award on the same subject matter in the same proceeding.[82] It was apparently believed by the Court in that case that the arbitrators could no longer perform their duties with the necessary degree of impartiality.

However, in a 1999 case the Court was also faced with the consequences on the arbitral tribunal of the annulment (on due process grounds) by a state court (the *Cour d'appel* of Paris) of a partial award rendered by a majority, leading to the necessity to render a new award on the same subject matter in the same proceedings. Faced with an application for the replacement of the tribunal (under both Article 11 and Article 12(2)) due to its alleged pre-judg-

---

80   *See* Section 13.10.

81   Derains & Schwartz 184.

82   *Id.* at 185.

ment of issues required to be decided *de novo*, and hence a perceived lack of impartiality, the Court nevertheless denied the application. As may thus be seen, the Court retains great discretion as to when the interest of arbitral justice requires replacement of an arbitrator or arbitrators, a discretion emphasized by the fact that the Court gives no reasons for its decision. Each decision will depend on the individual circumstances of the matter.

Court action under Article 12(2) will frequently be based on circumstances in which no fault is attributed to the arbitrator. Applications to remove arbitrators for fault in the conduct of the proceedings will usually be made by an Article 11 challenge. Nevertheless, the Court's powers under Article 12(2), to remove an arbitrator for not fulfilling his functions, also covers the broad category of misconduct of arbitrators whether that word is used in a pejorative sense or in a broad sense covering any procedural mishap in the conduct of the proceedings which leads the Court to conclude that arbitral justice requires replacement.[83] An attempt is made in Section 13.07 to define standards of conduct for arbitrators.

13.07   Standards of conduct for arbitrators during the proceedings

Little has been written about misconduct of ICC arbitrators during the course of proceedings. Few cases have been publicized where the Court of Arbitration, whether pursuant to challenge or on its own motion, has used its power to remove an arbitrator for specific misconduct. Instances of removal have tended to occur where the conduct of the arbitrators convinced the Court that an award would not be rendered if the tribunal continued under its original composition.

Since the sanction of removal does exist and is applied only after a pragmatic determination that the arbitrators are unable to render an award, the Court must be deemed to apply certain standards of conduct for arbitrators. The following discussion attempts to outline such standards.

Standards of conduct for arbitrators under ICC proceedings should be based on norms applied through the years on a case-by-case basis by leading ICC arbitrators and from the norms prevailing and required in the major national legal systems. There is no written code of conduct for arbitrators acting in ICC

---

83   A June 1975 ICC Working Group report commenting on the provision's recent incorporation into the 1975 Rules clarified that under the new provision, "an arbitrator who does not satisfactorily fulfill his functions (gross negligence, obvious partiality) or who does not observe the time limits set by the rules or by the Court can be replaced by a decision of the Court . . .". Report by Jean Robert, ICC document 420/179, 25th Congress of the ICC, Special Discussion Group No. 1, Tuesday 17th June, 3:30 p.m.–6:30 p.m.

proceedings.[84] Given the great diversity of nationalities of the arbitrators and of prevalent customs at the various seats of arbitration, it would be difficult to draft a comprehensive manual. An attempt to do so by an ICC working group in the late 1970's was never endorsed by the Court. Nevertheless, parties are entitled to expect that ICC arbitrators will respect the following general principles:

− An arbitrator communicating with a party in writing should address a copy of the communication to the other party, the other arbitrators, and the Secretariat of the Court.

− An arbitrator should not discuss the merits of the case or receive evidence or legal argument from a party in the absence of the other party and his fellow arbitrators.

− An arbitrator may communicate with a party regarding the fixing of procedural dates or other practical and material aspects of the arbitration, but the contents of such communication should immediately be made known to the other party and arbitrators.

− An arbitral tribunal should generally allow the parties to modify or adopt procedural rules, including ones that may be reached in the course of proceedings. For instance, if both parties agree, each party may communicate *ex parte* with the arbitrator it has named, particularly where the parties agree that such communication may favor a settlement.

− An arbitrator should not discuss the merits of the arbitration with another arbitrator in the absence of the third arbitrator, unless the latter has agreed and is informed of the subject of the discussion.

No general problem has been noted in the observance of these rules by presiding arbitrators. Most party-appointed arbitrators also have little difficulty in understanding that their exercise of quasi-judicial functions requires from them conduct which resembles the conduct of judges, albeit adapted to the circumstances. Furthermore, the legal training of arbitrators and counsel in many countries provides a set of values which discourages *ex parte* communications and other incidents of procedural unfairness.

Nevertheless, it is a fact of life that a few party-appointed arbitrators have honored these rules more in the breach than in the observance and have been know to discuss the merits of disputes—and sometimes tactics—with the party who appointed them. Some arbitrations may be facilitated by giving arbitrators freedom to communicate with the parties who appointed them; al-

---

84   For comparative purposes it is useful to consult the American Arbitration Association's *Code of Ethics for Arbitrators in Commercial Disputes* (1976) reprinted in H. Holtzmann, *The First Code of Ethics for Arbitrators in Commercial Disputes*, 33 BUSINESS LAWYER 309 (1977) and The International Bar Association's *Ethics for International Arbitrators* (1987) reprinted in 3 ARB. INT. 72 (1987); *see generally,* F. Nariman, *Standards of Behaviour of Arbitrators*, 4 ARB. INT. 311 (1988).

lowing such discussion of issues and evidence may ensure that the parties' views are correctly understood by the arbitral tribunal in its deliberations. Such a practice can be agreed by the parties. But what if the parties do not agree and, as is most usually the case, this delicate issue is never brought up? ICC litigants may find themselves in the following dilemma: if one of the parties maintains a purely judicial relationship with the arbitrator it nominated and makes no contact with him outside of the arbitral hearing but the other party communicates fully with "its" arbitrator and discusses the merits *ex parte*, is not the fundamental equilibrium of the proceedings threatened?

As long as the participants in ICC arbitration seek the many advantages of permitting two arbitrators to be selected freely by the parties, they will have to accept the risk that some party-nominated arbitrators may not abide by accepted minimum standards. The ICC Court of Arbitration has no doubt been reticent to publish a code of conduct that it cannot be confident of enforcing. It is true that in principle a disequilibrium in the arbitral process may be created by disrespect of procedural norms by one of the party- appointed arbitrators; however, the chairman of the tribunal will in practice normally be able to take into account such conduct and reestablish procedural equity. The Court of Arbitration should remove a party-nominated arbitrator only when his conduct manifests flagrant bias or abuse of procedure threatening the continuation or integrity of the proceedings.[85]

13.08   Replacement of arbitrators

Article 12(1) of the Rules,[86] provides:

> An arbitrator shall be replaced upon his death, upon the acceptance by the Court of the arbitrator's resignation, upon the acceptance by the Court of a challenge or upon the request of all the parties.

Article 12(2) of the Rules provides for replacement by the Court of an arbitrator when he is not fulfilling his functions in circumstances examined in Section 13.06.

It is only upon the acceptance of the challenge by the Court that the arbitrator's status is ended. The same is true of an arbitrator's resignation. It is only effective from the date of the Court's acceptance. By defining the effective date of a resignation, the Rules deal with what has appeared in some cases to

---

85   For comparative purposes, note the comments on the Buraimi Oasis Arbitration (*ad hoc*, 1955) between Saudi Arabia and the United Kingdom, reported in III Wetter, The International Arbi-tral Process 357-373 (1979) where it is suggested that the resignation of the British arbitrator as a reaction to alleged bias and *ex parte* communications by the Saudi arbitrator, which had the effect of suspending and finally frustrating the arbitration, was a remedy worse than the original ill.

86   Modifying and replacing Article 2(10) of the 1975 Rules (as amended in 1998). The phrase "or upon the request of all the parties" was added in 1998, thus reinforcing the liberty and inherent right of the parties to determine the procedure of the arbitration.

be the dilatory tactic of orchestrating the resignation of a party-nominated arbitrator. The fact that there must be an acceptance by the Court of Arbitration of the resignation gives the Court a mechanism to deal with the resigning arbitrator and some discretionary power.

The provision may also be useful in permitting the tribunal to continue to function following the submission of a completely *bona fide* resignation during the period prior to effective replacement of the arbitrator. The Court will ordinarily make its acceptance effective upon the date of replacement. In the meantime the work of the tribunal may proceed.

In cases where an arbitrator has died, resigned, or been replaced, the vacancy will ordinarily be filled by recourse to the nomination and appointment procedures set out in Articles 8 and 9 of the Rules. Replacement of sole and third arbitrators will be made by appointment of the Court following the recommendation of the same National Committee which was originally consulted. If a party-nominated arbitrator must be replaced, the same party may nominate his successor. Although this rule has potential for abuse (by repeated nomination of candidates who are unsuitable or prone to resign), it has, in practice, worked well enough in ICC arbitrations in most cases. Nevertheless, to be certain to provide a remedy in the case of abuse, or any other dysfunction, of the appointment process Article 12(4), added in 1998, provides (in part): "When an arbitrator is to be replaced, the Court has discretion to decide whether or not to follow the original nominating process . . . ."[87] Should the Court, in an exceptional case, decide that the original procedure of nomination by a party of an arbitrator for appointment by the Court was not to be followed it would make the appointment itself in the same way as if the party had defaulted in making a nomination. The new power given to the Court reflects practice in other modern international arbitration rules, notably those of the London Court of International Arbitration[88] (whose broader rules give

---

87 Article 12(4) replaces Article 2(12) of the 1975 Rules as amended in 1988, which did not allow for the Court to side-step the original nominating process in appropriate circumstances. This added provision should help avoid any dilatory tactics by the parties in situations where the original appointment of arbitrators had been delayed by disagreements between the parties and there is fear that the same could occur should the original nomination process be repeated. While the provision was intended to address any problem in the nomination of party-appointed arbitrators it could also find application where a contractually agreed method of arbitration was no longer appropriate.

88 Article 11(1) of the 1998 LCIA Arbitration Rules, which has the same text as Article 3(5) of the 1985 LCIA Rules which the Working Party of ICC International Arbitration Commission considered in making its recommendations for revision of the Rules provides: "In the event that the Court determines that a nominee is not suitable or independent or impartial, or if an appointed arbitrator is to be replaced, The Court shall have discretion to decide whether or not to follow the original nominating process."

the LCIA Court the possibility to appoint an arbitrator for a party even following upon the LCIA Court's rejection of an initial nomination) and the World International Property Organization.[89]

It should be noted that a challenge may be made at any time during the proceedings, subject to the notification time limits discussed in Section 13.10. If the challenge succeeds, there would have to be a substantial retrial of the case before a newly constituted tribunal. Once an award has been finally rendered and notified to the parties, however, the Court of Arbitration can no longer rule on pending or prospective challenges and is not competent to hear motions for rehearing or revision based on grounds for arbitrator disqualification. The Court's functions are terminated at the time the award is rendered and revision based on grounds for arbitrator disqualification can only be subsequently argued in national courts.

Since a party may raise a challenge at any time during the proceedings, it should be recognized that new grounds of challenge may arise well after the constitution of the tribunal. An example of such new grounds for challenge would be a disqualifying relationship between the arbitrator and a party established after the commencement of the proceedings.

A classic case was presented in an ICSID arbitration.[90] Sir John Foster, nominated as arbitrator by Occidental Petroleum Co., accepted an appointment to the board of directors of that company during the proceedings and consequently resigned from his position as arbitrator. Had he not done so he would certainly have been subject to challenge.

Failure of an arbitrator to reveal pertinent changes in his financial, professional or business relations with a party, or the development of certain kinds of conduct and contact with the party during the proceedings, can in themselves be sufficient cause for disqualification. Accordingly, challenges for disqualification made during the course of proceedings and prior to award have occasionally been successful.

Article 12(4) of the Rules provides that if an arbitrator is replaced in a situation where the original tribunal has made progress in the case, the new tribunal shall determine "if and to what extent prior proceedings shall be repeated

---

89   Article 33(b) of the 1994 WIPO Rules provides: "In the event that an arbitrator appointed by a party has either been successfully challenged on grounds which were known or should have been known to that party at the time of appointment, or has been released from appointment as arbitrator in accordance with Article 32 [because of *de facto* or *de jure* inability to perform the function] the Center shall have the discretion not to permit that party to make a new appointment. If it chooses to exercise this discretion, the Center shall make the substitute appointment."

90   Holiday Inns and Occidental Petroleum et al v. Morocco, reported in III Gillis Wetter, THE INTERNATIONAL ARBITRAL PROCESS 388-400 (1979) with comment by Frédéric Eisemann on the cause for disqualification and the strange consequence und the ICSID Rules that clamants lost their right to name a replacement arbitrator where, as occurred in the case, the remaining arbitrators refused to "consent" to the resignation.

before the reconstituted Arbitral Tribunal," after having invited the parties to comment on the issues. In many cases, particularly in view of the emphasis on written submissions in ICC proceedings, the new arbitrator will be able to obtain the necessary knowledge of the proceedings by reading the documents produced and briefs or memorials submitted by the parties. Where there has been substantial witness testimony on issues which remain to be decided, the tribunal will have to determine what, if any, repetition may be required. The fact that in most ICC proceedings no verbatim transcript is made of witness testimony or counsel's argument makes the decision more difficult than if the replacement arbitrator could read the testimony.[91] In any event the tribunal has discretion to determine the conduct of future proceedings, and may determine that rehearing witnesses is not required. Indeed, many ICC arbitrators from civil law jurisdictions remain skeptical of the importance of most witness testimony where alternative documentary evidence is available.

13.09 Non-replacement of arbitrators: the "truncated tribunal"

A new subsection was added to the Rules in 1998 permitting, in limited circumstances, the Court to refrain from replacing an arbitrator who has died, or been removed by the Court, and thus to allow the final award to be rendered by a tribunal composed of only two members . . . what has come to be known as a "truncated tribunal".

Article 12(5) provides:

> Subsequent to the closing of the proceedings, instead of replacing an arbitrator who has died or been removed by the Court pursuant to Articles 12(1) and 12(2), the Court may decide, when it considers it appropriate, that the remaining arbitrators shall continue the arbitration. In making such determination, the Court shall take into account the views of the remaining arbitrators and of the parties and such other matters that it considers appropriate in the circumstances.

The addition responded to a perceived need to deal with a situation that had manifested itself in a handful of cases which, while limited in number, had resulted in frustrating the arbitral process due to obstructive tactics of one member of a three person tribunal. The tactics were largely similar: towards the end of the arbitration, when the final outcome was beginning to take

---

91 For a case in which all members of a tribunal were replaced, and the tribunal revisited all prior determinations yet found that no repetition of the proceedings was required due to the adequacy of the documentary record, *see* ICC CASE 6476/1994, 8 ICC BULL. 59 (May 1997). For a description of alternative methods used for keeping an abbreviated record in ICC arbitral proceedings conducted with a heavy civil law influence, *see* A. Lowenfeld, *The Two-Way Mirror: International Arbitration as Comparative Procedure*, VII MICHIGAN YEARBOOK OF INTERNATIONAL LEGAL STUDIES 187 (1985). The description of the detailed witness summaries is not typical of contemporary ICC practice. It is worth noting, moreover, that in large cases verbatim transcripts are increasingly the rule.

shape within the confines of the tribunal, the arbitrator named by the losing party would engage in obstructive tactics with the purpose that no final award would be rendered. He might refuse to take place in final deliberations, absent himself for unexplained and unexplainable reasons, or simply "disappear." While the number of such cases remained small, the result was irritating as it could not only make a mockery of the arbitral process but also destroy the rights of the other party who had relied on the arbitration remedy to preserve contract rights.

There is no doubt that an arbitrator who without excuse refuses to participate in the final deliberations, or who persists in acting on his resignation as if effective when it has not been accepted by the Court, commits a wrong. The practice is well known in the context of public international law arbitrations where the politically charged atmosphere of disputes between states has led to more instances of purposeful attempts by an arbitrator to derail the arbitral process than is the case in commercial arbitration. The accepted remedy in such international law arbitrations was aptly summarized by Judge Schwebel (as he then was) of the International Court of Justice[92]:

— Withdrawal of an arbitrator from an international arbitral tribunal which is not authorized or approved by the tribunal is a wrong under customary international law and the general principles of law recognized and applied in the practice of international arbitration. It generally will constitute a violation of the treaty or contract constituting the tribunal, if not in terms then because the intention of the parties normally cannot be deemed to have authorized such withdrawal.

— Such a wrongful withdrawal may not, as a matter of international legal principle, debar an international arbitral tribunal from proceeding and rendering a valid award.

— While the precedents are not uniform, and the commentators are divided, the weight of international authority, to which the International Court of Justice has given its support, clearly favours the authority of an international arbitral tribunal from which an arbitrator has withdrawn to proceed and to render a valid award.

One remedy for an arbitrator's misconduct in the above circumstances is of course to remove and replace him. As described in Section 13.08 where the party can be considered the instigator of the arbitral misconduct, as well as in other appropriate circumstances, the Court is not required to request a nomination from that party and may make the appointment of an independent arbitrator on its own account.[93] But this remedy is not always efficacious and

---

92   Stephen Schwebel, INTERNATIONAL ARBITRATION: THREE SALIENT PROBLEMS 296 (Grotius Press 1987).

93   Article 12(4) of the Rules.

sometimes—in terms of delay of the rendering of a final award—could result in rewarding the obstructive party with the spoils of his misconduct.

For these reasons a number of institutional arbitration rules specifically provide for the valid continuation of arbitral proceedings by a truncated tribunal. The LCIA Rules (1998 edition) provide:

> Article 12.1. If any arbitrator on a three-member Arbitral Tribunal refuses or persistently fails to participate in its deliberations, the two other arbitrators shall have the power, upon their written notice of such refusal or failure to the LCIA Court, the parties and the third arbitrator, to continue the arbitration (including the making of any decision, ruling or award), not withstanding the absence of the third arbitrator.

The AAA International Arbitration Rules (1997 edition) have a similar provision:

> Article 11(1): If an arbitrator on a three-person tribunal fails to participate in the arbitration for reasons other than those identified in Article 10 [withdrawal after challenge, administrator's acceptance of challenge, administrator's acceptance of resignation, death of arbitrator], the two other arbitrators shall have the power in their sole discretion to continue the arbitration and to make any decision ruling or award, notwithstanding the failure of the third arbitrator to participate. . . .

Both of these articles go on to list the factors which the arbitrators must take into consideration in determining whether to proceed as a truncated tribunal or take other actions.

The approach of the ICC Rules is considerably more restrictive than that of the LCIA, the AAA and other institutions which have addressed the issue.[94] The ICC's approach is characterized by:

i) the late stage of the proceedings at which a truncated tribunal is permitted to operate: it is only "subsequent to the closing of the proceedings"[95] that the remaining members of the tribunal may proceed without the participation of the third arbitrator;

ii) the truncated tribunal may function only after the status of the defaulting or absent arbitrator has been terminated: Article 12(5) only applies where an arbitrator "has died or been removed by the Court." This condition distinguishes the situation under the ICC Rules from the situation under other arbitration rules where the status of the non-participating arbitrator is not formally determined leading to uncertainty as to his possible future participation.

---

94 In addition to those of the LCIA and the AAA, the rules of the World Intellectual Property Organization (WIPO) and the Permanent Court of Arbitration contain provisions for truncated tribunals.

95 For a description of the requirement under Article 22 of the Rules that the arbitral tribunal declare the proceedings closed, *see* Section 25.06.

iii) the Court, not the arbitral tribunal, decides whether the tribunal may proceed as a truncated tribunal: Article 12(5) provides that the Court "instead of replacing an arbitrator who has died or been removed" may decide to have the remaining arbitrators continue the arbitration.

The ICC's cautious approach to the truncated tribunal reflects, on the one hand, the fact that as the Rules provide a highly supervised system of arbitration there exist other solutions to the problems caused by the defaulting arbitrator, and, on the other hand, a concern—perhaps overemphasized—to avoid problems of enforcement in state courts of awards by truncated tribunals.

As noted earlier, the jurisprudence on truncated tribunals has been based largely on public international law arbitrations between states and more recently on the Iran-U.S. Claims Tribunal cases which, while resulting in decisions enforceable as commercial awards under the New York Convention, are of a hybrid nature and share many of the political and diplomatic issues of public international law arbitrations.[96] In those cases—particularly the public international law cases conducted before *ad hoc* tribunals—there is little alternative to having the truncated tribunal carry on. A state which withdraws its arbitrator because it is unwilling to accept the result of an award which is about to be delivered is unlikely to appoint a new arbitrator soon. In ICC proceedings there is an independent solution: the Court, exercising its supervisory and administrative role, after removal of a defaulting arbitrator, arranges for his replacement either by the original nominating process or by its own appointment where appropriate. Thus there is a solution, other than the truncated tribunal, which may not exist, as a practical matter, in many public international law arbitrations.

More generally, the revisers of the ICC Rules saw the truncated tribunal as a remedy to be used only in exceptional circumstances. Concern was voiced as to enforceability of an award rendered without the participation of the third arbitrator.[97] If considered as an award rendered by only two arbitrators it might conceivably violate legislative provisions in some states that tribunals may not be composed of an even number of members. The revisers were also aware that in a much criticized 1991 case[98] the Swiss Federal Tribunal had

---

96   The Iran-U.S. Claims Tribunal cases are reviewed in Stephen M. Schwebel, *The Validity of an Arbitral Award Rendered by a Truncated Tribunal*, 6 ICC BULL. 19 (November 1995).

97   The case where a defaulting arbitrator does not participate at all in the deliberations leading to an award, by a truncated tribunal, is to be distinguished from the case where an arbitrator participates in such deliberations but does not join in, or sign, the award. In the latter case, a majority award under Article 25(1) of the Rules will be entered. Such cases, which occur from time to time, have raised no significant problems. The mere failure of one arbitrator to sign the award has no significance as to its validity. While the Rules make no specific provision to this effect, it is recommended practice for the majority arbitrators to indicate the participation of the absent arbitrator in the deliberations and the fact that he was invited to sign the award.

98   *Tribunal fédéral Suisse*, First Civil Section, 30 April 1991, Ivan Milutinovic Pim v. Deutsche Babcock AG, BGE 1a 166, commented on at length by Stephen Schwebel, *The Validity of an Arbitral Award Rendered by a Truncated Tribunal*, 6 ICC BULL. 19 (November 1995).

found that an ICC award rendered by a truncated tribunal was invalid because it denied procedural equality to one party, thereby violating the guarantees of the Federal Constitution and the European Convention on Human Rights. Absent an explicit agreement by the parties, unequal distribution of party nominated arbitrators during arbitral deliberations was said to constitute a procedural inequity that violated due process.

The provisions of Article 12(5) present a reasonable solution to the difficult situation created by the non-participation of an arbitrator during final deliberations:

i) After having removed an arbitrator, it is for the Court—and not the remaining arbitrators—to decide whether final deliberations may go forward before only the two remaining arbitrators;

ii) The Court's power is limited: if the defaulting arbitrator has died or been removed by the Court prior to the closing of the proceedings replacement is the only solution;

iii) In exercising its power either to replace the defaulting arbitrator, or to allow the final deliberations to continue before a truncated tribunal, "the Court shall take into account the views of the remaining arbitrators and of the parties and such other matters that it considers appropriate in the circumstances."

iv) The agreement of the parties to the provisions in the Rules permitting continuation of final deliberations before a truncated tribunal may be sufficient to save the tribunal's decision from attack before state courts. In any event, the position of state courts relevant to any given arbitral proceeding—particularly the position of courts at the seat of arbitration—will be one of the factors that the Court takes into account in exercising its discretion, after the closing of proceedings, to replace a deceased or defaulting arbitrator or to permit the arbitration to continue before a truncated tribunal.

13.10   Time limits for challenge

Most objections to arbitrators are made at an early stage of the proceedings—indeed before the arbitrators have begun to exercise their functions. As noted in Section 13.04, the Secretariat communicates to the parties, prior to the Court's confirmation or appointment, any information relevant to the independence of the arbitrators.[99] This information usually consists of the *résumé* or *curriculum vitae* supplied by the arbitrator in addition to the Arbitrator's Statement of Independence in which he indicates his willingness to

---

99   Article 7(2): "Before appointment or confirmation by the Court, a prospective arbitrator shall sign a statement of independence and disclose in writing to the Secretariat any facts or circumstances which might be of such a nature as to call into question the arbitrator's independence in the eyes of the parties. The Secretariat shall provide such information to the parties in writing and fix a time limit for any comments from them."

serve and points out any circumstances relevant to his independence which should be brought to the attention of the parties. Pursuant to Article 7(2), the Secretariat fixes a time-limit for any comments.

Based on this information, a party may (within the time-limit set by the Secretariat) object to the proposal, such objection not yet amounting to a challenge (although having the same effect).

Once an arbitrator has been appointed, he may be challenged only within the time limitations specifically provided under the Rules. These limitations are found in Article 11(2) of the Rules:

> For a challenge to be admissible, it must be sent by a party either within 30 days from receipt by that party of the notification of the appointment or confirmation of the arbitrator, or within 30 days from the date when the party making the challenge was informed of the facts and circumstances on which the challenge is based if such date is subsequent to the receipt of such notification.

The intent in specifying a short time limitation is to require a party to act as soon as it has become aware of information about the arbitrator that it considers disqualifying and to provide a mechanism to deal with the problem which arises from the delayed presentation of such challenges. It had been the unfortunate experience of the Court that some parties, unhappy with the developments in an arbitration, challenge an arbitrator because of relationships they had known about from the outset. The provision[100] provides a deterrent to such challenges.

Article 11(2) is straightforward with respect to challenge at the time of appointment. The challenging party will have received from the Secretariat information concerning the arbitrator. In addition, the party may have personal knowledge of relationships or facts which in his opinion are disqualifying. In either event, a challenge must be made within 30 days of notification of receipt of the arbitrator's appointment. A party may also challenge later in the proceedings within 30 days of its discovery of the facts and circumstances on which it bases its challenge.

The procedure for removal of an arbitrator after confirmation presents more complexities than objection to a nomination because it encompasses two different grounds for removal: challenge for facts or relationships preexisting the arbitrator's appointment and challenge for facts or relationships arising subsequent to his appointment. In both cases the period of limitation is at least 30 days from the date when the party making the challenge was informed of the facts and circumstances on which the challenge is based. There is no limit to how far in advance of notification parties may become aware of

---

100 The time limit was first added in 1988 as Article 2(8) of the Rules. It is further reinforced by Article 33 (Waiver) of the Rules added in 1998.

disqualifying facts but they must use such facts in a challenge proceeding within 30 days of notification.

One might expect in the case of challenges based on facts preexisting the arbitrator's appointment that the challenging party would be charged with a duty of "due diligence", or at least expected to have a reasonable amount of curiosity to investigate. If an arbitrator's statement or curriculum vitae gives a straightforward listing of his activities and relationships (none of which he considers disqualifying), one might ask, should a party who suspects that closer examination of those relationships might lead to an undisclosed disqualifying relationship immediately request supplementary information from the arbitrator or should it make its own independent inquiry? The developing case law suggests that both these routes ought to be pursued. The time limitation of Article 11(2), however, by its terms only runs from the time when the challenging party "was informed of the facts and circumstances on which the challenge is based." Accordingly, a party challenging an arbitrator during the course of the proceedings should be required to allege on what date the facts and circumstances relied on came to its attention. If the challenge was made within 30 days from that day, it will be up to the Court of Arbitration to determine whether the allegation is credible, or whether in the circumstances, the knowledge must be considered to have been known, or deemed to have been known, at an earlier and disqualifying date. Parties who fail to challenge within the time limits not only risk adjudication by an inappropriate arbitrator, but may also waive the right to oppose recognition of, or seek judicial recourse from, the final award based on the composition of the arbitral tribunal. If a party remains silent throughout the arbitral proceedings with full knowledge of facts supporting arbitral disqualification, it should be held to waive the right to invoke such facts later as grounds for setting aside or refusal of recognition of an award.[101]

---

101 For typical case, see AAOT Foreign Economic Association (VO) Technostroy-export v. International Development and Trade Services, Inc., 139 F. 3d 982 (2nd Cir. 1998) ("where a party has knowledge of facts possibly indicating bias or partiality on the part of an arbitrator he cannot remain silent and later object to the award of the arbitrators on that ground."); Locabail (UK) Ltd. v. Bayfield Properties Ltd. and another, [2000] 1 ALL ER 65 ("If, appropriate disclosure having been made by the judge, a party raises no objection to the judge hearing or continuing to hear a case, that party cannot thereafter complain of the matter disclosed as giving rise to a real charge of bias. It would be unjust to the other party and undermine both the reality and the appearance of justice to allow him to do so.") Article 33 of the Rules, "Waiver," added in 1998, makes clear that a party loses its right to challenge an arbitrator, or to complain of procedural error, if complaint is not timely made.

CHAPTER 14

ADVANCE TO COVER COSTS

14.01   Determination of advances

i) Provisional advance ordered by the Secretary General

A key feature of ICC arbitration is the power given to the Court to determine the amount of arbitrators' fees and the ICC administrative expenses. This determination is to be made within the scope of a scale of charges (Appendix III of the Rules) based on the amount in dispute in the arbitration. The scale has a very broad range between the minimum and maximum fees and charges which may be set by the Court for any given amount in dispute. Where the sum in dispute is not stated, the Court may fix the costs and fees in its discretion.[1] In addition, the Court has the power to fix fees of the arbitrators at a figure higher or lower than those which would result from the application of the relevant scale based on the amount in dispute when so required by "the exceptional circumstances of the case."[2] An overview of the issues of costs in ICC arbitration is contained in Chapter 3, and consideration of how the Court makes its final determination of costs at the end of the arbitration and in conjunction with its scrutiny of the award is contained in Chapter 21. Here we consider the procedure for the determination by the Court of advances on costs since the Rules provide that the claimant and respondent are obliged to pay in equal shares at the outset of the arbitration the amount which the Court determines will be "likely to cover the fees and expenses of the arbitrators and the ICC administrative costs."[3] It is one of the considerable advantages of ICC arbitration that the entire matter of determining the amounts of arbitration fees and expenses, insuring that the amounts will in fact be available when needed, and undertaking the often difficult and time consuming

---

1   Appendix III, Article 2.

2   Rules, Article 31(2).

3   Rules, Article 30(2).

administrative steps with the parties to accomplish this, is taken out of the hands of the arbitrators and is handled by the arbitral institution through the Court and its Secretariat.

Once the Request and the Answer have been filed, and the process of forming the arbitral tribunal is under way, the Court will determine in accordance with Article 30(2) the appropriate advances to be made by the parties to cover the costs of arbitration. Some time may be required for this determination to be made and for payment of the advance by both parties to be received by the Secretariat (extensions of time may be requested for filing of the Answer and possible counterclaims, queries may be made by the Court as to the amount in dispute and some study required before fixing an amount which is intended to be valid for the entire arbitration, a respondent may be dilatory or may fail to file its Answer). Under prior versions of the Rules and Schedule of Costs, the file could not be distributed to the arbitrators until the total advance had been determined by the Court and 50% of these costs (25% to be paid by claimant and 25% by respondent) had been paid. This caused substantial delays in a number of cases. Accordingly, in order to expedite the arbitration and insure distribution of the file to the arbitrators as soon as possible, Article 30(1) of the Rules, added in 1998, provides that the Secretary General may fix a *provisional* advance to be paid by the claimant alone under the following terms:

> After receipt of the Request, the Secretary General may require the claimant to pay a provisional advance in an amount intended to cover the costs of arbitration until the Terms of Reference have been drawn up.

Five characteristics of the Secretary General's power to fix a provisional advance should be noted:

i) the Secretary General "may" fix a provisional advance: he is not required to do so and in an appropriate case may decide to submit the matter directly to the Court for the determination of the total advance;

ii) the provisional advance is payable by the claimant alone;

iii) the provisional advance is determined based on the amount of the claim and does not take into account the amounts of any counterclaims;[4]

iv) the advance is not to cover the costs of the entire arbitral proceedings but only "until the Terms of Reference have been drawn up";

v) the advance is provisional; it is replaced once the Court has determined the advance on costs under Article 30(3), with claimant's payment of the

---

4   While not explicit in the Rules, this is clear from the fact that the Secretary General may set a provisional advance prior to receipt of an Answer and is confirmed in the Schedule of Costs (Article 1(2) of Appendix III).

provisional advance considered as partial payment of the advance fixed by the Court.[5]

The Rules themselves do not set forth how the Secretary General is to determine the "amount intended to cover the costs of arbitration until the Terms of Reference have been drawn up." However, Article 1(2) of Appendix III provides:

> The provisional advance on costs fixed by the Secretary General according to Article 30(1) of the Rules shall normally not exceed the amount obtained by adding together the administrative expenses, the minimum of the fees (as set out in the scale hereinafter) based upon the amount of the claim and the expected reimbursable expenses of the Arbitral Tribunal incurred with respect to the drafting of the Terms of Reference. If such amount is not quantified, the provisional advance shall be fixed at the discretion of the Secretary General. Payment by the Claimant shall be credited to its share of the advance on costs fixed by the Court.

The provisional advance, which is based only on the amount of the claim, is intended to cover all the costs of the arbitration through to the Terms of Reference. In the past, however, where an arbitration has been abandoned or settled after the Terms of Reference had been prepared the fees payable to the arbitrators were based on 50 percent of the minimum fee for an amount in dispute based on the sum of the claims and the counterclaim. Early commentary suggested that to be able to preserve this practice it would be necessary for the Secretariat ordinarily to fix a provisional advance close to the maximum allowed under Article 1(2) of Appendix III.[6]

The ICC has recognized, however, that imposing excessive "front end loading" would result in controversy and defeat the purpose of the provisional advance to accelerate the arbitral process by rapid payment of an advance by the claimant alone. Accordingly, the Secretary General announced that in ordinary circumstances the provisional advance would be based on 50% of the ICC administrative expense for the amount in dispute according to the scale of charges therefore plus 50% of the minimum fee per arbitrator on the arbitrator's fee scale of charge for the amount in dispute according to the claim to which would be added an amount to cover the estimated reimbursable expenses of the arbitral tribunal through to the preparation of the Terms of Reference.[7]

One should note, however, that the advance is not strictly limited in this way. The Secretary General may set it at a higher amount (normally within the

---

5 Article 30(3) provides: ". . . Any provisional advances paid on the basis of Article 30(1) will be considered as a partial payment thereof."

6 DERAINS & SCHWARTZ, 308.

7 H. Grigera Naón, *The Powers of the ICC International Court of Arbitration Vis-à-Vis Parties and Arbitrators*, SPECIAL SUPPLEMENT ICC BULL. 60 (May 1999).

maximum limit provided for in Article 1(2) of Appendix III) when circumstances require. Concretely, the Secretary General must insure that there are sufficient funds on hand to pay the arbitrators and the ICC costs if the case is withdrawn prior to the drawing up of the Terms of Reference, or if the respondent defaults on payment after determination of the advance.

The concept of the provisional advance was developed to permit a claimant acting alone and without any cooperation from respondent to continue with arbitral proceedings in a rapid fashion. If a claimant feels the provisional advance is unfair it can refuse payment and await setting of the advance by the Court, but will lose the advantage of rapid distribution of the file to the arbitrators, and will be faced with the prospect of advancing 50% of the amount determined by the Court to cover the entire arbitration proceeding, a fee which may be based on a higher amount in dispute (if there are set-offs or counterclaims) and an amount on the scale substantially higher than the minimum.

ii) Advances on costs determined by the Court

The Court's responsibility for determining and if necessary readjusting advances on costs is set out in Article 30(2):

> As soon as practicable, the Court shall fix the advance on costs in an amount likely to cover the fees and expenses of the arbitrators and the ICC administrative costs for the claims and counterclaims which have been referred to it by the parties. This amount may be subject to readjustment at any time during the arbitration. Where, apart from the claims, counterclaims are submitted, the Court may fix separate advances on costs for the claims and the counterclaims.

The Court's decision will be made by a three person committee of the Court[8] after having received information and recommendations from the Secretariat, and ordinarily (except in default proceedings) with the knowledge of respondent's position regarding the place of arbitration and the number of arbitrators as well as its position on the claims and whether it has any counterclaims.[9]

The Court's determination of the amount of the advance "likely to cover the fees and expenses of the arbitrators and the ICC administrative costs for the claims and counterclaims which have been referred to it" (Article 30(2)) depends upon an estimate of the amount in dispute (App. III, Article 4). In some cases this is evident. When the claimant seeks relief in the form of liquidated

---

8   As authorized in Rules, Article 1(4) and Internal Rules, Article 4.

9   The Court is not required to await receipt of the respondent's Answer (for which substantial extensions of time are sometimes given) prior to setting the advance, but ordinarily will do so since, given the existence of the provisional advance mechanism, the arbitral proceedings will not be delayed.

damages which have been stipulated as a definite sum, that sum is the "amount in dispute" if there is no counterclaim.

In many cases, however, a specific amount of damages is not stipulated and determination of the amount claimed must await a requested accounting or expertise. In such a case, the Court must base the advance on its own estimate of the amount in dispute. It is free to revise this estimate during the course of the proceedings as further evidence or pleadings are produced which clarify the amount in dispute. The Secretariat will inform the Court of new information revealed in further documents filed in the case, or in the course of the Secretariat's communications with the arbitral tribunal. In large cases, where original estimates of the amount of the claim are frequently subject to modification, it is not unusual for the advance on costs to be increased several times during the proceedings.

When there is a counterclaim, the amount in dispute is the sum of the claim and the counterclaim. For example, a licensor may bring suit against a licensee for $500,000 in unpaid royalties and to confirm termination of the license agreement. If the licensee counterclaims, seeking to confirm the validity of the license agreement and an assessment of damages in the amount of $500,000 for interference with its contract rights, the amount in dispute is $1,000,000.

Counterclaimants have often opposed increases in fees based on the amount of the counterclaim on the ground that the counterclaim is merely the reflection of their defense against the claim. They have asserted that in their particular cases the tribunal would not be required to consider new evidence or arguments and the case will not be more complex by virtue of the counterclaim. They have argued further that in such circumstances the final award would be made in the amount of either the claim or the counterclaim, but never the sum of the two. Whatever the logical merit of such arguments, they have been rejected by the Court.

Respondents have a much stronger argument that amounts claimed only as defensive set-offs, and not as positive counterclaims, should not be considered as additional amounts in dispute and should not increase the advance on costs. Defensive set-offs serve to extinguish or reduce a claim, like any other defense, and cannot result in a positive award.[10] Article 30(5) of the Rules[11] provides:

> If one of the parties claims a right to a set-off with regard to either claims or counterclaims, such set-off shall be taken into account in determining the advance to cover the costs of arbitration in the same way as a separate claim insofar as it may require the Arbitral Tribunal to consider additional matters.

Unlike the situation of counterclaims, which are to be included in the amount in dispute whether or not they require the arbitral tribunal to consider additional matters, the amount of set-off claims (or, more properly, defenses) are only to be included "insofar as [they] may require the arbitral tribunal to consider additional matters." In the Court's practice (made after investigation by the Secretariat which will frequently have consulted with the arbitral tribunal) it is almost unheard of that set-off claims are not considered to require the arbitral tribunal to consider additional matters. Hence, the amounts of the claimed set-offs are almost always added to the amount in dispute.

To determine the appropriate advance the Court must determine not only the amount in dispute but also, based on that amount, an appropriate rate on the scale for setting arbitrators' fees. The Court must also estimate the expenses to be incurred by the arbitrators.

The amount in dispute is usually the sum of the principal amounts of the claims, counterclaims and set-offs. Interest on these amounts, whether claimed in specified amount or generally, is ordinarily not taken into account although exceptions may be made in unusual cases (e.g. where in a financial dispute the principal claim is for interest). In some exceptional arbitrations interest claims exceed the principal amount in dispute by a large measure. It would not be surprising to find that the Court would take these claims into consideration in fixing the advance (as it would for example if the amounts had been claimed as delay damages rather than moratory interest) although it does not appear to have a set position in the matter.

Claims by a party for the recovery of its costs of the arbitration, including the legal fees it will be required to expend for the arbitration, are not taken into account in estimating the amount in dispute.

Where the parties have not quantified their respective claims or counterclaims the Court will have to make an estimate for the purpose of calculating

---

10   For a comprehensive review of problems raised by set-off in arbitration, *see* K. Berger, *Set-off in International Arbitration*, 15 Arb. Int. 53, 80 (1999). The article also discusses problems arising from non-payment of advances in ICC arbitration by the party with a set-off claim, but fails to distinguish the differing consequences depending on whether separate advances have been established, discussed *infra*, Section 14.02.

11   Added to the Rules in 1998 and incorporating the same provision previously contained in the Internal Rules.

the advance. The issue is presented with considerable frequency as a claimant may present its claim as a request for "declarations" (in essence, seeking a declaratory award while reserving the right to quantify claims subsequently in the arbitration). Sometimes requests are presented in this way precisely to avoid having to invest too much at the outset of the arbitration as an advance on costs. The Court in the past has fairly regularly considered that unquantified claims should be considered to represent an amount in dispute of $ 1 million,[12] and advances determined based on that amount. In recent years, however, (and possibly in reaction to claimants' strategic choices for presenting unquantified claims in complex matters) the Court has been required to investigate more closely the background of such cases which has resulted in the fixing of higher (or very occasionally lower) estimates.

The determination of the amount in dispute does not by itself determine the amount which must be fixed to cover the expected arbitrators' fees since the scale has a very wide range between the minimum and maximum amounts provided (for instance, an arbitrator's fees may vary between $ 16,250 and $ 78,500 for a $ 2 million dispute). When arbitrators' fees are finally determined at the end of the arbitration the Court will take into account such factors as the complexity of the case, the time spent, the diligence of the arbitrators and similar factors in deciding the appropriate place in the allowable range to fix the arbitrator's fees (see Section 21.03, *infra*). These factors cannot be known at the very outset of the arbitration. Accordingly, in most cases the Court will set the advance to cover arbitrators' fees at the average amount allowable on the scale, so that in the example of a $ 2 million dispute the advance per arbitrator for fees would be $ 47,375 [($ 16,250 + $ 78,500)/2]. The Court is not, however, bound by this rule of thumb; in appropriate circumstances, it may fix a higher amount, and has occasionally done so. A table prepared by the authors permitting rapid calculation of probable advances on costs for various amounts in dispute is set out in Appendix I, Table 9B.

The advance will also include the amount to cover ICC administrative expenses provided on the scale for the amount in dispute.

As authorized by Article 30(2) the Court will also include in the amount of the required advance an amount to cover the arbitrators' expenses. The largest single element is travel expenses which can be very considerable when arbitrators are domiciled very distant from the seat of arbitration. Hearings, particularly where they are lengthy, add another significant element. The

---

12 Which would ordinarily represent an advance per arbitrator of $ 32,000 for arbitrators fees.

Secretariat is obliged to obtain from the arbitrators all relevant information so as to be able to make a reasonable estimate.[13]

iii) When separate advances may be authorized

According to Article 30(3) "[T]he advance on costs fixed by the Court shall be payable in equal shares. . .". It is an essential element of ICC arbitration that the parties are to contribute to advances on costs in equal portions. By accepting to submit their disputes to ICC arbitration the parties have contractually agreed to this. The consequences of default by a party to pay its share of the advance to cover global costs (including the right of the non-defaulting party to pay any unpaid amount of the global advance so as to progress the arbitration) are addressed in Section 14.02.

Despite the general principle of setting global advances only, Article 30(2) of the Rules[14] gives the power to the Court to fix separate advances for the claims and for the counterclaims. An interesting aspect of the setting of separate advances, when the Court accepts to do so, is that it inevitably leads to a large increase in the total amount of advances covering the total amount in dispute. This is because the separation of advances due for the claim and counterclaim leads to the loss of the advantage of the regressive nature of the scale of charges which causes a lower rate to be applicable to the aggregate amount in dispute than to each of the claims and counterclaims. Thus where there would be a claim of $ 1 million and a counterclaim of $ 5 million the advance for the $ 6 million amount in dispute (without taking into account an estimate of the tribunal's expenses) would for a three person tribunal be approximately $ 240,000. If separate advances were established the claimant would be required to advance approximately $ 115,000 for its $ 1 million claim and the respondent $ 230,000 for its $ 5 million counterclaim—an aggregate advance of $ 345,000. Parties have sometimes asked the Court to set the separate advances based on a lower percentage on the scale so as to avoid this seemingly anomalous result, but without success. It has been the view of the Court that each separate advance should be sufficient to fund the arbitration costs of the separate claim or counterclaim if the claims or counterclaims of the other party were withdrawn from the arbitration (as indeed sometimes occurs).

A separate advance is typically appropriate, and frequently requested, where a respondent makes a counterclaim, thereby increasing the amount in dispute and the advance, but is unwilling to contribute to the advance and thus

---

13   The amount of estimated expenses of the arbitral tribunal does not cover any costs of experts engaged by the tribunal. These are to be made the subject of arrangement between the arbitral tribunal and the parties. The tribunal should not engage such experts until the parties have made the required advances for this expense, Article 1(11), Appendix III.

14   ". . . where, apart from the claim, counterclaims are submitted, the Court may fix separate advances on costs for the claims and counterclaims."

adds to the burden of the claimant, if it must pay the amount due by the defaulting party. In a far fewer number of cases a claimant may lose interest in its claim, and by not contributing its share or adjusted share of the advance leave the arbitration suspended without the respondent able to obtain a ruling on its counterclaim. There are also cases where a respondent urges a counterclaim for an amount many times that of the originating claim. In view of this transformation of the scope of the arbitration brought by it, the claimant may wish to establish separate advances rather than have to contribute one-half of an advance to cover the expenses of an arbitration of a new dimension.

While Article 30(2) of the Rules puts no limit on the power of the Court to set separate advances on its own motion or at the request of a party, the Court does not favor the setting of separate advances. Generally, it does not do so on its own initiative, or even at the request of a party unless convinced that one of the parties will default in its obligation to pay one-half of the global advance and the other party will refuse to pay the advance of the defaulting party. It is evident that the Court prefers the setting and payment of a single advance in equal shares where this is possible and in case of default prefers the solution of payment by a party of the defaulting party's share of the single advance. Where the respondent accepts to pay nothing and its large counterclaim is part of a manifestly dilatory tactic, the claimant's refusal to pay for it may be expected and separate advances will be ordered. The situation is less clear where the respondent adds a disproportionate counterclaim to the arbitration, for which it is willing to advance its half of the global cost. Important questions arise. Must the claimant accept to pay half of the expected costs of a dispute which is no longer of the same nature as its claim? Is this not precisely the kind of situation that separate advances were designed to cover? Cannot the claimant ask that separate advances be established without first being considered in default of its obligation to contribute one-half of the global advance? A response to this point of view was expressed in one matter in an informal note by a member of the Secretariat stating:

> Please note that there is no provision of the Rules that could be construed as granting the parties the right to having the Court fixing separate advances on costs solely on the basis of a significant difference between the amount of the principal claims and the counterclaims.

The official position is not beyond dispute since the claimant had a legitimate interest to defend and arguably should not have been required to be declared in default of its arbitration agreement obligations to obtain it.

iv) Readjustment of advances by the Court

As an institution, the Court of Arbitration—and not the parties directly--is responsible for the remuneration of arbitrators. It must therefore ensure through the intervention of its Secretariat that the advances are paid as a condition to conducting the arbitral proceedings. It will verify that payment has been made at three stages in the proceedings: (i) at the time of the initial communication of the file to the arbitrators, (ii) when the Terms of Reference are notified to the Court, and (iii) prior to notification of the award.

Article 13 provides that the Secretariat shall transmit the file to the arbitral tribunal as soon as it has been constituted "provided the advance on costs requested by the Secretariat at this stage has been paid." In most cases this will mean the provisional advance to be paid by the claimant fixed by the Secretary General under Article 30(1). The whole purpose of adding this provisional payment mechanism to the Rules in 1998 was to expedite transmission of the file to the arbitral tribunal. In some (probably few) cases the provisional advance mechanism will not be used and the advance on costs for the entire proceeding will be set by the Court under Article 30(2). In such case the Secretariat will issue appropriate instructions to the parties as to the payments required to insure immediate transmission of the file to the arbitral tribunal. (Under prior practice, the file would be transmitted to the arbitrators as soon as 50% of the advance on costs had been made as a result of payments by one or both parties.) The Secretariat will not transmit the file to the arbitrators, and thus engage obligations for payment of their fees and expenses, until the appropriate advances have been paid to it.

The next formal occasion for verifying the situation of the advance on costs is when the Terms of Reference have been drawn up by the arbitral tribunal which will at the same time have drawn up a provisional timetable for the balance of the proceeding.[15] At this time the profile of the dispute will have become clearer, amounts in dispute may have been modified or supplemented,[16] and the Court will have fixed an amount for the advance designed to cover the whole arbitral proceeding. Indeed, this stage of the proceeding is so important that prior versions of the Rules provided that the Terms of Reference would not become operative for claims where the advance on costs had not been paid and which frequently had the effect of automatically suspending the proceedings.[17] Article 30(4) does away with this automatic suspension and simple provides:

> When a request for an advance on costs has not been complied with, and after consultation with the Arbitral Tribunal, the Secretary General may direct the Arbitral Tribunal to suspend its work . . .

This provision clearly improves on the automatic suspension provision of the prior Rules and also makes clear that it is not for the arbitral tribunal to take

---

15   Rules, Articles 18(3), 18(4).

16   Article 18(1) of the Rules provides that the Terms will be drawn up in the light of [the] most recent submissions" of the parties and should include "a summary of the parties' respective claims and of the relief sought by each party, with an indication to the extent possible of the amounts claimed or counterclaimed."

17   Article 9(4) of the 1975 edition of the Rules as amended in 1988.

the initiative to suspend due to non-payment of part of the advances: the responsibility is that of the Secretary General who of course should consult with the arbitral tribunal to understand all the circumstances of the case. On the other hand, in the interest of an orderly procedure, and in their own interest to assure that fees are calculated on revised amounts in dispute, it is the obligation of the arbitral tribunal on its own initiative to inform the Secretariat of changes in the amount in dispute.

The final verification of the payment of the advances on costs and their adequacy is made after the arbitrators have submitted their draft award to the Court for its scrutiny (see Chapter 20, *infra*). Article 28(1) states that no award may not be notified to the parties, and hence enter into effect, unless "the costs of arbitration have been fully paid to the ICC by the parties or one of them."

The Court's mission, accomplished with the assistance of the Secretariat, to assure the availability of the necessary financial resources to pay arbitration fees and expenses includes not only verifying that advances set by the Court have been paid but also taking the necessary steps to readjust the amounts of the advances as may be required by developments. Article 30(2) of the Rules specifically provides that the advance on costs "may be subject to readjustment at any time during the arbitration."[18] The Secretariat will remain in touch with the arbitral tribunal with regard to their expenses and time spent in the matter but it is the duty of the arbitral tribunal to advise as soon as possible of any changes in the amounts in dispute, or changes in the nature or complexity of the claims. The Court may make readjustments in the advances at any time based on these considerations, but it would be unfair to the parties to ask for new advances at the very end of the proceeding. Accordingly the Court has generally refused to increase advances (and hence refused to award arbitrators' fees in excess of the amount on deposit with the ICC) when the arbitral tribunal has failed to notify the Secretariat in timely fashion of increase in the amount in dispute and has only brought this fact to the attention of the Court at the time of submission of the draft award to the Court.

14.02 Consequences of default by one party

Respondent parties have the same obligation to pay the advance on costs as do claimant parties. By agreeing to ICC arbitration the parties have bound themselves to abide by the Rules. This clearly includes the payment of advances on costs, which is the obligation of both parties. The Secretary General of the Court of Arbitration has elaborated on this point, stating: "it is not an accepted practice in ICC arbitration for a party to refuse to pay all or part of its

---

18 *See also* Article 1(10) of Appendix III, Schedule of Arbitration Costs and Fees which provides that readjustments may cover, in particular, fluctuations in the amount in dispute, changes in the amount of the estimated expenses of the arbitrator or the evolving difficulty or complexity of arbitration proceedings.

share of the advance on costs and to leave it to the other party to pay for the defaulting party. . . . . The fact of non-payment will be brought to the attention of the arbitral tribunal so that it may be taken into account in fixing the final costs of the arbitration."[19]

Nevertheless, it is a fact that in a number of cases—fortunately a small minority—one of the parties will not make the required advance. Occasionally this is because of an inability to do so. More frequently, however, it is used as a dilatory tactic by a respondent wishing to obstruct the arbitral process. The ICC Rules provide mechanisms that deal with this possibility. The principal mechanism is Article 30(3), which provides in part that "any party shall be free to pay the whole of the advance on costs in respect of the principal claim or the counterclaim should the other party fail to pay its share."[20] Thus a claimant, faced with the possibility of delay due to default in payment by the respondent, may unblock the proceedings by paying the entire advance (its overpayment will be reimbursed if the defendant later complies).

Article 30(2) creates the possibility of separate deposits for the claim and counterclaim (*see* Section 14.01).

Absent such a possibility, an unscrupulous respondent faced with a claim of $1,000,000 would be tempted to lodge a groundless counterclaim of $10,000,000. The amount in dispute would then be $11,000,000, greatly increasing the arbitration costs which would ordinarily be fixed in equal amounts. The respondent, knowing that the Secretary General would be required to order the tribunal under Article 30(4) to suspend its work because of the non-compliance of a party to pay its share of the advance on costs, could refuse to pay its share of the arbitration costs. The arbitration would then be blocked until the whole advance was paid.

In this situation, the claimant could pay the entire advance on costs, pursuant to Article 30(3). As this would hardly be a sufficient remedy, it could instead request the fixing of separate advances under Article 30(2) and pay only the advance fixed for the claim. This is a common protective measure taken by claimants faced with a dilatory respondent who has also filed a counterclaim. If the respondent did not pay the advance fixed for the counterclaim, it would be considered withdrawn under Article 30(4), and the counterclaim would not be heard by the arbitral tribunal. The Respondent would,

---

19 Secretary General of the ICC Court of Arbitration, Communication of 1 January 1988, on costs and payment, Appendix II.

20 In fact when a party accepts to pay the unpaid portion on behalf of a defaulting party it does not make payment in respect of the principal claim *or* counterclaim but must pay the whole of the advance based on the total amount in dispute which includes the amount of the claim *and* counterclaim, if any. The present wording is misleading and it is surprising that it escaped the attention of the revisers of the 1998 Rules. *Accord*, DERAINS & SCHWARTZ, 317. The text would have been clearer if it simply stated: "However, any party shall be free to pay the whole of the advance on costs should the other party fail to pay its share."

however, be entitled to present its defense of the claim even though it had not paid any part of the advance. This is the rule whether or not separate advances have been fixed.

Article 30(4) sets out the general consequences of failure by a party to pay its share of the global advance or its separate advance as follows:

> When a request for an advance on costs has not been complied with, and after consultation with the Arbitral Tribunal, the Secretary General may direct the Arbitral Tribunal to suspend its work and set a time limit, which must be not less than 15 days, on the expiry of which the relevant claims, or counterclaims shall be considered as withdrawn. Should the party in question wish to object to this measure it must make a request within the aforementioned period for the matter to be decided by the court. Such party shall not be prevented on the ground of such withdrawal from reintroducing the same claims or counterclaims at a later date in another proceeding.

Several comments are in order:

> i) Where a respondent has paid no part of an advance fixed on the basis of a claim (with no counterclaim) the Rules provide no alternative for the claimant except to pay respondent's share of the advance if it wishes the arbitration to proceed;

> ii) Where a respondent has paid no part of an advance fixed on the basis of an aggregate amount in dispute including a claim and counterclaim the Rules provide no alternative, in the absence of redetermination of separate advances, for the claimant except to pay respondent's share of the global advance if it wishes the arbitration to proceed;

> iii) Where a respondent has paid no part of an advance fixed on the basis of a global amount in dispute including a claim and counterclaim, and the claimant has accepted to pay the defaulting party's share, then both the claim *and* counterclaim will be heard by the arbitral tribunal. It is only in the case that a separate advance has been established for the counterclaim and not paid, that the counterclaim will be barred.[21]

---

21 This result, which is confirmed by the constant practice of the Secretariat, is not always recognized by the parties or even experienced arbitrators because the wording of Article 30(4) of the Rules, and its predecessor, Article 15 of the 1980 Internal Rules, is not crystal clear. That article provides: "When a request for an advance on costs has not been complied with . . . the relevant claim or counterclaim shall be considered as withdrawn." However, where one party, to make up for the other's default, has paid the entire advance fixed on a global amount and the ICC has in hand funds to cover the expenses of the entire dispute, the request for an advance even on the opposing party's claim has in fact been complied with, and there is no reason to ask the tribunal to suspend its works or proceed with only part of the dispute. Moreover, where there is non-payment of one-half of a global advance it is not possible to say that a relevant claim or counterclaim has been withdrawn and the other paid for.

iv) Where separate advances have been determined and the respondent fails to pay the advance for its counterclaim, the counterclaim, after due notice has been given by the Secretary General, will be considered withdrawn and the arbitration will proceed on the claim only, if the claimant has paid its separate advance;

v) The same rules apply *pari passu* in the case of non-payment by a claimant, a less frequent occurrence.

vi) The formal final time limit for the payment of an advance (which pursuant to Article 30(4) must not be less than 15 days from the giving of notice thereof) is in fact set by the Secretary General only after lengthy investigations and discussions concerning any non-payment and its surrounding circumstances; in addition the non-paying party has the right to have the issue determined by the Court, but must make its request within the notice period;

vii) Withdrawal of a claim or a counterclaim is without prejudice; it may be reasserted, but not in the same arbitral proceeding.[22] If it is reintroduced before another arbitral tribunal, statute of limitation problems may arise.

viii) A party which has failed to contribute to a global advance on costs, or failed to pay a separate advance, is never prevented from defending against claims or counterclaims asserted against it and fully participating in the arbitral proceedings.

14.03   The use of bank guarantees for the advance on costs

Users of ICC arbitration services have frequently pointed out that a substantial part of the arbitration costs will only be paid out at the end of the arbitration, when the fees of the arbitrators are finally fixed, and payment made to them by the ICC. They have argued, therefore, that they should be able to satisfy the advance on costs obligation by furnishing a security device, such as a bank guarantee. Prior to 1986, parties occasionally reached agreement with the Secretariat on an *ad hoc* basis to furnish a bank guarantee in lieu of a cash payment. This was possible when the advance was very large or, more particularly, when it was necessary to cover the default of the opposing party. From July 1986 onwards the Court has advised parties by way of communications from the Secretary General of the circumstances in which bank guarantees would be accepted in lieu of cash.[23]

These conditions are now set out in Appendix III of the Rules, the Schedule of Arbitration Costs and Fees.

The general notion is that a party should be able to pay by way of bank guarantee any amounts in excess of its 50% share of the global advance estab-

---

22   Article 30(4).

23   Secretary General of the Court of Arbitration, communication of 1 January 1988, Note 19 *supra*.

lished by the Court, which it will have paid in cash. Thus, in case a party is required to pay the 50% share of the advance attributable to its defaulting opponent in order for the arbitration to proceed (Rules, Article 30(3)), this portion of the advance may be paid by bank guarantee (Appendix III, Article 1(5)). By the same token, where the separate advance that a party must pay exceeds one half of the aggregate advance (for the reasons set out in Section 14.01, *supra*) it may pay the excess by way of bank guarantee (Appendix III, Article 1(8)).

Where very large advances are required, the necessity of paying "up front" very large amounts which may not be disbursed for years may appear unduly burdensome. The Schedule of Arbitration Costs and Fees (Appendix III, Article 1(5)) provides some relief:

> Each party shall pay in cash its share of the total advance on costs. However, if its share exceeds an amount fixed from time to time by the Court, a party may post a bank guarantee for this additional amount.

In the past, the Court has accepted bank guarantees for the amounts of an advance payable by a party superior to $ 300,000, provided there were no special circumstances requiring large disbursements early in the arbitration. This remains a useful benchmark although the Court has not at present publicly fixed the amount in excess of which it will accept a guarantee. The matter should be taken up with the Secretariat by the concerned party at the appropriate time.

The Secretariat is entitled to establish the terms governing all bank guarantees (Appendix III, Article 1(9)) and the form of the bank guarantee will be supplied by the Secretariat upon request. In past years, on an *ad hoc* basis, the Secretariat accepted any unconditional bank guarantee payable on first demand on a first class, internationally recognized bank. With the increase in the number of requests to use bank guarantees, the Secretariat strongly prefers that the guarantee issued in its favor be made by the ICC's regular bank in Switzerland, leaving it to the party to make its own arrangements for bank-to-bank guarantees from its own bank. As these conditions may vary from time to time, parties seeking to use a bank guarantee to satisfy advance on costs obligations should contact the Secretariat as to the current requirements.

14.04   Other consequences of default by a party to pay advance on costs

i) Requiring payment by order, award or judgment

As noted above the Rules provide little relief in favor of a party which has been disadvantaged by having to pay its defaulting opponent's share of the advance on costs in order to progress the arbitration. Yet the defaulting party's refusal to pay its advance would ordinarily constitute a breach of contract since by agreeing to arbitration under the ICC Rules it has agreed to respect its provisions regarding advances on costs. While a refusal to pay an advance may occasionally be motivated by a principled legal position or a *bona fide* inability to pay, it is more often the case that the refusal reflects a desire to make the arbitration more difficult and more costly for the adversary. There is a growing sentiment that where this is the case there should be a remedy, either in the hands of the arbitral tribunal or the courts. The issue of the allocation of jurisdictional powers between courts and arbitral tribunals in respect to ancillary proceedings and interim measures is taken up in further detail in Chapters 26 and 27. We consider here some of the rather sparse and fragmented reactions by courts and arbitral tribunals to the failure of a party to contribute to the costs of the arbitration, and its consequences.

The most obvious option for the party seeking to reverse the consequences of its opponent's failure to pay its share of the advance on costs is for it to pay on behalf of the defaulting party and then to seek an interim award for immediate reimbursement of the sums which the party has been required to advance because of its adversary's default. All the conditions for an interim award seem fulfilled: immediate harm has been done to the non-defaulting party, the breach of the contractual obligation raises simple issues, the amount of damages are known and the claim is for a liquidated amount. The fact that the final determination of who shall pay the costs of the arbitration will only be known at the time of the final award is irrelevant: the breach of the obligation to pay the advance on costs is final and irrevocable and the damages to the paying party are known. The determination of final costs is an independent event giving rise to subsequent obligations.

Surprisingly, reported ICC awards (whether in their official "sanitized" versions published in the Yearbook or the Journal du droit international or otherwise) do not reveal any precedents of such successful interim awards, but there may well be unreported cases. In one unreported interim award commented on by a member of the Court[24] the arbitral tribunal found that the Rules "create a binding contractual obligation imposing on each of the parties payment of half of the advance" and that failure of the respondent to respect this obligation constituted a breach of contract. The tribunal had jurisdiction to determine the consequences of such breach. In that case, however, the tribunal did not make an interim award in favor of the claimant, finding that it had not established irreparable harm and that claimant was able to make the advance on behalf of the respondent without difficulty.[25] These do not appear to be particularly convincing reasons not to grant a monetary award for what is essentially a breach of contract claim. Nevertheless, a tribunal always has discretion whether to render interim awards, or to await the rendering of a single final award dealing with all issues, and it is the judge of determining when such an award will be opportune in view of all the circumstances of the case. The decision would seem to confirm the principle

---

24   D. Mitrovic, *Advance to Cover Costs of Arbitration*, 7 ICC BULL. 88 (December 1996).

25   *See* DERAINS & SCHWARTZ, 320.

that an arbitral tribunal may make an interim award against a defaulting party to require its payment (or reimbursement) of the default amount and one can expect to learn of such awards rendered in appropriate circumstances in the future.[26] An award for reimbursement to the party who had paid the advance on behalf of the defaulting party should be enforceable in national courts and under the New York Convention in the same way as any other award for a sum of money.

The party injured by an opponent's non-payment of the advance on costs may also seek interim relief from the arbitral tribunal by way of procedural order. This seems a less advisable tactic due to the difficulty of enforcement of such orders (*see* Chapter 26, *infra*).

Alternatively, the party seeking to obtain an effective order requiring the defaulting party to pay the required advance to the ICC may seek the intervention of a national court (usually the court at the domicile of the defaulting party) to obtain an injunction or similar order compelling such payment. Such relief falls within the traditional powers of national courts to grant provisional or interim measures in proceedings ancillary to arbitration. Obviously the prospects for success in obtaining an order of injunction depends upon the specific law of the concerned jurisdiction. A number of successful attempts have been reported in various jurisdictions.

In *Fertalage Industries (Algeria) v. Société Kaltenbach Thurin, S.A. (France)*[27] the claimant Algerian company had contributed its 50% share of the total advance on costs but the respondent French company had defaulted in payment and the claimant had refused to pay the defaulted amount. As a consequence, the ICC had ordered the arbitration withdrawn and refunded to the claimant its advance. Upon an action brought in the French court to enjoin the French company to make the required payment the President of the *Tribunal de grande instance* issued the required injunction in a *référé* (urgent measures) proceeding, subjecting the respondent to a fine (*astreinte*) of FF 10,000 per day if the order was not complied with. The court conditioned its injunction, and the respondent's obligations thereunder, upon the claimant having taken the necessary measures to have the arbitration actively reestablished with the ICC.

---

26 The claim for reimbursement of amounts paid on behalf of the defaulting party has a strong contractual flavor and poses fewer problems than where the non-defaulting party did not pay in place of its adversary and instead would seek an award requiring payment to the ICC. Framing the issue this way might be seen as more of a dispute between the arbitral institution and the parties using its services, than as a contractual dispute between the parties, *see* D. Mitrovic, *supra* n. 24 at p. 89.

27 *Tribunal de grande instance*, Beauvais, 9 April 1998 (unreported).

A similar result has been reported in a case brought before a state court in the United States.[28] In that case the order, obtained by default, required the respondent United States parties to pay their share of the advance on costs to the ICC within fourteen days.

ii) Treating non-payment as waiver of the right to require arbitration

One possible remedy for a party, when its adversary has defaulted in its obligation to pay its share of the advance on costs is to treat the arbitration agreement as terminated by breach and to bring suit in a national court. This tactic succeeded in *Société TRH Graphic v. Offset Aubin*[29] where a French party claimant was faced with the refusal by a British company respondent to contribute its share of the ICC advance on costs.

Declining to substitute payment for the defaulting respondent the claimant withdrew its arbitration claim and brought suit on the merits in a French court, which accepted jurisdiction, finding that the defaulting defendant had not, at the time, supplied any explanation of its default in payment, and had no right to claim the exclusivity of arbitral jurisdiction as it had paralyzed the arbitration by its dilatory attitude.

It is not certain that this solution would be followed by all courts as non-payment of an advance need not necessarily be considered waiver of the right to arbitrate, or such a breach of the arbitration agreement as to justify its termination.[30]

However, a respondent should understand that it takes substantial risks in failing to pay its share of an advance on costs contrary to its obligations under the arbitration agreement and contrary to the policies of the ICC as expressed by the Secretary General of the ICC Court.

iii) Impecuniosity of party as argument to avoid normal consequences of failure to pay advance

Claimant parties have occasionally sought to have the Court reduce or eliminate advances required by them on the grounds that their financial inability to make payment, and accordingly to prosecute their claims, rendered the arbitration agreement inequitable. The Court has not reacted favorably to such arguments.

Alternatively, claimants (and even occasionally respondents) have urged before national courts that because of their impecuniosity the arbitration agree-

---

28　Ulrich Schubert v. H.O. Engineering, Inc. et al, Order of the Superior Court of New Jersey, Middlesex County Docket No. L-4310-90 (4 March 1994), reported in DERAINS & SCHWARTZ, 320.

29　*Cour de cassation*, 19 November 1991, 1992 REV. ARB. 462.

30　Another question would be whether the issue of breach of the arbitration agreement and the consequences thereof should be considered by arbitrators and not a court.

ment should be considered frustrated,[31] the consequence alleged to be that the court should take jurisdiction over the merits of the dispute. A few cases of this nature have been known to have succeeded in the past when brought in Indian courts by Indian parties who alleged inability to pay advances (or sometimes to pay transportation and expenses for arbitrations to be held abroad), as well as inability to obtain Indian Central Bank authorization to obtain foreign exchange to pay advances.[32] This could be said to be based, in addition to sympathy for the Indian parties, on a certain hostility by the Indian courts to international arbitration in general as had been evidenced by their narrow construction of what matters should be considered "commercial" or "foreign" in such a way as to avoid the obligations of the New York Convention.[33]

More recently, however, in keeping with India's adoption of a modern arbitration law[34] covering and encouraging international arbitration, these protective practices seem to have ceased. Nevertheless, the courts will carefully examine whether any conduct by the non-Indian party may be considered to have added to the burden of the Indian party.

In one case[35] an Indian court rejected the Indian petitioner company's argument that the amount set for its separate advance on costs ($230,000) frustrated its agreement to arbitrate under the ICC Rules pursuant to which it had commenced an arbitration as claimant. The High Court investigated carefully whether the ICC Court had respected its Rules and the scale of charges and noted as well that the higher amount to be paid as a separate advance followed upon the claimant's failure to contribute its one half of the advance payable on the total amount in dispute. After observing that the petitioner had not given any consideration to reducing the amount of its damages claim so as to reduce the costs of arbitration, the Court found that the arbitration costs were in accordance with the agreement of the parties and that petitioner had not proved frustration.

---

31 Or "incapable of being performed" in the terms of Article II(3) of the New York Convention which provides an exception to the requirement of the courts in a Convention country to decline jurisdiction in view of an arbitration agreement and to send the parties to arbitration.

32 M/s V/o Tractoroexport v. M/s Taraporce and Co., I YEARBOOK 188 (1976) (Supreme Ct. India 1971); Indian Organic Chemicals v. Chemtex Fibres Inc., IV YEARBOOK 270 (1979) (High Court, Bombay, 1977); *see generally* Albert Jan van den Berg, THE NEW YORK ARBITRATION CONVENTION OF 1958, 160 (Kluwer 1981).

33 *See generally* Jan Paulsson, *The New York Convention's Misadventures in India*, 7 MEALEY'S INT. ARB. REP. (No. 6, 1992) 18; F.S. Nariman, *Finality in India: The Impossible Dream*, 10 ARB. INT. 373 (1994).

34 The Arbitration and Conciliation Act, 1996 (No. 26 of 1996).

35 E. Co. v. B. Co. (High Court, Delhi, 21 May 1998) (unreported).

In another recent case[36], an Indian appellate court rejected an application of an Indian company to suspend a pending ICC arbitration on the grounds that because of its financial circumstances it had filed an application under the Sick Industrial Companies Act, and that a Special Director had been appointed to prepare a rehabilitation scheme. The company sought the application of Section 22(1) of the Act which provided for suspension of any proceedings for winding up the company or for seizure or execution against its assets. The Court refused to broaden the statute to cover arbitration proceedings, and they were allowed to proceed.

iv) Alleged excessive nature of ICC costs

Very occasionally the costs of ICC arbitration (or of other institutional arbitration costs) may run afoul of legislation or policies designed for consumer protection. In one United States case, *Brower v. Gateway 2000*,[37] an ICC arbitration clause was included in sales documents shipped with a computer delivered to an individual pursuant to a mail order. The conditions of sale and arbitration obligations were said to be accepted if the computer was kept for more than 30 days. The consumer (together with a class of similarly situated buyers) brought suit in New York state court, in lieu of arbitration, arguing that the ICC arbitration clause, requiring the payment of a non-recoverable registration fee and the payment of ICC administrative expenses, was unjust and oppressive in view of the size of the claim. The New York Court followed the claimant in its argument that it was not required to participate in ICC arbitration. It did not, however, permit the party to avoid its arbitration obligation entirely and remitted it instead to *ad hoc* arbitration.[38]

While it may be debated whether the choice of ICC arbitration is appropriate for relatively small consumer transactions as in *Gateway*, and to what extent adhesion contracts will always be enforced in consumer transactions, the rationale of that case is unlikely to be applied to ICC arbitration clauses in normal international business transactions.

---

36   Burn, Standard Co., Ltd. v. McDermott International, Inc., (High Court Calcutta, Civil Appellate jurisdiction, 11 June 1997) (unreported).

37   676 N.Y.S. 2d 569 (1st Dept. 1998).

38   The decision is justly criticized in Hans Smit, *May An Arbitration Agreement Calling for Institutional Arbitration Be Denied Enforcement Because of the Cost Involved*, 8 AM. REV. INT. ARB. 167, (1999), who notes the court's failure to apply the applicable Federal Arbitration Act as well as its lack of understanding of the costs of ICC arbitration as compared with expected expenses of *ad hoc* arbitration. The facts of the case were extreme, however, and the ICC does not promote the use of its Rules for this kind of dispute.

CHAPTER 15

TERMS OF REFERENCE

15.01 Rationale

Once the file containing the initial submissions of both parties has been transmitted to the tribunal, the arbitrators' first duty is to draw up the Terms of Reference. Article 18 of the ICC Rules provides that this document should contain the following items:

a) the full names and descriptions of the parties;

b) the addresses of the parties to which notifications and communications arising in the course of the arbitration may be made;

c) a summary of the parties' respective claims and the relief sought by each party, with an indication to the extent possible of the amounts claimed or counterclaimed;

d) unless the arbitral tribunal considers it inappropriate, a list of issues to be determined;

e) the full names, descriptions[1] and addresses of the arbitrators;

f) the place of arbitration; and

g) particulars of the applicable procedural rules and, if such is the case, reference to the power conferred upon the arbitral tribunal to act as *amiable compositeur* or to decide *ex aequo et bono.*

The featuring of the Terms of Reference in successive versions of the ICC Rules derives from the procedural requirements of some legal systems—now largely modernized and replaced—which disfavored mandatory arbitration of future disputes by an arbitration clause and required that the parties enter into an agreement or *compromis* after the dispute had arisen. This special

---

[1]   The word "description" as found in the English version of Article 13 is a poor translation of "qualités" found in the French version, intended to refer to the arbitrator's profession, employment or status.

submission to arbitration (*see* Section 4.01) would define the issues to be decided in arbitration. Such was once the rule, for instance, under the French Code of Civil Procedure. It survives in a number of countries whose statutes were inspired by French law as it stood a few generations ago. In France, however, the requirement of a post dispute *compromis* has long been held inapplicable to international arbitrations and in any event has been eliminated as to both domestic and international arbitrations by provisions of the Code of Civil Procedure relating to arbitration.[2]

Even if no longer necessary to ensure compliance with national procedural laws requiring a *compromis*, the preparation of the Terms of Reference at the outset of the proceeding clarifies the issues to be decided by the arbitrators and the rules and powers they are to use in conducting the case. The existence of such a document further serves as a protection against attacks on an award on the grounds that the arbitrators had exceeded their authority or had ruled on issues not submitted to them. In fact, a clear statement of the claim in the Terms of Reference may avoid one of the jurisdictional grounds of attack—the defense of *ultra petita*: that an award has granted relief outside the scope of the pleadings.

The Terms of Reference may be drawn up by the arbitrators based on the pleadings and documents submitted to them[3] and then circulated to the parties for signature. The Terms of Reference may also be finalized during the tribunal's first meeting with the parties. This occasion should be used to agree upon various procedural matters. As in a pre-trial conference in ordinary court cases, the parties may also be expected to provide a realistic evaluation of the amount of time that their case will require, the number of witnesses they will present, the mode of exchanging documentary proof, the necessity of a site visit or technical expertise, and other related matters. While some of these items may be included in subsequent procedural orders by the tribunal rather than in the Terms of Reference, the preparation of the Terms of Reference marks the beginning of the proceedings before the arbitrators and provides a procedural framework for the dispute.

The Terms of Reference have been criticized as time consuming without bringing commensurate benefits.[4] Many such critics come from common-law countries, particularly the United States. Their opinion may be colored by

---

2   Amendments to the French Code of Civil Procedure by the Decrees of 14 May 1980 and 12 May 1981; *see* Articles 1442 (domestic arbitration) and 1492-1497 (international arbitration).

3   Note the provision of Article 18(1) that the Terms are to be drawn up in "the light of . . . [the] most recent submissions" of the parties. Thus it is possible to bring up new claims and issues after the Request and Answer. This has been confirmed in numerous ICC awards. *See e.g.* ICC Case No. 8197, affirmed *Cour d'appel*, Paris 19 May 1998, 13 MEALEY'S INT. ARB. REP. E-1 (July 1998).

4   Hans Smit, *The Future of International Commercial Arbitration: A Single Transnational Institution?*, 25 COLUMBIA JOURNAL OF TRANSNATIONAL LAW 9 at 26-27 (1986); Gillis Wetter, *The Present Status of the International Court of Arbitration of the ICC: An Appraisal*, 1 AM. REV. INT. ARB. 91 (1990).

rules of practice which encourage the discovery and development of facts after the exchange of initial pleadings and do not require an early definition of the issues by the parties. They may also underestimate the educational value of preparing the Terms of Reference when parties from widely differing legal and economic backgrounds are involved in the dispute. The authors have participated in some arbitrations where the meeting with the arbitrators to establish the Terms of Reference brought about the first effective realization by the respondent that an obligatory arbitral process was under way and that an award would ultimately be made on defined issues. Sometimes the discussion leading to agreement on the issues (or the effect on a party of the arbitrators' definition of the issues) has led to settlement. Thus the Terms of Reference may be useful as a protection of awards against attack, as a tool for organizing the future path of the arbitral proceedings, and sometimes as a means to *rapprochement* of the parties.

It would appear that these benefits of Terms of Reference have gained general acceptance among users of ICC arbitration. Resistance in common law countries, such as the United States, has diminished after increased familiarity with the international arbitration process. When national committees were consulted in connection with the 1998 Revision of the Rules on the issue of whether to continue to employ Terms of Reference, the response in favor of their continuation was (perhaps unexpectedly) almost unanimous in favor of retention.

One provision intended to lighten the requirements of the Terms was, however, introduced in the 1998 revision. Unlike the prior version of the Rules which required a "definition of the issues to be determined," Article 18(1)(d) is non-mandatory: "unless the Arbitral Tribunal considers it inappropriate, a list of issues to be determined." This removal of an obligation that the arbitral tribunal in all cases define issues in the Terms responded to criticism by many arbitrators that one could not, at this early stage of the proceedings, define issues in a complete or useful way.

The difficulty in defining issues early is even more pronounced under the 1998 Rules since the requirement for alleging in the Request a full statement of the claimant's case has been somewhat relaxed (*see* Section 10.04, *supra*). Issues, in any event, tend to evolve with the case. New issues which arise during the course of proceedings subsequent to the Terms of Reference are not excluded from consideration. Why not, practitioners argued, leave the necessity of a list of issues to be determined to the discretion of the arbitrator, since defining the issues may delay the arbitration?

Under the 1975 Rules, which required a description of the issues to be set out in the Terms of Reference, a significant number of arbitrators routinely avoided the requirement by utilizing a generic formula such as "The issues to be determined by the arbitrators will be those contained in the parties' pleadings and such other issues as may arise during the course of the arbitration." The Court did not object to such formulae when the Terms were transmitted to it.

The 1998 Rules give the arbitral tribunal discretion to go beyond this tolerated generic description of issues and to abandon any listing at all. Nevertheless, the provision that in ordinary cases the Terms shall contain a definition of issues reflects the ICC's recognition that the Terms remain an essential part of ICC arbitration and the desire that they be as meaningful as possible.

It may indeed be impossible, at the early stage of drafting the Terms, to be sure that one can define all the issues that may arise during the proceeding or that an issue, as it develops, has been correctly stated in the Terms. Fortunately, most case law tends to support the arbitral tribunal's power to treat any and all issues raised by the parties which are within the scope of the arbitration clause whether or not such issues are itemized in the Terms.[5] Nevertheless, it is recommended that the arbitrators when drafting the Terms take care to preserve this freedom. The ICC Practical Guide for the drafting of Terms of Reference suggests adding the following reservation: "The issues to be determined shall be those resulting from the parties' submissions and which are relevant to adjudication of the parties' respective claims and defenses. In particular, the Arbitral Tribunal may have to consider the following issues (but not necessarily all of these, and only these, and not in the following order . . .)."

15.02   Contents

The length and comprehensiveness of the Terms of Reference will depend upon the background and training of the arbitrators (particularly the presiding arbitrator, who usually drafts for the tribunal) and counsel, who may either present draft Terms of Reference to the tribunal or suggest modifications or additions to the tribunal's draft. The Terms of Reference may fulfill the requirements of the Rules and yet encompass only a few typewritten pages. They may also become very substantial documents if the claims, already

---

5   *See Cour de cassation, Première chambre civile*, 6 March 1996, Société Farhat Trading Co. v. Société Daewoo, 1997 REV. ARB. 69, Note J.J. Arnaldez (the extent of the arbitrator's jurisdiction is determined by the terms of the arbitration agreement. Within the scope of that jurisdiction the arbitrator may decide all issues which have been properly raised by the claims of the parties. The arbitrator is not limited to deciding only the issues set out in the Terms of Reference and does not decide in an unauthorized manner (*ultra petita*) when he decides additional issues within the scope of the arbitration clause); *compare* Steel Authority of India, Ltd. v. Hind Metal, Inc., [1984] 1 LLOYD'S L. REP. 405 (21 December 1993, Queen's Bench Division (Commercial Court)) (where an arbitrator fails to decide one of the issues specifically and unreservedly set out in the Terms of Reference the award is *infra petita* and, as not following the mission prescribed by the parties, may not be confirmed); *but see Cour supérieure de justice*, Luxembourg, 24 November 1993, Kersa Holding Company v. Infrancourtage, XXI YEARBOOK 617, 625 (1986) (holding that failure of arbitral tribunal to decide all the points in dispute not a ground for non-recognition of award under New York Convention.)

made in voluminous pleadings, are restated in detail and each litigious issue is separately defined in specific rather than general terms.

The Terms should follow the order set out in Article 18 but the form follows the particular inclinations and style of the arbitrators involved. A general tendency can be noted towards increased length and detail of the Terms, based on the increased experience level of arbitrators in ICC arbitrations who rely upon, and develop, precedents based on their previous experiences. Added length does not, however, necessarily make for a better Terms of Reference.

If the Request and the Answer are well drafted, the parties' respective claims may be sufficiently defined by a reference to those pleadings in the Terms of Reference. Where the pleadings are confused, the Terms of Reference should clearly summarize claims and defenses, and, where appropriate, set forth the issues to be determined. Experienced international arbitrators often call the attention of parties to issues which must be decided in order for the award to be enforceable but which parties have not specifically argued in submissions.

For the drafting of the summaries of the parties' claims and counterclaims required by Article 18(1)(c), the arbitrator frequently calls upon each of the parties to submit a draft summary of it own claims (or counterclaims) to be included, after appropriate revisions and additions by the arbitrator, in the Terms. It is the duty of the arbitrator to assure the parties that a statement of the position of each party in the Terms is in no way a recognition of its validity. A general clause accomplishing this, as well as avoiding any inappropriate limitation flowing from the drafting of a summary of claims, can be recommended for insertion in the Terms:

> The purpose of the following summary is to satisfy the requirements of Article 18(1)(c) of the ICC Rules (1998), without prejudice to any other or further allegations, arguments and contentions contained in the pleadings or submissions already filed and in such submissions as will be made in the course of this arbitration. Accordingly, the Tribunal shall be entitled, subject to Articles 15 and 19 of the ICC Rules and other applicable procedural requirements such as, *inter alia*, procedural time limits, to take into consideration further allegations, arguments, contentions and oral or written submissions. By signing these Terms of Reference, neither party subscribes to, or acquiesces in, the summary of the other party set forth below.

It is important that the statement of the claim or counterclaim in the Terms of Reference fully reflects the scope of the demand of each party: while new issues may be discussed, no new claim or counterclaim outside of the limits fixed in the Terms of Reference may be made during the proceedings without obtaining the authorization of the arbitral tribunal. Article 19 of the Rules provides:

> After the Terms of Reference have been signed or approved by the Court, no party shall make new claims or counterclaims which fall outside the limits of the Terms of Reference unless it has been authorized to do so by the Arbitral Tribunal, which shall consider the nature of such new claims or counterclaims, the stage of the arbitration and other relevant circumstances.

This provision is designed to prevent a party from adding new claims during the course of the proceedings unless so authorized by the arbitral tribunal. Without this provision, parties could delay the proceedings, hinder the preparation of a defense in an orderly way, or add a new cause of action which attaches a totally new monetary dimension to the dispute. Terms of Reference should be sufficiently broad to cover the full scope of the claims and counter-claims presented, and not exclude the development of more detailed claims during the proceedings, provided they reasonably fall within the general claims of the parties.

Under prior versions of the Rules, where new claims could not be included in the arbitration without the execution of a rider to the Terms of Reference, requiring the agreement of all parties, respondents were quick to argue that new allegations, or specifications of quantum, developed by claimants constituted new claims which the respondent would not agree to be added to the Terms. This spawned numerous arbitral rulings on the matter, with varied results.[6] The modification of the Rules to permit making of new claims within the discretion of the arbitrators (and not subject to veto by the adverse party) should largely remove the controversy over what constitutes a new claim. A party wishing to modify the nature or amount of its claim need not convince the arbitrators that the modifications do not constitute a new claim but only that the modifications, whether or not constituting a new claim, should in view of all the circumstances be permitted.

The Terms' summary of arguments in support of the claim and the defenses thereto should not be considered a limitation. Article 19 limits the adding of new claims but not the making of new arguments in support of claims generally set forth in the Terms, including new legal theories supporting the claim if based on the same alleged facts and circumstances.[7]

---

6   *Compare* ICC Case No. 4462/1985 XVI YEARBOOK 54 (1991) and ICC Case No. 6618/1991 8 ICC BULL. 70 (December 1997) (broad scope of claims modifications permitted without necessity of modifying terms) with ICC Case No. 6309/1991, III ICC AWARDS 459 (only narrow scope of claims modifications allowed).

7   *See, e.g.* ICC Case No. 6657/1993, 8 ICC BULL. 72 (December 1997), ICC Case No. 6618/1991, *id.* At 70, ICC Case No. 6223/1991, *id.* At 69.

Still, some drafters of Terms of Reference have felt it necessary to make this explicitly clear. For instance, in ICC Case 5302,[8] the drafters of the Terms stipulated:

> These Terms of Reference are designated to enable the parties and the Arbitral Tribunal to focus on the issues in this arbitration; they are not to be understood as foreclosing the making of arguments or introduction of evidence not expressly referred to herein.

To say that new claims may not be made (unless authorized by the arbitral tribunal) after the Terms of Reference have entered into effect is not to say that new calculations of damages or new theories of quantification may not be subsequently introduced without the necessity of requesting specific authorization. The Terms of Reference, after all, enter into effect at an early stage of the proceedings, usually long before a detailed economic analysis has been made of the consequences of breach and before experts have been consulted. Claimants, to be sure, are well advised to ensure that their claims, as restated in the Terms of Reference, are in general terms and refer to general theories of recovery, with amounts claimed as damages carefully designated as "estimates" or "provisional estimates." Failure to do so is not ordinarily fatal. New evidence and new quantification of damages does not constitute a new claim.[9]

In the *Carte Blanche* arbitration the claimant first sought to amend the Terms of Reference to increase the amount of approximately $6.7 million originally claimed so as to include additional consequential damages of some $3.5 million. After refusal of the respondent to agree to amendment of the Terms, the tribunal nevertheless permitted claimant to proceed with its claim of consequential and other damages, the total claimed amounting to over $16 million. Finding in favor of the claimant, the tribunal awarded it some $9 million in damages, of which approximately $5.1 million were consequential damages. Following notification of the award to the parties, the defendant sought to set aside the award in the United States on the ground that the award exceeded the arbitrators' powers. After reviewing the Terms of Reference and the claims made, a New York Federal District Court Judge confirmed the award, finding the arguments based on violation of the ICC Rules and the

---

8   Cited S. Jarvin, Note under ICC Case 4504, interim awards of 1985 and 1986, 1986 JDI, 1118, at 1128.

9   *Accord* DERAINS & SCHWARTZ, 250; *but see* FOUCHARD, GAILLARD, GOLDMAN ON INTERNATIONAL COMMERCIAL ARBITRATION (E. Gaillard and J. Savage, editors) 671 (Kluwer, 1999) (questioning the validity of the authors' statement in this text in the absence of some reservation or ambiguity in the Terms); *see* ICC Case No. 5514. 1990, III ICC AWARDS 459 (in a case governed by the 1975 Rules, where no new claims could be introduced without the agreement of the other party, the tribunal found that an increase in the amount of a claim is not a new claim, particularly where the Terms reserve the possibility of new quantification or where the claim has not been quantified).

Terms of Reference "unpersuasive."[10] Due regard should be given, however, to the fact that the Terms of Reference in that case were relatively broadly drafted, and that the U.S. Court, which recognized that its powers of review were limited, gave particular weight to the fact that the ICC Court of Arbitration, having scrutinized the award, found no violation of the Rules to bring to the attention of the arbitrators. To avoid any chance that a plea on similar grounds that the arbitral tribunal has neglected its duty of ensuring that all claims are within the scope of reference, might succeed, parties should be careful in their pleadings and in the drafting of the Terms of Reference.

The arbitrators' jurisdiction over the parties and the subject matter of the dispute should be among the issues defined in the Terms of Reference. Where a jurisdictional issue raises matters of exceptional complexity, two Terms of Reference may be conceivable: one to determine the jurisdictional questions and another concerning the merits of the dispute to be drafted subsequently if jurisdiction is found to exist. However, this approach is time-consuming and its acceptability to the Court of Arbitration is not certain. It is almost always a better practice to agree to Terms of Reference encompassing the entire dispute and, if appropriate, to provide therein for a preliminary decision on the issue of jurisdiction prior to submission of evidence and hearings on the merits.

The place of arbitration must be stipulated in the Terms of Reference. Ordinarily this will be the place of arbitration mentioned in the agreement containing an arbitration clause, or, when no place is stipulated in the agreement, the place designated by the Court of Arbitration under Article 14(1) of the Rules, which provides:

> The place of the arbitration shall be fixed by the Court, unless agreed upon by the parties.

However, in either case the parties can agree to another place of arbitration in the Terms, since such an agreement would either modify the original agreement to arbitrate, or obviate the Court of Arbitration's decision which, pursuant to Article 14(1), is to have effect only if the parties have not agreed. The parties should use the same care in deciding on a place of arbitration in the Terms as they would in the original agreement to arbitrate (*see* Section 7.02). The place of arbitration has important legal consequences. In a case known to the authors, the parties agreed, for reasons of convenience, to modify in the Terms the choice of venue provided in an arbitration clause. The clause was found in standard conditions incorporated by reference in the litigious contract. The unexpected consequence was to validate an arbitration clause which would most likely have been a nullity at the original seat of arbitration because neither the contract nor the referred to arbitration clause had been

---

10   Carte Blanche (Singapore) PTE Ltd. v. Carte Blanche International, Ltd., 683 F. Supp. 945, at 953-958 (SDNY 1988).

signed by the contracting parties, as required under the mandatory rules of procedure applicable there.

One of the most important items to be included in the Terms of Reference under Article 18(1)(g) of the ICC Rules is the "particulars of the applicable procedural rules. . ." This provision must be read in conjunction with the arbitrators' power to choose the applicable procedural rules and substantive law under Articles 15(1) and 17 (*see* Chapters 16 and 17), and the possible procedural imperatives of a national law in force at the seat of arbitration (*see* Section 16.02 as well as Part Five generally). Most modern legal systems recognize a large degree of party autonomy in determining procedural rules. It is usually unnecessary to settle the doctrinal dispute as to whether arbitrators' authority results from the international character of an arbitration or from the delegation of procedural powers to the parties by an applicable national procedural law.

The parties and the arbitrators should use the Terms of Reference to reach a common agreement on the basic procedure to be followed. They may agree to specific rules drafted for the dispute, or refer to other arbitral rules or to rules of national law. There is much to be said for trying to get the parties to agree to some specific aspects of the conduct of the proceedings at this preliminary stage. Whether specific procedural choices will favor one or the other party may be less predictable at this early stage; agreement may thus be more easily obtained.

Some of the procedural matters most frequently settled in the Terms of Reference include:

— language(s) of the proceedings,

— provisions as to general rules or principles for discovery of documents,

— provisions as to discovery of documents,

— provisions as to presentation of testimony in written form,

— provisions for the chairman of the tribunal to make procedural rulings alone (or after informal consultation with his fellow arbitrators),

— provision for interim awards, and

— empowering the arbitral tribunal to meet and hold hearings at venues other than the seat of arbitration.

The degree of procedural detail included in the Terms of Reference depends upon the outlook of the counsel and the arbitrators.[11] Some practitioners (of-

---

11 A substantial body of literature has been produced on the drafting of Terms of Reference, *see, e.g.*: Serge Lazareff (Chairman of the ICC Commission Working Group), *Practical Guide for Terms of Reference*, 3 ICC BULL 24 (1992), J.C. Goldsmith *How to Draft Terms of Reference*, 3 ARB. INT. 298 (1987).

ten Americans) seek to use the Terms of Reference as an opportunity to set forth a comprehensive procedural charter for the future conduct of the arbitration. This approach seldom results in consensus. Indeed, there are dangers in agreeing to precise procedural directions and deadlines (as opposed to rules or principles) in a document having the legal significance of the Terms of Reference: once provisions have been agreed by the parties and the arbitrators, they can be modified, in principle, only by a new agreement by the same persons. This may become impossible during the course of the arbitration. It is unwise to "lock in" procedural requirements which may become impossible in the light of changing circumstances but which, if not respected, would constitute a violation of the Terms of Reference. A particular hazard is the setting of a mandatory deadline for rendering the award. While well-intentioned counsel may have added such a clause in the hope of inspiring the arbitrators to celerity, if the arbitrators fail to render an award within the prescribed time, the result may be to put an end prematurely to the jurisdiction of the arbitrators and frustrate the intention of the parties.[12]

The 1998 Rules specifically empower the parties to shorten time limits otherwise specified under the Rules so as to provide for a party agreed "fast track" arbitration. Article 32(1) of the Rules provides:

> The parties may agree to shorten the various time limits set out in these Rules. Any such agreement entered into subsequent to the constitution of an Arbitral Tribunal shall become effective only upon the approval of the Arbitral Tribunal.

At the same time it was provided in Article 32(2) that the Court, despite the mandatory time limit agreed by the parties could extend any such time limit if "necessary to do so in order that the Arbitral Tribunal or the Court may fulfil their responsibilities in accordance with these Rules."

This desirable security device gives the Court the possibility to save the parties "from their own folly." Fear has been expressed in some quarters that giving this power to the Court guarantees that "fast track" arbitrations will automatically be converted into arbitrations on a slower track. So far, little evidence has surfaced to confirm this suspicion: the Court is mindful of its responsibility to maintain the parties' bargain and to put pressure on the parties to abide by the terms of their procedural agreement in the absence of exceptional circumstances. The Court retains the power to extend the time

---

12   For an example in rather special circumstances, *see* ICC Case 3383/1979, extracts *in* 1980 JDI 979; extracts in English *in* VII YEARBOOK 119 (1982), *see also Tribunal fédéral Suisse*, 24 March 1997, 1997 SWISS BULL. 316, with English translation in 12 MEALEY'S INT. ARB. REPORT, No. 9, pp. H1-H9) (September 10, 1999) (when a deadline imposed by the Terms for the filing of a Statement of Claim was extended by the Chairman of the Tribunal for several days, the ensuing award successfully resisted judicial nullification); *see generally*, Richard Kriendler and Timothy J. Kantz, *Agreed Deadlines and the Setting Aside of Arbitral Awards*, 1997 SWISS BULL. 576, discussed in Section 11.03.

limits agreed by the parties, but it has no obligation to do so. It should be noted that this exceptional power is vested only in the Court, and not in the arbitral tribunal.

Much difficulty can be avoided by stipulating that detailed procedural provisions (the order in which briefs and documents will be submitted, dates therefor, sequence and agenda of hearings, and the like) will be set forth in separate procedural orders by the arbitrators and adjusted as appropriate. At the time such orders become necessary, agreement of the parties is not indispensable although doubtless desirable. It should be accepted as ordinary ICC arbitration practice that the arbitral tribunal will include in the Terms of Reference only provisions which are intended to be unchangeable, using procedural orders, modifiable by the tribunal acting alone, for ordinary procedural items which by their nature can conceivably change. One of the items which should be made subject to change is the calendar of proceedings and the fixing of dates for specific actions (filing of memorials, evidence, witness statements, etc.) to be taken by the parties. The distinction between general procedural guidelines established in the Terms and calendar items to be established by procedural order is emphasized in Article 18(4) of the Rules which provides:

> When drawing up the Terms of Reference, or as soon as possible thereafter, the Arbitral Tribunal, after having consulted the parties, shall establish in a separate document a provisional timetable that it intends to follow for the conduct of the arbitration and shall communicate it to the Court and the parties. Any subsequent modifications of the provisional timetable shall be communicated to the Court and the parties.

By requiring that the provisional timetable be established in a "separate document" from the Terms, the Rules avoid any implication that the timetable has become part of the arbitration agreement or of the procedures agreed to by the parties and that any departure from the agreement could lead to the nullity of an award. At the same time, the Rules require the arbitrators to draw up a provisional timetable at the outset of proceedings which allows the Secretariat and the Court to ensure that the arbitration is progressing normally.

The parties may in the Terms define general procedural rules by referring to an existing body of arbitral rules or to the rules of a national procedural law (*see* Chapter 16). The inclusion of such rules in the Terms of Reference is more often the result of accepting a suggestion of the tribunal than an agreement between the parties. It is rare that parties will impose rules on a presiding arbitrator who expresses different preferences. Some of the criteria for choosing the procedural rules are referred to in Section 16.01 (*see also* Section 8.02). The decision is frequently made as a preliminary matter in the Terms of Reference.

It should be noted that the ICC Court has refused to accept Terms of Reference which purported to reverse the order of Article 15(1) of the Rules by stating that the proceedings were governed by any rules upon which the parties may agree and, where there is no such agreement, the ICC Rules. If the parties accept and prefer to follow all the customs and practices under the national law in effect at the seat of the arbitration, they may specifically refer to them as follows:

> The rules governing the proceedings shall be the ICC Rules of Arbitration and where these rules are silent, such other rules applicable under [English] law to arbitral proceedings taking place in [England].

If the parties are unfamiliar with procedural practices under the local law at the seat of arbitration and wish to be as free of such procedures as possible, they may provide:

> The rules governing the proceedings shall be the ICC Rules of Arbitration and where these rules are silent, such other rules as the arbitrators may from time to time settle.

It will then be up to the arbitrators to assure that the rules they settle do not conflict with any mandatory rules of national law applicable to international arbitrations in effect at the seat of arbitration, insofar as noncompliance therewith could endanger the enforceability of the award.

On 1 June 1999 the International Bar Association adopted Rules on the Taking of Evidence in International Commercial Arbitration ("IBA Rules of Evidence") designed to enable parties and arbitrators to conduct the evidence phase of international arbitration proceedings in an efficient and economical manner.[13] These Rules reflect an effort to suggest workable combinations of features from various national procedural systems. They may be looked to in the context of preparing Terms of Reference, which may profitably borrow from them. The Rules attempt to settle in a neutral fashion, acceptable to parties from both civil law and common law countries, issues relating to proof which have traditionally caused problems stemming from differences between the systems. They will appeal to parties who would prefer to have in advance a fairly detailed set of rules rather than to await the arbitrator's decision on issues as they arise. It has been the authors' experience that while the Rules offer useful precedents for dealing with various evidentiary issues that arise frequently in international arbitrations, it is rare that the parties or the arbitral tribunal adopts them *in toto* for application as such in the arbitration.

15.03   Default by party

The parties' participation in drafting the Terms of Reference is useful and important. However, if one of the parties refuses or fails to sign them, its default will not bring the proceedings to a halt. Article 18(3) provides that in case of default, the Terms of Reference are forwarded to the Court for review as soon

---

13   These Rules replace the IBA Supplementary Rules Governing the Reception of Evidence in International Commercial Arbitration originally issued in 1983. The Rules are available from the IBA and are also found in Appendix K to REDFERN & HUNTER.

as they have been signed by the arbitrators and the other party. If after such review the Court finds the Terms adequate (*i.e.* drawn up in accordance with the Rules) it will approve them and the arbitration will proceed.[14]

Similar to its power to appoint an arbitrator for a defaulting party, the power of the Court to approve the Terms of Reference upon a party's default is an important sanction of obstructive and dilatory tactics. At the same time, the Court's review constitutes an additional guarantee of procedural due process to the defaulting party.

It should be noted that where a party does not participate, the Terms of Reference should *not* include elements not agreed upon in the agreement to arbitrate but which in principle, *all* of the parties must agree upon, such as the law applicable to the dispute. These issues may only be determined in an arbitral award, based on a reasoned decision and after both parties have been given the opportunity to express their views. Similarly, adding the power of an arbitrator to act as *amiable compositeur*, or a shift in the agreed place of arbitration, cannot be included in the Terms of Reference which enter into effect according to the default procedures.

15.04   Entry Into effect

Once the Terms of Reference enter into effect the arbitrators are free to move forward. In order to avoid any undue delay in reaching this stage, Article 18(2) provides that the Terms of Reference signed by the parties and the members of the tribunal shall be transmitted to the Court within two months of the date of the tribunal's initial receipt of the file from the Secretariat, absent an extension of time by the Court (which may be granted upon a reasoned request from the arbitrator or on its own initiative if it decides it is necessary to do so).

The Terms of Reference ordinarily enter into effect on the date upon which the last signature of all parties and all members of the tribunal has been obtained. They are then transmitted to the Court, and no separate action of the Court is required. While no approval of the Court is required, however, and the Terms, where signed by all parties and the tribunal, will enter into effect prior to any review by the Court, the agreed Terms in fact are laid before the Court, after review by the Secretariat, which "takes note" of them. If there are fundamental errors in the drawing up of the Terms which could cause difficulties in the conduct of the proceedings or the enforcement of the awards, the Court will not take note of the Terms and will return them to the tribunal

---

14   For a detailed review of the Court's practices under the 1988 Rules in "taking note" of Terms of Reference which have been forwarded to it after having been signed by the parties and the arbitrators, and examining and approving Terms where there has been a default in signature, *see* Andreas Reiner, *Terms of Reference: The Function of the International Court of Arbitration and Application of Article 16 by the Arbitrators*, 7 ICC BULL. 59 (December 1996).

bringing the errors to the attention of the tribunal. This may require correction and new signatures by the arbitrators and the parties.[15] If a party has failed to sign the Terms of Reference, the Terms will enter into effect after approval by the Court and on the date of the notification to the tribunal by the Secretariat of the Court's approval. In the case of signature by a party of the Terms with reservations (e.g. not agreeing to certain of the issues defined in the Terms, or contesting the presence of one of the parties to the arbitration) the Court will ordinarily treat the case as default by a party. Unless signature is unconditional the procedure for approval by the Court must take place under Article 18(3) in the same way as where there is a refusal to sign the Terms.

15.05   Legal Effect

Terms of Reference are recognized as a required procedural step in ICC arbitration, their legal nature nevertheless is not easy to define. Two principal issues have arisen: are the arbitrators required to adhere to the prescriptions of the Terms, and do the Terms themselves constitute an agreement to arbitrate or *compromis* entered into after the dispute has arisen (as was originally provided for in early versions of the Rules to accommodate the former requirements of some legal systems)? As to the first question the answer is yes, subject nevertheless to the arbitrator's reasonable power of interpretation.[16] As to the second, the answer is less clear. The better view would be that the Terms only supplement the original agreement to arbitrate and only exceptionally constitute a novation and new agreement to arbitrate.

There is no doubt that the Terms of Reference, designed to be accepted and signed (subject to the default procedure described above) by the parties and the arbitrators, may have an important effect on the future conduct of the proceedings. This is particularly true in view of the provisions of Articles 15, 17 and 18 of the Rules confirming the power of the parties, and failing them the arbitrator, to agree on procedural rules, and stipulating what particulars must be put in the Terms. Parties may use the drafting of the Terms as an opportunity to expand (for instance by giving the arbitrator the powers of *amiable compositeur*) or to restrict (for instance by requiring an interim or preliminary award on specific issues) the arbitrator's authority.

---

15   *See* Andreas Reiner, *Terms of Reference: The Function of the International Court of Arbitration and Application of Article 16 by the Arbitrators*, 7 ICC BULL. 59 (December 1996); *see also* DERAINS & SCHWARTZ, 241-242.

16   A court reviewing an award may sometimes encounter ambiguity in Terms of Reference. This possibility is said to permit discretionary action by the tribunal and to avoid inequitable nullification of an award. For an argument in favor of the recognition of an inherent power of the arbitrator to settle procedural problems which the procedural agreement of the parties did not properly foresee, see Claude Reymond, *Réflexions sur quelques problèmes de l'arbitrage international, faiblesses, menaces et perspectives* in MELANGES EN HOMMAGE A FRANCOIS TARRE (Paris, 1999).

Where a requirement of the Terms is specific, and intended to be obligatory, the arbitral tribunal must respect it. The Court of Arbitration is cognizant of this requirement; its task of scrutiny of an award (*see* Chapter 20) includes comparing the award with the Terms. In the event the award does not respect a requirement of the Terms, the Court has the power to remit it to the arbitral tribunal, drawing its attention to the problem. A violation by the tribunal of a procedural imperative of the Terms may, in some circumstances, open the award to judicial review at the seat of arbitration or to defense against execution (on the grounds that the "arbitral procedure was not in accordance with the agreement of the parties," a permissible defense under Article V(1)(d) of the New York Convention).

An example may be found in the *SOFIDIF*[17] arbitration, a dispute involving the consequences of the withdrawal, following the Islamic revolution, of Iranian participation in uranium enrichment facilities to be constructed in France. An ICC tribunal sitting in Paris had entered an interim award, finding that it had jurisdiction over one of the French parties and one of the Iranian parties originally named, and that the Iranian party was liable in principle. The interim award also appointed experts to determine the quantum of damages. Earlier in the arbitration, by a procedural order issued contemporaneously with the Terms of Reference, the arbitrators had envisaged making an initial and separate award on the first two issues (jurisdiction and admissibility) prior to receiving further memorials and proof on the merits. Subsequently, after having received proof and written and oral argument on the issues of jurisdiction and admissibility, the tribunal revoked that portion of the first procedural order which provided for a preliminary award on the issues of jurisdiction and admissibility, joined these issues to the merits, and provided for further exchange of written pleadings, as well as oral argument on all issues. The interim award was then issued.

The Iranian party, OIETAI,[18] sought nullification of the award before the Paris Court of Appeal on a number of grounds. It maintained that the arbitral tribunal had failed to respect its mission when it failed to decide first and separately, in the form of an award, the issue of jurisdiction, as it claimed was required by the Terms of Reference. It was admitted that the tribunal had the power unilaterally to modify a procedural order but not, the Iranian party argued, the Terms of Reference, which it viewed as an agreement binding the tribunal and the parties.

---

17   *Cour d'appel*, Paris, 19 December 1986, SOFIDIF v. OIETAI and AEOI, 1987 Rev. Arb. 359.

18   The Organization for Investment and Economical and Technical Assistance of Iran.

The Court of Appeal accepted the reasoning of OIETAI on this issue and stated:

> [I]n joining the issue of jurisdiction to that of the merits, the arbitrators exceeded the limits of their mission;. . . they are held strictly to the provisions of the Terms of Reference and they may not, on their own motion, add to them. (Authors' translation.)[19]

Accordingly the ICC award was nullified. However, the French claimant then appealed to the *Cour de cassation*, France's highest court, on the grounds that the lower court had unreasonably restricted the power of the arbitrators to interpret the nature and effect of the Terms of Reference, which in fact had been drafted by the chairman of the tribunal and agreed by all the parties.

The *Cour de cassation* set aside the Court of Appeal's judgment, stating that while the mission confided to the arbitral tribunal could by its terms oblige the arbitrators to follow a particular procedure, notably to render separate awards on the issues of jurisdiction, admissibility, and the merits, this would be only on the condition "that these obligations result from express and precise clauses of the Terms of Reference." Given the complicated questions posed by the number of contracts and a diversity of arbitration clauses involved in the case, the *Cour de cassation* found that the Terms of Reference did in fact provide that the tribunal should initially determine the scope of its jurisdiction as a necessary prelude to deciding the merits. On the other hand, no particular form was required for this determination, and accordingly the tribunal was free to make a single award on both jurisdiction and the merits:

> [W]hile the Terms defining the mission of the arbitrators enumerated under four headings the points in dispute to be resolved, and provided for certain determinations to be made prior to others, they did not require at all that points I and II relative to jurisdiction and admissibility be decided by a distinct award rendered before the award on the merits.[20]

The *SOFIDIF* decisions illustrate the importance of the Terms of Reference and the care that should be taken in their drafting. If the parties require, and the arbitrators accept, that an interim award must be rendered prior to a determination on the merits, the Terms should clearly say so. Even where the Terms provide for separate awards, experienced arbitrators frequently seek to include an express exception so as to give them discretion to modify this requirement in certain circumstances. In one recent ICC case,[21] the Terms recog-

---

19   *Supra*, Note 17, at 365.

20   *Cour de cassation*, 8 March 1988, BULLETIN CIVIL I 64 (1988) at 42.

21   ICC Case 5754/1987 (unpublished).

nized the desire of the parties to have an interim award on the issues of jurisdiction, but added a reservation as follows:

> [T]he arbitrators will make an interim award as to jurisdictional issues before any consideration of substantive issues unless hereafter the arbitrators shall otherwise order for good reason shown.

By reason of that language the tribunal had discretion to join one of the jurisdictional issues to the merits. As it turned out, it did just that, for reasons given in a preliminary award, which nonetheless disposed of other jurisdictional issues.

The *SOFIDIF* case thus illustrates the importance of the Terms, and the fact that they may have the result of binding arbitrators to procedures described therein. It throws little light, however, on the issue whether ICC Terms of Reference may be deemed to be a submission agreement (*compromis*) constituting the reference to arbitration, and thus supplanting the arbitration clause as the source of arbitral authority, or whether they simply record a procedural agreement under the jurisdiction created by an arbitration clause. The better view would seem to be that the Terms of Reference should only exceptionally be considered an independent source of arbitral authority.

The issue may have more than theoretical significance. In the *SPP* case[22] an ICC tribunal had found that it had jurisdiction, not only over the respondent EGOTH, an Egyptian state organization, which had formally signed the arbitration agreement, but also over the Government of the Arab Republic of Egypt, because its Minister of Tourism had signed the Terms following the words "approved, agreed and ratified." The Government brought nullification proceedings at the place of arbitration before the Paris Court of Appeal. Opposing nullification, the claimants argued that the government was bound to abide by the arbitrators' determination of the jurisdiction issue. They argued that the government had signed the Terms of Reference and thus submitted the issue of jurisdiction to arbitrators who, having taken extensive evidence on the issue, had decided the issue of jurisdiction affirmatively. There was no doubt that the arbitrators had jurisdiction to determine their jurisdiction, but such a determination would ordinarily be subject to judicial review, either in nullification proceedings at the seat of arbitration, or in execution proceedings. Did the signature of Terms of Reference change this in any way? The Court of Appeal found that where the issue of jurisdiction was expressly reserved in the Terms, signature of the Terms in no way implied a definitive acceptance of the arbitral decision on the issue, and the national court was free

---

22   Arab Republic of Egypt v. Southern Pacific Properties, Ltd., *Cour d'appel*, Paris, 12 July 1984, 1985 JDI 129, 1986 REV. ARB. 75, English translation *in* 23 ILM 1048 (1984).

to examine the jurisdictional issue independently *de novo*. In the course of its decision, the Court of Appeal stated:

> [T]he respondents on appeal vainly argue that the Terms of Reference signed by the parties on 3 May 1980 are the equivalent of a submission (*compromis*) and that the A.R.E. is bound by the arbitrators' evaluation of the facts and documents submitted for their examination, notably those relative to their own jurisdiction.

> [T]he arbitration agreement could, in the circumstances, only have been constituted by the arbitration clause inserted in the contract of 12 December 1979 by virtue of which the Court of Arbitration of the ICC was seized of the dispute by the companies SPP and SPP-ME, and the arbitrators were designated in conformity with a set of rules which, moreover, distinguishes very clearly the agreement to arbitrate defined in Articles 7 and 8 [Article 6, 1998 Rules] from the Terms of Reference whose purpose is essentially to define the points in dispute and the mission of the arbitrator.[23]

In commenting on this decision, Professor Berthold Goldman highlighted the distinctions to be drawn between the Terms of Reference provided for in former Article 13 of the ICC Rules and a submission to arbitration (*compromis*). He pointed out that the Terms do not, as opposed to a *compromis* in civil law parlance, designate the arbitrators agreed by the parties. Under the ICC Rules, arbitrators are previously designated by the Court of Arbitration, and participate in drawing up the Terms. Moreover, a *compromis* is a contract which requires the agreement of both parties, while, under ICC Rule 18(3) Terms of Reference may be drawn up in the absence of a party; upon his default, they may nonetheless enter into effect after approval by the Court of Arbitration.

From such indicia Professor Goldman concluded that the equiparation of the Terms of Reference with an agreement to arbitrate or *compromis* is inexact.[24] Indeed, the very notion that the Terms of Reference somehow replace the original agreement to arbitrate (usually found in an arbitration clause in the litigious contract) is dangerous since ordinarily there is nothing to suggest that the parties have any intention to replace the original agreement or to vary its jurisdictional scope by signing the Terms under the ICC Rules (al-

---

23   *Supra*, Note 22. The decision of the Court of Appeal was sustained by the *Cour de cassation* which found that the court below had determined without manifest error that "an agreement to arbitrate could only be constituted by the arbitration clause inserted in the contract of 14 December 1974, and not the Terms of Reference whose purpose was only to define the points in issue. . .,"*Cour de cassation,* 6 January 1987, 1987 Rev. Arb. 468.

24   B. Goldman, 1985 JDI 129, 152 citing Section 15.03 of this book and the concording opinion of Y. Derains, 1984 JDI 913; *see also* F. Nicklisch, *Terms of Reference,* 1988 RIW (Recht der Internationalen Wirtschaft), Heft 10, p.763 (German law).

though they retain the right to do so, e.g. when parties agree to change the place of arbitration).[25]

An exception to the rule appears to exist where the Terms of Reference serve to take the place of a non-existent or defective arbitration clause, or to complete and widen the scope of a valid one. In *Société Kis France v. Société A.B.S.*[26] the intended Saudi Arabian distributor of a French company did not contend that a draft distribution agreement (which contained an ICC arbitration clause) had been signed, but maintained that the French company was liable in damages for abusive rupture of the negotiations. The respondent signed Terms of Reference without reservation as to the jurisdiction of the tribunal to adjudicate the dispute. The Terms stated that the French company "voluntarily submitted to the arbitral proceeding," while recording that such submission was not to be interpreted as acknowledging any contractual relationship with the claimants. In these circumstances, the arbitral tribunal found that it had jurisdiction over the dispute, confirmed that no contract had been entered into between the parties, but found that the abrupt and abusive breaking off of the contractual relationship by the French company made it liable to pay damages. On review, the Paris Court of Appeal found that respondent's reservation only concerned the merits of the issue of contractual liability, and not arbitral jurisdiction. It thus sustained the ICC award.[27]

It may thus be seen that in an exceptional case Terms of Reference signed by both parties, without reservation of objection to jurisdiction, may constitute an agreement to arbitrate, or *compromis* entered into after a dispute has arisen. These would appear to be rare circumstances. Some French authors nevertheless appear to see in the Terms a contractual document replacing the

---

25 Where there is a dispute over arbitral jurisdiction, some drafters of Terms of Reference insert a protective clause to the effect that "nothing in these Terms of Reference shall be construed to broaden, narrow, or change the scope of arbitral jurisdiction provided in the arbitration clause of the contract in dispute."

26 *Cour d'appel*, Paris, 19 March 1987, 1987 REV. ARB. 498.

27 To the same effect are *Cour d'appel*, Paris, 25 February 1993, Sansi Fruitgrowing Equipment SpA v. Semena I Possadatchen Material (unpublished) (when the parties sign an ICC Terms of Reference which unqualifiedly accepts arbitral jurisdiction the Terms serve as an agreement to arbitrate even though the exchange of telexes upon which the original claim of arbitral jurisdiction was based may have been insufficient to establish same) and *Cour d'appel*, Paris, 12 January 1988, Société anonyme Replor v. S.A.R.L. Ploemeloise de financement de participation, d'investissement, 1988 REV ARB. 691 (where an agreement between a French company and a private individual to arbitrate under the ICC Rules a future dispute in a domestic matter was null under the applicable French law. The nullity was cured by the unconditioned acceptance of arbitration in the post-dispute Terms of Reference which served as a *compromis*).

original agreement to arbitrate,[28] a characterization which would not be helpful to the practical implementation of ICC arbitration.[29]

It would be a mistake to weigh down the Terms of Reference with too much doctrinal baggage. Envisioned under the ICC Rules as a useful step in arbitral proceedings, they should not be construed as supplanting the original arbitration agreement itself.

In jurisdictions other than France, the issue of characterizing the Terms of Reference, which has preoccupied French legal scholars, does not appear to have arisen as a major issue.[30] The Terms are simply seen as a procedural step in the proceedings as provided in the Rules. This approach has avoided any of the theoretical problems arising out of the *compromis/clause compromissoire* distinction found in France and some other civil law countries. The practical findings in jurisdictions other than France and some civil law countries support an analysis of the Terms of Reference as a procedural tool. In the English case *Dalmia Dairy Industries, Ltd. v. National Bank of Pakistan*[31] a party had signed Terms of Reference although it contested ICC arbitral jurisdiction. On appeal, it was argued without success (as in the *SPP* case in France) that signature of the Terms constituted a binding agreement to accept the arbitrator's determination of the jurisdictional issue. The court found that neither signature of the Terms, nor appearance in the arbitration, could have the effect of conferring jurisdiction on an arbitrator if he was otherwise without jurisdiction. (On the facts of the case, the arbitrator's positive jurisdictional finding was sustained.)

---

28   In a comment to the Kis case, 1987 REV. ARB. 498 at 502, a retired Paris Court of Appeal Judge, M. Zollinger, stated that according to the most recent case law of that court as soon as Terms of Reference having the characteristics of a *compromis* (that is without reservation of jurisdiction and signed by both parties; *see* Art. 1473 NCPC) have been entered into, the original arbitration clause ceases to produce its effect. This comment seems overbroad, and inconsistent with the subsequent decision of France's highest court, the *Cour de cassation*, in SOFIDIF, *supra* Note 20, which reversed the Paris Court of Appeal's rigid interpretation of the effect of Terms of Reference. Other French authors have pointed out the contractual nature and consequence of the Terms, without going so far as to explicitly state that the Terms constitute a *compromis* supplanting the effect of the original agreement to arbitrate, *See* FOUCHARD, GAILLARD, GOLDMAN ON INTERNATIONAL COMMERCIAL ARBITRATION (E. Gaillard and J. Savage, editors) 672-673 (Kluwer 1999); E. Gaillard, *L'affaire Sofidif ou les difficultés de l'arbitrage multipartite*, 1987 REV. ARB. 275 at 289; J. C. Goldsmith, *How to Draft Terms of Reference*, 3 ARB. INT. 298 (1987).

29   Fear that the Terms could be construed as a *compromis*—or could constitute some other instrument acceding to the very arbitral jurisdiction that the party contests—has led some litigants, generally coming from states whose domestic law will not enforce an award based solely on an agreement to arbitrate future disputes, to refuse to sign the Terms (while participating, nonetheless, in their drafting). Their concern is that the formal attributes of the Terms might be deemed to fulfill the requirements of the law even though the jurisdictional position was reserved in the text of the Terms. While this cautious attitude will not prevent the arbitration from proceeding, it may cause delay, and should not be necessary if the party's position is spelled out in the Terms.

30   Nicklisch, *supra* note 24.

31   [1978] 2 LLOYD'S L. REP. 223

Common law courts have taken the position that ICC Terms of Reference have contractual significance and may constitute an agreement, or waiver of objection, to such issues as determination of the place of arbitration, the procedural rules to be applied, and the law applicable to the arbitration.[32] Procedural rules agreed to in the Terms, constituting a specific agreement by the parties, should take precedence over the general procedures set out in the Rules.[33]

---

32 *See* American Construction Machinery Equipment Corporation, Ltd. v. Mechanised Construction of Pakistan, Ltd., 659 F. Supp. 426 (SDNY, 1987).

33 La Pine Technology Corporation v. Kyocera Corporation, 130 F. 3d 884 (9th Cir. 1997), *see also* commentary in 12 MEALEY'S INT. ARB. REP. No. 12 (1997), p. 3. (The parties had agreed to a wider scope of judicial review of the arbitral award than provided under the Federal Arbitration Act. In response to the argument that this provision conflicted with former Article 24 (now Article 28 of the 1998 Rules) of the Rules, which provided that the parties would be deemed to have waived any right to judicial recourse to the extent such waiver was possible, the court stated: "It is true that Article 24 of the Rules of Arbitration of the International Chamber of Commerce, to which Kyocera agreed in the DA [Definitive Agreement], provides for finality of the arbitration award and waiver of judicial review. However, that article notwithstanding, the Terms of Reference, to which the Claimants, Kyocera, and the Tribunal all agreed and pursuant to which the arbitration was conducted, provided for judicial review in accordance with the terms of the DA. To the extent that they conflict with Article 24, the Terms of Reference control.") *La Pine id.* at 5 (For a contrasting French case which likewise found that the Terms of Reference bound the parties in the same way as an arbitration agreement but then found that an agreement purporting to extend the scope of judicial review provided by law was nevertheless null, see *Cour d'appel*, Paris, 27 October 1994, de Oiseno v. Mendes, 1995 REV. ARB. 263.) Such cases make it clear that the Terms, when signed by the parties without reservation, may constitute binding commitments by the parties complementary to the arbitration agreement.

CHAPTER 16

RULES GOVERNING THE PROCEEDINGS

16.01 Freedom of parties and arbitrators

Article 15(1) of the ICC Rules provides:

> The proceedings before the arbitral tribunal shall be governed by these
> Rules, and where these Rules are silent, by any rules which the parties
> or, failing them, the arbitral tribunal, may settle on, whether or not refer-
> ence is thereby made to the rules of procedure of a national law to be ap-
> plied to the arbitration.

The article provides a precedence for rules governing the proceedings: first
those set out in the Rules, then those agreed by the parties and finally those
agreed by the arbitrator. This might seem counterintuitive: one might think
that specific agreements by the parties as to procedure would take precedence
over those provided in the Rules which become applicable indirectly only because of the parties' general agreement to be bound by such Rules. The order
of precedence is the result of the institutional bias of ICC arbitration: the ICC
Court will only accept to administer and supervise arbitrations where the parties agree to be bound by all the principal dispositions of the Rules.[1] Conflict
between the Rules and procedures agreed by the parties or arbitrators are relatively infrequent: with respect to proceedings before the arbitral tribunal the
Rules are quite skeletal and do not in fact set out in any detail how they are to
be conducted. As a practical matter, Article 15(1) leaves many details of manner in which the arbitral proceedings shall be conducted completely in the
hands of the parties and the arbitrators. This is consistent with the aim of the
Rules to provide a universal procedure for the settlement of international dis-

---

1   *See* discussion of the subject in relation to the Terms of Reference, Sections 15.02 and 15.05, *su-
    pra* indicating circumstances where the parties specific agreement will take precedence over the
    general provisions of the Rules. The ICC Court will refuse to administer an arbitration with party
    agreed modifications to the Rules only when a fundamental characteristic of ICC arbitration
    (such as Court scrutiny of the award) is omitted.

putes detached, to the extent possible, from the particularities of national law (*see* Section 1.06).

Despite their international orientation, the ICC Rules do not take a position as to whether an arbitration may be completely detached from national laws governing arbitration as a legal institution, or governing the arbitration agreement itself, a subject discussed below in Chapter 28. Article 15(1) carefully distinguishes between the arbitrators' powers to make *rules* governing the proceedings and possible references to provisions of national arbitration law. Thus, the ICC Rules allow the arbitrators to settle rules directly and do not require them to choose a national law of procedure.[2] They leave unanswered the question whether the arbitrators' powers to set rules of procedure are derived directly from the agreement of the parties and their incorporation of the ICC Rules into that agreement, or must be found in national laws relating to arbitration in effect at the seat of arbitration.

The fact remains that the users of ICC arbitration generally seek a considerable degree of detachment from local procedural law. If there are any procedural requirements at the seat of arbitration, they would be those relating specifically to arbitration and not to court proceedings generally.[3] As a further limitation, such requirements must relate to international arbitration, and not domestic cases. Generally speaking, most jurisdictions give broad discretion to parties to determine the conduct of private arbitration proceedings, and many give especially wide latitude with respect to disputes that are international. If it is true that every State has the latent power to regulate and control arbitration activities within the limits of its territory,[4] the inquiry that must be made regarding the rules to be adopted by arbitrators is: has the state exercised this power, and if so to what extent?

---

2   This is to be contrasted with the requirements of the corresponding section under the 1955 Rules, which provided:

> The rules by which the arbitration proceedings shall be governed shall be these Rules and, in the event of no provisions being made in these Rules, those of the law of procedure chosen by the parties or, failing such a choice, those of the law of the country in which the arbitrator holds the proceedings.

3   This was made clear in ICC Case 5029/1986, XII YEARBOOK 113 (1987), where in an arbitration whose seat was in the Netherlands the tribunal rejected the argument that the contractual choice of Egyptian law to govern the contract should also govern the proceedings and found that the arbitration law of the Netherlands governed procedure: "The Arbitral Tribunal emphasizes that the applicability of Dutch arbitration law in the present case by no means implies that the Dutch rules concerning proceedings before Dutch State Courts are applicable. According to Dutch arbitration law, parties are free to agree on the rules of procedure and, failing such agreement, the arbitrator determines the conduct of the proceedings subject to a few necessary mandatory provisions . . . By referring to the Rules of the International Chamber of Commerce the parties have 'internationalized' the arbitration within this legal framework."

4   F.A. Mann, *Lex facit arbitrum*, in INTERNATIONAL ARBITRATION 159 (*Liber amicorum* for Martin Domke) (1967) p. 162, *reprinted in* 2 ARB. INT'L. 241 (1986).

16.02 Mandatory procedural requirements of national law

National laws often make it explicitly clear that arbitrators are free to settle procedural rules. In France, for instance, Article 1494 of the Code of Civil Procedure provides that for international arbitrations:

> The arbitration agreement may, directly or by reference to a set of arbitration rules, define the procedure to be followed in the arbitral proceedings; it may also subject it to a given procedural law.

> If the agreement is silent, the arbitrator, either directly or by reference to a law or a set of arbitration rules, shall establish such rules of procedure as may be necessary.

Article 182 of the Swiss Private International Law Act of 1987 governing international arbitration provides:

> The parties may, directly or by reference to arbitration rules, determine the arbitral procedure; they may also submit it to a procedural law of their choice.

> When the parties have not determined the procedure, the arbitral tribunal shall determine it to the extent necessary, either directly or by reference to a law or to arbitration rules.

> Whatever procedure is chosen, the arbitral tribunal shall assure equal treatment of the parties and the rights of the parties to be heard in an adversarial procedure.

Article 33(1) of the English Arbitration Act 1996, applicable to international and domestic arbitration alike, provides that the tribunal shall "adopt procedures suitable to the circumstances of the particular case, avoiding unnecessary delay or expense, so as to provide a fair means for the resolution of the matters falling to be determined."

The implicit doctrine of these provisions is that arbitrators should be allowed to settle procedural rules appropriate to the circumstances of the case and the parties before them. These rules may constitute a mixture of elements drawn from different practices and legal systems so as to establish equality and justice for the parties involved. In so doing, the arbitrators will accomplish what the parties reasonably expected when agreeing to ICC arbitration.

Without any sophisticated analysis, parties expect two things in practice: first, that by adopting an ICC clause in their contract, they will have escaped procedural particularities of local courts; and second, that international arbitrators will have the power to supplement the procedures set forth in the Rules. If the parties have not fixed the seat of arbitration in their contract and a neutral seat is fixed by the Court of Arbitration, it is clear that the national procedural law of the seat has no natural claim to govern the arbitral proceedings insofar as the intention of the parties is concerned. Even if the parties have chosen the place of arbitration in their contract, it is most doubtful that by such choice they intended to follow the rules of national procedure applicable to domestic arbitrations at the seat, let alone the practices followed in judicial proceedings there. More likely, they have chosen a site which is neutral and geographically convenient and has a reputation for the successful conduct of international commercial arbitrations. If chosen under wise counsel, the seat will have a legal system which does not forbid the application of the ICC Rules, nor of such supplementary rules within their framework as may be agreed by the arbitrators or the parties. (See the description of national law in five illustrative arbitral centers in Part V.)

The liberty given by the ICC Rules to parties and arbitrators to fix rules of arbitral procedure beyond the specific procedures of the Rules is nevertheless limited by the general command of Article 15(2) that "the Arbitral Tribunal shall act fairly and impartially and ensure that each party has a reasonable opportunity to present its case" and of Article 35 that the arbitrator "shall act in the spirit of these Rules and shall make every effort to make sure that the Award is enforceable at law."

The arbitrator thus has a duty to examine whether the proposed procedural rules may either open the possibility of challenge to the award before national courts at the seat of arbitration or pose a threat to execution of the award in other jurisdictions.

The role of the seat of arbitration has special significance, not so much because of the powers of *imperium* reserved to the State, whereby international arbitral proceedings failing to conform to local law could theoretically be forbidden, as because of the possibility of judicial review where the arbitration was held and the importance given to the law of the seat of arbitration by international conventions. For example, Article V(1)(e) of the New York Convention on the Recognition and Enforcement of Foreign Arbitral Awards provides that a contracting state may refuse recognition of an award if it:

> has not yet become binding on the parties, or has been set aside or suspended by a competent authority of the country in which, or under the laws of which, that award was made.

Accordingly, if disobedience of some mandatory law of local procedure results in a setting aside of an award at the seat of arbitration, the result is not only that the award is a dead letter in that country, but also that its international enforceability is greatly impaired.[5]

In fixing procedural rules, the ICC arbitrator should also keep in mind that recognition or enforcement of an award rendered pursuant to such rules must

---

[5]　Recent case law in France and the United States furnishes examples of exceptional precedents where awards set aside where rendered were in fact granted recognition and enforcement abroad. *See* discussion at Section 28.04(d), *infra*. It is reasonable to predict that such cases will remain rare.

not be "contrary to the public policy" of any country where execution may be sought. This is a ground for refusing to enforce awards under the New York Convention (Art. V(2)). While in reported cases this public policy exception has been narrowly prescribed, the arbitrator must assure that such standards of international due process as respect for basic procedural rights and the equality of the parties are maintained throughout the procedure.

16.03 Effect of choice of an a-national procedure

When drafting the Terms of Reference or in settling the rules governing the proceedings, should the parties or the arbitrators explicitly state that a national procedural law applies? It is one thing for the arbitrators to respect mandatory rules of law in force at the seat of arbitration (which in practice have the effect of assuring that broad considerations of public policy are respected) and another matter voluntarily to subject the arbitration to a national statutory framework.[6]

There is no doubt that such a choice can have a critical effect on how the arbitration will be treated in a given national legal system. (See Chapter 28.) The explicit choice of national procedural law may have the untoward consequence of subjecting an international commercial dispute, with arbitrators from the international community, to an overly narrow national procedure. Many experienced international arbitrators find such risks too great and abstain from expressly referring to any national procedural rules other than mandatory provisions of law which, unless observed, would endanger the award. Others who are at ease with the procedural law of the seat (particularly in jurisdictions which have modern legislation with respect to arbitration) feel free to make a specific choice of such procedural law. The solution adopted by ICC arbitrators may thus vary from the one extreme of following the rules used by courts at the seat of arbitration (an exceedingly rare occurrence) to the other extreme of expressly excluding any national procedural law.

The first extreme is illustrated by a case heard some years ago in London. The arbitrators and parties agreed in the Terms of Reference that the procedure would be governed by the Rules of the English Supreme Court. There the sole arbitrator was an English barrister and the parties (both non-English) were represented by English counsel. It is evident that the common nationality and legal background of counsel and the sole arbitrator led to a common decision to use formal legal rules with which all were familiar and comfortable. Never-

---

6   Where the seat of arbitration is a modern international arbitration center and the provisions of its arbitration law are well known, there may be an advantage to stipulating that in any event the arbitrators will follow the mandatory provisions of the arbitration law of the seat, to avoid any implication that another procedural law (for instance, that of the country whose substantive law applies) could possibly govern the procedure. Where the arbitration law of the seat is undeveloped, unclear or archaic, silence may be preferable.

theless, as a less formal approach to international arbitration has developed in England, it is unlikely that today the parties or arbitrators would voluntarily bind themselves to the formalism of court rules. Section 33(1)(a) of Arbitration Act 1996, *supra*, Section 16.02, mandates that the arbitrators consider less formal procedures and Article 15 of the Rules constitutes specific party agreement to the settling of rules by the arbitrators without reference to local procedures.

Most frequently the decision is to exclude the application of local rules. In an arbitration taking place in Paris, the Terms of Reference provided that the proceedings would be governed entirely by the ICC Rules and that:

> In accordance with Article 11 [Article 15(1), 1998 Rules] of those Rules, the Arbitrators and the Parties agree that the Arbitrators will have full freedom to organize the proceedings as they think fit, provided that the Parties be properly heard, and that, in particular, they will have authority to request production of any documents or other piece of evidence, whether documentary or testimonial, as they will find desirable for their findings, whether of fact or of law.

Another example is found in the Terms of Reference for an arbitration taking place in Paris between parties with a common-law background having contracted in English:

> The place of Arbitration shall be Paris. The language of the Arbitration shall be English. The procedure to be followed, including the rules of evidence which are to apply, will not be that of France, and instead shall be in accordance with ICC Rules, and to the extent not covered by such Rules, within the sound discretion of the Arbitrator.

While there are no statistics available, the authors would hazard a guess that parties or arbitrators specifically choose an applicable national procedural law in only a small percentage of ICC cases. By declining to make an explicit adoption of national procedural norms, the arbitrators retain a maximum degree of discretion to adopt procedures which are consistent with the requirements of international commerce and which may differ from the procedures normally in force.

16.04   Procedural rulings

The power to make rules necessarily carries with it the power to make rulings. In practice it is the procedural rulings of the tribunal on specific matters as they arise which fill out the framework in which the arbitration will proceed. The step by step approach to be taken by procedural rulings was emphasized in the Terms of Reference in an arbitration which provided:

> [T]he procedure will be governed by the Rules of the Court of Arbitration of the International Chamber of Commerce as well as by the decisions that the arbitral tribunal may take, from case to case, guided by

("*en s'inspirant de*") the principles of the law of civil procedure of Geneva. . .[7]

Where the Terms of Reference do not adopt the principles of a national procedural law, the arbitrators are free to make procedural rulings without reference to any national law provisions at all and, when parties come from jurisdictions having different systems of law, may decide to adopt solutions which borrow from both systems. Even when the parties are agreed on reference to national law procedures, the arbitrators have substantial flexibility to adapt these provisions to the needs of the arbitral process.

An illustration may be found in an arbitration having taken place in Geneva where the parties had agreed, subsidiarily, to the application of the procedural law of Geneva.[8] At issue was whether the arbitral tribunal was required to exclude from the arbitral procedure documents communicated by one of the parties more than a week after the extended deadline which had been accorded to it by the tribunal. The tribunal found that in all the circumstances the documents should be received, even if under the corresponding Geneva court procedure they would have been rejected:

> Whereas if, in strict application of the law, and before the judicial courts of Geneva, the argument of A [who sought to exclude the documents] is founded. . . it does not appear opportune to the arbitral tribunal to adopt it, in view of the character of arbitration, reinforced here by a clause of *amiable composition*, since A does not show that it has suffered a prejudice; it should be added, by analogy, that according to the case law of the Court of Appeal of Geneva, even the relative nullity of a procedural act may be pronounced only if the other party has suffered a prejudice thereby. . .

> Whereas, it is necessary to recall that the claimant has been able to reply on 6 April. . . without requesting an extension of this date and to provide oral explanation again on 21 and 22 May, and that thus the rights of due process have not been infringed.[9]

The arbitral tribunal's discretion to make procedural rulings is wide, and even more so where no national procedural law principles are referred to. In either case, however, there is a paramount limitation on its freedom and a norm which it must respect at all times, which is to preserve procedural due

---

7   ICC Case 4761/1984, 1986 JDI 1137. The difference between applying a procedural law and making rulings "guided by" the general principles of that law is clear. It is also of interest to note that while the principles of the procedural law of Geneva were chosen for the arbitration, the seat of the arbitration was in Paris.

8   ICC Case 3327/1981, 1982 JDI 971.

9   *Id.*

process. A succinct description of this limitation was given by Professor Berthold Goldman:

> [T]he details of mandatory public policy requirements concerning the arbitral hearing and related procedures. . . are so obvious. They lay down that each party's right to present its case and to discuss the position of the other party must be respected. . . these two requirements are not identical, since the first implies that every party must have the opportunity to develop fully its claims and arguments in defence, whilst the second ordains that no question shall be decided by the arbitrator until each party has been afforded the opportunity of discussing it.[10]

These principles have now been enshrined in Article 15(2) of the Rules adopted in 1998, even though their respect has always been required in ICC arbitration.

The application of these requirements has given rise from time to time to controversy, and challenge of arbitration awards before national courts in a number of cases involving such issues as fair notice, the setting of time limits and the handling of hearings and evidence.[11] Except in the most egregious cases, the wide discretion of arbitrators and the flexibility of the arbitral process have been confirmed by national courts which quite regularly reject the procedural arguments of disappointed parties.

The arbitrator's concern to respect procedural due process should not be permitted to lead to untoward delay, particularly at the instance of the dilatory litigant for whom delay may be viewed as an objective in itself. In practice it would appear that for every legitimate criticism that a given arbitration procedure risks jeopardizing the rights of a party, there are ten legitimate complaints that the procedures adopted by arbitral tribunals are too time consuming and do not provide a schedule to move the dispute to resolution in the shortest time frame consistent with due process.

It is the duty of the arbitrators to provide a reasonable schedule for the exchange of briefs, the production of evidence and the scheduling of hearings, and directions as to how those proceedings should be conducted.[12] These matters should be determined by procedural orders. Many tribunals choose to number their procedural orders consecutively so that the procedural framework of the arbitration can be easily referred to. The arbitrators should anticipate the difficulties that may arise, and provide for them in advance. It is frequently wise to have an informal hearing to discuss the principal proce-

---

10   60 YEARS OF ICC ARBITRATION, 267 (ICC Publishing, Paris, 1984).

11   Stephen Schwebel and Susan Lahne, *Public Policy and Arbitral Procedure*, report to the working group on public policy and arbitration, VIIIth International Congress of ICCA, New York, May 6-9, 1986, ICCA CONGRESS SERIES No. 3, at 205.

12   An example of such an order for the presentation of evidence and the conduct of hearings is found in Procedural Order of 4 September 1990, ICC case 6401, 1998 JDI 1058.

dural issues with the parties, the first occasion usually being at the stage of drafting and executing the Terms of Reference. The views of the parties may be requested on other issues from time to time. The tribunal should not, however, be passive and simply await requests by one or the other party. Experienced arbitrators know that the flexibility of arbitral procedures presents great advantages but also dangers of abuse. It is for the tribunal to anticipate procedural difficulties and, after any consultation required in the circumstances, set forth clearly the steps to be followed in the proceedings by each of the parties. In this way both parties, whatever their nationalities and legal background, will have the same expectations, and there will be no excuse for a party not to know whether a further reply is authorized, whether documents may be submitted after a certain date, how hearings will be conducted, or whether post-hearing briefs are permitted.[13] Procedural rulings, however, are not cast in stone. Unlike the Terms of Reference, which may be likened to a contract between the arbitrators and the parties, the arbitral tribunal is free to modify procedural orders without the consent of the parties. For good cause shown, the tribunal may envisage changes in procedures and provide additional opportunities for exchanges between the parties. What it should not do is to leave the parties in the dark as to the procedures to be followed, step by step, throughout the proceedings.

16.05 Representation and Rights of Audience

One of the most obvious advantages of international arbitration is the freedom it gives parties to select counsel of their own choice irrespective of where the dispute is heard. Recognition of the right is found in Article 21(4) of the Rules which provides: "The parties may appear in person or through duly authorized representatives. In addition, they may be assisted by advisers." An arbitral tribunal may ask for proof that an alleged representative of a party has in fact been duly authorized to act for the party. Similar proof may be asked of an adviser who most frequently will be a lawyer for the party although legal qualification is not required and parties to ICC arbitration have full freedom to choose whosoever they wish as advisers.[14]

---

13 A recurring problem in ICC arbitration has been the submission by a party, after final hearings have been held, of evidence or argument not specifically foreseen and authorized by the tribunal. Fearful of being accused of violating the right of a party to be heard, tribunals have tended to err in favor of admission of submissions, frequently leading to replies and rejoinders and consequent delay and confusion. The revisers of the 1998 Rules sought to clarify the situation by adding Article 22(1) providing: "When it is satisfied that the parties have had a reasonable opportunity to present their cases, the Arbitral Tribunal shall declare the proceeding closed. Thereafter, no further submission or argument may be made, or evidence produced, unless requested or authorized by the Arbitral Tribunal."

14 They may also appear directly without any representatives or advisers. Indeed Article 20(2) requires an arbitral tribunal to "hear the parties directly in person if any of them so requests."

With few exceptions it is accepted, and appears to be true at present in almost all the major international arbitration centers, that a foreign lawyer may represent his client in international arbitration without infringing on any local mandatory law at the place of arbitration concerning the practice of law.[15]

Accordingly, parties may choose counsel on the basis of any number of reasons, such as pre-existing knowledge of the file or specialty in a certain field, or general international arbitration expertise, even though counsel may have little or no connection with the place of arbitration itself.

This freedom of choice may be contrasted with the position of parties litigating before national courts, who are usually bound (by virtue of rules of court or other domestic legislation), to engage only lawyers qualified to practice in that particular jurisdiction.[16]

In practice it seems well settled that such restrictions should not apply to arbitrations, especially international ones, but the question of rights of audience in arbitration has received little legislative or judicial attention. Such legislation as there is tends to confirm the distinction. The authors know of no country in Europe, especially among those most frequently chosen as the seats of international arbitration, where it is considered imperative that parties to ICC arbitrations use locally qualified counsel. It nevertheless cannot be assumed that counsel wishing to advise and/or appear in a foreign jurisdiction unused to hosting international arbitrations will be immune from procedural challenges from local authorities or local counsel on the basis of local monopolies of rights of audience. Formal requirements for the right to appear could be imposed on one of two levels: either as a requirement of the procedural law chosen by the parties, or of mandatory law in force at the seat of arbitration. Challenges have occurred in isolated cases, with varied results.

In a number of jurisdictions where the issue had not been clearly addressed, legislation has arisen to confirm the established norm, an "open door policy" with few formal requirements except, in some instances, that parties' representatives be legally qualified as attorneys in at least one foreign jurisdiction, or, where the local law is also the law governing the contract, that local lawyers be engaged to represent the party together with the foreign lawyer.

---

15   "With exceedingly insignificant exceptions . . . the whole world has accepted the right for parties in international arbitrations to be represented by advocates without subjecting them to any formal or material requirements as to their competence . . . in legal systems permeated by the monopoly of lawyers, this is nothing less than a quiet revolution . . . Due to these circumstances, *inter alia*, an international corps of arbitration experts has emerged. To a large extent, its members have shared values and viewpoints, which in turn promotes the growth of a new, unitary international law of arbitration." J. G. Wetter, review of the first (1984) edition of this book, 1984 SVENSK JURISTTIDNING 156, at 160 (translation by the authors).

16   In most countries, domestic legislation imposes formal requirements on persons wishing to act as lawyers, generally demanding that they have formal certification of their knowledge of that forum's law and their fitness to advise on it.

Doubts had long been expressed in Japan, for instance, whether persons not locally qualified as attorneys could represent clients in arbitration in Japan.[17] The practical problems for a foreign lawyer in attempting to assist in the presentation of international arbitration matters in Japan have been well documented.[18] The formal issue of the right of representation has been mostly settled, however, through Law No. 65, which came into force on September 1, 1996. According to the Japan Commercial Arbitration Association[19]:

> By this amendment, a foreign lawyer practicing outside of Japan may represent a party to the proceedings of an arbitration case in regard to civil affairs where the place of arbitration is located in Japan and all or some of the parties have domicile (*jusho*) or principal place of business in a foreign country. A foreign law solicitor registered in Japan (*Gaikokuho-jimu-bengoshi*) may also represent a party in the above-mentioned case. The long pending issue of whether foreign lawyers may represent a party in international arbitral proceedings conducted in Japan in relation to conflicts with Japan's Lawyers' Law is considered to have been eventually settled.

In Thailand it is still unclear whether national legislation prohibiting foreign nationals from providing legal services or services in connection with legal disputes in Thailand[20] applies to arbitration. The prevailing view among legal scholars is that the Act should not apply to arbitration but legislative amendment is recommended to settle the issue.[21] The Ministry of Justice has in fact recommended legislation which would carve out an exception from any prohibition by the existing legislation and authorize foreign counsel to represent parties in arbitration in Thailand provided that local counsel has also been engaged.[22]

---

17 *See*, T. Doi, *National Report: Japan*, *in* IV YEARBOOK 115, at 129 (1976), concluding that it was "an open question whether a foreign party to an arbitration of international nature, which is to be held in Japan, may hire a non-Japanese attorney to represent him in the arbitration proceedings." *See also*, T. Sawada, *Practice of Arbitral Institutions in Japan*, 4 ARB. INT. 120, at 125 (1988), reaching no firm conclusion.

18 Charles Ragan, *Arbitration in Japan: Caveat Foreign Drafters and Other Lessons*, 7 ARB. INT. 93 (1991).

19 The Japan Commercial Arbitration Association, 1998, http://www.jcaa.or.jp/e/arbitration-e/kaiketsu-e/venue.html

20 *See* Alien Occupation Act of 1978 and Clause 39 of the Schedule to Royal Degree B.E. 2522 (1979).

21 *See*, for example, Judge Vichai Ariyanuntaka, *Thai Legal and Judicial System* (paper delivered at a seminar conducted by the Dhurakijpundit University Faculty of Law on 29-30 January 2000) which deals with the issue at pages 27-28.

22 If enacted in this form, the legislations would be more restrictive than that in Singapore which requires engagement of additional local counsel only if the contract at issue is governed by Singapore law. *See*, *infra*, text at n. 28.

In Hong Kong, the Arbitration Ordinance (as it appears in its updated 1997 version) explicitly recognizes the principle of free choice of counsel, providing in Section 2F that "For the avoidance of doubt, it is hereby declared that sections 44, 45, and 47 of the Legal Practitioners Ordinance (Cap 159) [limiting representation in domestic litigation] do not apply to—(a) arbitration proceedings."

Another illustration of legislation which specifically addresses the issue of representation in arbitration, the Australian International Arbitration Amendment Act (1989), provides a clear example of acceptance of the open door principle. Sections 29(2) and (3) state:

> (2) A party may appear in person before an arbitral tribunal and may be represented. . .
>
> > (b) by a duly qualified legal practitioner from any legal jurisdiction of that party's choice; or
> >
> > (c) by any other person of that party's choice.
>
> (3) A legal practitioner or a person, referred to in paragraphs (2)(b) or (c) respectively, while acting on behalf of a party to an arbitral proceeding to which Part III applies, including appearing before an arbitral tribunal, shall not thereby be taken to have breached any law regulating admission to, or the practice of, the profession of the law within the legal jurisdiction in which the arbitral proceedings are conducted.[23]

In England and Wales, where the local bar enjoys a near-monopoly on appearance rights before domestic courts, there are no restrictions on appearance before arbitral tribunals, and representation may include foreign counsel, local solicitors, or lay persons. Freedom of representation is guaranteed by section 36 of the 1996 Arbitration Act, restating prior law, which provides: "Unless otherwise agreed by the parties, a party to arbitral proceedings may be represented in the proceedings by a lawyer or other person chosen by him."[24] However, foreign parties wishing to retain local barristers have had problems in the past. Until 1985 in all cases, domestic or otherwise, due to

---

23 This provision was not included in the original draft of the legislation, but was introduced, it seems, as a result of the suggestions of various interest groups and commentators. (*See, e.g.*, J.C. Najar and M.A. Polkinghorne, *Australia's Adoption of the UNCITRAL Model Law*, 3 INT. ARB. REP. 21, at 27 (March 1989).) Another example is found in the Netherlands Arbitration Act (1986), Article 1038, which provides:

> 1. The parties may appear before the arbitral tribunal in person, be represented by a practicing lawyer, or be represented by any other person expressly authorized in writing for this purpose.
>
> 2. The parties may be assisted in the arbitral proceedings by any persons they may choose.

24 As English arbitration specialists put it: "A party to an arbitration may, in theory, be represented by his plumber, his dentist or anyone else of his choosing although the choice usually falls on a lawyer or specialist claims consultant in the relevant industry", A. Redfern and M. Hunter, LAW AND PRACTICE OF INTERNATIONAL COMMERCIAL ARBITRATION 331 (3d ed. 1999).

ethical rules of the profession, there was no direct right of access to local barristers; they could be retained only through a local solicitor who would then retain the barrister. This was considered expensive and unwieldy by parties who, having already engaged their own (foreign) advisors, would then have to incur fees in respect not only of the barrister, but further of a local solicitor as his conduit. Changes in the Overseas Practice Rules of the English bar in 1985 made it clear that local barristers could be retained through foreign qualified lawyers in the same manner as through a local solicitor. More recently, bar rules appear to permit clients abroad to engage English barristers directly.[25]

The small number of national courts which have dealt with the question of representation have been divided on the issue, and most rulings contrary to liberalization have been rendered moot by subsequent legislation.

The Paris *Cour de cassation* has long established that the monopoly of the French bar does not extend to international arbitral tribunals sitting in France. In a 19 June 1979 decision, concerning whether an arbitral award could be nullified because counsel for one of the parties was a *conseil juridique* (formerly a registered foreign lawyer not fully admitted to practice in France), the *Cour de cassation* affirmed that requirements for appearing before public courts "are not applicable concerning the assistance and representation of parties before arbitrators who are chosen by an agreement of the parties and whose decisions do not have, by themselves, enforcement provisions; as a consequence a *conseil juridique* could have been chosen by a party to represent it before an arbitral tribunal." In rendering its decision the court considered legal arguments put forth by the bar association of Paris and France of *avocats*, acting as *amicus curiae* in favor of greater restriction, as well as those of the National Association of *Conseils Juridiques* and the National Union of *Conseils Juridiques*, whose arguments for greater liberalization prevailed.[26]

Similarly, the High Court of Barbados has held that a party may use foreign counsel in arbitrations without breaching the qualification requirements imposed by that forum's Legal Profession Act.[27]

---

25 *See International Practice Rules*, amended 28 November 1998, section 3. Under certain conditions, mainly "where the lay client carries on business outside England and Wales or usually resides outside England and Wales," barristers may be retained directly by clients.

26 *Cour de cassation, Première Chambre civile*, 19 June 1979; 1979 REV. ARB. 487, 490-491.

27 In the Matter of an Arbitration between Lawler, Matusky and Skelly, Engineers and the Attorney General of Barbados, (No.320 of 1981), 22 August 1983, excerpts published in W. Michael Reisman, W. Laurence Craig, W. W. Park, & J. Paulsson, INTERNATIONAL COMMERCIAL ARBITRATION, Cases, Material and Notes, 892 (1997). The judgment endorsed, however, the arbitrator's ruling that the party's (foreign) counsel should be advised and assisted by a local lawyer throughout the course of the proceedings.

In contrast to the French and Barbados examples, the High Court of Singapore in 1988 ruled expressly in favor of extending local qualification requirements to international arbitration. In the controversial *Turner* case,[28] it held that foreign respondents were not entitled to engage a New York firm to represent them in arbitral proceedings in Singapore. The limitations imposed by the forum's Legal Profession Act (which imposed fines or imprisonment for unauthorized practice), the Court held, extended to the field of international arbitration.

The matter became somewhat of a *cause celèbre* because the foreign lawyers in question represented a substantial New York based international firm with a specific interest in international arbitration. Although the firm's representatives learned only of the decision while disembarking from their plane in Singapore, they were able to resolve their immediate problem by engaging local Singapore counsel for the proceedings. The decision was not appealed as the dispute was subsequently settled. The Singapore Court decision, however, which was obtained with the assistance of the Law Society of Singapore which intervened in favor of interdiction, left many international practitioners resolved not to designate Singapore as the seat of arbitration. In this way, the adverse comments generated in international circles as a result of the *Turner* decision had repercussions on the potential growth of Singapore as an arbitration center.

Subsequent to the *Turner* decision, Singapore legislators decided to change the policy on representation and legal assistance in international arbitration and enacted the March 1992 amendment to the Legal Profession Act.[29] Parties may now be represented by any person of their choice and representatives need not be lawyers. However, the 1992 reform states that if issues in dispute involve Singapore law, foreign lawyers appearing at the arbitration hearing must do so jointly with a Singapore lawyer.[30]

The possibility of a challenge to counsel remains to be considered by a party before agreeing to a place of arbitration with which it is not familiar, and militates in favor of choosing a place where the customs of international arbitral practice are well known. Indeed, this suggests that it is not in the long term interest of local lawyers or local bar associations to seek to limit or exclude the appearance of foreign counsel. There is no point in having a monopoly of

---

28   In the matter of an Arbitration between Builders Federal (Hong Kong) Limited and Joseph Gartner Co., and Turner (East Asia) Pte Ltd. (No. 90 of 1987, 30 March 1988, High Court of Singapore), 2 MALAYSIAN LAW JOURNAL 280 (1988); 4 MEALEY'S INT. ARB. REP. sec. C (1988), Case commentary p. 7. *See* comments by A. Lowenfeld, *Singapore and the Local Bar: Aberration or Ill Omen?*, 5 J. INT. ARB. 71 (1988); and M. A. Polkinghorne, *The Right of Representation in a Foreign Venue*, 4 ARB. INT. 333 (1988).

29   Sect. 34 A Legal Profession Act Cap. 161.

30   *See* Lawrence G.S. Boo, *Singapore*, ICCA INTERNATIONAL HANDBOOK ON COMMERCIAL ARBITRATION NATIONAL REPORTS, 26 (August 1996, Supplement 21).

non-existent business. Decisions such as the *Turner* case would clearly tend to lead contracting parties to look to other venues as the site of arbitration, and would inhibit any possible growth of the country in question as an arbitration center.

A strange footnote to the right of counsel from outside the jurisdiction to represent a client in arbitration is presented by the *Birbrower*[31] decision in California which involved a suit by New York lawyers to collect fees for services rendered to a California corporation, ESQ Business Services, Inc., in respect to its dispute with another company with principal place of business in California under a contract governed by California law. The dispute led to numerous negotiations culminating in the filing in San Francisco of an AAA arbitration on behalf of ESQ by the New York lawyers. The dispute was eventually settled but ESQ refused to pay its New York lawyers the fees contractually agreed to, alleging legal malpractice and relying on Section 6125 of the California Business and Profession Code, which states:

> No person shall practice law in California unless the person is an active member of the State Bar.

In a surprising decision the California Supreme Court found that a New York attorney's sustained participation in the preparation for arbitration, leading to the filing of a request for AAA arbitration in California, constituted the unauthorized practice of law and that therefore the fee agreement regarding that representation was invalid. The court noted, moreover, that the unauthorized "practice of law in California" constituted a misdemeanor.

The *Birbrower* case is of interest because it shows how in some circumstances local ethical concerns resulting in regulation of the practice of law in a jurisdiction may trump commercial policies favoring arbitration disputes, particularly those involving interstate and international commerce.

The decision was much criticized as constituting a threat to the free and open practice of arbitration. For international arbitration practitioners, it was thought to be a particularly embarrassing precedent since the United States has continuously pressed for the liberalization of the delivery of legal services and has opposed restrictive local bar measures.[32] Concern was manifested as to the Court's findings that:

> i) Practice of law "in California" could be infered from any sustained activity by out of state lawyers pertaining to California law, with the Cali-

---

31   Birbrower, Montalbano, Condon & Frank P.C. et al v. The Superior Court of Santa Clara County and ESQ Business Services, Inc., 17 Cal. 4th 119, 949 P. 2d 1 (Supreme Court, California, 5 January 1998).

32   The decision provided "fodder to foreign lawyers and government officials who resist liberalization of their systems by pointing to the irrationalities of American regulation". Donald H. Rivkin, *Transnational Legal Practice*, 33 INT'L LAWYER, 825, 828 (1999).

fornia client that created a continuing relationship with that client and which included legal duties and obligations;

ii) Accordingly, preparation for arbitration in California culminating in a trip to California by out of state lawyers to file a claim in arbitration constituted the unauthorized practice of law;

iii) No weight was given to the provision in the applicable AAA arbitration rules that a party could be represented "by counsel or other authorized representatives" thus permitting representation by non-lawyers or out-of-state attorneys;

iv) Despite a vigorous dissent on this issue, the Court was not inclined to follow New York precedent that participation in a private arbitration proceeding did not constitute the unauthorized practice of law.[33]

The concern about *Birbrower* was probably always overstated and in any event now seems resolved:

i) In the first place, the threat concerning unlicenced practice in California was never applicable to international arbitration. As the Court in *Birbrower* pointed out, California Code of Civil Procedure Section 1297.11 provides in respect to the arbitration of international commercial disputes: "The parties may appear in person or be represented or assisted by any person of their choice. A person assisting or representing a party need not be a member of the legal profession or licensed to practice law in California."

ii) The opinion only dealt with the right to enforce an agreement with out-of-state lawyers for payment for services rendered in California accessory to arbitration. It did not deal with an attempt to prevent the rendering of arbitration services (e.g. by enforcement of the misdemeanor legislation) or payment for services performed in arbitration proceedings themselves.

iii) In order to address the controversy surrounding *Birbrower* the California legislature enacted legislative Bill AB 2086 of 28 September 1998 which contains provisions permitting attorneys from "any other state" to appear in domestic arbitrations (thus preserving for domestic arbitration the freedom of choice of counsel already guaranteed in international arbitration).

---

33   Williamson v. John D. Quinn Construction Co., 537 F. Supp. 613, 616 (S.D.N.Y. 1982). The majority's rather lame reasoning was that in *Williamson* the out of state lawyer actually appeared in and conducted the arbitration while in *Birbrower* the unlicenced lawyer had primarily given counsel and advice culminating in the filing of a request for arbitration.

The result of all this is that after a number of (perhaps exaggerated) concerns about legal representation for arbitrations taking place in California, one can conclude that California now follows general United States practice:

> United States arbitration rules generally do not require a person who acts for another in an arbitration to have any particular legal training or be admitted to practice law at the place of arbitration.[34]

16.06   Confidentiality

If polled, the users of ICC arbitration would undoubtedly list confidentiality as one of the advantages which led them to choose arbitration over other forms of dispute resolution and particularly as compared to court litigation. If the subject were discussed further, however, it is by no means clear that they would want to see the principle of confidentiality in arbitration applied absolutely or that they, as parties to ICC arbitration, would be willing to bind themselves to secrecy in all circumstances; nor is it certain that they would have considered all the implications of an absolutist rule. In point of fact the ICC Rules have never set out absolute obligations of confidentiality binding on all participants in the arbitral process. They do, however, affirm that ICC arbitration is a private form of dispute resolution and that the public has no right to attend or be informed of arbitral proceedings (which may be the principal advantage that arbitration users are thinking of when they insist on the "confidentiality" of proceedings.)[35]

The ICC also represents that in its institutional role—the administration of international arbitrations—it will respect the confidentiality of the arbitral proceedings. Article 6 of the Statutes of the Court provides that the work of the Court is of a confidential nature and must be respected by anyone who participates in that work in whatever capacity. Article 1 of the Internal Rules of the Court is entitled "Confidential Character of the Work of the International Court of Arbitration" and assures the privacy of all sessions of the Court.[36]

The Secretariat, which "participates in the work of the Court" takes great pains to respect these obligations, to the extent of preserving the anonymity of participants in the arbitral process. Thus, to avoid divulging the names of the parties, arbitrations are usually referred to only by their docket numbers (e.g. ICC Arbitration No. 9191) without naming the parties involved, at least

---

34   Howard Holtzman and Donald Donovan, *United States*, ICCA INTERNATIONAL HANDBOOK ON COMMERCIAL ARBITRATION, NATIONAL REPORTS, 38 (January 1999, Supplement 28).

35   Article 21(3) of the Rules proves that: "The Arbitral Tribunal shall be in full charge of the hearings, at which all the parties shall be entitled to be present. Save with the approval of the Arbitral Tribunal and the parties, persons not involved in the proceedings shall not be admitted."

36   Article 3 of the Internal Rules also confirms that members of the Court must regard as confidential information that they will have learned in their status as Members, with a particular reminder that this obligation of non-communication extends to communications with their ICC National Committees.

when reference is made in places to which the public ordinarily has access.[37] By the same token when the Secretariat publishes syntheses of ICC awards for educational purposes, frequently in the ICC International Court of Arbitration Bulletin, reference is only made to docket number and the award is "sanitized" by removing the names of the parties and geographical and industrial facts which would risk identifying the case and its participants.

While there is no express article of the ICC Rules regarding their duty of confidentiality, arbitrators are informed of such duty in general terms when they accept appointment by the ICC. The ethical duty of confidentiality which they are expected to respect may be compared to that set out by the International Bar Association's Ethics for Arbitrators at Article 9:[38]

> The deliberations of the arbitral tribunal, and the contents of the award itself, remain confidential in perpetuity unless the parties release the arbitrators from this obligation. An arbitrator should not participate in, or give any information for the purpose of assistance in, any proceedings to consider the award unless, exceptionally, he considers it his duty to disclose any material misconduct or fraud on the part of his fellow arbitrators.

The obligation of confidentiality by the parties themselves, their counsel and witnesses and third party participants in the arbitral process, is less clear.

The parties themselves may, of course, agree to specific provisions concerning confidentiality and secrecy in their agreement to arbitrate and even provide specific contractual consequences or penalties if they are not respected. But in the absence of such an agreement may an absolute obligation of confidentiality be inferred?

A party may have legitimate needs, and sometimes a legal obligation, to reveal the fact of arbitral proceedings, the names of participants, the nature of the dispute and the possible financial consequences thereof. Obligations to auditors, to banks and other creditors, insurance companies and shareholders all spring to mind, as does the right of a sub-contractor to know the terms and circumstances of an arbitral dispute between the main contractor and the owner of the works.

Moreover, as international arbitration is increasingly recognized as the *ordinary* manner of settling international commercial disputes, and the number of pending ICC cases is in the hundreds (and international commercial arbi-

---

37   A similar respect for the confidentiality and privacy of arbitral proceedings should be accorded by arbitral tribunals (a duty usually assured by the tribunal's chairman) when they hold hearings in hotels, or institutional arbitration centers: notice of the hearing (on notice boards, at hotel reception desks and the like) should refer simply to "ICC Arbitration No. ___")

38   The duty, in principle, for an arbitrator to maintain confidentiality concerning the proceedings, the tribunal's deliberation, and its award is the most widely accepted aspect of confidentiality. *See e.g.*, Emmanuel Gaillard, *Le Principe de Confidentialité de l'Arbitrage Commercial International*, 1987, DALLOZ (chronique) 153.

tration cases generally in the thousands) is it possible to maintain absolute confidentiality, which is a regime of exception, particularly as transparency becomes the recognized and required norm of international corporate behavior today?

There is no easy answer to these questions and various national courts and arbitral institutions have answered them differently. At least one international arbitration institution has developed and applied detailed confidentiality rules[39] and some others have referred to the obligation at least generally.[40]

The issue of more expressly providing for and regulating confidentiality in ICC arbitration came up at the time of considering revision of the Rules and the adoption of what became the 1998 Rules.

The Court of Arbitration had proposed adding a general provision of confidentiality directed to all participants in the arbitral process (inspired in part by the WIPO Rules). The draft provided:

> Unless otherwise agreed by the parties, they and their counsel, the arbitrators, experts and any other persons associated with the arbitration proceeding shall respect the confidentiality of all information and documents produced during such proceedings, provided that such information or documents are not in the public domain by virtue of a law or judicial decision or not otherwise necessary in order for a party or third party to establish its rights. This obligation of confidentiality extends in the same manner to awards.

The International Arbitration Commission of the ICC, following the lead of the Working Party it had established to study revision of the Rules, and supported by comments of many of the National Committees, recognized that the

---

39 Particularly because of the nature of the disputes that it treats, the World Intellectual Property Organization ("WIPO") Rules of 1994 provides in Articles 73 to 76 separately for "Confidentiality of the Existence of the Arbitration", "Confidentiality of Disclosure Made During the Arbitration", "Confidentiality of the Award" and "Maintenance of Confidentiality by the Center and Arbitrator".

40 Article 34, AAA International Arbitration Rules (1997) provides, in part: ". . . Unless otherwise agreed by the parties, or required by applicable law, the members of the tribunal and the administrator shall keep confidential all matters relating to the arbitration or the award." Article 30, LCIA Rules (1998) provides, in part: ". . . [T]he parties undertake as a general principle to keep confidential all awards in their arbitration, together with all materials in the proceeding created for the purpose of the arbitration and all other documents produced by another in the proceedings not otherwise in the public domain—save and to the extent that disclosure may be required of a party by legal duty, to protect or pursue a legal right or to enforce or challenge an award in bona fide legal proceedings before a state court or other judicial authority." It also provides for the confidentiality of the arbitrators' deliberations and that the LCIA will not publish awards without the authorization of the parties. A complete survey and comparison of the rules governing confidentiality established by arbitral institutions and organizations is contained in the expert report of Julian Lew filed in the Esso/Australia v. Plowman case (discussed *infra* n. 41) and published in 11 ARB. INT. 337 (1995).

requirements of national law concerning confidentiality of arbitral proceedings were in a state of development and conflict.[41] They considered it dangerous to have the ICC set out mandatory rules of conduct which it would have no power to enforce (consider, for instance, the status of a third party witness) and which might be in conflict with relevant national laws (as, for instance, when a party, pursuant to subpoena or otherwise, would be required to communicate arbitration documents to a third party). In the end, the Commission recommended a more modest text, adding Article 20(7) to the Rules providing:

> The Arbitral Tribunal may take measures for protecting trade secrets and confidential information.

By restricting itself to providing that the arbitral tribunal may take measures for protecting trade secrets and confidential information, the section deals with concrete issues, principally that of how evidence presented in the arbitral proceedings relating to information which by its nature is confidential may be protected from disclosure.[42]

The arbitral tribunal may, however, take a broad view of what constitutes confidential information and be prepared to give instruction to the parties on maintaining confidentiality.

Whatever their sympathies with the principle of confidentiality arbitrators are likely to be prudent in the measures that they are willing to take to preserve it. They realize that the principle is not absolute and that in any event

---

41   Attention was focused particularly on the important case of Esso Australia Resources Ltd. v. Plowman, High Court of Australia, 7 April 1995, 128 ALR 391, summarized in XXI Yearbook 137 (1996) where it was held that parties to an arbitration are not held to an implied obligation of confidentiality preventing them from transmitting documents received in an arbitration to third parties. In that case the private party, Esso Australia, sought and failed to obtain declarations from the Supreme Court of Victoria that documents disclosed to the public utilities respondents in the arbitration could not be turned over by the respondents to their controlling body, the Minister for Energy and Materials. In rejecting the appeal the High Court, while recognizing privacy as an essential attribute of arbitration did not consider that in Australia "we are justified in concluding that confidentiality is an essential attribute of a private arbitration imposing an obligation on each party not to disclose the proceedings or documents and information provided in and for the purpose of the arbitration" (per Mason, C.J.). The case has given rise to substantial commentary including a Special Issue on the Confidentiality of International Commercial Arbitration, 11 ARB. INT'L. No. 3 (1995).

42   For development of the thesis that rules for confidentiality in arbitration can be developed from the law of trade secrets and proprietary rights to confidential information not in the public domain, see François Dessemontet, *Arbitration and Confidentiality* 7 AM. REV. INT. ARB. 299 (1996). Even before the adoption of Article 20(7) to the Rules, ICC arbitral tribunals had by procedural order taken specific steps to safeguard the confidentiality of specific documents, processes, trade secrets and industrial property rights. Such orders can limit the numbers and identity of persons, who may view disclosed documents and require such persons to sign a confidentiality agreement. For the text of such an order, see Arbitration Case 7893/1994, 1998 JDI 1069, Note D. Hascher.

they have no power of *imperium* over the parties and cannot punish a recalcitrant party for contempt.

An example of such a cautious approach is found in the *Amco Asia Corp. et al v. Republic of Indonesia* ICSID arbitration.[43]

The controlling shareholder of the claimants in that case, an investor in Indonesia, had informed a business newspaper of the claim in arbitration, and, according to the respondent Govenment of Indonesia, "recounted a one-sided version of the claimant's story in tones designed to be detrimental to international perceptions of the climate for foreign investment in Indonesia." Accordingly Indonesia asked that the tribunal recommend as a provisional measure that the claimants abstain from "presenting their case selectively outside this Tribunal." (Article 47 of the ICSID Convention allows arbitrators to "recommend" rather than *order* provisional measures).

Counsel to Indonesia argued that the claimant's actions had been "incompatible with the spirit of confidentiality which imbues these international arbitral proceedings" but could not point to any mandatory provision of the ICSID Rules to counter the argument made by claimants (after they first denied that their disclosures harmed Indonesia) that the ICSID Rules "do not prohibit individual parties from discussing the case and the status of the arbitration, publicly or otherwise."

The tribunal declined to make the recommendation requested by Indonesia. It stated that in the circumstances, there had been no transgression of "the good and fair practical rule, according to which both parties should refrain, in their own interest, to do anything that could aggravate or exacerbate the dispute." The reference to this "good and fair rule," however, hardly seems more substantial than Indonesia's reference to the "spirit of confidentiality." In fact, the arbitrators acknowledge that "it is right to say that the Convention and the Rules do not prevent the parties from revealing their case."

In effect, the arbitrators were not prepared to recognise an explicit duty to maintain confidentiality but only an implied duty not to exacerbate a dispute.

It is also possible that quite apart from the existence, or not, of specific rules on this aspect of confidentiality the arbitral tribunal was conscious of the fact that in a major investment dispute between a State and a foreign investor, it is highly unlikely that the elements of the dispute were confidential in nature or that aspects of it had not been the subject of public discussion and controversy.

---

43   Procedural Decision of 9 December 1983, 24 ILM 365 (1985). The decision is summarized in J. Paulsson and N. Rawding, *The Trouble With Confidentiality*, 5 ICC BULL 48 (May, 1994).

In an ICC arbitration in which one of the authors was involved some years ago involving competing petroleum interests, the point of view of one of the parties was regularly made known in commentary in an international newspaper (investors in that company also controlling the newspaper in question). The commentary in this newspaper reached its zenith, referring to the upcoming arbitration and the identity of the arbitrators, just as the hearing before the tribunal in Switzerland got underway. Counsel was preparing to make an impassioned plea for an immediate order to cease and desist this infringement of confidentiality when, on entering the hearing room, he observed that all three of the very eminent arbitrators were reading the offending article, were very interested in it, and highly amused that the case which they were presiding had achieved such notoriety. In the event, and particularly since many of the facts concerning the dispute were already before the public, counsel thought it wiser, at least for this instance, to consider confidentiality to be a principle to be weighed with all the circumstances of the case and not as an absolute criterion.

Against this rather caricaturial treatment of a confidentiality incident in arbitration there should be considered the recognition by a number of national courts that the agreement to arbitrate carries with it an implicit agreement by the parties to confidentiality, the reservation of some other national courts as to the existence and extent of such an obligation, and the recognized difficulties by all courts as to application of the principle in varied circumstances.

The principle was clearly recognized in France in *Aïter* v. *Ojjeh*[44] where a party sought to obtain annulment in France, before the *Cour d'appel* of Paris (a clearly incompetent jurisdiction), of an award rendered in London. The procedure had as a result that the award and its contents became public. Dismissing the recourse the *Cour d'appel* imposed substantial civil damages on the appellant for having "caused a public debate of facts which should remain confidential", thus infringing "the very nature of arbitral proceedings that they ensure the higest degree of discretion on the resolution of private disputes, as the two parties had agreed."

A similar sentiment has been expressed in the courts of England based on an implied agreement between the parties to confidentiality which must be accepted in principle, giving rise to a presumption of confidentiality which may be rebutted or overcome by considerations of public interest.[45]

---

44 *Cour d'appel*, Paris, 18 February 1986, 1986 REV. ARB. 583.

45 The leading case is Dolling-Baker v. Menett G Another [1990] 1 WLR 1205 where the Court of Appeal set aside a High Court order requiring disclosure of documents filed in a previous arbitration. In his opinion Parker C.J. found that the filing of the documents in the arbitration did not confer upon them any privilege or immunity but that there was an implied obligation of non-disclosure by the parties due to the very nature of arbitration. "As between parties to an arbitration, although the proceedings are consensual and may thus be regarded as wholly voluntary, their

The limited case law persuaded a leading English academician and arbitrator to comment:[46]

> "... [I]f I had to express my opinion as to the common perception of English lawyers and other professionals practicing in English arbitration and, speaking more broadly, about the common perception of those practicing in the field of international commercial arbitration, I would say that the common understanding has always been that not only are arbitrations to be held in private but that all information concerning them and what transpires in the arbitration room is to be treated as strictly confidential."

On the other hand, the denial by Australian courts of a general obligation of confidentiality inherent to the arbitral process as found in the *Esso Australia* case has been shared independently and pointedly by American courts as illustrated by the *Panhandle Eastern*[47] case. In that case the US government (acting to protect a security interest as guarantor of ship financing bonds) sought the production of documents relating to ICC proceedings in Geneva between a Panhandle subsidiary and Sonatrach, the Algerian national oil and gas company. The court found that the ICC Rules cited, those from the Internal Rules of the ICC Court, in particular Article 2, which provided that the "confidential character" of the work of the ICC Court "must be respected by anyone who participates in that work in any capacity," only pertained to members of the ICC Court. Absent a separate and specific agreement, "parties to arbitration proceedings or the independent arbitration tribunal which conducts those proceedings" were not bound to keep documents confidential.

One could almost say that these cases manifest a split between the "old world" and the "new world" as to whether a general rule of confidentiality must be inferred from the nature of the arbitral process or whether confidentiality is an exception to be narrowly circumscribed by specific agreement between the parties or special institutional rules for unusual kinds of disputes.

These conflicting cases support the ICC's conclusion, during the revision of the Rules in 1998, that there is insufficient consensus on the existence and extent of an implied agreement of confidentiality between the parties and also to what extent such an agreement can bind the other participants in the arbitral process (witnesses, experts, counsel, etc.).

---

very nature is such that there must ... be some implied obligation on both parties not to disclose or use for any other purpose any documents prepared for and used in the arbitration, or disclosed or produced in the course of the arbitration, or transcripts or notes of the evidence in the arbitration or the award, and indeed not to disclose in any other way what evidence had been given by any witness in the arbitration, save with the consent of the other party, or pursuant to an order or leave of the court."

46   Patrick Neill, Q.C., *Confidentiality in Arbitration*, 12 ARB. INT. 287 (1996).

47   United States v. Panhandle Eastern Corp. et al., 118 F.R.D. 346 (D. Del. 1988).

One thing is certain: almost all authorities recognize the principle of arbitrators' duty of confidentiality, and accept the arbitrators' corresponding right not to be questioned as to the content of the award or the deliberation and reason that led to it. Yet even this generally recognized principle can sometimes give rise to difficulties of application.[48]

---

48   In a Swedish case the U.S. counsel of one of the parties disclosed the text of an interim award on jurisdiction to Mealey's International Arbitration Report where it was published. After publication the Chairman of the arbitral tribunal disclosed the award to a member of the Supreme Court of Sweden because the Supreme Court was considering in another matter the same point of law. The offended party sought to overturn the award and disqualify the arbitrator. In a surprising decision the Stockholm City Court found that the party's breach of confidentiality entailed the nullification of the award. The Court of Appeal reversed the City Court's decision (Bulgarian Foreign Trade Bank, Ltd. v. A.I. Trade Finance, Inc., Case T 1092-98, Judgement of 30 March 1999, 14 MEALEY'S INT. ARB. REP. A-1 (No. 4, April 1999) finding that there was no statutory obligations of confidentiality for arbitration in Swedish law and while secrecy was an important attribute of arbitration, one could not say that there was an absolute and binding implied obligation of confidentiality. In the case it found that in any event any breach by the party revealing the award could be sanctioned by damages and that the invalidating of the arbitration award was not justified. It further found that the Chairman of the arbitral tribunal, who had revealed the award to a member of the Supreme Court purely for intellectual legal reasons, could not be disqualified (a point that was not ruled on by the court below). The Court of Appeal's decision seems to fall into the main line of confidentiality cases before national courts. However, the Swedish Supreme Court, which granted leave to appeal, will still have the last word. *See* Hans Bagner, *Confidentiality in International Commercial Arbitration Practice to be Considered by the Swedish Supreme Court*, 14 2MEALEY'S INT. ARB. REP. 9 (No. 9, September 1999).

CHAPTER 17

CHOICE OF SUBSTANTIVE LAW

17.01 Freedom of arbitrators to apply "appropriate" rules of law

i) Liberalization of choice of law process by the 1998 Rules

It is advisable to choose the applicable law in the principal agreement. Most systems of law give parties wide latitude to select the proper law of their contract. The various elements that should go into the exercise of their choice have been described in Section 7.04. When the parties fail to make an express choice, the arbitrators must deal with the issue. Article 17 of the Rules, as revised in 1998, gives the arbitrators wide discretion since they are permitted to choose the applicable law without reference to a particular system of choice of law; in addition they are allowed to apply "rules of law" as contrasted with a specific national law.

Article 17 of the ICC Rules provides, in part, that:

> (1) The parties shall be free to agree upon the rules of law to be applied by the arbitral tribunal to the merits of the dispute. In the absence of any such agreement, the arbitral tribunal shall apply the rules of law which it determines to be appropriate.

> (2) In all cases, the arbitral tribunal shall take account of the provisions of the contract and the relevant trade usage.

The modification of the Rules confirms the liberal power of the parties to determine the legal standards governing their obligations. While most contracts provide for the application of a single national law, parties sometimes choose independent rules of law such as the Vienna Sales Convention, or the UNIDROIT Principles of International Commercial Contracts, or "the rules of law governing contractual obligations common to England and France". Parties may also choose to apply "general principles of international law" or similar formulations (such as the principles of *lex mercatoria*), although it should be recognized that such formulations seldom supply sufficiently defined standards to resolve all the legal issues which may arise. The revised

Rules confirm that when parties act in this way arbitrators should accept their decision.

When the parties have not made any determination, Article 17(1) gives to the arbitral tribunal the power to apply "rules of law", thus a broader power than that granted by Article 13(3) of the 1975 Rules which implied a requirement to choose a single national law as the "proper law" of the contract designated by a rule of conflicts of law. This requirement was at odds with arbitral practices.

Even if in most cases where the parties have not designated the applicable rules of law it may be expected that the arbitral tribunal will choose a single national law as governing the obligations of the parties, Article 17(1) gives the arbitral tribunal a wider freedom in these circumstances than it theoretically enjoyed under the prior Rules. The arbitral tribunal is free to apply directly the law which it deems appropriate without any necessity to investigate any "rule of conflict", whether of a national law or otherwise, in making that determination. This empowerment to use the *"voie directe"* in choice of law also coincides with the tendencies of recent arbitral practice.

The freedom of the arbitral tribunal, like that of the parties, to apply rules of law other than those of a single state provides a flexibility to meet the intentions of the parties and to respond to all the circumstances of a case.

ii) Background of choice of law process in ICC arbitration

The choice of law process in international arbitration has attracted much scholarly writing.[1] The complexity of the process is such that in some cases an interim award may be required on the issue, preceded by full written and oral submissions. Such a process entails substantial additional expenses and delays, which could have been avoided had a law been designated in the principal agreement.[2]

---

1 *See* FOUCHARD GAILLARD AND GOLDMAN ON INTERNATIONAL COMMERCIAL ARBITRATION, PART V (Kluwer 1999); Berda Wortmann, *Choice of Law by Arbitrators: The Applicable Conflicts of Law System*, 14 ARB. INT. 97 (1998); M. Blessing, *Choice of Substantive Law in Arbitration*, 14 J. INT'L ARB. 339 (1997); Yves Derains, *The ICC Arbitral Process, Part VIII: Choice of Law Applicable to the Contract and International Arbitration*, 6 ICC BULL. 10 (May 1995); A.F.M. Maniruzzaman, *Conflict of Laws in International Arbitration: Practice and Trends*, 9 ARB. INT. 371 (1993); Horacio Grigera Naón, (Secretary General of the ICC Court of Arbitration 1997-__), CHOICE OF LAW PROBLEMS IN INTERNATIONAL ARBITRATION (J.C.B. Mohr 1992); O. Lando, *The Law Applicable to the Merits of the Dispute*, 2 ARB. INT. 104 (1988); Julian Lew, APPLICABLE LAW IN INTERNATIONAL ARBITRATION (1978).

2 Parties sometimes argue that it is indispensable for the arbitrators to render an interim award on applicable law, because they would otherwise be unduly burdened by having to present their case on the merits without being able to marshall their arguments in a coherent manner under the law which will ultimately govern the case. For an example of the arbitrators' rejection of such an argument (in a case where the parties "one after the other, but rather sporadically," invoked French and Tunisian law), see ICC Case 5103/1988, 1988 JDI 1207.

Prior to 1975, the ICC Rules contained no specific provisions on the choice of law or the arbitrators' powers to establish applicable law if the contract failed to stipulate it. In the absence of choice of law criteria in the Rules, ICC arbitrators tended to apply the conflict of laws rules of the law of the place of arbitration. The seat of arbitration was thus viewed as analogous to a judicial forum; the assumption followed that it was naturally the law of the place of arbitration, *lex fori*, which governed choice of law questions. This concept had been adopted in a 1957 resolution of the Institute of International Law, which declared: "The rule of choice of law in the seat of the arbitral tribunal must be followed to settle the law applicable to the substance of the difference."[3] Its application would usually result in giving the national law of the forum a general vocation in respect to arbitrations, not limited to procedural issues. By 1961, when the European Convention on International Arbitration was adopted, this concept had gone to an early grave.[4]

Article 13(3) of the 1975 ICC Rules, inspired by the European Convention, was aimed at liberating the choice of substantive law from national rules of conflict of laws, just as Article 11 liberated arbitrators from necessarily following national laws of procedure. One of the reasons for this liberalization was that if the seat of arbitration was picked by the ICC Court in the absence of agreement by the parties, such forum might have no connection with the parties or with the dispute. Worse, application of its conflict of laws system might result in application of a law unintended by either party. In a comment on the 1955 Rules,[5] Professor E. J. Cohn used the example of a dispute between a German firm and an English firm arising under a contract in which the parties chose neither the proper law of the contract nor the place of arbitration. If the Court of Arbitration had picked a city in a Swiss canton as the seat, Swiss choice of law rules would have designated German law as the proper law of the contract. However, under both German and English private international law, English law would have governed the contract. Professor Cohn, although devoted to the application of the procedural and choice of law rules of the seat, suggested that in such a situation the arbitrators should as an exceptional

---

3   1957 ANNUAIRE DE L'INSTITUT DU DROIT INTERNATIONAL 469.

4   Article VII(1) of the European Convention, 21 April 1961, UNTS vol. 464, p.364, No. 7041 (1963-64), gives arbitrators the freedom to choose any conflict of laws rules it deems appropriate. (*see generally* Section 37.03). The same approach is taken by Article 28(2) of the UNCITRAL Model Law (". . . the arbitral tribunal shall apply the law determined by the conflict of laws rules which it considers applicable.") Article 46(3) of the English Arbitration Act 1996 is to the same effect. Other laws (French, Dutch) do not require the arbitrators to apply any conflicts rule at all. Note that while conventions and arbitration laws of various countries may provide indications of choice of law rules to be applied by arbitrators, they are not mandatory. They all permit the parties to choose the rules of law applicable to their dispute either directly or indirectly by the adoption of institutional arbitration rules. By choosing the ICC Rules, the parties have made an indirect choice of law.

5   E.J. Cohn, *The Rules of Arbitration of the International Chamber of Commerce*, 14 INTERNATIONAL AND COMPARATIVE LAW QUARTERLY 132, 162 (1965).

matter be free to apply the choice of law rules common to the national conflict of laws systems of both parties.

The modern trend is to recognize that any perceived obligation to apply the choice of law rules of the seat stems from a false comparison of the seat of an arbitral tribunal with a judicial forum. A national court judge must apply the conflicts rules of the forum. He applies his own national law to determine the proper choice of law rules. These are the rules of the state upon which his powers depend, and may express the state's policies as to the correct determination of the extent of legislative jurisdiction of other states. The international arbitrator's powers, on the other hand, are derived from an arbitration agreement, and an arbitrator does not exercise public or institutional powers in the name of the state. As Pierre Lalive has written:

> The arbitrator exercises a private mission, conferred contractually, and it is only by a rather artificial interpretation that one can say that his powers arise from—and even then very indirectly—a tolerance of the state of the place of arbitration, or rather of the various states involved (states of the parties, of the *siége*, of the probable places of execution of the award), which accept the institution of arbitration, or of the community of nations, notably those which have ratified international treaties in the matter. Would it not be to force the international arbitrator into a kind of Procrustean bed[6] if he were assimilated to a state judge, who is imperatively bound to the system of private international law of the country where he sits and from which he derives his power of decision?[7]

Even before the adoption of the most recent ICC rules, ICC arbitrators had taken the position that an arbitrator should not be compared to a state court judge in the choice of law process since arbitrators have no obligation to apply the law of the seat as an assimilated *lex fori*. For example, an ICC arbitral award of 1970 held:

> The rules determining the applicable law vary from one country to the next. State judges derive them from their own national legislation, the *lex fori*. But an arbitral tribunal has no *lex fori* in the strict sense of the word, particularly when the arbitration case is of an international nature by virtue of the object of the dispute, the choice of the arbitrators, and

---

6   Readers will recall the myth of Procrustes, who seized unsuspecting travellers and made them fit his bed, cutting off their legs if they were long, stretching them if they were too short. *See* Jan Paulsson, *Arbitration Unbound*, 30 INTERNATIONAL AND COMPARATIVE LAW QUARTERLY 358, at 362 (1981).

7   Pierre Lalive, *Les règles de conflits de lois appliquées au fond du litige par l'arbitre international siégeant en Suisse*, 1976 REV. ARB. 155, at 159.

the organization itself which supervises the arbitration, in this instance the International Chamber of Commerce.[8]

The ICC Rules now recognize that it is undesirable to assimilate the arbitrator to a national judge in respect to choice of law rules. Article 17(1) of the Rules accordingly gives arbitrators freedom not only to apply choice of law rules other than those which would be applied by national courts at the seat of the arbitration but also to choose an applicable substantive law without the necessity of passing through the rules of a national choice of law system; they are also enabled to apply directly "rules of law". This last disposition opens the issue of whether ICC arbitrators may rule on a contractual dispute without regard to any national substantive law whatsoever. This topic will be discussed in Section 17.03 with respect to the concept of applying trade usages and *lex mercatoria*.

17.02   Choice of law criteria most frequently used in ICC arbitration

If the parties have not chosen the substantive law applicable to the contract, the arbitrators will generally determine the national law or laws pursuant to which the agreement should be interpreted and its performance weighed. This subject was introduced in Section 8.04.

A review of ICC arbitration practice reveals that the following methods are most frequently used by arbitrators to determine the proper law of the contract: (i) application of the choice of law systems in force at the seat; (ii) cumulative application of the choice of law system of the countries having a relation with the dispute; (iii) application of general principles of conflict of laws; and (iv) application of a rule of conflict chosen directly by the arbitrator.[9]

To these have been added the liberalizing effect of Article 17(1) of the 1998 Rules which permit the arbitral tribunal to apply directly "the rules of law which it determines to be appropriate" without reference to any system of conflicts.

i) Choice of law system in force at the seat

Since 1975 the ICC Rules have not required arbitrators to follow *the choice of law rules of the seat of arbitration*. However, even the most liberalized 1998 Rules do not prevent an arbitrator from using these rules if the arbitrator

---

8   ICC Case 1689/1970, reported by Yves Derains *in* 1972 REV. ARB. 104; *see also* ICC Case 1512/1971, extracts *in* I YEARBOOK 128 (1976); extracts in French translation *in* 1974 JDI 904, where the sole arbitrator (P. Lalive) declared: "The international arbitrator does not dispose of any *lex fori* from which he could borrow rules of conflicts of laws."

9   The following methods have occasionally been suggested, but by and large have been dismissed by ICC arbitrators: application of the conflicts of laws rules of the country of which the arbitrator is a national; application of the rules of the country whose courts would have had jurisdiction had there not been an agreement to arbitrate; and application of the rules of the country where the award would likely be executed. The difficulties of applying these methods to international as opposed to domestic arbitrations are reviewed *in* Lalive, *supra* note 7, at 160-164.

finds them appropriate for the particular dispute at hand. There may, however, be no significant relationship between the seat and the parties or the dispute; this is frequently the case where the Court of Arbitration fixes the place of arbitration. As a general proposition in such cases, there is less reason for applying the conflict of laws system at the seat of the arbitration than there is for applying its procedural rules (*see* Chapter 16). On the other hand, an arbitrator may find it appropriate to apply the choice of law rules of the venue if the arbitration agreement specifically stipulates the place of arbitration, particularly if there are other indices that this choice reflects a desire to implicate the legal order of that country.

The case for applying the conflicts rules of the seat of arbitration depends on the analogy of the seat to a judicial forum. In its most exaggerated form, such an analogy would lead to the direct application of the law of the seat as the proper law of the contract on the theory that a choice of forum implies a choice of its substantive law to govern the contract. A few ICC arbitral tribunals, in what appear today to be outdated cases, have taken this position.[10] In recent years, the substantive law of the place of arbitration has been applied in a few isolated cases. Such cases have been conditioned on the absence of preponderant connecting factors with another country, with the arbitrators concluding that in choosing the place of arbitration the parties manifested their lack of objection to application of the laws of that place as the proper law, particularly if local arbitrators were also chosen.[11]

The adoption of the conflict rules of the seat (and not directly its material law) is an attenuated form of the same approach.

An example of the recent application of the conflict rules of the seat of arbitration was supplied by *Westinghouse v. Republic of Philippines*[12] ICC arbitration chaired by a prominent Swiss arbitrator, Professor Claude Reymond. At issue was what law governed the performance and breach of a contract calling for the construction, equipment and supply of a nuclear power plant to the Philippines on a turnkey basis. While the parties had agreed that the construction and interpretation of the agreement was to be governed by

---

10 Those cases have taken as a starting point the maxim *qui elegit iudicem elegit ius* (who chooses the judge chooses the law) and have transferred it to the arbitral situation (*qui elegit arbitrum elegit ius*). Such a presumption has been applied with some regularity and logic where parties have chosen a national arbitral association encompassing a set of legal values, as in Eastern bloc arbitration associations. *See* Lew, *supra* Note 1, at 192. Lew also cites examples of some ICC awards in the 1950s in which Swiss arbitrators took a similar position. *Id.* at 192. A more recent example is found in ICC Case 2735/1976; extracts *in* 1977 JDI 947 (sales contracts between U.S. and Yugoslav parties; given the absence of any clear connecting factor with a specific legal system, the arbitrators concluded that the parties' choice of Paris as the place of arbitration at least meant they had *no objection* to the application of French law).

11 *See, e.g.* ICC Case 2391/1977, described by Yves Derains *in* Case Commentary, 1977 JDI 949.

12 Preliminary Award of 19 December 1991, ICC Arbitration No. 6401, 7 MEALEY'S INT. ARB. REP. B1 (January 1992).

Pennsylvania law, the domicile of Westinghouse, the negotiating history showed that the parties had been unable to agree on the law to govern validity, performance and breach. Exercising its power under Article 13(3) [Article 17 of the 1998 Rules] to determine the applicable law by selecting and applying the rules of conflict it deemed appropriate, the tribunal applied the provision of the Swiss Private International Law Act [SPILA] relative to arbitration stating:

> The arbitral tribunal shall decide the dispute according to the rules of law chosen by the parties or, in the absence of such choice, according to the rules of law with which the case has the closest connection.

The tribunal noted that this provision relating to the conduct of the arbitration did not itself provide all the elements necessary to determine the choice of law, notably how to determine the jurisdiction with which the case had the closest connection.[13] It accordingly turned to the general conflicts provisions of the SPILA which, while not mandatory with respect to international arbitration, clarified how the "closest connection" should be determined.

Article 117 of the SPILA provides that a contract is governed by the law of the state with which it is most closely connected which in turn is determined by the habitual residence of the party providing the "characteristic performance." In a construction contract the characteristic performance is clearly that of the supplier/builder. Application of these principles led to the application for the issues of validity and performance of the contract of the same Pennsylvanian law (habitual domicile of Westinghouse) as had been agreed by the parties for its construction and interpretation.

There are numerous ICC cases applying the private international law rules of the place of arbitration.[14] Some of the earlier examples of this choice were influenced by the linkage between the arbitration and the law of procedure at the place of arbitration under the 1955 Rules.[15] Others opted for local rules of conflict to avoid appearing to have an arbitrary preference;[16] they often did

---

13   The tribunal did not explore the idea that by having chosen the ICC Rules the parties had empowered the arbitrator (under the pre-1998 Rules) to choose the applicable law according to "the rule of conflict he deems appropriate" which theoretically might indicate a proper law or rules of law other than those with which the case has the closest connection, a rather theoretical exercise in any event.

14   *See* Lew, *supra* note 1, at 201- 202, 239-240, and 255-272.

15   The 1955 Rules provided that where rules governing the proceeding were not supplied by the Rules or a law of procedure chosen by the parties then the rules would be provided "by the law of the country in which the arbitrator holds the proceeding". While no similar provision existed for choice of law rules, many arbitrators found it natural to apply the same national law applicable to procedure. The mandatory linkage with the procedural law of the seat was abolished in the 1975 Rules and has been progressively deemphasized since.

16   This sentiment was expressed in a 1967 award in ICC case 1455, where a Swiss arbitrator sitting in Switzerland declared, in respect to a dispute between German and Yugoslav parties: "There is no such thing as potential rules of conflicts of laws which would tell an arbitrator from a third

not consider any alternatives apart from: a) applying the conflict rules of the place of arbitration, and b) adopting the conflict rules of the country of one of the parties.[17]

In practice today, relatively few ICC arbitrators rely solely upon the choice of law system of the seat of arbitration to determine the proper law of the contract.[18]

In those cases where weight is given to the conflicts system of the seat, it is usually reinforced by reference to other systems of conflict relevant to the dispute. Such is the cumulative approach, to be described next. Whether special weight will be given to the rules of conflict of the seat may well depend upon the nationality of the arbitrators. English arbitrators are more likely to give such emphasis since the law in which they are trained tends to consider arbitration as part of the national system of justice, whereas continental arbitrators are more likely to apply the cumulative system.

ii) Cumulative application of choice of law systems

The most frequent method used by ICC arbitrators to choose an appropriate conflict of laws rule is perhaps *the cumulative application of the different rules of conflict* of the countries having a relation to the dispute.[19] The approach is particularly satisfying to arbitrators when the different relevant conflict systems yield the same results.[20] Thus the comparative approach

---

country, without any link with the legal relationship between the parties, according to the private international law of what country he should determine the law applicable to the substance of the dispute. There is furthermore no criterion which could tilt the scales in favour of German private international law or Yugoslavian private international law. Application of either one would look like an arbitrary preference. Hence the solution which in actual practice is the most accessible is to refer to the rules of conflict of the *lex fori*," cited *in* Lew, *supra* Note 1, at 256-257.

17   *See, e.g.* the award in ICC Case 1455/1967, *id.*

18   *See, e.g.* ICC Case 1422/1966, *in* 1974 JDI 884, where the award states in respect to choice of a conflict system: "Considering that it is appropriate to eliminate forthwith the law of the forum, whose connection with the case is purely fortuitous." *Accord*, ICC Cases 4434/1983 JDI 893; 2730/1982, 1984 JDI 914. In light of this clear trend, the following statement by a sole arbitrator in ICC Case 5460/1987 appears aberrant and anachronistic: "The place of this arbitration is London, and on any question of choice of law I must therefore apply the relevant rules of the private international law of England," XIII YEARBOOK 104, at 106 (1988), particularly in light of the fact that the place of arbitration in that case had been established by the ICC rather than by agreement of the parties. Article 46(3) of the English Arbitration Act 1996 now makes clear that there is no obligation for an arbitral tribunal to apply English conflicts rules simply because the seat of arbitration is in England.

19   Among the published ICC decisions applying the cumulative approach to choice of law are: ICC Arbitration No. 4996/1985, 1986 JDI 1131, ICC Arbitration No. 4434/1983, 1983 JDI 893, ICC Arbitration No. 2879/1978, 1979 JDI 990; ICC Arbitration No. 2096/1972, quoted *in* Yves Derains, *L'application cumulative par l'arbitre des systèmes de conflits de lois intéressées au litige*, 1972 REV. ARB. 99, at 110.

20   *See, e.g.* ICC Case 3043/1978, *in* 1979 JDI 1000, where the arbitrator declared in passing that the result would not be different under any of the conflict systems of national laws having any connection with the controversy. When two laws with claims to applicability would lead to inconsis-

used by arbitrators resembles the approach used by many courts in determining applicable law: by examining the provisions of the various potentially applicable substantive laws, it may be determined that in fact there is no conflict and thus no need to make a choice.[21] For example, an arbitrator sitting in Switzerland to decide a dispute between an English and a French party might find that if the choice of law rules of England, France or Switzerland were applied successively, the same material law of the contract would always be chosen. The cumulative method is particularly apt for use in the arbitral process. By reference to the various potentially applicable rules of conflict, the arbitrators are able to infuse an international element into the proceedings and assure both parties that the issue has not been determined by the narrow application of the system of a single state, whose relationship to the dispute is not necessarily predominant.

iii) Application of general principles of conflict of laws

There is a divergence in the reasoning of different ICC tribunals in determining the jurisdictions which have a sufficient relation to the dispute to require that their conflicts system be taken into consideration. Tribunals which emphasize the contractual nature of the proceedings tend to give primacy to the laws of the parties to the dispute and those relating to the transaction.[22] Tribunals with a more procedural approach will consider the conflict system of the place of arbitration and in some cases refer to the laws of the parties to the transaction only to confirm primary reliance on the conflict system of the seat.[23]

Other arbitrators have eschewed both the seat-of-arbitration and the cumulative approaches, more broadly applying *"general principles of conflict of laws."*[24] Like the cumulative application of different systems, this method is based on a comparative approach but with decreased attention on the connection between the examined laws and the contractual relationship at issue.

In one ICC case, the arbitrator concluded that under "international conceptions of private law," the center of gravity of contractual relations was the place where a commercial agent exercised his activities; thus the law of that

---

tent results, ICC arbitrators have used their freedom to choose applicable law to favor the law under which contractual provisions are deemed valid, ICC Cases 4145/1984, 1985 JDI 985; 4996/1985, 1986 JDI 1132.

21 In ICC Case 1525/1969, cited *in* Derains, *supra* note 19, at 99, the arbitrators decided that it was unnecessary to determine whether the issue of prescription was governed by the statute of limitation of Turkey (one year) or Czechoslovakia (three years) since in any event a claim had been filed within the shorter period.

22 *See, e.g.* ICC Cases 1759 and 1990 of 1972, cited *in* Derains, *supra* note 19, at 105.

23 ICC Case 2438/1975, *in* 1976 JDI 969 (arbitrator in Switzerland confirmed choice of Spanish law by reference to conflict of laws systems of Switzerland, Italy and Spain).

24 ICC Case 2096/1972, cited in Derains, *supra* note 19, at 110.

country should be applied.[25] In other cases on similar grounds the law of the place of performance was chosen.[26] In another case, the arbitrator applied "criteria of localisation generally applied in private international law" in order to determine the jurisdiction with the closest connection to the transaction.[27] Sometimes an arbitrator will expressly state that he "does not deem it necessary to determine the applicable law according to any national system of conflict of laws," including those of the jurisdiction with the closest connection to the case;[28] instead, he will determine the applicable law by the criteria of "objective localization"[29] as permitted under generally accepted choice of law rules. A recognized source of general principles of conflicts of law is international conventions on the subject whether in force or not and whether or not the countries of which the parties to the arbitration are nationals are bound by the Convention.[30]

iv) Application of a conflict of laws rule chosen directly by the arbitrator

A fourth approach widely used by arbitrators is *to apply a conflict of laws rule directly*, without reference to a national law system or systems.[31] Thus, in determining whether a party had capacity to contract, the arbitrator would apply the conflict rule that questions of capacity are determined by the national laws of the person concerned, without seeking to demonstrate that that rule has a foundation in a specifically applicable national law.[32] Since this method requires at least an implicit recognition of what the arbitrator per-

---

25   ICC Case 2585/1977, cited *in* Y. Derains, Case Commentary, 1978 JDI 998. *See also* ICC Case 2680/1977, cited in *id.* at 997-998.

26   ICC Arbitration No. 3755/1988, 1 ICC BULL. 25 (December 1990) (turnkey contract); ICC Arbitration No. 6560/1990, XVII YEARBOOK 226 (1992).

27   ICC Case 2734/1977, cited *in* Y. Derains, *supra* note 25 at 998.

28   ICC Case 3043/1978, 1979 JDI 1000.

29   *Id.*

30   Conventions which are frequently referred to include the 1980 Rome Convention on the Law Applicable to Contractual Obligations, the Vienna Convention of 1980 on the International Sale of Goods, and the 1955 Hague Convention on the Law Applicable to the International Sale of Goods. For an example, *see* ICC Arbitration No. 7585/1994, 1995 JDI 1015, note Y. Derains (Application of the Vienna Convention of 11 April 1980 together with cumulative application of relevant national choice of law rules).

31   *See, e.g.* ICC Case 2879/1978, *in* 1979 JDI 990. In this particularly well-reasoned award, the arbitrators simply affirmed that they would apply the law of the place of performance of the contract, using this criterion without any indication of having found it in any particular national law or laws. This approach, as well as the free choice by an arbitrator without reference to any system of conflicts (*see* 17.02 v, *infra*) has been characterized by P. Lalive as the *voie directe*, in *Les règles de conflits de lois appliquées au fond du litige par l'arbitre international siégeant en Suisse*, *supra* note 7, at 181. *See also* ICC Cases 4132/1983, 1983 JDI 891; 3880/1983, 1983 JDI 897.

32   *See* ICC Case 2694/1977, *in* 1978 JDI 985.

ceives as universal norms or usages as concerns choice of law,[33] it may often be analyzed as a tacit adoption of "general principles."

v) Free choice by arbitrator without reference to any system of conflicts

A final approach, specifically recognized in Article 17(1) of the Rules and its provision that, in the absence of party choice, the arbitral tribunal may apply the rules of law "which it determines to be appropriate" is the choice by the arbitrator of the applicable law (or rules of law) without passing through any system of conflicts whatsoever. This possibility of *direct choice* of the applicable law permits arbitrators to choose rules of law appropriate for the very case before them, without concern for whether the same principles could be applied in another case. One of the factors which weighs on whether a law would be deemed appropriate is whether it would recognize and give force to the agreement between the parties. Where parties have entered into an agreement and entrusted its interpretation and enforcement to arbitrators it goes without saying that the arbitrators will favor the application of a law which permits its enforcement over one that will invalidate it.[34] Since arbitrators utilizing the *direct choice* method will generally seek to justify their choice by reference to principles of some kind, the method is not always distinguishable from the arbitrators' freedom *to apply a conflict of law rule directly*.[35] But the *direct choice* method in theory liberates the arbitrators from having to justify and explain their choice by the application of choice of laws principles. Nevertheless, in order to fulfill its obligation under Article 25(2) to give a reasoned award the arbitral tribunal should state why it found the rules of law it chose to be appropriate.

---

33 This recognition was entirely *explicit* in ICC Case 4650/1985, extracts *in* XII YEARBOOK 111 (1987), involving a U.S. architect and a Saudi Arabian company, where three arbitrators sitting in Geneva reasoned as follows, *id.* at 112:

> The arbitral tribunal does not deem it necessary in this case to decide on a specific rule of conflict to designate the proper law of the contract in view of the fact that most major rules in some form or other point to the place of the characteristic or dominant work and that in the opinion of the arbitral tribunal there can be no doubt that the dominant or characteristic work performed under the agreement was performed in Georgia, USA.

> The arbitral tribunal notes that a decision in favor of the laws of the State of Georgia would be consistent with international rules regarding the provision of engineering services.

34 *See* ICC Arbitration No. 4145/1984, XII YEARBOOK 97 (1987), 1985 JDI 985, note Y. Derains; *see generally*, FOUCHARD, GAILLARD, GOLDMAN ON INTERNATIONAL COMMERCIAL ARBITRATION 876 (Kluwer 1999).

35 *See* Pierre Lalive, *Les règles de conflits de lois appliquées au fond du litige par l'arbitre international siégant en Suisse*, 1976 REV. ARB. 155 and text at footnote 31, *supra*.

17.03   Application of contractual terms, relevant trade usage, and "lex mercatoria"

i) Application of contractual terms and relevant trade usage

In a review of the first edition of this book, J. G. Wetter wrote that

> . . . in practice (except in England and possibly also in the U.S.), international arbitral tribunals consider juridical issues as *questions of law* and not as facts to be proven by experts or otherwise. Such issues are then decided *directly* and are encompassed by the maxim *jura novit curia*. (In recent years, international law is increasingly invoked in awards. It is probably not unusual that arbitrators who rely on it and declare its contents lack academic training in the subject.) Be this as it may, there is no doubt that the first and most obvious duty of an international arbitral tribunal is to decide issues of law in accordance with applicable law, even if in a given case each arbitrator lacks practical as well as formal competence.[36]

This observation as to the "first and most obvious duty" of an international arbitrator should be recognized as a building block for analysis rather than as a final conclusion. It is commonplace for national laws to consider as a general rule that business contracts form the "law of the parties" (*pacta sunt servanda*), and national laws may take account of trade usages when evaluating the parties' undertakings and performance. To what extent will then the otherwise relevant rules of the applicable law give way to contractual

---

36   Book Review, 1984 SVENSK JURISTTIDNING 156, at 160, note 3. With regard to the question of how an ICC tribunal should inform itself as to the applicable law, *see* Case 5418/1987; XIII YEARBOOK 91 (1988), in which a tribunal presided by an Austrian chairman, sitting in Paris, dealt with a controversy with respect to the means of establishing the applicable (Hungarian) law as follows:

"When determining the law the tribunal may either make its own research or appoint an expert under Art. 14(2) of the [prior] Rules or may hear experts presented by the parties. It is a matter of the circumstances of the given case whether the tribunal assumes that one or the other way is more appropriate." *Id.* at 102.

Whichever alternative is used, the arbitral tribunal should take care to assure that the due process rights of the parties are preserved, and that each is given the opportunity to respond to the interpretation which is presented against it. In ICC Arbitration No. 5285, where the place of arbitration was Mexico City, the arbitral tribunal appointed its own expert on New York law but did not inform the parties of the identity of its expert or his conclusions. The award was attacked in New York on due process grounds, an attack which failed only because the complaining party had not objected to the procedure at the time and was held to have waived the objection, ISEC v. Bridas, 745 F. SUPP. 172 (S.D.N.Y. 1990), XVII YEARBOOK 639.

As to the situation in England, *cf.* the statement by the sole arbitrator in ICC Case 5460/1987, XIII YEARBOOK 104, at 106 (1988): "Under the rules of English private international law, foreign law is a question of fact, to be established by expert evidence; failing evidence to the contrary, English private international law compels me to assume that any foreign law is the same as English domestic law." Pursuant to Section 34 of English Arbitration Act 1996 an arbitral tribunal now has discretion as to procedural and evidential matters and hence may take the initiative, as permitted under the ICC Rules Article 17(1), to determine the choice of law issue without hearing expert testimony and without considering the choice of law issue as one of fact.

terms and to evidence of usages? Apart from this abstract question, international arbitrators have every reason to reflect on the practical reality that one of the reasons for choosing arbitration is to avoid an overly legalistic approach to the solution of commercial conflicts. Businessmen frequently feel that courts do not understand the realities of trade and commerce. Arbitrators, whose mission is derived entirely from the parties' contract, should, and generally do, give precedence to the rules the parties established for their relationship, *i.e.* the terms of their contract. It is for this reason that Article 17(2) of the ICC Rules provides that "*in all cases* the Arbitral Tribunal shall take account of the provision of the contract and the relevant trade usages." (Emphasis added.) At the time this formulation was included in the 1975 Rules, Jean Robert, Vice Chairman of the Court of Arbitration, stated: "It is legitimate here to think that this formula opens the way to a form of arbitration more or less unbound, in the future, from legalistic constraints."[37]

The requirements of Article 17(2) may be seen either as a complement to the provision of a national substantive law determined to be applicable to the contract, or as a substitute for application of a national substantive law.

Even where arbitrators have determined that a single national law governs the interpretation and execution of the contract in question, specific terms of the contract tend to take precedence over principles of statutory or case law, unless the legal provision is of mandatory effect (as for instance laws relating to the exercise of state power).

Reference to trade usages may frequently fill gaps in the applicable law, since usages in the world of international commerce may frequently develop more rapidly than the law.[38] Trade usage may be found in formalized rules such as the Incoterms published by the ICC and widely accepted in international sales and shipping contracts, the Uniform Rules and Practice for Documentary Credits (also published by the ICC), and the ICC rules governing standby letters of credit known as International Standby Practices (ISP 98).[39] They are also found in standardized conditions of contract applicable to certain industries, or included in widely accepted international treaties (such as the Hague Convention on Sales of 1955 or the 1980 Vienna Convention on the International

---

37   ICC Document No. 420/179, 25 May 1975.

38   An example of such a supplementary reference to trade usage is found in ICC Case 1472/1968, quoted *in* Yves Derains, *Le statut des usages du commerce international devant les juridictions arbitrales*, 1973 REV. ARB. 122, at 141. The tribunal in that case decided, for the interpretation and execution of the agreement, to "apply French national law, completed, if necessary, in supplementary fashion, by the rules and usages . . . applicable to international contracts." A more recent example is found in ICC Arbitration No. 8873/1997, 1998 JDI 1817, note Dominique Hascher.

39   For the DOCDEX Rules, see Section 38.09. The ISP 98 Rules were formulated by the ICC's Institute of International Law and Banking and were introduced to clarify the distinction between standby letters of credit and standard commercial (or documentary) letters of credit. The rules came into effect on January 1, 1999.

Sale of Goods) even though such treaties do not apply as a matter of law to the transaction. Numerous other trade usages or practices will be recognized according to the nature of the transaction and the field of activity.[40]

Arbitrators have referred to trade usages as a substitute for the application of a national law. Thus, in a claim by a French company against a Spanish company and a Bahamian company for reimbursement of expenses for the preparation of a submission for a public works project in Spain, the arbitral tribunal rejected the application of Spanish law to the interpretation of a series of contracts among different members of two international groups of companies.[41] While acknowledging that Spanish law and regulations would be applicable to corporate formalities and to the regulation of operations in Spain, the tribunal held that Spanish law would not be applicable either to the evaluation of the consequences of pre-operational negotiations between the parties or to the responsibility for preparing the preliminary study in question. In these circumstances, the tribunal found that the contractual relations among the parties were to be determined under general principles of law and international usages and customs.

The application of trade usages is consistent with the primacy of contractual terms. Usages may be deemed incorporated into the contract as a matter of specific intent (for instance, if reference is made in the contract to Incoterms, or contracting regulations), or by implication (a custom is not referred to but is deemed by the arbitrators to have been within the contemplation of the parties).[42] In this sense trade usage can be said to be internal to the contract and an expression of what the parties intended or can be deemed to have intended.

ii) Application of lex mercatoria

In addition to relevant trade usage which they are bound to apply under the Rules arbitrators may be led to apply what is sometimes referred to as the new *lex mercatoria*, or international law merchant (*see* Chapter 35). As has been seen in Section 7.04, parties occasionally enter into an explicit agreement that the norms of international commerce are to govern their contract.

---

40 *See* ICC Case 3202/1978, extracts *in* 1979 JDI 1003 (general conditions of factoring). An overview of the application of trade usage by arbitrators in ICC arbitration is found in Dossiers of the Institute, INTERNATIONAL TRADE USAGE, ICC Pub. No. 440/4.

41 ICC Case 2375/1975, extracts *in* 1976 JDI 973. *See also* ICC Case 1990/1972, extracts *in* 1974 JDI 897 and 1972 REV. ARB. 100; extracts in English *in* III YEARBOOK 217 (1978). In the latter case, having determined that all issues relating to the termination and adaptation of the contract due to external circumstances could be determined on the basis of the contract itself, the arbitrator found that it was nonetheless necessary to refer to provisions of national law to determine whether a charge of unfair competition was justified.

42 This statement is cited with approval by DERAINS & SCHWARTZ, 225, who attempt to distinguish between trade usage, said to be based on an agreement by which the parties observe the usual practices in their sector of business, and *lex mercatoria*, said to be legal rules arising out of international commerce independent of the agreement of the parties. There is, however, considerable overlap between the two concepts.

In the absence of a specific agreement, the arbitrators may nonetheless determine that such was the intent of the parties and submit the agreement to such international norms. This is not always a satisfactory solution as neither general principles of law nor trade usages present a complete system of law. Certain questions by their nature are ordinarily (but not exclusively) governed by a national law (such as capacity to contract, corporate powers, prescription, statutory interest, and the like). Nevertheless, in an increasing number of international disputes, arbitrators have ruled that the obligations of the parties are to be determined according to international trade usages and customs or general principles of law without reference to a specific national law. In many cases such awards may more nearly establish the real intent of the parties than would the application of a conflictualist approach which seeks to impose a single choice of national law.

Reference to general principles of law has a long tradition in international arbitration.[43] What has become more remarkable in ICC arbitral precedents is the readiness of some tribunals to state expressly that they have decided the case without reference whatsoever to any national law. One of the first such declarations of emancipation was the award rendered in ICC Case 1641/1969, where the tribunal baldly stated:

> The parties did not indicate in their agreements or their correspondence the national law to which they intended their relationship or their disputes might be subjected.

> They thus implicitly gave the arbitrator the discretion and the power, in order to interpret their obligations, to apply the norms of law and, in the absence thereof, commercial usages.[44]

In commenting on this decision, the then Secretary of the ICC Commission on International Arbitration noted that the expression "norms of law" was indistinguishable from expressions such as "general principles of law" or "rules common to civilized nations."[45] Over the thirty years since that decision, a number of ICC tribunals have found it possible and appropriate to base their decisions on general principles or usages without any reference to a single

---

43 Some of the famous early arbitral precedents which looked to the application of generally recognized international norms or a "common law of nations" include: Petroleum Development (Trucial Coast) Ltd. v. Sheik of Abu Dhabi, 2 INTERNATIONAL AND COMPARATIVE LAW QUARTERLY 247 (1952); S.E.E.E. v. Yugoslavia, Arbitral Award of 2 July 1956 of Messrs. Panchaud and Ripert, extracts *in* 1959 JDI 1074; the Aramco Case, 1963 REVUE CRITIQUE DE DROIT INTERNATIONAL PRIVÉ 272.

44 *See* extracts *in* 1974 JDI 888.

45 *See* Y. Derains, Case Commentary, 1974 JDI 890.

national governing law.[46] They have done so in cases where they had *amiable compositeur* powers and in cases where they did not.[47]

The concept of a legally binding resolution of contractual disputes not founded on a specific national proper law stirred controversy among scholars.[48] It may be of interest to consider how the issue has been dealt with by the courts in the few notable cases that have arisen in Austria, France and England.

In *Norsolor v. Pabalk Ticaret*,[49] Norsolor, a French company, had been held liable by ICC arbitrators for breach of contract with its Turkish commercial agent, and ordered to pay damages. Vienna had been selected by the ICC as the place of arbitration. No applicable national law had been agreed by the parties, nor had the parties given the arbitrators the power to act as *amiables compositeurs*.[50]

46　*See, e.g.,* ICC Case 3267/1979, extracts *in* 1980 JDI 961, where the arbitrator, having confirmed the absence of a choice of law clause in the contracts, and having noted that neither party had relied on a specific provision of national law, applied "the general principles widely admitted and regulating international commercial law, without reference to a particular system of law." A similar approach is found in ICC Case 1859/1973, extracts *in* 1973 REV. ARB. 133, where the arbitrator stated: "The contract was to be performed in three different countries . . .. it was clear that the parties intended to refer to the general principles and practices of international trade." *See also* ICC Arbitration No. 8365/1996, 1997 JDI 1078, note Jean Jacques Arnaldez (contract provided that applicable law was international law; arbitrator held that the reference to international law expressed parties' wish that contract be governed by no national law at all; held that contract was governed by *lex mercatoria*); ICC Arbitration No. 8385/1995, 1997 JDI 1061, note Yves Derains (application by sole arbitrator of *lex mercatoria* regarding piercing the corporate veil of a company).

47　*Amiable compositeur* awards *see* Chapter 18 (which are based on the premise that they need not be founded in law): ICC Cases 3267/1979, 1980 JDI 961, extracts in English *in* II YEARBOOK 96 (1982); 3540/1980, 1981 JDI 914, extracts in English *in* VII YEARBOOK 124 (1982); and an *ad hoc* award of 1977, 1980 REV. ARB. 560, extracts in English *in* VII YEARBOOK 77 (1982). Awards rendered by arbitrators not empowered to act as *amiables compositeurs*: ICC Cases 3131/1979 (*Norsolor*), IX YEARBOOK 109 (1984) (upheld by the Austrian Supreme Court, IX YEARBOOK 159 (1984) and enforced by the French Supreme Court, 24 ILM 360 (1985)); Fougerolles v. Banque du Proche Orient, unpublished award rendered in Geneva, enforced by the French *Cour de cassation*, 9 December 1981, 1982 JDI 931, 1982 REV. ARB. 183; 3820/1981, VII YEARBOOK 134 (1982); 4338/1984, 1985 JDI 981; and 5065/1986, 1987 JDI 1039. *See also* the award of 20 June 1980 rendered by arbitrators of the Netherlands Oils, Fats and Oilseeds Trade Association, extracts *in* VI YEARBOOK 144 (1981).

48　For contemporary restatements of the reluctance to embrace *lex mercatoria* as a juridical system giving rise to legal obligations, *see* P. Lagarde, *Approche critique de la lex mercatoria*, in LE DROIT DES RELATIONS ÉCONOMIQUES INTERNATIONALES, *supra* note 37, at 125; M. Mustill *The New Lex Mercatoria: The First Twenty-Five Years*, 4 ARB. INT. 86 (1988); *see also* J. Paulsson, *La lex mercatoria dans l'arbitrage CCI*, 1990 REV. ARB. 55 and Filip DeLy, INTERNATIONAL BUSINESS LAW AND LEX MERCATORIA (North Holland Press 1992).

49　Supreme Court, Austria, 18 November 1982, 1983 RECHT DER INTERNATIONAL EN WIRTSCHAFT 29, 868; excerpts in English *in* IX YEARBOOK 159 (1984).

50　ICC Arbitration No. 3131, IX YEARBOOK 109 (1984).

The arbitral tribunal had applied no single national law, whether French, Turkish, or Austrian, but had simply based its decision on its understanding of the agreement, on *lex mercatoria*, and on the principles of good faith dealings and mutual trust in business relations. The arbitrators affirmed that they understood *lex mercatoria* to include a rule that damages are payable if a contract is wrongfully terminated causing loss to the innocent party. In the award the word "equity" was used twice.

Norsolor sought to have the award set aside by the Austrian courts. The Court of Appeal of Vienna set aside a portion of the award (to wit the amount of damages),[51] reasoning that the arbitrators had failed to conform to the second sentence of Article 13(3) of the 1975 Rules:

> In the absence of any indication by the parties as to the applicable law, the arbitrator shall apply the law designated as the proper law by the rule of conflict which he deems appropriate.

The Court of Appeal deemed this sentence to require the arbitrators to ground their decision in a national law determined by a conflict-of-law analysis, (a requirement which no longer exists in the 1998 Rules); it was not permissible to refer to *lex mercatoria*. As the arbitral tribunal had not shown that French and Turkish law were identical with respect to the principal issues of the case, the Court of Appeal felt that the arbitrators had had a duty to determine which of the two laws was applicable.

The Austrian Supreme Court reversed the decision and reinstated the award.[52] It held in particular that the arbitrators had not violated any mandatory norms of law. Furthermore, the Supreme Court rejected the argument that the arbitrators had exceeded their jurisdictional powers. Although it recognized that the arbitral tribunal had applied principles of equity in awarding the sum of 800,000 French francs, and that the parties had not given to the arbitrators the powers of *amiables compositeurs* under Article 13(4) of the 1975 ICC Rules, the arbitrators' action was not in excess of their jurisdiction; the decision disposed of issues within the scope of the agreement to arbitrate.

Article 17(1) of the 1998 Rules (replacing Article 13(3) of the prior version of the Rules) is intended to confirm arbitrators' authority to follow the approach taken in this case, when it states that in the absence of agreement by the parties the tribunal "shall apply the rules of law which it determines to be appropriate."

---

51   Summarized *in* VIII YEARBOOK 365 (1983).

52   *Supra* note 49.

In a similar decision,[53] the French Supreme Court also upheld an ICC award rendered in Geneva where the arbitrators, having applied principles "generally applicable in international commerce," were accused by the losing party of having usurped the role of *amiables compositeurs*. The evolution of French case law led a respected commentator to affirm that henceforth there is no doubt that international *lex mercatoria* comports positive juridical norms.[54]

Indeed, French law now permits parties and arbitrators to subject an international contractual dispute to norms other than those provided by a single national legal system; rather than speaking of "the proper law" of contracts, Article 1496 of the Code of Civil Procedure as of 1981 provides:

> The arbitrator shall decide the dispute according to the *rules of law* chosen by the parties; in the absence of such a choice, he shall decide according to those he deems appropriate.

> He shall in all cases take into account trade usages. (Emphasis added.)[55]

In light of the fuller discussion in Chapter 35, the authors would sum up the present situation as follows. ICC arbitrators have the duty under Article 17(2) of the Rules to "take account of . . . the relevant trade usage" and may pursuant to Article 17(1) apply "rules of law" as opposed to a specific national law. To the extent that they refer to *lex mercatoria* in this limited sense, arbitrators may concomitantly be applying a national law. Indeed, it has become commonplace to find references in ICC awards to prior awards, and although one should be aware of the dangers of creating a context in which tribunals become concerned about the implications of their decisions for parties other than the ones before them (whose contract is, after all, the only source of the arbitrator's authority), the emergence of a body of arbitral precedents appears to have some utility, particularly in situations where the otherwise applicable law is difficult to determine.[56]

The controversy begins when arbitrators are invited to declare *lex mercatoria* or some other general set of rules to be the sole proper law. It is true that the

---

53   *Cour de cassation*, 9 December 1981, Fougerolle (France) v. Banque du Proche Orient (Lebanon) 1982 JDI 931; 1982 REV. ARB. 183. The *Norsolor* award itself was subsequently granted exequatur in France. *Tribunal de grande instance de Paris*, 20 June 1983, Société Norsolor S.A. v. Société Pabalk Ticaret Sirketi 1983 REV. ARB. 465.

54   B. Oppetit, Case Note, 1982 JDI 931, at 940.

55   Reproduced in the Annex to Chapter 30. As of 1986, Article 1052(2) of the Netherlands Code of Civil Procedure authorizes arbitrators, in the absence of a party stipulation of applicable law, to decide in accordance with "the rules of law" they consider "appropriate." The legislative history indicates that such "rules of law" need not be found in national legal systems but may be derived from *lex mercatoria*; A. J. van den Berg, *National Report*, XII YEARBOOK 3, at 25 (1987).

56   ICC Case 4761/1987 gave rise to Terms of Reference agreed by both parties (Italian and Libyan) to the effect that Libyan law was "in principle applicable to all aspects of the dispute," but that in the absence of proof of Libyan law, the tribunal "shall apply *lex mercatoria*, i.e. general principles of law," extracts *in* 1986 JDI 1137.

supreme courts of Austria (as the place of arbitration in the *Norsolor* case) and France (as the place of execution in the *Fougerolles* case) have appeared to accept the legitimacy of awards rendered on such a foundation. It is likewise true that the Court of Appeals of England accepted in 1988 to recognize such an ICC award rendered in Geneva,[57] stating: "By choosing to arbitrate under the Rules of the ICC and, in particular, Art. 13(3), the parties have left proper law to be decided by the arbitrators *and have not in terms confined the choice to national systems of law.*"[58] (Emphasis added.) There is thus increasing support for the proposition that lex mercatoria is more than an academic concept.[59]

One must immediately note, however, that the matter remains controversial and so invites litigation. In England, for example, the just-quoted decision has hardly generated enthusiasm for the proposition that arbitrators sitting in England may declare *lex mercatoria* as the proper law. To the contrary, commentators have questioned whether an award rendered under such circumstances would be consonant with English public policy, particularly in the absence of a stipulation by the parties in favor of *lex mercatoria* or some other form of general principles.[60] Whatever the arbitrator's private opinion about the normative comprehensiveness of *lex mercatoria* as a legal system, and irrespective of its attractiveness if the sole criterion is the appearance of neutrality, it is the present authors' view, as matters stand today in most countries, that ICC arbitrators run the risk of doing mischief if they declare *lex mercatoria* to be the governing law. The proper conduct would seem to be that of the tribunal in ICC Case 4650, which declined to accept *lex mercatoria* as the applicable law in the absence of any proof that the parties had so intended; "the choice of such a law would require an agreement between the parties . . ."[61] Arbitrators have considerable freedom under the ICC Rules. The authors are aware of no case in which an ICC award has been set aside on the grounds that the arbitrators made a mistaken choice of applicable law. ICC arbitrators may rely on usages and on arbitral precedents, irrespective of their determination of applicable law. Under these conditions, it would seem futile and imprudent to make abstract declarations to the effect that they have ren-

---

57   Deutsche Shachtbau- und Tiefbohrgesellschaft mbH v. Ras Al Khaimah National Oil Co. and Shell International Petroleum Co. Ltd., [1987] 2 LLOYD'S L. REP. 246, [1987] 2 ALL E.R. 769; extracts *in* XIII YEARBOOK 522 (1988); reversed on other grounds by the House of Lords, [1988] 2 ALL E.R. 833.

58   XIII YEARBOOK at 535 (1988).

59   *See e.g.* FOUCHARD, GAILLARD AND GOLDMAN ON INTERNATIONAL COMMERCIAL ARBITRATION, 945 (Kluwer 1999); E. Gaillard, *Thirty Years of Lex Mercatoria: Towards the Discriminating Application of Transnational Rules*, ICCA CONGRESS SERIES No. 7, 570 (Kluwer 1996).

60   *See, e.g.*, Mustill, *supra* note 48, at 108.

61   XII YEARBOOK 112 (1987). (A three-member tribunal sitting in Geneva and chaired by R. Briner.)

ered an award on a legal foundation whose legitimacy may still not be apparent to many national courts.[62]

17.04   Influence of public law and international public policy

Parties to international contracts often refer to arbitration as a conscious attempt to avoid the national courts of either party. The parties' choice of the proper law may also reflect a desire to avoid otherwise applicable national laws. In the absence of a specific choice of law by the parties, the application of the tribunals' choice of law rules may result in the designation of a proper law of contract foreign to one or both of the parties. The arbitrator will frequently be forced to decide whether the intent of the parties can be given full effect in the face of arguments by one of the parties that such application would contravene mandatory public laws.[63]

In this context, one problem can be easily disposed of. This is the doubt, occasionally raised in litigation before national courts, whether the parties are free to choose a law to govern their contract which has no rational relationship to the contract or the parties.[64]

Courts have generally recognized that conflict of laws rules give wide discretion to party autonomy as to the choice of law. On those few occasions where national courts have refused to recognize the parties' choice of law, it has almost always been because of the national court's desire to apply its own law, *lex fori*. An international arbitral tribunal, on the other hand, cannot be considered to have a *lex fori*. There is no reason for arbitrators to invalidate such a choice only because the chosen law has no nexus with the contract, the parties, or the dispute. International commercial contracts containing ICC arbitration clauses frequently stipulate a neutral foreign law as the proper law of the contract. The most frequently used laws in such circumstances appear to be those of England, France, and Switzerland. The authors are unaware of

---

62   As the then General Counsel of the ICC Court of Arbitration wrote in 1986, "by comparison with the number of cases submitted to (ICC) arbitration, *lex mercatoria* appears only rarely . . . one should not come away with the impression that most ICC arbitrations, or even a large proportion of them, refer to *lex mercatoria*," 1986 JDI at 1138. Indeed, an examination of the relevant arbitration clauses in 237 cases submitted to the ICC Court in 1987 revealed that only one provided that disputes should be settled "on the basis of international law," and *none* mentioned *lex mercatoria*, S. Bond, *How to Draft an Arbitration Clause*, paper given at a conference on the validity of arbitral awards (unpublished), Athens, 17 March 1988.

63   P. Mayer, *Mandatory Rules of Law in International Arbitration*, 2 ARB. INT. 274 (1986); *see also* M. Blessing, *Impact of Mandatory Rule, Sanctions, Competition Laws*, in INTRODUCTION TO ARBITRATION—SWISS AND INTERNATIONAL PERSPECTIVES (Swiss Commercial Law Series, Helbing & Lichtenhahn Verlag AG, Basle, 1999); M. Blessing, *Mandatory Rules of Law versus Party Autonomy in International Arbitration*, 14 J. INT. ARB. 23 (No. 4, 1997); S. Lazareff, *Mandatory Extraterritorial Application of National Law Rules*, ICCA CONGRESS SERIES No. 7, 538 (Kluwer 1996).

64   In England, *see* Vita Food Products v. Unus Shipping Co., 1939 A. C. 277 at 289; in France, *see* H. Battifol and P. Lagarde, DROIT INTERNATIONAL PRIVÉ, (6th edition) No. 544.

any ICC arbitration where the arbitrators have refused to recognize the parties' contractual choice of law.[65]

However, there may be circumstances in which arguments are raised to the effect that the law chosen by the parties or determined by the arbitrators to be applicable should be partially displaced by mandatory provisions of another law.

The issue is illustrated by a 1974 ICC arbitration award rendered by a sole arbitrator in a case involving the refusal of the National Bank of Pakistan to pay a guarantee in favor of an Indian party.[66] The guarantee was governed by Indian law and was payable in India. The Bank justified its non-payment on the grounds, *inter alia*, that it was forbidden by emergency Pakistani exchange controls from paying the guarantee due to the armed conflict which had broken out between India and Pakistan.

In ordering the Bank to make the payment, the arbitrator relied on the fact that the proper law of the contract was Indian law, which governed the creation, validity, extent, and extinction of the obligation. Under Indian law there was no excuse for non-payment. The defendant had relied on judicial precedents which indicated that an obligation of payment under the proper law of a contract should be disregarded where such payment was forbidden by the *lex loci solutionis*, the law of the place where the Bank had to take the necessary steps to effect payment. The arbitrator questioned this assumption in the award and ruled that, in any event, if the payment were required *both* under the proper law of the contract *and* the law of the contractually stipulated place of payment (India in both cases), such an obligation must be honored. In the award, he reasoned that:

> Sitting at Geneva, as an international arbitrator acting according to the Rules of the ICC, chosen by the parties, I do not consider myself bound by these decisions [reference had been made to English case law] as might be an English judge or arbitrator. Moreover, even if I were sitting in England, I would be reticent to decide that an illegality arising according to a foreign *lex loci solutionis* has any effect whatsoever where the proper law is a foreign law. . . The dominant tendency, however, in the absence of a direct precedent on this question seems clearly in favor of a negative response, that is to say that it is the proper law, and not that of the place of payment, that determines the question of whether a debtor is discharged by law of his contractual obligation.

---

65 For the proposition that the parties' freedom to choose the substantive law governing their contract is based on general principles of the law of international commerce, *see* ICC Arbitration No. 5865/1989, 1998 JDI 1008, note Dominique Hascher.

66 ICC Case 1512/1971, also discussed in Section 5.01, extracts *in* I YEARBOOK 128 (1976); extracts in French translation *in* 1974 JDI 904. Other awards deferring to laws of public policy in force at the place of performance include ICC Case 1859/1973, cited *in* Yves Derains, *supra* note 38; and ICC Case 3281/1981, extracts *in* 1982 JDI 990.

. . .Even if the issue of whether the foreign law of the place of performance (foreign in respect to the forum) determines this question, is doubtful, there seems to exist on one point at least unanimity when the contract is valid in virtue of the proper law and when this law is also that of the place of execution . . . However, in the present case the guarantee provides that payment would be made in India. In this case the arbitrator is of the opinion that Pakistan's law, the law of the residence of the debtor, is not to be applied.

The proper law of the contract may thus uphold contractually defined obligations despite alleged impossibility or illegality under the national laws of one of the parties, at least where the contract was not necessarily to be performed in the country whose law was alleged to treat such performance as illegal.

Accordingly, in the *Toprak v. Finagrain* arbitration,[67] Toprak, a Turkish State trading agency agreed, under a contract governed by English law, to purchase wheat at fixed prices and to open an irrevocable letter of credit with a first class United States or West European bank to cover payment. After a substantial drop in world market prices, the Turkish Ministry of Commerce instructed Toprak to renegotiate the contract at a lower price. When such renegotiation attempts failed, the Turkish Government refused to grant an import license to Toprak. Toprak had warranted that it would obtain required import authorizations. It was not contested that without such an import license, the buyer could not import the grain, nor establish a letter of credit.

The arbitral tribunal, sustained on appeal by the English Court of Appeal, found the Turkish state agency liable for breach of contract. The contract at signature was not intended to violate the laws of the country to which the goods were to be shipped. More importantly, the purchaser's obligation to supply a letter of credit, guaranteeing full payment of goods against documents, could have been performed outside of Turkey where no illegality could be claimed.

The power of the arbitrator to give effect to the proper law of the contract either chosen by the parties or indicated by the appropriate rule of conflict is an important factor in the efficacy of international arbitration. By choosing an international tribunal for the settlement of their disputes and by stipulating applicable law, parties seek to avoid the vagaries not only of their national courts, but also of national legislation. By nature a contractual institution, the arbitral tribunal will seek to give full effect to the contract, conceivably even at the risk of imperiling execution of the award in the territory of one of the parties. While Article 35 of the ICC Rules obliges the tribunal to use every

---

67 Toprak Mahsulleri Ofisi (Turkey) v. Finagrain (Switzerland), arbitration award of the Grain and Feed Trade Association (GAFTA) dated April 29, 1977; the award became a matter of public record in the course of judicial review in the English courts,[1979] 2 LLOYD'S L. REP. 98 (Court of Appeal, 26 January 1979).

effort to make sure that the award is enforceable at law, there may be occasions when this interest must give way to the need to render an award which conforms to the contractual intention of the parties, particularly if the award may be enforced in other jurisdictions.

This discussion should not lead to the easy conclusion that ICC arbitrators invariably apply the proper law of the contract to validate an obligation although performance thereof would be illegal at the intended place of performance. Despite respectable arguments to the contrary,[68] most international arbitral tribunals would in all likelihood be extremely reluctant to require a party to perform—or to pay damages for its failure to perform—when a mandatory national law in effect at the place of performance forbids such performance. The determination of this delicate issue would depend on the specific circumstances of the case (most importantly if there had been a contractual assumption of the risk of the legal impediment), the nature of the mandatory rules, and the consequences of their application.

The issue has arisen in several cases involving the enforceability of contracts where defendants have argued that the agreement is null because it violates the antitrust provisions of the EEC Convention. After finding that the dispute was arbitrable (*see* Section 5.07), the arbitrator in one illustrative ICC case reasoned that he had a duty to determine whether the defense of nullity was valid because he could not enforce a contract that was contrary to public policy. Under the circumstances of that case, he held that the contract was not contrary to public policy, and stated:

> A dispute relating essentially to the validity or to the nullity of a contract in light of Article 85 of the Treaty of Rome would be outside the jurisdic-

---

68 Professor L. Hjerner, *in Choice of Law Problems in International Arbitration with Particular Reference to Arbitration in Sweden*, 1982 YEARBOOK OF THE ARBITRATION INSTITUTE OF THE STOCKHOLM CHAMBER OF COMMERCE 18, took the position that the provisions of Article 13(3) [Article 17(1) of the 1998 Rules] confirming the powers of the parties to choose applicable law, and instructing the arbitrator, in the absence of such a choice, to apply the proper law according to such rules as he may "deem appropriate," constitute a mandate to the arbitrators to apply such law to the exclusion of mandatory provisions of other laws. He pointed out that the Swedish National Committee of the ICC has cautioned against the ICC Court's giving any instructions to arbitrators similar to the rule found in Article 7 of the European Economic Community Convention on the Law Applicable to Contractual and Non-Contractual Obligations, which provides:

(1) In the application of this Convention, effect may be given to the mandatory rules of the law of any country with which the situation has a significant connection, if and insofar as, under the law of that country, those rules must be applied whatever the law applicable to the contract. In considering whether to give effect to these mandatory rules, regard shall be had to their nature and purpose and to the consequences of their application or non-application.

(2) Nothing in paragraph (1) of this Article shall restrict the application of the rules of the law of the forum in a situation where they are mandatory irrespective of the law otherwise applicable to the contract.

There are at present no ICC directives or guidelines on conflict of law principles to be applied by arbitrators, nor is it expected that there will be any in the near future.

tion of arbitration, and no future disputes clause could substitute a private judge for a public judge in order to resolve a dispute which involves public policy *in se* and *per se*.

On the other hand, in a contractual dispute, if one party raises as a defense the nullity of the agreement upon which the other party bases his suit, the arbitrator has a duty under Article 85 of the Treaty of Rome to determine whether the factual and legal conditions which give rise to the application of the said article are met in the agreement.[69]

The power of the arbitrator to rule on the effect of competition laws at the place of performance even where the parties have agreed that the proper law of the contract is governed by the law of a third country (e.g. Swiss proper law in respect to the competition law of the European Union or the United States) is now beyond doubt. Few ICC tribunals today would deny that they have the power to decide the effect of such mandatory terms of competition law on the rights and obligations of the parties to the contract who have submitted a dispute to them (e.g. nullity, breach, damages, termination).[70] As early as 1975 a Swiss court had confirmed in respect to an ICC arbitration that an arbitrator had jurisdiction to consider whether the alleged violation of Article 85 of the Treaty of Rome by the contract in arbitration rendered that contract null.[71] Moreover, where national courts recognize that the effects of public policy issues defined by mandatory provisions of law are arbitrable the consequences must be taken into account by arbitrators.

The extension of the domain of arbitrable issues (*see generally* Section 5.07) has a direct and complicating effect on the law to be applied by international arbitrators. To put it in its simplest terms, when country A decides that its mandatory laws may be applied by arbitrators deciding a dispute under a contract otherwise governed by the laws of country B, the arbitral tribunal's task takes on an entirely new dimension.

In *Mitsubishi v. Soler Motors*,[72] the U.S. Supreme Court held that a counterclaim in arbitration that raised issues of U.S. antitrust law was subject to the jurisdiction of the arbitrators designated in the contract. The contract (an automobile distributorship agreement) was between a U.S. distributor and a Swiss joint venture subsidiary of Chrysler Motors and Mitsubishi Heavy In-

---

69 ICC Case 1397/1966, extracts *in* 1974 JDI 878. *See also* ICC Case 2811 of 1978, extracts *in* 1979 JDI 983; *and generally* Section 5.07.

70 *See ICC Awards on Arbitration and European Community Law*, 5 ICC BULL. 44 (November 1994); 6 ICC BULL. 52 (May 1995); Dossiers of the ICC Institute, COMPETITION AND ARBITRATION LAW (1993); *Special Supplement, International Commercial Arbitration in Europe*, ICC Publication Number 537, (1994) pp. 33-57.

71 *Chambre de recours*, Vaud, 28 October 1975, Ampaglas v. Sofia, 129 JOURNAL DES TRIBUNAUX, 1981-III-71.

72 473 U.S. 614 (1985). The *Mitsubishi* decision is discussed in detail in Sections 34.02(vi), and 34.04.

dustries. Swiss law was stipulated as applicable, and arbitration was to be held in Japan. Faced with arbitration in Japan before three Japanese arbitrators, and a claim that it had failed to take contractual deliveries, the distributor counterclaimed by alleging a conspiracy to divide markets and to restrain trade in violation of the Sherman Act. Such a claim, it further argued, could not be decided by arbitrators.

The Supreme Court disagreed. Without going into the details of a much-commented decision, one might simply describe the *Mitsubishi* policy as letting international arbitrators proceed to arbitrate all issues of a dispute even if they involve claims under U.S. law that purport to affect the validity of contractual provisions. This policy sees national courts limiting their involvement to an *a posteriori* control of any awards presented for enforcement in their jurisdiction by the criteria of their public policy.

In a few lines of the majority opinion in *Mitsubishi*, dictum was offered to the effect that the courts would have the opportunity to exercise their control function at the time of enforcement of the award:

> the national courts of the United States will have the opportunity at the award enforcement stage to ensure that the legitimate interest in the enforcement of antitrust laws has been addressed . . . [and] to ascertain that the [arbitral] tribunal took cognizance of the antitrust claims and actually decided them.

The *Mitsubishi* dictum (sometimes called the "second-look doctrine") suggests that it is now understood that international arbitrators have not only the right but the duty to examine the effect of mandatory legislation foreign to the law chosen by the parties and the law of the place of arbitration. This also seems to be what national courts at the seat of arbitration have concluded. For instance, in *G. SA v. SpA*[73] the Swiss Federal Tribunal set aside an award and remitted it to the arbitral tribunal for having failed to exercise its jurisdiction to determine whether the contract in question (a cooperation agreement between Belgian and Italian companies) complied with the obligations of the parties under Articles 85 and 86 of the Treaty of Rome. While in that case the proper law of the contract was the law of Belgium, all indications are that the result would have been the same even if the proper law was the law of Switzerland or one of its cantons.[74] The same duty is recognized in other jurisdictions.[75]

---

73   *Tribunal fédéral Suisse*, 28 April 1992, ATF 118 II 193.

74   *See* M. Blessing, *Impact of Mandatory Rules, Sanctions, Competition Law in* INTRODUCTION TO ARBITRATION—SWISS AND INTERNATIONAL PERSPECTIVES 247 (Swiss Commercial Law Series, Helbing & Lichtenhahn 1999).

75   *See e.g. Cour d'appel*, Paris, 19 May 1993, Société Labinal c/ Sociétés Mars et Westland Aerospace, note Charles Jarrosson, 1993 REV. ARB. 645.

While competition laws may present the most frequent occasions for arbitrators to have to consider the effect of mandatory public laws on a contract which has been specifically agreed by the parties to be governed by another law, there are others. What, for instance, is the effect of the agreement between a foreign manufacturer and its local distributor subjecting their distribution agreement to a third country's laws and a neutral place of arbitration on highly protective local legislation providing substantial indemnities for the distributor upon termination or non-renewal of distribution rights?[76]

Other examples involve exchange controls (as previously noted) and the effect on contracts of import and export restrictions, the United States Trading With The Enemy Act, and the interdiction of commerce and assets freeze orders edicted under United Nations or national (frequently U.S.) authority. In all these cases the arbitrator will have to deal with the contract at hand, the law applicable to the contract, the law of the place of performance and the law of the place of arbitration (*vis* where the award may be subject to judicial review) and the reasonable and legitimate expectations of the parties (they must have intended some consequences of choosing a law which is not that of the place of performance, and a neutral place of arbitration). The arbitrators will also have to take into account notions of international public policy.

As Professor Pierre Mayer has put it:

> Although arbitrators are neither guardians of the public order nor invested by the State with a mission of applying its mandatory rules, they ought nevertheless to have an incentive to do so out of a sense of duty to the survival of international arbitration as an institution.[77]

While in many cases the conflict between public policy considerations and the terms of the parties' agreement poses difficult questions, the issue of bribery is simple. International commercial arbitration may not permit itself to become an instrument of, and accomplice to, bribery. In a well-known ICC award rendered in 1963, a Swedish sole arbitrator sitting in France held that a contract which contemplated the making of illegal payments could not be enforced in international arbitration.[78] In that case, an Argentine national had intervened on behalf of a British company to obtain a contract with the Argentine government by means other than having the best or lowest tender. He was to receive 10% of the contract price for his services, out of which he was to make selected payments to high government officials. After the con-

---

76   *See* ICC Arbitration No. 6379/1990, 1992 YEARBOOK 212 (award did not apply the Belgian regulation).

77   *Supra* note 63, at 274.

78   ICC Case 1110/1963, excerpted and commented on by J. Lew, *supra* Note 1, at 553-555; *see also* J. Gillis Wetter, *Issues of Corruption Before International Arbitral Tribunals: The Authentic Text and True Meaning of Judge Gunnar Lagergren's 1963 Award in ICC Case No. 1110*, 10 ARB. INT. 277 (1994).

tract was obtained, the British company denied any obligation to pay, and ICC arbitration ensued. Neither party raised the issue of alleged illegality as a defense and both wished for the arbitration to proceed. Nevertheless, the sole arbitrator determined that he could not take jurisdiction over the case in view of clear violations of good morals and international public policy. His reasoning was, *inter alia*:

> Parties who involve themselves in an enterprise of the present nature must realize that they have forfeited any right to ask for the assistance of the machinery of justice (national courts or arbitral tribunals) in settling their dispute.[79]

More modern arbitral awards do not consider the claim of bribery (or the presence of bribery, even when not raised as a defense) as a jurisdictional issue. Most arbitrators would consider the issue of bribery as a defense to the enforcement of the contract, or a cause for the nullity of the contract. The issue of bribery and of the relevance and application of laws and regulations on commissions on government contracts have been considered in a number of ICC awards.[80] A distinction is made in a number of the cases between bribery, which is surely an infringement of international public policy, and failure to respect foreign procurement regulations, with respect to which the consequences may depend on the circumstances.[81] The issue of whether in-

---

79   For a discussion of this and more recent cases, *see* A. El Kosheri and P. Leboulanger, *L'arbitre face à la corruption et aux trafics d'influence*, 1984 REV. ARB. 3. The issue of corruption raises difficult issues of proof; *comp.* ICC Case 3916/1983, extracts in *id.*, at 9-10 (claim for commissions rejected) with ICC Case 4145/1984, extracts *in* XII YEARBOOK 97, at 100-107 (1987) (claim for commissions upheld), *see* José Rosell and Harvey Prager, *Illicit Commissions and International Arbitration: The Question of Proof*, 15 ARB. INT. 329 (1999) (containing a detailed analysis of several ICC awards on the subject).

80   *See e.g.* Westinghouse Electric Corp., Burns & Roe Enterprise, Inc. V. National Power Corp. and The Republic of the Philippines, ICC Arbitration No. 6401, Preliminary Award of 19 December 1991, 7 MEALEY'S INT. ARB. REP.; B1 (January 1992), pp. 721-737; *see generally* LES COMMISSIONS ILLICITES (Paris, ICC Publishing, 1992).

81   The difficulties in the appreciation of these circumstances is illustrated by the OTV v. Hilmarton matter where the award by arbitrators in Switzerland finding a commission agreement unenforceable because contrary to public policy was annulled by Swiss Courts (*Tribunal fédéral suisse*, 17 April 1990, 1993 REV. ARB. 315) but nevertheless recognized in France (*Cour d'appel*, Paris, 19 December 1991, 1993 REV. ARB. 300).

A second arbitration award rendered after the Swiss court's nullification of the first enforced the commission agreement but the award was denied recognition in France (*Cour de cassation*, 10 June 1997, 1997 REV. ARB. 376, note P. Fouchard) while it was recognized in England (Omnium de Traitement et de Valorisation S.A. v. Hilmarton Limited, Q.B. Div., 24 May 1999); *see* P. Lastenouse, *Le contrôle de l'Ordre Public Lors de l'Execution en Angleterre de la Seconde Sentence Hilmarton*, 1999 REV. ARB. 867); *see also* ICC Arbitration No. 8891 (unpublished), and other cases discussed *in* Rosell and Prager, *op. cit.* note 79, at 331; *see also* Northrop Corp. v. Triad International Marketing, 811 F. 2d 1265 (9th Cir. 1987), a decision by the U.S. Ninth Circuit Court of Appeals upholding an AAA award granting commissions under a contract governed by California law, the court refusing to accept that there was a "well-defined and dominant" public policy against enforcement of contracts for commissions in military sales to Saudi Arabia.

ternational public policy trumps the agreement of the parties is particularly difficult where neither of the parties has brought out the possible illegality of the agreement as part of a claim or defense. As an experienced English arbitrator once put it:[82]

> Suppose I have before me a case where an agent is claiming a commission from a supplier, expressed to be payable in the event that the supplier obtains a certain contract in a certain developing country. Suppose I begin to notice that both parties are carefully skating round the area of what the agent was actually supposed to do to earn his commission. Should I press them on it? Could it be that the reason why they have gone to arbitration rather than to law is precisely because that is an area they would prefer not to discuss in public? Of course, if I had positive evidence that the agent was supposed to bribe the Minister—or even just to encase the Minister's wife in expensive furs and jewels—I would be bound to dismiss the proceedings out of hand on the grounds of illegality, which is not at all what either of the parties wants me to do.

> In a case like that, is the arbitrator the servant of the parties, or of the truth? Whatever procedures he adopts, that is a question he can only decide for himself.

---

82   P. Sieghart, *Viewpoint*, 48 ARBITRATION 133, 135 (1982).

CHAPTER 18

"AMIABLE COMPOSITION"

18.01   Definition

Article 17(2) of the Rules requires that the arbitrator take into account the provisions of the contract and relevant trade usages. In the view of many arbitrators, this raises the possibility, where the parties have not otherwise agreed, of applying general principles of law and *lex mercatoria* to determine the contractual obligations of the parties. It certainly gives rise to a procedure significantly liberated from legalistic restraints. Nevertheless, such arbitration remains arbitration at law, and in most cases the tribunal will determine that a national law or laws underlie the obligations of the parties. Reference is made to such laws either as primary or supplementary sources of the tribunal's decision.

A greater divergence from the rule of law may be found when the arbitrator exercises the power of *amiable composition*. According to Article 17(3) of the Rules:

> The arbitral tribunal shall assume the powers of an *amiable compositeur* or decide *ex aequo et bono* only if the parties have agreed to give it such powers.

Such an agreement may either be contained in the original arbitration clause or reached at the time of drafting the Terms of Reference. Irrespective of when the parties have agreed to give the arbitrators powers to act as *amiable compositeurs*, the agreement must be specifically mentioned in the Terms of Reference (Article 18(1)(g) of the Rules).[1] In light of the analysis presented in Section 8.05, only a few general comments will be made to illustrate the concrete practice of *amiable composition* in ICC arbitration.

---

1   *See* ICC Case 7301/1993, XXIII YEARBOOK 47 (1998), where the arbitral tribunal in a construction dispute case was not given the *amiable composition* power and applied Swiss law in barring a late filed claim for defects. The tribunal stated: "Whether an amiable compositeurs approach might have led to a different solution is a question which must remain open."

The 1998 Rules modification added that the arbitral tribunal has the possibility to "decide *ex aequo et bono*" in addition to the possibility to decide as *amiable compositeur*. In either case this is only on the condition that "the parties have agreed to give it such powers." There is some dispute as to whether the powers of an arbitral tribunal acting as *amiable compositeur* or *ex aequo et bono* are coextensive or somewhat differing[2], a question which may depend on the law in effect at the place of arbitration. The Working Party which suggested the revision to the ICC Commission on International Arbitration considered the two terms to be synonymous.[3] The term *ex aequo et bono* is used by the UNCITRAL Rules as well as by some other institutional rules. Since ICC arbitration clauses from time to time refer to *ex aequo et bono* arbitration it was thought prudent to specifically provide for these powers in addition to those of *amiable composition* where the parties had so agreed.

The institution of *amiable composition* stems from civil law. As a departure from the ordinary rule that the arbitrator decides according to law, it permits an arbitrator to decide a case according to principles of equity and the arbitrator's conscience.[4] Legal systems providing for *amiable composition* specifically establish equitable as opposed to legal arbitration. With respect to the former, the arbitrator's decision is, as a practical matter, shielded from judicial review. It is unclear how such an institution is to be transposed into legal systems, such as the common-law system, which do not explicitly provide for this division into equitable and legal arbitration.

The arbitration laws in most civil law countries provide for arbitrators to decide as *amiable compositeurs* when the parties so agree. In addition to France, this is the case in Italy, Switzerland and the Netherlands, as well as in the countries having adopted the UNCITRAL Model Law.

English authors have often criticized the institution of *amiable composition*. In his commentary on the 1955 Rules, Professor E. J. Cohn went so far as to note that "the concept of *amiable composition* is happily unknown to English law."[5] If, however, the two principal characteristics of *amiable composition*

---

2   For a description of the possible differences, *see* M. Rubino-Sammartano, *Amiable Compositeur (Joint Mandate to Settle) and Ex Bono et Aequo (Discretionary Authority to Mitigate Strict Law - Apparent Synonyms Revisited*, 9 J. INT. ARB. No. 1 (1992) p. 5.

3   Some arbitrators have considered the terms synonymous as well, *see* ICC Case 4265/1984, 1984 JDI 923; ICC Case 4467/1984, 1984 JDI 925, ICC Case 6503/1990, 3 ICC AWARDS 613, commentaries Yves Derains.

4   The institution of *amiable composition* had its origins in the *Code Napoléon* and the French Code of Civil Procedure of 1806. The most recent modification (1980) of the French Code of Civil Procedure provides in Article 1474:

    "The arbitrator shall decide the case in conformity with rules of law, unless the parties have given him the power to decide as *amiable compositeur*." (authors' translation)

5   E.J. Cohn, *The Rules of Arbitration of the International Chamber of Commerce*, 14 INTERNATIONAL AND COMPARATIVE LAW QUARTERLY 156 (1965). More recent commentary also emphasizes the incompatibility with English law of a notion of arbitration outside of or contrary to the provisions

are the predominance of equity over law and restriction on the right of appeal, these features are known at common law albeit arrived at by other means and without specific claims that the arbitration is not being conducted under law. In England, for instance, prior to the 1979 amendment of the arbitration law,[6] arbitrators frequently refused officially[7] to give any reasons for the award. This kept courts from striking down an award for error of law on its face; the reasoning of the arbitrators in reaching their award was thus shielded from review. It has been suggested that by this device arbitrators were able to introduce equitable considerations into their awards. As stated by Lord Tangley, Chairman of the ICC Commission on International Arbitration at that time, and a former President of the Law Society:

> An error of law on the face of the award can be corrected by the Court and an arbitrator may be required to state a case on a point of law for the consideration of the Court. English law therefore frowns upon arbitration *ex aequo et bono* and will have nothing to do with that disreputable person the *amiable compositeur*. My continental friends regard this attitude as a typical piece of Anglo-Saxon hypocrisy. Only a minute proportion of matters dealt with by arbitration ever find their way to the Court. No experienced arbitrator will perpetrate an error of law on the face of the award, and no sensible arbitrator, unless he is called upon to state a special case, will give his reasons. Observing this facade, I strongly suspect that English arbitration is as successful as it is because arbitrators do act *ex aequo et bono* and behave as good and reliable *amiables compositeurs*.[8]

The situation in England has evolved. In principle arbitral tribunals are required to give reasons for their award (Arbitration Act 1996, Section 52) and while this provision may be waived under English law by specific agreement, this possibility is unavailing in ICC arbitration since Article 25(2) of the 1998 Rules provides that the award shall state the reasons upon which it is based, and this applies as much to *amiable composition* awards as to any others. Nevertheless, one can obtain much the same result the one approved by Lord Tangley since in international matters the parties may, by express agreement, exclude judicial review of the award for errors of law (Arbitration Act 1996,

---

of applicable law. *See* M.J. Mustill and S.C. Boyd, COMMERCIAL ARBITRATION, 74-86 (2d ed. 1989); Professor R. H. Christie, *Amiable Composition in French and English Law*, 58 ARBITRATION (No. 4) (1992) p. 377.

6 The Arbitration Act 1996, much as the previous 1979 law, now provides: "The Arbitral Tribunal shall contain the reasons for the award unless it is an agreed award or the parties have agreed to dispense with reasons." *See generally* Section 29.04.

7 The custom was frequently to deliver an official award containing the operative decision of the arbitrators, with separate unofficial and unsigned explanations of the reasoning. Such explanations could not be cited before any court.

8 *International Arbitration Today*, 15 INTERNATIONAL AND COMPARATIVE LAW QUARTERLY 719, 722 (1966).

Sections 69, 87). Moreover, Arbitration Act 1996 has taken some steps towards accommodation of *amiable composition* in Article 46(1), which provides:

The arbitral tribunal shall decide the dispute:

(a) in accordance with the law chosen by the parties as applicable to the substance of the dispute, or

(b) if the parties so agree, in accordance with such other considerations as are agreed by them or determined by the tribunal.

The DAC Report in support of the law[9] takes the position that the possibility to agree to "other considerations" covers the possibility of agreeing to equity clauses in general[10] and to *amiable composition* in particular.[11] Thus, for arbitrations taking place in England an English Court will recognize an agreement that the arbitrators will decide as *amiable compositeurs*. The agreement will also be recognized as an exclusion agreement hence effectively validating the award and shielding it from judicial review of points of law.[12]

If the parties desire *amiable composition*, it is probably wise to provide for the venue of the arbitration in a jurisdiction where the law specifically recognizes such powers. An *amiable composition* award valid where it is rendered will be entitled to recognition in other jurisdictions, particularly those which are parties to the New York Convention. The fact that the applicable rules of decision do not exist or are not available for arbitration taking place in the enforcement jurisdiction is not a ground for refusing to recognize a foreign award. This is the same principle which has permitted recognition and enforcement in England of foreign awards rendered by the application of a-national legal principles (such as *lex mercatoria*) whether or not such principles were a valid basis for an award under English law.[13] There is also authority for the recog-

---

9   Departmental Advisory Committee on Arbitration Law: Report on the Arbitration Bill, February 1996.

10   For the validity of the parties' agreement that the arbitrators shall decide "in equity" without reference to any provisions of law (a practice particularly used in reinsurance arbitration) *see* M. Kerr, *Equity Arbitration in England*, 2 AM. REV. INT. ARB. 377 (1991).

11   "Subsection [46](1) (b) recognizes that the parties may agree that their dispute is not to be decided in accordance with a recognized system of law but under what in this country are often called "equity clauses" or arbitration "*ex aequo et bono*" or "*amiable composition*", i.e. general considerations of justice and fairness, etc. It will be noted that we have avoided using this description in the Bill, just as we have avoided using the Latin and French expressions found in the Model Law. There appears to be no good reason to prevent parties from agreeing to equity clauses. However, it is to be noted that in agreeing that a dispute shall be resolved in this way, the parties are in effect excluding any right to appeal to the Court (there being "no question of law" to appeal)." (DAC Report at 223)

12   V.V. Veeder, *England* in ICCA HANDBOOK 53 (ARB. SUPP. 23, MARCH 1997).

13   *See* Deutsche Schactbau und Tiefbohrgesellschaft mbh v. Ras Al Khaima National Oil Company [1987] 2 LLOYD'S REP. 246, XII YEARBOOK 522 (1986); The Channel Tunnel Case [1993] AC 334, 368, XIX YEARBOOK 736 (1993).

nition of a foreign *amiable composition* award even though the jurisdiction where the award was rendered does not expressly recognize such powers.[14]

18.02 "Amiable Composition" and deciding "ex aequo et bono" under the ICC Rules

It is quite clear that under the 1998 Rules, the availability of *amiable composition* does not depend upon the procedural law of the seat of arbitration. This contrasts with the situation under the 1955 Rules, which provided in Article 19(3):

> The Court of Arbitration shall not give the arbitrator power to act as "amiable compositeur" unless the parties agree thereto, and *provided that it will not in any way interfere with the legal enforcement of the award*. (Emphasis added.)

The absence of any such qualification in the 1998 Rules confirms that the decision to give such extensive powers to the arbitrators lies solely in the hands of the parties without regard to local laws of procedure.

Parties to ICC arbitrations do grant this power to the arbitrators from time to time. One motivation is negative: unable to agree on applicable national law, the parties seek to shelter their relationship from an unforeseen national law chosen by the arbitrator, whose effect the parties feel unable to predict. The other motive, more positive, looks to the manner of judging or interpreting the rights and obligations of the parties and seeks to have a general standard of fairness applied in lieu of a legalistic approach.

Amiable composition is agreed far more frequently in long-term contracts than in contracts of short duration or simple sales transactions. In research at the ICC for a thesis on the subject, Eric Loquin found thirty- five examples of *amiable composition* arbitration, almost all in contracts of long duration, such as transfer of technology, turnkey industrial plant contracts, raw materials purchase or production, or economic development contracts.[15] The very nature of long-term contracts, the lack of developed principles or precedents in most national laws to deal with such complex agreements, and the economic interests at hand may commend an equitable solution to any dispute which may arise. *Amiable composition* is one method of securing such a resolution.

On the other hand, governments of developing countries, involved in such contracts directly or through State enterprises, are often reluctant to agree on

---

14 In Sweden, *see* A.B. Carl Engström v. N.V. Kunstmesthandel vorheen Hulshof, 1934 NYTT JURISDIKT ARKIV 491, cited *in* J. Paulsson, *The Role of Swedish Courts in Transnational Commercial Arbitration*, 21 VIRGINIA JOURNAL OF INTERNATIONAL LAW 211, 228 229 (1981); ARBITRATION IN SWEDEN 121 (Stockholm Chamber of Commerce Publication, 1977). A similar rationale was used by French courts to enforce in the *Norsolor* case a *lex mercatoria* award rendered in Austria whose law, according to its lower courts, did not permit *lex mercatoria* arbitration. *See* Section 17.03, *supra*.

15 E. Loquin, L'AMIABLE COMPOSITION EN DROIT COMPARÉ ET INTERNATIONAL, 145-154 (1980).

amiable composition if it means rejection of their own national law. They often feel that as a matter of principle their law should govern contracts essential to their economic development. This has occasionally led to combining a contractual choice of a national law with conferring the powers of *amiable compositeur* on the arbitrator. This practice is accepted by arbitrators and results in giving a single national law foundation to the contract, while still permitting the arbitrators to make an equitable application of national norms to the contract.[16]

Indeed, *amiable compositeurs* frequently prefer to investigate the underlying legal regime or regimes even when the contract is silent as to the applicability of any national law. As René David put it:

> In the vast majority of cases *amiables compositeurs* do not intend to work out a compromise, but they feel bound to decide as is prescribed by the law; they see in the law a kind of *ratio scripta* and do not find any good reason for departing from its application in particular cases. The *amiable compositeur* is in fact a judge, but one who enjoys greater flexibility in adopting the solution which he regards as best, even though from a strictly legal point of view it may not be absolutely correct.[17]

While an *amiable compositeur* arbitrator has very broad powers, his authority is not unlimited. It is said that the arbitrator's power is coextensive with the parties' capacity to settle a dispute by negotiation. Hence, in the proper exercise of his powers, the *amiable compositeur* will be loath to disregard mandatory provisions of law applicable in the place of contractual performance;[18] nor can he dismiss fundamental requirements of public policy.[19]

---

16   *See* ICC Case 2216/1974, extracts *in* 1975 JDI 917; E. Loquin, *supra* Note 15 at 161; and ICC Case 2879/1978, extracts *in* 1979 JDI 990 (where the parties during the arbitral proceedings asked the arbitrators to determine applicable law despite the existence of an *amiable composition* clause).

17   R. David, ARBITRATION IN INTERNATIONAL TRADE 355 (1985). Another definition is given in Mathieu de Boisséson, LE DROIT FRANCAIS DE L'ARBITRAGE 295 (1983): "A dispensation, foreseen by the case itself, from strictly applying the rules of law joined with the faculty of applying various criteria of interpretation and judgement, especially equity, commercial usages and the conscience of the arbitrator."

18   ICC Case 4265/1984, 1984 JDI 922; a sole arbitrator in France with powers of *amiable compositeur* refused to disregard a mandatory provision of the applicable Dutch law in respect to the period of time within which a claim for an agent's indemnity had to be filed. This rather narrow construction of the powers of *amiable composition* reflects French law concepts. Under Swiss law, such mandatory provisions of law can be disregarded as long as fundamental public policy concerns are protected; M. Blessing, *The New International Arbitration Law in Switzerland*, 5 J. INT. ARB. 9, 64 (1988).

19   ICC Case 2694/1977, 1978 JDI 985, 989. ICC arbitrators have in some cases found that their *amiable composition* powers were limited by mandatory provisions of the substantive law applicable to the contract; others have found limitations only in consideration of international public policy. For a review of the awards, *see* R. Briner, *Special Considerations Which May Affect the Procedure*, in ICCA CONGRESS SERIES No. 7, PLANNING EFFICIENT ARBITRATION PROCEEDINGS 362, 366-369 (1994).

It has also been held that while an *amiable compositeur* has the broadest powers to evaluate the performance or non-performance of contractual obligations, he does not have the power to disregard an express term of the contract, freely negotiated, nor to rewrite the contract, or adapt its terms to changed circumstances (*see* Section 8.05). This is particularly true in ICC arbitration since Article 17(2) of the Rules requires the arbitrator "[i]n all cases" to "take account of the provisions of the contract". Nevertheless, while respecting this obligation ICC arbitrators have found ways to moderate or attenuate the application of contractual provisions.[20]

Frequently, it is difficult to see how a decision which determines the respective obligations of the parties differs in ordinary cases as opposed to *amiable composition* cases. Perhaps the most marked difference is in evaluating the consequences of nonperformance. The *amiable compositeur* is much more at ease in establishing compensatory damages and awarding interest by the application of standards of commercial fairness than an ordinary arbitrator who must seek to justify his calculation by legal rules. It is perhaps in this field, more than any other, that the utilization of *amiable composition* powers may as a practical matter affect the outcome of a case.[21]

18.03 Scrutiny and review of awards rendered by amiables compositeurs

The most prominent legal effect of giving the arbitrator the powers of *amiable compositeur* is that an even greater shield from review is provided. This factor comes into play as early as during the course of scrutiny of the award by the Court of Arbitration pursuant to Article 27 (*see* Chapter 20). Awards that are rendered by an arbitrator with powers of *amiable compositeur* are distributed to the Rapporteur and to the members of the Court with the indication *amiable compositeur* stamped on the copy of the award as a reminder of the arbitral powers being exercised. The Court will use its power "to lay down modifications as to the form of the award," and to draw the attention of the arbitrator to points of substance, in a very sparing fashion. This does not exempt the *amiable compositeur* from being required to comply with fundamental notions of procedural fairness, nor from giving reasons for the award,[22]

---

20 *See* ICC Arbitration No. 4972/1989, 1989 JDI 1100, note G. Aguilar Alvarez; *see also* FOUCHARD, GAILLARD GOLDMAN ON INTERNATIONAL COMMERCIAL ARBITRATION 835-841 (Kluwer 1999).

21 ICC Case 6955/1993, XXIV YEARBOOK 107, 135 (1999): (claim by Swiss trading company against United States manufacturer for reimbursement for non-conforming goods, powers of *amiable compositeur* used to confirm an analysis of issues which relied on the United States Commercial Code); ICC Case 3267/1984, XII YEARBOOK 87, 93, 94-95 (1987): (claim by Mexican construction company against Belgian company concerning project in Saudi Arabia, powers of *amiable compositeur* used to evaluate justification for drawing down guarantee bond without detailed proof of damages incurred by wrongful termination); ICC Case 3327/1981, 1982 JDI 971,975: (extension of due dates for the payment of promissory notes by an African State in the context of a construction project); ICC Case 3344/1981, 1982 JDI 978: (determination of price in oil sales contract).

22 *See* new Article 25(2), 1998 Rules; *see* Chapter 20, *infra*.

and failure to do so may lead to a request by the Court for revision of the award.

The same is largely true in respect to judicial review. Thus in France, which has a legal system typical of the jurisdictions where *amiable composition* is specifically recognized, an action to annul the award will succeed whenever fundamental procedural fairness has not been respected or where the award violates public policy.[23] In particular, the *amiable compositeur* is not dispensed from having to give reasons for the award, which in France is a requirement of due process.[24]

Despite this possibility of limited judicial review it is clear that in France, as elsewhere, the giving of *amiable composition* powers to the arbitral tribunal serves to greatly reduce any possibility of attack on the award. In some respects it is curious that users of ICC arbitration, often quick to decry the "judicialisation" of international arbitration procedures, and the possibility of judicial interference, do not more frequently give to ICC arbitrators the power of *amiable composition*.

---

23   Articles 1484 (for domestic arbitrations) and 1502 and 1504 (for international arbitrations) of the French Code of Civil Procedure; English translation in the Annex to Chapter 30.

24   *Id.*, Articles 1471, 1480, 1502 and 1504. The necessity to give reasons does not, however, require the tribunal to set forth any basis at law for the award. *See Cour de cassation, Première chambre civile*, 19 November 1991, *Stapem S.A. v. Boccard S.A.*, (unpublished, appeal number 90-12.666) (reviewing an ICC award) (an arbitrator acting as *amiable compositeur* is entitled not to set forth the legal grounds on which he held a party responsible for breach of contract).

CHAPTER 19

ARBITRAL AWARDS

19.01   Time limits for awards

Article 24 of the ICC Rules provides:

(1) The time limit within which the Arbitral Tribunal must render its final award is six months. Such time limit shall start to run from the date of the last signature by the Arbitral Tribunal or of the parties of the Terms of Reference, or, in the case of application of Article 18(3), the date of the notification to the Arbitral Tribunal by the Secretariat of the approval of the Terms of Reference of the Court.

(2) The Court may extend this time limit, pursuant to a reasoned request from the Arbitral Tribunal or on its own initiative, if it decides it is necessary to do so.

Many national laws are hostile to arbitration procedures that are not subject to a fixed limitation of time.[1] While the parties may by common agreement extend a statutory time limit, many a claimant has found that the respondent is seldom willing to so agree when the expiration of the arbitration agreement may neutralize effective liability.

The solution of the ICC Rules is to establish a time limit six months from the entry into effect of the Terms of Reference but to give to the Court of Arbitra-

---

1   For instance, the French domestic arbitration law provides in Article 1456 of the Code of Civil Procedure:

If an arbitration agreement does not fix a time limit, the mission of the arbitrators shall continue only for six months from the day on which the last one of them accepted it. The legal or contractual time limit can be extended either by agreement of the parties, or, at the request of one of them or of the arbitral tribunal, by the presiding judge of the *Tribunal de grande instance* or . . . by the presiding judge of the *Tribunal de commerce*.

The time limit does not apply to international arbitrations, as has been confirmed by France's highest court. *Cour de cassation*, 15 June 1994, Sonidep v. Signoil, 1995 REV. ARB. 88. No time limit is stipulated in current Dutch, English, Swiss or Swedish (1999) legislation.

tion the power to extend it. Article 24(1) of the 1998 Rules spells out the date of entry into effect of the Terms of Reference[2] and hence the date from which the six month time limit will run. The date of the "rendering" of the final award is the date of the award's signature by the arbitrators (or a majority thereof) after the scrutiny and approval of the draft award by the ICC Court (*see* Article 27 of the Rules). Since the parties, by agreeing to arbitrate under ICC Rules, have agreed to the possibility of extensions and have vested authority in the Court of Arbitration to make such extensions, they will ordinarily be considered to have waived any time-limits that may be found in various national procedural laws.[3] French case law, which is of special interest since Paris is the site of approximately one-third of ICC arbitrations, has unequivocally confirmed the power of the ICC Court or the Committee of the Court to extend time limits within its discretion and without any requirement that it give reasons therefor.[4]

As previously noted, the six-month time limit for rendering of the final award is seldom adequate in major arbitrations. The Court therefore readily extends the time limit.

The Secretariat of the Court closely follows the calendar for each arbitration.[5] If the arbitrator fails to make a timely request for extension, the Secretariat will contact the presiding arbitrator or, if necessary, directly advise the Court of Arbitration of the problem.[6]

The question of extension of time is most frequently dealt with by the three-person Committee of the Court, which takes into account the arbitrator's estimate of the time required for further proceedings but will ordinarily not grant an extension of more than six months. Extensions of shorter periods of time will be granted where it is felt that this will encourage the arbitra-

---

2   This no longer includes the condition that payment of the total advance on costs be received as required under Article 18(3) of the prior version of the Rules. *See* Section 15.04, *supra*.

3   *See, e.g.*, to this effect, the decisions of 16 June 1976 of the French *Cour de cassation*, 1977 REV. ARB. 269.

4   *See* the decisions of the *Cour d'appel* of Paris of 3 December 1981, and 22 January 1982, *in* 1982 REV. ARB. 91; the latter case upheld by the *Cour de cassation*, 8 June 1983, 1987 REV. ARB. 309; *see also* P. Fouchard, *Les institutions permanentes d'arbitrage devant le juge étatique*, 1987 REV. ARB. 225, *see also*, FOUCHARD, GAILLARD GOLDMAN ON INTERNATIONAL COMMERCIAL ARBITRATION, 751-753 (Kluwer 1999). The decision of the ICC Court is considered to be administrative in nature and French courts will not review the desirability of such extensions for which no reasons are given by the ICC Court. *Cour d'appel*, Paris, 8 June 1983, *Société Appareils Dragon v. Empresa Central de Abastecimentos y Vantas de Equipos*, 1987 REV. ARB. 309.

5   The task of the Secretariat is facilitated by the imposition in Article 18(3) of the 1998 Rules of a requirement that the arbitral tribunal establish a provisional timetable for the conduct of the arbitration at the time of drawing up the Terms of Reference.

6   It has been held by French courts that the failure of the Court of Arbitration to inform the parties that it had extended the time for rendering the award does not infringe any procedural right of a party. *Cour d'appel*, Paris, 13 November 1992, *Casco Nobel France v. Sisco, Inc. and Kansa*, 1993 REV. ARB. 309.

tors to act quickly. The present practice is to grant three-month extensions generally; six-month extensions if the arbitrator provides a clear and convincing time schedule that reasonably requires more than three months; and twelve-month delays in very exceptional cases where all arbitrators and parties apply in writing with explanation of the need for such a long extension.[7]

The exercise by the Court of Arbitration of its discretion to extend limitations of time has been tested not only in the courts of France, but also in other jurisdictions. The cases are of interest because they properly characterize these powers as administrative, according to procedures agreed by the parties and hence, as long as exercised within the scope of the Rules, not subject to judicial review. In Switzerland, a petitioner attacked an ICC award alleged to have been rendered out of time, because the petitioner had not been given the opportunity to be heard on the issue of the extension of time within which to render an award, an extension which had been granted "automatically" by the Court of Arbitration. The Court of Appeal of the Canton of Bâle-ville rejected the recourse on the ground that the extension by the Court of Arbitration was not a reviewable act of procedure by an arbitrator or in the arbitration, but the performance of a contractual duty by a preconstituted third party in accordance with the agreement of the parties.[8] In Germany, as well, it has been held that the extension of the six month period may be made by the Court of Arbitration within its discretion, and that a party has no right to be heard on the issue.[9]

The powers given to the Court by the Rules, and the Court's practice thereunder, are designed to incite arbitral tribunals to proceed expeditiously and to avoid the risk of nullification of awards by a national court for failure to comply with prescribed time periods. The system broke down in one exceptional case: the French *Cour de cassation*[10] ultimately found cause to sustain the refusal of lower courts to enforce an ICC award alleged to have been rendered outside the contractually agreed time period. Under Article 18 of the prior Rules, the award in question was to have been rendered by the arbitrator prior to 31 December 1974; the award was in fact signed and submitted to the Court on 9 December 1974. However, since it was not approved by the Court until 22 January 1975, and since the Rules provide that the award is to be

---

7   A comment by a member of the ICC Court on the Court's practice in extending the six-month period for rendering an award is found in S. Bruna, *Control of Time Limits by the International Court of Arbitration*, 7 ICC BULL. 72 (December 1996).

8   *Cour d'appel*, 2 January 1984, Canton of Bâle-ville, 1985 SWISS BULL. 19, summary in Fouchard, Note 4 *supra*. The argument that an extension may be nullified in the absence of proof of exceptional circumstances, and an opportunity to be heard on the issue, accordingly failed in this case.

9   Federal Court, Third Civil Chamber, 14 April 1988, No. III ZR 12/87, 3 MEALEY'S INT. ARB. REP. 4 (No. 7, July 1988) (English translation)

10 27 April 1981 (*Société Ripolin*), 1981 GAZETTE DU PALAIS II.584.

signed and take effect only after scrutiny and approval of the award by the Court, it was found that the award could only have entered into effect after the time limitation, and was therefore not enforceable. This case fortunately appears unique.

In the 25 years since, the Secretariat has demonstrated great attentiveness to this aspect of the process, and, if a question arises in post-award national court proceedings, is prepared to produce records of the formal grant of final extensions by the Court.

19.02 Awards by consent

The interest of the parties in having a settlement incorporated in an award should be obvious. If agreed amounts are not paid voluntarily, a consent award would be granted recognition and be enforced as any other award. The enforcement procedures under the New York Convention and other bilateral and multilateral treaties make it easier for the parties to enforce an award than to bring suit in a national court under a settlement agreement. Accordingly, the ICC Rules provide in Article 26:

> If the parties reach a settlement after the file has been transmitted to the Arbitral Tribunal in accordance with Article 13, the settlement shall be recorded in the form of an Award made by consent of the parties if so requested by the parties and the Arbitral Tribunal agrees to do so.

The 1998 revision of the Rules make clear that a settlement will be recorded as an award only "if so requested by the parties". This is consistent with prior practice. Sometimes the parties see no need for an award.

The parties are in fact free, as part of the settlement agreement or separately, to withdraw the arbitration from the arbitral tribunal and the ICC. Just as the parties may agree to submit a dispute to ICC arbitration, they may agree to terminate any such submission; no consent award would then be issued. Such a result could be effected by the specific terms of a settlement agreement, withdrawing the pending case from arbitration. Parties may readily so agree when the settlement is self-executing (*i.e.,* when payment of any sums due is a condition precedent to the entering into effect of the settlement) or when there will be no sums to be paid in the future (*i.e.,* when each party drops its claim against the other). In other words, parties may disregard Article 26 of the Rules whenever they feel that the security of an award is not important to them.

The 1998 Revision, while confirming that a consent award would be made only on the request of the parties, also provided that such an award would be made only if "the arbitral tribunal agrees to do so." There are few cases where an arbitral tribunal would not acquiesce in the request of the parties to formalize their agreement as an award but the reserve is intended to assure that the consent award mechanism cannot be manipulated by the parties as an in-strument of fraud. One could imagine, for instance, the creation of a fictitious dispute designed to create a payment obligation for the purpose of tax deduct-ibility or money laundering. For the very reason that an arbitration award takes on international currency and can be enforced in most jurisdictions without the possibility of review of findings of fact or decision of law by the arbitrators, the tribunal must have the power to investigate and approve of the *bona fides* of the agreement submitted to them. The mere existence of the power of the arbitrators should be sufficient to assure that it will rarely be used.

A consent award, like any other ICC award, will be forwarded to the Court of Arbi-tration for its scrutiny. After its form has been approved by the Court (*see* Section 20.03) it will be notified to the parties by the Secretariat (*see* Section 22.02).

One motive for withdrawing claims as part of a settlement, rather than seek-ing a consent award, may be to reduce arbitration costs. Where a case is ter-minated prior to the rendering of an award, the full administrative expenses are not charged. The arbitrators' fees, fixed by the Court, depend on how much work was done by the arbitrators prior to the settlement. In the case of an award by consent, the arbitrators will spend some time drafting or exam-ining the award. This may lead to a greater allowance for arbitrators' fees than in cases where the claim is simply withdrawn, at least in those instances where the arbitrators themselves have been involved in the drafting of the consent award. In addition, in the case of a consent award, as is true for all awards, the Court has the power under Article 28(1) to withhold notification of the award until the full amount of costs have been paid by the parties or by one of them (*see generally* Section 22.02).

19.03   Interim and partial awards

i) Arbitral tribunal's power to render interim and partial awards

Ordinarily, it is desirable to determine all issues and decide all claims in a sin-gle award. However, an ICC tribunal has the power to render an award or awards prior to its final award.[11] Such preliminary awards, where required, may deal with such questions as jurisdiction, applicable law, prejudicial is-sues (*e.g.*, statutes of limitation, validity of contract, liability in principle), and decisions in respect to substantive claims.[12] The nomenclature of these

---

11   Article 2(3) of the Rules ("Definitions") defines "Award" to include "*inter alia*, an interim, partial or final Award." In addition to the usual reasons for which interim awards are given, the Rules now provide specifically at Article 23 for the arbitral tribunal's power to grant *interim measures* "in the form of an order, giving reasons, or of an Award, as the Arbitral Tribunal considers ap-propriate"; *see* discussion at Section 26.06, *infra*.

12   "Preliminary" indicates that it is not the tribunal's last award. An interim or partial award may be "final" in the sense that it is binding and enforceable, which would be the case of an award which disposed of one or more claims or such issues as the validity of the arbitral clause or the

preliminary awards is not homogenous and includes what have been termed interlocutory, interim, and partial awards. The term "interlocutory" is not favored as the description of a category of awards as it suggests a measure which is subject to change by the arbitrator, which would be a contradiction in terms with respect to an award. An ICC Committee found that the divergent usage of these terms in different countries made it impossible to find a universally acceptable terminology and that, in particular, the terms interim award and partial award were frequently used interchangeably.[13] Etymologically, it would seem preferable to reserve the term "partial award" for an award which disposes of one or more substantive claims, while the term "interim award" would have a broader scope, covering both partial awards and awards on jurisdiction or on prejudicial questions.

Any award, whether termed partial, or interim, is subject to the Court's scrutiny pursuant to Article 27, which contemplates that such awards may be made.[14] In fact, interim and partial awards are useful in many cases. They are permitted in ICC proceedings subject to the reservation in Article 35 that the arbitrator and the Court of Arbitration have the duty to "make every effort that the award is enforceable at law."[15]

Interim and partial awards are to be contrasted with interim decisions, given in the form of an order. A partial award, like a final award, must be forwarded to the Court of Arbitration for its scrutiny, and is notified to the parties by the Secretariat only after all formalities of an award have been complied with. An interim decision, however, is a procedural matter and is not subject to examination by the Court. It may be evidenced by simple orders or minutes of the tribunal. Many decisions of an interim nature may be made by an arbitral tribunal without an award even though they might affect the outcome of the case. Most procedural matters may be dealt with by decisions which do not become awards (unless incorporated in the final award), and need not be approved by the Court of Arbitration. Typical of such matters are motions seeking determinations such as the running of the statute of limitations or the

---

applicable law; indeed some courts and commentators refer to "partial final awards" to designate awards definitively disposing of part of a case which are subject to review and confirmation. Mettalgesellschaft A.G. v. M/V Capitaine Constante, 790 F2d 280 (2d Cir. 1986); C. Penna, *Partial Final Awards*, in ARBITRATION AND THE LAW, 1986 (AAA General Counsel's Annual Report) at 67.

13 WORKING PARTY ON PARTIAL AND INTERIM AWARDS AND DISSENTING OPINIONS, ICC COMMISSION ON INTERNATIONAL ARBITRATION, ICC Document No. 420/298 of 10 September 1987, No. 420/302 of 22 March 1988, and 420/305 Rev. of 20 March 1989 (Third Report of the Working Party, approved by the Commission, subject to minor modifications, on 19 April 1989).

14 Article 27 provides: "Before signing any Award, the Arbitral Tribunal shall submit it in draft form to the Court. The Court may lay down modifications as to the form of the Award and, without affecting the Arbitral Tribunal's liberty of decision, may also grant its attention to points of substance. No Award shall be rendered by the Arbitral Tribunal until it has been approved by the Court as to its form."

15 *See also* Article 6 of the Internal Rules of the Court of Arbitration.

failure of a request to state a claim at law. Unless granting such a motion would definitively dispose of a claim and thus require a final award, ICC arbitrators often choose not to make partial awards. Rather, they tend either to dispose of the question provisionally by a non-final written indication of their position (to be definitively determined and incorporated in the final award) or to refuse to rule on the question as a preliminary matter and reserve decision for the final award after submissions on all issues.

Subject to what is set forth below in sub-section ii, it is a matter of arbitral discretion as to whether, and in what circumstances, an interim or partial award should be made, unless the Terms of Reference have set forth a clear mandate that certain preliminary issues must or must not be determined in the form of an award.[16] Where there is no clear agreement by the parties on the matter, the arbitrator should decide whether a preliminary award will aid or impede the administration of arbitral justice, and particularly take into account whether the making of such an award will delay the overall conduct of the proceedings, and if so, whether such delay is justified.

ii) When arbitral tribunal must take decision by means of an award, not a procedural decision

For the most part, and as considered in the next sub-section, the arbitrator has discretion whether to make an intermediate decision by way of procedural decision, with the result to be incorporated in the final award as part of the tribunal's *ratio descendi*, or to make an interim award which creates a definitive title. It has been decided by national courts, however, that where a decision, while clothed in the form of a procedural decision, puts a definitive end to the claims of a party, then whatever its form it will be considered as an award, and will be subject to judicial review at the seat of arbitration.[17] These kind of cases have particular importance for ICC arbitration since all "awards" must be presented to the ICC Court for its review. If a decision framed as a procedural order is in fact considered by the national court as an award, this "award" will be defective for an additional reason: it will not have been scrutinized by the ICC Court, and accordingly, the arbitral procedure will

---

16   *Supra*, Section 15.05.

17   Defined as an award are "the decisions of arbitrators which decide in a definitive manner, all or part of a dispute which has been submitted to them, whether on the merits, on jurisdiction, or on a procedural issue which leads them to put an end to a proceeding . . ." *Cour d'appel*, Paris, 25 March 1994, Société Sardisud v. Société Technip, 1994 REV. ARB. 391. In another case, an ICC arbitral tribunal successfully defended that position that an interim and provisional decision that the statue of limitations had not run and that the arbitration should continue did not constitute a definitive decision requiring an interim award: The statue of limitations issue could be decided in the final award. *Cour d'appel*, Paris, 15 September 1998, Société Cubic Defense Systems Inc. v. Chambre de Commerce Internationale, 1999 REV ARB. 103.

not have been conducted according to the agreement of the parties.[18] Accordingly, ICC arbitral tribunals should take care to determine whether the procedural matter on which they rule definitively disposes of a claim or legal cause of action. If so, an arbitral award is required.

The same considerations are involved where the arbitral tribunal decides upon the correction or interpretation of an award pursuant to Article 29 of the Rules (*see* Section 22.05, *infra*). A decision to modify or correct the award takes the form of an addendum to the award which is submitted to the ICC Court for its scrutiny, then signed by the arbitrators and added to the award. Where the arbitral tribunal decides not to correct the Award, this will be encompassed in a document entitled "Decision," having all the characteristics and reasoning of an award, and submitted to the Court for its scrutiny. Such a decision puts an end to a claim or cause of action of a party and must be disposed of with the same formality as an award.

iii) Reasons for granting interim or partial awards

A common reason for requesting a preliminary award is to provide a ruling with respect to clear obligations (and to furnish a title upon which forcible execution may be granted) prior to resolution of other issues which may require lengthy proceedings. Examples would be a request for a preliminary determination that a contract is still in effect despite purported termination by one party (and hence that the parties have a continuing obligation to perform under the contract), or a determination that liquidated, payable debts should be satisfied even though the other party has formulated an off-setting claim or counterclaim for damages, the merits of which could be determined only after proceedings and hearings. In such cases, it is rare that both parties agree that a partial award be rendered; thus the party seeking an immediate ruling must persuade the arbitrators over the other party's objection that it is necessary to have a preliminary determination. Such occurrences are relatively rare.[19] Parties are more likely to reach consensus regarding the notion of partial awards with respect to issues having a less concrete impact, such as the determination of applicable law.

---

18   This was found to be the case in *Cour d'appel*, Paris, 1 July 1999, Société Braspetro Oil Services (Brasoil) v. GMRA, 1999 REV. ARB. 834, where an ICC arbitral tribunal had, by procedural order, found that Claimant's application for revision of a partial award, addressed to the tribunal, was inadmissible, hence putting an end to the revision proceedings (although not to the arbitration itself). The Court of Appeal considered the procedural order as if it were an award and set it aside because i) the award had not been subjected to the scrutiny of the ICC Court of Arbitration, a procedure agreed to by the parties when they accepted the ICC Rules; and ii) Claimant had not been given sufficient opportunity to prove the fraud upon which its application for revision was based.

19   *But see* an instance where an ICC tribunal sitting in Geneva and presided by a former Swiss federal judge rendered a partial award ordering payment of some US $26 million *the very first day of hearings*, reserving further issues of damages for the final award, *see* ICC Case 3093, 3100/1979, extracts *in* 1980 JDI 951; extracts *in* English *in* VII YEARBOOK 87 (1982).

The issue of jurisdiction may be made the subject of a preliminary award. More often, positive jurisdictional determinations are made by interlocutory orders or decisions which indicate the tribunal's disposition with respect to the jurisdictional issue by proceeding to hear the merits of the case but reserve final decision for the final award.[20] Nonetheless, parties occasionally provide for a partial award on jurisdiction in the Terms of Reference, and an arbitrator has discretion to render a jurisdictional award even in the absence of agreement. Some national arbitration laws provide that arbitral tribunals should ordinarily dispose of jurisdictional issues by preliminary decision or award.[21] This is the case, for instance, in Switzerland; Article 186 of the Private International Law Act provides:

The arbitral tribunal shall decide on its own jurisdiction.

Any objection to its jurisdiction must be raised prior to any defense on the merits.

The arbitral tribunal shall, as a rule,[22] decide on its jurisdiction by a preliminary decision.

National arbitration laws may also provide that positive decisions on jurisdiction, whether rendered by preliminary decision or award, are subject to judicial review. This is the case in Switzerland (Article 190, PILA) and under the UNCITRAL Model Law (Article 16(3)).

When an ICC arbitral tribunal intends to make a definitive and reasoned positive decision on jurisdiction in interlocutory fashion it should do so in the form of a preliminary award, even if a procedural decision to the same effect may be subject to judicial review under the law of the seat of arbitration. Any decision which the arbitral tribunal intends to have such finality as to permit judicial review should, in ICC arbitration, be presented to the ICC Court for its scrutiny and hence made in the form of an award.

In determining whether to make an interim award on jurisdiction, the arbitrator must take into account the delay that will ensue from the necessity of presenting the award to the Court of Arbitration for its scrutiny, and, more importantly, the frequently long period of time required where judicial review

---

20 Where a negative decision on jurisdiction puts an end to the arbitration, obviously a final award is required. Where arbitrators have definitively denied in interlocutory proceedings jurisdiction over some claims their decision will ordinarily take the form of a partial final award.

21 Some national laws, however, do not permit interlocutory judicial review of a positive finding of jurisdiction which may be reviewed only in connection with a subsequent final or partial final award. *See, e.g.,* the Netherlands Arbitration Act of 1986, Section 1052, XII YEARBOOK 379 (1987).

22 Note that the term "as a rule" indicates that the tribunal retains discretion not to issue an interim award confirming its jurisdiction if it finds that the plea was introduced for dilatory purposes only, or if the issue is so intimately linked with the facts that it is necessary to reserve the jurisdictional issue to be determined with the merits; M. Blessing, *The New International Arbitration Law in Switzerland,* 5 J. INT. ARB. 9, at 53 (1988).

is sought. Overall delay may be reduced if the arbitral proceedings on the merits are required to proceed while the appeal is pending. Under the laws of most jurisdictions—even those which stay the execution of an award pending judicial review—the issue of whether or not to suspend arbitral proceedings is entirely within the discretion of the arbitrator.[23] Obviously, the arbitrator will have to take seriously into consideration the expense and burden of further proceedings which would be wasted in the event the jurisdictional finding was not confirmed.

Partial awards may also be appropriate in complex contractual disputes with separable controversies. The authors are familiar with one ICC case involving a construction contract in a developing country where the arbitrators rendered fifteen partial awards on discrete disputes involving different phases of construction, and different sites and structures covered by the contract, prior to rendering a final award which disposed of the remaining miscellaneous disputes and costs. The entire arbitration lasted nearly five years, but the partial award mechanism permitted the injured party to recover damages immediately following hearings of evidence and argument on each of the sub-disputes. Equally important, this procedure allowed the project to go forward; as cash-flow is the life-blood of construction contractors, one may safely assume that in this case the project would have ground to a halt if major issues were left unresolved for five years pending a mammoth award that would have resembled more an autopsy than a diagnosis. Thus the rendering of partial awards, which requires confident, experienced, and authoritative arbitrators, may benefit both parties in the long run.

Generally, when arbitrators are requested to render a partial award, they must consider whether it will be more efficient to render a partial award or awards, requiring review by the Court of Arbitration, or to render only a single final award. Their discretionary authority in this regard is established by Article 15(1) of the Rules. They must also determine whether there is any impediment to the granting of partial awards by laws in force at the seat of arbitration.

19.04   Form of award

The ICC Rules contain no special provisions as to the form of the award but Article 25(2) of the 1998 Rules specifies that the award "shall state the reasons on which it is based," confirming prior practice required by the ICC Court. As to the form of the award, it is in the interest of the arbitral tribunal and of the Court of Arbitration that the award be considered by the parties to consti-

---

23   For France, *see Cour d'appel*, Paris, 7 July 1987, 1988 REV. ARB. 649, 653, note E. Mezger (pointing out that the ICC Rules agreed by the parties make no provision for suspension); for Switzerland, *see* Blessing, Note 22 *supra*, at 73. The stay of execution of an award is a limitation on the ordinary courts, which may not utilize enforcement powers pending appeal; it does not concern the arbitral tribunal's decision of whether to continue proceedings on the merits.

tute a fairly reasoned judgment on the issues and controversies presented. For this reason, the arbitral award should not only do justice to the parties, but should be so drafted that justice is seen to have been done. In addition, the tribunal must always keep in mind the directive of Article 35 to "make every effort to make sure that the Award is enforceable at law." For this reason, the arbitrators need to be certain not only that the merits of the dispute are sufficiently treated, but that a number of formal questions are treated in the award in order to facilitate recognition and enforcement of the award by national courts.

It is recommended that an award should ordinarily include the following items:[24]

i) The names and domiciles of the parties, and, where applicable, of their counsel or other representatives;

ii) The names of the arbitrators;

iii) A determination of the official place or seat of the arbitration;

iv) A recital of the essential milestones of the proceedings (dates of briefs and hearings) demonstrating the fact that the parties had adequate opportunity to present their case;

---

24 Some of these recommendations are drawn from the requirements of national legislation on arbitration procedure. While frequently these requirements are displaced, in international arbitration, by the agreement of the parties (either directly or by adoption of institutional arbitration rules) as to the form and contents of the award, which reduces formal requirements, prudence suggests that the additional formalities required by local laws be followed as well where possible. One of the duties of the Secretariat, in preparing the submission of arbitral awards for the scrutiny of the Court, is to determine whether there is any special requirement, at the seat of arbitration, for the form of the award, non respect of which might threaten the validity and enforceability of the award.

See, e.g., Article 1472 of the French Code of Civil Procedure, applicable to domestic arbitration (and which may also be applicable if the parties have agreed to adopt French procedural law) which requires:

The arbitral award should indicate:—the names of the arbitrators who rendered it;—its date;—the place where it was rendered;—the names, surnames, or appellation of the parties, as well as their domicile or corporate headquarters;—wherever appropriate, the name of the attorneys or other persons who have represented or assisted the parties.

See also Article 1057(4) of the Netherlands Arbitration Act of 1986 which provides:

In addition to the decision, the award shall contain in any case:

(a) the names and addresses of the arbitrator or arbitrators;

(b) the names and addresses of the parties;

(c) the date on which the award is made;

(d) the place where the award is made;

(e) the reasons for the decision, unless the award concerns merely the determination only of the quality or condition of goods . . . or the recording of a settlement. . .

v) The findings of the tribunal as to arbitral jurisdiction and reference to the arbitration agreement or clause upon which jurisdiction is based;

vi) Determination of the applicable substantive law or rules of law;

vii) If the arbitrators exercise the power of *amiable compositeur*, a reference to the agreement of the parties giving them such power;

viii) Reference to the respective claims and defenses of the parties and the issues to be determined;

ix) Reasoned resolution of the issues contained in the Terms of Reference;

x) A decision on each of the claims and, if applicable, counterclaims, and the reasons therefor;

xi) A determination of the monetary or other relief to be accorded, including damages, interest, and arbitration costs, including legal fees if appropriate; and

xii) Signature of the award by the arbitrators (or a majority of them; see Section 22.01) with the date of such award, following the scrutiny of the Court of Arbitration.

This list indicates only the most important items to be contained in an award. Generally, arbitrators must ensure that the award deals with all issues defined in the Terms of Reference. Some items found in the above list are specific requirements for arbitration awards under national procedural laws; adherence thereto facilitates international recognition of the award.[25]

The primary concern of ICC tribunals and the Court of Arbitration is to provide awards having international currency—awards which are recognized *de facto* in international business *milieux* as having the intrinsic value of persuasive and authoritative resolutions of disputes, and enforceable *de jure* in the greatest possible number of jurisdictions. Achieving this goal, which may well surpass the norms required for recognition of awards by particular national courts, is thought to be the best way of maintaining the traditionally high percentage of cases where the losing party voluntarily complies with the award. It should be recalled that in many jurisdictions, there is no require-

---

25   It should not, however, be concluded that non-respect of one of these procedural rules, even if considered "mandatory" under the laws of the country where the award was rendered, would necessarily have the effect that an ICC award rendered in one of these jurisdictions is unenforceable abroad. Art. V(1)(d) of the New York Convention provides as possible grounds for non-enforcement that "the arbitral procedure was not in accordance with the agreement of the parties, or, failing such agreement, was not in accordance with the law of the country where the arbitration took place." Given the precedence accorded to the "agreement of the parties" a forceful argument may be made that an award rendered in conformity with the ICC Rules and notified to the parties after scrutiny by the Court of Arbitration respects the procedure agreed to by the parties and must be enforced abroad even if not rendered in conformity with otherwise mandatory requirements of the national procedural law of the place of arbitration.

ment that an arbitrator give any reason for the award.[26] Furthermore, even in those jurisdictions where legislation requires reasoned awards, exception may be made for international awards as contrasted with domestic awards.[27] Finally, the New York Convention, which limits the grounds upon which a signatory country may refuse to recognize and execute a foreign award, does not allow the enforcement forum to insist that awards respect any particular form or that reasons be given; thus the absence of reasons is problematic under the New York Convention only if giving reasons is mandatory, and their absence therefore constitutes grounds of annulment at the seat of arbitration.[28]

This discussion becomes rather academic in the ICC context, where awards invariably state reasons, as now explicitly required by Article 25(2) of the Rules. Even arbitrators acting as *amiable compositeurs*, although sometimes considered as being dispensed from justifying their decision as a matter of law, are required to state their reasons in order that the parties and the Court be in a position to appraise the thoroughness of the arbitrators' treatment of the issues. (Often the decision in law is determined and *then* the powers of the *amiable compositeur* are applied.) The form of the reasoning of the award may vary greatly as a function of the legal background of the arbitrators, especially that of the presiding arbitrator, who normally plays the key role in drafting the award. Awards rendered by civil-law arbitrators tend to follow the example of civil-law court judgments, structured as an outline of tightly reasoned conclusions following legal and logical premises. Common-law arbitrators, on the other hand, tend to deal with the factual issues in much greater detail and to discuss and weigh the evidence at length. Nevertheless, it is neither necessary nor probably even desirable that an arbitrator attempt to summarize the evidence on each disputed factual issue. A judge must do so because his findings of fact are subject to appeal; gross factual errors, or mis-

---

26   This is so in the United States where neither federal nor state statutes take a position with respect to the need for arbitrators' statement of reasons. In practice, reasoned awards are rarely given in domestic commercial cases, and the Supreme Court has specifically ruled that arbitrators need not give reasons; Bernhardt v. Polygraphic Company, 350 U.S. 198 (1956).

    In England, the rendering of awards without giving reasons was traditional. The enactment of the Arbitration Act 1979 marked a shift to the system of reasoned awards which was confirmed by Arbitration Act 1996, Article 52(4) of which provides: "The award shall contain the reasons for the award unless it is an agreed award or the parties have agreed to dispense with reasons."

27   Thus, on one occasion, the courts of France recognized an English award which was not reasoned, and was not rendered pursuant to powers of *amiable composition*. The Court of Appeals stated that: ". . . the failure to give reasons, although contrary in principle to French procedure is not contrary to French international public policy, if it is permitted by the foreign law," *Cour d'appel* of Nancy, 29 January 1958, 1958 REVUE CRITIQUE DE DROIT INTERNATIONAL PRIVÉ 148; review (*cassation*) denied, *Cour de cassation* 14 June 1960, 1960 *id.* 393. To the same effect, *see also Cour de cassation*, 22 November 1966, 1967 REV. ARB. 9; and Provenda S.A. v. Alimenta S.A. decision of the Swiss Federal Tribunal, 12 December 1975, ARRÉTS DU TRIBUNAL FÉDÉRAL 101 Ia 521 (1976).

28   A.J. van den Berg, THE NEW YORK ARBITRATION CONVENTION OF 1958 381 (1981) updated in XXIV b YEARBOOK (1999).

takes in deciding mixed questions of fact and law, are intended to be corrected by appellate courts. This is not the case for the arbitrator, as ordinary appeal is meant to be excluded. While the arbitrator may be tempted to explain to the losing party why it lost, he should also keep in mind that disappointed parties will carefully examine even unnecessary or superfluous findings in search of means to continue the struggle. The award should, however, make it amply clear that the "rights of due process" have been fully respected, that the procedure was even-handed, and that the views of all members of the arbitral tribunal (especially a dissenting arbitrator) have been heard.

The variety of forms that ICC arbitral awards take may also be explained by the wide range of subject matters submitted to ICC arbitration. Nevertheless, common features of international commercial transactions lead to a certain similarity of approach in the motivation of awards whatever may be the origin and training of the arbitrators involved, and irrespective of the place of arbitration. In no event is the arbitrator bound to draft a decision in the same format as would a judicial tribunal.

A generous sampling of ICC arbitrators' reasoning may be found in extensive excerpts of ICC awards which have been published in recent years. Since 1974, excerpts of ICC awards in French have been published in the last issue of each volume of the JOURNAL DU DROIT INTERNATIONAL, with commentary by the present or former Secretary General or General Counsel of the Court of Arbitration. These awards and commentary have been gathered together in the COLLECTION OF ICC ARBITRAL AWARDS cited herein as ICC AWARDS, presently in three volumes covering the years 1975-1995. Since 1976, similar excerpts have been published in English in the ICCA YEARBOOK.

19.05   Majority awards and awards rendered by the chairman

For awards rendered by three arbitrators, Article 25(1) of the ICC Rules provides:

> When the Arbitral Tribunal is composed of more than one arbitrator, an Award is given by a majority decision. If there be no majority, the Award shall be made by the chairman of the Arbitral Tribunal alone.

It is a common feature of ICC arbitration practice that the arbitral tribunal makes substantial efforts to arrive at a unanimous decision. The winning party is frequently advantaged by a unanimous decision, even if it may feel that the consensus was obtained by a compromise which did not provide the full relief requested.[29] Unanimous decisions are more readily executed on a voluntary basis than those in which there is a dissenting arbitrator, and

---

29   For a pointed critique of the dynamics of compromise in arbitration, *see* J.G. Wetter, III *The International Arbitral Process* 347 *et seq.* (1979).

doubtless also facilitate national court recognition and execution of an award.

The arbitrators' deliberations are secret. The three arbitrators meet immediately following the close of the proceedings and tentatively agree on the main issues in the case. Next, the chairman submits a draft award to fellow arbitrators. The latter may suggest modifications or submit substitute drafts on certain points. While this is probably the most frequent procedure used by arbitral tribunals, the chairman may instead, after initial deliberations, ask each of the party-appointed arbitrators to submit a draft award with a view to developing a synthesis. Sometimes it is agreed that each arbitrator will submit a draft on certain issues, and a composite award will then be prepared by the chairman. Occasionally, when the chairman has difficulty in drafting in the official language of the arbitration, the arbitrators agree that one of the party-appointed arbitrators will initially draft the award. However, no details of the deliberative process are to be revealed to the parties. Individual positions are irrelevant; nothing significant is deemed to have occurred until the tribunal takes a position as an organic whole (even if the arbitrators are not unanimous).

This is not to suggest that failure to obtain unanimity prevents awards from being rendered. The provision in ICC arbitration for party-nominated arbitrators leads with some frequency to situations where an arbitrator refuses to join in an award against the party which nominated him. Article 25(1) of the Rules provides that with respect to tribunals composed of more than one arbitrator, the award is given by majority decision. Accordingly, any decision of the tribunal agreed by two out of three arbitrators may be forwarded as a majority award to the Court of Arbitration for its scrutiny. When approved, the award will be recirculated among the arbitrators and will enter into effect after it has been signed by at least the two arbitrators agreeing to the award (*see* Section 22.01).

In some cases, not even a majority view will emerge. This may be the case where each party-nominated arbitrator remains fairly close to the positions urged by "his" party and the chairman is unable to find common ground with either side. In such a case, Article 25(1) provides that the award shall be made by the chairman alone. This procedure is used extremely rarely in ICC practice as the arbitral process itself is an impetus for compromise and agreement. The fact is that most party-appointed arbitrators are aware of their obligation of independence and do not in fact conduct themselves as advocates for a party in the tribunal's deliberations. In addition, the very existence of the chairman's power to decide alone creates a significant incentive for at least one of the other arbitrators to compromise. It is the authors' firm opinion that this possibility of a decision by the chairman alone is highly appropriate in international arbitration.

When no majority may be found, the chairman alone drafts an award which, after scrutiny by the Court of Arbitration, will be notified to the parties as the chairman's award under Article 25(1). Ordinarily, the chairman's forwarding of the award to the Court will be preceded either by a confirmation by the other arbitrators that no agreement could be reached and that the chairman is to draft the award, or by the chairman having given the opportunity for the other arbitrators to join in the award and the latter confirming that no further deliberation could lead to a majority or unanimous award.

The chairman-alone mechanism is well illustrated in an ICC arbitration between an Egyptian state paper manufacturing company, RAKTA, and a U.S. construction company, Parsons & Whittemore, where each party nominated one of its nationals as arbitrator.[30] There were two awards in the case: a preliminary award denying the defendant's *force majeure* argument and a final award of damages. With respect to the preliminary award, the Egyptian arbitrator felt that the *force majeure* defense should be entirely rejected, while the American arbitrator considered it fully justified. The chairman, Judge Gunnar Lagergren of Sweden, held that the *force majeure* defense should be accepted since the difficulties of contractual performance were a result of the Israeli-Egyptian conflict of June 1967, but that it should be limited in time; in other words, the contractor had a duty to return to the site as soon as reasonably possible. As neither party-appointed arbitrator was willing to modify his position, the chairman decided alone over two dissenting opinions.[31] The process was repeated with respect to the final award: the American arbitrator refused to consider that there should be any damages for contractual non-performance, while the Egyptian arbitrator insisted on a far higher amount than the chairman was willing to grant.

The possibility under the ICC Rules of awards with which two of the three arbitrators disagree has been criticized in some quarters. However, while used only and exceptionally as a last resort, this procedure resembles a long tradition under prior English law which provided for calling in the third arbitrator to serve as an umpire, only after the two party appointed arbitrators had failed to arrive at a decision, and who ruled alone in the case of the continuing disagreement of the two party-appointed arbitrators.[32] It serves as additional insurance against paralysis of the arbitral process.

---

30   ICC Case 1703/1971, made public as result of enforcement proceedings in the U.S., 508 F. 2d 969 (2d. Cir. 1974); summarized *in* I YEARBOOK 205 (1976).

31   Extracts *in* I YEARBOOK 130 (1976); extracts in French *in* 1974 JDI 894, *see also* ICC Case 3381/1984, 1986 JDI 1096, 1099, where the chairman rendered the decision alone in view of the two dissenting opinions of the party-appointed arbitrators, one finding the damages awarded too high, the other too low. For another case where the chairman rendered an award alone, accompanied by two dissenting opinions, *see* ICC Case 3881/1994, 2 ICC AWARDS 257, note Sigvard Jarvin.

32   M.J. Mustill and S.C. Boyd, COMMERCIAL ARBITRATION 8 (2d ed. 1989).

19.06   Dissenting opinions

Whether it is a majority award or an award of the chairman alone, an ICC award must contain all the elements of an enforceable award. While the award may indicate that a particular arbitrator did not concur in the decision, a dissenting opinion *per se* does not ordinarily become part of the award, even though its contents may be made known to the parties.[33] A dissenting arbitrator may make his views known to the Court of Arbitration for its use in its scrutiny of the award. These views usually take the form of correspondence addressed to the Court, but they may be incorporated in a dissenting opinion.

Nothing in the Rules specifically prevents annexing a dissenting opinion to the award. The only inhibiting factor may be Article 35. Since Article 35 provides that both the tribunal and the Court of Arbitration shall make every effort that the award be enforceable at law, the award should conform as much as possible to the requirements of the jurisdictions in which arbitrations take place as well as those where awards may be enforced. As in the civil-law tradition there is no place for dissenting opinions in either judicial decisions or arbitral awards (apparently due to the fact that the deliberations of arbitrators and judges are secret and dissenting opinions tend to reveal the inner workings of the tribunal),[34] the practice of making dissenting opinions a part of an ICC award is not to be encouraged. This is all the more true since a great number of parties to ICC arbitration come from civil-law countries and there is always the possibility that an award may be presented for execution in a civil-law country where the defendant has assets. The silence of the Rules themselves regarding dissenting opinions, added to the notions in Article 25(1) that there may be a "majority decision" in the absence of unanimity, or a "sole decision" by the chairman in the absence of a majority, supports the view that there is only one award: the one that disposes of the case. A dissenting opinion is thus extraneous to *the* award.

---

33   *See generally*, F. Donovan *Dissenting Opinions*, 7 ICC Bull. 76 (December 1996).

34   René David, Arbitration In International Trade 326-7 (1985). In respect to dissenting opinions, the author states:

> French law does not allow them. An arbitrator may manifest his disagreement with the majority's decision in refusing to sign the award; he may not explain his position. That would be to contradict a principle considered fundamental in France, and that the new code of procedure (Article 1449) has expressly confirmed: the deliberations of the arbitrators are secret.

> Case law indicates, however, that violation of the secrecy of the deliberations has no effect on the award. Indeed, if it were a cause of nullity a party-appointed arbitrator would only have to publish his dissenting opinion to nullify an award of which he did not approve. *Cour d'appel*, Paris, 19 March 1981, 1982 Rev. Arb. 84. *See also* Noble China Inc. v. Lei, 42 Ontario Reports (3rd) 70, (Ontario Court (General Division) 1998), discussed in Section 16.06 *supra*, for an unusual case where the affidavit by a dissenting arbitrator furnished to support an attack on the award for bias by the majority arbitrators, and explaining the circumstances of the dissent, was rejected by the reviewing court because, *inter alia*, it infringed the secrecy of deliberations.

On the other hand, the procedural laws in many common-law countries permit dissenting opinions by arbitrators as well as by judges. Where the arbitration takes place in one of these countries, a common-law arbitrator may seek to have his dissenting opinion made known.[35] The proper procedure in such a case is for the dissenter to obtain the agreement of fellow arbitrators, expressed in the latter's majority decision, that the dissenting opinion may be annexed to the award.

As part of its review process, the Court of Arbitration may then decide to annex the dissenting opinion to the award, provided always that the enforceability of the award is not jeopardized. Article 6 of the Internal Rules of the Court provides:

> When the Court scrutinizes draft awards in accordance with Article 27 of the Rules, it considers to the extent practicable, the requirements as mandatory law at the place of arbitration.

In general, the Court of Arbitration makes its own determination of whether it considers that there is a legal impediment to communication of the dissenting opinion. However, it also considers that the arbitrators are free to interpret the law of the place of arbitration with regard to the communication of dissenting opinions. Where the majority of the tribunal considers the communication inadmissible under such law, the Court does not communicate the dissenting opinion with the award. When the Secretariat, acting for the Court, communicates the dissenting opinion to the parties with the award, it makes clear that it is not part of the award. Where the dissent is not communicated officially, there is nothing to prevent the dissenting arbitrator from communicating his opinion to the parties (and to the parties alone), provided that it takes place after the official notification of the award.[36]

---

35   For an example of a dissenting opinion in an ICC arbitration which became the subject of judicial review proceedings, *see* the Mobil Oil Indonesia case before the New York courts, where at the Appellate Division level, 392 N.Y.S. 2d 614 (1977), reference was made to a dissenting opinion rendered in the ICC arbitration by John Van Voorhis, a retired judge of the New York Court of Appeals. The rendering of a dissenting opinion in an ICC arbitration, and consideration of whether the majority arbitrators were required to meet to renew deliberations with the dissenter (no) was reviewed in detail by an English court in *Bank Mellat v. GAA Development & Construction Co.*, 2 LLOYD'S REP. 44, 49-51 (1988).

36   In the view of the authors, such a communication would not violate an arbitrator's obligation to respect the "secrecy of deliberations." Since the ICC Rules provide for majority awards, and an arbitrator may indicate that he is not part of the majority, there should be no impediment to his informal communication of his views. Such a communication would not constitute a violation of the "secrecy of deliberations" if it does not reveal the communications or thought processes of the other arbitrators. Such a communication after the notification of the award must be distinguished from the unauthorized communication by an arbitrator of his opinion, or of the majority opinion, prior to official notification of the final award. An initiative of this nature, possibly with the intent to derail the arbitral process, would be a serious breach of the arbitrator's obligations. *See* discussion at Section 16.06, *supra*, "Confidentiality." For an unusual case where an arbitrator, having rendered a dissenting opinion in an ICSID arbitration, subsequently, after annulment of the arbitral award, accepted to serve as counsel to the party having earlier appointed him, and

Because of the diversity of approaches of arbitral tribunals in dealing with dissenting opinions, and particularly because of conflict between civil law and common law concepts, a working committee of the ICC Commission on International Arbitration conducted a survey of the subject.[37] The opponents of dissenting opinions pointed out their disadvantages within the framework of the ICC Arbitration Rules, which provide for party-nominated arbitrators and scrutiny of awards by the Court of Arbitration. They argued that dissenting opinions underscore the link between the arbitrator and the party who nominates him, weaken the search for a unanimous position, and threaten to draw the Court of Arbitration into a debate—which is not its role—on the respective merits of the majority and dissenting views. Despite these negative views, a large majority of the Committee was strongly of the opinion that an arbitrator had a right to make his dissenting views known and that no steps should be taken to suppress dissenting opinions. It was recognized that it would nevertheless be desirable that a more uniform administrative approach be taken towards such opinions.

The Commission (whose views are only recommendations and not binding on the ICC Court) confirmed the Report encompassing the views of the majority.[38] The Report concluded that the dissenting opinion is not part of the award and that the Court of Arbitration is not required to scrutinize it under the Rules. It recommended, nevertheless, that the Court should continue its current practice of looking at the dissenting opinion at the same time that it scrutinizes the award, for any assistance that it may lend to such scrutiny.[39] The submission of a dissenting opinion should not occasion delay, and the chairman of the arbitral tribunal should fix an appropriate deadline for the dissenting opinion to be produced so that it may be dispatched simultaneously with the award to the Court of Arbitration. Frequently the majority arbitrators wish to see the dissenting opinion so that they may be sure to

---

thus to be in a position to utilize the information communicated to him by his earlier co-arbitrators, and to act against one of the parties that had earlier accepted his serving as arbitrator, *see* Klockner v. Cameroun, *ICSID arbitration* 81/2.

37 *Fourth Report on Dissenting and Separate Opinions*, WORKING PARTY ON PARTIAL AND INTERIM AWARDS AND DISSENTING OPINIONS, COMMISSION ON INTERNATIONAL ARBITRATION, Doc. No. 420/293 Rev. 2, 23 February 1988.

38 Commission on International Arbitration, Doc. No 420/1304, 25 May 1988.

39 A recent summary of the Court's practice concerning the place of dissenting opinions in the Court's scrutiny process was provided by F. Donovan (a member of the Court), Note 33 *supra*, 77: "Since, as has been pointed out, a dissenting opinion is not an award, its substance is not approved or disapproved by the Court. If the dissenting opinion is available at the same time as the ICC Court reviews the award, it is "laid" before the Court. On occasion, when the dissenting opinion appears strongly persuasive, particularly on points of interpretation of the applicable law, the Court may consider drawing the attention of the majority to such points (of substance) if it thinks there is some weakness in the reasoning of the majority thereof, as provided in Article 21 [Article 27 of the 1998 Rules]."

treat all questions raised in the draft award submitted. Once again, this should not be permitted to be the cause of needless delay.

The Report concluded that the general rule should be that the Court of Arbitration should notify dissenting opinions to the parties. In rare instances where such notification might imperil the award (and the Committee's survey found no country where this was certain to be the case), the practice of permitting a dissenting arbitrator informally to send his opinion to the parties should be maintained.

The practice of issuing opinions dissenting from ICC awards will remain controversial. There will continue to be cases where an arbitrator, as a matter of conscience, feels required to make known his views, especially if he believes that the award results in a miscarriage of justice. However, it would be unfortunate if these exceptional instances became commonplace. Party-nominated arbitrators should avoid the temptation of writing dissents only to justify their position. If they cannot bring themselves to accept the rule of consensus, it should be sufficient that the award indicate that it is made "by a majority." Ordinary issues of fact and law are not susceptible to judicial review; nor should they be if the institution of arbitration is to retain its vigor. The common-law rationale for dissenting opinions, namely that they usefully frame issues which appellate courts will settle in the interest of establishing the uniform application of legal principles throughout the jurisdiction, is thus inoperative in the context of arbitration. In these circumstances, one may feel that the Working Party's view that "the ICC should neither encourage nor discourage the giving of such opinions"[40] is too weak, and that, by its apparent neutrality, it might in fact lead to more dissenting opinions. The view of the present authors is that while dissenting opinions may exceptionally be justified, they are generally to be discouraged.

---

40   Fourth Report. Note 37 at p.2.

CHAPTER 20

THE COURT'S SCRUTINY OF AWARDS

20.01 The Court's role

Unlike the rules of some arbitral institutions, the ICC Rules do not provide for appellate review by a second-tier organ within the institution. While such institutional review may be appropriate where the first-tier arbitrators are lay arbitrators acting with great speed, this is not the case in the ICC context where the sole arbitrator or chairman is chosen for his or her established competence as an international arbitrator. Furthermore, ICC arbitration cases by their nature tend to be more time consuming and call for more careful deliberation than trade-association arbitrations.

On the other hand, the institution has an interest in ensuring that awards bearing the ICC *cachet* have international currency and be entitled to execution in the largest possible number of states. In view of the fact that ICC arbitral proceedings may in principle take place in any country, and that decisions are rendered by arbitrators of diverse nationalities and background, it is important that there be a central authority having experience with recognition and enforcement practices throughout the world to aid the arbitrators in issuing reliable awards.

This role of unification and verification is played by the Court of Arbitration (aided by its Secretariat), as provided for in Article 27 of the Rules:

> Before signing any Award, the Arbitral Tribunal shall submit it in draft form to the Court. The Court may lay down modifications as to the form of the Award and, without affecting the Arbitral Tribunal's liberty of decision, may also draw its attention to points of substance. No Award shall be rendered by the Arbitral Tribunal until it has been approved by the Court as to its form.

Special note should be made of the careful choice of words regarding the Court's powers: "scrutiny of the award" (in French, "*examen de la sentence*"). They are intended to reflect the supervisory, rather than arbitral or judicial, role of the Court. The award remains the product of the arbitral tribunal; if the Court feels substantive modifications are called for, it can only make suggestions to this effect to the arbitrators. The arbitrators cannot be forced to accept any modifications. (Since arbitrators cannot force the Court to approve their award either, there is a theoretical possibility of a deadlock; but this does not occur in practice.)

The make-up of the Court assures not only the availability of international expertise to assist in attaining optimal enforceability of the award, but it is also a guarantee of representative views in the international commercial community (*see* Section 2.03).

The procedures followed by the Court in scrutinizing awards merit attention. Prior to 1998, only the Court in plenary session could approve awards. This was the result of Article 11 of the prior version of the Internal Rules of the Court.[1] Now, under the power given to it by Article 4(5) of the 1998 Internal Rules, the Court has delegated to a three person committee of the Court the power to scrutinize and approve awards, which will allow earlier notification of a final award to the parties. Awards which raise particular problems or difficulties, and awards which did not receive a unanimous approval by a Committee of the Court, will continue to be scrutinized and approved at a plenary session of the Court.[2] In all cases the Secretariat will summarize for the members of the Court the procedure and circumstances of the case and award.

Where an award is to be presented to a plenary session of the Court, the Secretariat will ordinarily ask a member of the Court to act as *rapporteur* on such an award and to present it to the Court. *Rapporteurs* should be fluent in the language of the award and conversant with the law that governs the agreement, as well as any particularities of procedure either at the place of arbitration, or in jurisdictions likely to be relevant to any enforcement of the award. The *rapporteur* will ordinarily prepare both a written report (distributed to all members several days prior to the meeting) and an oral exposition for the meeting at which the award is considered.

The Secretariat's Counsel in charge of the file (*see* Section 2.04) is also available to assist the members of the Court, as is the Court's General Counsel, who studies all awards prior to the Court session at which the awards are discussed. Members of the Secretariat may not vote. However, the presence of Counsel of the Secretariat[3] may be most useful with respect to questions as to

---

1   Even then, however, routine awards (the so-called "B Awards") were presented to a three-person Committee of the Court for scrutiny. Where the Committee unanimously recommended approval, or other action, the recommendations were submitted to the whole Court, sitting in plenary session, but approval was considered only a formality.

2   *See* Robert Briner, *The Implementation of the 1998 ICC Rules of Arbitration*, 8 ICC BULL. 7, 9 (December 1997).

3   Internal Rules of the Court, Articles 1(1) and 1(2).

the precise status of the proceedings since they follow the file and have corresponded with the arbitrators, and frequently with counsel to the parties.

The Court spends considerable time in its scrutiny of awards. Some of the awards are, as one of the members of the Court put it, "so perfect that it calls for no comment other than the admiration of the members of the Court." Others give rise to lengthy discussions among the members, and subsequent correspondence between the Secretariat (acting upon instruction from the Court) and the arbitrators. Some arbitrators clearly feel that review by the Court is unnecessary and undesirable. The ICC believes, however, that this step is an important guarantee of the rights of the parties and of the reputation of the ICC arbitral process. It is given much of the credit for the belief that over 90% of ICC awards are respected voluntarily by the parties, and that ICC awards have a very good record of enforcement by national courts whenever they are challenged.

Article 27 reveals that in its scrutiny of the award the Court has both mandatory and advisory powers. The Court may "lay down" modifications as to the form of the award; it may merely "draw the [arbitral tribunal's] attention" to points of substance. A third power not specifically mentioned in Article 27, but explicit in Article 35, is that of assuring that the proceedings have respected the parties' fundamental right to be heard.

20.02 Review of procedural defects

In its review of the award submitted to it, or of correspondence concerning the award, the Court may become aware of a procedural defect not revealed on the face of the award. In other words, the process of scrutiny of the award may bring to light a defect in the arbitral process itself which may yet be curable. The issue most often raised before the Court at this stage is an alleged failure in the process of deliberations by the arbitrators.

This may occur if one of the arbitrators informs the Court that the draft decision contains elements which were not the subject of a discussion and deliberation among the arbitrators. In one case, the Court returned the award to the arbitrators for deliberation when it appeared that at the first meeting of the arbitrators, after the hearing, one arbitrator was presented by the chairman with a draft award already signed by the other two arbitrators and prior to discussion of any of the issues.

The Court must of course be wary of being led to delay proceedings by the unsupported allegations of procedural defect raised by a party or by an arbitrator. Chairmen of arbitral tribunals are well advised to keep minutes of both hearings and meetings of arbitrators so that a contemporaneous record is established and circulated to the other arbitrators. In this way, procedural controversies may be avoided. The absence of any such record may oblige the Court, when faced with an allegation of lack of deliberation, to return the matter to the tribunal. Such a step, however, seldom affects the final outcome; it merely inconveniences the prevailing party.

20.03   Modification of the form of awards

Without affecting the arbitrator's liberty of decision on the merits, the Court may, under Article 21 of the Rules, "lay down modifications as to the form of the award."

The Court's powers here are mandatory. It has a duty not to give finality to an ICC award until the formal prerequisites of a binding award have been complied with. Some of the formal requirements of an award have been set forth in Section 19.04. More generally, the Court reviews whether the arbitrators have adequately dealt with the issues presented to them and have given clear and noncontradictory reasons for their decision.

Some elements of this formal review are administrative—not to say clerical—in the strictest sense. Are the amounts awarded internally consistent? Do the items of damages awarded under each claim add up to the total amount of the award? Are the amounts awarded as interest consistent with the rate applied?

More generally, the review is intended to ensure the legal sufficiency of the award to accomplish the result intended by the arbitrators. The Court accordingly verifies those formal elements which should be contained in every ICC award. Moreover, it considers the appropriateness of compliance, where possible, with the formal requirements of national laws that may have an effect on the proceedings. Article 6 of the Internal Rules of the Court of Arbitration provides:

> When the Court scrutinizes draft awards in accordance with Article 27 of the Rules, it considers, to the extent practicable, the requirements of mandatory law at the place of arbitration.

If there appears to be a formal defect in the award, the Court, through its Secretariat, will advise the arbitrators of the modifications that should be incorporated in a new text of the award to be resubmitted by the arbitrators.

If the procedural defects are minor, the Court may approve the award subject to the notified specific modification being incorporated in the final award. In such a case, the final award—modified, dated, and signed—may simply be returned by the arbitrators to the Secretariat for direct notification to the parties. If the procedural defects are major, and substantial redrafting is required, the Court will require that the award be presented to it again for final approval.

The difference between modifications of form, as to which the Court has mandatory powers of revision, and of matters of substance, as to which it may only draw the arbitrator's attention, is not always clear. If findings of fact or law are questioned, a matter of substance is broached and the Court's power is in principle limited to bringing the matter to the arbitrator's attention. On the other hand, the Court may consider that contradictory findings in the substance of an award, or the failure of the reasons given to sustain the award rendered, are defects of form. In principle, the difference is difficult to articulate; in practice the distinction usually is readily perceived by experienced jurists accustomed to matters of degree.

20.04 Comments on points of substance

It is to be recalled that the Court does not act as a second-tier arbitration panel. In scrutinizing the award, it does not review the facts. Nor does the Court reexamine questions of law which may have been raised by the parties during the proceedings. What is studied is the award itself: the degree of coherence and consistency within the four corners of the award, and its conformity with the Terms of Reference.

The Court does not attempt to substitute its own appreciations for those of the arbitral tribunal as final trier of issues of fact and law. It must, however, assume that what appears to be an erroneous finding of fact (in contradiction with other findings of the award), or a conclusion as to the parties' obligations which is in opposition to clear contractual terms, may make the award unenforceable in national courts. Accordingly, it has the duty to bring such points to the attention of the arbitral tribunal for its consideration.

Ordinarily, this process is conducive to final awards which are well-fashioned to withstand the rigors of national-court enforcement proceedings. The arbitral tribunal is occasionally led by the Court to adopt substantive modifications in the award. More often, there is simply a new effort of draftsmanship and coherence, resulting in a better reasoned and more complete award. In all cases, the Court, as required by the Rules, will be scrupulous not to affect the arbitrator's liberty of decision on the substance of the award.

Most ICC arbitrators value the role of the Court in scrutinizing awards under Article 21 of the Rules.[4] It provides a "quality-control" device, permitting an international body, possessed of considerable practical experience and a diversity of technical expertise in arbitration matters, to draw the arbitrators' attention to problems of which they may not have been aware, and thus improve their product (the award) before it is delivered to customers of ICC arbitration. This may be particularly useful in cases where the arbitrators themselves, including the chairman, are not experienced in ICC arbitration. There is no doubt that the exercise by the Court of its Article 27 powers has

---

4 At least one arbitrator and commentator has taken the view that the review powers of the Court should be even broader. *See,* S. Goekjian, *Conducting an ICC Arbitration Proceeding,* MIDDLE EAST EXECUTIVE REPORTS 1, at 12 (February 1980); *ICC Arbitration from a Practitioner's Perspective,* 3 JOURNAL OF INTERNATIONAL LAW AND ECONOMICS 407, at 432 (1980).

avoided the issuance of flawed awards in many cases and has enhanced the acceptability of ICC awards both to the parties and to enforcement jurisdictions.

A few arbitrators nevertheless resent the institutional role given to the Court to scrutinize their awards, which they characterize as interference in their function. This is sometimes revealed in rather testy correspondence with the Secretariat replying to "observations" by the Court. This resentment has been given a theoretical underpinning by a doctrinal critique of the arbitration practices of the Court by Antoine Kassis, a Syrian lawyer and law professor.[5] Mr. Kassis takes the position that the Court's scrutiny of awards infringes the principles of secrecy of deliberations, the right of confrontation, and the independence of arbitrators, with the result, he claims, that ICC awards should be considered nullities, not enforceable by state courts under national law. The argument is based on the assumption that arbitral awards are binding upon the parties and enforceable under national law only if they conform to procedures defined by law for the conduct of judicial proceedings. This assumption cannot be substained; it seems to disregard half a century of progress in the field of international arbitration.[6] It is in fact now generally accepted that arbitration is a hybrid institution having both contractual and jurisdictional characteristics. More importantly, modern legislation dealing with arbitration procedure clearly gives broad discretionary power to the parties to determine how arbitration proceedings shall be conducted. The agreement of the parties to the ICC Rules, and the role of the Court of Arbitration specifically provided therein, constitutes clear acceptance of the Court's practice of scrutiny of awards under Article 27 of the Rules, which is a perfectly well known feature of ICC arbitrations. There is little reason, given the past record of national court decisions to be described in Section 20.05, to expect that national courts will be persuaded to call into question this seventy-five year old practice.

20.05   Court's scrutiny of awards as seen by national courts

Given the volume and stakes of ICC arbitrations, it is hardly surprising that national courts have often had the occasion, in the course of recognition and enforcement proceedings, to evaluate the Court of Arbitration's role of scrutiny of arbitrators' awards. By and large, they have sustained the Court against the attacks of imaginative litigants.

Since the Court does not act as an appellate jurisdiction, it rules only upon the formal sufficiency of the award. It reviews neither the merits of the decision, nor the written or oral pleadings of the parties before the arbitrators (*see* Sec-

---

5   A. Kassis, *Reflexions sur le reglement d'arbitrage de la Chambre de Commerce International* (L.G.D.J., Paris, 1988), summarized in Kassis, *The Questionable Validity of Arbitration and Awards under the Rules of the International Chamber of Commerce*, 6 J. INT. ARB. 79 1989.

6   For a more detailed refutation of Kassis' position *see* J. Paulsson, *Vicarious Hypochondria and Institutional Arbitration*, YEARBOOK OF THE ARBITRATION INSTITUTE OF THE STOCKHOLM CHAMBER OF COMMERCE 96 (1990).

tion 20.01). It is not obliged to examine written arguments addressed directly to the Court, although it frequently does. Oral argument before the Court is never permitted. These self-imposed restrictions have been the excuse for attacks by disappointed parties alleging that the administrative proceedings of the Court constitute a denial of due process. Other litigants have sought to characterize the administrative role of the Court as an interference in the independence of the arbitral tribunals.

Such attacks have consistently failed in France, as have attacks on the power of the Court to prolong the period of time within which arbitral awards must be rendered[7] (see Section 19.01). The same has been true in other jurisdictions.[8] The Court of Appeal of Paris,[9] approved by the *Cour de cassation*,[10] has specifically recognized that the Court of Arbitration does not exercise a second or appellate level of arbitral jurisdiction, and that it does not infringe upon the arbitrators' liberty of decision. Accordingly, it had no obligation to consider the written briefs that the parties had previously presented to the arbitrators.

A similar attack on the Court of Arbitration's review powers was rejected by the Superior Court of the Canton of Zurich,[11] which found that the powers of the Court did not constitute a forbidden interference in the freedom of decision of the arbitral tribunal. The court stated:

According to the terms of Article 21 [Article 27, 1998 Rules]of the Rules of Arbitration, the Court of Arbitration is juxtaposed with the arbitral tri-

---

7   *See* decisions of *Cour d'appel* of Paris, 3 December 1981, 22 January 1982 *in* 1982 REV. ARB. 91, note E. Mezger; 13 November 1992, Société Casco Nobel France v. SICO Inc. et Kansa, 1993 (REV. ARB. 632 (notice to parties not required for Court's extension of time limits for award).

8   *See e.g. Tribunal fédérale Suisse*, 16 July 1990, Syrian Petroleum Company (SPC) v. GTM Entrepose SA (the procedure of Article 21 [Article 27 of the 1998 Rules] of the ICC Rules of Conciliation and Arbitration pursuant to which the arbitral tribunal must submit a draft of any award to the International Court of Arbitration for approval does not violate the parties' due process rights, nor does it violate confidentiality, the arbitrators' independence, or the jurisdictional nature of arbitration; by choosing to have any dispute arbitrated by an ICC tribunal, the parties have consented that the ICC Court review the form of awards).

9   20 April 1972, Societe Schutte Lenz v. Veuve Gallais, 1973 REV. ARB. 84. *See also* 15 September 1998 Société Cubic Defense Systems Inc. v. Chambre de Commerce International, 1999 REV. ARB. 103, note Pierre Lalive, when the *Cour d'appel* in rejecting a claim for damages against the ICC goes to some pain to describe and defend the mission of the ICC Court of Arbitration.

10   23 January 1974; 1974 REV. ARB. 296. Kassis, *supra* Note 5 at 151, in support of a doctrinal attack on the arbitral institution's authority of scrutiny of the award, contends that the French cases do not clearly address themselves to the fundamental issue of the legitimacy and legality of the powers given to the Court of Arbitration under Article 27. In fact the modalities of the exercise of the power by the Court, and the method of the arbitral tribunal's proceedings following a request for modifications by the Court, have been reviewed by French courts, and neither the parties nor the courts have found any grounds to put into question the legitimacy of Article 27. *See, e.g., Cour de cassation*, 28 January 1981, 1982 REV. ARB. 425 (adequacy of deliberation of arbitral tribunal following exercise by the Court of its scrutiny function).

11   Superior Court of the Canton of Zurich, unpublished decision of 29 June 1979, Banque Yougoslave de l'Agriculture v. Robin International Inc. *et al.*

bunal and must be consulted by the latter before it renders its award. The fact that the parties may provide for such cooperation—or more exactly submit to rules which provide for it—must be recognized in the same way as the possibility of providing for an appeal before an appellate arbitral tribunal.

The Zurich Court accordingly denied the motion to set aside the award, finding that there was no violation of the procedural law of Zurich which prohibits interference by one level of jurisdiction with another jurisdiction.[12]

In the major international arbitration centers, the procedures of the ICC and the role of the Court of Arbitration are accepted without question as the regime chosen by the parties.[13]

The effect of a request by the Court of Arbitration for revisions to the text of an award, and the procedure to be followed by an arbitral tribunal following such a request, have, however, been the subject of litigation. Thus, in a 1988 English case[14] an application was made to set aside an award for arbitrator misconduct on the grounds that the members of the tribunal had not had a face to face deliberation following a request by the Court of Arbitration to provide it with strengthened reasoning concerning two issues raised in the award. In that case a draft majority award had been presented to the Court of Arbitration, and the Court's request for further explanation was made after it had received critical observations from the dissenting arbitrator. A revised majority award, responding to the points raised by the Court, was circulated to all the arbitrators, and the majority took into account the dissenting arbitrator's previous and renewed views, but further physical meetings for deliberation were not held. After a careful review of the allegations, the English court found that the opportunity to exchange further views by correspondence was more than adequate and that a requirement for a further meeting of the arbitrators would have imposed unrealistic and unnecessary requirements on international arbitrators coming from different countries.[15]

---

12   In the course of its decision, however, the Zurich court unflatteringly characterized the Court of Arbitration's review procedure, limited to the four corners of the award, as "devoid of interest" and "apparently having no other aim except to justify the administrative charge imposed by the ICC on each arbitration."

13   The only case known to the authors in which a national court has rejected an ICC award on the grounds that the ICC Court impermissibly interfered with arbitrators is the decision of 10 March 1976, of the Turkish Supreme Court in the infamous *Keban* case, reported in English *in* 46 ARBITRATION JOURNAL 241 (1981), which relieved a Turkish party from liability. (International arbitration has not fared well in the Turkish legal system.)

14·   Bank Mellat v. GAA Development Construction Company, [1988] 2 LLOYD'S L. REP. 44, Queen's Bench Division (Commercial Court), decision of 12 January 1988, summarized in 3 MEALEY'S INT. ARB. REP. 9 (1988).

15   The decision of the English court on this issue is exactly the same as the position of French courts, *see Cour de cassation*, 28 January 1981, *supra* Note 10.

In the course of his opinion, Mr. Justice Steyn[16], after reviewing the Court of Arbitration's practice in the scrutiny of awards,[17] analyzed the Court of Arbitration's function in the following terms:

> The supervisory function which is germane to the issues in the present case is the Court's power of scrutiny of awards before they are published. The power exists because the ICC system, the most truly international of all arbitral systems, provides for the conduct of arbitrations in most countries of the world, and the members of a three man tribunal frequently come from different continents, or at least from different countries, with fundamentally different legal systems. It is regarded as the first imperative of the ICC system that awards under it should be enforceable . . . The system of scrutiny of awards by the Court contributes to the enforceability of ICC awards. The Court has a mandatory power "to lay down modifications as to the form of the award." . . . The Court also has an advisory power. It may "without affecting the arbitrator's liberty of decision", draw the arbitrators' attention to "points of substance." . . . The process of scrutiny is directed at the internal coherence and consistency of the award. But it may also sometimes reveal a procedural flaw which can be corrected [citing an example of the exercise of this power given in the First Edition of this book, Section 20.02]. This is then a general description of the nature of *the system of scrutiny of awards which parties accept when they agree on arbitration in accordance with the ICC Rules.* (Emphasis added.)

---

16   Now Lord Steyn, a member of the judicial committee of the House of Lords.

17   Citing Sections 20.01 and 20.02 of the first edition of this book.

CHAPTER 21

DETERMINATION OF COSTS

21.01   General principles

Some elements relating to the cost of ICC arbitration, the advances for costs established under the Rules, and arbitrators' decisions as to the proportion of costs to be allocated among the parties, have been described in Chapters 3 and 14. This chapter describes the final determination of the costs, which, like the fixing of advances—and unlike the *award* of costs by the tribunal—is the duty of the Court (*see* Chapters 3 and 14, and Section 19.07). The Court assesses costs at the time of final approval of the award when all particular facts concerning the case—its degree of complexity, duration and any other circumstances—are known.

Articles 31(1) and 31(2) of the Rules set forth the powers of the Court to assess costs in the following terms:

(1) The costs of the arbitration shall include the fees and expenses of the arbitrators and the ICC administrative costs fixed by the Court, in accordance with the scale in force at the time of the commencement of the arbitral proceedings, as well as the fees and expenses of any experts appointed by the Arbitral Tribunal and the reasonable legal costs incurred by the parties for the arbitration.

(2) The Court may fix the fees of the arbitrators and others at a figure higher or lower than that which would result from the application of the scale should this be deemed necessary due to the exceptional circumstances of the case. Decisions on costs other than those fixed by the Court may be taken by the Arbitral Tribunal at any time during the proceedings.

It is improper for ICC arbitrators, in a draft award or otherwise, to purport to determine the amounts that will be paid to them. One of the advantages of the ICC arbitral process is to avoid the need for arbitrators to bargain with parties for their own fees, or worse, to seek to have them increased in the course of the proceedings, when the parties are under great pressure not to displease the tribunal which will judge them. The Court has an exclusive role in fixing the arbitrators' fees and expenses and separate fee arrangements between the parties and arbitrators are barred. Nothing would prevent, however, the parties, with the agreement of the arbitrators, to propose to the Court a fee arrangement different from the normal range of the scale. The Court retains absolute discretion whether or not to give effect to such a proposal. The ICC does not encourage such arrangements and very few in fact have been made.[1]

Arbitrators' expenses, as well as experts' fees, are by their nature reimbursable in their entirety and chargeable as such to the parties as arbitration costs. However, the Court retains the authority to approve or disapprove these charges. As noted earlier, the expenses of an expert investigation commissioned by the tribunal should be covered by a separate advance. Unusually large expenses (for instance, site visits or arrangements for very lengthy hearings) should also be agreed and paid for in advance by the parties, or at least notified to the Secretariat so that when necessary a supplementary advance may be set by the Court. Considering the fact that the Court ultimately must approve costs, parties should automatically notify the Court of any exceptional expenses. When the draft award is presented by the arbitrators to the Court, the Secretariat requires a detailed documentation of expenses. The Court's broad discretion is reflected in the significant variations permitted by the Schedule of Costs, as well as the power under Article 31(2) to depart from the scale in exceptional cases. The starting point for fixing the variable costs (*i.e.,* the administrative charge and arbitrators' fees and expenses) is the "sum in dispute" in the arbitration. Article 31(1) provides that these costs shall be "fixed by the Court, in accordance with the scale in force at the time of the commencement of the arbitral proceedings."

The Arbitration Costs and Fees in force from January 1, 1998 is annexed as Appendix III to the Rules. The scale is based on a degressive percentage applied to successive ranges of the amount in dispute. Composite tables to facilitate calculation of costs are reproduced in Table 9 of Appendix I to this book.

21.02   ICC administrative costs

With respect to the administrative charge, as opposed to arbitrators' fees, Appendix III, Arbitration Costs and Fees, does not on its face provide minimum-maximum percentages for each range of the sum in dispute. Rather, it provides a single percentage for each range, which (after a minimum lump

---

1   DERAINS AND SCHWARTZ (p. 304) citing this section from the previous edition of this work question whether the Court would currently consider favorably any special fee proposal by the parties. A 1998 addition to Appendix III of the Rules, "Arbitration Costs and Fees," confirms the hostility of the Court to special arrangements on fees but does not alter its discretion to consider proposals by the parties. Article 2 (4) of Appendix III provides: "The Arbitrator's fees and expenses shall be fixed exclusively by the Court as required by the Rules. Separate fee arrangements between the parties and the arbitrators are contrary to the Rules."

sum of $2,500 for the first $50,000 in dispute) degresses from 3.5% for the range for $50,000 to $100,000 to 0.06% for the range of sums in dispute in excess of $10,000,000 and up to $80,000,000. The administrative expense is "capped" at $75,800, so that no additional charge is made where the amount in dispute exceeds $80,000,000. The Scale set out in Appendix III of the Rules illustrates the following administrative charges:

SUM IN DISPUTE (in US Dollars)	ADMINISTRATIVE EXPENSES (in US Dollars)
50 000	2 500
500 000	11 050
1 000 000	16 800
10 000 000	33 800
50 000 000	57 800
80 000 000	75 800

In practice, the administrative fee becomes payable depending on how far the arbitration proceedings have advanced. If the administrative fee is fixed in connection with a final award, it almost invariably follows the Scale. Even in this instance, however, the Court may fix a higher or lower fee in exceptional circumstances. Article 2(5) of Appendix III to the Rules provides:

> . . . In exceptional circumstances, the Court may fix the administrative expenses at a lower or higher figure than that which would result from the application of such scale, provided that such expenses shall normally not exceed the maximum amount of the scale.

21.03 Arbitrators' fees

The Scale itself gives wide discretion with respect to arbitrators' fees, since the scale for a single arbitrator provides for a minimum or maximum percentage. While the permissible range varies among the different levels, on average the minimum-maximum variance is in the order of 1 to 3.5. In certain instances the proportion reaches 1 to 5. The ambit of discretion is even greater when the tribunal consists of three arbitrators, since Article 2(3) of Appendix III to the Rules provides:

> When a case is submitted to more than one arbitrator, the Court, at its discretion, shall have the right to increase the total fees up to a maximum which shall normally not exceed three times the fee of one arbitrator.

While the maximum payable to a three-man tribunal is three times the maximum fee of a sole arbitrator, the minimum is not specified and may thus be less than three times the minimum fee of a sole arbitrator. These rather esoteric provisions were doubtless intended to take into account the fact that a sole arbitrator may ordinarily be considered to have a more arduous task than the average member of a three-man tribunal.

The Scale gives ample leeway to the Court in fixing arbitrators' fees in ordinary cases. In exceptional circumstances, Article 31(2) of the Rules entitles the Court to abandon Appendix III to the Rules and fix arbitrators' fees either higher or lower, if this departure seems necessary. It is rare, however, that the Court finds divergence from the Scale necessary.

Some critics find the Court's discretion too great. An English commercial judge once stated:

> The Court fixes the fees payable to the ICC for its administration and other functions, as well as the fees of the arbitrators and umpires, in both cases by reference to a scale based on the amount in dispute but subject to a discretion. There are frequent criticisms of both levels of fees as being too high in the first case and too low or too unpredictable in the second.[2]

The Scale of Charges itself leaves a wide discretion between the minimum and maximum amounts which the Court of Arbitration may award as arbitrators' fees based on the amount in dispute, and further explanation is required. Appendix III to the Rules defines the factors which the Court takes into consideration in setting fees. Article 2(2) of Appendix III provides:

> In setting the arbitrator's fees, the Court shall take into consideration the diligence of the arbitrator, the time spent, the rapidity of the proceedings and the complexity of the dispute so as to arrive at a figure within the limits specified, or, in exceptional circumstances (Article 31(2) of the Rules) at a figure higher or lower than those limits.

The Rules acknowledge that the amount of time spent on a case is a relevant factor, but the effect thereof is limited to fixing the appropriate level within the minimum-maximum range of the Table attached to Appendix III.

Given this provision of Appendix III, the Secretariat has adopted the practice of requesting arbitrators to inform it of the amount of time spent on the arbitration. It does so immediately prior to the presentation of draft awards to the Court. When a case has been terminated by settlement or otherwise prior to the rendering of an award, the time spent will be particularly relevant: arbitrators' fees may be reduced from the amount called for by the Table attached to Appendix III, depending on how far the arbitration has progressed. This can be measured in terms of the stage of the proceedings attained (*i.e.,* have the Terms of Reference been signed, have there been hearings, or a draft or partial award?) as well as by time spent by the arbitrators.

---

2   M. Kerr, *International Arbitration v. Litigation, in* 3 INTERNATIONAL COMMERCIAL ARBITRATION, 141, 146 (1980). The criticism as to the level of the charge for administrative expenses appears exaggerated. Where disputes are submitted to a three-member tribunal the administrative expenses rarely exceed 15% of the fees for arbitrators, and the ICC charges for fees and expenses combined is a relatively low percentage of the total costs to the parties in bringing the arbitration.

Arbitrators from legal or professional *milieux* where the rule is to base fees on time spent have no difficulty in supplying the total number of hours spent and usually provide a breakdown of hours spent at hearings, at deliberations and other meetings of the arbitrators, studying the file, drafting the award, and the like. Other arbitrators—a minority—seem to find these requirements somewhat outlandish, and are able to supply only a very general estimate of time spent. Detailed estimates usually confirm the assumption that the chairman of a three-man tribunal has a heavier task than the other two arbitrators. He usually takes charge of the administrative and procedural work of the tribunal, and has a primary role in the drafting of the award. His greater effort and responsibility leads the Court almost invariably to provide a somewhat higher fee for the chairman than for his co-arbitrators (the usual ratio is 40/30/30).

When supplying data of the time they have spent on the arbitration, some arbitrators also advise the Court of the usual charges in their profession for services of that nature. This information may be useful, but is by no means determinative. It is perhaps valuable in the negative sense: it may demonstrate that fixing the fees based on the amount in dispute (perhaps even approaching the maximum of the scale) does not represent a windfall to the arbitrator. When parties appoint highly qualified arbitrators with a known usual cost based on hourly or daily rates, they cannot be shocked if the arbitrators' fees, based on the amount in dispute, are within the range of what the arbitrators would have received if they had devoted their time to their usual professional duties. On the other hand, there is no guarantee, nor should any exist, that an ICC arbitrator will receive as great a remuneration for services as arbitrator as for other professional services. This blunt fact is communicated to potential arbitrators during the selection process.

There is in fact no recognized world scale of acceptable hourly rates for arbitrators. Furthermore, in many parts of the world, particularly in State-controlled economies and in much of the developing world, hourly rates are not generally recognized. The ICC has no mission to impose the standards of certain countries and professions on others. It is for this, among other reasons (*see* Section 3.02), that ICC arbitrators' fees are still based on the amount in dispute.

Following the Scale of arbitrators' fees found in Appendix III to the Rules, an illustrative range of the fees of a sole arbitrator (or for each arbitrator of a three-person tribunal) would be as follows:

ARBITRATOR'S FEES (in US Dollars)		
Sum in Dispute	Minimum	Maximum
50 000	2 500	8 500
500 000	7 500	36 000
1 000 000	11 250	53 500
10 000 000	28 750	136 000

ARBITRATOR'S FEES (in US Dollars)		
Sum in Dispute	Minimum	Maximum
50 000 000	48 750	204 000
80 000 000	57 750	240 000

In some large cases of exceptional complexity and duration involving hundreds of millions of dollars, fees per arbitrator in multiples of $100,000 have been awarded. These are obviously unusual cases, although in view of the increasing number of large cases at the ICC more frequent than in the past. It should be noted that, given the amounts in dispute, the fees in these cases were nonetheless set well below the maximum fees allowed under the scale. When highly qualified arbitrators devote months to cases which regularly disrupt other activities over a course of several years, substantial fees are perfectly appropriate; in such arbitrations, it may be said that the arbitrators virtually "live" with the case. In average cases, it should always be kept in mind that the ICC system creates an incentive for efficiency; not being paid at a daily rate, ICC arbitrators have no hidden reason to prolong the case. Parties, if not always their lawyers, tend to value this feature of ICC arbitration once they have had experience with arbitration systems where proceedings seem never-ending. While some ICC arbitrations due to their complexity or other special factors have also been long-lasting at least parties can be assured that the remuneration system for the arbitrators provides no incentive for this to be the case.

It is rare that the Court feels obliged to exercise the discretion allowed under Article 31(2) to depart from the maximum or minimum amounts of the scale. The few cases in which departures from the minimum amounts are made usually involve very simple controversies with the result that application of even the minimum fee of the scale would result in an unwarranted windfall to the arbitrators.

There is no consensus among the consumers of ICC services (the parties to arbitrations) or its practitioners (arbitrators and counsel) whether ICC costs are good value for the money. Before criticizing the system as overly costly, one should bear in mind the following considerations:

i) in small arbitrations the arbitrator or arbitrators are likely to be under-compensated for their work;

ii) even in large cases, the arbitrators' remuneration will in many instances be lower than the fees based on hourly rates that leading counsel would receive in court litigation or as legal advisers in the most economically developed countries;

iii) it has not been demonstrated that *ad hoc* arbitration in cases of similar complexity results in lower fees, whereas the parties in such cases do not benefit from the ICC's *cachet* and supervision in administering the process in a manner likely to produce an enforceable award;

iv) the ICC probably receives the same number of complaints from arbitrators who find that the fees paid to them were not adequate compensation for their work as from parties who find the costs too high; and

v) a legitimate complaint can be made that where the amount in dispute is large, the parties pay to the ICC the entire estimated administrative expense and fees in advance at an early stage of the proceedings, usually by the time that the Terms of Reference have been executed, but receive no interest on these amounts. Steps taken to address this problem (notably the limited right to secure by bank guarantee an advance required to be made for a defaulting party, *see* Section 17.03) alleviate but do not eliminate the problem.

21.04 Arbitrators' allocation of costs between the parties

i) Arbitration costs and party costs

As noted earlier, the arbitral tribunal plays no role in the determination of the amount of the charge for ICC administrative expenses, or the amount of arbitrators' fees. These are determined by the Court. On the other hand, the arbitrators determine, subject to the Court's review and final approval, the other element of arbitration costs: tribunal expenses. This determination includes the ordinary expenses of the arbitrators (travel, accommodations, telephone, fax, etc.) and additional expenses chargeable to the parties, (translators' fees, rental of conference rooms, remuneration of experts, and the like).

The tribunal also determines the amount of party costs (legal fees paid by the parties and the like) recovered in the arbitration. It decides in what proportion the parties will be charged with the arbitration costs. It separately determines what party costs will be allowable. Articles 31(1) and 31(3) provide:

(1) The costs of the arbitration shall include the fees and expenses of the arbitrators and the ICC administrative costs fixed by the Court, in accordance with the scale in force at the time of the commencement of the arbitral proceedings, as well as the fees and expenses of any experts appointed by the Arbitral Tribunal and the reasonable legal and other costs incurred by the parties for the arbitration.

. . .

(3) The final Award shall fix the costs of the arbitration and decide which of the parties shall bear them or in what proportion they shall be borne by the parties.

While the nomenclature is somewhat confusing, the term "costs of the arbitration" is intended to cover two distinct kinds of costs: "arbitration costs" which are the administrative costs of the ICC and the fees and expenses of the arbitral tribunal and "party costs" which are the reasonable legal and other costs incurred by a party in the pursuit or defense of the claim in arbitration.

ii) Arbitration costs (costs incurred by the ICC and the arbitral tribunal)

The final award of the arbitrators, when signed by them and notified to the parties, will set forth the total amount of arbitration costs and will indicate what percentage of these costs each party must pay. (Costs are ordinarily not to be awarded in any interim or partial award.)[3] The mechanics of reaching that determination are not self-evident. In practice, the arbitral tribunal will submit a draft award to the Court, which leaves a blank for the amount of arbitration costs. At the same time, it will convey to the Court its accounting for expenses incurred by the arbitral tribunal since these are to be included in the costs fixed by the Court. Finally, it will determine in the draft award whether the costs should be borne entirely by one party or should be divided between them in some proportion.

Some reimbursable expenses that the arbitrators may incur are evident. International arbitration by its nature requires travel. Arbitrators will have transportation charges and hotel and restaurant bills. In addition, they may have secretarial, copying and other incidental expenses. More substantial disbursements include stenographic reporting services, translation services, and the fees and expenses of independent experts named by the tribunal. Because of the importance of these more substantial expenses, the arbitral tribunal will usually seek to have the views and, if possible, the agreement of the parties prior to officially submitting such expenses.

With the exception of the costs of experts, the charges will usually be paid directly by the Secretariat from the parties' advance to cover costs. The Secretariat of the Court communicates to arbitrators its standard rules (revised from time to time) for reimbursement of costs including class of air travel authorized, and limits of lodging and restaurant expenses.[4]

Since the costs of an independent expert may be particularly large, Article 1(ii) of Appendix III, Arbitration Costs and Fees, provides:

> Before any expertise ordered by the Arbitral Tribunal can be commenced, the parties, or one of them, shall pay an advance on costs fixed by the Arbitral Tribunal sufficient to cover the expected fees and expenses of the expert as determined by the Arbitral Tribunal . . .

---

3   The Court will not determine the final amount of allowable arbitration costs until the end of the proceeding. It would be possible, however, for the tribunal to award reimbursement of party costs thus far expended in an interim award. This is hardly ever done.

4   The most recent rules are found in the Secretariat's "Revised Notice to the Arbitrators: Personal and Arbitral Tribunal Expenses" of 1 January 1993. The Revised Notice provides for reimbursement of business class air fare for flights up to 6 hours and first class air fare for longer flights and a flat *per diem* expense of $400 for each day and night that the arbitrator is required to spend outside of his or her town of residence if hotel accommodation is required. The *per diem* may alternatively be increased to $500, in the same circumstances, if all expenses are itemized and justified by receipts. The Revised Notice gives examples of the kinds of out of pocket disbursements by arbitrators which are reimbursable.

Thus the tribunal may determine the costs of independent experts and fix a separate advance for such costs. The arbitral tribunal's final award will specify the final amount actually expended and allocate that cost between the parties, usually applying to some degree the principle "costs follow the event."

iii) Party costs

Article 31(1) permits arbitrators to include in recoverable arbitration costs "the reasonable legal and other costs incurred by the parties for the arbitration."[5] This explicit provision of the Rules provides a unifying element in what would otherwise be a chaotic situation, since the laws and practices of the diverse jurisdictions where an arbitration may take place (or where the parties are domiciled) may be in complete opposition: Some require the assessment of lawyers' fees as part of costs while others refuse to allow recovery of legal fees in any circumstances.

The specific provision in the Rules for recuperation of parties' legal costs has an extremely useful purpose as it constitutes party agreement on this issue which should withstand any argument that either the substantive law applicable to the agreement or the procedural law of the place of arbitration does not provide for or permit recovery of legal costs.[6]

Since the amounts claimed as legal and other costs incurred by a party for the arbitration can, where the amounts in dispute are substantial and the issues complex, themselves be very significant, it is important that due process be respected in the quantification of the amount to be awarded. The mere fact that the final amounts of legal costs can only be known at the very end of the proceedings raises practical problems. Arbitral tribunals have handled the procedure for claiming party costs in different ways. The most prevalent manner appears to be for the tribunal at the end of the final hearings in the matter

---

5   The prior version of the Rules provided for the recovery of the "normal legal costs" of the parties. The 1998 Rules provision is somewhat broader and authorizes recovery of payments made by a party to persons other than lawyers (*e.g.* technical experts, witnesses, and the like) and is closer to the prior (and current) French version of the Rules which permits recovery of *les frais normaux exposés par les parties pour leur défense* (the normal costs of the parties spent for their defense). There is no intended difference between "normal" and "reasonable" expenses.

6   Absent agreement by the parties, under the "American rule" the losing party is not required to reimburse the legal costs of the winner. Award of legal fees by an arbitrator in an arbitration taking place in New York under a contract governed by New York law has been disallowed in an arbitration under AAA rules which make no specific provision for the award of attorneys' fees. The United States District Court reviewing, under the Federal Arbitration Act, an award which had granted such fees assumed, *arguendo*, that the procedural prohibition under the New York Civil Procedure Act, which normally precludes an arbitrator from awarding attorneys' fees (NYCPLR Sec. 7513) was not applicable. The Court reasoned, however, that the arbitrator would only have the same powers as a judge. And under New York substantive law an award of legal fees in connection with a litigation is not authorized in the absence of a specific agreement to that effect. Asturiana De Zinc Marketing, Inc. v. Lasalle Rolling Mills, Inc., 97 Civ. 6053 (JSR), Mem. Order (per J. Rakoff, U.S.D.J.) (S.D.N.Y., 29 September 1998), 13 MEALEY'S INT'L ARB. REP. B-1 (No. 11, November 1998).

to request the parties to make simultaneous exchange of their respective costs claims, together with proof thereof, with the opportunity for each party to comment on the other's submission prior to the final close of proceedings. Prudent counsel will want to have the procedures for such submissions fixed well in advance so as to avoid surprise or foreclosure.

In one case where the parties' submissions on their legal costs were made at the very end of the case it appears that the arbitral tribunal submitted the draft award to the Court leaving a blank for the amount of the recoverable legal costs awarded. It subsequently added to the award the amount of party legal costs to be charged to the losing party *after* the award had been scrutinized by the Court (*i.e.*, filling in a blank space in the award prior to final signature of the award). The amount was substantial (nearly $ 1 million) and the losing party sought judicial review for denial of due process on the grounds that it had not been afforded proper opportunity by the tribunal to contest the amount and that the Court had "scrutinized" an incomplete award. The judicial recourse was denied,[7] but the procedure was unfortunate and obviously to be avoided in all future cases.

Recoverable party costs should be considered as similar to an item of damage suffered due to the breaches of contract or tortuous behavior of the other party, and the amounts claimed should be made the subject of proof like any other claim of damages. The arbitral tribunal will be most likely to award lawyers' fees in cases where the losing party either raised frivolous issues or adopted dilatory tactics significantly increasing the legal costs of the adversary, although it is not limited to these circumstances.

There is no hard and fast rule as to either the categories or amounts of "reasonable legal and other costs incurred by the parties for the arbitration which will be allowed." Much depends not only on verification and analysis of the expenses but also the equities of the underlying dispute. In the authors' experience, tribunals are more likely to allow costs disbursed for external consultants and advisers (lawyers, technical experts, economists and accountants) than to permit recoupment of a company's internal expenses whether allocated to its legal department or otherwise.[8] Tribunals may also tend to "cap" recoverable costs as a "reasonable" amount allowed based on relationship to the amount in dispute, the other party's claimed expenses for the same posts, and other equitable considerations. In some jurisdictions, lawyers in litigation before national courts are entitled to a fee based on the amount in dispute; they may seek to be paid by their client on this basis in arbitration

---

7   Compagnie de Bauxites de Guinée v. Hammermills, Inc., U.S. District Court, District of Columbia, C.A. No. 90-0169 (29 May 1992), see detailed discussion at Section 34.04(c).

8   Some awards have, however, allowed recoupment of costs of in-house legal counsel. Summaries of awards on the amount and allocation of legal costs are found in 4 ICC BULL. 43-48, (May 1993). Recoupment under this provision of legal costs incurred in judicial proceedings ancillary to the arbitration is not usually allowed (*see e.g.* ICC Case 6268/1990, 3 ICC AWARDS 68).

matters. Nevertheless, arbitrators are completely free to determine in their own discretion what they consider to be "reasonable."[9] Arbitral authority in rendering the award is usually exercised with moderation. Nevertheless, ICC arbitrators do award recovery of substantial legal fees in appropriate cases. After having reviewed credible proof of reasonably incurred legal expenses, arbitrators in many ICC cases have awarded recoveries of more than $500,000. In ICC Case 3493/1983,[10] the arbitrators awarded $730,704 on account of the prevailing claimant's legal costs, including lawyers' fees. Since then, awards of cost in excess of $1 million are unremarkable in the biggest cases. Where very substantial legal fees are awarded this may be the result of the tribunal's decision that the prevailing party had been put to great effort and excessive cost by the behaviour of the other party or because the amount of provable damage was small compared to the legal cost which had to be incurred by the prevailing party due to the obdurate position of its adversary.[11]

Despite the provision of the Rules that costs of the arbitration "shall include . . . the reasonable legal and other costs incurred by the parties for the arbitration" there is no obligation on the arbitrators to award such costs in favor of one or another party. In other words, having considered the evidence of each party as to their reasonable legal fees the arbitral tribunal is not obliged to allocate one party's costs to be recovered from the other. While the Rules authorize the arbitral tribunal to decide that "costs follow the event" they do not compel this solution. In fact, in many cases the arbitral tribunal, after allocating in favor of one party the burden of all, or the greater part, of the fees of arbitrators and ICC administrative costs, will decide, based on all the circumstances in the case, that each party will be responsible for its own legal costs, perhaps in order to avoid adding insult to injury. However, the tribunal should in its award note that it has considered this issue and give the reasons for its decisions. Some claims may succeed but not others, or the respondent may obtain recognition of certain rights by way of counterclaim or set-off. In these circumstances, arbitral tribunals tend either to apportion both the arbitration and party costs (*e.g.* 75%/25% or 60%/40%) or leave the costs to be split evenly between the parties.

---

9   In one arbitration award known to the authors, the winning party succeeded in all of its claims, and the loser was required to pay 100% of the direct ICC costs (administrative charge and arbitrators' fees). To obtain its victory, however, the winner claimed that it had expended over $200,000 in lawyers' fees and disbursements while the loser claimed it had spent approximately $25,000. The winner's recovery of its "reasonable" legal costs was limited to $50,000.

10   22 ILM 752 (1983).

11   For example, see Southern Pacific Properties Ltd. v. Egypt, ICSID Award of 20 May, 1992, 19 Yearbook 51, 82-83 (1994) in which the tribunal awarded $27.7 million in damages and $5 million for costs and attorneys' fees. For a good coverage of the general subject, with examples, *see* Y. Gotanda, *Awarding Costs and Attorneys' Fees in International Commercial Arbitration*, 21 MICHIGAN JOURNAL OF INTERNATIONAL LAW, (1999).

In one unpublished major arbitration lasting many years and where hundreds of millions of dollars were in dispute, the claimant obtained an award in its favor, but for a far smaller amount of damages than claimed. The tribunal stated that: "Despite the magnitude of the efforts and the resources deployed by the parties neither one nor the other has really obtained a victory." Accordingly, the tribunal found it equitable to divide equally the arbitration expenses, and to provide that each side would support its own legal fees. In other similar cases a tribunal might find that arbitration costs "follow the event" but that each side would bear its own party costs.

CHAPTER 22

ENTERING INTO EFFECT
OF THE AWARD

22.01   Signature of the award by arbitrators

Article 27 of the Rules provides:

> *Before signing any Award* , the Arbitral Tribunal shall submit it in draft form to the Court. . . . *No award shall be rendered by the Arbitral Tribunal until it has been approved by the Court as to its form.* (Emphasis added.)

Despite these clear terms of the Rules, a common error of arbitrators is to submit draft awards already signed. Awards have no legal effect until submitted to the Court for its approval. If the text is acceptable, a draft award may be approved at the Court's first consideration of it. Frequently, however, approval is given only at a subsequent session, after modifications of form by the arbitrators. It is only then that the date and signature of an award may be effective.

The legal effect of arbitrators' signatures is defined in Article 25(3) of the Rules:

> The Award shall be deemed to be made at the place of the arbitration and on the date stated therein.

The intent of this Article is to deny any importance to the actual place of signature of an award, and to make it unnecessary to reconvene the tribunal for signatures. Most frequently, the approved draft of an award will be circulated among the arbitrators at their respective domiciles. In these circumstances there is no common place of signature. The place where the instrument would be considered to take effect under ordinary rules of construction (*e.g.* the place where the last of the required signatures was obtained) might be wholly fortuitous.[1] Article 25(3), therefore, has the ef-

---

[1]   In the English House of Lords case Hicox v. Outhwaite [1991] 3 WLR 297, XVII YEARBOOK 599 (1992), the presiding arbitrator, an English Q.C., in arbitral proceedings whose seat was in England had drafted the award at his residence in Paris and after signing it there had sent it on to his

fect of deeming the award to be rendered at the place of arbitration (the *siége*[2] or "seat" of the arbitration), an important factor in its subsequent recognition and enforcement by national courts.

Since an award dated and signed before examination by the Court has no legal effect, such a signature does not count with respect to the time limit within which an award must be made.[3] Nor may such a draft be notified to the parties as an award, since it has not been issued according to the arbitration rules agreed to by them.

It is recognized that some arbitrators have adopted a practice, occasionally accepted by the Secretariat, of submitting to the Court signed but undated draft awards. The intent would seem to be on the one hand to indicate the formal agreement of the arbitrators to the draft submitted to the Court (avoiding a change of heart of an arbitrator with the passage of time) and, on the other hand, to avoid the need to recirculate the approved award, with consequent delay before the parties may receive the final award. As a practical matter, this procedure may be quite useful and appropriate, and seems to raise no legal difficulties. It must be kept in mind, however, that such a signed draft has no legal effect until approval of the Court, the dating of the award subsequent thereto, and the fulfillment of the other procedural conditions of Article 28 (*see* Section 22.02).

Once the award has been approved by the Court it should be signed by all the arbitrators even if they are not all in agreement with its terms (as would be the case of a majority award, or an award rendered by the Chairman of the Tribunal pursuant to Article 25(1) of the Rules). An arbitrator who is in disagreement with the award may note next to his signature "dissenting" or other words indicating his participation in the proceedings and deliberations while indicating that he disagrees with the result. Such an indication may or may not be accompanied by a separate dissenting opinion (*see* Section 19.06). Signature of the award is *prima facie* proof that the arbitrator participated in the deliberations and that the award was duly rendered. Refusal of an arbitrator to sign an award ordinarily is a breach of his obligations to the parties and to the arbitral process, but will not invalidate the award. It obviously would be inadmissible, and destructive of the entire institution of arbitration, if one of the arbitrators could nullify the entire proceed-

---

chambers in London for dispatch to the parties. The English court found that the award had been "rendered" in Paris and hence was a foreign award, which had consequences as to the regime of judicial review. The result has been reversed by provisions of the Arbitration Act 1996.

2   The French version of Article 25(3) provides:

     "La sentence est reputée rendue au siége de l'arbitrage à la date qu'elle mentionne."

3   *See* Section 19.01, and discussion therein of French case law to this effect; *Cour de cassation*, 27 April 1981, Arret No. 736, Société Ripolin, 1981.II GAZETTE DU PALAIS 584.

ings by the simple expedient of failing to sign the award.[4] On very rare occasions, however, a failure to sign may be justified if deliberations were not properly concluded.[5]

There have been described in Section 13.09 the power of the Court, in exceptional circumstances and after the closing of the proceedings, to remove an arbitrator and not replace him, thus creating a "truncated tribunal." In such a case the award would be signed only by the two remaining arbitrators and the circumstances would be described in the award.

22.02   Payment of costs and notification of award to parties

Article 28 of the Rules provides:

1) Once an Award has been made, the Secretariat shall notify to the parties the text signed by the Arbitral Tribunal, provided always that the costs of the arbitration have been fully paid to the ICC by the parties or by one of them.

2) Additional copies certified true by the Secretary General shall be made available on request and at any time to the parties, but to no one else.

---

4   In a number of cases arising before the Iran-United States Claims Tribunal, Iranian arbitrators have refused to sign awards with which they did not agree, *see* e.g. Cases No. 24, 129, and 298, XIII YEARBOOK 248, at 347-348 (1988). Nevertheless, such awards have been recognized as binding by the Tribunal, and awards made in such circumstances have been executed against the escrow fund provided by the Iran-United States agreements. A history of these cases, and of other international precedents, is set forth in detail in S. Schwebel, *The Authority of Truncated International Tribunals* in INTERNATIONAL ARBITRATION: THREE SALIENT PROBLEMS, Grotius Publications, Cambridge (1987).

5   In SEFRI S.A. v. Komgrap, *Tribunal fédéral Suisse, Première cour civile,* 23 October 1985, 1986 SWISS BULL. 77 a Yugoslav arbitrator, after having discussed two draft awards prepared by the majority arbitrators, announced his resignation from the tribunal, allegedly for health reasons, prior to the submission of the majority award to the Court of Arbitration. While the Court of Arbitration approved the majority award after minor modifications, the dissenting arbitrator refused to sign the award which was nevertheless signed by the majority and notified to the parties by the ICC Secretariat. The award was set aside by the Swiss Federal Tribunal on the grounds that there had not been an effective deliberation of the arbitrators in the particular circumstances of the case (while the arbitrators could have agreed that a final award would be reached by further circulation of drafts, in fact the tribunal had fixed a date for a further deliberation which was not held because of the dissenting arbitrator's "resignation"). The precedent would seem to create an incentive for dilatory tactics. A partial response may be found in Article 12(1) of the Rules providing that the resignation of an arbitrator becomes effective only upon its acceptance by the Court. In somewhat similar circumstances other national courts have sustained majority awards without requirement for further deliberations, *see e.g.* Bank Mellat v. GAA Development Construction Company, [1988] 2 LLOYD'S L. REP. 44, (Queen's Bench Division (Commercial Court), 12 January 1988), summarized in 3 MEALEY'S INT. ARB. REP. 9 (1988), Section 20.05, *supra* (in that case, however, the dissenting arbitrator had delivered a dissenting opinion). Note that the provisions of Article 12(5) of the 1998 Rules, permitting awards to be made by the two members of a "truncated tribunal" would not have saved the situation. That article only applies after the closing of the proceedings and in lieu of replacing an arbitrator who has died or been removed by the Court. Neither of these conditions had been fulfilled in the *Sefri* case.

3) By virtue of the notification made in accordance with Paragraph 1 of this Article, the parties waive any other form of notification or deposit on the part of the Arbitral Tribunal.

The final step in the process is the notification of the award to the parties by the Secretariat. Until such notification is made, the parties will know nothing of the contents of the award.[6] Given its exclusive role of notification, the Secretariat thus controls delivery of a legally binding document to the parties. Until a final award has been notified, a party has no document or title upon which an action for recognition and execution can be based.

Under Article 28, the Secretariat will refrain from notifying an award until all the costs assessed by the Court have been paid, thus using its power of notification as a security device. Ordinarily, this will not be necessary. The advances, in some cases increased during the proceedings, are generally sufficient to cover the final costs.

It may happen, however, that unexpected expenses, or more time consuming proceedings, have increased the costs beyond what was anticipated. A final assessment will be then made by the Court, which will have to be paid before the award is released. If one party refuses to pay the share allocated to it, the other will have to pay the full assessment before the award is released. In a few isolated instances parties have at this last stage hesitated to make final payment—sometimes because they were unsure whether they would be advantaged or disadvantaged by the award, sometimes because of changed financial circumstances—and the award has remained forever unnotified, the arbitral procedure a dead letter.

22.03 Finality and enforceability of award

When the award is notified to the parties (invariably by registered mail or courier service with receipt) it becomes a final arbitration award, the parties being deemed under Article 28(3) of the Rules to have waived any other form of deposit or notification which might otherwise be required for conclusion of the arbitral process. Local procedural laws may require deposit of the award with a local tribunal to trigger exceptional judicial remedies, or as a condition precedent to obtaining judicial recognition and enforcement in that jurisdiction. Such rules, however, are part of national enforcement systems rather than of the ICC arbitral process.

---

6   Cynics may claim that parties may have advance notice of the outcome by the indiscretions of party-appointed arbitrators. Such indiscretions cannot be completely excluded. In most cases, however, the secrecy of deliberations is maintained until the award is formally notified. Reputable arbitrators follow the Rules.

Article 28(6) provides:

> Every Award shall be binding on the parties.
>
> By submitting the dispute to arbitration under these Rules, the parties undertake to carry out any Award without delay and shall be deemed to have waived their right to any form of recourse insofar as such waiver can validly be made.

There is, in other words, no appellate arbitral procedure which prevents the entering into effect of the award. The parties are thus called upon to comply immediately with the award at the date of notification. The intent of Article 28(6) is also to supply a title with legal effect, ripe for enforcement before any national jurisdiction.

The 1998 Rules provide that "every Award shall be binding on the parties" rather than that "[t]he arbitral award shall be final" as under the previous Rules. The principal reason for the change was to clarify the relationship of the award with national court review and enforcement powers, and to be consistent with the New York Convention. Whether an award is "final" depends in the end on the specific provisions of recourse available from national courts. However, even if some (non-waivable) measure of judicial recourse remains open to the parties this does not prevent the award from being immediately binding and obligatory on the parties. Nor does it prevent the award from being immediately subject to recognition and enforcement as a foreign award under the New York Convention (Article V(1)(e) of which permits a defense that the award "has not yet become binding on the parties" but not one based on the non-finality of the award because judicial recourse is still open).[7]

Article 28(6) assures that no further arbitral procedure is necessary to ensure that the Award is binding upon the parties, and seeks to eliminate any ordinary judicial recourse. This neutralization of recourse to ordinary courts is obviously effective only to the extent that waiver of such recourse is permitted by the law applied by the court that is seized of the matter—as is explicitly recognized in the text of the Rules. In some jurisdictions, local procedural law treats arbitral awards, *in the absence of waiver of appeal*, in the same way as a judgment of an inferior court, with right of full—and sometimes *de novo*—review of legal and factual issues. Article 28(6) constitutes a waiver of any such ordinary appeal; few legal systems forbid waiver of appeal. Parties can hardly plead ignorance of this cornerstone of the ICC Rules to which they have agreed. Indeed, in one French case, the court as-

---

7   Article V(1) of the New York Convention provides: "Recognition and enforcement of the award may be refused, at the request of the party against whom it is invoked, only if that party furnishes to the competent authority where the recognition and enforcement is sought, proof that:

    . . . (e) The award has not yet become binding on the parties, or has been set aside or suspended by a competent authority of the country in which, or under the law of which, that award was made."

sessed civil damages for abusive procedure against a party which sought ordinary appeal from an ICC award.[8]

The 1998 Rules provide that the parties shall be deemed "to have waived their right to any form of recourse" rather than "their right to any form of appeal" under the former Rules. Reference to "any form of recourse" rather than "any form of appeal" was considered to be broader than the former language, and more in accordance with the terminology of modern arbitration statutes which generally permit access to the courts for the review of arbitration awards only on exceptional grounds—and do not permit "appeals" in which issues of law and fact may be relitigated. The modification is also consistent with the French language Rules which provide both in the 1975 and 1998 versions for the renunciation of "toutes voies de recours." "Recourse" would include "appeals" wherever they are permitted by national law. The extent to which recourse may be waived is a subject to be determined under the applicable national law.

As the Rules are incorporated by reference into the arbitration agreement, it is clear that the parties have consented to waive any ordinary form of recourse. Because of the breadth of the language, it should cover most circumstances where waiver may be expressed in any general way. If the objective intentions of the parties to an ICC arbitration clause are considered, based on the customs and usages of ICC arbitration, Article 28(6) should constitute a valid agreement to exclude all ordinary judicial appellate remedies. (National law rules for waiver of appeal are considered with respect to five illustrative legal systems in Part V.)

Waiver of "any form of recourse" cannot, however, act as a bar to nullification procedures established under national laws to void arbitral proceedings that have been conducted without jurisdiction or by fraud, or that are otherwise incompatible with international public policy.[9]

The effect of the waiver of appeal will operate differently depending on the country in which arbitration is conducted. For example in England, Article 28 of the ICC Rules will exclude appeals on points of law. *See* Section 69 of the 1996 Arbitration Act. The general waiver language of the Rules had the same

---

8   *Cour d'appel* of Paris, 22 April 1980, Victor Lebar v. Société Atlas Werk A.G., 1981 REV. ARB. 171 (the court pointed out that under the ICC Rules the appellant had renounced the right to appeal except in circumstances justifying the nullity of the award, not here alleged).

9   *See* Section 28.03; the effect of former Article 24(2) of the Rules was specifically considered in V. vs. S.C. Corporation, *Tribunal cantonal de Vaud,* 9 September 1980, unpublished, described and commented on *in* Jean-François Poudret, Claude Reymond and A. Wurzburger, L'APPLICATION DU CONCORDAT INTERCANTONAL SUR L'ARBITRAGE PAR LE TRIBUNAL CANTONAL VAUDOIS, 104-105 (1981). The Swiss court held that the parties could not waive the right to bring nullification procedures on the exceptional grounds listed in Article 36 of the Concordat.

effect under prior law.[10] However, challenge for excess of authority or serious procedural irregularity may not be excluded by contract. *See* Sections 67 and 68 of the 1996 Act[11]. In Switzerland, under federal arbitration law waiver of the right to challenge an award requires an explicit statement (*"déclaration expresse"*), which cannot be accomplished by reference to institutional rules.[12] If the parties elect cantonal law in Switzerland, any purported waiver of the appeal provided in Article 36 of the Intercantonal Concordat will be ineffective. In the United States it is clear that neither a special waiver or the general waiver contained in the Rules can bar appellate recourse on the limited grounds set out in the Federal Arbitration Act.[13] In the United States, the ICC waiver rule has become relevant in litigation where language added to an ICC arbitration clause purported to *expand* rather than restrict the scope of judicial review.[14]

By operation of Article 28(6), the parties "undertake to carry out any Award without delay . . ." Accordingly, an ICC award must be considered binding between the parties when rendered. It constitutes not only a moral obligation to comply with the terms of the award, but also a title from which legal rights flow. Thus, an award will ordinarily be considered to have *res judicata* effect from the date it is rendered.[15]

The fact that the ICC Rules comport an obligation on the parties to carry out the award has an effect on its immediate enforceability pursuant to the terms of international conventions. The New York Convention, for example, re-

---

10 *See* Arab African Energy Corp. (Arafenco) v. Olieprodukten Nederland B.V., Q.B., [1983] 2 LLOYD'S L. REP. 419.

11 By the same token, waiver of appeal language in the Rules will not exclude limited recourse from an award under the terms of the United States Arbitration Act.

12 *Tribunal fédérale Suisse*, 8 July 1992, Dragomand International AG v. Ital-Contractors Consortium of Condotte Partners (Applying Article 192, LDIP, the parties' choice of ICC Rules does not constitute a waiver of appeal under Swiss law), 9 April 1991, Clear Star Limited v. Centrala Morska Importoura-Eksportova "Centromor", 1991 REV. ARB. 709, note Tschantz.

13 M. & C. Corp. v. Erwin Behr GmbH & Co., K.G., 87 F.3d 844 (6th Cir. 1996).

14 *See* Lapine v. Kyocera, 130 F.3d 884 (9th Cir. 1997), where the Court of Appeal reversed a District Court decision which had refused to give effect to the specific terms of an arbitration clause providing for arbitration under the ICC Rules but calling for judicial review of conclusions of law that were "erroneous" and facts that "were not supported by the evidence". The Respondent argued that the waiver of any ground of appeal found in the ICC Rules precluded the Petitioner from seeking appeal based on the language of the arbitration clause. The resulting 2-1 appellate decision permitting the parties by agreement to expand the grounds of judicial review beyond those provided in the Federal Arbitration Act was controversial. However, its finding that the parties' specific agreement took precedence over the waiver of appeal provision in the prior version of the Rules was clearly correct.

15 Article 1476 of the French Code of Civil Procedure, for example, contains an explicit provision to this effect. For a lengthy consideration of whether an ICC award must be considered final and binding even though not filed or deposited pursuant to the requirements of the applicable (Indian) law, *see* Dalmia Dairy Industries Ltd. v. National Bank of Pakistan, [1978] 2 LLOYD'S L. REP. 223, (Court of Appeal of England, decision of 15 May 1977).

quires enforcement in a signatory State without the need for prior judicial recognition by the courts at the place of arbitration. A signatory State is not required to grant enforcement, however, if it can be shown that "[t]he award has not yet become binding on the parties."[16]

In the Gotaverken[17] case, *exequatur* was granted in Sweden to an ICC arbitration award rendered in Paris, despite the pendency of a suit in France to set aside the award. In applying statutory enforcement procedures based on the New York Convention, the Swedish Supreme Court gave weight to the waiver of appeal provisions of the ICC Rules, stating that:

> By the arbitration clause of the shipbuilding contracts, the parties agreed to comply with the award as finally binding and enforceable in matters submitted to the arbitrators. Further, the ICC Rules of Arbitration, under which the now relevant proceedings were conducted, contain a provision [Article 28(6), 1998 Rules] that the arbitral award shall be final.

> In consideration of the aforesaid, the present arbitral award must be considered to have become enforceable and binding on the parties in France, in the meaning intended by the [Swedish] Act concerning Foreign Arbitration Agreements and Awards, as of the moment and by virtue of the very fact that it was rendered. The fact that the buyer has subsequently challenged the award in France by "opposition" thereto has no effect in this respect.[18]

While the legal consequences of an ICC award may vary according to national laws (*see generally* Part V), as well as the availability of recognition and enforcement treaties, it is clear that by consenting to the ICC Rules, the parties agree to the extent possible that ICC awards are binding when rendered, and accept an obligation to respect them. Article 28(6) of the Rules is therefore perhaps the most significant factor in the estimated voluntary compliance with awards (according to the Secretariat) in more than 90% of ICC arbitrations.

22.04   Deposit of award and assistance of Secretariat

Articles 28(4) and (5) of the Rules provide:

> (4) An original of each Award made in accordance with the present Rules shall be deposited with the Secretariat.

---

16   New York Convention, Art. V(1)(e). *See generally,* A.J. van den Berg, THE NEW YORK ARBITRATION CONVENTION OF 1958, at 331 (1981).

17   Gotaverken v. GNMIC, Supreme Court, Sweden, 13 August 1979, 1979 *Nytt jurisdikt arkiv* 527; described *in* J. Paulsson, *The Role of Swedish Courts in Transnational Commercial Arbitration*, 21 VIRGINIA JOURNAL OF INTERNATIONAL LAW 211, at 236 *et seq.* (1981), with an English translation at 244.

18   *Id.* at 246.

(5) The Arbitral Tribunal and the Secretariat shall assist the parties in complying with whatever further formalities may be necessary.

Arbitral tribunals are ephemeral whereas the Court of Arbitration, with its Secretariat, is a permanent institution. By providing for the deposit of the award with the Secretariat, the Rules assure the preservation of the original award and proof of its authenticity.

The deposit of the award with the Secretariat in Paris and the notification of the award to the parties mark the close of the arbitration. This is not to be confused with new provisions under Article 22 of the 1998 Rules, "Closing of the Proceedings", which refers to a date fixed by the arbitral tribunal, after which the parties are blocked from further submissions. After that date the work of the arbitrators and the Court continues until a final award has been rendered and deposited with the Secretariat.

In most cases, the deposit of the award with the Secretariat of the ICC is the only deposit that will be made. As per Articles 28(4) and 28(5), the Secretariat will assist the parties in complying with whatever further formalities may be necessary. This includes not only providing certified copies of the award for use in enforcement proceedings (Article 28(2), but also taking all other steps to obtain recognition of the award, including providing records or explanations relating to the arbitral proceedings.

In fulfilling this task, the Secretariat has been recognized as part of an international institution whose mission is to assure the validity of awards rendered under its auspices. Its certification of the authenticity of awards and of the proper administration of the arbitration has generally been accepted by national courts. The Secretariat's experience and its ability to communicate in the languages of most national jurisdictions have facilitated the task of parties seeking enforcement of their awards.

The procedural law of the seat of arbitration may also call for the deposit of the award with a local court or its clerk, either as a prerequisite to enforcement of the award or to activate appeals or nullification procedures at the place of arbitration. It should not be considered a requirement to the international validity of the award, and failure to make such a deposit will not prevent the enforceability of the award abroad.

Parties to ICC arbitration should nevertheless consider whether they wish to deposit the award with a local court as a cumulative measure. In general, national law provisions for such a deposit are not mandatory and there is no sanction for failure to do so. The party wishing to ensure execution of the award should nonetheless ascertain that failure to register will not affect the validity of the award under the law of the place of arbitration.

The greatest advantage of registering an award with a local court is that this procedure ordinarily starts the running of the period of time within which any exceptional judicial appeal must be brought. A victorious party may therefore deposit the award in the hope that its adversary will fail to appeal within the brief period permitted, and the award will from then on be free from any potential challenge before the courts of the place of arbitration. In some places, the act of depositing the award triggers the obligation to pay a registration tax based on the value of the award. These amounts are very high in some jurisdictions and parties are accordingly dissuaded from depositing awards in such a jurisdiction if execution is not likely to be sought there.

22.05   Termination of arbitrators' powers

i) Functus Officio

In principle, the powers of the arbitrators cease with the rendering of the award after approval by the Court. The members of a tribunal are chosen for a single case with a mission only to determine the disputes thereunder, as defined in the Terms of Reference. Once a final award is rendered, they have fulfilled their mission and may be considered discharged of their office, or *functus officio*.[19] Given the ephemeral nature of arbitral tribunals, they cannot be expected to maintain an existence and be available indefinitely for motions for rehearing, rectification, correction, or reconsideration.

This general observation is especially pertinent to ICC arbitration since the Rules provide in Article 28(6) that the award notified to the parties shall be "binding on the parties." As a result, it may be immediately submitted to a national court for enforcement. It also has an administrative consequence in that, after notification of the award, no funds will be kept by the ICC for the costs of any further proceedings and any balance remaining from the advance will be returned to the parties after payment of the administrative expenses and arbitrators' fees (Article 31 of the Rules).

It is therefore clear that, as a general rule, once an ICC tribunal has rendered a final award, it has no jurisdiction to render a supplementary award, or to hear a motion for reconsideration, or reopening.[20] There are, however, limited exceptions.

ii) Correction and interpretation under Article 29 of the Rules

Prior to 1998, no provision of the Rules authorized an arbitral tribunal, after an award had been made and notified to the parties, to make any further ruling of any kind in respect to the award. While most other major international arbitration institutions by provisions in their rules authorized limited post

---

19   *Functus officio:* "(having discharged his duty), an expression applied to a judge, magistrate or arbitrator who has given a decision or made an order or award so that his authority is exhausted." JOWITT'S DICTIONARY OF ENGLISH LAW, (2d ed., 1977) (John Burke, ed.).

20   In addition to other bars to arbitral jurisdiction after the rendering and notification of a final award, in most cases the time limit of six months (Article 24(1) for rendering an award, and any extension thereof previously granted by the Court, will have expired by the time a request for reconsideration or rectification is lodged.

award corrections or interpretations by the tribunal,[21] such authority was thought to be unnecessary in the context of ICC arbitration because of the Court's scrutiny of the award. Scrutiny did not, however, invariably discover every mistake that could possibly be made by a tribunal, particularly those that were not revealed on the face of the award. Accordingly, in several matters where evident errors (of calculation and the like) were found in the final award, ICC arbitral tribunals, with the approval of the Court, proceeded to correct and modify the award.[22]

Article 29 of the 1998 revision provides positive, but limited, authority for a tribunal to make post-award corrections or interpretations. The principal characteristics of this provision are:

- the extremely limited time within which the tribunal may make a correction *sua sponte*, or within which a party may request a correction (30 days);

- authority for a party to request interpretation of the award also within a very limited time (30 days);

- absence of any express authority for the tribunal to make an additional award on any part of a claim which was not adjudicated;

- any decision to correct or interpret award is to be made in the form of an addendum to the award and to be scrutinized by the Court.

The full text of Article 29 reads:

29(1) On its own initiative, the Arbitral Tribunal may correct a clerical, computational or typographical error, or any errors of similar nature contained in an Award, provided such correction is submitted for approval to the Court within 30 days of the date of such Award.

29(2) Any application of a party for the correction of an error of the kind referred to in Article 29(1), or for the interpretation of an Award, must be made to the Secretariat within 30 days of the receipt of the Award by such party, in a number of copies as stated in Article 3(1). After transmittal of the application to the Arbitral Tribunal, it shall grant the other party a short time limit, normally not exceeding 30 days, from the receipt of the application by that party to submit any comments thereon. If the Arbitral Tribunal decides to correct or interpret the Award, it shall submit its decision in draft form to the Court not later than 30 days following the expiration of the time limit for the receipt of any comments from the other party or within such other period as the Court may decide.

---

21 UNCITRAL Rules (1976), Article 35 (interpretation), Article 36 (correction); LCIA Rules (1985), Article 17 (correction, and possibility for additional award on claims not dealt with); Stockholm Chamber of Commerce (1999), Section 31 (correction, interpretation); WIPO Rules (1994), Article 66 (correction).

22 ICC Case No. 6653/1993, III ICC AWARDS 512, note J.J. Arnaldez; *see* W. Kuhn, *Rectification and Interpretation of Arbitral Awards*, 7 ICC BULL. 78 (December 1996).

29(3) The decision to correct or to interpret the Award shall take the form of an addendum and shall constitute part of the Award. The provisions of Article 25, 27 and 28 shall apply *mutatis mutandis*.

The modification of the Rules to permit an arbitral tribunal to correct an award upon the request of a party or upon its own motion was not controversial. It confirmed a very limited practice which under the 1975 Rules had permitted correction of awards in exceptional circumstances. The power exists under most modern international arbitration rules.

Permitting interpretation was far more controversial. It was feared that the availability of the remedy would encourage parties to seek to reargue their case in applications for interpretation and in effect to solicit reconsideration by the tribunal of the merits of the case. The remedy described in the Rules is, however, surrounded by restrictions.

One of the principal safeguards against abuse of the interpretation remedy is that the arbitral tribunal is under no obligation to render a decision of interpretation. The purpose of the provision is to permit clarification of an award so as to permit its correct execution (as, for instance, if there would appear to be conflicting commands in the operative sections of the award). It is not to be used to require the tribunal to explain, or to reformulate, its reasons. It does not provide an occasion for the reconsideration by the tribunal of its decision. Should this be the basis of the party's application the tribunal will be quite justified in finding it unnecessary or inappropriate to render the requested "interpretation."

Another safeguard is inherent in the extremely short period of time within which an application can be made. Particularly in the case of interpretation it may well be that any conflict as to what the award means, or misunderstanding between the parties as to how it should be executed, only arises quite some time after the award was rendered. If such a question did arise in bona fide fashion after the 30-day period, and interpretation was clearly appropriate, could the Court of Arbitration, applying its broad discretionary powers under Article 35 (the "General Rules") nevertheless permit the arbitral tribunal to consider it? It is an open question but a good case can be made out that if the arbitral tribunal could, as a practical matter, be reconstituted, it would be appropriate in some cases for it to consider the application even if it was not made within the 30-day period provided by the Rules.

As noted above, Article 29(3) provides that where the tribunal decides to correct or interpret the award its decision shall take the form of an addendum to the award and be submitted to the same procedures and formalities within the ICC as an award. Nothing is said in the Rules as to what the arbitral tribunal should do if it refuses correction or interpretation. However, it is clear that such a decision puts an end to a claim by a party for a remedy provided under the Rules. Accordingly, such a final disposition should be made by a decision submitted to the Court with the same formality as an award and notified to the parties by the Secretariat. This has been confirmed by an instruction of the Secretariat dated 1 October 1999, and made available to all ICC tribunals.[23]

iii) Exceptional remedies under national law

A similar problem of reconstitution of an arbitral tribunal arises in those cases where a national court has set aside an award. In the ordinary case, the nullification of an award leaves intact the arbitration clause and the parties' obligation to arbitrate the dispute. Accordingly, the claimant is free to recommence arbitration by putting in motion the procedure to constitute a new arbitral tribunal.

In some jurisdictions, however, local procedural law provides for the return of the award to the initial arbitral tribunal for further proceedings.

For instance, Article 191 of the Swiss Private International Law Act, like Article 40 of the Swiss Intercantonal Arbitration Concordat, provides that where the arbitration award is annulled the matter will be remitted to the arbitral tribunal for further proceedings consistent with the setting aside action. The same dilemma presents itself: under the ICC Rules agreed by the parties the arbitral tribunal should be considered discharged of its obligations after having rendered its award. Can it be brought to life by the act of a State court?[24] Without further intervention by the Court of Arbitration, it would appear not. If an arbitral tribunal, having been discharged of its ICC mission, were to be reconvened without a new decision by the Court of Arbitration, its new award would not be an ICC award. Difficulties might be envisioned in its enforcement, at least outside of the place where it was rendered.

To avoid this problem, the Secretariat will confer with the parties to determine whether the original tribunal may be reconstituted (with the approval of the Court of Arbitration). If so, any new or revised award that it may render would be resubmitted to the Court for its scrutiny. In other cases, it may be necessary to constitute an entirely new tribunal. In all cases, the Court of Arbitration will seek to accommodate the requirements of its Rules with the exigencies of the national law at the seat of arbitration.

---

23 *Note of the Secretariat of the International Court of Arbitration of the International Chamber of Commerce regarding Correction and Interpretation of Awards,* 1 October 1999, which requires that the negative decision be submitted in a document entitled "Decision" which shall contain operative conclusions ("*dispositif* ") and reasons why the application is rejected. The Decision will be scrutinized by the Court, then signed by the arbitrators and notified to the parties.

24 If national courts send ICC awards back to the arbitrators for reconsideration, very complicated problems arise; fortunately, this situation is rare. For a discussion of the status and competence of arbitrators in Swiss and comparative law following the annulment of an award, *see* F.E. Klein, comment on Westland Helicopters Limited v. Arab Republic of Egypt, *Tribunal fédéral Suisse,* 24 September 1986, 1987 SWISS BULL. 12.

National law may also provide for exceptional remedies which may be addressed to the arbitral tribunal itself rather than to a national court.[25] This is the case of the remedy of revision which has a long history in public international law arbitrations[26] and which permits an arbitral tribunal in exceptional circumstances to withdraw the award that it has issued and to reissue a revised one. The principle has been echoed in a few precedents in national law. It is usually a condition of exercise of this remedy that the arbitral tribunal continue to be functioning or to be able to be reconstituted. The usual case will be when an arbitral tribunal remains in office (*i.e.,* after having rendered an interim award) but appears also to be available if the tribunal has disbanded but is capable of being reconstituted. The remedy remains very rare in international commercial arbitration but its existence was confirmed in two recent court decisions from two different jurisdictions. In France, the remedy of revision to be issued by the arbitral tribunal having rendered the disputed award has been confirmed provided that the original tribunal remains in existence or can be reconstituted. In such a case, the grounds permitting revision appear to be limited to fraud.[27] In Switzerland the grounds are somewhat broader including, in addition to fraud, new decisive facts in existence at the time of the award but discovered, without any fault attributable to the applicant, only subsequently. Under Swiss law, admissibility of an application for revision is determined by the Federal Tribunal and if admissible the application is remitted to the arbitral tribunal for determination whether revision is required.[28]

22.06   Exclusion of Liability

Prior to 1998 there was no provision in the ICC Rules seeking to provide immunity to arbitrators for the performance of their functions.

This was a source of considerable concern.[29] Since arbitration has increasingly become the normal mode of settlement of international commercial

---

25   The possibility is recognized by the ICC. The Secretariat's Note of 1 October 1999 provide at para. 2.3: "Where the relevant national law or court practice provide specific circumstances in which an Arbitral Tribunal may render certain decisions other than corrections of interpretations regarding an Award which has been approved and notified, such situations shall be treated in the spirit of this Note."

26   *See* Michael Reisman, NULLITY AND REVISIONS 208, 212 (Yale University Press 1971).

27   Fougerolle S.A. v. Procofrance S.A., *Cour de cassation,* 25 May 1992, 1992 JDI 974, note Loquin.

28   *Tribunal fédéral Suisse,* 9 July 1997, NKAP (Russia) v. E. (Hungary) and S. (Switzerland), 1997 SWISS BULL 506.

29   Studies of the problem include: A. Redfern, *The Immunity of Arbitrators,* in THE STATUS OF THE ARBITRATOR 121 (ICC Publishing, 1995); ICC Commission Working Party (Philip Fouchard, Chairman), *Final Report on the Status of the Arbitrator,* 7 ICC BULL . 27 (May 1996); E. Robine, *The Liability of Arbitrators and Arbitral Institutions in International Arbitrations Under French Law,* 5 ARB. INT . 323 (1989).

disputes, ICC arbitrators are faced with disputes involving larger and larger amounts and frequently intractable participants. The potential for attempts to engage the responsibility of the arbitrators or the arbitral institution for accepting to adjudicate a dispute which a party contends was not subject to arbitral jurisdiction, or for the unfavorable result obtained in arbitration, seems significant.[30]

Article 34 of the 1998 Rules provides:

> Neither the arbitrators, nor the Court and its members, nor the ICC and its employees, nor the ICC National Committees shall be liable to any person for any act or omission in connection with the arbitration.

The exclusion is broad in that it purports to exclude liability for any act or omission, without limitation, and that it extends not only to arbitrators but also to all participants in the administration of the ICC arbitration process. Most other arbitral institutions do not exclude arbitrator liability for "conscious and deliberate wrongdoing."[31] Except for this, Article 34 is consistent with the arbitration rules of other international institutions and provides some protection for arbitrators and other participants in the administration of ICC arbitration. As a rule agreed by the parties having accepted ICC arbitration, it binds the parties contractually. Stated in terms of an absolute exclusion of liability, its effectiveness may be limited by mandatory terms of applicable law, the provisions of such laws varying widely from jurisdiction to jurisdiction.[32] The clause should nevertheless have a salutary effect in deterring claims against arbitrators or the arbitral institution (compare the terms of Article 28(6)) regarding the parties' obligations concerning the enforceability of awards as to which the parties "shall be deemed to have waived their right to any form of recourse insofar as such waiver can be validly made").

The Working Party of the Arbitration Commission had initially proposed that any "deliberate wrong doing" be excluded from the arbitrator's exemption (Draft of 27 September 1996, ICC Doc. No. 420/15-015), to which was added the words "or gross negligence" (ICC Doc. No. 420/357 of 13 January 1997). However, after comments from National Committees indicating concern that the new rule might expand rather than restrict arbitrator liability (said to be

---

30 Fortunately, at present the problem still appears only to be potential. In their 1998 study, two former Secretaries General of the Court of Arbitration report to be unaware of any case in recent years where an ICC arbitrator has been successfully sued for damages. DERAINS & SCHWARTZ, 352. The ICC itself has been named as defendant in a number of cases in various jurisdictions, few of which have proceeded to final judgment. A judgment for $ 1,000,000 against the ICC by an Egyptian court because of an arbitral tribunal having exercised jurisdiction over the Egyptian state was withdrawn. A number of suits asserting claims against the ICC in Paris, which did proceed to final judgment, have all failed.

31 *See, e.g.* LCIA Rules (1998). Article 31.

32 Julian D. M. Lew, THE IMMUNITY OF ARBITRATORS (Lloyd's of London Press, 1990).

excluded absolutely under some national laws) the draft recommended by the Working Party and approved by the Arbitration Commission provided for absolute exclusion of liability. The ICC Court had opposed the exclusion of liability clause as recommended by the Arbitration Commission partially because of its absolute terms and partially because of its extension to the ICC Court and others with an administrative role who could not be considered to fall within the quasi-judicial function, and corresponding immunity, of arbitrators. The Court's position, in respect to not excluding liability for the administrative organs involved in the ICC arbitration process, would seem to be at odds with the practice of other arbitral institutions which have attempted in their rules[33] to extend immunity to cover the administrative acts of the arbitral institution. The English Arbitration Act 1996 (Section 74) has specifically extended immunity to arbitral institutions from any liability flowing from the appointment of arbitrators. Some national courts have on their own initiative extended immunity to cover institutional actions which are indispensable to the arbitral proceedings.[34] The ICC Council at its April 1997 meeting in Shanghai finally approved the absolute immunity text of the article, recognizing that in some jurisdictions, at least, mandatory provisions of national law might provide more restricted immunity.

The extension of absolute immunity to arbitrators has been criticized as being doubtful from a juridical point of view as well as on grounds of policy.[35] In recognition of the fact that most national legislations would impose civil responsibility on an arbitrator who caused harm by reason of intentional fault (or corrupt action) the usefulness of an addition to the Rules exempting an arbitrator from liability was questioned by one authority who wrote: "if the clause reserves the arbitrator's liability for such wrongful acts, it is unnecessary, and if it does not contain such a reservation, it is invalid."[36]

It was desired, however, by the revisers of the Rules to express clearly as a general principle the exemption from liability of an arbitrator for the performance of his arbitral duties. It was recognized and accepted that relevant na-

---

33   *See, e.g.* WIPO Rules (1994), Article 77, LCIA Rules (1998), Article 31.

34   *See* Corbin v. Washington Fire & Marine Insurance Co., 278 F. Supp. 393 (D.S.C. 1968), app'd 398 F. 2d 543 (4th Cir. 1968).

35   For a particularly acerbic criticism, *see* Pierre Lalive, *Sur l'irresponsabilité arbitral* in ETUDES DE PROCEDURE ET D'ARBITRAGE EN L'HONNEUR DE JEAN FRANCOIS POUDRET , 419, 420 (Faculté de Droit de l'Université de Lausanne, 1999). The author criticizes as well, with less support, the extension of exclusion of responsibility to the administrative organs of the ICC. The policy criticism, which deserves consideration, is whether the ICC, promoted as a superior and most reliable institution for arbitral dispute resolution, should encourage the exemption from liability of its arbitrators to the fullest extent allowed by law. The sentiment of the ICC Commission of Arbitration which sponsored the rule change would appear to have been affirmative. As another Swiss commentator put it "there was no reason why an ICC arbitrator should run more risks than another arbitrator," M. Blessing, *The ICC Arbitral Procedure Under the 1998 ICC Rules—What has Changed?* 8 ICC BULL. 16, 35 (December 1997).

36   P. Fouchard, *Final Report on the Status of the Arbitrator* 7 ICC BULL. 27, 31 (May 1996).

tional laws would restrict this exemption in extreme cases. But it was believed to be an error to set out in the Rules an independent contractual ground for liability in the case of some kinds of arbitrator misconduct in the performance of duties, which could be interpreted and applied, or perhaps misapplied, in different ways in any of the multitude of jurisdictions where an arbitrator's conduct in ICC arbitrations might become the subject of judicial proceedings. The precise definition of grounds for arbitrator liability was thought to create a target for the disappointed and disgruntled losing party to an arbitration.

Criticizing both the absolute exclusion of liability of arbitrators and the extension of the exclusion to the Court[37] and other administrative instances, Pierre Lalive states that the exclusion can be justified only on grounds of expediency and adds:[38]

> "One may admit, certainly, in the famous saying of Justice Holmes that 'the life of the law has not been logic, it has been experience' but even so . . . . Does not the attitude of these partisans of institutional irresponsibility make one think of the *Chauve-souris* [bat] in The Fable of La Fontaine?"[39]

Expedient or not, the exclusion of liability provision in the Rules, which no doubt would be ineffective to shield an arbitrator from intentional and conscious wrong doing, sets out a general principle applicable to ICC arbitration which is generally in conformity with the rules of other leading international arbitration institutions and conforms to the requirements of international commercial arbitration practices.

---

37 Which in various litigations has successfully resisted civil liability on the grounds that its mission is purely administrative and not jurisdictional.

38 Note 35 *supra* at 434.

39 La chauve-souris et les deux belettes, livre II, V: "Je suis oiseau; voyez mes ailes . . . je suis souris; vivent les rats."

Part IV

Hearings, Proof, and Ancillary Proceedings

CHAPTER 23

ICC ARBITRATORS' APPROACH TO FACT FINDING

23.01 Arbitrators' power to establish facts "by all appropriate means"

The parties may agree on specific rules of evidence to be applied by the arbitrator. They may do so in the agreement to arbitrate (*see* Sections 8.02 and 8.08), or in the Terms of Reference (*see* Section 15.02). They may thus establish rules for discovery and production of documents, for taking testimony, and for examination of witnesses. They may even agree that the arbitral proceedings shall follow the rules of a particular State court.

In fact, parties seldom do any of the above. Bringing up the subject of detailed procedures for future litigation would have a chilling effect on the negotiation of commercial agreements. Furthermore, parties agreeing to arbitration reasonably assume that in the event of a dispute procedural technicalities would largely be disregarded in the interest of expeditious proceedings under the agreed rules of arbitration.

In choosing ICC arbitration, the parties have opted for rules that establish only basic procedural guidelines for the arbitrator. The ICC Rules do not contain a detailed code of procedure. Articles 20(1)-20(7) supply the framework for the conduct of the proceedings and give wide powers to the arbitrator to fill gaps left by the Rules. Articles 20(1)-20(3) provide:

20(1) The arbitrator shall proceed within as short a time as possible to establish the facts of the case by all appropriate means.

20(2) After studying the written submissions of the parties and all documents relied upon, the Arbitral Tribunal shall hear the parties together in person if any of them so requests or, failing such a request, it may of its own motion decide to hear them.

20(3) The Arbitral Tribunal may decide to hear witnesses, experts appointed by the parties or any other person, in the presence of the parties, or in their absence provided they have been duly summoned.

The ICC arbitrator thus has the duty to ascertain the facts immediately, a burden which is not, strictly speaking, that of a common-law judge. In common-law adversary proceedings, the judge has the passive role of evaluating such evidence as the parties may see fit to present. In contrast, the ICC Rules suggest approval of the continental civil-law approach under which judges have a duty to "instruct" the case and actively investigate the facts. Under the Rules, ICC arbitrators are given broad discretion to establish the facts "by all appropriate means." The 1998 revision to the Rules in Article 20(5) adds the provision that at "any time during the proceedings, the arbitral tribunal may summon any party to provide additional evidence." Under previous versions of the Rules arbitrators were already entitled to order discovery pursuant to their general powers; the revision dispels any doubt on the subject. It also reflects the increasing number of requests for document production in ICC arbitration. *See* Section 26.01.

Articles 20(2) to 20(3) confer two specific powers on the arbitrator: to hear the parties and to hear witnesses. The concept of hearing parties contrasts with some national legal systems which bar parties from testifying on their own behalf. The ICC Rules conform to reasonable expectations in international transactions: the parties must be given an opportunity to explain their own case.[1] Article 20(2) of the Rules thus requires that the arbitrator shall hear a party at its request.

The arbitrator's power to hear witnesses distinguishes ICC arbitration from some types of arbitration, particularly those before commodities associations, whose arbitrators may be limited to examining samples and studying documents. The ICC arbitrator's power to hear witnesses is not necessarily a duty: the Rules state that the arbitrator "may" decide to hear third parties. Thus, by implication, the arbitrator is not required to hear third parties even if a party requests it.[2] Nevertheless, ICC arbitrators are generally hesitant to re-

---

1   Some legal systems make a distinction between "testimony" of third party witnesses given under oath and "statements" given by parties. The Rules do not reflect such a distinction. Most international commercial arbitrators are sufficiently experienced to evaluate the reliability of a party's statements, based on all the factors in the case. *See* Section 25.02.

2   In ICC Case 1512, Dalmia Dairy Industries, Ltd. (India) v. National Bank of Pakistan, Professor Pierre Lalive, sitting as sole arbitrator, refused to hear oral evidence proffered by the respondent Bank, whose argument was that a state of emergency justified its non-payment of a guarantee. It wished to present witnesses to explain the extent and practical consequences of hostilities. Having reviewed eight volumes of documents comprising more than a thousand pages, the sole arbitrator stated flatly that the presentation of witnesses was "completely unnecessary" since "the facts are simple and to a large extent undisputed." Professor Lalive's three carefully reasoned awards in the case, extracts in English in V YEARBOOK 170 and 174 (1980) (first and second preliminary awards) and I YEARBOOK 128 (1976) (award on the merits); extracts in French translation in 1974 JDI 904 (award on merits), were challenged in the courts of England, where the Bank resisted Dalmia's attempts to enforce the final award in the latter's favor. Continental practitioners noted with astonishment that English post-arbitral court proceedings, limited in principle to reviewing the *bona fides* of the award, were far more elaborate than the arbitration itself, with lengthy oral testimony from "competing" experts on Indian law, and resulted in a

fuse to hear any testimony whatsoever. Responsible arbitrators would want each party to be satisfied that it was given a fair opportunity to present its case.[3] Accordingly, the arbitrator's discretion not to hear witnesses is more frequently used to prevent cumulative testimony and to limit the scope of hearings than to bar witnesses altogether. The discretion of an arbitrator to refuse to receive otherwise admissible evidence, and its effect on an arbitral award, is an issue which has frequently been litigated in the United States.[4] The problem appears to have been raised less frequently elsewhere. Usually the problem is avoided by the arbitrator deciding to admit evidence for whatever it may be worth, as long as its admission will not unduly delay proceedings. Where witness testimony is involved, particular attention must be given by the arbitral tribunal to the time and cost involved, particularly where the offer of proof is cumulative.[5]

Because ICC arbitrators are given the discretionary power to establish the facts "by all appropriate means," many procedural issues are left open under the Rules. Nevertheless, as most ICC arbitrators are jurists, arbitrators act within a legal framework. They tend to apply procedures with which they are familiar and to look to the legal system which they know best, or is most closely connected to the dispute, in search of procedures to adopt by analogy. In referring to national law for guidance, ICC arbitrators make adjustments for the differing circumstances of international arbitration and seek the flexibility which is the essence of arbitration. (Even in domestic arbitration conducted entirely under national procedural law, arbitrators in most countries are not governed strictly by the procedural rigors of court proceedings.) Broadly speaking, the arbitrator has a choice of adopting either a common-law or a civil-law approach to fact-finding. There are substantial differ-

---

judgement of more than 120 pages. Of present interest is the fact that the Bank labeled the sole arbitrator's refusal to hear oral evidence as being "contrary to natural justice." The Court of Appeal upheld the arbitrator's exercise of his discretion, as defined in the ICC Rules, [1978] 2 LLOYD'S L. REP. 223.

3   Note the provision of Article 22 of the Rules, added in 1998, that the arbitral tribunal will close the arbitral proceedings "when it is satisfied that the parties have had a reasonable opportunity to present their cases."

4   *See e.g.* In re Arbitration Between InterCarbon Bermuda, Ltd. v. Caltex Trading and Transport Corp., 146 F.R.D. 64 (S.D.N.Y. 1993), summarized in XIX YEARBOOK 802 (1994) (confirming arbitrator's discretion to refuse to hear witnesses proposed by a party), *see also* M. Domke, COMMERCIAL ARBITRATION, Sec. 24.02 (Wilner, ed., 1999).

5   *See Cour d'appel*, Paris, 9 September 1997, Heilman v. Graziano Transmissions, 1998 REV. ARB. 712, where judicial recourse from an ICC award was denied. The arbitrators' refusal to cite additional witnesses employed by defendant company to be heard as witnesses at the request of claimant, without any representation as to the substance or relevance of their expected testimony, was not an abuse of discretion. In that case the arbitrators had heard five witnesses from a long list suggested by claimant and had offered to hear others for whom the claimant would have submitted a written version of their testimony prior to the hearing. They refused however to issue summons only to "hear witness after witness just to inquire whether someone, some place, in some manner would know something about something."

ences between the two traditions. It is therefore true that one encounters significant divergence where such factors as the nationality of the arbitrators, the seat of arbitration, or the applicable law lead to a procedure dominated by one rather than the other system.

23.02   Civil-law procedures

Civil-law proceedings are distinguished by an emphasis on documents. Witnesses, if any, are heard only after a series of exchanges of briefs and documents by both parties. Therefore, hearings are ordinarily much briefer than in common law arbitrations, and their function is only to emphasize and explore major disputed points already placed in their full context by documentary evidence and written briefs analyzing and interpreting such evidence.

Any proof admissible in court proceedings is accepted in arbitral proceedings. As is typical elsewhere with respect to commercial matters, documentary and testimonial proof is freely admitted as evidence. Arguments regarding the quality of proof tend to concern its credibility rather than its admissibility. Arbitrators following the continental system are thus largely unfettered by formal rules of evidence, and may evaluate proof as they see fit.

The principal characteristic of production of evidence in civil-law courts is the full exchange before hearings of documents upon which each party intends to rely. Court rules provide for the communication of documents so that each party is aware of its adversary's position in sufficient time to be able to respond. This principle of the adversarial process must be respected in arbitration under continental rules.

Arbitrators have the duty to evaluate not only the weight to be given to documents but also their authenticity.

Reports or certificates by experts may be received in written form. Such written statements, like written declarations of witnesses filed with the tribunal, are admissible but have only the weight of an oral declaration to the same effect.

Ordinarily, the parties should be given the opportunity to "confront" or question the expert (or to pose questions for the tribunal to ask if that is the mode of questioning adopted by the tribunal).

Unlike common-law proceedings, where the judge or arbitrator will hear only the witnesses whom the parties see fit to call, the arbitrator in civil- law proceedings, given his duty to "instruct" the case, may on his own motion call witnesses, order an expert evaluation, or decide upon an inspection or site visit.[6]

---

6   It is not usual, however, for a civil-law arbitrator to require additional evidence on his own motion. *See* C. Reymond, *Common Law and Civil Law Procedures: Which is the More Inquisitorial*, reproduced in 55 ARBITRATION 155 (1989).

While such practices differ in principle from those of the common-law arbitrator, the difference is attenuated in practice. The civil-law arbitrator ordinarily lacks any power to compel a witness to appear before him. Both civil-law and common-law arbitrators may explain to a party that certain witnesses or documents under its control appear useful to establish the truth. Failure of a party to comply with such a suggestion generally leads the arbitrator to draw adverse inferences. The only conclusion one may reasonably draw is that a civil-law arbitrator is more likely to take the initiative to make such a suggestion than his common-law counterpart.

To an outside observer, perhaps the most striking feature of witness testimony in continental judicial practice is the manner in which witnesses are examined.[7] In civil-law court proceedings, witnesses are called by the court rather than by the parties and are examined by the court itself, usually by the president of a three-member bench.[8] Counsel may put questions to witnesses only to adduce complementary testimony, and usually must address them to the tribunal. The role of counsel in examining witnesses, if not entirely passive, is thus secondary. While this may be the law applicable to court proceedings in civil-law jurisdictions, the flexibility of arbitration allows tribunals to relax this rule and permit counsel to examine witnesses directly.

23.03 Common-law procedures

Common-law proceedings place the emphasis on hearings, oral testimony, and the examination of witnesses. Having their origin in the right of trial by jury, common-law actions are adversarial in nature with each party presenting its witnesses. The principal mode of evidence—testimony under oath—is subject to verification by cross-examination. The secondary role of documentary and physical evidence is reflected by the fact that such evidence is presented during the hearing and authenticated by testimony at that time. Hence, the essence of a party's case in common-law proceedings is in the testimony of witnesses supported by documents, rather than in a file of documents which may or may not be explained by witnesses.

---

7   In France, for instance, Article 214 of the Code of Civil Procedure provides: "the parties must not interrupt, nor question, nor seek to influence witnesses who testify, nor address themselves directly to them, under pain of exclusion."

8   Another consequence of the witness being called by the tribunal and not by the party is the development of a professional tradition in some civil-law countries that counsel may not discuss testimony with a witness before the witness is called—a complete contradiction with the duty of a lawyer or solicitor in a common-law country to inform himself of the contents of the testimony of a witness called by his client. *See* C. Dieryck, *Procédure et Moyens de Preuve dans l'arbitrage commercial international*, 1988 REV. ARB. 267, 270. It seems largely accepted that these deontological restrictions should not apply to international arbitration proceedings. Article 4.3 of the 1999 IBA Rules of Evidence, which provides useful guidance of current thinking, takes the position that it is not improper for a party or its lawyers to interview a witness. *See* Section 24.05 *infra*.

Given the realities of modern commercial life, common-law judicial proceedings have strayed from this model. The jury has almost entirely disappeared in non-criminal proceedings in England. In the United States, it is frequently waived in commercial matters to avoid expense. In both countries, pre-trial discovery procedures permit the parties to examine documents in the possession of the adversary and pertinent to the case. Great quantities of documents may thus be discovered, and be produced later as evidence. Nevertheless, the jury tradition has left its mark on common-law proceedings, as reflected in the continued emphasis on the testimony and examination of witnesses, the oral presentation and authentication of documents, and the adversarial system of litigation. The predominance of oral testimony results in far longer hearings than in civil-law proceedings.

Another result of the trial-by-jury tradition is the existence of elaborate rules concerning the admissibility of evidence in court, designed to protect the trier of fact from the legerdemain of crafty lawyers. These exclusionary rules apply both as to documentary and testimonial proof. Particularly in the case of testimonial proof, such rules lead to elaborate rituals involving counsel and the court which most civil-law observers would be hard put to follow (for example, objections to hearsay evidence, to leading questions, to evidence which is not the "best evidence," and the like). Such rules, designed to keep untutored jurors from being led astray, have a very small function in proceedings before sophisticated international arbitrators.

In the United States it has been clearly established that arbitrators need not slavishly apply rules of court to exclude evidence on technical grounds. As Professor Martin Domke stated: Arbitration proceedings are not constrained by formal rules of procedure or evidence.[9]

Thus even where an arbitration follows the common-law model, the procedure is more flexible and less formal than in court proceedings. Rulings by arbitrators on the admissibility of evidence are not ordinarily subject to review by the courts.[10] Ruling on an appeal based on the wrongful admission of hearsay evidence in arbitration, a federal court of appeals in New York put it very well indeed:

> [T]he arbitrators appear to have accepted hearsay evidence as they were entitled to do. If parties wish to rely on such technical objections they should not include arbitration clauses in their contracts.[11]

---

9   Martin Domke, COMMERCIAL ARBITRATION, Sec. 24.02 (Wilner, ed., 1999). *See also* Brotherhood of Railroad Trainmen v. St. Louis Southwestern Railway Co., 252 F. Supp. 961 (D.D.C., 1996).

10   *One court refused to review evidentiary rulings, stating that such action would "result only in waste of time, the interruption of the arbitration proceeding, and encourage delaying tactics," Compania Panamena Maritima San Geressimo, S.A. v. J.E. Hurley Lumber Co., 244 F.2d 286, at 289 (2d. Cir. 1957).*

11   Petroleum Separating Co. v. Interamerican Refining Co., 296 F.2d 124 (2d. Cir. 1962).

It is difficult to conceive of an ICC award being vacated on the grounds that the arbitrator admitted proof which was excludable under some rule of evidence in court. On the other hand, an award may be vacated if the arbitrator wrongfully refused to receive pertinent and admissible evidence of such importance as to have prejudiced a party's right to present its case fairly.[12] Accordingly, a practice has developed in arbitration to admit evidence "for whatever it may be worth." This has the advantage of permitting parties to present their case without restraint. The arbitrator's freedom to weigh the evidence as he sees fit is preserved without risk of creating prejudicial error. He need only make certain that this flexibility is not abused by a party to delay or hinder the proceedings.

In England, in the past, the rules may have been stricter. According to the orthodox view expressed by the recognized authorities, Mustill and Boyd:

> It is widely believed that an arbitrator, merely because he is an arbitrator, is empowered to act on evidence which would not be strictly admissible in a Court of Law. This is not so. Arbitrators are bound by the law of England, and the rules regarding admissibility of evidence are part of that law. Thus, if an arbitrator admits evidence which is inadmissible, he commits an error of law which may be appealed against. Furthermore, if the arbitrator deliberately accepts evidence which is obviously inadmissible, he commits misconduct and the award will be set aside, at any rate if the evidence is important.[13]

However, Mustill and Boyd point out that this rule of law may be qualified if the parties, or the rules or customs of the arbitration institution, stipulate that strict rules of evidence do not apply or if objections to the admissibility of evidence have been waived. They also note that, in any event, courts are reluctant to set aside an award unless wrongly admitted evidence had a substantial bearing on the outcome of the case.

In the past, the authors recommended that if parties to an agreement providing for arbitration in England did not want strict English rules of evidence to apply, it would be wise for them to make that clear in the arbitration agreement[14] and clear agreement in advance of the procedures desired by the parties is always a good idea. However, even before the enactment of Arbitration Act 1996 the orthodox view expressed by Mustill and Boyd—that arbitrators were required to follow formal rules of evidence—was questioned, if not disregarded, by many experienced arbitrators.[15]

---

12 Martin Domke, COMMERCIAL ARBITRATION, sec. 24.02 (Wilner, ed. 1999).

13 Michael Mustill and Stewart Boyd, COMMERCIAL ARBITRATION 352 (2d. ed. 1989).

14 W. Laurence Craig, William W. Park and Jan Paulsson, INTERNATIONAL CHAMBER OF COMMERCE ARBITRATION, 380 (2d ed. 1990).

15 P. Sieghart, *Viewpoint*, 48 ARBITRATION 133, at 134 (1982): "One of the complaints about English arbitration for many years has been about delay, and the slavish application of the complex

The English Arbitration Act 1996 now makes clear that even where the parties have not waived the application of the English rules of evidence by express provision in the arbitration agreement or by adopting arbitration rules agreeing to, or giving the arbitrators power to set less formal rules, the arbitrators are statutorily empowered to do so. Section 34(1) gives the tribunal power to decide all procedural and evidential matters which are defined to include:[16]

> whether to apply strict rules of evidence (or any other rules) as to the admissibility, relevance or weight of any material (oral, written or other) on any matter of fact or opinion, and the time, manner and form in which such material should be exchanged and presented.

According to the statements in the DAC report accompanying the arbitration bill[17] this provision "makes it clear that arbitrators are not necessarily bound by the technical rules of evidence."

The provision of ICC Rules Article 15(1) clearly constitutes agreement by the parties that the arbitrators may settle rules governing the proceedings, including rules of evidence. The power given to the arbitrators by Article 20(1) "to establish the facts of the case by all appropriate means" should clearly constitute a waiver by the parties of the strict rules of evidence and an implicit consent to a customary informal evidentiary regime, provided only that the principles of due process ("natural justice") would continue to apply.

23.04   Generally recognized procedural principles

A party unfamiliar with the procedural system applied by the arbitrators is handicapped, particularly with respect to constraints on the admission of evidence. Lack of familiarity with the procedural principles adopted would also create a problem in the examination of witnesses and the production of documents. Are there universal rules of procedure that ICC arbitrators may apply in order to avoid unfairness to parties accustomed to different legal systems than the one the arbitrators are familiar with?

Rules of the Supreme Court—when the parties may well have chosen to go to arbitration rather than to law precisely in order to avoid just those things. How many English arbitrators, I wonder, realise that they are not under any obligation to apply or follow the Rules of the Supreme Court. All that the common law requires of them is to follow the ordinary rules of natural justice—in particular, to give both sides a fair hearing, and to allow no bias to creep into the proceedings. For that purpose, Section 12 of the [prior] 1950 Act gives arbitrators the power to examine the parties and witnesses on oath, and to call for the production of all the necessary documents. But beyond that, they are free to follow any procedure they please—subject of course to anything the parties may have agreed beforehand in the arbitration clause, or the submission, or in any standard arbitration rules which they have adopted."

16   Section 34(2)(f).

17   Departmental Advisory Committee on Arbitration Law, REPORT ON THE ARBITRATION BILL, February 1996, at Clause 34.

In some international arbitrations it may be obvious—from the nationality of the parties, a concordance of the place of arbitration with the substantive law of the contract, or other factors—that problems of proof and the conduct of the hearings should clearly follow either civil-law or common-law procedures. Even in these cases, ICC arbitrators have broad discretion to follow only those rules of court procedures which they find appropriate in the circumstances, and to adapt them to the informal and transnational character of arbitration. In other cases, however, there may be a real conflict, and whole-hearted adherence to one of the two systems will disappoint one of the parties and may in fact be unfair. In these circumstances, ICC arbitrators may choose to apply procedures which are common to the two systems or adopt certain features of each system.

Some commentators have inveighed against this temptation. Lord Mustill, after referring to the discretion of the arbitrator under the ICC Rules to temper the procedures of strict application of one of the two systems, once advised against combining features of both:

> [T]he arbitrators should not confuse *flexibility* with *compromise*. Having chosen one system, the arbitrators may modify it in the interests of efficiency, but should not try to marry it to the other system. Tribunals sometimes try to operate both systems at once, either out of mutual courtesy between the members of the tribunal, or because of the misplaced feeling that this will be more fair in cases where the parties come from countries with widely differing concepts of procedure. Experience shows that this attempt to amalgamate the two systems invariably produces a solution which embodies the weakest features of each system; and it almost always guarantees misunderstandings and confusion.[18]

While the learned judge's views are entitled to respect, it has been the authors' repeated experience in ICC arbitrations involving parties from common-law and civil-law backgrounds in the same case that the proceedings have been conducted in a manner which encompassed some of the attributes of each system. In particular, the civil-law custom of exchanging documents and written arguments before a hearing is frequently combined with the common-law practice of affording the opportunity to examine and cross-examine witnesses at the hearing.[19]

---

18 Michael Mustill, *Arbitral Proceedings*, paper given at ICC Arbitration Seminar in Malbun (Liechtenstein) on 24 November 1976, at 6. A more recent view to similar effect is found in Justin Thorens, *L'arbitre international au point de rencontrer des traditions du droit civil et de la common law*, in ETUDES DE DROIT INTERNATIONAL EN L'HONNEUR DE PIERRE LALIVE, 693 (Heilbing und Lichtenhahn, Bâle, 1993).

19 Other commentators have also witnessed a "procedural convergence" pursuant to which international commercial arbitrations tend to follow an increasingly uniform pattern: "The written stage is essentially based on continental procedure, whereas the oral stage has been influenced to a greater extent by Anglo-American techniques," FOUCHARD, GAILLARD, GOLDMAN ON INTERNATIONAL COMMERCIAL ARBITRATION 690 (Kluwer 1999).

In determining the procedure to be followed, ICC arbitrators look at the nature and complexity of the dispute, the desires of the parties, the contract underlying the dispute, and the Terms of Reference. In all cases the arbitrators must ensure that the essential elements of a fair procedure are respected so that the award may be enforceable. These elements comprise what one might call "arbitral due process." They include the right to be heard (*audi alteram partem*), the right to be informed of proofs and arguments of the other party in timely fashion (the *principe du contradictoire*), and the right to obtain an award based on the arbitrators' own opinion and judgment and not that of others.[20] These generally recognized principles are common to most systems of law. It is the arbitrator's task to apply them properly within the special context of international arbitration. While it would be erroneous to suggest that there exist generally recognized principles of international procedure that set forth specific steps an international arbitrator must take, the arbitrator's wide discretion within the ICC Rules should, in light of Article 35 requiring arbitrators to ensure enforceability at law, be exercised within the limits of certain general procedural principles recognized under all systems.

These principles may come into play at any stage of the proceedings, and the arbitrator should ensure their respect in all procedural contexts: the filing of documents, the order of argument, the taking of evidence and the examination of witnesses. International arbitrators are generally quite capable of deriving neutral principles for the presentation of evidence in international arbitration from general principles of procedural due process. In an article summarizing the studies of the International Council for Commercial Arbitration,[21] its first President, Jean Robert, stated that six general principles for taking evidence may be established for international commercial arbitration:

1) rules of procedure should not be copied from a single national court system but should be developed on a pragmatic basis to deal with the case at hand;

2) due to geographical distance generally separating the parties and the members of the tribunal, the importance of documents must be emphasized, and the arbitrators should not transfer their primary responsibility for interpreting them to witnesses;

3) since they are already informed of the nature of the dispute by prior examination of documents, the arbitrators may play a greater role in the conduct of the oral hearing than would be true in common-law court proceedings, and the hearing itself should play a secondary role in the development of evidence, with the opportunity of cross-examination granted on a pragmatic basis;

---

20   Rene David, ARBITRATION IN INTERNATIONAL TRADE 291 (1985).

21   J. Robert, *Administration of Evidence in International Commercial Arbitration*, 1 YEARBOOK 221 (1976).

4) affidavits should not be given great weight (*see* Section 24.04) unless accompanied by the right of subsequent examination of the witness;

5) the tribunal should decide which form of expert evaluation is most appropriate to the dispute: the expert-assessor attached to the tribunal and at its constant disposal, the neutral expert appointed by the tribunal to render a report and possibly to be available for examination, or expert witnesses of the parties; and

6) in all cases the parties should themselves agree, or permit the arbitrators to establish, the methods for taking evidence. This is the case in ICC arbitration, since Article 14(1) of the ICC Rules [Article 20(1) of the 1998 Rules] allows the arbitrators to establish the facts of the case "by all appropriate means." By referring to the ICC Rules, the parties have therefore agreed to let the arbitrators determine the appropriate manner of taking evidence and conducting hearings and other proceedings.

Mr. Robert concluded:

This enables the arbitrators to base themselves on the preceding principles. General acceptance of these principles would lead to a truly international custom with respect to the administration of evidence.[22]

It is true of course that these principles, while supplying a general framework, do not deal with the specifics of how evidence should be presented and how the facts should be determined. Indeed, the provisions of Articles 15(1) and (20)(1) of the Rules that procedures shall be those agreed by the parties and, if not by them, then by the arbitrators who have the power to develop the facts by all appropriate means, leave for determination on a case by case basis what should be done where neither the parties nor the arbitrators have agreed to anything in advance. Arbitrators (and for that matter parties when contemplating the drafting of arbitration clauses or the Terms of Reference) may refer usefully to the International Bar Association's *Rules on the Taking of Evidence in International Commercial Arbitration* (the "IBA Rules of Evidence").[23] The IBA Rules of Evidence, initially adopted in 1983 as "Supplementary Rules Governing the Presentation and Reception of Evidence in International Commercial Arbitration," were revised and renamed in 1999. They are intended to complement general rules applicable to arbitration such as the ICC Rules of Arbitration. The IBA Rules of Evidence deal not only with means of proof but more generally with the procedures by which facts are to be developed, and the powers of arbitrators relating thereto. They provide a

---

22   Id. at 226.

23   Reprinted in REDFERN & HUNTER, Appendix K, at 631. The IBA Working Group's *Commentary on the New IBA Rules of Evidence in International Commercial Arbitration* appeared in BUSINESS LAW INTERNATIONAL (IBA publication, January 2000), at 14. The Working Group describes the procedures reflected in the IBA Rules of Evidence as "initially developed in civil law systems, in common law systems, and even in international arbitration processes themselves."

description of what should be contained in the introductory submissions of each party, a procedure for production of documents (together with a limited right of discovery of documents in the hands of the opposite party), a procedure for the taking of evidence of witnesses, and a detailed list of arbitrators' powers in respect of the taking of evidence in general. Prepared by an IBA working group including lawyers from a variety of common-law and civil-law jurisdictions, the IBA Rules of Evidence were designed to define procedures acceptable to parties from diverse systems of law and to provide a general resolution of a number of problems that may arise in arbitral proceedings. Arbitrators may desire to adopt the IBA Rules of Evidence in whole or in part in a general procedural order relating to the conduct of the proceedings, although this is not a common practice. More frequently arbitrators refer to them for useful hints on how specific problems of establishing the facts of the case may be resolved.

The IBA Rules of Evidence are consistent with general ICC arbitration practice, which also avoids application of formal procedures appropriate for court proceedings but inappropriate for arbitration, as well as excessive reliance on any particular national system to provide the rules for proof of fact during the proceedings.[24] One of the advantages of a three-member ICC tribunal is that it is almost always cosmopolitan. Indeed, Article 9(5) provides that, as normal procedure and any time a party objects, the chairman of the tribunal shall be of a nationality other than those of the parties, unless the parties acquiesce in another choice. The result in practice is that the arbitrators tend to be deferential to each others' notions of fair procedure. Accordingly, procedural questions arising in the arbitration are resolved pragmatically rather than dogmatically. One may participate in many ICC arbitrations before hearing a reference to a single article of a national code of civil procedure. The prevailing rule is that of professional common sense, and good sense in this context tends to reflect an amalgam of three jurists' legal culture. It may confound theoreticians, but rarely causes a hitch in practice.

---

24   For a description of the practical workings of ICC arbitral tribunals composed of arbitrators from different legal systems, *see* A. Lowenfeld, *The Two-Way Mirror: International Arbitration as Comparative Procedure*, VII MICHIGAN YEARBOOK OF INTERNATIONAL LEGAL STUDIES 187 (1985).

CHAPTER 24

WRITTEN PROOF AND ARGUMENTS

24.01   Emphasis on written submissions in ICC arbitration

The continental civil-law system of proof is dominated by the exchange of documents between the parties. Hearings serve principally as an occasion for arguments based on facts revealed in written evidence already submitted. The common-law system, on the other hand, uses hearings to develop facts and to introduce documents into evidence.

The governing principles of the ICC Rules and the particularities of international disputes, where the parties and the arbitrators may be domiciled in different countries, favor the continental approach. Article 20(6) of the Rules provides: "The Arbitral Tribunal may decide the case solely on the documents submitted by the parties unless any of the parties requests a hearing." Pursuant to Articles 4 and 5 of the Rules, the Request for Arbitration and the Answer should contain a description of the nature and circumstances of the dispute giving rise to the claims as well as a statement of the relief sought, including, to the extent possible, an indication of any amount(s) claimed. After signature of the Terms of Reference, ICC arbitrators ordinarily provide for further exchanges of written submissions. Communication of documents is usually arranged *seriatim,* with each side also contributing briefs analyzing the evidence presented. These may take the form of an initial memorial to which the respondent will have the right to file a "counter-memorial" (memorandum of defense) in which the grounds of counterclaim, if any, are also set forth. A further exchange, consisting of a "replique" and a "duplique" accompanied by documents, is often necessary (see Chapter 15). Recognizing that a full statement of the claimant's case could prove burdensome in the early stages of arbitration, the drafters of the 1998 Rules provided in Article 4(3)(b) that the Request should contain "a description of the nature and circumstances of the dispute giving rise to the claims," rather than the particulars of all claims;[1] claims may be developed in subsequent written pleadings.

Proponents of oral proceedings argue that the examination and cross-examination of witnesses at length and at leisure by counsel is an important means of revealing the truth. Such tedious practices are largely unknown in ICC arbitration,[2] and would hardly be tolerated by continental arbitrators. Many experienced international arbitrators consider that a witness's essential contribution to the establishment of facts rarely requires more than a few hours of testimony. Arbitrators skeptical of the value of lengthy testimony in commercial cases would maintain that when all is said and done, after many days of observing an intelligent partisan witness on the stand, one knows little more than whether or not one likes him or her.

In any event, full-blown oral hearings are very lengthy. Examination of witnesses in a major commercial case in English courts may take many weeks, sometimes months. The process is somewhat less time-consuming in the United States, where there is extensive pre-trial deposition of witnesses by counsel prior to hearings. But such depositions demand enormous amounts of time of witnesses and counsel, although not of the court.

In international arbitration, extensive hearings are not practical. The site of arbitration will be foreign to at least one of the parties and usually to some or all of the arbitrators. The problems of arranging facilities for the hearing, hotel rooms, translators and stenographers (where required), and the discomfort for counsel working away from home offices contribute to make long hearings an unpleasant chore. The arbitrators usually have other functions which make it impossible for them to be exclusively available for long periods of time. As a result, hearings are seldom scheduled for a period of more than one or two weeks.[3] If further hearings are required, they ordinarily have to be separated in time.

It should not be forgotten that documents are of primary importance in commercial matters. They are relied on heavily even in court litigation. Whatever

---

[1]   The provision in the prior Rules that the Request should contain a "statement of the claimant's case" led to some confusion since some civil-law lawyers considered that a "statement of case" must require a detailed reference to what was expected to be proved and citation to the evidence therefor, while common law lawyers understood it to mean simply the pleading of issues sufficient to give notice of the elements of the claim with sufficient allegations of fact to make out a claim at law ("notice pleading").

[2]   The parties may, of course, agree that specific court rules or practices apply to an ICC arbitration. In one ICC case where the parties had agreed to apply the ordinary court rules of a specified common-law jurisdiction, one of the parties spent 20 hearing days reading documents into the record. Most practitioners (and all clients) would view this as a waste of the flexible and informal ICC mechanism.

[3]   In one case known to the authors, hearings extended over six consecutive weeks. In another case, extending over several years, there were more than 180 hearing days. Both cases were conducted under agreed common-law rules. They are quite exceptional.

may be the arguments in favor of oral proceedings in criminal litigation or in tort cases, they are far less relevant to an efficient system for the settlement of international commercial disputes by arbitration.

24.02 Documents

Since documents must be submitted in multiple copies (a minimum of five in proceedings with three arbitrators: one copy to each of the arbitrators, to the Secretariat, and to opposing counsel as provided for in Article 3(1)), original documents are usually not filed. Photocopies or other forms of copies are presumed authentic unless challenged. Questions of authenticity, like all questions of fact, are decided by the arbitral tribunal.

There is no standard form for submission of documents in ICC arbitrations. Americans often submit their numbered exhibits in bound volumes, or ring binders which permit individual exhibits to be removed if desired for closer examination. English lawyers frequently submit an agreed "bundle" of documents as is the norm in English practice.[4] Continental practitioners file *dossiers* in which exhibits are enclosed in individual titled folders.

Counsel are perfectly free to make submissions in whatever form they find most effective. Indeed, elements of different methods may be combined effectively. One prominent continental ICC arbitrator expresses a preference for the American system of bound and indexed exhibits for study prior to the hearing, but also likes to have during the hearing a separate unbound *dossier* containing the documents upon which counsel intends to rely in final argument in order to follow the oral exposition better. What is important is that the documents be submitted according to an orderly procedure consistent with the Rules, the Terms of Reference and such subsequent orders as are made by the arbitrators.

In technical cases such as licensing, manufacturing, or construction disputes, documents can be extremely voluminous and complex, including plans, formulae, engineering diagrams and computer accounting printouts. Furthermore, documents submitted are not always classified as "evidence." Excerpts of books or articles supporting a party's position may be submitted even if the author is not to appear as a witness.

The weight of documentary materials may be increased by the need to supply source materials relating to the applicable law. When a case is tried before na-

---

4   For a description of the use of the "agreed bundle" procedure in arbitration *see,* Michael Mustill & Stewart Boyd, COMMERCIAL ARBITRATION 326 (2d. ed. 1989). This is a useful procedure where counsel for the adverse parties agree on all the documents to be submitted to the tribunal and submit a single bundle of documents, in chronological order and numbered consecutively. While useful, the procedure is not required. Some well known ICC arbitral chairmen (not necessarily from common law countries), however, are persuaded of the utility of the system and will bring considerable pressure on parties to accept it.

tional courts whose own law governs the dispute, the judges are presumed to know the law and to have access to cases and materials relied upon by counsel. This is obviously not the case in international arbitration, where the arbitrators often come from countries other than the one whose law is to be applied.

Furthermore, ICC arbitrators have been called upon with increasing frequency to deal with problems arising from investments in and commerce with developing countries. The laws of those countries are often applicable to the dispute; it is therefore necessary to obtain and produce for the tribunal legal materials which are not always readily available. Extensive documentation on foreign laws and authorities, as well as expert opinions concerning their meaning, may thus constitute a substantial part of the documents submitted in arbitration.

Documents submitted *en masse*, without explanation or order, are meaningless to the arbitrators. The amount of time necessary to explain them at hearings is accordingly multiplied. Hence memorials and briefs prepared by the parties for the arbitration are of central importance, generally more so than oral argument. One of their key functions is to organize the evidence submitted and make clear its pertinence to disputed issues.

24.03 Memorials and briefs

The Request and Answer provided for in Articles 4 and 5 of the ICC Rules set the stage for the preparation of the Terms of Reference, which define the issues and establish procedures for their resolution.

Subsequent memorials or briefs address all issues of fact and law to be resolved in light of their definition in the Terms of Reference. They are prepared with a view to final resolution of the dispute after such hearings or oral argument as may be ordered.

Although other procedures may be agreed by the parties, the general rule in ICC arbitration is that the arbitrators read in detail all briefs and memorials submitted by the parties prior to hearings. The arbitrators thus come to the hearings fully aware of the documentary evidence submitted. Sometimes the parties will request, or the arbitrators require, that post-hearing memorials be filed by the parties, with the arbitrators sometimes identifying particular issues they would like to have briefed. In order to avoid delay, simultaneous, rather than consecutive, submissions are often ordered, sometimes with the right to file replies (also simultaneous).

While issues of law should be fully briefed, experience shows that it is by a cogent exposition of the facts, and a coherent synthesis of the documents in evidence, that briefs or memorials have their greatest impact. Experienced ICC arbitrators frequently find that they are able to resolve issues of law without the great amount of assistance that some parties are determined to give them;

but they admit they need and welcome the parties' guidance synthesizing and interpreting the facts.

The length of memorials and briefs depends on the complexity of the case. In major construction cases, the text of the memorials alone may exceed 1000 pages (evidentiary materials, of course, are likely to represent many times that quantity).

As stated in Section 24.01, most ICC arbitrators, following a continental approach, call for either one or two exchanges of documents and memorials between the parties prior to hearing and final argument. Occasionally, the hearings shed new light on issues previously treated as marginal. The arbitrators then invite the parties to prepare further written submissions, which in turn may require further response. As noted above, a party may seek to file a post-hearing memorial. Even if one of the parties opposes any post-hearing submissions, ICC arbitrators ordinarily are inclined to allow them, particularly if the party proposing such a submission agrees to be bound by an early deadline. To give some notion of the pre and post-hearing difference, pre-hearing memorials may be subject to deadlines of ten weeks or more while post-hearing submissions, frequently limited to particular issues which the arbitrators have found to require further development following the hearing, may have to be filed within thirty days, or even a shorter period.

24.04   Timeliness of submissions

All arbitral tribunals must be wary of dilatory tactics. One of the most difficult decisions that an arbitrator must make is to determine when "enough is enough." ICC tribunals are often indulgent in accepting submissions out of time, as long as the other party is given opportunity to reply. Time is seldom of essence in the final settlement of an international commercial dispute through arbitration; in a consensual dispute-resolution process, one should make every effort to leave each side with the feeling that it had full opportunity to present its case (and that due process was respected, rendering the award enforceable). The tribunal should nonetheless make a special ruling on any request for permission to file unscheduled pleadings or submissions. It should avoid the trap of prolonging proceedings in response to a deluge of new memoranda, pleadings, or evidence submitted by a party for which the arbitration has evolved unfavorably and which tries to make up for the weakness of its own case or its negligence in presenting it by abusing the flexibility and informality of arbitral proceedings.

Experienced arbitrators will not allow proceedings to get out of hand in this way and will make the requisite procedural orders to keep a reasonable time table.[5]

---

5   A fundamental mechanism in this connection is described in Section 25.06, *Closing the hearings*.

Some useful parallels may be drawn from practice before the Iran-U.S. Claims Tribunal where the issue of timeliness of submissions arose with particular acuteness, due in part to the underlying political and governmental interests.[6] That tribunal made a number of decisions (which, unlike ICC awards, are published) rejecting untimely submissions.[7] The criteria for such rejections have been described by Howard Holtzmann, a United States Member of the Tribunal, in the following terms:

> In deciding on whether to admit a late submission, the Tribunal has frequently referred to the requirements of equality and fairness, to the possible prejudice to other parties and to the fact that the orderly conduct of the proceedings requires that time limits be established and enforced.[8]

ICC arbitrators apply similar criteria in ruling on whether to receive documents filed out of time. When applying these principles, they take into account the character of the documents and the specific reasons given for the delay. It should be noted that the danger of prejudice is greater when an attempt is made to file new evidence as opposed to briefs and argument, and arbitrators will be reluctant to grant authorization in the former case without an exceptionally strong demonstration of justification.[9] In all cases, the task for the arbitrator and the parties is facilitated if the tribunal provides clearly by written procedural order the deadlines for filings by the parties.

24.05   Written statements of witnesses

One way to save time in arbitration is to convert oral testimony into written statements to be filed prior to the hearing. In some cases, written statements may entirely replace oral testimony, as the party against which the witness is proffered may conclude, without necessarily accepting the content of the statement, that cross-examination would not be productive.

---

6   In one arbitration before the Iran-U.S. Claims Tribunal with which the authors are familiar, and which took place during the early years of that Tribunal, the Iranian party submitted new briefs and evidence four months after the final hearing, even though witnesses had been heard and the case had been finally argued and closed, and although there had been exchanges of pre-hearing briefs and documents. In other cases before that tribunal, new evidence was filed by Iranian parties after final hearing and deliberations by the arbitrators, under circumstances that have led dispassionate practitioners to conclude that the evidence was intended to respond to points raised in the deliberations, and which could only have been known through ex-parte communications with an arbitrator. Obviously these kinds of abuses must be avoided in ICC arbitration.

7   *See e.g.*, Harris International Telecommunications, Inc. v. Iran, 17 Iran-U.S. C.T.R. 31 (Chamber One, 1987).

8   Howard Holtzmann, *Some Lessons of the Iran-United States Claims Tribunal*, in 1987 Symposium, PRIVATE INVESTORS ABROAD—PROBLEMS AND SOLUTIONS IN INTERNATIONAL BUSINESS, The Southwestern Legal Foundation, Section 16.04 (3) (a).

9   For a discussion of a particular case where the late filing of documents caused prejudice, *see* D. Branson, *Continuous Ownership of a Claim: A Hard Case at the Iran-United States Claims Tribunal Makes Bad Law*, 3 ARB. INT. 164 (1987).

Arbitrators often adopt this time-saving device, but are careful to ensure procedural due process. It is sometimes provided that witness statements will be produced by a party at the time of the submission of its documentary evidence and memorial. Some claimants may believe that giving prior notice of the contents of the testimony of its witnesses will give the respondent an unfair advantage in the preparation of the testimony of the latter's witnesses.[10] It is therefore frequently agreed (or ordered) that exchanges of written witness testimony be simultaneous rather than consecutive. The 1999 IBA Rules of Evidence suggest, in Article 4.6, two rounds of simultaneous exchanges, with the scope of the second round limited to rebuttal.

The form of written statements may be subject to an agreement or a procedural order. American practitioners, as well as those from many other common-law jurisdictions, expect written testimony to be submitted in the form of an affidavit under oath. In other jurisdictions, the concept of sworn statements may be unfamiliar. Indeed, it may be unclear in such jurisdictions which state officer has the right to administer an oath for a statement to be used in international arbitral proceedings. The best solution, reflected in Article 4 of the 1999 IBA Rules of Evidence, would be for the parties to agree that such evidence may be submitted with a simple signed declaration to the effect that the statement is true to the best of the witness' belief and knowledge (*see* Sec. 25.01).

Most parties agree to the submission of written statements by a witness on the condition that the witness be available for questioning at the request of the party against which the witness testifies. It is important and appropriate to be able to reserve the right of oral examination on significant or controversial evidence. For this reason, ICC tribunals usually impose as a condition of admission of written witness testimony that the witness be made available for questioning during hearings upon the demand of the other party. Unless there is an express agreement otherwise by the parties, the arbitral tribunal will ordinarily have discretion to determine under what circumstances a written statement of a witness will be admitted in evidence even though at the time of hearing the witness is unwilling or unable to appear in person.[11] Even when such a statement is admitted, the arbitral tribunal will ordinarily observe, in its award, that reliance on the statement is diminished because of the inability of the tribunal, and the adverse party, to question the witness on this statement.

---

10 A similar advantage may exist for the claimant who is respondent on a counterclaim in respect to written testimony submitted by the respondent-counterclaimant.

11 Article 4.7 of the 1999 IBA Rules of Evidence calls for witness statements to be disregarded if a witness refuses to attend the hearing, save "exceptional circumstances." Express provisions of national law, or accepted practice in a state, may also provide guidance. In his report on arbitration law in England (II ICCA HANDBOOK, Suppl. 23, March 1997), V.V. Veeder Q.C points out that "the Civil Evidence Acts 1968-1972 apply to arbitration, allowing written witness statements to

As a practical matter, the submission of written statements saves much time at hearings. The entire testimony of some witnesses and much of the testimony of others often goes unchallenged; thus written statements may stand alone. It is true that in many cases where the adversary wants a witness to appear for examination, the presenting party itself would have called the witness in order that his comportment and credibility be judged by the tribunal. Even with respect to such witnesses, however, submission of the prior written statement greatly shortens the examination of witnesses at hearings.

Article 15(1) of the ICC Rules recognizes the parties' right to establish procedural rules by agreement.[12] Thus where the parties agree to a procedure for submission of written evidence, or where the arbitrators provide for such a procedure because the subject has not been addressed by the parties, such an agreement should prevail and shelter the arbitration from any attack based on arguments that such a procedure is unknown or contrary to rules of judicial procedure at the seat of arbitration. The parties are said to have contractually agreed to this procedure in the same way that they agreed to arbitration.

The preparation of witness statements often involves drafting by lawyers who have interviewed the witness and submit a text for his or her approval. This presupposes contacts with the witness. The propriety of such contacts is established in contemporary international practice.[13]

It is a fortunate characteristic of international arbitration that the use of depositions is exceptional. Some commentators have gone so far as to say that depositions are "never" employed; the authors however agree with Messrs. Redfern and Hunter, who observe that "in some disputes . . . pre-trial depositions may be useful."[14] Certainly there have been instances in ICC arbitrations where witnesses were interrogated outside the presence of the tribunal.[15]

---

be addressed in evidence, without producing that witness for oral cross-examination where that witness is abroad." It is also the case that in the United States affidavits play a frequent and useful role in arbitration:

Rules of arbitration agencies rightly note that the arbitrator, in considering the weight to be given to such testimony by affidavit, should be aware that the absent witness was not subject to cross-examination and thus corroboration of oral testimony was lacking. But on occasion a party has no alternative and must make use of affidavits because the witness is not available for some valid reason. Martin Domke, COMMERCIAL ARBITRATION Sec. 24.02 (Wilner, ed., 1999).

12   Article 15(1) provides: "The proceedings before the Arbitral Tribunal shall be governed by these Rules, and where these Rules are silent, by any rules which the parties or, failing them, the Arbitral Tribunal, may settle on, whether or not reference is thereby made to the rules of procedure of a national law to be applied to the arbitration."

13   *See* Michael Schneider, *Witnesses in International Arbitration,* 1993 SWISS BULL. 302, at 306. The 1999 IBA Rules of Evidence confirm categorically in Article 4.3 that it is "not improper" for a party or its lawyers to interview proposed witnesses.

14   REDFERN & HUNTER, 72, at n. 83.

15   For the relevant procedural orders issued in ICC Case 7170/1993, where a witness apparently did not wish to leave his home in Italy, *see* ICC PROCEDURAL DECISIONS, 55.

CHAPTER 25

HEARINGS

25.01 Arbitrators' power of subpoena and to administer oath

The ICC arbitrator's powers are created only by the agreement of the parties, the ICC Rules agreed by them, and appointment by the ICC Court of Arbitration. Arbitrators possess no authority of compulsion, nor any other powers of *imperium* which are reserved to the State. As the Pope has no army, so the ICC arbitrator has no bailiff.

Accordingly, in many cases it does not occur to the ICC arbitrator to put a witness on oath (*i.e.* to instruct the witness to swear under oath that the testimony about to be given is true). The practice may be more frequent in some common law jurisdictions where witnesses in arbitrations routinely give testimony under oath.[1] If asked to do so by a party, he may well refuse. ICC arbitrators do not have any power to punish false testimony (*i.e.*, to hold a witness in contempt of court), nor derive from the Rules any power to subpoena witnesses or documents, even those in the hands of a party (although Article 20 does allow arbitrators to request, in the form of a summons, such witnesses or documents). The power of subpoena can only derive from national law. Most ICC arbitrators are reluctant to seek a source for their powers in state law rather than in the institutional rules and practices agreed by the parties. Therefore, in cases where an order of compulsion or enforcement is required, it may be necessary to approach a state court in ancillary proceedings in support of arbitration (*see* Chapter 27).

---

1   Statutes in many common law jurisdictions give power to arbitrators to administer the oath. *See e.g.* § 38(5) of English Arbitration Act 1996 which provides that the arbitral tribunal may direct that a party or witness be examined under oath and is given the power for that purpose to administer the oath. To the same effect are statutory provisions in a number of states of the United States *see* Uniform Arbitration Act § 7. Rather than to exercise such powers, where available, it is a much more frequent practice in ICC arbitration for the chairman or sole arbitrator to inform the witness that he has a duty to give truthful testimony and that he may be subject to criminal penalties for false testimony, and to secure the witness' acknowledgment of this duty. *Accord,* Article 4 of the 1999 IBA Rules of Evidence.

If, however, specific national legislation at the seat of arbitration empowers arbitrators to exercise specified delegated powers of the state, the ICC Rules do not prevent an ICC arbitrator from exercising such powers.

The issue arises most often in common-law jurisdictions. In the United States, for instance, the Federal Arbitration Act[2] as well as the provisions of the laws of a number of states give arbitrators the power to issue subpoenas to obtain material evidence. Such subpoenas may be addressed to the opposing party or third parties. Yet, refusal by an arbitrator to issue a subpoena at the request of a party is most unlikely to be deemed a denial of due process of such a degree as to jeopardize the award.[3] This conclusion is reinforced by the broad discretion given to arbitrators under the ICC Rules in procedural matters. In England, the arbitral tribunal may direct that a party or witness shall testify before it and that a party shall produce documents. (Arbitration Act 1996, Section 38). At the request of the arbitral tribunal (or by the parties, where agreed) the Court may exercise its powers of compulsion to obtain compliance. *Id.*, Sections 42, 43. In both the United States and the United Kingdom, however, if a person refuses to obey a subpoena or if a party refuses to produce a document under order, civil or penal sanctions for non- compliance may be imposed only by the ordinary courts and not by the arbitral tribunal.

In the United States, arbitrators may be given the power to put witnesses on oath by specific provisions of state legislation. An authoritative commentator recommends this formality as a way to indicate to the witness the importance of his testimony.[4] But refusal to administer an oath to a witness is not considered a procedural error; it could hardly be subject to judicial review in light of the arbitrators' broad discretionary powers under the ICC Rules. In England, the question of whether witnesses should be put on oath is a matter for the discretion of the arbitrator unless it is required by the arbitration agreement.[5]

In continental Europe, the power of an arbitrator to issue a subpoena or to administer oaths is largely unknown. Indeed, administering oaths may be considered a usurpation of judicial prerogatives, theoretically exposing the arbitrator to sanctions. For these reasons, most ICC arbitrators merely ask witnesses to declare that the testimony they give is the truth.[6] Arbitrators

---

2   9 U.S.C. Sec. 7

3   *See* Martin Domke, COMMERCIAL ARBITRATION Sec. 24.03 (Wilner, ed. 1999) and cases cited therein. For a detailed comment on the Sole Arbitrator's refusal to issue a *subpoena ad testificandum* under the Federal Arbitration Act, *see* ICC Arbitration No. 7453, 1997 JDI 1082, note D. Hascher.

4   Martin Domke, *supra* Note 31, Sec. 24.03.

5   V.V. Veeder, National Report, England *in* ICCA HANDBOOK 40 (Suppl. 23, March 1997). *See also* DAC REPORT ON THE ARBITRATION BILL (February 1996), Clause 43: "[Court Support] is not used to override any procedural method adopted by the tribunal, or agreed by the parties, for the arbitration."

6   ICC arbitrators might be advised to employ the non-controversial declaration (which avoids reference to any deity) which was adopted by the Iran-U.S. Claims Tribunal pursuant to Article 25

from civil-law countries, even when sitting on a tribunal in England or the United States, may not be comfortable with the concept of putting witnesses on oath and may therefore decline to do so even though authorized by legislation at the place of arbitration.[7]

25.02 Testimony

The structure of the ICC Rules is such that hearings and oral testimony take place at the end of a period of "instruction" of the case during which pleadings, documents, briefs and memoranda have been exchanged (*see* Section 24.01). The length of the hearings and oral testimony is thus normally shorter in ICC arbitration than during a common-law proceeding before a court. This does not mean that the presentation of testimony may not have significant impact.

Experienced arbitrators know that it is impossible to manage arbitral proceedings fairly and efficiently unless the tribunal controls the time spent in the examination of witnesses. Perhaps the simplest solution is also the best: to allocate a total amount of time equally between the two sides, and to charge time against the party which is actually using it, without regard to who called the witness. This practice became widespread as a result of the lessons of the Iran-US Claims Tribunal, where, as reported by Judge Pierre Bellet (a former President of the French Court of Cassation and subsequently a renowned international arbitrator):

> ". . . the time used by a party for the examination (and cross-examination) of witnesses was deducted from the time for its oral pleadings in order to ward off possible fraud consisting of making pleadings in between questions put to the witnesses."[8]

Distinctions between party witnesses and third-party witnesses, known in some national procedural regimes, are increasingly ignored in international arbitration. The authors agree with Mr. Hascher (now a judge at the influential Court of Appeal of Paris) when he writes:

> "Rather than drawing an artificial distinction between the corporate officers, and senior management or other directors who are regarded as party representatives and party employees, who are regarded as third

---

of its Rules and which provided that each witness shall declare: "I solemnly declare upon my honor and conscience that I will speak the truth, the whole truth and nothing but the truth," VIII YEARBOOK 248 (1983). *See also* Rule 34 of the ICSID Arbitration Rules.

7 An experienced French practitioner once wrote flatly: "In fact, whether parties or witnesses are heard in an arbitration, an oath will never be taken," J. Robert, *Administration of Evidence in International Commercial Arbitration* , I YEARBOOK 225 (1976). This statement may be too categorical for some venues of ICC arbitration. *See* Arbitration Act 1996 (England), 38(5).

8 *Presentation* in preface to ICC PROCEDURAL DECISIONS, at 15. For a characteristic example of what is sometimes eponymously known as the Böckstiegel Method applying this principle in ICC Case 7314/1996, *see id.* at 136.

party witnesses, it is preferable to hear all persons and evaluate the weight of their statements, having due regard to the nature and degree of the links between the deponents and the parties."[9]

Ideally, the rules for examination of witnesses should be established in the Terms of Reference or by a procedural order of the tribunal issued well before the presentation of witnesses. The method of hearing testimony should not be left unclear until witnesses are on the stand. An early definition of the manner in which witnesses are to be heard is necessary to permit the parties to prepare their case free from doubt or conflicting concepts concerning the procedure. Since the rules of evidence in international arbitration are relaxed,[10] the examination of witnesses is almost always quite informal even if common-law procedures are adopted as a general principle.

If the parties or the arbitrators have decided that the procedural law of the place of arbitration should apply, arbitrators should first examine any statutory provisions defining the procedure for arbitration. Failing that, they would refer to the rules of judicial procedure with respect to testimony. Such rules should be adapted so as to take into account the *desideratum* of informality in commercial arbitration. Unless the parties have otherwise agreed, court rules should not be applied blindly but "by analogy" insofar as appropriate to arbitration.[11] Modern arbitration laws make this clear. In France, for instance, the law provides that even if French procedural law has been agreed upon by the parties, the arbitrators need not follow court procedures except for fundamental rules of due process defined in designated rules of civil procedure.[12]

---

9   Explanatory Note to the tribunal's decision in ICC Case 7319/1994, ICC Procedural Decisions 96, at 97.

10   The parties could of course decide to conduct an arbitration exactly like a court proceeding but this is almost never intended. A more likely approach is to agree to specific evidentiary rules to be applied, and failing agreement to apply judicial rules only by analogy, *see generally*, Chapter 23.

11   *See, e.g.*, Articles 1494 and 1495 of the French Code of Civil Procedure. If the arbitration taking place in France is of an international nature, the procedure may be fixed by agreement of the parties or by the rules of an arbitration institution without reference to French procedural law. Even if French procedural law of arbitration is chosen, its provisions for the conduct of proceedings apply only in the absence of specific agreement by the parties on a rule of procedure governing the issue.

12   Article 1460 of the French Code of Civil Procedure provides: "The arbitrators shall determine the procedure for the arbitration without being bound by the rules established for the courts, unless the parties have provided otherwise in the arbitration agreement. Nevertheless, the guiding principles of litigation defined in Articles 4 to 10, 11 (paragraph 1) and 15 to 21 shall always be applicable to arbitral proceedings." These Articles defining "guiding principles" are translated in English in the Annex to Chapter 30, note 1.

Practitioners are well advised to consider in advance the position they wish to take with respect to the following procedural issues which frequently arise concerning the presentation of testimony in ICC arbitrations:[13]

i) *Examination by the tribunal*: Will the witness be called by the tribunal itself and will the principal examination be conducted by the presiding arbitrator? If so, do the parties have the right to question the witness freely after examination by the tribunal?

ii) *Examination by counsel*: If witnesses are to be presented and examined by a party and cross-examined by the adversary, are any specific limitations on the method of examination envisaged? It is current in ICC practice to permit a witness on direct examination to deliver an essentially narrative statement, punctuated by questions by the counsel who presented the witness.

iii) *Extent of cross-examination:* Whether examination of a witness is conducted principally by the tribunal or by counsel to the party presenting him, the adverse party is justified in requesting time and liberty to cross-examine the witness. In the absence of agreement by the parties, this issue is left to the discretion of the arbitrators. Contrary to the rumor that cross-examination is anathema to continental arbitrators, the authors' experience has been that most ICC arbitrators, irrespective of their origin, allow counsel a fair measure of cross-examination on all significant issues brought up in the witness' main statement.

iv) *Distinction between witnesses and party representatives*: Some national judicial rules make a theoretical distinction between party representatives and third-party witnesses. Generally, only the latter may give testimony under oath, whereas party representatives make declarations. This distinction seems to have little practical impact on the weight of statements made by witnesses or representatives of parties in ICC arbitration.[14] Nevertheless, it may be useful to clarify in advance whether any distinction is to be made in the presentation of these two kinds of statements. It should be recalled that whereas ICC arbitrators have discretion to hear witnesses, they are required to hear party representatives under Article 20(2).

---

13   For a practical review of a number of these issues from a comparative point of view, *see* A. Lowenfeld, *The Two Way Mirror: International Arbitration as Comparative Procedure*, VII MICHIGAN YEARBOOK OF INTERNATIONAL LEGAL STUDIES 187 (1985).

14   See text at Footnote 9, *supra*. This is similar to the result reached in the Iran-U.S. Claims Tribunal where parties and party representatives were not considered witnesses but were heard and questioned and awards could take into account what such interested persons said, provided the Tribunal believed it. *See* H. Holtzmann, *Some Lessons of the Iran-United States Claims Tribunal*, *in* 1987 Symposium, PRIVATE INVESTORS ABROAD—PROBLEMS AND SOLUTIONS IN INTERNATIONAL BUSINESS, The Southwestern Legal Foundation, Section 16.04(4). For the Iranian view that an issue of fact should not be determined solely on the basis of the statement of an interested person, *see* Economy Forms Corp. v. Iran, 5 IRAN-U.S. C.T.R. 1 (1983) (dissenting opinion of Mahmoud Kashari).

v) *Transcript or recording of testimony*: Full transcripts of oral proceedings may be made, by agreement of the parties or as ordered by the arbitrators. In some venues, the practical difficulties of obtaining competent stenographers to make a verbatim transcript in the language of the arbitration may be substantial. Parties therefore frequently dispense with the requirement of verbatim transcripts. Nonetheless, ICC tribunals often do order such a transcript if requested by a party for good reasons, even over the objection of the other side. ("Good reasons" may include the magnitude of a dispute, the controversial nature of anticipated statements of witnesses, or the likelihood of judicial review.) ICC arbitrators are reluctant to refuse a request for a transcript of testimony if the requesting party insists that it is an essential aid to arbitral due process. The costs of transcripts ordinarily become an arbitration expense to be paid by the ICC from the advances on costs; the final burden of the expense will be settled by the tribunal's allocation of arbitration costs in the final award (*see* Section 19.07). If hearing expenses are substantial, however, the parties may be invited to make direct payments rather than trigger a request for additional advances from the ICC. Even if a transcript is not ordered, the parties may request the arbitrators to arrange for a recording of the entire proceeding, from which a full or partial transcript may later be made if necessary, although experience teaches that reconstituted transcripts made in this way are seldom satisfactory.

vi) *Summary of testimony*: If no transcript or recording is made, it is often advisable that the tribunal prepare at least internal minutes of the testimony given. ICC arbitral tribunals may exceptionally request witnesses to examine, correct, and sign summaries of testimony prepared by the tribunal (usually by the chairman). In most cases where a transcript or recording is not made, however, the testimony of witnesses is not made part of the record and remains only in the memory of the arbitrators and in notes taken for their own use in deliberations.

vii) *Isolation of witnesses*: ICC tribunals occasionally rule that witnesses shall not appear in the hearing room until the moment of their testimony.[15] This reduces the possibility of witnesses adapting their testimony in light of testimony of other witnesses. Parties themselves (or the chief representative(s) of a corporate party) are entitled to be present throughout the hearing even if they intend to make declarations. In the latter case, the policy which supports isolation gives way to the policy of allowing a party to confront adverse testimony and evidence.

---

15 "The IBA Rules of Evidence do not say whether witnesses who have not yet testified may be in the hearing rooms or whether witnesses who have testified may remain. This is left for the arbitral tribunal to decide because it depends on the circumstances of the case, the nature of the dispute and of the persons involved," IBA Working Party, *Commentary on the New IBA Rules of Evidence in International Commercial Arbitration*, BUSINESS LAW INTERNATIONAL (IBA Publication, January 2000), 14, at 32.

Another exception to a request for isolation of a witness may be granted in the case of the principal expert consultant of a party. Such a consultant may aid counsel throughout a hearing where complex technical issues are involved, and counsel should not be deprived of this aid even though the expert will later testify on certain matters in the case. This practice is all the more justified since the expert will principally give his opinion on facts proved by others, rather than purport to prove the existence of facts.

viii) *Relation of counsel to witnesses:* Neither the ICC Rules nor any ICC code of ethics, custom or usage prevents counsel from consulting with witnesses with respect to the testimony they will give even when testimony of other witnesses has been heard by counsel.[16] In the authors' experience, counsel in most ICC arbitrations feel free to confer with witnesses and even to prepare their testimony. Rules to the contrary would in most cases be unrealistic. Where, however, a witness or expert is being examined by the arbitral tribunal, or cross-examined by counsel for the adverse party (or where there is a "confrontation" between experts), the tribunal may, when a recess is to be taken, order the witness not to discuss his testimony with counsel or representatives of the party calling him until his examination has been completed.

This practice may be contrasted with the ethical, and sometimes legal, requirements relating to communications between counsel and witnesses in court proceedings in certain jurisdictions. Thus it is the rule in France that *avocats* should not discuss with witnesses the testimony they intend to present in court proceedings. In other countries, professional ethics forbid barristers to discuss with a witness his testimony before the hearing, such preparation being reserved for solicitors.

In the major international arbitration centers at least, no mandatory provisions of national law apply such restrictions to international arbitral proceedings. This conclusion is buttressed by the fact that in most of these venues, foreign lawyers may represent their clients without limitations in international arbitration proceedings. It would be illogical and inequitable for an *avocat* or barrister to carry with him into international arbitration proceedings an ethical limitation on contacts with witnesses that lawyers or solicitors representing the other side do not share. The issue is not entirely free from doubt and may depend to some degree on whether the arbitration takes place within the jurisdiction where counsel is licensed to practice. Nevertheless, in the absence of some contrary obligatory rule of law at the site of arbitration, it appears that experienced ICC practitioners coming from diverse legal backgrounds feel free to adopt a rule of conduct in relation to witnesses that is appropriate to arbitral proceedings. They do not consider themselves bound by the limitations of their national bar in proceedings before national courts, particularly since the *raison d'être* of such limitations

---

16 *See* text at footnotes 13, *supra.*

disappears in international arbitral proceedings. The current international consensus is reflected in Article 4.3 of the 1999 IBA Rules of Evidence, which provide that it is "not improper" for a party or its lawyers to communicate with proposed witnesses.

25.03   Party experts

In common-law court cases involving technical matters, any party may call expert witnesses on its own behalf to provide evidence on technical questions in issue. "Battles of experts" ensue, with detailed examination and cross-examination by counsel. Oral testimony of experts presented by the parties is rare before the courts in civil-law countries, where tradition and applicable procedural codes provide for the appointment of one or more neutral experts by the court.

Under Article 20(4) of the ICC Rules, arbitrators may appoint neutral experts (*see* Section 26.04). In major cases involving technical isssues, however, both parties frequently wish to present evidence and testimony by experts whom they have consulted, whether the tribunal desires to be aided by a neutral expert or not.[17] This occurs irrespective of whether the parties come from civil-law or common-law jurisdictions. In fact, when the issues in dispute include the evaluation of construction, engineering, design, or mechanical and chemical processes, it is often indispensable for a party to consult experts outside its own organization. Such experts, while obviously paid for their work, do not have the same interest in the outcome of the litigation as a party's employee. Detached from the dispute, they can evaluate the issues more objectively. By the same token, their testimony may lend additional credibility to a party's case.

Even if they intend to appoint a neutral expert, ICC arbitrators are not well-advised to reject the presentation of expert testimony by the parties. In particular, parties from common-law countries view with great misgiving a procedure whereby the arbitrators receive all their technical briefing from someone who, perhaps by unfortunate accident, may turn out to be incompetent: such an "expert" could not easily be challenged because, while perfectly mistaken, he is also perfectly neutral in the sense that his erroneous conclusions were not intended to benefit either side.

Since the information to be given by a party's expert is ordinarily both detailed and technical, the expert's report is generally filed as a document with other written evidence in the case. The consultation should provide a resume of the qualifications of the expert as well as a summary of his *modus operandi* and the evidence examined in preparing his report.

---

17   Article 20(3) of the Rules, as modified in 1998, specifically provides that the tribunal may hear "experts appointed by the parties" although the tribunal retains its general discretion whether the hearing of such witnesses or experts is necessary.

The written report is the foundation upon which the expert's oral examination is built. He should be able to defend his views in response to questions from both the tribunal and opposing counsel. The flexible procedure of ICC arbitration and its relaxation of evidentiary rules provide a receptive framework for hearing party-produced experts, who can make significant contributions to the resolution of complex technical disputes.

Pre-hearing conferences among experts may be useful in some circumstances, and are contemplated in the 1999 IBA Rules of Evidence. The IBA Working Group explained its potential usefulness as follows:

> The practice suggested here, when deemed appropriate by the arbitral tribunal, can prove a valuable device to render the proceeding more economical. Respectable experts from the same trade, who are likely to know each other, can identify relatively quickly the reasons for their diverging conclusions and work towards finding areas of agreement. The arbitral tribunal may also direct party-appointed experts to state the rationale for any remaining disagreements. Where the experts have success and reach agreement, the parties and the arbitral tribunal will likely accept those findings, so that the arbitral process may proceed to the truly disputed aspects of the case.[18]

25.04 Demonstrative evidence

As ICC arbitration today tends to deal with increasingly complex factual issues, parties and arbitrators make use of the informality of arbitration procedures in novel ways. Demonstrative evidence,[19] while not easily accepted in judicial proceedings in continental countries, has been successfully used in numerous ICC arbitrations.

One case known to the authors involved the performance of an engine which was the subject of a license agreement between the parties; the engine was displayed in the hearing room for the arbitrators. In a similar case, a model of a mechanical device, produced in clear plastic so as to make visible the inner workings of the device, was used for purposes of demonstration. In another case, a visual display of sequences of enlarged photographs taken contemporaneously with the progress of construction work on an aborted hotel and resort project was mounted in a room adjacent to the hearing: the arbitrators could thus get a quick and concrete notion of what had in fact been done. Maps and elevations of the project area illustrated other disputed matters. All the maps and photographs had been submitted earlier as documentary proof,

---

18 *Commentary on the New IBA Rules of Evidence in International Commercial Arbitration*, BUSINESS LAW INTERNATIONAL (IBA publication, January 2000) 14 at 28.

19 Demonstrative evidence is that which appeals directly to the senses and thus does not need to be presented as part of testimony. It may be presented at any time during a hearing when the opportunity arises.

but it is difficult to testify, argue, or illustrate by reference to wallet-sized photographs or to maps presented in the format of typewriter paper. Displays mounted with some attention to graphics may reconstitute events in dispute much more effectively than is possible by using more traditional methods.[20]

Another example of effective use of demonstrative evidence in arbitration was where a party introduced its case by showing a film. Part of the film had been prepared for promotional purposes at the time of launching the investment project that had given rise to the dispute. Contemporaneous with the events in dispute, the film was credible evidence of the expectations of the parties. Another segment of the film showed the site of the proposed investment just prior to the arbitration, and demonstrated a number of points relevant to the dispute. This part of the film, which had been prepared for the purposes of the litigation, was not presented as evidence but rather as part of the opening statement of counsel; it constituted a striking demonstration of what the party intended to prove and provided in five minutes what two hours of description may not have conveyed.

Creative use of demonstrative evidence seems to be more often inspired by the parties than by their lawyers. Counsel, and sometimes arbitrators, are too frequently creatures of habit, acting as though their priority is to make the arbitral process conform to patterns of judicial proceedings (thus seeking to avoid any charge of procedural error). Overcautiousness in this respect can waste some of the advantages of the arbitral process, which should be used creatively to help solve complex technical and commercial problems with efficacity. It is precisely because of these advantages that many parties have turned away from formal court proceedings in favor of arbitration. Parties should be encouraged to exploit any such possibilities. Experienced ICC arbitrators are perfectly able to ensure that adversaries have an adequate opportunity to respond and that in all other respects the equal treatment of the parties is respected.

25.05   Oral argument

The priority given to written submissions in ICC arbitration (*see* Section 24.01) reduces the length and significance of oral testimony in comparison with court proceedings in common-law jurisdictions. However, oral argument by counsel, which is a central feature of both common-law and civil-law procedure, is given substantial weight. Counsel are given considerable time to "plead" their cases to the tribunal.

---

20   The Iran-U.S. Claims Tribunal has held that the showing of slides at the hearing by the Iranian party to explain and clarify earlier submitted evidence was not objectionable as long as it did not constitute new evidence submitted out of time. Oil Field of Texas, Inc. v. Iran, 12 IRAN-U.S. C.T.R. 308 (1986) (in the event, the issue of whether the slides constituted new evidence was not determined since the Tribunal did not rely on them).

In court proceedings under common-law rules, it is assumed that the court is substantially uninformed of the nature of the case prior to the hearing. It is thus usual for claimant's counsel to make an opening statement or speech prior to the presentation of its case, indicating the main argument of the case and what the testimony will prove. Then comes the presentation of each side's case, which may take a very long time. Counsel for respondent generally introduces respondent's evidence by an opening statement as well. At the close of all evidence, the respondent would be entitled to make a closing statement, following which the claimant is granted the "last word."

While this procedure is current not only in common-law court proceedings but also in English arbitral practice,[21] it should be modified in ICC arbitration. Although the ICC Rules provide no guidance as to the order of proceedings, it should be remembered that in ICC arbitrations memoranda will have been exchanged prior to the hearing and the arbitrators will already have read the documentary evidence submitted by the parties. Accordingly, opening statements by the parties (except for a brief introduction of witnesses) tend to be limited if not eliminated completely.

The tendency in ICC arbitration is to hear symmetrical presentation of argument, each party having the right to reply to pleas made by the other. Thus the respondent on each claim or counterclaim would tend to argue last. Nevertheless, ICC arbitrators sometimes vary this order by allowing the party having the burden of proof on a claim or counterclaim to have the last word in the form of brief rebuttal.

Oral argument in ICC arbitration generally commences after the end of all oral testimony (if there is any). The tribunal should obtain fairly firm commitments as to how much time each counsel will require. Even in large arbitrations, each side should be able to sum up in one day, or perhaps even in half a day. Counsel typically comment on the major items of documentary and testimonial evidence, and may illustrate arguments with charts, graphs, or other visual aids. It is in final argument that each side's theory of the case must be demonstrated and distilled, in some cases from a mass of evidence reflected in thousands of pages and representing long months of effort.

The following is a theoretical order of oral argument in a "model" ICC arbitration:

i) A presents the claim;

ii) B presents the defense and counterclaim (if any);

iii) A presents the defense to the counterclaim and rebuts the defense to the claim;

iv) B rebuts the defense to the counterclaim.

---

21 Michael Mustill and Stewart Boyd, COMMERCIAL ARBITRATION 346 (2d ed., 1989).

There may follow further rejoinders or surrebuttals as determined by the tribunal, always preserving the equality of the parties according to the bilateral procedures set forth above.

The above order of argument is illustrative and suggests a degree of formality rarely present in ICC arbitration. Ordinarily, the parties have no difficulty in agreeing with the arbitral tribunal on a rational order of argument and allocation of time between the parties.

25.06   Closing the proceedings

Until 1998 the Rules made no specific provision for the arbitrators to announce a formal closing of the proceedings (although nothing prevented them from so doing). The failure to establish formally when the proceedings were closed led in a number of cases to confusion, delay, and sometimes to claims of unfairness. Following a hearing, one party would insist on filing complementary evidence or argument, sometimes repetitively. The other party would insist on the right to reply, sometimes wishing to introduce new evidence as well. The tribunal, not wanting to give any cause for a complaint that the party had not been able to fully present its case, all too frequently acceded to the submission of such new evidence and argument with ensuing complications flowing from a right to response and the difficulty in determining how to bring the whole process to an end.

Article 22(1) of the Rules now provides:

> When it is satisfied that the parties have had a reasonable opportunity to present their case, the Arbitral Tribunal shall declare the proceedings closed. Thereafter, no further submission or argument may be made, or evidence produced, unless requested or authorized by the Arbitral Tribunal.

By setting out the "closing of the proceedings" as a mandatory decision to be made by the arbitral tribunal, the Rules attempt to impose some rigor in the post-hearing calendar for arbitral proceedings. Note the distinction to be drawn between "closing the hearings" and "closing the proceedings". Normally at the end of the oral hearings in the matter the arbitral tribunal will close the hearings, meaning that there are not more witnesses to be heard or oral argument to be expressed. Post-hearing procedural steps may remain to be accomplished which the tribunal will define by procedural order. There may be an exchange of post-hearing memorials, or the arbitrators may request the furnishing of a specific exhibit, or translation of a document or some such measure. Typically, statements of cost are more readily prepared at some short time after the hearings.

When the tribunal has decided that all such measures have been taken (and ruled, if necessary, on a party's demand that still further argument or evidence production be permitted) the time is ripe for it to enter an order declaring the proceedings closed. Before doing so the tribunal will satisfy itself that the parties have had a "reasonable opportunity" to present their cases.[22]

Article 22(1) does not require the tribunal to give notice to the parties of its intention to close the proceedings at some future date. Where post-hearing briefs are not considered necessary or appropriate the tribunal could very well, at the close of the hearing, declare the proceedings closed.

After the closure of the proceedings, nothing prevents the tribunal from asking a party to furnish a further document or information. However, a party may not provide further documents, information or argument without having been previously authorized by the tribunal. The tribunal should not authorize the reopening of the proceeding except for good cause.

After closing of the proceeding the tribunal will deliberate and then submit its draft award to the Court of Arbitration for this body's scrutiny of the award as provided in Article 27 of the Rules. At the time of closing the proceeding the tribunal must inform the Secretariat of the date upon which it expects to submit its draft award.[23]

---

22 The "reasonable opportunity" of Article 22(1) of the Rules reflects Article 15(2), also added in 1998, which provides: "In all cases, the arbitral tribunal shall act fairly and impartially and ensure that each party has a reasonable opportunity to present its case." The drafters of the revision made a conscious choice to use the terms "reasonable opportunity" rather than the term "full opportunity" as found in Article 15 of the UNCITRAL Arbitration Rules. A disappointed party may always believe that it should have still another opportunity to present its case, bring in new evidence, or reargue its case. The tribunal has full discretion to determine what is reasonable in the circumstances.

23 Article 22(2) of the Rules provides:

When the Arbitral Tribunal has declared the proceedings closed, it shall indicate to the Secretariat an approximate date by which the draft Award will be submitted to the Court for approval pursuant to Article 27. Any postponement of that date shall be communicated to the Secretariat by the Arbitral Tribunal.

This was another measure added in 1998 with the intent to expedite arbitral proceedings and to give more control (or at least information) by the Court and its Secretariat of the calendar of the proceeding.

CHAPTER 26

FACT FINDING AND INTERLOCUTORY MEASURES ORDERED BY ARBITRATORS

26.01 Production of documents

Arbitrators may order production of documents which are in the hands of a party or under its control. This authority is implicit in the arbitrator's mandate under Article 20(1) of the ICC Rules to establish the facts "by all appropriate means." ICC arbitrators, whether of civil law or common law persuasion, have, in the past, relied on this general rule to authorize them to order document discovery even though the Rules contained no express provision for discovery.[1]

Arbitrators' orders for the production of documents in ICC arbitration have nevertheless surprised parties on occasion, given that the custom in international arbitration has traditionally been for each side simply to present the documents and witnesses it relies on. To avoid any such misunderstanding, Article 20(5) was added to the 1998 Rules providing:

> At any time during the proceedings, the Arbitral Tribunal may summon any party to provide additional evidence.

---

1 *See e.g.*, discovery order in ICC Case 5542/1987, reported *in* ICC PROCEDURAL DECISIONS, 62-65, where arbitrators with civil law backgrounds acting in a dispute under a contract governed by Ethiopian law ordered production of specified documents but refused claimant's request for a general inspection of respondent's file. *See also*, ICC Case 6401/1991, ICC PROCEDURAL DECISIONS 192 for a procedural order setting out the circumstances in which a tribunal conducting an arbitration in Switzerland will request the assistance of Swiss courts to obtain discovery of documents in the possession of third parties. For an American case where New York courts refused to intervene in the arbitrator's decision to order discovery under inherent authority under the 1975 ICC Rules *see Mobil Oil v. Asamera*, 56 Appellate Division 2d 339; 392 N.Y.S. 2d 614 (1977); *rev'd* on other grounds 213 N.Y. 2d 276; 372 N.E. 2d 21 (1977).

With this provision the ICC joins the majority of international arbitral institutions which give arbitral tribunals the power to call on the parties to produce documents and witnesses, supply explanations, and provide experts.[2] Article 20(5) also responds to the increasing number of demands for discovery by ICC arbitration users and the more frequent use and normalization of the discovery process by ICC arbitral tribunals.[3] The power of ICC arbitral tribunals to order discovery is thus confirmed. This does not mean that a party has a *right* to document discovery or other discovery measures. The arbitral tribunal has discretion whether to require discovery and to what degree.

When issued by ICC arbitrators, orders for document discovery are generally rather limited in scope; the documents sought are identified with specificity and the reasons why their production is required are given. A typical case for ordering the production of documents is where the claimant seeks recovery of licence fees or royalties and the respondent-licensee refuses to give the licensor information regarding sales. Other instances may include possession of technical documents prepared in the execution of the contract, particularly where communication of such reports was a contractual obligation of the party against whom the order of discovery is sought.

ICC arbitrators typically decline to issue broad orders of discovery that would open the doors to "fishing expeditions" in which parties seek, pursuant to a general production order, to obtain documents favorable to their cause from which they can make out a case.[4] As previously noted, this reticence is also explained by the fact that ICC arbitrators have no power under the Rules to sanction a party for failure to comply.[5] A party which refuses to comply with an order, however, should be advised that the arbitrators are likely to conclude that the document in question is unfavorable to that party.[6] Other infer-

---

2   *See e.g.*, AAA International Rules (1997), Article 19; LCIA Rules (1998) Article 22; UNCITRAL Rules (1976), Article 24; ICSID Rules (1984), Rule 34(2).

3   Sigvard Jarvin, *Aspects of the Arbitral Proceedings*, ICC BULL. 38, 40 (Supplement 1997).

4   There are cases, however, where broad production orders are justified. In one ICC arbitration held in Switzerland, involving hundreds of millions of U.S. dollars, the arbitrators, relying on the Rules and the claim by one of the parties that it had a contractual right as a joint venture partner to examine the documents in the hands of the other partner, issued an order of production which had the result of permitting the requesting party to examine 18,000 pages of documents, of which it requested the copying for its use of some 5,000 pages. In another ICC arbitration involving responsibility for the failure of a plant to achieve the contractual production goal, the parties' agreement to produce documents corresponding to categories described in requests (and subject, if required, to confirming orders by the tribunal) resulted in the production on each side of a roomfull of documents.

5   The powers of courts under national law to order compliance with an arbitral tribunal's direction is taken up in Chapter 27.

6   For a case where the arbitrator warned the parties that a failure of a party to produce requested documents might result in drawing an inference adverse to that party, *see* ICC Case No. 8694/1996, 1997 JDI 1056, Note Y. Derains. *See also* ICC case 6497/1994, XXIVa YEARBOOK 71, 75-79 (1999) involving a claim for payment of services provided under a product agreement; re-

ences may also be drawn. To revert to the example of a royalty dispute, where the licensor has failed to produce the information regarding sales which were the subject of a discovery order, the tribunal may accept a presumption that sales continued at the same rate, at the rate of industry growth, or in conformity with other figures produced by the adversary. The effect of the possibility to draw adverse inferences is not without limit, however. There must be a logical nexus between the probable nature of the documents withheld and the inference derived therefrom. The arbitrators are not entitled to punish a recalcitrant party for poor procedural behavior by making adverse substantive findings in the award based only on such conduct.[7] In practice, parties almost always comply with arbitrators' production orders as they prefer not to antagonize the tribunal.[8]

Of course, the parties may agree either in the agreement to arbitrate, in the Terms of Reference, or elsewhere, to produce documents for examination and copying by the other party (*see* Sections 8.09 and 15.02). Thus, when one of the parties fails to respect its agreement, the arbitrators' authority to make an order for production is considerably reinforced by such a stipulation.

In deciding whether to grant an order for production, arbitrators may, in addition to relying on Article 20(5) of the Rules, consult the procedural law in effect at the seat of arbitration. The provisions of that law may apply directly if the arbitrators have determined under Article 15(1) that the national procedural law of the place of arbitration should apply or where the law of the seat considers them to be of mandatory application. They may apply indirectly and by analogy even when such a determination has not been made. Some

---

spondent argued that the services provided under the agreement consisted of bribing government officials, thereby rendering the agreement unenforceable under applicable Swiss law. The arbitral tribunal drew negative inferences from the claimant's refusal to allow an independent expert to examine records of payments to subcontractors. In light of the claimant's refusal, prior deception to the tribunal, and an unusually high commission awarded under the product agreement for unspecified "extraordinary services," the tribunal accepted the respondent's characterization of the contract, supported by the inference to be drawn from claimant's refusal to produce evidence, and rejected the claim for payment.

7   *See* Michael Mustill, *Commentary* in CONSERVATORY AND PROVISIONAL MEASURES IN INTERNATIONAL ARBITRATION 12 (ICC Publication No. 519, 1993)· "I must note a suggestion that arbitrators can compel obedience by making it clear that disobedience may have an adverse effect on the ultimate award. I must respectfully demur. If the merits are such that a party is entitled to win, then it is the arbitrator's duty to decide in his favour however recalcitrant he may have been during the arbitration."

8   An exception may exist in "political" cases where a State or a State agency resists a production order on the grounds of interference with its unlimited sovereignty (to which the reasonable answer, of course, is that routine commercial transactions are not sovereign acts). Requests made of Iranian companies and agencies to produce documents for use by the Iran-U.S. Claims Tribunal have seldom been successful. *See e.g.* INA Corporation v. Iran, 8 IRAN-U.S. C.T.R. 373, 382 (1985) (negative inference drawn from failure to produce).

national procedural laws give direct power to arbitrators to order production of documents.[9]

In the United States under the Federal Arbitration Act, and under New York State procedural law, arbitrators have the power to issue subpoenas and order production of documents.[10] Such powers are also reflected in some other states' procedural laws (*see* Section 25.01). In England, the same practice of discovery by list or "bundle" that is applicable in court proceedings is frequently also employed in arbitration. The issue of whether discovery shall be ordered and, if so, how much, remains within the power of the tribunal. The Arbitration Act of 1996 provides in Sec. 40(2)(d) that by signing an arbitration clause, the parties are deemed to have accepted to: "comply without delay with any determination of the tribunal as to procedural or evidential matters, or with any order or directions of tribunal . . . ." and that judges may sanction refusal by a party to comply with an arbitrator's order.

Quite apart from the question of whether the arbitrator has the power to order production of documents is the issue of whether to do so. Even where the arbitration takes place in a country whose arbitration law specifically empowers an arbitrator to order discovery similar to that permitted in court litigation, of every document in the possession or control of a party which has any bearing on the issues in the action, an arbitrator will almost never do so.[11] Arbitration is inherently a consensual process. The arbitrator should take into account that many parties to arbitration agreements (particularly, but not limited to, those from civil-law countries) would be shocked to learn that their agreement could have the effect of imposing on them a general obligation to disclose all relevant documents and indeed internal communications which would not be subject to disclosure under their own domestic laws.[12] Moreover, even in jurisdictions like the United States which provide the broadest scope of discovery in civil proceedings (depositions, document production, interrogatories, demand for admissions, etc.) the courts have

---

9   Article 1460 of the French New Code of Civil Procedure (NCPC) provides: "If a party is in possession of evidence, the arbitrator may also order him to produce it." The article applies to international arbitrations taking place in France, however, only if the parties have agreed to the application of French procedural law.

10   *See generally*, Gary Born, INTERNATIONAL COMMERCIAL ARBITRATION IN THE UNITED STATES 825-861 (Kluwer 1994) (Chapter 9, *Discovery and Disclosure in International Arbitration*).

11   "[T]he arbitrator should use discrimination in the employment of his power to order discovery. He should not feel that he is obliged to make any order for discovery at all, still less a full order. Conversely, he should not reject an order for discovery out of hand, simply because he regards it as legalistic and unfitted for the resolution of commercial disputes." Michael Mustill & Stewart Boyd, COMMERCIAL ARBITRATION 325 (2d ed., 1989); *see also* Croal, *Misconceptions about Discovery in English Arbitration*, 51 *Arbitration* 532 (1985).

12   "[M]any foreigners view with incredulity a system which requires them to produce (for example) documents passing within their own organization which were never intended for general distribution, and they point out with justice that the possibility of disclosure must serve to inhibit their freedom to express themselves frankly in writing." Mustill and Boyd, *supra* Note 11 at 325.

routinely upheld the right of arbitrators not to order any discovery whatsoever: if the parties had wanted to insist on the full panoply of procedures available at law they should not have decided on arbitration.[13]

In such an atmosphere, the arbitrator is bound to take into consideration the problem of non-compliance, or of compliance by only one of the parties, leading to a basic imbalance in the proceedings. Ordinarily, the arbitrator will find that the needs of arbitral justice will best be served by clearly drafted "rifle shot" discovery orders aimed at specified documents, or classes of documents, and that the "buck shot" approach is to be avoided.

The limited and discretionary power of arbitrator ordered discovery is seen as a compromise between common law and civil law proceedings. An example of this compromise is found in the International Bar Association's 1999 Rules of Evidence designed as supplementary rules which may be adopted in whole or in part by the parties for use in arbitral proceedings. The provisions for the request of document production is much more limited than would be found in judicial proceedings in common law jurisdictions:

Article 3—Documents . . .

3. A Request to Produce shall contain:

(a) (i) a description of a requested document sufficient to identify it, or (ii) a description in sufficient detail (including subject matter) of a narrow and specific requested category of documents that are reasonably believed to exist; (b) a description of how the documents requested are relevant and material to the outcome of the case; and (c) a statement that the documents requested are not in the possession, custody or control of the requesting Party, and of the reason why that Party assumes the documents requested to be in the possession, custody or control of the other Party.

. . .

6. The Arbitral Tribunal shall, in consultation with the Parties and in timely fashion, consider the Request to Produce and the objections. The Arbitral Tribunal may order the Party to whom such Request is addressed to produce to the Arbitral Tribunal and to the other Parties those requested

---

13   National courts have repeatedly held that discretionary decisions by arbitrators limiting or refusing requests for discovery do not constitute a ground for challenging an award. In England, *see,* Anangel Peace Compania Naviera S.A. v. Bacchus International, [1981] 1 LLOYD'S L. REP. 452 (Q.B. Div. (1980)). In France, I *Cour d'appel,* Paris, 21 January 1997, Société Nu Swift PLC v. Société White Knight et autres, 1997 REV. ARB. 429, note Y. Derains. In the United States, *see, e.g.,* Hyman v. Pottberg's Executors, 101 F. 2d 262 (2d Cir. 1939); Iron Ore Company of Canada v. Argonaut Shipping, Inc., XII YEARBOOK 173 (S.D.N.Y. 1985); Eddie S.S. Co. Ltd v. Czarnikow-Rionda Co., 480 F. Supp. 731 (S.D.N.Y. 1979); Standard Tankers (Bahamas) Co. v. Motor Tank Vessel, AKTI, 438 F. Supp. 153 (E.D.N.C. 1977); *but see* Chevron Transp. Corp. v. Astro Vencedor Compania Naviera, S.A., 300 F. Supp. 179 (S.D.N.Y. 1969).

documents in its possession, custody or control as to which the Arbitral Tribunal determines that (i) the issues that the requesting Party wishes to prove are relevant and material to the outcome of the case, and (ii) none of the reasons for objection set forth in Article 9.2 apply.

Despite the limitations to discovery set forth by the IBA Rules, the changes found in the 1999 version illustrate the increasing acceptance of more liberal discovery practices among practitioners of international arbitration. In 1983, when the IBA adopted the first version of the Rules, consensus did not extend further than to agree that international arbitrators could order a party to produce documents which "passed to or from such other party from or to a third party who is not a party to the arbitration."[14] In other words, purely *internal* documents were not susceptible to orders for production.

This limitation reflected a great reluctance on the part of civil law lawyers to accept a discovery practice which in their view would leave the international arbitral process on a slippery slope leading towards the excesses of Anglo-American discovery practices. In the intervening years, practitioners have seen that it is possible to control the process without allowing parties who are in sole possession of clearly relevant evidence to hide behind the "no internal documents" limitation.

Thus the 1999 IBA Rules of Evidence—which of course are consensual—authorize arbitrators to order the production of documents even if they were internally generated by a party, subject only to limitations defined in Article 3.6:

(i) the issues that the requesting Party wishes to prove are relevant and material to the outcome of the case, and

(ii) none of the reasons for objection set forth in Article 9.2 apply.

The "reasons for objection" of Article 9.2 are: lack of sufficient relevance or materiality, legal impediment or privilege, unreasonableness, loss or destruction of the document, confidentiality, compelling "political or institutional sensitivity," or compelling considerations of fairness. (The concept of "political or institutional sensitivity" was introduced after expressions of considerable concern from international organizations like the United Nations which were worried that extraordinarily sensitive documents might not qualify as *confidential* in the ordinary sense referring only to commercial or technical secrets.)

The IBA Rules also illustrate the slight relaxing of the specificity requirement in discovery requests. The 1999 revision accepted that requests could pertain to a "narrow and specific category of documents that are reasonably believed to exist" (Article 3.3(a)(ii)) whereas the 1983 Rules of Evidence contemplated only *individual documents*. There is no doubt that this was the most-debated

---

14   *See* David Shenton, *An Introduction to the IBA Rules of Evidence*, 1 ARB. INT. 118 (1985).

provision of the 1999 revision; it was illuminated by this explanation of the IBA Working Party:

> The description of an individual document is reasonably straightforward. The IBA Rules of Evidence simply require that the description be 'sufficient to identify' the document.
>
> Permitting parties to ask for documents by category, however, prompted more discussion. The Working Party did not want to open the door to 'fishing expeditions'. However, the Working Party understood that some documents would be relevant and material and properly produced to the other side, but they may not be capable of specific identification. Indeed, all members of the Working Party, from common law and civil law countries alike, recognized that arbitrators would generally accept such requests if they were carefully tailored to produce relevant documents. For example, if an arbitration involves the termination by one party of a joint venture agreement, the other party may know that the notice of the termination was given on a certain date, that the Board of the other party must have made the decision to terminate at a meeting shortly before that notice, that certain documents must have been prepared for the Board's consideration of that decision. The requesting party cannot identify the dates or the authors of such documents, but nevertheless can identify with some particularity the nature of the documents sought and the general time frame in which they would have been prepared. Such a request may qualify as a "narrow and specific category of documents," as permitted under Article 3.3(a)(ii).[15]

Another important comment made by the Working Party was this: "Because of the specificity required in the Request to Produce, it is likely that such a request will be made only after the issues have become sufficiently clear in the case."[16] While the importance of not allowing parties to disrupt the proceedings by trawling for "evidence" of irresponsible claims is fundamental, considerable professionalism and authority will be required of arbitrators to ensure that the proceedings are not derailed at a late stage by a party which argues that it was not previously in a position to see the real issues with sufficient clarity.

While the specific provision of the IBA Rules only apply directly where the parties have agreed (as a provision in the arbitration clause or elsewhere) to this procedure, they may be expected to have normative consequences as well.

---

15   *Commentary on the New IBA Rules of Evidence in International Commercial Arbitration*, BUSINESS LAW INTERNATIONAL (IBA publication, January 2000) 14, at 20.

16   *Id.* at 21.

Whether or not one accepts that the IBA Rules of Evidence have successfully encapsulated a workable international consensus, the fact remains that it has become a critical function of ICC arbitrators to deal with requests to order the production of documents.

Parties should be aware of the practical limitations on the arbitrator's power to order the production of documents or other evidence. In the first place, the ICC Rules do not provide any authority for an arbitrator to make any order of production involving a third party. Any such request would necessarily be based on statutory provision of national law and for enforcement require the intervention of a State court, and even there recourse may be limited.[17] In the second place, even in respect to the parties, the arbitrator has no real power of enforcement and thus the arbitrator's order may be disobeyed, or at least only half-heartedly obeyed, without fear of sanction. The power of the arbitrator to "draw adverse inferences" from non-production has substantial limitations. In some cases, as described earlier, it may be possible to conclude from the nature of the document requested what it must have revealed. In others, this is not the case. Where a party has not been able to sustain its claim, and the documents necessary to make out its cause of action are allegedly in the other party's possession, the failure of that party to produce, and the adverse inference drawn from it, is insufficient to sustain a claim or defense for which no evidence of record exists.[18] In other words, the "adverse inference" remedy may not be wholly sufficient.

This being said, the limitations on the arbitrator's powers may in most circumstances only be a theoretical drawback. Most parties will not want to displease the arbitral tribunal which has the full, and mostly unreviewable, power to decide all issues on the merits of the claims before it. Moreover, in the case of a refusal the arbitrator may not have to rely on the "adverse inferences" remedy and its limitations. The arbitrator's underlying appreciation of how the case should be decided—the arbitrator's *intime conviction*—may be fundamentally influenced by the obstinate party's conduct even if this never enters into the rationale given in the arbitrator's award.

---

17   *See* Chapter 27.

18   For statutory treatment of what an arbitrator is entitled to conclude from a party's non-production of evidence, *see* Arbitration Act 1996 (England), Article 41 (7):

> (7) If a party fails to comply with any other kind of peremptory order, then, without prejudice to section 42 (enforcement by court of tribunal's peremptory orders), the tribunal may do any of the following:-
>
>> (a) direct that the party in default shall not be entitled to rely upon any allegation or material which was the subject matter of the order;
>>
>> (b) draw such adverse inferences from the act of non-compliance as the circumstances justify;
>>
>> (c) proceed to an award on the basis of such materials as have been properly provided to it;
>>
>> (d) make such order as it thinks fit as to the payment of costs of the arbitration incurred in consequence of the non-compliance.

26.02 Depositions

A deposition is a written record of oral testimony given prior to hearing and without the presence of the tribunal. Both parties are represented at the taking of the deposition to examine and cross-examine the witness. The written record may be filed in the proceeding.

As a means of presenting testimony outside hearings and thus limiting their length, the deposition process is potentially of great interest in international arbitrations since the tribunal is generally unable to stay in session for weeks or months at a time. Furthermore, witnesses are often located throughout the world. The difficulty of assembling them all at one time to testify before the arbitrators may raise insurmountable problems of scheduling, not to mention great costs.

Parties occasionally agree to reciprocal depositions in ICC arbitration.[19] In a complex case, the parties may recognize that the submission of documents, including experts' reports, will not allow the parties to explore the witnesses' contributions to the degree desired. Yet it may be equally clear that it would be impractical to produce all the relevant witnesses at a distant place of arbitration. Accordingly, it may be agreed that each party has the right to depose witnesses, whether friendly or hostile. A stenographic record of their statements is filed in the arbitration and serves as the basis for comment in briefs and memoranda.

If the parties do not agree, can and should ICC arbitrators compel pre-trial testimony? In the absence of a specific statutory provision empowering them to compel testimony, arbitrators are generally extremely reluctant to order a party to depose in advance of hearing and the authors are not aware of instances where ICC arbitrators have ordered depositions over the objection of a party. The addition of Article 20(5) to the Rules in 1998, allowing the tribunal to request additional evidence "at any time during the proceedings," is not expected to bring about an appreciable change. The conduct of depositions

---

19 Several American practitioners insist that the right to take depositions should be routinely included in the Terms of Reference. S. Goekjian, *ICC Arbitration from a Practitioner's Perspective*, 14 JOURNAL OF INTERNATIONAL LAW AND ECONOMICS 407, at 421 (1980); A. McClelland, *International Arbitration: A Practical Guide for the Effective Use of the System for Litigation of Transnational Commercial Disputes*, 12 INTERNATIONAL LAWYER 83, at 91 (1978). According to Goekjian, *op. cit.*, "a practice has developed of providing in the Terms of Reference that witness testimony and cross-examination will be taken by depositions outside the presence of the Tribunal and that the depositions will be submitted to the Tribunal as part of the documentary evidence." In the authors' experience, such practice is rare. Counsel from non-common-law countries are very reluctant to agree to such a procedure at the early date of the Terms of Reference. However, if it becomes apparent upon the fixing of hearing dates that some of the witnesses will not be able to testify in person, and if the adverse party opposes the admission of written statements or affidavits without the right of cross-examination, a deposition procedure agreed by the parties or ordered by the Tribunal may solve many problems. If this can be agreed in the Terms of Reference, so much the better; it rarely happens that way.

outside the presence of the tribunal poses far more problems of control than does the production of documents. Furthermore, the tribunal has no legal power to compel testimony of third party witnesses. Accordingly, in the absence of agreement by the parties, or a court order requiring the preservation of testimony in support of the arbitration, it is unlikely, that an ICC arbitral tribunal will compel pre-hearing deposition of a witness.

26.03   Site visit

If necessary, arbitrators should be prepared to visit the site of operations to familiarize themselves with the technical issues and physical landscape of the dispute, particularly when disputes involve construction projects or the operation of industrial plants. Ordinarily, a site visit is initiated by the request of at least one of the parties.

The visit should be properly arranged so as to avoid *ex parte* communications with the arbitrators. Counsel and party representatives for both sides should be present throughout.

The site is likely to be under the control of one of the parties, whose employees will be present in various technical capacities. In the presence of a representative of the other party, the arbitrators may question such persons in connection with construction equipment, machines, or processes being observed. It should always be remembered, however, that remarks in this context are not testimony delivered in the controlled conditions of hearings and subject to cross-examination. Therefore, such statements should not be considered as direct evidence in the proceedings.

26.04   Experts appointed by the tribunal

The issue in major arbitrations is not usually whether there should be party experts or tribunal experts, but whether there should be tribunal experts *in addition to* party experts.

Parties sometimes oppose the appointment of tribunal experts. Having constituted an arbitral tribunal whose members they believe to be competent to comprehend and decide the issues in dispute, they do not wish to see an unknown expert take a predominant role in the decision-making process. Indeed, there is a fearful spectre of the "run-away expert" who, instead of giving precise and neutral answers to technical questions, makes value judgments and renders opinions on the ultimate issue in dispute. Concern also arises in some cases that the expert may add unnecessary cost to the arbitration which may be resented by the parties as a cost added by decision of the tribunal rather than arising from the independent decision of each party.

On the other hand, the arbitrators may be confused by contradictory evidence and opinions given by the parties' experts. They may wish to have recourse to a neutral expert who will be responsible to them and available to supply technical information and evaluation. The ICC Rules explicitly give the arbitrators the power to appoint neutral experts. Article 20(4) provides:

> The Arbitral Tribunal, after having consulted the parties, may appoint one or more experts, define their terms of reference and receive their reports. At the request of a party, the parties shall be given the opportunity to question at a hearing any such expert appointed by the Tribunal.

An arbitrator's refusal to appoint an expert is not a basis for challenging an award.[20]

The tribunal may appoint an expert known to the arbitrators, may seek to have an expert appointed under the ICC Rules for Technical Expertise (*see* Section 38.02), or may solicit the views of the parties as to the identity of a neutral expert. As with most procedural issues in ICC arbitration, it is desirable to obtain the agreement of the parties if possible. In some cases, the tribunal submits a list of experts to the parties and asks whether any experts are unacceptable to either party. If this approach works, the tribunal may then choose an expert acceptable to both sides. In other cases, the tribunal will solicit a list of experts from the parties and try to choose a mutually recommended candidate.

By careful drafting of the specific written instructions given to the expert (referred to in Article 20(4) as the experts' "terms of reference"), it is possible to preserve both the arbitrators' interest in having a neutral expert and that of a party who opposes the delegation of any decision-making function to a tribunal-appointed expert.[21] The observations of the parties should be solicited even though the power of the tribunal to make an appointment is not conditioned upon obtaining their agreement.

Any procedure established for an expert should reserve the parties' right to comment on the expert's report and to supply contradictory evidence.[22] The most common method is for the tribunal to prepare specific questions for the neutral expert who will be requested to respond on the basis of the evidence in the record and on the expert's own professional knowledge and experience. The written expertise then becomes an evidentiary document in the arbitration and the parties are free to argue the points and conclusions therein.

In addition to—or in lieu of—preparing written reports, neutral experts may be asked to attend the hearing, listen to the technical testimony of witnesses

---

20 PepsiCo, Inc v. Iran, 13 IRAN-U.S. C.T.R. 3, 17 (1986) (refusal to appoint expert); Arenco-BMD Maschinenfabrik GmbH v. Societa Ceramica Italiana Pozzi-Richard Ginori S.p.A., Court of Appeal of Milan (1984) XI YEARBOOK 511 (refusal to appoint expert did not invalidate award).

21 For examples of terms of reference for experts established in ICC arbitration, *see* ICC Case No. 6057, Procedural Order made in 1990, 1993 JDI 1068; ICC Case No. 5715, Procedural Order made in 1989, 1996 JDI 1050.

22 *See* J.F. Poudret, *Expertise et droit d'être entendu dans l'arbitrage international* in ETUDES DE DROIT INTERNATIONAL EN L'HONNEUR DE PIERRE LALIVE 608 (Bâle, 1993).

and party experts, and be available to answer questions of the tribunal. Such questions, however, should be asked during the hearing in the presence of the parties so that the parties will be in a position to comment on the answers.

In no case should the neutral expert(s) participate in the deliberation of the arbitrators on the merits of the case. The involvement of a fourth (or second) "arbitrator" would alter the fundamental nature of the arbitral process agreed by the parties and may be grounds for challenging the award.

26.05   Interim measures and other interlocutory relief ordered by arbitrators

i) Powers of the tribunal

ICC arbitrators have the inherent power to make interlocutory orders relevant to the arbitration and addressed to the parties.[23] Their authority does not extend to giving directions to third parties, nor do their orders to the parties have binding force. As with other orders by the tribunal, disobedience of an interlocutory order carries with it no immediate legal sanction for the recalcitrant party. In the absence of a particular provision of national law,[24] the courts at the seat of arbitration ordinarily are also not empowered to sanction non-compliance with arbitrators' interlocutory orders. Compliance is thus in a sense voluntary. Nevertheless, parties almost always comply with interlocutory orders of the arbitral tribunal since failure to do so is likely to be interpreted as an act of bad faith and influence the decision on the merits.

Interim measures are temporary in nature, limited in time by the length of the arbitration proceedings themselves, and limited as well by the scope of the underlying dispute. Interim measures are said to cover:

> those that have to do with the discovery, preservation and production of evidence concerning the dispute;

> those that have to do with preserving the subject matter of the dispute and avoiding prejudice to the rights of the parties during the pendency of the proceedings, and

> those that are destined to permit the effective execution of the award.

Together these powers might be called investigatory, preservatory (of the status quo) and conservatory (of the award to be rendered).

---

23   This power may also be buttressed by specific agreement by the parties giving interim measure powers to the arbitrators. *See* Section 8.07.

24   For instance, Article 183 of the 1987 Swiss Private International Law Act provides that arbitral tribunals have power "to order provisional or conservatory measures and request assistance of the courts if a party does not comply." Under Section 42 of the English Arbitration Act 1996 the High Court may make an order requiring a party to comply with a peremptory order made by the tribunal. An application to the court may be made by the arbitral tribunal or by a party with the agreement of the tribunal.

The tribunal's investigatory powers, which may be the basis of specific orders addressed to the parties and hence can also be considered as interim measures, have an independent basis. They are contained within the tribunal's general power under Article 20(1) of the Rules. The exercise of these powers is treated generally in Sections 26.01-26.04.

Prior to 1998 the ICC Rules did not contain a specific grant of authority to arbitral tribunals to grant interim and provisional measures. However ICC arbitral tribunals had consistently found an implied grant of such powers[25] from the provisions of Article 8(5) of the prior Rules which authorized parties to seek interim or conservatory measures from a national court but only, in the absence of exceptional circumstances, before the file was transmitted to the arbitrators.[26]

It remained, however, anomalous that the ICC Rules did not make specific provision for the grant of interim measures by its arbitrators as was the case with rules of other arbitration institutes. This is remedied by Article 23(1) of the 1998 Rules, which provides:

> Unless the parties have otherwise agreed, as soon as the file has been transmitted to it, the Arbitral Tribunal may, at the request of a party, order any interim or conservatory measure it deems appropriate. The Arbitral Tribunal may make the granting of any such measure subject to appropriate security being furnished by the requesting party. Any such measure shall take the form of an order, giving reasons, or of an Award, as the Arbitral Tribunal considers appropriate.

In addition to providing a direct and positive power to the arbitrators to order interim and conservatory measures, Article 23(1) also clarifies several issues which had not been entirely clear in prior practice: i) the arbitral tribunal may act as soon as the file has been transmitted to it (it need not wait, as had sometimes been contended, for the Terms of Reference to enter into effect); ii) the tribunal is empowered to condition its making of an interim order in favor of an applicant on the posting of security by that party to remedy any damage that may be caused to respondent if it is ultimately determined that

---

25   *See e.g.* the unpublished ICC award referred to in Eric Schwartz, *The Practices and Experiences of the ICC Court*, in CONSERVATORY AND PROVISIONAL MEASURES IN INTERNATIONAL ARBITRATION 45, 55 (ICC Publication No. 519, 1993) where the tribunal relied on Section 26.05 in a prior edition of this work for the proposition that "ICC arbitrators have the inherent power to make interlocutory orders relevant to the arbitration and addressed to the parties."

26   Article 8(5) of the 1975 Rules provided: *Before the file is transmitted to the arbitrator, and in exceptional circumstances even thereafter, the parties shall be at liberty to apply to any competent judicial authority for interim or conservatory measures, and they shall not by so doing be held to infringe the agreement to arbitrate or to affect the relevant powers reserved to the arbitrators..."* With some modifications this text is now found in Article 23(2) and is discussed in Chapter 27. The most important modification is that the new provision authorizes a party to apply to a national court in "appropriate" rather than "exceptional" circumstances.

the applicant is not entitled to relief; iii) the tribunal's decision may be made in the form of an order, giving reasons, or an award.

The arbitrator's powers to grant interlocutory relief should be seen as complementary to and independent of the powers of a court to grant interim or conservatory measures at the request of a party made, in compliance with Article 23(2) of the Rules, "before the file is transmitted to the Arbitral Tribunal, and in appropriate circumstances even thereafter."[27] The text of Article 23(2) of the Rules confirms the inherent powers of the arbitrator since it provides that any application to a court for interim relief will not "be deemed to be an infringement or a waiver of the arbitration agreement and shall not affect the relevant powers reserved to the Arbitral Tribunal."[28]

ii) Examples of interim measures

Interlocutory orders are usually intended to give all parties equal opportunity to present their cases to the tribunal, to preserve the status quo, or to permit other reasonable measures relating to performance under the contract pending final resolution of the dispute. The first category may be illustrated by an order directed to one party to permit its adversary to inspect goods, merchandise, or equipment within the former party's control. Absent such an order, the party without access to the disputed article may not be able to present substantial proof of its version of the facts. If the party in possession refuses to comply with the tribunal's order, the arbitrators would surely be justified in drawing adverse inferences and accepting as correct the facts alleged by the party denied the right of access.

Action to preserve the status quo is a more delicate matter. An order by a tribunal to a party to refrain from exercising an alleged contractual right prior to a final decision on the merits may prejudice that party. For example, if a party is ordered not to exercise its claimed right to end a contract and if the award ultimately confirms that it had the right to terminate at an earlier date, prejudice may have been caused by having prevented such party from immediately negotiating another contract. In appropriate cases, however, ICC tribunals may give such an order on the condition that the corresponding performance of the other party is likewise respected, particularly if such performance involves the payment of money, or by advancing security.

Arbitrators have an obligation to try to find an equitable and commercially practicable procedural solution to prevent irreparable and unnecessary injury to the parties. In one ICC case concerning a construction project in Africa, installment payments on the construction price were to be made by negotiable

---

27 *See* Chapter 27.

28 For an award holding that application for a prior court ordered expertise did not constitute a waiver of the agreement to arbitrate, *see* ICC Case 4156/1983, 1984 *JDI* 937. An arbitral tribunal cannot be expected to grant interim relief which contradicts or modifies interim measures ordered by a court at the seat of arbitration. *See* ICC Case 4998/1985, 1986 *JDI* 1139.

promissory notes. Alleging defective performance by the contractor, the defendant State entity stopped payment of the promissory notes. The contractor threatened to cease all work and commenced arbitration proceedings. Both parties manifested a desire to see the project completed. By an interlocutory order which was respected by both parties, the arbitral tribunal directed the State entity to pay the promissory notes into an escrow account controlled by the arbitral tribunal. From the escrow account, amounts were then paid to the contractor either as agreed by the parties or as the result of partial or final arbitral awards. In this manner, the contractual rights as well as the economic interests of both parties were preserved.

A similar result was reached in an ICC arbitration taking place in Switzerland[29] where a European builder of nuclear energy facilities for an Iranian government organization, having rescinded the agreement for non-payment by the purchaser, brought arbitration to recover sums allegedly due under the agreement. When the purchaser sought to draw down performance and completion guarantees issued by third party banks, the European party obtained an interlocutory order from the tribunal having the effect of preserving the *status quo*. The order took the form of a proposal addressed to both parties, which was contained in an interim award disposing of other issues, for the seller to withdraw its claim for a declaratory award that the attempt to call the bank guarantee was fraudulent and abusive, and for the purchaser formally to withdraw its call of the guarantees until the end of the arbitral procedure. The precatory nature of the tribunal's request may have been due to the presence of a State party in the arbitration. It was clear that the order had no compulsory effect, but it appears to have been accepted by the parties.

In the interest of preserving the status quo *pendente lite*, ICC tribunals have been willing to order a contract to be performed for a limited period even though one of the parties has claimed that the contract was rescinded.[30]

As can be seen from these examples, the arbitral tribunal seeks to the extent possible to obtain the mutual agreement of the parties to the proposed measures. Sometimes this result can best be achieved without recourse to the entry of reasoned procedural orders or interim awards as provided for in Article 23(1). One procedure which has been used to achieve consent to an interim measure is for the chairman of the arbitral tribunal, after consultation with the other arbitrators, to address a letter to the parties, expressing a provisional view of measures to be taken during the pendency of the arbitration, while allowing further comment by the parties and possible modification of

---

29   ICC Case 3896/1982, 1983 JDI 914, X YEARBOOK 47 (1985).

30   In ICC Arbitration Case 6503/1990, 1995 JDI 1022, the arbitral tribunal ordered that a long term contract should remain in existence, and the parties should execute its terms, during a period of one year after the claimed date of rescission to permit the arbitral tribunal to rule on the merits of the claimed rescission and to avoid unnecessary damage.

these views. The provisional nature of the chairman's views should be stressed in the letter.[31] Another interim measure of a persuasive nature is the attempt by arbitrators to encourage settlement negotiations. Such attempts which are generally accepted in ICC arbitration, may take the form of orders inviting the parties to participate in negotiation proceedings[32] Before issuing such orders, however, arbitrators should consider whether their attempt at reconciliation is permissible under the applicable law, keeping in mind that while a judge's attempt at reconciliation is often required in civil law systems, it is generally regarded as improper under common law systems.

iii) Procedural order or interim award?

Article 23(1) leaves it to the discretion of the tribunal whether interim measures will be taken in the form of a procedural order, with reasons, or an award. The possibility of taking interim measures by way of award is obviously intended to increase the chances of securing compliance with the arbitral tribunal's decision either voluntarily or, if need be, with the assistance of national courts. The fact that Article 23(1) contemplates the taking of interim measures by way of award emphasizes that the tribunal's decision is directed at the parties: an award by its nature finds the parties to the arbitrator and not third parties.

There are conceptual difficulties, however, for the tribunal to take its decision in the form of an award: while the tribunal no doubt intends to bind the parties with its decision, it is hard to conceive of the decision as finally disposing of a dispute between the parties. It was for this reason, as well as the practical problem of submitting the essentially summary proceedings for interlocutory orders to a regime appropriate to final disposition of a matter (reasoned award, scrutiny of the award by the Court), that a Working Party of the ICC Commission some years ago recommended that, in general, tribunal decisions concerning interim measures should *not* take the form of an award.[33] The Report also pointed to some practical problems in taking such decisions in the form of an award (for interim measures to be effective they must be rendered summarily; the necessity for fully reasoned awards, and the subsequent delay caused by the scrutiny process at the Court of Arbitration, risks rendering inefficacious interim relief ordered in the form of an award).

A further question arises whether the award format of interim measures entitles them to recognition and enforcement within the terms of the New York Convention.

---

31   For an example of this customized approach to procedure, *see* letter of the chairman in ICC case 6465/1004 reported in ICC Procedural Decisions 80.

32   *See* order inviting settlement, ICC case 5082/ 1994, reported in ICC Procedural Decisions 76-79.

33   ICC Working Party (Martin Hunter, Chairman), *Final Report on Interim and Partial Awards* 1 ICC Bull. 26, (December 1990).

In some circumstances interim measures have indeed been treated as awards, as was illustrated in an arbitration taking place in the United States.[34] In that case, an American contractor had given a $15 million "stand-by" letter of credit to guarantee performance of its contract with the Government of Israel. A dispute arose and the United States party started arbitration under the rules of the American Arbitration Association. The Government of Israel called upon the issuing bank to pay the letter of credit representing an unconditional guarantee. Payment was blocked momentarily by court-issued injunctions and attachments, both of which were vacated. The arbitrators then issued an interim award requiring the Government of Israel to pay the proceeds of the letter of credit into an escrow account owned by the two parties and to be disposed of either by agreement of the parties or by an award of the arbitral tribunal; failing either of these solutions, the matter was to be dealt with by order of a U.S. court having jurisdiction.[35] The interim award was found to be a final, albeit partial, award and was enforced under the New York Convention.[36] Although a final decision with respect to the letter of credit, the award clearly served primarily as a security device for a final award on the merits, and in this respect resembled the interlocutory orders described above.

Recognition and enforcement under the New York Convention of what is essentially an interlocutory order, modifiable by the arbitral tribunal in accordance with changes of circumstances but rendered in the form of awards must remain doubtful. There is a certain flaw in attempting to use the New York Convention, which was designed to insure enforcement of decision which put an end to a dispute between arbitrating parties, or at least part of a

---

34   Sperry International Trade v. Government of Israel, 532 F. Supp. 901 (S.D.N.Y. 1982).

35   The text of the award, as cited in the court's decision, *id.*, stated:

> 1. The proceeds of said letter of credit shall be paid into an escrow account . . . in the joint names of Claimant and Respondent . . .

> 2. Claimant and Respondent shall maintain the Escrow account in their joint names . . . and it . . . shall not be withdrawn . . . until Claimant and Respondent shall so agree in writing or by default of such agreement, this Tribunal or a Court in the State of New York or Federal Court in the United States of America shall finally so determine.

> 8. This order shall constitute an Award of the arbitrators and either party is at liberty to apply forthwith to the United States District Court for the Southern District of New York for confirmation and/or enforcement thereof.

36   Similar recognition has been given by a United States court of a preliminary award issued by arbitrators enjoining a party from exercising in full a maritime lien which would have prevented the conveyance of a ship to a mortgagee resulting in foreclosure of the party's interest in the ship. Southern Seas Navigation Ltd. v. Petroleas Mexicanas 606 F. Supp. 692 (S.D.N.Y. 1985). The injunction, it was said, was not "interim" in the sense that it was an "intermediate" step towards a further end but was rather an end in itself designed to clarify the parties' rights in the interim period prior to the final award. *See also* Yasuda Fire & Maine Insurance Company of Europe, 37 F.3d 345 (7th Cir. 1999) where a tribunal's interim order compelling respondent to deposit a letter of credit of $2.5 million to secure its possible liability on the award was considered to constitute an award and had sufficient finality to permit judicial review.

dispute, to secure enforcement of a decision which might, for instance, seek to preserve the status quo until a final arbitration award can be rendered. This flaw was precisely recognized in a much commented Australian case, *Resort Condominiums v. Bolwell*[37] where enforcement was denied to an arbitral award rendered in the United States in order to preserve the status quo between a United States licensor and an Australian licensee during the pendency of the arbitration. The award ordered the licensee not to enter into any competing arrangements and to require the deposit into an escrow account of all revenues received as a consequence of the license agreement. In refusing to enforce the award, Mr. Justice Lee of the Supreme Court of Queensland came to the conclusion that the so-called award was clearly of an interlocutory and procedural nature and did not finally put an end to any arbitral dispute or to establish the legal rights of the parties. According to the decision, the award was not enforceable under the New York Convention and indeed was not a final order subject to judicial review.

While authorities remain divided on whether awards basically granting interlocutory relief will be granted judicial recognition under the New York Convention, the strong logic of the *Resort Condominiums* case suggests that it would not be prudent to rely on the enforceability by national courts of such decisions as awards. This need not necessarily deter an ICC tribunal from using the award form. The added formality of a decision in this form may well have a positive effect in persuading the respondent party to comply with the decision or third parties to accept its consequences.

The award form has also been used to determine an amount due on a provisional basis between the parties while awaiting liquidation of accounts between the parties in a final award, as was the case in an ICC arbitration taking place in Geneva between a French corporate claimant and a Yugoslav enterprise acting as its subcontractor.[38] In response to the French contractor's suit for damages for faulty performance by its sub-contractor, the Yugoslav respondent raised a counterclaim for a fixed sum owed to it under the subcontract and requested immediate payment *par provision* (on account) of that amount pending the outcome of the arbitration on the principal claim. The arbitral tribunal noted that despite limitations under the Swiss Intercantonal Concordat on Arbitration on the power of arbitrators to grant interim measures,[39] it could enter an interim award ordering payment *par provision*,

---

37 MOT. No. 389 of 1993, 20 YEARBOOK 628 (1995) (Supreme Court of Queensland, 29 October 1993), commented on in M. Pryles, *The Case of Resort Condominiums v. Bolwell*, 10 ARB. INT. 385 (1994).

38 ICC Case 3540/1980, excerpts *in* 1981 JDI 914; excerpts *in* VII YEARBOOK 124 (1982).

39 Article 26 of the Swiss Intercantonal Concordat on Arbitration which applied at the time of the arbitration provided: "*Provisional orders.* The public judicial authorities alone have jurisdiction to make provisional orders. However, the parties may voluntarily submit to provisional orders proposed by the arbitral tribunal." Article 183 of the Swiss Private International Law Act of 1987, applicable to international arbitration as of 1 January 1989, provides that arbitral tribunals have power to order provisional or conservatory measures and may request assistance of the courts if a party does not comply.

upon the moving party giving adequate security, with damages between the parties to be liquidated definitively in the final award. In other words, interlocutory relief may be granted by an interim award. Any prohibition of arbitral provisional orders may thus be limited in its practical effect. The tribunal in the above case entered an interim award in favor of the Yugoslav respondent/counter claimant for the fixed sum due to it, but at the same time ruled that the French claimant had the right to setoff against the interim award any damages to which it might subsequently be held entitled. Pending the final award, the claimant's right to setoff was protected by requiring the posting of a bond, equal to any sum paid under the interim award.

iv) Security for costs

One of the issues that very occasionally comes up before an ICC tribunal is whether it has the power, on application of a party, to make an order for security for costs.[40] Such an order would condition the right of a claimant or counter-claimant to proceed on its claim upon the putting up of a bank guarantee or other form of surety to guarantee, in the case of lack of success, payment of the arbitration and party costs which the tribunal might order it to pay in a final award.

The existence of such an arbitral power in ICC arbitration seems clear, especially given the 1998 specification in Article 23(1) of arbitrators' interim measure powers. It is much less clear what exceptional circumstances would justify a tribunal to make an order for security for costs.

Even prior to the entering into effect of Article 23(1) of the Rules authorizing the ordering of "any interim or conservatory measure it deems appropriate" ICC tribunals had found that they had the power to grant security for costs as part of their inherent powers in connection with the conduct of arbitral proceedings. However, they were extremely reluctant to grant the remedy.[41]

While Article 23(1) does not specifically refer to security for costs it is quite certain that the Article was intended to include security for costs within the

---

40 Known as the *Cautio Judicatum Solvi* in civil law and also authorized under English law the security for costs device is designed to deter litigation and protect respondents from claims by financially irresponsible or insolvent claimants who will not be able to indemnify the respondent for legal costs which it incurs in a successful defense.

41 *See* ICC Case 7489/1992, 1993 JDI 1078, ICC PROCEDURAL DECISIONS 48, note Dominique Hascher (respondent counterclaimant requested tribunal to order claimant to furnish a bank guarantee to pay respondent's legal costs and secure the value of its counterclaim as a condition to proceeding with the claim; the tribunal, with its seat in France, considered that it had the power to order security, including security for costs, but found the request not justified); ICC Arbitration No. 7047/1994, 1995 SWISS BULL. 301 (refusal by tribunal to grant security for costs at the request of respondent state entities who had refused to contribute to ICC advance on costs of arbitration); ICC Case 6697, 1992 REV. ARB. 142 (constitution of guarantee ordered by arbitral tribunal due to exceptional circumstances involving the prospective insolvency of claimant). Other unpublished ICC awards on the issue are referred to in detail in A. Reiner, *Les mesures provisoires et conservatoires et l'arbitrage international, notamment l'arbitrage CCI*, 1998 JDI 855, 892.

ambit of interim measures. One of the national court decisions which had motivated the revisers of the Rules to confirm arbitrators' powers to order interim measures was the surprising House of Lords decision in the *Ken-Ren*[42] cases where the powers of an English court (as opposed to ICC arbitrators) to order security for costs in that case was confirmed, partially based on the court's doubt that ICC arbitrators enjoyed that power under the prior Rules. The case caused considerable adverse comment concerning undesirable court interference in international institutional arbitration[43] and the result has been modified for the future by the Arbitration Act 1996.[44]

The revisers accordingly were aware of the doubt expressed by the House of Lords with respect to arbitrators' powers under the ICC Rules to grant interim measures in general, and for security for costs in particular. Article 23(1) was designed to make clear arbitrators' powers for the entire domain.[45]

One of the reasons for not specifying security for costs as an interim measure is that many considered it undesirable to call attention to its availability or to suggest that it was a normal interim measure. The remedy is considered by many to be inappropriate in most circumstances for ICC arbitration, where specific provisions are made for the funding of arbitration costs by advances to be made by the parties in equal shares.[46] This expression of the contractual intent of the parties should be given effect and it may be said arguably to exclude additional measures to secure a party from the possibility that its adversary would not be able to pay a costs order made against it in a final award. In order for a claimant to pursue its claim in arbitration it will have al-

---

42   Coppée-Lavalin N.V. v. Ken-Ren Chemicals and Fertilizers, Ltd., Voest-Alpine Aktiengesellschaft v. Ken-Ren, [1995] 1 A.C. 38, [1994] 2 ALL E. R. 449, [1994] 2 LLOYD'S REP. 109, involving two ICC arbitrations held in London.

43   *See e.g.* J. Paulsson, *The Unwelcome Atavism of Ken-Ren: The House of Lords shows its Meddle*, 1994 SWISS BULL. 439; D. Branson, *The Ken-Ren Case: It is an Ado Where More Aid is Less Help*, 10 ARB. INT. 303 (1994). The criticism was particularly pointed in ICC circles because *Ken-Ren* effectively reversed the earlier holding of the Court of Appeal in Bank Mellat v. Helliniki Techniki, S.A. [1984] Q.B. 291 to the effect that in international arbitrations conducted under the ICC Rules in England the English courts should refrain in all circumstances from accepting to consider an application for security for costs.

44   Article 39 permits the parties to agree (by the adoption of institutional rules, or otherwise) that the tribunal shall have the power to make interim orders concerning costs; security for costs is not included within powers that may be exercised by the court in relation to arbitration.

45   *Accord*, M. Blessing, *Keynotes on Arbitral Decision Making*, ICC BULL. (Supplement 1997) ("The Working Party preferred not to make any specific reference in this respect, but the wording of Article 23 would seem broad enough to allow the making of an application for and the issuing of a ruling by the Tribunal on, the security for costs"); DERAINS AND SCHWARTZ, 274 ("Although not specifically mentioned, the drafters, thus, considered the wording of Article 23(1) to be broad enough to embrace applications for security for costs.").

46   ICC Arbitration 7137/1993, cited in Reiner, n. 41, *supra*, at p. 892 where the tribunal found that since the subject of arbitration costs was specifically provided for in Article 9 [Article 30 of the 1998 Rules] of the ICC Rules it was not for the arbitrators to envision other conservatory measures with respect to the same subject.

ready had to advance a substantial amount as fixed by the Secretariat or the ICC Court. It is not as if the claimant will not have been willing or required to make a substantial arbitration costs investment in the prosecution of its claim. The ICC practice of advances on costs offers a certain guarantee against abusive and extravagant claims.

An application for security for costs can be used with the motivation to deter or render impossible the prosecution of meritorious claims by claimants in reduced or precarious circumstances (sometimes such impecuniosity is claimed to be the direct result of the conduct of the respondent which is the subject of the arbitration claim). The effect is multiplied where the respondent comes from a highly developed state where the legitimate costs of defense may be particularly high (thereby adding to the overall cost of the arbitration). It is a question whether parties really intended, when they agreed to ICC arbitration, that a claimant would be required to provide security for such costs as a condition to proceeding to arbitration. Moreover, ICC arbitrators in many cases decide that each party will bear its own legal costs (*see* Section 21.04); this fact may suggest that it would be wrong to order pre-arbitration security based on the theory that an unsuccessful claimant would be liable for all its adversary's party costs. In recognition of this fact, even where security for costs is granted by the tribunal, there may be a tendency to "cap" the amount of security. In one recent case security was capped at 150% of the amount of the ICC advance on cost due from each party. (Each party was thus secured to obtain the reimbursement of its ICC advance on costs plus 50% of that amount for its party costs.) Finally, in a number of cases where an application for security was denied the Respondent had itself defaulted—on the ground that its adversary would be unable to indemnify it for its costs incurred—on its contractual and regulatory obligation to advance one-half of the amount fixed by the Court. In such circumstances the applicant for security, in default of its own contractual obligations, might be deemed to have "unclean hands."

It may be concluded that security for costs is not usually granted in ICC arbitration; nevertheless, the power exists and in some circumstances may be justified.

CHAPTER 27

ANCILLARY PROCEEDINGS BEFORE NATIONAL COURTS

27.01 Article 23(2) of the Rules: interim or conservatory measures

Article 23(2) provides in part:

> Before the file is transmitted to the Arbitral Tribunal, and in appropriate circumstances even thereafter, the parties may apply to any competent judicial authority for interim or conservatory measures. The application of a party to a judicial authority for such measures or for the implementation of any such measures ordered by an Arbitral Tribunal shall not be deemed to be an infringement or a waiver of the arbitration agreement and shall not affect the relevant powers reserved to the Arbitral Tribunal.

The article thus recognizes that even though a contract may provide for all disputes to be settled by ICC arbitration, the need for urgent interlocutory action may not always await the forming of the arbitral tribunal, a process which may take some time (particularly where one party defaults or is uncooperative). Moreover, certain interlocutory measures which are binding and enforceable, such as the issuance of an injunction or the attachment of funds, can only be decided by national courts. While the ultimate disposition of such interlocutory measures will be determined by the final award of the arbitrators, the parties to the arbitration, as well as third parties, will in the meantime be required to obey court mandates.

By explicitly referring to national court intervention as an available interlocutory step, the drafters recognized that the ICC Rules do not always provide expeditious or immediately enforceable remedies. The international arbitral process is relatively unsuited to rapid solutions, given the time necessary to convene an arbitral tribunal, the frequently dispersed domiciles of the tribunal's members, and the inability of the tribunal to enforce its own orders. The

ICC Commission on International Arbitration promulgated in 1990 Rules for a Pre-arbitral Referee Procedure[1] which permit parties to agree in advance that an arbitral referee may be appointed to make immediate provisional decisions upon the request of a party. The Pre-arbitral Referee procedure has not gained any substantial acceptance, however, and recourse to a competent national court remains the principal means of obtaining binding interlocutory action on an urgent basis. Furthermore, only a court order carries with it legal sanction against the person to whom it is directed.

A request for, and the grant of, interim or conservatory measures by nature will not prejudice a decision on the merits of a dispute, a decision which is the exclusive domain of the arbitral tribunal, nor will such a request constitute a waiver of the right to arbitrate.[2]

Before the arbitral tribunal has been constituted, the moving party seeking interim or conservatory measures has no alternative, absent a clause stipulating a Pre-arbitral Referee Procedure, but to address its request to a national court. Once a tribunal has been formed, an alternative exists since the arbitrators themselves have the inherent power to order parties to provide certain interlocutory relief (*see* Section 26.05) which is now made explicit by Article 23(1), although directions to third parties and measures requiring the sanction of immediate enforcement are beyond their authority. In view of the limitations on arbitral powers, Article 23(2) permits the parties to make application to a competent judicial authority not only before the file is transmitted to the arbitrators but also "in appropriate circumstances even thereafter." The substitution of the word "appropriate" in the 1998 Rules for the word "exceptional" in the previous version of the Rules is consistent with the specific grant of interim measures powers to arbitrators in Article 23(1). The article as a whole recognizes the complementary roles of arbitrators and the courts in assuring the effectiveness of the international arbitral process.[3]

---

1   *See* Section 38.03.

2   This is the specific premise of Article 23(2) of the Rules, consistent *inter alia* with Article VI(4) of the European Convention on International Commercial Arbitration (the Geneva Convention of 1961), which provides: "A request for interim measures or measures of conservation addressed to a judicial authority shall not be deemed incompatible with the arbitration agreement, or regarded as a submission of the substance of the case to the court." This general principle is recognized by all national courts. A requesting party must be careful not to seek final relief or final disposition of a matter as such requests could be found to constitute waiver of the right to arbitration. ICC arbitrators have consistently found that they retained arbitral jurisdiction over the merit of a dispute even though one party had sought extensive interim measures from a national court. *See e.g.* ICC case 4156/1983, 1984 JDI 937, commentary Sigvard Jarvin, ICC case 2444/1976, 1977 JDI 932, commentary Yves Derains.

3   On the subject generally, *see* Berthold Goldman, *The Complementary Roles of Judges and Arbitrators in Ensuring that International Commercial Arbitration is Effective* in 60 YEARS OF ICC ARBITRATION: A LOOK AT THE FUTURE 257 (ICC Publishing, 1984). In respect to interim measures, Lord Mustill has described the complementary role of judges and arbitrators as being like a relay race: at the outset, and before a tribunal has been appointed, the courts must have responsibility for

Whether applying to the tribunal or to a national court, the moving party must inform the ICC Court. Article 23(2) provides that:

Any such application and any measures taken by the judicial authority must be notified without delay to the Secretariat. The Secretariat shall inform the arbitrator thereof.[4]

27.02 Injunction, expertise, and other urgent measures

Whether a national court can enter orders in aid of arbitration is a matter of local law. Such orders are usually sought in the state where the arbitration is officially held (the "seat" of the arbitration). However, it is also possible that the courts of one state may be competent to make orders in aid of an arbitration conducted in another state.[5] Many international arbitration specialists generally favor the choice of a place of arbitration in countries whose courts are reluctant to intervene in the arbitral process, thereby reducing the potential for judicial interference with the arbitral tribunal. On the other hand, some degree of intervention by national courts may contribute to the efficacy of arbitration, whether by bringing to bear their powers of compulsion, which may be necessary to obtain or preserve evidence, or by frustrating dilatory tactics by ordering a recalcitrant party to comply with the procedural requirements of contractually stipulated rules of arbitration.

The power of a court in relation to the arbitral process may be found in a national law on arbitration, but can also be found in other statutes of general application giving courts exceptional jurisdiction to grant urgent and tempo-

---

urgent interim measures. After the tribunal has been named it should take on primary responsibility, even though recourse to the courts may be necessary for enforcement. After the award has been rendered the tribunal becomes *functus officio* and enforcement is up to the courts. Michael Mustill, *Comments and Conclusions in* CONSERVATORY AND PROVISIONAL MEASURES IN ARBITRATION 118, 119, (ICC Publication No. 519 (1993). *See also* D. Alan Redfern, *Arbitration and the Courts: Interim Measures of Protection—Is the Tide About to Turn?*, 30 TEXAS INT'L L.J. 71, 74 (1995).

4   In ICC Case 2444/1976, extracts *in* 1977 JDI 932, the arbitral tribunal held that the fact that a party failed to inform the ICC Court of Arbitration's Secretariat of its having requested a Yugoslav court to appoint an expert to make a pre-arbitration investigation of an allegedly defective turn-key plant was not prejudicial to the validity of said request. The then Secretary General of the Court commented that: "This administrative formality, intended to allow the Court of Arbitration to follow the evolution of proceedings submitted to it, is not required under pain of nullity." Yves Derains, Case Commentary, *id.* at 935; *accord,* ICC case 4415/1984, 1984 JDI 952, 957.

5   For instance at the situs of property attached to secure execution of an award to be obtained in a foreign jurisdiction. In *Channel Tunnel Group v. Balfour Beatty Ltd.* [1993] 1A.ER. 664 the House of Lords confirmed that English courts had jurisdiction to grant injunctive relief to a party in England in relation to a dispute to be ultimately resolved by a yet to be formed ICC tribunal in Belgium. The House of Lords found, however, that the exercise of such power could be justified only in exceptional circumstances which were not present in the case and when the "balance of advantage" or consideration of equity principles favored making an order. Article 44 of Arbitration Act 1996 now confirms the power of the High Court to grant injunctive relief (even where the seat of arbitration is abroad) where the arbitral tribunal does not have the power, or is unable, to act.

rary relief pending resolution of a dispute on the merits, and in the residual and discretionary powers of courts as developed in case law.[6]

English law is a useful point of reference because court powers are quite specific in this regard as a result of the revision and consolidation in 1996 of the laws concerning arbitration. Among other broad powers to control and assist arbitration, Section 42 of the Arbitration Act of 1996 gives the court power to enforce peremptory orders made by the tribunal and Section 44 gives it direct enforcement powers in the following terms:

(1) Unless otherwise agreed by the parties, the court has for the purposes of and in relation to arbitral proceedings the same power of making orders about the matters listed below as it has for the purposes of and in relation to legal proceedings.

Those matters are:

(a) the taking of the evidence of witnesses;

(b) the preservation of evidence;

(c) making orders relating to property which is the subject of the proceedings or as to which any question arises in the proceedings.

(i) for the inspection, photographing, preservation, custody or detention of the property, or

(ii) ordering that samples be taken from, or any observation be made of or experiment conducted upon, the property;

and for that purpose authorizing any person to enter any premises in the possession or control of a party to the arbitration

(d) the sale of any goods the subject of the proceedings;

(e) the granting of an interim injunction or the appointment of a receiver.

The fact that such explicit powers are found in the Arbitration Act is a manifestation of the close relationship between arbitration and the courts under English law and the feeling that the courts should be available to assist, but not interfere with, arbitrations taking place in England (*see generally* Chapter 29). It should be noted that under the English Arbitration Act 1996, the general powers exercisable by an arbitral tribunal, enumerated in Section 38, have been much expanded from prior law, including not only the power to request evidence but also to give directions in relation to property under dispute. The primary source for interim measures is intended to be the arbitral tribunal. The courts will enforce such interim measures but, under Section

---

6   *See generally* David Shenton and Wolfgang Kuhn, INTERIM COURT REMEDIES IN SUPPORT OF ARBITRATION: A COUNTRY-BY-COUNTRY ANALYSIS (London, International Bar Association 1987), and Reports of an IBA Sub-committee, *Interim Court Remedies in Support of Arbitration*, 3 INTERNATIONAL BUSINESS LAWYER 101-124 (1984).

42(3) of the Arbitration Act, English courts will not enforce peremptory orders of the tribunal until the applicant "has exhausted any available arbitral process in respect of failure to comply with the tribunal's order." The Arbitration Act thus seeks to increase the powers of the arbitral tribunal while limiting court intervention to what is necessary to assure their efficacy. The broad powers of the court set out in Section 44 may in case of urgency (for instance where the tribunal has not been constituted) be exercised directly on the application of a party or proposed party to the arbitration; if the case is not one of urgency, the court shall act only if the party's application is approved by the arbitral tribunal (or upon the agreement in writing of all parties).[7] The relationship between the court and the arbitral tribunal in relation to direct court intervention is well summarized in Section 44(5) which provides:

> In any case the court shall act only if or to the extent that the arbitral tribunal, and any arbitral or other institution or person vested by the parties with power in that regard, has no power or is unable for the time being to act effectively

As a result, as one commentator put it:

> "The overall effect is that the court has a far more limited role to play at the interlocutory stage of an arbitration than was the case under the 1950 Act, and is relevant only where the arbitrators themselves are contractually unable to act or where their orders are disobeyed for the most part in relation to evidence."[8]

The law in other jurisdictions is less explicit. In the United States, there is no specific provision in state arbitration statutes nor in the U.S. Arbitration Act allowing provisional remedies by courts when parties have agreed to settle their controversies by arbitration.[9] The availability of the principal provisional remedies of attachment and injunction must be determined according to general statutory rules of civil procedure relative to judicial proceedings and case law deciding the extent to which they can be applied in the arbitral context.[10]

In France, the arbitration part of the Code of Civil Procedure does not refer to provisional remedies. Nevertheless, the general power given to the courts to grant interim measures *en référé, i.e.,* on an urgent basis, without prejudicing the subsequent decision on the merits, clearly extends to disputes which are

---

7 Arbitration Act 1996, Article 44(3) and (4).

8 Robert Merkin, ARBITRATION ACT 1996 AN ANNOTATED GUIDE, footnote at 62 (1996).

9 M. Domke, *Commercial Arbitration,* Sec. 26.00 (Wilner, ed., 1999). Gary Born, INTERNATIONAL COMMERCIAL ARBITRATION IN THE UNITED STATES, 760 (Kluwer 1994). Note, however that Section 8 of Chapter 1 of the U.S. Arbitration Act provides for pre-arbitration attachment in maritime matters.

10 *See* Richard Hulbert, *The American Law Perspective* in CONSERVATORY AND PROVISIONAL MEASURES IN INTERNATIONAL ARBITRATION 93 (ICC Publishing, 1993).

the subject of arbitration as well as those before the courts.[11] The exceptional jurisdiction of the court to use its power to make summary orders that do not prejudice the merits is compatible with the parties' agreement to settle all disputes by arbitration and may be invoked even after an arbitral tribunal has been constituted. In the past a few commentators had questioned the legitimacy of the exercise of court power in the latter case (particularly on the grounds that prior Article 8(5) of the ICC Rules constituted an agreement between the parties that absent "exceptional circumstances" the parties would not seek interim measures from courts), but this interpretation did not prevail. In any event there seems to be little doubt now that when the parties have agreed to the 1998 ICC Rules and thus Article 23(2) of those Rules, they cannot protest if a court exercises its summary powers even after a tribunal has been constituted. French courts, moreover, have required very explicit language to constitute waiver of the right to seek interim measures from a court in relation to a dispute subject to international arbitration.[12]

General provisions of French procedural law providing for the *juge des référés* and the *juge de l'exécution* (established under the President of the Commercial Court in commercial cases) establish an institution for the taking of urgent measures which is applicable to disputes whose merits are to be decided in arbitration as well as those which are to be decided in court. The characteristic that distinguishes such jurisdiction is that decisions are designed to be of an interim nature and are not to be taken if they require determination of, or will prejudice, the merits of the dispute. Such proceedings are summary in nature. They have been resorted to in relation to arbitration in a variety of circumstances,[13] including:

— expertise

— preservation of evidence

11　*See, e.g. Cour de cassation, Première chambre civile*, 6 March 1990, 1990 REV. ARB. 633, note H. Gaudemet-Tallon; *see generally* Gérard Pluyette, *A French Perspective* in CONSERVATORY AND PROVISIONAL MEASURES IN INTERNATIONAL ARBITRATION 72 (ICC Publishing 1993); *see also* Philippe Ouakrat, *L'arbitrage commercial internationale et les mesures conservatoires: étude générale*, 1988 DROIT ET PRATIQUE DE COMMERCE INT. 239; Claude Goldman, *Mesures provisoires et arbitrage internationale*, 1993 INT BUS. L.J. 3.

12　*Cour de cassation*, 18 November 1986, Guinea and Soguipêche v. Atlantic Triton, 26 I.L.M. 373 (1986) (English translation). (The *Cour d'appel* had set aside the attachment in a French port of fishing vessels which was the subject of an ICSID arbitration on the grounds that Article 26 of the Washington Convention provided that consent to arbitration under the Convention would be "deemed to be consent to such arbitration to the exclusion of any other remedy." The *Cour de cassation* reversed the lower court's decision, finding that: ". . . given that the power of national courts to order conservatory measures, which is not preempted by the Washington Convention, can only be excluded by express consent of the parties or implied convention resulting from the adoption of arbitral rules calling for such waiver . . . the lower court's decision was in error.")

13　For a general treatment, *see* FOUCHARD GAILLARD AND GOLDMAN ON INTERNATIONAL COMMERCIAL ARBITRATION, Part IV, Chapter III, *Provisional and Conservatory Measures in the Course of the Arbitration Proceedings* (Kluwer, 1999).

− conservation of assets

− receivership

− injunction to prevent manifestly illicit conduct

− attachment; and

− (controversially), the granting of a *provision* or a judgment for an uncontested or uncontestable amount of a money claim included in a larger arbitral dispute.

In Switzerland, under the Private International Law Act of 1987, the arbitrators have power to order provisional or conservatory measures; if the party so ordered does not comply the arbitral tribunal may request assistance from the appropriate court.[14] However, the arbitrator's power to act on requests for provisional measures is not exclusive; there is nothing to prevent a party from addressing itself immediately to any competent state court without any requirement first to exhaust an arbitral remedy.[15]

Irrespective of the specific provisions of the national law, the general problem for most judges is whether justice requires their intervention, notwithstanding the existence of an arbitration clause.

The potential occasions for such intervention are many. The following example may be useful as an illustration. In the case of a contract containing an ICC arbitration clause for the purchase of ships, an Israeli buyer refused delivery of the ships from the French seller, claiming that performance criteria which were a condition of the purchase obligation had not been fulfilled. An impartial report of the ships' sea trials would have obviously been crucial evidence for arbitrators called upon to decide an action for rescinding the contract. It clearly would have taken some time for the arbitral tribunal to be formed and to decide on interim measures. The French seller thus obtained from the court of first instance of its domicile, which was also the place of sea trials and delivery under the contract, the appointment of a maritime expert to prepare an official report of the results of the sea trials. Such appointment of an expert by a French court sitting in urgent session

---

14   Article 183 provides:

Unless the parties have agreed otherwise, the arbitral tribunal may, at the request of a party, order provisional or conservatory measures. If the party so ordered does not comply voluntarily, the arbitral tribunal may request the assistance of the court. Such court shall apply its own law.

The arbitral tribunal or the court may make the granting of provisional or conservatory measures subject to appropriate sureties.

15   M. Blessing, *The New International Arbitration Law in Switzerland*, 5 J. INT. ARB. 9, at 49 (1988); *see generally* M. Blessing, *Interim Relief and Discovery in International Arbitration* in INTRODUCTION TO ARBITRATION—SWISS AND INTERNATIONAL PERSPECTIVES, Chapter X, pp. 273-278 (Swiss Commercial Law Series No. 10, 1999).

can be obtained within a few days. The report became an important item of evidence in the ensuing arbitration.[16]

Court intervention in aid of arbitration may also be useful and appropriate with respect to appointment of an expert to make a report at a stage of partial completion of a construction project. Evidence of a disputed construction technique or performance may soon be covered up by tons of cement or other building materials. While nothing prevents each side from preparing technical reports of their own (with photographs and other objective proof), the report of a neutral expert may be a more useful and convincing way of establishing the true situation. Such an appointment may be obtained fairly easily in most civil-law jurisdictions, but perhaps with more difficulty from common-law courts, which consider the appointment of a neutral expert to be exceptional, the marshaling of evidence being traditionally left to the initiative and resourcefulness of the parties. (For a description of such a procedure as a creation of contract within the ICC framework, *see* Section 38.02.)

It is important that the terms of reference for an expertise be carefully drafted so as to assure that the provisional measure does not touch upon, or prejudice, the substantive decision which is within the sole discretion of the arbitral tribunal. It has been argued (unsuccessfully) before the French courts that an interlocutory expertise should be limited to a simple *constat* as to material conditions at a given point of time and should not be permitted to require the expert's opinion as to the conformity of any fact to a technical standard or contract condition. Such an "opinion" addressed to a judge constitutes the intellectual elaboration of an opinion intended to convince a judge, and hence exceeds the domain of conservatory measures.[17] A leading case on the issue involved Eurodisney and contractors who had contracted with it (in a contract containing an ICC arbitration clause) to perform construction works at the theme park near Paris. Eurodisney had terminated the contract for (*inter alia*) failure of the contractors to meet contractual deadlines. Prior to the signature of the Terms of Reference by the parties and the arbitrators the contractors sought and obtained a court order for an expertise which required the expert not only to describe the works completed by the contractor as of the date of termination but also to "assess the extent of that work in light of the contractual stipulations [and] to state whether the work

---

16 This case from the authors' files is unreported. For a similar situation and the use by ICC arbitrators of the court-appointed expert's report, *see* ICC Cases 2444/1976, 1 ICC AWARDS 285 and 4156/1983, I ICC AWARDS 515.

17 *See* arguments made in EuroDisney SCA v. S.A. Gabo, S.A. Eremco and others, *Cour d'appel*, Paris, 22 May 1992 (*Quatorzième chambre B.*no 92/5759 and 5760) referred to in Gerard Pluyette, *A French Perspective* in CONSERVATORY AND PROVISIONAL MEASURES IN INTERNATIONAL ARBITRATION 72, 82 (ICC Publishing, 1993).

is in conformity with the initial forecasts . . ."[18] Eurodisney's argument that such a mission touched upon, and prejudiced, the substantive mission reserved to the arbitral tribunal was rejected. The decision is controversial.

Sale or other disposition of perishable goods is another area where courts may intervene despite the presence of an arbitration clause.[19] The dispute in arbitration in such cases would no longer concern title to the goods, but rather damages for financial loss.

An injunction or the appointment of a receiver may be available if its purpose is principally to preserve property pending the outcome of the dispute before the arbitral tribunal. In appropriate circumstances a court may grant an injunction to prevent the payment of a guarantee or the drawing down of a standby letter of credit if the payment might frustrate the arbitration and prejudice a party.[20]

In another case[21] involving a license given by an American manufacturer to a German licensee the manufacturer sought to terminate the license (which contained an ICC arbitration clause) and transfer its manufacturing assets to a third party. A United States Federal District Court had refused to grant an injunction at the request of the licensee. On appeal the Court of Appeal for the Seventh Circuit vacated the judgment and directed "the district court to enjoin White from repudiating the . . . contract and from transferring any of Sauer's claimed contractual rights to a third party until the London arbitration requested by Sauer . . . is completed and this lawsuit (including any appeals) is terminated."[22]

While in many jurisdictions injunctive relief is available to maintain the *status quo* generally, courts are wary about granting what in effect would be the very relief which is to be ultimately determined by arbitrators. In cases involving partnerships or joint ventures, where arbitration clauses are habitual, it may be necessary to seek the interim appointment of a receiver pending arbitration to run a business whose management might otherwise be paralyzed by the dispute.

---

18 *Cour de cassation*, 11 October 1995, Société Eurodisney v. Société Impresa Pizzarotti, 1996 REV. ARB. 228, 230.

19 Such intervention is provided for by legislation in some countries and by practice of the courts exercising summary jurisdiction in others. The United Kingdom is an example of the former, Arbitration Act 1996, Sec. 44(2)(d). France is an example of the latter.

20 *See* Rogers, Burgun, Shahine & Deschler, Inc. v. Dongsan Construction Co., 598 F. Supp. 754 (S.D.N.Y. 1984) (contractor enjoined from drawing down sub-contractor's letter of guarantee pending ICC arbitration).

21 Sauer-Getriebe KG v. White Hydraulics, Inc., 715 F. 2d 348 (7th Cir. 1983), cert. denied, 464 U.S. 1070.

22 *Id.* at 352.

27.03   Other interlocutory relief

Court intervention may also be sought when a party seeks to obtain payment of a debt whose amount is fixed, due, and payable without awaiting the outcome of arbitration. Alternatively, a party may request security for costs during arbitration.

The power of arbitrators to make interim or partial awards so as to liquidate fixed, due and payable sums prior to a final award on all issues has already been discussed in Section 26.05. In some legal systems, however, courts have concurrent jurisdiction to order interlocutory payment (*paiement par provision*), when the arbitral tribunal has not yet been constituted, and when urgency has been established.[23] In all cases, they must ensure that the exercise of their power does not interfere with the arbitral jurisdiction expressly agreed by the parties.

In France, the powers of the President of the court of first instance to grant a *provision* despite the existence of an arbitration clause would appear compatible with Article 23(2) of the ICC Rules, with the *caveat* that if a request for *provision* would require the judge to make a *prima facie* ruling on the merits, he may conclude that he is encroaching on the arbitrator's jurisdiction. Courts are quite properly reluctant to grant *provisions* if the arbitral tribunal has already been constituted or if court intervention may prejudice the merits or otherwise interfere with the arbitrators' powers.

In a prominent dispute between the French company EURODIF and an agency of the Iranian Government, the President of the *Tribunal de grande instance* of Paris denied EURODIF's request for a *provision* with respect to damages which were the subject of a pending ICC arbitration. The President referred to Article 8(5) of the ICC Rules (23(2) under the 1998 Rules) and to the fact that the request for damages was presently being considered by the arbitrators. He held:

> In these circumstances, and as EURODIF has invoked no element of fact or law justifying the exceptional character of its demand for a *provision*

---

23   *See* the decision of the French *Cour de cassation*, 9 July 1979, 1980 Rᴇᴠ. Aʀʙ. 79, holding that a lower court erred in refusing to grant a *provision* (payment on account) in a case where urgency was established as a matter of fact and where the amount payable was not seriously contested. This reasoning was applied by the *Cour d'appel* of Paris in an unpublished decision of 19 December 1980, to grant a *provision* pending an ICC arbitration (*see* P. Bertin, *L'intervention des juridictions au cours de la procédure arbitrale*, 1982 Rᴇᴠ. Aʀʙ. 331, 342) More recently, decisions of the *Cour de cassation* provide for a *provision* when creditors' claims "cannot seriously be contested", urgency exists, and the tribunal has not yet been constituted. *Cour de cassation*, 20 March 1989, Société the Authority for Supply Commodities Cairo Estran v. Société Ipitrade International, 1989 Rᴇᴠ. Aʀʙ. 494, and *Cour de cassation*, 29 November 1989, Société Horeva v. Société Sitas, 1990 Rᴇᴠ. Aʀʙ. 633. A similar system exists in the Netherlands.

brought before this court acting in urgent session, the court has no jurisdiction to act in the matter.[24]

The denial was affirmed by France's highest court, although commentators have warned that the decision cannot be read as general prohibition against the *référée-provision* device in connection with international commercial arbitration.[25]

Some national laws provide that litigants before the courts may, in certain circumstances, be required to provide security for legal fees and costs as a condition of proceeding with the action, particularly where the plaintiff is a foreign party. State courts should not exercise such powers to require security bonds relating to arbitration; such orders would interfere with the ICC's institutional processes. The ICC Rules require claimants to make an advance of arbitration costs (including those of the arbitrators and of the ICC) as a condition to proceeding in arbitration, a requirement which provides some protection against reckless and unsubstantiated claims. Moreover, ICC arbitrators have the possibility of ordering security for costs under their general authority to order interim measures under Article 23(1). *See*, Section 26.05, *supra*. Based on considerations such as these, the English Arbitration Act 1996 removed from the jurisdiction of courts the power to order security for costs in arbitral proceedings.[26] Before this legislative modification England had been one of the few jurisdictions (perhaps the only) to permit courts to order security for costs in arbitration proceedings.[27]

---

24 EURODIF v. OIAETI (the Iranian Organization for Investment, Economic and Technical Assistance), *Tribunal de grande instance*, Paris, 10 June 1982, by President Caratini. In an order handed down the same day in a related case, President Caratini denied a request for *provision* by the State of Iran in a claim against the French Atomic Energy Commission (CEA) (both orders unpublished).

25 *Cour de cassation*, *Première chambre civile*, 14 March 1984, 1985 REV. ARB. 69, note Couchez; *see also* FOUCHARD, GAILLARD, GOLDMAN ON INTERNATIONAL COMMERCIAL ARBITRATION 730, 731-733 (Kluwer 1999). From the case law that has developed since, and from informed commentary, it is fair to conclude that the *référé-provision* procedure is properly characterized as an interim measure and that accordingly the parties may have recourse to the courts within the limits of Article 23(2) of the Rules (and this despite language to the contrary in the 1984 decision by the High Court). French courts appear to require as a condition for application of the remedy that the arbitral tribunal has not been constituted or is incapable of acting, as well as the demonstration of urgency. To be considered an interim measure, any court order must be subject to being overruled by the tribunal in its award on the merits. For this reason it may be appropriate to require security from the party in whose favor a *provision* order is made.

26 This is the effect of Article 44 of the Act providing that the court shall enjoy the same powers in relation to arbitral proceedings as it has in relation to ordinary matters; a list of such matters is provided. Omitted from the list is security for costs. At the same time, Article 39 of the Act provides that the parties may agree (by agreement to institutional arbitration rules or otherwise) to empower arbitrators to order relief on a provisional basis specifically including "an order to make payment on account of the costs of arbitration." Article 38 additionally provides that an arbitral tribunal may order security for costs if the parties have not agreed otherwise.

27 Coppée-Lavalin SA/NV v. Ken Ren Chemicals and Fertilizers, Ltd. [1994] 2 W.L. R. 631; [1994] 2. ALL E.R. 449 (H.L. 1994), discussed *supra*, Section 26.05.

27.04   Attachments

Many jurisdictions allow conservatory attachment of assets pending arbitral proceedings and prior to an award.

In view of the fact that international arbitration is by its nature complex and time consuming, and that interlocutory orders rendered by arbitrators are not self-executing, it is appropriate that national legal systems provide a remedy to prevent recalcitrant defendants from frustrating the arbitral process by removing assets from the reach of effective execution following an award. Most national laws do provide such a remedy.

In many jurisdictions in continental Europe, conservatory attachments permit a claimant in arbitration to sequester assets of the defendant if it can demonstrate that there is reasonable cause to believe that its claim is founded and urgency exists. The precise conditions upon which such attachments may be granted are defined by law. Upon a showing of reasonable cause, attachments are routinely available in most countries. Such a provisional assessment by a national court of the possibility that the respondent may be indebted to the claimant and that the claim has some likelihood of success does not imply a prejudicial assessment by the court of the merits, the determination of which is reserved to the arbitrators.[28] Such attachments do not conflict with the obligations of the New York Convention to refer parties to arbitration[29] since attachment is only a provisional measure subject to an arbitration award which the State would later be obligated to execute.[30]

In England, there was substantial doubt for many years about the power of courts to grant attachments in support of arbitration except in admiralty cases[31] or cases involving right or title to a specific property or an identifiable

---

28   For an illustration of the interplay between national courts and ICC arbitrators in this regard, *see* the decision of 12 May 1977, of the Italian *Corte di cassazione*, Scherk Enterprises A.G. (Liechtenstein) v. Société des Grandes Marques (Italy), excerpts *in* IV YEARBOOK 285 (1979) (attachment in Italy pending arbitration in Zurich).

29   *Accord*, A.J. van den Berg, THE NEW YORK ARBITRATION CONVENTION OF 1958, 140 (1981). This position has been contested by some courts in the United States. *See* text at footnotes 37-44, *infra*.

30   For an example of French courts' approval of conservatory attachment in ICC proceedings, *see*, *Cour de cassation*, *Première chambre civile*, 20 March 1989, *République d'Iran v. Framatome et Eurodif*, 1989 REVUE TRIMESTRIELLE DU DROIT CIVILE 624, note R. Perrot, 1989 REV. ARB. 653, note P. Fouchard. *See also Cour de cassation*, 6 June 1990, Framatome S.A. (France) et al. v. Atomic Energy Organization of Iran (A.E.O.I.), 1990 BULLETIN DES ARRÊTS DE LA COUR DE CASSATION, PREMIÈRE PARTIE 100, commentary in RECUEIL DALLOZ 1990, Information rapides, 198. In *Framatome*, the highest French civil court of appeal considered whether the Atomic Energy Organization of Iran, financially dependant on the Iranian state, could be considered a part of the Iranian state, and thus immune from attachment proceedings on sovereign grounds. Ruling that it was not, the French court confirmed that parties to arbitration concerning private commercial disputes could be subject to attachment. Under French law a condition for attachment is that it be established that the claim appears to be "well founded in principle."

31   "There [was] no doubt that the Court [had] jurisdiction to arrest a vessel notwithstanding that the claim [fell] within an agreement to arbitrate," Michael Mustill & Stewart Boyd, COMMERCIAL ARBITRATION 339 (2d ed. 1989).

fund of money. As of 1975, however, it was possible to obtain so-called *Mareva* injunctions[32] in support of arbitration taking place in England, a power which English courts were apparently prepared to exercise as well in respect to foreign arbitrations, if other prerequisites to jurisdiction were established. Section 12(6)(f)(h) of the Arbitration Act 1950, which empowered the High Court to secure the amount in dispute and to grant injunctions, became the basis for the High Court's jurisdiction to issue a Mareva injunction freezing the respondent's assets pending the outcome of the hearing although cause had to be shown that the respondent was likely to seek to transfer assets out of England. Mareva injunctions restrained defendants from selling, disposing, or otherwise removing assets from the jurisdiction. For some time, it was thought that a Mareva injunction could be obtained only if the defendant was not domiciled in England. This limitation eventually disappeared; an injunction could be obtained in support of ICC arbitration in England even if the defendant was domiciled in England or elsewhere provided there was a risk that assets could have been transferred abroad. The power of courts to order Mareva injunctions in connection with arbitral proceedings was confirmed by Article 44(2)(e) of Arbitration Act 1996 which provides for "the granting of an interim injunction or the appointment of a receiver."[33]

In the United States, attachment is an ordinary and frequently granted provisional remedy in domestic arbitration[34] as well as in admiralty matters.[35] Thus it would not seem unreasonable to assume that pre-award attachment would be particularly favored in international arbitration, where the risks of flight and irreparable depletion of assets are probably higher than in domestic cases.[36] Surprisingly, however, the opposite is true. Of the 125 countries

---

32   So named after the case which established the injunctive device of restraining a party from removing from the jurisdiction or otherwise dealing with assets which could be used to satisfy a judgment or award, Mareva Compania Navierg S.A. v. International Bulk Carriers S.A., [1975] 2 LLOYD'S L. REP. 509.

33   Paragraph 214 of the DAC REPORT ON THE ARBITRATION BILL states:

"[T]he powers we have given the Court are intended to be used when the tribunal cannot act or act effectively, as subsection (5) makes clear. It is under this Clause that the Court has power to order *Mareva* or *Anton Piller* relief (*i.e.,* urgent protective measures to preserve assets or evidence) so as to help the arbitral process to operate effectively. Equally, there may be instances where a party seeks an order that will have an effect on a third party, which only the Court could grant. For the same reason the Court is given the other powers listed."

34   M. Domke, COMMERCIAL ARBITRATION, Sec. 26.02 (Wilner, ed. 1999): "Demands for attachments will be justified, as an aid to the arbitration process by preserving the subject matter or assets intact within the jurisdiction, thus making the award meaningful."

35   The United States Arbitration Act specifically provides for pre-arbitration attachments in admiralty matters: 9 U.S.C.A., Chap. 1, Sec. 8.

36   In fact, the leading federal case establishing that there is no inconsistency between seeking attachment from a court and requiring arbitration of the merits of the dispute involved an international dispute, Murray Oil Prods. Co. v. Mitsui & Co., 146 F. 2d 381 (2d. Cir. 1944) (per Learned Hand, J.). However, that case was decided prior to the entering into effect of the New York Con-

that have signed the New York Convention, the United States stands alone in having developed case-law to the effect that attachment pending international arbitration is somehow incompatible with the Convention. This view was adopted in 1974 in the leading federal case of *McCreary Tire & Rubber Co. (U.S.) v. CEAT S.p.A (Italy)*[37] which set aside an attachment granted by a lower court in favor of a United States distributor in connection with its dispute against an Italian manufacturer. The contract with the Italian manufacturer contained an ICC arbitration clause. The attachment had originally been granted in connection with a suit on the merits brought in federal court, in contravention of the arbitration clause. By the time the issue of the validity of the attachment came before the Court of Appeals, the ICC arbitration was actually under way. Finding that the suit on the merits in court had been brought in intentional contravention of the agreement to arbitrate, the Court of Appeals held that the attachment should fall with the dismissal of the suit. The Court of Appeals, rejecting the argument that the cause of action should only be stayed pending the outcome of arbitration and that the attachment should remain in force, found that:

> The Convention forbids the courts of a contracting state from entertaining a suit which violates an agreement to arbitrate. Thus the contention that arbitration is merely another method of trial, to which state provisional remedies should equally apply, is unavailable.

Despite the rather special facts upon which the decision was based, the *McCreary* case has stood as authority for what seems a dubious proposition: that an obligation to arbitrate and the duty of courts to refer parties to arbitration under Article II of the New York Convention somehow deprives the same courts of any power to take interim measures in aid of international arbitrations to which the New York Convention applies.

The *McCreary* proposition was resoundingly rejected in 1977 by the Federal District Court for the Northern District of California, which sustained a conservatory attachment of a US $85 million account receivable in support of international arbitration in the case of *Carolina Power and Light Co. v. Uranex*.[38] That case concerned the alleged breach of a long-term contract for the sale of uranium by a French seller to a United States utility company. It was alleged that the seller had no other assets within the United States and that the attachment would be not only security for execution of any arbitration award but also an incentive for the foreign seller to honor its obligation to arbitrate in New York.

---

vention.; *see also* Section 34.03(a), *infra*.

37 501 F.2d 1032 (3d Cir 1974); summarized *in* I YEARBOOK 204 (1976); for a critical analysis, *see* IX YEARBOOK 365-6 (1987).

38 451 F. Supp. 1044 (N.D. Cal. 1977); summarized *in* IV YEARBOOK 336 (1979).

The District Court found that "nothing in the text of the Convention itself suggests that it precludes prejudgment attachment." Refusing to follow *McCreary*, it permitted the attachment to stand. The case was settled prior to arbitration and hence the validity of the attachment was never ruled on by an appellate court.

After the *Uranex* decision, many commentators believed that United States case-law would develop along the lines of commercial practice in most jurisdictions and deem attachment in support of arbitration not to contravene the New York Convention.[39]

However, in 1981, the Fourth Circuit became the first federal appellate court to announce its unqualified support for the *McCreary* proposition in *I.T.A.D. Asso. v. Podar Bros*, 636 F.2d 75, 77 (4th cir. (S.C.) 1981).[40] The court, citing only *McCreary*, ordered the liquidation of an attachment placed by a district court on an Indian seller at the request of an American buyer, in connection with international arbitration proceedings. Other appellate decisions have mostly confirmed the *McCreary* doctrine[41], although the issue has not been treated yet at the appellate level in all jurisdictions, notably in the Ninth Circuit where the *Uranex* doctrine remains valid. The prediction of early reversal of the *McCreary* doctrine by the Supreme Court has so far not been confirmed, either because of lack of an appropriate case or for other reasons. Case law has tended to limit its effect, however.

McCreary has not been an obstacle to attachment in international maritime cases.[42] More generally, the only appellate court so far to call into question the *McCreary* doctrine has been the Fifth Circuit in *E.A.S.T., Inc. Of Stanford,*

---

39 In 1985 a knowledgeable practitioner wrote: "Given the diverse opinions of lower courts on the point it seems likely that the Supreme Court of the United States will be presented with the issue in due course. It seems equally likely that the *McCreary-Cooper* line of authority will be reversed." J. Becker, *Attachments in Aid of International Arbitration—The American Position*, 1 ARB. INT. 40, at 48 (1985); *see also*, C. Brower and W.M. Tupman, *Court Ordered Provisional Measures Under the New York Convention*, 80 AM. J. INT. L. 24 (1986).

40 Charles Brower, *What I Tell You Three Times is True: U.S. Courts and Pre-Award Interim Measures Under the New York Convention*, 35 VA. J. INT. LAW 971, 988 (1995).

41 In addition to cases in the 3rd and 4th circuits upholding *McCreary*, the highest court of the State of New York in a 4-3 decision refused to permit attachment in support of an ICC arbitration conducted in Zurich. Cooper v. Ateliers de la Motobecane, 57 N.Y. 2d 408, 456 N.Y.S. 2d. 728, 442 N.E. 2d 1239 (Court of Appeal 1982). The New York Convention prohibition was found to prevent application of New York procedural legislation (CPLR See 7502(c)) which specifically authorized attachments in aid of arbitration. While the New York decision is significant as precedent, state courts will not ordinarily be competent to rule on international arbitrations subject to the New York Convention since any party in such a case would have the right to remove the dispute from state courts to federal courts.

42 Andros Compania Maritima S.A. v. Andre and Cie. S.A., 430 F. Supp. 88 (S.D.N.Y. 1977); Atlas Chartering Services, Inc. v. World Trade Group, Inc., 453 F. Supp. 861 (S.D.N.Y. 1978); *but see* Metropolitan World Tanker Corp. v. P.N. Pertambangan Minjakdangas Bumi Nasional, 427 F. Supp. 3 (S.D.N.Y. 1975).

Conn. v. M/V Alaia, 876 F.2d 1168 (5th Cir. (La.) 1989). Finding that the arbitration in question was an admiralty matter, the court did not directly address *McCreary*, choosing instead to cite authority from the Second Circuit that the New York Convention allows attachment as an exception in admiralty cases. In dicta to its holding, however, citing a number of decisions and commentary critical of *McCreary*, the court observed that if the reasoning behind *McCreary* was valid, then it should apply to both admiralty as well as typical commercial disputes—since a treaty prohibition would override even a statutorily authorized attachment—, a view which the court chose not to adopt.

Most international practitioners would agree that since international arbitration has become a typical means to settle international disputes, claimants should not be deprived of security devices available through national courts since such devices may cause recalcitrant parties to cooperate in advancing the arbitral procedure as well as serve to ensure payment of awards. Should attachment be available only if parties have expressly accepted the possibility thereof in their contract (*see* Section 8.07)? Since national courts are expected, and indeed obligated, under the New York Convention to execute international awards, it is difficult to see why they should not be able to provide for attachment as security in advance of the award even in the absence of a contractual stipulation to that effect. No doubt the last chapter in this American saga has not been written; attachments continue to be granted by lower courts, particularly in the Second Circuit, an important venue for international commercial arbitrations and for business assets[43] although the Court of Appeal has not questioned the *McCreary* doctrine. Moreover, the New York Convention has not been deemed to be an impediment to the granting of injunctive relief.[44] The scope of any prohibition by the New York Convention on the granting of interim measures in support of arbitration will continue to be raised before federal courts of appeal in diverse circumstances.

27.05   Court ordered discovery and production of evidence

There has been considered above (Chapter 26) the role of the arbitrator in ordering the parties to produce documents or attend depositions in advance of hearings, and the possible recourse by the arbitrator, in many jurisdictions, to the courts when orders are not complied with. There also exists the possibility, although very narrowly restricted, for a party to bring ancillary proceedings in support of arbitration before a court to obtain discovery from a

---

43   *See e.g.*, Tampimex Oil Ltd. v. Latina Trading Corporation, 558 F. Supp. 1201 (S.D.N.Y. 1983) (refusal to vacate US $1,500,000 attachment as security for contractual claims subject to arbitration in London; the evidence included records of defendant's removal of assets to Switzerland).

44   *See* cases at footnotes 20-21, *supra*.

party, or for a party or the tribunal itself to seek judicial assistance to obtain evidence from a third party.

It is principally in common-law jurisdictions that this possibility, as narrow as it may be, has been exercised. In civil-law jurisdictions, the principal intervention by courts has been to order judicially supervised expert reports, on an urgent basis, to obtain an official finding of the facts at a particular moment (Section 27.02 *supra*). This is consistent with the fact that pre-trial discovery by judicial compulsion at the instance of a party is not a usual feature of the civil-law system. However, as will be seen, courts may assist an arbitral tribunal during the course of proceedings to obtain a document or witness statement, although this power is rarely utilized.

The ordinary rule in the United States is that "[d]iscovery under court supervision will not be granted except under extraordinary circumstances, and then only where it is shown to be absolutely necessary for the protection of the rights of a party. Necessity rather than convenience is the test."[45]

The law reports are replete with cases illustrating failed efforts of a party to an arbitration (frequently acting for a dilatory motive) to secure the assistance of the judiciary to obtain evidence for use in arbitral proceedings. It is a fair conclusion that United States courts in general "have concluded that allowing discovery on the merits of a case prior to arbitration is inconsistent with the aims of arbitration"[46] and that:

> "The availability of disclosure devices is a significant differentiating factor between judicial and arbitral proceedings. . . The courtroom may not be used as a convenient vestibule to the arbitration hall so as to allow a party to create his own unique structure combining litigation and arbitration."[47]

Accordingly, motions by a party made directly to a court to take depositions in another state, to order interrogatories, or to order production of documents in the hands of third parties (by way of subpoena or otherwise) are routinely denied.[48]

---

45   S. Stein and D. Watman, *The Arbitration Hearing* in International Commercial Arbitration in New York, 68 (J.S. McClendon and R. Everard Goodman, ed., 1986). *see also* Section 34.03(c), *infra*.

46   Mississippi Power Co. v. Peabody Coal Co., 69 F.R.D. 558, 567 (S.D. Miss. 1976) (citing numerous authorities).

47   De Sapio v. Kohlmeyer, 35 N.Y. 2d 402, 321 N.E. 2d 770 (1974).

48   Burton v. Bush, 614 F 2d 398, (4th Cir. 1980) (subpoena); Commercial Solvents Corp. v. Louisiana Liquid F. Co., 20 F.R.D. 359 (S.D.N.Y. 1957) (depositions); Penn Tanker Co. of Delaware v. C.H.Z. Rolimpex, Warszawa, 199 F. Supp 716 (S.D.N.Y. 1961) (written interrogatories and depositions), Oriental Commercial Shipping Co., Ltd. v. Rosseel, N.V. (No. 84-Civ. 7173, S.D.N.Y.), 4 Mealey's Int. Arb. Rep. Section B-1 (February 1989) (deposition concerning location of assets of Saudi Arabian defendant).

Relief has nevertheless been granted in a few exceptional cases, especially where the request is made prior to the constitution of the arbitral tribunal in the following circumstances:

(i) discovery on the issue of arbitral jurisdiction (*i.e.*, whether an arbitral agreement had been signed, or whether there was fraud in connection with the agreement to arbitrate);

(ii) discovery concerning arbitrability of the dispute;[49]

(iii) discovery to prevent disappearance of proof due to progress of the works (construction projects);[50]

(iv) discovery to prevent disappearance of witness testimony (witnesses on ships soon to set sail).[51]

If courts have been reluctant to intervene prior to the constitution of an arbitral tribunal to order pre-hearing discovery, it is logical that they would be even more reticent after constitution when a contractually agreed institution exists to engage in fact finding and to make the appropriate orders relating thereto. In addition, the ICC Rules agreed by the parties provide that after the file is transmitted to the arbitrator a party may apply to a judicial authority only in "appropriate circumstances."

Most United States courts accordingly refuse to intervene in the arbitral process to order pre-hearing discovery at the request of a party after the arbitral tribunal has been formed.[52] Where the arbitral tribunal itself has issued a subpoena or made an order to produce evidence for the arbitration hearing, a court may be called upon to ensure compliance, pursuant to specific state or federal legislative provisions.[53]

It is interesting to contrast these procedures with their counterparts under English law where pre-hearing discovery is more limited in scope (in principle

---

49　International Union of Elec., Radio Mach. Workers v. Westinghouse, 48 F.R.D. 298 (S.D.N.Y. 1969).

50　Vespe Contracting Co. v. Anvan Corp. 399 F. Supp. 516 (E.D.P. 1975). *See* Bigge Crane & Rigging Co. v. Docutel Corp., 371 F. Supp. 240 (S.D.N.Y. 1973).

51　Bergen Shipping Co. v. Japan Marine Serv., Ltd., 386 F. Supp. 450 (S.D.N.Y. 1984).

52　Burton v. Bush, 614 F. 2d 389, 390 (4th Cir. 1980); *see also* Hunt v. Mobil Oil Corporation, 583 F. Supp. 1092 (S.D.N.Y. 1984) (where the federal court enjoined state court proceedings having as their purpose the extensive discovery of facts since they were an unwarranted interference with the arbitration); for a discussion of the complicated relationship between state and federal rules of discovery for arbitration, *see* Willenken, *The Often Overlooked Use of Discovery in Aid of Arbitration and the Spread of the New York Rule to Federal Common Law*, 35 BUSINESS LAWYER 173 (1979).

53　*See e.g.*, USAA Sec. 7, New York CPLR Sec. 7505, California Civ. Proc. Code Sec. 1282- 1283. The subpoena power of arbitrators is described *in* M. Domke, COMMERCIAL ARBITRATION (Wilner ed., 1994), Sec. 24.03. An arbitrator's refusal to issue a subpoena will not be reversed by a court as the issuance is within the arbitrator's discretion. Thompson v. Zavin, 607 F. Supp. 780 (C.D. Cal. 1984).

no pre-hearing depositions are permitted) but where court intervention in support of arbitration is specifically provided for.

English court intervention authorized by law by way of discovery is broad and includes: The taking of the evidence of witnesses, inspection or photographing of the property in dispute, ordering that samples be taken from, or any observation be made of or experiment conducted upon, the property of parties, etc.[54] Most of these powers duplicate those given to an arbitrator, and ordinarily a party must address its request to the arbitral tribunal (if effectively constituted) and have recourse to the courts only if the arbitral tribunal's orders are ineffective.[55]

Under English law a party, consistent with the right of parties in normal court procedures, may issue a writ of subpoena[56] compelling a person to testify before an arbitral tribunal and to supply relevant documents related to the testimony. The subpoena should be used to obtain evidence actually needed at the hearing (fishing expeditions are not permitted) and has the advantage that it can be addressed to third parties, not subject to arbitral jurisdiction or requests from arbitrators. The courts will oversee the use of subpoenas (which, at the request of a party, are issued administratively without leave of court) to prevent abuse.[57] This contrasts with United States law where the power to issue subpoenas is, with some exceptions under state law, more generally given to the arbitral tribunal alone and is not much used.[58]

The issuing and executing of commissions rogatory to obtain evidence, where the arbitration takes place in one jurisdiction and the evidence is to be found in another, raise interesting questions. In civil-law jurisdictions the normal way for obtaining letters rogatory would be for the arbitral tribunal to request

---

54   Arbitration Act of 1996, Section 44(2).

55   Section 44(5) of the Arbitration Act provides: "In any case the Court shall act only if or to the extent that the arbitral tribunal, and any arbitral or other institution or person vested by the parties with power in that regard, has no power or is unable for the time being to act effectively."

56   Arbitration Act of 1996, Section 43(1).

57   For a helpful discussion of the issues, *see* Sunderland Steamship P and I Association v. Gatoil International Inc. (The "Lorenzo Halcoussi") [1988] 1 LLOYD'S L. REP. 180 (Q.B. Div., Mr. Justice Steyn) where a *subpoena duces tecum* addressed to a third party, in support of arbitration, sought to obtain extensive documents, including correspondence with one of the parties to the arbitration, for which the arbitrators had refused to issue a discovery order against the party. Under all the circumstances, the court found the terms of the subpoena overly broad and designed to obtain discovery in the nature of a fishing expedition. It was dismissed.

58   Section 7 of the Federal Arbitration Act gives arbitrators the power to issue subpoenas summoning witnesses to testify before them and in appropriate cases to produce books, records and documents deemed material as evidence. The arbitrators may petition the United States district court in the district in which they are sitting to enforce the subpoena if not voluntarily obeyed. The efficacy of the subpoena device is limited by the fact that it can only be served within the district where the arbitral tribunal is sitting. The mere fact that an arbitral tribunal will take the formal step of issuance of a subpoena may serve to persuade a witness to appear before an arbitral tribunal when requests by a party for voluntary appearance have failed.

the court at the seat of arbitration to obtain the evidence by issuing letters to a foreign court where some form of cooperation for obtaining evidence in civil proceedings exists. Article 184 of the 1987 Swiss Private International Law Act provides:

> Where the assistance of state authorities is needed for the taking of evidence, the arbitral tribunal *or a party with the consent of the arbitral tribunal* may request the assistance of the court at the seat of the arbitral tribunal . . . (Emphasis added.)

The Swiss law wisely provides a role for a party and sets out how it can act in the proceedings, since the tribunal itself, even if in a civil-law jurisdiction formally charged with developing the evidence in the case, cannot be expected to devote as much time and care in preparation of submissions to the local court as would be the party in whose interest the request is made.

In practice the letters rogatory procedure is cumbersome and is infrequently used in support of arbitral proceedings. Arbitrators rightly are seldom convinced that recourse to such a procedure is appropriate or required.[59] The authors are aware of one unusual case where the defendant party persuaded an ICC arbitral tribunal sitting in Geneva to request the cantonal court to issue letters rogatory to an Austrian court for the purpose of obtaining the evidence of a former co-manager of the defendant party, but who was allegedly no longer under the employment or control of the defendant and was hence a third party. The Swiss court granted the request. As predicted, the procedure was time consuming.

Another interesting question is whether a party or an arbitral tribunal may *directly* request a foreign court to assist in taking discovery or ordering the production of documents to be used in arbitration, without asking the court at the seat of arbitration to initiate a court-to-court request for cooperation. One such attempt was made for instance, by a party to an ICC arbitration, with seat in Geneva, to request directly from a United States federal court the production of documents held by the defendant U.S. company at its domicile within the court's jurisdiction. The request was based on 28 U.S.C. Section 1782(a), which provided:

> The district court of the district in which a person resides or is found may order him to give his testimony or statement or to produce a document or other thing for use in a proceeding in a foreign or international tribunal. The order may be made pursuant to a letter rogatory issued, or request made, by a foreign or international tribunal or upon the application of any interested person and may direct that the testimony or statement be

---

59 The considerations which an arbitral tribunal will take into account in deciding whether to seek the assistance of a Swiss court to obtain testimony from witnesses resident in Switzerland and those resident abroad is set out in documents excerpted from ICC Case 6401/1996, 1998 J.D.I. 1065, note Dominique Hascher.

given, or the document or other thing be produced, before a person appointed by the court.[60]

It was contended that the term "tribunal" as used in the statute was intended to have a very broad application and hence should cover ICC arbitral tribunals.[61] However, in the event, the defendant party "voluntarily" turned over the requested document. The issues before the court of the right of an arbitral tribunal, or of a party to the arbitral proceeding, directly to invoke the statute to obtain discovery in the United States of a document to be used abroad as evidence in a foreign arbitral proceeding thus became moot, and no decision was issued.

Several recent decisions, however, have treated the question of whether private arbitral tribunals can be included within the meaning of "international tribunals" under 28 U.S.C. Section 1782(a). In 1994 in the *Application of Technostroyexport*,[62] the federal district court for the Southern District of New York ruled that an arbitrator or arbitration panel constituted a "tribunal" within the meaning of 28 U.S.C. Section 1882(a); the court proceeded to issue an order for discovery. In 1998, however, a different judge on the same court in the *Bear Sterns* case quashed subpoenas issued in support of an ICC arbitration with its seat in Mexico on the ground that the term "foreign or international tribunal" as used in 28 U.S.C. Section 1782 authorizing district courts to assist discovery efforts in connection with proceedings before such tribunals did not encompass private international commercial arbitration.

The *Bear Sterns* decision was confirmed on appeal by the Second Circuit Court of Appeals.[63] In its opinion the Circuit Court showed considerable skepticism about the wisdom of expanding court ordered discovery in aid of arbitration.

> The legislative history's silence with respect to private tribunals is especially telling because we are confident that a significant congressional expansion of American judicial assistance to international arbitral panels created exclusively by private parties would not have been lightly un-

---

60 The text was amended on 10 February 1996 on procedural points; however, the term "foreign or international tribunal" remains.

61 The legislative history of the 1964 Amendment to the Section reveals that the word "tribunal" was used deliberately "to make it clear that assistance is not confined to proceedings before conventional courts [but extends to] proceedings before a foreign administrative tribunal or quasi-judicial agency. . .," cited *in* Fonsecie v. Blumenthal, 620 F. 2d 322, 323 (2d Cir. 1980) and *In re* Request from Ministry of Legal Affairs of Trinidad and Tobago, 848 F. 2d 1155 (11th Cir. 1988); *see* H. Smit, *International Litigation Under the United States Code*, 65 COLUM L. REV. 1015, 1026 at n. 71 (1964), taking the position that the word "tribunal" in the 1964 legislation of which he was one of the drafters, includes "arbitral tribunals."

62 853 F. Supp. 695, (S.D.N.Y. 1994)

63 National Broadcasting Company, Inc. and NBC Europe Inc. v. Bear Stearns & Co., Merrill Lynch & Co., Salomon Brothers Inc., SBC Warburg Inc.; Violy Byroum & Partners and T.V. Azteca S.A. de C.V., Docket No. 98-7468, 38 I.L.M. (1999) (Second Circuit, January 26, 1999 confirming order of Judge Sweet, S.D.N.Y., 16 January 1998, quashing subpoenas).

dertaken by Congress without at least a mention of this legislative intention.

The popularity of arbitration rests in considerable part on its asserted efficiency and cost-effectiveness—characteristics said to be at odds with full-scale litigation in the courts, and especially at odds with the broad-ranging discovery made possible by the Federal Rules of Civil Procedure. *See Allied-Bruce Terminix Cos. v. Dobson*, 513 U.S. 265, 280 (1995) (advantages of arbitration are that it is "usually cheaper and faster than litigation; . . . can have simpler procedural and evidentiary rules; . . . normally minimizes hostility and is less disruptive of ongoing and future business dealings among the parties") (quoting H.R. Rep. No. 97-542, at 13 (1982)). Few, if any, non-American tribunals of any kind, including arbitration panels created by private parties, provide for the kind of discovery that is commonplace in our federal courts and in most, if not all, state courts. If the parties to a private international arbitration make no provision for some degree of consensual discovery *inter se* in their agreement to arbitrate, the arbitrators control discovery, and neither party is deprived of its bargained-for efficient process by the other party's tactical use of discovery devices.

Citing the reasoning of the Second Circuit, the Fifth Circuit Court similarly refused to issue a discovery order to an individual who was not a party to an international arbitration between the Republic of Kazakhstan and Biedermann International [64]. The court made a distinction between public and private international tribunals and ruled that "the provision was enlarged to further comity among nations, not to complicate and undermine the salutary device of private international arbitration."

The Fifth Circuit Court found that from its adoption in 1855 through to its amendment in 1964, §1782 had permitted discovery assistance to parties only in proceedings before foreign courts; subsequent references to "international tribunals" were therefore intended to expand the discovery provision for "conventional courts" to include "foreign administrative and quasi-judicial agencies." The court added that "[t]here is no contemporaneous evidence that Congress contemplated extending §1782 to the then-novel arena of international commercial arbitration."

Liberal interpretation of §1782, the court pointed out, would create a conflict with Section 7 of the Federal Arbitration Act, under which "federal courts have a duty to enforce arbitrators' summons only within the federal district in which the arbitrators, or a majority of them, are sitting." The differences in available discovery options might then "create an entirely new category of disputes concerning the appointment of arbitrators and the characterization

---

[64] Application of the Republic of Kazakhstan v. Biedermann International, 98-21072 (Fifth Circuit, March 17, 1999), Stockholm Chamber of Commerce Arbitration

of arbitration disputes as domestic, foreign or international." Rather than aiding international arbitration, liberal interpretation of §1782, the Fifth Circuit warned, would empower "arbitrators or, worse, the parties, in private international disputes to seek ancillary discovery through the federal courts," a development which [would] "not benefit the arbitration process."

The recent decisions of the Second and Fifth Circuits show that United States courts now mostly exclude arbitration from the reach of §1782. Parties seeking discovery orders in the United States for use in arbitral proceedings taking place abroad must now request letters rogatory from a court at the place of arbitration, through application to the arbitral tribunal or directly to the court. Acceptance of the United States court to execute such letters rogatory would depend upon the existence and contents of treaty arrangements between the state of the requesting court and the United States.

PART V

THE IMPACT OF NATIONAL LAW

CHAPTER 28

NATIONAL CONSTRAINTS ON ICC ARBITRATION

28.01 Private Consent and Public Power

Arbitration arises from a contract to entrust the binding resolution of present or potential disputes to a private decision-maker rather than a court. Therefore it may seem puzzling that *national* procedural law should matter at all to *international* arbitration. After all, the purpose of an arbitration agreement, by its very nature, is to keep disputes away from judges.

Notwithstanding its consensual foundation, however, arbitration often proceeds in the shadow of state power. When one side to a dispute regrets its decision to renounce recourse to courts, the state lends its power to enforce the agreement to arbitrate. Judicial proceedings are stayed; arbitral awards are given *res judicata* effect; and the loser's assets may be seized.

An inevitable tension results from this mixture of private consent and public power. Aspirations toward delocalized dispute resolution collide with the national norms that must sometimes be invoked if an arbitration agreement is to be more than a piece of paper. Ironically, the idiosyncrasies of national law enter ICC arbitration precisely because the business community desires binding waiver of court litigation. When an unwilling defendant or a disappointed loser resists an arbitration agreement or award, judges often defer to the bargained-for arbitrator in a manner that interjects legal peculiarities of their own forum.

For example, in the well-known *Mitsubishi* case[1] the United State Supreme Court exacted a price for compelling arbitration between a Japanese auto manufacturer and its Puerto Rican distributor. The manufacturer had to stipulate that antitrust counterclaims would be considered under an American

---

1   *See* Section 33.02.

statute, the Sherman Act, despite the contract's explicit choice of Swiss governing law.[2] Moreover, the Court warned that an American judge asked to enforce any award resulting from the arbitration might have a second look at the process to insure that the United States' antitrust law had in fact been taken into account.[3]

Not only does national arbitration law affect ICC arbitration, but the ICC Rules in turn affect the application of national law. Many nations permit annulment or non-recognition of an award because the parties' agreement (which includes the ICC Rules[4]) was not followed with respect to the arbitral procedure[5] or the constitution of the arbitral tribunal.[6]

Sometimes the mandates of national arbitration law run parallel to the ICC Rules. For example, Article 15(2) of the Rules provides that the arbitral tribunal shall in all cases "act fairly and impartially and ensure that each party has a reasonable opportunity to present its case." This fundamental principle of ICC arbitration echoes analogous notions of due process and equal treatment contained in national law.[7]

28.02   Matters Affected by National Arbitration Law

Familiarity with national arbitration law commends itself both before and after a dispute has arisen. At the time the arbitration clause is drafted, lawyers should try to select an arbitral venue where the judiciary monitors an arbitration's fundamental procedural fairness, but does not review the merits of the arbitrator's conclusions of fact or law. The venue should also be in a country that adheres to the 1958 New York Arbitration Convention, which many nations apply only on the basis of reciprocity, to awards rendered in the territory of another contracting state.

---

2   *See* footnote 19 of Mitsubishi v. Soler, 473 U.S. 614 (1985). *See generally*, William W. Park, *Private Adjudicators and the Public Interest*, 12 BROOK. J. INT. L. 629 (1986).

3   The Court's problematic "second look" doctrine is discussed at 473 U.S. 614 (1985), pages 637-38.

4   For example, arbitrator independence would be incorporated into an arbitration clause by reference to the ICC Rules (see Article 7), regardless of whether the arbitral situs prohibits or allows arbitrator links with one of the parties.

5   *See* UNCITRAL Model Arbitration Law, Article 34(2)(a)(iv) and Article V(1)(d) of the New York Convention. *See also* 1996 English Arbitration Act, § 68(2)(c), defining serious irregularity for which an award may be challenged to include "failure by the tribunal to conduct the proceedings in accordance with the procedure agreed by the parties."

6   *See* French *NCPC* Article 1502(2), which permits annulment of an award if the arbitral tribunal was improperly constituted (*irrégulièrement composé*), and cases discussed in Matthieu de Boisséson, *LE DROIT FRANÇAIS DE L'ARBITRAGE* (1990), at paragraph 795 (pages 833-34).

7   *See e.g.*, 1996 English Arbitration Act § 68, French *NCPC* Article 1502(4), Swiss L.D.I.P. Article 190(2)(d), U.S. Federal Arbitration Act, § 10(a)(3) and UNCITRAL Model Arbitration Law, Article 34(a)(ii).

Later, after a claim has been filed, national arbitration law may become relevant if judicial proceedings are instituted to compel arbitration, to attach assets, to stay competing judicial proceedings, to remove biased arbitrators, or to obtain the production of evidence. Subsequent to the arbitration, courts may be asked to vacate, confirm or enforce an award on grounds as diverse (depending on the country) as a denial of due process, an excess of jurisdiction or even a mistake on a point of law.

The following five matters are among those aspects of national arbitration law which most frequently affect ICC arbitration.

(i) *The Validity of the Arbitration Agreement.* Like the New York Arbitration Convention, the laws at most major arbitral centers require arbitration agreements to be in writing, but may differ on how prominent the "writing" must be (first page in capitals? just above the signature?), whether it may be incorporated into a contract by reference to the rules of a trade association, or whether by its conduct a party may be deemed to have accepted a document containing an arbitration provision.

(ii) *Subject Matter Arbitrability.* Some countries require that disputes relating to public law matters (competition, patents, securities, discrimination) must be submitted to courts rather than arbitrators.

(iii) *Preconditions to Arbitration.* In some jurisdictions, only courts are empowered to determine whether arbitration claims have been filed within relevant express or implied time limits.

(iv) *Interim Measures.* To support arbitration, courts sometimes compel testimony, secure the attendance of witnesses, preserve evidence, arrange for sale of perishable goods, or remove non-performing arbitrators. In addition, courts of competent jurisdiction may deal directly with urgent matters such as the enforcement of confidentiality obligations or security agreements that have been excluded from the agreement to arbitrate, or are covered by Article 23(2) of the ICC Rules.

(v) *Review of Awards.* Courts at the arbitral seat generally may set aside an award if the proceedings are not fair or if the arbitrators exceed their mission. In some countries courts may also hear appeals on issues of law.

28.03   The Arbitral Situs

(a) The "Law of the Arbitration."

The arbitral situs—also called the arbitral "seat" or the place of arbitration—will be designated either in the arbitration agreement or by the ICC Court. Although the arbitral seat serves as the focal point for the proceedings, it is not always identical with the location of the hearings[8] or the deliberations,[9] which for reasons of convenience may be fixed elsewhere than the arbitration's juridical seat.

The role of the arbitral situs has attracted considerable scholarly attention,[10] with much spirited debate devoted to how far an international arbitration must or should fall under its tutelage.[11] The traditional premise that any arbitration should be subject to the law of the place of the proceedings[12] has begotten both critics[13] and defenders.[14]

Some countries have deliberately reduced the impact of local law on international arbitration. Prior to 1989, for example, international arbitrations in Switzerland were subject to the Intercantonal Arbitration Concordat, which

---

8   *See* Article 14(2) of the ICC Rules. With respect to a change of venue for the hearings the arbitrators must first consult with the parties, and may in no event ignore the parties' agreement on the matter.

9   Article 14(3) of the ICC Rules allows deliberations any place the arbitrators consider "appropriate."

10 *See generally*, William W. Park, *Duty and Discretion in International Arbitration*, 93 AM. J. INT'L ARB. 805 (1999). W. Laurence Craig, *International Ambition and National Restraints in ICC Arbitration*, 1 ARB. INT. 19 (1985); W. Laurence Craig, *The Uses and Abuses of Appeal in International Arbitration Awards*, 14 PRIVATE INVESTORS ABROAD (1987); William W. Park, *National Law and Commercial Justice*, 63 TULANE L. REV. 647 (1989); William W. Park, *The Lex Loci Arbitri and International Commercial Arbitration*, 32 INT. & COMP. L. Q. 21 (1983); Jan Paulsson, *Delocalization of International Commercial Arbitration*, 32 INT. & COMP. L.Q. 53 (1983); W. MICHAEL REISMAN, SYSTEMS OF CONTROL IN INTERNATIONAL ADJUDICATION AND ARBITRATION (1992); PHILIPPE FOUCHARD, EMMANUEL GAILLARD & BERTHOLD GOLDMAN, TRAITÉ DE L'ARBITRAGE COMMERCIAL INTERNATIONAL, paragraphs 44-50; REDFERN & HUNTER, pages 89-93; GARY BORN, INTERNATIONAL COMMERCIAL ARBITRATION IN THE UNITED STATES (1994) pages 3-4, 26-37.

11 For a classic articulation of the territorial seat theory of arbitration, see Miller v. Whitworth Street Estates, [1970] 1 All ER 796 (H.L.). English substantive law governed a contract giving rise to arbitration in Scotland. In light of the place of arbitration, the House of Lords upheld the arbitrator's refusal to present questions of law for judicial review under the "case stated" procedure, available under English law until 1979 but not then part of Scottish arbitration law.

12 This traditional view was articulated by the late Francis Mann, who argued that the pronouncements of an arbitral tribunal are without force unless linked to a specific system of national law. "Every right or power a private person enjoys," wrote Mann, "is inexorably conferred by or derived from a system of municipal law which may conveniently and in accordance with tradition be called *lex fori*, though it would be more exact (but also less familiar) to speak of the *lex arbitri*." F.A. MANN, *Lex Facit Arbitrum*, in INTERNATIONAL ARBITRATION: LIBER AMICORUM FOR MARTIN DOMKE 157 (P. Sanders, ed., 1967), at 159, reprinted in 2 ARB. INT. 241 (1986).

13 *See e.g.*, Jan Paulsson, *Arbitration Unbound: Award Detached from the Law of its Country of Origin*, 30 INT. & COMP. L. Q. 358 (1981); Jan Paulsson, *Delocalization of International Commercial Arbitration*, 32 INT. & COMP. L. Q. 53 (1983).

14 William W. Park, *The Lex Loci Arbitri and International Commercial Arbitration*, 32 INT. & COMP. L. Q. 21 (1983); William W. Park, *National Law and Commercial Justice*, 63 TUL. L. REV. 647 (1989).

fills procedural gaps in an arbitration by reference to Swiss federal law.[15] By contrast, analogous provisions of the currently applicable statute omit such reference.[16] The evolution of the ICC Rules shows a similar trend toward delocalization. While Article 16 of the Rules' 1955 version in some circumstances imposed the procedural law of "the country in which the arbitrator holds the proceedings", Article 15 of the current Rules establishes procedural autonomy for the parties and the arbitral tribunal.

Some scholars have suggested that mandatory norms of the arbitral situs constitute a *lex arbitri*,[17] or curial law.[18] This "law of the arbitration" is distinct from (i) the law applicable to the contract's validity and interpretation,[19] (ii) the internal procedural rules applied by the arbitrators to issues such as the admissibility of evidence, cross-examination or discovery,[20] and (iii) the treaties and statutes applicable to the recognition of foreign awards. While the *lex arbitri* bears upon an arbitration agreement's effectiveness, other legal systems may also affect the agreement's validity.[21] The curial law governs those aspects of the arbitration as to which the state perceives a regulatory right or duty, such as challenge of awards, consolidation of related proceedings, or the impartiality of the arbitrators.

(b) Why the Arbitral Situs Matters.

The practical importance of the arbitral situs rests on a twofold reality: (i) most national arbitration statutes provide some grounds for setting aside

---

15   See Concordat Article 24.

16   See Article 182, Swiss *Loi fédérale sur le droit international privé* (discussed in Chapter 33) and PIERRE LALIVE, JEAN-FRANÇOIS POUDRET & CLAUDE REYMOND, LE DROIT DE L'ARBITRAGE (1989), at 351-52

17   *See* REDFERN & HUNTER, at pages 78-84.

18   *See e.g.* Paul Smith Ltd. v. H & S International Holding Inc., [1991] 2 LLOYD'S L. REP. 127, where the Commercial Court referred to "the *lex arbitri*, the curial law or the law governing the arbitration" as concerning itself with matters such as interim measures of protection, vacancies in the arbitral tribunal and the removal of arbitrators for misconduct.

19   National law may apply directly to the substantive merits of the dispute, or may provide the choice-of-law principles determining the law applicable on the merits. In some cases, an arbitration agreement's validity may be determined under a law different from the one governing the dispute's merits. *See* discussion of the French *Cour de cassation* decision in the *Dalico* case, Section 31.02 (f).

20   For ICC arbitration, these internal procedural rules derive from the ICC Rules themselves, and when those Rules are silent, the rules agreed to by the parties or (failing agreement by the parties) decided upon by the arbitrators, as well any mandatory procedural norms imposed by the arbitral seat. *See* ICC Rules Article 15 (2). In some cases the national procedural norms applicable to an ICC arbitration may be expanded by contract. For example, in France NCPC Articles 1494 and 1495 make clear that parties to international arbitration may opt into French procedural law.

21   Thus *dictum* in an English Court of Appeal decision may go too far in suggesting that a London arbitral situs means that "English law is the proper law of the arbitration agreement." *See* ¶ 4, AT&T Corp. & Lucent Technologies Inc. v. Saudi Cable Co., Case No. QBCMF 1999/1200/A3, discussed in Chapter 13.

awards made within their territory, and (ii) annulment at the arbitral situs gives the loser a powerful argument for resisting the award's enforcement.[22] As the place where an award is "made" for purposes of the New York Convention's enforcement scheme,[23] the arbitral situs by vacatur of an award can impair,[24] though not necessarily destroy,[25] the award's international currency.[26]

To ignore the parties' choice of law could mean challenge of the award (for arbitrator excess of authority) at the place where it was rendered. But to apply the law might yield an unenforceable award if the party-chosen law violates the public policy of the place of performance. Moreover, in some cases multiple legal systems may vie with each other for even more direct control of an arbitration, with courts in the country of applicable law trying to enjoin arbitration conducted outside their borders.[27]

28.04   Award Annulment: Why and to What Effect

Assumptions about the law of the arbitral seat meet their most acute test when applied to annulment of awards. The traditional view that there exists a *lex arbitri,* or curial law of the arbitration, fixed by reference to the arbitral situs, has engendered considerable discussion. The matter of "delocalization" of awards raises four distinct but related issues: (a) Will and/or should the arbitration situs permit waiver of the right to challenge an award? (b) What national interests of the arbitral situs are furthered by an annulment procedure? (c) On what grounds may annulment be pronounced? (d) What effect should annulment of an award where rendered have when the award is presented for recognition in another country?

---

22   The vital role of the arbitral situs does not mean that procedural norms of other countries do not matter. For example, the place of the arbitration, the place of contract performance, the parties' residence and the *locus* of the loser's assets might also have an impact on whether a particular subject matter may be submitted to arbitration. *See generally* Eric Schwartz, *The Domain of Arbitration and Issues of Arbitrability: The View From the ICC,* 9 (No.1) ICSID REV. 17 (1994), at 24-30. Schwartz notes that arbitrators "generally seek to ensure that the claim before them is, in fact, arbitrable under all of the laws that may be relevant to that determination." *Id.* at 27.

23   Occasionally there may be divergence between the arbitral seat and the place the award is deemed made. *See* Hiscox v. Outhwaite, [1991] All ER 641, where an award signed in Paris was considered made in France under the New York Convention, while the seat of the arbitration remained in England for purposes of appeal. The result of this case has been overruled by the 1996 English Arbitration Act. *See* Chapter 30. For an early foreboding of the problems that might arise from disassociating the arbitral seat from the place of making the award, see Francis A. Mann, *Where is an Award Made?,* 1 ARB. INT. 107 (1985).

24   New York Arbitration Convention V(1)(e) provides that an award *may* be refused recognition and enforcement if set aside "by a competent authority of the country in which . . . that award was made." (Emphasis added.)

25   New York Arbitration Convention Article VII preserves the right to rely on awards under the local law of the enforcement forum, whatever that law might be.

26   *See* discussion *infra* at Section 28.04 (d).

27   *See* Section 28.05.

(a) Waiver of the Right to Challenge an Award.

The ICC Rules make clear that a choice of ICC arbitration operates to exclude appeal to national courts as far as possible. ICC Rules Article 28 provides that the parties "shall be deemed to have waived the right to any form of appeal insofar as such waiver can validly be made." The theory behind this rule is that parties to arbitration seek a reasonable measure of finality. On signing the arbitration agreement, the business managers do not expect that after a dispute has been decided by the arbitrator it will be tried yet again on the substantive merits before a judge.

The effect of Article 28 of the ICC Rules will function differently depending on the country in which an arbitration is conducted. For example, England allows appeal on points of English law to be excluded by contract, but does not allow a waiver of the right to challenge an award for serious procedural irregularity or excess of jurisdiction. See Chapter 30. By contrast, Swiss law in some situations does allow waiver of the right to challenge an award to extend to matters of procedural irregularity and public policy.[28]

(b) Public and Private Interests in Annulment Procedure.

An agreement to settle disputes under the ICC Rules implies that the parties have opted for the procedural neutrality of arbitration. Why then should courts at the arbitral situs interfere with an award? If actually asked to attach assets or stay a court action, a judge will have no alternative but to consider whether the award is worthy of enforcement or recognition. However, not every setting aside of an award implicates an attempt at enforcement or recognition. Some motions to vacate awards are more in the nature of requests for declaratory relief, seeking only that a court at the arbitral situs proclaim the award void, thereby reducing the prospect of its enforceability elsewhere.

In a transnational business dispute, the economic or social impact of an arbitration often occurs outside the country of the place of the proceedings. Few vital interests of the arbitral seat will be affected by the award unless one party or its property is found within the arbitration venue. If local substantive law applies to the merits of the case, perhaps the arbitral situs will care about the outcome of the dispute, but only tangentially by virtue of how it might fertilize local law through precedents that provide behavioral rules to guide business conduct outside the particular dispute.[29]

---

28 Swiss law requires an explicit statement (*déclaration expresse*), which cannot be incorporated by reference to the ICC Rules. For such a waiver to be valid, neither party may be resident or have a branch in Switzerland. *See* discussion of *L.D.I.P.* Article 192 in Chapter 33.

29 For this reason, until 1997 England restricted waiver of the right to appeal points of law in arbitrations arising out of admiralty, commodities and insurance contracts governed by English law, the so-called "special category" cases. To remain preeminent in these areas, it was assumed that English law had to be fed by judicial decisions dealing with modern day commercial controversies. *Compare* the so-called "public law model" of litigation, discussed in Robert G. Bone, *Lon Fuller's Theory of Adjudication and the False Dichotomy Between Dispute Resolution and Public Law Models of Litigation*, 75 B.U. L. Rev. 1273 (1995).

This does not mean that the arbitral situs will have no interest in exercising control over international arbitrations conducted within its borders. In some cases the arbitral situs might be the place of contract performance or the residence of one of the parties. Even if an arbitration does not have a direct effect at the place of the proceedings, nations that directly or indirectly give an arbitrator power to bring about legal consequences have generally felt an obligation to monitor at least the arbitration's procedural integrity. Since annulment at the arbitral situs constitutes a ground for award non-recognition under the New York Convention, any arbitration situs that allows an award to go unchallenged facilitates its enforcement in other jurisdictions.

Whether a national legal framework can be called favorable to arbitration depends in large part on one's perspective. The winner looks for speed, economy and finality, while the loser looks for judicial review to ensure that all aspects of the case have been fully and fairly considered. Although no national legal system will reconcile with complete satisfaction these inconsistent concerns of winner and loser, many now seek a middle ground. As discussed below, most major arbitral centers provide judicial review for the grosser forms of procedural injustice, while still leaving a large measure of discretion to the arbitral tribunal.

Conclusion about the costs and benefits of judicial review obviously depend on assumptions about the integrity of the judiciary. A right to challenge an award in court furthers procedural fairness in arbitration only if the judicial system itself is honest. In parts of the world that lack a tradition of judicial independence, or where judges are known to supplement their incomes through gifts from litigants, the business community may prefer to take its chances with potential misbehavior by arbitrators as the lesser of two evils.

(c) Models for Judicial Review.

Although the New York Arbitration Convention permits member states to refuse recognition to an award set aside where rendered, the Convention establishes no criteria for proper or improper vacatur.[30] Therefore judicial review of an award at the arbitral situs will be governed by the local arbitration law there in force.

Three statutory models have emerged for review of international arbitral awards at the seat of arbitration. The first provides for appeal on the legal merits of the dispute, coupled with a right to challenge awards for procedural defects in the arbitration such as arbitrator bias, excess of authority or denial of due process. Under the second paradigm, the loser has a right to challenge

---

30   *Compare* the approach of the European Arbitration Convention, discussed in Chapter 37, which defines acceptable grounds for award annulment that will justify non-recognition.

an award only for procedural defects, not error of law. A third model foresees no judicial review at all.[31]

Many countries have adopted hybrid régimes. For example England provides for challenge on both points of law and matters of procedural fairness, but allows the parties to opt out of review on questions of law. See Chapter 30. Switzerland permits a choice among all three régimes.[32] In the United States, some but not all federal courts have permitted the parties by contract to expand the scope of judicial review of awards beyond the procedural fairness grounds provided by the Federal Arbitration Act.[33]

While the trend in national law is toward greater autonomy for international arbitration, most major arbitral centers still provide some mandatory review for procedural irregularity. In its own way, each of the national arbitration régimes outlined in the following chapters gives the loser of an arbitration a right to challenge an award obtained by a fundamentally unfair procedure. In addition to making sure that the arbitral tribunal was properly constituted pursuant to a valid arbitration agreement, courts will hear challenges to awards for an arbitrator's excess of authority, bias, corruption or denial of one side's right to present its case.[34]

---

31 *See* Article 1717 of Belgian *Code judiciaire* before the 1998 amendments contained in Article 13 of *Loi du modifícant les dispositions du Code judiciaire relatives à l'arbitrage*. Dissatisfaction with the mandatory nature of judicial review led to its amendment so as to allow, but not impose, exclusion of court scrutiny. *See* Bernard Hanotiau & Guy Block, *La loi du 19 mai 1998 modifícant la législation belge relative à l'arbitrage*, 16 Swiss BULL. 528 (1998). The 1998 Belgian law was inspired by Article 192 of the Swiss *Loi fédérale sur le droit international privé*, discussed in Chapter 33.

32 The federal conflict of law code (*LDIP*) provides for review of procedural irregularity; cantonal law includes review of "arbitrary" awards that violate law; and if both parties are non-Swiss they may elect to exclude judicial review altogether. *See* Chapter 33.

33 The courts are divided on whether the grounds for judicial review enumerated in 9 U.S.C. § 10 constitute a floor or a ceiling. *See* Gateway Technologies v. MCI, 64 F. 3d 993 (5th Cir. 1995) (court allows de novo review of issues of law according to parties' agreement) and Fils et Cables d'Acier de Lens v. Midland Metals Corp, 584 F. Supp. 240 (S.D.N.Y. 1984) (arbitration clause held to have given court power to determine whether award supported by substantial evidence). *Contrast* Lapine Technology Corporation v. Kyocera, 909 F. Supp. 697 (N.D. Cal. 1995) (parties cannot by agreement alter scope of judicial review) and Chicago Typographical Union No. 16 v. Chicago Sun-Times, 935 F. 2d 1591 (7th Cir. 1995) (federal court review power cannot be created by contract).

34 Although France and Switzerland do not enumerate bias explicitly among grounds for vacatur, other statutory bases for award annulment would seem flexible enough to cover such a defect. For example, Swiss arbitration law includes in its list of award defects (i) irregular composition of the arbitral tribunal (L.D.I.P. Article 190(2)(a)) (ii) unequal treatment of the parties (L.D.I.P. Article 190(2)(d)) and (iii) violation of public policy (*ordre public*) (L.D.I.P. Article 190(2)(e)), all of which would arguably be implicated by appointment of a biased arbitrator. *See generally*, P. LALIVE, J.F. POUDRET, C. REYMOND, LE DROIT DE L'ARBITRAGE INTERNE ET INTERNATIONAL EN SUISSE (1989), pages 423-24.

One element in some legal systems that may be open to question is annulment for violation of the malleable catch-all notion "public policy."[35] Invocation of such a pliant concept would seem justified in connection with an award's enforcement where the loser has assets, but not necessarily award annulment at the arbitral situs. Judges will be understandably reluctant to attach property to enforce an arbitrator's decision that violates basic notions of justice. However, if neither party resides or has property at the arbitral situs, there may never be anything for courts there to enforce, and thus no reason to flirt with the risks of excessive judicial intervention that inhere in an abstraction as chameleon-like as public policy.[36]

(d) The Perspective of the Enforcement Forum.[37]

Issues presented in a motion to set aside an award at the arbitral seat intersect with questions raised later when the arbitrator's decision is presented for enforcement and/or recognition. For example, an award rendered in London may have to be enforced against the loser's bank accounts in Boston. If the award is set aside in London on the ground that the parties did not consent to arbitration, should enforcement be refused in the United States even if the American court sees no reason to question the validity of the arbitration agreement? What should an American court do if the English judge set aside the award for error of law, grounds for refusal of enforcement under neither American law nor the New York Convention?

Deference to the London nullification would be permitted but not required under New York Convention Article V(1)(e).[38] However, any interested party may still rely on an annulled award under the domestic law of the enforcement forum, whatever that might turn out to be in any given case.[39] Thus annulment will not necessarily uproot an award, making it invalid in all places

---

35 *See e.g.*, French NCPC Article 1502 (5)(*ordre public international*), Swiss L.D.I.P. Article 190 (*ordre public*) and UNCITRAL Model Arbitration Law Article 34(2)(b)(ii). *See also* 1996 English Arbitration Act § 68(2)(g), which includes in the list of serious irregularities justifying annulment "the award or the way in which it was procured being contrary to public policy."

36 By contrast, matters related to an arbitration's basic procedural integrity (*e.g.*, arbitrator impartiality and respect for the arbitral mission) touch on issues that are both more concrete and more universal, thus reducing the potential for mischief.

37 *See generally*, William W. Park, *Duty and Discretion in International Commercial Arbitration*, 93 Am. J. Int'l. L. 805 (1999).

38 The English text of Article V(1)(e) states that an award "may" be refused recognition and enforcement if set aside "by a competent authority of the country in which, or under the law of which, that award was made." The equally authoritative French version lends itself to a more forceful interpretation, providing that *"la reconnaissance et l'exécution de la sentence ne seront refusées que si la sentence . . . a été annulée ou suspendue."*

39 New York Arbitration Convention Article VII provides that the Convention would not "deprive any interested party of any right he may have to avail himself of an arbitral award in the manner and to the extent allowed by the law . . . of the country where such award is sought to be relied upon."

and at all times, but rather may impair its effectiveness depending on where enforcement is sought.

French case law has long held that an annulled award may be recognized under French domestic law, regardless of the Convention obligation. In the landmark case *Pabalk v. Norsolor* the French Cour de cassation held that the award set aside in Vienna qualified for enforcement under French law notwithstanding the annulment in Austria.[40]

A similar position was taken later in the many faceted saga of *Hilmarton v. OTV* with respect to an ICC arbitration in Geneva. After the arbitrator refused to give satisfaction to a claimant seeking to recover consulting services arising out of a contract to be performed in Algeria,[41] a Geneva cantonal court annulled the award.[42] Thereafter a second arbitral tribunal in the same matter issued an award for the claimant. The *French Cour de cassation* held that the first award, in favor of the defendant, was entitled to recognition (*exequatur*) notwithstanding annulment in Switzerland.[43] Another French court recognized the second award (in favor of the claimant) as well as the Swiss judicial annulment of the first award.[44] Finally, the French Cour de Cassation vacated the second lower court decision on the basis of *res judicata* (*"autorité de la chose jugée"*), stating that the existence of the first French judgment prevented later recognition of an incompatible foreign judicial or arbitral decision.[45]

---

40 *Cour de cassation*, 9 Oct. 1984, 1985 REV. ARB. 431, commentary by Berthold Goldman; 112 JDI 679 (1985), commentary by Philippe Kahn. Agency agreement between French and Turkish parties; later the Vienna annulment was itself reversed by the Austrian Supreme Court. *See also Cour de cassation*, 10 March 1993, Jolasry v. Polish Ocean Line, commentary by Jan Paulsson & Graham Coop, in 1 DISPUTE RESOLUTION UPDATE 9 (I.B.A. Committee D, 1994). *Compare Cour d'appel de Paris*, 12 February 1993, Société Unichips v. Gesnouin, 1993 REV. ARB. 255, commentary by Dominique Hascher.

41 The arbitrator found the contract illegal under Algerian law, and apparently believed that this illegality made the contract void as against Swiss public policy, thus requiring an award against the claimant.

42 The cantonal court, upheld by the Swiss *Tribunal fédéral*, found the Algerian illegality did not constitute a violation of Swiss public policy so as to justify refusal to enforce an otherwise valid contract. *See* 1993 REV. ARB. at 315 (*Court de Justice du Canton de Genève*, 17 November 1989) and at 322 (*Tribunal fédéral*, 17 April 1990). The award was rendered in August 1988, before entry into force of the *L.D.I.P.*, and thus challenged under Article 36 of the Intercantonal Concordat.

43 *Cour de cassation*, 23 March 1994, 1994 327 REV. ARB. (with commentary by Charles Jarrosson) and English translation in 9 MEALEY'S INT. ARB. REP. No. 5, at E-3 (1994) and 20 YEARBOOK 663. *See generally* Vincent Heuzé, *La Morale, L'Arbitre et Le Juge*, 1993 REV. ARB. 179.

44 The 1993 order of the *Tribunal de grande instance de Nanterre* which recognized the second award (as well as the Swiss court's annulment of the first award) was confirmed by the *Cour d'appel de Versailles* on 10 June 1997. *See* 1995 REV. ARB.639.

45 1997 REV. ARB. 376, with commentary by Philippe Fouchard. *See generally*, Philippe Fouchard, *La Portée internationale de l'annulation de la sentence arbitrale dans son pays d'origine*, 1997 REV. ARB. 329; Eric Schwartz, *French Supreme Court Renders Final Judgment in the Hilmarton Case*, [1997] INT. A. L.R. 45. By contrast, in England the High Court of Justice recognized the sec-

American courts have also been willing to enforce an annulled award on the foundation of internal law rather than international treaty commitment, much as they recognize foreign judgments on the discretionary basis of "comity," even though the United States is not a party to any foreign judgments treaty. In *Chromalloy Aeroservices v. Egypt,*[46] a Cairo court had annulled an award in favor of a company that had contracted for the maintenance of helicopters belonging to the Egyptian Air Force. A federal district court confirmed the award notwithstanding its annulment at the arbitral seat. The court reasoned (rightly or wrongly[47]) that such confirmation was permitted under the Federal Arbitration Act, and thus within the scope of New York Convention Article VII which foresees award enforcement as allowed under domestic law.[48]

The *Hilmarton* and *Chromalloy* cases have led to a lively exchange of views, some favorable to the decisions[49] and some skeptical of their wisdom.[50] At least one American court has forcefully rejected the *Chromalloy* reasoning.[51]

One approach would disregard annulment decisions not based on "international" standards,[52] defined to include the first four defenses to award enforcement under the New York Convention: invalid arbitration agreement, lack of opportunity to present one's case, arbitrator excess of jurisdiction and

---

ond (non-annulled) award in favor of claimant. *See* OTV v. Hilmarton, Q.B., 24 May 1999, 14 MEALEY'S INT. ARB. REP. Section A (June 1999).

46   939 F. Supp. 907 (D.D.C. 1996).

47   The extent to which the Federal Arbitration Act covers foreign awards is not self-evident, at least with respect to vacatur. In International Standard Electric Corporation v. Bridas Sociedad Anonima Petrolera, Industrial Y Comercial, 745 F. Supp. 172 (S.D.N.Y. 1990), the court held that the Federal Arbitration Act did not apply to allow vacatur of an award rendered in Mexico.

48   *Compare* the Belgian approach in SONATRACH v. Ford, Bacon & Davis, *T.P.I. de Bruxelles* (12è Ch.), 6 December 1988, affirmed *Cour d'appel de Bruxelles* (8è Ch.), 9 January 1990, 1990 J.T. 386; 15 YEARBOOK 370 (1990). Recognizing a 1985 ICC award annulled in Algiers, rendered against one of Algeria's most important state agencies, the court focused on the lack of any retroactive application of the New York Convention, which Algeria had not ratified until 1988.

49   *See* Philippe Fouchard, *La Portée internationale de l'annulation de la sentence arbitrale dans son pays d'origine*, [1997] REV. ARB. 329; Jan Paulsson, *Enforcing Arbitral Awards Notwithstanding a Local Standard Annulment*, 9 ICC BULL. 14 (May 1998); Gary Sampliner, *Enforcement of Nullified Foreign Arbitral Awards: Chromalloy Revisited*, 14 (No.3) J. INT. ARB.141 (1997) (hereinafter "Sampliner, *Chromalloy Revisited*").

50   *See generally* Jean-François Poudret, *Quelle Solution Pour en Finir avec L'Affaire Hilmarton?*, 1998 REV. ARB. 7 (1998). *See* Hamid Gharavi, *Chromalloy: Another View*, 12 MEALEY'S INT. ARB. REP., Commentary at page 1 (Jan. 1997) and *A Nightmare Called Hilmarton*, 12 MEALEY'S INT. ARB. REP 20 (Sept. 1997); Eric Schwartz, *A Comment on Chromalloy: Hilmarton à l'Américaine*, 14 (No. 2) J. INT. ARB. 125 (June 1997); Albert Jan van den Berg, *Annulment of Awards in International Arbitration*, in INTERNATIONAL ARBITRATION IN THE 21ST CENTURY 133, at 152 (Richard Lillich & Charles Brower eds., 1994).

51   *See* Baker Marine Ltd. v. Chevron Ltd. 191 F.3d 194 (2d. Cir. 1999).

52   *See* Jan Paulsson, *Enforcing Arbitral Awards Notwithstanding a Local Standard Annulment*, 9 ICC BULL. 14 (May 1998).

irregular composition of the arbitral tribunal.[53] Thus an annulment for error of law would be disregarded while an annulment for denial of due process would not.

In contrast, other commentators suggest that disregard of foreign annulments justifies itself only when the court order was procured in a way that violates the enforcement forum's public policy, for example by fraud or corruption, regardless of whether annulment is pronounced according to a local or an international standard.[54] Under this view, a local standard might further legitimate commercial goals and enhance respect for the parties' mutual expectations.[55]

In addition to recognition of awards set aside where rendered, an enforcement forum might also grapple with the arbitral seat's explicit refusal to set aside an award. Imagine for example that an English judge rejected a losing defendant's allegation that an arbitrator in London took a bribe. Should this determination be *res judicata* in New York when the award is there presented for enforcement? Thus far there is little case law on findings of non-nullity under the *lex loci arbitri*. However, an enforcement forum should in principle be free to exercise its own judgment under New York Arbitration Convention Article V, at least absent any applicable treaty on recognition of foreign judgments.

28.05   Multiple Procedural Norms

(a) Questions Incident to Enforcement.

In an ideal universe, lawyers might be able to take into account only one arbitration law for each arbitration. In the real world, however, two or more arbitration laws can come into play in a single international dispute. This happens most often when a basic legal issue arises incident to judicial actions to enforce the arbitration agreement and/or award at several different places.[56]

---

53   New York Convention Article V(1)(a)-(d).

54   *See* William W. Park, *National Law and Commercial Justice: Safeguarding Procedural Integrity in International Arbitration*, 63 TUL. L. REV. 647 (1989), at 688, distinguishing between "honest" and "dishonest" annulments; Pierre Karrer, *Judicial Review of International Arbitration Awards: Who Needs it?*, in TABLE TALK at 9 (International Arbitration Club, London, 1998), suggesting that "there is no presumption . . . that local annulment standards are bad *per se*." W. MICHAEL REISMAN, SYSTEMS OF CONTROL IN INTERNATIONAL ADJUDICATION AND ARBITRATION (1992), Chapter 4 Compare Michael Mustill, *Too Many Laws*, 63 ARBITRATION 248 (1997).

55   For example, London courts that decide appeals on points of English law (a local review standard) promote the development of a legal system on which many international business transactions rely. Litigants who choose London arbitration can by agreement exclude the default rule of merits appeal on English points of law. *See* § 69 of 1996 English Arbitration Act. When the parties have not excluded appeal, deference to English court orders arguably holds the parties to their bargain, furthering the same interests as award enforcement itself.

56   For example, Atlantic Richfield's attempt to enforce a 1977 award against the government of Libya for $80 million in favor of LIAMCO, a subsidiary established to hold and operate conces-

The existence of the agreement to arbitrate, for example, might be examined under contract law concepts of the defendant's country of residence (in a motion to compel arbitration[57]), the place of the arbitration (in an action to vacate the award) or the place where the loser has assets (in an attachment proceedings). Subject matter arbitrability could likewise be subject to scrutiny under public policy notions of each of these three legal systems.

(b) Choice of Law Issues.[58]

In most cases the arbitral situs will look to its own arbitration law to determine whether an arbitration should be allowed to proceed in the face of a challenge to the arbitration agreement. Sometimes, however, conflict-of-laws considerations require reference to another legal system. For example, in one recent case a court in New York stayed an arbitration being conducted there until the validity of the agreement to arbitrate was determined in Venezuela,[59] whose law had been selected to govern the principal contract.

To some extent, this risk can be reduced through drafting the arbitration clause to include language distinguishing the choices of substantive and procedural law. For example, the arbitration clause might provide:

> This Agreement shall be governed and construed according to the laws of Ruritania, provided that any dispute relating to the arbitration clause or any arbitration arising thereunder shall be governed by the law of the arbitral situs.

General choice-of-law rules may be hard to find with respect to many matters relating to the legal effectiveness of an arbitration clause, leaving arbitrators with little clear guidance from one case to another. For example, experts are divided among themselves on which law the arbitral tribunal should apply to determine arbitrability.[60] The legal systems that have been considered in-

---

sions in Libya, led to judicial action to attach Libyan assets in France, Sweden, Switzerland and the United States. *See* discussion at 20 ILM 1 (1981).

57   *See* discussion of Mitsubishi v. Soler in Sections 28.01 and 34.02.

58   *See generally*, Jonathan Hill, *Some Private International Law Aspects of the Arbitration Act 1996*, 46 INT'L & COMP. L.Q. 274 (1997), at pages 287-305.

59   *See* Pepsico v. Oficina Central de Asesoria, 945 F.Supp. 69 (S.D.N.Y. 1996). Subsequent motions dismissed in unpublished decision, 26 Nov. 1997, 2d Cir., No. 97-7318 and No. 97-7386. The district court stayed proceedings brought to compel arbitration in New York, so that a Venezuelan court could have the opportunity to determine arbitrability. Compare the approach in Rhone Mediterranée v. Achille Lauro, 712 F.2d 50, at 53 (3d Cir. 1983), determining the validity of an arbitration clause in an international contract by reference only to "internationally recognized defense[s] such as duress, mistake, fraud or waiver." A French court took a similar approach in the *Dalico* case, discussed in Section 31.02. *See also* Volt v. Stanford, 489 U.S. 468 (1989), where California state law was held to apply both the merits of the dispute and the arbitration procedure, with the consequence that an arbitration was stayed under California law, pending resolution of related litigation.

60   *See e.g.*, Karl-Heinz Böckstiegel, *Public Policy and Arbitrability*, 3 ICCA CONGRESS SERIES 177 (1986 ICCA Congress, P. Sanders, ed., 1987): "Agreement on the conclusion that there is dis-

clude *inter alia* the law governing the agreement,[61] the law of the place of arbitration and the law governing award enforcement.[62]

Occasionally the validity of an arbitration agreement or award will implicate the substantive as well as procedural law. For example, the merits of the dispute may raise mandatory norms (*lois de police*) of the place of contract performance,[63] sometimes supplanting the otherwise applicable law on a question such as competition law, bribery or boycotts.[64]

(c) Competing Curial Laws.

Rival procedural norms can also present themselves in more dramatic forms when more than one national judiciary proclaims its legal system to be the curial law governing the arbitration as a whole. This risk is particularly high when the contract, either intentionally or by inadvertence, refers directly or indirectly to a procedural law other than that of the arbitral situs. In several arbitrations conducted in England, a contract stipulation of the law of another country led to the argument (albeit unsuccessful) that the choice of non-English law deprived English courts of their curial jurisdiction.[65]

---

agreement seems to be the only common denominator that one can find between arbitrators, courts and publicists regarding the questions which is the applicable law on arbitrability." *Id.* at page 184.

61 *See* Bernard Hanotiau, *What Law Governs the Issue of Arbitrability*, 12 ARB. INT. 391 (1996) (". . . . the arbitral tribunal will decide the issue [arbitrability] by application of the law which governs the arbitration agreement," which Hanotiau considers will in most (but not all) cases be the "same domestic law as the main agreement.") *Id.* at 393-94.

62 *See* Eric Schwartz, *The Domain of Arbitration and Issues of Arbitrability*, 9 (No. 1) ICSID REV. 17 (1994): "Matters of arbitrability . . . should most appropriately be assessed, insofar as mandatory legal provisions are concerned, in accordance with the law of the state that has promulgated them." *Id.* at 25. Schwartz considers five sometimes overlapping laws that may be relevant to arbitrability: (i) the law governing the arbitration agreement, (ii) the law governing the principal contract, (iii) the law of the place of arbitration, (iv) the law of award enforcement and (v) the law governing the particular subject matter.

63 *See e.g.*, Swiss *LDIP*, Article 19; Rome Convention on Law Applicable to Contractual Obligations, Article 7; Mitsubishi v. Soler Motors, 473 U.S. 614 (1985), at footnote 19. *See generally*, Pierre Mayer, *Mandatory Rules of Law in International Arbitration*, 2 ARB. INT. 280 (1986); GIUDITTA CORDERO MOSS, INTERNATIONAL COMMERCIAL ARBITRATION: PARTY AUTONOMY AND MANDATORY RULES (1999).

64 Another area that has recently given rise to discussion in this area is the United States Racketeer Influenced and Corrupt Organizations Act (RICO), 18 USC §§ 1961-1968. *See e.g.* ICC Award No. 6320 (1992), discussed in Serge Lazareff, *Mandatory Extraterritorial Application of National Law Rules*, 11 ARB. INT. 137 (1995).

65 *See* Union of India v. McDonnell Douglas Corp., [1993] 2 LLOYD'S L. REP. 48, providing for application of the Indian Arbitration Act of 1940. *Compare* Sumitomo Heavy Industries v. Oil and Natural Gas Commission, [1994] 1 LLOYD'S L. REP. 45, where on the basis of a choice of Indian law defendants commenced an action in the High Court of Bombay to challenge the scope of an arbitration taking place in London. In both cases, the Commercial Court wisely affirmed its supervisory jurisdiction, making sense of the potential conflict by interpreting reference to Indian law in the first case as indicating procedural rules "internal" to the arbitral tribunal, and in the second case as applicable to the substance of the dispute.

In the United States courts have generally refrained from exercising jurisdiction over an arbitration based solely on a choice-of-law clause.[66] Courts of other nations, however, have occasionally taken a different view, and asserted power to annul awards made outside their borders, based only on a choice-of-law clause in the principal contract.[67]

In this connection, one must remember that the New York Arbitration Convention, for better or for worse, allows non-recognition of awards set aside by "a competent authority of the country in which, *or under the law of which*, that award was made."[68] Thus it is theoretically possible for an annulment in a country other than the arbitral situs to serve as a defense to award recognition under the Convention. This does not mean, however, that the exercise of jurisdiction by that other country is sound policy.

28.06   Keeping National Law in Perspective

The torrent of arbitration law reform during the past two decades[69] has often been fueled by expectations of "invisible exports," a euphemism for fees to arbitrators, lawyers and expert witnesses.[70]

---

66   *See* International Standard Electric Corporation (ISEC) v. Bridas Sociedad Anonima Petrolera, Industrial y Comercial, 745 F. Supp. 172 (S.D.N.Y. 1990). When an award was rendered in Mexico pursuant to a contract subject to New York substantive law, the loser sought to have it set aside in New York. The federal district court concluded that only Mexican courts had the power to vacate an award made in Mexico.

67   *See* Oil & Natural Gas Commission v. Western Company of North America, 1987 All India Reports SC 674, *excerpted in* 13 YEARBOOK 473 (1988); National Thermal Power Corporation v. Singer Corporation, Supreme Court of India, 18 YEARBOOK 403 (1993). *Compare* Renusager Power Co. Ltd. v. General Electric Co. (1993), *discussed in* Tony Khindria, *Enforcement of Arbitration Awards in India*, 23 INT. BUS. LAWYER 11 (January 1995). *See generally* Jan Paulsson, *The New York Convention's Misadventures in India*, 7 MEALEY'S INT. ARB. REP. at 3-8 (June 1992); J. Gillis Wetter & Charl Priem, *The 1993 General Electric Case: The Supreme Court of India's Re-Affirm Pro-Enforcement Policy Under the New York Convention*, 8 INT. ARB. REP. (December 1993); F.S. Nariman, *Finality in India: The Impossible Dream*, 10 ARB. INT. 373 (1994); Lawrence Ebb, *India Responds to the Critics of its Misadventures under the New York Convention: The 1996 Arbitration Ordinance*, 11 MEALEY'S INT. ARB. REP. 17 (1997).

68   New York Convention Article V(1)(e).

69   The chronicle of new arbitration statutes includes *inter alia* legislation in England (1979 and 1996), France (1981), Belgium (1985 and 1997), the Netherlands (1986), Portugal (1986), Switzerland (1987), Spain (1988), Hong Kong (1990, 1996 and 1997), Italy (1994), Germany (1997), as well as the UNCITRAL Model Law (1985) and its progeny. *See generally* Adam Samuel, *Arbitration in Western Europe: A Generation of Reform*, 7 ARB. INT. 319 (1991).

70   In connection with the 1996 English Arbitration Act, the Departmental Advisory Committee on Arbitration advised that "The fact is that this country has been very slow to modernize its arbitration law and this has done us no good in our endeavor to retain our pre-eminence in the field of international arbitration, a service which brings this country very substantial amounts indeed." 1996 Department of Trade and Industry, Departmental Advisory Report, paragraph 335, at 69. *See also* discussion of the movement to adopt the UNCITRAL Model Arbitration Law in the United States in Alan Scott Rau, *The UNCITRAL Model Law and Federal Courts: The Case of Waiver*, 6 AM. REV. INT. ARB. 223 (1995), in which Professor Rau refers to the "bizarre chapter of wishful thinking" that a state can attract international arbitration business simply through

How much the overhaul of a national legal régime will in fact increase the adopting country's selection as situs for ICC arbitration remains debatable. When, how and why legislative reform makes a country more desirable as an arbitral situs will depend not only on the stage of development of prior law, but also on the impact of non-legal influences. Geography and history often matter more to the choice of an arbitral situs than the efficiency of the legal environment, and may even trump the impact of a marginally less favorable statute, assuming consensus on what exactly constitutes a juridical environment favorable to arbitration.

More than one country has been a popular situs for international arbitration notwithstanding a legal régime which, at the relevant times, was generally considered as hostile to the business community's expectation of arbitrator autonomy. England attracted international arbitration (although not as much as some lawyers desired), even before the 1979 and 1996 reforms which made the legal framework for international arbitration more user friendly. Switzerland's popularity as an arbitral situs developed at a time when merits review of "arbitrary" awards prevailed under the *Intercantonal Concordat*.[71] Both nations gained favor as places to arbitrate due less to their national law than to factors such as England's central role in modern commercial and financial matters, and the Swiss reputation for neutrality and efficiency. The impetus for the reform in these jurisdictions came largely from lawyers and arbitrators who had already tasted the fruits of successful practice, and were anxious to keep business from going elsewhere.[72]

The role of historical accident does not mean that the quality of arbitration law does not matter, however. Particularly at the margins of venue selection, a reputation for a good or bad arbitration law will often cause a migration among otherwise plausible locations. Boston will not soon replace London or Paris as a center for international commercial arbitration, no matter how fine an arbitration statute the Commonwealth of Massachusetts adopts. However, costly judicial meddling in arbitration by English courts might well result in some arbitrations moving over the Channel to Paris or Geneva.

---

adoption of the Model Law.

71 Awards may be annulled if considered as "arbitrary" due to "violation of law or equity". *See* Article 36(f) of *Concordat Intercantonal sur l'Arbitrage*, which governed international arbitration in most Swiss cantons before the *Loi fédérale de droit international privé* took effect in 1989. Since 1989 the Concordat will apply only if the parties so elect in writing. *See LDIP* Article 176.

72 For the selection of England and Switzerland as locations for arbitration, *see* statistics on England and Switzerland as seats of arbitration in Appendix I of the first (1984) and second (1990) editions of W. Laurence Craig, William W. Park & Jan Paulsson, International Chamber of Commerce Arbitration.

28.07   Courts and Arbitral Jurisdiction[73]

While the parties to ICC arbitration expect the arbitrators to be the sole judges of the merits of the dispute, the same cannot necessarily be said about the limits of their own power. The interaction of national law and ICC arbitration implicates an allocation of functions between arbitrators and courts which can be both elusive and complex with respect to the when, how and by whom an arbitrator's jurisdiction will be determined.

Imagine for example.that a claim is made on the basis of an arbitration clause which the defendant says is invalid. Should the defendant be able to go to court at the outset of the proceedings to contest the arbitrators' jurisdiction? Or must the defendant wait until an award is rendered, and then move to have that award set aside? If an award has already been issued, what (if any) deference should a reviewing court show to the arbitrator's finding? If the arbitrator has found the principal contract invalid, will this necessarily entail invalidity of the arbitration clause? As discussed below, such questions are usually analyzed according to two oft-confused notions: *compétence-compétence* and separability.

(a) Compétence-Compétence.

The concept referred to as *compétence-compétence* (literally "jurisdiction concerning jurisdiction") links together a constellation of disparate notions about when arbitrators can rule on the limits of their own power.[74] Depending on the context, reference to an arbitrator's "jurisdiction to decide jurisdiction" has operated with three quite distinct practical consequences: (1) the arbitrators need not stop the arbitration when one party objects to their jurisdiction; (2) courts delay consideration of arbitral jurisdiction until an award is made; (3) arbitrators decide questions of their own jurisdiction bindingly, with no judicial review.

(i) No Need to Stop the Arbitration.

In its simplest formulation, *compétence-compétence* means no more than that arbitrators can look into their own jurisdiction without waiting for a court to do so. In other words, when one side says the arbitration clause is invalid, there is no need to halt proceedings and refer the question to a judge.[75] However, under this brand of *compétence-compétence* the arbitrators' determina-

---

73   *See generally*, William W. Park, *Determining Arbitral Jurisdiction*, 8 Am. Rev. Int'l Arb. 133 (1997).

74   *See generally*, Carlos Alfaro & Flavia Guimarey, *Who Should Determine Arbitrability?*, 12 Arb. Int. 415 (1996); William W. Park, *The Arbitrability Dicta in First Options v. Kaplan: What Sort of Kompetenz-Kompetenz Has Crossed the Atlantic?*, 12 Arb. Int. 137 (1996).

75   *See e.g.*, Christopher Brown Ltd v. Genossenschaft Oesterreifchischer Waldbesitzer, [1954] 1 Q.B. 8.; 1996 English Arbitration Act § 30.

tion about their power would be subject to judicial review at any time,[76] whether after an award is rendered[77] or when a motion is made to stay court proceedings or to compel arbitration.[78]

On this matter it is important not to confuse the allocation of functions between arbitrators and the ICC Court with the allocation of responsibility between arbitrators and national courts. Under Article 6 of the ICC Rules, if the ICC Court is "*prima facie* satisfied" that an arbitration agreement exists, any jurisdictional challenge of a deeper nature goes to the arbitrators. This does not mean, however, that national courts will be deprived of power to make jurisdictional determinations when asked to stay litigation, enjoin arbitration or vacate an award.[79]

(ii) Courts Consider Jurisdiction Only After Award.

French law goes further, however, and delays court review of arbitral jurisdiction until *after* an award is rendered. If an arbitral tribunal has already begun to hear a matter, courts must decline to hear the case. When an arbitral tribunal has not yet been constituted, court litigation will go forward only if the alleged arbitration agreement is clearly void (*manifestement nulle*).[80]

To some extent, what is at issue here is the timing of judicial review. Going to court at the beginning of the proceedings can save expense for a defendant improperly joined to the arbitration. On the other hand, judicial resources

---

76 The same English Arbitration Act that in § 30 provides for arbitrators to determine their own jurisdiction as a preliminary matter also permits judicial challenge of any jurisdictional determination (Act § 67) and provides for stay of litigation only if the court is satisfied that the arbitration agreement is not "null and void, inoperative or incapable of being performed" (Act § 9).

77 *See e.g* Swiss *Tribunal fédéral*, 17 August 1995, Vekoma v. Maran Coal Company, 14 SWISS BULL. 673 (1996) with commentary by Philippe Schweizer. ICC award rendered in Geneva, arising out of dispute over delivery of coke; courts in Switzerland will examine the arbitrators' jurisdictional determinations *de novo*.

78 *See e.g.* Three Valley Municipal Water District v. E.F. Hutton, 925 F. 2d 1136 (9th Cir. 1991) (held for the court to determine whether contracts were void because of signatory's lack of power to bind principals) and Engalla v. Permanente Med. Group, 938 P.2d 903 (Cal. 1997) (malpractice claim against a health care provider referred to *ad hoc* arbitration which left administration to the parties rather than an independent institution; Supreme Court of California found that the habitual delays in the process constituted evidence of fraud by health care provider). *See also* Swiss *Tribunal fédéral*, 16 Jan. 1995, Compagnie de Navigation et Transports v. Mediterranean Shipping Company, ATF 121 II 38, where the court called for a full examination of the scope of the arbitration clause before stay of judicial proceedings in favor of an arbitration outside of Switzerland, while admitting that in a domestic arbitration the court might be limited to a "*prima facie* review" of the arbitration agreement's validity.

79 *But see* Apollo v. Berg, 886 F. 2d 469 (1st Cir. 1989), where the court relied in part on what was then Article 8 of the ICC Rules (now Article 6(2)) to limit the court's own review function. After the defendant had questioned whether the arbitration clause remained valid after contract assignment, the federal court turned over to the arbitrators the question of the arbitration clause's validity. The decision has been questioned. *See* William W. Park, *The Arbitrability Dicta in First Options v. Kaplan* 12 ARB. INT. 137 (1996) at 147-48.

80 *See* Article 1458 of the *Nouveau code de procédure civile*, discussed in Chapter 31.

may be conserved by delaying review until the end of the process, when the parties may have settled. Article 16 of the UNCITRAL Model Arbitration Law constitutes what some see as a compromise, by giving the arbitral tribunal discretion to determine its jurisdiction in the form of an interim award, but giving the disappointed party only thirty (30) days to challenge such an award.

(iii) Courts Defer to Arbitrator's Jurisdictional Findings.

In the United States, a notion of "arbitrability arbitration" has emerged that might in some cases lead judges to defer to the arbitrators' jurisdictional findings. The much discussed Supreme Court *dictum* in *First Options v. Kaplan*[81] suggested that in some situations a contract might empower the arbitrators to rule on their own jurisdiction without subsequent *de novo* review. If "the arbitrability question itself" (the Supreme Court's way of talking about the arbitrator's power to hear a matter) is submitted to arbitration, courts must "give considerable leeway" to the arbitrators' jurisdictional decisions.[82]

The *First Options dictum* in some ways echoes German case law which, prior to Germany's adoption of the UNCITRAL Model Law, used the term *Kompetenz-Kompetenz* to describe an arbitral tribunal's power to rule on its own jurisdiction without subsequent judicial review.[83] The historic peculiarity of the German doctrine, however, argues against use of the term *Kompetenz-Kompetenz* except in its specific context.[84]

(iv) Hybrids.

Not surprisingly, the law in many jurisdictions deals in hybrid fashion with determinations of arbitral jurisdiction. For example, the 1996 English Arbitration Act gives the express right to challenge arbitral jurisdiction by declaration only to a person "who takes no part in the proceedings."[85] Otherwise the challenger must wait until an award has been rendered or apply for a deter-

---

81   514 U.S. 938 (1995). *See* discussion in § 33.04.

82   *Id*. at 943. For a recent case applying this "arbitrability *dicta*" see PaineWebber v. Elahi, 87 F.3d 589 (1st Cir. 1996), relating to time bars in securities arbitration.

83   *See* PETER SCHLOSSER, DAS RECHT DER INTERNATIONALEN PRIVATEN SCHIEDSGERICHTSBARKEIT (1989) at § 556. Adoption of the UNCITRAL Model Law in Germany would seem to have changed this situation. *See* Klaus-Peter Berger, *The Implementation of the UNCITRAL Model Law in Germany*, 13 MEALEY'S INT. ARB. REP. 38 (January 1998). *See also* ENTWURF EINES GESETZE ZUR NEUORDNUNG DES SCHIEDSVERFAHRENSRECHTS, July 1995, at 132.

84   Leading French scholars have underscored the danger of using the German expression. See PHILIPPE FOUCHARD, EMMANUEL GAILLARD & BERTHOLD GOLDMAN, TRAITÉ DE L'ARBITRAGE COMMERCIAL INTERNATIONAL (1996).

85   English Act § 72. Non-participants may challenge jurisdictional defects regardless of whether failure to participate was by choice or by inadvertence, and regardless of whether in hindsight non-participation seems justified. England's approach differs from that of Switzerland, where defendants may lose the right to challenge arbitral jurisdiction by boycotting the proceedings. *See* Swiss *Tribunal fédéral*, 19 April 1994, Westland Helicopters v. Emirates Arabs Unis et al., 120 II 155 ATF (1994), 12 SWISS BULL. 404 (1994).

mination on a preliminary point of jurisdiction.[86] Arbitral jurisdiction might also be tested before a judge if one party brings a court action for a claim which the other party says is covered by the arbitration agreement.[87]

(b) Separability.

Compétence-compétence analysis should not be confused with the principle of "separability" (sometimes called "autonomy"), by which the validity of an arbitration clause is determined independently from the validity of the basic commercial contract in which it is encapsulated. Established either by case law or by statute in most national arbitration laws,[88] the separability doctrine permits arbitrators to invalidate the main contract (e.g., for illegality or fraud in the inducement) without the risk that their decision will call into question the validity of the arbitration clause from which they derive their power. In other words, the separability doctrine gives arbitrators the tool with which to do their job, by examining fully the parties' agreement. Moreover, separability requires courts, when determining whether an arbitration should go forward at all, to look only to the validity of the arbitration agreement.[89]

Separability, however, says nothing about the validity of the arbitration clause itself, or by whom this validity is to be determined.[90] The fact that an arbitration clause *might* be valid notwithstanding infirmities in other terms of the contract does not mean that the clause necessarily will be valid, or that

---

86 *See* 1996 English Act §§ 67 (challenge to award) and 32 (preliminary jurisdictional question) discussed in Chapter 30. Moreover § 73 of the English Act provides for loss of the right to challenge arbitral jurisdiction if a party takes part in the proceedings without making timely objection, unless it did not know, and could not reasonably have discovered, the jurisdictional defect.

87 The 1996 English Arbitration Act § 9 requires a stay of proceedings only "so far as they concern that matter [to be referred to arbitration]" and only if the court is satisfied that the arbitration agreement is not "null and void, inoperative or incapable of being performed." Analogous provisions in Article 8 of the UNCITRAL Model Law envision the possibility of simultaneous proceedings by courts and arbitrators regarding the competence of the arbitral tribunal. See HOWARD HOLTZMANN & JOSEPH NEUHAUS, GUIDE TO THE UNCITRAL MODEL LAW ON INTERNATIONAL COMMERCIAL ARBITRATION (1989), at 306: "This provision provoked debate between those who considered that the court should have power to stay the arbitral proceedings in order to prevent potentially needless arbitration and those who would have . . . had the court suspend its own proceedings in order to avoid delay and needless court intervention."

88 In the United States, Prima Paint v. Flood & Conklin, 388 U.S. 395 (1967); in France, *Cour de Cassation*, 1ere civ., 7 May 1963, Gosset, (discussed in PHIIPPE FOUCHARD, EMMANUEL GAILLARD & BERTHOLD GOLDMAN, TRAITÉ DE L'ARBITRAGE COMMERCIAL INTERNATIONAL (1996)); in England, 1996 Arbitration Act § 7; in Switzerland, *LDIP* Article 178(3). *See also* UNCITRAL Model Arbitration Law, Article 16(1).

89 *See* Nicaragua v. Standard Fruit, 937 F. 2d 469 (9th Cir. 1991), involving an arbitration agreement in a "Memorandum of Intent."

90 Misunderstanding on the operation of separability, along with confusion about the meaning of *compétence-compétence*, has sometimes led commentators to question the social value of these doctrines, from concern that they may serve as roads to an arbitrator's improper arrogation of power.

an arbitrator's erroneous decision on the clause's validity will escape judicial scrutiny.

Separability and compétence-compétence intersect only in the sense that arbitrators who rule on their own jurisdiction will look to the arbitration clause alone, not to the entirety of the contract. The organization of some arbitration statutes puts separability and compétence-compétence in the same article or section.[91] Other statutes, however, are organized to separate the two doctrines.[92]

For example, an agreement between an American multinational and a business consultant might provide for the latter's assistance in obtaining an engineering contract in the Middle East. The Americans might resist paying the consultant on two grounds: (i) the person who signed the agreement allegedly on their behalf was not authorized to do so; and (ii) contract payments were earmarked to bribe government officials.

Separability notions would permit the arbitrators to find the main contract invalid (due to its illegal object of bribery), without thereby destroying their power to render an award pursuant to the arbitration clause. The separability doctrine would not, however, make the arbitration agreement itself valid if the individual who signed the agreement had no power to do so.

In turn, *compétence-compétence* principles would permit the arbitrators to examine the power of the person who signed the contract (although perhaps subject to subsequent court challenge). But under compétence-compétence principles standing alone, without the sister doctrine of separability, the arbitrators could not declare the main contract void for illegality without thereby undermining their jurisdiction to do so.

28.08   The Special Status of International Arbitration

The restraints imposed on international commercial arbitration have sometimes been less stringent than those applied to domestic dispute resolution. In France and Switzerland, for example, along with many jurisdictions that have adopted the UNCITRAL Model Arbitration Law, special legislation subjects awards in international disputes to a different form of judicial scrutiny than in domestic arbitration.[93] In the United States, case law considering

---

91   *See* UNCITRAL Model Arbitration Law, Article 16(1).

92   *See e.g.*, 1996 English Arbitration Act, which in § 7 says that an arbitration agreement "shall not be regarded as invalid, non-existent or ineffective because [another agreement of which it forms a part] is invalid or did not come into existence," but gives the arbitral tribunal power to rule on its own power (albeit subject to judicial scrutiny) in § 30.

93   *See* Chapters 29, 31, 32 and 33.

cross-border dispute resolution has permitted arbitration of what might otherwise have been non-arbitrable subject matters.[94]

Some lawyers see no need for such special treatment of international arbitration.[95] Moreover, some countries have retreated from divergent treatment of domestic and international arbitration,[96] due to concern that distinctions based on nationality might conflict with international commitments.[97]

However, there should no mystery about a special status for international arbitration. In cross-border business transactions, arbitration provides a neutral playing field that justifies itself primarily as a means of avoiding the "hometown justice" of the other party's judicial system. While some international transactions will go forward even if the parties' arbitration clause can be disregarded or eviscerated, in other cases the risk of a non-neutral forum will be unacceptable.[98]

The need for adjudicatory neutrality in international transactions often overrides any national interest in uniform application of law. The consequences to a Bostonian of litigation in Atlanta are far less fearsome than the prospect of court proceedings in Algiers or Athens. Potential litigants fear that court intervention in an arbitration may result in judicial proceedings in a foreign language, and perhaps before a xenophobic judge in a country without a tradition of judicial independence.

Although the reality of litigation bias against foreigners may often be less significant than the perception that such prejudice exists, the consequences for contract negotiation are the same, in the sense that some transactions will not go forward unless the parties have confidence in a reliable dispute resolution alternative to judicial litigation. A recent study found evidence that in federal civil actions in the United States, foreigners actually fare better than

---

94 *See* discussion in Chapter 34 of Scherk v. Alberto Culver (securities law claims), Mitsubishi v. Soler (antitrust claims) and Sonatrach v. Distrigas (claims in bankruptcy).

95 No less a scholar than Lord Mustill has written that he has "never understood why international arbitration should be different in principle from any other kind of arbitration." *See* Michael Mustill, *Cedric Barclay Memorial Lecture*, 58 ARBITRATION 159 (Aug. 1992) at 165.

96 Under the now superseded 1979 English Arbitration Act, pre-dispute waiver of appeal on points of law was not allowed between or among residents and/or citizens of the United Kingdom. The 1996 Arbitration Act contained similar provisions, which never entered into force due to a perceived conflict with obligations within the European Union. *See* § 3, Statutory Instrument 3146, providing that the Act would come into force "except sections 85 to 87" (relating to domestic arbitration).

97 *See e.g.*, Article 6 of the TREATY ESTABLISHING THE EUROPEAN COMMUNITY, as amended by the TREATY ON EUROPEAN UNION (Maastrich), which provides that "any discrimination on the grounds of nationality shall be prohibited."

98 On the effect of litigation risk aversion in international business, *see* William W. Park, *Neutrality, Predictability and Economic Cooperation*, 12 (No. 4) J. INT. ARB. 99 (1995).

domestic parties,[99] due in part to a fear of the American civil justice system that causes foreign litigants to continue to final judgment only when they have particularly strong cases.

A different standard for monitoring arbitration of domestic and international transactions requires criteria to distinguish one from another.[100] A party-oriented test to define international arbitration, which looks to the nationality and residence of the litigants, has been adopted in Belgium[101] and Switzerland.[102] A less mechanical approach, asking whether a transaction implicates international commerce, has been adopted by the French.[103] The United States[104] and the UNCITRAL Model Arbitration Law take a hybrid approach.[105]

---

99   *See* Kevin Clermont & Theodore Eisenberg, *Xenophilia in American Courts*, 109 HARV. L. REV. 1122 (1996); analysis of cases decided from 1986-94.

100 On characterization in conflict-of-laws, *see* Bernard Audit, *Qualification et Droit International Privé*, 18 DROITS: REVUE FRANÇAISE DE THÉORIE JURIDIQUE 55 (1993).

101 *See* Article 1717 of the Belgian *Code judiciaire*.

102 *See* Articles 176 and 192 of the Swiss *Loi fédérale sur le droit international privé*.

103 *See* French *NCPC*, Article 1492, which refers to disputes that "implicate international commerce." For a recent case testing this definition in the context of a consumer contract (where a pre-dispute arbitration clause would normally not be valid) *see Cour de cassation*, 21 May 1997, Meglio v. Société V2000, 1997 REV. ARB. 537, note Emmanuel Gaillard, and 1998 REV. CRIT. DR. INT'L PRIVÉ 86, note Vincent Heuzé. The *Cour de cassation* upheld the validity of an arbitration clause in an agreement for the purchase of a limited series Jaguar, finding that the contract implicated international commerce by virtue of a transfer of goods and funds between France and the United Kingdom.

104 The United States excludes from the scope of the New York Convention contracts between American citizens. However, an agreement between American citizens will be deemed to fall under the Convention if the parties' relationship "involves property located abroad, envisages performance or enforcement abroad or has some other reasonable relation with one or more foreign states." 9 U.S.C. § 202. *See* Lander v. MMP Investments, 107 F. 3d 476 (7th Cir. 1997), in which the Convention was applied between an American manufacturer and an American distributor in connection with their contract to distribute manufacturer's shampoo products in Poland. Moreover, the United States applies the New York Arbitration Convention to non-domestic awards rendered in the United States if the award was made within the legal framework of another country (*i.e.* foreign law) or involving parties domiciled or having their principal place of business outside the United States. *See* Bergesen v. Joseph Muller Corp., 710 F.2d 928 (2d Cir. 1983) at 932.

105 The Model Law characterizes an arbitration as international if either (i) the parties have places of business in different states, (ii) the transaction has some connection to a state other than the parties' place of business or (iii) the parties have opted to treat their agreement as international. *See* Model Law § 1(3). For a discussion of how this test is applied in practice, see decision by Mr. Justice Kaplan in Fung Sang Trading Ltd. v. Kai Sun Sea Products Ltd., Hong Kong Supreme Court, 29 October 1991,[1992] 1 HKLR 40, summarized with commentary in N. KAPLAN, J. SPRUCE AND M. MOSER, HONG KONG AND CHINA ARBITRATION 173 (1994), and discussed in note by Michael Pryles, in 2 WORLD ARBITRATION AND MEDIATION REPORT 329 (1991).

CHAPTER 29

THE UNCITRAL MODEL LAW

29.01 Statutory Framework

Alongside the 1958 New York Convention, the Model Law on International Commercial Arbitration has been one of two immensely important contributions made by the United Nations to the field of international commercial arbitration. It was adopted in 1985 by the United Nations Commission on International Trade Law (UNCITRAL) after several years' drafting efforts.[1]

The Model law is of course not a national law as such, but has served to inspire many national laws.[2] Some of these laws have incorporated the UNCITRAL text with no substantive modifications; others have significantly altered important provisions. What is common for all of the relevant countries is that they want to claim recognition as being true to the Model Law in order to gain international credibility and to entice foreigners to accept to arbitrate on their territory. Accordingly, some claims that a country has adopted the Model Law must be taken with a grain of salt, especially when they appear with qualifiers such as "*essentially* adopted" or "*substantially* inspired."

Most countries adopting the Model Law have however done so without such violations of its spirit. The result is to create an attractive perspective of convergence in comparative practice, as courts in numerous countries, when called upon to apply the same words, look to a common source. Some enact-

---

1 Text reprinted, *in* 2 ARB. INT. at 11 (1986), with a commentary by Gerold Herrmann, the UNCITRAL official who had primary responsibility for the project.

2 The following countries have adopted all or most of the Model Law: Canada (1986); Cyprus (1987); Bulgaria and Nigeria (1988); Australia and Hong Kong (1989); Scotland (1990); Peru (1992); Bermuda, Russia, Mexico, Tunisia (1993); Egypt and Ukraine (1994); India, Kenya, and Zimbabwe (1996); New Zealand (1997); and Germany (1998). In addition, eight of the United States have adopted the Model Law, including California and Texas. A South African enactment appears imminent. A number of the countries listed above have made the Model Law applicable to all arbitrations, international or domestic.

ments of the Model Law explicitly authorise courts to refer to the UNCITRAL *travaux préparatoires*[3] as an aid in interpretation.[4]

It is therefore important to understand the background and the purposes of the Model Law, which responded to a vision that the world would be a simpler place for practitioners of international arbitration if national legal systems treated the arbitral process in essentially similar ways. If the differences between national laws were eliminated with respect to the conditions under which courts may assist or interfere with the arbitral process, parties would be more carefree in choosing a place of arbitration. Less fearful of venturing from the traditional seats of arbitration, they could give priority to fairness and convenience rather than procedural considerations under local law.

The principal objectives of the Model Law may be said to be three-fold:

(1) To establish the freedom of parties to submit their disputes to arbitration according to whatever procedural rules may suit their specific needs, thus giving full effect to rules and policies appropriate in international practice;

(2) To define a nucleus of mandatory provisions, reflecting a consensus of international public policy, designed to ensure fairness and due process but to avoid the application of peculiar local rules unnecessary to the essential fairness of the arbitral process as conceived in international business relations; and

(3) To create a set of supplementary rules specifically geared to modern international practice, and available whenever parties do not choose another comprehensive body of rules of procedure.

The Model Law has two particular features thought to enhance its chances for success:

− It is not conceived as a treaty, and may therefore be adopted by national legislatures with whatever incidental wrinkles they require; the cumbersome process of ratification of international instruments is obviated; and

− Its scope is limited to disputes relating to *international* contracts, thus leaving national legal systems the option to retain their traditional regime for purely domestic arbitrations.

---

3   *See* HOWARD HOLTZMANN AND JOSEPH NEUHAUS, A GUIDE TO THE UNCITRAL MODEL LAW ON INTERNATIONAL COMMERCIAL ARBITRATION: LEGISLATIVE HISTORY AND COMMENTARY (1989) (hereinafter "HOLTZMANN AND NEUHAUS").

4   *See* A. Broches, *1985 Model Law on International Commercial Arbitration: An Exercise in International Legislation*, 18 NETHERLANDS YEARBOOK OF INTERNATIONAL LAW 3 (1987). To allow reference to *travaux préparatoires* as an aid to interpretation has not been allowed traditionally under the English tradition. It is therefore especially noteworthy that the following Commonwealth countries have so provided in their enactments of the Model Law: Australia, Canada, Hong Kong, Scotland, New Zealand and Zimbabwe.

The background, purposes, and leading principles of the Model Arbitration Law were reviewed in a comprehensive Report of the Secretary-General of the United Nations entitled "Possible Features of a Model Law of International Commercial Arbitration" and submitted to UNCITRAL's Fourteenth Session in June 1981.[5] The project involved extensive consultation with international bodies such as the International Council for Commercial Arbitration and the ICC's Court of Arbitration, as well as with the Asian-African Legal Consultative Committee (AALCC). It is thought likely to be acceptable in States with different legal, social and economic systems and of particular use to developing countries whose arbitration law is in need of modernisation and adaptation to international trade.[6]

The Secretary-General's Report set forth desiderata of great relevance to the very concept of *lex loci arbitri* (see Chapter 28) as relevant to international commercial arbitration:

> The ultimate goal of a model law would be to facilitate international commercial arbitration and to ensure its proper functioning and recognition. Its practical value would, in particular, depend on the extent to which it provides answers to the manifold problems and difficulties encountered in practice. Thus, in preparing the model law an attempt should be made to meet the concerns which have repeatedly been expressed in recent years, sometimes even labelled as "defects" or "pitfalls" in international commercial arbitration.

> A major complaint in this respect is that the expectations of parties as expressed in their agreements on arbitration procedure are often frustrated by conflicting mandatory provisions of the applicable law. To give only a few examples, such provisions may relate to, and be deemed to unduly restrict, the freedom of the parties to submit future disputes to arbitration, or the selection and appointment of arbitrators, or the competence of the arbitral tribunal to decide on its own competence or to conduct the proceedings as deemed appropriate taking into account the parties' wishes. Other such restrictions may relate to the choice of the applicable law, both the law gov-

---

5 Doc. A/CN.9/207, dated 14 May 1981.

6 The Venezuelan delegation, for one, expressed this view at the Fifteenth Session of UNCITRAL in New York (July-August 1982), reported *in* J.M.H. Hunter, *International Commercial Arbitration*, 1982 INT. BUS. LAW. 315. It is however remarkable that many of the developed countries embracing the Model Law were prepared to abandon highly sophisticated legal regimes built up over centuries; Australia, Canada, and Scotland in this respect stood out among the early adherents to the Model Law approach. Well later, this comment was written with respect to the influence of the Model Law on the progress of a working group charged with comprehensively reforming the German arbitration act: "The desire to draft a modern arbitration law suitable for national and international arbitration proceedings taking place in Germany has apparently been so strong that even basic concepts of the German law on arbitration have been abandoned in favour of an internationally accepted set of modern legal provisions," F.-B. Weigand, *The UNCITRAL Model Law: New Draft Arbitration Acts in Germany and Sweden*, 11 ARB. INT. 397, at 414 (1995).

erning the arbitral procedure and the one applicable to the substance of the dispute. Supervision and control by courts is another important feature not always welcomed by parties especially if exerted on the merits of the case.

These and other restrictive factors . . . tend to create the above disappointment with mandatory provisions of law. It is this concern which, for example, prompted the recommendation of the AALCC. . .: "Where the parties have adopted rules for the conduct of an arbitration between them, whether the rules are for *ad hoc* arbitration or for institutional arbitration, the arbitration proceedings should be conducted pursuant to those rules notwithstanding provisions to the contrary in municipal laws and the award rendered should be recognized and enforced by all Contracting States to the 1958 New York Convention".[7]

The Report went on to make clear that the UNCITRAL Secretariat did not advocate refusal of all mandatory laws, citing the AALCC's condemnation of awards "rendered under procedures which operate unfairly against either party," and suggesting they might be corrected by "mandatory provisions of the *lex loci arbitri* dealing with defects in the procedure, denial of justice, and lack of due process of law."[8]

In addition, the Report made the following important observations with respect to provisions of procedural law that are non-mandatory:

Another source of concern and of possibly unexpected legal consequences is the non-mandatory part of the applicable law. Although, by definition, such provisions may be derogated from and, thus, the effect of any undesired rule nullified, parties may not have made a contrary stipulation, in particular where they were not aware of such rule. Also, where parties have not agreed on a certain procedural point, yet another concern may arise from the fact that the applicable law does not contain a provision settling this point. The lack of such "supplementary" rule may create uncertainty and controversy detrimental to the smooth functioning of the arbitration proceedings.[9]

The Model Law's approach is to define a set of procedural rules that may—with the exception of fundamental principles of due process, such as the right to be heard—be freely altered by the parties. This approach is compatible with that of ICC arbitration (*see generally* Chapter 16).

The comments that follow in this Chapter are based on provisions in the Model Law as well as on caselaw applying various national enactments that faithfully follow the relevant Model Law provisions. They therefore do not necessarily apply to the law of all countries claiming to have adopted the Model Law, insofar as the latter may have varied the text.

---

7   Doc. A/CN.9/207, *supra* note 5, at paragraphs 9-11.

8   *Id.* at paragraph 12.

9   *Id.* at paragraph 13.

In federated states like Australia and Canada, the Model Law was first enacted by individual states, either because of the constitutional division of legislative authority or because proponents of international arbitration did not want to wait for federal legislation. This process seems to have created difficulties only in the United States, where a number of individual states have adopted the Model Law, notwithstanding the fact that most international cases would fall under the Federal Arbitration Act—which has not been reformed in line with the Model Law. The result has been to create thorny conceptual problems which fortunately have little impact in most cases.

29.02   The Agreement to Arbitrate

The way a legal system evokes issues regarding the validity of an arbitration agreement needs to be understood not only in terms of the *substantive* requirements, but also in terms of crucial *procedural* options. Let us first consider the latter.

If A brings an arbitration against B and B states that the arbitration agreement is invalid, must the arbitration be suspended while that issue is resolved in court? B may plausibly say that it would be wasteful to go through a lengthy and expensive arbitration only to find at the end that the entire exercise was a nullity. A may plausibly retort that the door to abuse would open if any respondent wishing to avoid arbitration could sidetrack the proceedings for several years, perhaps including the involvement of three levels of courts, simply by arguing that there was some defect in the arbitration agreement.

There are merits on both sides of this argument. It was one of the most discussed topics during the preparation of the Model law. The result is to be found in Article 16 of the Model Law, which intends to make it impossible to derail arbitral proceedings simply by raising an objection to the "existence or validity" of the arbitration agreement, while granting important discretion to the arbitral tribunal to proceed cautiously in the event it recognises the objection as a serious one, and wishes to avoid the risk of wasting its and the parties' efforts. The arbitral tribunal is, pursuant to Article 16(3), in a position to exercise this discretion at two decision points. First, it may decide to rule on the objection as a preliminary question, or leave the matter to be dealt with in the award on the merits. Second, in the event that the arbitral tribunal rejects the objection in a preliminary decision and the disappointed applicant takes the issue to court (which it must do within 30 days), the arbitral tribunal "may continue the arbitral proceedings and make an award."

In a word, Article 16 gives the arbitral tribunal considerable authority and responsibility to determine whether the objection justifies an interruption of the arbitral proceedings on the merits. It is a cornerstone of the Model Law.

There is another key procedural issue: what happens if a party (such as B in the example above) initiates a court case and resists an attempt by the other party to take the matter to arbitration on the grounds that there is no valid arbitration agreement? Should it be possible for B to have that issue adjudicated in court (including possible appeal) before an arbitral tribunal is named and has an opportunity to rule on it, and to avoid any arbitral proceedings as long as the matter is before the judge(s)? If so, the result would be to allow B to avoid Article 16 simply by getting into court before A has time to request arbitration.

The Model Law deals with this problem in a manner which ensures that A's access to arbitration cannot be stymied in this fashion, and that the discretion granted by Article 16 to the arbitral tribunal cannot be neutralised by winning a race to the courthouse. Thus, Article 8 provides:

> (1) A court before which an action is brought in a matter which is the subject of an arbitration agreement shall, if a party so requests not later than when submitting his first statement on the substance of the dispute, refer the parties to arbitration unless it finds that the agreement is null and void, inoperative or incapable of being performed.

> (2) Where an action referred to in paragraph (1) of this article has been brought, arbitral proceedings may nevertheless be commenced or continued, and an award may be made, while the issue is pending before the court.

Of course this provision does not assume that the court case initiated by B will vanish instantly upon A's request for arbitration. The court seized of the matter will not defer to the arbitral process unless it finds the arbitration agreement to be "null and void, inoperative or incapable of being performed." An example of how the Model Law works in this situation was given in a 1991 Hong Kong judgment[10] dealing with an objection to the effect that no contract had been concluded because the purported representative of one party did not have requisite authority, and that this was known to the other party. The objecting party therefore asked the court not to name an arbitrator, having refused to do so itself. The court rejected this plea, reasoning that it did not have to be entirely satisfied at this stage, as a "threshold test" had been met to the effect that there was an agreement to arbitrate. The court noted that if the objection was raised before the arbitrators and decided by them, it could be fully considered by the court thereafter pursuant to Article 16.[11]

As to the substantive requirements for arbitration agreements, Article 7(2) of the Model Law provides that they must be "in writing," defined as requiring the agreement to be

> . . . contained in a document signed by the parties or in an exchange of letters, telex, telegrams or other means of telecommunication which pro-

---

10   Fung Sang Trading Ltd. v. Kai Sun Sea Products & Food Co. Ltd., [1992] 1 HKLR 40, per Kaplan J.

11   *See* also Ocean Fisheries Ltd. v. Pacific Coast Fishermen's Mutual Marine Insurance Co., Federal Court of Canada, Trial Div., order for stay of 2 January 1997, 12 MEALEY'S INT. ARB. REP., (February 1997) at 9.

vide a record of the agreement, or in an exchange of statements of claim and defence in which the existence of an agreement is alleged by one party and not denied by another. The reference in a contract to a document containing an arbitration clause constitutes an arbitration agreement provided that the contract is in writing and the reference is such as to make that clause part of the contract.

This requirement is similar to that of Article II(2) of the New York Convention. It has been criticised as being inconsistent with commercial practice inasmuch as it enables a party to perform a contract, as set out in an order form or similar document, and nevertheless claim that an arbitration clause contained in the document is ineffective because that party did not sign it, or "exchange" any written message confirming it. This problem has come up on a number of occasions in Hong Kong. Judge Neil Kaplan (as he then was), who as High Court Judge in charge of the Constitution and Arbitration List decided most of the cases that arose under the first years of the Model Law in Hong Kong, believes that the drafters of both the Model Law and the New York Convention erred in failing to accommodate situations where contracts containing arbitration clauses have been accepted by conduct:

> . . . I find difficulty in seeing . . . why if one party is sent a contract which includes an arbitration clause and that party acts on that contract and thus adopts it without qualification, that party should be allowed to wash his hands of the arbitration clause but at the same time maintain an action for the price of the goods delivered or conversely sue for breach.[12]

In response, one might answer that the conclusion that a party has by its conduct accepted to sell certain goods does not necessarily mean that it also agrees to an arbitral mechanism proposed in the same document that contained the proposed business deal. As the Italian Supreme Court held in 1993,[13] arbitration clauses are to be analysed as autonomous (severable) elements of the contracts containing them, and therefore their validity must be ascertained independently of the validity of the contract as a whole.

In Hong Kong, Judge Kaplan's views prevailed and Article 7 was modified by the 1996 Arbitration Ordinance. See discussion in Chapter 32. The Ordinance eliminated the requirement of a writing, so that evidence by other means is acceptable to show an intent to arbitrate.

Although recognising the Model Law requirement as "fairly strict by international standards," the South African Law Commission nevertheless recom-

---

12 Neil Kaplan, *Is the Need for Writing as Expressed in the New York Convention and the Model Law Out of Step with Commercial Practice?* 12 ARB. INT. 27 at 29 (1996).

13 Decision of 28 October 1993; Robobar Ltd. v. Finncold; extracts *in* XX YEARBOOK 739 (1995).

mended that Article 7 be retained without change "in the interest of uniformity with most other Model Law countries."[14]

The New Zealand Arbitration Act, on the other hand, liberalised Article 7 by amending it to provide flatly that "An arbitration agreement may be made orally or in writing."[15]

This discussion of the validity of arbitration agreements under the Model Law would not be complete without considering the issue of arbitrability. Under Article 1(5), enactment of the Model Law does not affect any other laws which may restrict the scope of disputes which may be referred to arbitration. The UNCITRAL Secretariat noted from the outset that "national laws excluding certain subject matters—such as bankruptcy, antitrust, securities or patents—from the domain of arbitration are increasingly applied more leniently to international transactions than to purely domestic ones."[16] It was not however possible to provide an exhaustive list of nonarbitrable subject matters, nor perhaps desirable to do so, so as not to inhibit evolution (hopefully convergent) of the field of arbitrability.

29.03   Interlocutory matters

The central provision of the Model Law in this respect is Article 9, which provides that it is not incompatible with an arbitration agreement to request "interim measure[s] of protection" from a court before or during the arbitral proceedings. There is however no definition of such measures.

One of the commentaries on the Model Law observes as follows:

> Article 9 is not limited to any particular kind of interim measures. Thus it applies to measures to conserve the subject matter of the dispute; measures to protect trade secrets and proprietary information; measures to preserve evidence; pre-award attachments to secure an eventual award and similar seizures of assets; measures required from third parties; and enforcement of any interim measures ordered.[17]

The High Court of Hong Kong has held that Article 9 was intended to have a wider scope than orders simply preserving the subject matter of the dispute, and thus allowed the kind of third-party attachment known in English procedural parlance as a Mareva injunction:

> On the basis of the clear language used, I have no difficulty whatsoever in concluding that 'an interim measure of protection' is wide enough to cover a

---

14   Discussion Paper 69, A Draft International Arbitration Act for South Africa, at 25.

15   Reproduced in 12 ARB. INT. 67 at 71 (1996). An exception is made for "consumer arbitration agreements."

16   HOLTZMANN & NEUHAUS, at 331.

17   *Id.* at 332-333. HOLTZMANN & NEUHAUS also opine, at 333, that Article 9 may be excluded by agreement, but that conclusion is not free from doubt.

Mareva injunction. The protection afforded by a Mareva injunction is the reduction in the risk of the amount of the claim, or part of it, being dissipated or otherwise put out of the plaintiff's reach before the resolution of the dispute. If such an injunction is granted and, if obeyed, (and assuming that there were in fact sufficient assets in the defendant's possession to cover the plaintiff's claim or part thereof), the plaintiff is protected until trial against any steps the defendant may wish to take to render the judgment against him nugatory. This clearly protects the plaintiff during the period between the application and the resolution of the claim.[18]

Some common law jurisdictions (such as Scotland, New Zealand, and as appears likely South Africa) have considered it prudent to spell out the powers a court may exercise under Article 9, so that it becomes clear that intended measures are covered (e.g. orders securing the amount in dispute, like a Mareva injunction) and that unintended measures otherwise available under the general common law are excluded (e.g. review of procedural rulings while the arbitration is still in progress[19]).

While Article 9 of the Model Law deals with the power of court to order interim measures in connection with arbitral proceedings, Article 17 grants authority to the arbitral tribunal to order a party to carry out interim measures "in respect of the subject-matter of the dispute." (This authority may be excluded by agreement.) The Model Law does not establish enforcement mechanisms for such orders. Australia and Scotland amended the text to provide that they may be enforced as awards. Noting those examples, the South African Law Commission nevertheless recommended against such a change in that country's enactment on the basis that: "A party who foresees that it will be unable to enforce the tribunal's order would be well advised to apply directly to the court under Article 9."[20]

Court appointment of arbitrators is an interlocutory matter which is dealt with by the Model Law (Article 11), but under the ICC system this function is fulfilled by the arbitral institution (in a manner explicitly accepted in Article 11(2) of the Model Law) and so requires no comment here.

On the other hand, the Model Law does not allow the arbitral institution the final word if it rejects a challenge to an arbitrator (Article 13). In other words, while a decision by the ICC Court to remove an arbitrator is not reviewable by

---

18 Katran Shipping Co. Ltd. v. Keavea Transportation Ltd., unreported judgment of 29 June 1992, per Kaplan, J., extracts and quotation *in* NEIL KAPLAN, JILL SPRUCE AND MICHAEL MOSER, HONG KONG AND CHINA ARBITRATION 186, at 187 (1994).

19 *See, e.g.* Tuesday Industries Ltd. v. Condor Industries Ltd., 1978 4 SA 379 (South Africa, recognising the existence of the power but not exercising it). Kaplan et. al write, *supra* note 18, at 169: "The prospect of applications during the arbitration is not one which fits well to the non-interventionist role of the court."

20 Discussion Paper 69, *op. cit.* note 14, at 36.

any judicial authority, an *unsuccessful* challenge may be submitted to the ordinary courts. This principle, set down in Article 13(3), may not be varied by agreement (Article 13(1)).

By virtue of its crucial Article 16, discussed in Section 29.02, the Model Law leaves no room for argument that an arbitration should be stopped because the respondent wishes to plead before a court that the arbitral tribunal has no jurisdiction. Under Article 16, the arbitral tribunal itself has power to rule on such a plea, and furthermore has discretion whether to do so on an interim basis, and indeed whether in such a case to suspend the arbitral proceedings pending judicial review of that interim decision.

29.04   Review of awards

Since the New York Convention (Article V(1)(e)) allows enforcement fora to decline to enforce awards if they have been set aside in their country of origin (*see* Section 37.02), foreigners are loath to agree to arbitrate in countries which allow awards to be set aside because they are held defective under peculiar local criteria. This is why Article 34 of the Model Law, in defining the grounds on which an award may be set aside, simply repeats the most familiar of all international criteria for assessing the legitimacy of arbitral awards, namely those defined in Article V of the New York Convention (*see* Chapter 37) as permissible grounds for declining to engage a foreign award. (Ground (e) of the New York Convention's Article V(1) is not repeated because it is by definition inapplicable.)

A legal system that purports to adopt the Model Law and yet alters the scheme of Article 34 risks losing its reputation as a safe place to conduct international arbitrations. Certainly its claims to adhere to Model Law principles will be met with considerable skepticism. It is deeply misleading to make such a claim on the basis that 99% of the UNCITRAL text has been adopted, if the remaining 1% consists of a new qualification to the validity of arbitration agreements,[21] or the addition of "mistaken application of law" as a ground for setting aside awards.

Thus, Article 53(1) of Egypt's 1994 Law on Arbitration contains the two following uniquely local grounds for the annulment of awards in addition to those of Article 34 of the Model Law:

> (d) if the arbitral award fails to apply the law agreed by the parties to the subject matter of the dispute;
>
> . . .

---

[21] An example is the bill presented to the parliament (*majlis*) of Iran in 1993. It is said to "closely follow" the Model Law, yet it incorporates a prohibition against Iranian parties entering into arbitration agreements if the arbitral tribunal might be comprised of one or more arbitrators having the same nationality as a non-Iranian party to the dispute. To create such an uneven playing field is antithetical to the very fundaments of the Model Law.

(g) if nullity occurs in the arbitral award, or if the arbitral proceedings are tainted by nullity affecting the award.[22]

This kind of tampering was bound to lead to trouble,[23] and so it did: in the now-infamous *Chromalloy* case in which the Cairo Court of Appeal set aside an ICC award on the basis of paragraph (d).[24] To reach this result, the Court first determined that the contract properly fell under the category of administrative contracts, and that therefore the contractual reference to "Egypt Law" (sic) should be understood as an acceptance of the exclusive application of Egyptian administrative law. The arbitral tribunal had instead applied the Egyptian Civil Code. It had thus failed, in the Court's opinion, to apply the law agreed by the parties, and therefore run afoul of Article 53(1)(d). American[25] and French[26] courts, asked to enforce the award notwithstanding the Egyptian annulment, granted the applications, holding that the Egyptian court judgment did not impair the award for the purposes of the enforcement forum. Such international disharmony is naturally contrary to the aims of the Model Law.

---

22 This is the English translation that appeared in the dissenting opinion of the Egyptian arbitrator in the *Chromalloy* case; MEALEY'S INT. ARB REP., August 1996, at C-52. No particular elucidation is provided by the French translation published in 1994 REV. ARB. 763.

23 Eric Schwartz, *in A Comment on Chromalloy*, 14 J. INT. ARB. 124, at 135 (1997) writes of "regrettable modifications" and a result that will cause parties to consider Egypt to be "a less secure place to arbitrate than many other venues." Messrs B. Fillion-Dulfouleur and Ph. Leboulanger, in their commentary on *Le nouveau droit égyptien de l'arbitrage*, 1994 REV. ARB. 665, write that the circular and obscure text of paragraph (g) of Article 53(1) is likely to lead to applications for annulment.

24 By an order of 5 December 1995. *See* Jan Paulsson, *Enforcing Arbitral Awards Notwithstanding an LSA (Local Standard Annulment)*, 9 ICC BULL. 14 (May 1998).

25 Chromalloy Aeroservices v. Arab Republic of Egypt, 939 F. Supp. 907 (D.D.C. 1996).

26 Decision of 14 January 1997, MEALEY'S INT. ARB. REP. 395 (April 1997) B-1 (original text in French and English translation).

CHAPTER 30

ENGLISH LAW

30.01   Statutory Framework

(a) General Approach.

Replacing several centuries of piecemeal legislation and random judicial decisions, the 1996 English Arbitration Act[1] provides the first truly systematic and comprehensive legal framework for arbitration of commercial disputes in England.[2] The legislation caps almost two decades of flirting with (and skirmishing around) arbitration law reform,[3] beginning with the abolition in

---

[1]   The Act applies to proceedings commenced on or after 31 January 1997, regardless of the date of the arbitration agreement. Schedule 2, Statutory Instrument No. 3146 (c.96). For ICC Arbitration, the Act's first part, entitled "Arbitration Pursuant to an Arbitration Agreement," will do most of the work. Part II of the Act relates to problems peculiar to consumer, statutory and county court arbitrations. Part III applies to foreign awards. Part IV includes general provisions such as the meaning of "court" and provision for the Act's commencement.

[2]   See generally Mark Saville, *The Arbitration Act 1996 and its Effect on International Arbitration in England*, 63 ARBITRATION 104 (1997); Mark Saville, *The Origin of the New English Arbitration Act 1996: Reconciling Speed with Justice in the Decision-making Process*, 13 ARB. INT. 237 (1997); ROBERT MERKIN, ARBITRATION ACT OF 1996: AN ANNOTATED GUIDE (1996); V.V. Veeder, *La nouvelle loi anglaise sur l'arbitrage de 1996*, 1997 REV. ARB. 3; Martin Hunter, *The Procedural Powers of Arbitrators Under the English 1996 Act*, 13 ARB. INT. 345 (1997); Michael Mustill, *La nouvelle loi anglaise sur l'arbitrage de 1996: philosophie, inspiration, aspiration*, 1997 REV. ARB. 29; Claude Reymond, *L'Arbitration Act, 1996: convergence et originalité*, 1997 REV. ARB. 45; Arthur Marriott, *The New Arbitration Bill*, 62 ARBITRATION 97 (May 1996); MARGARET RUTHERFORD & JOHN SIMS, ARBITRATION ACT 1996: A PRACTICAL GUIDE (1996); RICHARD LORD & SIMON SALZEDO, GUIDE TO THE ARBITRATION ACT 1996 (1996); BRUCE HARRIS, ROWAN PLANTEROSE & JONATHAN TECKS, THE ARBITRATION ACT 1996 (1996); Jonathan Hill, *Some Private International Law Aspects of the Arbitration Act 1996*, 46 INT. & COMP. L. Q. 274 (1997).

[3]   For background on legislative initiatives, *see* Department of Trade and Industry, Departmental Advisory Committee on Arbitration Law, 1996 Report on the Arbitration Bill ("1996 DAC Report") and Supplementary Report of January 1997 ("1997 DAC Report"), *reprinted in* 13 ARB. INT. 275 (1997). *See also* 1994 Departmental Advisory Committee Consultation Paper on Draft Clauses of an Arbitration Bill, 10 ARB. INT. 189 (1994) and 1989 Departmental Advisory Committee Response to the UNCITRAL Model Law, 6 ARB. INT. 3 (1990). For a full list of all the DAC reports on the subject, *see* V.V. Veeder, National Report on England in ICCA INTERNATIONAL

1979 of the procedure by which awards had been subject to systematic review on their legal merits.[4] Some had felt that these statutory changes did not go far enough, and so a committee[5] was appointed to consider adoption of the Model Arbitration Law drafted by the United Nations Commission on International Trade Law. Although a decision was made not to import into England the Model Law,[6] its language and structure did exert a strong influence on the legislation that ultimately emerged from this reform process.[7]

The Act brings no radical departures from the basic principles that have governed arbitration in England since 1979. England's split-level approach to judicial review of awards continues to offer an optional right to appeal points of English law, coupled with a non-waivable opportunity to seek judicial review of an arbitration's fundamental procedural regularity. The Act thus balances the rival aspirations of finality and fairness in arbitration by supplementing the principle of party autonomy with reasonable default rules and mandatory safeguards for procedural integrity.

The Act's most significant achievement relates to form instead of substance, having put old wine into new and more user-friendly wineskins. This repackaging is no small feat, since practical application of even the best norms and traditions will depend on matters of language, organization and structure.[8]

The Act does introduce several important substantive innovations, however. Most notably, challenge of arbitrator misbehavior on the broad basis of "misconduct" has been replaced by detailed provisions for judicial review of arbitral excess of jurisdiction and lack of procedural integrity. In addition, the Act ends restrictions on the right to exclude judicial review of awards in admiralty, insurance and commodity market disputes. Finally, under the Act judges may no longer order security for costs in arbitration.

HANDBOOK ON COMMERCIAL ARBITRATION, at 10-11.

4   Before 1979, under the "case stated" procedure an arbitrator could be required to state a question of law for decision by the High Court, thus compromising the finality of the arbitration. *See generally* William W. Park, *Judicial Supervision of Transnational Commercial Arbitration*, 21 HARV. INT. LAW J. 87 (1980).

5   Departmental Advisory Committee, Department of Trade and Industry. Leadership of the Committee passed from Lord Mustill to Lord Steyn, and then to Lord Saville.

6   *See* 1989 Departmental Advisory Committee Response to the UNCITRAL Model Law, *reprinted in* 10 ARB. INT. 3 (1990).

7   Paragraph 108(7) of the 1989 Departmental Advisory Committee Report suggested that the new arbitration statute should draw upon the Model Law to enhance its accessibility.

8   Just to have the bulk of relevant rules in one handy statute will further their efficient implementation. The Act does not, however, purport to be a true codification, which the drafters rejected from fear of fossilizing a common law capable of adapting with relative ease to changing circumstances. *See* 1996 DAC Report, Section 9, at 8.

(b) Canons of Construction.

The 1996 Act opens with a tripartite articulation of fundamental precepts. The Act's interpretation is to be guided by the goals of procedural fairness, party autonomy and judicial restraint.[9] The first canon for construction of the Act calls for "fair resolution of disputes by an impartial tribunal without unnecessary delay or expense."[10] The practical application of this worthy objective will not always be self-evident, since fairness sometimes marries ill with speed and economy. What appears as undue delay to a claimant expecting an easy win may be dressed as essential due process or natural justice to a defendant anxious to present its case more fully. Indeed, how arbitrators and judges determine when delay and expense are warranted remains one of the most vital and elusive parts of any arbitration system.

The second of the Act's doctrinal foundations gives the parties freedom to agree how their disputes are resolved. Litigants will generally be held to their bargains on the mode for resolution of their controversies. Nevertheless certain mandatory rules, designed to safeguard both the public interest and the integrity of the arbitration, will sometimes trump the parties' desires. In particular, the Act requires an arbitrator to act impartially and to avoid unnecessary expense,[11] a dual mandate with an internal tension similar to that inherent in the first principle's aspiration toward fairness without delay. The statute's third interpretative principle admonishes judges against excessive zeal when dealing with arbitration-related matters. Judicial intervention is normally to be limited to measures prescribed in the Act. This does not, however, prohibit courts from exercising their inherent jurisdiction to relieve injustice in appropriate circumstances.[12]

(c) Scope.

Generally the Act governs arbitrations whenever the juridical seat of the arbitration is in England, Wales or Northern Ireland.[13] The seat of the arbitration

---

9   Act § 1.

10   For recent case law on arbitrator impartiality under English law, *see* AT&T Corp. & Lucent Technologies Inc. v. Saudi Cable Co., Case No. QBCMF 1999/1200/A3 (arbitrator's links to a competitor of one party in the arbitration), and Laker Airways v. FLS Aerospace Ltd., [1999] 2 LLOYD'S L. REP. 45 (arbitrator and advocate were barristers in the same chambers), both discussed in Chapter 13. *See also* Armen H. Merijan, *Caveat Arbitor: Laker Airways and the Appointing of Barristers as Arbitrators in Cases Involving Barrister-Advocates from the Same Chambers*, 17(1) J. INT. ARB. 31 (2000).

11   Act § 33.

12   The Act states that courts "*should* not," rather than "*shall* not," intervene except as provided by statute. *See* Nissan (UK) Ldt. v. Nissan Motor Company, discussed *infra* Section 30.03.

13   Act § 2. Since 1536 England and Wales have been part of the same legal system. Stat. 27 Hen. VIII, c. 26. To avoid the cumbersome expression "England and Wales or Northern Ireland," this article will generally indicate the scope of the Act by reference to the more convenient locations such as "English arbitration" or "arbitration in England."

(often but not always the place of the proceedings[14]) will be designated by the parties, the relevant arbitral institution, or the arbitral tribunal itself if so empowered.[15] Except with respect to certain consumer protection measures, the Act does not extend to Scotland, which has long had its own arbitration law.[16]

Some provisions of the Act may apply even if the seat of the arbitration is outside England. Judicial proceedings will be stayed in deference to arbitration abroad,[17] and in connection with foreign arbitration courts may secure assets by injunction and order the taking of evidence.[18] Moreover, when English law governs the arbitration agreement itself (as contrasted with the principal contract obligations), two rules apply regardless of the arbitral situs: an arbitration clause will be "separable" from the main contract, and the arbitration agreement will continue in effect even after death of a party.

(d) ICC Rules as an "Agreement Otherwise"

Litigants may choose to accept or to reject those of the Act's provisions hedged with qualifications such as "unless agreed otherwise" or "subject to any agreement of the parties." These provisions constitute default rules only. Whether reference to the ICC Rules will constitute an "agreement otherwise" for purposes of the Act depends on the particular question presented. For example, under Article 28 of the Rules the parties waive "any form of recourse [against the award] insofar as such waiver can validly be made." There should be no problem seeing this rule as an "agreement otherwise" for purposes of excluding merits review.[19]

The situation is less clear, however, with respect to other matters, particularly when the ICC Rules are silent. Imagine for example that during the proceedings one side requests a court determination of a *preliminary* point of law

---

14   *See generally* REDFERN & HUNTER, at 81-83. *See also* William W. Park, *National Law and Commercial Justice*, 63 TUL. LAW REV. 647, 679-83 (1989).

15   Act § 3. In the absence of such designating factors, the seat will be determined by reference to "the parties' agreement and all the relevant circumstances."

16   Act § 108. *See* Law Reform (Misc Provisions) (Scotland) Act 1990, §§ 66-67. *See generally* Lord Dervaird, *Scotland and the UNCITRAL Model Law: The Report to the Lord Advocate of the Scottish Advisory Committee on Arbitration Law*, 6 ARB. INT. 63 (1990). Scotland has adopted the UNCITRAL Model Arbitration Law with certain additions. For example, Article 34(2)(a)(v) of the Scottish version provides that "fraud bribery or corruption" will constitute grounds for the setting aside of an award.

17   Act § 2(2)(a) & (b).

18   Act § 2(3) says that powers conferred to support of arbitration under § 43 (attendance of witnesses) and § 44 (securing assets and taking evidence) will apply even if the seat of arbitration is outside England. Section 43, however, applies only if arbitral proceedings are being conducted in England.

19   Act § 69, which provides for appeal on points of law (defined as English law), begins with "unless otherwise agreed by the parties." By contrast, challenge for excess of authority and procedural irregularity under Act §§ 67 & 68 cannot be waived.

as allowed by § 45 of the Act. The waiver of "recourse" in Article 28 of the ICC Rules deals with awards rather than interlocutory questions. What the ICC Rules would mean for preliminary points of law will probably derive from invocation of the spirit of the rules rather than any concrete provision. Certainly the overall scheme of the rules contemplates that questions of law will be determined by the arbitral tribunal, subject to judicial review (if at all) only when encompassed in an interim or final award.[20]

Another illustration might be found in Act § 57, which permits the arbitrators to correct an award's clerical errors if the parties have not agreed otherwise. Clearly, the ICC Rules contemplate the arbitrators' right to deal with such accidental mistakes.[21]

Act § 57 does not, however, end with reference to minor slips and omissions. It goes on to allow arbitrators to make an "additional award" on matters not dealt with in the initial award.[22] Such supplementary awards are not dealt with in the ICC Rules.[23] Some have suggested that silence on arbitrator powers constitutes an "agreement otherwise" on such matters only if the relevant rules indicate that the arbitrators have no powers other than those expressly mentioned.[24] Since the ICC Rules do not state that the arbitrators' enumerated powers are exhaustive, this approach would lead to application of the Act's default rule on "additional awards," a result not free from doubt as a matter of policy in ICC Arbitration.

Ambiguity in terminology may also prove problematic. The Act allows arbitrators to decide in accordance with "such considerations" other than applicable law as are agreed by the parties.[25] Article 17 of the ICC Rules, for example, provides that the arbitrators shall in all cases take account of "relevant trade usages." Could an arbitrator apply the principles (or alleged principles) of the so-called *lex mercatoria*[26] on the theory that these are subsumed under "trade usages?" The answer would seem to depend on the particular issue, context and alleged principle.

---

20   Article 35 of the ICC Rules provides for gaps   to be filled "in the spirit of these Rules."

21   ICC Rules, Article 29.

22   The additional award must deal with a matter presented to the tribunal.

23   An arbitrator's decision interpreting an award or correcting an error must take the form of an addendum, considered part of the award itself. See Article 29(3) of the ICC Rules.

24   *See* Toby Landau, *The Effect of the New English Arbitration Act on Institutional Arbitration*, 13 J. INT. ARB. 113, at 119 (December 1996).

25   *See* Act § 46(1)(b). In applying this provision to an arbitration agreement made before the Act's entry into force, the agreement "shall have effect in accordance with the rules of law . . . as they stood immediately before the [effective] date." Statutory Instrument 3146, Schedule 2, paragraph 4. Thus language looking like an "equity clause" but interpreted differently prior to the Act will still be subject to the earlier interpretation if contained in pre-Act contracts. See 1997 DAC Report, paragraph 30.

26   See *generally* Chapter 35.

30.02   The Agreement to Arbitrate

(a) Definitions.

While an arbitration agreement is defined somewhat circularly as an agreement to submit to arbitration either present or future disputes, the Act attempts no characterization of arbitration itself. Thus the Act offers no help on the issue of how to distinguish arbitration from other binding private dispute resolution mechanisms such as expert evaluation.[27]

Like the New York Arbitration Convention, the Act requires an agreement in writing,[28] on the premise that "contracting out of the right to go to court [is of] such importance that it should be in some written form."[29] The definition of a writing, however, is broad enough to include most of the means of communication used today in international commerce, including unsigned documents[30] and reference (even oral) to institutional rules[31] or to documents containing an arbitration provision.[32]

(b) Separability.

The Act codifies the principle that an arbitration clause remains autonomous from the main commercial agreement in which it is found.[33] Unlike the UNCITRAL Model Arbitration Law,[34] however, the Act avoids affirming sepa-

---

27   The drafters were unconvinced that a definition would serve any useful purpose. *See* 1994 DAC Report, Section 18, at 10. For a general exploration of the characteristics of arbitration, *see* MICHAEL MUSTILL & STEWART BOYD, COMMERCIAL ARBITRATION 38-50 (2d edition 1989). On the role of experts in England, *see e.g.,* Jones v. Sherwood Computer Services, [1992] 1 WLR 277 (review of an expert's decision only for fraud or failure to perform correct function). *Compare* Mercury Communications v. General Telecommunications, [1996] 1 WLR 48 (House of Lords accepted review of expert's error). *See generally* JOHN KENDALL, EXPERT DETERMINATION (2d ed. 1996).

28   Act § 5.

29   1996 DAC Report, Section 33, at 14.

30   Act § 5(2)(a). For an example of an unsigned arbitration agreement, *see* Compagnie de Navigation et Transports. v. Mediterranean Shipping Company, Swiss ATF 121 II 38 (1995), discussed in Chapter 33 (bill of lading for maritime transports).

31   Act §5(3) provides that the parties make an agreement in writing when they "agree otherwise than in writing by reference to terms which are in writing."

32   § 6(2). For an example of incorporation of arbitration clauses by reference to other documents, *see, e.g.,* United States Fidelity & Guaranty Co. v. West Point Construction, 837 F. 2d 1507 (11th Cir. 1988) (performance bond incorporates arbitration provisions of subcontract). *See also* Bomar Oil v. Entreprise Tunisienne d'activité pétrolière (ETAP), French *Cour de cassation*, 11 Oct. 1989, XV YEARBOOK on International Arbitration 447 (1990), decision on rehearing, *Cour d'appel de Versailles*, 23 Jan. 1991, XVII Yearbook of International Arbitration 488 (1992), affirmed by the *Cour de cassation*, 9 Nov. 1993 (1ère Ch. Civ.).

33   Act § 7 provides that an arbitration clause "shall not be regarded as invalid, non-existent or ineffective because [the main agreement of which the arbitration clause forms a part] is invalid, or did not come into existence or has become ineffective...." For the prior law on separability, *see* Harbour Assurance v. Kansa [1993] QB 701.

34   The UNCITRAL Model Law amalgamates both separability and *compétence-compétence* notions in Article 16.

rability in the same section with reference to the arbitrator's power to decide jurisdictional questions,[35] thus resisting the tendency to confuse these two concepts.

The separability doctrine says that arbitrators can declare the principal agreement invalid (for example, due to illegality), without retroactively taking away their power to do so. On the other hand, the separability doctrine says nothing about how to determine whether the arbitrators' power existed in the first place. Nor does the doctrine of separability necessarily answer the question of whether assignment of the main agreement entails assignment of the arbitration clause.[36]

(c) "Special Category" Disputes.

The Act eliminates the restriction on arbitration of disputes arising out of admiralty, commodity market and insurance contracts governed by English law.[37] Prior legislation prohibited pre-dispute waiver of the right to appeal points of law in such "special category" cases, on the assumption that to remain preeminent in these areas English law required the fertilization of judicial decisions dealing with modern day commercial controversies. Litigation was seen not only as a way to settle a dispute, but also as a means to provide broader behavioral rules to guide business conduct outside the particular dispute.[38]

(d) Domestic Agreements.

The Act also departs from prior law in its lack of any special protection for domestic non-consumer arbitration. Careful readers will have seen that the text of the Act as it received Royal Assent on 17 June 1996 distinguished between domestic and international arbitration.[39] For example, the Act originally prohibited pre-dispute waiver of appeal on points of English law in non-international cases.[40] However, this special régime never entered into force due to hesitations about its wisdom.[41] Concern was expressed that distinctions

---

35 Arbitrators may rule on their jurisdiction either through an interim or a final award. Act § 31 (4), depending on the parties' agreement (if any) on the matters. In either case, a court may vary, confirm or set aside the award in whole or in part. Act § 67(3).

36 Although an early draft of the Act responded to this question in the affirmative, the Departmental Advisory Committee ultimately decided that the complexity of the issue could not be dealt with adequately in legislation covering exclusively arbitration. *See* 1996 DAC Report, page 17, at paragraphs 45-46.

37 On the background to this change, *see generally* the 1993 Departmental Advisory Committee Report on Special Categories under the Arbitration Act 1979, *reprinted in* 9 ARB. INT. 405 (1993).

38 Compare the so-called "public law model" of litigation, discussed in Robert G. Bone, *Lon Fuller's Theory of Adjudication and the False Dichotomy Between Dispute Resolution and Public Law Models of Litigation*, 75 BUL. REV. 1273 (1995).

39 Act §§ 85-87.

40 Act § 87.

41 *See* 1996 DAC Report, Clauses 317-31, at 66-69. The Secretary of State was given the right to order repeal or amendment of the domestic protective régime. Act § 88.

based on nationality conflicted with Britain's obligations within the European Union.[42] Consequently, in the end these protective provisions were not given effect.[43]

(e) Consumer Transactions.

The Act applies European Union consumer protection regulations[44] to arbitration agreements.[45] These regulations invalidate contract terms causing "significant imbalance in the parties' rights and obligations" to the consumer's detriment.[46]

One schedule to the Consumer Contract Regulations contains an illustrative list of terms that may be regarded as unfair, and therefore non-binding. These examples of unfairness include terms that require consumers to "take disputes exclusively to arbitration not covered by legal provisions."[47] The meaning of this curious phraseology (lifted verbatim from a European Council Directive) is not immediately clear, since any arbitration in England would seem by definition to be "covered by legal provisions," in the sense of being subject to the Act and its consumer protection scheme.[48]

30.03   Interlocutory Matters

(a) Jurisdictional Rulings.

Frequently during the proceedings one side will question the scope of the arbitration clause. The Act contemplates that the arbitral tribunal may decide such jurisdictional issues.[49] A court also may be called to examine the arbi-

---

42   Article 6 of the Treaty Establishing the European Union provides that "any discrimination on the grounds of nationality shall be prohibited." Shortly after adoption of the Act, the Court of Appeal expressed disapproval of a domestic protection scheme under the Consumer Arbitration Agreements Act 1988. *See* Phillip Alexander Securities & Futures Ltd. v. Bamberger, Court of Appeal, 12 July 1996, *reported in The Times*, 22 July 1996.

43   Section 3, Statutory Instrument 3146, provides that the Act would come into force "except sections 85 to 87."

44   Unfair Terms in Consumer Contracts Regulations of 1994, implementing European Council Directive 93/13/EEC (5 April 1993), OFFICIAL JOURNAL No. L95, 21 April 1993, page 29.

45   Act § 89.

46   Consumer Contract Regulations §§ 3 & 4. Consumers include individuals acting for purposes outside their business. *Id.*, § 2.

47   Schedule 3, § 1(q), Unfair Terms in Consumer Contracts Regulations 1994.

48   Several constructions of these words have been suggested, none entirely satisfactory: (1) arbitration agreements are *per se* invalid in all consumer transactions; (2) prohibition in consumer contracts of "equity clauses," by which an arbitrator decides without reference to a fixed legal system; (3) reference to small claims and statutory arbitration, covered later in the Act §§ 92 and 95-98; (4) consumers have no right to exclude appeal on questions of law.

49   Act § 30. The matter may be dealt with in a separate award on jurisdiction or in the final award on the merits. Act § 31(4). The Act refers to an "award" on jurisdiction, making clear that a jurisdictional decision will have the same force as any other award.

trators' decision pursuant to a subsequent challenge to the award,[50] provided the protesting party has not lost the right to object by failing to make a timely challenge in the arbitral proceedings themselves.[51]

Arbitral jurisdiction may also be relevant in a motion to stay legal proceedings, where a court must decide whether the agreement is "null and void, inoperative, or incapable of being performed," and whether the legal proceedings concern the matter to be referred to arbitration.[52] Case law subsequent to the Act, however, has made clear that a commitment to arbitrate may not be avoided by arguing that a "dispute" does not exist because the defendant has no sustainable defense.[53]

In some circumstances courts might also determine questions of jurisdiction as a preliminary matter, without waiting for an arbitrator's decision.[54] Such determinations may be made either by agreement of all the parties, or with the permission of the arbitral tribunal after satisfying the court that the determination will likely produce substantial cost savings.

(b) The Court's Supportive Powers.[55]

The judiciary will continue to play its traditional role of supporting the arbitral process. The Act makes clear that courts may secure assets[56] and assist in taking or preserving evidence, in support of arbitration both in England and abroad.[57] Courts may order compliance with the arbitrators' orders either on application of the arbitral tribunal itself or on request by a party to

---

50   Act § 67, discussed *infra* in Section 30.04. The DAC Advisory Committee noted, "Clearly the [arbitral] tribunal cannot be the final arbiter of a question of jurisdiction, for this would provide a classic case of pulling oneself up by one's own bootstraps . . . ." 1996 DAC Report, Section 138, at page 33.

51   Act § 73. Moreover, the right to challenge arbitral jurisdiction through injunction is given only to persons who take no part in the arbitral proceedings. Act § 72, discussed in Section 30.04.

52   Act § 9.

53   *See* Halki Shipping v. Sopex Oils, [1997] 3 ALL ER 833. Shipowner sued for demurrage under a charter party and court stayed legal proceedings. Whether contract defenses were doomed to fail was for the arbitrator to decide.

54   Act § 32.

55   The Act refers to "the court," regardless of whether jurisdiction lies with a county court or with the High Court in London. *See* Act § 105.

56   Under a so-called "Mareva injunction" an English court orders a defendant not to dispose of any of its assets located in England and Wales. In some cases the injunction may apply even extraterritorially. The injunction took its name from the decision of Lord Denning in Mareva Compania Naviera S.A. v. International Bulk Carriers S.A., [1975] 2 LLOYD'S REP. 509.

57   Act § 44. This power is in line with Article 9 of the UNCITRAL Model Arbitration Law, which provides that "it is not incompatible with an arbitration agreement" for a court to grant measures of interim protection. Act § 2(3) provides that the powers conferred on courts by § 44 may be exercised even when the arbitral seat is outside England and Wales.

the proceedings with the permission of the tribunal.[58] To secure the attendance of witnesses (assuming they can be found in the United Kingdom), the same procedures available in ordinary court proceedings may be used in arbitration.[59]

(c) The Arbitral Proceedings.

As a general rule, the arbitral procedure can be custom tailored to the parties' tastes. Either before or after the dispute arises, the parties may provide for matters such as consolidation of claims,[60] appointment of experts,[61] interim awards[62] or how to deal with delay.[63]

In one significant respect, however, the Act sets aside the principle of party autonomy. As mentioned earlier, no waiver is permitted with respect to the arbitrators' general duty of fairness.[64] An arbitral tribunal must give each party a reasonable opportunity to put forward its case, and must adopt procedures that both avoid delay and promote fair resolution of the dispute.

(d) Security for Costs.

The 1996 Act moves the power to order security for costs of arbitration from the court to the arbitral tribunal.[65] The arbitrators, however, may not exercise this power in a way that discriminates against foreign parties.[66]

This departure from prior law is significant in light of the much discussed *Ken-Ren* case, in which the House of Lords held that the High Court had power to order a claimant to provide security for costs in an ICC arbitration.[67] A bankrupt claimant was able to fund an arbitral proceeding, but not necessarily to pay the expenses that might be awarded if it lost.[68] The case was

---

58   Act § 41 permits the arbitral tribunal to deal with delay through what the Act calls "peremptory orders," which courts may enforce under Act § 42.

59   Act § 43. The exercise of these powers requires that the arbitral proceedings (to be distinguished from the seat of the arbitration) are conducted in England and that the witness be located in the United Kingdom.

60   Act § 35.

61   Act § 37.

62   Act § 39.

63   Act § 41.

64   Act § 33.

65   *See* Section 190-93 of 1996 DAC Report. *See generally*, Peter Fitzpatrick, *Security for Costs Under the Arbitration Act 1996*, 1998 INT. ARB. LAW REV. 139.

66   *See* Act § 38 & 44. Compare the court's power to order security for costs of challenge to awards under Act § 70(6).

67   Coppée Lavalin S.A. v. Ken-Ren Chemicals, House of Lords 5 May 1994, [1995] 1 A.C. 38. The case arose out of an arbitration pursuant to a contract for a chemical plant to be built in Kenya. *See generally* Claude Reymond, *Security for Costs in International Arbitration*, 110 LAW Q. REV. 501 (1994).

68   *See* Article 31 of the ICC Rules.

thus likely to evoke sympathy for the defendant. Nevertheless many felt that the interests of international arbitration in England were not furthered by such judicial intervention in a private procedure.[69]

(e) Inherent Jurisdiction.

After the Act courts are likely to be more careful exercising their inherent jurisdiction to control arbitration-related litigation. The power to do so, however, remains intact. The Act's basic interpretative principles instruct courts only that they "should not" intervene in matters covered by the Act (except as provided by statute), rather than that they "shall not" intervene.[70] The guideline's phrasing is hortatory rather than mandatory.

In the past, this power has been invoked, for example, to deal with non-signatories to an arbitration clause.[71] In *Nissan (UK) Ltd. v Nissan Motor Company*[72] the Court of Appeal stayed litigation pending the outcome of an arbitration even as against a company that was not a party to the arbitration agreement. A motor vehicle distributorship between a Japanese automobile manufacturer and an English company was supplemented by a second agreement with both the manufacturer and its subsidiary. The first but not the second agreement called for arbitration in Tokyo. When the Japanese terminated the relationship, the English company brought a court proceeding. This action was stayed against both the parent and its subsidiary pending the arbitration. Overlapping core issues, said the court, made the second contract merely "a side show."[73]

30.04   Review of Awards

(a) Statutory Skeleton.

What have been called "the active remedies" available to a party dissatisfied with the award[74] rest on a balanced approach to finality and fairness that includes: (i) a non-waivable right to challenge awards on matters of substan-

---

69   The 1996 DAC Report, Sections 193, notes that the *Ken-Ren* decision was greeted "with dismay" by those wishing to promote England as an arbitration center.

70   Act § 1(3). Compare Article 5 of the UNCITRAL Model Law, containing more forceful language to the effect that "no court *shall* intervene" in matters governed by the Model Law.

71   For another context case involving the court's "inherent powers" *see* Channel Tunnel Group v. Balfour Beatty Construction, [1993] A.C. 334 (H.L.). English courts were held to possess power to order interim injunctive relief with respect to ICC arbitration in Bruxelles, although the power was not exercised in that case.

72   Decision of 31 July 1991, Court of Appeal (Civil Division). Unpublished.

73   *Id.*, page 27. The court stayed the litigation in order to prevent injustice under power pursuant to "the inherent jurisdiction of the court."

74   *See generally* Anthony Diamond & V.V. Veeder, *The New English Arbitration Act 1996: Challenging an English Award Before the English Court*, 8 AM. REV. INT. ARB. 47 (1997). Diamond and Veeder distinguish between passive waiting for the opposing party to seek to enforce the award, and an active attack on the award at the seat of the arbitration in England.

tive jurisdiction and serious procedural irregularity; and (ii) a default rule that in some cases permits appeal on points of English law unless the parties agree otherwise, which will inevitably be the case in ICC arbitration.[75] The right to challenge an award with respect to matters of substantive jurisdiction or serious procedural irregularity is set forth in precise language,[76] a welcome advance over the prior law's amalgamation of a wide variety of bad behavior under the rubrics of "misconduct" or "mishap."[77]

The Act's most important structural innovation with respect to awards lies in a bifurcated approach to arbitral integrity, which separates disrespect for the arbitrator's mission from other procedural defects that affect the proceedings or the award. In both instances, courts may monitor arbitrations that lack propriety. However, since a procedural mistake may or may not be relevant to the outcome of the dispute, the Act incorporates a "substantial injustice" standard in determining whether or not irregularities fatally taint an award.[78]

On the other hand, jurisdictional excess is arguably more absolute in nature than other defects in the arbitration.[79] With respect to any specific issue, an arbitrator is unlikely to have just a little bit of jurisdiction any more than she might be just a little bit pregnant. Therefore the court has the right to set aside an award in whole or in part when arbitrators have exceeded their powers.

(b) Points of English Law.

The Act provides for appeal on question of law (defined as questions of English law[80]) but permits appeal to be waived either before or after the dispute arises.[81] This opportunity for waiver of merits review meets the goal of arbitral finality expected by those members of the international business community who arbitrate in London for reasons of convenience and expertise, rather

---

75 *See* Article 28(6) of the ICC Rules.

76 *See* Act §§ 30 and 67 (relating to substantive jurisdiction) and § 68 (serious procedural irregularity).

77 Arbitration Act 1950, § 23(2) permitted an award to be set aside "where an arbitrator or umpire has misconducted himself." "Procedural mishap" was a ground for remission of awards under controversial case law arising under § 22 of the 1950 Act. *See generally*, 1996 DAC report, Paragraph 281; Anthony Diamond & V.V. Veeder, *Arbitration and Adjudication After 1996* (Proceedings of Conference sponsored by Queen Mary and Westfield College, University of London, 1 May 1997), at page 59-60. *See also* V.V. Veeder, *Remedies Against Arbitral Awards: Setting Aside, Remission and Rehearing*, in 1993 YEARBOOK, ARBITRATION INSTITUTE, STOCKHOLM CHAMBER OF COMMERCE 125.

78 For example, one party's tardy submission of the cases on which it relies might constitute a procedural failing but not necessarily cause such injustice as to require annulment of the award.

79 *See* 1996 DAC Report, at 58.

80 Act § 82 defines a "question of law" to mean the law of England and Wales for courts in England and Wales, and the law of Northern Ireland for courts in Northern Ireland. Thus the arbitrators' conclusions on matters of foreign law will not be appealable.

81 Act § 69.

than to hear high-priced QC's engage in clever courtroom debate of matters already decided by the arbitrators.

As under prior law, exclusion of merits review can be made by reference to the ICC Rules, which automatically provide for waiver of appeal.[82] Agreeing to an award not accompanied by reasons (now commonplace in the United States) will also constitute waiver of appeal on points of law.[83]

Even if not excluded by contract, appeal on a question of law will be allowed only with the consent of the parties or by leave of the court.[84] Statutory criteria for allowing appeal are intended to discourage all but the most serious of challenges, when the arbitrator's decision is manifestly dysfunctional.[85] Leave to appeal will not be granted unless the arbitrators' decision is "obviously wrong," or the question is one of general public importance and the decision is "open to serious doubt."[86]

(c) Serious Procedural Irregularity.

The Act incorporates a useful though not exhaustive catalogue of defective arbitrator behavior comprised within the rubric of serious irregularity, an enumeration clearly better than the vague reference to "misconduct" and "mishap" under prior law.[87] This laundry list of improprieties includes failure to deal with all of the issues put to the tribunal; failure to conduct the proceedings according to the agreement of the parties; ambiguity in the award; and failure to comply with the general requirement that the arbitrator act fairly and impartially.[88] Any of these procedural flaws may result in an award being set aside in whole or in part or remitted to the arbitrators for reconsideration, but only if it has or will cause substantial injustice to the party challenging the award.[89]

---

82 Article 28 of the ICC Rules provides that the parties "shall be deemed to have waived their right to any form of recourse insofar as such waiver can validly be made." This principle was first elaborated in Arab African Energy Corp. v. Olie Produkten Nederland, [1983] 2 Lloyd's Rep. 419, interpreting reference to the ICC Rules as excluding appeal under the 1979 Arbitration Act.

83 Act § 69(1).

84 The provision for appeal of awards on questions of law operates in tandem with the possibility for courts to determine preliminary points of law under Act § 45, which, like appeal on the legal merits of award, can be waived.

85 The statutorily circumscribed conditions under which courts will grant leave to appeal derive in large measure from the guidelines set out in a House of Lords decision intended to restrict inappropriate appeals under the 1979 Act. See The Nema, [1982] A.C. 724.

86 Appeal must be brought within 28 days after the award or, as the case may be, notification of the result of an appeal within the arbitral process. Act § 70.

87 See Arbitration Act 1950, §§ 22 and 23, discussed supra.

88 Act § 33 amplifies the duty of fairness to include "giving each party a reasonable opportunity of putting his case and dealing with that of his opponent, and . . . avoiding unnecessary delay or expense . . . ."

89 The power to set an award aside is not to be exercised unless the court is satisfied that remission to the arbitrators would be inappropriate. Act § 68 (3).

Serious irregularity also includes an excess of power other than one related to substantive jurisdiction.[90] Such overreaching of a non-substantive nature might be found when arbitrators ignore limits set by the Act itself. For example, an arbitrator might order security for costs in a way that discriminates against foreigners, thus running afoul of the requirements of Act § 38. An excess of power under this provision might also occur if the arbitrator manifestly disregards the contractually stipulated governing law.

The catch-all talisman of "public policy" works its way into the Act § 68, where the examples of serious procedural irregularity that might permit challenge of an award include "the award or the way in which it was procured being contrary to public policy."[91] Although the malleable nature of public policy always creates a risk of misuse,[92] there is no reason at this time to suspect that English judges will greet public policy defenses with anything other than healthy skepticism.[93] However, if there is clear evidence of a contract's illegality at the place of performance, English courts generally will not enforce an award giving effect to the illicit agreement.[94]

If a concept as pliant and poorly defined as public policy is to be included in an arbitration statute, its invocation might be limited to situations in which judges are asked to enforce an award, as contrasted with setting an award aside. It is understandable that a court will be reluctant, for example, to at-

---

90   Act § 68 (2)(b). Substantive jurisdiction includes the validity and scope of the arbitration agreement as well as the proper constitution of the arbitral tribunal. Act §§ 30 & 67.

91   Act § 68(2)(g).

92   Similar concerns arise with respect to the UNCITRAL Model Arbitration Law and the arbitration statutes of countries such as France and Switzerland, which list violation of public policy as an explicit ground for award annulment.

93   For a case dealing with public policy in respect to a foreign award, see Westacre Investments v. Jugoimport, C.A., 12 May 1999, affirming Q.B., 19 December 1997 [1998] 3 WLR 770. Westacre concluded a consultancy agreement to assist Yugoslavia in selling military equipment. After obtaining a contract for the sale of tanks to Kuwait, Yugoslavia canceled the consultancy agreement on the ground that it contemplated bribery and was contrary to Kuwaiti law. In an award upheld by the Swiss *Tribunal fédéral*, an ICC arbitral tribunal found for Westacre. Nothing in the award itself suggested that the contract was against public policy. Refusing to look beyond the award and admit further evidence on the point, the court found that "the public policy of sustaining international arbitration awards on the facts of this case outweighs the public policy in discouraging international commercial corruption." *See also* DST v. Rakoil, [1987] 2 LLOYD'S REP. 246 and Dalmia Dairy Industries v. National Bank of Pakistan, [1978] 2 LLOYD'S REP. 223.

94   See Soleimany v. Soleimany, C.A., [1998] 3 WLR 811, discussed in Carol Mulcahy, *The Challenge to Enforcement of Awards on Grounds of Underlying Illegality*, 64 ARBITRATION 210 (1998). The Court of Appeal refused to enforce an award that gave effect to an illegal transaction. Father and son submitted a business dispute to a Beth Din, or court of Jewish law, which was characterized as an arbitral tribunal for purposes of the national arbitration statute. The award in favor of the son stated that the illegal nature of the underlying commercial activities—smuggling carpets out of Iran—was not relevant to the parties' rights under Jewish law. Quaere whether in this context it would have been appropriate for the Beth Din to apply the Jewish Law principle "*Dina De-Malkhuta Dina*," a conflict-of-laws rule by which the law of the land in some cases preempts Jewish law.

tach assets to give effect to an award that violates basic notions of justice. However, in many international arbitrations courts at the arbitral situs have no need to pass on public policy, unless either the loser has property there or legal proceedings are brought locally in conflict with the award.

(e) Substantive Jurisdiction.

The Act defines "substantive jurisdiction" capaciously to encompass not only the validity of the arbitration agreement, but also the proper constitution of the arbitral tribunal and the subject matter of the arbitration clause.[95] Arbitrators may rule on the extent of this jurisdiction either through an interim decision or in the final award on the merits.[96] In either case, a court may vary, confirm or set aside the award in whole or in part. Questions of arbitral jurisdiction may also be raised in a judicial action on the underlying dispute, when the party seeking to avoid arbitration asserts that the arbitration agreement is "null and void, inoperative or incapable of being performed."[97]

(f) Limits on Challenge.

No dispute resolution process will be well-served by expenditure of time and resources in its early stages which ultimately turn out to have been unnecessary. To reduce such waste and delay, the Act incorporates mechanisms that restrict the right to challenge awards if litigants should have acted sooner.

First, a "use it or lose it" principle requires that fundamental defects in the regularity of the proceedings be raised during the arbitration itself. Challenges both for excess of authority and for serious irregularity must be made "forthwith," or within the time provided by the arbitration agreement or the arbitral tribunal itself in appropriate situations.[98] To rebut the presumption that the right to object has been waived, the challenging party must show that it did not know, and could not with reasonable diligence have discovered, the grounds for objection.[99] Any ruling that the arbitrators have jurisdiction must be challenged directly or the right to object later will be lost.[100]

The Act provides a very important safeguard, however, for a person who takes no part in the arbitral proceedings. Non-participants may, through judicial proceedings for "declaration or injunction or other appropriate relief,"

---

95   Act § 30(1).

96   Act § 31 (4). The tribunal must follow the parties' agreement (if any) on whether an interim decision or an award on the merits is more appropriate. In the former case the Act speaks simply of a challenge, while in the latter case it calls for "an order declaring an award to be of no effect." Act § 67.

97   Act § 9(4).

98   Act § 73 (1).

99   In this respect, the Act is more severe than the analogous provisions in Article 4 of the UNCITRAL Model Arbitration Law, which covers only a party who actually "knows" of a procedural defect.

100 Id., § 73(2).

challenge the validity of the arbitration agreement, the constitution of the arbitral tribunal or the submission of particular matters to the arbitrators.[101] Challenge may be made regardless of whether failure to participate was by choice or by inadvertence, and regardless of whether in hindsight this non-participation proves justified. Thus the Act leads to a different result than in Switzerland, where defendants may lose their right to challenge an award's jurisdictional underpinnings by boycotting the proceedings.[102]

Second, a party seeking annulment of an arbitrator's decision for excess of jurisdiction or serious irregularity may do so only after attempting to remedy the problem through the appropriate arbitral procedures. In the interest of arbitral efficiency, court challenges to awards can only be brought after any available institutional review.[103]

(g) The "Making" of an Award.

Although the Act looks to the arbitral seat to determine the law governing the arbitration itself (as contrasted with the law applicable to the merits of the dispute), the New York Convention mandates enforcement of awards by reference to the place where an award is "made."[104] Under prior law, this difference between the arbitral seat and the place where the award is "made" had opened the door to confusion in a case where the arbitrator conducted the proceeding in London but signed the award on return home to Paris.[105] When the loser challenged the award on a point of law it became critical to determine whether the English arbitration statute applied. The House of Lords found both (i) that the award was "made" in Paris where signed, and (ii) that English courts could nevertheless hear appeals, given that the arbitration had its seat in England.

---

101 Act § 72. This protection comports with § 73, which takes away the right to object to jurisdictional defects only if a party "takes part, or continues to take part, in the proceedings" without making the appropriate objection.

102 *See* Westland Helicopters v. Emirates Arabs Unis, Arabie Saoudite, Etat du Qatar, ABH et Arab Organization for Industrialization (AOI), Swiss *Tribunal fédéral* decision of 19 April 1994, 120 II 155 ATF (1994), *also reported in* 12 SWISS BULL. 404 (1994).

103 Act § 70(2) speaks of "any available arbitral process of appeal or review." However, courts are not necessarily bound by the arbitral institution's decision on the matter. Challenge to an award must also be delayed until exhaustion of any application to correct an award under Act § 57, in default of the parties' agreement otherwise.

104 Convention Article I provides that the Convention shall apply to awards made in the territory of a State other than where recognition and enforcement are sought. Article V(1)(e) takes away the presumptive validity of an award set aside in the "country in which . . . the award was made."

105 *Hiscox v. Outhwaite,* House of Lords, [1991] A.E.R., 641; XVII YEARBOOK 599 (1992). The many commentaries on the case include Claude Reymond, *Where is an Arbitral Award Made?*, 108 LAW Q. REV. 1 (1992), and Michael Schneider, *Le lieu où la sentence est rendue*, 9 SWISS BULL. 279 (1991).

The Act reverses the first-mentioned holding in this case. Unless the parties agree otherwise, an arbitral seat in England will also be treated as the place the award was made, regardless of where it was signed or delivered.[106]

---

106 Act § 53.

CHAPTER 31

FRENCH LAW

31.01   Statutory framework

(a) Overview

French arbitration law has long recognized the distinction between domestic and international arbitration,[1] a differentiation codified in Articles 1442-1507 of the *Nouveau Code de Procédure Civile (NCPC)*. Introduced by decrees promulgated in 1980[2] (for domestic arbitration) and 1981[3] (for international arbitration), these provisions seek to balance arbitral autonomy with court scrutiny of an arbitration's procedural fairness.

The 1980 Decree codified several decades of judicial gloss on the basic French arbitration statute,[4] consolidating procedures for challenge of awards, reducing the use of dilatory tactics during arbitration, and limiting judicial interference during arbitral proceedings.

Most aspects of ICC arbitration conducted in France will be covered by the 1981 decree, encompassing *NCPC* Articles 1492–504. Moreover, the grounds for challenging awards rendered in international arbitration are a matter of mandatory public policy (see Section 31.04.), preventing parties from "opting into" the 1980 Decree on matters of judicial review.

---

1   *See generally*, MATTHIEU DE BOISSESON, DROIT FRANÇAIS DE L'ARBITRAGE INTERNE ET INTERNATIONAL (1990) (hereinafter "DE BOISSESON"); PHILIPPE FOUCHARD, EMMANUEL GAILLARD & BERTHOLD GOLDMAN, TRAITÉ DE L'ARBITRAGE COMMERCIAL INTERNATIONAL (1996) (hereinafter "FOUCHARD, GAILLARD & GOLDMAN").

2   Decree No. 80-354 of 14 May 1980, 1980 JOURNAL OFFICIEL DE LA RÉPUBLIQUE FRANÇAISE at 1238-40; 1980 RECUEIL DALLOZ SIREY, Legislation, at 207-09 (hereinafter "1980 Decree").

3   Decree No. 81-500 of 12 May 1981, 1981 JOURNAL OFFICIEL DE LA RÉPUBLIQUE FRANÇAISE at 1398-1406; RECUEIL DALLOZ SIREY, 28e CAHIER-CHRONIQUE, 9 Sept. 1981 (hereinafter "1981 Decree").

4   *See generally La réforme du droit français de l'arbitrage: Décret du 14 Mai 1980*, 1980 REV. ARB. 583.

The origin of the *NCPC* provisions applicable to international arbitration lies in two cases in which the Paris *Cour d'appel* held itself to lack jurisdiction to vacate ICC awards.[5] Subsequently, commentators urged legislative clarification of the role of courts with respect to international commercial arbitration in France.[6] Some feared that a completely *laissez-faire* approach, allowing international arbitration to be conducted in France with little or no judicial control, might lead foreign enforcement courts to be more exacting in monitoring the award, thereby impeding the efficient operation of cross-border arbitration.

(b) Contracts Implicating International Commerce

The Decree defines "international arbitration" by an economic standard. An arbitration is international if it "implicates international commercial interests."[7] Thus the fact that both parties are French does not deprive the arbitration of its international character.[8] For example, the Paris *Cour d'appel* recently held that an arbitration between attorneys of a French law firm implicated international commerce, given that the firm included American nationals practicing both in France and in the United States.[9]

Characterization of an arbitration as international can have significant effects, since a pre-dispute arbitration clause would normally be invalid in a consumer contract.[10] However, in *Meglio v. Société V2000*[11] the *Cour de cassation* upheld the validity of an arbitration clause in an agreement for the

---

5   *See Cour d'appel de Paris*, 21 Feb. 1980, Gen. Nat'l Maritime Transp. Co. v. Société Götaverken Arendal A.B., [1980] RECUEIL DALLOZ SIREY, JURISPRUDENCE 568; 1980 REV. ARB. 524; 1980 JDI 763. Jan Paulsson, *Arbitration Unbound: Award Detached from the Law of its Country of Origin*, 30 INT'L & COM. L. Q. 358, 385 (1981). *See also Cour d'appel de Paris*, 9 Dec. 1980, AKSA v. Norsolor, 1981 REV. ARB. 306; 20 ILM 887 (1981).

6   *See* Philippe Fouchard, *Les recours contre les sentences non françaises*, 1980 REV. ARB. 693, 694.

7   *NCPC* Article 1492.

8   *See generally*, FOUCHARD, GAILLARD & GOLDMAN at §§ 78 - 126; Philippe Fouchard, *Quand un arbitrage est-il international?*, 1970 REV. ARB. 59, 71-74. For the origin of this concept, *see Cour de cassation*, 19 Feb. 1930, Mardele v. Muller et Cie., 1933 RECUEIL SIREY GENERAL DES LOIS ET DES ARRÊTS, SIREY JURISPRUDENCE 41.

9   *See Cour d'appel de Paris*, 1 Dec. 1993, Rawlings v. Société Kevorkian, 1994 REV ARB. 695. The arbitration clause was contained in the law firm's basic constitutive document, the "*statuts*." In domestic arbitration, pre-dispute arbitration agreements are only allowed in contracts between *commerçants* (merchants), a category that does not include attorneys.

10   *See Code Civil*, Article 2061, generally prohibiting a pre-dispute arbitration clause (*clause compromissoire*). Compare *Code Civil* Article 2060, allowing post-dispute agreements to arbitrate (*compromis*) and *Code de commerce*, Article 63, allowing pre-dispute arbitration between merchants (*commerçants*). These provisions are reinforced by Loi no. 95-96, 1 February 1995, adding Article L.132-1 to the French *Code de la consommation* to implement the consumer protection scheme of European Council Directive 93/13/EEC, OFFICIAL JOURNAL No. L 95, 21 April 1993, at 29. *See generally*, Philippe Fouchard, *Clause abusives en matière d'arbitrage*, 1995 REV. ARB. 147.

11   *Cour de cassation*, 21 May 1997, 1997 REV. ARB. 537, note Emmanuel Gaillard, and 1998 REV. CRIT. DR. INT'L PRIVÉ 87, note Vincent Heuzé.

purchase of an automobile destined for personal use.[12] The court held that the contract implicated international commerce by virtue of a transfer of goods and funds between France and the United Kingdom, and by designating London as the arbitral situs.

(c) Party Autonomy

French law gives the parties wide freedom to define their arbitral procedure, provided they do not violate French notions of international public policy.[13] The agreement to arbitrate may stipulate the rules to be followed in the arbitration proceeding, as well as the procedural law (if any) to which the arbitration is to be subjected. In the event the parties have not agreed on these points, they may be fixed by the arbitral tribunal itself, provided there is no violation of fundamental procedural due process or international public policy.

The same principle of party autonomy applies to the choice of substantive law. The parties are free to designate the applicable law, or to authorize the arbitrators to decide as *amiable compositeurs*.[14] If no choice of law has been made by the parties, the arbitral tribunal may apply whatever legal system it deems appropriate, provided that it takes into account trade usages.[15] This provision accords with Article 17 of the ICC Rules, permitting applicable substantive law to be selected without reference to choice-of-law principles of the arbitral situs.[16]

31.02   The Agreement to Arbitrate

(a) Overview

In contrast to French domestic transactions, the validity of an agreement to arbitrate an international dispute does not depend on the distinction between post-dispute arbitration agreements (*compromis*) and pre-dispute arbitration clauses (*clauses compromissoires*). In France, therefore, the effectiveness of an ICC arbitration clause will be the same regardless of the stage at which the parties agreed to arbitration.

The arbitration clause is deemed to be independent from the main agreement, thus insulating the arbitrator's jurisdiction from attack solely due to a defect in the main contract.[17] In addition, the arbitration clause need not be subject to the law that governs the main contract. The validity of the agreement to arbitrate may even be established without reference to any national law, deter-

---

12   The purchase in question, it must be mentioned, related to a limited series Jaguar selling for £ 290,000, not the type of item normally arousing solicitude for the consumer.

13   *NCPC* Article 1494.

14   *NCPC* Article 1497.

15   *NCPC* Article 1496.

16   *NCPC* Articles 1494 and 1496.

17   *Cour de cassation,* 7 May 1963, Affaire Gosset, 1963 REV. CRIT. DR. INT'L PRIVÉ 615.

mined solely by reference to the parties' common will, and subject only to French concepts of international public policy.[18]

Assignment of a commercial agreement containing an arbitration clause will result in transfer of the arbitration clause itself. In a case involving claims against a defaulting debtor that were assigned to a French bank for collection, the *Cour de cassation* held the bank bound by the arbitration clause in the underlying commercial obligation.[19]

(b) Compétence-Compétence

French law explicitly adopts the principle whereby the arbitrators initially determine the limits of their jurisdiction.[20] *NCPC* Article 1466 provides:

> If one of the parties contests before the arbitral tribunal the scope of the tribunal's jurisdictional authority, the tribunal has power to rule upon the validity of the limits of its investiture.

In addition, French law delays court review of arbitral jurisdiction until *after* an award is rendered. When an arbitral tribunal has not yet been constituted, courts can hear a jurisdictional question only if the alleged arbitration agreement is clearly void (*manifestement nulle*) or when there has been difficulty in constituting the arbitral tribunal.[21] If an arbitral tribunal has already begun to consider a dispute (literally, been "seized" of the matter), courts must decline to hear the case.[22]

(c) State Contracts.

The general rule forbidding states and state entities to enter into arbitration agreements does not apply to an international arbitration.[23] Moreover, a for-

---

18   *See* discussion of the *Court de cassation* decision in the *Dalico* case, *infra* Section 31.02(f). *See also* FOUCHARD, GAILLARD & GOLDMAN at §§ 437, 594 and 597; *Cour d'appel de Paris*, 17 Dec. 1991, Société Gatoil v. National Iranian Cie., 1993 REV. ARB. 281, discussed in FOUCHARD, GAILLARD & GOLDMAN at §§ 436 and 545. *See also Cour de cassation*, 1ère Ch. Civ., 3 March 1992, Sonetex v. Charphil et Topkapi, 1993 JDI 141.

19   *See Cour de cassation*, 1re Ch. Civ., 5 Jan. 1999, Banque Worms v. Bellot, 149 DALLOZ AFFAIRES 291 (18 Feb. 1999), involving a *"cession Dailly"* (assignment in simplified form allowed by French statute, without need of the debtor's consent) arising from maritime repairs by a French shipyard for an Algerian company.

20   For example, *Cour de cassation, Ch. com.*, 21 Jan. 1992, Société Bail Line Shipping v. Société Recofi, 1995 REV. ARB. 57, where an arbitrator was held to have jurisdiction to determine whether or not the action was barred by preconditions established in the relevant contractual document.

21   *NCPC* Article 1458, held to apply to international arbitration in *Cour d'appel de Paris*, 20 Sept. 1995, Matra Hachette v. Reteitalia, 1995 REV. ARB. 87. For a summary of the law on this point, see *Cour de cassation 2ème Ch. Civ.*, 10 May 1995, Coprodag v. Bohin, 1995 REV. ARB. 617, note Emmanuel Gaillard.

22   *NCPC* Article 1458.

23   *See Cour d'appel de Paris*, 10 April 1957, Myrtoon Steamship, 1958 REV. CRIT. DR. INT'L PRIVÉ 120. This principle was confirmed by the *Cour de cassation*, 2 May 1966, Galakis, 1967 REV. CRIT. DR. INT'L PRIVÉ 553.

eign state, will not be allowed to invoke its own national law in order to avoid its commitment to arbitrate.[24]

Nevertheless, parties contemplating ICC arbitration in France must take care that any state intending to be bound by an arbitration clause so indicates clearly and unequivocally. This is one of the lessons to be learned from the decision in the well-known case *Arab Republic of Egypt v. Southern Pacific Property (Middle East) Ltd.*,[25] setting aside an ICC award against Egypt on the grounds that the arbitral tribunal decided in the absence of an arbitration agreement.[26]

(d) Waiver of Judicial Jurisdiction Based on Nationality.

An agreement to arbitrate has also been held to constitute a waiver of a French national's right to require the jurisdiction of French courts. Thus invocation of *Code civil* Articles 14 and 15, by which French courts are given jurisdiction over cases in which French citizens are either claimants or defendants, has been held not to constitute a matter of *ordre public*.[27]

(e) Subject Matter Arbitrability

French courts permit arbitration of many matters involving public policy,[28] including patents and antitrust,[29] but the arbitrability of employ-

---

24   *See Cour d'appel de Paris*, 17 Dec. 1991, Société Gatoil v. National Iranian Oil Company, 1993 REV. ARB. 281, at 285. *See also* FOUCHARD, GAILLARD & GOLDMAN, § 545.

25   *Cour d'appel de Paris*, 12 July 1984, 1985 JDI 129; affirmed by *Cour de cassation*, 6 Jan. 1987, 1987 REV. ARB. 469. English translations in 23 ILM 1048 (1984) and 26 ILM 1004 (1987). To provide for construction of a tourism complex near the Pyramids, a Hong Kong Company (SPP), Egypt's Minister of Tourism, and the Egyptian General Organization for Tourism and Hotels (EGOTH) concluded "Heads of Agreement" not providing for arbitration. Later in the year a subsequent agreement on the matter, which did contain an ICC arbitration clause, was also concluded. However, the Minister of Tourism signed this second contract with the mention "approved, agreed and ratified." After the project was cancelled due to public pressure, an ICC arbitral tribunal made an award in favor of SPP that found Egypt itself to be a party to the arbitration clause. On challenge of the award, the Paris *Cour d'appel* (affirmed by the *Cour de cassation*) interpreted the Minister's signature merely as a consent given in a supervisory capacity, which did not commit Egypt to arbitrate.

26   *See NCPC* Articles 1502 and 1504, discussed in Section 31.04.

27   *See* cases cited by FOUCHARD, GAILLARD & GOLDMAN at § 636, including *Cour de cassation*, 23 May 1963 (1964 REV. CRIT. DR. INT'L. PRIVE. 340, note Yves Loussouarn, 1964 JDI 113 note J.-B Sialelli), 9 Oct. 1967 (1968 JDI 913, note Jean-Denis Bredin) and 18 May 1994 (1995 DALLOZ 20, note Pierre Courbe).

28   *See Cour d'appel de Paris*, 23 March 1991, Société Ganz et autre v. Société Nationale des Chemins de Fers Tunisiens, 1991 REV. ARB. 479, holding that an arbitrator does not lose jurisdiction when the dispute's subject matter concerns a law deemed to be part of the French *ordre public*.

29   *See Cour d'appel de Paris*, 19 May 1993, Labinal v. Société Mors et Westland Aerospace, 1993 REV. ARB. 645 and *Cour d'appel de Paris*, 14 Oct. 1993, Aplix v. Velcro, 1994 REV. ARB. 165 (arbitrability of European Antitrust law); *Cour d'appel de Paris*, 24 March 1994, Société Deko v. G. Dingler et société Meva, 1994 REV. ARB. 514 (arbitrability of patents).

ment agreements is questionable.[30] An arbitrator may refuse to recognize the jurisdiction of a foreign trustee in bankruptcy when, in the arbitrators view, the bankruptcy was instigated for the purpose of disrupting the arbitral proceedings.[31]

(f) Existence and Validity of the Arbitral Agreement

French case law has been generous with respect to proof of an arbitration agreement's existence, recognizing an agreement to arbitrate created by reference to general conditions contained in a standard form. In *Bomar v. Entreprise Tunisienne d'activités pétrolières (ETAP)*,[32] the *Cour de cassation* has upheld an arbitral tribunal's jurisdiction with respect to a sale of crude oil, memorialized through an exchange of telexes referring to seller's standard contract terms, which provided for dispute resolution by arbitration in Paris. After an initial decision based on questionable reasoning,[33] a rehearing by the Versailles *Cour d'appel* led to proof of the arbitration clause under the liberal standards of evidence applicable between merchants (*commerçants*). In a decision upheld by the *Cour de cassation*, the court found evidence in inter-party communications of an intent that the parties be bound by reference to the standard form arbitration clause. Thus French law allows the existence of the arbitration clause to be demonstrated by the parties' course of conduct ("relations habituelles d'affaires").

In the *Dalico* decision, the *Cour de cassation* articulated an international standard for determining the validity of an arbitration clause.[34] The validity of the

---

30   *See generally* DE BOISSESON at § 586 and FOUCHARD, GAILLARD & GOLDMAN at §§ 559 - 579.

31   In *Cour d'appel de Paris*, Nov. 1993, République Côte d'Ivoire v. Norbert Beyrard, 1994 REV. ARB. 685, the court held that the refusal to recognize the foreign bankruptcy upheld the "international public policy principle of good faith execution of contracts" (*principe d'ordre public international de l'exécution de bonne foi des conventions*).

32   An arbitral award rendered on 2 July 1984 led to four decisions. *See Cour d'appel de Paris*, 20 Jan. 1987, Bomar v. Entreprise Tunisienne d'activités pétrolières (ETAP), 1987 REV. ARB. 482, note Catherine Kessedjian and 1987 JDI 934, note Eric Loquin; *Cour de cassation*, 11 Oct. 1989, 1990 REV. ARB. 134, note Catherine Kessedjian and 1990 JDI 633, note Eric Loquin; *Cour d'appel de Versailles*, 23 Jan. 1991, 1991 REV. ARB. 291, note Catherine Kessedjian; *Cour de cassation*, 9 Nov. 1993, 1994 REV. ARB. 108, note Catherine Kessedjian.

33   In an earlier stage the *Cour de cassation* had quashed a decision of the Paris *Cour d'appel* for failing to take into account the consensual nature of arbitration. The *Cour d'appel* had initially applied a test based on general custom and practice in the oil trade, rather than looking to the conduct between the parties themselves.

34   *Cour de cassation*, 1ère Ch. Civ, 20 Dec. 1993, Muncipalité de El Mergeb v. Dalico, 1994 REV. ARB. 116. The Court stated that an arbitration clause is "legally independent of the principal contract in which it is contained...and its existence is to be determined by the common will of the parties without the necessity of a reference to any national law" (*C'est d'après une règle matérielle du droit international de l'arbitrage que la clause compromissoire est indépendante juridiquement du contrat principal qui la contient . . . et que son existence et son efficacité s'apprécient d'après la commune volonté des parties, sans qu'il soit nécessaire de se référer à une loi étatique.) Id.* at 117. (Danish development of a water evacuation system in Libya; reference to arbitration in the annex of a contract's general conditions was deemed to evidence the parties' intent that arbitra-

clause, the Court said, could be evaluated solely according to the will of the parties alone, without reference to a national law.[35] The presumption in favor of the validity of a commitment to arbitrate was affirmed by the *Cour de cassation* in a decision upholding an arbitration clause in a Franco-Italian contract notwithstanding what would have been defects in a domestic agreement.[36]

Applying this standard, the *Cour de cassation* has allowed proof of an agreement to arbitrate by virtue of a clause on the back of sales confirmation orders,[37] stating that the form of an international arbitration agreement need not be in compliance with a national law. Rather, the validity of an international arbitration clause depends only on whether the party sought to be bound had real knowledge (*"connaissance effective"*) of the arbitration agreement before it signed the contract, and whether its acceptance of the agreement was indisputable (*"non-equivoque"*).

In determining the will of the parties with respect to the existence of an arbitration clause, French courts have on occasion pierced the corporate veil between shareholder and company. In particular, an arbitration agreement has been held to bind an individual who deceitfully used a corporate entity to conclude a commercial agreement.[38]

31.03   Interlocutory Matters

(a) Provisional and Conservatory Measures

French courts sitting *"en référé"* may order provisional measures in support of arbitration, including pre-award attachment (*"saisie-conservatoire")* of debts of French residents and other assets located in France.[39] A French judge may

---

tion preempt application of a court selection clause in the general terms themselves). See also *Cour d'appel de Paris*, 17 Dec. 1991, Société Gatoil v. National Iranian Cie., 1993 REV. ARB. 281; FOUCHARD, GAILLARD & GOLDMAN at §§ 436 and 545.

35   *See* FOUCHARD, GAILLARD & GOLDMAN at § 597. Compare *Cour de cassation*, 10 July 1990, Société libanaise L. et B. Cassia v. Société Pia Investment, 1990 REV. ARB. 851 and 1992 JDI 168, where it was held that the existence of the principal agreement containing the arbitration clause must itself be valid under the national legal system designated by the appropriate conflict-of-laws principles.

36   *Cour de cassation*, 5 Jan. 1999, Zanzi v. de Conick, 1999 REV. ARB, 260; note by Ph. Fouchard. *Cour de cassation* overturned lower court decision refusing to recognize arbitration clause in contract not characterized as "commercial" under French law. See *Code civil* Article 2061.

37   *Cour de cassation, 1ère Ch. Civ.*, 3 March 1992, Sonetex v. Charphil et Topkapi, 1993 JDI 141, involving an order of acrylic thread placed by a French company with the French agent of a Turkish entity. *See also* FOUCHARD, GAILLARD & GOLDMAN at §§ 491 - 496.

38   *Cour de cassation*, 11 June 1991, Orri v. Société des lubrifiants Elf Aquitaine, 1992 REV. ARB. 73. In connection with a corporate loan rescheduling, the shareholder in his individual capacity was held bound by an arbitration clause signed by the corporate entity.

39   *See NCPC Article 809*, concerning pre-award attachment. *See also Cour de cassation, 1ère Ch. civ.*, 20 March 1989, République Islamique d'Iran v. Société Framatom v. Eurodif, and 28 June 1989, Eurodif v. République Islamique d'Iran, 1989 REV. ARB. 653. *See generally* DE BOISSESSON at § 304.

also appoint experts to determine the condition of goods subject to dispute or evaluate other facts at issue in the arbitration.[40]

These procedures operate in tandem with Article 23(2) of the ICC Rules, which permits the parties to apply to competent judicial authorities for interim or conservatory measures. In France the competent judicial authority is the President of the *Tribunal de grande instance* or of the *Tribunal de commerce*, depending on whether French law characterizes the matter as commercial, for example because both parties are defined as merchants (*commerçants*) under the *Code de commerce*.[41]

By contrast, when the merits of a case are subject to arbitration, the *Cour de cassation* has restricted the use of a summary procedure called "*référé-provision,*"[42] whereby a judge would otherwise be able to grant money damages not seriously in dispute. Such a summary order for interlocutory payment of damages can only be made before constitution of the arbitral tribunal, and if the plaintiff demonstrates an urgency to its demand.[43]

(b) Appointment of Arbitrator

During the arbitral proceedings French courts defer to the ICC's appointment of arbitrators. Any judicial challenge to arbitrators must be put off until review of the award itself, at which time the ICC's decision will be monitored only on the narrow ground provided by *NCPC* Article 1502, concerning "regularity" of the arbitral tribunal's composition. This principle has been affirmed by the Paris *Cour d'appel*, in decisions holding that ICC removal of arbitrators is not subject to French judicial scrutiny during the arbitral proceedings.[44]

French courts can, however, intervene in case of difficulties related to the constitution of the arbitral tribunal.[45] The term "constitution" is interpreted broadly to allow judicial intervention even during the arbitral proceedings.[46]

---

40   *NCPC* Article 808. *See generally, Cour de cassation,* 11 Oct. 1995, Société Eurodisney v. Société Impresa Pizzarotti and Société Eurodisney v. Société Torno, 1996 REV. ARB. 228 and *Cour d'appel de Versailles*, 8 Oct. 1998, Société Akzo Nobel v. S.A. Elf Atochem, 1999 REV. ARB. 57.

41   *See* CODE DE COMMERCE, Article 631.

42   *Cour de cassation*, 14 March 1984, EURODIF *et al.* v. Islamic Republic of Iran *et al.*, 1985 REV. ARB. 65.

43   *See Cour de cassation, 1ère Ch. civ.*, 29 Nov. 1989, Société Balenciaga v. Société Allieri et Giovanozzi, and *Cour de cassation, 1ère Ch. civ.*, 6 March 1990, Société Horeva v. Société Sitas, 1990 REV. ARB. 633. *See also* FOUCHARD, GAILLARD & GOLDMAN at §§ 1339 - 1345.

44   *See Cour d'appel de Paris*, 15 May 1985, Raffineries de Pétrole d'Homs et de Banias v. ICC, 1985 REV. ARB. 147 (where the ICC was subject to a tort claim) and *Cour d'appel de Paris*, 15 Jan. 1985, Opinter France v. Dacomex, 1986 REV. ARB. 87, discussed in J.Y. Art, *Challenge of Arbitrators: Is an Institutional Decision Final?*, 2 ARB. INT. 261 (1986).

45   *NCPC* Article 1493.

46   Affaire La Belle Créole, 1990 REV. ARB. 176 (death of arbitrator required *Tribunal de Grande Instance de Paris* to appoint a new arbitrator). *See generally* Bruno Leurent, *L'intervention du Juge*, 1992 REV. ARB. 303; FOUCHARD, GAILLARD & GOLDMAN, § 868.

31.04   Review of Awards

(a) Grounds for Judicial Review

Striking a balance between the goals of arbitral autonomy and judicial scrutiny of an arbitration's basic procedural integrity,[47] French arbitration law allows courts to set aside international awards rendered in France only on statutorily limited grounds.[48] Thus ICC awards may not be set aside for failure to respect criteria applicable to domestic arbitration, such as time limits for rendering an award[49] or the need for physical meetings of the arbitrators.[50]

Annulment criteria for international arbitration are set forth in *NCPC* Article 1502, and include the following five grounds for challenging an award:

(1) If the arbitrator decided in the absence of an arbitration agreement or on the basis of a void or expired agreement;

(2) If the arbitral tribunal was irregularly composed or the sole arbitrator irregularly appointed;

(3) If the arbitrator violated the mission conferred on him;

(4) If due process [literally, the principle of adversarial process] was not respected;

(5) If the recognition or enforcement would be contrary to international public policy (*ordre public international*).

Considered to be a matter of public policy, these grounds for recourse cannot be contractually modified. Thus parties to ICC arbitration in France may neither opt out of application of the criteria in *NCPC* Article 1502, nor elect the wider appellate provisions for domestic arbitration contained in *NCPC* Articles 1481–1484.[51] Moreover, the right to challenge what is in substance an award (*sentence*) will not be lost because the arbitrators characterized the decision as a procedural order (*ordonnance*).[52]

Any potential ground for annulment should be brought to the arbitral tribunal's attention immediately, in order to avoid waiver of rights for failure to

---

47   *See generally* FOUCHARD. GAILLARD & GOLDMAN at §§ 1601 -1662.

48   *NCPC* Article 1502.

49   *See Cour de cassation*, 30 June 1976, Société Bruynzeel Deurenfabrieck N.V. v. Ministre d'Etat aux Affaires Etrangères de la République Malgache, 1976 BULL. CIV. I 198, 1977 REV. ARB. 137.

50   *Cour d'appel de Paris*, 22 Dec. 1978, Industrija Motora Rakovica v. Lynx Machinery Ltd., 1979 REV. ARB. 266, at 269.

51   In some cases French courts have voided arbitration clauses attempting to include overly expansive appellate review. *See Cour d'appel de Paris*, 27 Oct. 1994, Diseno v. Société Mendes, 1995 REV. ARB. 261. *See generally* cases cited in FOUCHARD, GAILLARD & GOLDMAN at 931, § 1597, notes 142-46. Compare the position in the United States as announced in Lapine v. Kyocera and related cases, discussed in Chapter 34.04.

52   Société Braspetro Oil Services (Brasoil) v. GMRA, 1999 REV. ARB. 834.

bring objections in a timely fashion. For example, a party with prior knowledge of a disqualifying link between an arbitrator and the opposing side must raise the matter during the arbitration, or risk being barred from later invoking the lack of independence to obtain award annulment.[53]

(b) A Case Study of French Judicial Review.

The judgment of the Paris *Cour d'appel* in *Torno v. Kumagai Gumi Ltd.*[54] illustrates in case study fashion the interaction of *NCPC* review criteria with the ICC Rules, and also confirms the healthy tendency of French courts to draw narrow limits around the grounds for award annulment.[55] A dispute between Italian and Japanese groups concerning a real estate development led to an ICC award ordering the Italians to buy out the Japanese stake in a joint venture company.

Resisting the obligation to acquire the Japanese investment, the Italian party first moved to have the award annulled under Article 1502(1)(void or expired arbitration agreement), on the ground that the award had been rendered more than six months after the Terms of Reference became effective, the normal time limit for awards under the ICC Rules.[56] The *Cour d'appel* dismissed this argument by noting that the ICC Rules allow an extension of time for the award, which in the case at hand had been granted by the ICC Court.

The Italian party also argued that the arbitrators had exceeded the scope of their jurisdiction, ground for annulment under Article 1502(3), by establishing the Terms of Reference without the signature of the Italian group. The Court had no trouble in rejecting this argument, again by reference to the provision in the ICC Rules allowing the Terms of Reference to enter into effect even absent one party's signature, after approval by the ICC Court.

Next it was argued that there had been a denial of due process (*principe de la contradiction*) under Article 1502(4), because the arbitrators had referred to notes taken during the hearing by counsel for the Japanese group. In dismissing this challenge, the *Cour d'appel* observed the parties' had failed to provide for a transcript (as requested by the arbitral tribunal), and found that the notes of counsel in no way constituted an official record of the proceedings.

---

53 *See Cour d'appel de Paris*, 12 Jan. 1995, Société Ardi v. Société Scapnor, 1996 REV. ARB. 72. This principle is reinforced by ICC Rules Article 11 (requiring challenge to an arbitrator within thirty days from notice of the appointment or knowledge of the facts on which challenge is based) and Article 33 (providing that a party who proceeds in an arbitration without raising objections to non-compliance with the ICC Rules is deemed to waive the right to object).

54 *Cour d'appel de Paris*, 1ère chambre, Section C, 19 May 1998.

55 The decision rejected all challenges to the award, which were based on four of the five grounds for recourse in Article 1502: paragraphs (1), (3), (4) and (5).

56 Article 24(1) of the ICC Rules provides for a final award within six months from the date of the last signature on the Terms of Reference, or from the date of notification of the Secretariat's approval of the Terms of Reference in the event one party refuses to sign.

Finally, the argument was made that the order for the transfer of shares violated international public policy,[57] since compelling specific performance is normally reserved to public authorities (*"l'imperium"*). To this the *Cour d'appel* correctly responded that the absence of public power restricts only the arbitrators' ability to take coercive measures to enforce their orders, not their right to make such orders.

(c) Recognition and Annulment Procedures.

The validity of an international award rendered in France may be established through judicial recognition (*exequatur*), granted by the *Tribunal de grande instance* with jurisdiction over the place where the award was rendered.[58] Execution is suspended during thirty days after *exequatur*, as well as during any subsequent challenge proceedings.[59]

The loser in an arbitration may challenge the award through a motion to vacate (*recours en annulation*),[60] made to the appropriate *Cour d'appel*[61] any time after the award has been rendered. However, an action for annulment must be brought no later than one month following notification of the award's judicial recognition (*signification de la sentence revêtue de l'exequatur*).[62] When an award has received *exequatur*, an annulment action is deemed to encompass an appeal of the *exequatur* order.

(d) Reasoned Awards.

The requirement of reasoned awards in domestic arbitration,[63] which may be waived in international arbitration,[64] is of only academic interest in ICC arbitration, where awards invariably set forth the tribunal's reasoning.[65] More importantly, French case law has made clear that courts will not allow arguments about inconsistencies in the awards's reasoning to serve as a back door for review of the award on the basis of the merits of the dispute.[66]

---

57   *NCPC* Article 1502(5).

58   *See NCPC* Article 1477. *NCPC* Article 1500 makes the provisions of Article 1476 through 1479 applicable to international arbitration.

59   *NCPC* Article 1506.

60   *NCPC* Article 1504.

61   As with motions for *exequatur*, the appropriate jurisdiction for challenge is determined by reference to the place where the award is rendered, deemed to be the arbitral seat fixed by the parties. *NCPC* Article 1505.

62   *NCPC* Article 1505.

63   *NCPC* Article 1471. *See also* DE BOISSESON, at §§ 386 and § 461; FOUCHARD, GAILLARD & GOLDMAN at § 1392.

64   *NCPC* Article 1495.

65   *See* ICC Rules, Article 25(2).

66   *See Cour de cassation 1ère Ch.Civ.*, 28 Feb. 1995, Société Générale pour l'Industrie v. Société Ewbank, 1995 REV. ARB. 597. With respect to a dispute arising from a joint venture subject to Swiss law, the *Cour de cassation* refused to review an award which the losing party argued was

(e) Due Process

French concepts of arbitral due process and "natural justice" derive from at least two sources. The more general foundation for procedural fairness lies in *NCPC* Article 1502(4), which imposes respect for "adversarial process" (*"principe de la contradiction"*).[67] An illustration of a violation of the *"principe de la contradiction"* would be a decision rendered by arbitrators who failed to hear the parties on the relevant point.[68]

Another basis for due process rights can be found in *NCPC* Article 1502(2), which requires proper composition of the arbitral tribunal. In the well-known *Dutco* case,[69] the *Cour de cassation* interpreted this provision to include equal treatment of the parties in nominating arbitrators. The dispute arose from a tripartite contract to construct a cement plant in Oman, providing that all disputes be settled by three arbitrators appointed under the ICC Rules.[70]

When one party brought a claim against the other two, the ICC required that a single arbitrator be nominated by the two defendants. Under protest the defendants chose a common arbitrator, but then challenged the award confirming arbitral jurisdiction. Each defendant argued that it should have the same opportunity as the plaintiff to nominate an arbitrator. The *Cour de cassation* held that the ICC practice violated the principle of "equality of the parties," which the Court held to be a matter of non-waivable public policy.

In response, the ICC Rules were modified to provide that when multiple parties cannot agree to a joint nomination of an arbitrator, the ICC may choose each member of the arbitral tribunal, designating individuals that it considers appropriate ("suitable" in English, *"apte"* in French).[71] Since the relevant inequality was the inability of each defendant to nominate an arbitrator as had the claimant, ICC choice of all arbitrators means that neither claimants nor defendants are favored.

---

based on the application of the wrong national law.

67   *See generally* Catherine Kessedjian, *Principe de la contradiction et arbitrage*, 1995 Rᴇᴠ. Aʀʙ. 381.

68 · *Cour d'appel de Paris*, 6 April 1995, Thyssen v. Maaden, 1995 Rᴇᴠ. Aʀʙ. 464, concerning the applicable interest rate.

69   *Cour de cassation*, 7 Jan. 1992, Siemens A.G. & BKMI Industrienlagen GmbH v. Dutco Consortium Construction Co., 1992 Rᴇᴠ. Aʀʙ. 470, note by Pierre Bellet. *See generally* Charles Jarrosson, Note, 119 JDI 726 (1992); Eric Schwartz, *Multi-party Arbitration and the ICC: In the Wake of Dutco*, 10 (No. 3) J. Iɴᴛ'ʟ Aʀʙ. 5 (1993); C.R. Seppala, *Multi-party Arbitrations at Risk in France*, Iɴᴛ. Fɪɴ. L. Rᴇᴠ. 33 (March 1993).

70   Article 2(2) of the ICC Rules in force at that time required disputes to be decided either by a sole arbitrator or a three-arbitrator panel. A similar provisions is contained in Article 8(1) of the current ICC Rules, although the ICC has discretion under Article 7(6) to approve a different arrangement.

71   ICC Rules, Article 10.

(f) Public Policy

NCPC Article 1502(5) provides for international awards rendered in France to be vacated for violation of international public policy (*ordre public international*). While both *international* and *domestic* public policy are creatures of French courts, the latter addresses policies relevant only in an internal context. The former implicate cross-border rather than purely French interests.[72] Thus an international commercial dispute may be arbitrable even though the principal contract from which it arises violates French domestic public policy.[73] Examples of violation of international public policy include procedural fraud (falsifying documents)[74] and improper extension of time limits for rendering an award.[75]

(g) Foreign Awards.

Although French courts may review foreign awards presented for recognition in France under Article V of New York Convention[76] (see Section 37.04), a party seeking a foreign award's recognition in France will benefit from provisions of French arbitration law that may be more favorable than the Convention. French case law, most notably *Hilmarton v. OTV* (discussed in Section 28.04), has been liberal in enforcing foreign awards under the *NCPC* notwithstanding arguable Convention grounds for non-recognition (annulment at the arbitral situs), reasoning that an international award exists independently from the national legal system of the place where rendered.

In determining whether an award was made in France or abroad,[77] French courts look to the arbitral situs (*"siège de l'arbitrage"*) as determined by the parties to the arbitration clause, rather than the place of the hearings. One recent case held that an award was made in Geneva, notwithstanding that

---

72 *See generally* HENRI BATIFFOL & PAUL LAGARDE, DROIT INTERNATIONAL PRIVÉ, § 363 (8th ed., 1993). *See also* BERNARD AUDIT, DROIT INTERNATIONAL PRIVÉ (1991), § 302, suggesting that a better terminology might be "public policy in the sense of private international law (*ordre public au sense du droit international privé*).

73 *See Cour de cassation*, 18 May 1971, Société Impex v. Société P.A.Z., 1972 D.S. JUR. 37, 1972 JDI 64.

74 *See Cour d'appel de Paris*, 30 Sept. 1993, Société European Gas Turbines SA v. Société Westman International Ltd., 1994 REV. ARB. 359, affirmed *Cour de cassation*, 19 Dec. 1995, 1996 REV. ARB. 49 (annulment of an award for commissions payable to promote a French company's services in Iran, where false expense statements had been provided). In the same action the court dismissed charges of *ordre public* violations due to an illegal object of the contract, finding that the alleged bribery had not been proven.

75 *Cour de cassation, 1ère Ch. Civ.*, 15 June 1994, Société Sonidep v. Société Sigmoil et Communauté urbaine de Casablanca, 1995 REV. ARB. 88.

76 The Convention's scope in France has been broadened by the withdrawal of the French reservation restricting the Convention to commercial transactions. *See* note by Philippe Fouchard, 1990 REV. ARB. 210.

77 In this connection, it is important to remember that *NCPC* Article 1504 provides that "An arbitral award rendered in France in international arbitral proceedings is subject to an action to set aside on the grounds set forth in Article 1502."

hearings were held and procedural orders signed in Paris.[78] The consequence was that French courts lacked jurisdiction to hear a challenge to the award.

Some commentators have questioned the compatibility of this case with the principle that an international award may be recognized notwithstanding its annulment at the arbitral situs. The argument runs that it is inconsistent to hold that the selection of a foreign arbitral situs links the resulting award to the foreign legal order so as to deprive French courts of power to annul the resulting award, and yet affirm (in recognizing an annulled award) that the award "is not integrated into the legal order of the country where rendered."[79]

(h) Arbitral Jurisdiction

In reviewing awards rendered in international cases, French courts do not normally tamper with the substantive merits of the dispute, even when the arbitrator has allegedly engaged in distortion (*dénaturation*) of the contract's substantive provisions.[80] The same cannot be said, however, when the very existence of the arbitration agreement is questioned. The *Cour de cassation* has affirmed the power of French courts to determine the validity of the arbitration agreement without deference to arbitral findings on the matter.[81]

---

78   *Cour d'appel de Paris*, 28 Oct. 1997, Sociétés de procédes de préfabrication pour le béton v. Libye, 1998 REV. ARB. 399.

79   *See* note by Bruno Lcurent, 1998 REV. ARB. 399, arguing that "to define the arbitral seat as the link established by the parties between their international arbitration and a legal system is inconsistent with the aggressive approach of the [*Cour de cassation* in *Hilmarton*] by which 'the international award [rendered in a given state] by definition is not integrated into the juridical order of the state where rendered.'" (*Il pourra sembler à d'aucuns que la définition du siège arbitral comme le lien juridique établi par les parties entre leur abitrage international et un système juridique s'accorde mal avec la formule militante de la Première Chambre civile* [in the *Hilmarton* case] *selon laquelle 'La sentence internationale [rendue dans un Etat déterminé] par définition n'est pas intégrée à l'ordre juridique de cet Etat où elle a été rendue.'*) Contrast the position of Philippe Fouchard, *La Portée internationale de l'annulation de la sentence arbitrale dans son pays d'origine*, 1997 REV. ARB. 329, discussed in Section 28.04.

80   See cases discussed in de BOISSÉSSON at § 794 and JEAN ROBERT, *La dénaturation par l'arbitre—réalité et perspectives*, 1982 REV. ARB. 405.

81   See discussion of Egypt v. SPP, Section 31.01, where the *Cour de cassation* stated, "Aucune limitation n'est apportée au pouvoir de cette juridiction [*i.e.* the lower court making the jurisdictional determination] de rechercher en droit et en fait tous les éléments concernant les vices en question."

CHAPTER 32

HONG KONG LAW

32.01   Statutory Framework

(a) The Amended Arbitration Ordinance.

Unless otherwise agreed by the parties,[1] ICC arbitrations in Hong Kong will normally[2] be subject to the United Nations Commission on International Trade Law (UNCITRAL) Model Law on International Commercial Arbitration.[3] Although the People's Republic of China (PRC) has resumed sovereignty over the former British colony, Hong Kong remains a Special Administrative Region (SAR) with its own legal system, and arbitration law.[4] Thus Hong Kong provides an arbitral system with which non-Chinese parties will feel relatively familiar.

The Model Law itself has been discussed earlier in Chapter 29, where readers will find an introduction to its basic principles and framework. The present chapter will highlight some of the ways in which the Model Law as adopted in

---

1   Section 2M of the Arbitration Ordinance, Hong Kong Laws Chapter 341, provides that the provisions on domestic rather than international arbitration shall apply to an international arbitration if the parties agree in writing (i) that Part II (§§ 22-34) of the Ordinance (governing domestic arbitration) shall apply, (ii) that the agreement shall be treated as a domestic arbitration agreement or (iii) that the dispute is to be arbitrated as a domestic arbitration. Sections 34A cross references this right to opt out of the provisions of the Model Law. In addition, the Ordinance permits parties to domestic arbitration to elect application of the UNCITRAL Model Law. See § 2L of the Arbitration Ordinance.

2   Arbitrations will be subject to the UNCITRAL Model Law if characterized as "international" (under criteria discussed below), which will almost always be the case for ICC arbitration. Although Article 1(1) of the ICC Rules does permit non-international disputes to be submitted to ICC arbitration, such submissions can be expected to be rare.

3   Adopted by the United Nations Commission on Trade Law on 21 June 1985. Domestic arbitrations will be subject to their own arbitration law.

4   See Basic Law of the Hong Kong Special Administrative Region of the People's Republic of China (4 April 1990) (hereinafter "Basic Law"), which constitutes Hong Kong as a separate law district within an otherwise unitary Chinese state. The separate legal régime is intended to last for a fifty-year transitional period ending 30 June 2047.

Hong Kong has been implemented and amplified by statute and interpreted by case law, as well as the enforcement in Hong Kong of awards made in Mainland China.[5]

Hong Kong adopted the UNCITRAL Model almost *verbatim*,[6] with the omission of only Articles 35 and 36 (dealing with recognition of foreign awards), which were considered unnecessary in light of the United Kingdom's accession to the New York Convention on behalf of Hong Kong. Hong Kong gave the Model Law a generous scope, making clear that its application was not limited to commercial arbitration.[7] In addition, the Arbitration Ordinance specifically gave the arbitrator power to make orders regarding costs and to award simple interest.[8]

The climate for ICC arbitration was improved by a subsequent legislative enactment referred to as the "Arbitration (Amendment) Ordinance 1996."[9] Inspired in large part by analogous reforms in England and Singapore, the 1996 Ordinance reduces many of the gaps between domestic and international arbitration in Hong Kong, by bringing the legal regime for the former in line with that of the latter. For example, the power of Hong Kong courts must now refer parties to arbitration in domestic cases pursuant to the same standards applicable under Article 8 of the UNCITRAL Model Law, which is to say, unless the agreement is "null, void, inoperative or incapable of being performed."[10]

For ICC arbitration, one of the most significant changes introduced by the 1996 Ordinance is a broader definition of arbitration agreement to include

---

5   *See generally*, NEIL KAPLAN, JILL SPRUCE & MICHAEL MOSER, HONG KONG AND CHINESE ARBITRATION: CASES AND MATERIALS (1994); Neil Kaplan, *An Update on Hong Kong's Arbitration Law*, INTERNATIONAL COMMERCIAL ARBITRATION IN ASIA 11 (ICC Bull. Special Supp., 1998) Neil Kaplan, *The Model Law in Hong Kong: Two Years On*, 8 ARB. INT. 223 (1992); ROBERT MORGAN, THE ARBITRATION ORDINANCE OF HONG KONG: A COMMENTARY (1997); Robert Morgan, *Hong Kong Arbitration in Transition: The Arbitration (Amendment Ordinance 1996*, 1997 INT. ARB. LAW REV. 19 and 1998 INT. ARB. LAW REV. 74(1998), reprinted 13 MEALEY'S INT. ARB. REP. 18(1998).

6   Arbitration Ordinance, Hong Kong Laws Chapter 341, which applies the UNCITRAL Model Law to arbitrations commenced after 6 April 1990. Part IIA (§§ 34A - 34D) of the Arbitration Ordinance incorporates the UNCITRAL Model Law, set forth in the Fifth Schedule of the Chapter 341 Ordinance. The Ordinance applies Chapters I through VII of the UNCITRAL Model Law. Although Hong Kong did not adopt Chapter VIII of the Model Law (award recognition), many of the provisions of Chapter VIII have been picked up in Part III (§§ 35-46) of the Ordinance, concerning enforcement of foreign awards.

7   Arbitration Ordinance, § 34C(2).

8   Arbitration Ordinance, § 34D. See also discussion of §§ 2GH and 2GI of the 1996 reforms, discussed *infra* in Section 32.04.

9   Although generally referred to as the "1996 Ordinance" the legislation was in fact given final approval by the Legislative Council only on 18 December 1997, to take effect retroactively as of 27 June 1997.

10 Arbitration Ordinance Section 6, as amended.

even documents not signed by the parties.[11] Thus for example, an arbitration clause will be valid if contained in an unsigned bill of lading, or in trade association rules to which reference is made in an oral contract. See discussion in Section 32.02 below.

Other changes effected by the 1996 Ordinance, applicable to both domestic and international arbitration in Hong Kong, include the following:

- the Hong Kong International Arbitration Centre (rather than a court) has power to make default appointments to arbitral tribunals;[12]

- the UNCITRAL rule that courts should not intervene in arbitration "except where so provided in [the] Law"[13] is reinforced by a more general principle that courts "should interfere in the arbitration of a dispute only as expressly provided by [the Arbitration] Ordinance;"[14]

- the arbitral tribunal is empowered to extend time for commencing arbitrations;[15]

- arbitrators may require claimants to give security for costs and order discovery of documents;[16]

- an arbitral tribunal may dismiss a claim for unreasonable delay in prosecuting the claim;[17]

- arbitrators are empowered to award compound interest;[18]

- arbitral tribunals are subject to an express duty both "to act fairly and impartially as between the parties, giving them a reasonable opportunity to present their cases" and to use appropriate procedures that avoid "unnecessary delay and expense."[19]

(b) What Is an "International" Arbitration?

In its first decision interpreting the UNCITRAL Model Law, the Hong Kong Supreme Court traced broad contours for the scope of the Model Law as applied in

---

11 Arbitration Ordinance Section 2AC excludes application of Article 7(2) of the Model Law.

12 Arbitration Ordinance Section 12 for domestic arbitration, and Section 34C(3) for international arbitration.

13 UNCITRAL Model Arbitration Law, Article 5.

14 Arbitration Ordinance Section 2AA.

15 Arbitration Ordinance Section 2GD.

16 Arbitration Ordinance Section 2GB.

17 Arbitration Ordinance Section 2GE.

18 Arbitration Ordinance Section 2GH.

19 Arbitration Ordinance 2GA. Compare Section 1 of the English Arbitration Act of 1996, discussed in Chapter 30.

Hong Kong. By its own terms, the Model Law covers commercial arbitrations defined as international according to several sometimes overlapping criteria:[20]

(a) the parties to an arbitration agreement have, at the time of the conclusion of that agreement, their places of business in different States[21]; or

(b) one of the following places is situated outside the State in which the parties have their places of business:

(i) the place of arbitration if determined in, or pursuant to, the arbitration agreement;

(ii) any place where a substantial part of the obligations of the commercial relationship is to be performed or the place with which the subject-matter of the dispute is most closely connected; or

(c) the parties have expressly agreed that the subject-matter of the arbitration agreement relates to more than one country.

In *Fung Sang Trading v. Kai Sun Sea Products & Food Co.*,[22] two Hong Kong companies had entered into a contract for the sale of Chinese soybean extract meal to be delivered FOB on a vessel named by buyer in the PRC, which at that time had not yet taken over the administration of Hong Kong from the British. In an opinion by Mr. Justice Kaplan, the Supreme Court focused on that portion of the Model Law which defines international by reference to the "place where a substantial part of the obligations of the commercial relationship is to be performed," and held the arbitration to be international because the buyers were to nominate a vessel to take delivery of the soybean extract in the PRC.

To determine coverage of the Model Law, Hong Kong will be considered a state unto itself.[23] For example, if one party has its place of business in Hong Kong and the other in Beijing, they will have places of business in "different States," thus triggering applicability of the Model Law. This does not necessarily mean, however, that the New York Convention will apply to enforcement in Hong Kong of an award rendered on the Mainland. As discussed in

---

20   *See* Model Law Article 1(3).

21   The Model Law, of course, uses "State" to refer to countries or nations, rather than the political *subdivisions of the United States' federal system* to which many North Americans often apply the term.

22   Supreme Court of Hong Kong, High Court, 29 October 1991, reprinted in XVII YEARBOOK 289 (1992).

23   Arbitration Ordinance Section 2(4).

Section 32.04, because Hong Kong is now a territory of the PRC, it will not be possible to argue that a Mainland award was "made in the territory of a State other than the State where the recognition and enforcement of such award."

(c) Liability of Institutions and Arbitrators.

Hong Kong has explicitly excluded liability for most acts and omissions of arbitrators[24] and supervisory arbitral institutions.[25] Liability will attach to their comportment only if an act was "done or omitted to be done dishonestly." In contrast to the English Act[26] the rule is stated in positive terms: an arbitrator or an appointing institution *is* liable for dishonest acts. Hong Kong law thus affirms the policy that neither the ICC nor its arbitrators should be threatened with litigation as a way to reopen questions of law or fact.

32.02 The Agreement to Arbitrate

The 1996 changes to the Arbitration Ordinance elaborate the scope of arbitration agreements that will be considered to be "in writing," and thus subject to the Model Law. A writing will now include:

- agreements in documents whether signed or not;

- agreements made by exchanges of written communications;

- reference to terms that are in writing;

- a non-written agreement later recorded, either by one of the parties or by a third person with the authority of both parties;

- an exchange of submissions in a court or arbitral proceeding in which one side alleges the existence of a non-written arbitration agreement not denied by the other side.

The 1996 amendments also state that a "writing" includes any means by which information can be recorded, and that an arbitration agreement can be incorporated into a contract by (i) reference to either a written form of arbitration clause (e.g., the "standard ICC arbitration clause" printed in the ICC's publication of its Arbitration Rules) or (ii) a document containing an arbitration clause.[27]

---

24 Arbitration Ordinance Section 2GM.

25 The Arbitration Ordinance speaks of a person "who appoints an arbitral tribunal" or "who exercises or performs any other functions of an administrative nature in connection with arbitration proceedings." Arbitration Ordinance Section 2GN.

26 See §§ 29 and 74 of the 1996 English Arbitration Act, discussed in Chapter 30, which provides that an arbitrator or an arbitral institution "is *not* liable for anything done or omitted . . . *unless* . . . shown to have been in bad faith."

27 Arbitration Ordinance Section 2AC(5), explicitly makes these provisions applicable notwithstanding the requirements of Article 7(2) of the UNCITRAL Model Law.

Hong Kong courts have usually interpreted Model Law Article 8 to require them to stay court proceedings in favor of arbitration notwithstanding the argument that there is no "genuine dispute." *Guangdong Agriculture Co. Ltd. v. Conagra International Ltd.*[28] involved a claim for damages arising from alleged short sale and delayed delivery of urea. Ordering a stay of litigation so the case could proceed to arbitration, Justice Barnett noted the hesitancy of judges to become involved in a detailed examination of the dispute, even if only as to a "short and simple" point of law. "What is 'short' or 'simple and clear,'" he wrote, "regrettably admits of varied interpretation."[29] Agreements to arbitrate, the court stated, should be enforced unless a claim in fact has been admitted by the party against which it is made.

Where the defendant, however, has made an unequivocal admission of liability and as to the quantum of damages, court actions will *not* be stayed in favor of arbitration, but rather summary judgment will be granted to the plaintiff.[30] However, not all proposals by a defendant to compensate a plaintiff will constitute admissions of liability and damages. In some cases, correspondence that might on its face appear as an admission will be treated merely as a commercial settlement offer.[31]

Hong Kong courts have show themselves willing to recognize even awkwardly drafted arbitration clauses that refer to a non-existent arbitral institution and lack reference to a specific arbitral situs. The case of *Lucky Goldstar International (H.K.) Ltd. v. Ng Moo Kee Engineering Ltd.*[32] arose out of a sale of elevators pursuant to a contract providing for arbitration in "a third country. . .and in accordance with the rules of procedure of the International Commercial Arbitration Association." The court held that the reference to an unspecified country and a non-existent institution did not render the arbitration agreement "null and void [or] inoperative," the Model Law criteria to determine whether parties should be referred to arbitration.[33] The arbitration could be held in any country other than where the parties had their places of business, which the court assumed would be chosen by the plaintiff. Indication of the non-existent arbitration institution was to be ignored, since no effect could be given to the reference.

---

28   Supreme Court of Hong Kong, 24 September 1992, reported in XVIII YEARBOOK 187 (1993).

29   Reported *id.* at 189.

30   *See* Joong & Shipping Co. Ltd. v. Choi Chong-sick & Chu Ghin Ho Co., High Court of Hong Kong, 31 March 1994, reported in abstract form in XX YEARBOOK 285 (1995). Claim for freight and demurrage which defendant had admitted in correspondence with plaintiff.

31   *See* Zhan Jiang E&T Dev Area Service Head v. An Hau Co. Ltd., High Court of Hong Kong, 21 January 1994, reported in abstract form in XX YEARBOOK 283 (1995).

32   High Court of Hong Kong, 5 May 1993(Kaplan, J.), [1993] 2 Hong Kong Law Reports 73, reported in abstract form in XX YEARBOOK 280 (1995) and 1994 ARB. & DISP. RES. J. 49 (March 1994).

33   Article 8, UNCITRAL Model Arbitration Law.

32.03 Interlocutory Matters

Hong Kong courts will have power to enforce a *subpoena duces tecum* to produce documents in the hands of a third party. In *Vibroflotation A.G. v. Express Builders Co. Ltd.*[34] a dispute arose between two subcontractors in which the plaintiff sought production of documents in the hands of the contractor. The court held that it had power to order such document production if requested by, or approved by, the arbitral tribunal.[35] The court presumed that in the instant case the arbitral tribunal had approved of the plaintiff's *subpoena*, since the tribunal had set a date for the document production. However, the court ultimately dismissed the application for enforcement of the *subpoena* as untimely, finding that the relevant evidentiary hearings were "months if not years away."

Hong Kong domestic arbitration law permits courts to order consolidation of arbitrations presenting common questions of law or fact.[36] However, the UNCITRAL Model Arbitration Law as enacted in Hong Kong contains no analogous provisions.

In connection with the interlocutory matter of appointing arbitrators, the role of the Hong Kong International Arbitration Centre (HKIAC) has been enhanced significantly under the 1996 amendments to the Arbitration Ordinance. To understand the function of the HKIAC, one must look briefly at the Model Law provisions on constitution of the arbitral tribunal—a task which in ICC arbitration will be carried out by the ICC Court. Model Law Article 11 contains provisions for appointment of arbitrators in the event the parties' agreement fails to provide a workable appointment mechanism.[37] Each country adopting the Model Law is to designate a court or "other authority" for constitution of the arbitral tribunal.[38] The HKIAC is now this "other authority" charged with arbitral appointments in problematic cases.[39] In addition, the HKIAC now has the power to decide whether there shall be one (1) or three (3) arbitrators when the arbitration clause is silent on the matter.[40]

Finally, the 1996 Ordinance makes clear that arbitrators need not apply formal rules of evidence. Section 2GA(2) provides that an arbitral tribunal is

---

34 High Court of Hong Kong, 15 August 1994, reported in abstract form, XX YEARBOOK 287 (1995).

35 *See* UNCITRAL Model Arbitration Law, Article 27, giving an arbitral tribunal power to request state assistance in the taking of evidence.

36 Arbitration Ordinance Section 6B.

37 Article 11 operates in situations both (i) where the appointment procedure established by the arbitration agreement breaks down (because a party, the party-nominated arbitrators or the contractually selected appointing authority fails to act or to agree) or where there has been no agreement on the appointment procedure.

38 UNCITRAL Model Law Article 6.

39 Arbitration Ordinance Section 34C(3), as amended by 1996 Ordinance Section 14.

40 Arbitration Ordinance Section 35C(5), as amended by 1996 Ordinance Section 14.

"not bound by the rules of evidence," but rather "can receive any evidence that it considers relevant to the proceedings," giving the evidence such weight as it considers appropriate.[41]

32.04   Review of Awards

(a) Awards Rendered in Hong Kong.

One attractive innovation added by the 1996 reforms is an explicit grant of authority for arbitrators to award "simple or compound interest from such dates, at such rates . . . as the [arbitral] tribunal considers appropriate."[42] An award of interest may cover any period ending not later than payment date, whether on monies awarded by the tribunal or on monies claimed in the arbitration but paid before the award was made.[43] If the arbitral tribunal does not deal with the matter, simple interest would still be payable from the date of the award, at the same rate as on a judgment debt.[44]

An international arbitration award rendered in Hong Kong may be set aside only on grounds that mirror the defenses to recognition of foreign awards contained in the New York Convention.[45] As set forth below, these include not only basic procedural defects to be proven by the party seeking annulment of the award (such as invalidity of the arbitration agreement, denial of due process and arbitrator excess of authority), but also a court's findings on its own motion that the subject matter is non-arbitrable or that the award conflicts with public policy of the country of the arbitral proceedings. The statutory list is exclusive.

The first group of grounds on which an award may be set aside provide that the party making the annulment application must furnish proof that:

> i. a party to the arbitration agreement . . . was under some incapacity; or the said agreement is not valid under the law to which the parties have subjected it or, failing any indication thereon, under the law of this State; or

> ii. the party making the application was not given proper notice of the appointment of an arbitrator or of the arbitral proceedings or was otherwise unable to present his case; or

---

41 To put this provision in context, it is important to remember that the preceding subsection of 2GA instructs the arbitral tribunal to "act fairly" and to use "appropriate" procedures so as to avoid "unnecessary delay and expense."

42 Arbitration Ordinance Section 2GH.

43 Prior law, under Ordinance Section 22A (now repealed), had limited arbitrators' power to simple interest. See Court of Appeal decision reversing the Supreme Court in *Attorney General v. Shimizu Corp.*, Nos. 185 and 186 of 1996 Hong Kong App.

44 Arbitration Ordinance Section 2GI provides for such interest "except when the award otherwise provides."

45 UNCITRAL Model Arbitration Law, Article 34. For comparison with Article V of the New York Convention, see discussion in Chapter 37.

iii. the award deals with a dispute not contemplated by or not falling within the terms of the submission to arbitration, or contains decisions on matters beyond the scope of the submission to arbitration, provided that, if the decisions on matters submitted to arbitration can be separated from those not so submitted, only that part of the award which contains decisions on matters not submitted to arbitration may be set aside; or

iv. the composition of the arbitral tribunal or the arbitral procedure was not in accordance with the agreement of the parties, unless such agreement was in conflict with a provision of this Law from which the parties cannot derogate, or, failing such agreement, was not in accordance with this Law.

In addition, a second set of grounds for annulment permit an award to be set aside if the court itself finds that:

i. the subject-matter of the dispute is not capable of settlement by arbitration under the law of this State; or

ii. the award is in conflict with the public policy of this State.

There is no reference to setting aside on grounds contained in Convention Article V(1)(e), which covers awards annulled at the place where made. It would be redundant for the statute to call for courts at the arbitral situs to vacate awards already set aside by local courts.

Since no application may be made for annulment because of an error of law, the legal framework for international arbitration in Hong Kong generally provides for more arbitral autonomy than the domestic arbitration regime.[46] However, award annulment is still possible on the basis of "public policy," a malleable notion whose effect on efficient arbitration depends on how it will be applied.[47] Recourse to public policy might, for example, be limited to matters such as bribery. Thus far Hong Kong case law indicates that judges will not allow public policy to be used as a catch-all to justify an inappropriate level of judicial intervention.[48] Here as elsewhere, the text of the law may prove conditioned by the context of its application. See discussion in Section 28.04.

---

46 *See* Arbitration Ordinance Section 23(2) (which provides for appeal of domestic awards on "any question of law arising out of an award made on an arbitration agreement." The parties to an arbitration may, however, exclude this right of appeal on points of law through an agreement in writing. *See* Arbitration Ordinance Section 23C.

47 For cases and discussion of the more limited role of procedural public policy in English arbitration law, see Chapter 30.

48 *See* decision by Justice Kaplan in Qinhuangdao Tongda Enterprise Development Co. v. Million basic Co., [1993] 1 HKLR 173 (reproduced in Neil Kaplan, Jill Spruce & Michael Moser, Hong Kong and China Arbitration 266(1994)), stating that public policy was to be "sparingly applied," and was not a "catch-all provision to be used wherever convenient." The case dealt with the scope of public policy as a defense to recognition of a foreign award, rather than in the context of judicial review of an award rendered in Hong Kong.

(b) Awards Rendered in Mainland China.[49]

Although the New York Convention has been extended to Hong Kong,[50] it is doubtful whether the Convention covers awards rendered in Mainland China and presented for enforcement in Hong Kong, and vice versa. This may turn out to be of no practical consequence, of course, when an award will be enforced outside China. Moreover, Mainland China and the Hong Kong SAR have concluded arrangements providing for reciprocal enforcement of awards on a basis similar to that under the New York Convention.[51]

Hebei Import & Export Corporation v. Polytek Engineering Company Ltd.[52] concerned a sale by a Hong Kong company (Polytek) to a Mainland company (Hebei) of equipment for producing rubber powder.[53] Following an allegation that the equipment was defective, an arbitral tribunal in Beijing, constituted under the rules of the China International Economic and Trade Arbitration Commission (CIETAC), ordered the seller to reimburse the purchase price of the equipment plus interest. Enforcement in Hong Kong was resisted on the ground of arbitrator misconduct, in that a site inspection was held without notice to the defendants. The Court of Final Appeal ultimately enforced the award, finding that Polytek failed to take measures to redress the situation.

---

49   *See* generally, Robert Morgan, *Enforcement of Chinese Awards in Hong Kong*, [1998] INT. ARB. LAW REV. (Issue 4) 157; Vivienne M. Ashman, New York Convention and China's "One Country, Two Systems," 220 (No. 2) NEW YORK LAW J. 1 (2 July 1998). For discussion of the relationship of Hong Kong to the rest of China for purposes of application of the UNCITRAL Model Law, see Section 32.01(ii). On arbitration in the PRC, *see* CHENG DEJUN, MICHAEL MOSER & WANG SHENGCHANG, INTERNATIONAL ARBITRATION IN THE PEOPLE'S REPUBLIC OF CHINA (1995); ARBITRATION LAWS OF CHINA, LEGISLATIVE AFFAIRS COMMISSION OF STANDING COMMITTEE OF NATIONAL PEOPLE'S CONGRESS of PRC.

50   *See* joint declaration of China (6 June 1997) and the United Kingdom (10 June 1997) notifying the United Nations that the New York Convention will be applied in the Hong Kong SAR. While the declaration expressly reserves Convention application in Hong Kong to awards made in the territory of another contracting state, nothing is said about the "commercial reservation" previously taken by China, leading some to suggest that the commercial reservation does not apply in China.

51   *See* Arrangement Concerning Mutual Enforcement of Arbitral Awards Between Mainland and Hong Kong Special Administrative Region, 21 June 1999. *See also* May Sin-mi Hon, *Deal Struck on Cross-Border Cases*, SOUTH CHINA MORNING POST, 16 December 1998; Robert Morgan, *Mutual Enforcement of Arbitral Awards Between Hong Kong and the People's Republic of China*, [1999] 2 INT. ARB. LAW. REP. 29.

52   Hong Kong Court of Final Appeal, 1999, 2 HK CFAR 111, reversing High Court of Hong Kong Special Administrative Region, Court of Appeal, Civil Appeal No. 116 (1997), 16 January 1998, 1 HKC 192 (1998), reprinted in 13 MEALEY'S INT. ARB. REP. (No. 2) E-1 (February 1998). *See generally*, Neil Kaplan, *Polytek Nearly Victorious: A Tale of Three Cities*, 66 ARBITRATION 25 (Feb. 2000).

53   Polytek, in turn, purchased the equipment from an American seller pursuant to a contract giving rise to its own CIETAC arbitration. *See* Polytek Engineering v. Jacobson Companies, 984 F. Supp. 1238 (D. Minn. 1997), ordering enforcement of an award against the American seller. By virtue of a provision stating that "all the terms and conditions should conform with the main contract [Polytek/Hebei] attached," the arbitration clause in the Polytek/Hebei agreement was deemed incorporated by reference into the purchase order concluded with the American seller.

In *dictum* the lower court had considered whether in Hong Kong the New York Convention would cover awards rendered on the Mainland *after* China's resumption of sovereignty. Since both Hong Kong and Beijing are now territories of the PRC, the answer would be "no" under the test of the first sentence of Article I of the Convention, which extends coverage to awards "made in the territory of a State other than the State where the recognition and enforcement of such awards are sought."

The Court went on to speculate about whether the award might be within the scope of the second sentence of Convention Article I, as an award "not considered domestic" where recognition is sought. Under the "one country two systems" concept, the Special Administrative Region of Hong Kong has a different legal system than that of the rest of China. Thus the decision suggested that "it can be strongly argued that a Beijing award would not be considered as a domestic award in Hong Kong."[54] The Court concluded, however, that the matter was not beyond doubt, making it "desirable that the relevant authority should consider appropriate amendments to the Arbitration Ordinance."[55]

As noted above, the problem has ben resolved in practice by a Memorandum of Understanding and implementing legislation that apply, as between Mainland China and Hong Kong SAR, the enforcement scheme of the New York Convention.

---

54 Hebei Import & Export Corporation v. Polytek Engineering Company, *supra*, at page E-4 of 13 MEALEY'S INT. ARB. REP. (Feb 1998).

55 *Id.*, at page E-5.

CHAPTER 33

SWISS LAW

33.01 Statutory Framework

(a) The Federal Statute: LDIP

The Swiss federal statute on private international law (*Loi fédérale sur le droit international privé*, or "*LDIP*") permits application of either cantonal or federal arbitration procedure to ICC arbitrations conducted in Switzerland.[1]

The scope of the *LDIP* is defined by a residence-oriented test, which applies the statute to an arbitration if at least one party is foreign, in the sense of being neither domiciled nor habitually resident in Switzerland. Whether or not an arbitration agreement is international in character, thus falling within the scope of the *LDIP*, will depend on the identities of the parties at the moment the arbitration clause is signed.[2] Thus it will not be possible to manipulate an arbitration into or out of the *LDIP* through assignment of the arbitration agreement.

There is only one federal court in Switzerland, the *Tribunal fédéral* or *Bundesgericht*, which sits in Lausanne. It may review cantonal court decisions when authorized to do so by the Federal Judiciary Act and may in some cases serve as a court of first instance. Since entry into force of the *LDIP*, the *Tribunal fédéral* hears challenges to arbitration awards covered by this statute.

---

1   Chapter 12, Articles 176-95, *Loi fédérale sur le droit international privé*. *See* generally P. LALIVE, J.F. POUDRET, C. REYMOND, LE DROIT DE L'ARBITRAGE INTERNE ET INTERNATIONAL EN SUISSE (1989). *See* also François Knoepfler & Philippe Schweizer, *Jurisprudence suisse en matière d'arbitrage international*, REVUE SUISSE DE DROIT INTERNATIONAL ET DE DROIT EUROPÉEN Vol. 1995 at 547, Vol 1996 at 539, Vol. 1997 at 587 and Vol. 1998 at 553.

2   *See Tribunal fédéral*, 27 Oct. 1995, Kolbrunner v. Federici.

(b) The Concordat

The Intercantonal Arbitration *Concordat* provides the cantonal law framework for an arbitral proceeding with its seat in one of Switzerland's cantons. However, ICC arbitration in Switzerland is usually international in nature,[3] and therefore subject to the *LDIP*.

To remove an arbitration from the scope of the *LDIP* the parties must in writing agree to exclude its provisions. *See LDIP* Article 176(2). Case law has made clear that a simple reference to the *Concordat* is not sufficient to displace the *LDIP*.[4] Rather the parties must explicitly express their intention that the *LDIP* not apply—a choice rarely made in international arbitration.

Since it is unlikely that cantonal procedure will be relevant to ICC arbitration, the following sections focus on the *LDIP*. Reference to judicial decisions arising out of application of the *Concordat* have been made only to explain attitudes of Swiss courts toward issues common to both the *Concordat* and the *LDIP*.[5]

Litigants that do contemplate application of the *Concordat* should be aware that judicial review of awards subject to its provisions is significantly more extensive than under the *LDIP*. Thirty-two of the *Concordat*'s forty-six articles contain mandatory provisions (*dispositions impératives*) dealing with matters such as the form of the arbitration agreement, revocation of arbitral authority, and challenge of the award's validity, which apply notwithstanding the parties' desire to tailor the arbitral proceedings otherwise. Some mandatory provisions are matters of fairness, such as the requirement that all arbitrators participate in the arbitral deliberations and decisions. Other provisions permit a substantial degree of judicial intervention in the merits of the dispute.

Under *Concordat* Article 36 an award may be set aside pursuant to a request for annulment (*recours en nullité*) on nine grounds: improper constitution of the arbitral tribunal; error as to the arbitral tribunal's jurisdiction; ruling by the arbitral tribunal on matters not submitted to it; violation of a party's right to due process; award on something other than what was claimed; "arbitrary" award; a ruling after expiration of the arbitral tribunal's mission; fail-

---

3   Although Article 1(1) of the ICC Rules permits coverage of "business disputes not of an international character," the resolution of non-international disputes under the ICC Rules is extremely rare.

4   *See Tribunal fédéral* I. SA v. T. SA, ATF 115 II 390 (1989); S. AG v. H. Ltd, ATF 116 I 721 (1990); *See also Tribunal de 1ère Instance de Genève*, 14 Sept. 1998, N. v. S..

5   For analysis of the *Concordat*, *see* PIERRE JOLIDON, COMMENTAIRE DU CONCORDAT SUISSE SUR L'ARBITRAGE; PIERRE LALIVE, JEAN-FRANÇOIS POUDRET & CLAUDE REYMOND, LE DROIT DE L'ARBITRAGE INTERNE ET INTERNATIONAL EN SUISSE.

ure by the arbitral tribunal to respect the provisions on the form of the award; or fees fixed at a manifestly excessive level.[6]

Many of these grounds for annulment comport with what one expects of a modern arbitration statute, in that they tend to promote the basic integrity of the award and the fundamental fairness of the proceedings. One ground that has engendered reservations, however, is "arbitrariness," given the capacious definition of the concept, which includes an award "manifestly contrary to the facts appearing on the file" or constituting a "clear violation of law or equity."[7]

If the *recours en nullité* is accepted, the court may set aside all or part of the award, or may return it to the arbitrators for correction.[8] The action for annulment must be made within thirty days of award notification, and may be heard only after the party has exhausted all appeals available under the arbitration agreement.[9]

33.02 The Agreement to Arbitrate

Federal law explicitly permits the arbitration clause to take any form (including telegram, telex or telecopy) permitting textual verification.[10]

The *Tribunal fédéral* has upheld the validity of the arbitration clause in a document signed by only one party, finding the requirement of a "writing" to be satisfied by a bill of lading that lacked the shipper's signature.[11] A French shipper had brought an action for goods damaged in transit, suing in Geneva notwithstanding a clause providing for arbitration in London. When the defendant moved to stay the litigation on the basis of the arbitration clause, the plaintiff argued that the arbitration agreement was invalid, since it had been signed only by the carrier. The court noted that the two merchants had a long course of dealing between themselves, and that the shipper had in fact filled out the bill of lading.

---

6   *Concordat*, Article 36.

7   *Concordat*, Article 36(f). "Equity" of course is used in the sense of fairness, rather than as one branch of Anglo-American law. Violation of equity becomes relevant only if the arbitral tribunal has been authorized to decide not in law but in equity, a notion sometimes allied with *amiable composition*. On distinctions between equity and *amiable composition*, *see* PIERRE LALIVE, JEAN-FRANÇOIS POUDRET & CLAUDE REYMOND, LE DROIT DE L'ARBITRAGE INTERNE ET INTERNATIONAL EN SUISSE at 172 and 215.

8   *Concordat*, Articles 39 and 40.

9   *Concordat*, Article 37.

10   *See LDIP* Art. 178(1).

11   ATF 121 II 38, 16 Jan. 1995, Compagnie de Navigation et Transports S.A. v. Mediterranean Shipping Company S.A., 13 SWISS BULL. 503 (1995).

The severability doctrine gives effect to an arbitration clause in a main agreement whose validity is contested.[12] The arbitration clause becomes void only if the reason for the contract's nullity also applies to the arbitration clause.

States and state agencies may not invoke their own national law to challenge their capacity to arbitrate,[13] thus settling the question raised in a case in which the Belgian government had invoked provisions of its own civil code in objecting to arbitral jurisdiction.[14] In addition, a more general rule contained earlier in the *LDIP* encourages security of transactions by limiting invocation of incapacity defenses under the law of a party's domicile, at least when the other side to the transaction could not in good faith have known of the incapacity.[15]

The *LDIP* contains broad provisions on subject-matter arbitrability. All claims are arbitrable if capable of being valued in money terms (*toute cause de nature patrimoine/jeder vermögensrechliche Anspruch*), as defined by Swiss jurisprudential concepts.[16]

An arbitration agreement entirely between non-Swiss parties may exclude all judicial review of the award if waiver of review is made expressly either in the arbitration clause or in a subsequent written agreement. *See* Section 33.04. The requirement that waiver of recourse be made by an express statement (*déclaration expresse*)[17] means that the model ICC arbitration clause must be augmented if the parties desire to exclude all judicial recourse against the award. To such an end, the clause might provide for example: "The parties hereby waive all right to judicial recourse against the award, and intend this clause to constitute a valid exclusion agreement in the sense of Article 192(1) of the Swiss Federal Statute on Private International Law."[18]

---

12   *LDIP* Art. 178(3).

13   *LDIP* Art. 177(2).

14   Benteler v. Belgium, *Journal des Tribunaux, Bruxelles*, No. 5289, 31 March 1984. Award rendered in Switzerland on 18 November 1983, arising out of a mining joint venture between Belgium and two West German companies. The arbitral tribunal refused to accept the Belgian government's objection to jurisdiction based on Art. 1672(2) of the Belgian *Code judiciaire*, limiting the capacity of state entities to conclude an arbitration agreement.

15   *LDIP* Article 36 provides: "La partie à un acte juridique qui est incapable selon le droit de l'Etat de son domicile ne peut pas invoquer cette incapacité si elle était capable selon le droit de l'Etat où l'acte a été accompli, à moins que l'autre partie niait connu ou dû connaître cette incapacité."

16   *See LDIP* Art. 177.

17   *See* ATF 116 II 639, 19 Dec. 1990, Sonatrach v. K.C.A. Drilling, JT 1991 I, 30 June 1991, in which the *Tribunal fédéral* confirmed that reference to the ICC Rules is not enough to constitute a waiver under *LDIP* Article 192 of the right to challenge an award in court.

18   For another suggested waiver formulation, *see* Marc Blessing, *The New International Arbitration Law in Switzerland*, 5 J. Int. Arb. No. 3, 9, at 75 (1988).

Swiss case law has been liberal in accepting the subject matter arbitrability of disputes that might implicate sensitive public policies.[19] The *Tribunal fédéral* has decided[20] that arbitrators sitting in Switzerland are not prohibited from reviewing the validity of a contract under the European Community's antitrust law.[21] The case involved a dispute arising out of a joint venture, governed by Belgian law, and raised antitrust questions under the law of the European Union. The Spanish company claimed that the agreement was contrary to Article 85 of the Treaty of Rome, which prohibits contracts that restrain or distort trade among Common Market Member States.

The *Tribunal fédéral* first noted that arbitrability is a matter covered by the *lex arbitri*, in this case Swiss law, which permits arbitration of matters related to property or pecuniary interests.[22] The Court discussed the opinions of experts in the field of European Community law, who supported the conclusion that national courts and arbitral tribunals are *not* precluded from reviewing the validity of an agreement under Article 85. Consequently, the *Tribunal fédéral* set aside the award, essentially telling the arbitrators that they were required to hear and to decide the antitrust matter.

33.03 Interlocutory Matters

The *LDIP* gives the arbitral tribunal authority to order interim measures of protection, and to have these orders enforced by courts of competent jurisdiction.[23] Swiss courts can thus be requested to grant interim relief either (i) directly, in their own right, when their help is requested by one of the parties,[24] or (ii) indirectly, to support the arbitral tribunal.[25]

Challenge to an arbitrator (*récusation*) at the arbitral seat is permitted either when the arbitrator fails to fulfill the qualifications set by the parties' agreement (either explicitly or by reference to the ICC Rules) or if circumstances permit doubt as to his independence. *See LDIP* Art. 180. The *LDIP* imposes a standard of independence, but not impartiality as required by the *Concordat*.

---

19 *LDIP* Article 177 limits arbitrability only in that the claim must in some way relate to property (*cause de nature patrimoine/vermögensrechtliche Anspruch*).

20 *Tribunal fédéral*, 1ère Cour civile, 28 April 1992, G.SA v. V.S.p.A., ATF 118 II, page 193, 1993 REV. ARB. 124. *See generally* Carlo Lombardini, *Effetti del Diritto Comunitario sui Contratti e Arbitrato del Commercio Internazionale*, 1993 DIRITTO DEL COMMERCIO INTERNAZIONALE 143.

21 *See also Tribunal fédéral*, 23 June 1992, Fincantieri-Cantieri Navali Italiani S.p.A v. OTO Melara S.p.A., ATF 188 II, 115 SEMAINE JUDICIAIRE 2 (1993), allowing arbitration of a dispute involving trade with Iraq in violation of the 1990 and 1991 United Nations Resolutions.

22 *LDIP* Article 177.

23 *LDIP* Article 183.

24 *LDIP* Article 10 provides that "Swiss judicial or administrative authorities may enter provisional orders even if they do not have jurisdiction on the merits."

25 *See* François Knoepfler, *Les mesures provisoires et l'arbitrage international*, in SCHIEDSGERICHTSBARKEIT (Andreas Kellerhals, Europa Institut Zürich, 1997) 307.

The arbitral tribunal has authority to fill gaps in the ICC Rules by adopting procedures it deems appropriate, as long as such matters have not been fixed by the parties themselves. However, these rules must guarantee procedural fairness in two respects: (i) equality between the parties, and (ii) the right to adversarial process (*"droit d'être entendu en procédure contradictoire"*). *See LDIP* Art. 182.

The LDIP contains a broad power for the judicial authorities to assist the arbitral tribunal "if necessary." In particular, the judge of the arbitral seat may assist the arbitrator in the taking of evidence. *See LDIP* Art. 184.

In determining whether to stay litigation in favor of arbitration, Swiss courts examining the validity of an arbitration agreement will apply a different level of scrutiny depending on whether the postulated arbitral proceedings are to take place inside or outside of Switzerland.[26] When an arbitration has its seat within Switzerland, a Swiss court asked to stay litigation will content itself with examination of the *prima facie* validity of the arbitration clause, at least if the arbitral tribunal has already been constituted.[27]

On the other hand, when the contested arbitration agreement provides for an arbitral seat outside Switzerland, courts have engaged in a full and complete examination of the agreement's validity.[28] Article 7 of the *LDIP* provides that courts should decline jurisdiction in deference to an arbitration agreement unless the agreement is "void, inoperative, or incapable of being performed,"[29] and contains no limit on the extent of the court's inquiry into the validity of the arbitration agreement.[30] In *Compagnie de Navigation et Trans-*

---

26   For an in-depth examination of the Swiss approach to determining who is bound to an arbitration clause, *see* Jean-François Poudret, *L'extension de la clause d'arbitrage: approches française et suisse*, 122 JOURNAL DU DROIT INTERNATIONAL 893 (1995).

27   *See Tribunal fédéral*, 29 April 1996, Fondation M. v. Banque X, ATF 122 II 139; 14 SWISS BULL. 527 (1996) and Note by Mayer at 361. The case involved an alleged defect in an arbitration clause based on limitations under Liechtenstein law on the powers of the foundation representative who had signed the agreement. The court concluded that when the arbitral seat is in Switzerland, "le juge étatique saisi pouvait admettre sans hésitation l'existence prima facie d'une convention d'arbitrage; il n'avait pas à examiner de surcroit si le droit liechtensteinois invoqué par la Fondation M restreignait les pouvoirs conférés expressément au mandataire. . . ."

28   *See generally* François Knoepfler & Philippe Schweizer, *Jurisprudence suisse en matière d'arbitrage international*, 1996 REVUE SUISSE DE DROIT INTERNATIONAL ET DE DROIT EUROPÉEN 539, 558. Knoepfler & Schweizer note that "lorsque le siège du tribunal arbitral est en Suisse, l'articulation entre les articles 7 LDIP et 179 LDIP est plus délicate." *Id.* at 565.

29   *LDIP* Article 7(b), covering agreements that are void, inoperative or incapable of being performed (*"caduque, inopérante ou non susceptible d'être appliquée"*/*"hinfällig, unwirksam oder nich erfüllbar"*).

30   By contrast, the provision of the *LDIP* dealing with appointment of arbitrators contains a significant qualification, instructing a court to appoint an arbitrator unless a "summary examination" (*"examen sommaire"* or *"summarische Prüfung"*) shows that no arbitration agreement exists.

ports S.A. v. MSC (Mediterranean Shipping Company) S.A.,[31] (discussed in Section 33.02 in connection with the requirement of a "writing"), the *Tribunal fédéral* affirmed that when arbitration occurs abroad a Swiss court should examine the validity of the arbitration clause "fully. . .without limiting itself to a prima facie examination" ("*avec plein pouvoir d'examen. . .sans pouvoir se limiter à un examen prima facie*").[32] The case involved a dispute between a French shipper (*Compagnie de Navigation et Transport*) and a Swiss carrier (MSC) for transport of merchandise from Marseille to Ile de la Réunion. The bill of lading provided for arbitration in London. When the goods were found to be damaged, the shipper brought suit in Geneva. The carrier moved to stay the litigation on the basis of the arbitration clause, which the shipper argued was invalid, since it had been signed only by the carrier.

The court held that a summary examination of the validity of the arbitration would be appropriate only if Swiss courts would later have a chance to correct an arbitrator's erroneous jurisdictional decision, which is to say, when the arbitration would be conducted in Switzerland. After examination the court found the clause valid on the basis of a long course of dealing between the parties.

An interim award on arbitral jurisdiction may be challenged for irregular composition of the arbitral tribunal or for an error on the jurisdictional issue itself.[33] The other grounds for challenge of an award (*see* Section 33.04) are not available at this stage.

The law applicable to the merits of the dispute may be chosen by the arbitral tribunal unless there has been a choice by the parties. In determining the applicable law in default of a choice by the parties, the arbitrators must look to the "legal rules with which the dispute is most closely linked" ("*les règles de droit avec lesquelles la cause présente les liens les plus étroits*").[34] *The term "legal rules" would seem broad enough to include* lex mercatoria (*see* Chapter

---

31 ATF 121 II 38, 16 Jan. 1995, 13 SWISS BULL. 503 (1995). For just such a case, when a Swiss court did examine the validity of an arbitration clause when hearing a challenge to an award, *see Vekoma v. Maran Coal Company*, discussed in Section 33.04. For scholarly commentary questioning the reasoning of the decision, see Jean-François Poudret and Gabriel Cottier, *Remarques sur l'Application de Article II de la Convention de New York*, 13 SWISS BULL. 383 (1985). ("Si cette solution doit certes être approuvée, la motivation qui la soutient repose toutefois sur une distinction peu convaincante et même infondée. . ." *Id.*, at 387.) For a less critical appraisal, see François Knoepfler & Philippe Schweizer, *Jurisprudence suisse en matière d'arbitrage international*, 1996 REVUE SUISSE DE DROIT INTERNATIONAL DE DE DROIT EUROPÉEN 539, page 558, at 565. *See also* Richard Hill, *Swiss Supreme Court Decision of 16 January 1995*, 14 SWISS BULL. 488 (1996).

32 The court added that the validity of the clause must be examined "in a free and unconstrained manner" ("*de manière complète et librement*"). *Id.* at 42.

33 *LDIP* Art. 190(2)(a) and (b).

34 *LDIP* Art. 187(1).

35).[35] The arbitrators may decide *ex aequo et bono* (*"statuer en équité"*) if so authorized.

It is not uncommon in many places to select judges as arbitrators. In Switzerland, however, the choice has been limited with respect to members of the federal judiciary. Judges sitting on the *Tribunal fédéral* can now accept appointment as arbitrators only if they will chair the tribunal or serve as sole arbitrator, or if the arbitral tribunal is composed entirely of members of the *Tribunal fédéral*.[36]

The *Tribunal fédéral* dealt with the matter of *litispendance* in arbitration.[37] An arbitration in Zürich had been begun notwithstanding that an existing court action was being heard on the same matter in Lima. The claimants in the Peruvian litigation challenged the Swiss proceedings on the basis of *litispendance*. The Swiss court held that the Lima action had been brought in violation of the contract's arbitration clause, and thus would have no effect on the arbitration in Switzerland. The Court noted that New York Convention Article II(3), like Swiss *LDIP* Article 7(b), requires courts to decline jurisdiction unless the arbitration agreement is found to be null and void, inoperative or incapable of being performed.

33.04   Review of Awards

An award rendered in Switzerland must contain reasons unless the parties have agreed otherwise. *See LDIP* Article 189. This requirement for a reasoned award is in line with Article 25(2) of the ICC Rules.

The *LDIP* provides five bases for challenge of awards:[38]

(1) irregular composition of the arbitral tribunal or irregular appointment of the sole arbitrator;

(2) an erroneous decision by the tribunal with respect to the tribunal's own jurisdiction;

(3) a decision beyond the matters submitted to the arbitrators, or failure to decide a matter within the request for arbitration;

(4) failure to respect the "equality of the parties" or the adversarial process (*"droit d'être entendu en procédure contradictoire"*);

---

35   Compare the French text, *"règles de droit,"* with the equally authoritative German text referring merely to *"Recht."*

36   *See* Règlement sur les activités accessoires des membres du Tribunal fédéral, 22 Feb. 1993, RO 1993, page 1352 and RS 173.113.1.

37   *Tribunal fédéral*, 1ère Cour civile, 19 Dec. 1997, Compañia Minera Condesa SA & Compañia Minas Buenaventura SA v. Bureau de Recherches Géologiques et Minières-Pérou, 1998 SEMAINE JUDICIAIRE 358.

38   *See generally* Gabrielle Kaufmann-Kohler, *Articles 190 et 191 LDIP: Les Recours Contre les Sentences Arbitrales*, 10 SWISS BULL. 64 (1992).

(5) incompatibility of the award with public policy (*ordre public*).

Interlocutory orders, however, may be appealed only for the first two grounds: defects in composition of the tribunal or an erroneous decision on jurisdiction.

Incompatibility with *ordre public*, the final ground for challenge of awards, might in some cases touch the merits of the award. However, Swiss conflict of laws principles distinguish between notions of *ordre public*, as applied to international transactions from "internal" public policy.

Moreover, Swiss courts have resisted an overly broad concept of public policy when presented as a defense to enforcement of an international contract.[39] In *Hilmarton v. OTV*[40] a Geneva cantonal court annulled an ICC award in which the arbitrator refused a claim for consulting services arising out of a contract to be performed in Algeria. The arbitrator had found the contract illegal under Algerian law, and mistakenly believed that this illegality made the contract void as against Swiss public policy.[41]

The *LDIP* provides two bases for judicial scrutiny of the arbitrators' jurisdiction. Article 190(2)(b) permits annulment where the tribunal "wrongly declared itself to have or not to have jurisdiction." Article 190(2)(c) deals with an arbitral tribunal that has "failed to decide a claim" or has "decided claims not submitted to it," sometimes referred to as awards *ultra petita* and *infra petita* (beyond and beneath the scope of the petition). The Swiss approach contrasts with that of the UNCITRAL Model Arbitration Law, which gives courts power to set aside an award only if the arbitrator

---

39   On substantive public policy as a ground for award annulment in Switzerland, *see* Homayoon Arfazadeh, *L'ordre public du fond et l'annulation des sentences arbitrales internationales en Suisse,* 1995 REVUE SUISSE DE DROIT INTERNATIONAL ET DE DROIT EUROPÉEN 223. *See also* François Knoepfler, *Corruption et arbitrage international,* in LES CONTRACTS DE DISTRIBUTION: CONTRIBUTIONS OFFERTES AU PROFESSEUR FRANÇOIS DESSEMONTET 357 (1998); *Tribunal fédéral,* 30 Dec. 1994 (1ère Cour Civile), 13 SWISS BULL. 217 (1995). An ICC arbitral tribunal sitting in Geneva (Hilmar Raeschke-Kessler, Jean Patry and Dobrosav Mitrovic) found no proof of bribery with respect to a contract for the sale of tanks to a foreign government. The court refused to annul the award, concluding that the findings of the arbitral tribunal had not resulted from any procedural irregularity (*"le tribunal arbitral n'a nullement violé l'ordre juridique procédural."*) *Id.* at 226. Subsequently this award was granted recognition in England. *See* Section 30.04, footnote 92.

40   The cantonal court, upheld by the Swiss *Tribunal fédéral,* found the alleged illegality of the contract under Algerian law did not constitute a violation of Swiss public policy. *See* 1993 REV. ARB. at 315 (*Cour de Justice du Canton de Genève,* 17 Nov. 1989) and at 322 (*Tribunal fédéral,* 17 April 1990).

41   Because the award was rendered before entry into force of the *LDIP,* challenge had been brought under Article 36 of the *Concordat,* permitting the court to correct what it perceived as the arbitrator's incorrect understanding of Swiss public policy. Thereafter a second arbitration tribunal issued an award for the claimant on the same matter. *See generally* discussion in Chapter 28.04, and Jean-François Poudret, *Quelle solution pour en finir avec l'affaire Hilmarton,* 1998 REV. ARB. 7.

wrongly exceeds his arbitral jurisdiction.[42] It also diverges from the broad French formulation providing for vacatur when the arbitrator "decided in a manner incompatible with the [arbitrator's] mission,"[43] and the general prohibition in the United States' Federal Arbitration Act covering arbitrators who "exceed their powers."[44]

In *G.S.A. v. V.SpA*,[45] the *Tribunal fédéral* exercised its power to annul an award on jurisdictional grounds relating to a claim's subject matter arbitrability. The case is intriguing as one of the few instances in which a court reversed an arbitral tribunal's determination that it did *not* have jurisdiction. In denying its jurisdiction to deal with the antitrust matter, the arbitral tribunal was found to have violated *LDIP* Article 190(2)(b), by "wrongly declaring itself to have or not to have jurisdiction." Far more typical, however, is the opposite situation where one side challenges the arbitrators' ruling that they do possess jurisdiction.

Nor does the *LDIP* explicitly list bias as grounds for annulment. Again, however, other statutory bases for award annulment would seem flexible enough to cover such a defect. Article 190(2) includes in its list of award defects (i) irregular composition of the arbitral tribunal (subsection a) (ii) failure to respect the principle of equal treatment of the parties (subsection d) and (iii) violation of public policy (*ordre public*) (subsection e), all of which might be implicated by appointment of a biased arbitrator.[46]

Challenge to the award must be made before the *Tribunal fédéral* in Lausanne unless the parties have expressly agreed to confer powers of review on the cantonal court of the arbitral seat.

---

42   *See* UNCITRAL Model Article 16(3) (the award may be challenged "if the arbitral tribunal rules as a preliminary matter that it has jurisdiction") and Article 34(2)(a)(iii) (the award may be set aside if it "deals with a dispute not contemplated by or not falling within the terms of the submission. . .or on matters beyond the scope of the submission"). Lord Wilberforce (observer for the Chartered Institute of Arbitrators at the discussions of the Model Law) objected to failure to permit judicial review of a decision to decline jurisdiction as "plac[ing] arbitrators in an impossible position," pushing them to favor their jurisdiction for fear of wrongly terminating one of the parties rights to arbitration. Cited in ADAM SAMUEL, JURISDICTIONAL PROBLEMS IN INTERNATIONAL COMMERCIAL ARBITRATION (1989), at 218-19.

43   *NCPC* Article 1502(3) and 1504.

44   9 U.S.C. § 10(a)(4).

45   *Tribunal fédéral*, 1ère Cour civile, 28 April 1992, G. SA v. V. SpA, ATF 118 II, page 193, 1993 REV. ARB. 124. *See* discussion in Section 33.02. *See generally*, Carlo Lombardini, *Effetti del Diritto Comunitario sui Contratti e Arbitrato del Commercio Internazionale*, 1993 DIRITTO DEL COMMERCIO INTERNAZIONALE 143.

46   On grounds for recusal of arbitrators at the time the arbitral tribunal is constituted, *see* Article 180 of the *LDIP*. *See generally*, P. LALIVE, J.F. POUDRET, C. REYMOND, LE DROIT DE L'ARBITRAGE INTERNE ET INTERNATIONAL EN SUISSE 423-4 (1989).

Timely challenge to defective awards (within thirty (30) days from notification of the award[47]) is imperative in Switzerland, as illustrated by the final stage of the multifaceted *Westland Helicopters* saga,[48] a case that highlights the dual dangers of boycotting an arbitration and taking too relaxed an attitude toward the requirements of local procedural law.[49] Egypt, United Arab Emirates, Saudi Arabia and Qatar had set up by treaty the Arab Organization for Industrialization (AOI) to build a unified Arab arms industry. AOI and a British company, Westland Helicopters, then created a jointly owned Egyptian company called the Arab British Helicopter Company, which in turn entered into a joint venture with Westland Helicopters to build helicopters in Egypt. The contracts, governed by Swiss law, provided for the arbitration of any disputes in Geneva under the ICC Rules.

In response to Egypt's 1979 peace treaty with Israel, the three other Arab states purported to terminate the existence of AOI, and Egypt in turn passed a law turning AOI into an Egyptian company. Westland Helicopters filed an ICC arbitration claim for breach of contract against the four Arab states, the Saudi-dominated AOI and the Arab British Helicopter Company. Egypt, alone among the four contracting states, objected in a timely fashion to the arbitrators' interim award finding jurisdiction over the member governments,[50] and was judicially discharged from the arbitration.[51]

Several years later a final award was rendered in favor of Westland Helicopters against the other three governments and the Riyadh-based AOI.[52] The *Tribunal fédéral* rejected as untimely the challenge for excess of authority un-

---

47 *See Concordat*, Article 37 and *LDIP* Article 191(1). The *LDIP* fixes challenge by reference to public law appeals (*recours de droit public*) under the *Loi d'organisation judiciaire*, set at thirty days by Article 89 of this latter law.

48 *Tribunal fédéral*, 19 April 1994, Westland Helicopters v. Emirats Arabes Unis, Arabie Saoudite, Etat du Qatar, ABH et Arab Organization for Industrialization (AOI), *ATF 120 II 155 (1994); 12 SWISS BULL.* 404 (1994). For earlier stages of the dispute, *see Tribunal fédéral*, 24 Sept. 1986, Westland Helicopters Ltd v. République Arabe d'Egypte, *ATF* 112 Ia 344, 109 SEMAINE JUDICIAIRE 1 (1987) (ICC Rule requiring challenge to an arbitrator to be brought before the ICC Court of Arbitration does not exclude recusation under the Concordat when the final award is presented for annulment).

49 By contrast, Sections 72 and 73 of the 1996 English Arbitration Act provide that non-participants in arbitration are not precluded from later challenging procedural and jurisdictional defects.

50 Award of 5 March 1994, ICC Case 3879, *reproduced in* 23 ILM 1071 (1985).

51 *Tribunal fédéral*, 19 July 1988, République arabe d'Egypte v. Westland Helicopters Limited, 28 ILM 687 (1989). The court stated that "taking into account the complete juridical independence resulting from the constituent instruments of AOI [the founding States] have manifestly shown that they did not want to be bound by the arbitration agreement." Translation by Georges Delaume.

52 Award of 28 June 1993, ICC Case No. 3879.

der *LDIP* Article 190(2)(b).[53] Attack on the interim jurisdictional award should have been made within the time provided under the law applicable at the time.[54]

Review of awards may be excluded by explicit agreement (*déclaration expresse*) in the arbitration clause if no party is resident in Switzerland (neither *domicile* nor *résidence habituelle*) nor has a Swiss branch. *LDIP* Article 192 provides:

> If neither of the parties has its domicile, its habitual residence or a business establishment in Switzerland, they may by express declaration in the arbitration agreement or in a subsequent written agreement waive all judicial recourse against the arbitral award; they may also waive judicial recourse for only one or some of the grounds enumerated in Article 190, paragraph 2.

Exclusion may be general, or may be limited to only some of the five aforementioned grounds for challenge. For example, parties to ICC arbitration in Switzerland might decide to exclude review relating to due process but not review of jurisdictional matters.

As mentioned in Section 33.02, waiver of the right to judicial review of the award requires an explicit exclusion agreement. Reference to the ICC Rules will not be sufficient to satisfy the requirements of *LDIP* Article 192.

A recent decision of the *Tribunal fédéral* dealt with the oft-vexed question of what deference (if any) a court should show to an arbitral tribunal's jurisdictional determination. As background, one must remember that the *LDIP* provides that an arbitral tribunal shall rule on its own jurisdiction in most cases ("*en général*"/"*in der Regel*") through an interlocutory decision, and that objections to arbitral jurisdiction must be raised prior to any defense on the merits. *LDIP* Article 186.

Swiss law, however, contains nothing equivalent to the French rule[55] requiring courts to refrain from hearing challenges to an arbitrator's jurisdiction until the end of the arbitration. On the contrary, Swiss courts will verify the existence of an arbitration clause when asked to hear a dispute allegedly covered by an agreement to arbitrate.[56] The depth of the court's initial jurisdictional investigation, however, may be more summary if the arbitration is

---

53   *Tribunal fédéral*, 19 April 1994, Westland Helicopters v. Emirats Arabes Unis, Arabie Saoudite, Etat du Qatar, ABH et Arab Organization for Industrialization (AOI), 120 II 155 ATF (1994), 12 SWISS BULL. 404 (1994).

54   The relevant arbitration law at that time, the Intercantonal Arbitration *Concordat*, provided thirty (30) days for an action to annul an award. *Concordat* Article 37.

55   *See* Article 1458 of the French *NCPC*.

56   *LDIP* Article 7.

conducted in Switzerland (thus leaving open a fuller examination after the award has been rendered) rather than abroad.[57]

On the other hand, after an award is rendered, Swiss courts will examine *de novo* the legal predicates of an arbitrator's jurisdiction. In a case that has engendered lively commentary, *Vekoma v. Maran Coal Company*,[58] the *Tribunal fédéral* invoked *LDIP* Article 190(2)(b) to annul an ICC arbitral award on jurisdiction, raising the issue of whether the arbitration had been brought within the contractually stipulated time limits.[59]

The background of this case involved a Dutch company that had undertaken to ship coke to an American coal corporation pursuant to a contract subject to Swiss law. Any dispute was to be resolved by ICC arbitration in Geneva, subject to the condition that the claim be filed "within thirty days after it was agreed that the difference or dispute cannot be resolved by negotiation."

Controversy led to an arbitration request in May 1992, resulting in an award for the claimant. The defendant challenged the award on the basis that the claim was not brought within the requisite contractual period of thirty days from breakdown of negotiations. The jurisdiction of the arbitrators depended upon the timeliness of the claim, which in turn depended upon how one interpreted the communication between the parties: i.e., when was there an "agreement to disagree," so as to trigger the thirty day period?

In the claimant's view, the view adopted by the arbitrators, settlement negotiations had broken down only in April, and therefore the arbitration was timely. The defendant took the position (with which the *Tribunal fédéral* agreed) that failure to settle occurred in January, when a letter from the claimants was met with silence.[60]

In finding for the defendant, the *Tribunal fédéral* held itself to have power to review the jurisdictional decision of the arbitral tribunal *de novo*, without the

---

57 *See* discussion of Compagnie de Navigation et Transport v. Mediterranean Shipping, *supra* Section 33.03.

58 *Tribunal fédéral*, 17 Aug. 1995, Transport-en Handelsmaatschappij "Vekoma" B.V. v. Maran Coal Company, 14 SWISS BULL. 673 (1996), with commentary by Philippe Schweizer. ICC Arbitration No. 7565/BGD.

59 *See generally* Paul Friedland, *The Swiss Supreme Court Sets Aside an ICC Award*, 13 (No. 1) J. INT. ARB. 111 (1996); Pierre Karrer & Claudia Kälin-Nauer, *Is There a Favor Iurisdictionis Arbitri?*, 13 (No. 3) J. INT. ARB. 31 (1996)(suggesting that the *Tribunal fédéral* should have given "somewhat more" deference to the arbitral tribunal's findings). The court's reasoning has been described as "unnecessarily subtle" (*inutilement subtile*) by François Knoepfler & Philippe Schweizer, *Jurisprudence suisse en matière d'arbitrage international*, 1996 REVUE SUISSE DE DROIT INTERNATIONAL ET DROIT EUROPÉEN 573.

60 The Americans had sent a settlement offer in January 1992, asking for a reply no later than 17 January. When no response was forthcoming from the Dutch, the Americans then sent a reminder notice three months later, to which the Dutch did reply (in the negative) on 13 April. A claim was filed with the ICC on 11 May.

type of deference to the arbitrator's findings that would normally be accorded a decision on the merits. The court then went on to find that the arbitration clause had lapsed by the time the claim was in fact filed several months later.

The reasoning of the *Tribunal fédéral* rests in large part on its distinction between an arbitrator's findings of fact and an arbitrator's conclusion of law.[61] The court deemed its review function to be more limited with respect to matters of fact than law.[62] In this connection, the *Tribunal fédéral* said that the parties' negotiation might have failed as a matter of either actual fact or legal norm ("*tatsächlich oder normativ*").[63] Finding that the claimant ought to have concluded from the defendant's silence that its January settlement offer had been refused, the court implied as a matter of law that negotiations had failed.

While the distinction between findings of fact and conclusions of law might be understandable in review of cantonal court decisions, it poses certain analytic paradoxes with respect to an arbitrator's jurisdictional decisions. An excess of jurisdiction would seem to be an excess of jurisdiction whether based on the wrong facts or the wrong law.[64] Yet the *Tribunal fédéral*'s review power will normally be exercised in the latter case but not the former. An alternative way to approach judicial review might be to ask whether the arbitrators' mistake concerns the merits of the case or their own jurisdiction, regardless of whether the mistake was one of law or of fact.[65]

Although the *LDIP* is silent on dissenting opinions, scholarly comment tends to admit that they may be included in awards and communicated to the par-

---

61   In this connection it is important to note that the procedure for an annulment action before the *Tribunal fédéral* is governed by norms applicable to public law challenges before the same court (*Loi d'organisation judiciaire, recours de droit public*). *See LDIP* Article 191(1). Karrer & Kälin-Nauer state that "When the Swiss Federal Supreme Court reviews a decision of an arbitral tribunal on its jurisdiction, it still fully reviews questions of law. By contrast, findings of fact by an arbitral tribunal are reviewable only where they are based on procedural errors which are themselves reviewable under Article 190, subsection 2, letter d of the PIL Statute [relating to equal treatment and right to be heard] and possibly letter e [public policy]." Pierre Karrer & Claudia Kälin-Nauer, *Is There a Favor Iurisdictionis Arbitri?*, 13 (No. 3) J. INT. ARB. 31, at 34 (1996).

62   *See* paragraph 3 of the opinion, found at 14 SWISS BULL. 676-77 (1996). *Compare Tribunal fédéral*, S.C.S. Ltd. v. C., C.S.A. & IHK-Schiedsgericht Zürich, ATF 117 II 94 (1991).

63   *Id.*, at paragraph 3(c), page 678.

64   *For example*, an arbitral tribunal might take jurisdiction over a parent corporation on the erroneous assumption that through its subsidiary the parent had entered into an arbitration agreement. The error might result from an incorrect understanding of the law (legal grounds for piercing the corporate veil) or the facts (capacity in which an individual signed the agreement), or both.

65   *See* e.g., LALIVE, POUDRET & REYMOND, *supra* note 1 (at page 439), to the effect that "De manière plus générale, nous pensons qu'il convient de distinguer. . . selon que l'examen [of the Tribunal fédéral] porte sur les motifs de recours prévus à l'article 190(2), auquel cas il est illimité. . . .

ties.[66] Some commentators suggest that it is up to the majority arbitrators to determine whether to include dissents in the award.[67]

Should the parties for any reason desire judicial registration of their award, they will find that Switzerland has become more user friendly in this respect. Some cantons have reduced the fees for such registration to an amount which, for most ICC arbitrations, will be *de minimis*.[68]

With respect to recognition and enforcement of foreign awards, the Swiss have given wide scope to the New York Convention. In 1992 Switzerland withdrew its reciprocity reservation to the New York Convention, by which the Convention had been applied to foreign awards only if rendered in the territory of another contracting state.[69]

The *LDIP* contains no explicit provisions analogous to those of the Concordat for "revision" of awards obtained by fraudulently procured evidence or rendered in ignorance of decisive evidentiary elements.[70] However, the *Tribunal fédéral* has exercised its power to fill what it perceives to be a gap ("*combler une lacune*") in the *LDIP*, by declaring itself to have power to hear requests for revision of awards based on false factual assumptions or influenced by a criminal offense.[71] *Révision* is available only with respect to facts occurring prior to the award but not known to the applicant during the proceedings. Should the *Tribunal fédéral* determine *révision* is justified, the matter would normally be remanded to the arbitrator who initially handled the case. A request for *révision* must be filed within ninety (90) days following discovery of the relevant facts.[72]

---

66   *See* Laurent Lévy, *Dissenting Opinions in International Arbitration in Switzerland*, 5 ARB. INT. 35 (1989), examining the issue under the *Concordat*. *See also* E. Bucher, *Arbitration under the ICC Rules in Switzerland*, in SWISS ESSAYS ON INTERNATIONAL ARBITRATION 127-37 (C. Reymond and E. Bucher, eds. 1984). *See generally* Working Party on Dissenting Opinions and Interim and Partial Awards, Adopted by the ICC Commission 21 April 1988, 2 ICC BULL. (No. 1)32 (1991).

67   PIERRE JOLIDON, COMMENTAIRE DU CONCORDAT SUISSE SUR L'ARBITRAGE (1984) 481.

68   *See Loi genevoise modifiant la loi sur les droits d'enregistrement (jugements arbitraux)*, 8 November 1996, amending Article 124(2)(b) of *Loi sur les droits d'enregistrement*. Registration fees are now fixed at a maximum of 1500 Swiss Francs.

69   *See Message concernant le retrait de quatre réserves faites à quatre conventions multilatérales en matière de droit international privé et de procédure civile internationale*, 19 February 1992, Conseil fédéral suisse (No. 92.023).

70   *Contrast Concordat* Article 41. The award must be affected by acts punishable under Swiss criminal law or rendered in ignorance of important facts in existence prior to the award, or evidence of decisive importance, which for some reason could not have been presented to the arbitrators during the proceedings.

71   *See* ATF 118 II 199 (1992), at 202-203, P. v. S., allowing the court to review a decision resting on findings "fausses ou influencées par un crime ou un délit." *See* commentary by Gabrielle Kaufmann & Laurent Lévy, 1998 INT. A. L.R. (No. 4) N-69. In the instant case, the court refused to find grounds for revision. *See also Tribunal fédéral*, Iére Cour Civile, 1 Nov. 1996, P. v. A, 15 SWISS BULL. 116 (1997).

72   *Tribunal fédéral*, 9 July 1997, N. Aluminum Plant v. Société E. et Société S., 15 SWISS BULL. 509 (1997).

If an award as to which review has been excluded under *LDIP* Article 192 is to be enforced in Switzerland, the provisions of the New York Convention relating to foreign awards will apply by analogy in any enforcement action.

CHAPTER 34

UNITED STATES LAW

34.01   Statutory Framework

(a) The Federal Arbitration Act

The Federal Arbitration Act (FAA)[1] applies to all international commercial arbitration conducted in the United States,[2] and vests federal courts with jurisdiction over cases arising under the New York Convention.[3] Although the UNCITRAL Model Arbitration Law has received attention from some arbitration specialists,[4] to date there have been no serious proposals for its adoption

---

[1]   9 U.S.C. Enacted in 1925, Chapter I of the FAA has remained basically unchanged except for two amendments added in 1988: § 15 (inapplicability of the Act of State Doctrine) and § 16 (appeals from district court orders). Chapter II (implementing the New York Convention) was enacted in 1970 and Chapter III (giving effect to the Panama Convention) in 1990. For a recent proposal to amend the FAA *see* Joseph Becker, *Fixing the Federal Arbitration Act by the Millenium*, 8 AM. REV. INT'L ARB. 75 (1997).

[2]   The Federal Arbitration Act includes within its scope "a written provision in any . . . contract evidencing a transaction involving [interstate or international] commerce," a notion to which the U.S. Supreme Court has given a broad interpretation. *See* Allied-Bruce Terminix v. Dobson, 513 U.S. 265 (1995). Non-binding arbitration has been held to come within the scope of the FAA. *See* Wolsey v. Foodmaker, 144 F.3d 1205 (9th Cir. 1998).

[3]   *See* 9 U.S.C. § 203. Any action arising under the New York Convention may be removed from a state to a federal court. *See* 9 U.S.C. § 205. Absent Convention coverage, federal courts do not have jurisdiction to hear a dispute about arbitration unless the dispute raises a question of federal law or implicates the court's "diversity" jurisdiction (e.g., dispute between citizens of different states or between a U.S. citizen and an alien). *See* PCS 2000 LP v. Romulus Telecommunications, 148 F.3d 32 (1st Cir. 1998). Thus the FAA is somewhat of an anomaly, in that it creates a body of federal law without creating any basis for federal court jurisdiction, except in international cases. *See* Moses H. Cone Memorial Hospital v. Mercury Construction Corp., 460 U.S. 1, n.32 (1983).

[4]   For commentary positive to the Model Law, *see* James Carter, *Federal Arbitration Act Seen as Out of Step with Modern Laws*, 5 NEWS AND NOTES FROM INSTITUTE FOR TRANSNATIONAL LAW 1 (1990); *Report of the Committee on State International Arbitration Statutes* (ABA Subcommittee, Section on International Law and Practice, March 1990). Compare the less favorable evaluation in David Rivkin & Frances Kellner, *In Support of the FAA: An Argument Against U.S. Adoption of the UNCITRAL Model Law*, 1 AM. REV. INT'L ARB. 535 (1990); *Report of the Washington Foreign Law*

on a federal level.[5] Labor arbitration rests on a statutory foundation different from commercial arbitration,[6] as does arbitration mandated by state consumer protection and malpractice schemes,[7] and so-called court-annexed arbitration.[8]

It is sometimes said that the FAA endorses a "pro-arbitration" policy.[9] Certainly American judges and legislators have manifested a benevolent attitude toward arbitration on many matters, such as arbitrator immunity,[10] immediate appeal of orders refusing to compel arbitration,[11] and presumptions about subject matter arbitrability.[12]

Society on the UNCITRAL Model Law on International Commercial Arbitration, reprinted in 3 OHIO ST. J. ON DISP. RESOL. 303 (1988); *Report of the Committee on Arbitration and Alternative Dispute Resolution, Association of the Bar of the City of New York, reprinted in* 1988-89 ARBITRATION AND THE LAW 250 (1989).

5   Several states, however, have adopted statutes patterned on the UNCITRAL Model.

6   29 U.S.C. § 185, codifying § 301 of the 1947 Taft Hartley Act. By its own terms the FAA excludes "contracts of employment" from its coverage. A broad interpretation would exclude all employment agreements. A narrower interpretation excludes only employment agreements arrived at by collective bargaining. The narrowest of all—at present the majority view—excludes only contracts involving classes of workers who are directly engaged in the transport of goods or the provision of services in foreign or interstate commerce. *See* Tenney Eng'g, Inc. v. United Elec., Radio & Mach. Workers, 207 F.2d 450 (3d Cir. 1953); Signal-Stat Corp. v. United Elec., etc., 235 F.2d 298 (2d Cir. 1956); Dickstein v. DuPont, 443 F.2d 783 (1st. Cir. 1971); Miller Brewing Co. v. Brewery Workers Local Union No. 9, 739 F.2d 1159 (7th Cir. 1984).

7   *See, e.g.,* Mass. Gen. Laws Ann. Ch. 90, §7N1/2 which requires all automobile manufacturers to submit to state-certified "new car arbitration" when a dispute exists as to a car's conformity to express or implied warranties that affect the safety, use or market value of the car. *See also* Maryland Health Care Malpractice Claims Act, Md. Code (1974, 1980 Rep. Vol., 1981 Cum. Supp.), §§ 3-2A-01 through 3-2A-09.

8   28 U.S.C. § 651. *See generally,* Lisa Bernstein, *Understanding the Limits of Court-Connected ADR: A Critique of Federal Court Annexed Arbitration Programs,* 141 U. PENN. L. REV. 2169 (1993).

9   *See* Mastrobuono v. Shearson Lehman Hutton, 514 U.S. 52, 56 & 62 (1995); Gilmer v. Interstate/ Johnson Lane Corp., 500 U.S. 20, 24 (1991); Mitsubishi Motors Corp. v. Soler Chrysler-Plymouth, Inc., 473 U.S. 614, 625 (1985); Dean Witter Reynolds Inc. v. Byrd, 470 U.S. 213, 219 - 221, and n.6 (1985); Moses H. Cone Hospital v. Mercury Construction Corp., 460 U.S. 1, 24 (1983); Scherk v. Alberto-Culver Co., 417 U.S. 506, 510, and n.4 (1974); Hewlett-Packard Co. v. Berg, 61 F.3d 101, 104 (1st Cir. 1995); Securities Indus. Assn. v. Connolly, 883 F.2d 1114, 1122 (1st Cir. 1989).

10   Generally, arbitrators in the United States (like judges) enjoy immunity from civil liability for acts performed in their decision-making capacity, even when incorrect or careless. *See* cases cited in David Branson & Richard Wallace, *Immunity of Arbitrators under United States Law,* in THE IMMUNITY OF ARBITRATORS 85 (Julian Lew, ed. 1990).

11   *See* discussion of 9 U.S.C. § 16 *infra* in Section 34.04.

12   *See* Mitsubishi Motors v. Soler Chrysler-Plymouth, 473 U.S. 614, 626 (1985) at 626 and First Options v. Kaplan, 514 U.S. 938, 943 (1995) (referring to how courts treat "silence or ambiguity about the question of whether a particular merits-related dispute is arbitrable.")

Generally, however, arbitration law in the United States provides neither incentives nor disincentives to arbitrate, but simply mandates enforcement of the parties' agreement. The FAA requires arbitration from business managers who have agreed to arbitrate, while allowing the proverbial day in court to those who have not done so.

(b) The Interaction of State and Federal Arbitration Law

Most states have enacted some form of the Uniform Arbitration Act (UAA),[13] sometimes supplemented by special statutes for international disputes.[14] The impact of state law is greatest on matters not covered by the FAA, for example the right to award legal fees.[15]

Federal arbitration law generally preempts inconsistent state statutes,[16] sometimes giving arbitration clauses greater enforceability than court selection agreements.[17] Nevertheless, state law consistent with the FAA may apply when (i) the parties agree to its application[18] or (ii) as the law of the ar-

---

13 The UAA has been adopted by all but four states (Alabama, Georgia, Idaho and Mississippi), as well as the District of Columbia, Puerto Rico, and the U.S. Virgin Islands. In 1996 the National Conference of Commissioners on Uniform Laws appointed a drafting committee to revise the Uniform Arbitration Act, which is considering *inter alia* provisions for consolidation of related arbitrations, arbitrator immunity, enforcement of interim arbitral rulings, and judicial review of questions of law if the parties so elect.

14 For example, California, Connecticut, Oregon and Texas have enacted international arbitration statutes inspired by the UNCITRAL Model Arbitration Act. *See* Cal. Code Civ. Proc. § 1297.11; Conn. Gen. Stat. § 50a-100; ORS § 36.450; Tex. Civ. Prac. & Rem. Code § 172.001. Some states, such as Florida, have adopted international arbitration statute not based on the UNCITRAL Model but incorporating many of its basic principles.

15 *See* Section 34.04.

16 *See* Allied-Bruce Terminix v. Dobson, 513 U.S. 265 (1995) where the U.S. Supreme Court reversed an Alabama decision holding that the FAA did not apply to an arbitration clause in a termite prevention contract. The Court interpreted the FAA to apply to all contracts which involve interstate commerce, rather than only to contracts which at formation "contemplated substantial interstate activity." 513 U.S. at 269. *See also* Southland Corp. v. Keating, 465 U.S. 1 (1984) (federal arbitration statute applied even with respect to claims under state regulatory regimes). *See generally* Alan Scott Rau, *The UNCITRAL Model Law in State and Federal Courts: The Case of Waiver*, 6 AM. REV. INT'L ARB. 223 (1995); Alan Scott Rau, *Does State Arbitration Law Matter At All?*, ADR Currents (AAA), June 1998, at 19; Rita Cain, *Preemption of State Arbitration Statutes: the Exaggerated Federal Policy Favoring Arbitration*, 19 J. CONTEMP. L. 1 (1993); Carlos Loumiet, Introductory Note to the Florida International Arbitration Act, 26 ILM 949 (1987).

17 *See* Doctor's Associates v. Hamilton, 150 F.3d 157 (2nd Cir. 1998) (dispute to be arbitrated under the rules of the American Arbitration Association), rejecting as "preempted by the FAA" the application of a New Jersey Supreme Court decision invalidating forum selection clauses in franchise agreements.

18 *See* Volt Information Sciences v. Board of Trustees, 489 U.S. 468 (1989), where parties provided that a construction contract would be governed by the law of "the place where the project is located," which was deemed to include California arbitration law providing stay of arbitration pending resolution of related litigation.

bitral situs it fills gaps in the FAA.[19] On some issues federal courts may be directed to look to state procedure,[20] or may adopt a choice-of-law analysis leading to application of foreign procedural norms.[21]

In practice, the rule that federal law preempts inconsistent state law does not always lend itself to simple application. Particularly when the FAA is silent, it is often less than self-evident exactly which state rules will be considered unduly restrictive. Some states, for example, specifically allow pre-award attachment,[22] permit consolidation of arbitrations arising out of related claims,[23] or restrict out-of-state lawyers' participation in arbitration.[24] All are matters on which the FAA contains no analogous provisions. Depending on perspective, these state dispositions may be perceived either to supplement [25] or to impede[26] the objectives of the FAA.[27]

---

19   *See* New England Energy, Inc. v. Keystone Shipping Co., 885 F.2d 1 (1st Cir. 1988), involving a provision of Massachusetts state law permitting courts to order consolidation of related arbitrations.

20   Under Federal Rule of Civil Procedure Rule No. 64, ". . . remedies providing for seizure of person or property. . . are available under the circumstances. . . provided by the law of the state" in which the federal court sits, unless an existing federal statute is otherwise applicable. *See generally* Lawrence Newman & Nancy Nelson, *Procedure of International Arbitration: Interim Measures of Protection, in* INTERNATIONAL COMMERCIAL ARBITRATION IN NEW YORK 99-113 (J.Stewart McClendon & Rosabel Everard Goodman eds., 1986).

21   *See* New England Utilities v. Hydro-Québec, 10 F. Supp. 2d 53 (D.Mass. 1998), where a federal court read the contract's choice-of-law clause to call for application of Québec's three-month period for award challenge, rather than the Massachusetts limit of thirty days. Surprisingly, in *dictum* the court said that the Federal Arbitration Act did not preempt state law on timeliness issues. Compare Westbrook Int'l v. Westbrook Technologies, 17 F.Supp.2d 621 (E.D. Mich. 1998) (Ontario law applicable to the merits of the dispute, but FAA governed arbitrability of claims).

22   *See, e.g.,* New York CPLR § 7502(c).

23   *See, e.g.,* Massachusetts General Laws ch. 251, § 2A.

24   *See e.g.* Birbrower, Montalbano, Condon & Frank v. Superior Court, 17 Cal. 4th 117, modified 17 Cal. 4th 563 (1998). An out-of-state law firm which represented a client in a California arbitration was held engaged in the unauthorized practice of law in California. The particular statute in question, however, contained an exception for international arbitration, and has subsequently been modified to allow nonresident attorneys to appear in California arbitrations upon filing an informational certificate with the arbitral tribunal and the local bar.

25   New England Energy, Inc. v. Keystone Shipping Co., 855 F.2d 1 (1st Cir. 1988), held that a federal court sitting in Massachusetts may order consolidation of related arbitrations pursuant to state statute.

26   In Cooper v. Ateliers de la Motobécane, S.A., 442 N.E.2d 1239 (N.Y. 1982), the New York provision on pre-award attachment was held inconsistent with the policies behind the Federal Arbitration Act and the New York Arbitration Convention. *See* discussion of federal law on pre-award attachment, Section 34.03.

27   A California court held that the Federal Arbitration Act did not preempt state law on view of awards. Siegel v. Prudential Insurance Co. of American, 67 Cal. App. 4th 1270, 79 Cal. Rptr 2d 726 (Court of Appeal 2nd Dist. 1998). An employer sought to vacate an award in favor of an employee on the basis of "manifest disregard of the law" (*see* discussion *infra* in Section 34.04) under the FAA. The California court held that state law precluded merits review of awards, and that to apply state law on this issue would not defeat the goals of the Federal Arbitration Act.

The interaction of federal and state arbitration law has been addressed in several U.S. Supreme Court decisions, not always consistent among themselves. In *Volt Information Sciences v. Board of Trustees*[28] the Court held that an arbitration in California could be stayed under provisions of state law pending resolution of related court proceedings. By their choice-of-law clause the parties were deemed to have incorporated California arbitration law into their contract.[29]

The Court's position on the effect of state law was revisited in *Mastrobuono v. Shearson Lehman Hutton*.[30] The Court upheld an arbitral award for punitive damages, notwithstanding that the relevant choice-of-law clause called for application of New York law, which prohibits arbitrators from awarding punitive damages. The contractual reference to New York was interpreted to include only substantive law, not "allocation of power between alternative tribunals." Not everyone has found it easy to square the *Volt* and *Mastrobuono* decisions.

Because the United States has no federal common law of contract, state law normally governs the formation of an arbitration agreement, just as it determines the validity of any other contract. Thus decisions about whether the parties agreed to submit to arbitration will be resolved by reference to "ordinary state law principles governing the formation of contracts."[31] Nevertheless, states may not single out arbitration clauses for threshold validity limitations more onerous than those imposed on other contracts. In *Doctor's Associates v. Casarotto*[32] the U.S. Supreme Court struck down a Montana requirement that arbitration clauses be in capital letters on the first page of the contract.

---

28   489 U.S. 468 (1989).

29   The majority stated that "where, as here, the parties have agreed to abide by state rules of arbitration, enforcing those rules according to the terms of the agreement is fully consistent with the goals of the FAA, even if the result is that the arbitration is stayed where the Act would otherwise permit it to go forward." Courts have refused to apply *Volt* to situations in which the choice of law clause impinges on the fundamental enforceability of the arbitration clause. *See* Securities Indus. Ass'n v. Connolly, 883 F.2d 1114 (1st Cir.1989) (state regulations limiting the right of securities brokers to require form arbitration agreements) and Doctor's Associate's v. Casarotto, 517 U.S. 681 (1996).

30   514 U.S. 52 (1995).

31   *See* First Options v. Kaplan, 514 U.S. 938, 943 (1995).

32   517 U.S. 681 (1996) (Federal Arbitration Act preempts Montana statute requiring arbitration clause to be "typed in underlined capitals on the first page of the contract;" dispute arising out of franchise to operate "sub" sandwich shop in Montana). A similar approach was taken by the First Circuit in Securities Industry Association v. Connolly, 883 F. 2d 1114 (1st Cir. 1989). *See also* Allied-Bruce Terminix v. Dobson, 513 U.S. 265 (1995), striking down an Alabama statute that made pre-dispute arbitration clauses unenforceable.

(c) Coverage of the New York Convention[33]

United States courts will not normally apply the Convention to agreements between Americans, unless the controversy involves foreign property, performance abroad or has "some other reasonable relation with one or more foreign states."[34] The consequence of this limitation can be significant, since the Convention extends the time normally allowed for award confirmation.[35] Accordingly, a recent ICC award rendered in the United States between two Americans was held to fall within the scope of the Convention because the contract provided for distribution of shampoo products in Poland.[36]

34.02   The Agreement to Arbitrate

(a) Basic Requirements

In the United States, the validity and scope of the arbitration agreement may be examined when motions are made to compel or to stay arbitral proceedings, or to stay a court action in favor of arbitration.[37] American courts generally will not order arbitration unless the agreement designates an arbitral seat in a country that has signed the New York Convention.[38]

Although an arbitration agreement must be in writing, it need not necessarily be signed.[39] However, performance pursuant to unsigned purchase orders

---

33   *See generally*, Alan S. Rau, *The New York Convention in American Courts*, 7 AM. REV. INT'L ARB. 213 (1996).

34   9 U.S.C. § 202. For the purpose of this section, a corporation is considered a citizen of the United States if it is incorporated or has its principal place of business in the United States. The United States applies the New York Convention subject to the two reservations. First, the Convention covers only awards made in the territory of another contracting state. Second, the Convention applies only to commercial transactions, a concept which United States courts have construed broadly, consistent with the policy of favoring arbitration.

35   Under 9 U.S.C. § 9 domestic awards may be confirmed within one year of being made, while under 9 U.S.C. § 207 courts may confirm Convention awards up to three years after being made. Different time limits apply to motions to vacate awards, which in practice often are heard at the same time as motions to confirm. If an award is made in the United States, federal courts may hear a motion to vacate within three months after the award has been delivered to the adverse party. 9 U.S.C. § 12.

36   Lander v. MMP Invs., 107 F.3d 476 (7th Cir. 1997), extending the broad coverage granted in Bergesen v. Joseph Muller Corp., 548 F. Supp. 650 (S.D.N.Y. 1982), *aff'd* 710 F.2d 928 (2d Cir. 1983) and Fuller Co. v. Compagnie des Bauxites de Guinée, 421 F. Supp. 938 (W.D. Pa. 1976). *Compare* Jones v. Sea Tow Servs., 30 F.3d 360 (2d Cir. 1994) (New York Convention held not to cover agreement between U.S. citizens just because contract provided for arbitration in London.)

37   *See* FAA §§ 3 and 4.

38   *See* National Iranian Oil Co. v. Ashland Oil, 817 F.2d 326 (5th Cir. 1987). In this connection one must remember that the United States acceded to the New York Convention subject to a "reciprocity reservation" applying the Convention only with respect to awards made in other Convention countries.

39   *See generally* Paul Friedland, *U.S. Courts' Misapplication of the "Agreement in Writing" Requirement for Enforcement of an Arbitration Agreement Under the New York Convention*, 3 INT. ARB. REP. 21 (1998).

containing an arbitration clause on their reverse sides has been deemed insufficient to meet the requirement of an "agreement in writing."[40]

(b) Separability

The legal autonomy of the arbitration clause has been well established since the U.S. Supreme Court in *Prima Paint Co. v. Flood & Conklin*.[41] Indeed, an agreement to arbitrate may be binding even when contained in an otherwise non-binding "Memorandum of Intent."[42]

(c) Repair of Defective Clauses

When the parties' expression of intent with respect to arbitration is incomplete, courts sometimes repair the arbitration clause. In *Jain v. Courier de Méré*,[43] a federal court was held to have the power to compel arbitration in its own district although the arbitration clause failed to specify either the location of the arbitration or the method of choosing arbitrators. In *Bauhinia Corp. v. China National Machinery & Equipment Import & Export Corp.*,[44] the court was confronted with two inconsistent arbitration clauses: one specifying arbitration in China, the other leaving the place of arbitration undetermined. On the assumption that an American court does not have the power to designate a foreign arbitral situs when the agreement fails to do so, the court ordered arbitration within its own district.

(d) "Non Signatories"[45]

American courts will not normally require arbitration with respect to a person that did not agree to arbitrate, even in a parent-subsidiary relation-

---

40 Kahn Lucas Lancaster v. Lark Int'l Ltd., 2d Cir. 1999, No. 97-9436. Federal law requirements may in some ways be less stringent than those of the New York Convention. *See* Sen Mar, Inc. v. Tiger Petroleum Corp., 774 F.Supp. 879 (S.D.N.Y. 1991).

41 388 U.S. 395 (1967).

42 In Republic of Nicaragua v. Standard Fruit Co., 937 F.2d 469 (9th Cir. 1991) the Court of Appeals held that the trial court had erred in determining the validity of an arbitration clause by looking to portions of the memorandum other than the arbitration clause.

43 51 F.3d 686 (7th Cir. 1995). The appeals court wrote, "Where. . . an arbitration agreement contains no provision for location, [9 U.S.C.] §4 would supplement §206 by giving a court the ability to compel arbitration in its own district." *Id.* at 689. Under 9 U.S.C. §5 courts have power to designate and appoint an arbitrator when no method has been specified by the parties.

44 819 F.2d 247 (9th Cir. 1987). Two of the three contracts contained two clauses which provided for arbitration in the event negotiations failed to settle disputes. The first clause stated "in case an arbitration is necessary and is to be held in Peking. . ." while the following clause provided "in case the Arbitration is to take place at [BLANK] . . . ."

45 Since the FAA does not require an arbitration clause to be signed (allowing an unsigned "written provision" to arbitrate, such as a telex exchange) it would be misleading to focus on lack of signature itself as tainting an arbitration clause. However, the term "nonsignatories" has long served as a useful shorthand reference to persons whose right or obligation to arbitrate may be problematic. With respect to sensitive areas such as consumer transactions and employment contracts, judicial analysis of whether a person has agreed to arbitration often interacts with issues of subject matter arbitrabilty. See discussion of "informed consent" *infra* at Section 34.02(f).

ship.[46] However, courts have occasionally extended the burdens and benefits of an arbitration clause by piercing the corporate veil or invoking theories of agency and equitable estoppel.[47]

(i) Piercing the Veil and Agency

While parent/subsidiary relationships sometimes lead courts to allow or to compel related companies to join an arbitration,[48] such joinder is by no means automatic.[49] Courts will enforce an award against a related company only when there is good reason to pierce the corporate veil. In *Carte Blanche (Singapore) v. Diners Club International*,[50] a franchisee brought an action to enforce an award against assets of the franchisor's parent corporation, Diners Club. Allowing enforcement the court noted that the parent had taken over all functions of its subsidiary, ignoring corporate formalities.[51]

The success of motions to pierce the veil will depend on the factual posture of the case. In *Ceska Sporitelina v. Unisys Corporation*,[52] the court refused to disregard the corporate structure when Unisys petitioned for arbitration pursuant to an agreement signed between a Czech financial institution and a

---

46   *See* Thomson-CSF v. American Arbitration Association, 64 F.3d 773 (2nd Cir. 1995) (recognizing five "exceptions" to the general rule that arbitration agreements do not bind non-signatories: incorporation by reference, assumption, agency, piercing of corporate veil and estoppel); Ceska Sporitelna, A.S. v. Unisys Corp., 1996 U.S. Dist. LEXIS 15435 (E.D. Pa. Oct. 10, 1996) at *12 (remarking that the general rule is "that only signatories to a contract can be bound by an arbitration clause found within the contract. . . .").

47   *See generally* John M. Townsend, *Nonsignatories and Arbitration: Agency, Alter Ego and Other Identity Issues*, 3 ADR CURRENTS 19 (September 1998).

48   *See, e.g.,* Dale Metals Corp. v. Kiwa Chemicals Industry Co., 442 F. Supp. 78 (S.D.N.Y. 1977). The federal district court held that a stay of litigation was appropriate even against companies that had not signed the arbitration agreement. The claims before the court and the claims subject to arbitration were substantially similar, and court proceedings had been commenced by a corporate affiliate of the entity that had agreed to arbitration.

49   See *Marathon Oil Co. v. Ruhrgas, A.G.*, 115 F.3d 315 (5th Cir. 1997), *rehearing en banc*, 145 F.3d 211 (5th Cir. 1998), *reversed and remanded*, 119 S. Ct. 1563 (1999), *action dismissed*, 182 F.3d 291 (5th Cir. 1999). *Amicus* brief filed on behalf of defendant, 9 WORLD ARB. & MEDIATION REP. 137 (1998), argued for broad scope for arbitration clause. American company claimed to have been fraudulently induced to invest in North Sea gas venture; removal of case from state to federal court under 9 U.S.C. § 205 (discussed *supra* note 3) depended on whether dispute was covered by arbitration clause signed by subsidiary of American plaintiff. The Circuit Court's first decision (later vacated) found that alleged fraud was independent of the contract containing the arbitration agreement. The Court subsequently held that German defendant lacked "minimum contacts" with forum necessary to justify court's personal jurisdiction. For another case finding lack of minimum contacts in the context of international arbitration, see Creighton Ltd. v. Government of Qatar, 181 F.3d 118 (D.C. Cir. 1999).

50   2 F.3d 24 (2d Cir. 1993).

51   *Id.* at 28. The court stated "[U]nder New York's law of piercing the corporate veil [enforcement of judgment against Diners Club] is not only appropriate, it is manifestly required in this case."

52 . 1996 U.S. Dist. LEXIS 15435 (E.D. Pa. Oct. 10, 1996), *stay denied, aff'd without op.*, 116 F.3d 467 (3d Cir. 1997), *mot. granted, cert. denied*, 118 S. Ct. 739 (1998).

Dutch subsidiary of Unisys. Similarly in *Dayhoff, Inc. v. H.J. Heinz Co.*,[53] the court found that unless an agency theory applied, only signatories could be bound by the arbitration and forum selection clauses.

In one case a court refused to compel a corporate parent to arbitrate, but went on to suggest that an award might be enforced against the parent either "as a guarantor . . . or on an *alter ego* theory." The court speculated that American construction companies might be bound by the results of an arbitration brought against a foreign subsidiary by subcontractors on a Singapore construction project.[54]

In some cases nonsignatories can be bound to arbitrate on an agency theory. In *Pritzker v. Merrill Lynch, Pierce, Fenner & Smith, Inc.*[55] an arbitration agreement was enforced as to a sister corporation on the basis that its interests were "directly related to" the conduct of the signatory.[56]

(ii) Equitable Estoppel

When legal and factual issues are substantially the same in related disputes, it may seem unfair to allow one side to pick and choose between judicial proceedings and arbitration with respect to several related adverse parties. In such cases courts sometimes order arbitration on a theory of "equitable estoppel." A claimant attempts to join a non-party "offensively," to include a defendant's parent with a deep financial pocket, while a respondent seeks a "defensive" joinder in the hope of making the award *res judicata* against the parent, thus forestalling a jury trial.

For example, in *Roberson v. The Money Tree of Alabama, Inc.*[57] the plaintiffs alleged that several defendants had acted in concert fraudulently to compel them to buy unnecessary loan insurance. Ordering the plaintiffs to arbitrate their claims against a defendant who had not signed the loan agreement, the court reasoned that the claims against the non-signatory were inextricably bound up with the loan agreement.[58] Another case, *Sunkist Soft Drinks, Inc.*

---

53 86 F.3d 1287 (3rd Cir. 1996), *amended, on reh'g,* 1996 U.S. App. LEXIS 18266 (3d Cir. Pa. July 24, 1996), *and cert. denied* 117 S. Ct. 583 (1996). The case arose out of the termination of three contracts between Dayhoff and Heinz Dolciaria S.p.A. following the sale of Heinz Dolciaria S.P.A. to Hershey. Hershey had argued that the arbitration and forum selection clauses applied to non-signatories to the agreements because "their conduct [was] so closely related to the contractual relationship between Heinz Dolciaria and Dayhoff. . . ." 86 F.3d at 1295.

54 Builders Federal (Hong Kong), Ltd. v. Turner Constr. Co., 655 F.Supp. 1400 (S.D.N.Y. 1987).

55 7 F.3d 1110 (3rd Cir. 1993).

56 *Id.* at 1122. The dispute arose out of a financial consultant's unauthorized purchase of risky investments for a pension plan. The nonsignatories whom the court ordered to arbitration were the financial consultant, and the sister corporation of the brokerage firm for whom the financial consultant worked.

57 954 F. Supp. 1519 (M.D. Ala. 1997).

58 954 F. Supp. at 1528.

v. Sunkist Grower,[59] involved a licensing agreement to market an orange drink. After a corporate licensee was purchased by another corporation, the licensor brought a claim against the new parent company for interference with the license agreement. The new owner successfully moved to compel arbitration on a theory of equitable estoppel, arguing that the claims were "intimately founded in and intertwined with" the license agreement.[60] And in *J.J. Ryan & Sons v. Rhone Poulenc Textile*[61] that court decided that arbitration clauses contained in distribution agreements with corporate affiliates required that charges against the parent should be referred to arbitration "[w]hen charges against a parent company and its subsidiary are based on the same facts and are inherently inseparable."[62]

(e) Preliminary Jurisdictional Determinations

In connection with a motion to compel arbitration or to stay litigation, the matter of who decides arbitral jurisdiction—courts or arbitrators—is not always clear.[63] In *Three Valleys Municipal Water District v. E.F. Hutton & Company, Inc.,*[64] several governmental bodies that had opened securities account agreements containing arbitration clauses brought a court action for wrongful conduct resulting in several million dollars in damages. The broker-dealer's motion to compel arbitration was opposed on the ground that the individual who signed the agreements lacked the authority to do so. The Court of Appeals held that judges rather than arbitrators must decide whether an arbitration agreement is binding in the context of a motion to compel arbitration.

---

59   10 F.3d 753 (11th Cir. 1993). Sunkist Soft Drinks was originally owned by General Cinema Corporation, and set up to market and produce an orange soda which would bear the "Sunkist" trademark owned by Sunkist Growers. Subsequently, Sunkist Soft Drinks was purchased by Del Monte.

60   *Id.* at 758. *See also* Gulf Guar. Life Ins. Co., v. Connecticut Gen. Life Ins. Co., 957 F. Supp. 839 (S.D. Miss. 1997).

61   863 F.2d 315 (4th Cir. 1988). When Rhone Poulenc Textile decided to have its affiliates distribute their own products it offered to buy Ryan. They were unable to decide upon a price because Ryan rejected Rhone Poulenc's valuation of its good will. Ryan alleged that Rhone Poulenc then influenced its affiliates to terminate their agreements with Ryan.

62   *See also* Lawson Fabrics, Inc. v. Akzona, Inc., 355 F. Supp. 1146 (S.D. N.Y. 1973); Sam Reisfeld & Son Import Co. v. S.A. Eteco, 530 F.2d 679 (5th Cir. 1976); Universal Am. Barge Corp. v. J-Chem, Inc., 946 F.2d 1131 (5th Cir. 1991) (action concerning fumigation liability for damage cargo; possible that arbitral award collaterally stopped action against nonparty fumigator); Usina Costa Pinto v. Louis Dreyfus Sugar Company, 933 F. Supp. 1170 (S.D.N.Y. 1996) (sugar trading company allegedly defrauded manufacturers before substituting in its place another company); American Bureau of Shipping v. Tencara Shipyard, 170 F.3d 349 (2d Cir. 1999) (yacht owners required to arbitrate under arbitration clause in shipbuilder's contract with ship classification society).

63   When the question is presented in the context of a motion to vacate an award, the matter has been addressed more squarely. *See* United States Supreme Court decision in *First Options v. Kaplan,* discussed in Section 34.04.

64   925 F.2d 1136 (9th Cir. 1991).

A different approach was taken in *Apollo Computer v. Berg*,[65] where a contract between a Massachusetts computer company and a Swedish distributor was terminated and the rights of the now bankrupt Swedish distributor were assigned to a third party. The court held that the validity of the ICC arbitration clause was a question for arbitrators themselves to decide, since the ICC rules called for the ICC to refer to the arbitrators any objections to the validity of an arbitration agreement as long as the ICC was "satisfied of the *prima facie* existence" of the arbitration agreement.[66]

At present, American courts disagree on whether judges or arbitrators should determine the threshold jurisdictional issue of whether time limits on the filing of arbitration claims have been met. In decisions involving considerable linguistic acrobatics, the Circuits have been evenly divided with respect to "eligibility requirements" in securities arbitration that require disputes to be brought within a fixed term after the controverted events.[67] Some have considered time limits contained in arbitration rules to constitute a jurisdictional prerequisite to be determined by courts, while others have held the matter to be for the arbitrator.[68]

Analogous issues related to statutes of limitations have sometimes been subject to a different approach. Generally judges determine the timeliness of a motion to compel arbitration,[69] while arbitrators determine the timeliness of

---

65   886 F.2d 469, 473 (1st Cir. 1989). Compare the approach in Société Générale de Surveillance v. Raytheon European Management & Systems Co., 643 F. 2d. 863 (1st Cir. 1981).

66   *See* Article 8(3) of the 1975 ICC Rules, in force at the time Apollo v. Berg was decided. Currently, this matter is dealt with in Article 6 (2) of the Rules, which contain a slightly different formulation of the same basic principle. The ICC must be *"prima facie* satisfied that an arbitration agreement may exist," rather than "satisfied of the *prima facie* existence" of the agreement. At least one commentator has asked whether the reasoning in *Apollo* might reveal itself to presume its own conclusion, since if on examination of the facts of the case the arbitration agreement revealed itself to have been invalid, then the ICC Arbitration Rules might be irrelevant. *See* William W. Park, *The Arbitrability Dicta in First Options v. Kaplan: What Sort of Kompetenz-Kompetenz Has Crossed the Atlantic?*, 12 ARB. INT. 137 (1996).

67   *See* Nat'l Ass'n of Sec. Dealers Code of Arb. Proc., Rule 10304 (formerly § 15) (providing that "no dispute, claim or controversy shall be eligible for submission to arbitration under this Code where six years have elapsed from the occurrence or event giving rise to the act or dispute, claim or controversy."). *See generally* Sean Costello, *Time Limits Under Rule 10304 of the NASD Code of Arbitration Procedure: Making Arbitrators More Like Judges or Judges More Like Arbitrators*, 52 BUS. LAW. 283 (1996); Lawrence W. Newman & Charles M. Davidson, *Arbitrability of Timeliness Defenses: Who Decides?*, 14 (No. 2) J. INT. ARB., June 1997, at 137; David Rivkin, *Courts Differ on Arbitrability of Time Limitations*, 1 ADR CURRENTS, Autumn 1996, at 21. Under recently proposed changes to the NASD rules, the six year eligibility rule would be suspended for a three year period.

68   *See* summary of cases in PaineWebber Inc. v. Elahi, 87 F.3d 589, 601 (1st Cir. 1996), holding that time bars applied to arbitrators, and citing language in NASD CODE OF ARBITRATION PROCE-DURE § 35 which permitted arbitrators to "interpret and determine the applicability of all provisions under this Code." *See* also discussion of *compétence-compétence* and First Options v. Kaplan, 514 U.S. 938 (1995), Section 34.4.

69   *See* National Iranian Oil Co. v. Mapco Int'l, Inc., 983 F.2d 485 at 491 (3d Cir. 1992) (looking to the Federal Arbitration Act). Since the FAA does not specify a statute of limitations, the court rea-

the underlying claim.[70] This approach assumes two separate time limits: one applicable to the principal agreement (to buy, sell, license, lease or lend) and one applicable to the agreement to arbitrate the dispute. Since the arbitrators' job is to apply the relevant substantive law to decide whether there should be recovery, the arbitral tribunal may be called to determine whether such recovery is permitted or barred under the statute of limitations contained in the applicable substantive law. In some cases, however, the applicable law might reserve to courts the matter of the claim's timeliness.[71]

Occasionally, the effect of one arbitrator's decision will become an issue in a subsequent arbitral proceeding. Courts in the United States have held that arbitrators rather than judges generally will decide whether to give *res judicata* effect to a prior award, at least if the parties have not manifested a contrary intent on the issue.[72]

(f) Subject Matter Arbitrability[73]

In the past American courts viewed many subjects as being of such vital public interest that resolution of related disputes was reserved for judges alone.[74] However, judicial resistance to arbitration of public law claims has eroded over the past twenty-five years.

---

soned that it must borrow the most closely analogous one from state law under the conflict of laws principles of the state in which the court sits.

70   *See id.* at 491. *See also* Avant Petroleum Inc. v. Pecten Arabian, Ltd., 696 F. Supp. 42 (S.D.N.Y. 1988).

71   *See* Smith Barney, Harris Upham & Co. v. Luckie, 85 N.Y.2d 193 (N.Y. 1995) (holding that N.Y. C.P.L.R. §§ 7502(b) and 7503(a) require courts to decide statute-of-limitations questions). *Contrast* PaineWebber Inc. v. Bybyk, 81 F.3d 1193, 1200 (2d Cir. 1996) (holding that the *Mastrobuono* reasoning requires the choice of New York law to be interpreted to refer to New York substantive law only, so as to exclude the New York procedural law that sends statute-of-limitations questions to courts).

72   *See* John Hancock Mut. Life. Ins. Co. v. Olick, 151 F. 3d 132 (3d Cir. 1998); Fire Ins. Co. v. National Gypsum Co., 101 F. 3d 813 (2nd Cir. 1996).

73   American courts often use the term "arbitrability" in speaking of the scope of the arbitration clause, as well as public policy limits on what subjects may be submitted to arbitrators at all. *See* discussion of First Options v. Kaplan, *infra* Section 34.04. To promote clarity, this chapter uses "arbitrability" only with respect to subject matter limits.

74   Such non-arbitrable subjects have at one time or another included securities regulation, patents, pension claims, the Racketeer Influenced and Corrupt Organizations Act, bankruptcy matters, the Commodities Exchange Act, the Civil Rights Act, competition law, state franchise law and punitive damages.

Significantly for ICC arbitration, the U.S. Supreme Court has ended federal limits on arbitrability of claims relating to securities regulation,[75] antitrust,[76] and maritime transport,[77] as well as many state restrictions on subject matter arbitrability.[78] Lower federal courts have shown an increasing willingness to allow arbitration even though one of the parties has filed for protection under the Bankruptcy Code.[79]

Certain subject matter limits on arbitrability remain, however. Most of these, however, will be relevant only to non-international disputes arising from consumer contracts and employment agreements.[80] Although age discrimination claims may be submitted to arbitration,[81] courts occasionally refuse to compel arbitration of employment discrimination claims,[82] sometimes due to

---

75   In 1989 the Supreme Court finally overruled its 1953 decision that had prohibited arbitration of securities disputes. *See* Rodriguez de Quijas v. Shearson/American Express, Inc. 490 U.S. 477 (1989). A double standard of arbitrability for securities disputes (whereby greater deference was accorded to arbitration of international than domestic disputes) had already been announced in 1974 by the Supreme Court in Scherk v. Alberto-Culver Co., 417 U.S. 506 (1974). *See generally* Matthew Press, *Arbitration of Claims Under the Securities Exchange Act of 1934*, 77 B.U.L.REV. 629 (1997).

76   *See* Mitsubishi Motors Corp. v. Soler Chrysler-Plymouth, Inc., 473 U.S. 614 (1985). An apparently routine termination of an automobile distributorship led the Supreme Court in a landmark decision to enforce an agreement to arbitrate all aspects of an international commercial dispute, including antitrust issues raised by the counterclaim.

77   *See* Vimar Seguros y Reaseguros, S.A. v. M/V Sky Reefer, 515 U.S. 528 (1995). A standard form bill of lading was issued in connection with the transport of a shipload of Moroccan oranges to Massachusetts. The purchaser and insurer opposed arbitration unsuccessfully on the basis that the Carriage of Good by Sea Act prohibits any "lessening of liability" for loss due to negligence or failure in duties under the Act, an argument which presumed that arbitrators might misapply the law in a way that reduced the carrier's responsibility.

78   *See* Southland v. Keating, 465 U.S. 1 (1984); KKN Enterprises v. Gloria Jean's Gourmet Coffees, 1st Cir. 1999, No. 98-2337. See generally § 34.01(b).

79   *See* Société Nationale Algérienne Pour La Recherche, etc. v. Distrigas Corp., 80 B.R. 606 (D. Mass. 1987); Mitsubishi Motors Corp. v. Soler Chrysler-Plymouth, Inc., 814 F.2d 844 (1st Cir. 1987). *See also*, Philip O'Neill, *Recent Developments in International Arbitration: An American Perspective*, 4 J. INT. ARB. (No. 1) 7, 15-20 (1987).

80   In some cases federal government agencies are by statute prohibited from agreeing to arbitration of contract disputes (Contract Disputes Act, 41 USC §§ 601 et seq.) except in the case of contracts with foreign government or international organizations 41 USC § 602(C)

81   *See* Gilmer v. Interstate/Johnson Lane Corp., 500 U.S. 20 (1991), distinguishing its previous holding in Alexander v. Gardner-Denver Co., 415 U.S. 36 (1974), which had held that an employee who arbitrates contractual rights under a collective-bargaining agreement is not precluded from asserting non-contractual statutory rights in court. *Gilmer* arose from an individual employment contract (rather than a collective-bargaining agreement) that gave the arbitrator broad power to arbitrate the statutory claims. See also Wright v. Universal Maritime Service Corp., 119 S.Ct. 391 (1998), concerning the adequacy of waiver of access to courts for statutory rights.

82   *See* Renteria v. Prudential Ins. Co. of Am., 113 F.3d 1104 (9th Cir. 1997), and Prudential Ins. Co. of Am. v. Lai 42 F.3d 1299 (9th Cir. 1994) (sexual harassment and discrimination claims), where it was held that there had been no knowing waiver of the right to litigate statutory claims also. *See also* Pryner v. Tractor Supply Co., 109 F.3d 354 (7th Cir. 1997), *cert. denied*, 118 S.Ct. 295

skepticism about the fairness of the arbitral process and the voluntariness ("informed consent") of the arbitration clause rather than the subject matter's arbitrability.[83] Courts have invalidated both a self-administered dispute resolution system[84] and an arbitral regime requiring a disproportionately high filing fee.[85]

One recent New York state decision struck down as "unconscionable" an ICC arbitration clause in a consumer sale of computer and software products, due to what the court considered the excessive costs of ICC arbitration in a consumer contract.[86] By contrast at least two decisions have enforced arbitration clauses packaged in boxes of mail-order goods.[87] Courts are divided in their

---

(1997) (discrimination claims related to race and age are arbitrable only if a worker explicitly consents; union cannot through collective bargaining agreement contract away an individual member's right to litigate statutory rights claims); Cole v. Burns Int. Sec. Serv., 105 F.3d 1465 (D.C. Cir. 1997) (racial discrimination claim subject to arbitration, but employer may not require employee to pay arbitrators' fees). The U.S. Equal Employment Opportunity Commission has also issued a policy statement taking the position that agreements which, as a condition of employment, impose binding arbitration of employment discrimination claims are "contrary to the fundamental principles evinced in" American employment discrimination laws. *See* EEOC Notice No. 915.002 (July 10, 1997). In at least one case the judge ordered discovery into the adequacy of the relevant arbitration rules to resolve claimants' discrimination claims.

83   *See* Rosenberg v. Merrill Lynch, 170 F.3d 1 (1st Cir. 1999), finding that Congress did not intend to preclude pre-dispute arbitration agreements with respect to discrimination claims, and that there was no "structural bias" in the NYSE arbitration system. However, Merrill Lynch had not familiarized the employee with the scope of the arbitration clause by providing her a copy of the NYSE rules. Consequently the employee did not "knowingly and voluntarily" consent to arbitration of the relevant claims.

84   *See* Engalla v. Permanente Med. Group, 938 P.2d 903 (Cal. 1997) (subjecting a malpractice claim against a health care provider in the Kaiser group to an arbitration clause). The *ad hoc* nature of the arbitration, which left administration to the parties rather than an independent institution, resulted in delay that caused a procedural asymmetry favoring the defendant health care provider. The trial court found fraud in the inducement, and thus allowed the deceased patient's heirs to rescind the agreement to arbitrate. The Court of Appeals decision to reverse the trial court was itself reversed by the Supreme Court of California, which remanded the case back to the trial court after finding that the habitual delays in the process constituted evidence of fraud by Kaiser.

85   *See* Teleserve Sys., Inc. v. MCI Telecommunications Corp., 230 A.D.2d 585 (N.Y. App. Div. 1997). Teleserve entered into an agreement to serve as MCI's agent in marketing MCI services. The court found unconscionable an agreement that included a clause providing for arbitration under the rules of an organization which required a filing fee based on the amount in dispute, which in the case at bar would have amounted to $ 204,000 on claimant's request for $ 40,000,000 in compensatory damages.

86   Brower v. Gateway 2000, 676 N.Y.S. 2d 569 (A.D. 1 Dept. 1998). Citing UCC § 2-302, the court noted that the deposit on costs was more than the cost of most of the manufacturer's products (*Id.* at 571), and expressed the opinion that the cost "necessarily entailed in arbitrating before the ICC is unreasonable and surely serves to deter the individual consumer from invoking the process." *Id.* at 574.

87   *See, e.g.*, Hill v. Gateway 2000, Inc., 105 F.3d 1147, 1148 (7th Cir. 1997) (arbitration clause in box containing computer ordered by mail and not returned within thirty days; court stated that "[a] contract need not be read to be effective."), *reh'g denied* 105 F.3d 1147 (7th Cir. 1997) *and cert. denied*, 118 S. Ct. 47 (1997); ProCD, Inc. v. Zeidenberg, 86 F.3d 1447 (7th Cir. 1996) (terms

willingness to enforce arbitration of consumer finance disputes[88] and malpractice claims.[89]

Unlike Europe[90] the United States has no comprehensive nation-wide legislative scheme for addressing potentially abusive arbitration clauses,[91] a gap that has led to a lively dialogue on the fairness of arbitration.[92] Complicating matters further is the fact that state law may not subject arbitration agreements to requirements inapplicable to other contracts.[93] Thus a state law requiring an arbitration clause to be signed by both parties would arguably be invalid, as singling out arbitration clauses for undue burdens.[94]

---

of arbitration clause inside software box).

88 *See* Bell v. Congress Mortgage Co., 24 Cal. App. 4th 1675 (1st Dist. 1994), *ordered depublished* 30 Cal. Rptr. 2d 205 (1994) (refusing to compel arbitration absent a "clear and informed" waiver of the right to a jury trial when a homeowner claims against mortgage lenders for fraudulent business practices); Lopez v. Plaza Finance Co., 1996 WL 210073 (N.D.Ill. April 25, 1996) (no enforcement of arbitration agreement in installment loan); Patterson v. ITT Consumer Fin. Corp., 14 Cal. App. 4th 1659 (1st. Dist. 1993) (arbitration clause used in documentation for relatively small loans was an unconscionable limit on the borrower's opportunity to be heard); Badie v. Bank of America, 67 Cal. App. 4th 779, 79 Cal. Rptr. 2d 273 (1998) (finding customer did not consent to bank's unilateral imposition of arbitration clause through "bill stuffer" notice with customer's monthly account statement), Court of Appeal reversed trial court decision in 1994 WL 660730 (Cal.Super. Aug. 18, 1994) (No. 944916) *not certified for publication.* Randolph v. Green Tree Financial Group, 11th Cir. 1999, No. 98-6055 (no arbitration of Truth in Lending Act claims). By contrast, arbitration clauses were enforced in McCarthy v. Providential Corp., 1994 WL 387852 (N.D. Cal. July 18, 1994) (senior citizen "reverse mortgage"); Meyers v. Univest Home Loan, 1993 WL 307747 (N.D.Cal. Aug. 5, 1993) (consumer loan).

89 *See* Wilson v. Kaiser Found. Hosps., 141 Cal. App. 3d 891 (3d Dist. 1983); Colorado Permanente Med. Group, P.C. v. Evans, 926 P.2d 1218 (Colo. 1996); Madden v. Kaiser Found. Hosp., 552 P.2d 1178 (Cal. 1976); Wheeler v. St. Joseph Hosp., 63 Cal. App. 3d 345 (4th Dist. 1976); Engalla v. Permanente Med. Group, Inc. 938 P.2d 903 (Cal. 1997).

90 *See* Council Directive 93/13/EEC, 1993 O.J. (L95) 29 (Apr. 21, 1993). *See also* English Arbitration Act, 1996, § 89, implementing U.K. Unfair Terms in Consumer Contracts Regulations (1994) §§ 3 & 4, and French Civil Code allowing only post-dispute agreements to arbitrate (*compromis*) (Code Civil Article 2060) unless the agreement has been concluded between merchants (*commerçants*) (Code de commerce Article 631).

91 In both the House and the Senate, however, bills are currently being considered to curb "involuntary application of arbitration" to employment discrimination claims. *See* Civil Rights Procedures Protection Act of 1997, S. 63 and H.R. 983, 105th Cong., 1st Sess., making, *inter alia*, the Federal Arbitration Act, 9 U.S.C. §§ 1-15 (1994), inapplicable to any claim of discrimination based on race, color, religion, sex, national origin, age or disability.

92 *See* Paul D. Carrington & Paul H. Haagen, *Contract and Jurisdiction*, 1996 SUP. CT. REV. 331 (1996); Thomas Carbonneau, *Arbitral Justice: The Demise of Due Process in American Law*, 70 TUL. L. REV. 1945 (1996); G. Richard Shell, *Fair Play, Consent and Securities Arbitration: A Comment on Speidel*, 62 BROOK. L. REV. 1365 (1996); Richard E. Speidel, *Contract Theory and Securities Arbitration: Whither Consent?*, 62 BROOK. L. REV. 1335 (1996); Jeffrey W. Stempel, *Bootstrapping and Slouching Toward Gomorrah: Arbitral Infatuation and the Decline of Consent*, 62 BROOK. L. REV. 1381 (1996); Stephen J. Ware, *Employment Arbitration and Voluntary Consent*, 25 HOFSTRA L. REV. 83 (1996).

93 *See* discussion of Doctor's Assoc. v. Casarotto, Section 34.01.

94 *See* Christine Williams v. Direct Cable and Beneficial National Bank, No. CV-97-009 (Ala. Cir. Ct. for Henry County, Aug. 13, 1997) in which an Alabama Circuit Court granted a motion to compel

Notwithstanding the benevolent judicial attitudes toward arbitration, courts continue to condemn as against public policy an arbitration clause that operates in tandem with a choice of law clause as a "prospective waiver" of the right to pursue statutory remedies for antitrust violations.[95] The extent of this "prospective waiver" doctrine was tested in a spate of cases involving clauses calling for resolution in England under English law of claims brought by American investors in the well-known Lloyd's insurance syndicates.[96] It had been argued that such forum selection mechanisms operated as *de facto* waivers of rights under the federal securities laws. To date, Circuit Courts have found the policies in favor of enforcing arbitration and court selection clauses to outweigh whatever benefit might obtain from having the disputes heard in United States courts. If a law less investor friendly than that of England is chosen, however, it might not be so clear that claimants have adequate remedies to vindicate their substantive legal rights.

(g) Class Actions

Generally a class action must be expressly authorized in the arbitration agreement or the applicable arbitration rules.[97] Under FAA § 4 courts have the power to enforce the parties agreement only as drafted, and thus will not order the claims to proceed on a class basis absent the parties' consent.[98]

---

arbitration pursuant to a "mail out change" to a credit agreement on the theory that to refuse enforcement to the modification would "place arbitration contracts in an inferior position to other contracts."

95   In *Mitsubishi* the Court insisted that in the case at bar the arbitrators should apply American antitrust law, despite the choice of law clause designating Swiss law. *Mitsubishi*, 473 U.S. 614, at 637, n.19.

96   *See* Riley v. Kingsley Underwriting Agencies, Ltd., 969 F.2d 953 (10th Cir. 1992); Roby v. Corporation of Lloyd's, 996 F.2d 1353 (2d Cir. 1993), Shell v. R.W. Sturge, Ltd. 55 F. 3d 1227 (6th Cir. 1995); Bonny v. Society of Lloyd's, 3 F.3d 156 (7th Cir. 1993); Allen v. Lloyd's of London, 94 F.3d 923 (4th Cir. 1996); Haynsworth v. Corporation, 121 F.3d 956 (5th Cir. 1997); Richards v. Lloyd's of London 107 F.3d 1422 (9th Cir. 1997), *reh'g en banc, granted* 121 F.3d 565 (1997), *and op. withdrawn, substituted op., on recons., en banc,* 135 F. 3d 1289 (1998).

97   *See* Champ v. Siegel Trading Co. Inc., 55 F.3d 269 (7th Cir. 1995); Gammaro v. Thorp Consumer Discount Co., 828 F. Supp. 673 (D. Minn. 1993); McCarthy v. Providential Corp., 1994 WL 387852 (N.D. Cal. July 18, 1994), *appeal dismissed,* 122 F.3d 1242 (1997), *motion for cert. filed* (May 26, 1998); Randolph v. Green Tree Fin. Corp., 991 F.Supp. 1410 (M.D. Ala. 1998). Some companies have put arbitration provisions in their consumer contracts as a defense against class actions. *See* Alan S. Kaplinsky and Mark J. Levin, *Excuse me but who's the predator: Banks can use arbitration clauses as a defense,* Business Law Today, May/June 1988 at 24.

98   Here as elsewhere, however, state law may play a role. *See* Blue Cross of California v. Superior Court, 67 Ca. App. 4th 42, 78 Cal. Rptr. 2nd 779 (1998), review denied 13 January 1999, where the California Court of Appeal allowed classwide arbitration under California law, on the theory that this aspect of state was not preempted by the Federal Arbitration Act. On the interaction of state and federal arbitration law, see generally Section 34.01(b).

34.03   Interlocutory Matters

(a) Assistance to the Arbitration

Although the FAA gives the arbitral tribunal wide powers to issue subpoenas for the production of witnesses and evidence,[99] the Act is silent on pre-award attachment in non-maritime cases.[100] Circuit courts are divided, therefore, on the judiciary's power to order interim measures such as pre-award attachment when the parties' agreement does not clearly cover the matter.

In this connection it is important to note that Article 23(2) of the ICC Rules provide that in some situations the parties may apply to a court for interim or conservatory measures. Some courts reason that by bargaining for arbitration the parties have implicitly excluded intervention by national courts until an award is rendered;[101] others view pre-award attachment as a way to maximize the efficiency of the arbitral process.[102] Depending on perspective, pre-award orders freezing assets either assist or disrupt the arbitral proceedings.

(b) Consolidation

The Federal Arbitration Act does not authorize forced joinder of different arbitrations arising out of related claims, even if they present similar questions of law and fact.[103] Thus consolidation remains problematic in the United States, except as agreed by the parties[104] or when conducted in a state that explicitly provides for joinder of related claims.[105]

---

99   9 U.S.C. § 7. *Compare* U.A.A. § 7; N.Y. Arbitration Law § 7505.

100   *See generally* David Wagoner, *Interim Relief in International Arbitration*, 51 J. DISP. RESOL. 68 (October 1996); Michael Hoellering, *Interim Measures and Arbitration: The Situation in the United States*, ARBITRATION AND THE LAW 154 (AAA, 1990-91). In admiralty cases the FAA allows attachment for the purpose of giving a court power to direct the parties to arbitrate. 9 U.S.C. § 8.

101   McCreary Tire & Rubber v. CEAT, S.p.A, 501 F.2d 1032 (3rd Cir. 1974). *See also* Cooper v. Ateliers de la Motobécane, S.A., 442 N.E.2d 1239 (1982).

102   Carolina Power & Light Co. v. Uranex, 451 F. Supp. 1044 (N.D. Cal. 1977); Andros Compania Maritima v. André & Cie, S.A., 430 F. Supp. 88 (S.D.N.Y. 1977).

103   *See* Government of U.K. of Gr. Brit. v. Boeing Co., 998 F.2d 68 (2nd Cir. 1993), denying consolidation of arbitrations with Boeing and Textron, Inc. relating to contract with the British Ministry of Defense to develop an electronic fuel system.

104   As between the same parties, Article 4(6) of the ICC Rules permits the Court to join claims until the signing of the Terms of Reference. Thereafter, addition of any new claim must be authorized by the arbitral tribunal. Compare Article 22(h) of the Arbitration Rules of the London Court of International Arbitration, permitting the arbitral tribunal to allow third persons to be joined in an arbitration provided the third person has consented in writing to joinder.

105   For example, Massachusetts Gen. Laws, c. 251, § 2A, calls for consolidation as provided in the Massachusetts Rules of Civil Procedure, which in Rule 42 permits joinder of actions "involving a common question of law or fact." New England Energy, Inc. v. Keystone Shipping Co., 855 F.2d 1 (1st Cir. 1988) has held that a federal court sitting in Massachusetts may order consolidation of related arbitrations pursuant to state statute Compare California Code of Civil Procedure, § 1281.3. Of course, when a dispute implicates a party that has not signed any arbitration clause at all, consolidation of claims may be impossible rather than just difficult.

(c) Discovery and Cross Examination

American courts will ordinarily hesitate to grant requests for broad discovery in arbitration.[106] Not all peculiarities of American procedure can be avoided, however. The right to cross examine witnesses, for example, has been held to be an essential element to a fair hearing.[107]

As a general matter U.S. courts may order discovery "for use in a proceeding in a foreign or international tribunal."[108] Some judicials decisions have held, however, that this provision does not cover arbitration.[109] In circumstances where discovery requests would be otherwise allowed, some courts require that a request come from the foreign tribunal,[110] while others have allowed a party (as an "interested person"[111]) to make the request.[112] The success of a request for a discovery order will not necessarily depend on whether the evidence is discoverable at the arbitral situs.[113]

---

106 *See* cases cited in Steven Stein & Daniel Watman, *The Arbitration Hearing, in* INTERNATIONAL COMMERCIAL ARBITRATION IN NEW YORK 88-90 (J.Stewart McClendon & Rosabel Everard Goodman eds., 1986).

107 *See* N.Y. C.P.L.R. § 7506(c); Nestel v. Nestel, 331 N.Y.2d. 241 (A.D., 1972).

108 28 U.S.C. § 1782.

109 *See* In re Application of National Broadcasting Co., 165 F. 3d 184 (2nd Cir. 1999), 1999 U.S. App. LEXIS 933. In connection with arbitration in Mexico, NBC directed subpoenas to bankers and advisers of Mexican television broadcasting company; held that for purposes of § 1782 an arbitral tribunal is not a "foreign or international tribunal"). *See also* In re Medway Power, 985 F. Supp. 402 (S.D.N.Y. 1997) (§ 1782 held not available for arbitration). *Compare* In re Application of Malev Hungarian Airlines, 964 F.2d 97 (2d Cir. 1992). *See* David Rivkin & Barton Legum, *Attempts to Use Section 1782 to Obtain U.S. Discovery in Aid of Foreign Arbitration*, 14 ARB. INT. 213 (1998); Eric Schwartz & Rolf Johnson, *Court Assisted Discovery in Aid of International Arbitrations*, 15 J. INT. ARB. 53 (1998); Hans Smit, *Assistance Rendered by the United States in Proceedings Before International Tribunals*, 62 COLUM. L. REV. 1264. (1962).

110 *See* In re Application of Technostroyexport, 853 F. Supp. 695 (S.D.N.Y. 1994) (arbitration pending in Moscow and Stockholm; *ex parte* discovery request refused without prejudice to a future application based on a ruling by an arbitral tribunal); Quijada v. Unifrutti of America, Inc. 22 Phila. 339 (1991); In re Zuhdi A. Bushnak, No.5: 96-MC-41-BR (E.D.N.C., Aug. 28, 1986).

111 "The order may be made pursuant to a . . . request made by a foreign or international tribunal or upon the application of any interested person. . . ." 28 U.S.C. § 1782.

112 John Deere, Ltd. v. Sperry Corp., 754 F.2d 132, 135 (3d Cir. 1985) (discovery request from an "interested person" allowed).

113 For cases deciding this issue in the context of requests from foreign courts, *see* In re Application of Aldunate, 3 F.3d 54 (2d Cir. 1993) (rejecting reciprocity requirement); Euromepa S.A. v. R. Emersian, Inc., 51 F.3d 1095 (2d Cir. 1995) (rejecting discovery reciprocity when assistance is court ordered); John Deere, Ltd. v. Sperry Corp., 754 F.2d 132, 135 (3d Cir. 1985) (rejecting discovery reciprocity for "interested persons"); United States v. Morris, 82 F.3d 590 (4th Cir. 1996) (rejecting reciprocity when a foreign court requests assistance in obtaining discovery); In re Letter Rogatory from First Court of First Instance in Civil Matters, Caracas, 42 F.3d 308, 311 (5th Cir. 1995) (no reciprocity requirement when request is from a foreign court). *Contrast* Lo Ka Chun v. Lo To, 858 F.2d 1564 (11th Cir. 1988) (requiring discovery reciprocity when request was from a private litigant); In re: Application Asta Medica, S.A., 981 F.2d 1 (1st. Cir. 1992) (requiring reciprocity in order to eliminate any unfair advantage use of US law would provide).

(d) Interim Procedural Questions

Which of several versions of the ICC Rules should be applied by the arbitrators was addressed in *Mobil Oil Indonesia, Inc. v. Asamera Oil (Indonesia), Ltd.*,[114] where arbitrators sitting in New York prepared Terms of Reference stating that the arbitral tribunal would apply the 1975 rather than the 1955 Rules.[115] The arbitrators concluded that the parties intended to refer to the Rules in effect when the Terms of Reference were to be drafted, rather than when the contract was signed. The New York State Appellate Division upheld the arbitrators reasoning that "[t]he parties agreed to be bound by the Rules of the ICC and it was for the arbitrators to determine which Rules of the ICC were intended."[116]

Sometimes a court may be required to decide the arbitration venue. In *Société Générale de Surveillance v. Raytheon European Management & Systems Co.*[117] the basic contract provided for ICC arbitration in Lausanne, Switzerland. A modification of the agreement ("change order") contained printed terms stipulating arbitration in Boston. The U.S. District Court of Massachusetts, upheld on appeal by the Court of Appeals for the First Circuit, found that the arbitration agreement in the basic contract prevailed over that on the change order and enjoined the Boston arbitration.

(e) Appeals from Court Orders

The FAA generally allows immediate appeals from district court orders adverse to arbitration, whereas appeal from orders favoring the arbitral process will not be allowed until the order is final.[118] Thus orders refusing to stay litigation, or denying a petition to compel arbitration, are immediately appealable.[119] By contrast, orders compelling arbitration or staying court proceedings are not appealable until the orders are of a final rather than interlocutory in nature.[120]

Generally, courts have considered pro-arbitration orders interlocutory (thus non-appealable) when "embedded" in actions that deal with claims unrelated

---

[114] 372 N.E.2d 21 (1977) discussed in Section 34.03.

[115] The contract had been signed in 1968, and the arbitration had commenced in 1974.

[116] 56 A.D. 2d 339, 342 (N.Y. 1977), *rev'd on other grounds*, 43 N.Y. 2d 276, 372 N.E. 2d 21 (1977). For a federal court sequel to this arbitration, *see* 487 F.Supp. 63 (S.D.N.Y. 1980), discussed in Section 34.04.

[117] 643 F.2d 863 (1st Cir. 1981).

[118] 9 U.S.C. § 16.

[119] 9 U.S.C. § 16 (a)(1). *See* Ballay v. Legg Mason Wood Walker, Inc. 878 F.2d 729 (3d Cir. 1989).

[120] FAA § 16 (b). *See* Adair Bus Sales v. Blue Bird Corp., 25 F.3d 953 (10th Cir. 1994). *Compare* S&L&H S.p.A. v. Miller-St. Nazianz, Inc., 988 F.2d 1518 (7th Cir. 1993), where arbitrability was the only issue before the court, thus qualifying the order as final rather than interlocutory.

to the arbitration question.[121] For example, an order to compel arbitration between an insurance underwriter and its policyholder was characterized as interlocutory, rather than final, by virtue of its link with the claims against the insurance adjuster, which had been consolidated in a single court action.[122]

34.04 Review of Awards

(a) Vacatur

(i) Overview.

In the arbitration end game, American courts have power to control the basic integrity of the arbitral process by vacating an award on the following grounds:

(1) Where the award was procured by corruption, fraud or undue means.

(2) Where there was evident partiality or corruption in the arbitrators, or either of them.

(3) Where the arbitrators were guilty of misconduct in refusing to postpone the hearing, upon sufficient cause shown, or in refusing to hear evidence pertinent and material to the controversy, or of any other misbehavior by which the rights of any party have been prejudiced.

(4) Where the arbitrators exceeded their powers, or so imperfectly executed them that a mutual, final, and definite award upon the subject matter submitted was not made.[123]

---

121 *See generally* Stedor Enterprises, Ltd. v. Armtex, Inc., 947 F.2d 727 (4th Cir. 1991) (action's sole purpose was to obtain an order compelling arbitration and thus order final and appealable);
 . Humphrey v. Prudential Secs., Inc., 4 F.3d 313 (4th Cir. 1993) (decision not final even when all the substantive issues have been compelled to arbitration); Perera v. Siegal Trading Co., 951 F.2d 780 (7th Cir. 1992); Filanto, S.p.A. v. Chilewich Int'l Corp., 984 F.2d 58 (2d Cir. 1993) (no appellate jurisdiction when a case has been closed but not dismissed). Circuits are divided as to whether dismissal of embedded proceedings without prejudice in deference to arbitration is a final decision. *Compare* Seacoast Motors v. Chrysler Corp., 143 F.3d 626 (1st Cir. 1998) (dismissal of embedded proceedings not a final decision) and Armijo v. Prudential Ins. Co., 72 F.3d 793 (10th Cir. 1995) (dismissed action appealable). *See also* Nationwide Ins. Co. v. Patterson, 953 F.2d 44 (3d Cir. 1991); Bradford-Scott Data Corp. v. Physician Computer Network, 128 F.3d 504 (7th Cir. 1997), *subsequent appeal*, 136 F.3d 1156 (7th Cir. 1998), *reh'g, en banc, denied*, 1998 U.S. App. LEXIS 5612 (7th Cir. Ind. Mar. 17, 1998)(granting a stay of court proceedings pending appeal of a determination that claim was not arbitrable). *See also* James R. Foley, Note, 13 OHIO ST. J. DISP. RESOL. 1071 (1998).

122 *See* McDermott Int'l, Inc. v. Underwriters at Lloyds, 981 F.2d 744 (5th Cir. 1993).

123 9 U.S.C. § 10(a) as its subsections were renumbered in 1990. For a recent survey of these grounds for vacatur, *see* Stephen L. Hayford, *A New Paradigm for Commercial Arbitration: Rethinking the Relationship Between Reasoned Awards and the Judicial Standards for Vacatur*, 66 GEO. WASH. L. REV. 443 (1998); Stephen L. Hayford & Scott Kenigan, *Vacatur: The Non-Statutory Grounds for Judicial Review of Commercial Awards*, 50 DISPUTE RESOLUTION J. 22 (Oct. 1996). By comparison the Uniform Arbitration Act in Section 12 provides for vacatur of an award (1) procured by corruption, fraud or under other means; (2) where there was evident partiality by an arbitrator appointed as a neutral, or corruption in any of the arbitrators, or misconduct prejudicing

Federal court power to review awards on these grounds will not be defeated by Article 28 of the ICC Rules by which the parties waive their rights of recourse against awards. In *M& C Corp. v. Erwin Behr GmbH,*[124] the Sixth Circuit held that a narrow interpretation must be given to the waiver provisions in order to preserve procedural safeguards. The court held that the ICC waiver of appeal provision "merely reflect[s] a contractual intent that the issues joined and resolved in the arbitration may not be tried de novo in any court"[125] but that awards cannot be insulated from review for fraud or other procedural irregularities.[126]

The Second Circuit has recently confirmed that the United States is free to apply its own standards for vacatur of awards made in the United States, notwithstanding that they may be covered by the New York Convention. The Court held that under the Convention scheme the country where the award is made is "free to set aside or modify an award in accordance with [the arbitral venue's] full panoply of express or implied grounds for relief."[127]

It is uncertain whether violation of substantive public policy constitutes a ground for vacatur in commercial arbitration.[128] Although labor cases permit

---

the rights of any party; (3) the arbitrators exceeded their powers; (4) the arbitrators refused to postpone the hearing upon sufficient cause being shown therefore or refused to hear material evidence; or (5) there was no arbitration agreement.

124 87 F.3d 844, 847 (6th Cir. 1996), *subsequent appeal,* 143 F.3d 1033 (1998), reversing district court stay of enforcement pending further arbitration. M & C Corp., doing business as Connelly Company, was an agent for a German manufacturer. After termination of an agency agreement by a German manufacturer, claims for unpaid commissions were sent to an ICC-appointed arbitrator in London.

125 87 F.3d at 847, quoting Iran Aircraft Industries v. Avco Corp., 980 F.2d 141, 145 (2nd Cir. 1992).

126 The court also held that (i) an American court had no power to vacate an award rendered outside the United States, (ii) "manifest disregard for the law" was not a ground for refusal to recognize a foreign award and (iii) a multiple damage award pursuant to state statute was not outside the terms of reference, and thus fell within the arbitrator's jurisdiction.

127 Yusuf Ahmed Alghanin & Sons v. Toys "R" Us, 126 F.3d 15, 23 (2d Cir. 1997). As to an award rendered in the United States in favor of foreign licensee, the district court was held to have power to set aside award for "manifest disregard of the law" (not found in instant case) even though not included in grounds for refusal of recognition to foreign awards under the New York Convention.

128 *See* Stephen L. Hayford, *Law in Disarray: Judicial Standards for Vacatur of Commercial Arbitration Awards,* 30 GA. L. REV. 731 (1996). In Northrop Corp. v. Triad Int'l Marketing, 811 F.2d 1265 (9th Cir. 1987), implicating alleged illegal commissions to intermediaries in armament contracts, Northrop had agreed to pay such commissions to Triad, but stopped after the 1975 Saudi decree declaring such fees "void and not binding." An arbitral tribunal in California interpreted California law (the governing law chosen by the parties) as permitting such commissions and made an award in favor of Triad. On motions to confirm (by Triad) and to vacate (by Northrop), a Federal District Court vacated the award as "contrary to law and public policy." The Court of Appeals reversed, holding that U.S. State Department policy was too ill-defined to impede confirmation, and that neither error as to interpretation of California law nor conflict with Saudi public policy could justify annulment of the award.

an award to be set aside for contravention of public policy,[129] the FAA contains no reference to public policy as ground for vacatur of an award.[130]

The general reluctance of federal courts to set aside arbitral awards can be illustrated by the case of *Mobil Oil Indonesia, Inc. v. Asamera Oil (Indonesia)*[131] involving a contract for exploration and production of petroleum in Indonesia. Mobil argued that the arbitrators had exceeded their power, essentially rewriting the contract between the parties, by interpreting "crude oil," on which royalties were payable, to include all hydrocarbons, despite the common sense definition of the term. The U.S. District Court for the Southern District of New York refused to vacate the award; the Court found it sufficient that the arbitrators statement of reasons contained a "barely colorable" justification for the outcome.[132]

(ii) Impartiality

In *Commonwealth Coatings Corp. v. Continental Casualty Co.*[133] the U.S. Supreme Court set aside an award of an arbitrator who had failed to disclose a prior business relationship with one of the litigants.[134] Impartiality, as interpreted by a plurality of the Court,[135] required arbitrators to "disclose to the parties any dealings that might create an impression of possible bias."[136] The concurring Justices added that an undisclosed business relationship should be grounds for disqualification of the arbitrator only if the relationship was substantial.[137] The dissent favored an actual bias standard, rather than one in which "innocent failure to volunteer information" constituted grounds to set aside an award."[138]

Arbitrators have a duty to disclose known facts, rather than a duty to investigate. In *Peoples Sec. Life Ins. v. Monumental Life Ins. Co.*[139] the court upheld

---

129 *See* United Paperworkers Int'l Union v. Misco, Inc. 484 U.S. 29 (1987).

130 It will be recalled that labor and commercial arbitration rest on different statutory foundations. *See* Section 34.01.

131 487 F. Supp. 63 (S.D.N.Y. 1980). The New York state court decision is 43 N.E.2d 276, 372 N.E.2d 21 (1977) discussed in Section 34.03.

132 *Id.* at 65.

133 393 U.S. 145 (1968).

134 A different standard may apply to party-nominated arbitrators. *See* Sunkist Soft Drinks, Inc. v. Sunkist Growers, Inc., 10 F.3d 753, 759 (1993) (differentiating between neutral and party appointed arbitrators then noting that the Rules of the AAA which applied to the party appointed arbitrator demanded that the arbitrator "act in good faith and with integrity and fairness" even if predisposed towards one of the parties).

135 Three Justices joined in one opinion and two in another. Three dissented.

136 393 U.S. at 149.

137 393 U.S. at 150 (J. Marshall and J. White concurring).

138 *Id.* at 154 (J. Fortas, J. Harlan and J. Stewart dissenting).

139 991 F.2d 141 (4th Cir. 1993).

the award of an arbitrator who was unaware that an attorney who represented one of the parties had joined a branch office of the arbitrator's law firm.[140]

Challenge to an arbitrator's integrity or independence should be made as soon as the protesting party becomes aware of the questionable behavior. Failure to make timely objection to arbitrator bias or corruption may constitute a waiver of the right to attack the award later.[141]

(iii) Arbitrator Misconduct

Decisions on the degree of misconduct necessary to justify vacatur of an award focus on refusal to postpone hearings[142] or to admit pertinent evidence.[143] Courts are generally hesitant to deprive arbitration of "speed and finality"[144] by interpreting the grounds for vacatur broadly.[145] It has been held that when an arbitrator has rendered a decision based on affidavits, rather than oral testimony, the parties have not been denied a "fundamentally fair hearing."[146] One example of conduct which *did* rise to the level of misconduct was the arbitrator's receipt of *ex parte* evidence when the applicable arbitration rules called for evidence to be taken in the presence of all parties.[147]

---

140 The party asserting partiality was unable to prove that a reasonable person would conclude that the arbitrator was partial. *Id.* at 146. *See also* Al-Harbi v. Citibank, N.A., 85 F.3d 680 (D.C. Cir. 1996) (determining that there was no basis for concluding there was "evident partiality" when an arbitrator did not know that arbitrator's former law firm had represented one of the parties).

141 *See* AAOT Foreign Economic Association (VO) Technostroyexport v. International Development and Trade Services, 139 F.3d 980 (2d Cir.1998). An attempt to test the integrity of a Russian arbitral tribunal allegedly led to an offer, from the Secretary to the arbitral institution, to fix the proceedings for $1 million. No payment was made, however, and the tribunal ultimately decided against the party that had discussed the bribe. The court refused to vacate the award, finding that the right to challenge the award for arbitrator corruption was waived by failure to notify opposing counsel of the problem. *See also* Fort Hill Builders v. National Grange Mutual Insurance Co., 866 F.2d 11 (1st Cir. 1989).

142 *See* Naing Int'l Enter.v. Ellsworth Assoc., 961 F. Supp. 1, 3 (D.D.C. 1997) (citations omitted).

143 In the context of a labor arbitration vacatur of an award was affirmed as the arbitrator had admitted a transcript but then refused to give it any weight. The Circuit Court stated that this effectively excluded evidence which was central to one of the party's case, thereby depriving them of a fair hearing. *See* Hoteles Condado Beach, La Concha and Convention Center v. Union de Tronquistas Local 901, 763 F.2d 34 (1st. Cir. 1985).

144 Newark Stereotypers' Union No. 18 v. Newark Morning Ledger Co., 397 F.2d 594, 598 (3rd Cir. 1968).

145 Consistent with courts efforts to not undermine the finality of arbitration awards §10(a)(3) has not been read to mean that "every failure to receive relevant evidence constitutes misconduct which will require the vacation of an arbitrator's award." *Id.* at 599.

146 Intercarbon Bermuda, Ltd. v. Caltex Trading & Transp. Corp., 146 F.R.D. 64, 72 (S.D.N.Y. 1993), quoting Roche v. Local 32B-32J Serv. Employees Int'l Union, 755 F.Supp. 622, 624 (S.D.N.Y. 1991).

147 Totem Marine Tug & Barge, Inc. v. North Am. Towing, 607 F.2d 649 (5th Cir. 1979).

(iv) "Manifest Disregard of the Law"

"Manifest disregard of the law"[148] constitutes what some commentators believe to be an independent (non-statutory) ground for annulment, while to others it appears as no more than one variety of arbitration excess of jurisdiction.[149] Clearly presupposing something beyond legal error[150] "manifest disregard of the law" might include an arbitrator's intentionally ignoring the correct governing law. An honest failure of interpreting the law is not enough.[151]

One First Circuit decision[152] discussed two classes of awards that might be vacated on grounds of "manifest disregard" for the law: awards "contrary to the plain language" of the agreement[153] and instances where it is clear from the record that the arbitrator "recognized the applicable law—and then ignored it."[154] In another case where the court vacated an arbitral award for "manifest disregard," the arbitral tribunal had noted an attorney's appeal to extra-legal justice, urging the tribunal to "do what is right and just and equitable in this case" rather than apply the law.[155]

---

148 Wilko v. Swan, 346 U.S. 427, at 436 (1953).

149 *See generally* Swift Indus., Inc. v. Botany Indus., Inc., 466 F.2d 1125 (3d Cir. 1972).

150 *See* Saxis S.S. Co. v. Multifacs Int'l Traders, Inc., 375 F.2d 577, 582 (2d Cir. 1967) (quoting San Martine Co. de Navigacion v. Saguenay Terminals, Ltd., 293 F.2d 796, 801 (9th Cir. 1961), the court refused to apply the concept of "manifest disregard"). *See also* Amicizia Societa Navegazione v. Chilean Nitrate & Iodine Sales Corp., 274 F.2d 805, 808 (2d Cir. 1960) (refusing to apply the "manifest disregard" concept to the facts at issue); Swift Indus., Inc. v. Botany Indus., Inc. 466 F.2d 1125 (3d Cir. 1972). In Sea Dragon, Inc. v. Gebr. Van Weelde Scheepvaartkantoor, B.V., 574 F. Supp. 367 (S.D.N.Y. 1983) the court vacated an award that would have directed violation of a Dutch injunction ordering charterer not to pay debt to vessel owner.

151 As a Second Circuit federal appeals judge put it: "Manifest disregard of the law may be found only where the arbitrators understood and correctly stated the law but proceeded to ignore it." Merrill Lynch, Pierce, Fenner & Smith, Inc. v. Bobker, 808 F.2d 930 (2d Cir. 1986). *See also* M & C Corp. v. Erwin Behr GmbH, 87 F.3d 8444 (6th Cir. 1996).

152 Advest, Inc. v. McCarthy, 914 F.2d 6 (1st Cir. 1990) (affirming a lower court refusal to vacate an award in a case wherein an investor alleged that a broker wrongfully liquidated his holdings). The investor had a margin account whereby the broker had loaned the customer part of the purchase price of the securities, which then served as collateral for the loan. The brokerage firm had demanded that the investor deposit more money after the mix of investments changed, saying that the additional funds were mandated by federal regulation when in fact the regulations were permissive. When the funds were not forthcoming the brokerage firm liquidated some of the investor's holdings. *See also* Prudential-Bache Sec., Inc. v. Tanner, 72 F.3d 234 (1st Cir. 1995), *subsequent appeal* 141 F.3d 1150 (1st. Cir. 1998).

153 914 F.2d 6, at 9.

154 For cases falling into this latter category, Judge Selya stated that "manifest disregard of the law" usually requires either a record demonstrating that the arbitrators knew the law and expressly ignored it, or a governing law with such clarity that a court could assume the arbitrators knew the rule and disregarded it.

155 Montes v. Shearson Lehman Bros., Inc., 128 F.3d 1456 (11th Cir. 1997). The Court stated,"We do not permit review [of an arbitration board's decision when its conclusion or reasoning is legally erroneous] and reject any argument that to err legally always equates to a "manifest disregard of law."

In one age discrimination case the court stated that the arbitrators' failure to make a reasoned award reinforced the court's suspicion that there had been manifest disregard of the law.[156] To some extent, one may be seeing the development of different standards for determining "manifest disregard of the law," with a more expansive interpretation given to the term in employment and consumer contracts than in commercial transactions.[157]

(v) Expanding Judicial Review to Cover Substantive Error

Although error of law and/or fact is not a ground for vacatur of awards under the FAA, the parties might sometimes want to provide by contract for judicial review on such grounds. Some courts allow parties to an arbitration to expand by contract the scope of judicial review,[158] while others view the practice with disfavor.[159]

(vi) Vacatur of Foreign Awards?

In a decision reaffirming the role of the arbitral situs, the United States District Court for the Southern District of New York held that an American court may hear an action to vacate an award only if made in the United States. *International Standard Electric Corp. v. Bridas Sociedad Anonima Petrolera, Indus. Y Comercial*[160] involved an ICC arbitration in Mexico City, between an Argentine corporation and an ITT subsidiary. The agreement itself was to be "governed by and construed under and in accordance with the laws of the State of New York." The losing party not only resisted enforcement of the award, but also moved to have it set aside.

---

156 Halligan v. Piper Jaffray, 148 F. 3d 197 (2nd Cir. 1998) cert. denied 119 S. Ct. 1286 (1999). (overturning the lower court's refusal to vacate an award in favor of employer). *See* generally Barry H. Garfinkel & Rona G. Shamoon, *A Dangerous Expansion of Manifest Disregard*, 3 ADR CURRENTS 1 (December 1998); Norman S. Poser, *Judicial Review of Arbitration Awards: Manifest Disregard of the Law*, 64 BROOKLYN L. REV. 471 (1998) (proposing an amendment to the FAA to permit awards to be overturned if "egregiously wrong").

157 Compare the approach in *Halligan*, with Willemijn Houdstermaatschappij BV v. Standard Microsystems Corp., 103 F.3d 9 (2nd Cir. 1997), where the Second Circuit vacated a lower court order vacating an award in a patent royalty case.

158 *See* Lapine Tech. Corp. v. Kyocera Corp., 130 F.3d 884 (9th Cir. 1997) *rev'g* 909 F. Supp. 697 (N.D. Cal. 1995) (parties permitted by agreement to expand scope of judicial review under FAA § 10); Gateway Technologies v. MCI Telecommunications Corp., 64 F.3d 993 (5th Cir. 1995) (court allows de novo review of issues of law according to parties' agreement); Fils et Cables d'Acier de Lens v. Midland Metals Corp, 584 F. Supp. 240 (S.D.N.Y. 1984) (court agrees to determine whether award supported by substantial evidence, as provided in parties' contract); New England Utilities v. Hydro-Quebec, 10 F. Supp. 2d 53 (D.Mass. 1998) (court allows contractual expansion of judicial review). *See also* Syncor International v. David MacLeish, 120 F. 3d 262 (4th Cir. 1997). *See generally,* Stephen A. Hochman, *Judicial Review to Correct Arbitral Error- An Option to Consider,* 13 OHIO ST. J. ON DISP. RESOL. 103 (1997); Andreas Lowenfeld, *Can Arbitration Coexist With Judicial Review?,* 3 ADR CURRENTS 1 (Sept. 1998).

159 *See* Chicago Typographical Union v. Chicago Sun-Times, 935 F.2d 1501 (7th Cir. 1995), stating that federal court review power cannot be created by contract.

160 745 F. Supp 172 (S.D.N.Y. 1990).

Focusing on the language of New York Convention Article V the Court concluded that it had no jurisdiction to vacate the award. Convention Article V(1)(e) permits refusal of recognition and enforcement to awards set aside by the "competent authority of the country in which, or under the law of which, the award was made." The expression "[the country] under the laws of which the award was made" referred to the procedural law of the arbitration, rather than the substantive law applicable to the merits of the dispute.[161]

A recent U.S. Supreme Court decision, however, makes application of this principle uncertain. In *Cortez Byrd Chips Inc. v. Bill Harbert Construction Company*,[162] the Court held that the venue provisions of FAA §§ 9-11 (allowing motions to confirm, vacate and modify awards at the arbitral situs) are only permissive. Consequently, motions to vacate may also be made in any federal district proper under the general venue statute (28 U.S.C. § 1391), including *inter alia* defendant's place of residence.

(b) Award Enforcement

Courts in the United States have shown a healthy skepticism of public policy defenses to the enforcement of foreign awards. In *Parsons & Whittemore Overseas Co. v. Société Générale de L'Industrie du Papier (RAKTA)*,[163] a U.S. company had contracted to build a paper mill plant in Egypt. When anti-American sentiment rose prior to the 1967 Arab-Israeli War and Egypt broke diplomatic ties with the U.S. they abandoned the site. The Egyptian company was granted an arbitral award in its favor for the U.S. company's breach of contract. The U.S. company defended against enforcement of the award arguing that to remain in Egypt would have been in defiance of U.S. national policy. The Second Circuit rejected the argument as a confusion of national and public policy. Public policy is narrow and only provides a ground to deny enforcement of a foreign arbitral award when enforcement "would violate the forum state's most basic notions of morality and justice."[164]

New York Convention defenses to recognition of foreign awards may serve as a basis on which to withhold confirmation of awards rendered in the United States.[165] They are not grounds for *vacatur* of an award, however. This may be significant in the context of the New York Arbitration Convention, which permits refusal of recognition to awards expressly annulled where rendered,

---

161 In the case at bar, that procedural law was the law of Mexico, notwithstanding the parties' choice of New York State law to govern the substantive interpretation of the contract.

162 120 S.Ct. 1331 (2000), to be published in 529 U.S. Reports. The Court states that a restrictive reading would "preclude any action under the FAA in courts of the United States to confirm, modify or vacate awards rendered in foreign arbitrations not covered by [the New York or Panama Convention]." 120 S. Ct. 1338.

163 508 F.2d 969 (2d Cir. 1974).

164 *Id.* at 974.

165 *See* 9 U.S.C. § 207.

but not to awards that have merely failed to receive court confirmation at the arbitral situs.

As a general rule American courts enforce foreign awards notwithstanding defenses based on sovereign immunity and "Act of State."[166]

In some cases, federal courts may stay confirmation of one award pending the outcome of a related arbitration. *Hewlett-Packard v. Berg*[167] involved disputes between American and Swedish companies arising out of two different contracts. After an ICC award in favor of the Swedes, the Americans paid the award less a set-off amount to which they believed they were entitled in the second arbitration. The Court of Appeals held that the District Court had the power to stay confirmation of the award pending outcome of the subsequent arbitration.

The decision doubtless was influenced by the insolvency of the Swedish party, which gave the Americans little assurance of collecting an award in their favor in the second arbitration. Understandable as this may be, not everyone has been able to reconcile the result with the New York Convention, which says nothing about stay of enforcement except when an application for setting aside or suspension of an award has been made at the place of arbitration.[168] The Court reasoned, however, that the Convention's listing of a single ground for stay should not be taken to exclude all other grounds.[169]

(c) The Second Look Doctrine

Courts reserve the right to have a second look at an award to insure that the public policy consequences of a dispute were properly considered.[170] As mentioned earlier[171] courts may refuse to enforce an agreement to arbitrate if the parties' contractual choice of law runs afoul of mandatory norms of the country of contract performance. In addition, at the stage when asked to recognize

---

166 *See* 28 U.S.C. §§ 1605(a)(6) & 1610(a)(6) and 9 U.S.C. § 16, respectively.

167 61 F. 3d 101 (1st Cir. 1995).

168 New York Convention Article VI. Although the award rendered in Boston did not qualify as a foreign award ("made in the territory of a state other than the state where the recognition and enforcement of such awards are sought"), the court seems to have considered whether it would fall within the scope of the Convention as an award "not considered as domestic." *See* Bergesen v. Joseph Muller Corp., 710 F. 2d 928 (2d Cir. 1983) and Lander Co. v. MMP Invs., 107 F.3d 476 (7th Cir. 1997).

169 The Court recognized the principle *expressio unius est exclusio alterius*, but called it "an aid to construction and not an inflexible rule." 61 F.3d 101, at 106. While recognizing the danger of abuse of judicial power to stay, the court said this risk argued "more for a cautious and prudent exercise of the power than for its elimination."

170 Mitsubishi Motors Corp. v. Soler Chrysler-Plymouth, Inc., 473 U.S. 614, 637 (1985).

171 *See* discussion of the "prospective waiver" doctrine announced in the *Mitsubishi* case *supra* Section 34.02 (vi).

the award itself, American judges might be called to determine whether the arbitrators have considered and respected mandatory norms.[172]

The so-called "second look doctrine" is of uncertain scope, leaving open whether judges should engage in a broad examination of the arbitrator's application of the law, or provide only a mechanical examination of whether the arbitrator in fact considered the mandatory statute. If a contract includes a choice-of-law clause explicitly selecting the legal system of a country with no antitrust law, an arbitrator mindful of the Supreme Court's caveat might decide the antitrust claims according to United States law. However, this departure from the parties' express choice of an applicable law (adjudication according to U.S. antitrust principles when the contract designated Swiss law) would increase the risk of successful challenge of the award outside the United States on the basis of excess of arbitral authority. The loser could first seek annulment of the award at the place where rendered, or another jurisdiction where the loser's assets are located, on the theory that the arbitrator decided inconsistently with the arbitral agreement.

As a practical matter, the "second look doctrine" is not likely to generate a great deal of case law. Any relatively experienced and thoughtful arbitrator who expects that his or her award may have to be enforced in the United States will at least mention the relevant American statutory issue, and then add a recital about how, after serious consideration, the American law was found inapplicable.

Finally, with respect to enforcement of foreign awards, at least one court in the United States has been willing to confirm an award annulled abroad in its country of origin.[173] The court reasoned that such confirmation was permitted under the Federal Arbitration Act, and thus within the scope of New York Convention Article VII which foresees award enforcement as allowed under domestic law.

(d) Punitive Damages

ICC arbitrators sitting in the United States should have the power to award "punitive" or "exemplary" damages unless the contract explicitly provides

---

172 *Dictum* in the *Mitsubishi* case reads in part as follows: "[T]he national courts of the United States will have the opportunity at the award enforcement stage to ensure that the legitimate interest in the enforcement of antitrust laws has been addressed . . . [and] to ascertain that the [arbitral] tribunal took cognizance of the antitrust claims and actually decided them." 473 U.S. at 638. The Court relied for this aspect of its decision on New York Convention Article V(2)(b) discussed in Chapter 37.

173 *See* Chromalloy Aeroservices v. Arab Republic, 939 F. Supp. 907 (D.D.C. 1996), involving an award rendered in Egypt, and annulled by a Cairo court, in favor of a company that had contracted for the maintenance of helicopters belonging to the Egyptian Air Force. *See* Chapter 28 and 37.

otherwise.[174] The U.S. Supreme Court decision in *Mastrobuono v. Shearson Lehman Hutton*[175] allowed an arbitral tribunal to award claimant investors $400,000 in punitive damages for alleged broker mishandling of a securities trading account—in addition to the $159,000 of compensatory damages. The contract called for application of New York law, which allowed courts alone to award punitive damages. The Supreme Court, however, read the applicable law stipulation to include only state substantive law.[176] Thus for those who wish to limit exposure to punitive damages, the path of prudence in light of *Mastrobuono* lies in drafting explicit exclusions, rather than relying on potentially unpredictable choice-of-law clauses.

(e) Attorney's Fees

While the Federal Arbitration Act is silent on the matter, the Uniform Arbitration Act provides that the arbitrator's power to grant costs does not include "counsel fees," subject to the proviso "unless otherwise provided in the agreement to arbitrat[e]."[177] In at least one case, the fact that both parties requested attorney's fees from the arbitral tribunal was taken as indicative that an award of fees was within the scope of the arbitration agreement.[178]

The ICC Rules, of course, provide that the costs of the arbitration may include "reasonable legal and other costs incurred by the parties for the arbitration."[179] And one federal court has held that an arbitrator may assess substantial attorneys' fees against the losing party even *after* ICC approval of the draft award. In *Compagnie des Bauxites de Guinee (CBG) v. Hammermills*[180] the arbitrator added nearly $1 million (a not *de minimis* amount) in attor-

---

174 Punitive damages give a winning claimant amounts over and above compensation for loss, such damages might be awarded where the wrong was aggravated by circumstances such as malice or wanton conduct.

175 514 U.S. 52 (1995). *See also* M & C Corp. v. Erwin Behr GmbH & Co., 87 F.3d 844 (6th Cir. 1996) (ICC arbitration in London; applicable Michigan law gave arbitration power to award double damages to sales representative).

176 Some subsequent state court decisions have distinguished *Mastrobuono* on its facts, so as to disallow punitive damages awarded by arbitrators. *See, e.g.,* Supreme Court of New York State, Dean Witter Reynolds Inc. v. Trimble, 631 N.Y.S. 2d 215 (Sup. Ct. 1995). *Compare* New York State Supreme Court decision Merrill Lynch, Pierce, Fenner & Smith, Inc. v. Levine, N.Y.L.J., July 5, 1995 (N.Y. Co.).

177 U.A.A. § 10. *See, e.g.,* Baxter Health Care Corp. v. Harvard Apparatus, 35 Mass. App. Ct. 204, 617 N.E.2d 1018 (1993); Floors, Inc. v. B.G. Danis of New England, 380 Mass. 91, 401 N.E.2d 839 (1980); Walker v. Warren, 7 Mass. L. Rptr. 453, 1997 WL 572936 (Mass. Super. Aug. 07, 1997) (No. Civ. A. 96-7022).

178 *See* Prudential-Bache Secs. v. Tanner, 72 F.3d 234 (1st Cir. 1995).

179 ICC Rules, Article 31.

180 1992 U.S. Dist. LEXIS 8046 (D.D.C. May 29, 1992). Alleging that Hammermills had supplied erroneous data used at the mining facility, CBG brought a $46 million breach of contract action against Hammermills. The sole arbitrator held for the defendant, denying the claim in its entirety.

neys' fees to be paid by the losing claimant.[181] In an action to vacate this portion of the award assessing legal costs, CBG argued that adding such fees to the draft award after its approval by the ICC Court violated ICC procedures by impairing the substantial completeness one expects of a draft award submitted for scrutiny, and that CBG had not been given an adequate opportunity to be heard on the issue of attorneys fees.[182] The U.S. district court rejected these arguments, stating that all parties should have known that the arbitrator had the power to assess legal costs.[183]

Surprisingly, the Court did not discuss the adequacy of the period during which the losing party had an opportunity to comment on the attorneys fees.[184] What was at issue was not whether an ICC arbitrator had the power to assess legal costs, but whether the prevailing party had in fact incurred the fees and whether these amounts were normal. An ICC arbitrator's authority to fix attorneys fees is not unfettered, but is limited to "normal" legal costs incurred by the parties. Moreover, it is fundamental to the scheme of the ICC Rules that each side should have an adequate opportunity to challenge the other side's proofs before submitting the draft award to the ICC Court for scrutiny.

(f) Arbitral Jurisdiction

In reviewing an award for excess of authority,[185] the United States Supreme Court has held that the scope of the arbitration agreement is normally a matter for courts to decide independently, without deference to the arbitral finding on the matter.[186] *First Options of Chicago v. Kaplan*[187] arose from an

---

181 Unlike the arbitrator's fees and the ICC administrative costs, which are fixed by the ICC Court, the quantum of legal costs is fixed by the arbitrator, as are the proportions in which the costs shall be born by the parties. *See* Article 31 of the ICC Rules.

182 The New York Convention defenses to enforcement of awards were implicated because Hammermills had sought confirmation of the award. Section 207 of the FAA directs federal courts to confirm awards unless the reviewing court finds one of the grounds for refusal of recognition set forth in Article V of the New York Convention. The due process concern (inability to present one's case) was covered by Convention Article V(1)(b), while the point relating the ICC procedures implicated Convention Article V(1)(d), which permits non-recognition of awards when "the arbitral procedure was not in accordance with the agreement of the parties." Although both Hammermills and CBG were incorporated in the United States the court accepted Convention application because the relationship involved property and envisaged performance abroad. *See* FAA § 202.

183 1992 U.S. Dist. LEXIS 8046, at *19.

184 On 21 October CBG received a copy of the statement of legal fees submitted by Hammermills. Sometime between the 19 October, when the draft award was approved by the ICC, and 26 October when the final award was signed and dated, the arbitrator added the legal fees to the award.

185 For the approach of federal courts to allocating jurisdictional functions in the context of motions to compel arbitration, *see* Section 34.02, discussing Apollo v. Berg, Three Valleys Mun. Water Dist. v. E.F. Hutton & Co., and PaineWebber v. Elahi.

186 The Supreme Court also held that when reviewing a district court decision confirming an arbitral award under the Federal Arbitration Act, a court of appeals should accept a district court's findings of fact unless "clearly erroneous," but that questions of law should be decided *de novo*.

187 514 U.S. 938 (1995).

arbitral award rendered against both an investment company and its owners with respect to debts owed to a securities clearing house. The owners argued that they had never signed the arbitration agreement, and consequently were not bound by its award.

The Supreme Court distinguished three elements in the interaction of judge and arbitrators in the case: the merits of the dispute (whether the Kaplans were personally liable for the investment company's debt); the arbitrability of the dispute (whether the Kaplans agreed to arbitrate the matter of their liability); and the allocation of functions between courts and arbitrators with respect to determinations of jurisdiction (whether courts show deference to arbitrators' ruling on their own power). On the last of these issues the Court held that the question of arbitral jurisdiction was for courts rather than arbitrators, and affirmed the Court of Appeals decision that the owners had not agreed to arbitrate.

In *dictum,* however, the Court suggested that in some situations (although not under the facts of *Kaplan*) what the Court called "the arbitrability question itself" (i.e., the arbitrator's jurisdiction) may be submitted to arbitration, in which case the courts must defer ("give considerable leeway") to arbitrators' decisions on the limits of their own jurisdiction.[188]

Thus an arbitration agreement covering the merits of the dispute could be supplemented by a submission of jurisdictional issues to arbitration, which would in some cases shield these jurisdictional determinations from independent judicial scrutiny. The proper application of this *dictum* will not always be clear. Since the Supreme Court in *Kaplan* affirms that in all circumstances awards may be reviewed under Section 10 of the FAA,[189] some consensual basis for arbitral authority must exist. Many of the cases interpreting this *dictum* have arisen in connection with time limits for bringing a claim (*see* Section 34.02) and the preclusive effect (sometimes called "collateral estoppel") of prior arbitral awards.[190]

---

188 The problematic language of the *dictum* (which in some situations may eclipse the holding of the case) says that if the parties have agreed to submit the arbitrability question to arbitration, then "the court's standard for reviewing the arbitrator's decision about the matter should not differ from the standard courts apply when they review any other matter that the parties have agreed to arbitrate. . . . That is to say, the court should give considerable leeway to the arbitrator, setting aside his or her decision only in certain narrow circumstances." *Id.* at 943.

189 *Id.* at 942.

190 *See*, e.g., National Union Fire Ins. v. Belco Petroleum Corp., 88 F.3d 129 (2d Cir. 1996); United States Fire Ins. Co. v. National Gypsum Co., 101 F.3d 813 (2d Cir. 1996), *cert. denied*, 117 S. Ct. 2512 (1997). *See* Gerard Sanders, *Rethinking Arbitral Preclusion*, 24 LAW & POLICY INT'L BUS. 101 (1992); Colin Hugh Buckley, *Issue Preclusion and Issue of Law: A Doctrinal Framework Based On Rules of Recognition, Jurisdiction & Legal History*, 24 HOUS. L. REV. 875 (1987); G. Richard Shell, *Res Judicata and Collateral Estoppel Effects of Commercial Arbitration*, 35 UCLA L. Rev. 623 (1988).

(g) Entry of Judgement Provisions

When drafting an arbitration agreement that may lead to an award which will have to be enforced in the United States, it is usually worth including an "entry of judgment" stipulation permitting courts to confirm the award. Although the portions of the FAA implementing the New York Convention should normally permit confirmation of a Convention award even absent such language,[191] needless litigation has sometimes resulted when lower court judges believed an arbitration clause must contain a "entry of judgment" provision.[192]

---

191 9 U.S.C. § 207.

192 *See* Daihatsu Motor Co., Ltd. v. Terrain Vehicles, 13 F.3d 196 (7th Cir. 1993) (interpreting 9 U.S.C. § 9).

PART VI

TRENDS IN INTERNATIONAL COMMERCIAL ARBITRATION

CHAPTER 35

LEX MERCATORIA

35.01 Three concepts of lex mercatoria

Lex mercatoria seems to mean different things to different people. The present authors suggest that the various notions may usefully be distinguished and grouped under three headings. First, the most ambitious concept of *lex mercatoria* is that of an autonomous legal order, created spontaneously by parties involved in international economic relations and existing independently of national legal orders. Second, *lex mercatoria* has been viewed as a body of rules sufficient to decide a dispute, operating as an alternative to an otherwise applicable national law. Third, it may be considered as a complement to otherwise applicable law, viewed as nothing more than the gradual consolidation of usage and settled expectations in international trade.

These concepts are sufficiently complex, and are so often encountered in commentary on ICC arbitration, that a description of their theoretical bases seems appropriate. In 1974, the ICC began to publish excerpts of awards, edited to preserve the anonymity of the parties, in the *Journal du droit international*. In the presentation of the initial small collection of awards, two ICC Court officials (Messrs Thompson and Derains) expressed a caveat. ICC arbitrators were not aware of awards rendered by other ICC arbitrators; since the ICC itself had neither the authority nor the wish to harmonize decisions of independent ICC arbitral tribunals, each award was rendered without regard to other awards. "One may thus hardly speak of an arbitral case law."[1]

That was a quarter of a century ago. Since then, similar selections of ICC awards have been published in French each year in the last issue of the *Journal du droit international*; in English, the *ICCA Yearbook Commercial Arbitration* has followed suit (beginning in 1976). Numerous other publications and books have helped create a substantial body of published ICC awards. The issues faced by ICC arbitrators also arise in non-ICC proceedings, and in-

---

1   1974 JDI 878.

deed the proliferation of published awards has extended to those rendered in such proceedings.

Concomitant with this development, ICC arbitrators have increasingly come to rely on previous awards to support their decisions. By 1981, in his introduction to the *Journal du droit international* digest of ICC awards, the then Secretary General of the ICC Court of Arbitration wrote that awards with increasing frequency referred to previous published awards.[2] Such references may be found not only in cases where arbitrators have been given the authority to act as *amiables compositeurs* and thus without founding their decision in law,[3] nor only in cases where the parties have stipulated by various formulations that general principles of law (rather than a specified national law) should apply,[4] but indeed in cases where a specific national law is acknowledged in principle as being applicable.[5] Given the fact that issues as to conflict of laws and the scope of arbitral jurisdiction often must be considered prior to the choice of the national law that may otherwise govern the contract, it is not surprising that ICC arbitrators' reference to prior awards is especially frequent in dealing with such preliminary issues.[6]

It has become commonplace for advocates to invoke arbitral precedents in memorials and oral argument. Whether one is a believer (*"lex mercatoria* is being continually reinforced")[7] or not ("the myth of arbitral precedents as a source of international commercial law"),[8] the trend cannot be ignored.

Reviewing the first edition of this book, the late eminent Swedish arbitration specialist Gillis Wetter suggested that we are witnessing the birth of something that should be called *the international law of arbitration* comprising both procedural and substantive elements and destined to grow in a manner similar to the common law in the United States, where "cases decided in a large number of jurisdictions, each of whose legal systems is sovereign, have come to create a common source of law which unites the various jurisdictions

---

2　Yves Derains, *Comment*, 1981 JDI 914. The same author repeated this observation more recently, *in Les tendances de la jurisprudence arbitrale internationale*, 1993 JDI 829.

3　*See, e.g.*, ICC Cases 3267/1979, I ICC AWARDS 76, 376; II ICC AWARDS 43; 5103/1988, II ICC AWARDS 361.

4　*See, e.g.*, ICC Case 3380/1980, I ICC AWARDS 96, 413.

5　*See, e.g.*, ICC Cases 3493/1983, I ICC AWARDS 124; 5073/1986, II ICC AWARDS 85; 2404/1975, I ICC AWARDS 280.

6　*See, e.g.*, ICC Cases 2930/1982, I ICC AWARDS 118; 4131/1982, I ICC AWARDS 146, 465; 4381/1986, II ICC AWARDS 264; 4237/1984, I ICC AWARDS 167; 4695/1984, II ICC AWARDS 33. *See also* Iran-US Claims Tribunal Cases 74 *et al.*, XIII YEARBOOK 288, at 292 (1988).

7　Yves Derains, Comment, 1981 JDI 914. *See also* Thomas Carbonneau, *Rendering Awards with Reasons: The Elaboration of a Common Law of International Transactions*, 23 COLUMBIA JOURNAL OF TRANSNATIONAL LAW 579 (1985).

8　Antoine Kassis, THEORIE GENERALE DES USAGES DU COMMERCE, at 501 (1984).

without disturbing their autonomy."[9] He wrote that the term *lex mercatoria* was inappropriate: at once too limited and overused.

While tempted to opt for a new expression and thus be free to define concepts afresh, upon reflection the present authors have not done so. Too much is written and said about *lex mercatoria* in the context of ICC arbitration for this book to skirt the subject. Yet Dr. Wetter was quite right in writing that the expression is over-burdened with meaning; the first task must be to understand the difference between the fundamentally disparate concepts behind the catch-phrase "*lex mercatoria*." The discussion can be meaningful only if the terms are defined.

For all of its intellectual fascination, the debate over lex mercatoria to date[10] does not appear to have had more than a marginal impact on the practice of international arbitration,[11] and this is even more true of the attitudes and conduct of parties to international contracts. It may, however, be argued that participants in the process apply and create *lex mercatoria* without knowing it. The proponents of *lex mercatoria* certainly have important and legitimate objectives: to discern rules for international commerce that conform to parties' expectations, and to avoid the trap created when the otherwise applicable national law appears uncertain, peculiar, dramatically amended since the date of the contract, or otherwise unpredictable and unjust in its application to foreigners. One problem is that the debate so far has involved only the members of a small group of specialists. Another is that when these specialists argue about *lex mercatoria*, they often are not talking about the same thing.

Proponents of *lex mercatoria* have the disconcerting habit of announcing the existence of an entire planet on little more evidence than blips on the radar screen, while detractors have adopted what one might call a posture of aggressive ignorance. The non-specialist, recoiling instantly from something which he recognizes as complicated and far removed from his every-day con-

---

9   J. Gillis Wetter, Book Review, 1984 SVENSK JURISTTIDNING 156, at 161.

10   The name most frequently associated with the doctrine of *lex mercatoria* is that of Professor Berthold Goldman, and his two leading essays, published with an interval of 15 years, are *Frontieres du droit et lex mercatoria in* ARCHIVES DE PHILOSOPHIE DU DROIT at 177 (1964), and *La lex mercatoria dans les contrats et l'arbitrage internationaux: realites et perspectives*, 1979 JDI 475. For a thorough review of the literature, *see* LE DROIT DES RELATIONS ECONOMIQUES INTERNATIONALES (1982), a collection of *liber amicorum* essays in honor of Prof. Goldman, which demonstrates that French legal scholars are not unanimously convinced that there has been a new dawning of *lex mercatoria; see, e.g.* Paul Lagarde, *Approche critique de la lex mercatoria*, at 125. *See generally*, LEX MERCATORIA AND ARBITRATION (T. Carbonneau ed., 2d ed. 1998); Emmanuel Gaillard, *Thirty Years of Lex Mercatoria: Toward the Selective Application of Transnational Rules* 10 ICSID REVIEW 208 (1995).

11   In 1986, the then General Counsel of the ICC Court of Arbitration noted that *lex mercatoria* "rarely appears" in ICC awards, Sigvard Jarvin, Comment, 1986 JDI 1138.

cerns, perhaps notes the catch-words for possible future reference, and goes on his way.

The discussion was revitalized in 1987 with the publication of a thoughtful and clear-eyed essay by Lord Mustill, "The New *Lex Mercatoria*."[12] It is a rare and fortunate contribution to the field: an effort of extensive research and analysis, examining the postulates and the evidence with a fresh mind. Moreover, it was undertaken by a jurist of the category most suitable to the task, but generally least likely to be in a position to carry it out: an experienced practitioner and magistrate at the height of professional life.

A principal merit of Mustill's essay is its demonstration of the disparate concepts that have been blurred in much of the previous literature. While acknowledging their intellectual debt to this learned judge, the present authors seek to spread neither conviction nor doubt. They aim simply to shed light on what may be relevant to current practice. They suggest that *lex mercatoria* is invoked to cover three different concepts, two of which are ideals rather than current realities. As for the third, which in the authors' view represents a useful evolution with a significant impact in practice, its contours are so modest that its very description may turn the tables: the theoreticians of *lex mercatoria* may deplore the banalization of their lofty constructs, while the scoffers might reflect that if this is all there is to it, they have been mercatorists all along.

(i) First concept: lex mercatoria as an autonomous legal order

The average international practitioner may have great difficulty finding his way through the arcane abstractions found in the literature. The present authors believe that the significant practical distinction is the one to be perceived between *the law of the arbitration*, that is to say the law (or laws) which determines the binding effect of the actions of the parties or the arbitrator (in agreeing to arbitrate, in choosing rules of procedure or the applicable substantive law, in determining jurisdiction or arbitrability, in issuing an award) and *the law under which the merits of the dispute are decided*. The latter is foremost in the minds of the parties when addressing the arbitral tribunal, because it establishes the nature and extent of their obligations; the former comes into play when facing national judges, because it determines what effect is to be given to an agreement to arbitrate, or to an arbitral award. (There are also occasions when arbitrators consider the effect of national laws other than the one they deem applicable to the contract, for example in determining the capacity of a party or the effect of mandatory rules of the country where the contract is to be performed. If one takes the U.S. legal system as an example, there has been an unmistakable extension of the ex-

---

12   *In* MAARTEN BOS & IAN BROWNLIE, eds., LIBER AMICORUM FOR LORD WILBERFORCE 149 (1987); reprinted in 4 ARB. INT. 86 (1988).

tra-contractual law arbitrators are expected to apply, from the validity of patents to the effect of antitrust laws; *see* Section 33.02.)

Given the fact that international business transactions by definition have connecting factors with more than one legal system, the distinction is at once natural and concrete.[13]

It is likely that every week an award is rendered in some Swiss city that applies a non-Swiss law, whether English, Brazilian, Iranian—or indeed *lex mercatoria*. But if that award is challenged before the Swiss judge, he will test it not under English, Brazilian, or Iranian law, nor under *lex mercatoria*, but according to the criteria of Swiss law. Thus, with respect to an ICC award which by its terms purports to decide the dispute by applying *lex mercatoria*, the question might arise whether the courts of the place of arbitration consider the award to be unlawful. Such a case has not arisen in England; some commentators there have expressed doubts as to the validity of such an award,[14] but those doubts were put to rest by Article 46(1)(b) of the Arbitration Act 1996, subject to the requirement that the parties so agree. The Supreme Court of Austria has faced this situation and upheld the award.[15] As of 1985, the courts of Belgium would not even have jurisdiction to hear such a challenge if no litigants were Belgian.[16] The point is that the relevant legal system for this purpose would be that of the U.K., Austria, or Belgium, respectively. Similarly, if an award is presented for enforcement in a country other than the one where it was rendered, it is the legal system of that country which determines the effects of the award.[17]

---

13   In a rigorous review of the theoretical literature, Professor Pierre Mayer has peeled off vast layers of cumbersome abstractions to reach the conclusion that "the ultimate legal source of an international relationship is to be found simultaneously in all the States whose courts may be called upon to hand down a decision with regard to it, either directly or on the occasion of granting leave to enforce an arbitral award. No legal order is fundamental for the relationship; the *Grundlegung* does not exist."

Le mythe de l'ordre juridique de base (ou Grundlegung), *in* LE DROIT DES RELATIONS ECONOMIQUES INTERNATIONALES 199, at 216 (LIBER AMICORUM FOR PROF. GOLDMAN, 1982).

14   *See, e.g.*, Michael J. Mustill, 4 ARB. INT. 86, at 108-9 (1988); Michael J. Mustill & Stewart C. Boyd, COMMERCIAL ARBITRATION 68-71 (2d ed. 1989), Martin Hunter, *Publication of Awards and Lex Mercatoria*, 57 ARBITRATION 55, at 57-58 and 67 (1988).

15   Norsolor S.A. v. Pabalk Ticaret, decision of 18 March 1982, in 1983 RECHT DER INTERNATIONALEN WURTSCHAFT 29, at 868; excerpts in English *in* IX YEARBOOK 159 (1984); discussed in Section 17.03.

16   *See* Jan Paulsson, *Arbitration Unbound in Belgium*, 2 ARB. INT. 68 (1986).

17   *See generally* Horacio Grigera Naón, *Enforceability of Awards Based on Transnational Rules under the New York, Panama, Geneva and Washington Conventions*, in TRANSNATIONAL RULES IN INTERNATIONAL COMMERCIAL ARBITRATION 89, ICC Publication No. 480/4 (1993). At the 65th International Law Association Conference in Cairo in 1992, a Resolution was adopted which recommended the following:

The fact that an international arbitrator has based an award on transnational rules (general principles of law, principles common to several jurisdictions, international law, usages of trade, etc.) rather than on one law of a particular State should not in itself affect the validity

627

If an international treaty such as the New York Convention applies, it does so because it has been made part of the national law of the enforcement forum. (The English courts have in fact held that an ICC award rendered in Switzerland and applying no national law as such, but "internationally accepted principles of law governing contractual relations," may be enforced.[18])

By contrast, the first concept covered by the expression *lex mercatoria* is that of an autonomous legal order which creates rules independent of any national legal order, and which govern the relationships of parties involved in international trade. As Lord Justice Mustill demonstrates after asking the simple question, "from where does its normative power arise?" the theoretical and practical difficulties of this concept are daunting. There exists no obligatory World Court of International Commerce. Disputants under an international contract may be confronted with one or more national judges or arbitrators, depending on the terms of the contract and on relevant rules of jurisdiction. At what point is one to suppose that a contractual relationship has fled the dominion of a national system to fall under an anational or transnational one? A cabinet maker in Lyon who has never set foot outside France may one day unthinkingly enter the realm of international commerce by accepting an order to send a table to London. Is it seriously meant that he therefore must suddenly be concerned not only with the French legal system (because he might be sued in Lyon if he fails to perform), and possibly the English legal system (because he may have to sue in London if he is not paid), but some *independent* legal order whose rules can be understood only if one is attuned to dominant principles of a host of national legal systems, conventions, form contracts devised by various organizations, and the like? Does the autonomous legal order come into play only when there is an arbitration clause? Or only if the contractual relationship is complex or of long duration—and if so where is the borderline? Is this legal order a matter of choice, available to parties who agree to refer to it, or is it obligatory whenever the relationship somehow has fallen within its ambit? When operating within this legal order, does an arbitrator apply existing law, or does he create it by rendering an award having precedential value? Mustill puts his finger on the di-

---

or enforceability of the award;

(1) where the parties have agreed that the arbitrator may apply transnational rules; or

(2) where the parties have remained silent concerning the applicable law.

18   In Deutsche Schachtbau- und Tiefbohrgesellschaft mbH v. Ras Al Khaimah National Oil Co. and Shell International Petroleum Co. Ltd., [1987] 2 LLOYD'S L. REP. 246, [1987] 2 ALL E.R. 769; extracts *in* XIII YEARBOOK 522 (1988); reversed on other grounds by the House of Lords, [1988] 2 LLOYD'S L. REP. 293, [1988] 2 ALL E.R. 833. The French courts have also enforced ICC awards applying *lex mercatoria* rendered in Austria and Switzerland; *see* Section 17.03.

lemma by using the illustration of an international arbitrator faced with a previous award which decided precisely the question of law at issue:

> If the arbitrator's function is simply that of an exponent, then the second arbitrator need do no more than pay appropriate respect to the reasons of his colleague, without being obliged to arrive at the same decision. If he thinks fit, he is at liberty to hold that his predecessor misunderstood the *lex mercatoria*. Again, at the other extreme, if the first arbitrator has exercised a creative function as a social engineer, his successor can fairly regard him as no more than a part of the self-regulating mechanism of the contract under which he acted, and can thus feel free to exercise the same function, in a different sense, under his own contract. But if the intermediate theory is correct, an award which enunciates a new rule thereby adds to the corpus; and since the *lex* is conceived to be a binding law, the subsequent arbitrator must apply it, whether he agrees with the conclusion or not.[19]

Perhaps the strongest objection to viewing *lex mercatoria* as a legal order is the fact that at present it is simply not sufficient to deal with all aspects of an international commercial dispute. For example, how is one to determine the *bona fides* of an act undertaken on behalf of a corporation? *Lex mercatoria*, understood as principles derived from shared expectations in the international community, may hold that the capacity of an entity is determined by the law under which it is constituted, but the fact is that there are no corporations created under *lex mercatoria*. In the same vein, Mustill writes:

> [I]t must be noted that the *lex mercatoria* has not yet laid claim to the whole territory of potential disputes arising from international commerce. Thus: (i) there appears to be no instance in which the *lex* has been invoked in a case of pure delict; (ii) the *lex* has rarely been applied where the issues are those of consent, fraud in the making of a contract, and so on; (iii) the *lex* has not, as far as the present author is aware, ever been credited in the literature with a power to create rights in *rem*, valid as against third parties—for example, by way of a transfer of title of corporeal assets, or pledge, or the creation of a monopoly such as patent or copyright . . . . once it is accepted that the *lex* may on occasion have to be applied to some aspects of a dispute, whereas national law is applied to others, the practical attractions seem less apparent.[20]

---

19   4 ARB. INT. 86, at 98 (1988).

20   *Id.* at 102. The best-known proponent of *lex mercatoria*, Berthold Goldman, has admitted that a number of lacunae of *lex mercatoria* (in particular the validity of consent, whether as a matter of capacity, authority or undue influence) are structural and not temporary, *in La lex mercatoria dans les contrats et l'arbitrage internationaux: realites et perspectives*, 1979 JDI 475, at 479-80. Commenting on this admission, Paul Lagarde infers that Goldman considers that such questions "naturally pertain to national legal orders," *in Approche critique de la lex mercatoria, supra* Note 10, at 141.

(ii) Second concept: lex mercatoria as a comprehensive body of substantive rules sufficient to decide a dispute

Hundreds of international arbitral awards have now been published, in whole or in part, either containing the whole record of the case or sanitized to protect the anonymity of the parties. As already noted, it is an everyday phenomenon in ICC arbitration that written memorials and pleaders refer to awards as precedents. The text of this book itself is replete with descriptions and citations of arbitral awards. Does this confirm *lex mercatoria's* existence as a body of laws sufficient to serve as the governing law of an international contract?

The present authors believe in the importance of arbitral precedents, but as shall be seen, in a more limited sense (the third concept). As matters stand today, it is difficult to maintain that *lex mercatoria* can govern a contract. As Mustill writes:

> The proponents of the *lex mercatoria* claim it to be the law of the international business community: which must mean the law unanimously adopted by all countries engaged upon international commerce. Such a claim would have been sustainable two centuries ago. But the international business community is now immeasurably enlarged. What principles of trade law, apart from those which are so general as to be useless, are common to the legal systems of the members of such a community? How could the arbitrators or the advocates who appear before them amass the necessary materials on the laws of, say, Brazil, China, Russia, Australia, Nigeria, and Iraq? How could any tribunal, however cosmopolitan and polyglot, hope to understand the nuances of the multifarious legal systems? In published awards the arbitrators occasionally make large claims about the universality of principles, but these are rarely if ever substantiated by citation of sources. Equally if not more important is the question: How could any adviser hope to predict what a tribunal not yet constituted might make of such a task in the future?[21]

---

21   4 ARB. INT. 89, at 92-3 (1988). The present authors wholly agree with the following observation by Lord Mustill:

> "In the literature, the use of legal encyclopaedias is sometimes advocated. I suggest that these are usually worse than useless for this particular purpose, unless the reader is guided by someone with direct knowledge: a little learning is indeed a dangerous thing. Anyone with practical experience of international disputes must acknowledge the difficulty of making an accurate assessment of the law of only one unfamiliar legal system, absent the kind of prolonged and expensive expert guidance which would be quite out of the question if dozens of different laws had to be assimilated."

Id. at 92, note 24. These types of considerations doubtless underlie the reluctance of many arbitrators to embrace *lex mercatoria* (second concept). Thus, in a case where the evidence seemed clear that the parties when contracting had not considered the matter of governing law, an ICC tribunal presided by one of the leading Swiss arbitrators (Dr. Briner, who in 1997 became Chairman of the ICC Court) declared its unwillingness to assume that *lex mercatoria* should apply: "the choice of such a law would require an agreement between the parties which in the present

Nor is Mustill satisfied with trade practice as a source of rules outside national law:

> The simple repetition of contracts on the same terms is as consistent with the exercise of freedom of contract as with subordination to a system of binding norms; indeed, far more so, since if the parties to a commodity transaction do not wish to bind themselves to, say, the GAFTA Contract Form No. 100, there is no legal or other institution which can compel them to do so. Moreover, the repetition of transactions in the same form could at most create a group of norms peculiar to the individual trade, thereby creating a network of para-legal systems. This is quite inconsistent with the theoretical premises of the *lex mercatoria*, which is that it springs spontaneously from the structure of international commerce—which is quite plainly regarded as an indivisible whole.[22]

Whatever one's views *de lege ferenda*, it would appear impossible to deny that Mustill's objections are well taken as a matter of current reality.[23] The present authors would add only these observations:

— At the time of the preparation of UNCITRAL's Model Law on International Commercial Arbitration,[24] there was much debate about what was to become Article 28(2), defining the law to be applied by the arbitrators when the parties have not stipulated applicable law. Proponents of *lex mercatoria* (second concept) wished the wording (following the example of recent arbitration laws in France and the Netherlands; *see* Section 17.03) to refer to "rules of law" rather than "the law" determined by applicable conflict rules. The purpose was to allow awards to be decided on the basis of *lex mercatoria*. This proposal was defeated.[25]

---

case was not reached," ICC Case 4650/1985, II ICC Awards 67, at 68.

22   4 Arb. Int. 86, at 95-6 (1988).

23   The French Supreme Court's decision in Compania Valenciana de Cementos Portland v. Primary Coal Inc., 22 Oct. 1991, 1992 Rev. Arb. 457 (upholding an ICC award rendered in Paris and applying general principles of "international trade") was heralded in some quarters as recognising the legal status of *lex mercatoria*, but in the opinion of the authors the judgment signifies only that the Court of Cassation refused to overrule the substantive determination of the arbitrators when the contract contained no choice-of-law clausse. If this latter view is correct, the debate over the "normative force" of *lex mercatoria* may as a practical matter be viewed as a tempest in a tea cup.

24   *See* Gerold Hermann, *The UNCITRAL Model Law—its Background, Salient Features and Purposes*, 1 Arb. Int. 6 (1985); same author, *UNCITRAL Adopts Model Law on International Commercial Arbitration*, 2 Arb. Int. 2 (1986); Jan Paulsson, *Report on the UNCITRAL Model Law as Adopted in Vienna on 21 June 1985*, 52 Arbitration 98 (1986).

25   On the other hand, Article 28(1) dealing with choice of law *by the parties* refers to "rules of law," which Professor Clive Schmitthoff has concluded authorizes arbitrations to apply *lex mercatoria* if the parties have so stipulated, International Trade Usages at 48 (ICC Publication No. 440/4, 1987). In commenting on the ILA Resolution quoted in Note 17, a leading international arbitrator, Prof. Karl-Heinz Böckstiegel, stated that: "the message of this resolution is not to tell parties to just use this and nothing else, but just to deal with a situation which does occur in practice."

‐ Awards handed down on the foundation of *lex mercatoria* can doubtless be things of beauty, if rendered by profoundly knowledgeable scholars of comparative law. But if correct application of *lex mercatoria* requires arbitrators of such calibre, there simply will be a shortage of qualified arbitrators. In addition, is it not a fair assumption that the best awards *from the viewpoint of the parties*, are rendered by persons experienced with the problem raised by the particular context and substance of the dispute (construction contracts, long-term supply agreements, charter parties, or insurance policies); and would it not be unfortunate if they would be disqualified or reluctant to accept appointment because they do not belong to the *lex mercatoria cognoscenti*?

‐ To those who would answer the last point by observing that one need not realistically fear a dearth of persons eager to act as international arbitrators, it must be responded that this fuels rather than allays one's apprehensions. In the hands of the untutored, authority to apply *lex mercatoria* may be a recipe for amateurism and arbitrariness. In some cases it may serve as a fig leaf for the arbitrator's private preferences, substituted for the parties' shared contractual expectations. Nothing is easier than to proclaim common principles on the basis of limited and superficial personal knowledge.[26] If enough awards are rendered by amateur mercatorists, there may well be pressure to reverse the international trend toward nonreviewability of arbitrators' findings of law.

In 1994, UNIDROIT came to the rescue of *lex mercatoria* by publishing Principles of International Commercial Contracts which seek to provide uniform substantive rules, dealing not only with general matters but also highly technical ones.[27]

Discussion of the ILA Resolution on Transnational Rules, 23 October 1992, in Transnational Rules in International Commercial Arbitration, ICC Publication No. 480/4, at 49 (1993).

26 Mustill, 4 Arb. Int. 86, at 113, note 195, describes ICC Case 2291/1975, 1976 JDI 989, as follows: "[A]n instructive example of the dangers of making unsupported generalizations. In the award and commentary we find that Anglo-Saxon law is 'plus accessible a la revision des contrats en cas de desequilibre meme pour la cause economique (clause de hardship)' [more open to the revision of contracts in the event of disruption of the contractural equilibrium even for economic causes] as well as reference to 'la presence presque automatique de clauses de ce type dans les contrats internationaux' [the nearly automatic presence of such clauses in international contracts]. The former is not a correct statement of the common law; and the inclusion of hardship and similar clauses in the routine type of transportation contract with which the arbitrators were concerned is almost, if not entirely, unknown."

27 Michael Bonell, *The UNIDROIT Principles in Practice: The Experience of the First Two Years*, 1 Uniform Law Review 30 (UNIDROIT, 1997), cites the award in ICC case 8128/1995, 123 JDI 812 (1996), where a sole arbitrator filled a gap in the otherwise applicable law with respect to the issue of interest by referring to Article 7.4.9(2) of the UNIDROIT Principles as a relevant "general principle" and therefore, in the circumstances, applied LIBOR plus two per cent. *See also* Klaus Peter Berger, *The Lex Mercatoria Doctrine and the UNIDROIT Principles of International Commercial Contracts*, 28 Law & Policy in International Business 943 (1997). For a more doubting view, see Hans van Houtte, *The UNIDROIT Principles of International Commercial Contracts*, 11 Arb. Int. 373, esp. 381-2 (1995). *See also*, The Unidroit Principles for International Commercial Contracts: A New Lex Mercatoria? (ICC Institute of International Business Law & Practice, 1995); Philippe Kahn, *Vers l'institutionnalisation de la lex mercatoria: à propos des principes*

If parties, arbitrators and courts come to refer to these Principles, however, it will not mean that they are embracing *lex mercatoria* as the accretion of a common law of international transactions, but by way of relying on what is in effect a fixed codification which itself contains lacunae and may—once accepted in various places—have some difficulty in evolving. The UNIDROIT Principles may thus turn out to be a competitor of *lex mercatoria*, not its savior. Or perhaps it will come to be accepted, atleast partially, as a snapshot of *lex mercatoria* as of 1994.[28]

(iii) Third concept: lex mercatoria as usage in international trade

Finally, the expression *lex mercatoria* may cover the notion of international trade usages sufficiently established to warrant that parties to international contracts—whether generally or by *category* of contracts—be considered bound by them. This is the concept that the present authors deem to be practically significant today.[29] They hold it to be important and useful, but recognize that this proposition may be so mundane that learned commentators would doubtless have found it unworthy of new schools of thought. Nor, apparently, would a skeptic like Mustill find in it the occasion to tax his wit and his pen, because he would accept it as the most natural thing in the world. In "The New *Lex Mercatoria*," he gives the concept but a passing glance:

> Nobody could deny that usage in this sense can be an important element in the assessment by a tribunal of the rights and duties created by the contract, either because in a codified or inexplicit form it is tacitly incorporated into the contract, or because it has been received into the relevant national law. But there is nothing special about international trade in this respect, nor anything special about arbitration.[30]

Mustill points out that Article 7(1) of the Geneva Convention of 1961, Article 33(3) of the UNCITRAL Arbitration Rules, and Article 13(5) of the ICC Rules (Article 17(2) in the 1998 revision) require trade usages to be taken into ac-

---

UNIDROIT (Commission Droit et Vie des Affaires, 1998); Klaus Peter Berger, *International Arbitral Practice and the UNIDROIT Principles of International Commercial Contracts*, 46 AM. J. COMP. L. 129 (1998); Detlev Vagts, *Arbitration and the UNIDROIT Principles*, CONTRATACIÓN INTERNACIONAL (Mexico 1998).

28 A similar venture has been undertaken by the Lando Commission which in May 1995 proposed "Principles of European Contract Law," a text which some hope may be precursor of a European Civil Code; *see* Ole Lando, *Principles of European Contract Law: An Alternative to or a Precursor of European Legislation?* 40 AMERICAN JOURNAL OF COMPARATIVE LAW 573 (1992).

29 Professor Clive Schmitthoff, who carried out an ICC research project begun in 1980 and terminated in 1987 with the publication of a report, INTERNATIONAL TRADE USAGES (ICC Publication No. 440/4) in reaching his conclusion that *lex mercatoria* is "a system of law" and not the reflection of authority to decide in equity, refers to *lex mercatoria* as "a universal trade usage," at 48. In fact it may be useful even if it is not a coherent "system," and even if it is not an impressively monolithic super-usage, but merely an incomplete concatenation of various usages. *See* Jan Paulsson, *La lex mercatoria dans l'arbitrage CCI*, 1990 REV. ARB. 55.

30 4 ARB. INT. 86, at 94 (1988).

count, and then says: "But the position would surely be just the same without them."[31] The justification for this assertion is, of course, *to be found in national laws*. The reader reflecting on his own national law will doubtless find support for the applicability of usages.[32] Indeed, the UNCITRAL Model Law on International Commercial Arbitration, which it should be recalled, *is a recommendation for harmonization of national laws* (and whose drafters, as seen, specifically declined to endorse the applicability, in the absence of agreement by the parties to that effect, of "rules of law" other than "the law"), firmly sets down, in Article 28(4):

> In all cases, the arbitral tribunal shall decide in accordance with the terms of the contract and shall take into account the usages of the trade applicable to the transaction.

Lex mercatoria in this modest sense may thus be seen essentially as an expansion of the notion of usages to encompass particular contracts whose specificity is that they are international. According to this view, the interpretation of international contracts requires recognition of the transnational context of the underlying transactions. The practical justification is not difficult to grasp. If international trade is to be facilitated, the regime of international contracts should not be a minefield of hidden provisions of

---

31   *Id.*, at note 33. Here Mustill may be underestimating the emphatic effect of what is now Article 17(2) of the ICC Rules providing that "[i]n all cases the arbitrator shall take account of the provisions of the contract and the relevant trade usages." For an instance where arbitrators relied on its precursor to establish a commission rate to replace a method for calculating remuneration which as a result of changed circumstances had become "excessive," *see* ICC Case 4145/1986, XII YEARBOOK 97, at 110 (1987).

32   Article 1135 of the French Civil Code states: "Contracts give rise not only to the obligations expressed therein, but also to all consequences which equity, usages or the law attach to that obligation in accordance with its nature." The position of French law finds numerous echoes not only in legal systems that have codified the law of obligations, but also in those of the common law. In England, usages fall under the category of "implied terms," and their claim to application was felicitously expressed one and a half centuries ago in Hutton v. Warren (1836), 1 MEESON & WELSBY'S EXCHEQUER REPORTS 466:

> "It has long been settled that in commercial transactions extrinsic evidence of custom and usage is admissible to annex incidents to written contracts in matters with respect to which they are silent. The same rule has also been applied to contracts in other transactions in life and this has been done upon the principle of presumption that, in such transactions, the parties did not mean to express in writing the whole of the contract by which they intended to be bound, but to contract with reference to those known usages."

Contemporary statutory law in the U.K. is quite to the point. Section 55(1) of the Sale of Goods Act 1979 provides:

> "[A]ny right, duty, or liability arising under a contract of sale by implication of law may be negatived or varied by usage if such as to bind both parties to the contract."

International contracts containing reference to the terms C.I.F. and F.O.B. have been cited as examples of usages that may, in light of §55(1), neutralize the application of the Sale of Goods Act even to contracts explicitly subject to English law.

For a fuller review of incorporation of usages into various national laws, based on an ICC research project, *see* Schmitthoff, *supra* Note 29.

national law. It is easy to say that no one should enter into a contract governed by, say, Finnish or Korean law without getting reliable and comprehensive legal advice, but if one adopts a position of absolute rigidity in this respect one is furthering the cause of lawyers rather than that of commerce. To do so would result in a situation where parties would view any foray into the international field as high adventure, particularly where the governing law is not specified in the contract. And as for parties who are active in a great number of countries, such as the licensor of widely desired technology, is it not healthy to start with the postulate that detailed standard contracts, developed over years of experience in various jurisdictions, should if at all possible be interpreted in a uniform manner, even though the judges of countries X, Y, and Z might have viewed the contracts differently if they had been concluded as a matter of purely domestic commercial relations between fellow nationals?

It would appear particularly appropriate to avoid unexpected peculiarities of a national law in the case where parties have not chosen the applicable law. In such a situation, one may often reasonably conclude that the parties have made a "negative choice." Each party proposed its own law, but each proposal was rejected; and finally neither law was stipulated. An arbitrator who then gives one of those laws primacy is in a sense doing just what the parties resolved should not be done. Another situation where the dominance of any national law seems doubtful is that of a contract to be performed in several countries.[33]

An example might be helpful. In ICC Case 2090,[34] a Pakistani party brought ICC arbitration against a French supplier under a C&F sales contract. An award was rendered by the three French arbitrators, sitting in Paris, in favor of the Pakistani buyer and against the French seller. It is clear that the tribunal took account of the practical difficulties a Third World party might face with respect to an arbitration to be conducted far away and under unfamiliar rules, as the following aspect of the case makes clear.

The French party had argued that under the contractually applicable French law, the buyer had failed to serve a "summons" as required by Article 1139 of the French Civil Code. Noting that Article 1139 refers to "a summons or any equivalent document," the arbitrators dismissed the technical argument. They felt it was appropriate to take into account the reasonable de-

---

33 *See* ICC Case 1859/1973, 1973 REV. ARB. 133, where the arbitrator stated: "The contract was to be performed in three different countries . . . it was clear that the parties intended to refer to the general principles and practices of international trade."

34 Award in ICC Case 2090/1976, I ICC AWARDS 56.

gree of familiarity by the Pakistani party of a foreign law it had accepted to
govern the contract:

> WHEREAS by law the judges are empowered to decide to what extent "an-
> other document" is "equivalent" to a summons;

> WHEREAS it is necessary to take into account the fact that the plaintiff,
> while it accepted to submit the dispute for solution under French law, is
> nonetheless a Pakistani company with its office in Karachi, and as such had
> little familiarities with technical precisions of French legal civil procedure;

> WHEREAS the claimant could have believed that it acted in good faith by
> contacting the French Commercial Counselor in Karachi on October 21,
> 1970, in order that he intercede with Defendant so that the latter would per-
> form the sales contract, and thus accomplishing an act or document which
> could be considered as a summons;

> WHEREAS in any case, it is necessary to consider as a document equivalent to
> a summons the letter from Claimant dated May 19, 1971, in which he informed
> the Defendant of his intention to seize the Arbitration Court with the "dispute
> arising from the nonperformance of the contract by the Defendant".[35]

The arbitrators thus took account of the international character of the contract in making allowances for the fact that the understanding of a Pakistani
party, used to particular customs in managing its contractual relationships,
might be quite different from that of a French party. The fact that the Pakistani party knows that a particular contract is governed by French (or Japanese or Brazilian) law will not necessarily change the instinctive reactions of
its personnel to given situations during the life of the contract. The international arbitrator should not necessarily draw the same inferences from the
acts or omissions of such a party as a French judge would when assessing the
conduct of a French party. This can hardly be controversial; a French judge
might well make the same allowances when dealing with an international
contract governed by French law but performed by foreigners. The ICC arbitrator, however, is more often called upon to reflect in this transnational
mode—and would be more suited to it if he has experience in international
practice. To insist that the international arbitrator should try to ascertain
how a judge of the country whose law he is applying would react, and then to
do exactly that, may finally lead to more controversy. To avoid violence to his
own sense of justice, the arbitrator would be tempted to reach for another applicable law. Although in most cases his "error" in determining the applicable
law would not be subject to review, this type of artifice appears less appealing

---

35   *Id.* at 132.

than the frank recognition that an international contract governed by French law may be viewed in a different light than a purely internal one.[36]

Viewed as usages specific to international contracts, *lex mercatoria* would have both negative and positive effects. The negative effect has just been illustrated with respect to ICC Case 2090: the avoidance of peculiarities demonstrably contrary to the reasonable expectations of the parties. The positive effect is to recognize that some rules applicable to international commercial relations are so pervasive that no particular references to sources in national laws are needed to justify application of the rules.[37]

This approach is particularly useful in cases where the governing law is unknown to the tribunal and the amount in dispute is so modest that it would be uneconomical for the parties to engage in research and offer detailed proof. It is even more useful when the governing law is that of a country whose sources of law are rudimentary. (In such a situation, the approach also has the salutary effects of making it easier for the arbitrator to accept the principle that the law of that country is applicable—thereby enhancing the legitimacy of the international arbitral process in the eyes of parties from that country—and, frequently, to avoid controversial references to the laws of former colonial powers as "ultimate" sources of the laws of developing countries.)

It is here, in the evolution of standards to which reference can be made directly, without invoking more specific sources of national law, that arbitral precedents come in. The observation that this third concept of *lex mercatoria* is banal should not obscure the fact that application of the usages of international contracts is a challenging one. The weight to be given to *lex mercatoria* applied in this sense would not be the same in every case, nor should it, in light of its ultimate justification as a matter of the parties' reasonable and le-

---

36 Since 1981, the date of a special French Decree on International Arbitration (*see* Section 30.01), Article 1496 of the French Code of Civil Procedure gives the following directive to international arbitrators:

"The arbitrator shall decide the dispute according to the rules of law chosen by the parties; in the absence of such a choice, he shall decide according to those he deems appropriate.

"In all cases he shall take into account trade usages." (Emphasis added.)

37 *See, e.g.*, ICC Case 4338/1984, I ICC AWARDS 555. A French court once made the following statement in rejecting an argument to the effect that the ICC Uniform Rules and Practice for Documentary Credit were "mere recommendations:"

"[T]hey cannot have the same binding character as the law, but they reflect usages which are recognized, particularly in commercial matters, as constituting a source of law, applying in the absence of any express reference by the parties, at least insofar as they have not excluded their application with respect to a given point."

Tribunal of Commerce of Paris, Judgment of 8 March 1976, 1977 REVUE DE LA JURISPRUDENCE COMMERCIALE 72. Since in the premises the parties had in fact made contractual reference to the Uniform Rules, this statement must be considered as *obiter dictum*. *See generally* Jean Stoufflet, *L'oeuvre normative internationale dans le domaine bancaire* in LE DROIT DES RELATIONS ECONOMIQUES INTERNATIONALES 361 (LIBER AMICORUM FOR PROF. GOLDMAN, 1982).

gitimate expectations. Thus, a foreign company which has long been established in France may appropriately be held to specifically French norms rather than international usages. And it may often be the case that with respect to certain categories of trade, the relevant usages are specific to that field of activity—different from general international usages and perhaps occasionally at variance with them.

One problem with the expression "usages" is that its primary meaning is that of conduct in the ordinary course of business, whereas the international arbitrator is looking for rules to be applied in a pathological situation: a dispute. There is no difficulty in applying usages in its ordinary sense to illuminate the meaning of contractual language (thus, for example, relevant usages may indicate whether "payment" was "made" at a particular date). But it is difficult to point to a dispositive "usage" when one party invokes a legal characterization of a situation (such as the neutralization of contractual duties due to an event of *force majeure*) which is challenged by the other. It is here that international arbitral awards may be seen to generate rules; the "usage" with respect to international contracts is that engendered by the existence of a body of arbitral precedents which may fairly be considered to fall within the scope of the settled and reasonable expectations of parties to international contracts. In this sense, "usages" may evolve into a type of customary law of international contracts, and it may be seen as creating useful and legitimate norms in the absence of contrary indications of otherwise applicable national law. The present authors would, however, express grave reservations with respect to any suggestions that "usages" created by arbitral precedents may *overrule* the explicit provisions of applicable national law. They are also mindful of the possible danger of arbitrators' inappropriately concerning themselves with implications of their decision beyond the parties before them.

One final reflection. National laws often give the judge (and by extension the arbitrator who may be applying them) wide powers to interpret contractual provisions and to apply them to the fact pattern at hand. When an international arbitrator exercises that authority, for example to establish the effect of an amendment on a prior contract or to determine whether an alleged event of *force majeure* was truly unavoidable, he does so (in conformity with whatever national law may be relevant) in light of all the circumstances. When those circumstances pertain to an international transaction, involving foreign states, foreign laws, foreign languages, and foreign currencies—not to mention foreigners—*a type of jurisprudence is generated, by repeated decisions dealing with similar transnational fact patterns, which by definition cannot be derived from a purely national context*. This, in the present authors' opinion, is a convincing rationale for the reference in ICC awards to arbitral precedents. As the unanimous ICC tribunal presided by Professor Pieter Sanders of the Netherlands put it in Case 4131/1982, after citing two prior ICC awards (relating to the possibility of inferring acceptance of arbitral jurisdiction from the conduct of parties in carrying out international contracts):

> The decisions of [ICC] tribunals progressively create caselaw which should be taken into account, because it draws conclusions from economic reality and conforms to the needs of international commerce, to which rules specific to international arbitration, themselves successively elaborated, should respond.[38]

35.02   ICC awards as precedents

The development of a mature body of authoritative rules requires that both businessmen and arbitrators view arbitral decisions as a confirmation of international commercial custom. By publishing awards rendered under its auspices, selecting especially those decisions that appear particularly independent of national law,[39] the ICC has contributed toward the development of *lex mercatoria*. It has become possible to discern a number of principles applied more because of their conformity to the parties' expectations than because they are compelled by specific national laws.

It was at this point of his reading of the first edition of this book that Gillis Wetter, who as noted in Section 35.01 is otherwise convinced of the potential significance of what he would prefer to call an "international law of arbitration," wrote that the authors' attempt to identify specific principles unintentionally caused the bubble to burst. The attempted demonstration, he concluded, revealed

> an unfortunately shriveled and meaningless remnant of what had appeared to be high-flying and beautifully shimmering juridico-technical structures, which scientific analysis reduces to a dozen or so obvious or exceedingly fuzzy juridical axioms of limited value.[40]

In light of this and many similar comments, the authors wish to emphasize the limited scope of their claims for these arguable norms of *lex mercatoria*. Certainly the "shimmering structures" of *lex mercatoria* (first concept) are not materialized here. And those who criticize *lex mercatoria* (second concept) on the grounds that it is far from able to deal with the full range of issues that arise in international business disputes may say with some force that as a system of jurisprudence, this is a "shriveled and meaningless" one. That leaves the "obvious" and the "fuzzy." In the view of the present authors, the significance of obvious or fuzzy norms should not be underesti-

---

38   I ICC AWARDS 146, 465.

39   The then Secretary General of the ICC Court of Arbitration wrote as follows in his introduction to the first award published in the digest of ICC awards appearing annually in the JOURNAL DE DROIT INTERNATIONAL: "Only those awards in which arbitrators have felt least constrained to apply national law have been published." 1974 JDI at 878. The introduction to the 1983 digest confirmed this guiding principle, 1983 JDI at 889.

40   *Supra* Note 9, at 160.

mated for the purposes of *lex mercatoria* (third concept). The question is whether a *lex mercatoria* of international usage has become so "obvious" with respect to a given principle that it may be applied without necessary reference to the otherwise applicable national law. If that has been the case, it is no mean achievement. Considering the cultural heterogeneity of the many significant actors in contemporary international trade, it would be unreasonable to expect that more than a handful of principles would reach this level of consensus. As for norms which appear "fuzzy," they obviously cannot be applied as long as the adjective fits. However, the frequency of attempts to apply them independently of national law suggests that it is an important matter in current practice; one should be attentive to their possible evolution into clearer norms.[41]

The following principles have been applied in ICC arbitration without reference to national law.

(i) Institutional freedom to regulate the conduct of arbitrators

Articles 11 and 12 of the ICC Rules establishes in very general terms standards for the conduct of arbitrators; an ICC arbitrator may be challenged if he is not "independent" of the parties, if he is "prevented *de jure* or *de facto* from fulfilling his functions," or if he is "not fulfilling his functions in accordance with the Rules or within the prescribed time-limits." The causes for removal of arbitrators are dealt with in Chapter 13. The point for present purposes is that rulings by the ICC on challenges of arbitrators are in most cases final[42] and may fairly be characterized as applying a set of uniform rules proper to ICC arbitration, rather than applying different national rules depending on the case. Thus, the standards discussed in Chapter 13 may be deemed to constitute norms germane to international arbitration.

---

41   An Indian author has expressed strong support for the development of *lex mercatoria* as a desideratum in terms of achieving greater acceptance of international arbitration by countries outside the industrialized world:

> "In international commerce and business, trade usages and customs familiar to the parties and accepted by them must retain the primacy of place and consideration . . . The harmonization of laws in international trade and practices in international arbitration will be the greatest factor, which will help the movement of arbitration and its adoption by trade in every country and region of the world. What is required in international trade is not laws tied to national or different systems of laws, but a legal system based on international trade laws and usages, customs and practices conducive to the development of a *lex mercatoria* for worldwide acceptance and practice."

N. Krishnamurthi, *Some Thoughts on a New Convention on Internation Arbitration*, in THE ART OF ARBITRATION 207, at 210 (LIBER AMICORUM FOR PIETER SANDERS, 1982).

42   *See* Jean-Yves Art, *Challenge of Arbitrators: Is an Institutional Decision Final?* 2 ARB. INT. 261 (1986).

(ii) Freedom to establish rules of procedure

Article 15(1) of the ICC Rules gives arbitrators the freedom (in the silence of the ICC Rules themselves and the absence of party agreement) to apply any rules of procedure they consider appropriate, "whether or not reference is thereby made to the Rules of procedure of a national law to be applied to the arbitration." This means that most of Parts III and IV of this book is evidence of commonly accepted principles, independent of national laws, as to the manner in which an international commercial arbitration should be conducted. (It may thus be taken as part of the *lex mercatoria* governing the arbitral process that arbitrators should first and foremost seek the parties' agreement when making procedural orders.) The fact that transgression of mandatory national rules of procedure may imperil the award does of course constrain prudent arbitrators, but it is rare that an arbitrator feels there is a conflict between such rules and his sense of the appropriate. At any rate, it does not alter the basic point that he may find a basis on which to make procedural rulings without looking to national law.

(iii) Freedom to establish applicable law

When the parties have not chosen applicable law, Article 17(1) of the ICC Rules provides that the "Arbitral Tribunal shall apply the rules of law which it determines to be appropriate." How arbitrators apply this rule is one of the most discussed aspects of ICC arbitration (*see* Chapter 17). It certainly is the point on which there is the greatest body of arbitral precedents, and which has given rise to the greatest number of instances in which ICC arbitrators cite previous published awards.[43] Chapter 17 of this book may thus be said to deal with the most developed category of principles elaborated independently of national law.

(iv) Arbitrators' authority to rule on their own jurisdiction

This principle, consecrated in ICC arbitration (*see* Section 11.03), is a widely recognized rule. Article 6(4) of the ICC Rules call on arbitrators to decide questions relating to their own jurisdiction, and countless ICC arbitrators have done just that.[44] In so doing, they have generally been upheld by national courts.[45]

---

43   *See, e.g.*, ICC Case 4237/1984, I ICC AWARDS 167.

44   *See, e.g.*, ICC Cases 3987/1983, I ICC AWARDS 521; 4367/1984, II ICC AWARDS 18; 4695/1984, II ICC AWARDS 33; 5065/1986, II ICC AWARDS 330; 5103/1988, II ICC AWARDS 361; 6268/1990, III ICC AWARDS 68; 6719/1991, II ICC AWARDS 567.

45   The references are too numerous to be cited. See generally the various *National Reports* published in the YEARBOOK. For a recent and thorough discussion at the highest level of a national court system, see the decision of the Supreme Court of India of 16 August 1984 in Renusugar Power Co. v. General Electric and International Chamber of Commerce, unpublished; extracts *in* X YEARBOOK 431 (1985).

(v) A State may not invoke its internal law to repudiate its agreement to arbitrate

As Judge Keba Mbaye (former Vice-President of the International Court of Justice and former First President of the Supreme Court of Senegal) put it: "A state must not be allowed to cite the provisions of its law in order to escape from an arbitration that it has already accepted."[46] The discussion in Section 5.02 demonstrates that this principle of good faith has been applied by ICC arbitrators as an imperative norm perceived without reference to any specific national law.[47]

It may be noted that by virtue of the new Swiss Federal Act on Private International Law, this principle has been incorporated into the national law of one of the leading venues for international arbitration.[48] This is a singular example—but perhaps a sign of things to come—of a national legal principle being derived from *lex mercatoria* rather than the other way round.

(vi) Pacta sunt servanda (contracts are to be enforced)

None of the first five principles discussed above relate to substantive matters, but rather to issues of procedure, applicable law, and jurisdiction. This is the first substantive principle. The classical basic postulate, it is given particular resonance by the ICC Rules themselves, which in Article 17(2) require arbitrators in all cases to take into account the provisions of the contract.[49]

For example, arbitrators presume that international businessmen negotiate contracts in awareness of the potential impact of price fluctuations and foreign exchange regulations. Unless the parties explicitly reallocate these risks, arbitrators hesitate to imply terms that alleviate a party's obligation to perform. Fluctuations of the currency in which a contract price is denominated changes the real value of contractual obligations. Parties may avoid this risk by using a currency stabilization clause, for example by indexing the cur-

---

46   *In* INTERNATIONAL ARBITRATION: 60 YEARS ON 293, at 296 (ICC Publication No. 412, 1984).

47   *See generally* Jan Paulsson, *May a State Invoke Its Internal Law to Repudiate Consent to International Commercial Arbitration?* 2 ARB. INT. 90 (1986). Michael Mustill, 4 ARB. INT. 86, at 112, note 91 (1988), writes: "Perhaps it should be classed as a principle of international *ordre public* rather than *lex mercatoria*." One might observe that to the extent that an international commercial arbitrator finds that he is authorized to apply international *ordre public*, he may be giving substance to *lex mercatoria* (first concept).

48   *See* Section 32.02.

49   As a U.S. court stated in upholding an agreement to arbitrate in the Netherlands against the complaint of a U.S. defendant that it would not have agreed to such an "onerous" condition as the obligation to arbitrate in a foreign country had it known that such an obligation was part of the "Conditions" referred to in an "Offer" it had accepted: "Parties, especially commercial parties, are generally held to their contracts whether they have read them or not. Were this not the law, there would be no certainty in contracts," JMA Investments *et al.* v. C. Rijkaart B.V. *et al.*, unpublished decision of 18 June 1985, USDC, E.D. Wash.; extracts *in* XI YEARBOOK 578, at 580 (1986).

rency to its gold value at the time of contracting.[50] ICC arbitrators have consistently enforced express currency stabilization clauses. In one case, for example, an Iranian purchaser was awarded damages for breach by the Yugoslavian seller in accordance with the contract's currency stabilization clause, without reference to the content of the contract's governing law.[51]

A party to an international contract generally must render payment in the designated currency even though its value has changed. In one ICC award,[52] the parties were required by contract to negotiate a new sales price should currency fluctuations cause an imbalance in the parties' obligations. When a devaluation of the U.S. dollar precipitated fruitless negotiations, the seller claimed that he had fulfilled his obligations. The arbitrator found that the clause required only that the parties undertake good faith negotiations, the failure of which meant that the contract was binding according to its original prices. Because the parties failed to provide an index to stabilize the price, the seller could arbitrate only the issue of the buyer's good faith.[53] The parties may have considered currency fluctuations, but they failed to create a currency stabilization clause. Instead they had drafted a type of hardship clause, ill-suited to currency stabilization.

The principle of *pacta sunt servanda* does not permit parties to be totally indifferent to the problems of their co-contractants when significant circumstances have rendered performance difficult. ICC arbitrators are not anxious to give the proverbial "pound of flesh." They find the *pacta sunt servanda* principle to be tempered by another rule; that of good faith.

(vii) Performance and renegotiation in good faith

Most national legal systems contain explicit legal texts to the effect, as the Egyptian Civil Code puts it in Article 148, that:

> A contract must be performed in accordance with its contents and in compliance with the requirements of good faith.

> A contract binds the contracting party not only as regards its expressed conditions but also as regards everything which, according to law, usage, and

---

50   Awards upholding "gold clauses" include, according to Mustill's enumeration, 4 ARB. INT. 86, at 112, note 94 (1988): ICC Cases 1512/1971, I ICC AWARDS 207; 1990/1972, I ICC AWARDS 20, 199; 2291/1975, I ICC AWARDS 274. Such a clause is only one of several mechanisms for adapting the contract to future circumstances. The more complex "hardship clause" calls for contractual adaption in the face of a wide variety of changed circumstances that may have made the contract onerous for one of the parties. The adaptation mechanism generally requires negotiation followed by arbitration, suitable for long-term development contracts rather than for sales contracts. *See* Bruno Oppetit, *L'adaptation des contrats internationaux aux changements de circonstances: la clause de "Hardship"*, 1974 JDI 794.

51   ICC Case 1717/1972, I ICC AWARDS 191. Iranian law had been found to govern the contract.

52   ICC Case 2478/1974, I ICC AWARDS 25, 233.

53   *Cf.* Note 84 *infra*.

equity, is deemed, in view of the nature of the obligation, to be a necessary sequel to the contract.[54]

To say that this principle has also evolved into a norm of *lex mercatoria* applicable "independently" of national laws may appear somewhat fatuous, since most national legal systems have long since erected it as a cornerstone of their law of obligations.[55] But beyond that, arbitral precedents provide illustrations of the "necessary sequels" that the requirement of good faith attach to international contracts.[56] Thus, the principle of good faith has been applied to hold an existing corporate entity bound by documents it signed on behalf of a company to be created,[57] to hold that the obligation by the supplier to install telecommunications equipment to be used in West Africa implied that the equipment "would be built with all specifications necessary for complying with the conditions prevailing at the site," and that in the circumstances of a case involving an international distribution agreement between U.S. and Argentine parties having had an initial two-year duration and having been extended for several shorter periods, a two-month notice of termination was wrongful and constituted a material breach.[58] In many cases, the issue of good faith may also be viewed in terms of estoppel (*see* paragraph xvii *infra*) as in the case of the corporate entity having signed on behalf of a yet-to-becreated company; having caused the other party to perform under the contract, it was estopped from seeking to avoid liability simply by failing to finalize the establishment of the company in whose name the contract had formally been signed.

While a party may ultimately insist on its contractual rights, it would be ill-advised to refuse even to discuss matters with a co-contractant harmed by substantially changed circumstances. Refusal to negotiate in good faith has been sanctioned by ICC arbitrators.[59]

---

54   Translation by Perrott, Fanner and Sims Marshall.

55   Some common lawyers seem to think that the good-faith obligation has no place in their law. The fact is that it does, but perhaps in so obvious a fashion that they do not recognize it when it appears—typically under the guise of implied terms. *See* STEPHEN BURTON and ERIC ANDERSEN, CONTRACTUAL GOOD FAITH (1995).

56   *But see*, for a sceptical view of the possibility of discerning useful transnational norms, Piero Bernardini, *Is the Duty to Cooperate in Long-term Contracts a Substantive Transnational Rule in International Commercial Arbitration? in* TRANSNATIONAL RULES IN INTERNATIONAL COMMERCIAL ARBITRATION 137, ICC Publication No. 480/4 (1993).

57   ICC Case 5065/1986, II ICC AWARDS 330.

58   ICC Case 5073/1986, II ICC AWARDS 85.

59   *See* ICC Case 3131/1979, extracts *in* I ICC AWARDS 122 but relevant passages only *in* 1983 REV. ARB. 525, at 531. *See also* Goldman, *supra* Note 10, 1979 JDI at 492; 2291/1975, I ICC AWARDS 274; ICC Cases 2478/1974, I ICC AWARDS 25, 233; 2508/1976, I ICC AWARDS 292; 5477/1988, II ICC AWARDS 358; and Note 84 *infra*.

(viii) Rules of force majeure

The defense of *force majeure* is often litigated in ICC arbitration. It breaks down into a number of sub-issues relating to the components of a valid defense, such as the meaning and scope of the requirements "insurmountability," "unforseeability" and "extraneousness." It can therefore not be encapsulated in a neat phrase. For this reason, and also because they provide a particularly rich field to observe arbitral jurisprudence in the making, the rules of *force majeure* are specially analyzed in Section 35.03.

(ix) Conduct may be deemed tacit acceptance of modifications of contract

The former Secretary General of the ICC Court of Arbitration has referred to:

> a consistent view by international commercial arbitrators that any act, or failure to act, that constitutes a divergence from the strict terms of contractual stipulations calls for an immediate reaction by the other contracting party, in the absence of which the latter is presumed to have waived any objection.[60]

The notion that the failure to act promptly may result in a waiver is frequently invoked as a defense against parties who allege failure of contractual performance but who had not, at the relevant time, promptly and clearly expressed their intention to consider the contract rescinded for breach. Their silence in effect created an ambiguous situation calculated to let them have it both ways. Under such circumstances, ICC tribunals have reduced damages.[61] In other situations, the claimant's failure to react in timely fashion (for example in inspecting goods) deprived the defendant of the possibility of early rectification of its deficient performance. To reduce the amount of awards on account of such failures appears consistent with the well established duty to mitigate damages. There are, however, difficulties in extending these concepts as far as the just-quoted passage might suggest. For if they are sought to be elevated to a general legal principle that "silence means acquiescence," it must be recognized as problematical.[62] These notions are better suited to the realm of arbitrators' discretion in evaluating facts, where they become matters of degree, than as coalescing into a legal principle which can hardly be articulated in general terms without generating controversy.

---

60   Yves Derains, *Comment*, I ICC AWARDS 447 (commenting ICC Case 3344/1981, *id.* at 440).

61   ICC Cases 2291/1975, I ICC AWARDS 274; 2520/1975, I ICC AWARDS 278; 3243/1981, I ICC AWARDS 429.

62   Lord Mustill writes flatly that it "is not consistent with the common law," 4 ARB. INT. 86, at 114, note 106 (1988).

(x) Ut res magis valeat quam pereat ("so that the thing be held valid rather than perish")

According to this principle, one should, when faced with contractual provisions which may have more than one interpretation, or which contradict one another, favor the interpretation which preserves meaning for each provision. In other words, interpretations which have the effect of cancelling contractual terms, or of making them redundant, are to be eschewed. In French, this is called the principle of the *effet utile*. ICC arbitrators have recognized it as being a "universally acknowledged principle of interpretation."[63]

(xi) The burden of proof of facts alleged to support a claim

The principle *actori incumbit probatio* has been applied by ICC arbitrators as a fundamental concept of the international legal community.[64]

(xii) Disregard of legal nomenclature misused by the parties

ICC arbitrators have refused to be bound by what the parties have seen fit to call their acts[65] or their contracts[66] if such expressions purport to create legal classifications that are wrong.

(xiii) Use of goods implies acceptance

It often happens that a buyer, while refusing to take delivery under contractual procedures, nonetheless utilizes equipment or goods and later claims to have reserved the right to challenge its quality. Absent other factors justifying the refusal of formal acceptance, ICC arbitrators have deemed use to be tantamount to acceptance.[67]

(xiv) Mitigation of damages

This principle, reaffirmed in 1987 in award which, pursuant to the parties' agreement, expressly applied *lex mercatoria*,[68] has become a consistently applied norm in ICC awards.[69]

---

63   ICC Case 1434/1975, I ICC AWARDS 263, at 267. *See also* ICC Cases 3460/1980, I ICC AWARDS 425; 5910/1988, II ICC AWARDS 371.

64   *See e.g.*, ICC Cases 1434/1975, I ICC AWARDS 263; 3344/1981, I ICC AWARDS 440; 6653/1993, III ICC AWARDS 513.

65·   ICC Case 3540/1980, I ICC AWARDS 105, 399.

66   ICC Case 3243/1981, I ICC AWARDS 429.

67   *Id.*

68   ICC Case 4761/1987, II ICC AWARDS 298, 302, 519.

69   See references given by Goldman, *supra* Note 10, 1979 JDI at 495; by Yves Derains, *Comment*, 1982 JDI 983, at 986; and in ICC Case 4761/1987, I ICC AWARDS 298, 302, 519. *See also* ICC Cases 4462/1987, III ICC AWARDS 17; 5910/1988, II ICC AWARDS 371; 5885/1989, III ICC AWARDS 40; 6069/1989, XV YEARBOOK 83 (1990); *and* Bernard Hanotiau, *La détermination du dommage réparable : principes généraux et principes en emergence, in* TRANSNATIONAL RULES IN INTERNATIONAL COMMERCIAL ARBITRATION 216-217, ICC Publication No. 480/4 (1993).

(xv) Damages for contractual breach are limited to foreseeable consequences

In evaluating damages, ICC tribunals have considered what was foreseeable in the ordinary course of events.[70] One commentator, noting that ICC arbitrators deem this principle to have an "international scope," concluded that the reasoning of the arbitrators was consonant with both the famous 19th-century English case of *Hadley v. Baxendale* and Article 1150 of the French Civil Code.[71]

(xvi) The availability of setoff or compensation

The right of a party to raise as a defense what common lawyers call setoff, and civil lawyers call compensation, is often an issue of surpassing practical importance in arbitration. Must the purchaser of goods pay immediately for certain shipments of goods notwithstanding his counterclaim on account of other defective deliveries under the same contract, or may his payment be suspended while the substance of his counterclaims is considered by the arbitral tribunal? May a nationalized concessionaire withhold taxes or royalties for minerals extracted because it has an unliquidated claim for compensation? The answer to these questions may be of no theoretical significance as to the merits of the dispute, but as a practical matter it may mean everything: if compensation is not available, the counterclaimant may be destroyed economically, or face such expenses, delays, or other difficulties of collection that he must accept a settlement for a fraction of that to which he is in principle entitled.

There is support for the proposition that a right to setoff of claims arising under the same contract is an established principle of international contractual usage irrespective of applicable national law; at least as long as the competing claims are to be heard by the same tribunal.[72] The usefulness of a rule in this connection is particularly great in view of the fact that the competing claims may otherwise be governed by different national laws containing different criteria for compensation. (The conclusion that the availability of setoff should be judged

---

70   ICC Cases 1526/1975, I ICC AWARDS 218, 290; 2404/1975, I ICC AWARDS 280; 5946/1990, III ICC AWARDS 46; *and* Hanotiau, *supra* Note 70 at 214-5.

71   Yves Derains, *Comment*, 1976 JDI 995, at 996.

72   ICC Case 3540/1980, I ICC AWARDS 105, 399. Mustill comments on this award as follows, 4 ARB. INT. 86, at 114, note 104: "the conditions ... resemble those for set-off 'in law' under English law, but are more restrictive than those of the set-off 'in equity'." *Cf.* ICC Case 5946/1990, III ICC AWARDS 46.

    Accord, award in Case 60/1980 of the Court of Arbitration at the Bulgarian Chamber of Commerce and Industry, XII YEARBOOK 84 (1987). For a case where setoff was denied because the claim in setoff was subject to another arbitral jurisdiction, *see* the award of 13 March 1984 of the Netherlands Royal Association of the Committee of Grain Traders, 1984 TIJDSCHRIFT VOOR ARBITRAGE 112; extracts in English *in* X YEARBOOK 79(1985). It appears that deductions from freight or hire by way of setoff are considered contrary to U.S. maritime law and custom absent agreement to the contrary; *see* Jerry Scrowcroft, Note, X YEARBOOK 101 (1985).

according to the law governing the claim sought to be extinguished has intuitive appeal but is not conclusive. If "the law of the counterclaim," as opposed to "the law of the claim," defines different criteria for claims that may be used to extinguish debts, there will inevitably be an argument.)

Hand in hand with the issue of setoff goes the doctrine of the *exceptio non adempleti contractus*. Contractual nonperformance is excusable as a reaction to failure of performance by the other contracting party. It is quite clear that this doctrine has particular legitimacy with respect to competing claims that may ultimately be used to offset each other and produce a single "net" debt. There is evidence for the proposition that the *exceptio* is an autonomous rule of international arbitration.[73] It would not seem misplaced to reflect that the *exceptio* was enshrined in Article 60 of the Vienna Convention on the Law of Treaties precisely because it was thought that in international conflicts, it would be unfair for the aggrieved party to have to continue to comply with a treaty which the other party is violating, and this for the duration of possibly lengthy proceedings;[74]

(xvii) Estoppel

The doctrine of *estoppel* is a creation of Anglo-American law. Moreover, it has not traditionally been listed among the perceived principles of *lex mercatoria*. Explicitly recognizing these two facts, Emmanuel Gaillard has nevertheless concluded that a rule to the effect that *no party may rely upon its own inconsistency to the detriment of another* may now be deemed elevated to the level of a "general principle applicable in international commercial arbitration."[75] Although Gaillard's main reference points are arbitral awards involving states,[76] he expresses the firm view that nothing in the sources or the scope of this "new principle" limits it to cases of State contracts.[77]

---

[73]   ICC Cases 2583/1976, I ICC AWARDS 304; 3540/1980, I ICC AWARDS 105, 399; *see also* P. O'Neill and N. Salam, *Is the Exceptio Non Adimpleti Contractus Part of the New Lex Mercatoria? in* TRANSNATIONAL RULES IN INTERNATIONAL COMMERCIAL ARBITRATION 147, ICC Publication No. 480/4 (1993).

[74]   Eduardo Jimenez de Arechaga, *International Law in the Past Third of a Century*, 1978-I RECUEIL DES COURS I, at 81. It should be noted that suspension of performance under this doctrine is at one's own risk; if it is ultimately decided that there was no material breach on the other side, the suspension itself may be a breach, *id.* the same reasoning would appear apposite to international contractual relations not *per se* governed by public international law.

[75]   *L'interdiction de se contredire au detriment d'autrui comme principe general du droit du commerce international*, 1985 REV. ARB. 241, at 258. *See also* Paul Bowden, *L'interdiction de se contredire au détriment d'autrui (estoppel) as a Substantive Transnational Rule in International Commercial Arbitration, in* TRANSNATIONAL RULES IN INTERNATIONAL COMMERCIAL ARBITRATION 125, ICC Publication No. 480/4 (1993).

[76]   Amco Asia Corp. et al. v. Republic of Indonesia, ICSID Award on Jurisdiction dated 25 September 1983, 23 ILM 351 (1984); Woodward-Clyde Consultants v. Islamic Republic of Iran and the Atomic Energy Organization of Iran, Iran-U.S. Claims Tribunal, Award of 2 September 1983, 3 IRAN-U.S. CLAIMS TRIBUNAL REPORTS 239 (1983-II).

[77]   1985 REV. ARB. 245. Gaillard particularly analyzes the similarity in comparative law of the doctrine of estoppel with those of apparence and *non concedit venire contra factum proprium*.

(xviii) Contracts are unenforceable if their purpose is contrary to international morality

As seen in Section 5.07, international arbitrators may consider a contract to be contrary to an imperative norm of international morality (*contra bonos mores*). In this connection, it should be noted that the Council of the ICC has adopted Rules of Conduct to Combat Extortion and Bribery, Article 1 of which provides simply "No one may demand or accept a bribe."[78]

In his important study, Lord Justice Mustill listed twenty rules "representing a tolerably complete account of the rules which are said to constitute the *lex mercatoria* in its present form."[79] Most of them have been discussed above. The rules falling in the following categories, although listed by Mustill, appear to be much more problematic, whether because they are "fuzzy" (to use Wetter's word) or because they are quite likely to be neutralized by conflicting norms—and therefore seem unlikely to escape analysis and ultimate disposition under applicable national laws.

Exceptions to pacta sunt servanda. The notion that contractual obligations may be attenuated or neutralized by a change of circumstances, or by a finding that the claimant has committed an abuse of right, or that the terms of the contract are unfair, are difficult enough to apply when they appear as part of a body of national law. Any attempt to introduce them as a general principle applicable by an ICC arbitrator would seem to open the door to subjectivism and unpredictability, and must be viewed with great reservations.[80]

In ICC Case 4667/1984, cited *in* Yves Derains, *Comment*, 1987 JDI 1043, at 1047-8, the arbitral tribunal stated that under the "usages" referred to in Article 13(5) of the ICC Rules, when a chief executive is assisted in negotiations by another representative of a company, the other party is entitled to believe that when the former leaves the table after having seen all documents ready for signature, the latter has authority to sign.

For an award holding an Austrian company bound by the signature of an unauthorized person who nonetheless had the appearance of authorization, *see* the award of 5 March 1980 of the Arbitration Court of the Chamber of Commerce and Industry of Czechoslavakia, unpublished, excerpts *in* XI YEARBOOK 112 (1986). *See also* the award in Case No. 255 of 26 April 1985 of the Iran-U.S. Claims Tribunal, XI YEARBOOK 332, at 336-337; Commentary, XI YEARBOOK 399, at 439 (1986).

78   ICC Publication, 1977. The same points may be made in this connection as were made in Note 47 *supra. See generally* Ahmed El Kosheri and Philippe Leboulanger, *L'arbitre face a la corruption et aux trafics d'influence*, 1984 REV. ARB. 3. *See also* United Nations Declaration against Corruption and Bribery in International Commercial Transactions, adopted 16 December 1996, 36 ILM 1044 (1997).

79   4 ARB. INT. 86, at 110 (1988).

80   "ICC arbitrators have only exceptionally admitted the application of the principle *rebus sic stantibus*," Werner Melis, *Force Majeure and Hardship Clauses in International Commercial Contracts in View of the Practice of the ICC Court of Arbitration*, 1 J. INT. ARB. 214, at 221 (1984). *See also* Hans van Houtte, *Changed Circumstances and Pacta Sunt Servanda, in* TRANSNATIONAL RULES IN INTERNATIONAL COMMERCIAL ARBITRATION 105, ICC Publication No. 480/4 (1993). For an illustration of the rejection by an ICC tribunal of an argument seeking to avoid contractual obligations under the notion of *rebus sic stantibus, see* ICC Case 2404/1975, I ICC AWARDS 280. *Ac-*

Culpa in contrahendo (wrongful acts while entering into a contractual relationship). While Mustill cites one commentator to the effect that *culpa in contrahendo* was recognized in ICC Case 2540/1976, he also notes that that particular case appears to have been decided in accordance with national law.[81] In addition, the notion of good faith in the negotiating process gives rise to remedies whose conditions are intricate and rather different as they appear under various national laws. One need only consider the vast learning in all developed legal systems on this topic, whether it appears under the headings of firm offers, mistake, misrepresentation (*dol*), negligence, estoppel, and implied contract.[82] Such tools require delicate handling in the best of cases, and do not readily lead to conclusions that there are transnational norms for pre-contractual behavior. In the case of arbitration, given its necessary foundation in contract, the difficulty is exacerbated.[83]

---

cord, ICC Cases 1512/1971, I ICC AWARDS 3, 33, 37, 207; 2216/1974, I ICC AWARDS 224; 5617/1989, III ICC AWARDS 537; award of 6 July 1983 in an *ad hoc* arbitration between Hungarian and Yugoslav parties (applying Swiss substantive law), unpublished; extracts *in* IX YEARBOOK 69, at 70 (1984); award No. 2049 of 21 December 1984 of the Society of Maritime Arbitrators, New York, Lygnos Brothers Shipping Inc. v. Gold Kist Inc., XI YEARBOOK 200 (1986). To the contrary, relief from contractual terms was granted under the facts of ICC Cases 4145/1986, I ICC AWARDS 559, II ICC AWARDS 53; 4761/1987, II ICC AWARDS 298, 302, 519; and the award of 25 September 1985 in Case No. 59, Iran-U.S. Claims Tribunal, XI YEARBOOK 283 (1986).

81   4 ARB. INT. 86, at 111, note 87 (1988).

82   A recent collection of essays by scholars and practitioners on this complex subject appeared *in* FORMATION OF CONTRACTS AND PRECONTRACTUAL LIABILITY, ICC Publication No. 440/9 (1990).

83   The situation is quite different—although no less complex—with respect to an admittedly valid contract which contains an undertaking to conduct further negotiations. The obligations, as a matter of international law, of *pacta de negotiando or pacta de contrahendo* were discussed in detail by the Arbitral Tribunal for the Agreement on German External Debt in the case of Greece v. Federal Republic of Germany, award of 26 January 1972, 47 INT. L. REP. 418 (holding past efforts by the parties to have been unsatisfactory and declaring the parties to be obliged to enter into "meaningful" negotiations, and not merely a "formal process . . . Meaningful negotiations cannot be conducted if either party insists upon its own position without contemplating any modification of it;" *id.* at 462). *See also* the following statement of the tribunal seized with a dispute under a nationalized oil concession in the *ad hoc* case of AMILOIL v. Kuwait, award of 24 March 1982, 21 ILM 976, at 1004 (1982):

> "An obligation to negotiate is not an obligation to agree. Yet the obligation to negotiate is not devoid of content, and when it exists within a well-defined juridical framework it can well involve precise requirements. In some cases the failure of the negotiations can be attributed to the conduct of one of the parties, and if so, the matter becomes transposed onto the plane of responsibility, and should find its solution there."

As Yves Derains, the then Secretary General of the ICC Court of Arbitration wrote in commenting on ICC Case 2508/1976, *in* I ICC AWARDS at 296, "the obligation to negotiate in good faith implies, among other things, that of 'refraining from making any manifestly unacceptable proposals that would necessarily lead to the failure of the discussions,'" citing *Les lettres d'intention dans la negociation des contrats internationaux*, 3 DROIT ET PRATIQUE DU COMMERCE INTERNATIONAL 73 (1977).

35.03 An illustration of the emergence of transnational norms: the issue of force majeure

ICC awards dealing with *force majeure* illustrate the way that the repeated use of certain analytical criteria in arbitral awards may create a recognized standard of international business behavior that is conducive to establishing authoritative customary rules of *lex mercatoria*.[84]

When considering the discussion that follows, the reader should be aware of the fact that many if not most cases deal with contracts that contain *force majeure* clauses, and thus do not necessarily support the proposition that there exists a general principle of *force majeure* independent of contractual stipulation. Rather, these cases suggest rules for interpreting *force majeure* clauses, which often follow standard forms and cannot be applied mechanically to the concrete situations that arise.

To raise a defense of *force majeure* the non-performing party must prove: (1) the impossibility or futility of performance; (2) the unforeseeability, at the time of signing the contract, of the circumstances that made performance impossible; and (3) prompt notification to the disappointed party of the inability to perform. Each of these elements reflects the needs and common practices of the international business community and will be discussed separately below.[85]

(i) Impossibility or futility

Arbitrators have distinguished impossibility from mere impracticality or onerousness. A party's inability to perform will not constitute impossibility if, in an objective sense, someone else could perform.

For example, in an ICC case[86] Jewish employees could not obtain the visas needed to perform services in an Arab country as required by their employer's contract with a Yugoslav firm. The arbitrator found that the employer, a German company, would have had to provide the services by employing non-Jewish workers if necessary. The Jewish employees' inability to perform

---

84 *See* Werner Melis, *Force Majeure and Hardship Clauses in International Commercial Contracts in View of the Practice of the ICC Court of Arbitration*, 1 J. INT. ARB. 214 (1984); David Rivkin, *Lex Mercatoria and Force Majeure, in* TRANSNATIONAL RULES IN INTERNATIONAL COMMERCIAL ARBITRATION 161, ICC Publication No. 480/4 (1993).

85 On *force majeure* in international transactions, *see generally* Harold Berman, *Excuse for Nonperformance in the Light of Contract Practices in International Trade*, COLUMBIA LAW REVIEW 1413 (1963); Georges Delaume, *Excuse for Non-performance and Force Majeure in Economic Development Agreements*, 10 COLUMBIA JOURNAL OF TRANSNATIONAL LAW REVIEW 242 (1971); Marcel Fontaine, *Les clauses de force majeure dans les contrats internationaux*, 5 DROIT ET PRATIQUE DU COMMERCE INTERNATIONAL 469 (1979).

86 ICC Case 1782/1973, 1 ICC AWARDS 230. The present interpretation does not necessarily follow from the published parts of the arbitrator's decision, but rather is expressed by Mr. Derains in his commentary, *id*. It is not clear whether Mr. Derains based his statements on unpublished parts of the award or whether he extrapolated from the award's reasoning.

did not support a finding of impossibility on behalf of their employer. The arbitrator held that if the German company itself could not perform, it was bound to engage another firm to fulfill its obligations. A standard of feasibility was derived from the business community as a whole rather than from the particular situation of the party obliged to perform.

In three related cases decided in 1974, a government, having nationalized a foreign corporation's source of raw materials, subsequently contracted to sell a quantity of the same material to another corporation.[87] The company suffering the nationalization threatened seizure of all such material sold by that government on the open market. The prospective buyer argued that the threats constituted *force majeure* and excused its non-compliance with the purchase agreement. Noting that others had purchased from the government, the arbitrators declined to make a finding of impossibility.

The award rendered against Parsons & Whittemore in favor of an Egyptian State entity similarly illustrates the difficulty of proving impossibility.[88] There the U.S. contractor in a turnkey project (paper mill) claimed that the Six Day War of 1967 excused non-performance because it made operations excessively dangerous. Although it found that a suspension of performance had been inevitable, the arbitral tribunal refused to find ultimate execution of the contract impossible.[89]

A written request from the Under-Secretary of a Ministry of the Indian government to give domestic requirements priority over exports, invoked by an Indian seller as an excuse for failure to make delivery under a commodity sales agreement, was not accepted as being an event of *force majeure* by another ICC tribunal.[90]

Back-to-back contracts are especially common in commodity contracts. The party in the middle—*i.e.* the buyer/reseller—is exposed to the risk that his supplier fails to perform. Unless the failure of delivery of a third-party upstream supplier is expressly stipulated as an event that discharges the obligation to deliver onward, the party in the middle will have a difficult defense. If

---

87   ICC Cases 2139/1974, I ICC AWARDS 23, 237; 2142/1974, I ICC AWARDS 7, 194.

88   ICC Case 1703/1971, I ICC AWARDS 6, 195; I YEARBOOK 130 (1976). *See also* 508 F.2d 969 (1974) (award enforced in the U.S.).

89   Accord, ICC Case 2546, unpublished; described and quoted *in* Melis, *supra* Note 85, at 217-218. *See also* Georges Delaume, *The Proper Law of State Contracts and the lex mercatoria: A Reappraisal*, 3 ICSID REVIEW—FOREIGN INVESTMENT LAW JOURNAL 79 (1988): "In the case of long-term State contracts, the normal consequence of force majeure events is suspension rather than termination of the agreement," *id.* at 93. For another award involving frustration of a contract due to the risks created by armed conflict, *see* ICC Case 5195/1986, II ICC AWARDS 101.

90   Case 3740, unpublished; described and quoted *in* Melis, *supra* Note 81, at 220. *See also* ICC Case 4237/1984, I ICC AWARDS 167 at 172: ". . . if every governmental reshuffle and accompanying public excitement constitutes *force majeure*, world trade would in modern times be bogged down by uncertainty."

the goods sold are fungible and available on the market, the defendant is not faced with an event of *force majeure*. In one ICC case, the defendant was held bound to perform irrespective of the fact that alternative suppliers would have demanded a premium of one-third above the market cost.[91]

A corollary to the impossibility requirement is that the alleged discharging event must be *extraneous* to the party invoking it. A party would be in bad faith if it first created the impossibility and then sought to rely on it as a defense. This concept is particularly relevant in the context of disputes involving public entities, where claimants often dispute the proposition that governmental intervention is entitled to recognition as a supervening event uncontrollable by the parties. The issue goes to the heart of the difficult matter of how to characterize the relationship between foreign public bodies and the government that created and controls them. Although it is a national court decision and not an arbitral award, the English House of Lords decision in *Czarnikow v. Rolimpex*[92] is well-known to international practitioners. There, a Polish foreign trade enterprise invoked as an event of *force majeure* a government ban, following a poor harvest, on all sugar exports. The English court held that although Rolimpex was bound to follow governmental directives, it was entitled to recognition as a separate legal entity. The court was satisfied that Rolimpex had sought to perform its contract but that its protests against the ban had been to no avail, and therefore upheld an award in favor of Rolimpex rendered by the Refined Sugar Association. In an often quoted passage, however, Lord Wilberforce stated: "I am not saying that there may not be cases when it is so clear that a foreign government is taking action purely in order to extricate a state enterprise from contractual liability, that it may be possible to deny to such action the character of government intervention . . ."[93] One limitation of the *Rolimpex* decision would thus be the factor of collusion. Another limitation was recognized by an *ad hoc* tribunal hearing a dispute between a West German supplier of industrial goods and a

---

91   Case 3952/1982, unpublished; described *in* Melis, *supra* Note 81, at 221. *See also* ICC Case 5195/1986, II ICC AWARDS 101 at 107: "Where events beyond the control of either party supervene which merely render performance financially more onerous for a contracting party he will not, under most systems of law, be excused from further performance or (in the absence of some special contractual or statutory provision—nowadays not infrequently to be found) entitled to insist upon extra compensation."

92   [1978] 2 ALL E.R. at 1043. See Joseph Becker, *The Rolimpex Exit from International Contract Responsibility*, 10 NEW YEW YORK UNIVERSITY J. INT. ARB. 214 (1978).

93   [1978] 2 ALL E.R. at 1047-48. An instance such as the one imagined by Lord Wilberforce was apparently faced by a tribunal comprised of Messrs Brunner (Netherlands), McCrindle (U.K.), and Vischer (Switzerland) in Case No. 723 of the Netherlands Arbitration Institute, Setenave v. Settebello. As reported in the Financial Times on 27 February 1986, the otherwise unpublished award unanimously refused to recognize a Portuguese decree designed to procure contractual benefits to a Portuguese State-owned shipyard in detriment to the rights of a foreign purchaser of a supertanker, holding that to do so would be contrary to "concepts of public policy and morality common to all trading nations," and this despite the fact that the contract was in principle governed by Portuguese law.

Polish buyer, whose contract for the construction of a fuel gas plant, signed in 1980, contained a *force majeure* clause giving the following illustrations: "natural disasters, fines, floods, earthquakes, strikes, war, mobilization, military actions of the enemy, requisitions, riot embargo, governmental order." In December 1981, the Polish Council of Ministers, "by virtue of the ordered state of war," banned the import of goods for 21 large industrial projects. The Polish buyer, which was a State-owned export trading company, contended that this was an event of *force majeure*. The two Swiss arbitrators, who rendered the award over the dissent of a Polish arbitrator, considered that the contractual reference to governmental orders as events of *force majeure* was "merely intended as an example;" the parties were using a standard clause and the tribunal found it "obvious that, by accepting this wording, claimant did not want to waive the defense of abuse of rights or a particular relationship of defendant to the ordering State."[94] Assessing this "defense" (a more appropriate term might have been "claim" or "contention") under the applicable Swiss law, and after many references to comparative law with respect to the issue of piercing the corporate veil of State enterprises, including the *Rolimpex* case, the tribunal reasoned as follows in rejecting the defense of *force majeure*:

> Where a State authority has the power to impose plan instructions on an enterprise, and this authority then imposes another instruction contradicting previous planning acts or does not permit execution of contracts entered into, it does not merely act by virtue of its function as a State organ, but also as an organ of the State enterprise having decision making and directive powers . . .

> Unilateral and specific interference of the State with contracts already entered into, by which the contracting parties are discharged of their contractual obligations is unacceptable under the principle of good faith according to Art. 2 Swiss Civil Code.

> When an enterprise is integrated in the State economic planning and enters into contracts within the objectives of the State economic planning, then modifications of the plan interfering with contracts entered into cannot be invoked as force majeure by the enterprise. Where, on the other hand, a Socialist State for other reasons issues a general order, which would affect a privately organized company in the same way as a State enterprise, and where the consequences of this order are not related to the specific nature of the State enterprise as a dependant enterprise, nothing would preclude reliance on force majeure.[95]

---

94   Interim award of 9 September 1983, XII YEARBOOK 63, at 67 (1987).

95   *Id.* at 74-75.

(ii) Unforeseeability

There is a presumed standard of foresight attributable to international businessmen. Thus the occurrence of a foreseeable event ignored by the contract does not relieve a party of its obligations.

International contracts are known to be particularly susceptible to price fluctuations and government regulations of foreign trade. Arbitrators accordingly hold international businessmen to a high level of sophistication in these matters.[96]

"A party is not liable for a failure to perform any of his obligations if he proves that the failure was due to an impediment beyond his control and that he *could not reasonably be expected to have taken the impediment into account at the time of the conclusion of the contract* or to have avoided or overcome it or its consequences." (Emphasis added.)

Price and currency fluctuations are inherent elements of international commerce. Thus, even a drastic price change will not generally constitute an unforeseeable event.[97] In a 1976 award, the arbitrator found that the increased market value of a product did not relieve the Belgian seller of its obligation to deliver it to a Japanese firm.[98] Referring to the price fluctuation, the arbitrator stated:

> Especially in the field of international commerce, circumstantial changes constitute one of the most important incentives for contracting, each party expecting to profit from changes in the market and at the same time implicitly accepting the risk that the change may be unfavorable.

Arbitrators may find government regulation of trade to be foreseeable and therefore not to constitute a valid defense. The fact that general legislation is

---

96   The wording of Article 70 of the 1980 Vienna Convention on Contracts for the International Sale of Goods is consistent with this observation:

97   It will be remarked that even if it were accepted that a spectacular price variation was of an unprecedented and reasonably unforeseeable magnitude, the obligor would also have to demonstrate that it rendered his performance possible. After all, a fixed price may be viewed as a reciprocal allocation of risk of price fluctuations—and the higher the variation, the greater the need for a reliable allocation. Legal systems which seek to alleviate the possibly harsh results of commercial bargains do so at great risk to contractual stability and predictability. In the U.S., for example, the doctrine of impracticability (as reflected in Restatement (Second) of Contracts § 261 and Section 2-615 of the Uniform Commercial Code) creates excuses on account of "the occurrence of an event the non-occurrence of which was a basic assumption on which the contract was made." As one might expect, what is or is not a "basic assumption" is in the eye of the beholder, making it difficult to make meaningful distinctions between valid and invalid defences. Thus, one court excused a contractor for having failed to remove all of an agreed quantity of gravel from the plaintiff's land because it could only have done so by the costly removal of gravel located under water, while another court enforced a contract to build two schools although the housing project that the schools had been intended to serve was cancelled; discussed *in* Rivkin, *supra* Note 85 at 166-8.

98   ICC Case 2708/1976, I ICC Awards 297.

potentially applicable to a party obliges that party to anticipate its actual application. In one case, a purchaser claimed *force majeure* as a defense because he could not obtain the foreign exchange needed to pay the seller.[99] Under regulations that antedated the contract, the central bank of the purchaser's country had the power to withhold foreign currency in times of foreign exchange shortages. The arbitral tribunal found the purchaser's inability to obtain foreign exchange foreseeable in light of the economic conditions existing at the time of contracting, and so rejected the defense.

Currency freezes may be foreseeable even in the absence of such general empowering legislation. In the *Dalmia Dairy Industries* award (Pierre Lalive, sole arbitrator)[100] the National Bank of Pakistan had guaranteed certain payments to an Indian company. Shortly thereafter war erupted between the two countries and Pakistan enacted emergency legislation that prevented the bank from complying with the guarantee. On the basis of "general principles of law," the arbitrator found that the bank had failed to prove the unforeseeability element of *force majeure*; since the war was predictable, the Pakistani bank should have foreseen the passage of emergency legislation.

In another case, however, the arbitrators found that subsequent government regulation could constitute *force majeure*.[101] The Rumanian government had cancelled the seller's export license. By failing to notify promptly his buyer of this development, the seller had, according to the buyer's argument, forfeited his *force majeure* defense. The arbitrators, however, declared the situation to constitute *force majeure* according to general principles of law without giving any further reasons for their finding.

A number of factors may distinguish the Rumanian exporter from the Pakistani bank. For example, the arbitrator may have decided that once the Rumanian government granted an export license, subsequent cancellation was less foreseeable than legislation passed in response to an imminent war. Unfortunately, the particular facts leading to the *force majeure* finding were not published in the case of the Rumanian exporter.

An illustration of a typical situation may be found in a 1984 award of the New York Society of Maritime Arbitrators. A charterer nominated a particular berth in the U.S. for the loading of coal. At the time of this nomination, the berth was being modified to be able to load. The construction was delayed by the Department of Environmental Conservation which intervened, following the expression of public concern, to evaluate the hazards of coal operations. The vessel had to wait for one month. As a result, the owner of the vessel claimed demurrage for delay. The charterer referred to a contractual clause excluding demur-

---

99   ICC Case 3093/1979, I ICC Awards 365.

100 ICC Case 1512/1971, I ICC Awards 3, 33, 206.

101 ICC Case 2478/1974, I ICC Awards 25, 233.

rage with respect to delays due to "any cause whatsoever beyond the control of the Charterer." This defense was rejected by the arbitrators, who stated that "the diligent exercise of [environmental conservation] procedures are foreseeable in the ordinary course by all prudent businessmen."[102]

Any reasonable standard of *force majeure* will involve scrutiny of the particular transaction in the context of the custom within a specific trade. For example, a short-term sales contract for fungible goods might justify a greater presumption of speculative intent, thus requiring a stricter standard of *force majeure*, than a contract involving long-term commitments to provide goods and services for which there may not be adequate substitutes.

ICC arbitrators necessarily use objective criteria to support presumptions of sophistication to discern the intent of the parties. In a 1974 award,[103] a Norwegian purchaser of oil claimed it had not contemplated a serious drop in prices when he entered into the contract. The arbitrator considered evidence as to what was actually within the purchaser's contemplation, and rejected the *force majeure* defense because the purchaser had in fact kept abreast of OPEC price meetings up to the time it signed the contract.

(iii) Prompt Notification

A duty to mitigate damages is consistently recognized in ICC awards. This stems from considerations of fairness, good faith, and a responsibility to carry out contractual obligations in a cooperative manner. The arbitrator in the previously mentioned Rumanian export dispute stated the concept as follows: "by virtue of general principles of law . . . it is the duty of the injured party to take all steps necessary to avoid an increase in damages."[104] In this dispute, the arbitrator referred to "general principles of law," but based his finding of a duty of prompt notification on a specific contractual provision.[105] Prompt notification of the impossibility of performance permits the other party to mitigate its damages by finding a suitable substitute at the earliest possible date.

35.04   Toward a concept of arbitral justice

Party autonomy, or freedom of contract, plays an important role in the creation of these norms. When private parties regulate their own legal relationships, the State has in essence delegated to individuals the power to establish law, within certain limits Party autonomy allows the international business community to create its own regulatory environment through con-

---

102 Award No. 2014, 13 September 1984, XI YEARBOOK 202 (1986).

103 ICC Case 2216/1974, I ICC AWARDS 224.

104 ICC Case 2478/1974, I ICC AWARDS 25, 233.

105 *See also* ICC Case 4237/1984, I ICC AWARDS 167; *ad hoc* award of 9 December 1983, *supra* Note 95.

tractual interaction, minimizing the impact of national law. Moreover, by means of contract, the business community can establish adjudicatory bodies both to interpret and apply a supplementary law based on non-national commercial custom.

Standardized contracts, seeking to crystallize customs and practices existing within a particular trade or commercial sector, have an important role to play in elevating these norms to a higher level of authority. When used frequently within a given commercial sector, these "self-regulatory" standardized contracts may provide stability that transcends a particular transaction and create a type of customary law.[106]

ICC arbitration seems particularly well suited to application of the new *lex mercatoria*. Drawn from a variety of countries, arbitrators are less preoccupied with national concerns than judges, and may be expected to possess a less parochial perspective, emphasizing good faith, general principles of law and the particular equities of the situation.

What can one say, finally, about the qualitative difference of the justice rendered by international arbitrators as compared with that of national judges? It is certainly true that arbitrators are less constrained by legal technicalities; in ICC cases, as in most international arbitrations, they do not live in fear of a court of appeal. Furthermore, the fact that both parties have often named an arbitrator may seem to have the practical effect that the psychological dynamics of arbitral tribunals militate in favor of "balanced" awards.

But that does not mean that arbitrators are to be confused with mediators. Their decision is to be justified as a matter of principle rather than accommodation or compromise.

On the question of liability, there is usually a clear winner. Arbitrators often find that one party has entirely succeeded as a matter of law and contract interpretation. The ruling on damages is frequently less categorical. It is thus perhaps with respect to quantum of damages that parties who have opted for arbitration are most likely to be dissatisfied, feeling that if they were clearly

---

106 An international construction law specialist has proposed the notion of a *lex construction* is as guidance in interpreting international contracts "as a reference, an aid, in deciding disputes when the applicable law is thin or non-existent." *Charles Molineaux, The FIDIC Conditions—Basis for a Construction Lex Mercatoria, A Lex Constructionis?* paper given at an LCIA/AAA Conference in Boston, 26-28 September 1996, p. 2. The author suggests ten common principles, such as "directed changes (or 'variations') do not amount to contract breach" and "the methods and sequences of construction shall be at the selection of the contractor unless there is a structural or other impact which is evident from a site investigation or noted in the tender document." *Id.* at 11. Molineaux's paper was developed in an article entitled *Moving Toward a Construction Lex Mercatoria*, 14 J. INT. ARB. 55 (1997).

Similar suggestions have been made in other domains by Aboubacar Fall, *Defence and Illustration of Lex Mercatoria in Maritime Arbitration* 15 J. INT. ARB. 83 (1998), and Doak Bishop, *International Arbitration of Petroleum Disputes: The Development of a Lex Petrolea*. XXIII YEARBOOK 1131 (1998).

right, they should have been awarded the full measure of damages requested. Failing that, they perceive arbitrators as too conciliatory, "splitting the difference" in the hopes of rendering an award acceptable to both parties rather than drawing the full consequences of their decision on the merits.

It may be true that at least with respect to lost profits, international arbitrators tend to be conservative. This attitude, however, may often be a consequence not so much of their being arbitrators as of the fact that their perspective is international. It is certainly true as a general proposition that international contracts are fraught with greater uncertainties than domestic ones. If arbitrators thus tend to discount theoretically impeccable demonstrations of *lucrum cessans*, are they not simply reflecting realistic expectations? The question cannot be answered in an absolute manner, since the parameters of what may reasonably be expected vary with the context of each case. Conversely, arbitrators may be persuaded to award some measure of damages, if they believe that in the normal course of events it was reasonable to anticipate some profits, even if those damages may not be proved to a mathematical certainty or by complete documentary proof.

The test of the international arbitrator finally remains the same: whether his decision reflects what the parties can fairly be held to have understood to be the consequences of their contractual undertaking. And if one is to recognize that an emerging arbitral justice as applied to international contracts is distinct from the justice of national courts, in the sense that three arbitrators of different nationalities sitting in London or Baghdad are unlikely to follow the same procedure, and to come out with exactly the same decision, as would English or Iraqi commercial judges applying the full panoply of local laws and technicalities, is that really contrary to what the parties expect?

CHAPTER 36

STATE CONTRACTS

36.01 International arbitration as a perceived menace to sovereignty

Economic development agreements between governments and foreign private enterprises, often referred to as "State contracts," include agreements to build and operate factories, airports, and harbors, or for the exploitation of natural resources. Such agreements generally provide for long-term collaboration, with the foreign enterprise becoming a partner in development, for example by making a direct investment in local joint ventures or undertaking to manage the project and provide technical training for indigenous personnel.[1]

International commercial arbitration is often the only adjudicatory process acceptable to both parties to State contracts. They may feel mutual mistrust of each other's national courts. A State may seek arbitration to avoid publicity, or to avoid subjection to a foreign State court which may appear as an affront to its sovereignty. The multinational enterprise may fear that the courts of the host country might be unduly influenced by the government, or that without submission to arbitration there may be no certainty of waiver of the State's immunity.

In the years following their independence (particularly in the 1970s), some developing nations manifested hostility toward settlement of disputes by tribunals other than their own. Negotiation of an arbitration clause in an agreement with a developing country or State agency requires sensitivity to Third World attitudes toward arbitration and their historical perspective, as well as the special problems that arise in connection with the arbitration of State contracts.

According to a report presented to the 1982 Montreal Conference of the International Law Association, ICC arbitration had by then become the preferred

---

1   See generally ESA PAASIVIRTA, PARTICIPATION OF STATES IN INTERNATIONAL CONTRACTS (Helsinki, 1990); Piero Bernardini, *Development Agreements with Host Governments, in* ROBERT PRITCHARD (ED.), ECONOMIC DEVELOPMENT, FOREIGN INVESTMENT AND THE LAW 161 (1996).

form of dispute resolution in North-South contractual relations.[2] It is certainly true that the posture of Third World parties in ICC arbitration has undergone a dramatic change.[3] This is apparent if one considers what is done in practice as opposed to what is said in various political contexts. Of the 11,143 parties involved in cases filed during the 11-year period 1989-1999, 2,531 (or 23%) were from developing countries.[4] Moreover, 1,073 of these parties (42%) were claimants, thereby destroying any perception that the Third World is a passive victim of arbitration as an eternally hapless defendant (*see generally* Section 1.04).

A related development concerns the composition of arbitral tribunals and the choice of the place of arbitration. It is obvious that Third World acceptance of arbitration would remain doubtful if tribunals were invariably chaired by Westerners. Since 1975, when the Lebanese Professor Sobhi Mahmassani was named sole arbitrator in the much-discussed *ad hoc* case between Libya and Atlantic Richfield (through its subsidiary LIAMCO),[5] it has become common to entrust the chairmanship of tribunals to non-Western arbitrators. In particular, of the 837 African, Asian, Latin American, and Mid-Eastern nationals named ICC arbitrators in the 1989-1999 period, 186 (20%) were designated by the ICC Court of Arbitration rather than by parties. Given the limited reservoir of experienced jurists in certain regions of the world, the process is by necessity a gradual one. The same may be said for fixing the seat of arbitration in the Third World. The ICC may already confidently be said to have the greatest experience in this regard, an African, Asian, Latin American or Mid-Eastern city having been established as the place of ICC arbitration 323 times during the 1989-1999 period, in no less than 40 different countries, including remote locales such as Laos and Paraguay. (By country, the leading venues were Singapore (60), Mexico (27), Egypt (13) and Tunisia (9 times).

Although there is a significant participation of Third World countries in the ICC institution generally, and although indeed a slight majority of the members of the ICC Court come from developing countries—including three Vice-Presidents—the most active participants within the ICC structure are clearly those from the industrialized countries. Since the ICC aspires to universality, it does more than keep the door open; it actively promotes greater participation by the Third World within its structure. Naturally, the process is circular: the greater the universality of the institution, the greater its perceived usefulness and legitimacy; the greater its usefulness and legitimacy in

---

2   *Arbitration between Parties from Industrialized and Less Developed Countries*, (report of the Committee on International Commercial Arbitration; Karl-Heinz Bockstiegel, rapporteur).

3   *See generally* Jan Paulsson, *Third World Participation in International Investment Arbitration*, 1987 ICSID REVIEW—FOREIGN INVESTMENT LAW JOURNAL 19.

4   Detailed statistics concerning the ICC caseload may be found in Appendix I.

5   The Mahmassani award has been published in 20 ILM 1(1981); extracts in French appeared *in* 1980 REV. ARB. 132.

the eyes of parties who are only beginning to become "insiders," the greater their incentive to play a role in the institution as such.

The mistrust of international arbitration that characterized many developing countries' attitudes into the 1970's seems to have given way to a greater measure of pragmatism and confidence in accepting neutral dispute resolution. For example, very little is heard today of the 1974 United Nations Charter of Economic Rights and Duties of States, at least in terms of its purported status as the expression of mandatory international norms prohibiting reference to international arbitration to resolve nationalization disputes. The following statement of Judge Keba Mbaye, former Vice-President of the International Court of Justice and former First President of the Supreme Court of Senegal, reflects the contemporary attitude:

> For a long time the French-speaking countries of Africa, following the French example, had thought that they could avoid arbitration, by citing procedural rules forbidding them to agree to international arbitration . . . This situation . . . was sapping the confidence of the economic partners of these countries. It was a question of pure good faith. A state must not be allowed to cite the provisions of its law in order to escape from an arbitration that it has already accepted.[6]

In the end, the perception of fairness is paramount. As it was put in 1984 by Fali Nariman, a Senior Advocate of the Supreme Court of India who was to become the first non-Western President of ICCA, while "judges and lawyers are now increasingly impressed by reasoned decisions of foreign arbitral tribunals" and businessmen "no longer complain (even when they lose) about the absence of a right of appeal," the road had not been an easy one:

> In the early years we had a rough time coping with International Commercial Arbitration—its novelty baffled us, made us suspicious. We stumbled, nearly floundered—but we have pulled through. We are now realizing its usefulness. And then, fairness begets fairness. A recent decision of a foreign court (the U.S. District Court of Ohio), in the case of India's largest public sector company (the Fertilizer Corporation of India) has created a very favorable impression both in commercial and legal circles.[7]

36.02 Arbitration without privity

Ordinarily international arbitrations are conducted between parties who have signed an arbitration agreement. But a trend has emerged for states to grant

---

6   IN 60 YEARS ON: A LOOK AT THE FUTURE (ICC Publication No. 412, 1984, a collection of papers from the 60th anniversary of the ICC Court of Arbitration) at 296. *Cf.* Jan Paulsson, *May a State Invoke its Internal Law to Repudiate Consent to International Commercial Arbitration?* 2 ARB. INT. 90 (1986).

7   ICC Publication No. 412, note 6 *supra*, at 90. The case Mr. Nariman was referring to is Fertilizer Corp. of India v. IDI Management, Inc. 517 F. Supp. 948 (S.D. Ohio 1981).

foreign parties the right to initiate international arbitrations against the state even if they have signed no arbitration agreement. Such claims seek relief on account of alleged violations by the state of laws or treaties which protect the rights of third-party foreigners, such as investors.[8]

The principle that national investment laws may create compulsory arbitration without privity is beyond cavil. The Report of the Executive Directors of the World Bank that accompanied the 1965 Convention on the Settlement of Investment Disputes between States and Nationals of Other States (the "ICSID Convention") stated in paragraph 24:

> ". . . a host State might in its investment promotion legislation offer to submit disputes arising out of certain classes of investments to the jurisdiction ‘of the Centre, and the investor might give his consent thereto in writing."

In other words, unless the law is abrogated in the interim, an investor may wait *until a dispute has arisen* to announce its intention to avail itself of the arbitral mechanism—which until that moment is compulsory only as to the State.

If this principle is not understood or accepted, one must conclude that the 129 States that have bound themselves to the ICSID Convention (as of the beginning of 1998) did so in ignorance. (Of course a State would be perfectly free to sign the ICSID Convention with the firm intention *never* to refer to ICSID in an investment law. It is only the *possibility* of using the mechanism which is at issue here.)

This does not however mean that the existence and scope of "offers to submit" contained in national legislation are uncontroversial.

In the *Pyramids Oasis* case,[9] for example, the claimant relied on a provision in a 1974 Egyptian investment law to the effect that:

> "Investment disputes in respect of the implementation of the provisions of this Law shall be settled . . . within the framework of the Convention for the Settlement of Investment Disputes between the State and the nationals of other countries [*sic*] to which Egypt has adhered by virtue of law no. 90 of 1971, where it applies."

---

8   *See generally* Jan Paulsson, *Arbitration Without Privity*, 10 ICSID REVIEW—FOREIGN INVESTMENT LAW JOURNAL 232 (1995); Antonio Parra, *The Scope of New Investment Law and International Instruments, in* ROBERT PRITCHARD (ED.), ECONOMIC DEVELOPMENT, FOREIGN INVESTMENT AND THE LAW 27 (1996); Jacques Werner, *The Trade Explosion and Some Likely Effects on International Arbitration*, 14 J. INT. ARB. 5 (1997).

9   Southern Pacific Properties v. Arab Republic of Egypt; of the many episodes of this dispute, the only one relevant for present purposes is the Decision on Jurisdiction handed down by the ICSID tribunal presided by Judge Jiménez de Aréchaga on 14 April 1988, excerpts of which were published in XVI YEARBOOK 28 (1991).

The Government of Egypt contended that this text was insufficient to create compulsory jurisdiction. For one thing, although the just-quoted passage was published in English by the General Authority for Investment in brochures made available to investors, the Government argued that only the official Arabic text of the investment law should be given weight, and thus initiated a scholarly debate on the correctness of the imperative form of the verb "shall."

The Government also argued that use of the expression "within the framework of the Convention" and "where it applies" each implied the need for separate consent to ICSID jurisdiction. Furthermore, it took the position that the simple reference to the Convention was insufficient to create compulsory arbitral jurisdiction since the Convention provides for conciliation as well as arbitration.

Each of these objections was rejected by the arbitral tribunal.

It is widely understood that in a later case involving the Republic of Egypt, another claimant investor also relied on this form of legislative consent to ICSID, but the dispute was settled before any decision with regard to jurisdiction.[10]

The claimant in the case of *Gaith Pharaon v. Republic of Tunisia* similarly relied on an article in the 1969 Tunisian Investment Code as a foundation for ICSID jurisdiction. Here too, as the result of a settlement of the case, the objections raised by the State were never decided.[11]

The potential operation of bilateral investment treaties (BITs) in this context was illustrated in the ICSID case of *Asian Agricultural Products Ltd. v. Republic of Sri Lanka*, where the claimant, a Hong Kong company, took the position that Sri Lanka had made an undertaking to arbitrate claims by investors by virtue of Art. 8(1) of the UK/Sri Lanka BIT. The Centre's jurisdiction was not challenged by the respondent. The Tribunal noted that claimant's claim for compensation remained outstanding without reply for more than the cool-down period defined in the BIT and that "hence AAPL became entitled to institute the ICSID arbitration proceedings." The case thus went forward, and an award was rendered in favor of the investor to compensate for the destruction of a shrimp farm, which had been occupied by governmental security forces in violation of the State's duty under the treaty to provide protection and security.[12]

---

10 Manufacturers Hanover Trust Company v. Arab Republic of Egypt and General Authority for Investment and Free Zones, Order of Discontinuance dated 24 June 1993 cited *in* ICSID CASES, 31 March 1994, at page 27.

11 Order of Discontinuance dated 21 November 1988 cited in *id.*, at page 24. In December 1994, an ICSID arbitration was initiated against the State of Albania by Tradex Hellas, a Greek investor, on the basis of an arbitration provision in the Albanian investment law.

12 6 ICSID REVIEW—FOREIGN INVESTMENT LAW JOURNAL 526 (1991); 30 ILM 577 (1991); 17 YEARBOOK 106 (1992); excerpts in French translation in 119 JDI 217 (1992). A similar ICSID case, American Manufacturing & Trading Inc. v. Republic of Zaire, 12 MEALEY'S INT. ARB. REP. A-1

A host of similar BIT provisions seek to create international arbitral jurisdiction. It would be exceedingly difficult to prepare an inventory of them all.[13] Even if the exercise were limited to the 100 countries most active in international trade[14] the task of determining the potential existence of 5,000 inter-State agreements would be overwhelming, and even more difficult to catalogue for the following two reasons:

> 1) the contents of BITs vary greatly; as much as any individual country might like to impose its own idea of a standard BIT, the varying negotiating strength of the other side has the effect of rendering most countries' portfolios of BITs quite heterogeneous;

> 2) in particular, the scope and nature of third-party access to international arbitration through BIT mechanisms are so different from one BIT to the next that one cannot speak of a dominant practice; each BIT must be examined on its own.

To take the case of France, the simplest situation is one where the BIT has been signed with a country which is very eager to receive investment (and perhaps from which France perceives it is unlikely to *receive* investments) and is willing to extend very wide and unqualified access to international arbitration. Thus, Article 8 of the Franco-Paraguayan BIT of 1978 gives investors in simple unqualified language the right to seek ICSID arbitration. Similarly, though with a slight nuance, Article 10 of the Franco-Czechoslovak BIT of 1990 entitles an investor to seek ICSID arbitration (or UNCITRAL arbitration if either relevant State is not an ICSID member at the relevant time) if it has not been given satisfaction within six months of raising a complaint.

A different situation arises when one or both signatory States are more selective, perhaps because neither wishes to undertake in advance that every investor will be able to bring an international case against the host State. One response is to give *qualified* access to international arbitration.

Thus, Article 8 of the Franco-Polish BIT of 1989 gives an investor the right to seek ad hoc arbitration if it has not been given satisfaction within six

---

(March 1997), resulted in a monetary award to the investor on account of destruction of property by armed insurrection, held by the arbitrators to trigger the host state's liability under a 1984 BIT with the United States. Six other ICSID arbitrations have been brought by investors invoking BITs, against Albania, Argentina (two), Chile, Malaysia and Ukraine.

13   *See generally* Antonio Parra, *Provisions on the Settlement of Investment Disputes in Modern Investment Laws, Bilateral Investment Treaties and Multilateral Instruments on Investment*, 12 ICSID REVIEW—FOREIGN INVESTMENT LAW JOURNAL 287 (1997), M. SORNARAJAH, THE INTERNATIONAL LAW ON FOREIGN INVESTMENT, Chapter 6 (1994); Paul Peters, *Dispute Settlement Arrangements in International Treaties*, 22 NETHERLANDS YEARBOOK INTERNATIONAL LAW 91 (1991).

14   It is not preposterous to consider that 100 countries might be relevant; quite small countries may be involved in significant international disputes. An indication to this effect is the fact that in 1993 parties from 94 different countries had recourse to arbitration under the Rules of the International Chamber of Commerce (Chronique, 1994 JDI 1032).

months of raising a complaint, *but this right relates only to disputes concerning expropriation.*

Similarly, Article 10 of the Franco-Moroccan BIT of 1975 also gives investors the right to seek ICSID arbitration, provided that the matter:

− concerns a "productive investment" having been approved by the host State and guaranteed by the State of the investor;

− is of a legal nature and concerns reparations for violations of provisions of the agreement that establish rights to be compensated in the event of expropriation, to repatriate revenues or capital, and to use expatriate personnel; and

− has not been dealt with satisfactorily by "internal recourse" within a two-year period.

To take yet another example in this vein, Article 8 (combined with para. 4 of the Annex) of the PRC-France BIT of 1984 gives an investor the right to seek UNCITRAL arbitration if it has not been given satisfaction within six months of raising a complaint, but this right relates only to disputes concerning the "amount of compensation" to be paid in the event of expropriation. (Article 4 requires compensation to be "appropriate," "without delay," "practically feasible" and "freely transferable.")

It cannot be said that there is today a coherent *corpus* of BITs that allow arbitration without privity. Some allow arbitration only in relation to specifically approved investments. Other BITs, as typified by most such treaties entered into by the PRC, limit arbitrability only to certain types of disputes, and even then only subject to certain procedural preconditions. Yet Mr Sornarajah is plainly mistaken when he affirms that the foreign investor's right to use the remedy exists only if there is *also* an arbitration clause in "the contract" concluded by the foreign party.[15] His assertion is backed by neither authority nor textual analysis. If such a remarkable limitation had been envisaged by the drafters of BITs, it would have been explicit. BITs most often do not require any State-investor contract at all. They typically specify the type of arbitration which would be available to aggrieved investors. If Mr Sornarajah were right, BITs would simply refer, e.g., to "such reference to arbitration as may have been defined in the approved investment contract." But an overwhelming majority of BITs reviewed by the present author go much farther.[16] Per-

---

15 *Op. cit.* Note 13, at 267. Mr Sornarajah would thus reduce the entire purpose of the frequently appearing provisions envisaging arbitration of investors' grievances to that of transforming a State's breach of a contractual obligation to arbitrate, owed to the investor, into a corresponding breach of a treaty obligation owed to the investor's home State.

16 This conclusion is shared by Professor Patrick Juillard of France, a knowledgeable and prudent specialist in the field of international economic law: *Les conventions bilatérales d'investissement conclues par la France*, 1979 JDI 274, at 289. Accord, Geneviève Burdeau, *Nouvelles perspectives pour l'arbitrage dans le contentieux économique intéressant l'Etat*, 1995 REV. ARB. 3, at 14.

sons who find it hard to accept that a State might have to account for its actions before an international tribunal would doubtless, if given the power to write BITs as they fancy, have charted the road to arbitration through the eye of their thinnest needle. But that is not what has happened.

The wave of the future in this connection may be the development of *multilateral* treaties. The arbitration mechanism provided for in the North American Free Trade Agreement is a significant example; a more recent development is Article 26 of the Energy Charter Treaty.[17] The latter is remarkably far-reaching; indeed, as compared with the gradual development of national protection laws and BITs, it represents a quantum leap—both in terms of the mechanisms it makes available to the complainant and in terms of the magnitude of their potential application. They should be considered in light of the equally significant fact that 41 States signed the Treaty on 17 December 1994, including major producing or purchasing powers in the energy field—e.g. France, Germany, Italy, Japan, Kazakhstan, the Netherlands, Russia, Spain and the United Kingdom. Japan and Norway (among others) made statements to the effect that they expected to sign in 1995; the same position was understood to be taken by Uzbekistan and Turkmenistan. The stated reason why the United States initially declined to sign is not that the Energy Charter Treaty went too far, but that it fell short of ensuring investors' substantive rights to the same extent as BITs concluded by the US.[18]

The operation of Article 26 may be generally described as follows:

- an investor who is a national of a signatory state may use the mechanism for any claimed violation of Part III of the Treaty (entitled "Investment Promotion and Protection");

- there is a cooling period of three months (relatively short in comparison to most similar provisions in BITs);

- if the investor is not satisfied, it has a wide range of options with respect to where it may seek redress: the courts or administrative tribunals of the host state, any jurisdiction provided for by a previous agreement, or arbitration under the Treaty;

- if the investor wishes to avail itself of arbitration under the Treaty, it has the further option of choosing among three sets of rules: those of ICSID (either those of the ICSID Convention or the ICSID Additional Facility), UNCITRAL, and the Arbitration Institute of the Stockholm Chamber of Commerce;

---

17   *See generally* THOMAS WÄLDE (ED.), THE ENERGY CHARTER TREATY: AN EAST-WEST GATEWAY FOR INVESTMENT AND TRADE (1996); Esa Paasivirta, *The European Union and the Energy Sector: The Case of the Energy Charter Treaty*, *in* M. KOSKENNIEMI (Ed.) INTERNATIONAL LAW ASPECTS OF THE EUROPEAN UNION 197 (1998).

18   US Government Statement, European Energy Charter Treaty Meeting, Lisbon, 15 December 1994, 34 INT. LEGAL MATERIALS 556 (1995).

⁻irrespective of the type of arbitration chosen, the dispute must, under Article 26(6) be decided "in accordance with this Treaty and applicable rules and principles of international law;"

⁻signatory states may make two types of limited reservation (viz. to exclude disputes already submitted by the investor to a competent forum, or to exclude claims under specific contracts between the defendant State and the investor).

The unmistakable thrust of Article 26 is to eliminate procedural or jurisdictional wrangling by creating a regime that strongly favors the use of neutral arbitration to sanction violation of the Treaty to the detriment of investors. This can be seen in the wide range of options granted to the claimant. For example, reference to a previously agreed forum is only a possibility, but not a requirement. This means that a defendant minded to be obstreperous will find no comfort in the fact that a dispute is only *partially* covered by a contract containing an arbitration clause; a claimant apprehensive of the limited authority of arbitrators operating under such a clause may wipe the slate clean and opt for one of the three types of arbitration defined in Article 26 without regard to what had been agreed before. Indeed, any defect in an arbitration clause might be cured in this manner by relying on Article 26.[19]

It is too early to tell whether this new field of international arbitration will fundamentally alter practice, or remain a marginal feature. What is already clear however is that this is not a subgenre of an existing discipline. It is dramatically different from anything previously known in the international sphere. It could presage an epochal extension of compulsory arbitral jurisdiction over States, at the behest of private litigants who wish to rely on governmental undertakings even though they have not contracted for a forum. The aim here is not to take anything away from States, but to help ensure that foreigners have faith in their promises. The objective is not arbitration that *favors the foreigner*, but one that simply favors *neutrality*. This is what the Guidelines submitted to the Fall 1992 meeting of the Development Committee of the Board of Governors of the IMF and the World Bank refer to as *independent* arbitration, further defined in Section V(2) as a process where "the majority of the arbitrators are not solely appointed by one party to the dispute."

The OECD Multilateral Investment Agreement under the joint consideration of the Committee on International Investments and Multinational Enterprises and the Committee on Capital Movements and Invisible Transactions may be the next great advance. The fundamental idea is to create a new multilateral

---

19 If there is an issue whether arbitrators operating under Article 26 are authorized or required to admit counterclaims, the fact that the claimant had chosen to disregard a pre-existing arbitration clause under which the new respondent could have brought a claim would intuitively weigh in favor of admissibility. The opposite conclusion could lead to unattractive situations of the respondent state initiating a *second* arbitration under the original clause, each proceeding thus casting a shadow on the other.

treaty with "legally binding obligations and enforcement proceedings;" its framework is described as possibly encompassing "liberalisation, investment protection and dispute settlement;" it is intended for OECD member States and non-member States alike. Such a document would then supplant BITs, which are threatening to create confusion by the variety of their formulations. In other words, what is envisaged is a *global charter* for a legal regime applicable to all types of investments, overarching both regional and sectorial treaties—such as NAFTA and the Energy Charter Treaty. One of five Working Groups is concentrating solely on "dispute settlement." While specific mechanisms are still under study, the Working Group has explicitly referred to the "ample precedents in BITs and other investment agreements."

So far, access to arbitration without privity has tended to be more frequently envisaged by reference to the ICSID or the UNCITRAL mechanisms rather than to ICC arbitration. The principle however is the same.

36.03   Sovereign immunity and acts of State

Arbitration agreements serve to stabilize contract terms. A governmental attempt to impose altered terms on a preexisting arrangement with a multinational enterprise, for example, may be countered by the commencement of arbitral proceedings. Whereas judicial action might be dismissed due to the sovereign immunity of the defendant government, an arbitration clause is generally deemed to constitute a waiver of immunity (*see* Section 8.13).[20] If a State has agreed to arbitration and then refuses to participate, the arbitration proceeds unilaterally.

The sometimes confusing interplay between the doctrines of sovereign immunity and acts of State is beyond the scope of this book and has been dealt with exhaustively elsewhere. A brief summary of the contours of these doctrines must suffice for present purposes.

The sovereignty of a foreign nation traditionally raised a bar to a court's exercise of jurisdiction against the State to adjudicate a claim or to enforce a judgment or award. State agencies, as well as the government itself, may benefit from immunity. The modern development of the doctrine, codified in the United States' Foreign Sovereign Immunities Act[21] and its U.K. analogue, the State Immunities Act,[22] follows a "restricted" doctrine of immunity that denies immunity to acts that are "commercial" in character. The commercial character of the act is determined according to its nature rather than its purpose.

---

20   *See also* Georges Delaume, *State Contracts and Transnational Arbitration*, 75 AMERICAN JOURNAL OF INTERNATIONAL LAW 784 (1981).

21   28 U.S.C. ÃÃ1602-1611, as implemented by Department of State Regulations, 22 C.F.R. Ã93.1, 93.2 (1977), amended in 1988, 124 CONGRESSIONAL RECORD S.17209.

22   Reprinted *in* 48 HALSBURY'S STATUTES OF ENGLAND (3d ed.) 85.

A State may waive its immunity even as to non-commercial matters. The Foreign Sovereign Immunities Act denies immunity when a foreign State has "waived its immunity either explicitly or by implication, notwithstanding any withdrawal of the waiver."[23] The U.K. State Immunities Act similarly provides that a State is not immune from judicial process if it has submitted to the jurisdiction of the courts of the United Kingdom "after the dispute . . . has arisen or by a prior written agreement."[24]

The so-called "act of State" doctrine bars adjudication of claims or enforcement of an award resulting from an act done by a sovereign power, within its territory, of a governmental rather than commercial nature. The nationalization of alien owned property by legislative decree constitutes the quintessential "act of State." Of the several justifications for the doctrine, the one most worthy of consideration is perhaps that the national judiciary should not risk embarrassing the executive arm of the government in its conduct of foreign affairs.[25] Another explanation is that the doctrine merely gives effect to the traditional choice of law rule that title to personal property is determined according to local law—the *lex situs*.

A series of cases that arose in the District of Columbia illustrate the interplay of sovereign immunity and the act of State doctrine. In *Ipitrade v. Nigeria*,[26] a French company had won an ICC arbitration, conducted in Switzerland and under Swiss law, for breach of a contract for the sale of cement to Nigeria. Nigeria did not satisfy the $9 million award, and Ipitrade brought suit in the District of Columbia. The federal court confirmed the award on the ground that in agreeing to arbitration Nigeria implicitly waived sovereign immunity and could not unilaterally revoke such waiver.

---

23   28 U.S.C. §1605(a).

24   Section 2(1)(2), State Immunities Act. *See generally* Hazel Fox, *States and the Undertaking to Arbitrate*, 37 INTERNATIONAL & COMPARATIVE LAW QUARTERLY 1 (1988).

25   *See* the U.S. Supreme Court's discussion of the doctrine in Banco Nacional de Cuba v. Sabbatino, 376 U.S. 398 (1964). On the "commercial" exception to the Act of State doctrine, *see* Alfred Dunhill v. Cuba, 425 U.S. 682 (1976). An early trace of the doctrine is to be found in *Blad's Case* of 1673:

". . . the Plaintiff hath proved letters patent from the King of Denmark for the sole trade of Iceland; a seizure by virtue of that patent; a sentence upon that seizure; a confirmation of that sentence by the Chancellor of Denmark; an execution of that sentence after confirmation; and a payment of two-thirds to the King of Denmark after that execution. Now, after all this, to send it to a trial at law, where either the Court must pretend to judge of the validity of the king's letter patent in Denmark, or of the exposition and meaning of the articles of peace; or that a common jury should try whether the English have a right to trade in Iceland, is monstrous and absurd."

26   465 F. Supp. 824 (D.D.C. 1978).

In *LIAMCO v. Libya*,[27] however, the award creditor fared less well. An American oil company brought suit to enforce an arbitral award against Libya, which in 1973 and 1974 had nationalized rights in petroleum concessions and equipment. Libya had refused to participate in the proceedings. The award was rendered in Geneva in 1977 by Dr. Sobhi Mahmassani, sole arbitrator, in the amount of US $80 million. Relying on the *Ipitrade* precedent, the oil company sought to have the award recognized in the District of Columbia. The judge of the federal court of first instance agreed that he had jurisdiction over the claim under the Foreign Sovereign Immunities Act. As in *Ipitrade*, the State had implicitly waived its sovereign immunity by agreeing to arbitration. He nevertheless declined to exercise his jurisdiction on the grounds of the act of State doctrine. In refusing to confirm the award, the judge referred to Article V(2)(a) of the New York Convention, which allows courts to refuse to recognize foreign awards the "subject matter of which is not capable of arbitration under the law of that country." In this judge's view, an act of State could not lead to an arbitrable claim.

LIAMCO would seem to render a contract claim non-arbitrable, despite a waiver of immunity, if the breach took the form of a legislative act. Nigeria's breach of contract in *Ipitrade* was not—as the Libyan breach was—couched in the trappings of a legislative act. If a government can circumvent the Sovereign Immunities Act by breach of contract through legislative act, waiver of sovereign immunity may quickly become an empty construct. There may be little difference between breaking a contract and enacting legislation preventing its performance.[28]

It is noteworthy that in the *LIAMCO* case, the United States Department of State submitted an *amicus curiae* brief in support of the oil company's appeal, indicating that the President would not invoke his power under the "Hickenlooper Amendment" to oust the court of jurisdiction when required by foreign policy considerations.[29] Settlement out of court, however, prevented the hearing of LIAMCO's appeal. After settlement, the Court of Appeals vacated the District Court's decision.[30] Only six months later, a decision of the U.S. District Court for the District of Columbia ignored the *LIAMCO* decision

---

27   482 F. Supp. 1175 (D.D.C. 1980), *dismissed as moot*, Order, D.C. Cir. Nos 80-1207 and 80-1252 (6 May 1981); summarized *in* VII YEARBOOK 382(1982). *See also supra*, Note 5.

28   *See* Judge Lauterpacht's opinion in the "Norwegian Loans" case, France v. Norway, INTERNATIONAL COURT OF JUSTICE REPORTS (1957), at 9; discussed *in* Jennings, 7 INTERNATIONAL & COMPARATIVE LAW QUARTERLY 349 (1958). The *LIAMCO* ruling was reversed by a legislative amendment to the Act in 1988; *see* Note 38 *infra*.

29   *See* 20 ILM 161 (1981) for excerpts from the State Department's brief.

30   The Court's Order, D.C. Cir. No. 80-1207 (May 6, 1981), provides that "the order filed by the District Court on January 18, 1980, shall be and is hereby vacated."

and recognized an award in favor of insurance companies seeking compensation for nationalization of their Iranian business.[31]

LIAMCO also attempted attachment against Libyan assets in France. Sweden and Switzerland. In France, recognition of the award (*exequatur*) was granted by the *Tribunal de grande instance* in Paris,[32] only to be followed by a lifting of the attachment orders less than one month later. LIAMCO obtained twenty-nine attachment orders against French assets of Libya and companies claimed to be emanations of the Libyan State. The French authorities, however, in the person of the *Procureur de la Republique*, joined the Libyan parties in asking the court to lift the attachment orders. The court did so,[33] but granted LIAMCO the right to further proceedings to establish whether any of the assets were not exempt from immunity. The out-of-court settlement interrupted the work of a three-member court-appointed commission established to investigate the nature of the assets seized.

In Sweden, the Court of Appeal of Svea granted a motion for the award's enforcement.[34] The Court held that Libya had waived its immunity entirely by signing an arbitration agreement. No distinction was made between immunity from jurisdiction and immunity from execution.[35]

In Switzerland, the Federal Tribunal overturned an attachment order that LIAMCO had secured from the Zurich District Court against Libyan assets in six local banks.[36] The federal court did not challenge the validity of the arbitral award itself, but ruled rather that the Zurich tribunal had no jurisdiction to order attachments against a State when the litigation lacks a "sufficient domestic relationship." Such a relationship might be established, for example, by activities that justify jurisdictional venue in Switzerland. Neither the location of assets in Switzerland, nor the choice of Geneva as the arbitral seat, established a "sufficient domestic relationship" in the *LIAMCO* case.

---

31 American International Group v. Iran, 493 F. Supp. 522 (D.D.C. 1980). Other contemporaneous American cases dealing with sovereign immunity included Maritime International Nominees v. Guinea, 505 F. Supp. 141 (D.D.C. 1981); Birch Shipping v. Tanzania, 507 F. Supp. 311 (D.D.C. 1980); Texas Trading v. Nigeria, 500 F. Supp. 320 (S.D.N.Y. 1980).

32 Judgment of 7 February 1979, *President du Tribunal de grande instance*, Paris. discussed *in* P. Rambaud, *Suites d'un differend petrolier: l'affaire LIAMCO devant le juge francais*, 25 ANNUAIRE FRANCAIS DE DROIT INTERNATIONAL 820 (1979).

33 Judgment of 5 March 1979, *Tribunal de grande instance*, Paris, 1979 JDI 857.

34 Judgment of 18 June 1980, Court of Appeal of Svea (Stockholm), reprinted (in French translation) and discussed *in* Jan Paulsson, *L'immunite restreinte enterinée par la jurisprudence suédoise*, 108 JDI 545 (1981).

35 One of the authors suggested that the decision may have been too broad on the issue of immunity from execution; Paulsson, *id.* at 548.

36 Judgment of 19 June 1980, *Tribunal federal*, 106 BGE Ia at 142; ILM 15 (1981), VI YEARBOOK 151 (1981) (summary in English), 75 AMERICAN JOURNAL OF INTERNATIONAL LAW 153 (1981) (summary in English).

The *LIAMCO* saga illustrates the lack of consensus and predictability of national laws with respect to enforcement of awards against foreign sovereigns.[37] The latest legislative development in the United States was the passage in 1988 of amendments to the Foreign Sovereign Immunities Act,[38] which in particular establish that the act of State doctrine is not to be applied to bar the enforcement of arbitration agreements or the confirmation of awards. (It also notably makes it possible to execute arbitral awards against the commercial property of foreign States whether or not it was used in the commercial activity that gave rise to the arbitration.)

The discussion above has focused on the possible effects of the doctrines of sovereign immunity and acts of State at the stage of enforcing awards. The question may be asked whether these doctrines may or should also be applied as part of the substantive determination made in international arbitral awards.

The matter of sovereign immunity is rather easy to dispose of. Either the arbitral tribunal has jurisdiction or it has not. If it does, by definition the State has consented to arbitration and thus waived claims of immunity it may otherwise have raised. In other words, the issue in arbitration is whether the State has validly consented to arbitration; there is ordinarily no reason to consider issues of sovereign immunity.

The matter of acts of State is more difficult. One should distinguish cases in which the relevant State is a party to the dispute from those where it is not.

If the State is a party to the dispute, it would be logical to conclude that any of its acts must necessarily be subject to the judgment of the arbitrators insofar as they pertain to the assessment of compliance with contractual duties. Logic gives way to reality, however; there comes a point at which acts of a State go so far beyond the sphere of the particular contractual relationship under consideration, partaking of sovereign legislative or regulatory prerogatives in the general interest, that the authority of an arbitrator to rule on their validity becomes problematic. Such cases may be resolved by taking the act of State as a given, and simply assessing its contractual consequences in terms of an obligation to make compensation.[39]

---

37   *See generally* Hazel Fox, *State Immunity and Enforcement of Arbitral Awards: Do We Need an UNCITRAL Model Law Mark II for Execution Against State Property?* 12 ARB. INT. 89 (1996).

38   S. 2204, 124 *Congressional Record* S.17209 (21 October 1988). In July 1999, the US Court of Appeals for the District of Columbia held, in considering an action to enforce an ICC award rendered in Paris, that although the Foreign Sovereign Immunities Act of 1979 ensured subject matter jurisdiction it preserved the Constitutional defense of lack of personal jurisdiction, and thus denied enforcement, Creighton Ltd. V. Government of the State of Qatar, 181F 3d 118 (D.C. Cir. 2 July 1999). If this decision holds, it will create serious obstacles to enforcement of foreign awards in the United States against Foreign Sovereigns who, like Qatar, have not signed the New York Convention.

39   *See* the awards in AMINOIL v. State of Kuwait, 21 ILM 976 (1982); SPP (Middle East) *et al.* v. Arab Republic of Egypt *et al.*, ICC case 3493/1983, 22 ILM 752 (1983). *Cf.* Paasivirta, Note 1 *supra* at 306: "the will of the parties, or reasonable expectations, does not seem to be a satisfactory

If the State is *not* a party to the arbitration, the difficulty is exacerbated. To put it simply, it is difficult for private arbitrators to take on the task of assessing the legitimacy of the sovereign acts of a State which has not consented to their jurisdiction. If they were to disregard the act of State, their awards may be fragile. Yet there are circumstances in which arbitrators are unwilling to accept acts of State as establishing valid defenses of *force majeure* particularly in light of evidence of close connections between the respondent and the State in question.[40] This is a difficult and recurring issue in the context of contracts signed by State enterprises, and is beyond the scope of this book.[41] There have been two notable instances of international arbitrators refusing to accept the validity of acts of State. The first was the ICC award in the case of *SGTM v. Bangladesh*,[42] where the original respondent, a wholly-owned state entity called the East Pakistan Investment Development Corporation (EPIDC), had been dissolved by a decree which purported to vest all its assets, but none of its liabilities, in a new state-owned entity. Finding that this decree was an unacceptable attempt by the Bangladesh government to neutralize the contractual obligations of EPIDC, the sole arbitrator asserted jurisdiction over both the State of Bangladesh and EPIDC's successor entity, and held them liable. The award was subsequently set aside by the Swiss courts on the grounds that the arbitrator had exceeded his powers.[43] In the *Settebello v. Setenave* case, decided by three eminent international arbitrators under the rules of the Netherlands Arbitration Institute, a decree by the Portuguese government was disregarded, reportedly on the grounds that its application would be "contrary to generally accepted principles of international law and . . . concepts of public policy and morality common to all trading nations."[44] The case involved a tanker to be built by the Portuguese state-owned shipyard Setenave. At the relevant time, the market value of the tanker had fallen sharply and it appeared likely, given delays in completion of the vessel, that the buyer would invoke a cancellation clause in the contract. The contract was subject to Portuguese law. The government enacted the contested decree,

---

ground for the enforcement of State contracts in international law. Instead, reliance and rendering of benefits provide more weighty reasons . . . ." He notes that purely executory contracts ("i.e. contracts unperformed or upon which there has been no reliance") are "prime examples of the will-theory of contracts" and affirms that to his knowledge such contracts have never in practice been accorded equal protection with executed contracts under international law; *id.* at 307.

40 *See* the *ad hoc* interim award of 9 September 1983 between an unnamed West German engineering company and an unnamed Polish State export trading company, extracts *in* XII YEARBOOK 63 (1987).

41 *See generally* KARL-HEINZ BÖCKSTIEGEL, ARBITRATION AND STATE ENTERPRISES (1984).

42 ICC Case 1803/1972, V YEARBOOK 177 (1980).

43 Decision of 5 May 1976 of the Swiss *Tribunal federal*, extracts in V YEARBOOK 217 (1980).

44 Quoted *in* THE FINANCIAL TIMES, 27 February 1986 (Business Law section).

which declared that contractual rights to cancel on the grounds of delays in delivery could be neutralized provided that delivery were effected within a further two years. The arbitrators refused to take account of the decree and held Settebello entitled to cancel as per the terms of the contract. The award was reportedly challenged before the Dutch courts on the grounds that the arbitrators were bound by the decree, but a subsequent settlement apparently ended the dispute before that challenge was resolved.

Given the likely resistance by non-party States to findings by a foreign arbitral tribunal to the effect that the corporate veil of a State enterprise is to be disregarded, or that an act of the State is to be denied effect as an event of *force majeure*, or is to be held to be an abuse of right, arbitrators require especially convincing evidence before so holding.

36.04   The ability of developing countries to deal with transnational disputes

There has been a dramatic increase in recent years in the numbers of parties from the Third World participating in the ICC arbitral process. Tables 5 and 6 of Appendix I are revealing: while during a 1972-75 three-year time period the African country with the most nationals represented in ICC arbitrations was Algeria with five, 19 African nationalities equalled or exceeded this total in 1980-88 and 22 in 1989-1999. As for the Middle East and Asia, Iran, Israel, and Japan were the most active in the earlier period with six parties each; no less than 25 countries reached or surpassed this total in 1980-88, and 30 in 1989-1999 (*see also* Section 1.04).

That the Third World participates in the ICC arbitral process is therefore clear, and, as has been seen in Section 36.01, this participation has had the result that more ICC arbitrations are conducted in developing countries and more nationals of Third World countries now serve as arbitrators.

It remains to be seen, however, to what extent parties from developing countries are able to present their cases in an effective and confident way. Here too there seems to have been a significant change,[45] reflected *inter alia* in the facts that ten out of twenty-five Third World parties to ICC arbitrations commenced in 1986 were claimants and not defendants, and during the entire subsequent 1989-1999 period that proportion rose above 40%.[46]

One of the authors has attempted to make a qualitative analysis of how well litigants from developing countries are able to defend their interests in inter-

---

45   *See* Philippe Leboulanger, *L'arbitrage international Nord-Sud, in* ETUDES OFFERTES À PIERRE BELLET 323 (1991).

46   *See* Appendix I, Table 5.

national arbitrations.[47] (A quantitative study appeared beyond reach, as it is nearly impossible to tell from a simple reading of an award which party obtained the greatest satisfaction. The *Aminoil* award.[48] for example, formally obliged the Government of Kuwait to pay damages to the nationalized concessionaire, but the amount awarded was only a small part of the claim, and the award recognized the essential legitimacy of the nationalization of an oil field.) The study showed that Third World litigants have successfully argued to the international arbitrator that he should apply their own national law in cases where rules of conflict so dictate, recognize the purpose of an investment agreement as an element of its interpretation, and order Western defendants to respect performance bonds immediately irrespective of the argument that there were valid counterclaims which ought to offset payment under the bonds. Indeed, the arbitral mechanism is no longer limited to North-South relationships; a major ICC arbitration involved two African parties.[49] Furthermore, a clear trend was observed toward charging competent professionals with the task of preparing arbitrations. Many developing countries by now have experienced and proficient advocates among their own nationals; others have recourse to international firms. At any rate, the days of the 1960's, when Third World parties not only were almost exclusively defendants but frequently lost by default, are over. In sum, these parties appear to have measured the stakes and in many instances generated the capabilities to meet the challenge.

---

47   Paulsson, *supra* Note 3.

48   ILM 976 (1982) (original English text); translated into French *in* 1982 JDI 869.

49   1980 JDI 951 (1980); extracts in English *in* VII YEARBOOK 87 (1982). In this case, the arbitral tribunal presided by the Swiss professor Robert Party rendered a provisional award of some US $26 million the very day of the first hearings. *See also* the Dalmia Dairy Industries award, ICC Case 1512/1971, extracts *in* I YEARBOOK 128 (1976); extracts in French translation *in* 1974 JDI 904.

Moreover, the study showed that parties from developing countries have been willing and able to pursue Western defendants into their home courts to obtain forcible execution of ICC awards. Such initiatives have, in particular, routinely succeeded in the U.S.[50] and France.[51] And while parties from developing countries understandably want the increase in numbers of Third World presiding arbitrators to accelerate, there is no dearth of awards rendered by European arbitrators in favor of Third World parties.

---

50 *See, e.g.*, RAKTA (Egypt) v. Parsons & Whittemore Inc., 508 F. 2d 969 (2d Cir. 1974); I YEARBOOK 205 (1976); Ethiopia v. Baruch Foster Corp., 535 F. 2d 334 (5th Cir. 1976); II YEARBOOK 252 (1977); Fertilizer Corporation of India v. IDI Management, Inc., 517 F. Supp. 948 (1981), VII YEARBOOK 382(1982), *reconsideration denied*, 530 F. Supp. 542(1982), VIII YEARBOOK 419 (1983); National Oil Corp. (Libya) v. Libyan Sun Oil Co. (US), 733 F. Supp. 800 (DC Del. 1990), XVI YEARBOOK 651 (1991); International Standard Electric Corp. v. Bridas S.A. (Argentina), 745 F. Supp. 172 (SDNY, 1990), XVII YEARBOOK 639 (1992); Ukrvneshprom State Foreign Economic Enterprise (Ukraine) v. Tradeway, Inc. (US), No. 95 Civ. 10278 (RPP), 1996 WL 107285 (SDNY, 12 March 1996), XXII YEARBOOK 958 (1997); Anhui Provincial Import & Export Corp. (People's Republic of China) v. Hart Enterprises Int., Inc. (US), No. 96 Civ. 128 (LAK), 1996 WL 229872 (SDNY, 7 May 1996), XXII YEARBOOK 979 (1997) (enforcement of a CIETAC award rendered in Beijing by default); Agroengineering (Russia) v. American Custom Service, Inc. (US), 7 June 1996, EDNY, 95 Civ. 2238, XXII YEARBOOK 990 (1997) (enforcement of an FTAC award rendered in Moscow by default); Yusuf Ahmed Alghanim & Sons W.L.L. (Kuwait) v. Toys 'R' Us Inc. (US) *et al.*, 126 F. 3d 15 (2d Cir. 1997), *cert. den.*, 118 S.Ct. 1042 (1998) ("non-domestic" AAA award in the amount of US $46.4 million enforced).

51 Compagnie de Saint-Gobain-Pont-a-Mousson v. Fertilizer Corporation of India. *Cour d'appel*, Paris, 10 May 1974; 1971 REV. ARB. 111; I YEARBOOK 184(1976); Comptoirs Industriels Reunis Blachere (France) v. Societe de Developpement Viticole (SODEVI) (Morocco), *Cour d'appel*, Paris, 3 December 1981, 1982 REV. ARB. 92; Societe Appareils Dragons (France) v. Empresa Central de Abastecimientos y Ventas de Equipos y Piezas de la Construccion (Construimport) (Cuba), *Cour d'appel*, Paris, 22 January, 1982, 1982 REV. ARB. 92; affirmed, *Cour de cassation*, 8 June 1983 (unpublished).

CHAPTER 37

ICC ARBITRATION AND THE
NEW YORK CONVENTION

37.01   Background

In almost one hundred and twenty countries,[1] the Convention on the Recognition and Enforcement of Foreign Arbitral Awards[2] implements the business managers' bargain to waive judicial jurisdiction in favor of private justice. Generally referred to as the New York Arbitration Convention (or sometimes the "United Nations Convention") this multilateral agreement provides for recognition of both the arbitration clause and the resulting award, even in countries that have resisted analogous treaties to enforce court selection agreements and foreign judgments.

The genesis of the New York Convention lies in a 1953 report of the International Chamber of Commerce (ICC)[3] underscoring the commercial community's need for arbitral awards that are transportable from one country to another. The report suggested a new treaty that would liberate foreign arbitral awards from the burdensome enforcement procedures of the Geneva Convention,[4] which had been read to require what was called "double *exequatur*,"

---

1   As of the date of this writing, one hundred and twenty (120) jurisdictions have adhered to the New York Convention, either by ratification, accession or succession.

2   330 U.N.T.S. 38, 21 U.S.T. 2517, T.I.A.S. No. 6997 (1958) [hereinafter "The Convention"]. *See generally* ALBERT JAN VAN DEN BERG, THE NEW YORK ARBITRATION CONVENTION OF 1958 (1981). For an illustrative discussion of one country's adoption and implementation of the Convention, see John P. McMahon, *Implementation of the United Nations Convention on Foreign Arbitral Awards in the United States*, 2 J. MARITIME L. & COMMERCE 735 (1971) and Alan S. Rau, *The New York Convention in American Courts*, 7 AMER. REV. INT'L ARB. 213 (1996).

3   International Chamber of Commerce, Enforcement of International Arbitral Awards: Report and Preliminary Draft Convention, ICC Brochure No. 174 (1953), *reprinted in* U.N. DOC. E/C.2/373 *and in* 9 ICC BULL.32 (May 1998).

4   Convention on the Execution of Foreign Arbitral Awards (Geneva 1927), 92 L.N.T.S. 301. The Geneva Convention applied to awards made in pursuance to an agreement covered by the 1923

judicial recognition orders in both the country where the award was made and the enforcement forum.[5] Thus an award rendered in Boston had to be confirmed by a court in Massachusetts before enforcement in Montréal.

The ICC proposed streamlining award enforcement by eliminating the "double *exequatur*" requirement and shifting key burdens of proof from the party seeking award enforcement to the party resisting its recognition. For example, under the Geneva Convention the party relying on the award had to present documentary evidence that the award had not been annulled where rendered.[6] In contrast, the ICC draft treaty required that award annulment be invoked by the party resisting recognition.[7]

The United Nations Economic and Social Council (ECOSOC) reworked the ICC draft into a convention that was in some ways less ambitious. For example, the United Nations version focuses on "foreign" awards (made in a country other than the enforcement forum), rather than the broader notion of "international" awards favored by the ICC. Following a three week conference of governments and non-governmental organizations, a compromise version was adopted at the United Nations' New York headquarters on 10 June 1958.

37.02 Framework

The New York Convention operates both to enforce arbitration agreements and to promote recognition of awards at the place where the loser has assets. The Convention requires courts of contracting states to refer the parties to arbitration when a dispute is subject to a written arbitration agreement that is not "null and void, inoperative or incapable of being performed."[8] Although this duty to refer the parties to arbitration will apply to judicial actions, the arbitration clause will not necessarily bar administrative proceedings.[9]

Geneva Protocol on Arbitration Clauses, 27 L.N.T.S. 157, which had provided for stay of court proceedings at the arbitration situs, much as would a uniform arbitration law.

5   The party relying on the award had to provide documentary evidence that the award "not be considered . . . open to *opposition*, *appel* or *pourvoi en cassation*" and that there not exist "any proceedings for the purpose of contesting the validity of the award are pending." See Geneva Convention Article 4(2), with cross-reference to the requirements of Convention 1(d). Moreover, Geneva Convention Article 4(1) required the party relying on the arbitrators' decision to provide an award "duly authenticated according to the requirements of the law of the country in which it was made."

6   1927 Convention, Article 4(3), with cross reference to requirements of Article 2(a).

7   *See* Article IV of the "Preliminary Draft Convention" included in the International Chamber of Commerce Report on Enforcement of International Arbitral Awards, ICC Brochure No. 174 (1953).

8   New York Arbitration Convention, Article II (3).

9   *See* Farrel Corp. v. United States ITC, 949 F.2d 1147 (Fed. Cir. 1991). When a dispute arose between an United States manufacturer and an Italian licensee of rubber mixing technology, the licensor began litigation in the United States, notwithstanding the contract's arbitration clause providing for ICC arbitration in Geneva. Although judicial proceedings were dismissed, the plaintiff was allowed to file a complaint with the International Trade Commission (ITC) alleging trade secret misappropriation. The court reasoned that the arbitration agreement operated as a waiver

In addition, courts must recognize foreign awards as they would domestic ones.[10] The Convention provides that awards shall be enforced "in accordance with the rules of procedure of the territory where the award is relied upon," subject to no conditions more onerous than those imposed on domestic awards.

37.03   Scope

(a) Nationality Generally Irrelevant

There is no requirement that the contracting parties or the litigants (usually but not always the same) come from different states, or that the party seeking to enforce an award be from a country that has adhered to the Convention. Citizenship is relevant to Convention coverage only indirectly, when the parties' different nationalities add an element indicating an award is "not domestic," as discussed below.[11]

(b) Awards

Geography is the principal trigger for application of the Convention, which covers primarily foreign awards.[12] Under this test, an award rendered in New York would be covered by the Convention when presented for enforcement against assets in Zürich, Paris or London, but not when recognition is sought before courts in Atlanta or Los Angeles.

Inability to meet the geographical test, however, does not mean the award creditor is entirely out of luck. The Convention will also apply to "awards not considered as domestic," a subtle and multi-faceted notion. Thus in the above scenario, a New York award might be considered by a United States court as "not domestic" if the factual configuration of the case contained foreign parties or other significant cross-border elements.

The concept of a "non-domestic" award was recently given a wide scope in a decision holding that United States courts could apply the Convention to awards rendered in the United States in disputes entirely between United

---

of access to a judicial rather than an administrative forum.

10   New York Arbitration Convention, Article III.

11   In some countries, however, national legislation implementing the Convention might restrict its application as between citizens of the same country. *See, e.g.,* § 202 of the United States Federal Arbitration Act.

12   The first sentence of Convention Article I(1) refers to awards "made in the territory of a State other than the State where the recognition and enforcement of such awards are sought."

States corporations.[13] Part of the contract was to be performed abroad, leading the court to consider the dispute within the scope of the Convention.

(c) Agreements

For better or for worse, the Convention is less precise with respect to its coverage of arbitration agreements than awards. The Convention requires only that the agreement to arbitrate be in writing, and that it cover disputes "in respect to a defined legal relationship" (whether or not contractual) concerning a "subject matter capable of settlement by arbitration."[14]

Whether through design or inadvertence, the Convention drafters did not indicate further limitations on the type of arbitration agreements covered. Commentators have suggested, however, that Convention coverage of arbitration agreements should be interpreted consistently with its scope as to awards.[15] Applying by analogy the general provisions on Convention coverage of awards, the Convention would apply to agreements (i) providing for foreign arbitration (in a country other than the one in which the arbitration clause is invoked) and (ii) sufficiently international to be "not domestic."

(d) Requirement of a Writing

The requirement that the arbitration agreement be in written form does not mean that the agreement must necessarily be signed. Convention Article II defines an agreement in writing to include a contract either signed by the parties or "contained in an exchange of letters or telegrams" whether signed or not. Thus, for example, New York Convention coverage has been extended to a dispute arising out of a purchase of oil, where telexes exchanged between the buyer and the seller referred to seller's standard contract terms which provided for arbitration.[16]

The requirement of a "writing" is similar (though by no means identical) to that contained in many national arbitration statutes.[17] Likewise, Article 7(2)

---

13   In *Lander Co. v. MMP, Invs.*, an ICC arbitration in New York arose from a contract between two United States businesses to distribute shampoo products in Poland. 107 F. 3d 476 (7th Cir. 1997), *cert. denied*, 139 L. Ed. 2d 19 (1997). The *Lander* decision extends the principle endorsed in an earlier United States case which characterized as "not domestic" an award made in New York between two foreign parties. *See* Bergesen v. Joseph Muller Corp., 710 F.2d 928 (2d Cir. 1983).

14   New York Convention, Article II (2).

15   *See, e.g.,* ALBERT JAN VAN DEN BERG, THE NEW YORK ARBITRATION CONVENTION OF 1958, § I-2.1, 57 (1981).

16   *See* Bomar v. ETAP, *Cour de Cassation* (Cass. 1e civ., 9 Nov. 1993), 1994 REV. ARB. 108, note Catherine Kessedjian.

17   *See, e.g.,* § 5 of English Arbitration Act of 1996, Article 178 Swiss *Loi fédérale sur le droit international privé* and § 2 of United States Federal Arbitration Act. For a critique of national judicial interpretation of the writing requirement as applied to international arbitration, see Paul D. Friedland, *U.S. Courts' Misapplication of the "Agreement in Writing" Requirement for Enforcement of an Arbitration Agreement Under the New York Convention*, 13 MEALEY'S INT. ARB. REP. 21

of the UNCITRAL Model Arbitration Law provides that arbitration agreements must be ". . . contained in a document signed by the parties or in an exchange of letters, telex, telegrams or other means of telecommunication which provide a record of the agreement, or in an exchange of statements of claim and defense in which the existence of an agreement is alleged by one party and not denied by another."

Some commentators have questioned whether the requirement of either a signed document or an "exchange" is consistent with good commercial practice. A contracting party might benefit from a form contract (perhaps in a purchase order) and then after performance resist enforcement of the arbitration clause by arguing that one side had failed to sign the form.[18] In response one might suggest that acceptance of a condition on price or quantity of goods does not necessarily imply an agreement on other terms, particularly a stipulation as important as a waiver of the right to go to court.

Sophisticated judges have given a wide scope to the writing requirement. For example, in a case where an agreement to arbitrate was contained in a bill of lading signed only by the carrier, the Swiss *Tribunal fédéral* held the clause valid on the basis of a long course of dealing between the parties. The shipper of goods had brought a court action in Geneva notwithstanding that the bill of lading provided for arbitration in London.[19]

(e) Reservations

The Convention allows contracting states to make two reservations.[20] The first is a requirement of territorial reciprocity, which applies the treaty only to awards rendered in another Convention country. Thus the winner of an arbitration in Iran (which to date has not adhered to the Convention) could not use the Convention to enforce its award in the United States, which has made the reciprocity reservation. A contracting state may also reserve Convention application to differences arising exclusively out of commercial relationships.

(May 1998).

18 See Neil Kaplan, *Is the Need for Writing as Expressed in the New York Convention and the Model Law Out of Step with Commercial Practice?* 12 ARB. INT. 27, 29 (1996), in which the author asks "why if one party is sent a contract which includes an arbitration clause and that party acts on that contract and thus adopts it without qualification, that party should be allowed to wash his hands of the arbitration clause but at the same time maintain an action for the price of the goods delivered or conversely sue for breach."

19 *Compagnie de Navigation et Transports S.A. v. MSC (Mediterranean Shipping Company) S.A.* ATF 121 II 38 (16 Jan. 1995); 13 SWISS BULL. 503 (1995).

20 New York Convention, Article I (3).

37.04   Defenses to Recognition and Enforcement

A court of a Convention country may refuse recognition and enforcement to awards only on the basis of a limited list of procedural defenses.[21] Divided into two groups, one relating mainly to procedural defects in the arbitral process (protecting the loser's interests), and the other permitting courts to decline enforcement to awards that contravene their fundamental notions of public policy (protecting the forum's own vital interests).

With respect to the latter set of defenses a court may refuse to enforce an award (i) whose subject matter is not arbitrable or (ii) which violates the forum's public policy (*ordre public*).[22] These defenses may be raised by a court on its own motion, without any proof by the party resisting the award. Traditionally courts have given a narrow scope to the Convention's "public policy" defense,[23] interpreting policy violations to include only breach of the forum's "most basic notions of morality and justice."[24] A broad interpretation would defeat the Convention's purpose of permitting parties to international transactions to promote neutral dispute resolution.

The other group of defenses, intended principally to safeguard the parties against injustice, must be asserted and proven by the party resisting the award. The initial four subdivisions of this group permit an award to be refused recognition on the basis that the fundamental fairness of the arbitration was in question. In summary form, these defenses cover (i) an invalid arbitration

---

21 On the stay of enforcement of one award pending the result in a second arbitration, see *Hewlett-Packard v. Berg*, discussed in Chapter 34.04.

22 New York Arbitration Convention, Article V(2).

23 For a survey of the public policy defense, *see* Audley Sheppard (Rapporteur), *Public Policy as a Ground for refusing Enforcement of Foreign Arbitral Awards*, INTERNATIONAL LAW ASSOCIATION, COMMITTEE ON INTERNATIONAL COMMERCIAL ARBITRATION, TAIPEI CONFERENCE (1998). *See also* REDFERN & HUNTER, at 471-74; ALBERT JAN VAN DEN BERG, THE NEW YORK ARBITRATION CONVENTION OF 1958 (1981).

24 *See* Parsons & Whittemore Overseas Co. v. Société Générale de l'Industrie du Papier (RAKTA), 508 F.2d 969, 974 (2d Cir. 1974) (rejecting a public policy defense related to a rupture in diplomatic relations between Egypt and the United States). The public policy defense was also dismissed in Fertilizer Corp. of India v. IDI Management, Inc., 530 F. Supp. 542 (S.D. Ohio 1982) (arbitrator's lack of independence from one party); Antco Shipping Co. v. Sidermar, 417 F. Supp. 207 (S.D.N.Y. 1976) (participation in the Arab boycott of Israel); Biotronik GmbH v. Medford Medical Instrument Co., 415 F. Supp. 133, 139 (D.N.J. 1976) (passively misleading the arbitral tribunal did not to trigger public policy defense, although *dictum* suggested that active fraud such as perjury might violate public policy). For one aberrant case in which an award *was* refused enforcement on public policy grounds (where French law called for a particularly high interest rate on late payment) see Laminoirs-Trefileries-Cableries de Lens, S.A. v. Southwire Co., 484 F. Supp. 1063 (N.D. Ga. 1980).

agreement, (ii) lack of opportunity to present one's case, (iii) arbitrator excess of jurisdiction and (iv) irregular composition of the arbitral tribunal.[25]

A final ground in the "party oriented" set of defenses permits courts' refusal of enforcement to awards set aside where rendered. Thus annulment of an award at the arbitral situs gives the loser a powerful argument for resisting the award's enforcement.

It is important to remember, however, that the New York Arbitration Convention establishes no criteria for proper or improper vacatur at the arbitral situs.[26] Judicial review of an award at the place where made will be governed by the local arbitration law there in force, which may provide for award vacatur on any ground it sees fit, or for no vacatur at all. See Chapters 28-34.

Although vacatur at the arbitral situs can impair the award's international currency under the Convention, it will not necessarily foreclose enforcement in all jurisdictions. The English text of Convention Article V(1)(e) provides an award "may" (not "must") be refused recognition if set aside where the award was made.[27] Moreover, any interested party may still enforce an annulled award under the domestic law of the recognition forum, whatever that law might turn out to be. Convention Article VII provides that the Convention would not "deprive any interested party of any right he may have to avail himself of an arbitral award in the manner and to the extent allowed by the law . . . of the country where such award is sought to be relied upon."

Thus a New York court asked to enforce a London award presented for enforcement against the loser's American bank account would be permitted either to defer to the English nullification or (if allowed under the Federal Arbitration Act) to enforce the award. And indeed, courts in the United States and France have invoked domestic arbitration law to recognize Convention awards annulled where rendered, a practice raising policy concerns that have divided commentators.[28]

---

25 New York Arbitration Convention, Article V(1)(a)-(d). For a case dealing with the opportunity to present one's case in the matter of allocation of attorney's fees in ICC arbitration, see discussion of *CBG v. Hammermill*, discussed in Chapter 34.04.

26 Compare the approach of the European Arbitration Convention (Geneva 1961), which in Article IX defines acceptable grounds for award annulment that will justify non-recognition.

27 The equally authoritative French version lends itself to a more forceful interpretation, providing that *"la reconnaissance et l'exécution de la sentence ne seront refusées que si la sentence . . . a été annulée ou suspendue."*

28 *See* discussion of the *Chromalloy* and *Hilmarton* cases, Chapter 28.04. In addition, a Belgian court enforced an award annulled in Algeria in *SONATRACH v. Ford, Bacon & Davis* (also discussed in Chapter 28.04), although relying on the lack of any retroactive application of the New York Convention (which Algeria had yet not ratified at the relevant time) and thus being distinguishable from the French and American approaches.

37.05   Interaction with Other Treaties

When a nation adheres to the New York Convention as well as another treaty that might influence ICC arbitration, ordering principles are needed. In some cases the hierarchy of treaty provisions will be relatively simple and uncontroversial, while in other contexts the interaction may be more complex. The present section sketches the interaction of the New York Convention with five other treaties which, depending on the circumstances, may have an effect effect on cross-border commercial dispute resolution: the Geneva Protocol, the Geneva Convention, the European Convention, the Panama Convention and the Bruxelles Convention. In addition, readers are minded that arbitration provisions are contained in many bilateral trade and investment treaties,[29] as well as in the United Nations Convention on the Carriage of Goods by Sea (relevant to charter-parties)[30] and the Inter-American Convention on Extraterritorial Validity of Foreign Judgments and Arbitral Awards.[31]

(a) The Geneva Protocol and The Geneva Convention

The New York Convention replaces the 1923 Geneva Protocol and the 1927 Geneva Convention as between countries that are parties to both treaties, regardless of what the nationality of the parties to the dispute might be. New York Convention Article VII provides that both the Geneva Protocol and the Geneva Convention "shall cease to have effect between Contracting States on their becoming bound and to the extent that they become bound by this Convention."

(b) The European Convention

The European Convention supplements the New York Convention in disputes only among persons which, at the time the arbitration agreement was concluded, had their "habitual place of residence or their seat in different Contracting States."[32] This can sometimes be quite significant, since under Article IX of the European Convention annulment of an award in its country of origin will constitute a ground for refusal of recognition *only* if based on one of the Convention-approved grounds: invalid arbitration agreement, lack of proper notice, arbitral excess of authority and improper constitution of the arbitral tribunal. Thus if an award made in London is vacated for error of law, the enforceability of the award under the Convention would not be impaired. Similar treatment would be reserved for an award rendered in Paris and set aside under NCPC Article 1502 for violation of public policy (*ordre public*).

---

29   *See generally* RUDOLF DOLZER & MARGRETE STEVENS, BILATERAL INVESTMENT TREATIES (1995).

30   Hamburg, 31 March 1978. See Convention Article 22.

31   Montevideo, 8 May 1979. See discussion in INTERNATIONAL ARBITRATION TREATIES (Hans Smit & Vratislav Pechota, eds. 1998), at 219-230.

32   *See* Article I of the 1961 European Convention on International Commercial Arbitration.

(c) The Panama Convention

In Latin American countries, the Panama Convention[33] mirrors much of the New York Arbitration Convention. However, the Panama Convention provides that execution and recognition of an award "may" be ordered, as contrasted with the New York Arbitration Convention's mandate that a contracting state "shall" recognize and enforce awards. Moreover, the Panama Convention does not distinguish between foreign and domestic awards, and provides that the parties' failure to select procedural rules results in automatic application of the arbitration rules of the Inter-American Commercial Arbitration Association.[34]

To determine whether the Panama Convention substitutes for the New York Convention, one must first count the parties. When a majority of those who agreed to arbitration are citizens of states that have adhered to the Panama convention and are members of the Organization of American States, then the Panama Convention will usually apply.[35]

(d) The Bruxelles Convention

The Bruxelles Convention on Jurisdiction and Judgments in Civil and Commercial Matters implicitly endorses the recognition of arbitration clauses and awards by excluding arbitration from its scope, which covers allocation of judicial competence and enforcement of court judgments among members of the European Union.[36] A parallel treaty signed in Lugano extends similar principles to nations belonging to the European Free Trade Association (EFTA).[37]

Whether this exclusion covers collateral proceedings related to the validity of the arbitration clause itself was not always been clear. A broad view of the exclusion would carve out from the Bruxelles Convention coverage *all* disputes related to an arbitration, including ancillary controversies relating to the validity of the agreement to arbitrate. A narrower view would make the Conven-

---

33 Officially titled the Inter-American Convention on International Commercial Arbitration, the treaty was signed in Panama in 1975.

34 *See generally* David W. Rivkin, *International Arbitration and Dispute Resolution*, PLI Commercial Law & Practice Course Handbook, 765 PLI/Comm 183 (1998), at 222-223.

35 *See* 9 U.S.C § 305. *Compare* Skandia Am. Reinsurance Corp. v. CAJA Nacional De Ahorro Y Segoro, 96 Civ. 2301, 1997 U.S. Dist. LEXIS 7221, at *3 n.4 (S.D.N.Y. May 21, 1997), in which the judge in *dictum* presumed it would be possible to enforce an award under both treaties. Because neither party raised the question of the Panama Convention, the enforcement was analyzed only from the perspective of the New York Convention.

36 Art. I (4) ("The Convention shall not apply to . . . arbitration.") Matters of status, matrimonial relationships and succession, as well as bankruptcy and social security, are also excluded from coverage.

37 *See* Lugano Convention of 16 September 1988. EFTA includes Switzerland, one of the most important ICC arbitration venues.

tion inapplicable only to arbitration proceedings themselves, or in litigation connected directly with judicial recognition of an award.[38]

The European Court of Justice (ECJ) took the broader view in a decision known as *The Atlantic Emperor*.[39] A Swiss buyer of oil claimed the oil was seriously contaminated, and began arbitration against the Italian seller in London, as provided in the contract. A court in London was asked to assist in the appointment of an arbitrator, as provided under the English arbitration law as then in force. The Italians commenced a rival proceeding in Italy, claiming that under the Bruxelles Convention only courts at the Italian defendant's residence were competent to hear the dispute.

As a general rule, the Bruxelles Convention permits residents of a contracting state to be sued only at their domicile.[40] The real dispute (said the Italian seller) was over the validity of the arbitration clause; if this issue were to be decided in the negative by Italian courts, English courts would have no jurisdiction to appoint an arbitrator.

Invoking "the principle of legal certainty," the ECJ determined the Convention's scope solely by reference to the litigation subject matter, arbitration. The Court reasoned that it would reduce the reliability of arbitration if the Convention scope could "vary according to the existence or otherwise of a preliminary issue that could be raised at any time by the parties." Consequently, the preliminary issue of whether an arbitration agreement exists at all were excluded from the Convention's scope. The English proceeding for the appointment of arbitrators therefore could go forward, notwithstanding the Italian litigation.[41]

While supportive of arbitration, *The Atlantic Emperor* raised the prospect of multiple decisions on the validity of an arbitration agreement. One country's

---

38   For a discussion of the merits of these competing views, see His Hon. Judge Zuleeg *Report for the Hearing*, 7 ARB. INT. 187 (1991); Marco Darmon, *Marc Rich Co., A.G. v. Società Italiana Impianti P.A.: Opinion of the Advocate General*. 7 ARB. INT. at 197; Professor Peter Schlosser, *1968 Brussels Convention and Arbitration*, 7 ARB. INT. at 227; Paul Jerard, *Opinion*, 7 ARB. INT. at 243.

39   Marc Rich & Co., A.G. v. Società Italiana Impianti P.A., European Court of Justice, 25 July 1991, EC Case No. C-190/89, *reprinted in* 7 ARB. INT. 251 (1991) and XVII YEARBOOK 233 (A.J. van den Berg, ed., 1992). For an American report of the case, see ARB. TIMES, *Important Ruling for ADR in Europe*, Spring 1992, at 8. *See generally*, Bernard Audit, *Arbitration and the Brussels Convention* 9 ARB. INT. 1 (1993); comment by Wolfram Krohn, 86 AM. J. INT'L L. 134 (1992). For the English aspect of the case, see Marc Rich & Co. v. Società Italian Impianti (The Atlantic Emperor) [1989] 1 LLOYD'S REP. 548. The Court of Appeal referred to question to the European Court of Justice under the 1957 Treaty of Rome establishing the Common Market.

40   Bruxelles Convention, Article 2(1).

41   ECJ Case C - 190/89, *reprinted in* 7 ARB. INT. 251, 256 (1991). Moreover, it was pointed out by the Advocate General of the European Community that if the Convention applied to arbitration-related court proceedings, this would amount to an international recognition of judgments annulling arbitral awards, which would deprive courts at the arbitral seat of their curial jurisdiction. *See* Darmon Opinion, ¶ 77, at 219-220.

court might consider an arbitration clause valid, thereby assisting in the constitution of the arbitral tribunal, while another country's judge, competent to hear a dispute under the Bruxelles Convention, might find an arbitration clause void.

At least one national judicial decision has held that courts in different Bruxelles Convention states must recognize each others' decisions on the validity of arbitration clauses. A recent judgment of the English High Court[42] dealt with a case in which a cargo ship's collision with a jetty near Bordeaux resulted in a multiparty dispute. The vessel owners began an arbitration in London based on a charter party arbitration clause allegedly incorporated by reference into the bill of lading. The Bordeaux *Tribunal de commerce,* however, decided that the bill of lading did not so incorporate the arbitration clause.[43] The London High Court felt required to give *res judicata* effect to this earlier French decision, pursuant to provisions of the Bruxelles Convention calling for recognition of judgments rendered in other contracting states.[44]

---

42 *The Heidberg*, [1994] 2 LLOYD'S L. REP. 287.

43 Judgment of 23 September 1993, *reported in* Dominique Hascher, *Recognition and Enforcement of Judgments on the Existence and Validity of an Arbitration Clause under the Brussels Convention*, 13 ARB. INT. 33 n.37 (1997).

44 Bruxelles Convention, Articles 25-30.

NEW YORK CONVENTION ON THE RECOGNITION AND ENFORCEMENT OF FOREIGN ARBITRAL AWARDS

New York, 10 June 1958

21 U.S.T. 2517 (1970)

Article I

1. This Convention shall apply to the recognition and enforcement of arbitral awards made in the territory of a State other than the State where the recognition and enforcement of such awards are sought, and arising out of differences between persons, whether physical or legal. It shall also apply to arbitral awards not considered as domestic awards in the State where their recognition and enforcement are sought.

2. The term "arbitral awards" shall include not only awards made by arbitrators appointed for each case but also those made by permanent arbitral bodies to which the parties have submitted.

3. When signing, ratifying or acceding to this Convention, or notifying extension under article X hereof, any State may on the basis of reciprocity declare that it will apply the Convention to the recognition and enforcement of awards made only in the territory of another Contracting State. It may also declare that it will apply the Convention only to differences arising out of legal relationships, whether contractual or not, which are considered as commercial under the national law of the State making such declaration.

Article II

1. Each Contracting State shall recognize an agreement in writing under which the parties undertake to submit to arbitration all or any differences which have arisen or which may arise between them in respect of a defined legal relationship, whether contractual or not, concerning a subject matter capable of settlement by arbitration.

2. The term "agreement in writing" shall include an arbitral clause in a contract or an arbitration agreement, signed by the parties or contained in an exchange of letters or telegrams.

3. The court of a Contracting State, when seized of an action in a matter in respect of which the parties have made an agreement within the meaning of this article, [shall],[1] at the request of one of the parties, refer the parties to arbitration, unless it finds that the said agreement is null and void, inoperative or incapable of being performed.

Article III

Each Contracting State shall recognize arbitral awards as binding and enforce them in accordance with the rules of procedure of the territory where the award is relied upon, under the conditions laid down in the following articles. There shall not be imposed substantially more onerous conditions or higher fees or charges on the recognition or enforcement of arbitral awards to which this Convention applies than are imposed on the recognition or enforcement of domestic arbitral awards.

Article IV

1. To obtain the recognition and enforcement mentioned in the preceding article, the party applying for recognition and enforcement shall, at the time of the application, supply:

(*a*) The duly authenticated original award or a duly certified copy thereof;

(*b*) The original agreement referred to in article II or a duly certified copy thereof.

2. If the said award or agreement is not made in an official language of the country in which the award is relied upon, the party applying for recognition and enforcement of the award shall produce a translation of these documents into such language. The translation shall be certified by an official or sworn translator or by a diplomatic or consular agent.

Article V

1. Recognition and enforcement of the award may be refused, at the request of the party against whom it is invoked, only if that party furnishes to the competent authority where the recognition and enforcement is sought, proof that:

(*a*) The parties to the agreement referred to in article II were, under the law applicable to them, under some incapacity, or the said agreement is not valid under the law to which the parties have subjected it or, failing any in-

---

1   The word "shall" does not appear, as it manifestly should, in the text of Article II(3) of the Convention as published in 330 *United Nations Treaty Series* (1959) p. 38 at p. 39. The Final Act of the New York Conference of 1958 includes the word "shall" (UN-DOC/E/CONF.26/8/Rev. 1 and E/CONF.26/9/Rev. 1, p. 9).

dication thereon, under the law of the country where the award was made; or

(*b*) The party against whom the award is invoked was not given proper notice of the appointment of the arbitrator or of the arbitration proceedings or was otherwise unable to present his case; or

(*c*) The award deals with a difference not contemplated by or not falling within the terms of the submission to arbitration, or it contains decisions on matters beyond the scope of the submission to arbitration, provided that, if the decisions on matters submitted to arbitration can be separated from those not so submitted, that part of the award which contains decisions on matters submitted to arbitration may be recognized and enforced; or

(*d*) The composition of the arbitral authority or the arbitral procedure was not in accordance with the agreement of the parties, or, failing such agreement, was not in accordance with the law of the country where the arbitration took place; or

(*e*) The award has not yet become binding on the parties, or has been set aside or suspended by a competent authority of the country in which, or under the law of which, that award was made.

2. Recognition and enforcement of an arbitral award may also be refused if the competent authority in the country where recognition and enforcement is sought finds that:

(*a*) The subject matter of the difference is not capable of settlement by arbitration under the law of that country; or

(*b*) The recognition or enforcement of the award would be contrary to the public policy of that country.

Article VI

If an application for the setting aside or suspension of the award has been made to a competent authority referred to in article V(1)(*e*), the authority before which the award is sought to be relied upon may, if it considers it proper, adjourn the decision on the enforcement of the award and may also, on the application of the party claiming enforcement of the award, order the other party to give suitable security.

Article VII

1. The provisions of the present Convention shall not affect the validity of multilateral or bilateral agreements concerning the recognition and enforcement of arbitral awards entered into by the Contracting States nor deprive any interested party of any right he may have to avail himself of an arbitral award in the manner and to the extent allowed by the law or the treaties of the country where such award is sought to be relied upon.

2. The Geneva Protocol on Arbitration Clauses of 1923 and the Geneva Convention on the Execution of Foreign Arbitral Awards of 1927 shall cease to have effect between Contracting States on their becoming bound and to the extent that they become bound, by this Convention.

Article VIII

1. This Convention shall be open until 31 December 1958 for signature on behalf of any Member of the United Nations and also on behalf of any other State which is or hereafter becomes a member of any specialized agency of the United Nations, or which is or hereafter becomes a party to the Statute of the International Court of Justice, or any other State to which an invitation has been addressed by the General Assembly of the United Nations.

2. This Convention shall be ratified and the instrument of ratification shall be deposited with the Secretary-General of the United Nations.

Article IX

1. This Convention shall be open for accession to all States referred to in article VIII.

2. Accession shall be effected by the deposit of an instrument of accession with the Secretary-General of the United Nations.

Article X

1. Any State may, at the time of signature, ratification or accession, declare that this Convention shall extend to all or any of the territories for the international relations of which it is responsible. Such a declaration shall take effect when the Convention enters into force for the State concerned.

2. At any time thereafter any such extension shall be made by notification addressed to the Secretary-General of the United Nations and shall take effect as from the ninetieth day after the day of receipt by the Secretary-General of the United Nations of this notification, or as from the date of entry into force of the Convention for the State concerned, whichever is the later.

3. With respect to those territories to which this Convention is not extended at the time of signature, ratification or accession, each State concerned shall consider the possibility of taking the necessary steps in order to extend the application of this Convention to such territories, subject, where necessary for constitutional reasons, to the consent of the Governments of such territories.

Article XI

In the case of a federal or non-unitary State, the following provisions shall apply:

(*a*) With respect to those articles of this Convention that come within the legislative jurisdiction of the federal authority, the obligations of the federal Government shall to this extent be the same as those of Contracting States which are not federal States:

(*b*) With respect to those articles of this Convention that come within the legislative jurisdiction of constituent states or provinces which are not, under the constitutional system of the federation, bound to take legislative action, the federal Government shall bring such articles with a favourable recommendation to the notice of the appropriate authorities of constituent states or provinces at the earliest possible moment;

(*c*) A federal State Party to this Convention shall, at the request of any other Contracting State transmitted through the Secretary-General of the United Nations, supply a statement of the law and practice of the federation and its constituent units in regard to any particular provision of this Convention, showing the extent to which effect has been given to that provision by legislative or other action.

Article XII

1. This Convention shall come into force on the ninetieth day following the date of deposit of the third instrument of ratification or accession.

2. For each State ratifying or acceeding to this Convention after the deposit of the third instrument of ratification or accession, this Convention shall enter into force on the ninetieth day after deposit of such State of its instrument of ratification or accession.

Article XIII

1. Any Contracting State may denounce this Convention by a written notification to the Secretary-General of the United Nations. Denunciation shall take effect one year after the date of receipt of the notification by the Secretary-General.

2. Any State which has made a declaration or notification under article X may, at any time thereafter, by notification to the Secretary-General of the United Nations, declare that this Convention shall cease to extend to the territory concerned one year after the date of the receipt of the notification by the Secretary-General.

3. This Convention shall continue to be applicable to arbitral awards in respect of which recognition or enforcement proceedings have been instituted before the denunciation takes effect.

Article XIV

A Contracting State shall not be entitled to avail itself of the present Convention against other Contracting States except to the extent that it is itself bound to apply the Convention.

Article XV

The Secretary-General of the United Nations shall notify the States contemplated in article VIII of the following:

(*a*) Signatures and ratifications in accordance with article VIII;

(*b*) Accessions in accordance with article IX;

(*c*) Declarations and notifications under articles I, X and XI;

(*d*) The date upon which this Convention enters into force in accordance with article XII;

(*e*) Denunciations and notifications in accordance with article XIII.

Article XVI

1. This Convention, of which the Chinese, English, French, Russian and Spanish texts shall be equally authentic, shall be deposited in the archives of the United Nations.

2. The Secretary-General of the United Nations shall transmit a certified copy of this Convention to the States contemplated in article VIII.

CHAPTER 38

ADDITIONAL ICC DISPUTE RESOLVING MECHANISMS

38.01 Conciliation

In principle, conciliation plays an important role in the ICC approach to dispute resolution, as suggested until the publication of the new ICC Rules of Arbitration in 1998, by the very name "ICC Rules of Conciliation and Arbitration." In reality, ICC conciliation has been a very poor cousin of ICC arbitration. Only seven conciliation requests were received in 1999 as compared to 529 requests for arbitration.[1] As contrasted with the Arbitration Rules, the Conciliation Rules were until 1988 inflexible and outdated. For example, it appeared unavoidable that three conciliators be appointed, that they be appointed by the President of ICC (not by the Court or one of its officials), and that they all be residents of Paris. There was no provision for fees, with the result that it was difficult to imagine that competent volunteers could be found for a constant and significant stream of cases. These anomalous features of the process were to be explained by history, as described by a former Secretary General of the Court:

> When the ICC was founded, some 60 years ago, the Secretary-General was assisted by an Administrative Commission composed of the permanent representatives of nearly all National Committees of the ICC in Europe and overseas who were resident in Paris. These Commissioners were expected and ready, as part of their functions, occasionally to lend their experience as international lawyers or businessmen to merchants having recourse to the conciliation facilities offered by the ICC. They read

---

1   Similarly, over a five-year period ending in 1994, the ratio of requests for arbitration as compared with requests for conciliation was 2000/60, i.e. 3%, *see* Eric Schwartz, *International Conciliation and the ICC*, 5 ICC BULL. 5 (December 1994). It must also be pointed out that following the 8 requests received in 1997, four conciliation procedures were in fact aborted due to one party's unwillingness to proceed, *see* 9 ICC BULL. 9 (May 1998).

the statements and documents filed and heard the parties at ICC Headquarters before formulating, after a meeting of normally half a day, their
proposal for an amicable settlement. The parties had no administrative
charge to pay until after the end of World War II and they have still no
fee to pay to the conciliators. The classical Commissioners have practically disappeared because of the modern conditions of transport and
communications. The conciliation system still exists because members
of the ICC Court of Arbitration and representatives of embassies concerned continued to act free of charge as conciliators in the few cases
which currently are submitted to ICC conciliation: in 1979 some 300 requests for arbitration were filed and only 5 requests for conciliation.
True, in the pre-war period when the ICC registered up to 100 cases per
year, the great majority was settled by conciliation; but then the disputes
were of a quite different kind concerning less complex agency or sales
contracts, and the average amount at stake was at least a hundred times
lower than in the present-day cases of turn-key contracts, oil deliveries,
investments etc.[2]

In 1988, entirely revised Conciliation Rules went into effect. They were designed as a flexible framework intended to maximize the chances of reaching
a solution agreeable to both sides. The concept of a three-member Conciliation Committee was abandoned in favor of that of a sole conciliator. The Secretary General of the Court of Arbitration was given a crucial role in setting
the mechanisms in motion. He appoints the conciliator, using his judgment
as to substantive and diplomatic skills required for a particular case, and he
establishes costs and fees. He is not restricted to appointing residents of
Paris. As for the conciliator, he may proceed entirely as he sees fit. The
pre-1988 Committees had to prepare proposed Terms of Settlement for the
parties to accept or reject, no matter how artificial the exercise might seem.
The post-1988 conciliator may view himself as a prodder or cheerleader on
the sidelines, encouraging the parties to reach common ground by direct negotiations, or he may take a more directive role, telling the parties what he
thinks ought to be a reasonable settlement (typically on the basis of his expectation of what would realistically happen if the dispute were continued to
the bitter end) and forcing them to take a position. If he determines that the
attempt at conciliation will not succeed, he simply ends the process by filing a
report to that effect. Article 7(b) provides that the report should not contain
reasons. The conciliator's authority to rule that the attempt has failed is a
safeguard against manoeuvres by respondents who might otherwise be
tempted to submit a never-ending series of ostensible new proposals in order

---

2   Frédéric Eisemann, *Conciliation as a Means of Settlement of International Business Disputes: the
     UNCITRAL Rules as Compared with the ICC System*, in THE ART OF ARBITRATION (LIBER AMICORUM
     FOR PIETER SANDERS) 121, at 127 (1982).

to argue that conciliation is still pending, and thus stave off formal claims before the downstream arbitrator or judge.

Conciliation should not be confused with amicable settlements reached before arbitrators. Although an agreement reached in conciliation is legally binding, it is not enforceable as an award under Article 17 of the Arbitration Rules. If a party fails to respect a conciliation agreement, the party wishing to rely on it would have to present a claim before the competent arbitrator or judge. Conciliation proceedings are intrinsically divorced from arbitration proceedings. The arbitrator must decide the parties' rights and therefore looks to the law or to principles of fairness; the conciliator looks to what both parties might accept, irrespective of how it might be justified in principle. Thus conciliation may have a certain pragmatic appeal.

A request for conciliation does not require an arbitration clause or any other special agreement to have been negotiated. Nor does the existence of an arbitration clause *preclude* a request for conciliation. It thus follows that the respondent has no obligation to accept any procedure for conciliation. (In consequence, there is substantial doubt that a request for conciliation will toll statutes of limitations.)

A different situation theoretically arises where the contract contains a clause requiring the parties to participate in conciliation prior to litigation, whether before an arbitral tribunal or ordinary courts. Nevertheless, it would seem impossible that failure to respect such an obligation would lead to sanctions within the framework of the conciliation process, since any disposition of a dispute by way of conciliation must be by mutual agreement. Perhaps failure to cooperate in conciliation may be analyzed as a breach of contract to be sanctioned by "downstream" arbitrators or judges; but while a party having refused even to go through the motions of conciliation may have impaired its credibility, it is difficult to imagine cases where parties conduct themselves so obstreperously that their failure to cooperate in conciliation in and of itself triggers any significant sanction (*see generally* Section 8.01). Article 11 of the Conciliation Rules, providing that no views expressed, suggestions made, proposals put forward, or positions taken in the course of the conciliation proceedings may be referred to at the stage of arbitration, reinforces this conclusion.

At most, contractual undertakings to conciliate would generally have the effect that arbitration may not be instituted until conciliation (however half-hearted) has been attempted (*see* Section 8.01).

Conciliators need not be overly concerned with procedural niceties, since by definition their proposals must be accepted by mutual agreement. For example, they may hear parties separately or take other initiatives in the interest of settlement that would be out of the question in arbitration, where binding awards are issued irrespective of the parties' agreement and where therefore failure to respect basic principles of the adversarial process may result in challenges to the award. Of course it would be counterproductive to adopt a type of procedure over the stated objections of a party, as this would obviously reduce the likelihood of the conciliation finally succeeding.

As mentioned above, Article 11 of the Conciliation Rules precludes any effect on arbitration of anything that may have occurred during the conciliation attempt. This principle is designed to enhance parties' willingness to participate constructively and flexibly in the conciliation, without fear that they will later be held to have made irreversible concessions. To this end, Article 10 prohibits the appointment as arbitrator—and indeed as representative or counsel of a party—of a person having sat on a conciliation committee involving the same dispute.

As for the costs of conciliation, the Schedule of Conciliation Costs provides that each party is required to make an advance payment of US$ 500 towards the administrative expenses, failing which the request will not be registered by the Secretariat of the Court. This sum is to be paid to the Secretariat and is not refundable but will be deducted from the total administrative costs. The administrative costs of a conciliation shall be fixed at one-quarter of the rate applicable for arbitrations according to the amount in dispute. When the amount is not specified, the Secretariat fixes the costs at its discretion. On the other hand, conciliators' fees have no relation to the scale of arbitrators' fees, but are fixed by the Secretary General of the Court "taking into consideration the time spent, the complexity of the dispute and any other relevant circumstances."

Under Article 9 of the Conciliation Rules, advances for costs are to be paid in equal shares by the parties. Presumably, the failure of a respondent to pay its share does not create the type of dilemma that occurs in arbitrations (*see* Section 14.02). Such a failure would appear to make it so improbable that conciliation could succeed that the process would never get under way at all.

Whether under the ICC Rules or otherwise, conciliation is more often talked about than attempted. Once a dispute has arisen, many claimants are convinced that they have already exhausted all possibilities of reaching amicable settlement and are impatient to start adversarial proceedings. They suspect that conciliation would be a waste of time and money, and works only to the advantage of the respondent by postponing the ultimate day of reckoning. Such skepticism may be warranted in many cases, but the present authors' experience has convinced them that in many cases conciliation could be used more effectively than most claimants imagine. An adept conciliator may calm the ardours of both parties. He may cause the claimant to take account not only of weaknesses of its case, but the value of immediate payment of a lesser but certain amount. He may cause the respondent to question the invincibility of its imagined defenses. The cool-headed view of an objective third party may convince top management on both sides to make some discount for the exuberance and subjectivity of the persons directly involved in the dispute.

The 1988 reform of the ICC Conciliation Rules thus set the stage for what may become a more useful dispute resolution mechanism. It all depends on parties' awareness of its availability, and their conviction that it may be cost-efficient. In fact, only one of the ICC conciliations commenced in the 1988-1994 period cost the parties more than $14,000 on account of conciliator fees and ICC charges; "most cases were completed within a few months of receipt of the file by the conciliator."[3]

38.02 Expertise

The word "expertise" in this context is not used in the ordinary English sense of skill or knowledge as the attribute of a person, but rather, borrowing from the French, is used to refer to a *procedure* whereby a party may obtain an expert evaluation before proceeding on the merits of a dispute. An *expertise* in this meaning is often ordered by a court to establish facts (e.g. that goods have perished), causation (e.g. why the site was polluted), or a technical proposition (e.g. it is necessary to rebuild a wall) in circumstances where some urgency dictates that one not await an initiative by the jurisdiction competent to hear the merits of a dispute.

The ICC's International Centre for Expertise was established in December 1976 as an organ independent of the Court of Arbitration. After a few years of initial inactivity, during which practitioners became aware of the existence and uses of the Centre, this institution now seems to have an increased practical impact, particularly in connection with large construction disputes. The authors have seen an increasing number of references to the Centre in recently negotiated contracts.

The first interventions by experts acting under the aegis of the Centre occurred during the 1980-1982 period, when parties from Algeria, Austria, Belgium, Canada, Finland, France, India, Italy, Iraq, Sweden, Syria, Tunisia, the United Kingdom, the United States, and Yugoslavia asked the Centre for prompt appointment of technical experts. The disputes involved, for example, textile and chemical plants, the quality of powdered milk, purification plants, a bakery, and a cement factory.

According to the ICC's 1982 Annual Report (at page 24):

> Disputes submitted (to the Centre in 1982) were almost always settled as soon as the expert had been appointed. It seemed that the mere fact of one party deciding to call for expertise had the effect of bringing the parties to a negotiated settlement of their dispute.

---

3 Schwartz, *supra* Note 1, at 11. Reviewing what he terms the "successful application" of the ICC Conciliation Rules, the author concludes, at 16: "I suspect that it could be usefully attempted much more often than is the case at present."

The number of requests to the Centre increased over the succeeding years, and has averaged almost ten per year since 1985 (19 general cases in 1997 and 10 requests for documentary credit cases), and the total number of requests has now reached 161. The ICC is convinced of the usefulness of the Centre, and modified its Rules in 1993 to reflect experience in the Centre's first 12 years of operations. It was noted that most of the requests to the Centre have been submitted by the mutual agreement of parties to contracts which did not contain any clause referring to the Centre. This suggests insufficient awareness of the Centre by contract negotiators.[4] The new Rules have wider scope, and are supported by a reinforced structure. In addition to the Secretariat, a permanent Standing Committee has been created, composed of five members of different nationalities, each being a qualified expert.[5]

The Centre does not itself employ experts on a permanent basis, nor does it have a formal list of experts. Rather, it cooperates directly with a number of professional organizations to obtain advice on an *ad hoc* basis in light of the requirements of each particular case. That this is the most practical way of operating would seem apparent when one considers the wide range of fields in which the Centre has been requested to intervene, including "desert irrigation, ship-building, glass-making, sugar refining, boilermaking, to name but a few."[6]

One obvious reason to call upon the Centre is to obtain an expert opinion as to contractual compliance or adjustments in performance in cases of great technical complexity. Such an opinion would stop short of resolving legal issues of liability or fashioning ultimate remedies, which would be left to whichever jurisdiction has authority to decide the merits of a dispute (such as an arbitral tribunal). If the parties so agree, a case before the Centre may result in findings and even recommendations that are binding (provided they fall within the scope of the expert's mission). That is to say, the technical conclusions or solutions reached by the expert would not be subject to challenge before a tribunal called upon to make a final legal disposition of the case.

Another *raison d'etre* for the Centre, less obvious but certainly no less important than relieving jurist arbitrators of the task of making technical determi-

---

4   As the Chairman of the Centre's Standing Committee put it in 1995: "The present task facing the International Centre for Expertise, which is the only organisation of this type in the world with some experience, is to make itself better known. It deserves to be, in view of what it is already doing and in view of what it hopes to achieve in the future." Hervé Charrin, *The ICC International Centre for Expertise: Realities and Prospects*, ICC BULL. 33, at 46 (December 1995).

5   The Standing Committee is composed of a Frenchman (the Chairman), an American, an Englishman, a Japanese and a Swiss national, nominated for 3 renewable years.

6   Michael Bühler, *Technical Expertise: An Additional Means for Preventing or Settling Commercial Disputes*, 6 J. INT. ARB. 135, at 150 (1989). For a more recent description of the Centre's activities, *see* Jean-François Bourque, *L'expérience du Centre International d'Expertise de la CCI et le développement de l'expertise international*, 1995 REV. ARB. 231.

nations, is the fact that it may be used to resolve practical problems much sooner—perhaps years sooner—than an arbitral tribunal. In other words, expertise under the Centre may be a *pre-arbitral* solution, which in the best of cases would make arbitration unnecessary. Although technical expertise is by definition non-legal, it undeniably has a great impact on the potential decision of subsequent arbitrators; technical experts may verify the state of execution of a contract or ascertain the conformity of goods or equipment at delivery.

In this context, it is relevant to note that practice in international construction contracts over the past decade has tended to place less reliance on the concept of an "independent" engineer standing between owner and contractor to issue rapid orders in case of controversy, full-scale arbitration thus being required only when the decision of the engineer is contested. Such engineers have been perceived by contractors as unable to keep an adequate distance from the owner; indeed, Article 2(1) of the 1977 FIDIC conditions for civil engineering construction contracts appeared to acknowledge the engineer's ultimate subordination to the owner, a state of affairs that would disqualify the former from deciding disputes between the owner and the contractor. The unease created by this state of affairs caused the 1988 FIDIC conditions to provide in Article 2.6 for the engineer "to act impartially," but many contractors remain unconvinced. If the institution of the independent engineer is seen as illusory, a void would be created; the lifeblood of construction projects is cashflow and the resolution of disputes must be managed efficiently. Great complaint about the system is inevitable if all disputes are to await the outcome of full arbitration. Technical expertise may to some extent fill this void.

A concrete illustration of the Centre's possibilities may be found in the case of a poorly performing factory.[7] The contract made clear that it was the owner's duty to build the foundations, including particular welding work. Observing progress, the builder informed the owner that the welding performed by the latter was incompatible with technical requirements for the rest of the plant, and that if another type of (more expensive) process were not adopted, the functioning of the factory would be threatened by vibration problems. The owner refused to accept this contention, and completed the foundations as he saw fit. The builder protested in writing to protect his legal position. Three years later, the factory was ready to be commissioned, but performance levels could not be reached. The builder alleged that the cause was the defective nature of the welding, but the owner rejected this contention and accordingly refused to take final delivery of the factory.

---

7   This example was suggested by Yves Derains *in Expertise technique et référé arbitral*, 1982 REV. ARB. 239, at 240.

Having foreseen nothing but the traditional mechanism of arbitration, the parties would now be faced with a situation in which justice may be rendered only in an approximative fashion. The arbitrators may appoint an expert to assist them (Article 20(4) of the Rules of Arbitration), but it may be too late for such an expert to assess the technical context at the relevant time. (In the example given, one might even imagine the absurdity that he would have to order the partial destruction of the factory's foundations to evaluate the quality of the welding.) The alternative is no more satisfactory: to rely on the parties' past unilateral declarations, possibly confirmed or contradicted by testimony. And no matter what the legal solution (the award) turns out to be, the opportunity to avoid a technical disaster, unfortunate for both parties, would have been missed years before.

In this type of a case, it may be very useful to have obtained an expert opinion at the time of the initial controversy. The owner may have found out that his welding was substandard in the eyes of a neutral expert; alternatively, the builder may have been told that his complaint about the welding was unfounded, and that he therefore would have no excuse on that ground if the factory's performance turned out not to meet contract specifications. In either case. an independent expert's opinion would go a long way toward an early and persuasive clarification of litigious issues, thereby creating an incentive for settlement as opposed to arbitration. For even if the expert's opinion does not formally bind arbitrators, most parties would correctly conclude that no unilaterally generated document or other proof would have as great an impact on a future arbitral tribunal as the report of a competent neutral expert.

As the above discussion suggests, the two fundamental criteria upon which the Centre will be judged are the efficiency of the procedure of technical expertise and the quality of the experts operating under the Centre. The more sophisticated the area, the more limited the range of choices of possible experts. In some specialized industries, it is very difficult to find a high- level expert who has not had some professional relationship with one of the litigants or their affiliates. The Centre has made efforts, drawing on the ICC's worldwide network of contacts, to establish extensive files on experienced experts.

The Centre's model clause is worded as follows:

> The parties to this agreement agree to have recourse, if the need arises, to the International Centre for Expertise of the International Chamber of Commerce (ICC), in accordance with the ICC's Rules for Expertise.

The parties may wish to provide for further details concerning the procedure and object of the expertise. This calls for an appreciation of the interplay between the specific technical context of their transactions and the Rules for the Centre (*see* Appendix III). A detailed discussion of the possible approaches is beyond the scope of this book. Needless to say, any additions to the model clause should be carefully examined; since it is difficult to impeach an expert's opinion, it would be most frustrating to find that the expertise obtained seemed to miss the point. Some factors to bear in mind when drafting a clause referring to the Centre are the following:

− whether the expertise should be combined with the downstream possibility of regular ICC arbitration (this ordinarily makes sense);

− whether the expert should be given the authority to supervise contractual performance;

− whether the expert should actually be named in the contract, in order that he monitor progress and be in a position to make near - immediate decisions (this is a costly option, and in any event it should be made clear that in case the named expert is not in a position to act when called upon, the Centre's ordinary procedure should be followed); and

− whether the expert may make binding recommendations.

The notion that an expert's recommendations may be binding gives rise to the question whether his decision is tantamount to an award and enforceable in the same manner as an award, including recognition and enforcement under international conventions.

It may not be in the best interest of technical expertise as an institution that it seek to have the same effects as an award. Proper arbitration is conducted with a degree of procedural rigor that is commensurate with the claim of arbitration to replace ordinary courts in finally settling disputes. If expert proceedings seek to achieve similar results, they would doubtless become overly legalistic, losing flexibility and efficiency. If, on the other hand, they fail to observe procedural rigor but nonetheless seek to have the effect of awards, they are likely to be discredited in the eyes of ordinary courts.

The best view may therefore be to consider the results of technical expertise, when the parties have made an express stipulation to that effect, to be binding as a matter of fact upon the ultimately competent jurisdiction (whether an ordinary court or an arbitral tribunal), but leaving the latter to establish legal inferences and in particular to render decisions that purport to be final dispositions of the contractual relationship.

This view seems consistent with the following view of a leading commentator on the New York Convention, who observed that:

> It was never the intention to widen the scope of the Convention to the effect that procedures akin to arbitration would be included. Decisions like the Dutch *bindend advies* (binding opinion), the German *Schiedsgutachten* and the English valuation are not regarded as arbitration proper. Under the applicable rules of national law these decisions cannot be enforced as an award.[8]

---

8   Pieter Sanders, *Commentary on court decisions on the New York Convention*, IV YEARBOOK 233 (1979).

38.03   Pre-arbitral Referee

In late 1989, the Commission on International Arbitration concluded several years' effort by adopting Rules for a Pre-arbitral Referee Procedure which, following approval by the ICC Executive Board and Council, entered into force in 1990. It was an excellent idea which thus far has not worked.

The Pre-arbitral Referee Procedure was intended to create an exceptionally rapid remedy within the ICC framework. While a significant range of pre- arbitration solutions may be obtained by recourse to the Centre for Technical Expertise (see Section 38.02), it was perceived that some urgent measures required legal interpretations beyond the scope of technical expertise, as well as a number of authoritative decisions intended to replace court-ordered injunctions or conservatory measures. Rapid interventions of this type appeared particularly necessary in the context of construction contracts,[9] where disputes often arise as to compliance with contractual obligations, the scope of contracted works, whether progress payments are due, whether payment under performance bonds is justified, and the like; as well as more generally in the context of all types of long-term transactions.

In some cases, the fullblown procedure of arbitration may be unsatisfactory, notwithstanding the theoretical possibility under the Rules for arbitrators to grant provisional relief (*see* Chapter 26). In the first place, arbitrators are generally disinclined to grant such relief, either because they do not wish to appear to favor one litigant at an early stage of the proceedings, or because they are precluded by applicable procedural law. But more importantly, for ordinary arbitrators to take such action the arbitral tribunal must already have been constituted, and this in and of itself may imply time consuming nomination procedures. Truly urgent measures are in fact incompatible with the concept of three-member tribunals, since it is the rule rather than the exception that ICC arbitrators are residents of different countries and cannot convene on an instant basis. At any rate, Article 2.4.1 of the Referee Rules make clear that "once the competent jurisdiction becomes seized of the case it alone may order any further provisional or conservatory measures that it considers necessary."

In practice, despite the existence of the Pre-arbitral Referee Rules, many requests for provisional measures were brought before a third party other than an arbitrator, especially under Article 8.5 of the former ICC Rules of Arbitration (now Article 23(2)).

The ICC Pre-arbitral Referee Procedure is not to be confused with the types of expedited arbitral proceedings envisaged in various arbitral centers that call

---

9   *See* J. Goedel, *Aspekte der Streiterledigung bei internationalen Bauverträgen und das Arbitral Referee Verfahren*, 4 SCHRIFTENREIHE DES DEUTSCHEN INSTITUTS FÜR SCHIEDSGERICHTWEGEN 33, with English summary at 55 (publication of the German Institute of Arbitration, 1984).

for full disposition of cases and the rendering of final awards on an especially rapid basis (such as the "Short Procedure" defined in Article 20 of the 1983 Arbitration Procedure of the Institution of Civil Engineers (ICE)). ICC referees would in fact act rapidly, but their decisions would by definition be provisional. As it was stated in an explanatory note to the Commission draft of October 1988, a referee would be:

> empowered to make an order designed to meet the urgent problem at hand, including the power to order the preservation or recording of evidence. The order should therefore provide a temporary resolution of the dispute and may lay the foundations for its final settlement either by agreement or otherwise.

Urgent measures are thought necessary to conserve or establish ephemeral evidence or to order provisional measures to avoid irreparable harm. In addition, they may dispose of minor disputes that otherwise would cause disproportionate trouble in a greater context, for example in situations where a squabble as to who is bound to perform a $250,000 reparation sours the contractor-owner relationship in a $100,000,000 project.

The ICC Pre-arbitral Referee Procedure is directly inspired by the French institution of the *juge des référés*, which might be translated as "a court sitting in urgent session."[10] Under the French judicial system, a party may approach an individual magistrate (whereas decisions on the merits of important civil litigation are generally rendered by three-judge tribunals, even at the level of courts of initial jurisdiction) to request urgent measures (such as conservatory attachments, but going as far as ordering immediate payments of apparent debts), on the ground that such measures are required to prevent irreparable harm. It must moreover appear that the immediate decision requested (referred to as made *en référé*) will not definitively affect the substantial rights of the parties; those rights are to be determined by the full proceedings on the merits of the controversy. To prevail *en référé*, a litigant must convince the magistrate that his claim is well founded in principle.

Article 2.1 of the Pre-arbitral Referee Rules (see Appendix III) defines the powers of the referee as follows:

> a) To order any conservatory measures or any measures of restoration that are urgently necessary either to prevent immediate damage or irreparable loss and so to safeguard any of the rights or property of one of the parties;

> b) To order a party to make to any other party or to another person any payment which ought to be made;

---

10   *See generally* Yves Derains, *supra* Note 3, at 244.

c) To order a party to take any step which ought to be taken according to the contract between the parties, including the signing or delivery of any document or the procuring by a party of the signature or delivery of a document;

d) To order any measures necessary to preserve or establish evidence.

Under Article 6 of the Rules, the referee is called up to render an "order" within 30 days. It should be noted that one of the central issues dealt with by the Commission was thus resolved by not calling the referee's decision an "award." Referees' orders will thus not be scrutinized and approved by the ICC Court as are awards (*see* Chapter 20): nor will they be enforceable before national courts in the same ways as awards. Indeed, Article 6.3 states explicity that:

> ·The Referee's order does not pre-judge the substance of the case nor shall it bind any competent jurisdiction which may hear any question, issue or dispute in respect of which the order has been made. The order of the Referees shall however remain in force unless and until the Referee or the competent jurisdiction has decided otherwise.

The Pre-arbitral Referee Procedure may have some interplay with the expertise in that the referee may control abuse of the latter. The referee may have a direct influence on procedural aspects of full-scale arbitration, for example by ordering the payment of deposits.[11] Although the referee's decision does not bind the downstream arbitrators, the referee's decision clearly has some teeth. Yves Derains, who was instrumental in the ICC's work on the referee concept, has suggested that the referee's decision as a contractual matter binds the parties to act or refrain from acting in accordance therewith: it is thus qualitatively different from experts' reports or conciliators' proposals.[12] The decision is furthermore definitive as a matter of fact, without prejudice to issues of liability. As an example, Mr. Derains refers to a case where the referee might decide whether construction should be halted due to a shortage of specified material, or whether inferior substituted material should be used. If the referee decides on the latter option, it must be accepted as definitive with respect to the limited question of whether it was appropriate to proceed with the substituted material. However, the referee's decision would not preclude future arbitrators from deciding that the contractor had assumed the risk of shortage, or conversely that the owner had prevented completion of construction prior to the shortage, and awarding or refusing to award damages accordingly.

---

11   *Id.* at 245.

12   *Id.* at 248. With respect to experts' reports, the situation is different if the parties have expressly stipulated that the expert shall render recommendations of a binding nature. In such a case, the expert's decision would appear to have the same weight as that of a referee. *See generally* Section 38.02.

One may object to the concept of Pre-arbitral Referees on the ground that an ordinary judge, given the institutions of effective execution available to him, is better suited to grant provisional measures. Whatever the merits of this observation, it is a fact that not all ordinary courts readily grant provisional relief in the context of an international arbitration (see Section 8.07). Furthermore, in many contexts the relevant national court would not be a neutral one. The new ICC mechanism thus seeks to allow effective and rapid intervention (including visits to the site of works, or other investigations) by a neutral referee appointed by a neutral international institution. It should also be noted that the Referee Rules themselves attempt to provide sanctions for failure to comply with a referee's order, or for abuse of the Rules. Article 6.8.1 provides that the court or (more probably) the arbitral tribunal having jurisdiction over the ultimate dispute may determine whether a party is liable for loss or damage suffered by any other party on account of disobedience of a referee's order; Article 6.8.2 envisages that liability may also arise if damages were caused by a wrongfully requested order. Whether these provisions will in fact lead to referee orders' becoming *de facto* enforceable remains to be seen. Their degree of effectiveness is likely to depend on the particular circumstances of a given case.

The ambitious scope of the Referee Rules becomes clear when one compares them to the Rules for Technical Expertise (see Section 38.02). The expert operating under the latter would intervene essentially to establish facts at a particular time or, if the parties have so agreed, making recommendations of a technical nature. The expert would not interpret contractual rights or duties, and would not order provisional payments. The referee, on the other hand, would be an alternative to a court in fashioning injunctive or conservatory relief. He would make provisional determinations of a legal nature. Pre-arbitral referees will therefore in all likelihood be lawyers; as may indeed be inferred from Article 5.3 of the Referee Rules, which entitles them *inter alia* to obtain "the report of an expert."

A crucial consideration will naturally be the proficiency of the referees themselves. One possibility would be for the parties jointly to name a referee at the time of agreement; he would then follow the evolution of performance and be prepared to make near-instant decisions at any time. This alternative may be a costly one, since it requires that a permanently available referee keep himself informed of performance under the contract, whether his intervention is required or not. The other possibility would be for the ICC to develop a "stable" of willing and able referees to be assigned to disputes as they arise.

38.04 Adaptation of contracts

In cases of unforeseeable difficulties during the life of international contracts, especially those of long duration, the parties may find that their agreements are silent as to how such difficulties are to be solved. Alternatively, one of the parties may claim that the unforeseen event—whether or not it qualifies as one of *force majeure* excusing performance as a matter of law—as a practical matter prevents performance of the contracts as defined.

The ICC in 1978 thus established Rules for the Regulation of Contractual Relations, creating a procedure by which contracts may be modified and adapted to circumstances. Such adaptation is in fact occasionally explicitly contemplated in sophisticated international contracts and variously referred to as "hardship," "revision," "reopening," "adjustment clause," or the like. Depending on the legal system that may be brought to bear on the case, the task of adaptation may in fact be entrusted to arbitrators operating under the standard ICC Rules of Arbitration; their decision would accordingly purport to be an enforceable award (*see generally* section 8.06). But pending universal acceptance of the notion that arbitral awards may effect modification of contract, the ICC procedure of adaptation under the aegis of the Standing Committee for the Regulation of Contractual Relations aimed to reach the result of a binding adjustment of contracts that does not take the form of an award.

Reference to the adaptation procedure was deemed compatible with a parallel reference to ordinary ICC arbitration. The ICC's model adaptation clause was worded in alternative forms, depending on whether the parties wanted the procedure to result in (A) recommendations or (B) a binding contractual change:

> In the event that the parties are unable to agree to apply all or any of the provisions of Article _____ of this contract (or any other appropriate wording chosen by the parties in the particular circumstances of the contract) they shall apply to the Standing Committee for the Regulation of Contractual Relations of the International Chamber of Commerce (ICC) in order that a third person who shall be appointed in accordance with the Rules on the Regulation of Contractual Relations of the ICC, and who shall carry out his mission in accordance with the said Rules . . . (A) may issue a recommendation. Or. . . (B) may on their behalf make a final decision which shall be binding on the parties and shall be deemed to be incorporated in the contract.

Article 9(3) and 9(4) of the Rules established the principles of an adversarial process and the right to a hearing. It was assumed that written and oral presentations would be designed to convince the third person of the fairness of a proposal for adaptation in light of legitimate expectations, based on trade practice and economic factors (as opposed to legal analysis). At any rate, the central Article 11(3) provided:

> When the third person takes a decision, that decision is binding on the parties to the same extent as the contract in which it is deemed to be incorporated. The parties agree to give effect to such a decision as if it were the expression of their own will.

Under Article 12(1), the third person is in principle required to fulfill his mission within 90 days from the date of his receipt of the file.

The Rules for the Regulation of Contractual Relations were not welcomed with unanimous enthusiasm, even within the ICC structure. The Swedish National Committee, for example, explained its skepticism on three grounds:[13]

— The contemplated procedure may create greater problems than those which parties intend to resolve by drafting various forms of hardship or adjustment clauses; the conditions of applicability of the ICC adaptation procedure appear confused.

— The legally binding nature of the adaptation process is doubtful outside the confines of arbitration proper.

— As a matter of pragmatic business sense, it may be preferable that the parties make every effort to foresee potential difficulties of contractual performance and, in the event modification of their agreements turns out to be required, that the parties themselves agree to the conditions for their future relationship rather than leaving the matter to a third party.

Some of these objections may be answered, at least in theoretical terms. The ICC itself, in the Introduction to its booklet *Adaptation of Contracts* (ICC Publication No. 326), stated explicitly at page 8 that the adaptation procedure was "clearly of a contractual nature," and that in the ICC's view the decision of the "third person" with respect to the adaptation of the relevant contract "is inserted into the contract and is as binding on the parties as the contract" and is not the equivalent of an award. Furthermore, the existence of the adaptation process creates a contractual tool whose potential usefulness should not be dismissed out of hand by stating the platitude that it is generally preferable for parties to foresee everything in their contracts.

Whatever its theoretical merits, this concept failed in practice. The Rules for the Regulation of Contractual Relations were never used. In 1994, Yves Derains (who was to become Co-chairman of the Working Party that prepared drafts of the 1998 Arbitration Rules) examined the causes of this failure and published his conclusions.[14] In particular, he mentioned the facts that parties did not understand how these Rules fit in with other ICC mechanisms, and tended to see them as either a useless complication or, worse, a dangerous intrusion into the contractual relationship. While the ICC will undoubtedly honor any unexpected requests to use this mechanism on the strength of clauses drafted in the past, it is no longer recommended; the ICC has ceased publishing the Rules. On the other hand, the widespread use of adaptation clauses is a relatively recent phenomenon, whose significance may become

---

13   Lars Hjerner, INTERNATIONELLA HANDELSKAMMARENS FÖRLIKNINGS OCH SKILJEDOMSREGLER 13 (1981).

14   *In A Report on the ICC Rules of Contractual Relations*, 5 ICC BULL. 31 (December 1994).

apparent in years to come, as the contracts in which they are found become the focus for litigation.

38.05　Maritime and aviation arbitration

Although the usual ICC arbitration procedure may be used in maritime cases, it was thought appropriate to devise an alternative set of rules containing certain modifications intended better to reflect the needs and usages of international maritime litigation. The ICC accordingly collaborated with the international association of maritime lawyers, the *Comité Maritime International* (CMI), to develop what are called "The ICC-CMI International Maritime Arbitration Rules." They were established in 1978 (reproduced in Appendix III).[15] The ICC-CMI Rules are designed not only for conflicts involving maritime law *strictu sensu* but also for disputes relating to shipbuilding, carriage of goods, chartering and contracts of carriage by sea.

The principal difference between standard ICC arbitration and the ICC-CMI Rules relates to the role of the ICC's Court of Arbitration, which is eliminated in ICC-CMI cases. The latter are administered by the permanent "International Maritime Arbitration Committee," whose 12 members are evenly divided between ICC appointees and CMI appointees having experience with maritime disputes. This Committee designates chairmen as well as arbitrators on behalf of defaulting parties. It further supervises the proceedings, grants time extensions where appropriate, decides challenges to arbitrators, and establishes the amount of deposits for costs. On the other hand, the arbitrators establish their own fees, subject only to the parties' right to have them finally reviewed by the Committee.

Furthermore, the ICC-CMI Rules do not call for the preparation of Terms of Reference. Nor are ICC-CMI awards reviewed even with respect to matters of form either by the Court of Arbitration or the Maritime Arbitration Committee. In other words, ICC-CMI proceedings are more autonomous from the permanent ICC structure than are ordinary ICC arbitrations.

The jurisdiction of an ICC-CMI tribunal depends on the parties' specific consent. While the Secretariat of the ICC Court of Arbitration may call the parties' attention to the fact that their dispute is of such a nature that it could be handled under the ICC-CMI Rules, a contract containing an ICC arbitration clause cannot be subjected to ICC-CMI arbitration against a party's wishes and vice versa.

The ICC-CMI Rules are the same as those of ordinary ICC arbitration with respect to questions of procedure before the arbitrators and applicable law (Articles 9 and 10, respectively). The reader is accordingly referred to the general commentary of this book.

15　ICC Publication No. 324.

In spite of these statements, the first request for arbitration under the ICC-CMI Rules was not registered until 1985, prompting the ICC headquarters to consider the need to be more effective in informing practitioners of the availability of the International Maritime Arbitration Services. In the past ten years, 9 disputes were submitted to the Standing Committee, suggesting that the ICC-CMI Rules are neither revitalized nor totally forgotten.

In 1997, the ICC and the International Air Transport Association (IATA) developed draft Rules of Arbitration for international airline passenger liability claims. The interest of the ICC/ IATA Draft Rules is to promote a dispute resolution procedure for disputes relating to the passengers' claims over the quantum of damages against air carriers and/or their insurance companies in the context of an international air transport accident as defined in the 1929 Warsaw Convention, with enforceable arbitral awards. The dispute is to be administered by a Standing Committee composed jointly by the ICC and the IATA.

As of the present writing, however, the draft is still subject to requests for fundamental revisions. A useful discussion of its provisions would be impossible at this stage; nor can any assessment be made as to its prospective impact in practice.

38.06 Specialized commissions

The various mechanisms described in the five preceding sections comprise, in addition to that of arbitration itself, all of the means by which parties might ask ICC organs to deal directly with their disputes.

There are however, several other ICC organs (see Table 1 of Appendix 1) which, while not directly charged with responsibility for settling disputes between two parties engaged in international trade, may be of considerable interest to litigants in various contexts. Thus the work of the International Panel on Extortion and Bribery in Business Transactions (which gave rise to the creation under the 1996 revised ICC Rules on Extortion and Bribery of a Standing Committee on Extortion and Bribery in order to combat such practices) may be relevant to parties alleging that their adversaries' claims are based on illegal contracts, particularly in the area of commissions related to government purchasing. More generally, the analysis of trade practices and occasionally the establishment of norms (particularly in the area of transportation and banking: the familiar INCOTERMS)[16] by these organs are often highly useful in demonstrating the "relevant trade usages" which ICC arbitrators are required, under Article 17(2) of the Rules, to take into account "in all cases."

---

16 In this connection, the Uniform Customs and Practice for Documentary Credits also merit mention. *See generally* the series of articles in English and French appearing in the sections entitled *Les pratiques commerciales internationales* and *Les pratiques bancaires, in* HOMMAGE À FREDERIC EISEMANN (ICC Publication No. 321, 1978); Jean Stoufflet, *L'oeuvre normative de la Chambre de commerce internationale dans le domaine bancaire, in* LE DROIT DES RELATIONS ÉCONOMIQUES INTERNATIONALES (*LIBER AMICORUM* FOR BERTHOLD GOLDMAN) 361 (1982).

38.07   Appointing authority

To parties who do not wish to call upon the full range of arbitration services provided under the aegis of the ICC Court of Arbitration, the ICC is still willing to offer its experience in finding qualified arbitrators.

This service may be particularly relevant with respect to arbitrations conducted under the UNCITRAL Rules of Arbitration, established in 1976 by the United Nations Commission on International Trade Law. The UNCITRAL Rules are designed to work largely on an *ad hoc* basis (*see* Section 4.03), but contemplate the intervention of an "appointing authority" to nominate arbitrators, and to rule on challenges to arbitrators, in the event the parties do not agree to the composition of the arbitral tribunal. The parties may, under the UNCITRAL Rules, designate such appointing authority in advance. (Failing designation by the parties, the appointing authority would if necessary be chosen by the Secretary-General of the Permanent Court of Arbitration at the Hague.) In 1997, the ICC received 3 requests for appointment under the UNCITRAL Rules.

In order to avoid inconsistency between contractual language and the organization of the ICC, which may be modified over time, the following formulation would seem effective in an UNCITRAL arbitration clause:

> The appointing authority shall be the Chairman of the Court of Arbitration of the International Chamber of Commerce, or in the event of his unavailability to act, the International Chamber of Commerce, acting in accordance with such rules as it may from time to time adopt for this purpose.

A formal exposition of the procedure the ICC would follow as appointing authority under UNCITRAL Arbitration Rules has now been published by the ICC.[17] The ICC's practice is to consider for appointment as UNCITRAL arbitrators only persons having a significant professional and business background, primarily from among those having experience as ICC arbitrators, respecting the principle of neutrality of nationality where chairmen or sole arbitrators are concerned. The designation process is directly supervised by the Chairman of the ICC Court.

Challenges to arbitrators would probably be decided in the same manner as is done in full ICC arbitration proceedings in the context of its own fully supervised cases, that is to say in plenary sessions of the Court and on the basis of a report by one of its members.

When parties resort to *ad hoc* arbitration under rules other than those of UNCITRAL, they have nevertheless the option of requesting that the ICC con-

---

17   In ICC Publication No. 409.

stitute an arbitral tribunal, or designate arbitrators in place of defaulting parties. In 1997, the ICC received 5 requests for such a nomination.

38.08 Supervising arbitration applying non-ICC rules

As repeatedly noted, the ICC Arbitration Rules are flexible, inspired by the fundamental principle that the parties are free to decide rules of procedure (*see* Article 11 of the Rules, further described in Section 16.01).

There is thus no objection in principle to the parties' stipulation in the arbitration clause that the arbitration follow a set of more complete rules, such as the UNCITRAL Arbitration Rules or those of a trade association active in the relevant trade. Indeed, such a stipulation may have the positive effect of relieving the arbitral tribunal later from having to choose rules of procedure against the wishes of a party (or perhaps both parties).

On the other hand, reference to two different sets of arbitration rules must be made with great care so as to avoid the type of inconsistency that would render the arbitration inoperative (see Chapter 9). For example, a stipulation that the parties wish to have an ICC-administered arbitration applying UNCITRAL Rules is of doubtful efficacy. There are significant potential inconsistencies between the two, notably the fact that ICC awards are necessarily scrutinized for approval by the ICC Court of Arbitration while the UNCITRAL Rules contemplate no such step in the process. The ICC is unwilling to administer proceedings fundamentally different from its own basic concepts; it does not wish to lend its authority to an arbitration that does not allow the ICC Court to exercise its customary control.

To be certain that the procedure is operational, it is thus adviseable to make clear that in an ICC-administered arbitration the ICC Rules take precedence, and that additional rules of procedure are referred to only to fill gaps. This might be accomplished with the following formulation:

> In matters of procedure with respect to which the ICC Rules are silent, the arbitral tribunal shall follow the rules of procedure established by. . .

38.09 Documentary Credit Disputes.

The International Chamber of Commerce offers parties to documentary credit transactions not only the possibility of arbitrating their disputes under its arbitration rules, but also the opportunity to settle controversies through a panel of experts. Developed through almost two years of intensive deliberation by an ICC working party, the "Documentary Credit Dispute Expertise Rules" (DOCDEX) were approved in final form by the ICC Banking Commission in November 1996 and took effect in October 1997. The rules are reproduced in Appendix III. The procedure will be administered by the ICC Centre for Expertise in collaboration with the Banking Commission.[18]

Under the DOCDEX rules, a request for dispute resolution may be filed unilaterally by an aggrieved party, or jointly by all parties to the dispute. Such disputes typically deal with alleged discrepancies in documentary credits and can usually be resolved without a hearing. The ICC will appoint three independent experts from a list maintained by the ICC Banking Commission. After payment of the advance on costs, the ICC Centre for Expertise will transmit the file to the experts for a decision, made on the basis of documents alone. The Rules cover only issues arising under the Uniform Customs and Practices for Documentary Credits or the Uniform Rules for Bank-to-Bank Reimbursement under Documentary Credits ("URR"). Thus an allegation of fraud would fall outside the scope of the expert's mission.

The DOCDEX Rules state that the experts' decision "is not intended to conform with any legal requirements of an arbitration award." Therefore it is doubtful that very many courts would subject the decision to arbitration statutes or treaties, even if one of the parties so requested. The parties are free to consider it legally binding or as having moral force only. If the parties fail to state how they will characterize the decision, the default rule presumes bindingness.

The International Center for Expertise received a significant number of requests for DOCDEX in its first year of operation. The parties involved in these cases came from fifteen different countries, and the proposed or appointed experts from fourteen countries.

The need for such rules can be illustrated by a recent case of *Clarendon v. State Bank of Saurashtra*.[19] For pedagogical value, *Clarendon* could hardly have been excelled even if scholars had tried to construct a hypothetical example of the hazards of going to court over a documentary credit dispute. A Swiss beneficiary of a $2.2 million letter of credit issued by a state bank in India had to pursue almost four years of judicial proceedings, with three different court decisions, merely to obtain an appellate order remanding the case to a lower court for disposition on the merits of the documentary credit claim.

To the beneficiary, the legal questions raised in the case could hardly have seemed other than arcane and irrelevant to interpretation of the letter of credit itself: federal court subject matter jurisdiction, the Foreign Sovereign Immunities Act, and the applicant's status as an indispensable party to the litigation under the Federal Rules of Civil Procedure. The merits of the case

---

18   *See* Jean-François Bourque, *New System to Resolve L/C Disputes through Expertise*, 7 ICC BULL. 12 (May 1996); William W. Park, *Documentary Credit Dispute Resolution: The Role of Arbitrators and Experts*, 12 MEALEY'S INT. ARB. REP. 15 (Nov. 1997); *see also News*, 8 ICC BULL. 3, at 12 (May 1997): "In the U.K., it is estimated that 50% of letters of credit contain discrepancies."

19   77 F.3d 631 (2d Cir. 1996).

hinged on whether the Uniform Customs and Practices for Documentary Credits requires (as it does) that an issuing bank give prompt notice of refusal to honor a credit by reason of discrepant documents, in the instant case a bill of lading dated a day earlier than called for in the credit.

The types of dispute suitable for DOCDEX might implicate not only controversies between issuing and confirming banks, but also bank/customer litigation. Complications might arise out of alleged fraud by the seller; use of buyer's funds to offset indebtedness to the issuing bank, or simple disagreement about how to interpret the terms of the letter of credit.

APPENDIX I

STATISTICS AND GENERAL INFORMATION

TABLE OF CONTENTS

Appendix I: **Statistics and General Information**

Table 1   Composition of ICC Commissions and Working Groups. 721

Table 2   Composition of the Court of Arbitration. 724

Table 3   Nationalities of Arbitrators 727

Table 4   Nationalities of Arbitrators
              Selected in 1989-1999 (11 Years). 728

Table 5   Nationalities of Parties
              to Arbitration Filed in 1989-1999 (11 Years). 732

Table 6   Regional Leaders. 737

Table 7   Places of Arbitration Established
              in 1989-1999 (11 Years) 738

Table 8   Amounts in Dispute 743

Table 9A   Calculating ICC Administrative Expenses and Fees of
              Arbitrators According to the ICC Schedule 744

Table 9B   Estimating Costs and the Advance on Costs. 745

Table 10   Signatories to the 1958 New York Convention on the
              Recognition and Enforcement of Foreign Arbitral Awards 748

Appendix II:

Rules of Optional Conciliation 753

Rules of Arbitration of the International Chamber of Commerce. 756

Statutes of the International Court of Arbitration of the ICC 771

Internal Rules of the International Court of Arbitration of the ICC 773

Arbitration Costs and Fees 776

Destination table: From 1975 Arbitration Rules to
1998 Arbitration Rules. 781

Derivative table: From 1998 Arbitration Rules to
1975 Arbitration Rules. 784

Appendix III:

ICC Rules for Expertise. 789

ICC Rules for Documentary Credit Dispute Resolution Expertise
DOCDEX Rules 793

Appendix to the ICC DOCDEX Rules 798

ICC/CMI Rules for International Maritime Arbitration. 800

ICC Rules for a Pre-Arbitral Referee Procedure 808

APPENDIX: Costs and Payment for the
ICC Pre-arbitral Referee Procedure 813

TABLE 1

COMPOSITION OF ICC COMMISSIONS AND WORKING GROUPS

(Excluding the Secretary General's Office
and the Court of Arbitration)
(Dated May 1998)

1. Commission on Banking Technique and Practice.

Chair: Dieter Kiefer, Managing Director, UBS (Switzerland).

2. Commission on Corporate Economists Advisory Group.

Chair: Klaus Friedrich, Chief Economist, Dresdner Bank AG (Germany).

3. Commission on Electronic Commerce Project.

(Subgroups: Working Group on Electronic Trade Practices, Working Group on Information Security, Working Group on E-terms).

Chair: Ake Nilson, Director, Marinade Ltd (UK).

4. Commission on Energy.

(Subgroups: Working Party on Liberalisation and Privatisation of the Energy Markets, Joint Working Party on Climate Change, Working Party on Business Perspectives on Energy).

Chair: Juhani Santaholma, Executive Vice-President, Fortnum Power & Heat Division (Helsinki).

5. Commission on Environment.

(Subgroups: Environmental Management Systems, Sustainable Development, Joint Working Party on Waste Management, Joint Working Party on Climate Change, Joint Working Party on Trade and Environment, Joint Working Party on Taxes and Charges, Joint Working Party on Forest, Joint Working Party on BioSociety.

Chair: Lord Holme of Cheltenham, Adviser to the Chairman, Rio Tinto (UK).

6. Standing Committee on Extortion and Bribery.

(Subgroups: Subcommittee on the Promotion of the ICC Rules on Extortion and Bribery, Subcommittee on Company Practices against Extortion and Bribery, Subcommittee on International Organisations, Subcommitte on Private-Private Bribery).

Chair: François Vincke, Secretary General, Petrofina SA (Belgium).

7. Commission on Financial Services and Insurance.

(Subgroups: Committee on Insurance Issues, Working Party on Pension Reform).

Chair: Coley Clark, Senior Vice-President, Electronic Data Systems (USA).

8. Commission on Intellectual and Industrial Property.

(Subgroups: Ad Hoc Working Party on Interface between Intellectual Property, Development and the Protection of the Environment, Ad Hoc Working Party on Future Intellectual Property Issues for Business, Ad Hoc Working Party on Utility Models).

Chair: Ashok S. Ganguly, Chairman, ICI India Ltd (India).

9. Commission on International Arbitration.

(Subgroups: Working Party on Adaption, Extension and Promotion of ICC ADR Services).

Chair: Paul A. Gélinas, Partner, Baudel, Delclaux, Landon and Gélinas (France).

10. Commission on International Commercial Practice.

(Subgroups: Working Party on Transfer of Ownership, Working Party on Franchising, Working Party on Trade Terms—Incoterms, Working Party on Intermediaries, Working Party on Commercial Agency & Distributorship).

Chair: Fabio Bortolotti, Professor, Bortolotti, Mathis & Associati (Italy).

11. Commission on International Trade and Investment Policy.

(Subgroups: Committee on Customs and Trade Regulations, Joint Working Party on Trade and Environment, Joint Working Party on Competition and International Trade, Joint Working Party on BioSociety).

Chair: Arthur Dunkel, Former Director General of the GATT, Consultant, Member of the Board of Nestlé and Crédit Suisse Holding (Switzerland).

12. Commission on Law and Practices relating to Competition.

Subgroups: Joint Working Party on Competition and International Trade, Working Party on Vertical Agreements, Working Party on Information Exchange between Antitrust Authorities).

Chair: Ferdinand Hermanns, Attorney-at-Law (Germany).

TABLE 1   APPENDIX I

13. Commission on Marketing, Advertising and Distribution.

(Subgroups: Working Party on Postal Services, Working Party on Advertising in the Interactive Media, Code Revision Task Force, Joint Working Party on BioSociety, Ad Hoc Working Group on ICMP).

Chair: John F. Manfredi, Executive Vice President, Corporate Affairs, Nabisco Inc. (United States).

14. Commission on Taxation.

(Subgroups: Ad Hoc Working Party on Environmental Taxes and Charges, Ad Hoc Working Party on Taxation Issues Arising from Electronic Commerce, Ad Hoc Working Party on Abuse of Tax Provisions, Ad Hoc Working Party on the Introduction of Arbitration clauses for the resolution of International Tax conflicts, Ad Hoc Working Party on the Spread of VAT Regimes).

Chair: Karel Koojiman, Head of Taxation and Corporate Structure Division, Shell International (Netherlands).

15. Commission on Telecommunications and Information Technologies.

(Subgroups: Working Party on Telecommunications, Working Party on Privacy and Data Protection, Working Party on Computing and IT).

Chair: Peter Gerard, Member of the Executive Board, Mannesmann (Germany).

16. Commission on Transport.

Commission on Air Transport.
(Subgroups: Working Party on Air Law, Ad Hoc Working Group on Revisions to the Warsaw Liability System).
Chair: Jeffrey N. Shane, Partner, Wilmer, Cutler and Pickering (United States).

Committee on Air Cargo Transport.
Chair: Anton van der Lande, Vice-President, Public Affairs International United Parcel Service, Brussels (United States).

Cargo Coordinating Forum.
(Subgroup: Ad Hoc Working Group on Multimodal Transport Law and Practice).
Chair: To be announced.

Commission on Maritime Transport.
Chair: Knud Pontoppidan, Executive Vice President, A.P. Møller (Denmark).

Commission on Surface Transport
Chair: Rune Svensson, Senior Advisor, Volvo Transport Corporation (Sweden).

TABLE 2

COMPOSITION OF THE COURT OF ARBITRATION
(Term January 1, 2000 - December 31, 2002)

Officers

Chairman	Robert Briner (Switzerland)
Vice-Chairmen	Gerald Aksen (United States)
	Michel Aurillac (France)
	Piero Bernardini (Italy)
	Francis P. Donovan (Australia)
	Ahmed S. El-Kosheri (Egypt)
	Ottoarndt Glossner (Germany)
	Carlos Henrique de C. Fróes (Brazil)
	Michael J. Mustill (United Kingdom)
	Fali S. Nariman (India)
	Toshio Sawada (Japan)
Secretary General	Horacio A. Grigera Naón (Argentina)
Deputy Secretary General	Anne Marie Whitesell (United States)
General Counsel	Fabien Gélinas (Canada)
Counsel	Denis Bensaude (France)
	Andrea Carlevaris (Italy)
	Brooks W. Daly (United States)
	Katherine Gonzalez Arrocha (Panama)
	Detlev Kühner (Germany)
	Eduardo Silva Romero (Colombia)

Members

Argentina	Sergio Le Pera
	Ernesto O'Farrell (Alternate member)
Australia	Garry Downes
	Karyl Nairn (Alternate member)
Austria	Günther Frosch
	Christian Herbst (Alternate member)
Bahrain	Hassan Ali Radhi
	Sheikha Hayya bint Rashid Al Khalifa (Alternate member)
Bangladesh	M. Zahir
Belgium	Pierre Gabriel
Brazil	Luiz Fernando Teixeira Pinto
	Maximiano Mafra de Laet (Alternate member)

TABLE 2   APPENDIX I

Burkina Faso	Harouna Sawadogo
Cameroon	Gaston Kenfack Douajni
Canada	Robert Knutson
Chile	Carlos Eugenio Jorquiera M. José Luis López Blanco (Alternate member)
Colombia	Fernando Mantilla-Serrano
Cyprus	Antis A. Triantafyllides
Czech Rep.	Jana Doskova
Denmark	P.R. Meurs-Gerken
Ecuador	José Ramon Jiminez Carbo
Egypt	Yehia El Gamal Borham Atallah (Alternate member)
Finland	Robert Mattson
France	Patrice Level Philippe Boivin (Alternate member)
Germany	Fabian von Schlabrendorff Michaël Bühler (Alternate member)
Ghana	Samuel K. B. Asante
Greece	Epaminondas Spiliotopoulos
Hungary	Ivan Szasz
Iceland	Baldvin B. Harladsson
India	D. M. Popat Sarosh R. Zaiwalla (Alternate member)
Iran	Mohammad H. Tammadon Mohsen Mohebi (Alternate member)
Ireland	Roderick H. Murphy S.C. Michael W. Carrigan (Alternate member)
Israel	Michel A. Calvo Mayer Gabay (Alternate member)
Italy	Renzo Morera Loretta Malintoppi (Alternate member)
Ivory Coast	Léon Boissier-Palun
Japan	Kazuo Takayanagi
Jordan	Rajai K.W. Dajani
Korea	Lee Jay Ki
Kuwait	Anwar Al-Fuzaie Youssef Mohamad Al-Ali (Alternate member)
Lebanon	Ghaleb S. Muhmassani Mouhieddine Kaissi (Alternate member)
Luxembourg	Pierre Seimetz
Madagascar	Raymond Ranjeva
Mexico	Julio C. Treviño Fernando Estavillo Castro (Alternate member)
Morocco	Hamid Andaloussi Abdelaziz Souhair (Alternate member)

Netherlands	Sierk Bruna
New Zealand	David A. R. Williams
	Jason A. Fry (Alternate member)
Nigeria	Bola Ajibola
	H. Odein Ajumogobia (Alternate member)
Norway	Gunnar Nerdrum
Pakistan	M.A.K. Afridi
	Mohamed J. Jaffer
Peru	Eduardo Ferrero
Philippines	Floretino P. Feliciano
Portugal	Joâo Luís Pinheiro Lopes dos Reis
	Manuel Cavaleiro Brandao (Alternate member)
Saudi Arabia	Abdelrahman A. Abbar
Singapore	K.S. Chung
South Africa	Mervyn King S.C.
Spain	Juan Antonio Cremades
	Mercedes Tarrazón Rodón (Alternate member)
Sweden	Hans Bagner
Switzerland	Pierre Neiger
Syria	Faez Anjak
Thailand	Kiat Sittheeamorn
Togo	Wle-Mbanewar Bataka
Trinidad and Tobago	Alcade Warner
Tunisia	Salah Mejri
Turkey	Turgut Kalpsüz
	Turgul Ansay (Alternate member)
Ukraine	Vasyl Marmazov
United Kingdom	Michael Lee
	David St. John Sutton (Alternate member)
United States	Carl F. Salans
	Axel H. Baum (Alternate member)
Uruguay	Paul Arrighi Bustamante
Venezuela	James Otis Rodner
	Alfredo Zuloaga (Alternate member)

TABLE 3

NATIONALITIES OF ARBITRATORS

	1980-1988		1989-1999	
	Chosen by the ICC	Chosen by parties	Chosen by the ICC	Chosen by parties
Austria	81	45	87	108
Belgium	147	71	144	120
France	205	558	315	678
Germany	78	210	167	413
Italy	62	89	110	270
Netherlands	47	66	42	107
Spain	17	21	33	91
Sweden	21	24	40	80
Switzerland	361	382	387	726
U.K.	153	280	234	484
U.S.A.	62	212	108	484

TABLE 4

NATIONALITIES OF ARBITRATORS
SELECTED IN 1989-1999 (11 YEARS)

Total arbitrators: 6,853 (including 2,832 sole arbitrators and 458 arbitrators nominated for defaulting parties.)

The number in parenthesis indicates the number of arbitrators chosen by parties having a nationality different than that of the arbitrators in question.[1]

Chosen by:	Claimant	Defendant	Jointly	ICC	Total
Africa					
Algeria	13 (4)	21 (5)	4	1	39
Angola	0	1	0	0	1
Benin	0	2 (2)	0	1	3
Burkina Faso	0	1	0	0	1
Cameroon	1	2	0	1	4
Ethiopia	0	3	0	0	3
Ghana	0	3 (1)	0	1	4
Ivory Coast	0	1	0	0	1
Kenya	0	0	1	0	1
Liberia	0	1	0	0	1
Libya	2(1)	9 (1)	0	0	11
Mauritania	1	1	0	0	2
Mauritius	1	0	0	0	1
Morocco	7 (1)	9 (2)	0	7	23
Mozambique	0	2 (2)	0	0	2
Nigeria	3	0	0	2	5
Senegal	1 (1)	0	1	0	2
South Africa	2 (1)	3	2	3	10
Sudan	2 (2)	2	0	0	4
Tunisia	9	9 (3)	0	20	38
Zaire	1	1	0	1	3
TOTAL	**43**	**71**	**8**	**37**	**159**

1   For arbitrations filed until 31 December 1997 under the old ICC Rules of Conciliation and Arbitration.

TABLE 4   APPENDIX I

Chosen by:	Claimant	Defendant	Jointly	ICC	Total
Latin America					
Argentina	9 (3)	13 (4)	3	5	30
Brazil	5 (1)	3 (1)	0	1	9
Chile	3	1	1	0	5
Colombia	5	4	5	8	22
Cuba	3	5	0	0	8
Dominican Republic	1	0	0	0	1
Ecuador	1	0	0	0	1
Guyana	0	1	0	0	1
Mexico	16 (4)	19 (6)	9	28	72
Panama	2	0	1	0	3
Paraguay	0	1	0	0	1
Peru	2	2	0	1	5
Uruguay	2 (1)	1 (1)	0	2	5
Venezuela	1	1	0	3	5
TOTAL	**50**	**51**	**19**	**48**	**168**
North America					
Canada	37 (20)	39 (15)	32	95	203
U.S.A.	211 (98)	200 (79)	73	108	592
TOTAL	**248**	**239**	**105**	**203**	**795**
Asia					
Bangladesh	1	6	1	2	10
China	1	3	0	1	5
Hong Kong	1	2 (1)	1	0	4
India	21 (8)	25 (10)	7	18	71
Indonesia	4	3 (1)	1	0	8
Japan	6 (1)	7	1	2	16
Malaysia	8 (3)	6	2	6	22
Nepal	1	3	0	0	4
Pakistan	4 (1)	3	0	2	9
Philippines	4	4	0	0	8
Singapore	14 (8)	15 (6)	6	28	63
South Korea	4 (1)	8	2	0	14
Sri Lanka	2 (1)	5	0	1	8
Taiwan	1	1 (1)	1	0	3
Thailand	4	8	2	3	17
Vietnam	0	3	0	0	3
TOTAL	**76**	**102**	**24**	**63**	**265**

Chosen by:	Claimant	Defendant	Jointly	ICC	Total
Eastern Europe					
Belarus	0	1 (1)	0	0	1
Bulgaria	5	8	0	1	14
Croatia	3	2	0	0	5
Czech Republic	8 (1)	5	2	0	15
Estonia	0	0	1	0	1
Hungary	6	9 (1)	8	1	24
Latvia	0	1	0	0	1
Poland	14 (3)	12	3	0	29
Romania	10 (1)	7	0	1	18
Russian Federation	7 (3)	10	2	0	19
Slovakia	0	1 (1)	1	0	2
Slovenia	0	5	1	0	6
Yugoslavia	27 (2)	19 (1)	2	6	54
TOTAL	**80**	**80**	**20**	**9**	**189**
Western Europe					
Austria	46 (27)	43 (22)	19	87	195
Belgium	49 (28)	41 (18)	30	144	264
Cyprus	0	1	8	2	11
Denmark	21 (13)	11 (4)	8	20	60
Finland	3(1)	3	0	12	18
France	289 (126)	256 (112)	133	315	993
Germany	169 (130)	146 (92)	98	167	580
Greece	20 (4)	23 (5)	4	11	58
Ireland	5(2)	3 (1)	7	30	45
Italy	126 (32)	102 (26)	42	110	380
Liechtenstein	0	1 (1)	0	0	1
Luxembourg	3 (1)	1 (1)	3	25	32
Netherlands	39 (27)	39 (25)	29	42	149
Norway	8 (2)	8 (3)	2	11	29
Portugal	12 (1)	15 (2)	5	9	41
Spain	41 (14)	37 (8)	13	33	124
Sweden	32 (9)	27 (7)	21	40	120
Switzerland	258 (169)	237 (151)	231	387	1113
Turkey	12 (1)	22	2	8	44
United Kingdom	196 (138)	166 (108)	122	234	718
TOTAL	**1329**	**1182**	**777**	**1687**	**4975**
Middle East					
Bahrain	0	3 (1)	0	1	4
Egypt	29 (6)	49 (11)	1	8	87

TABLE 4   APPENDIX I

Chosen by:	Claimant	Defendant	Jointly	ICC	Total
Iran	13 (3)	6 (2)	2	0	21
Iraq	1 (1)	0	0	0	1
Israel	2 (1)	1	1	1	5
Jordan	1	3 (1)	0	2	6
Kuwait	1	1	0	1	3
Lebanon	33 (26)	17 (9)	0	24	74
Saudi Arabia	7 (4)	2	0	0	9
Syria	15 (7)	13 (3)	4	1	33
U.A.E.	1	1	0	0	2
TOTAL	**103**	**96**	**8**	**38**	**245**

Oceana					
Australia	6 (5)	9 (7)	6	26	47
New Zealand	1 (1)	1(1)	3	5	10
TOTAL	**7**	**10**	**9**	**31**	**57**

TABLE 5

NATIONALITIES OF PARTIES
TO ARBITRATION FILED IN 1989-1999 (11 YEARS)

Total parties: 11,143

	Claimant	Defendant	Total
Africa			
Algeria	19	23	42
Angola	0	3	3
Benin	1	0	1
Botswana	3	1	4
Burkina Faso	3	3	6
Cameroon	3	12	15
Cape Verde	0	1	1
Chad	0	1	1
Congo	4	6	10
Djibouti	0	2	2
Ethiopia	2	29	31
Gabon	5	6	11
Gambia	1	1	2
Ghana	1	12	13
Guinea	3	6	9
Ivory Coast	6	2	8
Kenya	5	8	13
Lesotho	0	1	1
Liberia	9	6	15
Libya	2	19	21
Madagascar	2	3	5
Malawi	0	4	4
Mali	0	4	4
Mauritania	2	2	4
Mauritius	2	1	3
Monaco	4	0	4
Morocco	23	33	56
Mozambique	0	4	4
Niger	1	1	2

TABLE 5   APPENDIX I

	Claimant	Defendant	Total
Nigeria	19	11	30
Rwanda	0	1	1
Senegal	3	4	7
Seychelles	2	1	3
South Africa	14	16	30
Sudan	4	5	9
Swaziland	1	2	3
Sao Tome and Principe	0	4	4
Tanzania	1	11	12
Transkei (Rep. of)	0	2	2
Togo	2	0	2
Tunisia	29	22	51
Uganda	4	9	13
Zaire	3	12	15
Zambia	0	2	2
Zimbabwe	3	2	5
TOTAL	**186**	**298**	**484**

Latin America

	Claimant	Defendant	Total
Argentina	36	35	71
Bolivia	2	5	7
Brazil	19	36	55
Chile	10	7	17
Colombia	9	17	26
Costa Rica	2	0	2
Cuba	3	7	10
Ecuador	1	3	4
El Salvador	1	3	4
Guatemala	0	7	7
Guyana	0	10	10
Mexico	71	109	180
Panama	71	22	93
Paraguay	1	2	3
Peru	6	8	14
Uruguay	2	2	4
Venezuela	7	33	40
TOTAL	**241**	**306**	**547**

	Claimant	Defendant	Total
North America			
Canada	95	86	181
U.S.A.	574	628	1202
TOTAL	**669**	**714**	**1383**
Asia			
Afghanistan	1	0	1
Bangladesh	4	9	13
Brunei	0	1	1
China	19	42	61
Hong Kong	51	45	96
India	122	168	290
Indonesia	25	32	57
Japan	86	79	165
Laos	1	3	4
Malaysia	17	34	51
Nepal	2	7	9
North Korea	1	7	8
Pakistan	19	30	49
Philippines	13	43	56
Singapore	43	51	94
South Korea	55	87	142
Sri Lanka	6	31	37
Taiwan	12	24	36
Thailand	29	48	77
Vietnam	3	7	10
TOTAL	**509**	**748**	**1257**
Caribbean			
Antigua and Barbados	2	0	2
Aruba	1	1	2
Bahamas	9	4	13
Barbados	2	1	3
Belize	0	1	1
Bermuda	18	14	32
British Virgin Islands	27	11	38
Cayman Islands	15	8	23
Dominican Republic	0	7	7
Haiti	0	1	1
Jamaica	3	2	5
Netherlands Antilles	24	12	36
Puerto Rico	1	1	2

TABLE 5   APPENDIX I

	Claimant	Defendant	Total
Saint-Lucia	0	1	1
Trinidad and Tobago	2	4	6
TOTAL	**104**	**68**	**172**

Eastern Europe

	Claimant	Defendant	Total
Albania	3	10	13
Armenia	0	1	1
Belarus	1	3	4
Bosnia-Herzegovina	2	0	2
Bulgaria	26	29	55
Croatia	7	4	11
Czech Republic	24	43	67
Georgia	0	1	1
Hungáry	43	36	79
Kazakhstan	5	4	9
Latvia	1	2	3
Lithuania	0	7	7
Macedonia	1	8	9
Poland	32	41	73
Romania	64	39	103
Russian Federation	28	73	101
Serbia	0	1	1
Slovakia	5	11	16
Slovenia	11	10	21
Turkmenistan	2	14	16
Ukraine	8	5	13
USSR	3	5	8
Uzbekistan	0	1	1
Yugoslavia	68	49	117
TOTAL	**334**	**397**	**731**

Western Europe

	Claimant	Defendant	Total
Andorra	1	2	3
Austria	94	115	209
Belgium	113	98	211
Channel Islands	5	1	6
Cyprus	17	18	35
Denmark	45	46	91
Finland	44	38	82
France	710	677	1387
Germany	433	500	933
Greece	63	54	117

	Claimant	Defendant	Total
Iceland	1	1	2
Ireland	32	18	50
Italy	349	356	705
Liechtenstein	26	20	46
Luxembourg	35	31	66
Malta	6	4	10
Monaco	6	3	9
Netherlands	151	148	299
Norway	36	35	71
Portugal	35	31	66
Spain	106	201	307
Sweden	81	73	154
Switzerland	223	175	398
Turkey	51	77	128
United Kingdom	290	326	616
TOTAL	2953	3048	6001

Middle East

	Claimant	Defendant	Total
Bahrain	4	7	11
Egypt	42	61	103
Iran	26	15	41
Iraq	3	11	14
Israel	17	18	35
Jordan	4	10	14
Kuwait	16	15	31
Lebanon	21	11	32
Oman	0	3	3
Qatar	9	10	19
Saudi Arabia	30	42	72
Syria	27	14	41
U.A.E.	22	24	46
Yemen	4	8	12
TOTAL	225	249	474

Oceana

	Claimant	Defendant	Total
Australia	30	40	70
Fiji	0	2	2
New Zealand	4	3	7
Vanuatu	5	7	12
Western Samoa	1	2	3
TOTAL	40	54	94

TABLE 6

REGIONAL LEADERS

(most frequently involved nationalities)

	1980-1988	1989-1999
Europe		
France	892	1387
Germany	522	933
Italy	297	705
United Kingdom	275	616
Africa		
Algeria	62	42
Libya	55	21
Morocco	30	56
Tunisia	36	51
Middle East		
Egypt	122	103
Iran	48	41
Lebanon	52	32
Israel	22	35
Asia		
Japan	52	165
India	49	290
South Korea	49	142
Americas		
U.S.A.	634	1202
Canada	60	181
Mexico	16	180
Panama	46	93

TABLE 7

PLACES OF ARBITRATION ESTABLISHED
IN 1989-1999 (11 YEARS)

Total choices: 3393

	Agreed between parties	Fixed by the ICC	Total	Percentage (rounded)
In Africa				
Algeria	6	0	6	
Ethiopia	2	0	2	
Ivory Coast	1	0	1	
Kenya	0	2	2	
Mozambique	1	0	1	
Nigeria	1	1	2	
South Africa	1	0	1	
Tunisia	1	8	9	
Zaire	1	0	1	
TOTAL	**14**	**11**	**25**	**0.75%**
In Latin America				
Argentina	11	0	11	
Brazil	3	0	3	
Chile	2	0	2	
Colombia	2	0	2	
Equador	1	0	1	
Mexico	22	5	27	0.5%
Panama	0	1	1	
Paraguay	1	0	1	
Peru	1	0	1	
Venezuela	1	0	1	
TOTAL	**44**	**6**	**50**	**1.0%**
In North America				
Canada	24	17	41	1.25%
Calgary	3-0			
Dorval	1-0			

TABLE 7   APPENDIX I

	Agreed between parties	Fixed by the ICC	Total	Percentage (rounded)
Montreal	8-8			
Ottawa	2-2			
Saint John's	1-0			
Toronto	8-1			
Vancouver	1-6			
U.S.A	213	34	247	5.25%
Atlanta	3-0			
Austin	0-1			
Baltimore	0-1			
Boston	4-0			
Buffalo	1-0			
Chicago	22-1			
Cleveland	2-0			
Columbus	2-1			
Dallas	5-0			
Dayton	1-0			
Denver	1-2			
Detroit	1-1			
Guam	0-1			
Honolulu	3-0			
Houston	18-0			
Hutchinson	1-0			
Indianapolis	1-0			
Irvine	1-0			
Little Rock	0-1			
Los Angeles	27-5			
Meadville	1-0			
Memphis	0-1			
Miami	9-1			
Minneapolis	1-1			
Nashville	1-0			
Newark	1-0			
New Orleans	1-1			
New York	61-10			
Orlando	1-0			
Petaluma	1-0			
Philadelphia	5-0			
Pittsburgh	1-1			
Pullman	1-0			
Redmond	1-0			
Richmond	1-0			
Saint Louis	3-0			

	Agreed between parties	Fixed by the ICC	Total	Percentage (rounded)
San Antonio	1-0			
San Diego, Cal.	4-0			
San Francisco	5-2			
San Jose, Cal.	4-2			
Santa Barbara	2-0			
Seattle	3-1			
Topeka	1-0			
Washington	10-0			
Wilmington	1-0			
TOTAL	**237**	**51**	**288**	**6.5%**
In Asia				
Bangladesh	5	0	5	
China	2	0	2	
Hong Kong	32	2	34	0.75%
India	27	4	31	
Indonesia	7	1	8	
Laos	2	0	2	
Japan	9	3	12	
Malaysia	6	2	8	
Nepal	6	0	6	
Pakistan	2	2	4	
Philippines	5	0	5	
Singapore	50	10	60	1.25%
South Korea	10	0	10	
Sri Lanka	8	2	10	
Taiwan	7	0	7	
Thailand	8	3	11	
Vietnam	0	1	1	
TOTAL	**186**	**30**	**216**	**5.0%**
In Caribbean				
Bahamas	0	1	1	
Barbados	1	0	1	
Bermuda	1	0	1	
Netherlands Antilles	1	0	1	
Puerto Rico	1	0	1	
TOTAL	**4**	**1**	**5**	**0.25%**
In Europe				
Austria	78	16	94	3.0%

	Agreed between parties	Fixed by the ICC	Total	Percentage (rounded)
Belgium	40	14	54	2.0%
Bulgaria	1	0	1	
Cyprus	0	10	10	
Czech Republic	3	0	3	
Denmark	12	6	18	0.5%
Finland	3	1	4	
France	858	198	1056	33.0%
Germany	111	27	138	4.5%
Greece	12	6	18	0.5%
Hungary	5	0	5	
Ireland	0	1	1	
Italy	41	19	60	2.5%
Liechtenstein	3	0	3	
Lithuania	2	0	2	
Luxembourg	11	15	26	1.0%
Netherlands	46	18	64	2.0%
Norway	4	0	4	
Poland	4	0	4	
Portugal	6	0	6	
Romania	1	1	2	
Russian Federation	1	0	1	
Spain	15	3	18	0.5%
Sweden	65	5	70	2.0%
Switzerland	693	80	773	25.0%
Basel	5-6			
Bern	21-1			
Geneva	340-42			
Lausanne	31-5			
Lugano	13-1			
Zurich	283-25			
Turkey	9	3	12	
United Kingdom	273	45	318	8.5%
Yugoslavia (Rep. of)	2	0	2	
TOTAL	**2299**	**468**	**2767**	**85.0%**

In Middle East

Bahrain	2	1	3	
Egypt	13	1	13	
Jordan	1	0	1	
Kuwait	0	1	1	

	Agreed between parties	Fixed by the ICC	Total	Percentage (rounded)
Lebanon	1	0	1	
Oman	2	0	2	
Qatar	1	0	1	
Saudi Arabia	1	0	1	
Syria	6	1	7	
U.A.E.	2	0	2	
TOTAL	29	3	32	1.0%
In Oceana				
Australia	4	3	7	
New Zealand	1	1	2	
Vanuatu	0	1	1	
TOTAL	5	5	10	0.5%
GRAND TOTAL	2818	575	3393	100.0%

TABLE 8[2]

AMOUNTS IN DISPUTE

(Percentage per category)

	1988	1989	1990	1991	1992	1993	1994	1995	1996	1997	1998
Under US $ 50,000	5.8	5.0	4.0	4.7	5.6	4.5	5.5	2.5	3.5	2.9	3.3
US $ 50,000 to 200,000	15.1	14.5	12.5	10.4	12.1	11.5	9.5	11.2	11.9	15.9	8.5
US $ 200,000 to 1 million	20.6	25.5	30.0	25.2	19.6	22.6	29.5	24.1	23.2	18.9	27.1
US $ 1 million to 10 million	39.9	34.1	30.0	28.4	37.0	40.0	32.5	37.1	36.8	32.1	34.9
More than US $ 10 million	7.4	12.7	11.3	13.7	19.7	13.3	12.4	13.4	12.4	15.8	19.8
Amount not indicated	11.2	8.2	12.2	17.6	6.0	8.1	10.6	11.7	12.2	14.4	6.4

2   Unlike other materials in the Appendix, this table has not been developed by specific research for this book. These statistics were taken from tables published in the ICC BULLETIN each year, and in the annual review of selected ICC arbitration awards found in the JOURNAL DE DROIT INTERNATIONAL. The figures are somewhat approximate and certainly understated, since amounts in dispute are frequently increased as arbitrations proceed. The fact that costs of ICC arbitration are proportional to the amounts in dispute accounts for a reluctance by parties to announce their full claim immediately. Moreover, cases frequently come to the Court with no clearly stated amount in dispute.

TABLE 9A

CALCULATING ICC ADMINISTRATIVE EXPENSES AND FEES OF ARBITRATORS ACCORDING TO THE ICC SCHEDULE*

(Amounts in U.S. dollars)

SUM IN DISPUTE	ADMINISTRATIVE EXPENSES	FEES PER ARBITRATOR	
		Minimum	Maximum
Up to 50,000	2,500	2,500	17%
50,001 to 100,000	2,500 plus (3.5% x amount in excess of 50,000)	2,500 plus (2.0% x amount in excess of 50,000)	8,500 plus (11% x amount in excess of 50,000)
100,001 to 500,000	4,250 plus (1.7% x amount in excess of 100,000)	3,500 plus (1.0% x amount in excess of 100,000)	14,000 plus (5.5% x amount in excess of 100,000)
500,001 to 1,000,000	11,050 plus (1.15% x amount in excess of 500,000)	7,500 plus (0.75% x amount in excess of 500,000)	36,000 plus (3.5% x amount in excess of 500,000)
1,000,001 to 2,000,000	16,800 plus (0.6% x amount in excess of 1,000,000)	11,250 plus (0.5% x amount in excess of 1,000,000)	53,500 plus (2.5% x amount in excess of 1,000,000)
2,000,001 to 5,000,000	22,800 plus (0.2% x amount in excess of 2,000,000)	16,250 plus (0.25% x amount in excess of 2,000,000)	78,500 plus (1.0% x amount in excess of 2,000,000)
5,000,001 to 10,000,000	28,800 plus (0.1% x amount in excess of 5,000,000)	23,750 plus (0.1% x amount in excess of 5,000,000)	108,500 plus (0.55% x amount in excess of 5,000,000)
10,000,001 to 50,000,000	33,800 plus (0.06% x amount in excess of 10,000,000)	28,750 plus (0.05% x amount in excess of 10,000,000)	136,000 plus (0.17% x amount in excess of 10,000,000)
50,000,001 to 80,000,000	57,800 plus (0.06% x amount in excess of 50,000,000)	48,750 plus (0.03% x amount in excess of 50,000,000)	204,000 plus (0.12% x amount in excess of 50,000,000)
80,000,001 to 100,000,000	75,800	57,750 plus (0.02% x amount in excess of 80,000,000)	240,000 plus (0.1% x amount in excess of 80,000,000)
100,000,000 and up	75,800	61,750 plus (0.01% x amount in excess of 100,000,000)	260,000 plus (0.05% x amount in excess of 100,000,000)

* Calculated from the Revised Schedule of Arbitration Costs, effective from January 1, 1998 and confirmed in the New ICC Rules in force as from January 1, 1998. This revised schedule will apply to all cases received as from January 1, 1998, but will not affect cases received prior to that date.

TABLE 9B

ESTIMATING COSTS AND THE ADVANCE ON COSTS

| SUM IN DISPUTE | ADMINISTRATIVE EXPENSES | FEES PER ARBITRATOR | | TOTAL COSTS administrative charges plus fees of arbitrator(s) | | | | | |
| | | | | ONE ARBITRATOR | | THREE ARBITRATORS | | | |
		Min.	Max.	Min.	Max.	Min.	Max.		
50,000	2,500	2,500	8,500	5,000	11,000	10,000	28,000
100,000	4,250	3,500	14,000	7,750	18,250	14,750	46,250
200,000	5,950	4,500	19,500	10,450	25,450	19,450	64,450
300,000	7,650	5,500	25,000	13,150	32,650	24,150	82,650
400,000	9,350	6,500	30,500	15,850	39,850	28,850	100,850
500,000	11,050	7,500	36,000	18,550	43,500	33,550	119,050
600,000	12,200	8,250	39,500	20,450	51,700	36,950	130,700
700,000	13,350	9,000	43,000	22,350	56,350	40,350	142,350
800,000	14,500	9,750	46,500	24,250	61,000	43,750	154,000
900,000	15,650	10,500	50,000	26,150	65,650	47,150	165,650
1,000,000	16,800	11,250	53,500	28,050	70,300	50,550	177,300

SUM IN DISPUTE	ADMINISTRATIVE EXPENSES	FEES PER ARBITRATOR		TOTAL COSTS administrative charges plus fees of arbitrator(s)			
				ONE ARBITRATOR		THREE ARBITRATORS	
		Min.	Max.	Min.	Max.	Min.	Max.
2,000,000	22,800	16,250	78,500	39,050	101,300	71,550	258,300
3,000,000	24,800	18,750	88,500	43,550	113,300	81,050	290,300
4,000,000	26,800	21,250	98,500	48,050	125,300	90,550	322,300
5,000,000	28,800	23,750	108,500	52,550	137,300	100,050	354,300
6,000,000	29,800	24,750	114,000	54,550	143,800	104,050	371,800
7,000,000	30,800	25,750	119,500	56,550	150,300	108,050	389,300
8,000,000	31,800	26,750	125,000	58,550	156,800	112,050	406,800
9,000,000	32,800	27,750	130,500	60,550	163,300	116,050	424,300
10,000,000	33,800	28,750	136,000	62,550	169,800	120,050	441,800
15,000,000	36,800	31,250	144,500	68,050	181,300	130,550	470,300
20,000,000	39,800	33,750	153,000	73,550	192,800	141,050	498,800
25,000,000	42,800	36,250	161,500	79,050	197,750	151,550	527,300
30,000,000	45,800	38,750	170,000	84,550	215,800	162,050	555,800
35,000,000	48,800	41,250	178,500	90,050	227,300	172,550	584,300
40,000,000	51,800	43,750	187,000	95,550	238,800	183,050	612,800
45,000,000	54,800	46,250	195,500	101,050	250,300	193,550	641,300
50,000,000	57,800	48,750	204,000	106,550	261,800	204,050	669,800
60,000,000	63,800	51,750	216,000	115,550	267,750	219,050	711,800
70,000,000	69,800	54,750	228,000	124,550	297,800	234,050	753,800
80,000,000	75,800	57,750	240,000	133,550	315,800	249,050	795,800

SUM IN DISPUTE	ADMINISTRATIVE EXPENSES	FEES PER ARBITRATOR		TOTAL COSTS administrative charges plus fees of arbitrator(s)			
				ONE ARBITRATOR		THREE ARBITRATORS	
		Min.	Max.	Min.	Max.	Min.	Max.
90,000,000	75,800	59,750	250,000	135,550	325,800	255,050	825,800
100,000,000	75,800	61,750	260,000	137,550	335,800	261,050	855,800
Over 100,000,000	75,800	61,750	260,000	137,550	335,800	261,050	855,800
		plus (0.01% x amount in excess of 100,000,000)	plus (0.05% x amount in excess of 100,000,000)	plus (0.01% x amount in excess of 100,000,000)	plus (0.05% x amount in excess of 100,000,000)	plus (0.3% x amount in excess of 100,000,000)	plus (0.15% x amount in excess of 100,000,000)

* This table has been prepared by the authors as a rough guide for planning purposes at the outset of an arbitration. The advance on costs is set by the Court, usually after the receipt of both the Request and Answer (including counterclaims, if any). Nevertheless, under the 1998 Rules, the Secretary General has the discretion to fix a provisional advance. As regards the calculation of the advance, the Court's general practice is to set an amount between the minimum and the maximum total costs set forth in the appropriate column above. Increases in the advance may be fixed by the Court in accordance with the fluctuation of the sum in dispute during the course of the arbitration, exceptional expenses of the arbitrators, or the complexity and length of the proceedings.

TABLE 10

SIGNATORIES TO THE 1958 NEW YORK CONVENTION ON THE RECOGNITION AND ENFORCEMENT OF FOREIGN ARBITRAL AWARDS

(as of October 1999)

Country	Year of ratification, accession (a), or succession (s)	Reservation(*)
Algeria	1989 (a)	1-2
Antigua and Barbuda	1989 (a)	1-2
Argentina	1989	1-2
Armenia	1997 (a)	1-2
Australia	1975 (a)	none
Austria	1961 (a)	none
Bahrain	1988 (a)	1-2
Bangladesh	1992 (a)	none
Barbados	1993 (a)	2
Belarus	1960	1
Belgium	1975	1
Benin	1974 (a)	none
Bolivia	1995 (a)	none
Bosnia and Herzegovina	1992 (s)	1-2
Botswana	1971 (a)	1-2
Brunei Darussalam	1996 (a)	1
Bulgaria	1961	1
Burkina Faso	1987 (a)	none
Cambodia	1960 (a)	none
Cameroon	1988 (a)	none
Canada	1986 (a)	2(**)
Central African Republic	1962 (a)	1-2
Chile	1975 (a)	none

TABLE 10   APPENDIX I

Country	Year of ratification, accession (a), or succession (s)	Reservation(*)
China	1987 (a)	1-2
Colombia	1979 (a)	none
Costa Rica	1987	none
Croatia	1993 (s)	1-2
Cuba	1974 (a)	1-2
Cyprus	1980 (a)	1-2
Czech Republic	1993 (s)	1
Denmark	1972 (a)	1-2
Djibouti	1983 (a)	none
Dominica	1988 (a)	none
Ecuador	1962	1-2
Egypt	1959 (a)	none
El Salvador	1998	none
Estonia	1993 (a)	none
Finland	1962	none
France	1959	1
Georgia	1994 (a)	none
Germany	1961	1
Ghana	1968 (a)	none
Greece	1962 (a)	1-2
Guatemala	1984 (a)	1-2
Guinea	1991 (a)	none
Haiti	1983 (a)	none
Holy See	1975 (a)	1-2
Hungary	1962 (a)	1-2
India	1960	1-2
Indonesia	1981 (a)	1-2
Ireland	1981 (a)	1
Israel	1959	none
Italy	1969 (a)	none
Ivory Coast	1991 (a)	none
Japan	1961 (a)	1
Jordan	1979	none
Kazakstan	1995 (a)	none
Kenya	1989 (a)	1
Kuwait	1978 (a)	1

Country	Year of ratification, accession (a), or succession (s)	Reservation(*)
Kyrgyzstan	1996 (a)	none
Laos	1998 (a)	none
Latvia	1992 (a)	none
Lesotho	1989 (a)	none
Lithuania	1995 (a)	1-2
Luxembourg	1983	1
Madagascar	1962 (a)	1-2
Malaysia	1985 (a)	1-2
Mali	1994 (a)	none
Mauritania	1997 (a)	none
Mauritius	1996 (a)	1-2
Mexico	1971 (a)	none
Moldova	1998 (a)	1
Monaco	1982	1-2
Mongolia	1994 (a)	1-2
Morocco	1959 (a)	1
Mozambique	1998 (a)	none
Nepal	1998 (a)	1-2
Netherlands	1964	1
New Zealand	1983 (a)	1
Niger	1964 (a)	none
Nigeria	1970 (a)	1-2
Norway	1961 (a)	1
Oman	1999 (a)	none
Panama	1984 (a)	none
Paraguay	1997 (a)	none
Peru	1988 (a)	none
Philippines	1967	1-2
Poland	1961	1-2
Portugal	1994 (a)	1
Republic of Korea	1973 (a)	1-2
Romania	1961 (a)	1-2
Russian Federation	1960	1
San Marino	1979 (a)	none
Saudi Arabia	1994 (a)	1
Senegal	1994 (a)	none

TABLE 10   APPENDIX I

Country	Year of ratification, accession (a), or succession (s)	Reservation(*)
Singapore	1986 (a)	1
Slovakia	1993 (s)	none
Slovenia	1991 (s)	1-2
South Africa	1976 (a)	none
Spain	1977 (a)	none
Sri Lanka	1962	none
Suriname	1964	1
Sweden	1972	none
Switzerland	1965	none
Syria	1959 (a)	none
Tanzania	1964 (a)	1
Thailand	1959 (a)	none
Trinidad and Tobago	1966 (a)	1-2
Tunisia	1967 (a)	1-2
Turkey	1992 (a)	1-2
Uganda	1992 (a)	1
Ukraine	1960	1
United Kingdom	1975 (a)	1
United States of America	1970 (a)	1-2
Uruguay	1983 (a)	none
Uzbekistan	1996 (a)	none
Venezuela	1995 (a)	1-2
Vietnam	1995 (a)	1-2
The Former Yugoslavian Republic of Macedonia	1994 (s)	none
Yugoslavia	1982 (a)	1-2
Zimbabwe	1994 (a)	none

* The first reservation is the so-called "reciprocity reservation" (at present made by 66 States). The second is the so-called "commercial reservation" (at present made by 42 States).
** The commercial reservation does not apply to the Province of Quebec

Appendix II

ICC Rules of Conciliation

ICC Rules of Arbitration Including the Statutes and the Internal Rules of the Court of Arbitration in Force as from 1 January 1998

Conversion Tables Between 1975 and 1998 ICC Arbitration Rules

Arbitration Costs and Fees

Effective as of January 1, 1998

Rules of Optional Conciliation

Preamble

Settlement is a desirable solution for business disputes of an international character. The International Chamber of Commerce therefore sets out these Rules of Optional Conciliation in order to facilitate the amicable settlement of such disputes.

Article 1

All business disputes of an international character may be submitted to conciliation by a sole conciliator appointed by the International Chamber of Commerce.

Article 2

The party requesting conciliation shall apply to the Secretariat of the International Court of Arbitration of the International Chamber of Commerce setting out succinctly the purpose of the request and accompanying it with the fee required to open the file, as set out in Appendix III hereto.

Article 3

The Secretariat of the International Court of Arbitration shall, as soon as possible, inform the other party of the request for conciliation. That party will be given a period of 15 days to inform the Secretariat whether it agrees or declines to participate in the attempt to conciliate.

If the other party agrees to participate in the attempt to conciliate, it shall so inform the Secretariat within such period.

In the absence of any reply within such period or in the case of a negative reply, the request for conciliation shall be deemed to have been declined. The Secretariat shall, as soon as possible, so inform the party which had requested conciliation.

Article 4

Upon receipt of an agreement to attempt conciliation, the Secretary General of the International Court of arbitration shall appoint a conciliator as soon as possible. The Conciliator shall inform the parties of his appointment and set a time-limit for the parties to present their respective arguments to him.

Article 5

The conciliator shall conduct the conciliation process as he thinks fit, guided by the principles of impartiality, equity and justice.

With the agreement of the parties, the conciliator shall fix the place for conciliation.

The conciliator may at any time during the conciliation process request a party to submit to him such additional information as he deems necessary.

The parties may, if they so wish, be assisted by counsel of their choice.

Article 6

The confidential nature of the conciliation process shall be respected by every person who is involved in it in whatever capacity.

Article 7

The conciliation process shall come to an end:

a) Upon the parties signing an agreement. The parties shall be bound by such agreement. The agreement shall remain confidential unless and to the extent that its execution or application require disclosure.

b) Upon the production by the conciliator of a report recording that the attempt to conciliate has not been successful. Such report shall not contain reasons.

c) Upon notification to the conciliator by one or more parties at any time during the conciliation process of an intention no longer to pursue the conciliation process.

Article 8

Upon termination of the conciliation, the conciliator shall provide the Secretariat of the International Court of Arbitration with the settlement agreement signed by the parties or with his report of lack of success or with a notice from one or more parties of the intention no longer to pursue the conciliation process.

Article 9

Upon the file being opened, the Secretariat of the International Court of Arbitration shall fix the sum required to permit the process to proceed, taking into consideration the nature and importance of the dispute. Such sum shall be paid in equal shares by the parties.

This sum shall cover the estimated fees of the conciliator, expenses of the conciliation, and the administrative expenses as set out in Appendix III hereto.

In any case where, in course of the conciliation process, the Secretariat of the Court shall decide that the sum originally paid is insufficient to cover the likely total costs of the conciliation, the Secretariat shall require the provision of an additional amount which shall be paid in equal shares by the parties.

Upon termination of the conciliation, the Secretariat shall settle the total costs of the process and advise the parties in writing.

All above costs shall be borne in equal shares by the parties except and insofar as a settlement agreement provides otherwise.

A party's other expenditures shall remain the responsibility of that party.

Article 10

Unless the parties agree otherwise, a conciliator shall not act in any judicial or arbitration proceeding relating to the dispute which has been the subject of the conciliation process whether as an arbitrator, representative or counsel of a party.

The parties mutually undertake not to call the conciliator as a witness in any such proceedings, unless otherwise agreed between them.

Article 11

The parties agree not to introduce in any judicial or arbitration proceeding as evidence or in any manner whatsoever:

a) any views expressed or suggestions made by any party with regard to the possible settlement of the dispute;

b) any proposals put forward by the conciliator;

c) the fact that a party had indicated that it was ready to accept some proposal for a settlement put forward by the conciliator.

Rules of Arbitration of the International Chamber of Commerce

Introductory provisions

Article 1: International Court of Arbitration

1. The International Court of Arbitration (the "Court") of the International Chamber of Commerce (the "ICC") is the arbitration body attached to the ICC. The statutes of the Court are set forth in Appendix I. Members of the Court are appointed by the Council of the ICC. The function of the Court is to provide for the settlement by arbitration of business disputes of an international character in accordance with the Rules of Arbitration of the International Chamber of Commerce (the "Rules"). If so empowered by an arbitration agreement, the Court shall also provide for the settlement by arbitration in accordance with these Rules of business disputes not of an international character.

2. The Court does not itself settle disputes. It has the function of ensuring the application of these Rules. It draws up to its own Internal Rules (Appendix II).

3. The Chairman of the Court, or, in the Chairman's absence or otherwise at his request, one of its Vice-Chairmen shall have the power to take urgent decisions on behalf of the Court, provided that any such decision is reported to the Court at its next session.

4. As provided for in its Internal Rules, the Court may delegate to one or more committees composed of its members the power to take certain decisions, provided that any such decision is reported to the Court at its next session.

5. The Secretariat of the Court (the "Secretariat") under the direction of its Secretary General (the "Secretary General") shall have its seat at the headquarters of the ICC.

Article 2: Definitions

In these Rules:

(i) "Arbitral Tribunal" includes one or more arbitrators.

(ii) "Claimant" includes one or more claimants and "respondent" includes one or more respondents.

(iii) "Award" includes, inter alia, an interim, partial or final Award.

Article 3: Written Notifications or Communications; Time Limits

1. All pleadings and other written communications submitted by any party, as well as all documents annexed thereto, shall be supplied in a number of copies sufficient to provide one copy for each party, plus one for each arbitrator, and one for the Secretariat. A copy of any communication from the Arbitral Tribunal to the parties shall be sent to the Secretariat.

2. All notifications or communications from the Secretariat and the Arbitral Tribunal shall be made to the last address of the party or its representative for

756

whom the same are intended, as notified either by the party. Such notification or communication may be made by delivery against receipt, registered post, courier, facsimile transmission, telex, telegram or any other means of telecommunication that provides a record of the sending thereof;

3. A notification or communication shall be deemed to have been made on the day it was received by the party itself or by its representative, or would have been received if made in accordance with the preceding paragraph.

4. Periods of time specified in, or fixed under the present Rules, shall start to run on the day following the date a notification or communication is deemed to have been made in accordance with the preceding paragraph. When the day next following such date is an official holiday, or a non-business day in the country where the notification or communication is deemed to have been made, the period of time shall commence on the first following business day. Official holidays and non-business days are included in the calculation of the period of time. If the last day of the relevant period of time granted is an official holiday or a non-business day in the country where the notification or communication is deemed to have been made, the period of time shall expire at the end of the first following business day.

Commencing the arbitration

Article 4: Request for Arbitration

1. A party wishing to have recourse to arbitration under these Rules shall submit its Request for Arbitration (the "Request") to the Secretariat, which shall notify the Claimant and Respondent of the receipt of the Request and the date of such receipt.

2. The date on which the Request is received by the Secretariat shall, for all purposes, be deemed to be the date of the commencement of the arbitral proceedings.

3. The Request shall, inter alia, contain the following information:

   a) the name in full, description and address of each of the parties;

   b) a description of the nature and circumstances of the dispute giving rise to the claims;

   c) a statement of the relief sought, including, to the extent possible, an indication of any amount(s) claimed;

   d) the relevant agreements and, in particular, the arbitration agreement;

   e) all relevant particulars concerning the number of arbitrators and their choice in accordance with the provisions of Articles 8, 9 and 10, and any nomination of a arbitrator required thereby; and

   f) any comments as to the place of arbitration, the applicable rules of law and the language of the arbitration.

4. Together with the Request, the Claimant shall submit the number of copies thereof required by Article 3(1) and shall make the advance payment on administrative expenses required by Appendix III ("Arbitration Costs and Fees") in force on the date the Request is submitted. In the event that the Claimant fails to comply with either of these requirements, the Secretariat may fix a time limit within which the Claimant must comply, failing which the file shall be closed without prejudice to the right of the Claimant to submit the same claims at a later date in another Request.

5. The Secretariat shall send a copy of the Request and the documents annexed thereto to the Respondent for its Answer to the Request once the Secretariat has sufficient copies of the Request and the required advance payment.

6. When a party submits a Request in connection with a legal relationship in respect of which arbitration proceedings between the same parties are already pending under these Rules, the Court may, at the request of a party, decide to include the claims contained in the request in the pending proceedings provided that the Terms of Reference have not been signed or approved by the Court. Once the Terms of Reference have been signed or approved by the Court, claims may only be included in the pending proceedings subject to the provisions of article 19.

Article 5: Answer to the Request; Counterclaims

1. Within 30 days from the receipt of the Request from the Secretariat, the respondent shall file an Answer (the "Answer") which shall, inter alia, contain the following information:

   a) the name in full, description and address of each of the parties;

   b) a description of the nature and circumstances of the dispute giving rise to the claims;

   c) its response to the relief sought;

   d) any comments concerning the number of arbitrators and their choice in light of the Claimant's proposals and in accordance with the provisions of Articles 8, 9 and 10, and any nomination of an arbitrator required thereby; and

   e) any comments as to the place of arbitration, the applicable rules of law and the language of the arbitration.

2. The Secretariat may grant the Respondent an extension of the time for filing the Answer, provided the application for such an extension contains the Respondent's comments concerning the number of arbitrators and their choice, and, where required by Articles 8, 9 and 10, the nomination of an arbitrator. If the Respondent fails to do so, the Court shall proceed in accordance with these Rules.

3. The Answer shall be supplied to the Secretariat in the number of copies specified by Article 3(1).

4. A copy of the Answer and the documents annexed thereto shall be communicated by the Secretariat to the Claimant.

5. Any counterclaim(s) made by the Respondent shall be filed with its Answer and shall provide:

a) a description of the nature and circumstances of the dispute giving rise to the counterclaim(s); and

b) a statement of the relief sought, including, to the extent possible, an indication of any amount(s) counterclaimed.

6. The Claimant shall file a Reply to any counterclaim within 30 days from the date of receipt of the counterclaim(s) communicated by the Secretariat. The Secretariat may grant the Claimant an extension of time for filing the Reply.

Article 6: Effect of the Arbitration Agreement

1. Where the parties have agreed to submit to arbitration under the Rules, they shall be deemed to have submitted ipso facto to the Rules in effect on the date of commencement of the arbitration proceedings unless they have agreed to submit to the Rules in effect on the date of their arbitration agreement.

2. If the Respondent does not file an Answer, as provided by Article 5, or if any party raises one or more pleas concerning the existence, validity or scope of the arbitration agreement, the Court may decide, without prejudice to the admissibility or merits of the plea or pleas, that the arbitration shall proceed if it is prima facie satisfied that an arbitration agreement under the Rules may exist. In such a case, any decision as to the jurisdiction of the Arbitral Tribunal shall be taken by the Arbitral Tribunal itself. If the Court is not so satisfied, the parties shall be notified that the arbitration cannot proceed. In such a case, any party retains the right to ask any court having jurisdiction whether or not there is a binding arbitration agreement.

3. If any of the parties refuses or fails to take part in the arbitration or any stage thereof, the arbitration shall proceed notwithstanding such refusal or failure.

4. Unless otherwise agreed, the Arbitral Tribunal shall not cease to have jurisdiction by reason of any claim that the contract is null and void or allegation that it is non-existent provided that the Arbitral Tribunal upholds the validity of the arbitration agreement. The Arbitral Tribunal shall continue to have jurisdiction to determine the respective rights of the parties and to adjudicate their claims and pleas even though the contract itself may be non-existent or null and void.

The Arbitral Tribunal

Article 7: General Provision

1. Every arbitrator must be and remain independent of the parties involved in the arbitration.

2. Before appointment or confirmation, a prospective arbitrator shall sign a statement of independence and disclose in writing to the Secretariat any facts or circumstances which might be of such a nature as to call into question the arbitrator's independence in the eyes of the parties. The Secretariat shall provide such information to the parties. The Secretariat shall provide such information to the parties in writing and fix the time limit for any comments from them.

3. An arbitrator shall immediately disclose in writing to the Secretariat and to the parties any facts or circumstances of a similar nature which may arise during the arbitration.

4. The decisions of the Court as to the appointmentconfirmation, challenge or replacement of an arbitrator shall be final and the reasons for such decisions shall not be communicated.

5. By accepting to serve, every arbitrator undertakes to carry out his responsibilities in accordance with these Rules.

6. Insofar as the parties have not provided otherwise, the Arbitral Tribunal shall be constituted in accordance with the provisions of Articles 8, 9 and 10.

Article 8: Number of Arbitrators

1. The disputes shall be decided by a sole arbitrator or by three arbitrators.

2. Where the parties have not agreed upon the number of arbitrators, the Court shall appoint a sole arbitrator, save where it appears to the Court that the dispute is such as to warrant the appointment of three arbitrators. In such case, the Claimant shall nominate an arbitrator within a period of 15 days from the receipt of the notification of the notification of the nomination made by the Claimant.

3. Where the parties have agreed that the dispute shall be settled by a sole arbitrator, they may, by agreement, nominate the sole arbitrator for confirmation. If the parties fail to nominate a sole arbitrator within 30 days from the date when the Claimant's Request for arbitration has been received by the other party, or within such additional time as may be allowed by the Secretariat, the sole arbitrator shall be appointed by the Court.

4. Where the dispute is to be referred to three arbitrators, each party shall nominate in the Request and the Answer, respectively, one arbitrator for confirmation by the Court. if a party fails to nominate an arbitrator, the appointment shall be made by the Court. The third arbitrator, who will act as chairman of the arbitral Tribunal, shall be appointed by the Court, unless the

parties have agreed upon another procedure for such appointment, in which case the nomination will be subject to confirmation pursuant to Article 9. Should such procedure not result in a nomination within the time limit fixed by the parties or the Court, the third arbitrator shall be appointed by the Court.

Article 9: Appointment and Confirmation of the Arbitrators

1. In confirming or appointing arbitrators, the Court shall consider the prospective arbitrator's nationality, residence and other relationships with the countries of which the parties or the other arbitrators are nationals and the prospective arbitrator's availability and ability to conduct the arbitration in accordance with these Rules. The same shall apply where the Secretary general confirms arbitrators pursuant to Article 9(2).

2. The Secretary General may confirm as co-arbitrators, sole arbitrators and chairmen of Arbitral Tribunals persons nominated by the parties or pursuant to their particular agreements, provided they have filed a statement of independence without qualification or a qualified statement of independence has not given rise to objections. Such confirmation shall be reported to the Court at its next session. If the Secretary General considers that a co-arbitrator, sole arbitrator or chairman of an Arbitral Tribunal should not be confirmed, the matter shall be submitted to the Court.

3. Where the Court is to appoint a sole arbitrator or the chairman of an Arbitral Tribunal, it shall make the appointment upon a proposal of a National Committee of the ICC that it considers to be appropriate. If the Court does not accept the proposal made, or if the National Committee fails to make the proposal requested within the time limit fixed by the Court, the Court may repeat its request or may request a proposal from another National Committee that it considers to be appropriate.

4. Where the Court considers that the circumstances so demand, it may choose the sole arbitrator or the chairman of the Arbitral Tribunal from a country where there is no National Committee, provided that neither of the parties objects within the time limit fixed by the Court.

5. The sole arbitrator or the chairman of the Arbitral tribunal shall be of a nationality other than those of the parties. However, in suitable circumstances and provided that neither of the parties objects within the time limit fixed by the Court, the sole arbitrator or the chairman of the Arbitral Tribunal may be chosen from a country of which any of the parties is a national.

6. Where the Court is to appoint an arbitrator on behalf of a party which has failed to nominate one, it shall make the appointment upon a proposal of the National Committee of the country of which that party is a national. If the Court does not accept the proposal made, or if the National Committee fails to make the proposal requested within the time limit fixed by the Court, or if the country of which the said party is a national has no National Committee, the

Court shall be at liberty to choose any person whom it regards as suitable. The Secretariat shall inform the National Committee, if one exists, of the country of which such person is a national.

Article 10: Multiple Parties

1. Where there are multiple parties, whether as Claimant or as Respondent, and where the dispute is to be referred to three arbitrators, the multiple Claimants, jointly and the multiple Respondents, jointly, shall nominate an arbitrator for confirmation pursuant to Article 9.

2. In the absence of such a joint nomination and where all parties are unable to agree to a method for the constitution of the Arbitral Tribunal, the Court may appoint each member of the Arbitral Tribunal and shall designate one of them to act as chairman. In such case, the Court shall be at liberty to choose any person it regards as suitable to act as arbitrator, applying Article 9 when it considers this appropriate.

Article 11: Challenge of Arbitrators

1. A challenge of an arbitrator, whether for an alleged lack of independence or otherwise, shall be made by the submission to the Secretariat of a written statement specifying the facts and circumstances on which the challenge is based.

2. For a challenge to be admissible, it must be sent by a party either within 30 days from receipt by that party of the notification of the appointment or confirmation of the arbitrator, or within 30 days from the date when the party making the challenge was informed of the facts and circumstances on which the challenge is based, if such date is subsequent to the receipt of such notification.

3. The Court shall decide on the admissibility, and, at the same time if necessary, on the merits of a challenge after the Secretariat has afforded an opportunity for the arbitrator concerned, the other party or parties and any other members of the Arbitral Tribunal, to comment in writing within a suitable period of time. Such comments shall be communicated to the parties and to the arbitrators.

Article 12: Replacement of Arbitrators

1. An arbitrator shall be replaced upon his death, upon the acceptance by the Court of the arbitrator's resignation, upon acceptance by the Court of a challenge or upon the request of all the parties.

2. An arbitrator shall also be replaced on the Court's own initiative when it decides that he is prevented de jure or de facto from fulfilling his functions, or that he is not fulfilling his functions in accordance with the Rules or within the prescribed time limits.

3. When, on the basis of information that has come to its attention, the Court considers applying Article 12(2), it shall decide on the matter after the arbitrator concerned, the parties and any other members of the Arbitral tribunal have had an opportunity to comment in writing within a suitable period of time. Such comments shall be communicated to the parties and to the arbitrators.

4. When an arbitrators is to be replaced, the Court has discretion to decide whether or not to follow the original nominating process. Once reconstituted, and after having invited the parties to comment, the Arbitral Tribunal shall determine if and to what extent prior proceedings shall be repeated before the reconstituted Arbitral Tribunal.

5. Subsequent to the closing of the proceedings, instead of replacing an arbitrator who has died or been removed by the Court pursuant to Articles 12(1) and 12(2), the Court may decide, when it considers it appropriate, that the remaining arbitrators shall continue the arbitration. In making such determination, the Court shall take into account the views of the remaining arbitrators and of the parties and such other matters that it considers appropriate in the circumstances.

The Arbitral Proceedings

Article 13: Transmission of the File to the Arbitral Tribunal

The Secretariat shall transmit the file to the Arbitral Tribunal as soon as it has been constituted, provided the advance on costs requested by the Secretariat at this stage has been paid.

Article 14: Place of the Arbitration

1. The place of the arbitration shall be fixed by the Court unless agreed upon the parties.

2. The Arbitral Tribunal may, after consultation with the parties, conduct hearings and meetings at any location it considers appropriate unless otherwise agreed by parties.

3. The Arbitral tribunal may deliberate at any location it considers appropriate.

Article 15: Rules Governing the Proceedings

1. The proceedings before the Arbitral Tribunal shall be governed by these Rules, and, where these Rules are silent, by any rules which the parties or, failing themthe Arbitral Tribunal may settle on, whether or not reference is thereby made to the rules of procedure of a national law to be applied to the arbitration.

In all cases, the Arbitral Tribunal shall act fairly and impartially and ensure that each party has a reasonable opportunity to present its case.

Article 16: Language of the Arbitration

In the absence of an agreement by the parties, the Arbitral Tribunal shall determine the language or languages of the arbitration, due regard being given to all relevant circumstances, including the language of the contract.

Article 17: Applicable Rules of Law

1. The parties shall be free to agree upon the rules of law to applied by the Arbitral Tribunal to the merits of the dispute. In the absence of any such agreement, the Arbitral Tribunal shall apply the rules of law which it determines to be appropriate.

2. In all cases, the Arbitral Tribunal shall take account of the provisions of the contract and the relevant trade usages.

3. The Arbitral Tribunal shall assume the powers of an amiable compositeur or decide *ex aequo et bono* only if the parties have agreed to give it such powers.

Article 18: Terms of Reference; Procedural Timetable

1. As soon as it has received the file from the Secretariat, the arbitral Tribunal shall draw up, on the basis of documents or in the presence of the parties and in the light of their most recent submissions, a document defining its Terms of Reference. This document shall include the following particulars:

  a) the full names and descriptions of the parties;

  b) the addresses of the parties to which notifications and communications arising in the course of the arbitration may be made;

  c) a summary of the parties' respective claims and of the relief sought by each party, with an indication to the extent possible of the amounts claimed or counterclaimed;

  d) unless the Arbitral Tribunal considers it inappropriate, a list of issues to be determined;

  e) the full names, descriptions and addresses of the arbitration; and

  f) particulars of the applicable procedural rules and, if such is the case, reference to the power conferred upon the Arbitral Tribunal to act as amiable compositeur or to decide ex aequo et bono.

2. The Terms of Reference shall be signed by the parties and the Arbitral Tribunal. Within the two month of the date on which the file has been transmitted to it, the Arbitral Tribunal shall transmit to the Court the Terms of Reference signed by it and by the parties. The court may extend this time limit pursuant to a reasoned request from the Arbitral Tribunal or on its own initiative if it decides it is necessary to do so.

3. If any of the parties refuses to take part in the drawing up of the Terms of Reference or to sign the same they shall be submitted to the Court for ap-

proval. When the Terms of Reference are signed in accordance with Article 18(2) or approved by the Court, the arbitration shall proceed.

4. When drawing up the Terms of Reference, or as soon as possible thereafter, the Arbitral Tribunal, after having consulted the parties, shall establish in a separate document a provisional timetable that intends to follow for the conduct of the arbitration and shall communicate it to the Court and the parties. Any subsequent modifications of the provisional timetable shall be communicated to the Court and the parties.

Article 19: New Claims

After the Terms of Reference have been signed or approved by the Court, no party shall make new claims or counterclaims which fall outside the limits of the Terms of Reference unless it has been authorized to do so by the Arbitral Tribunal, which shall consider the nature of such new claims or counterclaims, the stage of the arbitration and other relevant circumstances.

Article 20: Establishing the Facts of the case

1. The Arbitral Tribunal shall proceed within as short a time as possible to establish the facts of the case by all appropriate means.

2. After studying the written submissions of the parties and all documents relied upon, the Arbitral Tribunal shall hear the parties together in person if any of them so requests or, failing such a request, it may of its own motion decide to hear them.

3. The Arbitral Tribunal may decide to hear witnesses, experts appointed by the parties or any person, in the presence of the parties, or in their absence provided they have been duly summoned.

4. The Arbitral Tribunal, after having consulted the parties, may appoint one or more experts, define their terms of reference and receive their reports. At the request of a party, the parties shall be given the opportunity to question at a hearing any such expert appointed by the Tribunal.

5. At any time during the proceedings, the Arbitral Tribunal may summon any party to provide additional evidence.

6. The Arbitral Tribunal may decide the case solely on the documents submitted by the parties unless any of the parties request a hearing.

7. The Arbitral Tribunal may take measures for protecting trade secrets and confidential information.

Article 21: Hearings

1. When a hearing is to be held, the Arbitral Tribunal, giving reasonable notice, shall summon the parties to appear before it on the day at the place fixed by it.

2. If any of the parties, although duly summoned, fails to appear without valid excuse, the Arbitral Tribunal shall have the power to proceed with the hearing.

3. The Arbitral Tribunal shall be in full charge of the hearings, at which all the parties shall be entitled to be present. Save with the approval of the Arbitral Tribunal and the parties, persons not involved in the proceedings shall not be admitted.

4. The parties may appear in person or through duly authorized representatives. In addition, they may be assisted by advisers.

Article 22: Closing of the Proceedings

1. When it is satisfied that the parties have had a reasonable opportunity to present their cases, the Arbitral Tribunal shall declare the proceedings closed. Thereafter, no further submission or argument may be made, or evidence produced, unless requested or authorized by the Arbitral Tribunal.

2. When the Arbitral Tribunal has declared the proceedings closed, it shall indicate to the Secretariat at an approximate date by which the draft Award will be submitted to the Court for approval pursuant to Article 27. Any postponement of that date shall be communicated to the Secretariat by the Arbitral Tribunal.

Article 23: Conservatory and Interim Measures

1. Unless the parties have otherwise agreed, as soon as the file has been transmitted to it, the Arbitral Tribunal may, at the request of a party, order any interim or conservatory measure it deems appropriate. The Arbitral Tribunal may make the granting of any such measure subject to appropriate security being furnished by the requesting party. Any such measure shall take the form of an order, giving reasons, or of an Award, as the Arbitral Tribunal considers appropriate.

2. Before the file is transmitted to the Arbitral Tribunal; and in appropriate circumstances even thereafter, the parties may apply to any competent judicial authority for interim or conservatory measures. The application of a party to a judicial authority for such measures or for the implementation of any such measures ordered by an Arbitral Tribunal shall not be deemed to be an infringement or a waiver of the arbitration agreement and shall not affect the relevant powers reserved to the Arbitral Tribunal. Any such application and any measures taken by the judicial authority must be notified without delay to the Secretariat. The Secretariat shall inform the Arbitral Tribunal thereof.

Awards

Article 24: Time Limit for the Award

1. The time limit within which the Arbitral Tribunal must render its final Award is six months. Such time limit shall start to run from the date of the last signature by the Arbitral Tribunal or of the parties of the Terms of Reference, or, in the case of application of Article 18(3), the date of the notification to the Arbitral Tribunal by the Secretariat of the approval of the Terms of Reference by the Court.

2. The Court may extend this time limit pursuant to a reasoned request from the Arbitral tribunal or on its own initiative if it decides it is necessary to do so.

Article 25: Making of the Award

1. When the Arbitral Tribunal is composed of more than one arbitrator, an Award is given by a majority decision. If there be no majority, the Award shall be made by the chairman of the Arbitral Tribunal alone.

2. The Award shall state the reasons upon which it is based.

3. The Award shall be deemed to be made at the place of the arbitration and on the date stated therein.

Article 26: Award by Consent

If the parties reach a settlement after the file has been transmitted to the Arbitral Tribunal in accordance with Article 13, the settlement shall be recorded in the form of an Award made by consent of the parties if so requested by the parties and if the Arbitral Tribunal agrees to do so.

Article 27: Scrutiny of the Award by the Court

Before signing any Award, the Arbitral Tribunal shall submit it in draft form to the Court. The Court may lay down modifications as to the form of the Award and, without affecting the Arbitral Tribunal's liberty of decision, may also draw its attention to points of substance. No Award shall be rendered by the Arbitral Tribunal until it has been approved by the Court as to its form.

Article 28: Notification, Deposit and Enforceability of the Award

1. Once an Award has been made, the Secretariat shall notify to the parties the text signed by the Arbitral Tribunal, provided always that the costs of the arbitration have been fully paid to the ICC by the parties or by one of them.

2. Additional copies certified true by the Secretary general shall be made available on request and at any time to the parties, but to no one else.

3. By virtue of the notification made in accordance with Paragraph 1 of this Article, the parties waive any other form of notification or deposit on the part of the Arbitral Tribunal.

4. An original of each Award made in accordance with the present Rules shall be deposited with the Secretariat.

5. The Arbitral Tribunal and the Secretariat shall assist the parties in complying with whatever further formalities may be necessary.

Every Award shall be binding on the parties. By submitting the dispute to arbitration under these Rules, the parties undertake to carry out any Award without delay and shall be deemed to have waived their right to any form of recourse insofar as such waiver can validly be made.

Article 29: Correction and Interpretation of the Award

1. On its own initiative, the Arbitral Tribunal may correct a clerical, computational or typographical error, or any errors of similar nature contained in an Award, provided such correction is submitted for approval to the Court within 30 days of the date of such Award.

2. Any application of a party for the correction of an error of the kind referred to in Article 29(1), or for the interpretation of an Award, must be made to the Secretariat within 30 days of the receipt of the Award by such party, in a number of copies as stated in Article 3(1). After transmittal of the application to the Arbitral Tribunal, it shall grant the other party a short time limit, normally not exceeding 30 days, from the receipt of the application by that party to submit any comments thereon. If the Arbitral Tribunal decides to correct or interpret the Award, it shall submit its decision in draft form to the Court not later than 30 days following the expiration of the time limit for the receipt of any comments from the other party or within such other period as the Court may decide.

3. The decision to correct or to interpret the Award shall take the form of an addendum and shall constitute part of the Award. The provisions of Articles 25, 27 and 28 shall apply mutatis mutandis.

Costs

Article 30: Advance to Cover the Costs of the Arbitration

1. After receipt of the Request, the Secretary General may request the Claimant to pay a provisional advance in an amount intended to cover the costs of arbitration until the Terms of Reference have been drawn up.

2. As soon as practicable, the Court shall fix the advance on costs in an amount likely to cover the fees and expenses of the arbitrators and the ICC administrative costs for the claims and counterclaims which have been referred to it by the parties. This amount may be subject to readjustment at any time during the arbitration. Where, apart from the claims, counterclaims are submitted, the Court may fix separate advances on costs for the claims and the counterclaims.

3. The advance on costs fixed by the Court shall be payable in equal shares by the Claimant and the Respondent. Any provisional advance paid on the basis of Article 30(1) will be considered as a partial payment thereof. Howeverany party shall be free to pay the whole of the advance on costs in respect of the principal claim or the counterclaim should the other party fail to pay its share. When the Court has set separate advances on costs in accordance with Article 30(2), each of the parties shall pay the advance on costs corresponding to its claims.

4. When a request for an advance on costs has not been complied with, and after consultation with the Arbitral Tribunal, the Secretary General may direct the Arbitral Tribunal to suspend its work and set a time limit, which must be not less than 15 days, on the expiry of which the relevant claims, or counterclaims, shall be considered as withdrawn. Should the party in question wish to object to this measure it must make a request within the aforementioned period for the matter to be decided by the Court. Such party shall not be prevented on the ground of such withdrawal from reintroducing the same claims or counterclaims at a later date in another proceeding.

5. If one of the parties claims a right to a set-off regard to either claims or counterclaims, such set-off shall be taken into account in determining the advance to cover the costs of arbitration in the same way as a separate claim insofar as it may require the Arbitral Tribunal to consider additional matters.

Article 31: Decision as to the Costs of the Arbitration

1. The costs of the arbitration shall include the fees and expenses o the arbitrators and the ICC administrative costs fixed by the Court, in accordance with the scale in force at the time of the commencement of the arbitral proceedings, as well as the fees and expenses of any experts appointed by the Arbitral Tribunal and the reasonable legal and other costs incurred by the parties for the arbitration.

2. The Court may fix the fees of the arbitrators at a figure higher or lower than that which would result from the application of the relevant scale should this be deemed necessary due to the exceptional circumstances of the case. Decisions on costs other than those fixed by the Court may be taken by the Arbitral Tribunal at any time during the proceedings.

3. The final Award shall fix the costs of the arbitration and decide which of the parties shall bear them or in what proportion they shall be borne by the parties.

Miscellaneous

Article 32: Modified Time Limits

1. The parties may agree to shorten the various time limits set out in these Rules. Any such agreement entered into subsequent to the constitution of an

Arbitral Tribunal shall become effective only upon the approval of the Arbitral Tribunal.

2. The Court, on its own initiative, may extend any time limit which has been modified pursuant to Article 32(1) if it decides that it is necessary to do so in order that the arbitral Tribunal or the Court may fulfil their responsibilities in accordance with these Rules.

Article 33: Waiver

A party which proceeds with the arbitration without raising its objection to a failure to comply with any provision of these Rules, or of any other rules applicable to the proceedings, any direction given by the Arbitral Tribunal, or any requirement under the arbitration agreement relating to the constitution of the Arbitral Tribunal, or to the conduct of the proceedings, shall be deemed to have waived its right to object.

Article 34: Exclusion of Liability

Neither the arbitrators, nor the Court and its members, nor the ICC and its employees, nor the ICC National Committees shall be liable to any person for any act or omission in connection with the arbitration.

Article 35: General Rule

In all matters not expressly provided for in these Rules, the Court and the Arbitral Tribunal shall act in the spirit of these Rules and shall make every effort to make sure that the Award is enforceable at law.

Statutes of the International Court of Arbitration of the ICC

Article 1: Function

1. The function of the International Court of Arbitration of the International Chamber of Commerce (the court) is to ensure the application of the Rules of Arbitration and the Rules of Conciliation of the International Chamber of Commerce, and it has all the necessary powers for that purpose.

2. As an autonomous body, it carries out these functions in complete independence from the ICC and its organs.

Its members are independent from the ICC National Committees.

Article 2: Composition of the Court

The Court shall consist of a Chairman, Vice-Chairmenand members and alternate members (collectively designated at members). In its work it is assisted by its Secretariat (Secretariat of the Court).

Article 3: Appointment

1. The Chairman is elected by the ICC Council upon recommendation of the Executive Board of the ICC.

2. The ICC Council appoints the Vice-Chairman of the Court from among the members of the Court or otherwise.

3. Its members are appointed by the ICC Council on the proposal of the National Committees, one member for each Committee.

4. On the proposal of the Chairman of the Court, the Council may appoint alternate members.

5. The term of office of all members is three years. If a member is no longer in a position to exercise his functions, his successor is appointed by the Council for the remainder of the term.

Article 4: Plenary Session of the Court

The Plenary Sessions of the Court are presided over by the Chairman, or, in his absence, by one of the Vice-Chairmen, designated by him. The deliberations shall be valid when at least six members are present. Decisions are taken by a majority vote, the Chairman having a casting vote in the event of a tie.

Article 5: Committees

The Court may set up one or more Committees and establish the functions and organization of such Committees.

Article 6: Confidentiality

The work of the Court is of a confidential nature and must be respected by everyone who participates in that work in whatever capacity. The Court lays down the rules regarding the persons who can attend the meetings of the Court and its Committees and who are entitled to have access to the materials submitted to the Court and its Secretariat.

Internal Rules of the International Court of Arbitration of the ICC

Article 1: Confidential Character of the Work of the International Court of Arbitration

1. The sessions of the Court, whether plenary or those of a Committee of the Court, are open only to its members and to the Secretariat.

2. However, in exceptional circumstances, the Chairman of the Court may invite other persons to attend. Such persons must respect the confidential nature of the work of the Court.

3. The documents submitted to the Court, or drawn up by it in the course of its proceedings, are communicated only to the members of the Court and to the Secretariat and to persons authorized by he Chairman to attend Court sessions.

4. The Chairman or the Secretary General of the Court may authorize researchers undertaking work of a scientific nature on international trade law to acquaint themselves with awards and other documents of general interest, with the exception of memoranda, notes, statements and documents remitted by the parties within the framework of arbitration proceedings.

5. Such authorization shall not be given unless the beneficiary has undertaken to respect the confidential character of the documents made available and to refrain from any publication in their respect without having previously submitted the text for approval to the Secretary General of the Court.

6. The Secretariat will in each case submitted to arbitration under the Rules retain in the archives of the Court all awards, terms of reference, and decisions of the Court as well as copies of the pertinent correspondence of the Secretariat.

7. Any documents, communications or correspondence submitted by the parties or the arbitrators may be destroyed unless a party or an arbitrator requests in writing within a period fixed by the Secretariat the return of such documents. All related costs and expenses for the return of those documents shall be paid by such party or arbitrator.

Article 2: Participation of Members of the International Court of Arbitration in ICC Arbitration

1. The Chairman and the members of the Secretariat of the Court may not act as arbitrators or as counsel in cases submitted to ICC arbitration.

2. The Court shall not appoint Vice-Chairmen, or members of the Court as arbitrators. They may, however, be proposed for such duties by one or more of the parties, or pursuant to any other procedure agreed upon by the parties, subject to confirmation by the Court.

3. When the Chairman, a Vice-Chairman or a member of the Court or of the Secretariat is involved in any capacity whatsoever in proceedings pending before the Court, such person must inform the Secretary General of the Court upon becoming aware of such involvement.

4. Such person must refrain from participating in the discussions or in the decisions of the Court concerning the proceedings and must be absent from the courtroom whenever the matter is considered.

5. Such person will not receive any material documentation or information pertaining to such proceedings.

Article 3: Relations between the Members of the Court and the ICC National Committees

1. By virtue of their capacity, the members of the Court are independent of the ICC National Committees which proposed them for appointment by the ICC Council.

2. Furthermore, they must regard as confidential, vis-à-vis the said National Committees, any information concerning individual cases with which they have become acquainted in their capacity as members of the Court, except when they have been requested by the Chairman of the Court or by its Secretary General to communicate specific information to their respective National Committee.

Article 4: Committee of the Court

1. In accordance with the provisions of Article 1(4) of the Rules and Article 5 of its Statutes (Appendix I), the Court hereby establishes a Committee of the Court.

2. The members of the Committee consist of a Chairman and at least two other members. The Chairman of the Court acts as the Chairman of the Committee. If absent, the Chairman may designate a Vice-Chairman of the Court or, in exceptional circumstances, another member of the Court as Chairman of the Committee.

3. The other two members of the Committee are appointed by the Court from among the Vice-Chairmen or other members of the Court. At each Plenary Session the Court appoints the members who are to attend the meetings of the Committee to be held before the next Plenary Session.

4. The Committee meets when convened by its Chairman. Two members constitute a quorum.

5. (a) The Court shall determine the decisions that may be taken by the Committee.

(b) The decisions of the Committee are taken unanimously.

(c) When the Committee cannot reach a decision or deems it preferable to abstain, it transfers the case to the next Plenary Session, making any suggestions it deems appropriate.

(d) The Committee's decisions are brought to the notice of the Court at its next Plenary Session.

Article 5: Court Secretariat

1. In case of absence, the Secretary General may delegate to the General Counsel and Deputy Secretary General the authority to confirm arbitrators, to certify true copies of awards and to request the payment of a provisional advance, respectively provided for in Articles 9(2), 28(2) and 30(1) of the Rules.

2. The Secretariat may, with the approval of the Court, issue notes and other documents for the information of the parties and the arbitrators, or as necessary for the proper conduct of the arbitral proceedings.

Article 6: Scrutiny of Arbitral Awards

When the Court scrutinizes draft awards in accordance with Article 27 of the Rules, it considers, to the extent practicable, the requirements of mandatory law at the place of arbitration.

Arbitration Costs and Fees

Article 1: Advance on Costs

1. Each request to commence an arbitration pursuant to the Rules must be accompanied by an advance payment of US$ 2,500 on the administrative expenses. Such payment is non-refundable, and shall be credited to the Claimant's portion of the advance on costs.

2. The provisional advance on costs fixed by the Secretary General according to Article 30(1) of the Rules shall normally not exceed the amount obtained by adding together the administrative expenses, the minimum of the fees (as set out in the scale hereinafter) based upon the amount of the claim and the expected reimbursable expenses of the Arbitral Tribunal incurred with respect to the drafting of the Terms of Reference. If such amount is not quantified, the provisional advance shall be fixed at the discretion of the Secretary General. Payment by the Claimant shall be credited to its share of the advance on costs fixed by the Court.

3. In general, after the Terms of Reference have been signed or approved by the Court and the provisional timetable has been established, the Arbitral Tribunal shall, in accordance with Article 30(4) of the Rules, proceed only with respect to those claims or counterclaims in regard to which the whole of the advance on costs has been paid.

4. The advance on costs fixed by the Court according to Article 30(2) of the Rules comprises the fees of the arbitrator or arbitrators (hereinafter referred to as "arbitrator"), any arbitration-related expenses of the arbitrator and the administrative expenses.

5. Each party shall pay in cash its share of the total advance on costs. However, if its share exceeds an amount fixed from time to time by the Court, a party may post a bank guarantee for this additional amount.

6. A party that has already paid in full its share of the advance on costs fixed by the Court may, in accordance with Article 30(3) of the Rules, pay the unpaid portion of the advance owned by the defaulting party by posting a bank guarantee.

7. When the Court has fixed separate advances on costs pursuant to Article 30(2) of the Rules, the Secretariat shall invite each party to pay the amount of the advance corresponding to its respective claims.

8. When, as a result of the fixing of separate advances on costs, the separate advance fixed for the claim of either party exceeds one-half of such global advance as was previously fixed (in respect of the same claims and counterclaims that are the object of separate advances), a bank guarantee may be posted to cover any such excess amount. In the event that the amount of the

separate advance is subsequently increased, at least one-half of the increase shall be paid in cash.

9. The Secretariat shall establish the terms governing all bank guarantees which the parties may post pursuant to the above provisions.

10. As provided in Article 30(2) of the Rules, the advance on costs may be subject to readjustment at any time during the arbitration, in particular to take into account fluctuations in the amount in dispute, changes in the amount of the estimated expenses of the arbitrator, or the evolving difficulty or complexity of arbitration proceedings.

11. Before any expertise ordered by the Arbitral Tribunal can be commenced, the parties, or one of them, shall pay an advance on costs fixed by the Arbitral Tribunal sufficient to cover the expected fees and expenses of the expert as determined by the Arbitral Tribunal. The Arbitral Tribunal shall be responsible for ensuring the payment by the parties of such fees and expenses.

Article 2: Costs and Fees

1. Subject to Article 31(2) of the Rules, the Court shall fix the fees of the arbitrator in accordance with the scale hereinafter set out, or, where the sum in dispute is not stated, at its discretion.

2. In setting the arbitrator's fees, the Court shall take into consideration the diligence of the arbitrator, the time spent, the rapidity of the proceedings, and complexity of the dispute so as to arrive at a figure within the limits specified, or, in exceptional circumstances (Article 31(2) of the Rules), at a figure higher or lower than those limits.

3. When a case is submitted to more than one arbitrator, the Court, at its discretion, shall have the right to increase the total fees up to a maximum which shall normally not exceed three times the fees of one arbitrator.

4. The arbitrator's fees and expenses shall be fixed exclusively by the Court as required by the Rules. Separate fee arrangements between the parties and the arbitrator are contrary to the Rules.

5. The Court shall fix the administrative expenses of each arbitration in accordance with the scale hereinafter set out, or, where the sum in dispute is not stated, at its discretion. In exceptional circumstances, the Court may fix the administrative expenses at a lower or higher figure than that which would result from the application of such scaleprovided that such expenses shall normally not exceed the maximum amount of the scale. Further, the Court may require the payment of administrative expenses in addition to those provided in scale of administrative expenses as a condition to holding an arbitration in abeyance at the request of the parties or of one of them with the acquiescence of the other.

6. If an arbitration terminates before the rendering of a final award, the Court shall fix the costs of the arbitration at its discretion, taking into account the

stage attained by the arbitral proceedings and any other relevant circumstances.

7. In the case of an application under Article 29(2) of the Rules, the Court may fix an advance to cover additional fees and expenses of the Arbitral Tribunal and may subordinate the transmission of such application to the Arbitral Tribunal to the prior cash payment in full to the ICC of such advance. The Court shall fix at its discretion any possible fees of the arbitrator when approving the decision of the Arbitral Tribunal.

8. When an arbitration is preceded by attempted conciliation, one-half of the administrative expenses paid for such conciliation shall be credited to the administrative expenses of the arbitration.

9. Amounts paid to the arbitrator do not include any possible value-added taxes (VAT) or other taxes or charges and imposts applicable to the arbitrator's fees or charges and imposts applicable to the arbitrator's fees. Parties are expected to pay any such taxes or changes; however, the recovery of any such charges or taxes is a matter solely between the arbitrator and the parties.

Article 3: Appointment of Arbitrators

1. A registration fee normally not exceeding US$ 2,500 is payable by the requesting party in respect of each request made to the ICC to appoint an arbitrator for any arbitration not conducted under the Rules. No requests for appointment of an arbitrator will be considered unless accompanied by the said fee, which is not recoverable and becomes the property of the ICC.

2. The said fee shall cover any additional services rendered by the ICC regarding the appointment, such as decisions on a challenge of an arbitrator and the appointment of a substitute arbitrator.

Article 4: Scales of Administrative Expenses and of Arbitrator's Fees

1. The Scales of Administrative Expenses and Arbitrator's Fees set forth below shall be effective as of January 1, 1998 in respect of all arbitrations commenced on or after such date, irrespective of the version of the Rules applying to such arbitrations.

2. To calculate the administrative expenses and the arbitrator's fees, the amounts calculated for each successive slice of the sum in dispute must be added together, except that where the sum in dispute is over US$ 80 million, a flat amount of US$ 75,800 shall constitute the entirety of the administrative expenses.

a) Administrative expenses

Sum in dispute (in US dollars)		Administrative expenses (*)
Up to	50,000	$2,500
From	50,001 to 100,000	3.50%
From	100,001 to 500,000	1.70%
From	500,001 to 1,000,000	1.15%
From	1,000,001 to 2,000,000	0.60%
From	2,000,001 to 5,000,000	0.20%
From	5,000,001 to 10,000,000	0.10%
From	10,000,000 to 50,000,000	0.06%
From	50,000,001 to 80,000,000	0.06%
Over	80,000,000	$75,800

(*) (For illustrative purposes only,, the table on the following page indicates the resulting administrative expenses in US $ when the proper calculations have been made.)

b) Arbitrator's Fees

Sum in (dispute in US Dollars)		Fees (**)	
		Minimum	Maximum
Up to	50,000	$2,500	17.00%
From	50,001 to 100,000	2.00%	11.00%
From	100,001 to 500,000	1.00%	5.50%
From	500,001 to 1,000,000	0.75%	3.50%
From	1,000,001 to 2,000,000	0.50%	2.50%
From	2,000,001 to 5,000,000	0.25%	1.00%
From	5,000,001 to 10,000,000	0.10%	0.55%
From	10,000,001 to 50,000,000	0.05%	0.17%
From	50,000,001 to 80,000,000	0.03%	0.12%
From	80,000,001 to 100,000,000	0.02%	0.10%
Over	100,000,000	0.01%	0.05%

(**) (For illustrative purpose only,, the table on the following page indicates the resulting range of fees when the proper calculations have been made.)

SUM IN DISPUTE (IN US DOLLARS)	A. ADMINISTRATIVE EXPENSES (*) (IN US DOLLARS) ADMINISTRATIVE EXPENSES	B. ARBITRATOR'S FEES (**) (IN US DOLLARS) MINIMUM	MAXIMUM
UP TO 50,000	2,500	2,500	17.00% OF THE SUM IN DISPUTE
FROM 50,001 TO 100,000	2,500 + 3.50% OF AMT. OVER 50,000	2,500 + 2.00% OF AMT. OVER 50,000	8,500 + 11.00% OF AMT. OVER 50,000
FROM 100,001 TO 500,000	4,250 + 1.70% OF AMT. OVER 100,000	3,500 + 1.00% OF AMT. OVER 100,000	14,000 + 5.50% OF AMT. OVER 100,000
FROM 500,001 TO 1,000,000	11,050 + 1.15% OF AMT. OVER 500,000	7,500 + 0.75% OF AMT. OVER 500,000	36,000 + 3.50% OF AMT. OVER 500,000
FROM 1,000,001 TO 2,000,000	16,800 + 0.60% OF AMT. OVER 1,000,000	11,250 + 0.50% OF AMT. OVER 1,000,000	53,500 + 2.50% OF AMT. OVER 1,000,000
FROM 2,000,001 TO 5,000,000	22,800 + 0.20% OF AMT. OVER 2,000,000	16,250 + 0.25% OF AMT. OVER 2,000,000	78,500 + 1.00% OF AMT. OVER 2,000,000
FROM 5,000,001 TO 10,000,000	28,800 + 0.10% OF AMT. OVER 5,000,000	23,750 + 0.10% OF AMT. OVER 5,000,000	108,500 + 0.55% OF AMT. OVER 5,000,000
FROM 10,000,001 TO 50,000,000	33,800 + 0.06% OF AMT. OVER 10,000,000	28,750 + 0.05% OF AMT. OVER 10,000,000	136,000 + 0.17% OF AMT. OVER 10,000,000
FROM 50,000,001 TO 80,000,000	57,800 + 0.06% OF AMT. OVER 50,000,000	48,750 + 0.03% OF AMT. OVER 50,000,000	204,000 + 0.12% OF AMT OVER 50,000,000
FROM 80,000,000 TO 100,000,000	75,800	57,750 + 0.02% OF AMT. OVER 80,000,000	240,000 + 0.10% OF AMT. OVER 80,000,000
OVER 100,000,000	75,800	61,750 + 0.01% OF AMT. OVER 100,000,000	260,000 + 0.05% OF AMT. OVER 100,000,000

Destination table: From 1975 Arbitration Rules to 1998 Arbitration Rules

Table A

TABLE A	
From: 1975 ARBITRATION RULES	To: 1998 ARBITRATION RULES
ARTICLE 1: INTERNATIONAL COURT OF ARBITRATION	
Article 1(1)	Article 1(1)
Article 1(2)	Article 1(2)
Article 1(3)	Article 1(3)
Article 1(4)	Article 1(4)
Article 1(5)	Article 1(5)
ARTICLE 2: THE ARBITRAL TRIBUNAL	
Article 2(1)	Article 1(2); Article 7(6); Article 9(1)
Article 2(2)	Article 2(i); Article 8(1)
Article 2(3)	Article 8(3)
Article 2(4)	Article 8(4)
Article 2(5)	Article 8(2)
Article 2(6)	Article 9(3); Article 9(4); Article 9(5); Article 9(6)
Article 2(7)	Article 7(1); Article 7(2); Article 7(3)
Article 2(8)	Article 11(1); Article 11(2)
Article 2(9)	Article 11(3)
Article 2(10)	Article 12(1)
Article 2(11)	Article 12(2); Article 12(3)
Article 2(12)	Article 12(4)
Article 2(13)	Article 7(4)
ARTICLE 3: REQUEST FOR ARBITRATION	
Article 3(1)	Article 4(1); Article 4(2)
Article 3(2)	Article 4(3)
Article 3(3)	Article 4(5)
ARTICLE 4: ANSWER TO THE REQUEST	
Article 4(1)	Article 5(1); Article 5(2)
Article 4(2)	Article 5(4)
ARTICLE 5: COUNTER-CLAIM	
Article 5(1)	Article 5(5)
Article 5(2)	Article 5(6)
ARTICLE 6: PLEADINGS AND WRITTEN STATEMENTS, NOTIFICATIONS OR COMMUNICATIONS	
Article 6(1)	Article 3(1)

TABLE A	
From: 1975 ARBITRATION RULES	**To: 1998 ARBITRATION RULES**
Article 6(2)	Article 3(2)
Article 6(3)	Article 3(3)
Article 6(4)	Article 3(4)
ARTICLE 7: ABSENCE OF AGREEEMENT TO ARBITRATE	
Article 7	Article 6(2)
ARTICLE 8: EFFECT OF THE AGREEMENT TO ARBITRATE	
Article 8(1)	Article 6(1)
Article 8(2)	Article 6(3)
Article 8(3)	Article 6(2)
Article 8(4)	Article 6(4)
Article 8(5)	Article 23(2)
ARTICLE 9: ADVANCE TO COVER COSTS OF ARBITRATION	
Article 9(1)	Article 30(2)
Article 9(2)	Article 30(3)
Article 9(3)	Article 13; Article 30(4)
Article 9(4)	Article 30(4)
ARTICLE 10: TRANSMISSION OF THE FILE TO THE ARBITRATOR	
Article 10	Article 13
ARTICLE 11: RULES GOVERNING THE PROCEEDIINGS	
Article 11	Article 15(1)
ARTICLE 12: PLACE OF ARBITRATION	
Article 12	Article 14(1)
ARTICLE 13: TERMS OF REFERENCE	
Article 13(1)	Article 18(1)
Article 13(2)	Article 18(2); Article 18(3)
Article 13(3)	Article 17(1)
Article 13(4)	Article 17(3)
Article 13(5)	Article 17(2)
ARTICLE 14: THE ARBITRAL PROCEEDINGS	
Article 14(1)	Article 20(1); Article 20(2); Article 20(3)
Article 14(2)	Article 20(4)
Article 14(3)	Article 20(6)
ARTICLE 15	
Article 15(1)	Article 21(1)
Article 15(2)	Article 21(2)
Article 15(3)	Article 16
Article 15(4)	Article 21(3)

TABLE A	
From: 1975 ARBITRATION RULES	**To: 1998 ARBITRATION RULES**
Article 15(5)	Article 21(4)
ARTICLE 16	
Article 16	Article 19
ARTICLE 17: AWARD BY CONSENT	
Article 17	Article 26
ARTICLE 18: TIME-LIMIT FOR AWARD	
Article 18(1)	Article 24(1)
Article 18(2)	Article 24(2)
Article 18(3)	N.A.
ARTICLE 19: AWARD BY THREE ARBITRATORS	
Article 19	Article 25(1)
ARTICLE 20: DECISION AS TO COSTS OF ARBITRATION	
Article 20(1)	Article 31(3)
Article 20(2)	Article 31(1)
Article 20(3)	Article 31(2)
ARTICLE 21: SCRUTINY OF AWARD BY THE COURT	
Article 21	Article 27
ARTICLE 22: MAKING OF AWARD	
Article 22	Article 25(3)
ARTICLE 23: NOTIFICATION OF AWARD TO PARTIES	
Article 23(1)	Article 28(1)
Article 23(2)	Article 28(2)
Article 23(3)	Article 28(3)
ARTICLE 24: FINALITY AND ENFORCEABILITY OF AWARD	
Article 24(1)	Article 28(6)
Article 24(2)	Article 28(6)
ARTICLE 25: DEPOSIT OF AWARD	
Article 25	Article 28(4); Article 28(5)
ARTICLE 26: GENERAL RULE	
Article 26	Article 35

Derivative table: From 1998 Arbitration Rules to 1975 Arbitration Rules

Table B

TABLE B	
From: 1998 ARBITRATION RULES	**To: 1975 ARBITRATION RULES**
INTRODUCTORY PROVISIONS	
ARTICLE 1: INTERNATIONAL COURT OF ARBITRATION	
Article 1(1)	Article 1(1); Article 1, Internal Rules
Article 1(2)	Article 2(1); Article 1(2)
Article 1(3)	Article 1(3)
Article 1(4)	Article 1(4)
Article 1(5)	Article 1(5)
ARTICLE 2: DEFINITIONS	
Article 2(i)	Article 2(2)
Article 2(ii)	NEW
Article 2(iii)	NEW
ARTICLE 3: WRITTEN NOTIFICATIONS OR COMMUNICATIONS; TIME LIMITS	
Article 3(1)	Article 6(1); NEW
Article 3(2)	Article 6(2)
Article 3(3)	Article 6(3)
Article 3(4)	Article 6(4)
COMMENCING THE ARBITRATION	
ARTICLE 4: REQUEST FOR ARBITRATION	
Article 4(1)	Article 3(1)
Article 4(2)	Article 3(1)
Article 4(3)	Article 3(2)
Article 4(4)	NEW
Article 4(5)	Article 3(3)
Article 4(6)	Article 13, Internal Rules
ARTICLE 5: ANSWER TO THE REQUEST; COUNTERCLAIMS	
Article 5(1)	Article 4(1)
Article 5(2)	Article 4(1)
Article 5(3)	NEW
Article 5(4)	Article 4(2)
Article 5(5)	Article 5(1)
Article 5(6)	Article 5(2)
ARTICLE 6: EFFECT OF THE ARBITRATION AGREEMENT	
Article 6(1)	Article 8(1)

TABLE B	
From: 1998 ARBITRATION RULES	**To: 1975 ARBITRATION RULES**
Article 6(2)	Article 8(3); Article 7; Article 12, Internal Rules
Article 6(3)	Article 8(2)
Article 6(4)	Article 8(4)
THE ARBITRAL TRIBUNAL	
ARTICLE 7: GENERAL PROVISIONS	
Article 7(1)	Article 2(7)
Article 7(2)	Article 2(7)
Article 7(3)	Article 2(7)
Article 7(4)	Article 2(13)
Article 7(5)	NEW
Article 7(6)	Article 2(1)
ARTICLE 8: NUMBER OF ARBITRATORS	
Article 8(1)	Article 2(2)
Article 8(2)	Article 2(5)
Article 8(3)	Article 2(3)
Article 8(4)	Article 2(4)
ARTICLE 9: APPOINTMENT AND CONFIRMATION OF THE ARBITRATORS	
Article 9(1)	Article 2(1)
Article 9(2)	NEW
Article 9(3)	Article 2(6)
Article 9(4)	Article 2(6)
Article 9(5)	Article 2(6)
Article 9(6)	Article 2(6)
ARTICLE 10: MULTIPLE PARTIES	
Article 10(1)	NEW
Article 10(2)	NEW
ARTICLE 11: CHALLENGE OF ARBITRATORS	
Article 11(1)	Article 2(8)
Article 11(2)	Article 2(8)
Article 11(3)	Article 2(9)
ARTICLE 12: REPLACEMENT OF ARBITRATORS	
Article 12(1)	Article 2(10)
Article 12(2)	Article 2(11)
Article 12(3)	Article 2(11)
Article 12(4)	Article 2(12)
Article 12(5)	NEW

TABLE B	
From: 1998 ARBITRATION RULES	**To: 1975 ARBITRATION RULES**
THE ARBITRAL PROCEEDINGS	
ARTICLE 13: TRANSMISSION OF THE FILE TO THE ARBITRAL TRIBUNAL	
Article 13	Article 9(3); Article 10
ARTICLE 14: PLACE OF THE ARBITRATION	
Article 14(1)	Article 12
Article 14(2)	NEW
Article 14(3)	NEW
ARTICLE 15: RULES GOVERNING THE PROCEEDINGS	
Article 15(1)	Article 11
Article 15(2)	NEW
ARTICLE 16: LANGUAGE OF THE ARBITRATION	
Article 16	Article 15(3)
ARTICLE 17: APPLICABLE RULES OF LAW	
Article 17(1)	Article 13(3)
Article 17(2)	Article 13(5)
Article 17(3)	Article 13(4)
ARTICLE 18: TERMS OF REFERENCE; PROCEDURAL TIMETABLE	
Article 18(1)	Article 13(1)
Article 18(2)	Article 13(2)
Article 18(3)	Article 13(2)
Article 18(4)	NEW
ARTICLE 19: NEW CLAIMS	
Article 19	Article 16
ARTICLE 20: ESTABLISHING THE FACTS OF THE CASE	
Article 20(1)	Article 14(1)
Article 20(2)	Article 14(1)
Article 20(3)	Article 14(1)
Article 20(4)	Article 14(2)
Article 20(5)	NEW
Article 20(6)	Article 14(3)
Article 20(7)	NEW
ARTICLE 21: HEARINGS	
Article 21(1)	Article 15(1)
Article 21(2)	Article 15(2)
Article 21(3)	Article 15(4)
Article 21(4)	Article 15(5)

TABLE B	
From: 1998 ARBITRATION RULES	**To: 1975 ARBITRATION RULES**
ARTICLE 22: CLOSING OF THE PROCEEDINGS	
Article 22(1)	NEW
Article 22(2)	NEW
ARTICLE 23: CONSERVATORY AND INTERIM MEASURES	
Article 23(1)	NEW
Article 23(2)	NEW; Article 8(5)
AWARDS	
ARTICLE 24: TIME LIMIT FOR THE AWARD	
Article 24(1)	Article 18(1)
Article 24(2)	Article 18(2)
ARTICLE 25: MAKING OF THE AWARD	
Article 25(1)	Article 19
Article 25(2)	NEW
Article 25(3)	Article 22
ARTICLE 26: AWARD BY CONSENT	
Article 26	Article 17
ARTICLE 27: SCRUTINY OF THE AWARD BY THE COURT	
Article 27	Article 21
ARTICLE 28: NOTIFICATION, DEPOSIT AND ENFORCEABILITY OF THE AWARD	
Article 28(1)	Article 23(1)
Article 28(2)	Article 23(2)
Article 28(3)	Article 23(3)
Article 28(4)	Article 25
Article 28(5)	Article 25
Article 28(6)	Article 24(1); Article 24(2)
ARTICLE 29: CORRECTION AND INTERPRETATION OF THE AWARD	
Article 29(1)	NEW
Article 29(2)	NEW
Article 29(3)	NEW
COSTS	
ARTICLE 30: ADVANCE TO COVER THE COSTS OF THE ARBITRATION	
Article 30(1)	NEW
Article 30(2)	Article 9(1)
Article 30(3)	Article 9(2); Article 14, Internal Rules
Article 30(4)	Article 9(3); Article 15, Internal Rules
Article 30(5)	Article 16, Internal Rules

TABLE B	
From: 1998 ARBITRATION RULES	To: 1975 ARBITRATION RULES
ARTICLE 31: DECISION AS TO THE COSTS OF THE ARBITRATION	
Article 31(1)	Article 20(2)
Article 31(2)	Article 20(3)
Article 31(3)	Article 20(1)
MISCELLANEOUS	
ARTICLE 32: MODIFIED TIME LIMITS	
Article 32(1)	NEW
Article 32(2)	NEW
ARTICLE 33: WAIVER	
Article 33	NEW
ARTICLE 34: EXCLUSION OF LIABILITY	
Article 34	NEW
ARTICLE 35: GENERAL RULE	
Article 35	Article 26

Appendix III

ICC Rules for Expertise

ICC Rules for Documentary
Credit Dispute Resolution
Expertise (Docdex Rules)

ICC/CMI Rules for International
Maritime Arbitration

ICC Pre-Arbitral Referee
Procedure

ICC Rules for Expertise

SECTION 1: General Provisions

Article 1: The International Court for Expertise

1. The International Centre for Expertise which was established by the International Chamber of Commerce (ICC) has for its function the appointment or the proposal of experts in connection with international business transactions.

2. The Centre consists of a Standing Committee and a Secretariat.

The Standing Committee is composed of five members (a chairman and four members) of different nationalities all of whom are appointed by the ICC for a three year renewable term.

The Secretariat of the Centre is assumed by the ICC.

Article 2: Recourse to the International Centre for Expertise

1. Any request for the appointment or proposal of an expert shall be submitted to the ICC International Centre for Expertise, at the ICC Headquarters in Paris.

2. The request shall contain inter alia the following information:

− names, description and addresses of the parties involved

− where applicable, a copy of the parties' agreement to have recourse to the ICC International Centre for Expertise

− any relevant indications concerning the choice of an expert

− a descriptive summary of the expert's brief.

Article 3: Manner in which an Expert is Chosen

Any appointment or proposal of an expert as well as any decision on the replacement of an expert, in accordance with Articles 4, 5 and 7, shall be made as quickly as possible by the Chairman of the Standing Committee after consultation with members of the Standing Committee.

SECTION 2: Proposal of an Expert

Article 4:

At the request of an arbitral tribunal or any person, the Chairman of the Standing Committee may propose the name(s) of one or more experts.

The Centre's intervention ends on notification of the proposal.

SECTION 3: Appointment of an Expert and Expertise Procedure

Article 5: Appointment of an Expert

1. Where the parties have agreed to have recourse to the ICC International Centre for Expertise, one or more parties may request the Centre to appoint an

expert. If the request for appointment is not made jointly by all the parties to the agreement, the Secretariat of the Centre shall send a copy of the request to the other party or parties who may make representations within a time limit fixed by the Secretariat according to the circumstances of the case.

2. Subject to Article 6, the Chairman of the Standing Committee shall confirm the choice of the expert nominated by the parties by mutual consent. Failing such an agreement, the Chairman shall appoint an expert.

Article 6: the Expert's Independence

Prior to an appointment, the Centre shall invite the prospective expert to submit a declaration confirming his independence of the parties.

Article 7: Replacement of an Expert

1. The Chairman of the Standing Committee shall decide on the replacement of an expert who has died or resigns or is unable to carry out his functions.

The Chairman may replace the expert, after having considered the expert's observations, if any, where objections are made by one of the parties concerning the person appointed as expert.

2. The Chairman may also replace the expert if he should find, after having considered the expert's observations, if any, that the expert is not fulfilling his functions in accordance with the Rules or within any prescribed time limits.

Article 8: The Expert's Brief

1.

a) The expert is empowered to make findings within the limits set by the request for expertise, after giving the parties an opportunity to make submissions.

b) The expert may also be empowered, by express agreement between the parties, either in a prior agreement or in their request for the appointment of an expert, to:

– recommend, as needed, those measures which he deems most appropriate for the performance of the contract and/or those which would be necessary in order to safeguard the subject matter supervise the carrying out of the contractual operations.

2. In agreeing to the applications of theses Rules the parties undertake to provide the expert with all the facilities in order to implement his Brief and, in particular, to make available all documents he may consider necessary and also to grant him free access to any place where the expertise operations are being carried out. The information given to the expert will be used only for the purpose of the expertise and shall remain confidential.

3. Unless otherwise agreed the findings or recommendations of the expert shall not be binding upon the parties.

Article 9: Notification of the Expert's Report

The expert shall send his report to the centre in as many copies as there are parties plus one for the Centre. Thereafter, the Centre shall notify the expert's report to the parties.

SECTION 4: Costs of the Expertise

Article 10: Costs Where an Expert is Proposed

Each request for the proposal of an expert shall be accompanied by an amount of US $ 1,000. This amount represents the total administrative costs for any proposal of experts.

Article 11: Costs Where an Expert is Appointed

1. Each request for the appointment of an expert shall be accompanied by an amount of US $ 1,000. This amount, which is not refundable, shall be credited to the Centre's administrative costs.

2.

a) The costs of the expertise, where an expert is appointed under these Rules, comprise the expert's fees and expenses, and the administrative cost of the ICC International Centre for Expertise.

b) Before the appointment of the expert, the Chairman of the Standing Committee, following consultation with the expert and the requesting party(ies) shall determine the basis upon which the expert's fees and expenses are to be calculated.

c) The Chairman of the Standing Committee shall determine the amount of the administrative costs which in any case shall be neither greater than 15 % of the expert's fees nor less than US $ 1,000.

3. The estimated costs for the expertise as fixed by the Chairman of the Standing Committee are payable to the Centre by the party or parties requesting the appointment prior to the commencement of the expertise operations. This estimated amount may be readjusted by the Chairman of the Standing Committee in the course of the expertise.

4. The amount of costs shall be fixed by the Chairman of the Standing Committee upon conclusion of the expertise operations and the balance, if any, shall be payable before the notification of the Report to the parties.

Model Expertise Clause

"The parties to this agreement agree to have recourse, if the need arises, to the International Centre for Expertise of the International Chamber of Commerce in accordance with the ICC's Rules for Expertise".

Request for the Centre's Intervention

Parties wishing to use the Centre's services should contact:

The ICC International Centre for Expertise
38, Cours Albert 1er
75008 Paris FRANCE

ICC Rules for Documentary Credit Dispute Resolution Expertise
DOCDEX RULES

Article 1: Dispute Resolution Service

1.1 These Rules concern a service called the "Documentary Credit Dispute Expertise" (DOCDEX) which is available in connection with any dispute related to

− a documentary credit incorporating the Uniform Customs and Practice for Documentary Credits (UCP), and

− the application of the UCP and/or of the Uniform Rules for Bank-to-Bank Reimbursement under Documentary Credits (URR).

1.2 DOCDEX is made available by the International Chamber of Commerce (ICC) through its International Centre for Expertise (Centre) under the auspices of the ICC Commission on Banking Technique and Practice (Banking Commission).

1.3 When a dispute is submitted to the Centre in accordance with these Rules, the Centre shall appoint three experts from a list of experts maintained by the Banking Commission. These three experts (Appointed Experts) shall make a decision which, after consultation with the Technical Adviser of the Banking Commission, shall be rendered by the Centre as a DOCDEX Decision in accordance with these Rules. The DOCDEX Decision is not intended to conform with any legal requirements of an arbitration award.

1.4 Unless otherwise agreed, a DOCDEX Decision shall not be binding upon the parties.

1.5 In the DOCDEX procedure the communication with the Centre shall be conducted exclusively in writing, i.e. by communication received in a form that provides a complete record thereof, via teletransmission or other expeditious means.

Article 2: Request

2.1 The Initiator shall apply for a DOCDEX Decision by submission of a request (Request). The Initiator may be one of the parties to the dispute applying individually, or more or all parties to the dispute submitting jointly a single Request. The Request, including all documents annexed thereto, shall be supplied to the Centre in Paris, France, in four copies.

2.2 A Request shall be concise and contain all necessary information clearly presented, in particular the following:

2.2.1 full name and address of the Initiator, clearly stating such Initiator's function(s) in connection with the documentary credit, and

2.2.2 full name and address of any other party to the dispute (Respondent), clearly stating such Respondent's function(s) in connection with the documentary credit, where the Request is not submitted jointly by all parties to the dispute, and

2.2.3 a statement of the Initiator formally requesting a DOCDEX Decision in accordance with the ICC Documentary Credit Dispute Expertise Rules, ICC Publication No. 577, and

2.2.4 a summary of the dispute and of the Initiator's claims, clearly identifying all issues related to the documentary credit and the UCP and/or URR to be determined, and

2.2.5 copies of the documentary credit in dispute, all amendments thereto, and all documents deemed necessary to establish the relevant circumstances, and

2.2.6 a statement by the Initiator that a copy of such Request, including all documents annexed thereto, has been sent to each Respondent named in the Request.

2.3 The Request must be accompanied by the payment of the Standard Fee as per the Appendix hereto.

Article 3: Answer

3.1 The Respondent may submit an Answer to the Initiator's Request. The Respondent may be one or more of the parties to the dispute named in the Request as Respondent, each submitting an individual Answer or submitting only a single Answer. The Answer must be received by the Centre within the period stipulated in the Centre's Acknowledgement of the Request (*see Article 5*). The Answer, including all documents annexed thereto, shall be supplied to the Centre in Paris, France in four copies.

3.2 An Answer shall be concise and contain all necessary information clearly presented, in particular the following:

3.2.1 name and address of the Initiator, and

3.2.2 date of the relevant Request, and

3.2.3 a statement of the Respondent formally requesting a DOCDEX Decision in accordance with the ICC Documentary Credit Dispute Expertise Rules, ICC Publication No. 577, and

3.2.4 a summary of the Respondent's claims, clearly referring to all issues related to the documentary credit and the UCP and/or URR to be determined, and

3.2.5 copies of all additional documents deemed necessary to establish the relevant circumstances, and

3.2.6 a statement of the Respondent that a copy of such Answer, including all documents annexed thereto, has been sent in writing to the Initiator and to the other Respondent named in the Request.

3.3 If the Respondent does not provide a statement pursuant to Art. 3.2.3, then the final DOCDEX Decision will not be made available to him.

Article 4: Supplements

4.1 Request, Answers and Supplements shall be final as received.

4.2 The Centre may ask the Initiator and Respondent, by way of an Invitation, to submit specific supplementary information, including copies of documents, relevant to the DOCDEX Decision (Supplement).

4.3 Supplements must be received by the Centre in four copies within the period stipulated in the Invitation. The Supplement shall be concise and contain all necessary information clearly presented and include copies of relevant documents. It shall also contain:

4.3.1 date and reference as stated in the Invitation, and

4.3.2 name and address of the issuer of such Supplement, and

4.3.3 a statement of the issuer of such Supplement that a copy of the Supplement, including all documents annexed thereto, has been sent to the Initiator or Respondent.

4.4 Supplements shall only be submitted to the Centre upon and in accordance with an Invitation issued by the Centre.

Article 5: Acknowledgements and Rejections

5.1 The Centre shall confirm the receipt of Requests, Answers and Supplements to the Initiator and Respondent (Acknowledgement).

5.2 The Centre will stipulate a reasonable period of time within which each Answer or Supplement must be received by the Centre. The stipulated time should not exceed 30 days after the date of the Acknowledgement of the receipt of a Request or 14 days after the date of an Invitation to submit a Supplement.

5.3 Any Answer or Supplement received by the Centre after expiry of the period of time specified in the relevant Acknowledgement or Invitation, or any communication not solicited by the Centre, shall be disregarded.

5.4 By advice to the Initiator and Respondent, the Centre may reject at any time, before or after its Acknowledgement, any Request, Answer or Supplement, in whole or part,

5.4.1 where the Centre or Appointed Experts deem any issue to be determined to be unrelated to a documentary credit and the UCP and/or URR, or

5.4.2 which in other respects does not fulfil the requirements of these Rules, or

5.4.3 in respect of which the Standard Fee has not been received by the Centre within 14 days after the date of the Request.

5.5 Periods of time specified in these Rules or in any Acknowledgement or Invitation referring to days shall be deemed to refer to consecutive calendar days and shall start to run on the day following the date of issuance stated in the relevant Acknowledgment or Invitation. If the last day of the relevant period of time is, or any fixed day falls on, a non-business day in Paris, France, then the period of time shall expire at the end of the first following business day in Paris.

Article 6: Appointment of Experts

6.1 The Banking Commission will maintain an internal list of experts having profound experience and knowledge of documentary credits and the UCP and/or URR.

6.2 Upon receipt of a Request, the Centre shall appoint three independent experts from the list. Each Appointed Expert shall declare his independence of the parties indicated in the Request. The Centre shall designate one of the three Appointed Experts to act as their Chair.

6.3 An Appointed Expert shall at all times keep strictly confidential all information and documents related to any DOCDEX case.

6.4 Where an Appointed Expert deems that he is unable to carry out his functions, he shall immediately give notice of termination to the Centre. Where the Centre deems that an Appointed Expert is unable to carry out his functions, it shall immediately give notice of termination to such Appointed Expert. In either case, such Appointed Expert shall immediately return to the Centre the Request, Answer(s) and Supplement(s) received, including all documents annexed thereto, and the Centre shall inform the other Appointed Experts of such termination.

6.5 The Centre shall, without delay, replace an Appointed Expert whose appointment is prematurely terminated pursuant to Article 6.4 of these Rules and the Centre shall inform the other Appointed Experts accordingly.

Article 7: Appointed Experts' Procedure

7.1 Upon receipt of the Standard Fee, the Centre shall submit to the Appointed Experts the Request, Answer(s) and Supplement(s) received in connection therewith.

7.2 The Appointed Experts shall render their decision impartially and exclusively on the basis of the Request, Answer(s) and Supplement(s) thereto, the documentary credit, and the UCP and/or URR.

7.3 Where it is deemed necessary by the Appointed Experts, their Chair may ask the Centre to invite the Initiator and Respondent, pursuant to Article 4 of these Rules, to provide additional information and/or copies of documents.

7.4 Within 30 days after they have received all information and documents deemed by them to be necessary and appropriate to the issues to be determined, the Appointed Experts shall draft a decision and their Chair shall submit the decision to the Centre.

7.5 Neither the Initiator nor the Respondent shall

— seek an oral hearing in front of the Appointed Experts.

— request the ICC to reveal the name of any Appointed Expert,

— seek to have an Appointed Expert or officer of the Banking Commission called as witness, expert or in any similar function to an arbitral tribunal or a court of law hearing the dispute in connection with which such Appointed Expert or officer of the Banking Commission participated by rendering a DOCDEX Decision.

Article 8: DOCDEX Decision

8.1 Upon receipt of the decision of the Appointed Experts, the Centre shall consult with the Technical Adviser of the Banking Commission or his nominated delegate, to ascertain that the DOCDEX Decision will be in line with the UCP and/or URR and their interpretation by the Banking Commission. Amendments suggested by the Technical Adviser (or his delegate) shall be subject to the consent of the majority of the Appointed Experts.

8.2 Subject to Article 10.2 of these Rules, the Centre will issue and make available the DOCDEX Decision without delay to

8.2.1 the Initiator and

8.2.2 the Respondent who has requested, pursuant to Article 3.2.3, a DOCDEX Decision in accordance with the ICC Documentary Credit Dispute Expertise Rules, ICC Publication No. 577.

8.3 The DOCDEX Decision shall be issued by the Centre in the English language, unless Appointed Experts decide otherwise, and shall contain, *inter alia*, the following

8.3.1 names of the Initiator and Respondent, and

8.3.2 summary of the representations relevant to the issues determined, and

8.3.3 determination of the issues and the decisions taken with succinctly stated reasons therefor, and

8.3.4 date of issuance and signature for and on behalf of the Centre.

8.4 The DOCDEX Decision shall be deemed to be made at Paris, France, and on the date of its issuance by the Centre.

Article 9: Deposit and publication of the DOCDEX Decision

9.1 An original of each DOCDEX Decision shall be deposited with the Centre and shall be kept there for 10 years.

9.2 the ICC may publish any DOCDEX Decision, provided always the identities of the parties to the dispute are not disclosed.

Article 10: Costs of DOCDEX

10.1 The costs of the DOCDEX service shall be the Standard Fee set out in the Appendix. The Standard Fee shall not be recoverable. In exceptional circumstances, an Additional Fee may be payable which shall be fixed by the centre at its discretion, taking into account the complexity of the issue and subject to the ceiling set out in the Appendix under "Additional Fee". Such Additional Fee shall be invoiced to the Initiator within a reasonable time, at the latest within 45 days or after the date of the Acknowledgement of the Request. No Additional Fee will be charged where the amount of the letter of credit in dispute does not exceed the minimum amount stated in the Appendix.

10.2 The DOCDEX Decision shall not be issued until the Centre has received the Standard Fee and, if invoice, any Additional Fee.

Article 11: General

11.1 In all matters not expressly provided for in these Rules, the Centre, experts, Appointed Experts, officers, officials and employees of the ICC shall adhere to strict confidentiality and shall act in the spirit of these Rules.

11.2 Appointed Experts, officers, officials and employees of the ICC assume no liability or responsibility for the consequences arising out of delay and/or loss in transit of any message(s), letter(s), or document(s), or for delay, mutilation or other error(s) arising in the transmission of any telecommunication, or for errors in translation and/or interpretation of technical terms.

11.3 Appointed Experts, officers, officials and employees of the ICC assume no liability or responsibility for the discharge or purported discharge of their functions in connection with any DOCDEX Decision, unless the act or omission is shown not to have been in good faith.

Appendix to the ICC DOCDEX Rules

1. Standard fee:

The Standard Fee, which includes administrative expenses and expert fees, is USD 5,000.

2. Additional fee:

Pursuant to Article 10.1 of these Rules the Centre may, if the amount of the letter of credit exceeds USD 100,000, charge an Additional Fee of up to 100% of the Standard Fee.

3. Payment

Any payment made towards such fees shall be made in United States Dollars to the International Chamber of Commerce in Paris

− by credit transfer to

> Bank SARASIN, Elisabethenstrasse, No.62,
> Postfach CH 4002 Basel
> Account No.0.25047-0 30 01, or

− by cheque payable to the International Chamber of Commerce, or

− by Visa Card stating
Expiration date...
Visa Card Number.......................................
Name on card ....
Signature..Date................

4. Transmission:

Any such payment shall be accompanied by an advice in writing to the

> International Chamber of Commerce
> International Centre for Expertise
> 38, Cours Albert 1er
> F-75008 Paris
> France
> Fax: 33 1 49 53 28 59

stating the following data

− Name:..

− Business Title: ....

− Company: ....

− Address: ....

− Code/ Postal code: ....

− Date of Request: ....

5. General:

This Appendix is subject to change without notice. Please enquire with the International Chamber of Commerce as to the applicable version of this Appendix.

ICC/CMI Rules for International Maritime Arbitration

The ICC-CMI Arbitral Organization

Article 1

The International Chamber of Commerce (ICC) and the Comité Maritime International (CMI) have jointly decided, with a view to providing a service to the maritime world at large, to issue rules for the conduct of arbitration disputes relating to maritime affairs including inter alia contracts of chartering, contracts of carriage by sea or of combined transport, contracts of marine insurance, salvage, general average, shipbuilding and ship repairing contracts, contracts of sale of vessels and other contracts creating rights in vessels.

Article 2

1. An institutional body known as the "Standing Committee on Maritime Arbitration" (hereinafter referred to as the Standing Committee) will have the duty of ensuring the application of these Rules.

2. The Standing Committee shall be composed of twelve members: six appointed by the ICC and six by the CMI.

The members of the Standing Committee shall be appointed for three years.

3. The Chairman of the Standing Committee, selected from among its members, shall be appointed jointly by the ICC and the CMI.

Likewise from among the members of the Standing Committee, two Vice-Chairmen shall be appointed: one by the ICC and one by the CMI.

4. The Secretariat of the Standing Committee shall be provided by the ICC and its costs shall be met by the parties seeking arbitration under these Rules.

The seat of the Standing Committee will be 38, Cours Albert ler, 75008 Paris (France), where the meetings of the Standing Committee will be held unless otherwise agreed.

5. The Standing Committee shall have power to deliberate when at least two of the members appointed by the ICC and two of the members appointed by the CMI are present. Decisions shall be taken within the Committee by a simple majority. If no majority is attained, the Chairman of the meeting shall have a casting vote.

Request for arbitration and Defendant's answer

Article 3

1. Where the parties have agreed that disputes between them shall be referred to arbitration under these Rules, such disputes shall be settled in accordance with these Rules subject to such modification as the parties may agree.

2. A party wishing to have recourse to ICC-CMI maritime arbitration shall submit its Request to the Secretariat of the Standing Committee with a copy of it to the Defendant.

The date when the Request is received by the Secretariat shall be deemed, for all purposes, to be the date of commencement of the arbitration proceedings.

3. The Request for arbitration shall contain the following information:

a) names in full, description, and addresses of the parties

b) a summary of the claimant's points of claim

c) the document containing the arbitration clause or the arbitration agreement

d) such documents as are deemed relevant to clarify the subject matter of the dispute

e) all relevant particulars concerning the number and appointment of arbitrators.

4. Disputes shall be settled by a sole arbitrator or by three arbitrators if circumstances so require. In the following Articles, the word "arbitrator" denotes a single arbitrator or three arbitrators as the case may be.

Article 4

1. The Defendant shall within 21 days from the date on which he receives the Claimant's request for arbitration state whether he agrees that the dispute be submitted to arbitration according to these Rules and, if so, comment on the proposals made concerning the number and appointment of arbitrators and, where appropriate, nominate an arbitrator.

2. If the Defendant objects to submitting the dispute to arbitration according to these Rules, the Claimant shall have a period of 15 days from the day such objection is communicated to him to comment on the Defendant's objection. If the Claimant agrees that there is no agreement that the dispute be submitted to arbitration under these Rules, the parties will be informed by the Secretariat that the proceedings are discontinued. If the Claimant maintains that there is a valid arbitration agreement, the matter shall be referred to the Standing Committee and resolved according to the provisions of Art. 5.

3. The Defendant's failure to reply within the time mentioned above to the Claimant's request for arbitration shall be considered as an objection to the request.

4. The Defendant shall have a period of 30 days from the date when he has notified the Secretariat of his agreement to the Claimant's request for arbitration or, failing such agreement, from the date when he has received notice of the Standing Committee's decision that the arbitration shall proceed, to file his defence and supply relevant documents.

5. Within the last-mentioned time limit the Defendant may in his defence make a counter-claim to which the Claimant may file a reply within 21 days from the date it was communicated to him.

6. The time limits stipulated in this Article may, upon the request of either party, be extended by the Secretariat but not for more than an additional period of 30 days unless the parties otherwise agree. If a longer extension is requested, or failing such an agreement if the Secretariat refuses to grant an extension, the request shall be submitted to the Standing Committee.

Validity of the arbitration agreement

Article 5

1. Should one of the parties raise one or more pleas concerning the existence or validity of the agreement to arbitrate, and should the Standing Committee be satisfied of the prima facie existence of such an agreement, the Standing Committee may, without prejudice to the admissibility or merits of the plea or pleas, decide that the arbitration shall proceed. In such a case any decision as to the arbitrator's jurisdiction shall be taken by the arbitrator himself.

2. Unless otherwise provided, the arbitrator shall not cease to have jurisdiction by reason of any claim that the contract containing the arbitration agreement is null and void or allegation that it is non-existent provided that he upholds the validity of the agreement to arbitrate. He shall continue to have jurisdiction, even though the contract itself may be non-existent or null and void, to determine the respective rights of the parties and to adjudicate upon their claims and pleas.

3. If one of the parties refuses or fails to take part in the arbitration, the arbitration shall proceed notwithstanding such refusal or failure.

Constitution of the Arbitral Tribunal

Article 6

1. Insofar as the parties have not themselves appointed arbitrators, and unless the parties have otherwise agreed, the Standing Committee shall appoint arbitrators in accordance with the provisions of this Article.

2. Where the parties have agreed that the disputes shall be settled by a sole arbitrator and fail so to nominate him within 30 days from the date when the Claimant's Request for Arbitration has been communicated to the other party, the sole arbitrator shall be appointed by the Standing Committee.

3. Where the dispute is to be referred to three arbitrators, each party shall nominate in the Request for Arbitration and in the Answer thereto one arbitrator. Such person shall be independent of the party nominating him. If a party fails to nominate an arbitrator, the appointment shall be made by the Standing Committee. The third arbitrator, who will act as chairman of the arbitral tribunal, shall be appointed by the arbitrators nominated by the parties

(unless the parties have nominated such third arbitrator) within a fixed time limit. Should the two arbitrators fail, within the time limit fixed by the parties or the Standing Committee, to reach agreement on the third arbitrator, he shall be appointed by the Standing Committee.

4. Where the parties have not agreed upon the number of arbitrators, the Standing Committee shall appoint a sole arbitrator, save where it appears to the Standing Committee that the dispute is such as to warrant the appointment of three arbitrators. In such a case the parties shall each have a period of 21 days within which to nominate an arbitrator.

5. Where the Standing Committee is to appoint a sole arbitrator or the Chairman of an arbitral tribunal, the sole arbitrator or the Chairman of an arbitral tribunal shall be chosen from a country other than those of which the parties are nationals. However, in suitable circumstances and provided that neither of the parties objects, the sole arbitrator or the Chairman of the arbitral tribunal may be chosen from a country of which any one of the parties is a national.

6. Should an arbitrator be challenged by one of the parties, the Standing Committee, as sole judge of the grounds of challenge shall make a decision which shall be final.

7. If an arbitrator dies or is prevented from carrying out his functions or has to resign consequent upon a challenge or for any other reason, or if the Standing Committee, after having considered the arbitrator's observations, decides that the arbitrator is not fulfilling his functions in accordance with the Rules or within the prescribed time limits, he shall be replaced. In all such cases the procedure indicated in the preceding paragraphs 2, 3 and 5 shall be followed.

When an arbitrator is replaced, prior hearings may be repeated at the discretion of the new arbitral tribunal.

Deposit of costs

Article 7

1. The Standing Committee shall fix the amount of the deposit in a sum likely to cover the administrative costs of arbitration of the claims which have been referred to it and, after consulting the arbitrator, his fee and costs.

Where, apart from the principal claim, one or more counterclaims are submitted, the Standing Committee may fix separate deposits for the principal claim and the counterclaim or counterclaims.

2. It is for the Claimant or Counter-claimant as the case may be to make the deposit(s) referred to in (1) above.

3. The Secretariat may make the transmission of documents to the arbitrator conditional upon the payment by the parties or one of them of the whole or part of the deposit to the Secretariat of the Standing Committee.

4. Before proceeding to establish the facts of the case, in accordance with the provisions of Article 11, the arbitrator shall inquire of the Secretariat whether the requests for deposit have been complied with.

The arbitrator shall only proceed in respect of those claims for which he has received confirmation from the Secretariat of the payment of the deposit.

Place of Arbitration, Procedure and Applicable Law

Article 8

The place of arbitration shall be that agreed by the parties. In the absence of such an agreement, the place of arbitration will be fixed by the Standing Committee.

Article 9

Unless otherwise agreed, the Rules governing the proceedings before the arbitrator shall be those set out in these Rules and, where these Rules are silent, any Rules which the parties (or, failing them, the arbitrator) may settle.

Article 10

1. The parties shall be free to determine the law to be applied by the arbitrator to the merits of the dispute. In the absence of any indication by the parties as to the applicable law, the arbitrator shall apply the law designated as the proper law by the rule of conflict of laws which he deems appropriate.

2. The arbitrator shall assume the powers of an amiable compositeur only if the parties have agreed to give him such powers.

Arbitration proceedings

Article 11

1. All pleadings and written statements submitted by the parties, as well as all documents annexed thereto, shall be sent with one copy of each to the Secretariat, the other party and the arbitrator. When the arbitrator has not yet been appointed the copies intended for him shall be sent to the Secretariat which, subject to the provisions of Art. 7 (3), shall transmit them to the arbitrator when appointed.

All notifications or communications from the parties, the Secretariat and the arbitrator shall be validly made if they are delivered against receipt or forwarded by registered post to the address or last known address of the party for whom the same are intended.

Notification or communication shall be deemed to have been effected on the day when it was received, or should, if made in accordance with the preceding paragraph, have been received by the party itself or by its representative.

2. The parties shall be at liberty to apply to any competent judicial authority for such measures as are outside the jurisdiction of the arbitrator and they

shall not by so doing be held to infringe the agreement to arbitrate or to affect the relevant powers reserved to the arbitrator.

3. The arbitrator shall proceed within as short a time as possible to establish the facts of the case. He may fix time limits. After study of the written submissions of the parties and of all documents relied upon, the arbitrator shall hear the parties if one of the parties so requests failing such a request he may of his own motion decide to hear them.

In addition, the arbitrator may decide to hear any other person in the presence of the parties or in their absence provided they have been duly summoned.

4. The arbitrator may appoint one or more experts, define their terms of reference, receive their reports and/or hear them in person in the presence of the parties or in their absence provided they have been duly summoned.

5. The arbitrator may decide the case on the relevant documents alone if the parties so request or agree.

6. At the request of one of the parties or if necessary on his own initiative, the arbitrator, giving reasonable notice, shall summon the parties to appear before him on the day and at the place appointed by him and shall so inform the Secretariat.

7. If one of the parties, although duly summoned, fails to appear, the arbitrator, if he is satisfied that the summons was duly received and the party is absent without valid excuse, shall have power to proceed with the arbitration.

Such proceedings shall then be deemed to have been conducted in the presence of all parties.

8. The arbitrator shall determine the language or languages of the arbitration, due regard being paid to all the relevant circumstances and in particular to the language of the contract.

9. The arbitrator shall be in full charge of the hearings, at which all the parties shall be entitled to be present. Save with the approval of the arbitrator and of the parties, person not involved in the proceedings shall not be admitted.

10. The parties may appear in person or through duly appointed representatives. In addition, they may be assisted by advisers.

The Arbitration award

Article 12

1. If the parties reach a settlement the same shall, if the parties so request and the arbitrators agree, be recorded in the form of an arbitral award made by consent of the parties.

2. The arbitrator shall make his award within six months after the date for the constitution of the arbitral tribunal. The Standing Committee may, if necessary, extend this time.

3. Where no such extension is granted and, if appropriate, after application of the provisions of Art. 6 (7), the Standing Committee shall determine the manner in which the dispute is to be resolved.

4. When three arbitrators have been appointed, the award is given by a majority decision. If there be no majority, the award shall be made by the chairman of the arbitral tribunal.

5. The arbitrator's award shall, in addition to dealing with the merits of the case, fix the costs of the arbitration and decide which of the parties shall bear the costs or in what proportions the costs shall be borne by the parties.

The costs of the arbitration shall include the arbitrator's costs and fees, the fees and expenses of any experts, the normal legal costs incurred by the parties, and the administrative costs fixed by the Standing Committee.

6. The arbitrator shall, when fixing his fee, take into account the complexity of the subject matter and the time spent.

The arbitrator's decision on his own fees may be appealed to the Standing Committee within 30 days after the notification of the award.

Article 13
The arbitral award shall be deemed to be made at the place of the arbitration proceedings and on the date when it is signed by the arbitrator.

Article 14
1. Once an award has been made, the Secretariat shall notify to the parties the text signed by the arbitrator, provided always that the costs of the arbitration have been fully paid by the parties or by one of them.

2. Additional copies certified as true by the Secretariat shall be made available, on request and at any time, to the parties but to no one else.

3. By virtue of the notification made in accordance with (1) of this article, the parties waive any other form of notification or deposit of the award.

Article 15
1. The arbitral award shall be final.

2. By submitting the dispute to the ICC-CMI International Maritime Arbitration Rules, the parties shall be deemed to have undertaken to carry out the resulting award without delay and to have waived their right to any form of appeal insofar as such waiver can validly be made.

Article 16
An original of each award made in accordance with the present Rules shall be deposited with the Secretariat.

The Secretariat and when requested by the Secretariat, the arbitrator shall assist the parties in complying with whatever further formalities may be necessary.

Article 17

In all matters not expressly provided for in these Rules, the Standing Committee and the arbitrator shall act in the spirit of these Rules and shall make every effort to make sure that the award is enforceable at law.

Arbitration costs

1. Each party to a dispute submitted to the ICC-CMI International Maritime Arbitration Rules shall be liable for a registration fee of US $1,000. No application will be entertained unless accompanied by this payment.

The registration fee is not recoverable and becomes the property of the Secretariat of the Standing Committee.

2. The parties are responsible for paying to the Secretariat of the Standing Committee a sum intended to cover the arbitrator(s) fees, the administrative charge, the arbitrator(s) personal expenses and, should the case arise, the costs of any expertise procedure and all other similar expenses.

3. The arbitrator(s) set(s) (his) (their) own fees taking into account the complexity of the subject matter and the time spent thereon. However, the fees of the arbitrator(s) may be appealed to the Standing Committee within 30 days after notification of the award. The final decision with respect to determination of the fees of arbitrators lies with the Standing Committee in the event of appeal.

4. The amount of the administrative charge is calculated as set forth in the following table:

Sum in Dispute (in US dollars)	Administrative charge (in US dollars)
0 - 100,000	2.5%
100,000 - 500,000	2,500 + 1.5% of amount over 100,000
500,000 - 1,000,000	8,500 + 1.0% of amount over 500,000
1,000,000 - 10,000,000	13,500 + 0.3% of amount over 1,000,000
over 10,000,000	40,500 + 0.1% of amount over 10,000,000

ICC Rules for a Pre-Arbitral Referee Procedure

Introduction

During the course of many contracts, especially those made for long-term transactions, problems can arise which require an urgent response. It is frequently not possible to obtain in the time required a final decision from an arbitral tribunal or from a court.

Accordingly, the International Chamber of Commerce (ICC) has set out the following Rules for a Pre-arbitral Referee Procedure in order to enable parties which have so agreed to have rapid recourse to a person (called a "Referee") empowered to make an order designed to meet the urgent problem in issue, including the power to order the preservation or recording of evidence. The order should therefore provide a temporary resolution of the dispute and may lay the foundations for its final settlement either by agreement or otherwise.

Use of the Pre-arbitral Referee Procedure does not usurp the jurisdiction of any entity (whether arbitral tribunal or national court) that is ultimately responsible for deciding the merits of any underlying dispute.

Article 1. Definitions

1.1. These Rules concern a procedure called the "Pre-arbitral Referee Procedure" which provides for the immediate appointment of a person ("the Referee") who has the power to make certain orders prior to the arbitral tribunal or national court competent to deal with the case ("the competent jurisdiction") being seized of it.

1.2. The Secretariat of the ICC International Court of Arbitration ("the Secretariat") shall act as the Secretariat of the Pre-arbitral Referee Procedure.

1.3. (a) In these Rules any reference to a party includes a party's employees or agents. (b) Any reference to the "Chairman" means the Chairman of the ICC International Court of Arbitration or includes, in his absence, a Vice-Chairman.

Article 2. Powers of the Referee

2.1. The powers of the Referee are:

(a) To order any conservatory measures or any measures of restoration that are urgently necessary either to prevent immediate damage or irreparable loss and so to safeguard any of the rights or property of one of the parties

(b) to order a party to make to any other party or to another person any payment which ought to be made

(c) To order a party to take any step which ought to be taken according to the contract between the parties, including the signing or delivery of any document or the procuring by a party of the signature or delivery of a document:

(d) To order any measures necessary to preserve or establish evidence.

2.1.1. These powers may be altered by express written agreement between the parties.

2.2. The Referee shall not have power to make any order other than that requested by any party in accordance with Article 3.

2.3. Unless the parties otherwise agree in writing, a Referee appointed in accordance with these Rules shall not act as arbitrator in any subsequent proceedings between those parties or in any other proceedings in which there is any issue or question which is the same as or connected with any which had been raised in the proceedings before the Referee.

2.4. If the competent jurisdiction becomes seized of the case after the appointment of the Referee, the Referee shall nevertheless retain the power to make an order within the time provided by Article 6.2 unless the parties otherwise agree or the competent jurisdiction orders otherwise.

2.4.1. Except as provided in Article 2.4 above or by the relevant rules of the competent jurisdiction, once the competent jurisdiction becomes seized of the case it alone may order any further provisional or conservatory measures that it considers necessary.

For such purpose the competent jurisdiction, if its rules so permit, shall be deemed to have been authorised by the parties to exercise the powers conferred on the Referee by Article 2.1.

Article 3. Request for Referee and Answer

3.1. An agreement to use the Pre-arbitral Referee Procedure must be in writing.

3.2. A party who requires the appointment of a Referee must send two copies of its Request and of any annexed documents to the Secretariat. Such party must at the same time notify the other party or parties of the Request by the quickest method of delivery available, including telefax.

3.2.1. Each such Request must be accompanied by the amount required to open the file, as set out in Article B.1 of the Appendix to these Rules.

3.2.2. The Request must be drawn up in whatever language may have been agreed upon in writing by the parties or, in the absence of any such agreement, in the same language as the agreement to use the Pre-arbitral Referee Procedure. If this language is not English, French or German, a translation of the Request into one of these language must accompany the Request. The annexed documents may be submitted in their original language without translation except where it is necessary in order to under the Request. The Request shall be in writing and shall contain in particular:

   (a) the names and addresses of the parties to the agreement together with a brief description of the legal relationships between the parties

   (b) a copy of the agreement on which the Request is based

(c) the order or orders requested and an explanation of the grounds relied on so as to show that the Request falls within Article 2.1

(d) as the case may be, the name of the Referee chosen by agreement of the parties

(e) any information concerning the choice of the Referee required to be appointed, including, as appropriate, technical or professional qualifications, nationality and language requirements

(f) confirmation that the request has been sent to every other party, stating the means by which this has been done and enclosing proof of transmission, such as postal registration form. receipt from a private courier, or telefax receipt.

3.3. The requesting party shall, if required by the Secretariat, establish when a copy of the Request was received by each party to whom it was sent or when it should be treated as having been received by said party.

3.4. The other party or parties must submit to the Secretariat in writing an Answer to the Request within 8 days from receipt of the copy of the Request sent in accordance with Article 3.2 above, and must send at the same time a copy to the requesting party and to any other party, using the quickest method of delivery available, including telefax. The Answer must state any order requested by that party or parties.

Article 4. Appointment of the Referee and Transmission of File

4.1. The Referee may be chosen by the parties by agreement before or after a Request is made pursuant to Article 3, in which case the name and address of the Referee shall be sent immediately to the Secretariat. Upon receipt of the Answer or upon the expiry of the time limit set out in Article 3.1. whichever is sooner, and having verified the prima facie existence of the agreement of the parties, the Chairman shall appoint the Referee agreed upon.

4.2. If a Referee is to be appointed under Article 3.2.2 (e), the Chairman shall, upon the expiry of the time limit set out in Article 3.4. appoint the Referee in the shortest time possible, taking account of his technical or professional qualifications, his nationality, residence, other relationships with the countries in which the parties are established or with which they are otherwise connected, and any submissions of any party concerning the choice of a Referee.

4.3. Once the Referee has been appointed, the Secretariat shall notify the parties that he has been appointed and shall transmit the file to him. Thereafter all documentation from the parties must be sent directly to the Referee with a copy to the Secretariat. All documentation from the Referee to the parties must be copied to the Secretariat.

4.4. Any party may challenge a Referee appointed under Article 4.2. In such case the Chairman, after giving the other party and the Referee an opportunity to comment, shall take within the shortest time possible a final decision as to the validity of the challenge. His decision shall be within his sole discretion and shall not itself be subject to challenge or appeal by any party.

4.5. Another person shall be appointed (a) where a Referee dies or is prevented or unable to carry out his functions, or (b) it is decided under Article 4.4. that a challenge is valid or (c) if the Chairman decides, after giving the Referee an opportunity to comment, that he is not fulfilling his functions in accordance with the Rules or within any applicable time limit. Such an appointment shall be made in accordance with Article 4.2 (but subject to Article 4.4). In such case the new Referee shall proceed afresh.

4.6. The reasons for any decision about an appointment, challenge or replacement of any Referee shall not be disclosed.

Article 5. The Proceedings

5.1 If any party shall not have presented an Answer by the time the file has been transmitted to the Referee then the requesting party may be required by the Referee to establish to his satisfaction that a copy of the Request was received or should be treated as having been received by that party before he proceeds further. If the Referee is not so satisfied he shall notify the relevant party of his right to submit an Answer and shall set a time limit within which the Answer shall be submitted. Any such action by the arbitral Referee shall not affect the validity of his appointment.

5.2. Any decision as to the Referee's jurisdiction shall be taken by the Referee.

5.3. Within the limits of the powers conferred on him by Article 2.1. and subject to any agreement of the parties the Referee shall conduct the proceedings in the manner which he considers appropriate for the purpose for which he was appointed including:

− considering the written documents submitted by the parties,

− informing the parties of any further investigation or inquiry that he may consider necessary,

− making such further investigation or inquiry, which may include him visiting any place where the contract is being carried out or the establishments of the parties or any other relevant place, obtaining the report of an expert, and hearing any person he chooses in connection with the dispute, either in the presence of the parties or, if they have been duly convened, in their absence. The results of these investigations and inquiries shall be communicated to the parties for comment.

5.4. In acceding to these Rules the parties undertake to provide the Referee with every facility to implement his terms of reference and, in particular, to make available to him all documents which he may consider necessary and also to grant free access to any place for the purpose of any investigation or inquiry. The information given to the Referee shall remain confidential between the parties and the Referee.

5.5. The Referee may convene the parties to appear before him within the shortest time limit possible on a date and at a place fixed by him.

5.6. If one of the parties does not make a submission, comment or appear as required by the Referee, and the Referee is satisfied that the party concerned has received or should have received the relevant communication he may nonetheless continue with the proceedings and may make his order.

Article 6. The order

6.1. The decisions taken by the Referee shall be sent by him to the Secretariat in the form of an order giving reasons.

6.2. The Referee shall make and send the order within 30 days from the date on which the file was transmitted to him. This time limit may be extended by the Chairman upon a reasoned request from the Referee or on his own initiative if he thinks it is necessary to do so.

6.3. The Referee's order does not pre-judge the substance of the case nor shall it bind any competent jurisdiction which may hear any question, issue or dispute in respect of which the order has been made. The order of the Referee shall however remain in force unless and until the Referee or the competent jurisdiction has decided otherwise.

6.4. The Referee may make the carrying out of his order subject to such conditions as he thinks fit including (a) that a party shall commence proceedings before the competent jurisdiction on the substance of the case within a specified period, (b) that a party for whose benefit an order is made shall provide adequate security.

6.5. The Secretariat shall notify the parties of the order of the Referee provided that it shall have received the full amount of the advance on costs fixed by the Secretariat. Only orders so notified are binding upon the parties.

6.6. The parties agree to carry out the Referee's order without delay and waive their right to all means of appeal or recourse or opposition to a request to a Court or to any other authority to implement the order, insofar as such waiver can validly be made.

6.7. Unless otherwise agreed between the parties and subject to any mandatory order, any submissions, communications or documents (other than the order) established or made solely for the purposes of the Pre-arbitral Referee Procedure shall be confidential and shall not be given to the competent jurisdiction.

6.8. The Referee shall not be obliged to explain or give further additional reasons for any order after it has been notified by the Secretariat under Article 6.5. Neither the ICC nor any of its employees or persons acting as Chairman or Vice-Chairman, nor any person acting as Referee shall be liable to any person for any loss or damage arising out of any act or omission in connection with the Rules except that the Referee may be liable for the consequences of conscious and deliberate wrongdoing.

6.8.1. The competent jurisdiction may determine whether any party who refuses or fail to carry out an order of the Referee is liable to any other party for loss or damage caused by such refusal or failure.

6.8.2. The competent jurisdiction may determine whether a party who requested the Referee to issue an order the carrying out of which caused damage to another party carrying out the order is liable to such other party.

Article 7. Costs

7.1. The costs of the Pre-arbitral Referee Procedure comprise: (a) an administrative charge as set out in the Appendix to these Rules, (b) the fees and expenses of the Referee to be determined as set out in the Appendix and (c) the costs of any expert. The Referee's order shall state who should bear the costs of the Pre-arbitral Referee Procedure and in what proportion. A party who made an advance or other payment in respect of costs which it was not liable to have made under the Referee's order shall be entitled to recover the amount paid from the party who ought to have made the payment.

7.2. The costs of and payment for any procedure under these Rules are as set out in the Appendix hereto.

APPENDIX: Costs and Payment for the ICC Pre-arbitral Referee Procedure

A. Costs

1. An administrative charge of US$ 1,500 is payable by the requesting party in respect of each request made to the ICC to appoint a Referee or to administer a Pre-arbitral Referee Procedure.

The charge covers all services rendered by the ICC that may be required by the Rules, but not any services required by alterations to or extensions of the Procedure. The administrative charge is not refundable and becomes the property of the ICC.

2. The amount of the fees and expenses of the Referee shall be fixed by the Secretary General of the ICC Court of Arbitration. The amount shall be reasonable, taking into consideration the time spent, the complexity of the matter and any other relevant circumstances.

3. The costs of the procedure shall also include any fees and expenses of any expert.

B. Payment

1. The amount required to open the file (Article 3.2.1 of the Rules) is US$ 4,000 of which $1,500 constitutes the administrative charge as set out above and $2,500 constitutes an advance on the fees and expenses of the Referee

and any expert. No request for the appointment of a Referee or for the administration of an ICC Pre-arbitral Referee Procedure will be entertained unless accompanied by this amount.

2. As soon as possible after the file has been sent to the Referee and after such consultation as is possible with the Referee and the parties, the Secretariat shall fix an advance on costs to cover the estimated costs of the Pre-arbitral Referee Procedure (Art. 7.1 of the Rules). Such advance on costs is subject to re-adjustment by the Secretariat.

The requesting party shall pay the whole of this advance on costs except insofar as the Secretariat may request the other party or parties to contribute to the advance on costs in the light of any request for an order by the Referee which any other party may have made.

3. No order of the Referee shall be notified by the Secretariat or be valid unless the advance on costs has been received (Art.6.5). Where two or more parties have been asked to contribute to the advance on costs and have not paid their contribution, only the order requested by the party or parties who have fully paid the advance or contribution shall be notified and be valid.

TABLES

TABLE OF CASES

TABLE OF ARBITRAL AWARDS

TABLE OF AUTHORITIES

TABLE OF ARTICLES OF THE 1998 ICC ARBITRATION RULES

TABLE OF CASES

AAOT Foreign Economic Association (VO) Technostroy-export v. International Development and Trade Services, Inc., Court of Appeals, 2d Cir (United States), 1998, 139 F.3d 980: pages 251 (footnote 101), 613 (footnote 141).

A.B. Carl Engström v. N.V. Kunstmesthandel vorheen Hulshof, Supreme Court (Sweden) 1934 NYTT JURISKIKT ARKIV 491: page 351 (footnote 14).

Abu Dhabi Gas Liquefaction Company Ltd. v. Eastern Bechtel Corp. and Chiyoda Chemical Engineering & Construction Co. Ltd., *Court of Appeal* (England) 1982, 2 LLOYD'S L. REP. 425, 21 ILM 1057 (1982); 1983 REV. ARB. 119: page 81 (footnote 116).

Adair Bus Sales v. Blue Bird Corp., Court of Appeals, 10th Cir. (United States) 1994, 25 F.3d 953: page 609 (footnote 120).

Advest, Inc. v. McCarthy, Court of Appeals, 1st Cir. (United States) 1990, 914 F.2d 6: page 614 (footnotes 152, 153).

Agrimpex S.A. v. J.V. Braun & Sons Inc., *Areios Pagos* (Supreme Court) (Greece), 14 January 1977, 25 NOMIKON VIMA (1977) 1126, IV YEARBOOK 269 (1979): page 47 (footnote 7).

Agroengineering v. American Custom Service, Inc., District Court, E.D.N.Y. (United States), 7 June 1996, 95 Civ. 2238, XXII YEARBOOK 990 (1997): page 678 (footnote 50).

Aiter v. Ojjeh, *Cour d'appel*, Paris, (France), 18 February 1986, 1986 REV. ARB. 583: page 316 (text and footnote 44).

AKSA v. Norsolor, *Cour d'appel de Paris* (France), 9 December 1980, 1981 REV. ARB. 306, 20 ILM 887 (1981): page 550 (footnote 5).

Aldunate, *In re* Application of, Court of Appeals, 2d Cir. (United States), 1993, 3 F.3d 54: page 608 (footnote 113).

Alexander v. Gardner-Denver Co., Supreme Court (United States), 1974, 415 U.S. 36: page 603 (footnote 81).

Alfred Dunhill v. Cuba, Supreme Court (United States), 1976, 425 U.S. 682 : page 671 (footnote 25).

Al-Harbi v. Citibank, Court of Appeals, D.C. Cir. (United States), 1996, 85 F.3d 680: page 613 (footnote 140).

Allen v. Lloyd's of London, Court of Appeals, 4th Cir. (United States), 1996, 94 F.3d 923: page 606 (footnote 96).

Allied-Bruce Terminix v. Dobson, Supreme Court (United States), 1995, 513 U.S. 265: pages 492, 591 (footnote 2), 593 (footnote 16), 595 (footnote 32).

Almira Films v. Pierrel, *Cour de cassation* (France), 5 February 1991, 1991 REV. ARB. 625: pages 68 (footnote 70), 69 (footnote 72).

Amicizia Societa Navegazione v. Chilean Nitrate & Iodine Sales Corp., Court of Appeals, 2d Cir. (United States), 1960, 274 F.2d 805: page 614 (footnote 150).

American Bureau of Shipping v. Tencara Shipyard, Court of Appeals, 2d Cir. (United States) 170 F.3d 349: page 600 (footnote 62).

American Construction Machinery Equipment Corporation, Ltd. v. Mechanised Construction of Pakistan, Ltd., District Court, S.D.N.Y. (United States) 1987, 659 F. Supp. 426: page 293 (footnote 32).

American International Group v. Iran, District Court, D.C. (United States), 1980, 493 F. Supp. 522: page 673 (footnote 31).

American Manufacturing & Trading Inc. v. Republic of Zaire, 12 MEALY'S INT. ARB. REP. A-1 (March 1997): page 665 (footnote 12).

Ampaglas S.p.A. v. Sofia S.A., *Tribunal cantonal,* Vaud (Switzerland), 28 October 1975, JOURNAL DES TRIBUNAUX 1981 III: pages 67 (footnote 65), 342 (footnote 71).

Anangel Peace Compania Naviera S.A. v. Bacchus International, Queen's Bench Division (England) [1981] 1 LLOYD'S L. REP. 452: page 453 (footnote 13).

Andersen Consulting v. Andersen Worldwide Société Coopérative and Arthur Andersen LLP, District Court, S.D.N.Y. (United States), 1998, 1998 WL 122590: page 170 (footnote 38).

Andros Compania Maritima v. André & Cie, S.A., District Court, S.D.N.Y. (United States), 1977, 430 F. Supp. 88: pages 485 (footnote 42), 607 (footnote 102).

Animalfeeds International Corp. v. S.A.A. Becker et Cie., *Tribunal de grande instance,* Strasbourg (France), 9 October 1970, 1970 REV. ARB. 166; II YEARBOOK 244 (1977): page 121 (footnote 34).

Antco Shipping Co. Ltd. *et al.* v. Sidermar S.p.A., District Court, S.D.N.Y. (United States), 1976, 417 F. Supp. 207; II YEARBOOK 251 (1977): pages 69 (footnote 76), 79 (footnote 110), 83 (footnote 119, 120), 684 (footnote 24).

Aplix v. Velcro, *Cour d'appel de Paris* (France), 14 October 1993, 1994 REV. ARB. 165: page 553 (footnote 29).

Apollo Computer v. Berg, Court of Appeals, 1st Cir. (United States), 1989, 886 F.2d 469: pages 157 (footnote 6), 160 (footnote 13), 170 (footnotes 37, 38), 176 (footnote 51), 513 (footnote 79), 601 (text and footnotes 65, 66), 620 (footnote 185).

Application of the Republic of Kazakhstan v. Biedermann International, 98-21072, Fifth Circuit, March 17, 1999, Stockholm Chamber of Commerce Arbitration (Sweden): page 492 (text and footnote 64).

Arab African Energy Corp. v. Olie Produkten Nederland, Queen's Bench Division, Commercial Court (England), 6 May 1983, [1983] 2 LLOYD'S L. REP. 419: pages 403 (footnote 10), 543 (footnote 82).

Aramco Case, (France) 1963 REVUE CRITIQUE DE DROIT INTERNATIONAL PRIVE 272: page 333 (footnote 43).

Arbitration Between Intercarbon Bermuda, Ltd., In re v. Caltex Trading and Transport Corp., District Court, S.D.N.Y. (United States), 1993, 146 F.R.D. 64, XIX YEARBOOK 802 (1994): pages 417 (footnote 4), 613 (footnote 146).

Arenco-BMD Maschinenfabrik GmbH v. Sociéta Ceramica Italiana Pozzi-Richard Ginori S.p.A., Court of Appeal of Milan (Italy), (1984) XI YEARBOOK 511: page 459 (footnote 20).

Armijo v. Prudential Ins. Co., Court of Appeals, 10th Cir. (United States), 1995, 72 F.3d 793: page 610 (footnote 121).

Asta Medica, S.A., In re Application of, Court of Appeals, 1st Cir. (United States), 1992, 981 F.2d 1: page 608 (footnote 113).

Asturiana DeZinc Marketing, Inc. v. Lasalle Rolling Mills, Inc., 97 Civ. 6053 (JSR), Mem. Order (Per J. Rakoff, U.S.D.J.) S.D.N.Y. (United States), 29 September 1998, 13 MEALY'S INT. ARB. REP. B-1 (No. 11, November 1998): page 393 (footnote 6).

AT&T Corporation and Lucent Technologies, Inc. v. Saudi Cable Company, Court of Appeal (England), Case No. QBCMF 1999/1200/A3,15 May 2000, 2000 WL 571190: pages 207 (footnote 13), 216 (text and footnote 32), 217, 218, 219, 222, 226 (footnote 51).

Atlas Chartering Services, Inc. v. World Trade Group, Inc. District Court, S.D.N.Y. (United States) 1978, 453 F. Supp. 861: page 485 (footnote 42).

Attorney General v. Shimizu Corp., Court of Appeal (Hong Kong), 1996, 1996 Hong Kong App. No. 185 and No. 186: page 570 (footnote 43).

Audi NSU Auto Union A.G. v. Overseas Motors, Inc., District Court, E.D. Mich. (United States), 1976, 418 F. Supp. 982, II YEARBOOK 252 (1977): page 119 (footnote 28).

Audi NSU Auto Union A.G. v. S.A. Adelin Petit & Cie, Cour de cassation (Belgium), 28 June 1979, V YEARBOOK 257 (1980): page 70 (footnote 79).

Avant Petroleum Inc. v. Pecten Arabian, Ltd., District Court, S.D.N.Y. (United States), 1988, 696 F. Supp. 42: page 602 (footnote 70).

Badie v. Bank of America, California Court of Appeal (United States) 67 Cal. App 4th 779, 79 Cal Reptr. 2d 273 (1998): page 605 (footnote 88).

Baker Marine, Ltd. v. Chevron, Ltd., Court of Appeals, 2d Cir. (United States) 1999, 191 F.3d 194: page 506 (footnote 51).

Ballay v. Legg Mason Wood Walker, Inc., Court of Appeals, 3rd Cir. (United States), 1989, 878 F.2d 729: page 609 (footnote 119).

Banco Nacional de Cuba v. Sabbatino, Supreme Court (United States), 1964, 376 U.S. 398: page 671 (footnote 25).

Bank Mellat v. GAA Development & Construction Co., Queen's Bench Division, Commercial Court (England), 12 January 1988, 3 MEALY'S INT. ARB. REP. 9, 2 LLOYD'S L. REP. 44: pages 372 (footnote 35), 382 (footnote 14), 399 (footnote 5).

Bank Mellat v. Helliniki Techniki, S.A., Court of Appeal (England) [1984] Q.B. 291: page 468 (footnote 43).

Banque Worms v. Bellot, *Cour de cassation* (France), 5 January 1999, 149 DALLOZ AFFAIRES 291 (18 February 1999): page 552 (footnote 19).

Banque Yougoslave de l'Agriculture v. Robin International Inc. et al., Superior Court of the Canton of Zurich (Switzerland), unpublished decision of 29 June 1979: pages 381 (footnote 11), 382 (text and footnote 12).

Bauhinia Corp. v. China National Machinery & Equipment Import & Export Corp., Court of Appeals, 9th Cir. (United States), 1987, 819 F.2d 247: page 597 (text and footnote 44).

Baxter Health Care Corp. v. Harvard Apparatus, Massachusetts Appeals Court (United States), 1993, 35 Mass. App. Ct. 204, 617 N.E.2d 1018: page 619 (footnote 177).

BEC-GTAF v. State of Tunisia, *Tribunal de première instance* (Tunisia), 17 October 1987; *Cour d'appel* Tunis (Tunisia), 1 February 1988; 1988 REV. ARB. 732: pages 45 (footnote 5), 71 (footnote 84).

Bell v. Congress Mortgage Co., California Appellate Court (United States), 1994, 24 Cal. App. 4th 1675; *ordered depublished,* 30 Cal. Rptr. 2d 205 (1994): page 605 (footnote 88).

Ben Nasser et al. v. BNP and Crédit Lyonnais, *Cour d'appel* (France) 1994 REV. ARB. 380: page 232 (footnote 63).

Benteler v. Belgium, Journal des Tribunaux, Bruxelles (Switzerland), No. 5289, 31 March 1984: page 578 (footnote 14).

Bergen Shipping Co. v. Japan Marine Serv., Ltd., District Court, S.D.N.Y. (United States) 1984, 386 F. Supp. 450: page 488 (footnote 51).

Bergesen v. Joseph Muller Corp., District Court, S.D.N.Y. (United States), 1982, 548 F. Supp. 650; *aff'd,* Court of Appeals, 2d Cir., 1983, 710 F.2d 928: pages 518 (footnote 104), 596 (footnote 36), 617 (footnote 168), 682 (footnote 13).

Bernhardt v. Polygraphic Company, Supreme Court (United States) 1956, 350 U.S. 198: page 367 (footnote 26).

BGD Transport-en Handelsmaatschappij "Vekoma" B.V. v. Maran Coal Company, *Tribunal fédéral* (Switzerland), 17 August 1995, 14 SWISS BULL. 673 (1996): pages 513 (footnote 77), 581 (footnote 31), 587 (text and footnote 58), 588 (footnote 62).

Bigge Crane & Rigging Co. v. Docutel Corp., District Court, S.D.N.Y. (United States) 1973, 371 F. Supp. 240: page 488 (footnote 50).

Birbrower, Montalbano, Condon & Frank P.C. et al v. The Superior Court of Santa Clara County and ESQ Business Services, Inc., California Supreme Court (United States), 1998, 17 Cal. 4th 117, 949 P.2d 1; *modified,* 17 Cal. 4th 563 (1998): pages 309 (text and footnote 31), 310 (text and footnote 33), 594 (footnote 24).

Birch Shipping v. Tanzania, District Court, D.C. (United States) 1980, 507 F. Supp. 311: page 673 (footnote 31).

Biotronik GmbH v. Medford Medical Instrument Co., District Court, D.N.J. (United States), 1976, 415 F. Supp. 133: page 684 (footnote 24).

Blad's Case, (England) (1673) 3 Swan 603, 36 ER 991: page 671 (footnote 25).

Blue Cross of California v. Superior Court, California Court of Appeal (United States) 1998, 67 Ca. App. 4th 42, 78 Cal. Rptr. 2nd 779: page 606 (footnote 98).

Bomar v. Entreprise Tunisienne d 'activités pétrolières (ETAP), *Cour d'appel de Paris* (France), 20 Jan. 1987, 1987 REV. ARB. 482, 1987 JDI 934; *Cour de cassation (France)*, 11 Oct. 1989, 1990 REV. ARB. 134, 1990 JDI 633; *Cour d'appel de Versailles* (France), 23 Jan. 1991, 1991 REV. ARB. 291; *Cour de cassation (France)*, 9 Nov. 1993, 1994 REV. ARB. 108, XX YEARBOOK 660 (1995): pages 74 (text and footnote 95), 536 (footnote 32), 554 (text and footnotes 32, 33), 682 (footnote 16).

Bonny v. Society of Lloyd's, Court of Appeals, 7th Cir. (United States), 1993, 3 F.3d 156: page 606 (footnote 96).

Bradford-Scott Data Corp. v. Physician Computer Network, Court of Appeals, 7th Cir. (United States), 1997, 128 F.3d 504; *subsequent appeal*, 7th Cir.,

1998, 136 F.3d 1156; *reh'g, en banc, denied,* 1998 U.S. App. LEXIS 5612: page 610 (footnote 121).

Bremer Vulkan (FRG) v. South India Shipping Co., House of Lords (England) [1981] 1 ALL E.R. 298: page 153 (footnote 32).

Brotherhood of Railroad Trainmen v. St. Louis Southwestern Railway Co., District Court, D.D.C. (United States) 1996, 252 F. Supp. 961: page 420 (footnote 9).

Brower v. Gateway 2000, New York State Court, 1st Dept. (United States) 1998, 676 N.Y.S. 2d 569: pages 272 (text and footnote 37), 604 (footnote 86).

Builders Federal (Hong Kong), Ltd. v. Turner Constr. Co., District Court, S.D.N.Y. (United States), 1987, 655 F. Supp. 1400: page 177 (footnote 54).

Builders Federal (Hong Kong) Ltd. v. Joseph Gartner Co., and Turner (East Asia) Pte Ltd., High Court of Singapore, No. 90 of 1987 (Singapore) 30 March 1988, 2 MALAYSIAN LAW JOURNAL 280 (1988): pages 305 (footnote 22), 308 (text and footnote 28), 309.

Bulgarian Foreign Trade Bank, Ltd. v. A.I. Trade Finance, Inc., Court of Appeal, Stockholm (Sweden), Case T 1092-98 (Sweden) Judgment of 30 March 1999, 14 MEALY'S INT. ARB. REP. A-1 (No. 4 April 1999): page 318 (footnote 48).

Bureau de recherches géologiques et minières (BRGM) *et al.* v. Patino Tinto International N.V., *Cour d 'appel,* Paris (France), 11 December 1981, 1982 RECUEIL DALLOZ SIREY 387: page 88 (footnote 8).

Burgmeister & Wain Engineering Co. Ltd. v. Creusot Loire *et al., Cour d'appel* (France), 21 December 1979, 1981 REV. ARB. 155; *Cour de cassation* (France), 8 November 1982, 1983 REV. ARB. 177: page 83 (footnote 121).

Burn, Standard Co., Ltd. v. McDermott International, Inc., High Court Calcutta, Civil Appellate jurisdiction (India), 11 June 1997: page 272 (footnote 36).

Burton v. Bush, Court of Appeals, 4th Cir. (United States), 1980, 614 F.2d 389: pages 487 (footnote 48), 488 (footnote 52).

C.A. Embotelladora Caracas v. Pepsi-Cola Panamericana S.A., Second Court of First Instance, Caracas (Venezuela), 24 January 1997, 12 MEALEY'S INT. ARB. REP. G-3 (Jan. 1997): page 133 (footnote 13).

Campaniello Imports Ltd. v. Saporiti Italia S.p.A., Court of Appeals, 2d Cir. (United States), 1997, 117 F.3d 655: page 51 (footnote 16).

Canada Packers Inc. *et al.* v. Terra Nova Tankers Inc. *et al.,* Ontario Court of Justice (Canada), 1 October 1992, XII YEARBOOK 669 (1997): page 66 (footnote 61).

Carbomin S.A. v. Ekton Corp., *Cour de justice,* Geneva (Switzerland), 14 April 1983, 106 LA SEMAINE JUDICIAIRE 37 (1984); XII YEARBOOK 502 (1987): page 56 (footnote 30).

Carte Blanche (Singapore) v. Diners Club International, Court of Appeals, 2d Cir. (United States), 1993, 2 F.3d 24: pages 177 (footnote 54), 598 (text and footnotes 50, 51).

Carte Blanche (Singapore) PTE Ltd. v. Carte Blanche International, Ltd., District Court, S.D.N.Y. (United States) 1988, 683 F. Supp. 945: pages 279, 280 (footnote 10).

Carolina Power and Light Co. v. Uranex, District Court, N.D.C.A. (United States) 1977, 451 F. Supp. 1044; summarized in IV YEARBOOK 336 (1979): pages 484 (text and footnote 38), 485, 607 (footnote 102).

Casco Nobel France v. SICO, Inc. and Kansa, *Cour d'appel,* Paris (France), 1993 REV. ARB. 309: page 356 (footnote 6).

Cekobanka v. ICC, *Tribunal de grande instance,* Paris (France), 8 October 1986, 1987 REV. ARB. 367: pages 159 (footnote 10), 160 (text and footnote 14), 161.

Cereali Mallozzi S.p.A. v. Agenzia Marittima Albano e Avallone *et al.,* Court of First Instance, Naples (Italy), 7 April 1982, 90 IL DIRITTO MARITTIMO 341 (1983); XII YEARBOOK 492 (1987): page 56 (footnote 31).

Cerealsarda di A. Casillo & Co. S.a.S. v. Ditta Otello Mantovani, Court of Appeal, Venice (Italy), 26 January 1983, 68 RIV. DIR. INT. 204 (1985); XII YEARBOOK 493 (1987): page 56 (footnote 31).

Ceska Sporitelina, A.S. v. Unisys Corporation, District Court, E.D. Pa. (United States), Oct. 10, 1996, 1996 U.S. Dist. LEXIS 15435; *stay denied, aff'd without op ,* Court of Appeals, 3d Cir., 1997, 116 F.3d 467; *mot. granted, cert. denied,* Supreme Court, 1998, 118 S. Ct. 739: page 598 (text and footnotes 46, 52).

Champ v. Siegel Trading Co. Inc., Court of Appeals, 7th Cir. (United States), 1995, 55 F.3d 269: page 606 (footnote 97).

Channel Tunnel Group v. Balfour Beatty Ltd., House of Lords (England), [1993] 1 ALL ER 664, [1993] AC 334, 368, XIX YEARBOOK 736 (1993): pages 350 (footnote 13), 473 (footnote 5), 541 (footnote 71).

Chevron Transp. Corp. v. Astro Vencedor Compania Naviera, S.A., District Court, S.D.N.Y. (United States) 1969, 300 F. Supp. 179: page 453 (footnote 13).

Chicago Typographical Union No. 16 v. Chicago Sun-Times, Court of Appeals, 7th Cir. (United States), 1995, 935 F.2d 1501: pages 503 (footnote 33), 615 (footnote 159).

Christine Williams v. Direct Cable and Beneficial National Bank, Alabama Circuit Court, Henry County (United States), Aug. 13, 1997, No. CV-97-009: page 605 (footnote 94).

Christopher Brown Ltd. v. Genossenschaft Oesterreifchischer Waldbesitzer, Queen's Bench, Commercial Court (England), 1954, [1954] 1 Q.B. 8: page 512 (footnote 75).

Chromalloy Aeroservices v. Arab Republic of Egypt. District Court, D.D.C. (United States), 1996, 939 F. Supp. 907; *Cour d'appel de Paris* (France), 14 January 1997, 1997 REV. ARB. 395: pages 506 (footnote 46), 529 (text and footnotes 22, 25, 26), 618 (footnote 173), 685 (footnote 28).

Clarendon v. State Bank of Saurashtra, Court of Appeals, 2d Cir. (United States), 1996, 77 F.3d 631: page 716 (text and footnote 19).

Clear-Star Limited v. Centrala Morska Importoura-Eksportova "Centromor", (Switzerland) *Note* Tschantz, 9 April 1991, 1991 REV. ARB. 709: page 403 (footnote 12).

Coastal States Trading Inc. v. Zenith Navigation S.A., District Court, S.D.N.Y. (United States), 1977, 446 F. Supp. 330; IV YEARBOOK 329 (1979): page 75 (footnote 97).

Cole v. Burns Int. Sec. Serv., Court of Appeals, D.C. Cir. (United States), 1997, 105 F.3d 1465: page 604 (footnote 82).

Colin Reid Sellar v. The Highland Railway Company & Others, House of Lords (England) [1919] S.C. (H.L.) 19: page 226 (footnotes 51, 52).

Colorado Permanente Med. Group, P.C. v. Evans, Colorado Supreme Court (United States), 1996, 926 P.2d 1218: page 605 (footnote 89).

Cominco France S.A. v. Soquiber S.L., Spanish Supreme Court (Spain) (unpublished), extracts *in* VIII YEARBOOK 408 (1983): page 152 (footnote 28).

Commercial Solvents Corp. v. Louisiana Liquid F. Co., District Court, S.D.N.Y. (United States) 1957, 20 F.R.D. 359: page 487 (footnote 48).

Commonwealth Coating Corp. v. Continental Casualty Co., Supreme Court (United States), 1968, 393 U.S. 145: pages 210 (text and footnote 21), 216 (footnote 31), 612 (text and footnotes 133, 136, 137, 138), 613 (footnote 140).

Compagnia Generale Construzione "COGECO" S.p.A. v. Piersanti, *Corte di Cassazione* (Italy), 27 April 1979, 15 RIV. DIR. INT. 565 (1979); VI YEARBOOK 229 (1981): pages 45 (footnote 3), 70 (footnote 77).

Compagnie de Navigation et Transports, S.A. v. MSC (Mediterranean Shipping Company), S.A., *Tribunal fédéral* (Switzerland), 16 January 1995, ATF 121 II 38; 13 SWISS BULL. 503 (1995): pages 513 (footnote 78), 536 (footnote 30), 577 (footnote 11), 580, 581 (text and footnote 31), 587 (footnote 57), 683 (footnote 19).

Compagnie des Bauxites de Guinee (CBG) v. Hammermills, District Court, D.D.C. (United States), May 29, 1992, 1992 U.S. Dist. LEXIS 8046: pages 394 (footnote 7), 619 (text and footnote 180), 620 (footnote 183), 685 (footnote 25).

Compagnie Saint Gobain Pont-'a-Mousson v. Fertilizer Corporation of India Ltd., High Court, Delhi (India), 28 August 1970, II YEARBOOK 245 (1977); *Cour d 'appel* Paris (France), 10 May 1974, 1971 REV. ARB. 111, I YEARBOOK 184 (1976): pages 96 (footnote 12), 678 (footnote 51).

Compania Espanola de Petroles S.A. v. Nereus Shipping S.A., Court of Appeals, 2d Cir. (United States), 1975, 527 F.2d 99: page 80 (footnote 111).

Compania Panamena Maritima San Geressimo, S.A. v. J.E. Hurley Lumber Co., Court of Appeals, 2d Cir. (United States), 1957, 244 F.2d 286: page 420 (footnote 10).

Compania Valenciana de Cementos Portland v. Primary Coal Inc., Supreme Court (France), 22 October 1991, 1992 REV. ARB. 457: page 631 (footnote 23).

Compañia Minera Condesa S.A. & Compañia Minas Buenaventura, S.A. v. Bureau de Recherches Géologiques et Minières-Pérou, *Tribunal fédéral* (Switzerland), 19 December 1997, 1998 SEMAINE JUDICIAIRE 358: page 582 (footnote 37).

Comptoirs Industriels Réunis Blachère v. Société de Developpement Viticole, *Cour d 'appel,* Paris (France), 3 December 1981, 1982 REV. ARB. 92: page 678 (footnote 51).

Confex v. Ets. Dahan, *Cour de cassation* (France), 25 February 1986, 1986 JDI 735; XII YEARBOOK 484 (1986): pages 54 (footnote 26), 57 (footnote 31).

Consorts Ury v. Galeries Lafayette, *Cour de cassation*, 13 April 1972, 1975 REV. ARB. 235: page 216 (footnote 31).

Continaf B.V. v. Polycoton S.A., *Tribunal de première instance,* Geneva (Switzerland), 21 May 1987, XIII YEARBOOK 516 (1988): page 64 (footnote 56).

Cooper v. Ateliers de la Motobécane, S.A., New York Court of Appeals (United States), 1982, 442 N.E.2d 1239, 57 N.Y. 2d 408, 456 N.Y. S. 2d 728: pages 485 (footnote 39, 41), 594 (footnote 26), 607 (footnote 101).

Copal Co. Ltd. v. Fotochrome Inc., District Court, E.D.N.Y. (United States), 1974, 337 F. Supp. 26; Court of Appeals, 2d Cir., 1975, 517 F.2d 512, I YEARBOOK 202 (1976): page 68 (footnote 71).

Coppée-Lavalin N.V. v. Ken-Ren Chemicals and Fertilizers, Ltd., Voest-Alpine Aktiengesellschaft v. Ken-Ren, House of Lords (England), [1995] 1 A.C. 38, [1994] 2 LLOYD'S L. REP. 109: pages 468 (text and footnote 42), 540 (text and footnote 67), 541 (footnote 69).

Coppée-Lavalin SA/NV v. Ken Ren Chemicals and Fertilizers, Ltd., House of Lords (England), [1994] 2 W.L. R. 631; [1994] 1 AC 38, 2 ALL E.R. 449: pages 468 (text and footnote 42), 481 (footnote 27).

Coprodag v. Bohin, *Cour de cassation* (France), 10 May 1995, 1995 REV. ARB. 617: page 552 (footnote 21).

Corbin v. Washington Fire & Marine Insurance Co., District Court, D.S.C. (United States) 1968, 278 F. Supp. 393; app'd Court of Appeals, 4th Cir., 1968, 398 F.2d 543: page 412 (footnote 34).

Cortez Byrd Chips, Inc. v. Bill Harbert Construction Co., Supreme Court (United States) 2000, 120 S. Ct. 1331: page 616 (text and footnote 162).

Cosiac v. Luchetti *et al., Cour de cassation* (France), 10 May 1988, 1988 REV. ARB. 639: page 52 (footnote 17).

Cour d'appel, Canton of Bâle-ville (France) 2 January 1984, 1985 SWISS BULL. 19: page 357 (footnote 8).

Cour d'appel, Grenoble (France), 13 September 1993, 1994 REV. ARB. 337, *Note* Moreau: pages 71, 140 (footnote 6).

Cour d'appel, Nancy (France), 29 January 1958, 1958 REVUE CRITIQUE DE DROIT INTERNATIONAL PRIVÉ 148: page 367 (footnote 27).

Cour d'appel, Paris (France), 19 December 1980 (unpublished): page 480 (footnote 23).

Cour d'appel, Paris (France), 19 March 1981, 1982 REV. ARB. 84: page 371 (footnote 34).

Cour d'appel, Paris (France), 3 December 1981, 22 January 1982 in 1982 REV. ARB. 91, *Note* E. Mezger: pages 356 (footnote 4), 381 (footnote 7).

Cour d'appel, Paris (France), 15 January 1985, 1986 REV. ARB. 87: page 207 (footnote 13).

Cour d'appel, Paris (France), 7 July 1987, 1988 REV. ARB. 649: page 364 (footnote 23).

Cour d'appel, Paris (France), 12 January 1996, 1996 REV. ARB. 437: page 233 (text and footnote 66).

Cour d'appel, Paris (Franace), 13 June 1996, 1997 JDI 151: page 142 (footnote 10).

Cour d'appel, Versailles (France), 10 June 1997, 1995 REV. ARB. 639: page 505 (footnote 44).

Cour de cassation, (France), 14 June 1960, 1960 REVUE CRITIQUE DE DROIT INTERNATIONAL PRIVÉ 393: page 367 (footnote 27).

Cour de cassation, (France) 23 May 1963, 1964 Rev. Crit. Dr. Int'l Privé 340: page 553 (footnote 27).

Cour de cassation, (France), 22 November 1966, 1967 Rev. Arb. 9: page 367 (footnote 27).

Cour de cassation, (France), 23 January 1974, 1974 Rev. Arb. 296: page 381 (footnote 10).

Cour de cassation (France), 16 June 1976, 1977 Rev. Arb. 269: page 356 (footnote 3).

Cour de cassation, (France), 28 January 1981, 1982 Rev. Arb. 425: pages 381 (footnote 10), 382 (footnote 15).

Cour de cassation (France), 9 July 1979, 1980 Rev. Arb. 79: page 480 (footnote 23).

Cour de cassation (France), 8 March 1988, Bull Civ. I 64 (1988): pages 288 (footnote 20), 292 (footnote 28).

Cour de cassation, Deuxième chambre civile (France), 7 October 1987, 1987 Rev. Arb. 179: page 207 (footnote 13).

Cour de cassation, Première chambre civile (France), 19 June 1979, 1979 Rev. Arb. 487: page 307 (footnote 26).

Cour de cassation, Première chambre civile (France), 14 March 1984, 1985 Rev. Arb. 69, *Note* Couchez: page 481 (footnote 25).

Cour de cassation, Première chambre civile (France), 6 March 1990, 1990 Rev. Arb. 633, *Note* H. Gaudemet-Tallon: page 476 (footnote 11).

Cour de cassation, Première chambre civil (France), 16 March 1999, 1999 Rev. Arb. 308: page 234 (footnote 67).

Crédit populaire d'Algérie v. Sapvin, French *Cour de cassation* (France), February 14, 1978, 1980 Revue critique du droit international privé 707: page 211 (footnote 23).

Creighton Ltd. v. Government of the State of Qatar, Court of Appeals, D.C. Cir., (United States), 1999, 181 F.3d 118: pages 598 (footnote 49), 674 (footnote 38).

Czarnikow v. Rolimpex, House of Lords (England), 1978, [1978] 2 All E.R. 1043: pages 211 (footnote 23), 653 (text and footnotes 91, 92), 654.

DST v. Rakoil, Court of Appeal (England), March 1987, [1987] 2 Lloyd's L. Rep. 246, [1987] 2 All E.R. 769; *rev'd* House of Lords [1988] 2 Lloyd's L. Rep. 293, [1988] 2 All ER 833: page 544 (footnote 93).

Daihatsu Motor Co., Ltd. v. Terrain Vehicles, Court of Appeals, 7th Cir. (United States), 1993, 13 F.3d 196: page 622 (footnote 192).

Dale Metals Corp. v. Kiwa Chemicals Industry Co., District Court, S.D.N.Y. (United States), 1977, 442 F. Supp. 78: pages 82 (text and footnote 118), 178 (footnote 57), 598 (footnote 48).

Dalmia Dairy Industries Ltd. v. National Bank of Pakistan, Court of Appeal (England), 18 May 1977, [1978] 2 LLOYD'S L. REP. 287: pages 63 (footnote 51), 162 (footnote 20), 292.

Dalmia Dairy Industries v. National Bank of Pakistan, Court of Appeal (England), 1977, [1978] 2 LLOYD'S L. REP. 223: pages 403 (footnote 15), 417 (footnote 2), 544 (footnote 93).

Dayhoff, Inc. v. H.J. Heinz Co, Court of Appeals, 3d Cir. (United States), 1996, 86 F.3d 1287; *amended, on reh'g,* Court of Appeals, 3d Cir., 1996 U.S. App. LEXIS 18266; *cert. denied,* Supreme Court, 1996, 117 S. Ct. 583: page 599 (text and footnote 53).

De Oiseno v. Mendes, *Cour d'appel*, Paris (France), 27 October 1994, 1995 REV. ARB. 263: page 293 (footnote 33).

De Sapio v. Kohlmeyer, New York Court of Appeals (United States) 1974, 35 N.Y. 2d 402, 321 N.E. 2d 770: page 487 (footnote 47).

Dean Witter Reynolds Inc. v. Byrd, Supreme Court (United States), 1985, 470 U.S. 213 (1985): page 592 (footnote 9).

Dean Witter Reynolds Inc. v. Trimble, New York Supreme Court (United States), 1995, 631 N.Y.S.2d 215: page 619 (footnote 176).

Deutsche Shachtbau-und Tiefbohrgesellschaft mbH v. Ras Al Khaimah National Oil Co. *et al.,* Court of Appeal (England), 24 March 1987, [1987] 2 LLOYD'S L. REP. 246, [1987] 2 ALL E.R. 769, XIII YEARBOOK 522 (1988); House of Lords (England), 1988, [1988] 2 LLOYD'S L. REP. 293, 2 ALL E.R 833: pages 54 (footnote 23), 337 (footnote 57), 350 (footnote 13).

Dickstein v. DuPont, Court of Appeals, 1st Cir. (United States), 1971, 443 F.2d 783: page 592 (footnote 6).

Diseno v. Société Mendes, *Cour d'appel de Paris* (France), 27 October 1994, 1995 REV. ARB. 261: page 557 (footnote 51).

Ditte Frey, Milota, Seitelberger v. Ditte F. Cuccaro e figli, Court of Appeal, Naples (Italy), 13 December 1974, 11 RIV. DIR. INT. 552 (1975); ICA NY CONVENTION V.22; I YEARBOOK 193 (1976): page 55 (footnote 29).

Doctor's Associate's v. Casarotto, Supreme Court (United States), 1996, 517 U.S. 681: pages 595 (text and footnotes 29, 32), 605 (footnote 93).

Doctor's Associates v. Hamilton, Court of Appeals, 2d Cir. (United States), 1998, 150 F.3d 157: page 593 (footnote 17).

Dolling-Baker v. Mennet G Another, Court of Appeal (England) [1990] I WLR 1205: page 316 (footnote 45).

Dragomand International AG v. Ital-Contractors Consortium of Condotte Partners, *Tribunal fédérale Suisse* (Switzerland), 8 July 1992 (applying Article 192, LDIP): page 403 (footnote 12).

E. Co. v. B. Co., High Court, Delhi (India), 21 May 1998): page 271 (footnote 35).

E.A.S.T., Inc. of Stanford, Conn. v. M/V Alaia, Court of Appeals, 5th Cir. (United States) 1989, 876 F.2d 1168: pages 485, 486.

Economy Forms Corp. v. Iran, (Iran) 5 Iran-U.S. C.T.R. 1 (1983): page 439 (footnote 14).

Eddie S.S. Co. Ltd. v. Czarnikow-Rionda Co., District Court, S.D.N.Y. (United States) 1979, 480 F. Supp. 731: page 453 (footnote 13).

Engalla v. Permanente Med. Group, Inc., California Supreme Court (United States), 1997, 938 P.2d 903: pages 513 (footnote 78), 604 (footnote 84), 605 (footnote 89).

Esso Australia Resources Ltd. v. Plowman, High Court of Australia (Australia), 7 April 1995, 128 ALR 391, 11 ARB. INT. 337 (1995); summarized in XXI YEARBOOK 137 (1996): pages 313 (footnote 40), 314 (footnote 41), 317.

Ethiopia v. Baruch Foster Corp., Court of Appeals, 5th Cir. (United States), 1976, 535 F.2d 334; II YEARBOOK 252 (1977): page 678 (footnote 50).

Eurodif v. Islamic Republic of Iran, *Cour de cassation* (France), 14 March 1984, 1985 REV. ARB. 65; *Cour de cassation* (France), 28 June 1989, 1989 REV. ARB. 653: pages 555 (footnote 39), 556 (footnote 42).

Eurodif v. OIAETI (the Iranian Organization for Investment, Economic and Technical Assistance), *Tribunal de grande instance*, Paris (Franace), 10 June 1982, by President Caratini: pages 480, 481 (footnote 24).

Euro Disney SCA v. S.A. Gabo, S.A. Erenco and others, *Cour d'appel*, Paris (France), 22 May 1992 (*Quatorzième chambre B* no 92/5759 and 5760) referred to in Gerard Pluyette, *A French Perspective* in CONSERVATORY AND PROVISIONAL MEASURES IN INTERNATIONAL ARBITRATION 72, 82 (ICC Publishing, 1993): page 478 (footnote 17).

Euromepa, S.A. v. R. Emersian, Inc., Court of Appeals, 2d Cir. (United States), 1995, 51 F.3d 1095: page 608 (footnote 113).

European Gas Turbines S.A. v. Westman Int. Ltd., *Cour d'appel,* Paris (France), 30 September 1993, 1994 REV. ARB. 359: page 64 (footnote 56).

Ex parte Pinochet Ugarte (No. 2), House of Lords (England) [1999] 1 ALL ER 577 (H.L.): page 236 (footnote 75).

Farrel Corp. v. United States ITC, Court of Appeals, Fed. Cir. (United States), 1991, 949 F.2d 1147: page 680 (footnote 9).

Federal Court, Third Civil Chamber, Court of Arbitration (Germany), 14 April 1988, No. III ZR 12/87, 3 MEALEY'S INT. ARB. REP. 4 (July 1988): page 357 (footnote 9).

Fertalage Industries (Algeria) v. Société Kaltenbach Thurin, S.A. (France), *Tribunal de grande instance*, Beauvais, 9 April 1988 (unreported): page 269 (text and footnote 27).

Fertilizer Corporation of India *et al.* v. IDI Management Inc., District Court, S.D. Ohio (United States), 1981, 517 F. Supp. 948, VII YEARBOOK 382 (1982); 1982, 530 F. Supp. 542, VIII YEARBOOK 419 (1983): pages 87 (footnote 4), 93 (footnote 2), 120 (footnote 29), 209 (footnote 19), 210 (footnote 20), 224 (footnote 50), 228 (footnote 55), 663 (footnote 7), 678 (footnote 50), 684 (footnote 24).

Ferrara S.p.A. *et al.* v. United Grain Growers Ltd., District Court, S.D.N.Y. (United States), 1977, 441 F. Supp. 778; IV YEARBOOK 331 (1979): page 57 (footnote 32), 73 (footnote 93).

Filanto, S.p.A. v. Chilewich Int'l Corp., Court of Appeals, 2d Cir. (United States), 1993, 984 F.2d 58: page 610 (footnote 121).

Fils et Cables d'Acier de Lens v. Midland Metals Corp., District Court, S.D.N.Y. (United States), 1984, 584 F. Supp. 240: page 503 (footnote 33), 615 (footnote 158).

Fincantieri-Cantieri Navali Italiani S.p.A v. OTO Melara S.p.A., *Tribunal fédéral* (Switzerland), 23 June 1992, ATF 188 II, 115 SEMAINE JUDICIAIRE 2 (1993): page 579 (footnote 21).

First Options of Chicago v. Kaplan, Supreme Court (United States), 1995, 514 U.S. 938: pages 60 (footnote 43), 514 (text and footnotes 81, 82), 592 (footnote 12), 595 (footnote 31), 600 (footnote 63), 601 (footnote 68), 602 (footnote 73), 620 (text and footnote 187), 621 (text and footnotes 188, 189).

Flood and Conklin Manufacturing v. Prima Paint, Supreme Court (United States) 1967, 388 U.S. 395: page 169 (text and footnote 34).

Floors, Inc. v. B.G. Danis of New England, Massachusetts Supreme Judicial Court (United States), 1980, 380 Mass. 91, 401 N.E.2d 839: page 619 (footnote 177).

Fondation M. v. Banque X, *Tribunal fédéral* (Switzerland), 29 April 1996, ATF 122 II, 139; 14 SWISS BULL. 527 (1996): page 580 (footnote 27).

Fonsecie v. Blumenthal, Court of Appeals, 2d Cir. (United States), 1980, 620 F.2d 322: page 491 (footnote 61).

Fort Hill Builders v. National Grange Mutual Insurance Co.,Court of Appeals, 1st Cir. (United States), 1989, 866 F.2d 11: page 613 (footnote 141).

Fougerolle (France) v. Banque du Proche Orient (Lebanon), unpublished award rendered in Geneva, enforced by the French *Cour de cassation* (France), 9 December 1981, 1982 JDI 931, 1982 REV. ARB. 183: pages 334 (footnote 47), 336 (footnote 53), 337.

Fougerolle S.A. v. Procofrance S.A., *Cour de cassation, Première chambre civile*, 25 May 1992, 1992 JDI 974: page 410 (footnote 27).

Framatome S.A. (France) et al. v. Atomic Energy Organization of Iran (A.E.O.I.), *Cour de cassation* (France), 1990 BULLETIN DES ARRETS DE LA COUR DE CASSATION, PREMIERE PARTIE 100, commentary in RECUEIL DALLOZ 1990, Information rapides, 198: page 482 (footnote 30).

Fuller Co. v. Compagnie des Bauxites de Guinée, District Court, W.D. Pa. (United States), 1976, 421 F. Supp. 938: page 596 (footnote 36).

Fung Sang Trading Ltd. v. Kai Sun Sea Products & Food Co. Ltd., Supreme Court (Hong Kong), 29 Oct. 1991, [1992] 1 HKLR 40, XVII YEARBOOK 289 (1992): pages 518 (footnote105), 524 (footnote 10), 566 (text and footnote 22).

G. S.A. v. V. S.p.A., *Tribunal fédéral Suisse* (Switzerland), 28 April 1992, ATF 118 II 193; 1993 REV. ARB. 124: pages 343 (text and footnote 73), 579 (footnote 20), 584 (text and footnote 45).

Gaetano Butera v. Pietro e Romano Pagnan, Supreme Court (Italy), 18 September 1978, 15 RIV. DIR. INT. 525 (1979); IV YEARBOOK 296 (1979): page 59 (footnote 40).

Galakis, *Court de cassation (France)*, 2 May 1966, 1967 REV. CRIT. DR. INT'L PRIVÉ 553, 1966 BULLETIN CIVIL I-199: pages 45 (footnote 5), 552 (footnote 23).

Gammaro v. Thorp Consumer Discount Co., District Court, D. Minn. (United States), 1993, 828 F. Supp. 673: page 606 (footnote 97).

Gateway Technologies v. MCI Telecommunications Corp., Court of Appeals, 5th Cir. (United States), 1995, 64 F.3d 993: pages 503 (footnote 33), 615 (footnote 158).

Gemanco v. S.A.E.P.A. and S.I.A.P.E., *Cour d'appel*, Paris (France), 2 June 1989, 1991 REV. ARB. 92: page 227 (footnote 53).

Gen. Nat'l Maritime Transp. Co. v. Société Götaverken Arendal A.B., *Cour d'appel de Paris* (France), 21 Feb. 1980, *Recueil Dalloz Sirey Jurisprudence* 568: page 550 (footnote 5).

Genesco Inc. v. T.F. Kakiuchi Co. and T. Kakiuchi America Inc., Court of Appeals, 2d Cir. (United States), 1987, 815 F.2d 840: page 66 (footnote 62).

George Fischer Foundry Systems Inc. v. Adolph H. Hottinger Maschinenbau GmbH, Court of Appeals, 6th Cir. (United States), 7 June 1995, 1995-1 Trade Cases (CCH) Sec. 70019, 1995 U.S. App. LEXIS 13757: page 66 (footnote 64).

Getreide Import Gesellschaft mbH v. Fratelli Casillo, Court of Appeal, Bari (Italy), 28 November 1977, 61 RIV. DIR. INT. 820 (1978), VII YEARBOOK 342 (1982) ; *Corte de Cassazione* (Italy), 7 October 1980, 1980 RIV. DIR. INT. 76, VII YEARBOOK 342 (1982): pages 58 (footnotes 36, 37), 71 (footnotes 83, 86), 73 (footnote 93).

Gilmer v. Interstate/Johnson Lane Corp., Supreme Court (United States), 1991, 500 U.S. 20: pages 592 (footnote 9), 603 (footnote 81).

Gosset, *Cour de cassation* (France), 7 May 1963, 1963 REV. CRIT. DR. INT'L PRIVÉ 615: pages 515 (footnote 88), 551 (footnote 17).

Gotaverken v. GNMIC, Supreme Court (Sweden), 13 August 1979, 1979 NYTT JURISDIKT ARKIV 527: page 404 (text and footnote 17).

Government of New Zealand v. Mobil Oil New Zealand Ltd. *et al.,* High Court, Wellington (New Zealand), 1987, XIII YEARBOOK 638 (1988): page 66 (footnote 63).

Government of United Kingdom v. Boeing Co., Court of Appeals, 2d Cir. (United States), 1993, 998 F.2d 68: page 607 (footnote 103).

Gregg and Others (U.K.) v. Raytheon Ltd. (U.S.), Court of Appeal, Opinion of Lord Denning, M.R. and Lord Justice Roskill (England), [1980] 1 ALL E.R.: page 153 (footnote 32).

Guangdong Agriculture Co. Ltd. v. Conagra International Ltd., High Court of Hong Kong (Hong Kong), 24 Sept. 1992, XVIII YEARBOOK 187 (1993): page 568 (text and footnotes 28, 29).

Guinea and Soguipêche v. Atlantic Triton, *Cour de cassation* (France), 18 November 1986, 26 ILM 373 (1986) (English translation): page 476 (footnote 12).

Gulf Guar. Life Ins. Co., v. Connecticut Gen. Life Ins. Co., District Court, S.D. Miss. (United States), 1997, 957 F. Supp. 839: page 600 (footnote 60).

Hadley v. Baxendale, (England), 9 Ex. 341, 156 Eng. Rep. 145 (1854): page 647.

Halki Shipping v. Sopex Oils, Queen's Bench Division, Admiralty Court (England), 1997, [1997] 3 ALL ER 833: page 539 (footnote 53).

Halligan v. Piper Jaffray, Court of Appeals, 2d Cir. (United States), 1998, 148 F.3d 197: page 615 (footnotes 156, 157).

Harbour Assurance v. Kansa, Court of Appeal (England), 1993, [1993] Q.B. 701: page 536 (footnote 34).

Harris International Telecommunications, Inc. v. Iran, (Iran) 17 Iran-U.S. C.T.R. 31 (Chamber One, 1987): page 432 (footnote 7).

Haynsworth v. Corporation, Court of Appeals, 5th Cir. (United States), 1997, 121 F.3d 956: page 606 (footnote 96).

Hebei Import & Export Corporation v. Polytek Engineering Company Ltd., Hong Kong Court of Final Appeal (Hong Kong), 1999, 2 HKCFAR 111; *reversing* Court of Appeal, Hong Kong Special Administrative Region, 1998, 1 HKC 192 (1998), 13 MEALEY'S INT. ARB. REP. (No. 2) E-1 (Feb. 1998): pages 572 (text and footnote 52), 573 (footnotes 54, 55).

Hecht v. Soc. Buismans, *Cour d'appel,* Paris (France), 1970, 1972 REV. ARB. 67; *Cour de cassation* (France), 4 July 1972, 1972 JDI 843, 1974 REVUE CRITIQUE DE DROIT INTERNATIONAL PRIVÉ 82, 1974 REV. ARB. 67: pages 46 (footnote 6), 53 (footnote 22), 62 (footnote 50), 99 (footnote 15), 141 (footnote 7).

Heidberg, High Court (England), [1994] 2 LLOYD'S L. REP. 287: page 689 (footnote 42).

Heilman v. Graziano Transmissions, *Cour d'appel,* Paris (France), 9 September 1997, 1998 REV. ARB. 712: page 417 (footnote 5).

Hewlett-Packard Co. v. Berg, Court of Appeals, 1st Cir. (United States), 1995, 61 F.3d 101: pages 592 (footnote 9), 617 (text and footnotes 167, 169), 684 (footnote 21).

Heyman v. Darwins Ltd., House of Lords (England), 1942 A.C. 356; 1 ALL E.R. 337: page 169 (text and footnote 35).

Hill v. Gateway 2000 Inc., Court of Appeals, 7th Cir. (United States), 1997, 105 F.3d 1147: pages 55 (footnote 26), 604 (footnote 87).

Hilmarton v. OTV. *Cour de Justice du Canton de Genève* (Switzerland), 17 November 1989, 1993 REV. ARB. 315 and *Tribunal fédéral,* 17 April 1990, 1993 REV. ARB. 315; *Cour de cassation* (France), 1994 REV. ARB. 327 and 1997 REV. ARB. 376; High Court of Justice, Q.B. (England), 24 May 1999, 14 MEALEY'S INT. ARB. REP. Section A (June 1999): pages 65 (footnote 58), 345 (footnote 81), 505 (text and footnotes 42, 43, 45), 506 (footnote 45), 561, 562 (footnote 79), 583 (text and footnote 40), 685 (footnote 28).

Hirschfeld Productions Inc. v. Edwin Mirvich *et al.,* Court of Appeals, N.Y. (United States), 22 October 1996, 11 MEALEY'S INT. ARB. REP. B-1 (Nov. 1996): page 79 (footnote 109).

Hiscox v. Outhwaite, House of Lords (England), 1991, [1991] 3 ALL ER, 641; XVII YEARBOOK 599 (1992); 3 WLR 297: pages 397 (footnote 1), 500 (footnote 23), 546 (footnote 105).

Hoogovens BV v. MV Sea Catteleya, District Court, S.D.N.Y. (United States), 3 May 1994, No. 93 Civ. 3859; XXII YEARBOOK 881: page 134 (footnote 15).

Hoteles Condado Beach, La Concha and Convention Center v. Union de Tronquistas Local 901, Court of Appeals, 1st Cir. (United States), 1985, 763 F.2d 34: page 613 (footnote 143).

Humetrix, Inc. v. Gemplus SCA, District Court, California (United States), 11 November 1997 (unpublished): page 178 (footnote 57).

Humphrey v. Prudential Secs., Inc., Court of Appeals, 4th Cir. (United States), 1993, 4 F.3d 313: page 610 (footnote 121).

Hunt v. Mobil Oil Corp., District Court, S.D.N.Y. (United States) 1984, 583 F. Supp. 1092; *aff'd* S.D.N.Y., 1987, 654 F. Supp. 1487: pages 207 (footnote 13), 488 (footnote 52).

Hutton v. Warren, (England), 1836, 1 MESSON & WELSBY'S EXCHEQUER REPORTS 466: page 634 (footnote 32).

Hyman v. Pottberg's Executors, Court of Appeals, 2d Cir., (United States), 1939, 101 F.2d 262: page 453 (footnote 13).

I. SA v. T. SA, *Tribunal fédéral* (Switzerland), ATF 115 II 390 (1989): page 576 (footnote 4).

Imperial Ethiopian Government v. Baruch Foster Corp., Court of Appeals, 5th Cir. (United States), 1976, 535 F.2d 334: page 6 (footnote 5).

INA Corporation v. Iran, (Iran) 1985, 8 Iran-U.S. C.T.R. 373: page 451 (footnote 8).

Indian Organic Chemicals Ltd. v. Chemtex Fibres Inc. *et al.*, High Court, Bombay (India), 1977, IV YEARBOOK 271 (1979): pages 83 (footnote 121), 95 (footnote 11), 271 (footnote 32).

Industrija Motora Rakovica (I.M.R.) v. Lynx Machinery Ltd., *Cour d'appel de Paris* (France), 22 December 1978, 1979 REV. ARB. 266: page 557 (footnote 50).

Intercarbon Bermuda, Ltd. v. Caltex Trading & Transp. Corp., District Court, S.D.N.Y. (United States), 1993, 146 F.R.D. 64: page 613 (footnote 146).

International Cultural Property Society, Inc. v. Walter de Gruyter & Co., New York Supreme Court (United States) Index No. 121566/99, 14 MEALY'S INT. ARB. REP. 3 (No. 11, November 1999): page 141 (footnote 10).

International Standard Electric Corp. v. Bridas S.A., District Court, S.D.N.Y. (United States), 1990, 745 F. Supp. 172; XVII YEARBOOK 639 (1992): pages 330 (footnote 36), 506 (footnote 47), 510 (footnote 66), 615 (text and footnote 160), 678 (footnote 50).

International Union of Elec., Radio Mach. Workers v. Westinghouse, District Court, S.D.N.Y. (United States) 1969, 48 F.R.D. 298: page 488 (footnote 49).

Ipitrade International S.A. v. Federal Republic of Nigeria, District Court, D.C. (United States), 1978, 465 F. Supp. 824; 13 ILM 1395 (1978); IV YEARBOOK 337 (1979): pages 4 (footnote 3), 46 (footnote 5), 671 (text and footnote 26), 672.

Iran Aircraft Industries v. Avco Corp., Court of Appeals, 2d Cir. (United States), 1992, 980 F.2d 141: page 611 (footnote 125).

Iron Ore Company of Canada v. Argonaut Shipping, Inc., District Court, S.D.N.Y. (United States) 1985, XII YEARBOOK 173: page 453 (footnote 13).

Isover St. Gobain v. Dow Chemical France *et al., Cour d'appel,* Paris (France), 21 October 1983, 1984 REV. ARB. 98; IX YEARBOOK 132 (1984): pages 52 (footnote 19), 75 (text and footnote 98), 76.

Israel Chemical Phosphates Ltd. v. N.V. Algemene Oliehandel, Court of First Instance, Rotterdam (The Netherlands), 26 June 1970, 1971 NETHERLANDSE JURISPRUDENTIE 1372; ICA NY CONVENTION V.9; I YEARBOOK 195 (1976): page 56 (footnote 29).

I.T.A.D. Asso. v. Podar Bros, Court of Appeals, 4th Cir. (United States), 1981, 636 F.2d 75: page 485.

J.A. van Walsum N.V. v. Chevelines S.A., *Tribunal cantonal,* Geneva (Switzerland), 6 June 1967, 64 SCHWEIZERISCHE JURISTEN-ZEITUNG 56 (1968); ICA NY CONVENTION V.2; I YEARBOOK 199 (1976): page 55 (footnote 29).

J.J. Ryan & Sons Inc. v. Rhone Poulenc Textile S.A., Court of Appeals, 4th Cir. (United States), 1988, 863 F.2d 315: pages 89 (footnote 9), 178 (footnote 57), 600 (text and footnote 61).

Jain v. Courier de Méré, Court of Appeals, 7th Cir. (United States), 1995, 51 F.3d 686: page 597 (text and footnote 43).

Japan Time v. Kienzle France and the International Chamber of Commerce, *Cour d'appel,* Paris (France), 11 July 1980 (unpublished): pages 139 (footnote 3), 161 (footnote 17).

JMA Investments *et al.* v. C. Rijkaart B.V. *et al.,* District Court, E.D. Wash. (United States), 18 June 1985, XI YEARBOOK 578 (1986): pages 57 (footnote 31), 642 (footnote 49).

John Deere, Ltd. v. Sperry Corp., Court of Appeals, 3d Cir. (United States), 1985, 754 F.2d 132: page 608 (footnotes 112, 113).

John Hancock Mutual Life Insurance Co. v. Olick, Court of Appeals, 3d Cir. (United States), 1998, 151 F.3d 132: page 602 (footnote 72).

Jolasry v. Polish Ocean Line, *Court de cassation (France),* 10 March 1993, 1 DISP. RESOL. UPDATE 9 (I.B.A. Committee D, 1994): page 505 (footnote 40).

Jones v. Sea Tow Servs., Court of Appeals, 2d Cir. (United States), 1994, 30 F.3d 360: page 596 (footnote 36).

Jones v. Sherwood Computer Services, Court of Appeal (England), [1992] 1 W.L.R. 277: page 536 (footnote 27).

Joong & Shipping Co. Ltd. v. Choi Chong-sick & Chu Ghin Ho Co., High Court of Hong Kong (Hong Kong), 31 March 1994, XX YEARBOOK 285 (1995): page 568 (footnote 30).

Josef Meissner GmbH & Co. v. Kanoria Chemicals & Industries Ltd., High Court, Calcutta (India), 1986, 1986 ALL INDIA REPORTS CALCUTTA 45; XIII YEAR-BOOK 497 (1988): page 80 (footnote 111).

Kabushiki Kaisha Ameroido Nihon v. Drew Chemical Corp., District Court, Yo-kohama (Japan), 1980, 1981 JAPANESE COMMERCIAL ARBITRATION ASSOCIATION QUARTERLY 81-82; VIII YEARBOOK 394 (1983): page 59 (footnote 41).

Kahn Lucas Lancaster, Inc. v. Lark International Ltd., District Court, S.D.N.Y. (United States), 1997, 1997 WL 458785; rev'd Court of Appeals, 2d Cir., 1999, No. 97-9436: pages 55 (footnote 26), 597 (footnote 40).

Katran Shipping Co. Ltd. v. Keavea Transportation Ltd., High Court of Hong Kong (Hong Kong), 29 June 1992, extracted in NEIL KAPLAN, JILL SPRUCE AND MICHAEL MOSER, HONG KONG AND CHINA ARBITRATION 186 (1994): page 527 (footnote 18).

KCA Drilling v. Sonatrach, Tribunal fédéral (Switzerland), 15 March 1990, ARRÊTS DU TRIBUNAL FÉDÉRAL 116 I a 56: page 80 (footnote 114).

Keban, Turkish Supreme Court (Turkey), 46 ARBITRATION JOURNAL 241 (1981): page 382 (footnote 13).

Kersa Holding Company v. Infrancourtage, Cour supérieure de justice (Lux-embourg), 24 November 1993, XXI YEARBOOK 617 (1986): page 276 (foot-note 5).

Khoms El Mergeb v. Société Dalico, Cour de cassation (France), 20 December 1993, 1994 JDI 432; 1994 REV. ARB. 116: page 53 (footnote 22).

Kinoshita, In re, Court of Appeals, 2d Cir. (United States), 1961, 287 F.2d 951: page 89 (footnote 9).

Kis France S.A. v. S.A. Société Générale, Cour d'appel, Paris (France), 31 Octo-ber 1989, 1992 REV. ARB. 90; XVI YEARBOOK 145 (1991): page 77 (foot-note 101).

KKN Enterprises v. Gloria Jean's Gourmet Coffees, Court of Appeals, 1st Cir. (United States) 1999, No. 98-2337: page 603 (footnote 78).

Kolbrunner v. Federici, Tribunal fédéral (Switzerland), 27 October 1995: page 575 (footnote 2).

Komplex v. Voest-Alpine Stahl, Tribunal fédéral Suisse (Switzerland), 14 June 1990, 1994 SWISS BULL. 226, Note S. Besson: page 145 (footnote 20).

Laker Airways Incorporated v. FLS Aerospace Limited, Queen's Bench (Eng-land), [1999] 2 LLOYD'S L. REP. 45, 26 April 1999 (Opinion of Mr. Justin Rix): pages 228 (footnote 56), 533 (footnote 10).

Laminoirs-Trefileries-Cableries de Lens, S.A. v. Southwire Co., District Court, N.D. Ga. (United States), 1980, 484 F. Supp. 1063; VI YEARBOOK 247 (1981): pages 87(footnote 4), 117 (footnote 24), 684 (footnote 24).

Lander Co. v. MMP Invs., Court of Appeals, 7th Cir. (United States), 1997, 107 F.3d 476: pages 518 (footnote 104), 596 (footnote 36), 617 (footnote 168), 682 (footnote 13).

Lapine Technology Corporation. v. Kyocera Corporation., Court of Appeals, 9th Cir. (United States), 1997, 130 F.3d 884; commentary in 12 MEALY'S INT. ARB. REP. No. 12 (1997); *rev'g* 909 F Supp 697, N.D. Cal. 199: pages 293 (footnote 33), 403 (footnote 14), 503 (footnote 33), 557 (footnote 51), 615 (footnote 158).

Lawler, Matusky and Skelly, Engineers v. Attorney General of Barbados, High Court of Barbados (Barbados), (No. 320 of 1981), 22 August 1983, (unpublished): page 307 (footnote 27).

Lawson Fabrics, Inc. v. Akzona, Inc., District Court, S.D.N.Y. (United States), 1973, 355 F. Supp. 1146: page 600 (footnote 62).

Letter Rogatory from First Court of First Instance in Civil Matters, *In re*, Caracas, Federal Court of Appeals, 5th Cir. (Caracas), 1995, 42 F.3d 308: page 608 (footnote 113).

LIAMCO v. Libya, District Court, D.C. (United States), 1980, 482 F. Supp. 1175; Court of Appeals (United States), 6 May 1981, D.C. Cir. No. 80-1207, VII YEARBOOK 382 (1982); *Tribunal de grande instance,* Paris (France), 7 February 1979; *Tribunal de grande instance,* Paris (France), 5 March 1979, 1979 JDI 857; Court of Appeal, Svea (Sweden), 18 June 1980, 20 ILM 893, VII YEARBOOK 359 (1982); *Tribunal fédéral* (Switzerland), 19 June 1980, 106 BGE IA, ILM 15 (1981), VI YEARBOOK 151 (1981), 75 AMERICAN JOURNAL OF INTERNATIONAL LAW 153 (1981): pages 123 (footnote 41), 672 (text and footnotes 27, 28, 30), 673 (text and footnotes 32, 33, 34, 36), 674.

Libyan National Oil Company v. WETCO, *Tribunal fédéral* (Switzerland), 1975, ARRÊTS DU TRIBUNAL FÉDÉRAL 101.III.58 (1975): page 131 (footnote 9).

Locabail (UK) Ltd. v. Bayfield Properties Ltd., Court of Appeal (England), 17 November 1999, [2000] 1 ALL ER 65: pages 229 (footnote 57), 251 (footnote 101).

Lo Ka Chun v. Lo To, Court of Appeals, 11th Cir. (United States), 1988, 858 F.2d 1564: page 608 (footnote 113).

Lonrho Ltd. *et al.* v. Shell Petroleum Company Ltd. *et al.,* Chancery Division (England), 1978, IV YEARBOOK 320 (1979): pages 65 (footnote 59), 86 (text and footnote 2), 87 (text and footnote 3).

Lopez v. Plaza Finance Co., District Court, N.D. Ill. (United States), Apr. 25, 1996, 1996 WL 210073: page 605 (footnote 88).

LTDC v. R.J. Reynolds Tobacco Int., *Cour d'appel,* Paris (France), 27 October 1994, 1994 REV. ARB. 695: page 61 (footnote 47).

Lucky Goldstar International Ltd. v. Ng Moo Kee Engineering Ltd., High Court of Hong Kong (Hong Kong), 5 May 1993, [1993] 2 HKLR 73, XX YEARBOOK 280 (1995) and March 1994 ARB. & DISP. RES. L. J. 49: page 568 (text and footnote 32).

M & C Corp. v. Erwin Behr GmbH, Court of Appeals, 6th Cir. (United States), 1996, 87 F.3d 844, *subsequent appeal,* 6th Cir., 1998, 143 F.3d 1033: pages 403 (footnote 13), 611 (text and footnotes 124, 125), 614 (footnote 151), 619 (footnote 175).

Madden v. Kaiser Found. Hosp., California Supreme Court (United States), 1976, 552 P.2d 1178: page 605 (footnote 89).

Malev Hungarian Airlines, *In re* Application of, Court of Appeals, 2d Cir. (United States), 1992, 964 F.2d 97: page 608 (footnote 109).

Marathon Oil Co. v. Ruhrgas, *A.G.,* Court of Appeals, 5th Cir. (United States), 1997, 115 F.3d 315, *rehearing en banc,* 145 F.3d 211, *reversed and remanded,* Supreme Court, 1999, 119 S. Ct. 1563, *action dismissed,* 5th Cir., 1999, 182 F.3d 291: pages 83 (footnote 119), 598 (footnote 49).

Marc Rich & Co., A.G. v. Società Italiana Impianti P.A., Court of Appeal (England), 25 July 1991, EC Case No. C-190/89, 7 ARB. INT. 251 (1991), XVII YEARBOOK 233, 1 LLOYD'S L. REP. 548: page 688 (text and footnote 39).

Mardele v. Mulle, *Cour de cassation* (France), 19 February 1930, 1933 RECUEIL SIREY GENERAL DES LOIS ET DES ARRÊTS, SIREY JURISPRUDENCE 41: page 550 (footnote 8).

Maritime International Nominees v. Guinea, District Court, D.C. (United States), 1981, 505 F. Supp. 141: page 673 (footnote 31).

Martine Co. de Navigacion v. Saguenay Terminals, Ltd., Fedeal Court of Appeals, 9th Cir. (United States), 1961, 293 F.2d 796: page 614 (footnote 150).

Mauritius Sugar Syndicate *et al.* v. Black Lion Shipping Co. S.A. *et al.* ("The Rena K"), Queen's Bench Division (England), 1978, [1978] 1 LLOYD'S L. REP. 545; IV YEARBOOK 323 (1979): page 73 (footnote 93).

Mareva Compania Naviera, S.A. v. International Bulk Carriers, S.A., Court of Appeal (England), 1975, [1975] 2 LLOYD'S L. REP. 509: pages 483 (text and footnote 32), 539 (footnote 56).

Mastrobuono v. Shearson Lehman Hutton, Supreme Court (United States), 1995, 514 U.S. 52: pages 592 (footnote 9), 595 (text and footnote 30), 602 (footnote 71), 619 (text and footnotes 175, 176).

Matra Hachette v. Reteitalia, *Cour d'appel de Paris* (France), 20 September 1995, 1995 REV. ARB. 87: page 552 (footnote 21).

McCarthy v. Providential Corp., District Court, N.D. Cal. (United States), July 18, 1994, 1994 U.S. Dist. LEXIS 10122, *appeal dismissed*, Court of Appeals, 9th Cir. (United States), 1997, 122 F.3d 1242: pages 605 (footnote 88), 606 (footnote 97).

McCreary Tire & Rubber v. CEAT, S.p.A, Court of Appeals, 3d Cir. (United States), 1974, 501 F.2d 1032: pages 484 (text and footnote 37), 485 (text and footnotes 39, 41), 486, 607 (footnote 101).

McDermott Int'l, Inc. v. Underwriters at Lloyds, Court of Appeals, 5th Cir. (United States), 1993, 981 F.2d 744: page 610 (footnote 122).

McDonnell Douglas Corp. v. Kingdom of Denmark, District Court, E.D. Miss. (United States), 1985, 607 F. Supp. 1016; XI YEARBOOK 581 (1986): page 88 (footnote 7).

Meadows Indemnity Co. Ltd. v. Baccala & Shoop Insurance Services Inc. *et al.*, District Court, E.D.N.Y. (United States), 1991, 760 F. Supp. 1036; XVII YEARBOOK 686 (1992): page 72 (footnote 92).

Mediterranean Enterprises Inc. v. Ssangyong Corp., Court of Appeals, 9th Cir. (United States), 1993, 708 F.2d 1458: page 89 (footnote 9).

Mediterranean Shipping Co. v. GALF Assurance *et al., Cour de cassation* (France), 20 June 1995, 1995 REV. ARB. 622: page 56 (footnote 29).

Medway Power, *In re*, District Court, S.D.N.Y. (United States), 1997, 985 F. Supp. 402: page 608 (footnote 109).

Meglio v. Société V2000 *et al. Cour de cassation* (France), 21 May 1997, BULL. CIV. 1 No. 159, 107; 1997 REV. ARB. 537; 1998 REVUE CRITIQUE DE DROIT INTERNATIONAL PRIVÉ 87: pages 46 (footnote 6), 71 (footnote 82), 518 (footnote 103), 550 (text and footnote 11).

Meiki Co. Ltd. v. Bucher-Guyer S.A., *Tribunal fédéral* (Switzerland), 17 March 1976, ARRÊTS DU TRIBUNAL FÉDÉRAL 102 IA 493; V YEARBOOK 220 (1980): page 91 (footnote 1).

Menicucci v. Mahieux, *Cour d'appel*, Paris (France), 13 December 1975, 1976 JDI 106: page 72 (footnote 91).

Mercury Communications v. General Telecommunications, House of Lords (England), 1995, [1996] 1 W L R 48: page 536 (footnote 27).

Merrill Lynch, Pierce, Fenner & Smith, Inc. v. Bobker, Court of Appeals, 2d Cir. (United States), 1986, 808 F.2d 930: page 614 (footnote 151).

Merrill Lynch, Pierce, Fenner & Smith, Inc. v. Levine, New York County Court (United States), N.Y. L. J., 5 July 1995 (N.Y. Co.): page 619 (footnote 176).

Metallgesellschaft A.G. v. Motosi Aldo *et al., Corte de Cassazione* (Italy), 19 November 1978, VI YEARBOOK 232 (1981): page 48 (footnote 9).

Mettalgesellschaft A.G. v. M/V Capitaine Constante, Court of Appeals, 2d Cir. (United States), 1986, 790 F.2d 280: page 360 (footnote 12).

Metex v. T.E.K. Directorate, Supreme Court (Turkey), 1 March 1995: page 100.

Metropolitan World Tanker Corp. v. P.N. Pertambangan Minjakdangas Bumi Nasional, District Court, S.D.N.Y. (United States) 1975, 427 F. Supp. 3: page 485 (footnote 42).

Meyers v. Univest Home Loan, District Court, N.D. Cal. (United States), Aug. 5, 1993, 1993 WL 307747: page 605 (footnote 88).

Miller v. Whitworth Street Estates, House of Lords (England), [1970] 1 ALL ER 796: page 498 (footnote 11).

Miller Brewing Co. v. Brewery Workers Local Union No. 9, Court of Appeals, 7th Cir. (United States), 1984, 739 F.2d 1159: page 592 (footnote 6).

Mississippi Power Co. v. Peabody Coal Co., District Court, S.D. Miss. (United States) 1976, 69 F.R.D. 558: page 487 (footnote 46).

Mitsubishi Motors Corp. v. Soler Chrysler-Plymouth, Inc., Supreme Court (United States), 1985, 473 U.S. 614: pages 44 (footnote 1), 61 (text and footnote 47), 66 (text and footnote 64), 67 (footnote 64), 68, 170, 342 (footnote 72), 343, 495, 496 (footnotes 2, 3), 508 (footnote 57), 509 (footnote 63), 517 (footnote 94), 592 (footnotes 9, 12), 603 (footnote 76), 606 (footnote 95), 617 (footnote 170).

Mitsubishi Motors Corp. v. Soler Chrysler-Plymouth, Inc., Court of Appeals, 1st Cir. (United States), 1987, 814 F.2d 844: pages 603 (footnote 79), 617 (footnote 171), 618 (footnote 172).

Mobil Oil Indonesia v. Asamera Oil (Indonesia) Ltd., N.Y. Supreme Court, Appellate Division (United States) 1977, 487 F. Supp. 63, 56 A.D. 2d 339; 392 N.Y.S. 2d 614; New York Court of Appeals (United States), 1977, 43 N.Y. 2d 276, 372 N.E.2d 21: pages 144 (footnotes 18, 19), 372 (footnote 35), 449 (footnote 1), 609 (text and footnotes 114, 116), 612 (text and footnotes 131, 132).

Montes v. Shearson Lehman Bros., Inc., Court of Appeals, 11th Cir. (United States), 1997, 128 F.3d 1456: page 614 (footnote 155).

Moses H. Cone Memorial Hospital v. Mercury Construction Corp., Supreme Court (United States), 1983, 460 U.S. 1: page 44 (footnote 1), 591 (footnote 3), 592 (footnote 9).

Motoren-, Turbinen-, und Pumpen AG v. Ministry of War of Egypt *et al.*, *Tribunal fédéral* (Switzerland), 1967, ARRÊTS DU TRIBUNAL FÉDÉRAL 93.I.345 (1967): page 131 (footnote 8).

M/s V/O Tractoroexport v. M/s Tarapore and Co., Supreme Court (India), 1971, 58 ALL INDIA REPORTER S.C.I. pt. 685, January 1971; I YEARBOOK 188, 66 AM. J. INT'L. 627 (1976): pages 95 (footnote 10), 271 (footnote 32).

Municipalité de El Mergeb v. Dalico, *Cour de cassation* (France) 20 December 1993, 1994 REV. ARB. 116: pages 165 (footnote 25), 499 (footnote 19), 508 (footnote 59), 552 (footnote 18), 554 (text and footnote 34).

Murray Oil Prods. Co. v. Mitsui & Co., Court of Appeals, 2d Cir. (United States) 1944, 146 F.2d 381: page 483 (footnote 36).

Myrtoon Steamship, *Cour d'appel de Paris* (France), 10 April 1957, 1958 REV. CRIT. DR. INT'L PRIVÉ 120: page 552 (footnote 23).

Naing Int'l Enter.v. Ellsworth Assoc., District Court, D.D.C. (United States), 1997, 961 F. Supp. 1: page 613 (footnote 142).

National Broadcasting Co., *In re* Application of, District Court, S.D.N.Y. (United States), Jan. 16, 1998, 1998 U.S. Dist. LEXIS 385, *aff'g* 165 F.3d 184 (2nd Cir 1999): page 608 (footnote 109).

National Broadcasting Company, Inc. and NBC Europe Inc. v. Bear Stearns & Co., Merrill Lynch & Co., Salomon Brothers Inc., SBC Warburg Inc. Violy Byroun & Partners and T.V. Azteca S.A. de C.V., District Court, S.D.N.Y. (United States), 16 January 1998, No. 98-7468; 2d Cir., January 26, 1999 confirming order of Judge Sweet, quashing subpoenas: page 491 (text and footnote 63).

National Iranian Oil Co. v. Ashland Oil, Court of Appeals, 5th Cir. (United States), 1987, 817 F.2d 326: page 596 (footnote 38).

National Iranian Oil Co. v. Mapco Int'l, Inc., Court of Appeals, 3d Cir. (United States), 1992, 983 F.2d 485: pages 601 (footnote 69), 602 (footnote 70).

National Metal Converters, Inc. v. I/S Stavborg, Court of Appeals, 2d Cir. (United States), 1974, 500 F.2d 424: page 119 (footnote 28).

National Oil Corp. v. Libyan Sun Oil Co., District Court, D. Del. (United States), 1990, 733 F. Supp. 800; XVI YEARBOOK 651 (1990): page 678 (footnote 50).

National Thermal Power Corporation v. Singer Corporation, Supreme Court (India), 1992, XVIII YEARBOOK 403 (1993): page 510 (footnote 67).

National Union Fire Ins. v. Belco Petroleum Corp., Court of Appeals, 2d Cir. (United States), 1996, 88 F.3d 129: page 621 (footnote 190).

Nationwide Ins. Co. v. Patterson, Court of Appeals, 3d Cir. (United States), 1991, 953 F.2d 44: page 610 (footnote 121).

Naviera Amazonica Peruana S.A. v. Compania International de Seguros del Peru, Court of Appeal (England), 1987, [1988] 1 FTLR 100; XIII YEARBOOK 156 (1988): page 107 (footnote 5).

Nema, The (Pioneer Shipping v. B.T.P. Tioxide), House of Lords (England), 1981, [1982] A.C. 724: page 543 (footnote 85).

Nestel v. Nestel, New York Supreme Court, Appellate Division (United States) 1972, 331 N.Y.2d 241: page 608 (footnote 107).

New England Energy, Inc. v. Keystone Shipping Co., Court of Appeals, 1st Cir. (United States), 1988, 855 F.2d 1: pages 594 (footnotes 19, 25), 607 (footnote 105).

New England Utilities v. Hydro-Quebec, District Court, D. Mass. (United States), 1998, 10 F. Supp. 2d 53: pages 594 (footnote 21), 615 (footnote 158).

Newark Stereotypers' Union No. 18 v. Newark Morning Ledger Co., Court of Appeals, 3d Cir. (United States), 1968, 397 F.2d 594: page 613 (footnotes 144, 145).

Nissan (UK) Ltd. v. Nissan Motor Company, Court of Appeal, Civil Division (England), 31 July 1991 (Unpublished): pages 533 (footnote 12), 541 (text and footnote 72).

NKAP (Russia) v. E. (Hungary) and S. (Switzerland), *Tribunal fédéral Suisse, Première cour civile* (Switzerland), 9 July 1997, 1997 SWISS BULL. 506: pages 410 (footnote 28), 589 (footnote 72).

Noble China Inc. v. Lei, Ontario Court, General Division (Canada) 1998, 42 ONTARIO REPORTS (3rd) 70: page 371 (footnote 34).

Nordsee v. Reederei Mond and Reederei Friedrich Busse, Court of Justice of the European Communities, 23 March 1982, 1982 EUROPEAN COURT REPORTS 1112; VIII YEARBOOK 183 (1983): pages 61 (footnote 46), 67 (footnote 66).

Norsolor S.A. v. Pabalk Ticaret Ltd., Court of Appeal, Vienna (Austria), 18 November 1982, 1983 RECHT DER INTERNATIONALEN WURTSCHAFT 29; IX YEARBOOK 159 (1984); VIII YEARBOOK 365 (1983), 1983 REV. ARB. 465: pages 334 (text and footnote 49), 335 (text and footnotes 49, 51), 336 (footnote 53), 337, 627 (footnote 15).

Northrop Corp. v. Triad International Marketing S.A., Court of Appeals, 9th Cir. (United States), 1987, 811 F.2d 1265: pages 64 (footnote 56), 345 (footnote 81), 611 (footnote 128).

Norwegian Loans, France v. Norway, International Court of Justice, 1957, INTERNATIONAL COURT OF JUSTICE REPORTS (1957): page 672 (footnote 28).

Nova (Jersey) Knit Ltd. v. Kammgarn Spinnerei GmbH, House of Lords (England), 16 February 1977, [1977] 1 LLOYD'S L. REP. 163; [1977] 2 ALL E.R. 465; IV YEARBOOK 314 (1979): pages 75 (footnote 96), 80 (footnote 112), 87 (footnote 5).

Ocean Fisheries Ltd. v. Pacific Coast Fishermen's Mutual Marine Insurance Co., Federal Court of Canada, Trial Division (Canada), order for stay of 2 January 1997, 12 MEALEY'S INT. ARB. REP. 9 (Feb. 1997): page 524 (footnote 11).

Oddmund Grundstad v. Joseph Ritt *et al.,* Court of Appeals, 7th Cir. (United States), 1997, 106 F.3d 201: page 80 (footnote 111).

Offshore International v. Banco Central, [1976] 2 LLOYD'S L. REP. 402: page 145 (footnote 20).

OIAETI ET SOFIDIF V. COGEMA, SERU, EURODIF, CEA, *Cour d'appel*, Versailles (France), 7 MARCH 1990, 1991 REV. ARB. 326, *Note* Eric Loquin: pages 176 (footnote 52), 181 (text and footnotes 64, 65), 182 (footnote 66).

Oil & Natural Gas Commission v. Western Company of North America, (India) 1987 All India Reports SC 674, XIII YEARBOOK 473 (1988): page 510 (footnote 67).

Oil Field of Texas, Inc. v. Iran, (Iran) 12 Iran-U.S. C.T.R. 308 (1986): page 444 (footnote 20).

Omnium de Traitement et de Valorisation S.A. v. Hilmarton Ltd., Queen's Bench Division (England), 24 May 1999: page 345 (footnote 81).

Omnium français des pétroles v. Giannoti, (Switzerland), VII ANNUAIRE SUISSE DE DROIT INTERNATIONAL 128 (1950): page 88 (footnote 8).

Opinter France v. Dacomex, *Cour d'appel de Paris* (France), 15 January 1985, 1986 REV. ARB. 87: page 556 (footnote 44).

Orazio Torrisi v. Friedrich Kern, Supreme Court (Italy), 15 March 1986; XII YEARBOOK 497 (1987): page 58 (footnote 36).

Orbis, *Tribunal fédéral Suisse* (Switzerland), 26 October 1966, ATF 92 I 271: page 216 (footnote 31).

Organisation de l'Energie Atomique de l'Iran (O.E.A.I.) v. Eurodif S.A., SOFIDIF, *et al.* (unpublished); *Tribunal de grande* instance of Paris (France), 25 June 1980: page 161 (footnote 17).

Oriental Commercial and Shipping Co. *et al.* v. Rosseel N.V., District Court, S.D.N.Y. (United States), 1985, 609 F. Supp. 75; XII YEARBOOK 532 (1987): pages 44 (footnote 2), 53 (footnote 22), 76 (footnote 100).

Oriental Commercial Shipping Co. Ltd. v. Rosseel, N.V. District Court, S.D.N.Y., No. 84-Civ 7173 (United States) 1989, 4 MEALEY'S INT. ARB. REP. Section B-1 (Febraury 1989): page 487 (footnote 48).

Orri v. Société des Lubrifiants Elf Aquitaine, *Cour de cassation* (France), 11 June 1991, 1992 REV. ARB. 73: pages 178 (footnote 56), 555 (footnote 38).

Overseas Cosmos Inc. v. NR Vessel Corp., District Court, S.D.N.Y. (United States), 1998, 97 Civ. 5898; 13 MEALEY'S INT. ARB. REP. B-11 (May 1998): page 55 (footnote 28).

P. v. A, *Tribunal fédéral* (Switzerland), 1 November 1996, 15 SWISS BULL. 116 (1997): page 589 (footnote 71).

P. v. S., *Tribunal fédéral* (Switzerland), ATF 118 II 199 (1992): page 589 (footnote 71).

PCS 2000 LP v. Romulus Telecommunications, Court of Appeals, 1st Cir. (United States), 1998, 148 F.3d 32: page 591 (footnote 3).

Pabalk v. Norsolor, *Cour de cassation* (France), 9 October 1984, 1985 REV. ARB. 431 and 112 J. DR. INT'L PRIVÉ 679 (1985): page 505 (text and footnote 40).

PaineWebber Inc. v. Bybyk, Court of Appeals, 2d Cir. (United States), 1996, 81 F.3d 1193: page 602 (footnote 71).

PaineWebber Inc. v. Elahi, Court of Appeals, 1st Cir. (United States), 1996, 87 F.3d 589: pages 170 (footnote 37), 514 (footnote 82), 601 (footnote 68), 620 (footnote 185).

Paperconsult AG v. CEPAL *et al.*, *Tribunal fédéral* (Switzerland), 1962, ARRÊTS DU TRIBUNAL FÉDÉRAL 88.I.100 (1962): page 131 (footnote 7).

Parsons & Whittemore Overseas Co. Inc. v. Société Générale de l'Industrie du Papier (RAKTA), Court of Appeals, 2d Cir. (United States), 1974, 508 F.2d 969; I YEARBOOK 205 (1976): pages 6 (footnote 5), 42 (footnote 10), 616 (text and footnotes 163, 164), 652 (text and footnote 87), 678 (footnote 50), 684 (footnote 24).

Patterson v. ITT Consumer Fin. Corp., California Appellate Court, 1st Dist. (United States), 1993, 14 Cal. App. 4th 1659: page 605 (footnote 88).

Paul Smith, Ltd. v. H & S International Holding, Inc., Commercial Court (England) [1991] 2 LLOYD'S L. REP. 127: page 499 (footnote 18).

Penn Tanker Co. of Delaware v. C.H.Z. Rolimpex, Warszawa, District Court, S.D.N.Y. (United States) 1961, 199 F. Supp 716: page 487 (footnote 48).

Pennzoil Exploration and Production Co. *et al.* v. Ramco Hazar Energy Ltd., Court of Appeals, 5th Cir. (United States), 13 May 1998, 13 MEALEY'S INT. ARB. REP. F-3 (May 1998): page 88 (footnote 7).

Peoples Sec. Life Ins. v. Monumental Life Ins. Co., Court of Appeals, 4th Cir. (United States), 1993, 991 F.2d 141: page 612 (text and footnote 139).

P.E.P. Shipping v. Noramco Shipping Corp., District Court, E.D.La. (United States), 1997, 1997 WL 358118: page 55 (footnote 28).

Pepsico Inc. and Pepsi-Cola Panamericana S.A. v. Oficina Central De Asesoria y Ayuda Tecnica C.A. *et al.,* District Court, S.D.N.Y. (United States), 1996, 945 F. Supp. 69; 11 MEALEY'S INT. ARB. REP. D-1 (Nov. 1996): page 508 (footnote 59).

Perera v. Siegal Trading Co., Court of Appeals, 7th Cir. (United States), 1992, 951 F.2d 780: page 610 (footnote 121).

Petroleum Separating Co. v. Interamerican Refining Co., Court of Appeals, 2d Cir. (United States), 1962, 296 F.2d 124: page 420 (text and footnote 11).

Phillip Alexander Securities & Futures Ltd. v. Bamberger, Court of Appeal (England), 12 July 1996, THE TIMES, 22 July 1996: page 538 (footnote 42).

Pierreux NV v. Transportmaschinen Handelshaus GmbH, *Tribunal de commerce,* Brussels (Belgium), 6 May 1993, XXII YEARBOOK 631 (1997): pages 46 (footnote 6), 70 (footnote 80).

Pinochet Ugarte (No. 2), House of Lords (England) [1999] 1 ALL ER 577: page 226 (footnote 51).

Polytek Engineering v. Jacobson Companies, District Court, D. Minn. (United States), 1997, 984 F. Supp. 1238: page 572 (footnote 53).

Prima Paint Co. v. Flood & Conklin, Supreme Court (United States), 1967, 388 U.S. 395: pages 51 (text and footnote 16), 515 (footnote 88), 597 (text and footnote 41).

Primex International Corp. v. Wal-Mart Stores Inc., Court of Appeals, 2d Cir. (United States), 27 March 1997, 89 N.Y. 2d 594; 657 N.Y.S. 2d 385: page 80 (footnote 113).

Pritzker v. Merrill Lynch, Pierce, Fenner & Smith, Inc., Court of Appeals, 3d Cir. (United States), 1993, 7 F.3d 1110: page 599 (text and footnotes 55, 56).

ProCD, Inc. v. Zeidenberg, Court of Appeals, 7th Cir. (United States), 1996, 86 F.3d 1447: page 604 (footnote 87).

Prograph International v. Barhydt, District Court N.D. Cal. (United States) 1996), 928 F. Supp. 983: page 140 (footnote 6).

Provenda S.A. v. Alimenta S.A., Swiss Federal Tribunal (Switzerland), 12 December 1975, ARRÊTS DU TRIBUNAL FÉDÉRAL 101 Ia 521 (1976): page 367 (footnote 27).

Provincial Import & Export Co. v. Hart Enterprises Int., Inc., District Court, S.D.N.Y. (United States), 6 May 1996, No. 96 Civ. 128 (LAK); XXII YEARBOOK 979 (1997), 1996 WL 229872: page 678 (footnote 50).

Prudential Ins. Co. of Am. v. Lai, Court of Appeals, 9th Cir. (United States), 1994, 42 F.3d 1299: page 603 (footnote 82).

Prudential-Bache Sec., Inc. v. Tanner, Court of Appeals, 1st Cir. (United States), 1995, 72 F.3d 234, *subsequent appeal,* 1st Cir, 1998, 141 F.3d 1150: pages 614 (footnote 152), 619 (footnote 178).

Pryner v. Tractor Supply Co., Court of Appeals, 7th Cir. (United States), 1997, 109 F.3d 354, *cert. denied,* Supreme Court, 1997, 118 S. Ct. 295: page 603 (footnote 82).

Psichikon Compania Naviera Panama v. Société Industrielle des Engrais de la Réunion, *Cour de cassation* (France), 7 January 1992, 1992 REV. ARB. 553: page 74 (footnote 95).

Quijada v. Unifrutti of America, Inc., Common Pleas Court of Philadelphia County, Pennsylvania (United States), 1991, 22 Phila. 339: page 608 (footnote 110).

Quintette Coal Ltd. v. Nippon Steel Corp., Court of Appeal, British Columbia (Canada), 1990, 50 BCLR (2d) 207; 1991 1 WWR 219: page 72 (footnote 92).

Qinhuangdao Tongda Enterprise Development Co. v. Million Basic Co., (Hong Kong) [1993] 1 HKLR 173: page 571 (footnote 48).

R. v. Bow Street Metropolitan Stipendiary Magistrate, (England), [1999] 1 ALL ER 577: page 226 (footnote 51).

R. v. Gough, Court of Appeal (England), [1993] AC 646: pages 219 (text and footnote 39), 220 (footnote 42).

R. v. Sussex Justices, ex parte McCarthy, (England), [1924] 1 KB 256: page 219 (footnote 41).

Raffineries de Pétrole d'Homs et de Banias v. ICC, *Cour d'appel de Paris* (France), 1985 REV. ARB. 147: page 556 (footnote 44).

RAKTA v. Parsons & Whitemore Inc., Court of Appeals, 2d Cir. (United States), 1974, 508 F.2d 969; I YEARBOOK 205 (1976): page 370 (footnote 30).

Randolph v. Green Tree Fin. Corp., District Court, M.D. Ala. (United States), Nov. 26, 1997, No. 96-D-11-N, 1997 U.S. Dist. LEXIS 21721; *recons. denied,* M.D. Ala., 991 F. Supp. 1410: pages 605 (footnote 88), 606 (footnote 97).

Rawlings v. Société Kevorkian, *Cour d'appel de Paris* (France), 1 December 1993, 1994 REV. ARB. 695: page 550 (footnote 9).

R.E.D.E.C. et Pharaon v. Unzinexport et Chambre de Commerce Internationale, *Tribunal de grande instance,* Paris (France), 13 July 1988, 1989 REV. ARB. 97: pages 159 (footnote 10), 161 (text and footnote 16).

Renteria v. Prudential Ins. Co. of Am., Court of Appeals, 9th Cir. (United States), 1997, 113 F.3d 1104: page 603 (footnote 82).

Renusager Power Co. v. General Electric Co. and the ICC, Supreme Court (India), 16 August 1984, X YEARBOOK 431 (1985): pages 44 (footnote 2), 53 (footnote 22), 80 (footnote 112), 88 (footnote 7), 510 (footnote 67), 641 (footnote 45).

Republic of Nicaragua v. Standard Fruit Co., Court of Appeals, 9th Cir. (United States), 1991, 937 F.2d 469: pages 48 (footnote 8), 515 (footnote 8), 597 (footnote 42).

Republique arabe d'Egypte v. Western Helicopters Ltd., *Cour de justice de Genève* (Switzerland), 26 November 1982, *aff'd Tribunal fédéral Suisse*, 16 May 1983: page 201 (footnote 26).

République Côte d'Ivoire v. Norbert Beyrard, *Cour d'appel de Paris* (France), 12 November 1993, 1994 REV. ARB. 685: pages 68 (footnote 71), 554 (footnote 31).

République Islamique d'Iran v. Société Framatom et Eurodif, *Cour de cassation* (France), 20 March 1989, 1989 REV. ARB. 653, *Note* P. Fouchard, 1989 REVUE TRIMESTRIELLE DU DROIT CIVILE 624, *Note* R. Perrot: pages 482 (footnote 30), 555 (footnote 39).

Request from Ministry of Legal Affairs of Trinidad and Tobago, *In re*, Court of Appeals, 11th Cir. (United States), 1988, 848 F.2d 1155: page 491 (footnote 61).

Resort Condominiums v. Bolwell, MOT No. 389, Supreme Court of Queensland (Australia), 29 October 1993, 20 YEARBOOK 628 (1995): page 466 (text and footnote 37).

Rhône Mediterranée v. Achille Lauro, Court of Appeals, 3d Cir. (United States), 1983, 712 F.2d 50: pages 165 (footnote 25), 508 (footnote 59).

Richards v. Lloyd's of London, Court of Appeals, 9th Cir. (United States), 1997, 107 F.3d 1422, *reh'g en banc granted*, 1997, 121 F.3d 565, *op. withdrawn & substituted op. on recons. en banc,* 1998, 135 F.3d 1289: page 606 (footnote 96).

Riley v. Kingsley Underwriting Agencies, Ltd., Court of Appeals, 10th Cir. (United States), 1992, 969 F.2d 953: page 606 (footnote 96).

Roberson v. The Money Tree of Alabama, Inc., District Court, M.D. Ala. (United States), 1997, 954 F. Supp. 1519: page 599 (text and footnotes 57, 58).

Robobar, Ltd. v. Finncold, Supreme Court (Italy), 28 October 1993, XX YEARBOOK 739 (1995): page 525 (footnote 13).

Roby v. Corporation of Lloyd's, Court of Appeals, 2d Cir. (United States), 1993, 996 F.2d 1353: page 606 (footnote 96).

Roche v. Local 32B-321 Serv. Employees Int'l Union, District Court, S.D.N.Y. (United States) 1991, 755 F. Supp 622: page 613 (footnote 146).

Rodriguez de Quijas v. Shearson/American Express, Supreme Court (United States), 1989, 490 U.S. 477: pages 69 (footnotes 73, 75), 603 (footnote 75).

Roger Jakubowski v. Nora Beverages, Inc., New York Supreme Court (United States), 21 November 1995 (unpublished): page 178 (footnote 55).

Rogers, Burgun, Shahine & Deschler, Inc. v. Dongsan Construction Co., District Court, S.D.N.Y. (United States) 1984, 598 F. Supp. 754: pages 479 (footnote 20), 486 (footnote 44).

Rosenberg v. Merrill Lynch, Pierce, Fenner & Smith, Inc., Court of Appeals, 1st Cir. (United States), 1997, 170 F.3d 1: page 604 (footnote 83).

Roussel-Uclaf v. G.D. Searle & Co. Ltd. *et al.,* Chancery Division (England), 1977, 1 LLOYD'S L. REP. 225; IV YEARBOOK 317 (1979): pages 68 (footnote 69), 74 (footnote 96), 75 (footnote 96).

S.A. Agima v. Smith Industries Ltd., *Tribunal de commerce,* Brussels (Belgium), 1975, VIII YEARBOOK 360 (1983): page 70 (footnote 79).

S.A. Assicuriazioni e Riassicurazioni "Lloyd Continental" S.p.A. v. Navigazione Alga, *Corte di cassazione* (Italy), 11 September 1979, 1980 RIV. DIR. INT. p.p. 425; VI YEARBOOK 230 (1981): pages 58 (footnote 38), 78 (footnote 107).

SAEPA & SIRPE v. Germanco srl, Supreme Court (Italy), 1996, XXII YEARBOOK 737 (1997): pages 46 (footnote 5), 71 (footnote 84).

S. AG v. H. Ltd., *Tribunal fédéral* (Switzerland), ATF 116 I 721 (1990): page 576 (footnote 4).

S.A. Mineraçao da Trinedade-Samitri v. Utah International Inc., Court of Appeals, 2d Cir. (United States), 1984, 745 F.2d 190; XI YEARBOOK 572 (1986): pages 66 (footnote 60), 89 (footnote 9).

S.A. Tradax v. S.p.A. Carapelli, *Corte di Appello,* Florence (Italy), 22 October 1976, III YEARBOOK 279 (1978): page 65 (footnote 59).

S.C.S., Ltd. v. C., C.S.A. & IHK-Schiedsgericht Zurich (Switzerland), ATF 117 II 94 (1991): page 588 (footnotes 62, 63).

S&L&H, S.p.A. v. Miller-St. Nazianz, Inc., Court of Appeals, 7th Cir. (United States), 1993, 988 F.2d 1518: page 609 (footnote 120).

Sam Reisfeld & Son Import Co. v. S.A. Eteco, Court of Appeals, 5th Cir. (United States), 1976, 530 F.2d 679: page 600 (footnote 62).

Sansi Fruitgrowing Equipment SpA v. Semena I Possadatchen Material, *Cour d'appel* (France), 25 February 1993 (unpublished): page 291 (footnote 27).

Sauer-Getriebe KG v. White Hydraulics, Inc., Court of Appeals, 7th Cir. (United States), 1983, 715 F.2d 348, *cert. denied* Supreme Court, 464 U.S. 1070: pages 479 (text and footnotes 21, 22), 486 (footnote 44).

Saxis S.S. Co. v. Multifacs Int'l Traders, Inc., Court of Appeals, 2d Cir. (United States), 1967, 375 F.2d 577: page 614 (footnote 150).

Scheepvaartkantoor Holwerda v. S.p.A. Esperia de Navigazione, Court of Appeal, Naples (Italy), 17 March 1979, 1979 IL DIRITTO MARITTIMO 377; VII YEAR-BOOK 337 (1982): pages 47 (footnote 7), 95 (footnote 8).

Scherk v. Alberto-Culver Co., Supreme Court (United States), 1974, 417 U.S. 506; ICA NY CONVENTION V.54; I YEARBOOK 203 (1976); *rehearing denied*, 419 US 885 (1974): pages 57 (footnote 33), 63 (footnote 53), 69 (footnote 74), 71(footnote 85), 120 (footnote 29), 517 (footnote 94), 592 (footnote 9), 603 (footnote 75).

Scherk Enterprises A.G. (Liechtenstein) v. Société des Grandes Marques (Italy), *Corte di cassazione*, 12 May 1977, excerptes *in* IV YEARBOOK 285 (1979): page 482 (footnote 28).

Sea Dragon, Inc. v. Gebr. Van Weelde Scheepvaartkantoor, B.V., District Court, S.D.N.Y. (United States), 1983, 574 F. Supp. 367, X YEARBOOK 94 (1985): pages 64 (footnote 56), 614 (footnote 150).

Seacoast Motors v. Chrysler Corp., Court of Appeals, 1st Cir. (United States), May 13, 1998, 143 F.3d 626: page 610 (footnote 121).

Securities Indus. Ass'n v. Connolly, Court of Appeals, 1st Cir. (United States), 1989, 883 F.2d 1114: pages 592 (footnote 9), 595 (footnotes 29, 32).

SEFRI S.A. v. Komgrap, *Tribunal fédéral Suisse, Première cour civil* (Switzerland)*e*, 23 October 1985, 1986 SWISS BULL. 77: page 399 (footnote 5).

Sen Mar, Inc. v. Tiger Petroleum Corp., District Court, S.D.N.Y. (United States), 1991, 774 F. Supp. 879: page 597 (footnote 40).

Setec v. SICCA, *Tribunal de grande instance*, Paris (France), 13 January 1986, 1987 REV. ARB. 63, *Note* P. Bellet: page 233 (footnote 65).

Shell v. R.W. Sturge, Ltd., Court of Appeals, 6th Cir. (United States), 1995, 55 F.3d 1227: page 606 (footnote 96).

Siegel v. Prudential Insurance Co. of America,California Court of Appeal (United States) 1998, 67 Cal. App. 4th 1270, 79 Cal. Rptr. 2d 726: page 594 (footnote 27).

Siemens A.G. & BKMI Industrienlagen GmbH v. Dutco Consortium Construction Co., *Cour de cassation* (France), 7 January 1992, 1992 REV. ARB. 470: pages 199, 200 (text and footnote 24), 201, 560 (footnote 69).

Signal-Stat Corp. v. United Elec., Court of Appeals, 2d Cir. (United States), 1956, 235 F.2d 298: page 592 (footnote 6).

Skandia Am. Reinsurance Corp. v. CAJA Nacional De Ahorro Y Segoro, District Court, S.D.N.Y. (United States), May 21, 1997, 96 Civ. 2301, 1997 U.S. Dist. LEXIS 7221: page 687 (footnote 35).

Smith Barney, Harris Upham & Co. v. Luckie, New York Court of Appeals (United States), 1995, 85 N.Y.2d 193: page 602 (footnote 71).

Société Akzo Nobel v. S.A. Elf Atochem, *Cour d'appel de Versailles* (France), 8 October 1998, 1999 REV. ARB. 57: page 556 (footnote 40).

Société anonyme Replor v. S.A.R.L., *Cour d'appel*, Paris (France), 12 January 1988, 1988 REV. ARB. 691: page 291 (footnote 27).

Société Appareils Dragons v. Empresa Central de Abastecimientos y Ventas de Equipos y Piezas de la Construccion, *Cour d'appel*, Paris (France), 22 January 1982, 1982 REV. ARB. 92; *Cour de cassation* (France), 8 June 1983, 1987 REV. ARB. 309: pages 356 (footnote 4), 678 (footnote 51).

Société Ardi v. Société Scapnor, *Cour d'appel de Paris* (France), 12 January 1995, 1996 REV. ARB. 72: page 558 (footnote 53).

Société Bail Line Shipping v. Société Recofi, *Cour de cassation* (France), 21 January 1992, 1995 REV. ARB. 57: page 552 (footnote 20).

Société Balenciaga v. Société Allieri et Giovanozzi, *Cour de cassation* (France), 29 November 1989, 1990 REV. ARB. 633: page 556 (footnote 43).

Société Braspetro Oil Services (Brasoil) v. GMRA, *Cour d'appel*, Paris (France), 1 July 1999, 1999 REV. ARB. 834: page 362 (footnote 18).

Société Bruynzeel Deurenfabrieck N.V. v. Ministre d'Etat aux Affaires Etrangères de la République Malgache, *Cour de cassation* (France), 30 June 1976, 1976 BULL. CIV. I 198, 1977 REV. ARB. 137: page 557 (footnote 49).

Société CFTE v. Dechavanne, *Cour d'appel,* Grenoble (France), 13 September 1993, 1994 REV. ARB. 336: pages 70 (footnote 77), 71 (footnote 82).

Société Château Tour Saint Christophe v. Astrom, *Cour de cassation* (*Chambre sociale*), 16 February 1999, 1999 REV. ARB. 290: page 140 (footnote 6).

Société Confex v. Etablissements Dahan, *Cour de cassation* (France), 25 February 1986, 1986 JDI 735; XII YEARBOOK 484 (1987): page 73 (footnote 94).

Société Cubic Defense System, Inc. v. Chambre de Commerce Internationale, *Cour d'appel*, Paris (France), 15 September 1998, 1999 REV. ARB. 103, *Note* P. Lalive: pages 361 (footnote 17), 381 (footnote 9).

Société Deko v. G. Dingler et Société Meva, *Cour d'appel de Paris* (France), 24 March 1994, 1994 REV. ARB. 514: page 553 (footnote 29).

Société Eurodisney v. Société Impresa Pizzarotti & Société Torno, *Cour de cassation* (France), 11 October 1995, 1996 REV. ARB. 228: pages 479 (footnote 18), 556 (footnote 40).

Société European Gas Turbines, S.A. v. Société Westman International Ltd., *Cour d'appel de Paris* (France), 30 September 1993, 1994 REV. ARB. 359, *aff'd,*

Court de cassation (France), 19 December 1995, 1996 REV. ARB. 49: page 561 (footnote 74).

Société Farhat Trading Co. v. Société Daewoo, *Cour de cassation, Première chambre civile* (France), 6 March 1996, 1997 REV. ARB. 69, *Note* J.J. Arnaldez: page 276 (footnote 5).

Société Ganz v. Société Nationale des Chemins de Fers Tunisiens, *Cour d'appel de Paris* (France), 29 March 1991, 1991 REV. ARB. 478: pages 64 (footnote 56), 553 (footnote 28).

Société Gatoil v. National Iranian Cie., *Cour d'appel de Paris* (France), 17 December 1991, 1993 REV. ARB. 281: pages 552 (footnote 18), 553 (footnote 24), 555 (footnote 34).

Société Générale pour l'Industrie v. Société Ewbank, *Cour de Cassation* (France), 28 February 1995, 1995 REV. ARB. 597: page 559 (footnote 66).

Société Générale de Surveillance (SGS) v. Raytheon European Management & Systems Co., Court of Appeals, 1st Cir. (United States), 1981, 643 F.2d 863: pages 80 (footnote 112), 601 (footnote 65), 609 (text and footnote 117).

Société des Grands Travaux de Marseille v. People's Republic of Bangladesh *et al., Tribunal fédéral* (Switzerland), 5 May 1976, ARRÊTS DU TRIBUNAL FÉDÉRAL 102 IA 574; V YEARBOOK 217 (1980): pages 45 (footnote 3), 675 (text and footnote 43).

Société Horeva v. Société Sitas, *Cour de Cassation* (France), 6 March 1990, 1990 REV. ARB. 633: pages 480 (footnote 23), 556 (footnote 43).

Société Icori v. Kuwait Foreign Trading Contracting & Investment Co., *Tribunal de grande instance*, Paris (France), 24 February 1992, 1994 REV. ARB. 557: page 228 (footnote 56).

Société Impex v. Société P.A.Z., *Cour de cassation* (France), 18 May 1971, 1972 JDI 64: page 561 (footnote 73).

Société Kis France v. Société A.B.S., *Cour d'appel*, Paris (France), 19 March 1987, 1987 REV. ARB. 498: pages 291 (text and footnote 26), 292 (footnote 28).

Société Labinal v. Sociétés Mars and Westland Aerospace, *Cour d'appel* (France), 19 May 1993, 1993 REV. ARB. 645; 120 JDI 957 (1993); 8 MEALEY'S INT. ARB. REP. 7 (July 1993): pages 66, 67 (footnote 64), 343 (footnote 75), 553 (footnote 29).

Société LeGant Nicolet v. SAFIC, *Cour de cassation* (France) June 1956, 1957 REV. ARB. 14: page 163 (footnote 21).

Société Libanaise L. et B. Cassia v. Société Pia Investment, *Cour de Cassation* (France), 10 July 1990, 1990 REV. ARB. 851, 1992 JDI 168: page 555 (footnote 35).

Société Nationale Algérienne Pour La Recherche et Transport (Sonatrach) v. Distrigas Corp., District Court, D. Mass. (United States), 1987, 80 B.R. 606: pages 517 (footnote 94), 603 (footnote 79).

Société Nationale v. Shaheen Natural Resources, District Court, S.D.N.Y. (United States) 1985, 585 F. Supp. 57: page 177 (footnote 54).

Société Nu Swift PLC v. Société White Knight et autres, *Cour d'appel*, Paris (France), 21 January 1997, 1997 REV. ARB. 429: page 453 (footnote 13).

Société Ripolin, *Cour de cassation* (France), 27 April 1981, Arret No. 736, 1981 GAZETTE DU PALAIS II.584: pages 357 (footnote 10), 398 (footnote 3).

Société Sardisud v. Société Technip, *Cour d'appel*, Paris (France), 25 March 1994, 1994 REV. ARB. 391: page 361 (footnote 17).

Société Schutte Lenz v. Veuve Gallais, *Cour d'appel Paris* (France) 20 April 1972, 1973 REV. ARB. 84: page 381 (footnote 9).

Société Sonidep v. Société Sigmoil et Communauté urbaine de Casablanca, *Cour de cassation* (France), 15 June 1994, 1995 REV. ARB. 88: pages 355 (footnote 1), 561 (footnote 75).

Société the Authority for Supply Commodities Cairo Estran v. Société Ipitrade International, *Cour de cassation* (France) 20 March 1989, 1989 REV. ARB. 494: page 480 (footnote 23).

Société TRH Graphic v. Offset Aubin, *Cour de cassation* (France), 19 November 1991, 1992 REV. ARB. 462: page 270 (text and footnote 29).

Société Tunisienne d'Electricité et de Gaz (STEG) v. Société Entrepose, *Tribunal de grande instance* (France), 22 March 1976, 1976 REV. ARB. 268; III YEARBOOK 283 (1978): pages 45 (footnote 5), 71 (footnote 84).

Société Unichips v. Gesnouin, *Cour d'appel de Paris* (France), 12 Feb. 1993, 1993 REV. ARB. 255: page 505 (footnote 40).

Sociétés de procédes de préfabrication pour le béton v. Libye, *Cour d'appel de Paris* (France), 28 October 1997, 1998 REV. ARB. 399: pages 186 (footnote 2), 188 (text and footnote 7), 189 (footnote 8), 562 (footnote 78).

SOFIDIF v. OIETAI and AEOI, *Cour d'appel*, Paris (France), 19 December 1986, 1987 REV. ARB. 359: pages 287 (text and footnote 17), 288 (text and footnote 19), 289.

Soleimany v. Soleimany, Court of Appeal (England), 1998, [1998] 3 W.L.R. 811: page 544 (footnote 94).

Sonatrach v. Ford, Bacon & Davis, *Trib. de 1ère Instance de Bruxelles* (Belgium), 23 July 1987 & *Trib. de 1ère Instance de Bruxelles*, 6 Dec. 1988, 1990 *Annales de droit de Liège* 267, 7 SWISS BULL. 213 (1989), XV YEARBOOK COMM. ARB. 370 (1990); *aff'd*, *Cour d'Appel de Bruxelles*, 9 Jan. 1990 (8è Ch) 1990 J. T. 386: pages 506 (footnote 48), 685 (footnote 28).

Sonatrach v. General Tire & Rubber Co., District Court, S.D.N.Y. (United States), 1977, 430 F. Supp. 1332: pages 83 (footnote 119), 178 (footnote 57).

Sonatrach v. K.C.A. Drilling, *Tribunal fédéral* (Switzerland), 19 December 1990, ATF 116 II 639: page 578 (footnote 17).

Sonetex v. Charphil et Topkapi, *Cour de cassation* (France), 3 March 1992, 1993 JDI 141: pages 552 (footnote 18), 555 (footnote 37).

Sopac Italiana S.p.A. v. Bukama GmbH and FIMM, *Tribunale,* Milan (Italy), 22 March 1976, 12 RIVISTA DI DIRITTO PRIVATO (1976); II YEARBOOK 248 (1977): pages 83 (footnote 121), 87 (footnote 3).

Southern Pacific Properties Ltd. v. Arab Republic of Egypt, *Cour d'appel*, Paris (France), 12 July 1984, 23 ILM 1048 (1984) (English translation), decision upheld, *Cour de cassation*, 6 January 1987, 26 ILM 1004 (English translation); XIII YEARBOOK 158, ICSID decision, XVI YEARBOOK 16 (1993); Arab Republic of Egypt v. Southern Pacific Property (Middle East) Ltd., *Cour d'appel de Paris* (France), 12 July 1984, 1985 JDI 129; *aff'd*, *Court de cassation (France)*, 6 January 1987, 1987 REV. ARB. 469; translation in 23 ILM 1048 (1984) and 26 ILM 1004 (1987): pages 76 (footnote 100), 179 (footnote 58), 289 (text and footnote 22), 290 (footnote 23), 292 (text and footnote 31), 553 (text and footnote 25), 562 (footnote 81), 664 (footnote 9).

Southern Seas Navigation Ltd. v. Petroleas Mexicanas, District Court, S.D.N.Y. (United States) 1985, 606 F Supp. 692: page 465 (footnote 36).

Southland Corp. v. Keating, Supreme Court (United States), 1984, 465 U.S. 1: pages 593 (footnote 16), 603 (footnote 78).

S.p.A. Carapelli v. Ditta Otello Mantovani, Court of Appeal, Venice (Italy), 26 April 1980, 82 IL DIRITTO MARITTIMO 256 (1980); VII YEARBOOK 340 (1982): pages 57 (footnote 31), 58 (footnote 37).

Sperry International Trade v. Government of Israel, District Court, S.D.N.Y. (United States) 1982, 532 F. Supp. 901: page 465 (footnotes 34, 35).

Splosna Plovba v. Agrelak Steamship Corp., District Court, S.D.N.Y. (United States), 1974, 381 F. Supp. 1368; I YEARBOOK 204 (1976): page 120 (footnote 33).

Standard Tankers (Bahamas) Co. v. Motor Tank Vessel, AKTI, District Court, E.D.N.C. (United States) 1977, 438 F. Supp. 153: page 453 (footnote 13).

Stapem S.A. v. Boccard S.A., *Cour de cassation*, *Première chambre civile* (France), 19 November 1991 (unpublished): page 354 (footnote 24).

Stedor Enterprises, Ltd. v. Armtex, Inc., Court of Appeals, 4th Cir. (United States), 1991, 947 F.2d 727: page 610 (footnote 121).

Steel Authority of India, Ltd. v. Hind Metal, Inc., Queen's Bench Division, Commercial Court (England) 1983, [1984] 1 LLOYD'S L. REP. 405: page 276 (footnote 5).

Succula Ltd. and Pomona Shipping Co. Ltd. v. Harland and Wolff Ltd., Queen's Bench Division (England), 1980, [1980] 2 LLOYD'S L. REP. 381: page 30 (footnote 1).

Sumitomo Corp. *et al.* v. Parakopi Compania Maritima S.A., District Court, S.D.N.Y. (United States), 1979, 477 F. Supp. 737; VI YEARBOOK 245 (1981): page 93 (footnote 3).

Sumitomo Heavy Industries Ltd. v. Oil and Natural Gas Commission, Queen's Bench (England), 23 July 1993, [1994] 1 LLOYD'S L. REP. 45; (1998) 1 SUPREME COURT CASES 305: pages 90 (footnote 14), 100 (footnote 18), 108 (footnote 6), 509 (footnote 65).

Sunderland Steamship P and I Association v. Gatoil International Inc. (The "Lorenzo Halcoussi"), Queen's Bench Division (England), [1988] 1 LLOYD'S L. REP. 180: page 489 (footnote 57).

Sunkist Soft Drinks Inc. v. Sunkist Growers Inc., Court of Appeals, 11th Cir. (United States), 1993, 10 F.3d 753; Supreme Court, 1994, 115 S. Ct. 190: pages 48 (footnote 8), 599, 600 (text and footnotes 59, 60), 612 (footnote 134).

Swift Indus., Inc. v. Botany Indus., Inc., Court of Appeals, 3d Cir. (United States), 1972, 466 F.2d 1125: page 614 (footnotes 149, 150).

Syncor International v. David MacLeish, Court of Appeals, 4th Cir. (United States), 1997, 120 F.3d 262: page 615 (footnote 158).

Syrian Petroleum Company (SPC) v. GTM Entrepose SA, *Tribunal fédéral Suisse* (Switzerland), 16 July 1990: page 381 (footnote 8).

Tampimex Oil Ltd. v. Latina Trading Corp, District Court, S.D.N.Y. (United States) 1983, 558 F. Supp. 1201: page 486 (footnote 43).

Technostroyexport, *In re* Application of, District Court, S.D.N.Y. (United States), 1994, 853 F. Supp. 695: pages 491 (text and footnote 62), 608 (footnote 110).

Telefunken v. *Cour de Justice*, Geneve & N.V. Phillips, *Tribunal fédéral* (Switzerland), 1952, ARRÊTS DU TRIBUNAL FÉDÉRAL 78.1.352 (1952): page 131 (footnote 7).

Teleserve Sys., Inc. v. MCI Telecommunications Corp., New York Supreme Court, Appellate Division (United States), 1997, 230 A.D.2d 585: page 604 (footnote 85).

Tenney Eng'g, Inc, v. United Elec., Radio & Mach. Workers, Court of Appeals, 3d Cir. (United States), 1953, 207 F.2d 450: page 592 (footnote 6).

Texas Trading v. Nigeria, District Court, S.D.N.Y. (United States), 1980, 500 F. Supp. 320: page 673 (footnote 31).

Thiokol Corp. v. Certain Underwriters at Lloyd's of London, District Court, D.C. Utah, North Div. (United States), 6 May 1997, 1:96-CV-028B: page 129 (footnote 4).

Thompson v. Zavin, District Court, C.D. Cal. (United States) 1984, 607 F. Supp. 780: page 488 (footnote 53).

Thomson C.S.F. v. Frontier AG Bern, Federal Tribunal (Switzerland), 28 January 1997, 16 SWISS BULL. 118 (1998): page 64 (footnote 56).

Thomson-CSF v. American Arbitration Association, Court of Appeals, 2d Cir. (United States), 1995, 64 F.3d 773: page 598 (footnote 46).

Thyssen v. Maaden, *Cour d'appel de Paris* (France), 6 April 1995, 1995 REV. ARB. 464: page 560 (footnote 68).

Three Valleys Municipal Water District v. E.F. Hutton & Company, Inc., Court of Appeals, 9th Cir. (United States), 1991, 925 F.2d 1136: pages 170 (footnote 37), 513 (footnote 78), 600 (text and footnote 64), 620 (footnote 185).

Toprak Mahsulleri Ofisi (Turkey) v. Finagrain (Switzerland) (GAFTA) April 29, 1977, [1979] 2 LLOYD'S L. REP. 98 (Court of Appeal, 26 January 1979): page 340 (text and footnote 67).

Total Soc. It. p.a. v. Achille Lauro, *Corte di cassazione* (Italy), 25 January 1977, 17 RASSEGNA DELL'ARBITRATO 94 (1977); IV YEARBOOK 284 (1979): page 47 (footnote 7).

Torno v. Kumagai Gumi Ltd., *Cour d'appel de Paris* (France), 19 May 1998: page 558 (footnote 54).

Totem Marine Tug & Barge, Inc. v. North Am. Towing, Court of Appeals, 5th Cir. (United States), 1979, 607 F.2d 649: page 613 (footnote 147).

Tracomin S.A. v. Sudan Oil Seeds Co., Federal Supreme Court (Switzerland), 5 November 1985, 1985 ARRÊTS DU TRIBUNAL FÉDÉRAL 3IB 253; XII YEARBOOK 511 (1987): pages 54 (footnote 26), 56 (footnote 30), 58 (footnote 36).

Tradax Export S.A. v. Amoco Iran Oil Co., *Tribunal fédéral* (Switzerland), 7 February 1984, XI YEARBOOK 532 (1986): page 78 (footnote 107).

Tuesday Industries Ltd. v. Condor Industries Ltd. (South Africa) 4 S.A. 379 (1978): page 527 (footnote 19).

Tribunal fédéral Suisse (Switzerland), 24 March 1997, 1997 SWISS BULL. 316, with English translation in 12 MEALEY'S INT'L ARB. REP, No. 9, pp. H1-H (September 10, 1999): page 282 (footnote 12).

Tribunal de grande instance, Paris (France), 28 March 1984, 1985 REV. ARB. 141: page 207 (footnote 13).

Twi Lite International Inc. v. Anam Pacific Corp. *et al.,* District Court, N.D. Calif. (United States), 1996, 11 MEALEY'S INT. ARB. REP. E-1 (November 1996): page 51 (footnote 16).

Ukrvneshprom State Foreign Economic Enterprise v. Tradeway, Inc., District Court, S.D.N.Y. (United States), 11 March 1996, No. 95 Civ. 10278 (RPP); 1996 WL 107285, XXII YEARBOOK 958 (1997): page 678 (footnote 50).

Ulrich Schubert v. H.O. Engineering, Inc. et al, Order of the Superior Court of New Jersey, Middlesex County Docket No. L-4310-90 (United States) 4 March 1994: page 270 (footnote 28).

Union of India v. McDonnell Douglas Corp., Queen's Bench Division, Commercial Court (England), 1992, [1993] 2 LLOYD'S L. REP. 48: page 509 (footnote 65).

United Paperworkers Int'l Union v. Misco, Inc., Supreme Court (United States), 1987, 484 U.S. 29: page 612 (footnote 129).

United States v. Morris, Court of Appeals, 4th Cir. (United States), 1996, 82 F.3d 590: page 608 (footnote 113).

United States v. Panhandle Eastern Corp. et al., Delaware Supreme Court (United States) 1988, 118 F.R.D. 346: page 317 (text and footnote 47).

United States Fidelity Co. v. West Point Construction Co., Court of Appeals, 11th Cir. (United States), 1988, 837 F.2d 1507: pages 80 (footnote 111), 536 (footnote 32).

United States Fire Ins. Co. v. National Gypsum Co., Court of Appeals, 2d Cir. (United States), 1996, 101 F.3d 813, *cert. denied,* Supreme Court, 1997, 117 S. Ct. 2512: pages 602 (footnote 72), 621 (footnote 190).

Universal American Barge Corp. v. J-Chem, Inc., Court of Appeals, 5th Cir. (United States), 1991, 946 F.2d 1131: page 600 (footnote 62).

Universal Pictures v. Inex Film and Inter-Export, *Cour d'appel,* Paris (France), 1978, 1978 REV. ARB. 515; *Cour de cassation* (France), 1980, JURISCLASSEUR PERIODIQUE No. 27-28, 9 July 1980, Part IV, 257: pages 79 (text and footnote 110), 196 (footnote 18), 230 (text and footnote 58).

Usina Costa Pino S.A. v. Louis Dreyfus Sugar Co., District Court, S.D.N.Y. (United States), 1996, 933 F. Supp. 1170: pages 48 (footnote 8), 600 (footnote 62).

V. v. S.C. Corporation, *Tribunal cantonal de Vaud* (Switzerland), 9 September 1980 (unpublished): page 402 (footnote 9).

Van Hopplynus S.A. v. Coherent Inc., *Tribunal de commerce,* Brussels (Belgium), 5 October 1994, 1995 REV. ARB. 311; XXII YEARBOOK 637 (1997): page 70 (footnote 80).

Varley v. Tarrytown Associates Inc., Court of Appeals, 2d Cir. (United States), 1973, 477 F.2d 208: page 119 (footnote 27).

Vendome Holding and Cartier v. Horowitz, *Tribunal fédéral Suisse* (Switzerland), 10 October 1979, 1981 *Journal des Tribunaux* 61-127: page 173 (footnote 42).

Verlinden B.V. v. Central Bank of Nigeria, Court of Appeals, 2d Cir. (United States), 1981, 647 F.2d 320: page 4 (footnote 3).

Vespe Contracting Co. v. Anvan Corp., District Court, E.D.P. (United States) 1975, 399 F. Supp. 516: page 488 (footnote 50).

Vibroflotation A.G. v. Express Builders Co. Ltd., High Court of Hong Kong (Hong Kong), 15 August 1994, XX YEARBOOK 287 (1995): page 569 (text and footnote 34).

Victor Leber v. Société Atlas Werk A.G., *Cour d'appel*, Paris (France), 22 April 1980, 1981 REV. ARB. 71: page 402 (footnote 8).

Victrix Steamship Co. v. Salen Dry Cargo AB, District Court, S.D.N.Y. (United States), 28 August 1986, XIII YEARBOOK 537 (1988); Court of Appeals, 2d Cir. (United States), 1987, 825 F.2d 709, XV YEARBOOK 534 (1990): page 68 (footnote 71).

Vimar Seguros y Reaseguros, S.A. v. M/V Sky Reefer, Supreme Court (United States), 1995, 515 U.S. 528: pages 56 (footnote 29), 603 (footnote 77).

Vita Food Products v. Unus Shipping Co., (England) 1939 A.C. 277: page 338 (footnote 64).

Volt Information Sciences v. Board of Trustees, Supreme Court (United States), 1989, 489 U.S. 468: pages 508 (footnote 59), 593 (footnote 18), 595 (text and footnotes 28, 29).

Walker v. Warren, Massachusetts Superior Court (United States), 1997, 7 Mass. L. Rptr. 453, 1997 WL 572936: page 619 (footnote 177).

Westacre Investments v. Jugoimport. Commercial Court, Q.B. (England), 12 May 1999, [1999] Q.B. 740; *Tribunal fédéral* (Switzerland), 30 December 1994 (1ère Cour Civile), 13 SWISS BULL. 217 (1995): pages 544 (footnote 93), 583 (footnote 39).

Westbrook Int'l v. Westbrook Technologies, District Court, E.D. Mich. (United States), 1998, 17 F. Supp. 2d 681: page 594 (footnote 21).

Westinghouse v. Republic of Philippines, Preliminary Award of 19 December 1991, ICC Arbitration No. 6401, 7 MEALEY'S INT'L ARB. REP. B1 (January 1992): pages 65 (footnote 57), 324 (footnote 12).

Westland Helicopters Ltd. v. République Arabe d'Egypte, *Tribunal fédéral Suisse* (Switzerland), 24 September 1986, 1987 SWISS BULL. 12, ATF 112 Ia

344, 109 SEMAINE JUDICIAIRE 1 (1987), XII YEARBOOK 186 (1987): pages 207 (footnote 13), 409 (footnote 24), 585 (footnote 48).

Westland Helicopters v. Emirates Arabs Unis, Arabie Saoudite, Etat du Qatar, ABH et Arab Organization for Industrialization (AOI), *Tribunal fédéral* (Switzerland) 19 April 1994, ATF 120 II 155 (1994),12 SWISS BULL. 404 (1994): pages 514 (footnote 85), 546 (footnote 102), 585 (text and footnote 48), 586 (footnote 53).

Westland Helicopters, Ltd. (U.K.) v. A.O.I. *et al.*, *Tribunal fédéral Suisse*, 19 July 1988, 1988 SWISS BULL. 220, 28 ILM 687: pages 174 (footnote 48), 585 (footnote 51).

Wheeler v. St. Joseph Hosp., California Appellate Court, 4th Dist. (United States), 1976, 63 Cal. App. 3d 345: page 605 (footnote 89).

Wilko v. Swan, Supreme Court (United States), 1953, 346 U.S. 427: pages 69 (footnote 73), 614 (footnote 148).

Williamson v. John D. Quinn Construction Co., District Court, S.D.N.Y. (United States) 1982, 537 F. Supp. 613: page 310 (footnote 33).

Wilson v. Kaiser Found. Hosps., California Appellate Court, 3d Dist. (United States), 1983, 141 Cal. App. 3d 891: page 605 (footnote 89).

Wolsey v. Foodmaker, Court of Appeals, 9th Cir. (United States), 1998, 144 F.3d 1205: page 591 (footnote 2).

Wren Distributors, Inc. and Innovative Marketing Concepts, Inc. v. Phone-Mate, Inc. District Court, S.D.N.Y. (United States) 1985, 600 F. Supp. 1576: page 178 (footnote 55).

Wright v. Universal Maritime Service Corp., Supreme Court (United States) 119 S. Ct. 391 (1998): page 603 (footnote 81).

X v. Y, *Bundesgericht* (Federal Republic of Germany), 6 March 1969, 1969 WERTPAPIER MITTEILUNGEN 671; II YEARBOOK 235 (1977): page 41 (footnote 8).

X v. Y, *Bundesgericht* (Federal Republic of Germany), 25 May 1970, 1970 WERTPAPIER MITTEILUNGEN 1050, II YEARBOOK 237 (1977): pages 55 (footnote 29), 59 (footnote 42).

X v. Y, *Bundesgericht* (Federal Republic of Germany), 12 February 1976, 1976 WERTPAPIER MITTEILUNGEN 435; II YEARBOOK 242 (1977): page 135 (footnote 17).

X v. Y, *Bundesgericht* (Federal Republic of Germany), 9 March 1978, 1978 WERTPAPIER MITTEILUNGEN 573; IV YEARBOOK 264 (1979): page 40 (footnote 6)

X v. Y, Case No. 565, *Areios Pagos* (Supreme Court) (Greece), 1965, 1966 EPHIMERIS ELLION NOMIKON 289: page 46 (footnote 5).

X v. Y, *Cour d'appel* (France), 11 December 1981, 1982 RECUEIL DALLOZ SIREY 389: page 66 (footnote 60).

X v. Y, *Cour de cassation* (France), 11 October 1954, 1982 RECUEIL DALLOZ SIREY 388: page 65 (footnote 59).

X v. Y, Court of Appeal, Venice (Italy), 21 May 1976, 1976 RIV. DIR. INT. 850; III YEARBOOK 277 (1978): page 41 (footnote 7).

X v. Y, *Landgericht*, Bremen (Federal Republic of Germany), 8 June 1967, DIE DEUTSCHE RECHTSPRECHUNG AUF DEM GEBIETE DES INTERNATIONALEN PRIVATRECHTS IN DEN JAHREN 1966 UND 1967, 860; ICA NY CONVENTION V. 46; II YEARBOOK 234 (1977): pages 55 (footnote 27), 68 (footnote 71).

X v. Y, *Landgericht*, Bremen (Federal Republic of Germany), 20 January 1983, XII YEARBOOK 486 (1987): page 68 (footnote 71).

X v. Y, *Landgericht*, Hamburg (Federal Republic of Germany), 19 December 1967, 1968 ARBITRALE RECHTSPRAAK 139; ICA NY CONVENTION V.47; II YEARBOOK 235 (1977): page 55 (footnote 28).

X v. Y, *Landgericht*, Hamburg (Federal Republic of Germany), 16 March 1977, III YEARBOOK 274 (1978): page 47 (footnote 7).

X v. Y, *Landgericht*, Hamburg (Federal Republic of Germany), 20 April 1977, IV YEARBOOK 261 (1979): page 66 (footnote 61).

X v. Y, *Landgericht*, Heidelberg (Federal Republic of Germany), 23 October 1972; *Oberlandesgericht*, Karlsruhe (Federal Republic of Germany), 13 March 1973; II YEARBOOK 239 (1977): pages 106 (footnote 2), 129 (footnote 4).

X v. Y, *Oberlandesgericht*, Düsseldorf (Federal Republic of Germany), 8 November 1971, DIE DEUTSCHE RECHTSPRECHUNG AUF DEM GEBIETE DES INTERNATIONALEN PRIVATRECHTS IN DEN JAHREN 1971 (1971) 492; ICA NY CONVENTION V.50; II YEARBOOK 238 (1977): pages 55 (footnote 29), 59 (footnotes 40, 42).

X v. Y, *Oberlandesgericht*, Celle (Federal Republic of Germany), 5 June 1981, VII YEARBOOK 322 (1982): page 60 (footnote 42).

X v. Y, *Oberlandesgericht*, Hamm (Federal Republic of Germany), 15 November 1994, XXII YEARBOOK 707 (1997): pages 85 (footnote 1), 86 (footnote 1), 89 (footnote 11).

X v. Y, *Oberlandesgericht*, Dresden (Federal Republic of Germany), 5 December 1995, XXII YEARBOOK 266 (1997): pages 85 (footnote 1), 89 (footnote 11).

X v. Y, *Oberster Gerichtshof* (Supreme Court) (Austria), 17 November 1971, 96 JURISTISCHE BLATTER 629 (1974); ICA NY CONVENTION V.29; I YEARBOOK 183 (1979): page 58 (footnote 38).

X v. Y, *Pretore*, Genoa (Italy), 30 April 1980, 16 RIV. DIR. INT. 458 (1980); VII YEARBOOK 342 (1982): page 70 (footnote 77).

X v. Y, Supreme Court (Lebanon), 27 April 1987, 1988 REV. ARB. 723 (unpublished): page 134 (footnote 14).

X v. Y, *Tribunal cantonal,* Vaud (Switzerland), 20 November 1946, JOURNAL DES TRIBUNAUX 1947 III 59: page 51 (footnote 16).

X v. Y, *Tribunal de commerce,* Paris (France), 8 March 1976, 1977 REVUE DE LA JURISPRUDENCE COMMERCIALE 72: page 637 (footnote 37).

X v. Y, *Tribunal de grande instance,* Paris (France), 1 February 1979, 1980 REV. ARB. 97: page 128 (footnote 3).

X v. Y, *Tribunal de grande instance,* Paris (France), 16 October 1979, 1980 REV. ARB. 101: page 128 (footnote 3).

X v. Y, *Tribunal fédéral* (Switzerland), 28 April 1992, 9 SWISS BULL. 368 (1992); 1993 REV. ARB. 124; XVIII YEARBOOK 143 (1993): page 67 (footnote 66).

X v. Y, *Tribunal fédéral* (Switzerland), 21 March 1995, XXII YEARBOOK 800 (1997): page 54 (footnote 25).

X v. Y, *Tribunal Superior* (Supreme Court) (Spain), 11 February 1981, LA LEY, 27 April 1981, No. 146; VII YEARBOOK 356 (1982): page 47 (footnote 7).

Yasuda Fire & Maine Insurance Company of Europe, Court of Appeals, 7th Cir. (United States), 1999, 37 F.3d 345: page 465 (footnote 36).

Yusuf Ahmed Alghanim & Sons W.L.L. v. Toys -R- Us Inc. *et al.,* Court of Appeals, 2d Cir. (United States), 1997, 126 F.3d 15: pages 611 (footnote 127), 678 (footnote 50).

Zanzi v. De Coninck, *Cour de cassation* (France), 5 January 1999, 1999 REV. ARB. 260: pages 141 (footnote 10), 555 (footnote 36).

Zhan Jiang E&T Dev Area Service Head v. An Hau Co. Ltd., High Court of Hong Kong (Hong Kong), 21 Jan. 1994, XX YEARBOOK 283 (1995): page 568 (footnote 31).

Zuhdi A. Bushnak, *In re,* District Court, E.D.N.C. (United States) 28 August 1986, No. 5: 96-MC-41-BR: page 608 (footnote 110).

Table of Arbitral Awards

ICC Awards

1007/1959, cited *in* P. Sanders, *L'autonomie de la cause compromissoire, in* Hommage à Frédéric Eisemann 39 (ICC Publication No. 321, 1978): page 163 (text and footnote 21).

1024/1959, cited *in* P. Sanders, *L'autonomie de la cause compromissoire, in* Hommage à Frédéric Eisemann 39 (ICC Publication No. 321, 1978): page 164 (footnote 22).

1110/1963, G. Wetter, *Issues of Corruption before International Tribunals: The Authentic Text and True Meaning of Judge Gunnar Lagergren's 1963 Award in ICC Case No. 1110*, 10 Arb. Int. 277 (1994): pages 63 (footnote 54), 344 (footnote 78).

1250/1964, I ICC Awards 30: pages 109 (footnote 9), 123.

1397/1966, I ICC Awards 179, 1974 JDI 878: pages 66 (footnote 63), 342 (footnote 69).

1422/1966, 1974 JDI 884: page 326 (footnote 18).

1434/1975, I ICC Awards 263: pages 78 (text and footnote 104), 103, 646 (footnotes 62, 63).

1455/1967, cited in J. Lew, Applicable Law in International Arbitration (1978): pages 325 (footnotes 16, 17), 326 (footnote 17).

1472/1968, quoted *in* Y. Derains, *Le statut dezs usages du commerce international devant les juridictions arbitrales*, 1973 Rev. Arb. 122: page 331 (footnote 38).

1512/1971 (Dalmia Dairy Industries v. National Bank of Pakistan), I ICC Awards 3, 33, 37, 207; I Yearbook 128 (1976); comments by P. Lalive, 1974 JDI 904: pages 53 (footnote 22), 63 (footnote 51), 72 (footnote 87), 109 (footnote 9), 123, 323 (footnote 8), 339 (footnote 66), 416 (footnote 2), 643 (footnote 50), 650 (footnote 79), 656 (footnote 99), 677 (footnote 49).

1525/1969, quoted *in* Y. Derains, *L'application cumulative par l'arbitre des systèmes de conflits de lois intéressées au litige*, 1972 Rev. Arb. 99: page 327 (footnote 21).

1526/1968/1975, extracts *in* 1974 JDI 915, I ICC AWARDS 218 ; comment by Y. Derains 1974 JDI 918: pages 164 (text and footnote 23, 24), 647 (footnote 69).

1641/1969, extracts *in* 1974 JDI 888: page 333 (text and footnote 44).

1677/1975, I ICC AWARDS 20: pages 63 (footnote 54), 113 (footnote 15).

1689/1970, reported by Y. Derains in 1972 REV. ARB. 104: page 323 (footnote 8).

1703/1971 (Parsons & Whittemore v. RAKTA), I ICC AWARDS 6, 195; I YEARBOOK 130 (1976); made public as result of enforcement proceedings in the U.S. 508 F.2d 969 (2d. Cir. 1974); summarized in I YEARBOOK 205 (1976): pages 370 (footnote 30), 652 (footnote 87).

1717/1972, I ICC AWARDS 191: page 643 (footnote 51).

1759/1972, quoted *in* Y. Derains, *L'application cumulative par l'arbitre des systèmes de conflits de lois intéressées au litige*, 1972 REV. ARB. 99: page 327 (footnote 22).

1782/1973, I ICC AWARDS 230: page 651 (footnote 85).

1803/1972 (Société des Grands Travaux de Marseille v. East Pakistan Industrial Development Corp.), I ICC AWARDS 40; V cited *in* P. Sanders, *L'autonomie de la cause compromissoire*, *in* HOMMAGE À FRÉDÉRIC EISEMANN 39 (ICC Publication No. 321, 1978) 177 (1980): pages 45 (footnote 4), 103 (footnote 28), 173 (footnote 45), 675 (footnote 42).

1859/1973, 1973 REV. ARB. 133; cited in Y. Derains, 1974 JDI 890: pages 334 (footnote 46), 339 (footnote 66), 635 (footnote 33).

1939/1971, cited by Y. Derains, 1973 REV. ARB. 145: page 45 (footnote 4).

1955/1973, cited *in* P. Sanders, *L'autonomie de la cause compromissoire*, *in* HOMMAGE À FRÉDÉRIC EISEMANN 39 (ICC Publication No. 321, 1978): page 165 (footnote 26).

1990/1972, I ICC AWARDS 20, 199; extracts *in* 1974 JDI 897, 1972 REV. ARB. 100; extracts in English in III YEARBOOK 217 (1978); quoted *in* Y. Derains, *L'application cumulative par l'arbitre des systèmes de conflits de lois intéressées au litige*, 1972 REV. ARB. 99: pages 327 (footnote 22), 332 (footnote 41), 643 (footnote 50).

2090/1976, I ICC AWARDS 56: pages 635 (text and footnote 34), 636 (footnote 35), 637.

2096/1972, quoted *in* Y. Derains, *L'application cumulative par l'arbitre des systèmes de conflits de lois intéressées au litige*, 1972 REV. ARB. 99: pages 326 (footnote 19), 327 (footnote 24).

2114/1972 (Meiki Co. Ltd. v. Bucher-Guyer S.A.), I ICC AWARDS 49: pages 91 (footnote 1), 132 (footnote 11).

2138/1974, I ICC AWARDS 242: page 76 (text and footnote 100).

2139/1974, I ICC AWARDS 23, 237: pages 68 (footnote 71), 652 (footnote 86).

2142/1974, I ICC AWARDS 7, 194: page 652 (footnote 86).

2216/1974, ICC AWARDS 28, 224, 1975 JDI 917: pages 352 (footnote 16), 650 (footnote 79), 657 (footnote 102).

2272/1975, I ICC CASES 11: page 81 (text and footnote 115).

2291/1975, I ICC AWARDS 274, 1976 JDI 1989: pages 632 (footnote 26), 643 (footnote 50), 644 (footnote 59), 645 (footnote 60).

2321/1974 (Solel Boneh v. Republic of Uganda), I ICC AWARDS 8: pages 44 (footnote 2), 53 (footnote 22), 122 (footnote 38), 123 (footnote 39), 132 (footnote 10).

2375/1975, I ICC AWARDS 257, 1976 JDI 973: pages 77 (text and footnote 102, 103), 332 (footnote 41).

2391/1977, described by Y. Derains in *Case Note*, 1977 JDI 949: page 324 (footnote 11).

2404/1975, I ICC AWARDS 280: pages 624 (footnote 5), 647 (footnote 69), 649 (footnote 79).

2438/1975, 1976 JDI 969: page 327 (footnote 23).

2444/1976, I ICC AWARDS 285; extracts in 1977 JDI 932: pages 472 (footnotes 2, 4), 478 (footnote 16).

2476/1976, I ICC AWARDS 289: pages 165 (footnote 27), 166 (footnote 28).

2478/1974, I ICC AWARDS 25, 233, 1975 JDI 926, III YEARBOOK 222 (1978): pages 105 (footnote 1), 643 (footnote 52), 644 (footnote 59), 656 (footnote 100), 657 (footnote 103).

2508/1976, I ICC AWARDS 292: pages 644 (footnote 59), 650 (footnote 82).

2520/1975, I ICC AWARDS 278: page 645 (footnote 60).

2540/1976, 4 ARB. INT. 86: page 650 (text and footnote 80).

2546 (unpublished): page 652 (footnote 88).

2583/1976, I ICC AWARDS 304: page 648 (footnote 72).

2585/1977, cited in Y. Derains, *Case Note*, 1978 JDI 998: page 328 (footnote 25).

2637/1975, I ICC AWARDS 13: pages 97 (footnote 13), 109 (footnote 9), 123.

2671/1976 (Mobil Oil Indonesia v. Asamera Oil (Indonesia) Ltd.), interim award of March 30, 1976; referred to in review proceedings in New York courts, N.Y. LAW JOURNAL, Oct. 28, 1976, p. 10, col. 4: page 144 (footnotes 16, 17).

2680/1977, cited *in* Y. Derains, *Case Note*, 1978 JDI 998: page 328 (footnote 25).

2694/1977, 1978 JDI 985: pages 328 (footnote 32), 352 (footnote 19).

2708/1976, I ICC AWARDS 297: page 655 (footnote 97).

2730/1982, 1984 JDI 914: pages 64 (footnote 56), 326 (footnote 18).

2734/1977, cited *in* Y. Derains, *Case Note*, 1978 JDI 998: page 328 (footnote 27).

2735/1976; extracts *in* 1977 JDI 947: page 324 (footnote 10).

2811/1978, I ICC AWARDS 164, 456, 1979 JDI 983: pages 66 (footnote 63), 342 (footnote 69).

2879/1978, 1979 JDI 990: pages 326 (footnote 19), 328 (footnote 31), 352 (footnote 16).

2930/1982, I ICC AWARDS 118; IX YEARBOOK 105: pages 64 (footnote 56), 624 (footnote 6).

3043/1978, 1979 JDI 1000: pages 326 (footnote 20), 328 (footnotes 28, 29).

3093/1979, I ICC AWARDS 365, VII YEARBOOK 87 (1982): pages 362 (footnote 19), 656 (footnote 98).

3100/1979, I ICC AWARDS 365, VII YEARBOOK 87 (1982): page 362 (footnote 19).

3130/1980, I ICC AWARDS 417: page 138 (footnote 2).

3131/1979 (Norsolor v. Pabalk Ticaret), I ICC AWARDS 122, 1983 REV. ARB. 525, IX YEARBOOK 109 (1984); upheld by the Austrian Supreme Court, IX YEARBOOK 159 (1984); enforced by the French Supreme Court, 24 ILM 360 (1985): pages 334 (footnotes 47, 50), 336 (footnote 53), 644 (footnote 59).

3202/1978, extracts *in* 1979 JDI 1003: page 332 (footnote 40).

3243/1981, I ICC AWARDS 429: pages 645 (footnote 60), 646 (footnotes 65, 66).

3267/1979 (Servicios Profesionales Construccion v. Eurosystem hospitalier en faillite), I ICC AWARDS 76, 376; II ICC AWARDS 43; 1980 JDI 961, VII YEARBOOK 96 (1982), XII YEARBOOK 87 (1987): pages 113 (footnote 15), 334 (footnotes 46, 47), 353 (footnote 21), 624 (footnote 3).

3281/1981, 1982 JDI 990: page 339 (footnote 66).

3327/1981, I ICC AWARDS 433: pages 45 (footnote 4), 301 (footnotes 8, 9), 353 (footnote 21).

3344/1981, I ICC AWARDS 440: pages 353 (footnote 21), 645 (footnote 59), 646 (footnote 63).

3380/1980, I ICC AWARDS 96, 413: pages 102 (footnote 22), 624 (footnote 4).

3381/1984, 1986 JDI **1096: page 370 (footnote 31).**

3383/1979, I ICC AWARDS 100, 394; extracts in **1980 JDI 979; extracts in Eng**lish *in* VII YEARBOOK 119 (1982): pages 38 (footnote 2), 40 (footnote 5), 48 (footnote 10), 135 (footnote 16), 167 (footnote 30), 282 (footnote 12).

3460/1980, I ICC AWARDS 425: page 646 (footnote 62).

3493/1983 (Southern Pacific Properties (M.E.) *et al.* v. Arab Republic of Egypt *et al.*); subsequent court proceedings, I ICC AWARDS 124, 22 ILM 752 (1983), 1986 REV. ARB. 75: pages 173 (footnote 45), 395 (text and footnote 10), 624 (footnote 5), 674 (footnote 39).

3540/1980, I ICC AWARDS 105, 399, 1981 JDI 914, VII YEARBOOK 124 (1982): pages 101 (footnote 20), 109 (footnote 9), 123, 334 (footnote 47), 466 (footnote 38), 646 (footnote 64), 647 (footnote 71), 648 (footnote 72).

3683/1982, interim award of 25 April 1985, reported in *Cour d'appel*, Paris, 19 December 1986, 1987 REV. ARB. 359 (setting aside the award on unrelated grounds). *Cour de cassation*, 8 March 19888, 1989 REV. ARB. 481 (annulling the Paris *Cour d'appel* decision); *Cour d'appel*, Versailles, 7 March 1990, 1991 REV. ARB. 326: page 176 (footnote 52).

3740 (unpublished): page 652 (footnote 89).

3742/1983, I ICC AWARDS 486: page 76 (footnote 100).

3755/1988, 1 ICC BULL 25 (December 1990): page 328 (footnote 26).

3820/1981, VII YEARBOOK 134 (1982): page 334 (footnote 47).

3879/1984 (Westland Helicopters, Ltd. v. AOI *et al.*), II ICC AWARDS 11, 23 ILM 1071 (1984), XI YEARBOOK 127 (1986): pages 174 (footnote 48), 585 (footnotes 50, 52).

3880/1983, 1983 JDI 897: page 328 (footnote 31).

3881/1994, II ICC AWARDS 257, *Note* S. Jarvin: page 370 (footnote 31).

3896/1982, I ICC AWARDS 161, X YEARBOOK 47 (1985): pages 45 (footnote 4), 80 (footnote 111), 463 (footnote 29).

3916/1982/1983, I ICC AWARDS 507; extracts in 1984 REV. ARB. 3: pages 63 (footnote 54), 65 (footnote 58), 345 (footnote 79).

3938/1982, I ICC AWARDS 503: page 115 (footnote 20).

3952/1982 (unpublished): page 653 (footnote 90).

3987/1983, I ICC AWARDS 521: pages 94 (footnote 4), 641 (footnote 44).

4023/1984, ICC AWARDS 528: page 186 (footnote 2).

4131/1982/1984 (Isover St. Gobain v. Dow Chemical France), I ICC AWARDS 146, 465, 1984 REV. ARB. 137, IX YEARBOOK 131 (1984): pages 52 (footnote 19), 54 (footnote 24), 75 (footnote 98), 76, 108 (footnote 8), 173 (footnote 46), 177 (text and footnote 53), 638, 639 (footnote 38).

4132/1983, 1983 JDI 891: page 328 (footnote 31).

4145/1983-84-86, I ICC AWARDS 53, 558, II ICC AWARDS 53, XII YEARBOOK 97 (1987), 1985 JDI 985, *Note* Y. Derains: pages 44 (footnote 2), 52 (footnote 17), 53 (footnote 22), 65 (footnote 58), 128 (footnote 2), 327 (footnote 20), 329 (footnote 34), 345 (footnote 79), 634 (footnote 31), 650 (footnote 79).

4156/1983, I ICC AWARDS 515, 1984 JDI 937: pages 462 (footnote 28), 472 (footnote 2), 478 (footnote 16).

4237/1984, I ICC AWARDS 167: pages 624 (footnote 6), 641 (footnote 43), 652 (footnote 89), 657 (footnote 104).

4265/1984, 1984 JDI 922: pages 348 (footnote 3), 352 (footnote 18).

4338/1984, I ICC AWARDS 555, 1985 JDI 981: pages 334 (footnote 47), 637 (footnote 37).

4367/1984, II ICC AWARDS 18: page 641 (footnote 44).

4381/1986, II ICC AWARDS 264, 1986 JDI 1103: pages 44 (footnote 3), 45 (footnote 4), 53 (footnote 20), 54 (footnote 24), 130 (footnote 6), 165 (footnote 25), 624 (footnote 6).

4392/1983, I ICC AWARDS 473: pages 44 (footnote 2), 53 (footnote 22), 80 (footnote 111).

4402/1983, I ICC AWARDS 153, VIII YEARBOOK 204 (1983), IX YEARBOOK 138 (1984): pages 76 (footnote 100), 78 (footnote 106), 172.

4415/1984, I ICC AWARDS 530, 1984 JDI 952: pages 68 (footnote 71), 473 (footnote 4).

4434/1983, 1983 JDI 893: page 326 (footnotes 18, 19).

4462/1985/1987, III ICC AWARDS 17 (1987), XVI YEARBOOK 54 (1991): pages 278 (footnote 6), 646 (footnote 68).

4467/1984, 1984 JDI 925: page 348 (footnote 3).

4472/1984, I ICC AWARDS 525: pages 54 (footnote 25), 128 (footnote 2), 132 (footnote 11).

4491/1984, I ICC AWARDS 539: page 94 (footnote 5).

4504/1985/1986, II ICC AWARDS 279, 1986 JDI 1118: pages 76 (footnote 100), 78 (footnote 106), 166 (footnote 29), 174 (footnote 47), 279 (footnote 8).

4555/1985, I ICC AWARDS 536, II ICC AWARDS 24: page 52 (footnote 17).

4589/1984, II ICC AWARDS 32, 454: page 71 (footnote 81).

4604/1984, I ICC AWARDS 546: pages 53 (footnote 20), 66 (footnote 63).

4650/1985, II ICC AWARDS 67; extracts in XII YEARBOOK 111 (1987): pages 329 (footnote 33), 337 (text and footnote 61), 631 (footnote 21).

4667/1984 (unpublished), quoted in Y. Derains, Note, II ICC AWARDS 297, 338: pages 48 (footnote 8), 649 (footnote 76).

4695/1984, II ICC AWARDS 33, XI YEARBOOK 149 (1986): pages 53 (footnote 20), 71 (footnote 81), 165 (footnote 25), 624 (footnote 6), 641 (footnote 44).

4761/1987, II ICC AWARDS, 298, 302, 519, 1986 JDI 1137: pages 115 (footnote 20), 301 (footnote 7), 336 (footnote 56), 646 (footnotes 67, 68), 650 (footnote 79).

4862/1986, II ICC AWARDS 308: page 171 (footnote 39).

4972/1989, 1989 JDI 1100, *Note* G.A. Alvarez: page 353 (footnote 20).

4996/1985, 1986 JDI 1131: pages 326 (footnote 19), 327 (footnote 20).

4998/1985, 1986 JDI 1139: page 462 (footnote 28).

5029/1986, II ICC AWARDS 69, 480; XII YEARBOOK 113 (1987): pages 44 (footnote 2), 53 (footnote 22), 85, 296 (footnote 3).

5065/1986, II ICC AWARDS 330, 1987 JDI 1039: pages 48 (footnote 8), 165 (footnote 25), 173 (footnote 44), 334 (footnote 47), 641 (footnote 44), 644 (footnote 57).

5073/1986, II ICC AWARDS 85: pages 624 (footnote 5), 644 (footnote 58).

5082/1994, ICC PROCEDURAL DECISIONS 76-79: page 464 (footnote 32).

5103/1988, II ICC AWARDS 361: pages 45 (footnote 4), 65 (footnote 59), 78 (footnote 104), 86, 128 (footnote 2), 320 (footnote 2), 624 (footnote 3), 641 (footnote 44).

5195/1986, II ICC AWARDS 101: pages 652 (footnote 88), 653 (footnote 90).

5285 (ISEC v. Bridas, 745 F Supp. 172 (S.D.N.Y. 1990)), XVII YEARBOOK 639: page 330 (footnote 36).

5302, cited S. Jarvin, *Note* under ICC Case 4504; interim awards of 1985 and 1986, 1986 JDI 1118: page 279.

5418/1987, XIII YEARBOOK 91 (1988): page 330 (footnote 36).

5423/1987, II ICC AWARDS 339: pages 128 (footnote 2), 138 (footnote 2).

5460/1987, XIII YEARBOOK 104 (1988): pages 326 (footnote 18), 330 (footnote 36).

5477/1988, II ICC AWARDS 358: pages 65 (footnote 59), 644 (footnote 59).

5514/1990, III ICC AWARDS 459: page 279 (footnote 9).

5542/1987, reported in D. Hascher, ICC PROCEDURAL DECISIONS 62-65: page 449 (footnote 1).

5617/1989, III ICC AWARDS 537: page 650 (footnote 79).

5622/1992, 8 ICC BULL 52 (May 1997): pages 143 (text and footnote 13), 145 (footnote 20).

5625/1987, II ICC AWARDS 484: page 151 (footnote 26).

5651/1988, (unpublished): page 80 (footnote 114).

5715/1989, 1996 JDI 1050: page 459 (footnote 21).

5721/1990, 117 JDI 1020: page 78 (footnote 105).

5730/1988, 24 August 1988, Société de Lubrifiante Elf Aquitaine v. Orri, 1992 REV. ARB. 125; *Cour d'appel*, Paris, 11 January 1991, 1992 REV. ARB. 95; *Cour de cassasion civile*, 11 June 1991, 1992 REV. ARB. 73: page 178 (footnote 56).

5754/1987 (unpublished): pages 90 (footnote 12), 115 (footnote 21), 288 (footnote 21).

5832/1988, ICC CASES 352, 536: page 48 (footnote 8).

5865/1989, 1998 JDI 1008, *Note* D. Hascher: page 339 (footnote 65).

5885/1989, III ICC AWARDS 40: page 646 (footnote 68).

5910/1988, II ICC AWARDS 371, 1988 JDI 1216: pages 138 (footnote 2), 646 (footnotes 62, 68).

5946/1990, III ICC AWARDS 46: page 647 (footnotes 69, 71).

5989/1989, XV YEARBOOK 74 (1990); 1997 JDI 1046, *Note* D. Hascher: page 181 (footnote 62).

6057/1990, 1993 JDI 1068: page 459 (footnote 21).

6069/1989, XV YEARBOOK 83 (1990): page 646 (footnote 68).

6106/1990, ICC BULL. SPECIAL SUPPLEMENT: INTERNATIONAL COMMERCIAL ARBITRATION IN EUROPE 34 (1994): page 66 (footnote 63).

6223/1991, 8 ICC BULL 69: page 278 (footnote 7).

6259/1990, interim award of 20 September 1990, Helge Berg and Lars Arvid Skoog v. Apollo Computer, Inc. (unpublished): page 176 (footnote 51).

6268/1990, III ICC AWARDS 68: pages 394 (footnote 8), 641 (footnote 44).

6309/1991, III ICC AWARDS 459: page 278 (footnote 6).

6320/1992, III ICC AWARDS 336, 577: pages 87 (footnote 4), 509 (footnote 64).

6379/1990, III ICC AWARDS 134: pages 70 (footnote 80), 344 (footnote 76).

6401 (Westinghouse v. National Power Corp. of the Philippines), 7 MEALY'S INT. ARB. REP. B-1 (1991-2), 1998 JDI 1058; *Note* D. Hascher, ICC PROCEDURAL DECISIONS 192: pages 65 (footnote 57), 302 (footnote 12), 324 (footnote 12), 345 (footnote 80), 449 (footnote 1), 490 (footnote 59).

6437/1990, 8 ICC BULL 68 (May 1997): page 165 (footnote 25).

6465/1004, ICC PROCEDURAL DECISIONS 80: page 464 (footnote 31).

6475/1994, 6 ICC BULL. 52 (May 1995): page 66 (footnote 63).

6476/1994, 8 ICC BULL. 59 (May 1997): page 245 (footnote 91).

6497/1994, XXIV-a YEARBOOK 71: page 450 (footnote 6).

6503/1990, 3 ICC AWARDS 613; 1995 JDI 1022, commentary Y. Derains: pages 348 (footnote 3), 463 (footnote 30).

6519/1991, III ICC AWARDS 420, *Note* Y. Derains: page 177 (footnote 54).

6560/1990, XVII YEARBOOK 226 (1992): page 328 (footnote 26).

6610/1991, XIX YEARBOOK 162 (1994): page 78 (footnote 105).

6618/1991, 8 ICC BULL 70 (December 1997): page 278 (footnotes 6, 7).

6653/1993, III ICC AWARDS 512, *Note* J.J. Arnaldez: pages 407 (footnote 22), 646 (footnote 63).

6657/1993, 8 ICC BULL 72 (December 1997): page 278 (footnote 7).

6697/1990, 1992 REV. ARB. 135: pages 68 (footnote 71), 467 (footnote 41).

6709/1991, III ICC AWARDS 435, 119 JDI 998 (1992): pages 68 (footnote 69), 171 (footnote 39).

6719/1991, II ICC AWARDS 567: page 641 (footnote 44).

6752, III ICC AWARDS 195: page 177 (footnote 54).

6784/1990, 8 ICC BULL 53 (May 1997): pages 146 (footnote 22), 148 (footnote 24).

6955/1993, XXIV YEARBOOK 107 (1999): page 353 (footnote 21).

7047/1994, 1995 SWISS BULL 301: page 467 (footnote 41).

7076/1993, 8 ICC BULL 66 (May 1997): page 150 (footnote 25).

7097/1993, ICC BULL. SPECIAL SUPPLEMENT: INTERNATIONAL COMMERCIAL ARBITRATION IN EUROPE 39 (1994): page 66 (footnote 63).

7137/1993, cited in A. Reiner, *Les mesures provisoires et conservatoires et l'arbitrage international notamment l'arbitrae CCI*, 1998 JDI 855: page 468 (footnote 46).

7154/1993, III ICC AWARDS 555: page 78 (footnote 107).

7155/1993, 1996 JDI 1037: page 177 (footnote 54).

7170/ 1993, ICC PROCEDURAL DECISIONS 55: page 434 (footnote 15).

7237/1993, 8 ICC BULL 65 (May 1997): page 150 (footnote 25).

7245/1991, Société Procédés de Préfabrication pour le Béton c/Libye, setting aside refused, *Cour d'appel*, Paris, 1998 REV. ARB. 399, *Note* B. Leurent: page 186 (footnote 2).

7263/1994, XXII YEARBOOK 92 (1997): pages 45 (footnote 4), 48 (footnote 8).

7301/1993, XXIII YEARBOOK 47 (1998): page 347 (footnote 1).

7314/1996, ICC PROCEDURAL DECISIONS 136: page 437 (footnote 8).

7319/1994, ICC PROCEDURAL DECISIONS 96: pages 438 (footnote 9), 439 (footnote14).

7375/1996 (Iran v. Westinghouse Electric Corp.), 11 MEALEY'S INT. ARB. REP. A-1 (December 1996): page 80 (footnote 114).

7453/1997, 1997 JDI 1082, *Note* D. Hascher: page 436 (footnote 3).

7489/1992, 1993 JDI 1078, *Note* D. Hascher: page 467 (footnote 41).

7565/1995 (Vekoma B.V. v. Maran Coal Company): page 587 (footnote 58).

7585/1994, 1995 JDI 1015, *Note* Y. Derains (Application of the Vienna Convention of 11 April 1980 together with cumulatiave application of relevant national choice of law rules): page 328 (footnote 30).

7604/1995, 1998 JDI 1027, *Note* D. Hascher: pages 165 (footnote 25), 177 (footnote 54).

7610/1995, 1998 JDI 1027, *Note* D. Hascher: pages 165 (footnote 25), 177 (footnote 54).

7673/1993, ICC BULL. SPECIAL SUPPLEMENT: INTERNATIONAL COMMERCIAL ARBITRATION IN EUROPE 36 (1994): page 66 (footnote 63).

7893/1994, 1998 JDI 1069: page 314 (footnote 42).

8128/1995, 123 JDI 812 (1996): page 632 (footnote 27).

8197/1998, affirmed *Cour d'appel*, Paris 19 May 1998, 13 MEALEY'S INT. ARB. REP. E-1 (July 1998): page 274 (footnote 3).

8365/1996, 1997 JDI 1078, *Note* J.J. Arnaldez: page 334 (footnote 46).

8385/1995, 1997 JDI 1061, *Note* Y. Derains: pages 177 (footnote 54), 334 (footnote 46).

8694/1996, 1997 JDI 1056, *Note* Y. Derains: page 450 (footnote 6).

8742/1996, 1999 JDI 1066, *Note* D. Hascher: page 141 (footnotes 8, 9).

8873/1997, 1998 JDI 1817, *Note* D. Hascher: page 331 (footnote 38).

8891 (unpublished): page 345 (footnote 81).

AAA

Revere Copper and Brass v. Overseas Private Investment Corp. (United States), 24 August 1978, 17 ILM 1321 (1978); V YEARBOOK 202 (1980): pages 45 (footnote 4), 104 (footnote 29).

Ad Hoc Awards

1977, 1980 REV. ARB. 560, extracts in English *in* VII YEARBOOK 77 (1982): page 334 (footnote 47).

30 June 1994, 13 SWISS BULL. 269 (1995): pages 61 (footnote 46), 66 (footnote 63), 67 (footnote 66).

American Independent Oil Co. (AMINOIL) v. Kuwait, 24 March 1982, IX YEARBOOK 71 (1984); 21 ILM 976 (1982): pages 104 (footnote 28), 650 (footnote 82), 677 (text and footnote 48).

British Petroleum Co. (B.P.) v. Libya, 10 October 1973, 53 INTERNATIONAL LAW REPORTS 297 (1979); 1977 JDI 350; 17 ILM 3 (1978): pages 104 (footnote 29), 109 (footnote 9), 123.

Buraimi Oasis Arbitration (1955) between Saudi Arabia and the United Kingdom, reported in Gillis Wetter, III THE INTERNATIONAL ARBITRAL PROCESS 357-373 (1979): page 242 (footnote 85).

Czarnikow v. Rolimpex, Interim award of 9 September 1983, XII YEARBOOK 63 (1987): pages 654 (text and footnotes 93, 94), 675 (footnote 40).

Libyan American Oil Co. (LIAMCO) v. Libya, 1977, 20 ILM 1 (1981): pages 104 (footnote 29), 507 (footnote 56), 662 (text and footnote 5).

Petroleum Development (Trucial Coast) Ltd. v. Sheik of Abu Dhabi, 2 INTERNATIONAL AND COMPARATIVE LAW QUARTERLY 247 (1952): page 333 (footnote 43)

Sapphire International Petroleums Ltd. v. National Iranian Oil Co., 1963, 1964 INTERNATIONAL AND COMPARATIVE LAW QUARTERLY 1001: page 103 (footnote 26).

Saudi Arabia v. Arabian American Oil Co. (ARAMCO), 1958, 1963 INTERNATIONAL LEGAL REPORTS 117: page 103 (footnote 27).

S.E.E.E. v. Yugoslavia, Award of 2 July of Messrs. Panchaud and Ripert, extracts in 1959 JDI 1074: page 333 (footnote 43).

Texaco Overseas Petroleum Co./California Asiatic Oil Co. v. Libya ("Texaco-Calasiatic Award"), 1977 JDI 350: page 104 (footnote 29).

X (Hungarian) v. Y (Yugolsav), 6 July 1983, IX YEARBOOK 69 (1984): page 650 (footnote 79).

X (West German) v. Y (Polish), 9 September 1983, XII YEARBOOK 63 (1987): pages 654 (footnotes 93, 94), 675 (footnote 40).

Arbitration Court—Bulgarian Chamber of Commerce and Industry

Case 60/1980, XII YEARBOOK 84 (1987): page 647 (footnote 71).

Arbitration Court—Chamber of Commerce and Industry, Czechoslovakia

5 March 1980, XI YEARBOOK 112 (1986): pages 48 (footnote 8), 649 (footnote 76).

Arbitration Court—Chamber of Commerce and Industry, Sofia

1 October 1980, XII YEARBOOK 84 (1987): page 80 (footnote 111).

Arbitration Court—Chamber of Foreign Trade, Berlin (GDR)

Case No. 12, 1974, I YEARBOOK 127 (1976): page 59 (footnote 39).

Arbitration Court—Japan Shipping Exchange

X v. Y, 1 September 1981, XI YEARBOOK 193 (1986): page 134 (footnote 14).

Arbitral Tribunal—Agreement on German External Debt

Greece v. Federal Republic of Germany, 26 January 1972, 47 INTERNATIONAL LAW REPORT 418: page 650 (footnote 82).

Arbitral Tribunal—Hamburg Commodity Exchange Grain Merchants' Association

7 December 1995, XXII YEARBOOK 55 (1997): page 54 (footnote 26).

Graphic Industry Award (The Netherlands)

X v. Y, 6 March 1973, III YEARBOOK 224 (1978): page 73 (footnote 94).

ICSID

Amco Asia Corp. *et al.* v. Republic of Indonesia, 25 September 1983, 23 ILM 351 (1984): pages 44 (footnote 2), 53 (footnote 22), 648 (footnote 75).

Amco Asia Corp, et al v. Republic of Indonesia, Procedural Decision of 9 December 1983, 24 ILM 365 (1985): page 315 (text and footnote 43).

American Manufacturing & Trading Inc. v. Republic of Zaire, 21 February 1997, 12 INT. ARB. REP. A-1 (March 1997): page 665 (footnote 12).

Asian Agricultural Products Ltd. v. Republic of Sri Lanka, 27 June 1990, 6 ICSID REVIEW-FOREIGN INVESTMENT LAW JOURNAL 526 (1991); 30 ILM 577 (1991); XVII YEARBOOK 106 (1992): page 665 (text and footnote 12).

Gaith Pharaon v. Republic of Tunisia, 21 November 1988; ICSID CASES, 31 March 1994, 24: page 665 (text and footnote 11).

Klockner v. Cameroun, *ICSID arbitration* 81/2: page 373 (footnote 36).

Manufacturers Hanover Trust Co. v. Arab Republic of Egypt and General Authority for Investment and Free Zones, 24 June 1993, ICSID CASES, 31 March 1994: page 665 (footnote 10).

SOABI v. Republic of Senegal, 1 August 1984, XVIII YEARBOOK 42 (1992): page 80 (footnote 114).

Southern Pacific Properties, Ltd. v. Arab Republic of Egypt (Decision on Jurisdiction), 14 April 1988, XVI YEARBOOK 28 (1991): page 664 (footnote 9).

Southern Pacific Properties, Ltd. v. Arab Republic of Egypt, 20 May 1992, XIX YEARBOOK 51 (1994): page 395 (footnote 11).

Iran-U.S. Claims Tribunal

Case No. 24, XIII YEARBOOK 248 (1988): page 399 (footnote 4).

Case No. 43, 8 October 1986, XII YEARBOOK 287 (1987): page 65 (footnote 58).

Case No. 59, 25 September 1985, XI YEARBOOK 283 (1986): page 650 (footnote 79).

Case No. 74, 14 July 1987, XIII YEARBOOK 288 (1988): page 624 (footnote 6).

Case No. 129, XIII YEARBOOK 248 (1988): page 399 (footnote 4).

Case No. 255, 26 April 1985, XI YEARBOOK 332 (1986): page 649 (footnote 76).

Case No. 298, XIII YEARBOOK 248 (1988): page 399 (footnote 4).

Pepsico, Inc. v. Iran, 13 Iran-U.S. C.T.R. 3 (1986): page 459 (footnote 20).

Woodward-Clyde Consultants v. Islamic Republic of Iran and the Atomic Energy Organization of Iran, 2 September 1983, 3 IRAN-U.S. CLAIMS TRIBUNAL REPORTS 239 (1983-II): page 648 (footnote 75).

Netherlands Arbitration Institute

Setenave v. Settebello (Case No. 723), 1986, Financial Times, 27 February 1986: pages 104 (footnote 28), 653 (footnote 92), 675.

Netherlands Oils, Fats and Oilseeds Trade Association (NOFOTA),

5 September 1977, IV YEARBOOK 218 (1979): page 72 (footnote 90).

20 June 1980, VI YEARBOOK 144 (1981): page 334 (footnote 47).

Netherlands Royal Association of the Committee of Grain Traders

X v. Y, 13 March 1984, 1984 TIJDSCHRIFT VOOR ARBITRAGE 112; X YEARBOOK 79 (1985): page 647 (footnote 71).

Paris Chamber of Arbitration

Case No. 9246, 8 March 1996, XXII YEARBOOK 30 (1997): page 47 (footnote 8).

Society of Maritime Arbitrators of New York

MAP Tankers Inc. v. MOBIL Tankers Ltd., 28 November 1980, VII YEARBOOK 151 (1982): page 76 (footnote 99).

No. 2014, 13 September 1984, XI YEARBOOK 202 (1986): pages 656, 657 (footnote 101).

No. 2049, 21 December 1984, XI YEARBOOK 200 (1986): page 650 (footnote 79).

No. 2068, 5 September 1984, XI YEARBOOK 205 (1986): page 64 (footnote 56).

No. 2068A, 28 August 1981, XI YEARBOOK 205 (1986): page 64 (footnote 56).

TABLE OF AUTHORITIES

Carlos Alfaro & Flavia Guimarey, *Who Should Determine Arbitrability?* 12 ARB. INT. 415 (1996): page 512 (footnote 74).

Guillermo Aguilar Alvarez, Note, II ICC AWARDS 356: page 48 (footnote 8).

The American Arbitration Association, *Code of ethics for Arbitrators in Commercial Disputes* (1976) reprinted in Holtzmann, *The First Code of Ethics for Arbitrators in Commercial Disputes*, 33 BUSINESS LAWYER 309 (1977): pages 214 (footnote 28), 241 (footnote 84).

Pascal Ancel, *Case Note, Parodi v. Annecy et France Boissons, Court of Appeal of Lyon*, 3 REV. ARB. 402 (1997): page 79 (footnote 108).

ANNUAIRE DE L'INSTITUT DU DROIT INTERNATIONAL 469 (1957): page 321 (footnote 3).

Arbitrator's Declaration of Independence, reprinted in 6 ICC BULL. 77 (November 1995): page 195 (footnote 17).

Homayoon Arfazadeh, *L'ordre public du fond et l'annulation des sentences arbitrales internationales en Suisse,* 1995 REVUE SUISSE DE DROIT INTERNATIONAL, ET DE DROIT EUROPÉEN 223: page 583 (footnote 39).

Hon. Judge Vichai Ariyanuntaka, *Thai Legal and Judicial System*, (paper delivered at a seminar conducted by the Dhurakijpundit University Faculty of Law on 29-30 January 2000) 27-28: page 305 (footnote 21).

Arnaldez and Jakande, *Les amendements apportés au Règlement d'Arbitrage de la Chambre de Commerce International (C.C.I.),* 1988 REV. ARB. 67: pages 192 (footnote 14), 238 (footnote 79).

Jasana Arsic, *International Commercial Arbitration on the Internet—Has the Future Come Too Early?* 14 J. INT. ARB. 209 (September 1997): page 56 (footnote 30).

Jean-Yves Art, *Challenge of Arbitrators: Is an Institutional Decision Final?* 2 ARB. INT. 261 (1986): pages 207 (footnote 13), 556 (footnote 44), 640 (footnote 42).

Vivienne M. Ashman, *New York Convention and China's "One Country, Two Systems"*, 220 (No. 2) NEW YORK L. J. 1 (2 July 1998): page 572 (footnote 49).

Bernard Audit, *Arbitration and the Brussels Convention*, 9 ARB. INT. 1 (1993); *comment by* Wolfram Krohn, 86 AM. J. INT. L. 134 (1992): page 688 (footnote 39).

BERNARD AUDIT, DROIT INTERNATIONAL PRIVÉ (1991): page 561 (footnote 72).

Bernard Audit, *Qualification et Droit International Privé*, 18 DROITS: REVUE FRANÇAISE DE THÉORIE JURIDIQUE 55 (1993): page 518 (footnote 100).

Hans Bagner, *Confidentiality in International Commercial Arbitration Practice to be Considered by the Swedish Supreme Court*, 14 INT'L ARB. REP. 29 (No. 9, September 1999): page 318 (footnote 48).

Henri Battifol, *Arbitration Clauses Concluded between French Government-Owned Enterprises and Foreign Private Parties*, 7 COLUM. J. TRANSNAT'L L. 32 (1968): page 45 (footnote 5).

HENRI BATTIFFOL & PAUL LAGARDE, DROIT INT. PRIVÉ (8th ed., 1993): pages 338 (footnote 64), 561 (footnote 72).

Joseph Becker, *Attachments in Aid of International Arbitration-The American Position*, 1 ARB. INT. 40 (1985): page 485 (footnote 39).

Joseph Becker, *Fixing the Federal Arbitration Act by the Millennium*, 8 AM. REV. INT. ARB. 75 (1997): page 591 (footnote 1).

Joseph Becker, *The Rolimpex Exit from International Contract Responsibility*, 10 N.Y.U. J. INT'L ARB. 214 (1978): page 653 (footnote 91).

John Beechey, *Arbitrability of Anti-trust/Competition Law Issues—Common Law*, 12 ARB. INT. 179 (1996): page 66 (footnote 63).

Pierre Bellet, *Intervention*, in E. Minoli, *Relations entre partie et arbitre*, 1970 REV. ARB. 221: page 211 (footnote 22).

Pierre Bellet, *Presentation* in preface to ICC PROCEDURAL DECISIONS: pages 434 (footnote 15), 437 (text and footnote 8), 438 (footnote 9).

Jean Benglia, *Inaccurate References to the ICC*, 7 ICC BULL. 11 (December 1996): pages 157 (footnote 5), 186 (footnote 2).

Klaus-Peter Berger, *The Implementation of the UNCITRAL Model Law in Germany*, 13 MEALEY'S INT. ARB. REP. 38 (Jan. 1998): page 514 (footnote 83).

Klaus-Peter Berger, *International Arbitral Practice and the UNIDROIT Principles of International Commercial Contracts*, 46 AM. J. COMP. L. 129 (1998): page 633 (footnote 27).

Klaus-Peter Berger, *The Lex Mercatoria Doctrine and the UNIDROIT Principles of International Commercial Contracts*, 28 LAW & POLICY IN INTERNATIONAL BUSINESS 943 (1997): page 632 (footnote 27).

Klaus-Peter Berger, *Set-off in International Arbitration*, 15 ARB. INT. 53 (1999): page 258 (footnote 10).

Harold Berman, *Excuse for Nonperformance in the Light of Contract Practices in International Trade,* COLUMBIA LAW REVIEW 1413 (1963): page 651 (footnote 84).

Piero Bernardini, *Development Agencies with Host Governments,* ECONOMIC DEVELOPMENT, FOREIGN INVESTMENT AND THE LAW 161 (Robert Pritchard, Ed., 1996): page 661 (footnote 1).

Piero Bernardini, *Is the Duty to Cooperate in Long-term Contracts a Substantive Transnational Rule in International Commercial Arbitration?* TRANSNATIONAL RULES IN INTERNATIONAL COMMERCIAL ARBITRATION 137 (ICC PUBLICATION No. 480/4, 1993): page 644 (footnote 56).

Lisa Bernstein, *Understanding the Limits of Court-Connected ADR: A Critique of Federal Court Annexed Arbitration Programs,* 141 U. PA. L. REV. 2169 (1993): page 592 (footnote 8).

P. Bertin, *L'intervention des juridictions au cours de la procédure arbitrale,* 1982 REV. ARB. 331: page 480 (footnote 23).

Doak Bishop, *International Arbitration of Petroleum Disputes: The Development of a Lex Petrolea,* XXIII YEARBOOK 1131 (1998): page 658 (footnote 105).

Doak Bishop and L. Reed, *Practical Guidelines for Interviewing, Selecting and Challenging Party-Appointed Arbitrators in International Commercial Arbitration,* 14 ARB. INT. 395 (1998): page 213 (footnote 25).

Marc Blessing, *Arbitrability of Intellectual Property Disputes,* 12 ARB. INT. 191 (1996): page 67 (footnote 67).

Marc Blessing, *Choice of Substantive Law in Arbitration,* 14 J. INT'L ARB. 339 (1997): page 320 (footnote 1).

Marc Blessing, *The ICC Arbitral Procedure Under the 1998 ICC Rules-What has Changed?* 8 ICC BULL. 16 (December 1997): page 412 (footnote 35).

Marc Blessing, *Impact of Mandatory Rule, Sanctions, Competition Laws,* INTRODUCTION TO ARBITRATION—SWISS AND INTERNATIONAL PERSPECTIVES 247 (SWISS COMMERCIAL LAW SERIES, HELBING & LICHTENHAHN VERLAG AG, BASLE, 1999): pages 338 (footnote 63), 343 (footnote 74).

Marc Blessing, *Interim Relief and Discovery in International Arbitration,* in INTRODUCTION TO ARBITRATION—SWISS AND INTERNATIONAL PERSPECTIVES (Swiss Commercial Law Series No.10, 1999): page 477 (footnote 15).

Marc Blessing, *Keynotes on Arbitral Decision Making,* ICC BULL. (Supplement 1997): page 468 (footnote 45).

Marc Blessing, *Mandatory Rules of Law versus Party Autonomy in International Arbitration,* 14 J. INT'L ARB. 23 (No. 4, 1997): page 338 (footnote 63).

Marc Blessing, *The New International Arbitration Law in Switzerland*, 5 J. INT. ARB. No. 3 (1988): pages 352 (footnote 18), 363 (footnote 22), 364 (footnote 23), 477 (footnote 15), 578 (footnote 18).

Karl-Heinz Böckstiegel, ARBITRATION AND STATE ENTERPRISES (1984): page 675 (footnote 41).

Karl-Heinz Böckstiegel, *rapporteur, Arbitration between Parties from Industrialized and Less Developed Countries*, 60 INTERNATIONAL LAW ASSOCIATION, REPORT OF CONGRESS 269: pages 39 (footnote 3), 662 (footnote 2).

Karl-Heinz Böckstiegel, *Discussion of the ILA Resolution on Transnational Rules, 23 October 1992*, TRANSNATIONAL RULES IN INTERNATIONAL COMMERCIAL ARBITRATION (ICC Publication No. 480/4, 1993): page 631 (footnote 25).

Karl-Heinz Böckstiegel, *Public Policy and Arbitrability*, 3 ICCA CONGRESS SERIES 177 (1986 ICCA Congress, P. Sanders ed., 1987): page 508 (footnote 60).

Stephen Bond, *The Constitution of the Arbitral Tribunal*, ICC BULL. 23 (Supplement, 1997): page 197 (footnote 19).

Stephen Bond, *The Experience of the ICC International Court of Arbitration*, MULTI-PARTY ARBITRATION, (ICC PUBLISHING, 1991): page 151 (footnote 26).

Stephen Bond, *The Experience of the ICC in the Confirmation/Appointment Stage of an Arbitration*, in THE ARBITRAL PROCESS AND THE INDEPENDENCE OF ARBITRATORS, ICC Publication No. 472 (1991) (Sixth Joint ICC/ICSID/AAA Colloquium on International Arbitration, ICC, Paris, 27 October 1988): pages 196 (footnote 18), 204 (footnotes 5, 6), 212 (footnote 24), 214 (footnote 27).

Stephen Bond, *How to Draft an Arbitration Clause*, 6 J. INT. ARB. 65 (June 1989): pages 89 (footnote 10), 102 (footnote 23).

Stephen Bond, *How to Draft an Arbitration Clause*, (Paper given at a conference on the validity of arbitral awards (unpublished), Athens, 17 March 1988: page 338 (footnote 62).

Stephen Bond, *The Selection of ICC Arbitrators and the Requirement of Independence*, 4 ARB. INT. 300 (1988): page 195 (footnote 17).

Robert G. Bone, *Lon Fuller's Theory of Adjudication and the False Dichotomy Between Dispute Resolution and Public Law Models of Litigation*, 75 B.U. L. REV. 1273 (1995): pages 501 (footnote 29), 537 (footnote 38).

Michael Bonell, *The UNIDROIT Principles in Practice: The Experience of the First Two Years*, 1 UNIFORM LAW REVIEW 30 (UNIDROIT, 1997): page 632 (footnote 27).

Lawrence G.S. Boo, *Singapore*, ICCA INTERNATIONAL HANDBOOK ON COMMERCIAL ARBITRATION NATIONAL REPORTS, 26 (August 1996, Supplement 21): pages 51 (footnote 16), 308 (footnote 30).

Gary Born, INTERNATIONAL COMMERCIAL ARBITRATION IN THE UNITED STATES 825-861 (Kluwer 1994): pages 452 (footnote 10), 475 (footnote 9), 498 (footnote 10).

Pierre Bourel, *Arbitrage international et immunités des états étrangers,* 1982 REV. ARB. 119: pages 123 (footnote 40), 124 (footnote 45).

Jean-François Bourque, *L'expérience du Centre International d'Expertise de la CCI et le développement de l'expertise international,* 1995 REV. ARB. 231: page 702 (footnote 6).

Jean-François Bourque, *New System to Resolve L/C Disputes through Expertise,* 7 ICC BULL. 12 (May 1996): page 716 (footnote 18).

Paul Bowden, *L'interdiction de se contredire au détriment d'autrui (estoppel) as a Substantive Transnational Rule in International Commercial Arbitration,* TRANSNATIONAL RULES IN INTERNATIONAL COMMERCIAL ARBITRATION 125 (ICC Publication No. 480/4, 1993): page 648 (footnote 74).

David Branson, *Continuous Ownership of a Claim: A Hard Case at the Iran-United States Claims Tribunal Makes Bad Law,* 3 ARB. INT. 164 (1987): page 432 (footnote 9).

David Branson, *The Ken-Ren Case: It is an Ado Where More Aid is Less Help,* 10 ARB. INT. 303 (1994): page 468 (footnote 43).

David Branson & Richard Wallace, *Immunity of Arbitrators under United States Law, in* THE IMMUNITY OF ARBITRATORS 85 (Julian Lew, ed. 1990): page 592 (footnote 10).

Robert Briner, *The Implementation of the 1998 ICC Rules of Arbitration,* 8 ICC BULL. 7 (December 1997): pages 158 (footnote 9), 205 (footnote 10), 376 (footnote 2).

Robert Briner, *Special Considerations Which May Affect the Procedure,* ICCA CONGRESS SERIES NO. 7, PLANNING EFFICIENT ARBITRATION PROCEEDINGS (1994): page 352 (footnote 19).

Robert Briner, *Switzerland,* III ICCA HANDBOOK SUPPL. (13 September 1992): page 115 (footnote 19).

A. Broches, *1985 Model Law on International Commercial Arbitration: An Exercise in International Legislation,* 18 NETHERLANDS YEARBOOK OF INT. L. 3 (1987): page 520 (footnote 4).

Charles Brower, *What I Tell You Three Times is True: U.S. Courts and Pre-Award Interim Measures Under the New York Convention,* 35 VA. J. INT. LAW 971 (1995): page 485 (footnote 40).

Charles Brower and W.M. Tupman, *Court Ordered Provisional Measures Under the New York Convention,* 80 AM. J. INT'L 24 (1986): page 485 (footnote 39).

S. Bruna, *Control of Time Limits by the International Court of Arbitration*, 7 ICC BULL. 72 (December 1996): page 357 (footnote 7).

Eugene Bucher, *Arbitration under the ICC Rules in Switzerland*, SWISS ESSAYS ON INTERNATIONAL ARBITRATION 127 (C. Reymond and E. Bucher eds., 1984): page 589 (footnote 66).

Colin Hugh Buckley, *Issue Preclusion and Issue of Law: A Doctrinal Framework Based On Rules of Recognition, Jurisdiction & Legal History*, 24 HOUS. L. REV. 875 (1987): page 621 (footnote 190).

Michael Bühler, *Technical Expertise: An Additional Means for Preventing or Settling Commercial Disputes*, 6 J. INT. ARB. 135 (1989): page 702 (footnote 6).

Geneviève Burdeau, *Nouvelles perspectives pour l'arbitrage dans le contentieux économique intéressant l'Etat*, 1995 REV. ARB. 3: page 667 (footnote 16).

John Burke, ed. JOWITT'S DICTIONARY OF ENGLISH LAW (2d ed., 1977): page 406 (footnote 19).

STEPHEN BURTON AND ERIC ANDERSON, CONTRACTUAL GOOD FAITH (1995): page 644 (footnote 55)

P. Cahier, *The Strengths and Weaknesses of International Arbitration Involving a State as a Party*, *in* Julian Lew, ed., CONTEMPORARY PROBLEMS IN INTERNATIONAL ARBITRATION (Martinus, Nijhoff 1987): page 179 (footnote 59).

Rita Cain, *Preemption of State Arbitration Statutes: the Exaggerated Federal Policy Favoring Arbitration*, 19 J. CONTEMP. L. 1 (1993): page 593 (footnote 16).

M. Calvo, *The Challenge of ICC Arbitrators—Theory and Practice*, 15 J. INT. ARB. No. 4, (1998): pages 224 (footnote 49), 230 (footnote 59), 235 (footnotes 70, 71).

Thomas Carbonneau, *Arbitral Justice: The Demise of Due Process in American Law*, 70 TUL. L. REV. 1945 (1996): page 605 (footnote 92).

THOMAS CARBONNEAU, ED., LEX MERCATORIA AND ARBITRATION (1990): page 625 (footnote 10).

Thomas Carbonneau, *Rendering Awards with Reasons: The Elaboration of a Common Law of International Transactions*, 23 COLUM. J. TRANSNAT'L L. 579 (1985): page 624 (footnote 7).

Paul D. Carrington & Paul H. Haagen, *Contract and Jurisdiction*, 1996 SUP. CT. REV. 331 (1996): page 605 (footnote 92).

James Carter, *Federal Arbitration Act Seen as Out of Step with Modern Laws*, 5 NEWS & NOTES FROM INST. FOR TRANSNAT'L L. 1 (1990): page 591 (footnote 4).

B. Chapman, *FOSFA International Arbitration*, 4. ARB. INT. 323 (1986): pages 10 (footnote 10), 13 (footnote 11).

Hervé Charrin, *The ICC International Centre for Expertise: Realities and Prospects*, ICC BULL. 33 (December 1995): page 702 (footnote 4).

R.H. Christie, *Amiable Composition in French and English Law*, 58 ARBITRATION (No. 4) (1992): page 349 (footnote 5).

Kevin Clermont & Theodore Eisenberg, *Xenophilia in American Courts*, 109 HARV. L. REV. 1122 (1996): page 518 (footnote 99).

E.J. Cohn, *The Rules of Arbitration of the International Chamber of Commerce*, 14 INT'L & COMP. L. QUARTERLY 132 (1965): pages 321 (footnote 5), 348 (footnote 5).

Commission on International Arbitration, Doc. No. 420/1304, 25 May 1988: page 373 (footnote 38).

Sean Costello, *Time Limits Under Rule 10304 of the NASD Code of Arbitration Procedure: Making Arbitrators More Like Judges or Judges More Like Arbitrators*, 52 BUS. LAW. 283 (1996): page 601 (footnote 67).

W. Laurence Craig, William W. Park, and Jan Paulsson, translation of Book IV of the French Civil Code of Procedure, *The Arbitration Law of France*, VII YEARBOOK 271 (1982): page 138 (footnote 1).

W. Laurence Craig, *International Ambition and National Restraint in ICC Arbitration*, 1 ARB. INT. 19 (1985): pages 10 (footnote 9), 498 (footnote 10).

W. Laurence Craig, *The Uses and Abuses of Appeal in International Arbitration Awards*, 14 PRIVATE INVESTORS ABROAD (1987): page 498 (footnote 10).

W. Laurence Craig, *Uses and Abuses of Appeals from Awards*, 4 ARB. INT. 174 (1988): page 8 (footnote 7).

W. LAURENCE CRAIG, WILLIAM W. PARK AND JAN PAULSSON, ANNOTATED GUIDE TO THE 1998 ICC ARBITRATION RULES, WITH COMMENTARY (Oceana Publications/ICC Publishing S.A. 1998): pages 142 (footnote 11), 186 (footnote 3), 201 (footnote 25).

W. LAURENCE CRAIG, WILLIAM W. PARK AND JAN PAULSSON, INTERNATIONAL CHAMBER OF COMMERCE ARBITRATION, 380 (2d ed. 1990): pages 421 (footnote 14), 511 (footnote 72).

BERNARDO CREMADES, ESTUDIOS SOBRE EL ARBITRAJE (1977): page 46 (footnote 5).

Bernardo Cremades, *Spain*, III ICCA HANDBOOK SUPPL. (13 September 1992): page 115 (footnote 19).

J. Cremades, *Problems that Arise from Changes Affecting one of the Signatories to the Arbitration Clause*, 7 ICC BULL. 29 (December 1996): page 176 (footnote 50).

Philip M. Croal, *Misconceptions about Discovery in English Arbitration*, 51 AR-BITRATION 532 (1985): page 452 (footnote 11).

Departmental Advisory Committee on Arbitration Law, REPORT ON THE ARBI-TRATION BILL SECTION 104 (1996): pages 208 (footnote 16), 350 (footnotes 9, 11), 422 (footnote 17), 436 (footnote 5), 483 (footnote 33), 531 (footnote 3), 532 (footnote 8), 536 (footnote 29), 537 (footnotes 36, 41), 539 (footnote 50), 540 (footnote 65), 541 (footnote 69), 542 (footnotes 77, 79).

Departmental Advisory Committee on Arbitration Law (1997), Supplementary Report of January 1997, 13 ARB. INT. 275 (1997): pages 531 (footnote 3), 535 (footnote 25).

Departmental Advisory Committee Consultation Paper on Draft Clauses of an Arbitration Bill (1994), 10 ARB. INT. 189 (1994): pages 531 (footnote 3), 536 (footnote 27).

DEPARTMENTAL ADVISORY COMMITTEE REPORT ON SPECIAL CATEGORIES UNDER THE ARBITRATION ACT 1979 (1993), 9 ARB. INT. 405 (1993): page 537 (footnote 37).

DEPARTMENTAL ADVISORY COMMITTEE RESPONSE TO THE UNCITRAL MODEL LAW, 6 ARB. INT. 3 (1990): pages 531 (footnote 3), 532 (footnotes 6, 7).

Jan Dalhuisen, *The Arbitrability of Competition Issues,* 11 ARB. INT. 151 (1995): page 61 (footnote 45).

Marco Darmon, *Marc Rich Co., A.G. v. Società Italiana Impianti P.A.: Opinion of the Advocate General,* 7 ARB. INT. 197 (1991): page 688 (footnote 38).

RENÉ DAVID, ARBITRATION IN INTERNATIONAL TRADE (1985): pages 38 (footnote 1), 95 (footnote 10), 352 (text and footnote 17), 371 (footnote 34), 424 (footnote 20).

Eduardo Jimenez de Arechaga, *International Law in the Past Third of a Century,* 1978-I RECUEIL DES COURS I: page 648 (footnote 73).

MATTHIEU DE BOISSESON, DROIT FRANÇAIS DE L'ARBITRAGE: INTERNE ET INTERNA-TIONAL (2d ed. 1990): pages 352 (footnote 17), 496 (footnote 6), 549 (footnote 1), 555 (footnote 39), 559 (footnote 63), 562 (footnote 80).

CHENG DEJUN, MICHAEL MOSER & WANG SHENGCHANG, INTERNATIONAL ARBITRA-TION IN THE PEOPLE'S REPUBLIC OF CHINA (1995): page 572 (footnote 49).

Georges Delaume, *Excuse for Non-performance and Force Majeure in Economic Development Agreements,* 10 COLUM. J. TRANSNAT'L L. REV. 242 (1971): page 651 (footnote 84).

Georges Delaume, *The Proper Law of State Contracts and the Lex Mercatoria: A Reappraisal,* 3 ICSID REVIEW—FOREIGN INVESTMENT LAW JOURNAL 79 (1988): page 652 (footnote 88).

Georges Delaume, *State Contracts and Transnational Arbitration,* 75 AM. J. INT'L L. 784 (1981): page 670 (footnote 20).

Jean-Louis Delvolvé, *Multipartisme: the Dutco Decision of the French Cour de Cassation*, 9 ARB. INT. 197 (1993): page 200 (footnote 24).

FILIP DE LY, INTERNATIONAL BUSINESS LAW AND LEX MERCATORIA (North Holland Press 1992): page 334 (footnote 48).

Yves Derains, *Case Note*, 1974 JDI 890: page 333 (footnote 45).

Yves Derains, *Case Note*, 1977 JDI 932: page 473 (footnote 4).

Yves Derains, *Note*, 1976 JDI 995: page 647 (footnote 70).

Yves Derains, *Note*, 1981 JDI 914: page 624 (footnotes 2, 7).

Yves Derains, *Note*, 1982 JDI 983: page 646 (footnote 68).

Yves Derains, *Note*, 1987 JDI 1043: page 649 (footnote 76).

Yves Derains, *Note*, I ICC AWARDS 296: page 650 (footnote 82).

Yves Derains, *Comment on ICC Case 3344/1981*, I ICC AWARDS 447: page 650 (footnote 82).

Yves Derains, *Expertise technique et référé arbitral*, 1982 REV. ARB. 239: pages 703 (footnote 7), 707 (footnote 10), 708 (text and footnotes 11, 12).

Yves Derains, *The ICC Arbitral Process, Part VIII: Choice of Law Applicable to the Contract and International Arbitration*, 6 ICC BULL. 10 (May 1995): page 320 (footnote 1).

Yves Derains, *L'application cumulative par l'arbitre des systèmes de conflits de lois interessées au litige*, 1972 REV. ARB. 99: pages 102 (footnote 24), 326 (footnote 19), 327 (footnotes 21, 22, 24).

Yves Derains, *L'expérience de la Chambre de commerce internationale en matière de propriété industrielle*, 1997 REV. ARB. 40: page 67 (footnote 67).

Yves Derains, *Le statut des usages du commerce international devant les juridictions arbitrale*, 1973 REV. ARB. 122: page 331 (footnote 38).

Yves Derains, *Les tendances de la jurisprudence arbitrale internationale*, 1993 JDI 829: page 624 (footnote 2).

Yves Derains, *Note*, 1983 JDI 905: page 77 (footnote 101).

Yves Derains, *Note*, 1987 JDI 1039: page 160 (footnote 15).

Yves Derains, *Opinion*, 1984 JDI 913: page 290 (footnote 24).

Y. DERAINS AND E. SCHWARTZ, A GUIDE TO THE NEW ICC RULES OF ARBITRATION (Kluwer 1998): pages 90 (footnote 13), 140 (footnote 6), 142 (footnote 11), 151 (footnote 26), 160 (footnote 12), 181 (footnote 62), 192 (footnote 14), 201 (footnote 25), 212 (footnote 24), 239 (footnotes 81, 82), 255 (footnote 6), 264 (footnote 20), 268 (footnote 25), 270 (footnote 28), 279 (footnote 9), 286 (footnote 15), 332 (footnote 42), 386 (footnote 1), 411 (footnote 30), 468 (footnote 45).

Lord Dervaird, *Scotland and the UNCITRAL Model Law: The Report to the Lord Advocate of the Scottish Advisory Committee on Arbitration Law*, 6 ARB. INT. 63 (1990): page 534 (footnote 16).

François Dessemontet, *Arbitration and Confidentiality*, 7 AM. REV. INT. ARB. 299 (1996): page 314 (footnote 42).

Anthony Diamond & V.V. Veeder, *Arbitration and Adjudication After 1996* (Proceedings of Conference sponsored by Queen Mary and Westfield College, University of London) 1 May 1997: page 542 (footnote 77).

Anthony Diamond & V.V. Veeder, *The New English Arbitration Act 1996: Challenging an English Award Before the English Court*, 8 AM. REV. INT. ARB. 47 (1997): page 541 (footnote 74).

C. Dieryck, *Procédure et moyens de preuve dans l'arbitrage commercial international*, 1988 REV. ARB. 267: page 419 (footnote 8).

A. Dimolitsa, *Issues Concerning the Existence, Validity and Effectiveness of the Arbitration Agreement*, 7 ICC BULL. 14 (December 1996): pages 157 (footnote 8), 159 (footnote 10), 160 (footnote 12).

T. Doi, *National Report: Japan*, IV YEARBOOK 115: page 305 (footnote 17).

RUDOLF DOLZER & MARGRETE STEVENS, BILATERAL INVESTMENT TREATIES (1995): page 686 (footnote 29).

M. DOMKE, COMMERCIAL ARBITRATION, Sec. 24.02 (Wilner, ed., 1994 Supp): pages 417 (footnote 4), 420 (text and footnote 9), 421 (footnote 12), 434 (footnote 11), 436 (footnotes 3, 4), 475 (footnote 9), 483 (footnote 34), 488 (footnote 53).

F. Donovan, *Dissenting Opinions*, 7 ICC BULL. 76 (December 1996): pages 371 (footnote 33), 373 (footnote 39).

DOSSIERS OF THE ICC INSTITUTE, COMPETITION AND ARBITRATION LAW (1993): page 342 (footnote 70).

DOSSIERS OF THE ICC INSTITUTE, INTERNATIONAL TRADE USAGE, ICC PUB NO. 440/4: page 332 (footnote 40)

Lawrence Ebb, *India responds to the Critics of its Misadventures under the New York Convention: The 1996 Arbitration Act*, 11 MEALEY'S INT. ARB. REP. 17 (Mar. 1996): page 510 (footnote 67).

Frédéric Eisemann, *Conciliation as a Means of Settlement of International Business Disputes: the UNCITRAL Rules as Compared with the ICC System*, THE ART OF ARBITRATION 121 (LIBER AMICORUM FOR PIETER SANDERS, 1982): page 698 (footnote 2).

Frédéric Eisemann, *La déontologie de l'arbitre commercial international*, 1969 REV. ARB. 217: page 212 (footnote 24).

Frédéric Eisemann, *La double sanction prévue par la Convention de la BIRD en cas de collusion ou d'ententes similaires entre un arbitre et une partie qui l'a désigné*, 23 ANNUAIRE FRANÇAISE DE DROIT INTERNATIONAL at No. 16: page 216 (footnote 31).

Frédéric Eisemann, *La clause d'arbitrage pathologique*, ARBITRAGE COMMER-CIAL: ESSAIS IN MEMORIAM EUGENIO MINOLI (1974): page 127 (footnote 1).

Jacques el-Hakim, *National Report, Syria*, VII YEARBOOK 35 (1982): page 71 (footnote 86).

Ahmed El Kosheri and Philippe Leboulanger, *L'arbitre face à la corruption et aux trafics d'influence*, 1984 REV. ARB. 3: pages 64 (footnote 56), 345 (foot-note 79), 649 (footnote 77).

Aboubacar Fall, *Defence and Illustration of Lex Mercatoria in Maritime Arbi-tration*, 15 J. INT. ARB. 83 (1998): page 658 (footnote 105).

B. Fillion-Dulfouleur & Philippe Leboulanger, *Le nouveau droit égyptien de l'arbitrage*, 1994 REV. ARB. 665: page 529 (footnote 23).

Peter Fitzpatrick, *Security for Costs Under the Arbitration Act 1996*, 1998 INT. ARB. L. REV. 139: page 540 (footnote 65).

James R. Foley, *Note*, 13 OHIO ST. J. DISP. RESOL. 1071 (1998): page 610 (foot-note 121).

Marcel Fontaine, *Les clauses de force majeure dans les contrats internationaux*, 5 DROIT ET PRATIQUE DU COMMERCE INTERNATIONAL 469 (1979): page 651 (footnote 84).

FORMATION OF CONTRACTS AND PRECONTRACTUAL LIABILITY (ICC Publication No. 440/9, 1990): page 650 (footnote 81).

Fourth Report on Dissenting and Separate Opinions, WORKING PARTY ON PAR-TIAL AND INTERIM AWARDS AND DISSENTING OPINIONS, COMMISSION ON INTERNA-TIONAL ARBITRATION, DOC. No. 420/293 Rev. 2, 23 February 1988: pages 373 (footnote 37), 374 (footnote 40).

PHILIPPE FOUCHARD, ARBITRAGE COMMERCIAL INTERNATIONAL (1965): page 113 (footnote 15).

Philippe Fouchard, *Clause abusives en matière d'arbitrage*, 1995 REV. ARB. 147: page 550 (footnote 10).

Philippe Fouchard, *Note*, 1979 REV. ARB. 339: page 128 (footnote 3).

Philippe Fouchard, *Note*, 1990 REV. ARB. 571: page 70 (footnote 78).

Philippe Fouchard, *Final Report on the Status of the Arbitrator*, 7 ICC BULL. 27 (May 1996): pages 410 (footnote 29), 412 (footnote 36).

Philippe Fouchard, *La Portée internationale de l'annulation de la sentence arbitrale dans son pays d'origine*, 1997 REV. ARB. 329: pages 505 (footnote 45), 506 (footnote 49), 562 (footnote 79).

Philippe Fouchard, *Les institutions permanentes d'arbitrages devant le juge étatique*, 1987 REV. ARB. 225: pages 160 (footnote 14), 236 (footnote 74), 356 (footnote 4), 357 (footnote 8).

Philippe Fouchard, *Les recours contre les sentences non françaises*, 1980 REV. ARB. 693: page 550 (footnote 6).

Philippe Fouchard, *Note on commercial reservation to New York Convention*, 1990 REV. ARB. 210: page 561 (footnote 76).

Philippe Fouchard, *Quand un arbitrage est-il international?* 1970 REV. ARB. 59: page 550 (footnote 8).

PHILIPPE FOUCHARD, EMMANUEL GAILLARD & BERTHOLD GOLDMAN, INTERNATIONAL COMMERCIAL ARBITRATION (E. Gaillard and J. Savage, editors) 671 (Kluwer, 1999): pages 279 (footnote 9), 292 (footnote 28), 320 (footnote 1), 329 (footnote 34), 337 (footnote 59), 353 (footnote 20), 356 (footnote 4), 423 (footnote 19), 476 (footnote 13), 481 (footnote 25).

PHILIPPE FOUCHARD, EMMANUEL GAILLARD & BERTHOLD GOLDMAN, TRAITE DE L'ARBITRAGE COMMERCIAL INTERNATIONAL (1996): pages 68 (footnote 68), 80 (footnote 113), 498 (footnote 10), 514 (footnote 84), 515 (footnote 88), 549 (footnote 1), 550 (footnote 8), 552 (footnote 18), 553 (footnotes 24, 27), 554 (footnote 30), 555 (footnotes 34, 35, 37), 556 (footnotes 43, 46), 557 (footnotes 47, 51), 559 (footnote 63).

ANGHELOS C. FOUSTOUCOS, L'ARBITRAGE INTERNE ET INTERNATIONAL EN DROIT PRIVÉ HELLENIQUE (1976): page 46 (footnote 5).

Hazel Fox, *State Immunity and Enforcement of Arbitral Awards: Do We Need an UNCITRAL Model Law Mark II for Execution Against State Property?* 12 ARB. INT. 89 (1996): page 674 (footnote 37).

Hazel Fox, *States and the Undertaking to Arbitrate,* 37 INTERNATIONAL & COMPARATIVE LAW QUARTERLY 1 (1988): page 671 (footnote 24).

THE FRESHFIELDS GUIDE TO ARBITRATION AND ADR CLAUSES IN INTERNATIONAL CONTRACTS 88 (2d edition 1999): page 117 (footnote 23).

Paul Friedland, *The Swiss Supreme Court Sets Aside an ICC Award*, 13 (No. 1) J. INT. ARB. 111 (1996): page 587 (footnote 59).

Paul Friedland, *U.S. Courts' Misapplication of the "Agreement in Writing" Requirement for Enforcement of an Arbitration Agreement under the New York Convention,* 13 MEALEY'S INT. ARB. REP. 21 (May 1998): pages 55 (footnote 26), 596 (footnote 39), 682 (footnote 17).

Emmanuel Gaillard, *L'affaire SOFIDIF ou les difficultés de l'arbitrage multipartite*, 1987 REV. ARB. 275: pages 181 (footnote 65), 292 (footnote 28).

EMMANUEL GAILLARD, LE PRINCIPE DE CONFIDENTIALITE DE L'ARBITRAGE COMMERCIAL INTERNATIONAL, 1987 DALLOZ (chronique) 153: page 312 (footnote 38).

Emmanuel Gaillard, *Les manœuvres dilatoires des parties et des arbitres dans l'arbitrage commercial international*, 1990 REV. ARB. 570: page 204 (footnote 8).

Emmanuel Gaillard, *L'interdiction de se contredire au détriment d'autrui comme principe général du droit du commerce international*, 1985 REV. ARB. 241: page 648 (text and footnotes 74, 76).

Emmanuel Gaillard, *Note on Meglio v. Société V2000*, 1997 REV. ARB. 537: page 46 (footnote 6).

Emmanuel Gaillard, *Thirty Years of Lex Mercatoria: Towards the Discriminating Application of Transnational Rules*, ICC CONGRESS SERIES No. 7 (Kluwer 1996): page 337 (footnote 59).

Emmanuel Gaillard, *Thirty Years of Lex Mercatoria: Toward the Selective Application of Transitional Rules*, 10 ICSID REVIEW 208 (1995): page 625 (footnote 10).

Barry H. Garfinkel & Rona G. Shamoon, *A Dangerous Expansion of Manifest Disregard*, 3 ADR CURRENTS 1 (December 1998): page 615 (footnote 156).

M. Gaudet, *La coopération des jurisdictions étatiques à l'arbitrage institutional*, 1988 SWISS BULL. 90: page 236 (footnote 74).

Fabien Gélinas, *The Application of the ICC Rules by the Court: 1998 Overview*, 10 ICC BULL. 11 (Spring 1999): page 159 (footnote 11).

Hamid Gharavi, *A Nightmare Called Hilmarton*, 12 MEALEY'S INT. ARB. REP. 20 (Sept. 1997): page 506 (footnote 50).

Hamid Gharavi, *Chromalloy: Another View*, 12 MEALEY'S INT. ARB. REP. 1 (Jan. 1997): page 506 (footnote 50).

Daniel Girsberger and Christian Hausmaninger, *Assignment of Rights and Agreement to Arbitrate*, 8 ARB. INT. 123 (1992): page 176 (footnote 50).

O. Glossner, *Sociological aspects of international commercial arbitration*, in THE ART OF ARBITRATION (Liber Amicorum for Pieter Sanders) (1982): pages 215 (footnotes 29, 30), 231 (footnotes 60, 61), 232 (footnote 62).

J. Goedel, *Aspekte der Streiterledigung bei internationalen Bauerverträgen und das Arbitral Referee Verfahren*, 4 SCHRIFTENREIHE DES DEUTSCHEN INSTITUTS FUR SCHIEDSGERICHTWEGEN 33: page 706 (footnote 9).

S. Goekjian, *Conducting an ICC Arbitration Proceeding*, MIDDLE EAST EXECUTIVE REPORTS 1 (February 1980): page 379 (footnote 4).

S. Goekjian, *ICC Arbitration from a Practitioner's Perspective*, 3 JOURNAL OF INTERNATIONAL LAW AND ECONOMICS 407 (1980): pages 379 (footnote 4), 457 (footnote 19).

Berthold Goldman, Note, 1985 JDI 129: page 290 (text and footnote 24).

Berthold Goldman, *The Complementary Roles of Judges and Arbitrators in Ensuring that International Commercial Arbitration is Effective*, 60 YEARS OF ICC ARBITRTIATIONS: A LOOK AT THE FUTURE 257 (ICC Publishing, 1984): pages 302 (text and footnote 10), 472 (footnote 3), 663 (footnote 6).

Berthold Goldman, *Frontières du droit et lex mercatoria*, ARCHIVES DE PHILOSOPHIE DU DROIT 177 (1964): pages 625 (footnote 10), 644 (footnote 59).

Berthold Goldman, Intervention, Symposium of 20 November 1970 on *Qualification de l'arbitre international*, 1970 REV. ARB. 203: pages 216 (footnote 31), 227 (footnote 54).

Berthold Goldman, *La lex mercatoria dans les contrats et l'arbitrage internationaux: réalités et perspectives*, 1979 JDI 475: pages 625 (footnote 10), 629 (footnote 20).

Claude Goldman, *Measures provisoires et arbitrage internationale*, 1993 INT. BUS. L. J. 3: page 476 (footnote 11).

J.C. Goldsmith, *How to Draft Terms of Reference*, 3 ARB. INT. 298 (1987): pages 281 (footnote 11), 292 (footnote 28).

Jean-Louis Goutal, *La clause compromissoire dans les connaissements*, 1996 REV. ARB. 605: page 56 (footnote 29).

Serge Gravel and Patricia Peterson, *French Law and Arbitration Clauses-Distinguishing Scope from Validity: Comment on I.C.C. Case No. 6519 Final Award*, 37 McGILL L. J. 510 (1992): page 156 (footnote 3).

Horacio Grigera Naón, *Enforceability of Awards Based on Transnational Rules under the New York, Panama, Geneva and Washington Conventions*, TRANSNATIONAL RULES IN INTERNATIONAL COMMERCIAL ARBITRATION 89 (ICC Publication No. 480/4, 1993): page 627 (footnote 17).

Horacio A. Grigera Naón, *The Role of the Secretariat of the International Court of Arbitration*, ICC. BULL. SPECIAL SUPPLEMENT: THE NEW 1998 RULES OF ARBITRATION 18 (1997): page 26 (footnote 8).

Bernard Hanotiau, *L'arbitrabilité et la favor arbitrandum: un réexamen*, 121 JDI 899 (1994): page 62 (footnote 49).

Bernard Hanotiau, *La détermination du dommage réparable: principes généraux et principes en emergence*, TRANSNATIONAL RULES IN INTERNATIONAL COMMERCIAL ARBITRATION 216 (ICC Publication No. 480/4, 1993): pages 646 (footnote 68), 647 (footnote 69).

Bernard Hanotiau, *What Law Governs the Issue of Arbitrability?* 12 ARB. INT. 391 (1996): pages 60 (footnote 44), 62 (footnote 48), 70 (footnote 80), 509 (footnote 61).

Bernard Hanotiau & Guy Block, *La loi du 19 mai 1998 modifiant la législation belge relative à l'arbitrage,* 16 SWISS BULL. 528 (1998): page 503 (footnote 31).

BRUCE HARRIS, ROWAN PLANTEROSE & JONATHAN TECKS, THE ARBITRATION ACT 1996 (1996): page 531 (footnote 2).

Dominique Hascher, *ICC Practice in Relation to the Appointment, Confirmation, Challenge and Replacement of Arbitrators,* 6 ICC BULL. 4 (November 1995): pages 195 (footnote 17), 204 (footnotes 7, 8), 207 (footnote 13), 227 (footnote 53), 235 (footnote 71), 237 (footnote 77).

Dominique Hascher, *Recognition and Enforcement of Judgments on the Existence and Validity of an Arbitration Clause under the Brussels Convention,* 13 ARB. INT. 33 (1997): page 689 (footnote 43).

I. Hautot, *Les pouvoirs de la Cour d'arbitrage de la C.C.I. de décider ou non d'organiser l'arbitrage,* 1990 SWISS BULL. 12: page 159 (footnote 10).

Stephen L. Hayford, *A New Paradigm for Commercial Arbitration: Rethinking the Relationship Between Reasoned Awards and the Judicial Standards for Vacatur,* 66 GEO. WASH. L. REV. 443 (1998): page 610 (footnote 123).

Stephen L. Hayford, *Law in Disarray: Judicial Standards for Vacatur of Commercial Arbitration Awards,* 30 GA. L. REV. 731 (1996): page 611 (footnote 128).

Stephen L. Hayford & Scott Kenigan, *Vacatur: The Non-Statutory Grounds for Judicial Review of Commercial Awards,* 50 DISP. RESOL. J. 22 (Oct. 1996): page 610 (footnote 123).

Gerold Hermann, *The UNCITRAL Model Law—its Background, Salient Features and Purposes,* 1 ARB. INT. 6 (1985): page 631 (footnote 24).

Gerold Hermann, *UNCITRAL Adopts Model Law on International Commercial Arbitration,* 2 ARB. INT. 2 (1986): page 519 (footnote 1).

Vincent Heuzé, *Note* on Meglio v. Société V2000, 1998 REV. CRIT. DR. INT. PRIVÉ 87: page 46 (footnote 6).

Jonathan Hill, *Some Private International Law Aspects of the Arbitration Act 1996,* 46 INT. & COMP. L.Q. 274 (1997): pages 508 (footnote 58), 531 (footnote 2).

Richard Hill, *Formal Requirements for Arbitration Agreements: Does Kahn Lucas Lancaster v. Lark International Open Pandora's Box?* 12 MEALEY'S INT. ARB. REP. 18 (October 1997): page 55 (footnote 26).

Richard Hill, *Swiss Supreme Court Decision of 16 January 1995*, 14 SWISS BULL. 488 (1966): page 581 (footnote 31).

Lars Hjerner, *Choice of Law Problems in International Arbitration with Particular Reference to Arbitration in Sweden*, 1982 YEARBOOK OF THE ARBITRATION INSTITUTE OF THE STOCKHOLM CHAMBER OF COMMERCE 18: page 341 (footnote 68).

LARS HJERNER, INTERNATIONELLA HANDELSKAMMARENS FORLIKNINGS OCH SKILJEDOMSREGLER 13 (1981): pages 66 (footnote 60), 711 (footnote 13).

Stephen A. Hochman, *Judicial Review to Correct Arbitral Error-An Option to Consider*, 13 OHIO ST. J. DISP. RESOL. 103 (1997): page 615 (footnote 158).

Michael Hoellering, *Arbitration of Patent Disputes*, ARBITRATION & THE LAW 1987-88: page 67 (footnote 67).

Michael Hoellering, *Interim Measures and Arbitration: The Situation in the United States*, ARBITRATION AND THE LAW 154 (AAA, 1990-91): page 607 (footnote 100).

Howard M. Holtzmann, *Some Lessons of the Iran-United States Claims Tribunal*, in 1987 Symposium, PRIVATE INVESTORS ABROAD-PROBLEMS AND SOLUTIONS IN INTERNATIONAL BUSINESS, The Southwestern Legal Foundation, Section 16.04 (3)(a): pages 432 (text and footnote 8), 439 (footnote 14).

Howard M. Holtzmann, *United States*, IV ICCA HANDBOOK, SUPPL. (September 1992): page 120 (footnote 30).

Howard M. Holtzmann & Donald Donovan, *United States*, ICCA HANDBOOK, 38 (January 1999, Supplement 28): page 311 (footnote 34).

HOWARD HOLTZMANN & JOSEPH NEUHAUS, A GUIDE TO THE UNCITRAL MODEL LAW ON INTERNATIONAL COMMERCIAL ARBITRATION (1989): pages 515 (footnote 87), 520 (footnote 3), 526 (footnotes 16, 17).

HOMMAGE A FRÉDÉRIC EISEMANN (ICC Publication No. 321, 1978): page 713 (footnote 16).

R. Horning, *Has HAL Signed a Contract?* 12 SANTA CLARA COMPUTER & HIGH TECH. L. J. 290 (1996): page 56 (footnote 30).

Richard Hulbert, *The American Law Perspective*, CONSERVATORY AND PROVISIONAL MEASURES IN INTERNATIONAL ARBITRATION 93 (ICC Publishing, 1993): page 475 (footnote 10).

Martin Hunter, *International Commercial Arbitration*, 1982 INT. BUS. LAW 315: page 521 (footnote 6).

Martin Hunter, *Case* Note, 1988 LLOYD'S MARITIME AND COMMERCIAL LAW QUARTERLY REVIEW 23: pages 107 (footnote 5), 133 (footnote 12).

Martin Hunter, *Ethics of the International Arbitrator*, 1987 J. CHARTERED INSTITUTE OF ARBITRATORS 219: page 227 (footnote 53).

Martin Hunter, *The Procedural Powers of Arbitrators Under the English 1996 Act*, 13 ARB. INT. 345 (1997): page 531 (footnote 2).

Martin Hunter, *Publication of Awards and Lex Mercatoria,* 57 ARBITRATION 55 (1988): page 627 (footnote 14).

Martin Hunter and Jan Paulsson, *Note on the 1985 Rules of the LCIA,* X YEARBOOK 167 (1985): page 75 (footnote 96).

IBA, *Note on the New IBA Rules of Evidence in International Commercial Arbitration*, BUSINESS LAW INTERNATIONAL (IBA Publication, January 2000) 14: pages 443 (footnote 18), 455 (footnotes 15, 16).

IBA Working Group's *Note* on the New IBA Rules of Evidence, INTERNATIONAL COMMERCIAL ARBITRATION, IN BUSINESS LAW INTERNATIONAL (IBA Publication, January 2000): pages 425 (footnote 23), 440 (footnote 15).

ICC Awards on Arbitration and European Community Law, 5 ICC BULL. 44 (November 1994): page 342 (footnote 70).

ICC Court of Arbitration (General Counsel, 1986), *Lex Mercatoria*, 1986 JDI 1138: page 338 (footnote 62).

ICC Document No. 420/179, INTERNATIONAL ARBITRATION, 1975.05.25, *The Revised ICC Rules of Arbitration*, report of Jean Robert, Rapporteur of the ICC Commission on International Arbitration: pages 193 (footnote 15), 331 (footnote 37).

ICC Document No. 420/357 of 13 January 1997: page 411.

ICC 1997 Statistical Report, 9 ICC BULL. 6 (May 1998): page 190 (footnote 13).

ICC Publishing, LES COMMISSIONS ILLICITES (Paris, 1992): page 345 (footnote 80).

ICC Working Party (Martin Hunter, Chairman), *Final Report on Interim and Partial Awards*, 1 ICC BULL. 26 (December 1990): page 464 (footnote 33).

C. Imhoos, *Constitution of the Arbitral Tribunal,* 2 ICC BULL. 3 (November 1991): page 190 (footnote 12).

INTERNATIONAL ARBITRATION TREATIES (HANS SMIT & VRATISLAV PECHOTA, EDS 1998): page 686 (footnote 31).

The International Bar Association, *Ethics for International Arbitration* (1987), 2 INT. ARB. REP. 287, 3 ARB. INT. 72 (1987): pages 194 (footnote 16), 214 (footnote 28), 241 (footnote 84).

Iran U.S. Claims Tribunal Oath, VIII YEARBOOK 248 (1983): page 436 (footnote 6).

M. Issad, *L'arbitrage en Algerie,* 1977 REV. ARB. 219, 236: pages 46 (footnote 5), 71 (footnote 86).

Japan Commercial Arbitration Association, 1998, http://www.jcaa.or.jp/e/arbitration-e/kaiketsu-e/venue.html: page 305 (footnote 19).

Charles Jarrosson, *L'arbitrage et la Convention Européenne des droits de l'homme* 1989 REV. ARB. 573: pages 234 (footnote 69), 236 (footnote 73).

Charles Jarrosson, *Note,* 1993 REV. ARB. 645: page 343 (footnote 75).

Charles Jarrosson, *Note on Siemens A.G. & BKMI GmbH v. Dutco Co.*, 119 JDI 726 (1992): page 560 (footnote 69).

Sigvard Jarvin, *Aspects of the Arbitral Proceedings*, ICC BULL 38 (Supplement 1997): page 450 (footnote 3).

Sigvard Jarvin, *Note,* 1986 JDI 1138: page 625 (footnote 11).

Sigvard Jarvin, *Comments on a September 1982 Decision by the Chairman,* VIII YEARBOOK 206 (1983): page 20 (footnote 2).

Sigvard Jarvin, *Participation à l'arbitrage C.C.I. des Etats et entreprise publiques*, 1995 REV. ARB. 585: page 179 (footnote 59).

Sigvard Jarvin, *The Place of Arbitration—A Review of the ICC Court's Guiding Principles and Practice when Fixing the Place of Arbitration*, 7 ICC BULL. 54 (December 1996): page 190 (footnote 11).

Jennings, 7 INTERNATIONAL & COMPARATIVE LAW QUARTERLY 349 (1958): page 672 (footnote 28).

Paul Jerard, *Opinion*, 7 ARB. INT. 243 (1991): page 688 (footnote 38).

PIERRE JOLIDON, COMMENTAIRE DU CONCORDAT SUISSE SUR L'ARBITRAGE (1984): pages 576 (footnote 5), 589 (footnote 67).

Patrick Juillard, *Les conventions bilatérales d'investissement conclues par la France,* 1979 JDI 274: page 667 (footnote 16).

Philippe Kahn, *Vers l'institutionnalisation de la lex mercatoria: à propos des principes UNIDROIT,* Commission Droit et Vie des Affaires, 1998: page 632 (footnote 27).

Neil Kaplan, *An Update on Hong Kong's Arbitration Law*, INTERNATIONAL COMMERCIAL ARBITRATION IN ASIA 11 (ICC BULL. SPECIAL SUPP., 1998): page 564 (footnote 5).

Neil Kaplan, *Is the Need for Writing as Expressed in the New York Convention and the Model Law Out of Step with Commercial Practice?* 12 ARB. INT. 27 (1996): pages 55 (footnote 26), 525 (footnote 12), 683 (footnote 18).

Neil Kaplan, *The Model Law in Hong Kong: Two Years On,* 8 ARB. INT. 223 (1992): page 564 (footnote 5).

Neil Kaplan, *Polytek Nearly Victorious: A Tale of Three Cities*, 66 ARBITRATION 25 (Feb. 2000): page 572 (footnote 52).

NEIL KAPLAN, JILL SPRUCE & MICHAEL MOSER, HONG KONG AND CHINESE ARBITRATION: CASES AND MATERIALS (1994): pages 518 (footnote 105), 527 (footnote 18), 564 (footnote 5), 571 (footnote 48).

Alan S. Kaplinsky and Mark J. Levin, *Excuse me but who's the predator: Banks can use arbitration clauses as a defense*, 1988 BUS. L. TODAY, MAY/JUNE: page 606 (footnote 97).

Pierre Karrer, *Judicial Review of International Arbitration Awards: Who Needs it?* 1998 TABLE TALK 9 (International Arbitration Club, London): page 507 (footnote 54).

Pierre Karrer & Claudia Kälin-Nauer, *Is There a Favor Iurisdictionis Arbitri?* 13 (No. 3) J. INT. ARB. 31 (1996): pages 587 (footnote 59), 588 (footnote 61).

Antoine Kassis, *The Questionable Validity of Arbitration and Awards under the Rules of the International Chamber of Commerce*, 6 J. INT. ARB. 79 (1989): page 380 (footnote 5).

Antoine Kassis, *Reflexions sur le reglement d'arbitrage de la Chambre de Commerce International*, (L.G.D.J., Paris, 1988): pages 380 (footnote 5), 381 (footnote 10).

ANTOINE KASSIS, THEORIE GENERALE DES USAGES DU COMMERCE (1984): page 624 (footnote 8).

Gabrielle Kaufmann & Laurent Lévy, *Note*, 1998 INT. A.L.R. (No. 4) N-69: page 589 (footnote 71).

Gabrielle Kaufmann, *Articles 190 et 191 LDIP: Les Recours Contre les Sentences Arbitrales*, 10 SWISS BULL. 64 (1992): page 582 (footnote 38).

John Kendall, EXPERT DETERMINATION (2d ed. 1996): page 536 (footnote 27).

John Kerr, *Arbitrability of Securities Law Claims in Common Law Nations*, 12 ARB. INT. 171 (1996): page 69 (footnote 75).

Michael Kerr, *Concord and Conflict in International Arbitration*, 13 ARB. INT. 137 (1997): page 108 (footnote 6).

Michael Kerr, *Equity Arbitration in England*, 2 AM REV. INT. ARB. 377 (1991): page 350 (footnote 10).

Michael Kerr, *International Arbitration v. Litigation*, 3 INTERNATIONAL COMMERCIAL ARBITRATION, 141 (1980): page 388 (footnote 2).

Catherine Kessedjian, *Note on Bomar v. Entreprise Tunisienne d'activités pétrolières (ETAP)*, 1994 REV. ARB. 108: page 682 (footnote 16).

Catherine Kessedjian, *Principe de la contradiction et arbitrage*, 1995 REV. ARB. 381: page 560 (footnote 67).

Tony Khindria, *Enforcement of Arbitration Awards in India,* 23 INT. BUS. LAW-YER 11 (January 1995): page 510 (footnote 67).

Antoine Kirry, *Arbitrability: Current Trends in Europe,* 12 ARB. INT. 373 (1996): page 67 (footnote 64).

F.E. Klein, *Comment on Westland Helicopters, Ltd. V. Arab Republic of Egypt,* 1987 SWISS BULL 12: page 409 (footnote 24).

Theodore Klein, *Disagreement on the Scope of an Arbitration Clause,* 7 ICC BULL. 24 (December 1996): pages 156 (footnote 3), 181 (footnote 62).

François Knoepfler, *Corruption et arbitrage international,* LES CONTRACTS DE DISTRIBUTION: CONTRIBUTIONS OFFERTES AU PROFESSEUR FRANCOIS DESSEMONTET 357 (1998): page 583 (footnote 39).

François Knoepfler, *Les mesures provisoires et l'arbitrage international,* SCHIEDSGERICHTSBARKEIT (ANDREAS KELLERHALS, EUROPA INSTITUT Zürich, 1997): page 579 (footnote 25).

François Knoepfler & Philippe Schweizer, *Jurisprudence suisse en matière d'arbitrage international,* 1996 REVUE SUISSE DE DROIT INTERNATIONAL ET DE DROIT EUROPÉEN 539: pages 580 (footnote 28), 581 (footnote 31), 587 (footnote 59).

Richard Kriendler and Timothy J. Kantz, *Agreed Deadlines and the Setting Aside of Arbitral Awards,* 1997 SWISS BULL. 576: page 282 (footnote 12).

N. Krishnamurthi, *Some Thoughts on a New Convention on International Arbitration,* THE ART OF ARBITRATION 207 (1982): pages 95 (footnote 7), 99 (footnote 14), 640 (footnote 41).

W. Kuhn, *Rectification and Interpretation of Arbitral Awards,* 7 ICC BULL. 78 (December 1996): page 407 (footnote 2).

Paul Lagarde, *Approche critique de la lex mercatoria,* LE DROIT DES RELATIONS ECONOMIQUES INTERNATIONALES: page 334 (footnote 48).

Paul Lagarde, *Approche critique de la lex mercatoria,* LIBER AMICORUM FOR PROF. GOLDMAN, 1982: pages 625 (footnote 10), 629 (footnote 20).

Pierre Lalive, *Arbitration with Foreign States or State-Controlled Entities: Some Practical Questions* in J. Lew, ed. CONTEMPORARY PROBLEMS IN INTERNATIONAL ARBITRATION, (Queen Mary's College, University of London 1986): page 211 (footnote 23).

Pierre Lalive, *Avantages et inconvénients de l'arbitrage ad hoc,* ETUDES OFFERTES À PIERRE BELLET 301 (1991): page 39 (footnote 4).

Pierre Lalive, *Les règles de conflits de lois appliquées au fond du litige par l'arbitre international siégeant en Suisse,* 1976 REV. ARB. 155: pages 322 (footnote 7), 323 (footnote 9), 328 (footnote 31), 329 (footnote 35).

Pierre Lalive, *Sur la Bonne Foi dans l'Exécution des Contrats d'Etat* in MELANGES OFFERTS À RAYMOND VANDER ELST 425 (Editions Nemesis, Brussels, 1986), p. 425: page 211 (footnote 23).

Pierre Lalive, *Sur l'irresponsabilité arbitral*, ETUDES DE PROCEDURE ET D'ARBITRAGE EN L'HONNEUR DE JEAN FRANCOIS POUDRET (Faculté de Droit de L'Université de Lausanne, 1999): pages 412 (footnote 35), 413 (footnote 38).

PIERRE LALIVE, JEAN-FRANÇOIS POUDRET & CLAUDE REYMOND, LE DROIT DE L'ARBITRAGE INTERNE ET INTERNATIONAL EN SUISSE 339 (Lausanne, 1989): pages 235 (footnote 72), 499 (footnote 16), 503 (footnote 34), 575 (footnote 1), 576 (footnote 5), 577 (footnote 7), 584 (footnote 46), 588 (footnote 65).

Toby Landau, *The Effect of the New English Arbitration Act on Institutional Arbitration*, 13 J. INT. ARB. 113 (Dec. 1996): page 535 (footnote 24).

Ole Lando, *The Law Applicable to the Merits of the Dispute*, 2 ARB. INT. 104 (1988): page 320 (footnote 1).

Ole Lando, *Principles of European Contract Law: An Alternative to or a Precursor of European Legislation?* 40 AM. J. COMP. L. 573 (1992): page 633 (footnote 28).

P. Lastenouse, *Le Contrôle de l'Ordre Public Lors de l'Execution en Angleterre de la Seconde Sentence Hilmarton*, 1999 REV. ARB. 867: page 345 (footnote 81).

Serge Lazareff, *Mandatory Extraterritorial Application of National Law*, 11 ARB. INT. 137 (1995), (ICC CONGRESS SERIES No. 7, 538 (Kluwer 1996): pages 72 (footnote 90), 338 (footnote 63), 509 (footnote 64).

Serge Lazareff (Chairman of the ICC Commission Working Group), *Practical Guide for Terms of Reference*, 3 ICC BULL. 24 (1992): page 281 (footnote 11).

Philippe Leboulanger, *L'arbitrage international Nord-Sud*, ETUDES OFFERTES À PIERRE BELLET 323 (1991): page 676 (footnote 45).

Philippe Leboulanger, *Multi-Contract Arbitration*, 13 J. INT. ARB. No. 4 (1996): page 183 (footnote 68).

Bruno Leurent, *L'intervention du Juge*, 1992 REV. ARB. 303: page 556 (footnote 46).

Bruno Leurent, *Note on Sociétés de procédes de préfabrication pour le béton v. Libye*, 1998 REV. ARB. 399: page 562 (footnote 79).

Laurent, Lévy, *Dissenting Opinions in International Arbitration in Switzerland*, 5 ARB. INT. 35 (1989): page 589 (footnote 66).

JULIAN LEW, APPLICABLE LAW IN INTERNATIONAL COMMERCIAL ARBITRATION (1978): pages 111 (footnote 13), 320 (footnote 1), 324 (footnote 10), 325 (footnote 14), 326 (footnote 16), 344 (footnote 78).

Julian Lew, *ICC Working Party on Intellectual Property Disputes and Arbitration,* SWISS ARBITRATION ASSOCIATION SPECIAL SERIES No. 6, 44 (1994): page 67 (footnote 67).

JULIAN LEW, THE IMMUNITY OF ARBITRATORS (Lloyd's of London Press, 1990): page 411 (footnote 32).

Julian Lew, *Report,* 11 ARB. INT. 337 (1995): page 313 (footnote 40).

Carlo Lombardini, *Effetti del Diritto Comunitario sui Contratti e Arbitrato del Commercio Internazionale,* 1993 DIRITTO DEL COMMERCIO INTERNAZIONALE 143: pages 579 (footnote 20), 584 (footnote 45).

ERIC LOQUIN, L'AIMABLE COMPOSITION EN DROIT COMPARÉ ET INTERNATIONAL (1980): pages 110 (text and footnote 10), 351 (footnote 15), 352 (footnote 16).

Eric Loquin, *Note,* 1991 REV. ARB. 326: pages 181 (footnote 64), 182 (footnote 66).

Eric Loquin, *Note,* 1992 JDI 974: page 410 (footnote 27).

Andreas Lowenfeld, *Singapore and the Local Bar: Aberration or Ill Omen?* 5 J. INT. ARB. 71 (1988): pages 305 (footnote 22), 308 (footnote 28).

Andreas Lowenfeld, *The Two-Way Mirror: International Arbitration as Comparative Procedure,* VII MICHIGAN YEARBOOK OF INTERNATIONAL LEGAL STUDIES 187 (1985): pages 245 (footnote 91), 426 (footnote 24), 439 (footnote 13), 441 (footnote 16).

Fernando Mantilla Serrano, *International Arbitration and Insolvency Proceedings,* 11 ARB. INT. 51 (1995): page 68 (footnote 71).

RICHARD LORD & SIMON SALZEDO, GUIDE TO THE ARBITRATION ACT 1996 (1996): page 531 (footnote 2).

Carlos Loumiet, *Introductory Note to the Florida International Arbitration Act,* 26 ILM 949 (1987): page 593 (footnote 16).

Yves Loussouarn, *Note,* 1964 JDI 113: page 553 (footnote 27).

Andreas Lowenfeld, *Can Arbitration Coexist With Judicial Review?* 3 ADR CURRENTS 1 (Sept. 1998): page 615 (footnote 158).

A.F.M. Maniruzzaman, *Conflict of Laws in International Arbitration: Practice and Trends,* 9 ARB. INT. 371 (1993): page 320 (footnote 1).

Francis A. Mann, *Lex facit arbitrum,* INTERNATIONAL ARBITRATION 159 (*Liber amicorum* for Martin Domke) (1967): pages 296 (footnote 4), 498 (footnote 12).

Francis A. Mann, *Where is an Award Made?* 1 ARB. INT. 107 (1985): page 500 (footnote 23).

Arthur Marriott, *The New Arbitration Bill*, 62 ARBITRATION 97 (1996): page 531 (footnote 2).

Pierre Mayer, *La neutralisation du pouvoir normatif de l'Etat en matière de contrats d'Etat*, 1986 JDI 5: page 103 (footnote 25).

Pierre Mayer, *La sentence contraire à l'ordre public au fond*, 1994 REV. ARB. 615: page 61 (footnote 47).

Pierre Mayer, *L'Autonomie de l'arbitre international dans l'appréciation de sa propre compétence*, 217 RECUEIL DES COURS 323 (1989): page 169 (footnote 33).

Pierre Mayer, *Le mythe de l'ordre juridique de base (ou Grundlegung)*, LE DROIT DES RELATIONS ECONOMIQUES INTERNATIONALES 199 (LIBER AMICORUM FOR PROF. GOLDMAN, 1982): page 627 (footnote 13).

Pierre Mayer, *Les limites de la séparabilité de la clause compromissoire*, 1998 REV. ARB. 359: page 49 (footnote 11).

Pierre Mayer, *Mandatory Rules of Law in International Arbitration*, 2 ARB. INT. 274 (1986): pages 101 (footnote 19), 338 (footnote 63), 344 (text and footnote 77), 509 (footnote 63).

Pierre Mayer, *Note*, Crédit populaire d'Algérie v. Sapvin, French *Cour de cassation*, February 14, 1978, 1980 REVUE CRITIQUE DU DROIT INTERNATIONAL PRIVÉ 707: page 211 (footnote 23).

KEBA MBAYE, INTERNATIONAL ARBITRATION: 60 YEARS ON 293 (ICC Publication No. 412, 1984): pages 642 (footnote 46), 663 (footnote 6).

A. McClelland, *International Arbitration: A Practical Guide for the Effective Use of the System for Litigation of Transnational Commercial Disputes*, 12 INTERNATIONAL LAWYER 83 (1978): page 457 (footnote 19).

J.S. MCCLENDON AND R. EVERARD GOODMAN, Eds., INTERNATIONAL COMMERCIAL ARBITRATION IN NEW YORK (The World Arbitration Institute New York, 1986): page 120 (footnote 31).

Joseph McLaughlin, *Arbitrability: Current Trends in the United States*, 12 ARB. INT. 113 (1996): page 61 (footnote 45).

John P. McMahon, *Implementation of the United Nations Convention on Foreign Arbitral Awards in the United States*, 2 J. MARITIME L. & COMM. 735 (1971): page 679 (footnote 2).

Werner Melis, *Force Majeure and Hardship Clauses in International Commercial Contracts in View of the Practice of the ICC Court of Arbitration*, 1 J. INT. ARB. 214 (1984): pages 643 (footnote 53), 644 (footnote 59), 649 (footnote 79), 651 (footnote 83), 652 (footnotes 88, 89), 653 (footnote 90).

Armen Merijan, *Caveat Arbitor: Laker Airways and the Appointing of Barristers as Arbitrators in Cases Involving Barrister-Advocates from the Same Chambers*, 17(1) J. INT. ARB. 31 (2000): page 533 (footnote 10).

ROBERT MERKIN, ARBITRATION ACT OF 1996: AN ANNOTATED GUIDE (1996): pages 475 (footnote 8), 531 (footnote 2).

Ernest Mezger, *Case Note*, 1982 REV. ARB. 220: page 111 (footnote 12).

Ernest Mezger, *Case Note*, 1988 REV. ARB. 649: page 364 (footnote 23).

G. Mirabelli, *Application of the New York Convention by the Italian Courts*, IV YEARBOOK 362 (1979): page 58 (footnote 35).

D. Mitrovic, *Advance to Cover Costs of Arbitration*, 7 ICC BULL. 88 (December 1996): pages 268 (footnote 24), 269 (footnote 26).

Jean-Hubert Moitry, *L'arbitre international et l'obligation de boycottage imposée par un Etat*, 1991 JDI 349: page 69 (footnote 76).

Charles Molineaux, *The FIDIC Conditions—Basis for a Construction Lex Mercatoria, A Lex Constructionis?* LCIA/AAA CONFERENCE IN BOSTON, (26-28 September 1996): page 658 (footnote 105).

Charles Molineaux, *Moving Toward a Construction Lex Mercatoria*, 14 J. INT. ARB. 55 (1997): page 658 (footnote 105).

Robert Morgan, THE ARBITRATION ORDINANCE OF HONG KONG: A COMMENTARY (1997): pages 82 (footnote 117), 564 (footnote 5).

Robert Morgan, Enforcement of Chinese Awards in Hong Kong, 1998 (No. 4) INT. A.L.R. 157: page 572 (footnote 49).

Robert Morgan, *Hong Kong Arbitration in Transition: The Arbitration (Amendment Ordinance 1996)*, 1997 INT. ARB. LAW REV. 19, 1998 INT. ARB. LAW REV. 74 (1998), 13 MEALY'S INT. ARB. REP. 18 (1998): page 564 (footnote 5).

Robert Morgan, *Mutual Enforcement of Arbitral Awards Between Hong Kong and the People's Republic of China*, 1999 INT. ARB. LAW. REP. 29: page 572 (footnote 51).

Giuditta Cordero Moss, INTERNATIONAL COMMERCIAL ARBITRATION: PARTY AUTONOMY AND MANDATORY RULES (1999): page 509 (footnote 63).

Carol Mulcahy, *The Challenge to Enforcement of Awards on Grounds of Underlying Illegality*, 64 ARBITRATION 210 (1998): page 544 (footnote 94).

Michael J. Mustill, *The New Lex Mercatoria,* LIBER AMICORUM FOR LORD WILBERFORCE 149 (Maarten Bos & Ian Brownlie, Eds., 1987); 4 ARB. INT. 86 (1988): pages 626 (text and footnote 12), 627 (footnote 14), 628, 629 (text and footnotes 19, 20), 630 (text and footnote 21), 631 (text and footnote 22), 632 (footnote 26), 633 (text and footnote 30), 642 (footnote 47), 643 (footnote 50), 645 (footnote 61), 647 (footnote 71), 649 (text and footnote 78), 653 (text and footnote 92).

Michael J. Mustill, *Arbitral Proceedings*, paper given at ICC Arbitration Seminar in Malbun (Liechtenstein) on 24 November 1976: page 423 (text and footnote 18).

Michael J. Mustill, *Cedric Barclay Memorial Lecture*, 58 ARBITRATION 159 (Aug. 1992): page 517 (footnote 95).

Michael J. Mustill, *Note*, CONSERVATORY AND PROVISIONAL MEASURES IN ARBITRATION 12 (ICC Publication No. 519, 1993): page 451 (footnote 7).

Michael J. Mustill, *Comments and Conclusions*, CONSERVATORY AND PROVISIONAL MEASURES IN INTERNATIONAL ARBITRATION 118 (ICC Publication No.519 (1993)): pages 472 (footnote 3), 473 (footnote 3).

Michael J. Mustill, *La nouvelle loi anglaise sur l'arbitrage de 1996: philosophie, inspiration, aspiration*, 1997 REV. ARB. 29: page 531 (footnote 2).

Michael J. Mustill, *The New Lex Mercatoria: The First Twenty-Five Years*, 4 ARB. INT. 86 (1988): pages 334 (footnote 48), 337 (footnote 60).

Michael J. Mustill, *Too Many Laws*, 63 ARBITRATION 248 (1997): page 507 (footnote 54).

MICHAEL J. MUSTILL & STEWART C. BOYD, COMMERCIAL ARBITRATION (2d Ed. 1989): pages 114 (footnote 16), 349 (footnote 5), 370 (footnote 32), 421 (text and footnote 13), 429 (footnote 4), 445 (footnote 21), 452 (footnotes 11, 12), 482 (footnote31), 536 (footnote 27), 627 (footnote 14).

Horacio Grigera Naon, (Secretary General of the ICC Court of Arbitration 1997-), CHOICE OF LAW PROBLEMS IN INTERNATIONAL ARBITRATION (J.C.B. Mohr 1992): page 320 (footnote 1).

Horacio Grigera Naon, *The Powers of the ICC International Court of Arbitration Vis-à-Vis Parties and Arbitrators*, SPECIAL SUPPLEMENT ICC BULL. 60 (May 1999): page 255 (footnote 7).

Jean-Claude Najar and Michael A. Polkinghorne, *Australia's Adoption of the UNCITRAL Model Law*, 3 INT. ARB. REP. 21 (March 1989): page 306 (footnote 23).

F.S. Nariman, *Finality in India: The Impossible Dream*, 10 ARB. INT. 373 (1994): pages 271 (footnote 33), 510 (footnote 67).

F.S. Nariman, *Standards of Behaviour of Arbitrators*, 4 ARB. INT. 311 (1988): page 241 (footnote 84).

Patrick Neill, Q.C., *Confidentiality in Arbitration*, 12 ARB. INT. 287 (1996): page 317 (footnote 46).

Lawrence W. Newman & Charles M. Davidson, *Arbitrability of Timeliness Defenses: Who Decides?* 14 (No. 2) J. INT. ARB. 137 (1997): page 601 (footnote 67).

Lawrence W. Newman & Nancy Nelson, *Procedure of International Arbitration: Interim Measures of Protection*, INTERNATIONAL COMMERCIAL ARBITRATION IN NEW YORK 99 (J. Stewart McClendon & Rosabel Everard Goodman eds., 1986): page 594 (footnote 20).

F. Nicklisch, *Terms of Reference*, 1988 RIW (RECHT DER INTERNATIONALEN WIRTSCHAFT), HEFT 10, p. 763 (German law): pages 290 (footnote 24), 292 (footnote 30).

O'Conor, *Enforcement of Arbitration Awards: Arbitration Rules for the Time Being*, 1 INTERNATIONAL ARBITRATION LAW REVIEW 42 (1977): page 145 (footnote 21).

P. O'Neill and N. Salam, *Is the Exceptio Non Adimpleti Contractus Part of the New Lex Mercatoria?* TRANSNATIONAL RULES IN INTERNATIONAL COMMERCIAL ARBITRATION 147 (ICC Publication No. 480/4, 1993): page 648 (footnote 72).

Philip O'Neill, *Recent Developments in International Arbitration: An American Perspective*, 4 (No. 1) J. INT. ARB. 7 (1987): page 603 (footnote 79).

Bruno Oppetit, *Arbitrage juridictionnel et arbitrage contractuel*, 1977 REV. ARB. 315: page 115 (footnote 19).

Bruno Oppetit, *Case Note*, 1982 JDI 931: page 336 (footnote 54).

Bruno Oppetit, *L'adaptation des contrats internationaux aux changements de circonstances: la clause de "Hardship"*, 1974 JDI 794: page 643 (footnote 50).

Philippe Ouakrat, *L'arbitrage commercial internationale et les mesures conservatoires: étude générale*, 1988 DROIT ET PRATIQUE DE COMMERCE INT. 239: page 476 (footnote 11).

Esa Paasivirta, *The European Union and the Energy Sector: The Case of the Energy Charter Treaty*, INTERNATIONAL LAW ASPECTS OF THE EUROPEAN UNION 197 (M. Koskenniemi, Ed., 1998): page 668 (footnote 17).

ESA PAASIVIRTA, PARTICIPATION OF STATES IN INTERNATIONAL CONTRACTS (Helsinki, 1990): pages 661 (footnote 1), 674 (footnote 39).

Judge Panchaud, *Intervention, Symposium on Qualification de l'arbitre international*, 1970 REV. ARB. 203: page 216 (footnote 31).

William W. Park, *The Arbitrability Dicta in First Options v. Kaplan: What Sort of Kompetenz-Kompetenz Has Crossed the Atlantic?* 12 ARB. INT. 137 (1996): pages 50 (footnote 14), 60 (footnote 43), 512 (footnote 74), 513 (footnote 79), 601 (footnote 66).

William W. Park, *Determining Arbitral Jurisdiction*, 8 AM. REV. INT'L ARB. 133 (1997): page 512 (footnote 73).

William W. Park, *Documentary Credit Dispute Resolution: The Role of Arbitrators and Experts*, 12 INT. ARB. REP. 15 (Nov. 1997): page 716 (footnote 18).

William W. Park, *Duty and Discretion in International Arbitration*, 93 AM J. INT'L LAW 805 (1999): pages 498 (footnote 10), 504 (footnote 37).

William W. Park, *Judicial Supervision of Transnational Commercial Arbitration*, 21 HARV. INT. L. J. 87 (1980): page 532 (footnote 4).

William W. Park, *The Lex Loci Arbitri and International Commercial Arbitration*, 32 INT. & COMP. L.Q. 21 (1983): page 498 (footnotes 10, 14).

William W. Park, *National Law and Commercial Justice: Safeguarding Procedural Integrity in International Arbitration*, 63 TUL. L. REV. 647 (1989): pages 61 (footnote 47), 498 (footnotes 10, 14), 507 (footnote 54), 534 (footnote 14).

William W. Park, *Neutrality, Predictability and Economic Cooperation*, 12 (No. 4) J. INT. ARB. 99 (1995): page 517 (footnote 98).

William W. Park, *Private Adjudicators and the Public Interest*, 12 BROOK. J. INT. L. 629 (1986): page 496 (footnote 2).

William W. Park and Jan Paulsson, *The Binding Force of International Arbitral Awards*, 23 VA. J. INT'L L. 253 (1983): page 106 (footnote 4).

Antonio Parra, *Provisions on the Settlement of Investment Disputes in Modern Investment Laws, Bilateral Investment Treaties and Multilateral Instruments on Investment*, 12 ICSID REVIEW—FOREIGN INVESTMENT LAW JOURNAL 287 (1997): page 666 (footnote 13).

Antonio Parra, *The Scope of New Investment Law and International Instruments*, ECONOMIC DEVELOPMENT, FOREIGN INVESTMENT AND THE LAW 27 (Robert Pritchard, Ed., 1996): page 664 (footnote 8).

Jan Paulsson, *Arbitration Unbound: Award Detached from the Law of its Country of Origin*, 30 INTERNATIONAL AND COMPARATIVE LAW QUARTERLY 358 (1981): pages 8 (footnote 7), 71 (footnote 82), 106 (footnote 3), 322 (footnote 6), 498 (footnote 13), 550 (footnote 5).

Jan Paulsson, *Arbitration Unbound in Belgium*, 2 ARB. INT. 68 (1986): page 627 (footnote 16).

Jan Paulsson, *Arbitration Without Privity*, 10 ICSID REVIEW—FOREIGN INVESTMENT LAW JOURNAL 232 (1995): page 664 (footnote 8).

Jan Paulsson, *Delocalization of International Commercial Arbitration*, 32 INT. & COMP. L. Q. 53 (1983): pages 498 (footnotes 10, 13).

Jan Paulsson, *Enforcing Arbitral Awards Notwithstanding an LSA (Local Standard Annulment)*, 9 ICC BULL. No. 1 (May 1998): pages 8 (footnote 7), 506 (footnotes 49, 52), 529 (footnote 24).

Jan Paulsson, *Ethics, Eligibility, Elitism,* 14 J. INT. ARB. 13 (1997): page 27 (footnote 9).

Jan Paulsson, *La lex mercatoria dans l'arbitrage CCI,* 1990 REV. ARB. 55: pages 334 (footnote 48), 633 (footnote 29).

Jan Paulsson, *La réforme de l'arbitrage en Inde,* 1996 REV. ARB. 597: page 100 (footnote 17).

Jan Paulsson, *L'immunité restreinte enterinée par la justice suédoise dans le cadre de l'exéquatur d'une sentence arbitrale etrangère rendue à l'encontre d'un Etat,* 1981 JDI 544: pages 124 (footnote 41), 673 (footnotes 34, 35).

Jan Paulsson, *May a State Invoke Its Internal Law to Repudiate Consent to International Commercial Arbitration?* 2 ARB. INT. 90 (1986): pages 46 (footnote 5), 125 (footnote 46), 642 (footnote 47), 663 (footnote 6).

Jan Paulsson, *The New York Convention's Misadventures in India,* 7 MEALY'S INTERNATIONAL ARBITRATION REPORT 3 (June 1992): pages 99 (footnote 16), 108 (footnote 6), 271 (footnote 33), 510 (footnote 67).

Jan Paulsson, *Report on the UNCITRAL Model Law as Adopted in Vienna on 21 June 1985,* 52 ARBITRATION 98 (1986): page 631 (footnote 24).

Jan Paulsson, *The Role of Swedish Courts in Transnational Commercial Arbitration,* 21 VA. J. INT'L L. 211 (1981): pages 351 (footnote 14), 404 (footnotes 17, 18).

Jan Paulsson, *Sovereign Immunity: French Caselaw Revisited,* 19 INTERNATIONAL LAWYER 277 (1985): page 124 (footnote 45).

Jan Paulsson, *Sovereign Immunity from Execution in France,* 11 INTERNATIONAL LAWYER 673 (1977): page 124 (footnote 45).

Jan Paulsson, *Third World Participation in International Investment Arbitration,* 1987 ICSID REVIEW-FOREIGN INVESTMENT LAW JOURNAL 19: pages 6 (footnote 5), 78 (footnote 105), 662 (footnote 3), 677 (footnote 47).

Jan Paulsson, *The Unwelcome Atavism of Ken-Ren: The House of Lords shows its Meddle,* 1994 SWISS BULL. 439: page 468 (footnote 43).

Jan Paulsson, *Vicarious Hypochondria and Institutional Arbitration,* YEARBOOK OF THE ARBITRATION INSTITUTE OF THE STOCKHOLM CHAMBER OF COMMERCE 96 (1990): page 380 (footnote 6).

Jan Paulsson and Nigel Rawding, *The Trouble With Confidentiality,* 5 ICC BULL. 48 (May, 1994): page 315 (footnote 43).

C. Penna, *Partial Final Awards,* ARBITRATION AND THE LAW 1986 (AAA General Counsel's Annual Report): page 360 (footnote 12).

WOLFGANG PETER, ARBITRATION AND RENEGOTIATION OF INTERNATIONAL INVESTMENT AGREEMENTS (2d Ed. 1995): page 114 (footnote 18).

Paul Peters, *Dispute Settlement Arrangements in International Treaties*, 22 NETHERLANDS YEARBOOK INTERNATIONAL LAW 91 (1991): page 666 (footnote 13).

Gérard Pluyette, *A French Perspective*, CONSERVATORY AND PROVISIONAL MEASURES IN INTERNATIONAL ARBITRATION 72 (ICC Publishing 1993): pages 476 (footnote 11), 478 (footnote 17).

Michael A. Polkinghorne, *The Right of Representation in a Foreign Venue*, 4 ARB. INT. 333 (1988): pages 305 (footnote 22), 308 (footnote 28).

Norman S. Poser, *Judicial Review of Arbitration Awards: Manifest Disregard of the Law*, 64 BROOKLYN L. REV. 471 (1998): page 615 (footnote 156).

Jean-François Poudret, *Expertise et droit d'être entendu dans l'arbitrage international*, ETUDES DE DROIT INTERNATIONAL EN L'HONNEUR DE PIERRE LALIVE 608 (Bâle, 1993): page 459 (footnote 22).

Jean-François Poudret, *L'extension de la clause d'arbitrage: approches française et suisse*, 122 JDI 893 (1995): page 580 (footnote 26).

Jean-François Poudret, *Quelle Solution Pour en Finir avec L'Affaire Hilmarton?* 1998 REV. ARB. 7 (1998): pages 506 (footnote 50), 583 (footnote 41).

Jean-François Poudret, C. Reymond and A. Wurzburger, *L'application du Concordat intercantonal sur l'arbitrage par le Tribunal cantonal vaudois*, 104-105 (1981): page 402 (footnote 9).

Jean-François Poudret and Gabriel Cottier, *Remarques sur l'Application de Article II de la Convention de New York*, 13 SWISS BULL. 383 (1985): page 581 (footnote 31).

Matthew Press, *Arbitration of Claims Under the Securities Exchange Act of 1934*, 77 B.U.L. REV. 629 (1997): page 603 (footnote 75).

Michael Pryles, *The Case of Resort Condominiums v. Bolwell*, 10 ARB. INT. 385 (1994): page 466 (footnote 37).

Michael Pryles, *Note*, 2 WORLD ARBITRATION AND MEDIATION REPORT 329 (1991): page 518 (footnote 105).

Charles Ragan, *Arbitration in Japan: Caveat Foreign Drafters and Other Lessons*, 7 ARB. INT. 93 (1991): page 305 (footnote 18).

P. Rambaud, *Suites d'un differend pétrolier: l'affaire LIAMCO devant le juge français*, 25 ANNUAIRE FRANÇAIS DE DROIT INTERNATIONAL 820 (1979): page 673 (footnote 32).

Alan Scott Rau, *Does State Arbitration Law Matter At All?* 3 ADR CURRENTS 19 (June 1998): page 593 (footnote 16).

Alan Scot Rau, *The New York Convention in American Courts*, 7 AM. REV. INT. ARB. 213 (1996): pages 596 (footnote 33), 679 (footnote 2).

Alan Scott Rau, *On Integrity in Private Judging*, 14 ARB. INT'L. 115: page 201 (footnote 27).

Alan Scott Rau, *The UNCITRAL Model Law in State and Federal Courts: The Case of Waiver*, 6 AM. REV. INT. ARB. 223 (1995): pages 510 (footnote 70), 593 (footnote 16).

Alan Redfern & Martin Hunter, *Consultation Document on Proposed Clauses and Schedules for an Arbitration Bill,* 10 ARB. INT. 189 (1994): pages 60 (footnote 43), 110 (footnote 11).

Alan Redfern, *Arbitration and the Courts: Interim Measures of Protection-Is the Tide About to Turn?* 30 TEXAS INT. L.J. 71 (1995): page 473 (footnote 3).

Alan Redfern, *The Immunity of Arbitrators*, THE STATUS OF THE ARBITRATOR 121 (ICC Publishing, 1995): page 410 (footnote 29).

ALAN REDFERN & MARTIN HUNTER, LAW AND PRACTICE OF INTERNATIONAL COMMERCIAL ARBITRATION (3d ed. 1999): pages 60 (footnote 43), 115 (footnote 21), 306 (footnote 24), 425 (text and footnote 23), 434 (footnote 14), 498 (footnote 10), 499 (footnote 17), 534 (footnote 14), 684 (footnote 23).

Andreas Reiner, *Le règlement d'arbitrage de la CCI, version 1998*, 1998 REV. ARB. 3: page 201 (footnote 25).

Andreas Reiner, *Les mesures provisoires et conservatoires et l'arbitratrage international, notamment l'arbitrage CCI*, 1998 JDI 855: pages 467 (footnote 41), 468 (footnote 46).

Andreas Reiner, *Terms of Reference: The Function of the International Court of Arbitration and Application of Article 16 by the Arbitrators*, 7 ICC BULL. 59 (December 1996): pages 285 (footnote 14), 286 (footnote 15).

W. MICHAEL REISMAN, NULLITY AND REVISIONS (1971): page 410 (footnote 26).

W. MICHAEL REISMAN, SYSTEMS OF CONTROL IN INTERNATIONAL ADJUDICATION AND ARBITRATION (1992): pages 498 (footnote 10), 507 (footnote 54).

W. MICHAEL REISMAN, W. LAURENCE CRAIG, WILLIAM W. PARK & JAN PAULSSON, INTERNATIONAL COMMERCIAL ARBITRATION: CASE MATERIALS AND NOTES ON THE RESOLUTION OF INTERNATIONAL BUSINESS DISPUTES (Foundation Press 1997): pages 99 (footnote 16), 127 (footnote 1), 169 (footnote 33), 307 (footnote 27).

Report on the ICC Rules of Contractual Relations, 5 ICC BULL. 31 (December 1994): page 711 (footnote 14).

Reports of an IBA Sub-Committee, *Interim Court Remedies in Support of Arbitration*, 3 INTERNATIONAL BUSINESS LAWYER 101-124 (1984): page 474 (footnote 6).

Claude Reymond, *Common Law and Civil Law Procedures: Which is the More Inquisitorial*, 55 ARBITRATION 155 (1989): page 418 (footnote 6).

Claude Reymond, *Des connaissances personnelles de l'arbitre à son informa-tion privilégiée: reflexions sur quelques arrêts récents*, 1991 REV. ARB. 3: page 233 (footnote 64).

Claude Reymond, *L'Arbitration Act, 1996: Convergence et originalité*, 1997 REV. ARB. 45: page 531 (footnote 2).

Claude Reymond, *Problèmes actuels de l'arbitrage commercial international*, 1982 REVUE ECONOMIQUE ET SOCIALE 5: page 116 (footnote 22).

Claude Reymond, *Reflexions sur quelques problèmes de l'arbitrage interna-tional, faiblesses, menances et perspectives*, MELANGES EN HOMMAGE A FRANCOIS TARRE (Paris, 1999): page 286 (footnote 16).

Claude Reymond, *Security for Costs in International Arbitration*, 110 L. Q. REV. 501 (1994): page 540 (footnote 67).

Claude Reymond, *Where is an Arbitral Award Made?* 108 L. Q. REV. 1 (1992): page 546 (footnote 105).

Joanne Riches, Comment [1999] SWEET & MAXWELL, INT. A.L.R. 175: page 228 (footnote 56).

David W. Rivkin, *Courts Differ on Arbitrability of Time Limitations*, 1 ADR CURRENTS 21 (Autumn 1996): page 601 (footnote 67).

David W. Rivkin, *International Arbitration and Dispute Resolution*, PLI Com-mercial Law & Practice Course Handbook, 765 PLI/Comm. 183 (1998): page 687 (footnote 34).

David Rivkin, *Lex Mercatoria and Force Majeure*, TRANSNATIONAL RULES IN IN-TERNATIONAL COMMERCIAL ARBITRATION 161 (ICC Publication No. 480/4, 1993): pages 643 (footnote 53), 644 (footnote 59), 651 (footnote 83), 655 (foot-note 96).

David Rivkin & Barton Legum, *Attempts to Use Section 1782 to Obtain U.S. Discovery in Aid of Foreign Arbitration*, 14 ARB. INT. 213 (1998): page 608 (footnote 109).

David Rivkin & Frances Kellner, *In Support of the FAA: An Argument Against U.S. Adoption of the UNCITRAL Model Law*, 1 AM. REV. INT. ARB. 535 (1990): page 591 (footnote 4).

Donald H. Rivkin, *Transnational Legal Practice*, 33 INT'L LAWYER 825 (1999): page 309 (footnote 32).

Jean Robert, *Administration of Evidence in International Commercial Arbitra-tion*, I YEARBOOK 221 (1976): pages 424 (text and footnote 21), 425 (text and footnote 22), 437 (footnote 7).

Jean Robert, *La dénaturation par l'arbitre—réalité et perspectives*, 1982 REV. ARB. 405: page 562 (footnote 80).

Jean Robert, Report, ICC Document 420/179, 25th Congress of the ICC, Special Discussion Group No 1, Tuesday 17th June, 3:30 p.m.-6:30 p.m.: page 240 (footnote 83).

E. Robine, *The Liability of Arbitrators and Arbitral Institutions in International Arbitrations Under French Law*, 5 ARB. INT. 323 (1989): page 410 (footnote 29).

Andrew Rogers, *Arbitrability,* 10 ARB. INT. 263 (1994): page 66 (footnote 63).

Andrew Rogers, *Forum Non Conveniens in Arbitration,* 4 ARB. INT. 240 (1988): page 95 (footnote 9).

Andrew Rogers & Rachel Launders, *Separability—the Indestructible Arbitration Clause,* 10 ARB. INT. 77 (1994): page 49 (footnote 11).

José Rosell and Harvey Prager, *Illicit Commissions and International Arbitration: The Question of Proof,* 15 ARB. INT. 329 (1999): page 345 (footnotes 79, 81).

Jacqueline Rubellin-Devichi, *De l'effectivité de la clause compromissoire en cas de pluralité de défendeurs ou d'appel en garantie dans la jurisprudence récente,* 1981 REV. ARB. 29: page 83 (footnote 121).

M. Rubino-Sammartano, *Amiable Compositeur (Joint Mandate to Settle) and Ex Bono et Aequo (Discretional Authority to Mitigate Strict Law-Apparent Synonyms Revisited,* 9 J. INT'L. ARB. No. 1 (1992): page 348 (footnote 2).

MARGARET RUTHERFORD & JOHN SIMS, ARBITRATION ACT 1996: A PRACTICAL GUIDE (1996): page 531 (footnote 2).

Adam Samuel, *Arbitration in Western Europe: A Generation of Reform*, 7 ARB. INT. 319 (1991): page 510 (footnote 69).

ADAM SAMUEL, JURISDICTIONAL PROBLEMS IN INTERNATIONAL COMMERCIAL ARBITRATION (1989): page 584 (footnote 42).

Gerard Sanders, *Rethinking Arbitral Preclusion*, 24 L. & POLICY INT. BUS. 101 (1992): page 621 (footnote 190).

Pieter Sanders, *Note on Court Decisions on New York Convention 1958,* I YEARBOOK 207 (1976): pages 58 (footnote 38), 120 (footnote 31).

Pieter Sanders, *Note on Court Decisions on the New York Convention,* IV YEARBOOK 233 (1979): pages 58 (footnote 38), 705 (footnote 8).

Pieter Sanders, *Note on UNCITRAL Arbitration Rules,* II YEARBOOK 172 (1977): page 52 (footnote 17).

Pieter Sanders, *L'autonomie de la clause compromissoire*, HOMMAGE A FRÉDÉRIC EISEMANN 39 (ICC Publication No. 321, 1978): pages 163 (footnote 21), 164 (footnote 22), 165 (footnote 26), 167 (footnote 31).

Pieter Sanders, *The New Dutch Arbitration Act,* 3 ARB. INT. 194 (1987): page 82 (footnote 117).

P. Sargos, *Droit à un tribunal impartial,* Report of the *conseiller à la Cour de cassation, Assemblée plénière,* 6 Nov. 1998, J.C.P. II 10198: pages 234 (footnote 69), 236 (footnote 73).

Mark Saville, *The Arbitration Act 1996 and its Effect on International Arbitration in England,* 63 ARBITRATION 104 (1997): page 531 (footnote 2).

Mark Saville, *The Origin of the New English Arbitration Act 1996: Reconciling Speed with Justice in the Decision-making Process,* 13 ARB. INT. 237 (1997): page 531 (footnote 2).

T. Sawada, *Practice of Arbitral Institutions in Japan,* 4 ARB. INT. 120 (1988): page 305 (footnote 17).

PETER SCHLOSSER, DAS RECHT DER INTERNATIONALEN PRIVATEN SCHIEDSGERICHTS-BARKEIT (1989): page 514 (footnote 83).

Peter Schlosser, *1968 Brussels Convention and Arbitration,* 7 ARB. INT. 227: page 688 (footnote 38).

Peter Schlosser, *Right and Remedy in Common Law Arbitration and in German Arbitration Law,* 4 J. INT. ARB. 27 (1987): page 115 (footnote 19).

Clive Schmitthoff, INTERNATIONAL TRADE USAGES 48 (ICC Publication No. 440/4, 1987): pages 631 (footnote 25), 633 (footnote 29), 634 (footnote 32).

Michael Schneider, *Le lieu où la sentence est rendue,* 9 SWISS BULL. 279 (1991): page 546 (footnote 105).

Michael Schneider, *Witnesses in International Arbitration,* 1993 SWISS BULL. 302: page 434 (footnote 13).

Eric Schwartz, *A Comment on Chromalloy: Hilmarton a' l'Americaine,* 14 J. INT. ARB. 125 (1997): pages 506 (footnote 50), 529 (footnote 23).

Eric Schwartz, *The Domain of Arbitration and Issues of Arbitrability: The View from the ICC,* 9 ICSID REVIEW-FOREIGN INVESTMENT LAW JOURNAL 17 (1994): pages 62 (footnote 48), 500 (footnote 22), 509 (footnote 62).

Eric Schwartz, *French Supreme Court Renders Final Judgment in the Hilmarton Case,* 1997 INT. ARB. LAW. REV. 45: page 505 (footnote 45).

Eric Schwartz, *International Conciliation and the ICC,* 5 ICC BULL. 5 (December 1994): pages 697 (footnote 1), 701 (footnote 3).

Eric Schwartz, *Multi-party Arbitration and the ICC—In the Wake of Dutco,* 10 (No. 3) J. INT. ARB. 5 (1993): page 560 (footnote 69).

Eric Schwartz, *The Practices and Experiences of the ICC Court,* CONSERVATORY AND PROVISIONAL MEASURES IN INTERNATIONAL ARBITRATION, ICC Publication No. 519 (1993): page 461 (footnote 25).

Eric Schwartz, *The Rights and Duties of ICC Arbitrators*, THE STATUS OF ARBITRATORS, ICC Publication No. 564 (1995): page 235 (footnote 71).

Eric Schwartz & Rolf Johnson, *Court Assisted Discovery in Aid of International Arbitrations*, 15 J. INT. ARB. 53 (1998): page 608 (footnote 109).

Stephen Schwebel, INTERNATIONAL ARBITRATION: THREE SALIENT PROBLEMS (Grotius Press 1987): pages 49 (footnote 12), 50 (footnotes 13, 14), 123 (footnote 40), 246 (footnote 92), 399 (footnote 4).

Stephen Schwebel, *The Validity of an Arbitral Award Rendered by a Truncated Tribunal*, 6 ICC BULL. 19 (November 1995): page 248 (footnotes 96, 98).

Stephen Schwebel and S. Lahne, *Public Policy and Arbitral Procedure*, REPORT TO THE WORKING GROUP ON PUBLIC POLICY AND ARBITRAITON, VIIIth INTERNATIONAL CONGRESS OF ICCA, New York, May 6-9, 1986: page 302 (footnote 11).

Jerry Scowcroft, *Note,* X YEARBOOK 101 (1985): page 647 (footnote 71).

Jerry Scowcroft, *Note,* XIII YEARBOOK 128 (1988): page 82 (footnote 117).

Secretariat of the International Court of Arbitration of the International Chamber of Commerce regarding Correction and Interpretation of Awards, *Note*: page 409 (footnote 23).

Secretary General of the ICC Court of Arbitration, Communication of 1 January 1988, Modifying July 1, 1986 communication on costs and payment, Appendix II: pages 264 (footnote 19), 266 (footnote 23).

Christopher R. Seppala, *Multi-party Arbitrations at Risk in France*, INT. FIN. L. REV. 33 (Mar. 1993): page 560 (footnote 69).

David Shenton, *An Introduction to the IBA Rules of Evidence*, 1 ARB. INT. 118 (1985): page 454 (footnote 14).

David Shenton and Wolfgang Kuhn, INTERIM COURT REMEDIES IN SUPPORT OF ARBITRATION: A COUNTRY-BY-COUNTRY ANALYSIS (London, International Bar Association 1987): page 474 (footnote 6).

P. Sieghart, *Viewpoint*, 48 ARBITRATION 133: pages 346 (footnote 82), 421 (footnote 15).

May Sin-mi-Hon, *Deal Struck on Cross-Border Cases*, SOUTH CHINA MORNING POST, 16 DECEMBER 1998: page 572 (footnote 51).

Special Supplement, International Commercial Arbitration in Europe, ICC Publication No. 537 (1994) pp. 33-57: page 342 (footnote 70).

Stewart Shackleton, *The Applicable Law in International Arbitration Under the New English Arbitration Act 1996*, 13 ARB. INT. 375 (1997): page 110 (footnote 11).

G. Richard Shell, *Fair Play, Consent and Securities Arbitration: A Comment on Speidel*, 62 BROOK. L. REV. 1365 (1996): page 605 (footnote 92).

G. Richard Shell, *Res Judicata and Collateral Estoppel Effects of Commercial Arbitration*, 35 UCLA L. REV. 623 (1988): page 621 (footnote 190).

Audley Sheppard (Rapporteur), *Public Policy as a Ground for refusing Enforcement of Foreign Arbitral Awards*, INTERNATIONAL LAW ASSOCIATION, COMMITTEE ON INTERNATIONAL COMMERCIAL ARBITRATION, TAIPEI CONFERENCE (1998): page 684 (footnote 23).

Alan Shilston, *A View from the 1981 Annual Conference of the Chartered Institute of Arbitrators*, 47 ARBITRATION 255 (1982): pages 24 (footnote 6), 25 (footnote 7).

Hans Smit, *Assistance Rendered by the United States in Proceedings Before International Tribunals*, 62 COLUM. L. REV. 1264 (1962): page 608 (footnote 109).

Hans Smit, *The Future of International Commercial Arbitration: A Single Transnational Institution?* 25 COLUM. J. TRANSNAT'L L. 9 (1986): page 274 (footnote 4).

Hans Smit, *International Litigation Under the United States Code*, 65 COLUM. L. REV. 1015 (1964): page 491 (footnote 61).

Hans Smit, *May An Arbitration Agreement Calling for Institutional Arbitration Be Denied Enforcement Because of the Cost Involved*, 8 AM REV. INT. ARB. 167 (1999): page 272 (footnote 38).

M. SORNARAJAH, THE INTERNATIONAL LAW ON FOREIGN INVESTMENT (1994): pages 666 (footnote 13), 667 (footnote 15).

Special Issue on the Confidentiality of International Commercial Arbitration, 11 ARB. INT'L No. 3 (1995): page 314 (footnote 41).

Richard E. Speidel, *Contract Theory and Securities Arbitration: Whither Consent?* 62 BROOK. L. REV. 1335 (1996): page 605 (footnote 92).

Steven Stein & Daniel Watman, *The Arbitration Hearing*, INTERNATIONAL COMMERCIAL ARBITRATION IN NEW YORK 68 (J.Stewart McClendon & Rosabel Everard Goodman eds., 1986): pages 487 (footnote 45), 608 (footnote 106).

Jeffrey W. Stempel, *Bootstrapping and Slouching Toward Gomorrah: Arbitral Infatuation and the Decline of Consent*, 62 BROOK. L. REV. 1381 (1996): page 605 (footnote 92).

C. Stippl, *International Multi Party Arbitration: The Role of Party Autonomy*, 7 AMERICAN REVIEW OF INTERNATIONAL ARBITRATION 47 (1996): pages 81 (footnote 115), 666 (footnote 13), 667 (footnote 15).

Stockholm Chamber of Commerce Publication, ARBITRATION IN SWEDEN 121 (1977): page 351 (footnote 14).

Jean Stoufflet, *L'œuvre normative de la Chambre de commerce internationale dans le domaine bancaire*, LE DROIT DES RELATIONS ECONOMIQUES

INTERNATIONALES 361 (LIBER AMICORUM FOR PROF. GOLDMAN, 1982): pages 625 (footnote 10), 637 (footnote 37), 646 (footnote 68), 713 (footnote 16).

R. Straus, *The General Consensus on International Commercial Arbitration*, 68 AM. J. INT'L L. 709 (1974): page 194 (footnote 16).

Summaries of Awards, 4 ICC BULL 43-48 (May 1993): page 394 (footnote 8).

Lord Tangley, *International Arbitration Today*, 15 INTERNATIONAL AND COMPARATIVE LAW QUARTERLY 719 (1966): page 349 (text and footnote 8).

Justin Thorens, *L'arbitre international au point de rencontrer des traditions du droit civil et de la common law*, ETUDES DE DROIT INTERNATIONAL EN L'HONNEUR DE PIERRE LALIAVE 693 (Heilbing und Lichtenhahn, Bâle, 1993): page 423 (footnote 18).

John M. Townsend, *Nonsignatories and Arbitration: Agency, Alter Ego and Other Identity Issues*, 3 ADR CURRENTS 19 (Sept. 1998): page 598 (footnote 47).

UNIDROIT PRINCIPLES OF INTERNATIONAL COMMERCIAL CONTRACTS (International Institute for the Unification of Private Law 1994): page 632 (footnote 27).

Detlev Vagts, *Arbitration and the UNIDROIT Principles*, CONTRACTACION INTERNACIONAL (MEXICO) 1998: page 633 (footnote 27).

Albert Jan van den Berg, *Annulment of Awards in International Arbitration*, in INTERNATIONAL ARBITRATION IN THE 21ST CENTURY (Richard Lillich & Charles Brower eds., 1994): page 506 (footnote 50).

Albert Jan van den Berg, *Note of Court Decisions on the 1958 New York Convention*, VII YEARBOOK 290 (1982): page 95 (footnote 8).

Albert Jan van den Berg, *Court Decisions on the New York Convention 1958, Consolidated Note*, XXI YEARBOOK 394 (1996): page 140 (footnote 6).

Albert Jan van den Berg, *National Report*, XII YEARBOOK 3 (1987): page 336 (footnote 55).

Albert Jan van den Berg, *The Netherlands*, III ICCA HANDBOOK SUPPL. (7 April 1987): page 115 (footnote 19).

ALBERT JAN VAN DEN BERG, THE NEW YORK ARBITRATION CONVENTION OF 1958 (1981), XXIV B YEARBOOK (1999): pages 73 (footnote 93), 95, 271 (footnote 32), 367 (footnote 28), 404 (footnote 16), 482 (footnote 29), 679 (footnote 2), 682 (footnote 15), 684 (footnote 23).

Hans van Houtte, *Arbitrability Involving Securities Transactions*, 12 ARB. INT. 405 (1996): page 69 (footnote 75).

Hans van Houtte, *Changed Circumstances and Pacta Sunt Servanda*, TRANSNATIONAL RULES IN INTERNATIONAL COMMERCIAL ARBITRATION 105 (ICC Publication No. 480/4, 1993): page 649 (footnote 79).

Hans van Houtte *The UNIDROIT Principles of International Commercial Contracts*, 11 ARB. INT. 373 (1995): page 632 (footnote 27).

V.V. Veeder, *England,* ICCA HANDBOOK 53 (Supplement March 1997): pages 115 (footnote 19), 350 (footnote 12), 433 (footnote 11).

V.V. Veeder, *La nouvelle loi anglaise sur l'arbitrage de 1996*, 1997 REV. ARB. 3: page 531 (footnote 2).

V.V. Veeder, National Report, England, ICCA HANDBOOK 40 (Suppl. 23 March 1997): pages 436 (footnote 5), 531 (footnote 3).

V.V. Veeder, *Remedies Against Arbitral Awards: Setting Aside, Remission and Rehearing*, 1993 YEARBOOK, ARBITRATION INSTITUTE, STOCKHOLM CHAMBER OF COMMERCE 125: page 542 (footnote 77).

H. Verbist, *The Practice of the ICC International Court of Arbitration With Regard to the Fixing of the Place of Arbitration*, 12 ARB. INT. 347 (1996): page 186 (footnote 1).

David Wagoner, *Interim Relief in International Arbitration*, 51 DISP. RESOL. J. 68 (Oct. 1996): page 607 (footnote 100).

THOMAS WALDE (Ed.), THE ENERGY CHARTER TREATY: AN EAST-WEST GATEWAY FOR INVESTMENT AND TRADE (1996): page 668 (footnote 17).

Stephen J. Ware, *Employment Arbitration and Voluntary Consent*, 25 HOFSTRA L. REV. 83 (1996): page 605 (footnote 92).

F.B. Weigand, *The UNCITRAL Model Law: New Draft Arbitration Acts in Germany and Sweden*, 11 ARB. INT. 397 (1995): page 521 (footnote 6).

Wilhelm Wengler, *Les principes généraux du droit en tant que loi du contrat*, 1982 REVUE CRITIQUE DE DROIT INTERNATIONAL PRIVÉ 496: pages 102 (footnote 21), 112 (footnote 14).

Jacques Werner, *The Trade Explosion and Some Likely Effects on International Arbitration*, 14 J. INT. ARB. 5 (1997): page 664 (footnote 8).

J. Gillis Wetter, *A Multi-party Arbitration Scheme for International Joint Ventures*, 3 ARB. INT. 2 (1987): page 126 (footnote 48).

J. Gillis Wetter, *Book Review*, 1984 SVENSK JURISTTIDNING 156: pages 304 (footnote 15), 330 (footnote 36), 624, 625 (text and footnote 9), 639 (text and footnote 40).

J. GILLIS WETTER, THE INTERNATIONAL ARBITRAL PROCESS (1979): pages 24 (footnote 5), 34 (footnote 2), 242 (footnote 85), 244 (footnote 90), 368 (footnote 29).

J. Gillis Wetter, *The Internationalization of International Arbitration,* 11 ARB. INT. 117 (1995): page 62 (footnote 48).

J. Gillis Wetter, *The Present Status of the International Court of Arbitration of the ICC: An Appraisal*, AM REV. INT. ARB. 91 (1990): page 274 (footnote 4).

J. Gillis Wetter & Charl Priem, *The 1993 General Electric Case: The Supreme Court of India's Re-Affirm Pro-Enforcement Policy Under the New York Convention*, 8 MEALEY'S INT. ARB. REP. (Dec. 1993): page 510 (footnote 67).

Willenken, *The Often Overlooked Use of Discovery in Aid of Arbitration and the Spread of the New York Rule to Federal Common Law*, 35 BUSINESS LAWYER 173 (1979): page 488 (footnote 52).

Working Party Draft, ICC Doc. No. 420/15-15 of 8 October 1996: page 201 (footnote 25).

Working Party Draft, ICC Doc. No. 420/15-15 of 27 September 1996: page 411.

Working Party on Partial and Interim Awards of the ICC Commission on International Arbitration, ICC Document No. 420/298 of 10 September 1987, No. 420/302 of 22 March 1988: page 360 (footnote 13).

Working Party (Third Report) 420/305 Rev. of 20 March 1989: page 360 (footnote 13).

Berda Wortmann, *Choice of Law by Arbitrators: The Applicable Conflicts of Law System*, 14 ARB. INT. 97 (1998): page 320 (footnote 1).

TABLE OF ARTICLES OF THE 1998 ICC ARBITRATION RULES

Introductory Provisions

Article 1: International Court of Arbitration

Article 1(1): pages 90 (footnote 13), 138-140, 145, 563 (footnote 2), 576 (footnote 3).

Article 1(2): page 207.

Article 1(3): page 20 (text and footnote 2).

Article 1(4): page 256 (footnote 8).

Article 2: Definitions

Article 2: page 216.

Article 2(2): pages 199 (footnote 23), 359 (footnote 11), 560 (footnote 70).

Article 3: Written Notifications or Communications; Time Limits

Article 3: page 35.

Article 3(1): pages 149, 407, 429.

Article 3(2): pages 153, 154 (footnote 33).

Article 3(4): page 154.

Commencing the Arbitration

Article 4: Request for Arbitration

Article 4: pages 20, 145, 427, 430.

Article 4(1): page 145.

Article 4(2): page 146.

Article 4(3): pages 146, 148.

Article 4(3)(a): pages 147, 148.

Article 4(3)(b): page 427.

Article 4(3)(c): page 149.

Article 4(3)(e): page 149.

Article 4(3)(f): pages 147, 148.

Article 4(5): pages 149, 153, 376.

Article 4(6): pages 182, 183, 607 (footnote 104).

Article 5: Answer to the Request; Counterclaims
Article 5: pages 149, 189 (footnote 10), 427, 430.

Article 5(1): pages 150, 158.

Article 5(2): page 150.

Article 5(5): page 150 (text and footnote 25).

Article 6: Effect of the Arbitration Agreement
Article 6: pages 290, 513, 708.

Article 6(1): page 142.

Article 6(2): pages 21, 26, 59, 85, 149, 154 (footnote 33), 155, 156, 158, 159 (footnote 11), 161, 164 (footnote 25), 170 (footnote 38), 171, 172, 513 (footnote 79).

Article 6(3): pages 54, 152, 153, 708.

Article 6(4): pages 21, 51, 61, 161, 162, 164, 166, 170 (text and footnote 38), 171, 641.

The Arbitral Tribunal
Article 7: General Provisions
Article 7: pages 208, 496 (footnote 4).

Article 7(1): pages 27, 194, 203 (footnote 1), 207, 208 (footnote 18).

Article 7(2): pages 22, 194, 204, 213, 214, 249 (footnote 99), 250.

Article 7(3): page 213.

Article 7(4): pages 22, 23, 195, 206, 207 (text and footnote 14), 220.

Article 7(6): page 560 (footnote 70).

Article 8: Number of Arbitrators
Article 8: pages 146, 185, 243.

Article 8(1): pages 81, 189 (footnote 9), 199 (footnote 22), 560 (footnote 70).

Article 8(2): pages 91, 149, 189.

Article 8(3): page 156 (footnote 3).

Article 8(4): pages 52 (footnote 17), 132, 152, 191, 197.

Article 9: Appointment and Confirmation of the Arbitrators
Article 9: pages 146, 185, 198, 199, 243, 312.

Article 9(2): pages 195, 205 (footnote 9).

Article 9(3): pages 191, 192, 710.

Article 9(4): pages 192, 710.

Article 9(5): pages 193, 224, 426.

Article 9(6): pages 21, 152, 197 (text and footnote 20), 198.

Article 10: Mutual Parties

Article 10: pages 22, 126, 146, 189 (footnote 9), 198-200, 560 (footnote 71).

Article 10(1): pages 198, 200.

Article 10(2): pages 198-200, 201 (text and footnote 25).

Article 11: Challenge of Arbitrators

Article 11: pages 203, 237, 239, 240, 321, 640, 715.

Article 11(1): pages 203 (footnote 1), 204, 205, 207, 223, 243 (footnote 88).

Article 11(2): pages 204, 206 (footnote 12), 250, 251.

Article 11(3): pages 203 (footnote 1), 205 (text and footnote 11), 206, 710.

Article 12: Replacement of Arbitrators

Article 12: page 640.

Article 12(1): pages 203 (text and footnote 1), 237 (footnote 76), 242, 245, 399 (footnote 5), 711.

Article 12(2): pages 204 (footnote 4), 237-240, 242, 245.

Article 12(4): pages 143 (footnote 14), 243 (text and footnote 87), 244, 246.

Article 12(5): pages 24, 245, 399 (footnote 5), 247-249.

The Arbitral Proceedings

Article 13: Transmission of the File to the Arbitral Tribunal

Article 13: pages 262, 273, 358.

Article 13(1): page 144.

Article 14: Place of Arbitration

Article 14: pages 11, 185-188.

Article 14(1): pages 188, 206, 280.

Article 14(2): pages 187, 188 (text and footnote 5), 498 (footnote 8).

Article 14(3): pages 187, 188 (footnote 5), 498 (footnote 9).

Article 15: Rules Governing the Proceedings

Article 15: pages 9, 99, 277, 286, 300, 499.

Article 15(1): pages 9, 61, 106, 117, 144 (footnote 15), 281, 283, 295, 296, 300, 364, 422, 425, 434 (text and footnote 12), 451, 641.

Article 15(2): pages 223, 234, 298, 302, 447 (footnote 22), 496, 499 (footnote 20).

Article 16: Language of the Arbitration
Article 16: page 96.

Article 17: Applicable Rules of Law
Article 17: pages 281, 286, 319, 325, 535, 551, 699.

Article 17(1): pages 61, 102, 109 (text and footnote 9), 319, 320, 323, 329, 330 (footnote 36), 335, 336, 341 (footnote 68), 641.

Article 17(2): pages 98, 100, 102 (text and footnote 22), 111, 319, 331, 336, 347, 353, 633, 634 (footnote 31), 642, 713.

Article 17(3): page 347.

Article 18: Terms of Reference; Procedural Timetable
Article 18: pages 23, 150 (footnote 25), 273, 277, 286.

Article 18(1): pages 262 (footnote 16), 274 (footnote 3).

Article 18(1)(c): page 277.

Article 18(1)(d): page 275.

Article 18(1)(g): pages 112, 281, 347.

Article 18(2): pages 23, 285.

Article 18(3): pages 152, 262 (footnote 15), 284, 286, 355, 356 (footnote 5).

Article 18(4): pages 262 (footnote 15), 283.

Article 19: New Claims
Article 19: pages 150 (footnote 25), 183, 277, 278.

Article 20: Establishing the Facts of the Case
Article 20: pages 153 (footnote 30), 435.

Article 20(1): pages 34, 415, 422, 425, 449, 461.

Article 20(2): pages 303 (footnote 14), 415, 416, 439.

Article 20(3): pages 415, 416, 442 (footnote 17).

Article 20(4): pages 415, 442, 459.

Article 20(5): pages 415, 416, 449-451, 457.

Article 20(6): pages 118, 415, 427.

Article 20(7): pages 314 (text and footnote 42), 415.

Article 21: Hearings

Article 21: pages 378, 379.

Article 21(3): pages 2 (footnote 1), 311 (footnote 35).

Article 21(4): page 303.

Article 22: Closing of the Proceedings

Article 22: pages 247 (footnote 95), 405, 417 (footnote 3).

Article 22(1): pages 303 (footnote 13), 446, 447 (text and footnote 22).

Article 22(2): page 447 (footnote 23).

Article 23: Conservatory and Interim Measures

Article 23: pages 116, 117 (footnote 23), 359 (footnote 11), 468 (footnote 45).

Article 23(1): pages 116, 461, 463, 464, 467, 468 (text and footnote 45), 472, 481.

Article 23(2): pages 116, 461 (footnote 26), 462, 471, 472 (text and footnote 2), 473, 476, 480, 481 (footnote 25), 497, 556, 607, 706.

Article 24: Time Limit for the Award

Article 24: pages 237, 355.

Article 24(1): pages 13, 23, 135, 355, 356, 406, 558 (footnote 56).

Article 24(2): pages 13, 135, 355.

Article 25: Making of the Award

Article 25: page 408.

Article 25(1): pages 248 (footnote 97), 368-371, 398.

Article 25(2): pages 153 (footnote 31), 329, 349, 353, 364, 367, 559 (footnote 65), 582.

Article 25(3): pages 397, 398 (footnote 2).

Article 26: Award by Consent

Article 26: page 358.

Article 27: Scrutiny of the Award by the Court

Article 27: pages 24, 35, 353, 356, 360 (text and footnote 14), 372, 373 (footnote 39), 375, 377-380, 381 (text and footnotes 8, 10), 397, 408, 447 (text and footnote 23).

Article 28: Notification, Deposit and Enforceability of the Award

Article 28: pages 119, 293 (footnote 33), 398-400, 402, 408, 501, 534, 535, 543 (footnote 82), 611.

Article 28(1): pages 35, 263, 359, 399.

Article 28(2): pages 2 (footnote 1), 399, 405.

Article 28(3): page 400.

Article 28(4): pages 404, 405.

Article 28(5): pages 404, 405.

Article 28(6): pages 121, 401-404, 406, 411, 542 (footnote 75).

Article 29: Correction and Interpretation of the Award
Article 29: pages 24 (footnote 4), 362, 406, 407, 535 (footnote 21).

Article 29(1): page 407.

Article 29(2): page 407.

Article 29(3): pages 408, 535 (footnote 23).

Article 30: Advance to Cover the Costs of the Arbitration
Article 30: page 468 (footnote 46).

Article 30(1): pages 25, 36, 254, 255 (text and footnote 5), 262.

Article 30(2): pages 35, 36, 253 (footnote 2), 254, 256, 259, 260 (text and footnote 14), 261-264.

Article 30(3): pages 34, 254, 255 (footnote 5), 260, 264, 267.

Article 30(4): pages 25, 152 (footnote 29), 262, 264, 265 (text and footnote 21), 266 (text and footnote 22).

Article 30(5): page 258 (text and footnote 11).

Article 31: Decision as to the Costs of the Arbitration
Article 31: pages 112 (footnote 14), 118, 406, 540 (footnote 68), 619 (footnote 179), 620 (footnote 181).

Article 31(1): pages 143 (footnote 12), 385, 386, 391, 393.

Article 31(2): pages 32, 253 (footnote 2), 385-388, 390.

Article 31(3): page 391.

Miscellaneous
Article 32: Modified Time Limits
Article 32(1): page 282.

Article 32(2): page 282.

Article 33: Waiver
Article 33: pages 251 (footnote 101), 558 (footnote 53).

Article 34: Exclusion of Liability
Article 34: page 411.

Article 35: General Rule

Article 35: pages 9, 24, 54, 187 (footnote 3), 209, 298, 340, 360, 365, 371, 377, 408, 424, 535 (footnote 20).

INDEX

A

AAA
See American Arbitration Association (AAA)

Adaptation of contracts, 114-116, 709-712

Additional elements, arbitration, 91-104
applicable law, 97-104
language of arbitration, 96-97
nationality of arbitrators, 92-93
number of arbitrators, 91-92
place of arbitration, 93-96
qualifications of arbitrators, 93

Ad hoc **proceedings, 30, 31, 38-40**

Advances to cover costs, 253-272
bank guarantees, 266-267
cost reforms, 36
counterclaims, 257
default, consequences, 263-266
excessive nature of costs, alleged, 272
impecuniosity of party as argument to avoid consequences, 270-272
payment by order, award or judgment, 267-270
waiver of right to require arbitration, treating non-payment as, 270
defensive set-offs, 258-259
determination of, 253-263
court's responsibility, 256-260
dispute, amount, 258
excessive nature of costs, alleged, 272
failure to contribute, consequences, 34-35
problems of, 33-34
provisional advance, 253-256
readjustment by Court, 261-263
Schedule of Arbitration Costs and Fees, 266-267
Secretary General, provisional advance ordered by, 253-256
separate advances authorized, 260-261

Africa
arbitration, avoidance of, 663
arbitrators, interim measures, 462-463
jurisdiction issues, 164

Agency
arbitration agreements, United States law, 598-599

Algeria
awards, annulment, 505

Alter-ego approach, parent and subsidiary, 177-178

American Arbitration Association (AAA), 10, 146-147
Center for Dispute Resolution, 3
Code of Ethics, 215
truncated tribunal, 247

American Deputy Secretary General, 24

"American rule," 393 n.6

Amiable compositeur, **110-114, 273, 335-336, 347-354**
awards, 366-367
review of awards, 353-354
default by party, 285
definition, 347-351
ICC rules, under, 351-353
party autonomy, 551
powers of, 286
scrutiny, 353-354

Amiable composition
See Amiable compositeur

Ancillary proceedings before national courts, 471-493
    attachments, 482-486
    conservatory measures, 471-473
    discovery, court-ordered, 486-493
    evidence, court-ordered production of, 486-493
    expertise, 473-479
    injunction, 473-479
    interim measures, 471-473
    interlocutory relief, 480-481

Annual Conference, ICC, 18

Answer
    and counterclaim, 150-151
    failure or refusal, 151-153

Appeals
    court orders, from
        United States law, 609-610
    waiver of, 121-122

Applicable law, merits of the dispute, 97-104

Apportionment of costs, 118-119

Appropriate rules of law, freedom of arbitrators to apply, 319-323

Arbitrability
    See Arbitration agreement

Arbitral awards
    See Awards

Arbitral jurisdiction
    See Jurisdiction

Arbitral justice concept, 657-659

Arbitral Tribunal, 51-52
    advances to cover costs, 262
    amiable compositeur, 110-114
    applicable law, 98
    awards
        interim and partial awards, 359-361
        time limits, 355

confidentiality, 314
    constituting, 185-202
    fact finding, 416
        production of documents, 449
    hearings, closing proceedings, 446
    jurisdiction issues, 159, 166, 171
    multi-party arbitrations, 198-202
    rules or law of procedure, 106
    written proof, 427

Arbitration Act 1996
    See English Arbitration Act 1996

Arbitration agreements, 43-83
    ad hoc (non-administered) arbitration, 38-40
    arbitrability, 60-72
        bankruptcy, 68-69
        claims sounding in tort, 65-66
        commercial and non-commercial transactions, distinctions, 70
        competition law, 66-67
        consumer transactions, 69
        contracts contra bonos mores, 63-64
        control of judges and, 63
        defined, 60
        delictual liability, 65-66
        employment agreements, 69
        European Convention of 1961, 61-72
        internal transactions, international context, 62
        patents, 67-68
        personal status, matters of, 69
        public policy, 69
        securities law, 69
        trade boycott, 69
        trademarks, 67-68
    Arbitral Tribunal, 51-52
    arbitration clause
        autonomy, 48-52
        related agreements not containing, 79-80

assignments of contract, 78-79
authority to represent parties, 46-48
Belgian law, 52, 503 n.31
bills of lading, 56 n.29
capacity of the parties, 44-46
compétence-compétence, 48-49. *See also* main entry for *Compétence-compétence*
compromis, 37
contractual clause, 37-38
defective clauses, repair of
    United States law, 597
English law, 536-538
    consumer transactions, 538
    definitions, 536
    domestic agreements, 537-538
    separability, 536-537
    "special category" disputes, 537
estoppel, 48 n. 8
European Convention of 1961, 61-72
favor validitas approach, 43
form of agreement to arbitrate, 54-59
freedom of parties, 72
French law, 52-53, 551-555
    clauses compromissoires, 551-552
    existence of arbitral agreement, 554-555
    jurisdiction based on nationality, waiver of, 553
    state contracts, 552-553
    subject matter arbitrability, 553-554
    validity of arbitral agreement, 554-555
good faith, 45
grain-trade arbitration, 58 n.36
Hong Kong law, 567-568
immunity, 46 n.5
incorporation by reference, 73-74
institutional arbitration, 40-41
    supervised institutional arbitration, 41-42
international *ordre public*, 45

Italian law, 57, 58
jurisdiction over parties who have not signed, 171-179
law applicable, 52-54
law governing, 107-108
locus regit actum, 47
multi-party disputes, 81-83
New York law. *See* New York Convention on the Recognition and Enforcement of Foreign Arbitral Awards(1958)
related agreements not containing arbitration clause,79-80
related parties not having signed, 74-79
    assignments of contract, 78-79
    group of companies doctrine, 75-78
separability, 48-49 n.11
supervised institutional arbitration, 41-42
Swiss law, 577-578
types of, 37-42
United States law, 596-606
    agency, 598-599
    basic requirements, 596-597
    class actions, 606
    defective clauses, repair of, 597
    equitable estoppel, 599-600
    jurisdiction, preliminary determinations, 600-602
    non-signatories, 597-600
    piercing the veil, 598-599
    separability, 597
    statutes of limitations, 601-602
    subject matter arbitrability, 602-606
validity, 43-83, 497, 577-578
writing, in, 59

Arbitration clause
    autonomy, 48-52
    related agreements not containing, 79-80

Arbitration costs, 391-393

Arbitration under ICC, generally, 1-15
See also specific topics
amounts involved, 3-4
arbitrators, choice of, 9-13
basic principles, 1-2
cases submitted
amounts involved, 3-4
subject matter, typical, 6-7
volume of, 2-3
categories, 6
delocalization, 7-9
geographic adaptability, 1
institutional supervision, 1
length of proceedings, 13-14
maritime disputes, 6
1998 rules
liberalization of choice of law
process, 319-320
overview, 142-143
openness, 1
parties, typical, 4-6
political sensitivity, 4
procedural flexibility, 1
rules, overview, 137-154
answer and counterclaim,
150-151
business disputes, 138-142
communications, 153-154
counterclaim, 150-151
default, 152-153
edition of ICC rules applicable,
142-145
1998 rules, 142-143
non-business disputes, 140-141
notifications, 153-154
refusal or failure to answer,
151-153
request for arbitration, 145-149
time periods, calculations of,
153-154
universality, 1, 3
venue, choice of, 9-13

volume of cases, 2-3

Arbitrators, 26-28
allocation of costs between parties,
391-396
appointment of, 21-22, 27
French law, 556
appropriate rules of law, freedom to
apply, 319-323
awards
signature, 397-399
termination of arbitrators' powers,
406-410
bias, 230-232
appearance of, 214
bona fide fear of partiality, 215
chairman of tribunal, 27
challenge, 23, 203-206
bias, 230-232
direct interest in subject matter of
arbitration, 225-226
due process violations, 234-235
failure of disclosure as ground,
215
financial relationship with parties,
226-230
grounds for, 223-236
national court precedents, use of,
235-236
nationality as grounds, 224-225
nemo debet esse judex in propria
causa, 225-226
party-nominated v. third or sole
arbitrators, 223-224
previously expressed opinion,
230-232
related proceedings, serving as
arbitrator in, 232-234
subordinate relationship with
party, 226-230
Swiss law, 579
time limits, 249-251
choice of, 9-13
conclusion of arbitration, authorizing,
24

confirmation of, 204-205
    refusals, 207-208
conflict of laws, 328-329
curriculum vitae, 249, 251
death of, 242
disclosure, duty of, 213-223
    failure of disclosure as ground for challenge, 215
    "in the eyes of the parties," 213-214
    "might be of such a nature," 213-214
    National Court precedents, 216-223
    rule requirement, 213-215
disqualification, 203-206
droits de la contradiction, 234
droits de la défense, 233, 234
due process violations, 234-235
ex officio powers of court to remove, 237
expenses, determination of, 23
fact finding, 415-426, 449-460
    approach to, 415-426
    "by all appropriate means," 415-418
    civil-law procedures, 418-419
    common-law procedures, 419-422
    compromise, 423
    depositions, 457-458
    experts appointed by tribunal, 458-560
    flexibility, 423
    procedural principles, 422-426
    production of documents, 449-456
    right to be heard, 424
    site visit, 458
failure of party to nominate, 197-198
fees, 29, 31-32
    determination of, 385, 387-391
    discretion of Court, 390
    minimum-maximum range, 388-390

financial relationship with parties, 226-229
    prior relationship, 229-230
free choice of law, 329
freedom of parties and arbitrators, 295-296
Hong Kong law, liability, 567
impartiality, 208 n.16
incapacity of, 203-251
independence, 204, 207-208
    defined, 27, 210-211
    lack of, 223
    requirement, overview, 209-213
independent party-nominated arbitrators, 195-196
institutional freedom, 640
interim measures, 460-469
    costs, security for, 467-469
    examples of, 462-464
    procedural order or interim award, 464-467
interlocutory relief, 460-469
    tribunal, powers of, 460-462
jurisdiction, authority, 161-171, 641
legal training, 241
misconduct, 240, 246, 610, 613
nationality of, 224-225
non-replacement of, 245-249
oath, power to administer, 435-437
objections to, 204
party-nominated, 194-196, 223-224
previously expressed opinion, 230-232
rejection of nomination, 203-206
related proceedings, serving as arbitrator in, 232-234
removal of, 217-218, 237-240
replacement of, 242-245
resignation of, 243
résumé, 249
sole arbitrators. *See* Sole arbitrators
standards for, 204, 207-209, 240-242

subordinate relationship with party, 226-229
>prior relationship, 229-230
subpoena, 435-437
supervision by Court, 207 n.13
Terms of Reference, approval of, 23
truncated tribunal, 245-249
· windfalls to, 32

Arguments, written proof and, 427-434

Asia, situs of cases, 7

Attachments
>ancillary proceedings before national courts, 482-486

Attorneys' fees, 395-396
See also Costs
>United States law, 619-620

Australia
>awards, 466
confidentiality, 317
rights of audience, 306
UNCITRAL Model Law and, 527

Australian International Arbitration Amendment, 306

Austria, 4
>arbitration agreements, 48 n. 8
arbitrators, 27
lex mercatoria, 335

Authority
>appointing, 714-715
arbitrators, jurisdiction, 161-171, 641
non-existent authority, 129-132
representation of parties, arbitration agreements, 46-48

Aviation arbitration, 712-713

Awards, 355-383
>*amiable compositeur*, rendered by, 353-354
"a-national" nature of, 8

annulment, 500-507
>enforcement forum, 504-507
French law, 559
judicial review, models for, 502-504
private interests in procedure, 501-502
public interests in procedure, 501-502
United States law, 614-615
waiver of right to challenge award, 501
approval of, 24
attorneys' fees, United States law, 619-620
chairman, awards rendered by, 368-370
consent, by, 358-359
correction, 406-409
costs, payment of, 399-400
Court's scrutiny of, 375-383
>legal sufficiency, ensuring, 378
modification of form of award, 378-379
national courts, as seen by, 380-383
procedural defects, review of, 377-378
rapporteur, Court as, 376
role of Court, 375-377
substance, comments on points of, 379-380
"deliberate wrongdoing," 411-412
deposit of, 404-406
disclosure, United States law, 612-613
dissenting opinions, 371-374
due process, 560
enforceability of, 400-404
English law, 541-547
>challenge, limits on, 545-546
jurisdiction, 545
making of award, 546-547
points of law, 542-543

procedural irregularity, 543-545

statutory skeleton, 541-542

entering into effect of, 397-413

finality of, 400-404

foreign awards, French law, 561-562

form of award, 364-368

modification of, 378-379

French law

annulment, 559

case study, 558

due process, 560

foreign awards, 561-562

judicial review, grounds for, 557-558

jurisdiction, 562

public policy, 561

reasoned awards, 559

recognition, 559

review of, 557-562

functus officio, 408

Hong Kong law

annulment, 570-571

Hong Kong, awards rendered in, 570-571

Mainland China, awards rendered in, 572-573

review of, 570-573

interim awards, 359-364, 464-467

Swiss law, 581

interpretation under Article 29, 406-409

judicial review

French law, 557-558

United States law, 615

jurisdiction

considered only after award, 513-514

French law, 562

lex mercatoria, as precedent to, 639-650

liability, exclusion of, 410-413

local law, enforcement of awards, 401

Mainland China, awards rendered in, 572-573

majority awards, 368-370

national law

constraints on ICC arbitration, 497

exceptional remedies under, 409

New York Convention, 681-682

1998 Rules

form of award, 364

time limit, 358

notification to parties, 399-400

partial awards, 359-364

procedural defects, review of, 377-378

recognition, 559

review of

French law, 557-562

Hong Kong law, 570-573

national law, constraints on ICC arbitration, 497

United States law, 610-622

second look doctrine, 617-618

secrecy of deliberations, 372 n.36

signature by arbitrators, 397-399

substance, comments on points of, 379-380

Swiss law

annulment, 576

interim awards, 581

review of, 582-591

termination of arbitrators' powers, 406-410

time limits, 355-358

extension of time, 356-357

unanimity and, 369

UNCITRAL Model Law, review of awards, 528-529

United States law, 610-622

annulment, 614-615

arbitral jurisdiction, 620-621

attorneys' fees, 619-620

disclosure, duty, 612-613

enforcement of award, 616-617

entry of judgment provisions, 622

excess of authority, award for, 620-621

foreign awards, enforcement, 617

foreign awards, vacatur, 615-616

impartiality, 612-613

judicial review, 615

jurisdiction, 620-621

manifest disregard of the law, 614-615

misconduct, arbitrators, 610, 613

punitive damages, 618-619

second look doctrine, 617-618

substantial error, 615

vacatur, 610-616

waiver of right to recourse, 402

B

Back-to-back contracts, 652-653

Bank guarantees, advances to cover costs, 266-267

Bankruptcy, arbitration agreement, 68-69

Barbados, Legal Profession Act, 307

Belgian law, 503 n.31
arbitration agreements, 50, 52
arbitrators, 27
public law, 343
site of arbitration, 13

Belgian Law on Exclusive Distributorships (1971), 70

Belgium, 4
See also Belgian law

Bellet, Judge Pierre, 437

Bensaud, Denis, 25

Bias
arbitrators, 214, 230-232
awards, review of, United States law, 612-613

Bilateral investment treaties (BITs), 665-668

Bills of lading, arbitration clauses, 56 n.29

BITs
See Bilateral investment treaties (BITs)

Bombay, arbitration agreement, 83

Bonos mores, 63-64

Bordeaux Tribunal de commerce, 689

Boyd, Stewart, 421

Briefs, 430-431

Briner, Robert, 20

Brussels, arbitration agreement, 81

Bruxelles Convention, New York Convention and, 687-689

Bundesgericht (Switzerland), 575

Business disputes, 138-142

C

California
ancillary proceedings, attachments, 484
rights of audience, 309-310

Canada, 4
arbitrator, removal of, 217-218
site of arbitration, 11
situs of cases, 7

Capacity of the parties, arbitration agreements, 44-46

Carlevaris, Andrea, 25

Cattaui, Maria Livanos, 17

Cautio Judicatum Solvi, 467 n.40

Center for Dispute Resolution of the American Arbitration Association, 3

Chairman, awards rendered by, 368-370

Challenge
  arbitrators. *See* Arbitrators
  awards, English law, 545-546

China International Economic and Trade Arbitration Commission (CIETAC), 3, 572

Choice of law
  See also Substantive law, choice of
  absence of, 98
  national law, constraints on ICC arbitration, 508-509

CIETAC
  See China International Economic and Trade Arbitration Commission (CIETAC)

Citizens of United States, corporations as, 596 n.34

Claims sounding in tort, 65-66

Class actions, United States law, 606

Clauses compromissoires, 551-552

Closing proceedings, hearings, 446-447

Cohn, Professor E. J., 321, 348-349

Comité Maritime International (CMI), 712-713

Commerce Act 1986, New Zealand, 66 n.63

Commission on International Arbitration, 19

Commissions of ICC, 18

Common-law procedures
  fact finding, 419-422
  hearings
    oral argument, 445
    subpoenas, 436

Communications, 153-154

Compensation, availability, 647-648

Compétence-compétence, 48-49, 162, 512-515, 552

Competition law, arbitration agreement and, 66-67

Compromis, 37, 274, 286

Compromise, inappropriate, 132-133

Conciliation, 697-701
  adapting contract and, 115-116
  as precondition, 105-106

Conciliation Committee, 698

Conciliation Rules, 698, 700

Concordat (Switzerland), 576-577

Confidentiality, 311-318

Conflict of laws
  See also Substantive law, choice of
  cumulative application of the different rules of conflict, 326-327
  general principles of, 327-328
    arbitrator, chosen by, 328-329
  rules of, 108-109

Congresses of ICC, 18

Connivance, nationality of arbitrators and, 92

Consent, awards by, 358-359

Conservatory measures, ancillary proceedings before national courts, 471-473

Consolidation
  jurisdiction
    multiple contracts between same parties, 180-182
    related arbitration proceedings, 182-183
  United States law, 607

Constitutional Law of the Islamic Republic of Iran, 72

Construction industry
  jurisdiction, third parties, 180

Consumer Contract Regulations, 538

Consumer transactions
    arbitration agreement, 69

Contra bonos mores, 649

**Contracts, adaptation of, 114-116,
709-712**

**Contracts between States or State
entities, 102-104**

Contracts contra bonos mores, 63-64

Contractual breach, damages, 647

**Contractual clause, arbitration
agreements, 37-38**

**Contractual terms, application of,
330-332**

**Convention on the Recognition and
Enforcement of Foreign Arbitral
Awards (1958)**
See New York Convention on the
Recognition and Enforcement of
Foreign Arbitral Awards (1958)

**Convention on the Settlement of
Investment Disputes Between States
and Nationals of Other States (1965),
163**

Corporate group
See **Group of companies doctrine**

Cost reforms, 35-36

Costs, 29-36
    See also Fees
    ad hoc proceedings, 30, 31
    administrative costs, determination
        of, 386-387
    advances to cover, 253-272. *See also*
    Advances to cover costs
        cost reforms, 36
        failure to contribute,
            consequences, 34-35
        problems of, 33-34
    allocation of costs between parties,
        arbitrators', 391-396
    "American rule," 393 n.6

arbitration costs, 391-393
assessment, 29
awards, payment of costs, 399-400
capping of administrative costs,
    386-387
comparisons, 31
complex litigation, 30-31
determination of, 385-396
    allocation of costs between
        parties, arbitrators',391-396
    general principles, 385-386
    ICC administrative costs, 386-387
drafting, minimization of costs and,
    32-33
evaluation in relation to alternatives,
    29-33
failure to contribute, consequences,
    34-35
party costs, 393-396
payment-for-services rendered, 31-32
per diem system, 31
provisional advances, 34
reforms, 35-36
service-mindedness and, 32
windfalls to arbitrators, 32

Costs, security for, 467-469
    English law, 468, 540-541

Counsel, hearings
    examination, 439
    witnesses, relation to, 441

Counterclaims, 150-151
    Terms of Reference, 276-277

Cour d'appel, **550, 554, 558**

Cour de cassation
    agreement to arbitrate, 552, 553
        n.25, 554-555
        jurisdiction, 164
        validity, 65-66
    awards, 381
        annulment, 505
        time limits for, 357

French bar, monopoly of, 307
Terms of Reference, 288

Court of Arbitration, 19-24
advances to cover costs. *See* Advances
to cover costs
arbitrators
appointment of, 21-22
challenges against, determination,
23
conclusion of arbitration,
authorizing, 24
expenses, determination of, 23
incapacity or disqualification of,
203-251
Terms of Reference, approval of,
23
awards. *See* Awards
Commission on International
Arbitration, 19
establishment of, 2
failure of party to nominate
arbitrator, 197-198
fees, determination of, 23
International Centre for Expertise, 19
International Maritime Arbitration
Organization (IMAO), 19
jurisdiction
prima facie agreement to arbitrate,
155-157, 166
procedure for raising issues,
158-161
plenary session, 19-20
prima facie agreement to arbitrate
determination of, 21
jurisdiction, 155-157, 166
sole arbitrator, appointment of, 192
time limits, extension of, 23
truncated tribunals, 24
venue, determination of, 23

Court orders, appeals from
United States law, 609-610

Credit disputes, 715-717

Cross-examination, hearings, 439

**Cumulative application of the different
rules of conflict, 326-327**

Curial laws, competing, 509-510

Currency fluctuations, 642-643, 655

Curriculum vitae, arbitrators, 249, 251

Cyprus, 11

D

Daly, Brooks, 25

Damages
contractual breach, 647
mitigation, 646
United States law, punitive damages,
618-619

David, René, 352, 371 n.34

Default
advances, consequences, 263-266
excessive nature of costs, alleged,
272
impecuniosity of party as
argument to avoidconsequences,
270-272
payment by order, award or
judgment, 267-270
waiver of right to require arbitration,
treating non-payment as, 270
consequences, 152-153
Terms of Reference, 284-285

Defendants
advances, failure to contribute, 34-35

**Defensive set-offs, advances to cover
costs, 257-258**

"Deliberate wrongdoing"
awards, 411-412

Delictual liability, 65-66

Delocalization, 7-9

Depositions
defined, 457
fact finding, arbitrators, 457-458
reciprocal depositions, 457

Deposits
See Advances to cover costs

Derains, Yves, 164

Developing countries
See Third World countries

Disclosure
arbitrators, duty of, 213-223
failure of disclosure as ground for challenge, 215
"in the eyes of the parties," 213
"might be of such a nature," 213
National Court precedents, 216-223
rule requirement, 213-215
awards, United States law, 612-613

Discovery, 118
court-ordered, 486-493
United States law, 608

Dispute resolving mechanisms, 697-717
adaptation of contracts, 709-712
appointing authority, 714-715
aviation arbitration, 712-713
conciliation, 697-701
documentary credit disputes, 715-717
expertise, 701-705
maritime arbitration, 712-713
pre-arbitral referee, 706-709
specialized commissions, 713
supervising arbitration, 715

Dissenting opinions, awards, 371-374

District of Columbia, sovereign immunity, 671

Documentary Credit Dispute Expertise Rules (DOCDEX), 715-717

Documents, 429-430
fact finding, production of documents, 449-456. *See also* Production of documents

Domke, Martin, 420

Donovan, F., 373 n.39

Dossiers, 429

Double *exequatur*, 8, 120, 679-680

Drafting, cost minimization and, 32-33

***Droits de la contradiction*, 234**
See also Due process.

***Droits de la défense*, 233, 234**
See also Due process.

Due process
arbitrator disqualification, 234-235
in England,
judicial review for "serious procedural irregularity", 543-44,
arbitrators' duty of fairness under English arbitration law, 543, n. 8
duty to challenge serious procedural irregularity in timely fashion, 545
in France,
judicial review for denial of *principe de la contradiction* 1502 (4), 557-558
French concepts of due process, including equal treatment, 560-61
in general,
reasonable opportunity to present case under ICC Rules Article 15, 496
award annulment for denial of due process, 497
judicial review for denial of due process, 502
due process as goal of UNCITRAL Model Law, 520,

in Switzerland,
> award review for failure to respect adversarial process, 576
> award review for failure to respect equality of the parties, 582
> exclusion of right to challenge award for due process, 586

in United States
> right to fair hearing and cross-examination of witnesses, 608
> misbehavior by which rights prejudiced, 610
> fundamentally fair hearing, 613

under the New York Convention
> defenses to recognition, 684
> lack of opportunity to present case, 685

interaction with European Convention, 686

Dutch Chamber of Commerce, 128-129

E

East Europe, arbitrators, 211

ECJ
See **European Court of Justice (ECJ)**

EFTA
See **European Free Trade Association (EFTA)**

EGOTH
See **Egyptian General Organization for Tourism and Hotels (EGOTH)**

Egypt, 5
> awards, 370
> Civil Code, 529, 643
> Israel, peace treaty, 585
> Israel-Egypt conflict, 1967, 370
> Law on Arbitration (1994), 528

Egyptian General Organization for Tourism and Hotels (EGOTH), 289, 553 n.25

Elements of arbitration
> additional elements, 91-104
> indispensable elements, 85-90
> occasionally useful elements, 105-126
> pathological elements, 127-135

Employment agreements, arbitration agreement, 69

Employment discrimination, 452 n.11

England
See also **English law; United Kingdom**
> ancillary proceedings, attachments, 482
> appeal, waiver of, 121
> arbitration agreement, assignments of contract, 80
> choice of national procedure, effect of, 299-300
> confidentiality, 316-317
> fact finding, arbitrators' approach to, 420, 421-422
> hearings, subpoenas, 436
> interim measures, 468
> jurisdiction issues, 168, 169
> *lex mercatoria*, 337
> liberalization of choice of law process, 319
> rights of audience, 306-307
> Terms of Reference, 292

English, as official language, 96

English Arbitration Act 1950
> ancillary proceedings, attachments, 483

English Arbitration Act 1979, 121

English Arbitration Act 1996, 50, 168, 187, 208 n.16, 297, 531-547
> additional awards, 535
> "agreement otherwise," 534-535
> agreement to arbitrate, 536-538
> *amiable compositeur*, 350
> awards, 541-547

construction, 533

fact finding, arbitrators' approach to, 421-422

injunction or expertise, 474-475

interlocutory matters, 538-541

interlocutory relief, 481

scope, 533-534

English Court of Appeals

arbitrators, duty of disclosure, 216-223

English House of Lords, 169, 653

English law, 531-547

See also England; United Kingdom

additional awards, 535

"agreement otherwise," 534-535

agreement to arbitrate, 536-538

consumer transactions, 538

definitions, 536

domestic agreements, 537-538

separability, 536-537

"special category" disputes, 537

ancillary proceedings, injunction or expertise, 474-475

arbitral proceedings, 540

awards, 541-547

challenge, limits on, 545-546

jurisdiction, 545

making of award, 546-547

points of law, 542-543

procedural irregularity, 543-545

statutory skeleton, 541-542

construction, 533

costs, security for, 540-541

discovery, court-ordered, 488-489

interlocutory matters, 538-541

jurisdiction, 538-539

awards, 545

inherent jurisdiction, 541

scope, 533-534

statutory framework, 531-535

supportive powers of court, 539-540

Entry into effect, 285-286

Entry-of-judgment, 119-120, 622

Equitable estoppel

arbitration agreements, United States law, 599-600

Equivocation, 128-129

Estoppel, 48 n. 8, 599-600

lex mercatoria, 648

Ethiopia, 5

EURODIF dispute, 480-481

Europe

ancillary proceedings, attachments, 482

hearings

oaths, 436-437

subpoenas, 436-437

European Convention on International Arbitration, 321, 472 n.2

New York Convention and, 686

European Court of Justice (ECJ), 688

European Free Trade Association (EFTA), 687

European Wholesale Potato Trade Rules (RUCIP), 40

Evidence

See also Fact finding, arbitrators

contradictory, experts, 458-459

court-ordered production of, 486-493

hearings, demonstrative evidence, 443-444

Ex aequo et bono, 273, 348, 582

ICC rules, under, 351-353

Exceptio nonadempleti contractus, 648

Exclusion agreement, 121

Expenses, arbitrators, 23

Expertise, 701-705
    ancillary proceedings before national
        courts, 473-479

Experts
    fact finding
        by arbitrators, 458-560
        and questioning, 418
    fees, 386, 392
    hearings, 442-443

F

FAA
    See Federal Arbitration Act (United
    States)

**Fact finding, arbitrators, 415-426,
449-460**
    "by all appropriate means," 415-418
    civil-law procedures, 418-419
    common-law procedures, 419-422
    compromise, 423
    depositions, 457-458
    experts appointed by tribunal,
        458-560
    flexibility, 423
    procedural principles, 422-426
    production of documents, 449-456
        confidentiality, 454
        discovery, limitations, 454
        employment discrimination, 452
            n.11
        extraordinary services, 451 n.6
        noncompliance, 453
        "political" cases, 451 n.8
    right to be heard, 424
    site visit, 458

**Federal Arbitration Act (United States),
170, 436, 591-593**
    See also United States law
    awards
        annulment, 502, 506 n.47
        judicial review, 615

    court orders, appeals from, 609-610
    employment contracts, 592 n.6
    entry-of-judgment provisions, 119,
        622
    evidence, court-ordered production of,
        489 n.58, 492-493
    fact finding, production of
        documents, 452
    interlocutory matters
        assistance to arbitration, 607
        consolidation, 607

Fees
    arbitrators', 29, 31-32
        determination of, 385, 387-391
        discretion of Court, 390
        minimum-maximum range,
            388-390
    Court of Arbitration, determination
        by, 23
    experts, 386, 392

**Fifth International Arbitration Congress
(1975)**
    New Delhi, 122

Force majeure, **370**
    lex mercatoria, 645, 651-657
    sovereign immunity, 676

Foreign investments, 140

Foreign lawyers, exclusion of, 94

Foreign Sovereign Immunities Act, 672

Foster, Sir John, 244

France, 4
    See also French law; Paris
    ancillary proceedings
        injunction or expertise, 475-477
        interlocutory relief, 480-481
    arbitration agreements, 45 n.5, 71
        arbitrability, 65-66
        related parties not having signed,
            77
        separability, 48-49 n.11

awards
    annulment, 503 n.34
    Court's scrutiny of, 381
    time limits, 357
bilateral investment treaties (BITs), 666-667
business disputes, 139
confidentiality, 316
conflict of laws, rules of, 109
constraints on ICC arbitration, 516
equivocation, 128
fact finding, arbitrators' approach to, 419 n.7
hearings, testimony, 438
jurisdiction issues, 161, 163, 164, 168, 172
    multiple contracts between same parties, 181, 182
liberalization of choice of law process, 319
procedural requirements, 297
Procédure arbitrale, 106
public law, 344
référé provision, 481
rights of audience, 307
site of arbitration, 11, 12, 13
situs of cases, 7
sovereign immunity, waiver of, 124
Taiwan, sale of military vessels, 64 n.56
Tribunal de commerce, 556
Tribunal de grande instance, 480, 556

Freedom of choice, 304

Freedom of parties and arbitrators, 295-296

Freezing assets, United States law, 607

Freezing law of contracting state, 104

Freezing of legal relationship, 125

French, as official language, 96

French Code of Civil Procedure, 438 n.12

French Court of First Instance, 230

French law, 549-562
  See also **France; Paris**
  agreement to arbitrate, 551-555
    clauses compromissoires, 551-552
    existence of arbitral agreement, 554-555
    jurisdiction based on nationality, waiver of, 553
    state contracts, 552-553
    subject matter arbitrability, 553-554
    validity of arbitral agreement, 554-555
  amiable compositeur. See Amiable compositeur
  arbitration agreement, 52-53
  arbitrators, appointment of, 556
  awards
    annulment, 505, 559
    case study, 558
    dissenting opinions, 371 n.34
    due process, 560
    foreign awards, 561-562
    judicial review, grounds for, 557-558
    jurisdiction, 562
    public policy, 561
    reasoned awards, 559
    recognition, 559
    review of awards, 557-562
    time limits, 356
  compétence-compétence. See Compétence-compétence
  compromise, inappropriate, 132
  conservatory measures, 555-556
  contracts implying international commerce, 550-551
  interlocutory matters, 555-556
  jurisdiction, agreement to arbitrate, 553
  lex mercatoria, 635-636

Nouveau Code de Procédure Civile (NCPC), 549, 557
party autonomy, 551
provisional measures, 555-556
state contracts, 552-553
statutory framework, 549-551

Functus officio, awards, 408

Futility, *lex mercatoria*, 651-654

G

Gélinas, Fabien, 25

General principles of law, 101-102

Geneva
compromise, inappropriate, 132
procedural law of, 301
World Economic Forum, 17-18

Geneva Convention of 1961
lex mercatoria, 633
New York Convention and, 686

Geneva Protocol (1923)
New York Convention and, 686

German law
See also Germany
choice of law processes, 321
jurisdiction, first options dictum, 514

Germany, 4
See also German law
awards, time limits, 357
entry-of-judgment stipulation, 119
equivocation, 128-129
jurisdiction issues, 163
site of arbitration, 11, 12, 13
situs of cases, 8

Goldman, Professor Berthold, 290, 625 n.10

Gonzalez-Arrocha, Katherine, 25

Good faith
arbitration agreements, 45
lex mercatoria, 643-644

Grain-trade arbitration, 58 n.36

Greece, arbitration agreements, 46 n.5, 47 n. 7

Group of companies doctrine, 75-78

H

Hague Convention on Sales (1955), 331

Hascher, Mr., 437-438

Hearings, 435-447
closing proceedings, 446-447
counsel, examination by, 439
cross-examination, extent of, 439
demonstrative evidence, 443-444
experts, 442-443
oath, arbitrators' power to administer, 435-437
oral argument, 444-446
oral hearings, 428
party experts, 442-443
pre-hearing conferences, 443
recording of testimony, 440
subpoena, arbitrators' power of, 435-437
summary of testimony, 440
testimony, 437-442
transcript of testimony, 440
tribunal, examination by, 439
witnesses
counsel, relation to, 441
isolation of, 440-441
party representatives, distinction, 439

Hong Kong
See also Hong Kong law
bilateral investment treaties (BITs), 665

rights of audience, 306
UNCITRAL Model Law, 524-525
  interlocutory matters, 526-527

Hong Kong International Arbitration Centre (HKIAC), 569

Hong Kong law, 563-573
See also Hong Kong
agreement to arbitrate, 567-568
amended arbitration ordinance, 563-565
awards
  annulment, 570-571
  Hong Kong, awards rendered in, 570-571
  Mainland China, awards rendered in, 572-573
  review of, 570-573
interlocutory matters, 569-570
international arbitration, defined, 565-566
International Arbitration Centre, 565
liability of institutions and arbitrators, 567
New York Convention and, 566-567, 573
statutory framework, 563-567
UNCITRAL Model Law, 563-566

I

ICC
See International Chamber of Commerce

ICC Arbitration rules, overview
See Arbitration under ICC, generally

ICC Court of Arbitration
See Arbitration under ICC, generally

ICC Model Clause, 88-90
adapting contract, 115
number of arbitrators, 91, 189

ICSID
See International Centre for Settlement of Investment Disputes (ICSID)

IMAO
See International Maritime Arbitration Organization (IMAO)

Immunity
See also Sovereign immunity
arbitration agreements, 46 n.5

Impartiality
awards, United States law, 612-613

Imperium, **298**

Incorporation by reference, arbitration agreement, 73-74

Independence of arbitrators. defined, 27

Independent party-nominated arbitrators, 195-196

India, 4
applicable law, 99-100
arbitration agreement, law governing, 108
default, advances to cover costs, 271-272
ICC award rendered, challenge of, 209
ICC Model Clause, 88
1996 Arbitration Act, 100
place of arbitration and, 95
public law, 339
sovereign immunity, waiver of, 122

Indispensable elements, arbitration, 85-90
ICC Model Clause. *See* ICC Model Clause
scope of dispute, 86-88
unambiguous references, 85-86

Indonèsia, confidentiality, 315

Injunctions
ancillary proceedings before national courts, 473-479
Mareva injunctions, 483, 526-527

Inoperative reference, 130

Institute of International Business Law and Practice
Academic Council, 18-19

Institutional arbitration, 40-41
supervised, 41-42

Institutional freedom, 640

Institutional supervision, 1

Institutions, insufficient specification, 133-134

Interim awards, 359-364, 464-467

Interim measures
ancillary proceedings before national courts, 471-473
arbitrators, 460-469
costs, security for, 467-469
examples of, 462-464
procedural order or interim award, 464-467
national law, constraints on ICC arbitration, 497

Interim procedural questions, United States law, 609

Interlocutory matters
English law, 538-541
French law, 555-556
Hong Kong law, 569-570
Swiss law, 579-582
UNCITRAL Model Law, 526-528
United States law, 607-610
assistance to arbitration, 607
consolidation, 607
court orders, appeals from, 609-610
discovery, 608
freezing assets, 607
interim procedural questions, 609

Interlocutory relief
arbitrators, 460-469
tribunal, powers of, 460-462
national courts, 480-481

International Air Transport Association (IATA), 713

International Bar Association
Ethics for Arbitrators, 312
Rules on the Taking of Evidence in International Commercial Arbitration, 425-426, 443
production of documents, 454-455
Supplementary Rules Governing the Presentation and Reception of Evidence in International Commercial Arbitration (IBA Rules of Evidence), 118, 425
Taking of Evidence, 284

International Centre for Expertise, 19, 701-704, 716

International Centre for Settlement of Investment Disputes (ICSID), 7

International Chamber of Commerce
annual conference, 18
arbitration, generally. See Arbitration under ICC, generally
Commissions, 18
Congresses, 18
Court of Arbitration. See Court of Arbitration
Institute of International Business Law and Practice, Academic Council, 18-19
Joint Working Parties, 18
national committees, 17-19
nominations by, 20
organizational framework, 17-28. See also Organizational framework of ICC

International Chamber of Commerce in Geneva
references to, 85

International Council for Commercial Arbitration, 424

International Court of Justice, 130

International Law Association
Montreal Conference of 1982, 39, 661-662

International Maritime Arbitration Organization (IMAO), 19

International Maritime Arbitration Services, 713

International *ordre public*, 45

International Panel on Extortion and Bribery in Business Transactions, 713

International public policy, 338-346

International Standby Practices (ISP 98), 331

International Wool Agreement of 1965, 55

Iran
ancillary proceedings, interlocutory relief, 480
arbitration agreement, 72
jurisdiction issues, 181
SOFIDIF decisions, 287-289

Iran-U.S. Claims Tribunal, 20

Israel
awards, procedural order or interim award, 465
Egypt, peace treaty, 585
Egypt-Israel Conflict, 1967, 370

Italian Code of Civil Procedure, 165

Italian law
arbitration agreement, 45 n.3, 47-48, 55 n.29, 57, 58, 71
incorporation by reference, 73

Italy, 4
jurisdiction issues, 165

J

Japan, 4
arbitration agreement, multi-party disputes, 82
rights of audience, 305

Japan Commercial Arbitration Association, 305

Joint Working Parties of ICC, 18

Judicial review, awards
French law, 557-558
United States law, 615

Juge de l'exécution, 476

Juge des référés, 476, 707

Julliard, Patrick, 667 n.16

Jurisdiction, 155-183
arbitration agreements
French law, 553
parties who have not signed, 171-179
preliminary determinations, United States law, 600-602
arbitrators, authority, 161-171, 641
awards
French law, 562
United States law, 620-621
compétence-compétence. See *Compétence-compétence*
consolidation
multiple contracts between same parties, 180-182
related arbitration proceedings, 182-183
de facto consolidation, 180-183
English law, 538-539
inherent jurisdiction, 541
first options dictum, 514
hybrids, 514-515
national law, constraints on ICC arbitration, 512-516

non-signatories, 174-179

prima facie agreement to arbitrate, 155-157, 166

    determination of, 21

procedure for raising issues, 158-161

third parties, addition to proceedings, 179-180

Jurit novit curia, 330

Jury trial
    fact finding, arbitrators' approach to, 420

K

Kaplan, Judge Neil, 525

Kassis, Antoine, 380

Kazakhstan, Republic of, 492

Kuala Lumpur, site of arbitration, 12

Küner, Detlev, 25

Kuwait City, site of arbitration, 12

L

Lagergren, Judge Gunnar, 63

Lalive, Pierre, 49, 322, 413, 416 n.2

Language
    of arbitration, 96-97
        adapting contract, 115
        Request for Arbitration, 147-148

Latin America, 5
    situs of cases, 7

Law of the parties, 330

LDIP
    See Loi fédérale sur le droit international privé (LDIP)

Legal certainty, principle of, 688

Length of proceedings, generally, 13-14

Lex arbitri, 499, 500

Lex fori, 321, 322, 338

Lex loci arbitri, 521-522

Lex mercatoria, 319, 332-338, 350, 623-659
    applicable law, freedom to establish, 641
    application of, 102, 110, 323
    arbitral justice concept, 657-659
    autonomous legal order, as, 626-629
    awards as precedence, 639-650
    back-to-back contracts, 652-653
    burden of proof, 646
    compensation, availability, 647-648
    comprehensive body of substantive rules, as, 630-633
    concepts of, 623-639
        autonomous legal order, as, 626-629
        comprehensive body of substantive rules, as, 630-633
        international trade, as usage in, 633-639
    culpa in contrahendo, 650
    currency fluctuations, 642-643, 655
    damages
        contractual breach, 647
        mitigation, 646
    definition, 347
    enforcement of contracts, 642-643
    English law, 535
    estoppel, 648
    force majeure, 645, 651-657
    futility, 651-654
    gold clauses, 643 n.50
    good faith, 643-644
    ICC awards as precedence, 639-650
    institutional freedom, 640
    internal law of state and, 642
    international trade, as usage in, 633-639

jurisdiction, authority of arbitrators to rule on own, 641

legal nomenclature missed by parties, 646

modifications of contract, conduct as acceptance, 645

morality, contract unenforceable if purpose contrary to, 649-650

notification, 657

obvious and fuzzy norms, 639-640

pacta sunt servanda, 642-643
  exceptions to, 649

price variations, 655

rules of procedure, freedom to establish, 641

setoff, availability, 647-648

trade practice, 631

UNCITRAL Model Law, 631, 634

unforseeability, 655-657

UNIDROIT and, 632-633

use of goods as acceptance, 646

validity, 646

LIAMCO, 672-674

Liberalization of choice of law process, 319-320

Libya
  inoperative reference, 130
  sovereign immunity, 672-673

Locus regit actum, 47

Loi fédérale sur le droit international privé (LDIP), 503 n.52, 575
  See also Swiss law
  arbitration agreements, 43, 44
  awards, review of, 582-590
  interlocutory matters, 579
  scope of, 576

London
  See also England; English law; United Kingdom
  arbitrators, challenge, 236
  awards, annulment, 504

choice of national procedure, effect of, 299-300

place of arbitration and, 95

London Court of International Arbitration, 3, 243-244
  arbitrators' fees, 31-32

Long-term projects, adapting contract, 114

Loquin, Eric, 351

M

Mahmassani, Sobhi, 672

Mainland China, awards rendered in, 572-573

Majlis, 72

Majority awards, 368-370

Manifest disregard of the law, 614-615

Manifestement nulle, 513

Mareva injunctions, 483, 526-527

Maritime arbitration, 712-713

Maritime disputes, 6

Martin, Andrew, 144

Massachusetts, consolidation, 607 n.105

Mayer, Professor Pierre, 344, 627 n.13

Mbaye, Judge Keba, 642, 663

Mediation as precondition, 105-106

Memorials, 430-431

Mexico, 4
  site of arbitration, 11, 12

Middle East, situs of cases, 7

Misconduct, arbitrators, 240, 246, 610, 613

Model Clause
  See ICC Model Clause

Montreal Conference of the International Law Association (1982), 39, 661-662

Morality, contract unenforceable if purpose contrary to, 649-650

Moscow, place of arbitration, 95

Multilateral treaties, 668

Multi-party arbitrations, Arbitral Tribunal, 198-202

Multi-party disputes
accommodation for, 125-126
arbitration agreement, 81-83
non-signatories, 81

Multiple contracts between same parties
jurisdiction, 180-182

Mustill, Michael, 421, 423
lex mercatoria, 626, 628-631, 634, 643 n.50
culpa in contrahendo, 650

N

Naón, Horacio Grigera, 24

Nariman, Fali, 663

National arbitration associations, 10

National arbitration law
See National law

National Bank of Pakistan, 339

National committees, 17-19
arbitrators, appointment of, 21-22, 27, 33
cost reforms and, 35
failure of party to nominate arbitrator, 197-198
nominations by, 20
sole arbitrator, appointment of, 192

National courts
ancillary proceedings before, 471-493
attachments, 482-486
conservatory measures, 471-473
discovery, court-ordered, 486-493
evidence, court-ordered production of, 486-493
expertise, 473-479
injunction, 473-479
interim measures, 471-473
interlocutory relief, 480-481
arbitrators, duty of disclosure, 216-223

Nationality of arbitrators, 92-93

National law
awards
exceptional remedies under, 409
time limits, 355
choice of national procedure, effect of, 299-300
constraints on ICC arbitration, 495-518
arbitral situs, 497-500
arbitration agreement, validity, 497
award annulment, 500-507
awards, review of, 497
choice of law issues, 508-509
compétence-compétence, 512-515
curial laws, competing, 509-510
enforcement, questions incident to, 507-508
interim measures, 497
jurisdiction, 512-516
law reform and, 510-511
matters affected by national arbitration law, 496-497
multiple procedural norms, 507-510
preconditions to arbitration, 497
private consent, 495-496
public power, 495-496
separability, 515-516

subject matter arbitrability, 497

mandatory procedural requirements, 297-299

NCPC
See Nouveau Code de Procédure Civile (NCPC)

Negotiation as precondition, 105-106

Nemo debet esse judex in propria causa, **225-226**

The Netherlands, 4
site of arbitration, 11

Netherlands Arbitration Institute, 675

New Delhi
Fifth International Arbitration Congress (1975), 122

New York
arbitrators, challenge, 236
fact finding, arbitrators' approach to, 420
interim procedural questions, 609
subject matter arbitrability, 604

New York Convention on the Recognition and Enforcement of Foreign Arbitral Awards (1958), 8, 679-696
adherence to, 496
agreements, 682
amiable compositeur, 350
annex, 691-696
arbitration agreement, 43, 53
form of agreement to arbitrate, 54-55, 57
incorporation by reference, 73
non-commercial matters, 70
arbitrators, truncated tribunal, 248
articles, 691-696
attachments, 482, 484
awards, 500 n.24, 681-682
annulment, 502, 504, 507
consent, by, 358

enforcement of, 401 n.7, 403-404, 616
non-recognition, 510
procedural order or interim award, 464-466
review of, 616
background, 679-680
Bruxelles Convention, interaction, 687-689
business disputes, 141
capacity of the parties, 44 n.3
double *exequatur,* 679-680
enforcement, defenses, 684-685
entry-of-judgment stipulation, 119-120
European Convention on International Arbitration, interaction, 686
failure to meet requirements, 59
foreign awards, 561
framework, 680-681
Geneva Convention, replacement, 686
Geneva Protocol, replacement, 686
Hong Kong law and, 566-567, 573
nationality, irrelevance of, 681
other treaties, interaction with, 686-689
Panama Convention, interaction, 687
place of arbitration and, 95
recognition
of award, refusal of, 298
defenses, 684-685
reservations, 683
rules or law of procedure, 107
scope of, 681-683
Swiss law and, 589-590
United States law, coverage, 596
writing, requirement of, 682-683

New York law
See New York Convention on the Recognition and Enforcement of Foreign Arbitral Awards (1958)

New York Society of Maritime Arbitrators, 656

New York State law, fact finding production of documents, 452

New York Supreme Court of New York County, 144

New Zealand, arbitration agreement, 66 n.63

New Zealand Arbitration Act, 526

Nigeria, 4

Non-business disputes, 140-141

Non-existent authority, 129-132

Non-signatories
    arbitration agreements, United States law, 597-600
    jurisdiction, 174-179
        parent and subsidiary, 177-178
    multi-party disputes, 81

Notifications, 153-154
    lex mercatoria, 657

Nouveau Code de Procédure Civile (NCPC), 549, 557

Number of arbitrators, 91-92, 189-191

O

Oaths, hearings
    arbitrators' power to administer, 435-437

Objections to arbitrators, 204

Occasionally useful elements, arbitration, 105-126
    adapting contract, powers, 114-116
    amiable compositeur, 110-114
    apportionment of costs, 118-119
    arbitration agreement, law governing, 107-108
    conciliation as precondition, 105-106
    conflict of laws, rules of, 108-109
    discovery, 118
    entry-of-judgment stipulations, 119-120
    mediation as precondition, 105-126
    multi-party disputes, accommodation for, 125-126
    negotiation as precondition, 105-106
    procedural details, 117-118
    provisional relief, powers and procedures, 116-117
    rules or law of procedure, 106-107
    waivers
        appeals, 121-122
        sovereign immunity, 122-125

OECD Multilateral Investment Agreement, 668-669

Oral hearings, 428, 444-446

Organizational framework of ICC, 17-28
    arbitrators, 26-28. *See also* Arbitrators
    Court of Arbitration, 19-24
    national committees, 17-19
    Secretariat, 24-26. *See also* Secretariat of International Court of Arbitration

P

Pacta sunt servanda, 642-643
    exceptions to, 649

Pakistan
    arbitration agreement, law governing, 108
    lex mercatoria, 635-636
    public law, 339-340

Pakistani law, 100

Panama Convention, New York Convention and, 687

Panchaud, Judge, 216 n.31

Parent corporations
  jurisdiction, non-signatory parties,
    177-178

Paris
  See also France; French law
  arbitration agreement, 52, 62 n.50
  arbitrators, removal of, 239-240
  Chamber of Arbitration, 47 n. 8
  choice of national procedure, effect of,
    300
  Cour d'appel, 550, 554, 558
  Cour de cassation, 65-66, 164, 288,
    307, 552, 553 n.25, 554-555
    awards, 381, 505
    time limits for awards, 357
  Court of Appeal, 52
  General Secretariat, 17
  place of arbitration, 187, 188
  situs of cases, 7, 8
  Tribunal de grande instance, 161

Partial awards, 359-364

Parties
  regional origins, 4-5
  time limits, extension of, 23
  typical, 4-6

**Partnership agreements, assignments of
  contract, 80**

Party costs, 393-396

Party-nominated arbitrators, 194-196

Patents, arbitration agreement, 67-68

**Pathological elements of arbitration,
  127-135**
  compromise, inappropriate, 132-133
  equivocation, 128-129
  hasty resolutions, 135
  illusory arbitration clause, 134
  institutions, insufficient *specification*,
    133-134
  non-existent authority, 129-132
  specificity, overdoing, 135

Pendente lite, 463

Pennsylvania law, 325

People's Republic of China, 563

Per diem system, costs, 31

Personal status, matters of
  arbitration agreement, 69

Photocopies, 429

Piercing the veil, 598-599

**Place of arbitration, 93-96, 185-189,
  280-281**

Poland, *lex mercatoria*, 654

**Politics, arbitration under ICC, generally,
  4**

Pre-arbitral referee, 706-709

Preconditions to arbitration, 497

**Previously expressed opinion,
  arbitrators, 230-232**

Price variations, *lex mercatoria*, 655

Prima facie **agreement to arbitrate**
  determination of, 21
  jurisdiction, 155-157, 166

Private consent
  national law, constraints on ICC
    arbitration, 495-496

Privity, arbitration without, 663-670

Procedural details, 117-118

Proceedings, rules governing, 295-318
  confidentiality, 311-318
  freedom of parties and arbitrators,
    295-296
  national law
    choice of national procedure,
      effect of, 299-300
    mandatory procedural
      requirements, 297-299
  representation, 303-311

rights of audience, 303-311

rulings, 300-303

Production of documents

confidentiality, 454

discovery, limitations, 454

employment discrimination, 452 n.11

extraordinary services, 451 n.6

fact finding, 449-456

noncompliance, 453

"political" cases, 451 n.8

Proof

lex mercatoria, burden of proof, 646

written. *See* Written proof

Provisional Advances, 36

Provisional relief, powers and procedures, 116-117

Public law, 338-346

Public policy

arbitration agreement, 69

English law and, 544

French law and, 561

New York Convention and, 684

Q

Qatar, arbitrators, 233

Qualifications of arbitrators, 93

R

Recognition of award, refusal of, 298

Recours en nullité, Swiss law, 577

Référé provision (France), 481, 555-556

Referee Rules, 706-709

Reforms, cost, 35-36

Related agreements, controversies, 86-87

Related parties

arbitration agreement, not having signed, 74-79

assignments of contract, 78-79

group of companies doctrine, 75-78

Renvoi mechanism, 99

Representation, 303-311

Request and Answer

provisional advance following, 254

written proof, 430-431

Request for Arbitration, 25-26

cost

determining beforehand, 29

reforms, 35

language, 147-148

number of arbitrators, 189

overview, 145-149

Request to Produce, 455

Res judicata

arbitration agreement, multi-party disputes, 82

Reymond, Professor Claude, 323

Rhodesia, 86

Rights of audience, 303-311

Robert, Jean, 424-425

Rome, public law, 341-342

Romero, Edouardo Silva, 25

RUCIP

See European Wholesale Potato Trade Rules (RUCIP)

Rules and Schedule of Costs, 254

Rules for the Regulation of Contractual Relations, 711

Rules of Conduct to Combat Extortion and Bribery, 65

Rules of conflict, 102

Rules of ICC
See Arbitration under ICC, generally

Rules or law of procedure, 106-107

S

Sanders, Professor Pieter, 52, 638-639

Saudi Arabia
arbitrators, duty of disclosure, 217
Terms of Reference, 291

Saudi Arabian Council of Ministers'
Decision, 72

Schedule of Arbitration Costs and Fees,
266-267

Schedule of Conciliation costs, 700

Schmitthoff, Clive, 633 n.29

Schwebel, Judge Stephen, 49

Scope of dispute, specificity, 86-88

Scotland, UNCITRAL Model Law and, 527

Scrutiny, *amiable compositeur*, 353-354

Seat of arbitration
choice of law system in force,
323-326
injunction, 473
national law, constraints on ICC
arbitration, 497-500

Second look doctrine, 617-618

Secrecy of deliberations, awards, 372
n.36
Court's scrutiny of, 376

Secretariat of International Court of
Arbitration, 24-26
advances to cover costs, 262-263
bank guarantees, 266
American Deputy Secretary General,
24-25
arbitrators, appointment of, 22

awards
deposit of, 404-406
time limits, 356, 358
costs, determining, 29
liaisons, 26
Paris-based, 7, 17
Request for Arbitration, 25-26, 149
requests received, number of, 2

Secretary General, 24-25
advances to cover costs, 262
bank guarantees, 266
default, notice given, 266
provisional advance ordered by,
253-256

Securities law, arbitration agreement, 69

Separability
arbitration agreements
English law, 516 n.92, 536-537
French law, 48-49 n.11
United States law, 597
national law, constraints on ICC
arbitration, 515-516

Setoff, availability, 647-648

"Shall," wording, 139-140

Sherman Act, 496

Signature, arbitrators, 397-399

Singapore
rights of audience, 308
site of arbitration, 11, 12

Site visit, 458

Society of Maritime Arbitrators, 76

SOFIDIF decisions, 287-289

Sole arbitrators
appointment of, 191-194
challenge, 223-224
fees, 29
nationality, 92

Sornarajah, M., 667

South African law, UNCITRAL Model Law and, 525-526, 527

Sovereign immunity
    acts of state and, 670-676
    force majeure, 676
    waiver of, 122-125

Sovereignty, 109
    international arbitration as menace to, 661-663

Spain, 4
    arbitration agreement, related parties not having signed, 77
    conflict of laws, rules of, 109

Spanish law, relevant trade, 332

Specificity, overdoing, 135

Stand-by letter of credit, 465

Standing Committee for the Regulation of Contractual Relations, 710

Standing Committee on Extortion and Bribery, 713

State contracts, 661-678
    bilateral investment treaties (BITs), 665-668
    developing countries, transnational disputes, 676-678
    multilateral treaties, 668-669
    privity, arbitration without, 663-670
    sovereign immunity and acts of state, 670-676
    sovereignty, international arbitration as menace to, 661-663
    United Nations Charter of Economic Rights and Duties of States (1974), 663

Statutes of limitations
    arbitration agreements, United States law, 601-602

Steyn, Mr. Justice, 383

Subject matter arbitrability, 497
    French law, 553-554
    United States law, 602-606

Subject matter of cases, typical, 6-7

Subpoena, arbitrators' power of, 435-437

Subsidiaries
    jurisdiction, non-signatory parties, 177-178

Substantive law, choice of, 319-346
    appropriate rules of law, freedom of arbitrators to apply, 319-323
    background of choice of law processes, 320-323
    contractual terms, application of, 330-332
    criteria most frequently used, 323-329
    cumulative application of systems, 326-327
    free choice of law by arbitrator, 329
    general principals of conflict of laws, 326-327
        arbitrator, chosen by, 328-329
    international public policy, 338-346
    lex mercatoria. See Lex mercatoria
    public law, influence of, 338-346
    seat of arbitration, choice of law system in force, 323-326
    trade usage, 330-332

Sui generis administration, 31

Supervised institutional arbitration, 41-42

Sweden, 4
    See also Swedish law
    appeals, waivers of, 122
    arbitration agreement, 63
    awards, enforcement, 404
    sovereign immunity, 673
        waiver of, 122-123

Swedish law, 102
    See also Sweden

Swiss Code of Obligations, 101

Swiss Federal Statute on Private
International Law, 578
See also Swiss law

Swiss Federal Tribunal, 248-249
See also Swiss law

Swiss Intercantonal Concordat on
Arbitration
See also Swiss law
awards
annulment, 505 n.42
procedural order or interim award,
466
seat of arbitration, 498-499

Swiss law, 575-590
*See also Loi fédérale sur le droit
international privé (LDIP);* Swiss
Intercantonal Concordat on Arbitration;
Swiss Private International Law Act of
1987; Swiss Tribunal; Switzerland;
Switzerland Private International Law
Act
agreement to arbitrate, 577-578
validity, 577-578
awards
annulment, 501 n. 28, 576
interim awards, 581
review of, 582-591
compromise, inappropriate, 132
Concordat, 576-577
déclaration expresse, 578
evidence, court-ordered production of,
490
interlocutory matters, 579-582
New York Convention and, 589-590
ordre public, 583
recours en nullité, 577
statutory framework, 575-577

Swiss Private International Law Act of
1987, 297, 363, 409
See also Swiss law

Switzerland, 4, 673
See also Swiss law
ancillary proceedings, injunction or
expertise, 477
appeal, waiver of, 121-122
applicable law, 100-101
arbitration agreement, 55 n.29
arbitrators, 27, 235
interim measures, 463
awards
annulment, 503 n.34
challenges, limits on, 546
exceptional remedies, 409
interim or partial awards, 363
time limits, 357
Bundesgericht, 575
confidentiality, 316
constraints on ICC arbitration, 516
jurisdiction issues, 167
Private International Law Act of
1987, 477
procedural requirements, 297
provisional relief, 116
public law, 342-343
site of arbitration, 11, 12, 498-499
Tribunal fédéral, 505 n.42, 575,
583-589, 683
arbitrability, 579
arbitration agreements, 577
interlocutory matters, 582

T

Taiwan
French military vessels, sale of, 64
n.56

Tangley, Lord, 349

Technical expertise, adapting contract
and, 115-116

Technical legal questions, qualifications
of arbitrators, 93

Terms of Reference, 273-293
    advances to cover costs, 261-262
        provisional advance, 255
    amiable compositeur, 347-351
    awards
        French law, 558
        time limits, 355-356
    claims, 276-277
    consolidation, 607 n.104
    contents, 276-284
    cost reforms and, 36
    costs of drafting, 32
    counterclaims, 276-277
    default by party, 284-285
    entry into effect, 285-286
    fact finding
        approach to, 415
        production of documents, 451
    hearings, testimony, 438
    interim procedural questions, 609
    jurisdiction, consolidation, 182-183
    language or arbitration, 97
    legal effect, 286-293
    national law, 299-300
    particulars of the applicable
      procedural rules, 281-284
    place of arbitration, 187, 280-281
    procedural details, 117
    procedural rules, 281-284, 300-301
    provisional advances, 34
    rationale, 273-276
    summary of arguments, 277-278
    written proof, 427, 430

Testimony, hearings, 437-442

Thailand, rights of audience, 305

Third World countries
    claimants, 5
    ICC arbitration, 662
    site of arbitration, 11-12, 12
    transnational disputes, 676-678

Thompson, Robert, 209-210

Three-member tribunals, 194
    arbitrators' fees, 387

Three-sided arbitration, 151

Time periods, calculations of, 153-154

Trade boycott, arbitration agreement, 69

Trademarks, arbitration agreement, 67-68

Trade secrets, 314

Trade usage, 330-332

Treaty of Rome, 341-342, 343

***Tribunal de commerce* (France), 556**

***Tribunal de grande instance* (France), 480, 556**

***Tribunal fédéral* (Switzerland), 505 n.42, 575, 683**
    arbitrability, 579
    arbitration agreements, 577
    awards
        annulment, 505 n.42
        review of, 583-589
    interlocutory matters, 582

Tri-partite joint venture contract, 199-200

Truncated tribunals, 24, 245-249

Tunis, site of arbitration, 12

Tunisia
    arbitration agreement, 71
    site of arbitration, 11

Turkish law, 100, 340

Two-sided arbitration, 151

Two-tiered arbitration, 121

U

Uganda, waiver of sovereign immunity, 122

Ultra petitoa, 274

Unambiguous references, importance of, 85-86

UNCITRAL Model Law, 50 n.15, 169, 519-529
See also UNCITRAL rules
  adoption of, 591-592
  agreement to arbitrate, 523-526
  amiable compositeur, 348
  awards
    interim or partial awards, 363
    review of, 528-529
  Hong Kong law, 563-566
  interlocutory matters, 526-528
  jurisdiction, 514
  lex mercatoria, 631, 634
  New York Convention and, 683
  objectives of, 520
  statutory framework, 519-523

UNCITRAL Rules, 532
See also UNCITRAL Model Law
  adoption of, 107
  appointing authority, 714
  commencement of arbitration proceedings, 147
  entry-of-judgment stipulation, 120
  ex aequo et bono, 348
  hearings, closing proceedings, 447 n.22
  jurisdiction, 162-163
  · supervising arbitration, 715

Unforseeability, *lex mercatoria*, 655-657

UNIDROIT Principles of International Commercial Contracts, 319, 632-633

Uniform Arbitration Act (UAA), 593
  attorneys' fees, 619-620

Uniform Customs and Practices for Documentary Credits, 716, 717

Uniform rules and Practice for Documentary Credits, 331

Uniform Rules for Bank-to-Bank Reimbursement under Documentary Credit (URR), 716

United Kingdom, 4
See also England; English law; London
  site of arbitration, 11, 12, 13
  sovereign immunity, waiver of, 124

United Nations Charter of Economic Rights and Duties of States (1974), 663

United Nations Commission on International Trade Law
See UNCITRAL Rules
  Model Law on International Commercial Arbitration. *See* UNCITRAL Model Law

United Nations Convention
See New York Convention on the Recognition and Enforcement of Foreign Arbitral Awards (1958)

United States, 4
See also United States law
  ancillary proceedings, attachments, 483
  arbitration agreement, 71
  arbitrators, 28
  constraints on ICC arbitration, 516-518
  discovery, court-ordered, 487
  fact finding, arbitrators' approach to, 420
  hearings
    oaths, 436
    subpoenas, 436
  jurisdiction issues, 170
  site of arbitration, 11, 12, 13
  situs of cases, 7
  Trading with the Enemy Act, 344

United States law, 591-622
See also Federal Arbitration Act (United States); United States
  agreement to arbitrate, 596-606
    agency, 598-599

basic requirements, 596-597

class actions, 606

defective clauses, repair of, 597

equitable estoppel, 599-600

jurisdiction, preliminary
determinations, 600-602

non-signatories, 597-600

piercing the veil, 598-599

separability, 597

statutes of limitations, 601-602

subject matter arbitrability,
602-606

ancillary proceedings, injunction or
expertise, 475

attorneys' fees, 619-620

awards, review of, 610-622

annulment, 614-615

arbitral jurisdiction, 620-621

attorneys' fees, 619-620

disclosure, duty, 612-613

enforcement of award, 616-617

entry of judgment provisions, 622

excess of authority, award for,
620-621

foreign awards, enforcement, 617

foreign awards, vacatur, 615-616

impartiality, 612-613

judicial review, 615

jurisdiction, 620-621

manifest disregard of the law,
614-615

misconduct, arbitrators, 610, 613

punitive damages, 618-619

second look doctrine, 617-618

substantial error, 615

vacatur, 610-616

citizens of United States, corporations
as, 596 n.34

consolidation, 607

court orders, appeals from, 609-610

discovery, 608

interim procedural questions, 609

interlocutory matters, 607-610

assistance to arbitration, 607

consolidation, 607

court orders, appeals from,
609-610

discovery, 608

freezing assets, 607

interim procedural questions, 609

New York Convention, coverage of,
596

state and federal arbitration law,
interaction of, 593-595

statutory framework, 591-596

V

Vacatur

awards, United States law, 610-616

Venezuela

compromise, inappropriate, 132-133

Venue

choice of, 9-13

Court of Arbitration, determination
by, 23

delocalization, 7-9

**Vienna Convention on the International
Sale of Goods (1968), 331-332**

**Vienna Convention on the Law of
Treaties, 648**

Vienna Sales Convention, 319

W

Waivers

appeals, 121-122

sovereign immunity, 122-125

Wales, rights of audience, 306-307

Western Europe, 4-5

West Gronkshire Traders' Association, 8